JAVA

HOW TO PROGRAM
FIFTH EDITION

Deitel™ Books, Cyber Classrooms, Complete Tra
published by

How To Program Series

Advanced Java™ 2 Platform How to Program

C How to Program, 3/E

C++ How to Program, 4/E

C# How to Program

e-Business and e-Commerce How to Program

Internet and World Wide Web How to Program, 2/E

Java™ How to Program, 5/E

Perl How to Program

Python How to Program

Visual Basic® 6 How to Program

Visual Basic® .NET How to Program, 2/E

Wireless Internet & Mobile Business How to Program

XML How to Program

Deitel™ Developer Series

C# A Programmer's Introduction
C# for Experienced Programmers
Java™ Web Services for Experienced Programmers
Web Services A Technical Introduction
Visual C++ .NET for Experienced Programmers

.NET How to Program Series

C# How to Program
Visual Basic® .NET How to Program, 2/E

For Managers Series

e-Business and e-Commerce for Managers

Visual Studio® Series

C# How to Program
Visual Basic® .NET How to Program, 2/E
Getting Started with Microsoft® Visual C++® 6 with an Introduction to MFC
Visual Basic® 6 How to Program

Coming Soon

e-books and e-whitepapers
Premium CourseCompass, WebCT and Blackboard Multimedia Cyber Classroom versions

Multimedia Cyber Classroom and Web-Based Training Series

C++ Multimedia Cyber Classroom, 4/E
C# Multimedia Cyber Classroom
e-Business and e-Commerce Multimedia Cyber Classroom
Internet and World Wide Web Multimedia Cyber Classroom, 2/E
Java™ 2 Multimedia Cyber Classroom, 5/E
Perl Multimedia Cyber Classroom
Python Multimedia Cyber Classroom
Visual Basic® 6 Multimedia Cyber Classroom
Visual Basic® .NET Multimedia Cyber Classroom, 2/E
Wireless Internet & Mobile Business Programming Multimedia Cyber Classroom
XML Multimedia Cyber Classroom

The Complete Training Course Series

The Complete C++ Training Course, 4/E
The Complete C# Training Course
The Complete e-Business and e-Commerce Programming Training Course
The Complete Internet and World Wide Web Programming Training Course, 2/E
The Complete Java™ 2 Training Course, 5/E
The Complete Perl Training Course
The Complete Python Training Course
The Complete Visual Basic® 6 Training Course
The Complete Visual Basic® .NET Training Course, 2/E
The Complete Wireless Internet & Mobile Business Programming Training Course
The Complete XML Programming Training Course

To follow the Deitel publishing program, please register at:

www.deitel.com/newsletter/subscribe.html

for the *DEITEL™ BUZZ ONLINE* e-mail newsletter.

To communicate with the authors, send e-mail to:

deitel@deitel.com

For information on corporate on-site seminars offered by Deitel & Associates, Inc. worldwide, visit:

www.deitel.com

For continuing updates on Prentice Hall and Deitel publications visit:

www.deitel.com,
www.prenhall.com/deitel or
www.InformIT.com/deitel

Library of Congress Cataloging-in-Publication Data

On file

Vice President and Editorial Director, ECS: *Marcia J. Horton*
Acquisitions Editor: *Petra J. Recter*
Assistant Editor: *Sarah Parker*
Project Manager: *Jennifer Cappello*
Vice President and Director of Production and Manufacturing, ESM: *David W. Riccardi*
Executive Managing Editor: *Vince O'Brien*
Managing Editor: *Tom Manshreck*
Production Editor: *John F. Lovell*
Director of Creative Services: *Paul Belfanti*
Creative Director: *Carole Anson*
Chapter Opener and Cover Designer: *Tamara L. Newnam, Dr. Harvey Deitel*
Interior Design Assistance: *Geoffrey Cassar*
Manufacturing Manager: *Trudy Pisciotti*
Manufacturing Buyer: *Lisa McDowell*
Marketing Manager: *Pamela Shaffer*
Marketing Assistant: *Barrie Reinhold*

© 2003 by Pearson Education, Inc.
Upper Saddle River, New Jersey 07458

10 9 8 7 6 5 4 3 2

ISBN 0-13-101621-0
ISBN 0-13-183661-7

Pearson Education Ltd., *London*
Pearson Education Australia Pty. Ltd., *Sydney*
Pearson Education Singapore, Pte. Ltd.
Pearson Education North Asia Ltd., *Hong Kong*
Pearson Education Canada, Inc., *Toronto*
Pearson Educacion de Mexico, S.A. de C.V.
Pearson Education–Japan, *Tokyo*
Pearson Education Malaysia, Pte. Ltd.
Pearson Education, Inc., *Upper Saddle River, New Jersey*

JAVA

HOW TO PROGRAM
FIFTH EDITION

H. M. Deitel
Deitel & Associates, Inc.

P. J. Deitel
Deitel & Associates, Inc.

PRENTICE HALL, Upper Saddle River, New Jersey 07458

Trademarks

To Terrell Hull and James Huddleston:

For your steadfast commitment to excellence in teaching and writing about Java and object technology.

For your extraordinary contributions as reviewers and for your insistence that we "get it right."

Thank you for being our mentors, our colleagues and our friends.

It is a privilege to work with consummate software professionals.

Harvey and Paul Deitel

Contents

24   Servlets   1220

25   JavaServer Pages (JSP)   1261

Preface

Welcome to Java! At Deitel & Associates, we write college-level programming-language textbooks and professional books and work hard to keep our books up-to-date. Writing *Java How to Program, Fifth Edition, (5/e* for short), was a joy. This book and its support materials have everything instructors and students need for an informative, interesting, challenging and entertaining Java educational experience. As the book goes to publication, it is compliant with the latest version of Java—the *Java 2 Platform, Standard Edition (J2SE), version 1.4.1*—and with object-oriented design using the latest version of the *UML (Unified Modeling Language)* from the Object Management Group (OMG). We tuned the writing, the pedagogy, our coding style, the book's ancillary package and added a substantial treatment of developing database-driven Internet- and Web-based applications. We moved the *Tour of the Book* to the Preface. The tour will help instructors, students and professionals get a sense of the rich coverage the book provides of Java object-oriented programming, object-oriented design with the UML, and developing Internet- and Web-based applications. If you are evaluating the book, please be sure to read the *Tour of the Book*, which starts on page xxxvi.

Whether you are an instructor, a student, an experienced professional or a novice programmer, this book has much to offer. Java is a world-class programming language for developing industrial-strength computer applications for devices ranging from cell phones and PDAs to the largest enterprise servers. We carefully audited the manuscript against the *Java Language Specification*,[1] which defines Java. As a result, the programs you create by studying this text should work with any J2SE 1.4.1 compatible Java platform.

In this Preface, we overview *Java How to Program, 5/e*'s comprehensive suite of educational materials that help instructors maximize their students' Java learning experience. We explain conventions we use, such as syntax coloring the code examples, "code washing" and highlighting important code segments to help focus students' attention on the key con-

---

1. Electronic HTML and PDF copies of the *Java Language Specification* are available free at the Sun Microsystem's Java Web site at `java.sun.com/docs/books/jls/index.html`.

cepts introduced in each chapter. We overview the new features of *Java How to Program, 5/e*, including our enhanced treatment of object-oriented programming, Web-application development with servlets and JSP, the enhanced optional elevator-simulation object-oriented design (OOD) case study with the UML, the overview of design patterns and the extensive use of UML diagrams that have been upgraded to UML version 1.4 standards.

Prentice Hall has bundled a CD with the text that contains Sun Microsystem's *J2SE 1.4.1 Software Development Kit* (J2SDK) and their *Sun ONE Studio 4 (Community Edition)*, integrated development environment (IDE). To further support novice programmers, we offer several free *DIVE-INTO™ Series* publications that explain how to compile, execute and debug Java programs using the J2SDK, Sun ONE Studio (Community Edition) and Borland's *JBuilder Personal* edition. These publications are located at www.deitel.com/books/downloads.html with the resources for *Java How to Program, 5/e*.

We overview the complete package of ancillary materials available to instructors and students using *Java How to Program, 5/e*. These include an *Instructor's Resource CD* with solutions to most of the book's chapter exercises and a *Test-Item File* with hundreds of multiple-choice questions and answers. Additional instructor resources are available at the book's Companion Web Site (www.prenhall.com/deitel), which includes a *Syllabus Manager* and customizable PowerPoint® Lecture Notes. Numerous support materials are available for students at the Companion Web Site, as well. For instructors who want to hold closed-lab sessions (or highly structured homework assignments), we provide a lab manual, *Java in the Lab, Lab Manual to Accompany Java How to Program, Fifth Edition*. This publication includes carefully constructed Prelab Activities, Lab Exercises and Postlab Activities for a closed lab setting. Instructors can obtain the solutions manual to *Java in the Lab* from their regular Prentice Hall representatives.

We overview *The Java 2 Multimedia Cyber Classroom, 5/e*—an interactive, multimedia CD-based version of the book. This learning aid provides extensive interactivity features including hyperlinking, text search, audio "walkthroughs" of programs, Flash® animations and hundreds of exercises and solutions. We describe how to order both the *Cyber Classroom* and *The Complete Java 2 Training Course, 5/e*, boxed product, which contains the *Cyber Classroom* and the textbook later in the preface.

We discuss several DEITEL™ e-learning initiatives, including an explanation of Deitel content available for the *Blackboard, CourseCompass* and *WebCT* Course Management Systems, each of which supports *Java How to Program, 5/e*. *Premium CourseCompass*, which offers enhanced Deitel content based on *The Java 2 Multimedia Cyber Classroom, 5/e*, will be available for Summer 2003 courses.

In preparation for this edition, *Java How to Program, 4/e*, was reviewed by 35 distinguished academics and industry professionals. After applying their comments, the manuscript for *Java How to Program, 5/e*, was reviewed by 44 distinguished academics and industry professionals. We list all the reviewers names and affiliations in the acknowledgements. The Preface concludes with information about the authors and about Deitel & Associates, Inc. Please send an e-mail to deitel@deitel.com if you have questions as you read this book; we will respond promptly. Please visit our Web site, www.deitel.com, regularly and be sure to sign up for the *DEITEL™ BUZZ ONLINE* e-mail newsletter at www.deitel.com/newsletter/subscribe.html. We use the Web site and the newsletter to keep our readers current on *Java How to Program, 5/e*, and all other DEITEL™ publications and services.

New Features in Java How to Program, Fifth Edition

This edition contains many new features and enhancements including:

Full-Color Presentation

This book is in full color to show programs and their outputs as they typically appear on a computer screen. We syntax color all the Java code, as do most Java integrated-development environments and code editors. This greatly improves code readability—an especially important goal, given that this book contains over 23,000 lines of code. Our syntax-coloring conventions are as follows:

```
comments appear in green
keywords appear in dark blue
errors and JSP scriptlet delimiters appear in red
constants and literal values appear in light blue
all other code appears in black
```

Code Highlighting

We have added extensive code highlighting. In our code walkthroughs, we have eliminated most of the "redundant" code snippets that appeared inline in the text in earlier editions. We kept them in the earliest portion of the book as a pedagogic device to help novices. We want the reader to see all new code features in context, so from Chapter 4 forward, our code walkthroughs simply refer to the line numbers of the new code segments inside complete source programs. To make it easier for readers to spot the featured segments, we highlight them in bright yellow. This helps students review the material rapidly when preparing for exams or labs.

"Code Washing"

Code washing is our term for applying extensive comments, using meaningful identifiers, applying indentation and using vertical spacing to separate meaningful program units. This process results in programs that are much more readable and self-documenting. We have done extensive "code washing" of all the source code programs in the text, the lab manual, the ancillaries and the *Cyber Classroom*.

Tuned Treatment of Object-Oriented Programming in Chapters 9 and 10

This is one of the most significant improvements in this new edition. We performed a high-precision upgrade of *Java How to Program, 4/e*, Chapter 9 and split it into two chapters. The improvements make the material clearer and more accessible to students and professionals, especially those studying object-oriented programming for the first time.

Chapter 9, Object-Oriented Programming: Inheritance. The new Chapter 9 carefully walks the reader through a five-example sequence that demonstrates `private` data, `protected` data and software reuse via inheritance. We begin by demonstrating a class with `private` instance variables and `public` methods to manipulate that data. Next, we implement a second class with several additional capabilities. To do this, we duplicate much of the first example's code. In our third example, we begin our discussion of inheritance and software reuse—we use the class from the first example as a superclass and inherit its data and functionality into a new subclass. This example introduces the inheritance mechanism and demonstrates that a subclass cannot access its superclass's `private` members directly. This motivates our fourth example, in which we introduce `protected` data in the superclass and demonstrate that the subclass can indeed access the `protected` data inherited from the superclass. The last example in the sequence demonstrates proper software engineering by defining the superclass's data as `private` and using the superclass's `public` methods (that were inherited by the subclass) to manipulate the superclass's `private` data from the subclass. We follow the five-part introduction with a three-level class hierarchy that employs the software engineering techniques introduced earlier in the chapter. The chapter closes with a discussion of software engineering with inheritance.

Chapter 10, Object-Oriented Programming: Polymorphism. The new Chapter 10 builds on the inheritance concepts presented in Chapter 9 and focuses on the relationships among classes in a class hierarchy. Chapter 10 uses a three-example sequence to present the powerful processing capabilities that these relationships enable. We begin with an example that illustrates the "is-a" relationship between a subclass object and its superclass type. This relationship enables the subclass object to be treated as an object of its superclass. We show that we are able to assign a subclass object's reference to a superclass variable and invoke the superclass's methods on that object. This example uses polymorphism, which enables a program to process objects of classes related by a class hierarchy as objects of their superclass type. When a method is invoked via a superclass variable, the subclass-specific version of that method is invoked. In our second example, we demonstrate that the reverse is not true—a superclass object is not considered to be an object of its subclass type—and we show that compiler errors occur if a program attempts to manipulate a superclass object in this manner. Our third example demonstrates that the only methods which can be invoked through a superclass variable are those methods defined by the superclass type. The example shows that attempts to invoke subclass-only methods result in compilation errors. The chapter continues with a case study on polymorphism in which we process an array of variables that contain references to objects. All the objects referenced by the elements of the array have a common abstract superclass containing the set of methods common to every class in the hierarchy. We conclude with a case study that demonstrates how a program that processes objects polymorphically can still perform type-specific processing by determining the type of the object currently being processed.

Java New I/O (NIO) APIs

Java's New I/O APIs are significant new additions to J2SE 1.4. We overview portions of these APIs in sections of three chapters. Section 11.8 demonstrates NIO's regular expression capabilities, which enable programs to search strings for character patterns. Section 17.13 introduces NIO's high-performance I/O classes that enable developers to take advantage of buffers, channels, charsets and more. This section also presents an example of using channels and buffers to write data to, and read data from, a file. Section 18.11 continues our discussion of the NIO APIs with an introduction to selectors and non-blocking I/O for implementing high-performance network servers. We then implement a distributed chat program that demonstrates these capabilities. Sections 11.8 and 17.13 also provide Web links for further study of the NIO APIs.

Database and Web-Applications Development with JDBC, Servlets and JSP

By popular demand, we have returned several topics to *Java How to Program, Fifth Edition.* Chapter 23, Java Database Connectivity with JDBC, demonstrates how to build data-driven applications with the JDBC™ API. Chapter 24, Servlets, and Chapter 25, JavaServer Pages™ (JSP), expand our treatment of Internet and Web programming topics and have everything readers need to begin developing their own Web-based applications that will run on the Internet! Readers will learn how to build so-called *n*-tier applications, in which the functionality provided by each tier can be distributed to separate computers across the Internet or executed on the same computer. In particular, we build a three-tier Web-based survey application and a three-tier Web-based guestbook application. Each application's information is stored in the application's data tier—in this book, a database implemented with IBM's Java-based Cloudscape database product (a trial version is on the CD that accompanies this book). The user enters requests and receives responses at each application's client tier, which is typically a computer running a Web browser such as Microsoft Internet Explorer or Netscape. Web browsers, of course, know how to communicate with Web sites throughout the Internet. The middle tier contains both a Web server and one or more application-specific servlets (in the case of our survey application) or JavaServer Pages (in the case of our guestbook application). We use Apache's Tomcat Web server as our application server for these examples. Tomcat, which is the reference implementation for the servlets and JavaServer Pages technologies, is included on the CD that accompanies this book and is available free for download from www.apache.org. Tomcat communicates with the client tier across the Internet using the HyperText Transfer Protocol (HTTP). We discuss the crucial role of the Web server in Web programming and provide many examples demonstrating interactions between a Web browser and a Web server.

Unified Modeling Language™ (UML)

The Unified Modeling Language™ (UML) has become the preferred graphical modeling language for designing object-oriented systems. In *Java How to Program, Fourth Edition*, we used the UML in optional sections only, and we used conventional flowchart segments and inheritance diagrams to reinforce the explanations. We have fully converted the diagrams in the book to be UML 1.4 compliant. In particular, we upgraded all the figures in the UML/OOD Elevator Simulation case study; we converted all the flowcharts in Chapters 4 and 5 on Control Statements, to UML activity diagrams; and we converted all the inheritance diagrams in Chapters 9, 10, 12–13 and 15 to UML class diagrams.

This *Fifth Edition* carefully tunes the optional (but highly recommended) case study we present on object-oriented design using the UML. The case study was submitted to a distinguished team of OOD/UML reviewers, including leaders in the field from Rational (the creators of the UML) and the Object Management Group (responsible for maintaining and evolving the UML). In the case study, we fully implement an elevator simulation. In the "Thinking About Objects" sections at the ends of Chapters 1–8, 10–14, 16 and 19, we present a carefully paced introduction to object-oriented design using the UML. We present a concise, simplified subset of the UML then guide the reader through a first design experience intended for the novice object-oriented designer/programmer. The case study is fully solved. It is not an exercise; rather, it is an end-to-end learning experience that concludes with a detailed walkthrough of the Java code. In each of the first five chapters, we concentrate on the "conventional" methodology of structured programming, because the objects that we build will use these structured-program pieces. We conclude each chapter with a "Thinking About Objects" section, in which we present an introduction to object-oriented design (OOD) using the UML. These "Thinking About Objects" sections help students develop an object-oriented design, so that they immediately can use the object-oriented programming concepts they begin learning in Chapter 8. In the first of these sections at the end of Chapter 1, we introduce basic concepts and terminology of OOD. In the optional

"Thinking About Objects" sections at the ends of Chapters 2–5, we consider more substantial issues, as we undertake a challenging problem with the techniques of OOD. We analyze a typical problem statement that requires a system to be built, determine the objects needed to implement that system, determine the attributes these objects need to have, determine the behaviors these objects need to exhibit and specify how the objects need to interact with one another to meet the system requirements. We accomplish this even before we discuss how to write Java programs. In Appendices D–F, we include a Java implementation of the object-oriented system we designed in the earlier chapters. This case study will help prepare students for the kinds of substantial projects they will encounter in industry. We employ a carefully developed, incremental object-oriented design process to produce a UML model for our elevator simulator. From this design, we produce a substantial working Java implementation using key programming notions, including classes, objects, encapsulation, visibility, composition and inheritance.

Discovering Design Patterns

These optional sections introduce popular object-oriented design patterns. Over the past decade, the software engineering industry has made significant progress in the field of *design patterns*—proven architectures for constructing flexible and maintainable object-oriented software.[2] Using design patterns can substantially reduce the complexity of the design process. We present several design patterns in Java, but these can be implemented in any object-oriented language, such as C++, C# or Visual Basic .NET. We describe several design patterns used by Sun Microsystems in the Java API. We use design patterns in many programs in this book, which we will identify in our "Discovering Design Patterns" sections. These programs provide examples of using design patterns to construct reliable, robust object-oriented software.

Teaching Approach

Java How to Program, Fifth Edition contains a rich collection of examples, exercises, and projects drawn from many fields to provide the student with a chance to solve interesting real-world problems. The book concentrates on the principles of good software engineering and stresses program clarity. We avoid arcane terminology and syntax specifications in favor of teaching by example. Our code examples have been tested on popular Java platforms. We are educators who teach edge-of-the-practice topics in industry classrooms worldwide. The text emphasizes good pedagogy.

Learning Java via the LIVE-CODE™ Approach

Java How to Program, 5/e, is loaded with LIVE-CODE™ examples. Each new concept is presented in the context of a complete, working example that is immediately followed by one or more sample executions showing the program's input/output dialog. This style exemplifies the way we teach and write about programming and is the focus of our multimedia *Cyber Classrooms* and Web-based training courses. We call this method of teaching and writing the LIVE-CODE™ *Approach. We use programming languages to teach pro-*

---

2.   Gamma, Erich, Richard Helm, Ralph Johnson, and John Vlissides. *Design Patterns; Elements of Reusable Object-Oriented Software.* (Massachusetts: Addison-Wesley, 1995).

gramming languages. Reading the examples in the text is much like typing and running them on a computer. We provide all the source code for the book's examples on both the accompanying CD and at www.deitel.com. We encourage you to run every example.

Java Programming with Applications and Swing from Chapter Two!
Java How to Program, 5/e, "jumps right into" programming Java applications with the Swing GUI components from Chapter 2. There is great stuff to be done in Java so let's get right to it! Java is not trivial by any means, but it's fun to program with and students can see immediate results. Students can get graphical, animated, multimedia-based, audio-intensive, multithreaded, database-intensive, network-based programs running quickly through Java's extensive class libraries of reusable components. They can implement impressive projects. They are typically more creative and productive in a one- or two-semester course than in C and C++ introductory courses.

World Wide Web Access
All of the source-code examples for *Java How to Program, 5/e,* (and our other publications) are available on the Internet as downloads from the following Web sites:

> www.deitel.com
> www.prenhall.com/deitel

Registration is quick and easy and the downloads are free. We suggest downloading all the examples, then running each program as you read the corresponding text. Making changes to the examples and immediately seeing the effects of those changes is a great way to enhance your Java learning experience.

Objectives
Each chapter begins with objectives that inform students of what to expect and give them an opportunity, after reading the chapter, to determine whether they have met the intended objectives. The objectives serve as confidence builders.

Quotations
The chapter objectives are followed by sets of quotations. Some are humorous, some are philosophical and some offer interesting insights. We have found that students enjoy relating the quotations to the chapter material. Many of the quotations are worth a second look *after* you read the chapters.

Outline
The chapter outline enables students to approach the material in a top-down fashion. Along with the chapter objectives, the outline helps students anticipate future topics and set a comfortable and effective learning pace.

23,341 Lines of Code in 219 Example Programs (with Program Outputs)
We present Java features in the context of complete, working Java programs. These LIVE-CODE™ programs range in size from just a few lines of code to substantial examples containing hundreds of lines of code. Each program is followed by a window containing the outputs produced when the program is run, so students can confirm that the programs run as expected. Relating outputs back to the program statements that produce those outputs is

an excellent way to learn and to reinforce concepts. Our programs exercise the diverse features of Java. The code is syntax colored with Java keywords, comments and other program text each appearing in different colors. This facilitates reading the code—students especially will appreciate the syntax coloring when they read the larger programs we present.

615 Illustrations/Figures

An abundance of charts, line drawings, programs and program outputs is included. We have converted all flowcharts to UML activity diagrams. We also use UML class diagrams to model the relationships between classes throughout the text.

534 Programming Tips

We have included programming tips to help students focus on important aspects of program development. We highlight hundreds of these tips in the form of *Good Programming Practices*, *Common Programming Errors*, *Error-Prevention Tips*, *Look-and-Feel Observations*, *Performance Tips*, *Portability Tips* and *Software Engineering Observations*. These tips and practices represent the best we have gleaned from a combined six decades of programming and teaching experience. One of our students—a mathematics major—told us that she feels this approach is like the highlighting of axioms, theorems, and corollaries in mathematics books; it provides a basis on which to build good software.

82 Good Programming Practices

Good Programming Practices are tips that call attention to techniques for writing clear programs. These techniques help students produce programs that are more readable, self-documenting and easier to maintain.

156 Common Programming Errors

Students learning a language—especially in their first programming course—tend to make certain kinds of errors frequently. Focusing on these Common Programming Errors reduces the likelihood that students will makes the same mistakes. It also shortens long lines outside instructors' offices during office hours!

50 Error-Prevention Tips

When we first designed this "tip type," we thought we would use it strictly to tell people how to test and debug Java programs. In fact, many of the tips describe aspects of Java that reduce the likelihood of "bugs" and thus simplify the testing and debugging processes.

36 Look-and-Feel Observations

We provide Look-and-Feel Observations to highlight graphical user interface conventions. These observations help students design their own graphical user interfaces in conformance with industry norms.

52 Performance Tips

In our experience, teaching students to write clear and understandable programs is by far the most important goal for a first programming course. But students want to write the programs that run the fastest, use the least memory, require the smallest number of keystrokes, or dazzle in other nifty ways. Students really care about performance. They want to know what they can do to "turbo charge" their programs. So we highlight opportunities for improving program performance—making programs run faster or minimizing the amount of memory that they occupy.

23 Portability Tips

One of Java's "claims to fame" is "universal" portability, so some programmers assume that if they implement an application in Java, the application will automatically be "perfect-ly" portable across all Java platforms. Unfortunately, this is not always the case. We include Portability Tips to help students write portable code and to provide insights on how Java achieves its high degree of portability. We had many more portability tips in our books, C How to Program *and* C++ How to Program. Java How to Program *has fewer of these tips be-cause Java is designed to be portable top-to-bottom (for the most part)—much less effort is required on the Java programmer's part to achieve portability than with C or C++.*

135 Software Engineering Observations

The object-oriented programming paradigm requires a complete rethinking about the way we build software. Java is an effective language for performing good software engineering. The Software Engineering Observations *highlight architectural and design issues that affect the construction of software systems, especially large-scale systems. Much of what the stu-dent learns here will be useful in upper-level courses and in industry as the student begins to work with large, complex real-world systems.*

Summary (954 Summary bullets)

Each chapter ends with additional pedagogical devices. We present a thorough, bullet-list-style summary of the chapter. On average, there are 38 summary bullets per chapter. This helps the students review and reinforce key concepts.

Terminology (2166 Terms)

We include in a *Terminology* section an alphabetized list of the important terms defined in the chapter—again, further reinforcement. On average, there are 87 terms per chapter.

437 Self-Review Exercises and Answers (Count Includes Separate Parts)

Extensive self-review exercises and answers are included for self-study. This gives the stu-dent a chance to build confidence with the material and prepare for the regular exercises. Students should be encouraged to do all the self-review exercises and check their answers.

858 Exercises (Count Includes Separate Parts)

Each chapter concludes with a set of exercises, including simple recall of important termi-nology and concepts; writing individual Java statements; writing small portions of Java methods and classes; writing complete Java methods, classes, applications and applets; and writing major term projects. The large number of exercises across a wide variety of areas enables instructors to tailor their courses to the unique needs of their audiences and to vary course assignments each semester. Instructors can use these exercises to form homework as-signments, short quizzes and major examinations. The solutions for most of the exercises are included on the *Instructor's Resource CD,* which is *available only to instructors* through their Prentice Hall representatives. [**NOTE: Please do not write to us requesting the In-structor's CD. Distribution of this ancillary is limited strictly to college professors teaching from the book. Instructors may obtain the solutions manual only from their Prentice Hall representatives.**] Students and professional readers can obtain solutions to approximately half the exercises in the book by purchasing the optional *Java 2 Multimedia Cyber Classroom, 5/e. The Cyber Classroom* offers many other features and is ideal for self study and reference. Also available is the boxed product, *The Complete Java 2 Training*

Course, 5/e, which includes both our textbook, *Java How to Program, 5/e*, and the *Java 2 Multimedia Cyber Classroom, 5/e*. All of our *Complete Training Course* products are available at bookstores and online booksellers, including www.informIT.com. If you already have the textbook, you can purchase the *Java 2 Multimedia Cyber Classroom, 5/e* (ISBN# 0-13-101769-1), separately at www.InformIT.com/cyberclassrooms.

Approximately 4800 Index Entries (with approximately 8000 Page References)

We have included an extensive *Index* at the back of the book. Using this resource, readers can search for any term or concept by keyword. The *Index* is useful to people reading the book for the first time and is especially useful to professional programmers who use the book as a reference. These index entries also appear as hyperlinks in the *Java 2 Multimedia Cyber Classroom, 5/e*.

"Double Indexing" of Java LIVE-CODE™ Examples

We have "double indexed" *Java How to Program*'s 219 LIVE-CODE™ examples. For every Java source-code program in the book, we took the figure caption and indexed it both alphabetically and as a subindex item under "Examples." This makes it easier to find examples using particular features.

Bibliography

An extensive bibliography of books, articles and Sun Microsystems Java 2 documentation is included to encourage further reading.

Software Included with Java How to Program, Fifth Edition

There are a number of for-sale Java development tools available. However, you do not need them to get started with Java. We wrote *Java How to Program, 5/e*, using only the *Java 2 Standard Edition Software Development Kit (J2SDK), version 1.4.1*. For your convenience, Sun's J2SDK 1.4.1 is included on the CD that accompanies this book. The current J2SDK version can always be downloaded from Sun's Java Web site java.sun.com/j2se. This site also contains the J2SDK documentation downloads.

With Sun's cooperation, we also were able to include on the CD a powerful Java integrated development environment (IDE)—*Sun ONE™ Studio 4, Community Edition*. *Sun ONE™ Studio 4, Community Edition*, is a professional IDE written in Java that includes a graphical user interface designer, code editor, compiler, visual debugger and more. The J2SDK must be installed before installing *Sun ONE™ Studio 4 Community Edition*. If you have any questions about using this software, please read the documentation on the CD, or read our *DIVE-INTO™ Series* publication *Dive Into Sun ONE Studio 4, Community Edition*. This document is available with the resources for *Java How to Program, 5/e*, at www.deitel.com/books/downloads.html.

The CD contains the book's examples (including the Elevator Case Study implementation) and an HTML Web page with links to the Deitel & Associates, Inc. Web site and the Prentice Hall Web site. If you have access to the Internet, this Web page can be loaded into your Web browser to give you quick access to all the resources. In addition, we provide several chapters and appendices from other Deitel publications. These include material on XHTML and Cascading Style Sheets (for use with Chapter 24, Servlets, and Chapter 25, JavaServer Pages), and material on Extensible Markup Language (XML) and Java's XML-processing APIs, which are now part of J2SE 1.4.

Ancillary Package for Java How to Program, Fifth Edition

Java How to Program, 5/e, has extensive ancillary materials for instructors. The *Instructor's Resource CD (IRCD)* contains the *Instructor's Manual* with solutions to the vast majority of the end-of-chapter exercises and a *Test Item File* of multiple-choice questions (approximately two per book section). In addition, we provide PowerPoint slides containing all the code and figures in the text, and bulleted items that summarize the key points in the text. Instructors can customize the slides. The PowerPoint slides are downloadable from www.deitel.com and are available as part of Prentice Hall's *Companion Web Site* (www.prenhall.com/deitel) for *Java How to Program, 5/e*, which offers resources for both instructors and students. For instructors, the *Companion Web Site* offers a *Syllabus Manager*, which helps instructors plan courses interactively and create online syllabi.

Students also benefit from the functionality of the *Companion Web Site*. Book-specific resources for students include:

- Customizable PowerPoint® slides
- Example source code
- Reference materials from the book appendices (such as operator-precedence chart, character set and Web resources)

Chapter-specific resources available for students include:

- Chapter objectives
- Highlights (e.g., chapter summary)
- Outline
- Tips (e.g., *Common Programming Errors*, *Error-Prevention Tips*, *Good Programming Practices*, *Look-and-Feel Observations*, *Portability Tips*, *Performance Tips* and *Software Engineering Observations*)
- Online Study Guide—contains additional short-answer self-review exercises (e.g., true/false) with answers and provides immediate feedback to the student

Students can track their results and course performance on quizzes using the *Student Profile* feature, which records and manages all feedback and results from tests taken on the *Companion Web Site*. To access the *Companion Web Site*, visit www.prenhall.com/deitel.

Java in the Lab

This lab manual (full title: *Java in the Lab, Lab Manual to Accompany Java How to Program, 5/e*; ISBN# is 0-13-101631-8[3]) complements *Java How to Program, 5/e*, and the optional *Java 2 Multimedia Cyber Classroom, 5/e*, with hands-on lab assignments designed to reinforce students' understanding of lecture material. This lab manual is designed for closed laboratories, which are regularly scheduled classes supervised by an instructor. Closed laboratories provide an excellent learning environment because students can use concepts presented in class to solve carefully designed lab problems. Instructors are better able to gauge the students' understanding of the material by monitoring the students' progress in lab. This lab manual also can be used for open laboratories, homework and for self-study.

---

3. *Java How to Program, 5/e*, and the lab manual also are available together in a value pack (ISBN# 0-13-102719-0).

Java in the Lab focuses on Chapters 1–12, 15 and 17 of *Java How to Program, 5/e*. Each chapter in the lab manual is divided into *Prelab Activities*, *Lab Exercises* and *Postlab Activities*.[4] Each chapter contains objectives that introduce the lab's key topics and an assignment checklist that allows students to mark which exercises the instructor has assigned. The lab manual pages are perforated, so students can submit their answers (if required).

Solutions to the lab manual's *Prelab Activities*, *Lab Exercises* and *Postlab Activities* are available in electronic form. Instructors can obtain these materials from their regular Prentice Hall representatives; the solutions are not available to students.

Prelab Activities

Prelab Activities are intended to be completed by students after studying each chapter in *Java How to Program, 5/e*. *Prelab Activities* test students' understanding of the material presented in the textbook, and prepare students for the programming exercises in the lab session. The exercises focus on important terminology and programming concepts and are effective for self-review. Prelab Activities include *Matching Exercises*, *Fill-in-the-Blank Exercises*, *Short-Answer Questions*, *Programming-Output Exercises* (determine what short code segments do without actually running the program) and *Correct-the-Code Exercises* (identify and correct all errors in short code segments).

Lab Exercises

The most important section in each chapter is the Lab Exercises. These exercises teach students how to apply the material learned in *Java How to Program, 5/e*, and prepare them for writing Java programs. Each lab contains one or more lab exercises and a debugging problem. The *Lab Exercises* contain the following:

- *Lab Objectives* highlight specific concepts on which the lab exercise focuses.
- *Problem Descriptions* provide the details of the exercise and hints to help students implement the program.
- *Sample Outputs* illustrate the desired program behavior, which further clarifies the problem descriptions and aids the students with writing programs.
- *Program Templates* take complete Java programs and replace key lines of code with comments describing the missing code.
- *Problem-Solving Tips* highlight key issues that students need to consider when solving the lab exercises.
- *Follow-Up Questions and Activities* ask students to modify solutions to lab exercises, write new programs that are similar to their lab-exercise solutions or explain the implementation choices that were made when solving lab exercises.
- *Debugging Problems* consist of blocks of code that contain syntax errors and/or logic errors. These alert students to the types of errors they are likely to encounter while programming.

---

4. We expect few introductory classes to advance beyond Chapter 11 of this lab manual. For this reason, the labs in Chapters 12, 15 and 17 do not contain the extensive sets of activities available in the previous chapters. Nevertheless, instructors will be able to conduct effective labs using the exercises we have included on these more complex topics. Instructors with special requirements should write to deitel@deitel.com.

Postlab Activities

Professors typically assign *Postlab Activities* to reinforce key concepts or to provide students with more programming experience outside the lab. *Postlab Activities* test the students' understanding of the *Prelab* and *Lab Exercise* material, and ask students to apply the knowledge to creating programs from scratch. The section provides two types of programming activities: coding exercises and programming challenges. Coding exercises are short and serve as review after the *Prelab Activities* and *Lab Exercises* have been completed. These ask students to write programs or program segments using key concepts from the textbook. *Programming Challenges* allow students to apply the knowledge they have gained in class to substantial programming exercises. Hints, sample outputs and/or pseudocode are provided to aid students with these problems. Students who complete the *Programming Challenges* for a chapter successfully have mastered the chapter material. Answers to the programming challenges are available at www.deitel.com/books/downloads.html.

Java 2 Multimedia Cyber Classroom, 5/e, and *The Complete Java 2 Training Course, 5/e*

We have updated our optional interactive multimedia version of the book—*The Java 2 Multimedia Cyber Classroom, 5/e* (CD for Windows®)—with considerable additional audio, including the new material on database development with JDBC and Web-applications development with servlets and JavaServer Pages. This resource is loaded with electronic learning and reference features. The *Cyber Classroom* is packaged with the textbook at a discount in *The Complete Java 2 Training Course, 5/e* (ISBN# 0-13-101766-7). If you already have the book and would like to purchase the *Cyber Classroom* separately, please visit www.InformIT.com/cyberclassrooms; the ISBN number for the *Cyber Classroom* is 0-13-101769-1. Deitel™ *Cyber Classrooms* are generally available in CD and various popular Web-based training formats.

The CD provides an introduction in which the authors overview the *Cyber Classroom*'s features. The textbook's 219 LIVE-CODE™ example Java programs truly "come alive" in the *Cyber Classroom*. When viewing a program, simply click the lightning-bolt icon to run the program. You will immediately see the program's output. If you want to modify a program and see the effects of your changes, simply clicking the floppy-disk icon causes the source code to be "lifted off" the CD and "dropped into" one of your own directories so you can edit the code, recompile the program and run your new version. Click the audio icon to hear one of the authors "walk you through" the code. In addition, the *Cyber Classroom* contains the full-text of *Java How to Program, 5/e*, in fully-searchable format.

The *Cyber Classroom* also provides post-assessment exams (with answers) for each chapter in the book. These exams are powerful features that allow users to gauge their understanding of the programming concepts presented in the chapters. Each exam question hyperlinks to the section in the book from which the question was derived. This allows users to review the appropriate chapter material before or after answering the question. A chart is provided that summarizes the user's exam results by chapter.

The *Cyber Classroom* also provides navigational aids, including extensive additional hyperlinking for easy navigation. The *Cyber Classroom* is browser based, so it remembers sections that you have visited recently and allows you to move forward or backward among them. The thousands of index entries are hyperlinked to their text occurrences. You can use the "find" feature to locate occurrences of a term throughout the text. The Table of Contents entries are "hot," so clicking a chapter or section name takes you immediately to that chapter or section.

Students like the fact that solutions to approximately half the exercises in the book are included with the *Cyber Classroom*. Studying and running these extra programs is a nice way for students to enhance their LIVE-CODE™ learning experience.

Students and professional users of our *Cyber Classrooms* tell us that they like the interactivity and that the *Cyber Classroom* is a powerful reference tool. We received an e-mail from a person who said that he lives "in the boonies" and cannot take a live course at a university, so the *Cyber Classroom* provided a nice solution to his educational needs.

Professors tell us that their students enjoy using the *Cyber Classroom*, and consequently spend more time on the courses, mastering more of the material than in textbook-only courses. For a complete list of the available and forthcoming *Cyber Classrooms* and *Complete Training Courses*, see the *Deitel™ Series* page at the beginning of this book, the product listing and ordering information at the end of this book or visit www.deitel.com, www.prenhall.com/deitel or www.InformIT.com/deitel.

Advanced Java™ 2 Platform How to Program

Our companion book—***Advanced Java 2 Platform How to Program***—focuses on the ***Java 2 Platform, Enterprise Edition (J2EE)***, presents advanced Java 2 Platform Standard Edition features and introduces the ***Java 2 Platform, Micro Edition (J2ME)***. This book is intended for developers and upper-level university students in advanced courses who already know Java and want a deeper treatment and understanding of the language. The book features our signature LIVE-CODE™ approach of complete working programs and contains over 37,000 lines of code. The programs are more substantial than those presented in *Java How to Program, Fifth Edition*. The book expands the coverage of Java Database Connectivity (JDBC), servlets and JavaServer Pages (JSP) from *Java How to Program, Fifth Edition*. The book also covers emerging and more advanced Java technologies of concern to enterprise application developers, including Model-View-Controller; Java 2D and Java 3D; JavaBeans Component Model; Security; Java 2 Micro Edition (J2ME) and Wireless Internet; Remote Method Invocation (RMI); Enterprise JavaBeans (EJBs); Java Message Service (JMS); Jini; JavaSpaces; Jiro; Java Management Extensions (JMX); Common Object Request Broker Architecture (CORBA); Peer-to-Peer Networking; Web Services; XML and Java Native Interface (JNI).

Java Web Services for Experienced Programmers

Part of the new *Deitel Developer Series* for computer professionals, Java *Web Services for Experienced Programmers* uses our proven LIVE-CODE™ approach to teach the latest XML and Java technologies for building and integrating Web services, including the *Java Web Services Developer Pack*. This book is designed for industry professionals who require in-depth coverage of Java Web-services technologies. The book is also suitable for upper-level computer science courses in Web services or as a supplement to courses in distributed computing and advanced Java programming. Instructors should contact their Prentice Hall representatives to obtain examination copies. Topics covered include XML; Document Type Definitions (DTDs); Document Object Model (DOM™) and the Java API for XML Processing (JAXP); eXtensible Stylesheets Transformations (XSLT™) and the Transformation API for XML (TrAX); Simple Object Access Protocol (SOAP); Web Services Description Language (WSDL); Universal Description, Discovery and Integration (UDDI) and the Java API for XML Registries (JAXR); Java API for XML-based Remote Procedure Calls (JAX-RPC); Java API for XML Messaging (JAXM) and the SOAP with Attachments API for Java (SAAJ); Web Services Security with Secure Sockets Layer (SSL), XML Signature, XML Encryption, XML Key Management Specification (XKMS), Security Assertions Markup Language (SAML) and eXtensible Access Control Markup Language (XACML); and Wireless Web Services with Java 2 Micro Edition (J2ME™).

Course Management Systems: Blackboard™, WebCT™, CourseCompass ^SM^ and Premium CourseCompass ^SM^

Selected content from the Deitels' introductory programming language *How to Program* series, including *Java How to Program, 5/e*,[5] is available to integrate into various popular course management systems, including CourseCompass, Blackboard and WebCT. An enhanced version of CourseCompass, called Premium CourseCompass, will be available for *Java How to Program, 5/e*, for Summer 2003 courses. Course management systems help faculty create, manage and use sophisticated Web-based educational tools and programs. Instructors can save hours of inputting data by using Deitel course-management-systems content.

Blackboard, CourseCompass and WebCT offer:

- **Features to create and customize an online course**, such as areas to post course information (e.g., policies, syllabi, announcements, assignments, grades, performance evaluations and progress tracking), class and student management tools, a gradebook, reporting tools, page tracking, a calendar and assignments.

- **Communication tools** to help create and maintain interpersonal relationships between students and instructors, including chat rooms, whiteboards, document sharing, bulletin boards and private e-mail.

- **Flexible testing tools** that allow an instructor to create online quizzes and tests from questions directly linked to the text, and that grade and track results effectively. All tests can be inputted into the gradebook for efficient course management. WebCT also allows instructors to administer timed online quizzes.

- **Support materials** for instructors are available in print and online formats.

In addition to the types of tools found in Blackboard and WebCT, CourseCompass from Prentice Hall includes:

- **CourseCompass course home page**, which makes the course as easy to navigate as a book. An expandable table of contents allows instructors to view course content at a glance and to link to any section.

- **Hosting on Prentice Hall's centralized servers**, which allows course administrators to avoid separate licensing fees or server-space issues. Access to Prentice Hall technical support is available.

---

5. The entire text of *Java How to Program, 5/e*, is included in the e-Book included with Premium CourseCompass.

- **"How Do I" online-support sections** are available for users who need help personalizing course sites, including step-by-step instructions for adding PowerPoint® slides, video and more.

- **Instructor Quick Start Guide** helps instructors create online courses using a simple, step-by-step process.

Premium CourseCompass Course Management System

Premium CourseCompass integrates content from several sources, including Deitel *Cyber Classrooms*, *How to Program* books and *Companion Web Sites* with CourseCompass courseware—providing enhanced content to CourseCompass users. Premium CourseCompass includes:

- **Pre-Loaded DEITEL™ Content in a Customizable Interface.** An instructor can aggregate and customize all course materials. This feature includes the e-Book, a searchable digital version of *Java How to Program, 5/e*, including full-color graphics and downloadable PowerPoint® slides.

- **All the Interactivity of the *Cyber Classroom*.** Students can work with code and receive the added benefit of 17+ hours of detailed audio descriptions of thousands of lines of code to help reinforce concepts. Every code example from *Java How to Program, 5/e*, is included.

- **Abundant Self-Assessment and Complete *Test-Item File*.** Use or edit hundreds of pre-loaded assessments, or upload your own. Assessments include self-review exercises, programming exercises (half with answers included) and test questions. Instructors choose which questions to assign, and students receive immediate feedback. Instructors can collect students' work and track their progress in an online gradebook.

To view free online demonstrations and learn more about these Course Management Systems, that support Deitel content, visit the following Web sites:

- Blackboard: `www.blackboard.com` and `www.prenhall.com/blackboard`

- WebCT: `www.webct.com` and `www.prenhall.com/webct`

- CourseCompass: `www.coursecompass.com` and `www.prenhall.com/coursecompass`

Computer Science AP Courses Switching to Java in Fall 2003

The AP Computer Science Program recently decided to move the AP computer science curriculum from C++ to Java starting with classes in the Fall of 2003. The first Java-based AP Computer-Science exams will be administered in the Spring of 2004. *Java How to Program, 5/e*, is a suitable textbook for instructors teaching AP Computer-Science classes and for preparing students to take the corresponding exams. While writing this book, we carefully reviewed the goals of the AP Computer Science A and AB exams, to ensure that *Java How to Program, 5/e*, covers the information required for the exams. At the time of this publication, the syllabi for the these exams had not yet been finalized. Instructors and students interested in preparing for these exams should visit:

`www.deitel.com/books/jHTP5/Java_AP_Exam.html`

dedicated to the use of *Java How to Program, 5/e*, in the Computer Science AP curriculum. We will update this site regularly with additional information about the exams. For detailed information on the Computer Science AP curriculum, please visit

apcentral.collegeboard.com

Deitel e-Learning Initiatives

e-Books and Support for Wireless Devices

Wireless devices will have an enormous role in the future of the Internet. Given recent bandwidth enhancements and the emergence of 2.5 and 3G technologies, it is projected that, within a few years, more people will access the Internet through wireless devices than through desktop computers. Deitel & Associates is committed to wireless accessibility and recently published *Wireless Internet & Mobile Business How to Program*. To fulfill the needs of a wide range of customers, we currently are developing our content both in traditional print formats and in newly developed electronic formats, such as wireless e-books so that students and professors can access content virtually anytime, anywhere. For periodic updates on these initiatives subscribe to the *Deitel™ Buzz Online* e-mail newsletter, www.deitel.com/newsletter/subscribe.html or visit www.deitel.com.

e-Matter

Deitel & Associates is partnering with Prentice Hall's parent company, Pearson PLC, and its information technology Web site, www.InformIT.com, to launch the DEITEL™ e-Matter series at www.InformIT.com/deitel in 2003. This series will provide professors, students and professionals with an additional source of information on programming and software topics. e-Matter consists of stand-alone sections taken from published texts, forthcoming texts or pieces written during the Deitel research-and-development process. Developing e-Matter based on pre-publication books allows us to offer significant amounts of the material to early adopters for use in academic and corporate courses.

Deitel and InformIT Newsletters

Deitel Newsletter

Our own free e-mail newsletter, the *DEITEL™ BUZZ ONLINE*, includes commentary on industry trends and developments, links to free articles and resources from our published books and upcoming publications, product-release schedules, challenges, anecdotes, information on our corporate instructor-led training courses and more. To subscribe, visit

www.deitel.com/newsletter/subscribe.html

Deitel Column in the InformIT Newsletters

Deitel & Associates, Inc., contributes to two free *InformIT* weekly e-mail newsletters, currently subscribed to by more than 1,000,000 IT professionals worldwide.

- *Editorial Newsletter*—Contains dozens of new articles per week on various IT topics, including programming, advanced computing, networking, business, Web development, software engineering, operating systems and more. Deitel & Associates contributes 2–3 articles per week taken from our extensive content base or from material being created during our research and development process.

- *Promotional Newsletter*—Features weekly specials and discounts on most Pearson publications. Each week a new DEITEL™ product is featured along with information about our corporate instructor-led training courses.

To subscribe, visit `www.InformIT.com`.

The New DEITEL™ Developer Series

Deitel & Associates, Inc., is making a major commitment to covering leading-edge technologies for industry software professionals through the launch of our *DEITEL™ Developer Series*. *Web Services A Technical Introduction* and *Java Web Services for Experienced Programmers* are among the first books in the series. These will be followed by *Java 2 Enterprise Edition, Java 2 Micro Edition, .NET A Technical Introduction, ASP .NET with Visual Basic .NET for Experienced Programmers, ASP .NET with C# for Experienced Programmers* and many more. Please visit `www.deitel.com` for continuous updates on all published and forthcoming *DEITEL™ Developer Series* titles.

The *DEITEL™ Developer Series* is divided into three subseries. The *A Technical Introduction* subseries provides IT managers and developers with detailed overviews of emerging technologies. The *A Programmer's Introduction* subseries is designed to teach the fundamentals of new languages and software technologies to programmers and novices from the ground up; these books discuss programming fundamentals, followed by brief introductions to more sophisticated topics. The *For Experienced Programmers* subseries is designed for seasoned developers seeking an intermediate-level treatment of new programming languages and technologies, without the encumbrance of introductory material; the books in this subseries move quickly to in-depth coverage of the features of the programming languages and software technologies being covered.

Tour of the Book

You are about to study one of today's most exciting and rapidly developing computer programming languages. Mastering Java will help you develop powerful business and personal computer-applications software. In this section, we take a tour of the many capabilities of Java you will study in *Java How to Program, Fifth Edition*.

Chapter 1—Introduction to Computers, the Internet and the Web—discusses what computers are, how they work and how they are programmed. The chapter gives a brief history of the development of programming languages from machine languages, to assembly languages, to high-level languages. The origin of the Java programming language is discussed. The chapter includes an introduction to a typical Java programming environment. The chapter also introduces object technology, the Unified Modeling Language and design patterns.

Chapter 2—Introduction to Java Applications—provides a lightweight introduction to programming *applications* in the Java programming language. The chapter introduces nonprogrammers to basic programming concepts and constructs. The programs in this chapter illustrate how to display data on the screen to the user and how to obtain data from the user at the keyboard. Some of the input and output is performed by using *graphical user interface (GUI)* components. Chapter 2 also provides detailed treatments of *decision making* and *arithmetic operations*.

Chapter 3—Introduction to Java Applets—introduces Java *applets*, which are Java programs designed to be transported over the Internet and executed in Web browsers (like Netscape Navigator and Microsoft Internet Explorer). The chapter shows several of the demonstration applets supplied with the J2SDK. We then write Java applets that perform tasks similar to the programs of Chapter 2, and we explain the similarities and differences between applets and applications.

Chapter 4—Control Statements: Part 1—focuses on the program-development process. The chapter discusses how to take a *problem statement* and from it develop a working Java program, including performing intermediate steps in *pseudocode*. The chapter introduces some primitive types and simple control statements for decision making (`if` and `if...else`) and repetition (`while`). We examine counter-controlled repetition and sentinel-controlled repetition, and introduce Java's increment, decrement and assignment operators. The chapter uses simple UML activity diagrams to show the flow of control through each of the control statements.

Chapter 5—Control Statements: Part 2—continues the discussions of Java control statements with examples of the `for` repetition statement, the `do...while` repetition statement, the `switch` selection statement, the `break` statement and the `continue` statement. The chapter also contains a discussion of Java logical operators.

Chapter 6—Methods—takes a deeper look inside objects. Objects contain data called fields and executable units called methods. We discuss class-library methods and build our own methods. For computer-science courses, the chapter also presents a discussion of recursion. The techniques presented in Chapter 6 are essential to the production of properly structured programs, especially the larger programs that system programmers and application programmers are likely to develop. The topic of method overloading (i.e., allowing multiple methods to have the same name as long as they have different "signatures") is motivated and explained clearly. We also introduce *events* and *event handling*.

Chapter 7—Arrays—explores processing lists and tables of values. Arrays in Java are objects, further evidence of Java's commitment to object orientation. We discuss the structuring of data into arrays of data items of the same type. The chapter presents numerous examples of both single-dimensional arrays and multidimensional arrays. Examples in the chapter investigate common array manipulations, printing histograms, passing arrays to methods and an introduction to the field of survey data analysis (with simple statistics). A feature of this chapter is the discussion of elementary sorting and searching techniques and the presentation of binary searching as a dramatic improvement over linear searching.

Chapter 8—Object-Based Programming—begins our deeper discussion of classes. The chapter represents a wonderful opportunity for teaching data abstraction the "right way"—through a language (Java) expressly devoted to implementing new types. The chapter focuses on the essence and terminology of classes and objects. The chapter discusses implementing Java classes, accessing class members, enforcing information hiding with access modifiers, separating interface from implementation, using access methods and utility methods and initializing objects with constructors. The chapter discusses declaring and using constants, *composition*, the `this` reference, `static` class members and examples of popular abstract data types such as stacks and queues. The chapter introduces the `package` statement and discusses how to create reusable packages.

Chapter 9—Object-Oriented Programming: Inheritance—introduces one of the most fundamental capabilities of object-oriented programming languages, inheritance, which is a form of software reusability in which new classes are developed quickly and easily by absorbing the capabilities of existing classes and adding appropriate new capabilities. The chapter discusses the notions of superclasses and subclasses, access modifier `protected`, direct superclasses, indirect superclasses, use of constructors in superclasses and subclasses, and software engineering with inheritance. The chapter compares inheritance ("is a" relationships) with composition ("has a" relationships).

Chapter 10—Object-Oriented Programming: Polymorphism—deals with another fundamental capability of object-oriented programming, namely polymorphic behavior. This style of programming is typically used to implement today's popular GUI frameworks, such as Java's Swing. This chapter distinguishes between `abstract` classes and concrete classes, and introduces interfaces—Java's replacement for the dangerous (albeit powerful) feature of C++ called multiple inheritance. The chapter presents the powerful concept of *nested classes* that help hide implementation details. Then, the chapter demonstrates our first GUI-based applications as part of a more complete introduction to event handling. In this section, we use nested classes to define the event handlers for several GUI components. A feature of this chapter is its three polymorphism case studies—a payroll system, a shape hierarchy headed up by an `abstract` class and a shape hierarchy headed up by an interface.

Chapter 11—Strings and Characters—deals with processing words, sentences, characters and groups of characters. We present classes `String`, `StringBuffer`, `Character` and `StringTokenizer`. We also present Java's API for regular expressions (new to J2SE 1.4), which enables programs to search strings for sequences of characters that match specified patterns.

Chapter 12—Graphics and Java2D—is the first of several chapters that present Java's graphical and multimedia capabilities. We discuss graphics contexts and graphics objects; drawing strings, characters and bytes; color and font control; screen manipulation and paint modes and drawing lines, rectangles, rounded rectangles, three-dimensional rectangles, ovals, arcs and polygons. We introduce the Java2D API, which provides powerful graphics capabilities. Figure 12.22 is an example of how easy it is to use the Java2D API to create complex graphics effects such as textures and gradients.[6]

Chapter 13—Graphical User Interface Components: Part 1—introduces several of Java's *Swing components* for creating programs with user-friendly graphical user interfaces (GUIs). These *platform-independent* GUI components are written entirely in Java, providing them with great flexibility. Swing components can be customized to look like the computer platform on which the program executes, or they can use the standard Java look-and-feel to provide an identical user interface on all computer platforms. GUI development is a huge topic, so we divided it into two chapters. These chapters cover the material in sufficient depth to enable you to build rich user interfaces. The chapter illustrates GUI principles, the `javax.swing` hierarchy, labels, buttons, lists, textfields, combo boxes, checkboxes, radio buttons, panels, handling mouse events, handling keyboard events and layout managers to position components. The chapter enhances our discussions of event handling.

Chapter 14—Graphical User Interface Components: Part 2—continues the Swing discussion started in Chapter 13. Through its programs, tables and line drawings, the

---

6.   Our companion book, *Advanced Java 2 Platform How to Program*, presents the Java 3D API for building three-dimensional worlds.

chapter illustrates GUI design principles, textareas, extending Swing components, sliders, windows, menus, pop-up menus, changing the look-and-feel, multiple-document interfaces, tabbed panes and using advanced layout managers.[7]

Chapter 15—Exception Handling—is one of the most important chapters in the book from the standpoint of building "mission-critical" or "business-critical" applications. Programmers need to be concerned with, "What happens when the component I call on to do a job experiences difficulty? How will that component signal that it had a problem?" To use a Java component, you need to know not only how that component behaves when "things go well," but also what *exceptions* that component *throws* when "things go poorly." The chapter distinguishes between rather serious system `Errors` and `Exceptions`. The chapter discusses the vocabulary of exception handling, including *try blocks*, *catch clauses* and *finally clauses*. The chapter also introduces the new chained-exception facility in J2SE 1.4. The material in this chapter is crucial to many of the examples in the remainder of the book.

Chapter 16—Multithreading—deals with developing Java programs that can perform multiple activities concurrently. Computers used to be built with a single, rather expensive processor. Today, processors are becoming so inexpensive that it is possible to build computers with many processors that work in parallel—such computers are called *multiprocessors*. The trend is clearly towards computers that can perform many tasks in parallel. As we will see, multithreading is effective even on single-processor systems. This chapter presents multithreaded programs that demonstrate the problems that can occur in concurrent programming. A feature of the chapter is the extensive set of examples that show these problems and how to solve them. The chapter discusses threads and thread methods. It walks through the various thread states and state transitions with a graphical representation of a thread's life cycle. We discuss thread priorities and thread scheduling. We examine a producer/consumer relationship without synchronization, observe the problems that occur and solve the problem with thread synchronization. We implement a producer/consumer relationship with a circular buffer and proper synchronization with a monitor. We discuss daemon threads that "hang around" and perform tasks when processor time is available. We discuss interface `Runnable` which enables objects to run as threads without having to subclass class `Thread`.

Chapter 17—Files and Streams—deals with input/output that is accomplished through streams of data directed to and from files. In this chapter, we translate objects into a persistent format. Being able to store data in files or move it across networks (Chapter 18) makes it possible for programs to save data and to communicate with each other. The chapter begins with an introduction to the data hierarchy from bits, to bytes, to fields, to records, to files. Next, Java's simple view of files and streams is presented. We show how programs pass data to secondary storage devices, like disks, and how programs retrieve data already stored on those devices. We discuss class `File` which programs use to obtain information about files and directories. We explain how objects can be output to, and input from, secondary storage devices. We also introduce the high-performance, New I/O (NIO) APIs (introduced in J2SE 1.4).

---

7. Chapters 1–6 of *Advanced Java 2 Platform How to Program* present more advanced GUI concepts.

Chapter 18—Networking—deals with Java programs that communicate over computer networks. This chapter presents Java's lowest level networking capabilities. The chapter examples illustrate an applet interacting with the browser in which it executes, creating a mini Web browser, communicating between two Java programs using streams-based sockets and communicating between two Java programs using packets of data. A key feature of the chapter is the implementation of a collaborative client/server Tic-Tac-Toe game in which two clients play Tic-Tac-Toe against each other arbitrated by a multi-threaded server—great stuff! The capstone example in the chapter is the Deitel Messenger case study, which simulates many of today's popular instant-messaging applications that enable computer users to communicate with friends, relatives and coworkers over the Internet. This 1,130-line, multithreaded, client/server case study uses most of the programming techniques presented up to this point in the book. The chapter also continues our discussion of J2SE 1.4's NIO APIs with an introduction to selectors and non-blocking I/O for implementing high-performance network servers.[8]

Chapter 19—Multimedia: Images, Animation and Audio—presents some of Java's capabilities for making programs come alive through multimedia. The chapter discusses images and image manipulation, audio and animation. We present a LIVE-CODE image-map application with the icons from the programming tips shown earlier in the preface and that appear throughout the book. As the user moves the mouse pointer across the icons, the tip type is displayed. Once you have read the chapter, you will be eager to try out all these techniques, so we have included many exercises to challenge and entertain you.

Chapter 20—Data Structures—is particularly valuable in second- and third-level university courses. The chapter discusses the techniques used to create and manipulate dynamic data structures, such as linked lists, stacks, queues and trees. For each type of data structure, we present examples with sample outputs. Although it is valuable to know how these classes are implemented, Java programmers will quickly discover that most of the data structures they need are available in class libraries, such as Java's own `java.util` that we discuss in Chapters 21–22.

Chapter 21—Java Utilities Package and Bit Manipulation—presents several `java.util` classes and discusses Java's bit-manipulation operators. One particularly useful class is `Vector`—a dynamic array that can grow and shrink as necessary. We also discuss `Stack`, `Hashtable`, `Properties`, `Random` and `BitSet`.

Chapter 22—Collections—discusses the `java.util` classes of the Collections API that provide predefined implementations of many of the data structures discussed in Chapter 20. Collections provide Java programmers with a standard set of data structures for storing and retrieving data and a standard set of algorithms (i.e., procedures) that allow programmers to manipulate the data (such as searching for particular data items and sorting data into ascending or descending order). The chapter examples demonstrate collections, such as linked lists, trees, maps and sets, and algorithms for searching, sorting, finding the maximum value, finding the minimum value and so on.

Chapter 23—Java Database Connectivity with JDBC™—discusses Java's support for databases. Today's most popular database systems are relational databases. We present

---

8. Our companion book, *Advanced Java 2 Platform How to Program*, offers a much deeper treatment of networking and distributed computing, with topics including remote method invocation (RMI), Java 2 Enterprise Edition, wireless Java (and the Java 2 Micro Edition) and Common Object Request Broker Architecture (CORBA).

examples using IBM's Cloudscape—a pure-Java database management system. This chapter introduces JDBC and uses it to connect to a Cloudscape database, then to manipulate its content. We use the Structured Query Language (SQL) to extract information from, and insert information into, a database. The following chapters on servlets and JavaServer Pages use the techniques shown in this chapter to build data-driven Web applications.

Chapter 24—Servlets—discusses servlets, which typically extend the functionality of Web servers. Servlets are effective for developing Web-based solutions that interact with databases on behalf of clients, dynamically generate custom content to be displayed by browsers, and maintain unique session information for each client. The Java servlet API allows developers to add functionality to Web servers for handling client requests. Servlets also are reusable across Web servers and across platforms. This chapter demonstrates the Web's request/response mechanism (primarily with HTTP `get` and `post` requests), redirecting requests to other resources and interacting with databases through JDBC. The chapter features three-tier client/server application that tracks users' responses to a survey.

Chapter 25—JavaServer Pages (JSP)—introduces an extension of servlet technology called JavaServer Pages (JSP). JSPs enable delivery of dynamically generated Web content and are used primarily by Web designers and others who are not familiar with Java programming. JSPs may contain Java code in the form of scriptlets. To increase performance, each JSP is compiled into a Java servlet—this normally occurs the first time a JSP is requested by a client. Subsequent client requests are fulfilled by the compiled servlet. This chapter features a three-tier client/server guest-book application that stores guest information in a database.

Appendix A—Operator Precedence Chart—lists each of the Java operators and indicates their relative precedence and associativity.

Appendix B—ASCII Character Set—lists the characters of the ASCII (American Standard Code for Information Interchange) character set and indicates the character code value for each. Java uses the Unicode character set with 16-bit characters for representing all of the characters in the world's "commercially significant" languages. Unicode includes ASCII as a subset.

Appendix C—Number Systems—discusses the binary (base 2), decimal (base 10), octal (base 8) and hexadecimal (base 16) number systems. This material is valuable for introductory courses in computer science and computer engineering.

Appendices D–F contain the implementation of our case study on Object-Oriented Design with the UML. These are discussed in the overview of the case study.

Appendix G—Unicode—discusses the Unicode character set, which enables Java to display information in many languages. The appendix provides a sample Java program that displays "Welcome to Unicode" in several different languages.

(Optional) A Tour of the Case Study on Object-Oriented Design with the UML

In this and the next section, we tour the two optional major features of the book—the optional case study of object-oriented design with the UML and our introduction to design patterns. The case study involving object-oriented design with the UML is an important addition to *Java How to Program, Fifth Edition*. This tour previews the contents of the "Thinking About Objects" sections and discusses how they relate to the case study. After completing this case study, you will have completed an object-oriented design and implementation for a significant Java application.

Section 1.15—*Thinking About Objects: Introduction to Object Technology and the Unified Modeling Language*

This section introduces the object-oriented design case study with the UML. We provide a general background of what objects are and how they interact with other objects. We also discuss briefly the state of the software-engineering industry and how the UML has influenced object-oriented analysis and design processes.

Section 2.9—*(Optional Case Study) Thinking About Objects: Examining the Problem Statement*

Our case study begins with a *problem statement* that specifies the requirements for a system that we will create. In this case study, we design and implement a simulation of an elevator system in a two-story building. We provide the design of our elevator system after investigating the structure and behavior of object-oriented systems in general. We discuss how the UML will facilitate the design process in subsequent "Thinking About Objects" sections by providing us with several types of diagrams to model our system. Finally, we provide a list of URL and book references on object-oriented design with the UML. You might find these references helpful as you proceed through our case-study presentation.

Section 3.7—*(Optional Case Study) Thinking About Objects: Identifying the Classes in the Problem Statement*

In this section, we begin to design the elevator simulation. We identify the classes, or "building blocks," of our simulation by extracting the nouns and noun phrases from the problem statement. We arrange these classes into a UML class diagram that describes the class structure of our simulation. The class diagram also describes relationships, known as *associations*, among classes (for example, a person has an association with the elevator, because the person rides the elevator).

Section 4.14—*(Optional Case Study) Thinking About Objects: Identifying Class Attributes*

A class contains both *attributes* (data) and *operations* (behaviors). This section focuses on the attributes of the classes discussed in Section 3.7. As we see in later sections, changes in an object's attributes often affect the behavior of that object. To determine the attributes for the classes in our case study, we extract the adjectives describing the nouns and noun phrases (which defined our classes) from the problem statement, then place the attributes in the class diagram we create in Section 3.7.

Section 5.11—*(Optional Case Study) Thinking About Objects: Identifying Objects' States and Activities*

An object, at any given time, occupies a specific condition called a *state*. A *state transition* occurs when that object receives a message to change state. The UML provides the *state-chart diagram*, which identifies the set of possible states that an object may occupy and models that object's state transitions. An object also has an *activity*—the work performed by an object in its lifetime. The UML provides the *activity diagram*—a flowchart that models an object's *activity*. In this section, we use both types of diagrams to begin modeling specific behavioral aspects of our elevator simulation, such as how a person rides the elevator and how the elevator responds when a button is pressed on a given floor.

Section 6.15—(Optional Case Study) Thinking About Objects: Identifying Class Operations

In this section, we identify the operations, or services, of our classes. We extract from the problem statement the verbs and verb phrases that specify the operations for each class. We then modify the class diagram of Section 3.7 to include each operation with its associated class. At this point in the case study, we will have gathered all information possible from the problem statement. However, as future chapters introduce such topics as inheritance, event-handling and multithreading, we will modify our classes and diagrams.

Section 7.10—(Optional Case Study) Thinking About Objects: Collaboration Among Objects

At this point, we have created a "rough sketch" of the model for our elevator system. In this section, we see how it works. We investigate the behavior of the simulation by discussing *collaborations*—messages that objects send to each other to communicate. The class operations that we discovered in Section 6.15 turn out to be the collaborations among the objects in our system. We determine the collaborations in our system, then collect them into a *collaboration diagram*—the UML diagram for modeling collaborations. This diagram reveals which objects collaborate and when. We present a collaboration diagram of the people entering and exiting the elevator.

Section 8.17—(Optional Case Study) Thinking About Objects: Starting to Program the Classes for the Elevator Simulation

In this section, we take a break from designing the behavior of our system. We begin the implementation process to emphasize the material discussed in Chapter 8. Using the UML class diagram of Section 3.7 and the attributes and operations discussed in Sections 4.14 and 6.15, we show how to implement a class in Java from a design. We do not implement all classes—because we have not completed the design process. Working from our UML diagrams, we create code for the `Elevator` class.

Section 10.12—(Optional Case Study) Thinking About Objects: Incorporating Inheritance into the Elevator Simulation

Chapters 9–10 discuss object-oriented programming. We consider inheritance—classes sharing similar characteristics may inherit attributes and operations from a "base" class. In this section, we investigate how our elevator simulation can benefit from using inheritance. We document our discoveries in a class diagram that models inheritance relationships—the UML refers to these relationships as *generalizations*. We modify the class diagram of Section 3.7 by using inheritance to group classes with similar characteristics.

Section 11.9—(Optional Case Study) Thinking About Objects: Event Handling

In this section, we include interfaces necessary for the objects in our elevator simulation to send messages to other objects. In Java, objects often communicate by sending an *event*—a notification that some action has occurred. The object receiving the event then performs an action in response to the type of event received—this is known as *event handling*. In Section 7.10, we outlined the message passing, or the collaborations, in our model, using a collaboration diagram. We now modify this diagram to include event handling, and, as an example, we explain in detail how doors in our simulation open upon the elevator's arrival.

Section 12.9—(Optional Case Study) Thinking About Objects: Designing Interfaces with the UML

In this section, we design a class diagram that models the relationships between classes and interfaces in our simulation—the UML refers to these relationships as *realizations*. In addition, we list all operations that each interface provides to the classes. Lastly, we show how to create the Java classes that implement these interfaces.

Section 13.17 - (Optional Case Study) Thinking About Objects: Use Cases

Chapter 13 discusses user interfaces that enable a user to interact with a program. In this section, we discuss the interaction between our elevator simulation and its user. Specifically, we investigate the scenarios that may occur between the application user and the simulation itself—this set of scenarios is called a *use case*. We model these interactions, using *use-case diagrams* of the UML.

Section 14.13—(Optional Case Study) Thinking About Objects: Model-View-Controller

We designed our system to consist of three components, each having a distinct responsibility. By this point in the case study, we have almost completed the first component, called the *model*, which contains data that represent the simulation. We design the *view*—the second component, dealing with how the model is displayed—in Section 19.7. We design the *controller*—the component that allows the user to control the model—in this section. A system such as ours that uses the model, view and controller components is said to adhere to *Model-View-Controller* (*MVC*) architecture. In this section, we explain the advantages of using this architecture to design software. We use the UML *component diagram* to model the three components, then implement this diagram as Java code.

Section 16.11—(Optional Case Study) Thinking About Objects: Multithreading

In this section, we declare certain objects as "threads" to enable these objects to operate concurrently. We modify the collaboration diagram originally presented in Section 7.10 (and modified in Section 11.9) to incorporate multithreading. We present the UML *sequence diagram* for modeling interactions in a system. This diagram emphasizes the chronological ordering of messages. We use a sequence diagram to model how a person inside the simulation interacts with the elevator. This section concludes the design of the model portion of our simulation. We design how this model is displayed in Section 19.7, then implement this model as Java code in Appendix E.

Section 19.7—(Optional Case Study) Thinking About Objects: Animation and Sound in the View

This section designs the view, which specifies how the model portion of the simulation is displayed. Chapter 19 presents several techniques for integrating sound and animation in programs. This section uses some of these techniques to incorporate sound and animation into our elevator simulation. Specifically, this section deals with animating the movements of people and our elevator, generating sound effects and playing "elevator music" when a person rides the elevator. This section concludes the design of our elevator simulation. Appendices D, E and F implement this design as a 3,320-line, fully operational Java program.

Appendix D—Elevator Events and Listener Interfaces

[Note: This appendix is on the CD that accompanies this book.] As we discussed in Section 11.9, several objects in our simulation interact with each other by sending messages, called events, to other objects wishing to receive these events. The objects receiving the events are called *listener objects*—these must implement *listener interfaces*. In this appendix, we implement all event classes and listener interfaces used by the objects in our simulation.

Appendix E—Elevator Model

[Note: This appendix is on the CD that accompanies this book.] The majority of the case study involved designing the model (i.e., the data and logic) of the elevator simulation. In this appendix, we implement that model in Java. Using all the UML diagrams we created, we present the Java classes necessary to implement the model. We apply the concepts of object-oriented design with the UML and object-oriented programming and Java that you learned in the chapters.

Appendix F—Elevator View

[Note: This appendix is on the CD that accompanies this book.] This final appendix implements our display of the elevator simulation. We use the same approach to implement the view as we used to implement the model—we create all the classes required to run the view, using the UML diagrams and key concepts discussed in the chapters. By the end of this appendix, you will have completed an "industrial-strength" design and implementation of a large-scale system. You should feel confident tackling larger systems, such as the 10,000-line Enterprise Java case study we present in our companion book *Advanced Java 2 Platform How to Program* and the kinds of applications that professional software engineers build. Hopefully, you will move on to even deeper study of object-oriented design with the UML.

(Optional) A Tour of the "Discovering Design Patterns" Sections

Our treatment of design patterns is spread over five optional sections of the book. We overview those sections here.

Section 10.12—(Optional) Discovering Design Patterns: Introducing Creational, Structural and Behavioral Design Patterns

This section lists the sections in which we discuss the various design patterns. We divide the discussion of each section into creational, structural and behavioral design patterns. Creational patterns provide ways to instantiate objects, structural patterns deal with organizing objects and behavioral patterns deal with interactions between objects. The remainder of the section introduces some of these design patterns, such as the Singleton, Proxy, Memento and State design patterns. Finally, we provide several URLs for further study on design patterns.

Section 14.14—(Optional) Discovering Design Patterns: Design Patterns Used in Packages `java.awt` *and* `javax.swing`

This section contains most of our design-patterns discussion. Using the material on Java Swing GUI components in Chapters 13 and 14, we investigate some examples of pattern use in packages `java.awt` and `javax.swing`. We discuss how these classes use the Factory Method, Adapter, Bridge, Composite, Chain-of-Responsibility, Command, Observer, Strategy and Template Method design patterns. We motivate each pattern and present examples of how to apply them.

Section 16.12—(Optional) Discovering Design Patterns: Concurrent Design Patterns

Developers have discovered several design patterns since those described by the gang of four. In this section, we discuss concurrency design patterns, including Single-Threaded Execution, Guarded Suspension, Balking, Read/Write Lock and Two-Phase Termination—these solve various design problems in multithreaded systems. We investigate how class `java.lang.Thread` uses concurrency patterns.

Section 18.12—(Optional) Discovering Design Patterns: Design Patterns Used in Packages `java.io` *and* `java.net`

Using the material on files, streams and networking in Chapters 17 and 18, we investigate some examples of pattern use in packages `java.io` and `java.net`. We discuss how these classes use the Abstract Factory, Decorator and Facade design patterns. We also consider architectural patterns, which specify a set of subsystems—aggregates of objects that each collectively comprise a major system responsibility—and how these subsystems interact with each other. We discuss the popular Model-View-Controller and Layers architectural patterns.

Section 22.12—(Optional) Discovering Design Patterns: Design Patterns Used in Package `java.util`

Using the material on data structures and collections in Chapters 20–22, we investigate pattern use in package `java.util`. We discuss how these classes use the Prototype and Iterator design patterns. This section concludes the discussion on design patterns. After finishing the *Discovering Design Patterns* material, you should be able to recognize and use key design patterns and have a better understanding of the workings of the Java API. After completing this material, we recommend that you move on to the Gang-of-Four book.

Acknowledgments

One of the great pleasures of writing a textbook is acknowledging the efforts of the many people whose names may not appear on the cover, but whose hard work, cooperation, friendship, and understanding were crucial to the production of the book.

Several people at Deitel & Associates, Inc. devoted long hours to this project. We would like to acknowledge the efforts of our full-time Deitel & Associates, Inc. colleagues Tem Nieto, Sean Santry, Su Zhang and Jeff Listfield.

- Tem Nieto is a graduate of the Massachusetts Institute of Technology. Tem teaches XML, Java, Internet and Web, C, C++ and Visual Basic seminars and works with us on textbook writing, course development and multimedia authoring efforts. He is co-author with us of several books, including *Internet & World Wide Web How to Program (Second Edition), XML How to Program, Visual Basic*

.NET How to Program and *C# How to Program*. In *Java How to Program, Fifth Edition* Tem co-authored Chapters 12–14 and 22 and the Special Section entitled "Building Your Own Compiler" in Chapter 20.

- Sean Santry, a graduate of Boston College (Computer Science and Philosophy) and co-author of *Advanced Java 2 Platform How to Program* and *Java Web Services for Experienced Programmers*, edited the entire manuscript, designed and implemented the Deitel Messenger networking application in Chapter 18 (Networking), contributed to the design and updated the optional case study on OOD/UML and updated the optional design patterns introduction.

- Su Zhang holds B.Sc and a M.Sc degrees in Computer Science from McGill University. Her graduate research included modeling and simulation, real-time systems and Java technology. She is co-author with us on *Java Web Services for Experienced Programmers* and has contributed to other Deitel publications, including *Advanced Java 2 Platform How to Program* and *Python How to Program*. Su helped update several chapters and created the examples that introduce features new to Java 1.4, such as the New I/O APIs (covered in Chapters 17 and 18) and chained exceptions (covered in Chapter 15).

- Jeff Listfield is a Computer Science graduate of Harvard College. His course work included classes in computer graphics, networks and computational theory and he has programming experience in C, C++, C#, Java, Perl and Lisp. Jeff is our co-author on *C# How to Program, C# A Programmer's Introduction* and *C# for Experienced Programmers*, and contributed to *Perl How to Program*. Jeff helped update several chapters in the book, and wrote new examples and sections on regular expressions in Chapter 11, sorting in Chapter 22 and parts of the New I/O API sections in Chapters 17 and 18).

We are fortunate to have been able to work on this project with the talented and dedicated team of publishing professionals at Prentice Hall. We especially appreciate the extraordinary efforts of our computer science editor, Petra Recter and her boss—our mentor in publishing—Marcia Horton, Editorial Director of Prentice-Hall's Engineering and Computer Science team. Tom Manshreck did a marvelous job as production manager. Jennifer Cappello did a wonderful job managing the review process.

The *Java 2 Multimedia Cyber Classroom, Fifth Edition* was developed in parallel with *Java How to Program, Fifth Edition*. We sincerely appreciate the "new media" insight, savvy and technical expertise of our e-media editor-in-chief, mentor and friend Mark Taub. He and our e-media editor, Karen Mclean, did a remarkable job bringing the *Java 2 Multimedia Cyber Classroom, Fifth Edition* to publication under a tight schedule.

We owe special thanks to Tamara Newnam (`smart_art@earthlink.net`) who did the art work for our programming tips icons and the cover. She created the delightful bug creature who shares with you the book's programming tips.

We sincerely appreciate the efforts of our 70 fourth edition post-publication reviewers and our fifth edition reviewers:

Sun Microsystems Reviewers
Dibyendu Baksi (Sun Microsystems)
Konstantin Kladko (Sun Microsystems)

Doug Kohlert (Sun Microsystems)
Peter Jones (Sun Microsystems)
Paul Monday (Sun Microsystems)
Tomas Pavek (Sun Microsystems)
Brandon Taylor (Sun Microsystems)

Academic Reviewers
Rekha Bhowmik (St. Cloud State University)
Clint Bickmore (Front Range Community College)
Brian Blake (Georgetown University)
Ayad Boudiab (Georgia Perimiter College)
Chadi Boudiab (Georgia Perimiter College)
Michael Buckley (State University of New York-Buffalo)
James Chegwidden (Tarrant County College)
Deborah Coleman (Rochester Institute of Technology)
Don Francis Costello (University of Nebraska)
Balazs Csizmazia (University of Klagenfurt)
Tamara Dinev (Florida Atlantic University)
Sarah Fix (The Career Center High School)
Bill Freitas (The Lawrenceville School)
Thomas Graffte (Strayer University)
Balaji Janamanchi (Texas Tech University)
Charles Lake (Faulkner State Community College)
Brian Larson (Modesto Junior College)
Hong Lin (DeVry University)
David McKain (Lakota East High School)
Andy Novobilski (University of Tennessee-Chattanooga)
Richard Ord (University of California, San Diego)
Gavin Osborne (Saskatchewan Institute of Applied Sci.& Tech.)
Merrill Parker (Chattanooga State Technical Community College)
Donna Reese (Mississippi State University)
Craig Slinkman (University of Texas, Arlington)
Gidget Smith (Arkansas State University)
Ron Sones (James Madison University)
Mahendran Velauthapillai (Georgetown University)
Loran Walker (Lawrence Technological University)
Warren Wiltsie (Fairleigh Dickinson University)

Other Industry Reviewers
Shishir Abhyanker (Accenture)
Sinan Alhir (Independent Consultant)
Richard Bonneau (IONA Technologies)
Columbus Brown (IBM)
Carl Burnham (Southpoint)
Brian Cook (Zurich Insurance)
Jonathan Earl (Independent Consultant)
Ron Felice (Omniware Development)

Karl Frank (TogetherSoft Corporation)
Kyle Gabhart (Independent Consultant)
Johan Galle (E2S)
Mark Grand (ClickBlocks, LLC)
Ajay Gupta (American Airlines, Inc.)
Kevlin Henney (Curbralan, Ltd.)
Ethan Henry (Sitraka)
Anne Horton (AT&T Laboratories)
James Huddleston (Independent Consultant)
Terrell Hull (Sun Certified Java Architect, Rational Qualified Practitioner)
Sachin Korgaonkar (Idealake Technologies, Pvt. Ltd.)
Don Kostuch (You Can C Clearly Now)
Krishna Kunchithapadam (Oracle Corporation)
Paul McLachlan (Compuware Corporation)
Davyd Norris (Rational)
Bill O'Farrell (IBM)
Praveen Sadhu (Infodat Solutions, Inc.)
Cameron Skinner (Embarcadero Technologies/OMG)
Stephen Tockey (Construx Software/OMG)
Kim Topley (Keyboard Edge, Ltd.)
Sudhir Upadhyay (BEA Systems, Inc.)
John Varghese (UBS Warburg)
Bing Xue (Siemens)
Hadar Ziv (eBuilt, Inc.)

Under a tight time schedule, they scrutinized every aspect of the text and made countless suggestions for improving the accuracy and completeness of the presentation.

Well, there you have it! We have worked hard to create this book and its optional Cyber Classroom version. The book is loaded with LIVE-CODE™ examples, programming tips, self-review exercises and answers, challenging exercises and projects, and numerous study aids to help you master the material. Java is a powerful programming language that will help you write programs quickly and effectively. And Java is a language that scales nicely into the realm of enterprise-systems development to help organizations build their key information systems. As you read the book, we would sincerely appreciate your comments, criticisms, corrections and suggestions for improving the text. Please address all correspondence to:

deitel@deitel.com

We will respond promptly, and we will post corrections and clarifications on our Web site,

www.deitel.com

We hope you enjoy learning with *Java How to Program, Fifth Edition* as much as we enjoyed writing it!

Dr. Harvey M. Deitel
Paul J. Deitel

About the Authors

Dr. Harvey M. Deitel, Chairman of Deitel & Associates, Inc., has 40 years experience in the computing field including extensive industry and academic experience. He is one of the world's leading computer science instructors and seminar presenters. Dr. Deitel earned B.S. and M.S. degrees from the Massachusetts Institute of Technology and a Ph.D. from Boston University. He has 20 years of college teaching experience including earning tenure and serving as the Chairman of the Computer Science Department at Boston College before founding Deitel & Associates, Inc. with his son Paul J. Deitel. He is author or co-author of several dozen books and multimedia packages. With translations published in Japanese, Russian, Spanish, Italian, Basic Chinese, Traditional Chinese, Korean, French, Polish, Turkish, Urdu, Greek, and Portuguese, Dr. Deitel's texts have earned international recognition. Dr. Deitel has delivered professional seminars internationally to major corporations, government organizations and various branches of the military.

    Paul J. Deitel, CEO of Deitel & Associates, Inc., is a graduate of the Massachusetts Institute of Technology's Sloan School of Management where he studied Information Technology. Through Deitel & Associates, Inc. he has delivered programming-language seminars to major corporations, government organizations and various branches of the military. He has lectured on Java and C++ for the Boston Chapter of the Association for Computing Machinery, and has taught satellite-based courses through a cooperative venture of Deitel & Associates, Inc., Prentice Hall and the Technology Education Network. He and his father, Dr. Harvey M. Deitel, are the world's best-selling Computer Science textbook authors.

About Deitel & Associates, Inc.

Deitel & Associates, Inc. is an internationally recognized corporate training and content-creation organization specializing in Internet/World Wide Web software technology, e-business/e-commerce software technology and computer programming languages education. The company provides courses on Internet and World Wide Web programming, object technology and major programming languages. The founders of Deitel & Associates, Inc. are Dr. Harvey M. Deitel and Paul J. Deitel. The company's clients include many of the world's largest computer companies, government agencies, branches of the military and business organizations. Through its publishing partnership with Prentice Hall, Deitel & Associates, Inc. publishes leading-edge programming textbooks, professional books, interactive CD-ROM-based multimedia *Cyber Classrooms*, satellite courses and Web-based training courses. Deitel & Associates, Inc. and the authors can be reached via e-mail at

```
deitel@deitel.com
```

To learn more about Deitel & Associates, Inc., its publications and its worldwide corporate on-site curriculum, see the last few pages of this book, visit:

```
www.deitel.com
```

and subscribe to the free *DEITEL BUZZ ONLINE* e-mail newsletter at

```
www.deitel.com/newsletter/subscribe.html
```

Individuals wishing to purchase Deitel books, Cyber Classrooms, Complete Training Courses and Web-based training courses can do so through

```
www.deitel.com/books/index.html
```

Bulk orders by corporations and academic institutions should be placed directly with Prentice Hall. See the last few pages of this book for worldwide ordering details.

1

Introduction to Computers, the Internet and the Web

Objectives

- To understand basic computer science concepts.
- To become familiar with different types of programming languages.
- To introduce a typical Java development environment.
- To understand Java's role in developing distributed client/server applications for the Internet and Web.
- To introduce object-oriented design with the UML and design patterns.

Our life is frittered away by detail … Simplify, simplify.
Henry Thoreau

High thoughts must have high language.
Aristophanes

The chief merit of language is clearness.
Galen

My object all sublime
I shall achieve in time.
W. S. Gilbert

He had a wonderful talent for packing thought close, and rendering it portable.
Thomas Babington Macaulay

Egad, I think the interpreter is the hardest to be understood of the two!
Richard Brinsley Sheridan

Outline

1.1 Introduction

Welcome to Java! We have worked hard to create what we hope will be an informative, entertaining and challenging learning experience for you. Java is a powerful computer programming language that is fun for novices to use and appropriate for experienced programmers building substantial information systems. *Java How to Program, Fifth Edition*, is designed to be an effective learning tool for each of these audiences.

How can one book appeal to both groups? The answer is that the common core of the book emphasizes achieving program *clarity* through the proven techniques of *object-oriented programming*. Nonprogrammers will learn programming the right way from the beginning. We have attempted to write in a clear and straightforward manner. The book is abundantly illustrated. Perhaps most importantly, the book presents hundreds of working Java programs and shows the outputs produced when those programs are run on a computer. We teach Java features in the context of complete working Java programs. We call this the LIVE-CODE™ *approach*. These examples are available from several locations—they are on the CD that accompanies this book, they may be downloaded from www.deitel.com or www.prenhall.com/deitel, and they are available on our interactive CD product, the *Java 2 Multimedia Cyber Classroom, Fifth Edition*.

The early chapters introduce the fundamentals of computers, computer programming and the Java computer programming language. The material in these chapters presents a solid foundation for the deeper treatment of Java in the later chapters. Experienced programmers tend to read the early chapters quickly and find the treatment of Java in the later chapters rigorous and challenging.

Most people are familiar with the exciting tasks computers perform. Using this textbook, you will learn how to command computers to perform those tasks. It is *software* (i.e., the instructions you write to command computers to perform *actions* and make *decisions*) that controls computers (often referred to as *hardware*). Java, developed by Sun Microsystems, is one of today's most popular software-development languages.

This book is based on the *Java 2 Platform, Standard Edition*, which describes the Java language, libraries and tools. Other vendors can implement *Java development kits* based on the *Java 2 Platform*. Sun provides an implementation of the *Java 2 Platform, Standard Edition* called the *Java 2 Software Development Kit, Standard Edition (J2SDK)* that includes the minimum set of tools you need to write software in Java. We used J2SDK version 1.4.1, which is included on the accompanying CD, to implement and test the programs in this book. Future updates to the J2SDK can be downloaded from `java.sun.com/j2se`.[1]

Computer use is increasing in almost every field of endeavor. In an era of steadily rising costs, computing costs have been decreasing dramatically due to rapid developments in both hardware and software technologies. Computers that might have filled large rooms and cost millions of dollars two decades ago can now be inscribed on the surfaces of silicon chips smaller than a fingernail, costing perhaps a few dollars each. Ironically, silicon is one of the most abundant materials on earth—it is an ingredient in common sand. Silicon-chip technology has made computing so economical that hundreds of millions of general-purpose computers are in use worldwide helping people in business, industry and government, and in their personal lives. That number could easily double in the next few years.

Over the years, many programmers learned the programming methodology called *structured programming*. You will learn structured programming and the exciting newer methodology, *object-oriented programming*. Why do we teach both? Object-orientation is the key programming methodology used by programmers today. You will create and work with many *objects* in this course. But you will discover that the internal structure of those objects often is built using structured-programming techniques. Also, the logic of manipulating objects occasionally is expressed with structured programming.

Java has become the language of choice for implementing Internet-based and intranet-based applications and software for devices that communicate over a network. Do not be surprised when your new stereo and other devices in your home become networked together by Java technology! Also, do not be surprised when your wireless devices, like cell phones, pagers and personal digital assistants (PDAs) communicate over the so-called Wireless Internet via the kind of Java-based networking applications that you will learn in this book and its companion *Advanced Java 2 Platform How to Program*. Java has evolved rapidly into the large-scale applications arena. It is no longer a language used simply to make World Wide Web pages "come alive." Java has become the preferred language for meeting many organizations' programming needs.

Java continues to evolve rapidly, so we wrote this fifth edition of *Java How to Program* just six years after the first edition was published. This edition is based on the *Java 2 Platform, Standard Edition (J2SE)*. Java has grown so rapidly over the last several years that it

---

1. Sun revises the J2SDK on a regular basis. Check their Web site for updates.

now has two other editions. The *Java 2 Platform, Enterprise Edition* (*J2EE*) is geared toward developing large-scale, distributed networking applications and Web-based applications. The *Java 2 Platform, Micro Edition* (*J2ME*) is geared toward development of applications for small, memory-constrained devices, such as cell phones, pagers and PDAs. The number of topics to cover in Java has become far too large for one book. For this reason, we published *Advanced Java 2 Platform How to Program*, which emphasizes developing applications with J2EE and provides coverage of several high-end topics from the J2SE. This book also includes substantial materials on J2ME and wireless-application development.

You are about to start on a challenging and rewarding path. As you proceed, if you would like to communicate with us, please send e-mail to

deitel@deitel.com

or browse our World Wide Web site at

www.deitel.com

We will respond promptly. To keep up to date with Java developments at Deitel & Associates, please register for our e-mail newsletter, *The Deitel Buzz Online* at

www.deitel.com/newsletter/subscribe.html

We hope you enjoy learning with *Java How to Program*. You may want to consider using the interactive CD-ROM version of the book called the *Java 2 Multimedia Cyber Classroom, Fifth Edition*. Ordering instructions for this product appear at the end of this book. If you purchased *The Complete Java 2 Training Course, Fifth Edition*, you already own the *Java 2 Multimedia Cyber Classroom, Fifth Edition*.

1.2 What Is a Computer?

A *computer* is a device capable of performing computations and making logical decisions at speeds millions (even billions) of times faster than human beings can. For example, many of today's personal computers can perform a billion additions per second. A person operating a desk calculator might require a lifetime to complete the same number of calculations a powerful personal computer can perform in one second. (Points to ponder: How would you know whether the person added the numbers correctly? How would you know whether the computer added the numbers correctly?) Today's fastest *supercomputers* can perform hundreds of billions of additions per second! And trillion-instruction-per-second computers are already functioning in research laboratories!

Computers process *data* under the control of sets of instructions called *computer programs*. These computer programs guide the computer through orderly sets of actions specified by people called *computer programmers*.

A computer is comprised of various devices (such as the keyboard, screen, "mouse," disks, memory, DVD, CD-ROM and processing units) that are referred to as *hardware*. The computer programs that run on a computer are referred to as *software*. Hardware costs have been declining dramatically in recent years, to the point that personal computers have become commodities. Unfortunately, software-development costs have been rising steadily as programmers develop ever more powerful and complex applications, without significantly improved technology for software development. In this book, you will learn proven software-development methods that can reduce software-development costs—structured programming, top-down stepwise refinement, functionalization, object-based programming, object-oriented programming and object-oriented design.

1.3 Computer Organization

Regardless of differences in physical appearance, virtually every computer may be envisioned as being divided into six *logical units* or sections:

1. *Input unit.* This is the "receiving" section of the computer. It obtains information (data and computer programs) from *input devices* and places this information at the disposal of the other units so that the information can be processed. Most information is entered into computers through keyboards and mouse devices. Information also can be entered by speaking to your computer, by scanning images and by having your computer receive information from a network, such as the Internet.

2. *Output unit.* This is the "shipping" section of the computer. It takes information that has been processed by the computer and places it on various *output devices* to make the information available for use outside the computer. Most information output from computers today is displayed on screens, printed on paper or used to control other devices. Computers also can output their information to networks, such as the Internet.

3. *Memory unit.* This is the rapid access, relatively low-capacity "warehouse" section of the computer. It retains information that has been entered through the input unit, so the information may be made immediately available for processing when it is needed. The memory unit also retains processed information until that information can be placed on output devices by the output unit. The memory unit is often called either *memory* or *primary memory*.

4. *Arithmetic and logic unit (ALU).* This is the "manufacturing" section of the computer. It is responsible for performing calculations such as addition, subtraction, multiplication and division. It contains the decision mechanisms that allow the computer, for example, to compare two items from the memory unit to determine whether they are equal.

5. *Central processing unit (CPU).* This is the "administrative" section of the computer. It is the computer's coordinator and is responsible for supervising the operation of the other sections. The CPU tells the input unit when information should be read into the memory unit, tells the ALU when information from the memory unit should be used in calculations and tells the output unit when to send information from the memory unit to certain output devices. Many of today's computers have multiple processing units and, hence, can perform many operations simultaneously—such computers are called *multiprocessors*.

6. *Secondary storage unit.* This is the long-term, high-capacity "warehousing" section of the computer. Programs or data not actively being used by the other units normally are placed on secondary storage devices (such as disks) until they are again needed, possibly hours, days, months or even years later. Information in secondary storage takes much longer to access than information in primary memory, but the cost per unit of secondary storage is much less than the cost per unit of primary memory.

1.4 Evolution of Operating Systems

Early computers were capable of performing only one *job* or *task* at a time. This form of computer operation is often called single-user *batch processing*. The computer runs a single program at a time while processing data in groups or *batches*. In these early systems, users generally submitted their jobs to a computer center on decks of punched cards. Users often had to wait hours or even days before printouts were returned to their desks.

Software systems called *operating systems* were developed to help make it more convenient to use computers. Early operating systems managed the smooth transition between jobs. This minimized the time it took for computer operators to switch between jobs and hence increased the amount of work, or *throughput*, computers could process.

As computers became more powerful, it became evident that single-user batch processing rarely utilized the computer's resources efficiently because most of the time was spent waiting for slow input/output devices to complete their tasks. Instead, it was thought that many jobs or tasks could be made to *share* the resources of the computer to achieve better utilization. This is called *multiprogramming*. Multiprogramming involves the "simultaneous" operation of many jobs on the computer—the computer shares its resources among the jobs competing for its attention. With early multiprogramming operating systems, users still submitted jobs on decks of punched cards and waited hours or days for results.

In the 1960s, several groups in industry and the universities pioneered *timesharing* operating systems. Timesharing is a special case of multiprogramming, in which users access the computer through *terminals*, typically devices with keyboards and screens. In a typical timesharing computer system, there may be dozens or even hundreds of users sharing the computer at once. The computer actually does not run all the users simultaneously. Rather, it runs a small portion of one user's job then moves on to service the next user. The computer does this so quickly that it may provide service to each user several times per second. Thus, the users' programs *appear* to be running simultaneously. An advantage of timesharing is that the user receives almost immediate responses to requests rather than having to wait long periods for results as with previous modes of computing.

1.5 Personal, Distributed and Client/Server Computing

In 1977, Apple Computer popularized the phenomenon of *personal computing*. Initially, it was a hobbyist's dream. Computers became economical enough for people to buy them for their own personal or business use. In 1981, IBM, the world's largest computer vendor, introduced the IBM Personal Computer. This quickly legitimized personal computing in business, industry and government organizations.

These computers were "standalone" units—people did their work on their own computers then transported disks back and forth to share information (often called "sneakernet"). Although early personal computers were not powerful enough to timeshare several users, these machines could be linked together in computer networks, sometimes over telephone lines and sometimes in *local area networks (LANs)* within an organization. This led to the phenomenon of *distributed computing,* in which an organization's computing, instead of being performed strictly at some central computer installation, is distributed over networks to the sites at which the work of the organization is performed. Personal computers were powerful enough to handle the computing requirements of individual users, and to handle the basic communications tasks of passing information between one another electronically.

Today's personal computers are as powerful as the million dollar machines of just a decade ago. The most powerful desktop machines—called *workstations*—provide individual users with enormous capabilities. Information is shared easily across computer networks where computers called *file servers* offer a common store data that may be used by *client* computers distributed throughout the network, hence the term *client/server computing*. Java has become widely used for writing software for computer networking and for distributed client/server applications. Today's popular operating systems such as UNIX, Linux, Mac OS X (pronounced "OS ten") and Windows provide the kinds of capabilities discussed in this section.

1.6 Machine Languages, Assembly Languages and High-Level Languages

Programmers write instructions in various programming languages, some directly understandable by computers and others that require intermediate *translation* steps. Hundreds of computer languages are in use today. These may be divided into three general types:

1. Machine languages

2. Assembly languages

3. High-level languages

Any computer can directly understand only its own *machine language*. Machine language is the "natural language" of a particular computer. It is defined by the hardware design of that computer. Machine languages generally consist of strings of numbers (ultimately reduced to 1s and 0s) that instruct computers to perform their most elementary operations one at a time. Machine languages are *machine dependent* (i.e., a particular machine language can be used on only one type of computer). Such languages are cumbersome for humans, as can be seen by the following section of a machine-language program that adds overtime pay to base pay and stores the result in gross pay:

```
+1300042774
+1400593419
+1200274027
```

Machine-language programming was simply too slow and tedious for most programmers. Instead of using the strings of numbers that computers could directly understand, programmers began using English-like abbreviations to represent elementary operations. These abbreviations formed the basis of *assembly languages*. *Translator programs* called *assemblers* were developed to convert assembly-language programs to machine language at computer speeds. The following section of an assembly-language program also adds overtime pay to base pay and stores the result in gross pay, but more clearly than its machine-language equivalent:

```
LOAD    BASEPAY
ADD     OVERPAY
STORE   GROSSPAY
```

Although such code is clearer to humans, it is incomprehensible to computers until translated to machine language.

Computer usage increased rapidly with the advent of assembly languages, but programming in these languages still required many instructions to accomplish even the simplest tasks. To speed the programming process, *high-level languages* were developed in which single statements could be written to accomplish substantial tasks. The translator programs that convert high-level language programs into machine language are called *compilers*. High-level languages allow programmers to write instructions that look almost like everyday English and contain commonly used mathematical notations. A payroll program written in a high-level language might contain a statement such as

```
grossPay = basePay + overTimePay
```

Obviously, high-level languages are much more desirable from the programmer's standpoint than either machine languages or assembly languages. C, C++ and Java are among the most powerful and most widely used high-level programming languages.

The process of compiling a high-level language program into machine language can take a considerable amount of computer time. *Interpreter* programs were developed to execute high-level language programs directly without the need for compiling those programs into machine language. Although compiled programs execute much faster than interpreted programs, interpreters are popular in program-development environments in which programs are recompiled frequently as new features are added and errors are corrected. Once a program is developed, a compiled version can be produced to run most efficiently.

1.7 History of C++

C++ evolved from C, which evolved from two previous languages, BCPL and B. BCPL was developed in 1967 by Martin Richards as a language for writing operating-systems software and compilers. Ken Thompson modeled many features in his language B after their counterparts in BCPL and used B to create early versions of the UNIX operating system at Bell Laboratories in 1970.

The C language was evolved from B by Dennis Ritchie at Bell Laboratories and was originally implemented in 1972. C initially became widely known as the development language of the UNIX operating system. Today, virtually all new major operating systems are written in C or C++.

The widespread use of C with various types of computers (sometimes called *hardware platforms*) led to many variations. These were similar, but often incompatible. This was a serious problem for programmers who needed to write portable programs that would run on several platforms. It became clear that a standard version of C was needed. In 1983, the X3J11 technical committee was created under the American National Standards Committee on Computers and Information Processing (X3) to "provide an unambiguous and machine-independent definition of the language." In 1989, the standard was approved. The American National Standards Institute (ANSI) cooperated with the International Organization for Standardization (ISO) to standardize C worldwide; the joint standard document was published in 1990 and is referred to as ANSI/ISO 9899: 1990. The second edition of Kernighan and Ritchie,[2] published in 1988, reflects this version called ANSI C, a version of the language still used worldwide.

C++, an extension of C, was developed by Bjarne Stroustrup in the early 1980s at Bell Laboratories. C++ provides a number of features that "spruce up" the C language, but more

---

2.   Kernighan, B. W., and D. M. Ritchie. *The C Programming Language: Second Edition.* Englewood Cliffs, NJ: Prentice Hall, 1988.

importantly, it provides capabilities for *object-oriented programming* (discussed in more detail in Section 1.15). C++ was also standardized by the ANSI and ISO committees.

There is a revolution brewing in the software community. Building software quickly, correctly and economically remains an elusive goal, and this at a time when demands for new and more powerful software are soaring. *Objects* are essentially reusable software components that model pieces of software programs in terms of *properties* (such as name, color and size) and *behaviors* (such as calculating, moving and communicating). Software developers are discovering that using a modular, object-oriented design and implementation approach can make software-development groups much more productive than is possible with previous popular programming techniques such as structured programming. Object-oriented programs are often easier to understand, correct and modify.

Many other object-oriented languages have been developed, including Smalltalk, developed at Xerox's Palo Alto Research Center (PARC). Smalltalk is a pure object-oriented language—literally everything is an object. C++ is a hybrid language—it is possible to program in either a C-like style, an object-oriented style or both.

1.8 History of Java

Perhaps the microprocessor revolution's most important contribution to date is that it made possible the development of personal computers, which now number in the hundreds of millions worldwide. Personal computers have had a profound impact on people's lives and the ways organizations conduct and manage their business.

Many people believe that the next major area in which microprocessors will have a profound impact is in intelligent consumer-electronic devices. Recognizing this, Sun Microsystems funded an internal corporate research project code-named Green in 1991. The project resulted in the development of a C++-based language that its creator, James Gosling, called Oak after an oak tree outside his window at Sun. It was later discovered that there already was a computer language called Oak. When a group of Sun people visited a local coffee shop, the name Java was suggested, and it stuck.

The Green project ran into some difficulties. The marketplace for intelligent consumer-electronic devices was not developing as quickly as Sun had anticipated. Worse yet, a major contract for which Sun competed was awarded to another company. The project was in danger of being canceled. By sheer good fortune, the World Wide Web exploded in popularity in 1993, and Sun people saw the immediate potential of using Java to add *dynamic content* and animations to Web pages. This breathed new life into the project.

Sun formally announced Java at a major conference in May 1995. Ordinarily, an event like this would not have generated much attention. However, Java generated immediate interest in the business community because of the phenomenal interest in the World Wide Web. Java is now used to develop large-scale enterprise applications, to enhance the functionality of World Wide Web servers (the computers that provide the content we see in our Web browsers), to provide applications for consumer devices (such as cell phones, pagers and personal digital assistants) and for many other purposes.

1.9 Java Class Libraries

Java programs consist of pieces called *classes*. Classes include pieces called *methods* that perform tasks and return information when they complete those tasks. You can create each piece you need to form a Java program. However, most Java programmers take advantage of rich collections of existing classes in the *Java class libraries*, which are also known as the *Java APIs (Application Programming Interfaces)*. Thus, there are really two pieces to learning the Java "world." The first is the Java language itself so that you can program your own classes; the second is the classes in the extensive Java class libraries. Throughout this book, we discuss many library classes. Class libraries are provided primarily by compiler vendors, but many class libraries are supplied by independent software vendors (ISVs).

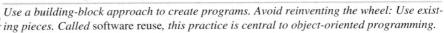

Software Engineering Observation 1.1

Use a building-block approach to create programs. Avoid reinventing the wheel: Use existing pieces. Called software reuse, *this practice is central to object-oriented programming.*

[*Note*: We include many of *Software Engineering Observations* throughout this text to explain concepts that affect and improve the overall architecture and quality of software systems, and particularly of large-scale software systems. We also highlight *Good Programming Practices* (to help you write programs that are clearer, more understandable, more maintainable and easier to test and *debug*, or remove programming errors), *Common Programming Errors* (problems to watch out for so that you do not make these same errors in your programs), *Performance Tips* (techniques that will help you write programs that run faster and use less memory), *Portability Tips* (techniques that will help you write programs that can run, with little or no modifications, on a variety of computers; these tips also include general observations about how Java achieves its high degree of portability), *Error-Prevention Tips* (techniques that will help you remove bugs from your programs and, more important, techniques that will help you write bug-free programs) and *Look and Feel Observations* (techniques that will help you design the "look" and "feel" of your graphical user interfaces for appearance and ease of use). Many of these techniques and practices are only guidelines; you will, no doubt, develop your own preferred programming style.]

Software Engineering Observation 1.2

When programming in Java, you will typically use the following building blocks: Classes from class libraries, classes and methods you create yourself and classes and methods others create and make available to you.

The advantage of creating your own classes and methods is that you know exactly how they work and you can examine the Java code. The disadvantage is the time-consuming and complex effort that goes into designing and developing new classes and methods.

Performance Tip 1.1

Using Java API classes and methods instead of writing your own versions can improve program performance, because these classes and methods are carefully written to perform efficiently. This technique also improves the prototyping speed of program development (i.e., the time it takes to develop a new program and get its first version running).

Portability Tip 1.1

Using classes and methods from the Java API instead of writing your own improves program portability, because these classes and methods are included in every Java implementation.

Software Engineering Observation 1.3

Extensive class libraries of reusable software components are available over the Internet and the Web. Many of these libraries are available at no charge.

1.10 FORTRAN, COBOL, Pascal and Ada

Hundreds of high-level languages have been developed, but only a few have achieved broad acceptance. *FORTRAN* (FORmula TRANslator) was developed by IBM Corporation in the 1950s to be used for scientific and engineering applications that require complex mathematical computations. FORTRAN is still widely used, especially in engineering applications.

COBOL (COmmon Business Oriented Language) was developed in 1959 by computer manufacturers, the government and industrial computer users. COBOL is used for commercial applications that require precise and efficient manipulation of large amounts of data. By some estimates, more than half of all business software is still programmed in COBOL.

During the 1960s, many large software-development efforts encountered severe difficulties. Software schedules were typically late, costs greatly exceeded budgets and the finished products were unreliable. People began to realize that software development was a far more complex activity than they had imagined. Research activity in the 1960s resulted in the evolution of *structured programming*—a disciplined approach to writing programs that are clearer than unstructured programs, easier to test and debug and easier to modify.

One of the more tangible results of this research was the development of the Pascal programming language by Professor Niklaus Wirth in 1971. Pascal, named after the seventeenth-century mathematician and philosopher Blaise Pascal, was designed for teaching structured programming in academic environments and rapidly became the preferred programming language in most universities. Unfortunately, the language lacks many features needed to make it useful in commercial, industrial and government applications, so it has not been widely accepted in these environments.

The *Ada* programming language was developed under the sponsorship of the U.S. Department of Defense (DOD) during the 1970s and early 1980s. Hundreds of separate languages were being used to produce the DOD's massive command-and-control software systems. The DOD wanted a single language that would fill most of its needs. The language was named after Lady Ada Lovelace, daughter of the poet Lord Byron. Lady Lovelace is credited with writing the world's first computer program in the early 1800s (for the Analytical Engine mechanical computing device designed by Charles Babbage). One important capability of Ada is called *multitasking*, which allows programmers to specify that many activities are to occur in parallel. Java, through a technique we will explain called *multithreading*, also enables programmers to write programs with parallel activities.

1.11 BASIC, Visual Basic, Visual C++, C# and .NET

The BASIC (Beginner's All-Purpose Symbolic Instruction Code) programming language was developed in the mid-1960s by Professors John Kemeny and Thomas Kurtz of Dartmouth College as a language for writing simple programs. BASIC's primary purpose was to familiarize novices with programming techniques. Visual Basic was introduced in 1991 to simplify the process of developing Microsoft Windows applications.

Visual Basic .NET [3] is designed for Microsoft's new programming platform, .NET. Earlier versions of Visual Basic provided object-oriented capabilities, but Visual Basic

---

3. The reader interested in Visual Basic .NET may want to consider our book, *Visual Basic .NET How to Program, Second Edition.*

.NET offers enhanced object orientation and makes use of .NET's powerful library of reusable software components called the Framework Class Library (FCL).

Visual C++ is a Microsoft implementation of C++ that includes Microsoft's own extensions to the language. Early graphics and GUI programming in Visual C++ was implemented using the Microsoft Foundation Classes (MFC). Now, with the introduction of .NET, Microsoft provides a common library (the FCL) for implementing GUI, graphics, networking, multithreading and other capabilities. This library is shared among Visual Basic, Visual C++, C# (Microsoft's new language) and many other languages that Microsoft and other software vendors are making available for .NET.

The advancement of programming tools (e.g., C++ and Java) and consumer-electronic devices (e.g., cell phones and PDAs) created problems and new requirements. The integration of software components from various languages proved difficult, and installation problems were common because new versions of shared components were incompatible with old software. Developers also discovered they needed Web-based applications that could be accessed and used via the Internet. As a result of the popularity of mobile electronic devices, developers recognized the need for software that was accessible to anyone and available via almost any type of device. To address these needs, Microsoft announced its *.NET* (pronounced "dot-net") *initiative* and the *C#* (pronounced "C-Sharp") programming language.

Comparably to Java, the *.NET platform* enables Web-based applications to be distributed to many devices (even cell phones) and to desktop computers. The C# programming language, developed at Microsoft by a team led by Anders Hejlsberg and Scott Wiltamuth, was designed specifically for the .NET platform as a language that would enable programmers to migrate easily to .NET.

1.12 The Internet and the World Wide Web

The *Internet*—a global network of computers—was developed more than four decades ago with funding supplied by the Department of Defense. Originally designed to connect the main computer systems of about a dozen universities and research organizations, the Internet today is accessible by hundreds of millions of computers worldwide.

With the introduction of the *World Wide Web*—which allows computer users to locate and view multimedia-based documents on almost any subject over the Internet—the Internet has exploded into one of the world's premier communication mechanisms.

The Internet and the World Wide Web are surely among humankind's most important and profound creations. In the past, most computer applications ran on computers that were not connected to one another. Today's applications can be written to communicate among the world's hundreds of millions of computers. The Internet mixes computing and communications technologies. It makes our work easier. It makes information instantly and conveniently accessible worldwide. It makes it possible for individuals and local small businesses to get worldwide exposure. It is changing the nature of the way business is done. People can search for the best prices on virtually any product or service. Special-interest communities can stay in touch with one another. Researchers can be made instantly aware of the latest breakthroughs.

Java How to Program, Fifth Edition, presents programming techniques that allow Java applications to use the Internet and the Web to interact with other applications. These capabilities, and the ones discussed in our book *Advanced Java 2 Platform How to Program*, allow Java programmers to develop the kind of enterprise-level distributed applications that are used in industry today. Java applications can be written to execute on any computer platform, yielding major savings in systems development time and cost for corporations. If you are interested in developing applications to run over the Internet and the Web, learning Java may be the key to challenging and rewarding career opportunities for you.

1.13 Basics of a Typical Java Environment

The following discussion explains the typical steps for creating and executing a Java program using a Java development environment. The steps are shown in Fig. 1.1 and are explained in the following text.

Java programs normally go through five phases to be executed (Fig. 1.1). These are *edit, compile, load, verify* and *execute*. We discuss these concepts in the context of the *Java 2 Software Development Kit (J2SDK) version 1.4.1*, which is included on the CD that accompanies this book. *Carefully follow the installation instructions for the J2SDK provided on the CD to ensure that you set up your computer properly to compile and execute Java programs.* Complete installation instructions for the J2SDK can be found on Sun's Java Web site at

```
developer.java.sun.com/developer/onlineTraining/new2java/
    programming/learn/
```

[*Note*: The preceding Web site[4] provides installation instructions for UNIX/Linux, Windows and Mac OS. If you are not using one of these operating systems, refer to the manuals for your system's Java environment or ask your instructor how to accomplish these tasks in your environment.]

Phase 1 consists of editing a file. This is accomplished with an *editor program* (normally known as an *editor*). The programmer types a Java program, using the editor, and makes corrections, if necessary. When the programmer specifies that the file in the editor should be saved, the program is stored on a secondary storage device, such as a disk. Java program file names end with the `.java` *extension*. An extension is the portion of a file name that identifies the type of data the file contains. The `.java` file-name extension indicates that a file contains source code in the Java programming language. Two editors widely used on UNIX/Linux systems are `vi` and `emacs`. On Windows, simple editing programs like Windows Notepad will suffice. Java integrated development environments (IDEs), such as Sun™ ONE Studio[5] have text editors that are integrated into the programming environment. We assume that the reader knows how to edit a file.

---

4. Web links occasionally break as companies enhance their Web sites. If you encounter a problem with any links in this book, please check our Web site `www.deitel.com` for errata, and please notify us by e-mail at `deitel@deitel.com`.
5. *Sun™ ONE Studio, Community Edition* is included on the CD that accompanies this book. *Sun ONE Studio, Community Edition* executes on most major platforms. Our example programs should operate properly with any Java integrated development environment that supports the Java 2 Platform, Standard Edition, version 1.4.1.

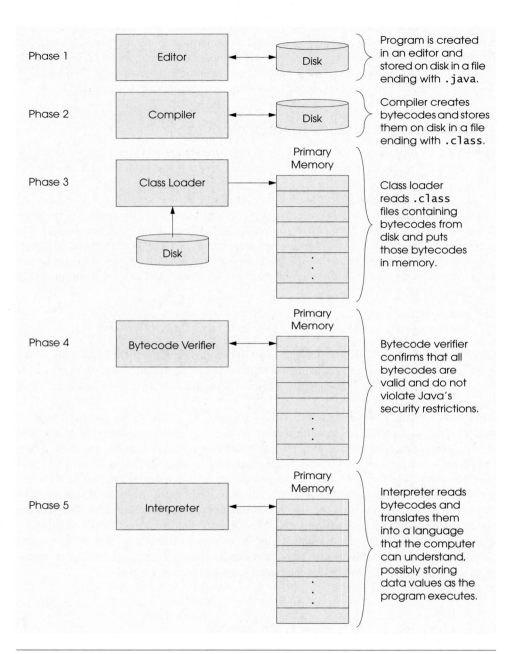

Fig. 1.1   Typical Java environment.

In Phase 2 (discussed in more detail in Chapter 2 and Chapter 3), the programmer gives the command *javac* to *compile* the program. The Java compiler translates the Java program into *bytecodes*—the instructions understood by the Java interpreter. To compile a program called Welcome.java, type

```
javac Welcome.java
```

at the command window of your system (i.e., the *MS-DOS prompt* in Windows 95/98/ME, the *Command Prompt* in Windows NT/2000/XP or the *shell prompt* in UNIX/Linux). If the program compiles correctly, the compiler produces a file called `Welcome.class`. This file contains the bytecodes that will be interpreted during the execution phase.

Phase 3 is called *loading*. The program must first be placed in memory before it can be executed. This is done by the *class loader,* which takes the `.class` files containing the bytecodes and transfers them to primary memory. The `.class` file can be loaded from a disk on your system or over a network (such as your local university or company network or even the Internet).

As the classes are loaded, their bytecodes are verified by the *bytecode verifier* in Phase 4. This verification ensures that the bytecodes for classes are valid and that they do not violate Java's security restrictions. Java enforces strong security, because Java programs arriving over the network should not be able to damage your files and your system (as computer viruses might). Note that bytecode verification also occurs in applications that download classes from a network.

Finally, in Phase 5, the interpreter, under the control of the operating system, interprets the program one bytecode at a time, thus performing the actions specified by the program. There are two types of programs for which this process occurs: *applications* and *applets*.[6] An application is a program (such as a word-processor program, a spreadsheet program, a drawing program or an e-mail program) that normally is stored and executed from the user's local computer. An applet is a small program that normally is stored on a remote computer that users connect to via a World Wide Web browser. The remote computer is known as a *Web server*. Applets are loaded from a remote computer into the browser, executed in the browser and discarded when execution completes. To execute an applet again, the user must point a browser at the appropriate location on the World Wide Web and reload the program into the browser.

Applications are loaded into memory and executed by using the *Java interpreter* via the command *java*. When executing a Java application called `Welcome`, the command

```
java Welcome
```

invokes the interpreter for the `Welcome` application and causes the class loader to load information used in the `Welcome` program. [*Note*: The Java interpreter is also called the *Java Virtual Machine* or the *JVM*.]

Web browsers such as *Netscape* or *Microsoft Internet Explorer* are used to view documents on the World Wide Web called *Hypertext Markup Language (HTML)* documents. HTML describes the format of a document in a manner that is understood by the browser application. We introduce HTML in Section 3.4; for a detailed treatment of HTML and other Internet programming technologies, please see our text *Internet and World Wide Web How to Program, Second Edition*.) An HTML document may contain a Java applet. When the browser sees an applet referenced in an HTML document, the browser launches the Java class loader to load the applet (normally from the location where the HTML document is stored). Each browser that supports Java has a built-in Java interpreter (i.e., JVM). After the applet loads, the browser's Java interpreter executes the applet. Applets also can exe-

---

6.   In later chapters, we discuss another type of Java program called a "servlet," which extends the
      functionality of a Web server.

cute from the command line, using the *appletviewer command* provided with the J2SDK—the set of tools including the compiler (`javac`), interpreter (`java`), `appletviewer` and other tools used by Java programmers. Like Netscape and Microsoft Internet Explorer, the `appletviewer` requires an HTML document in order to invoke an applet. For example, if the `Welcome.html` file refers to the `Welcome` applet, the `appletviewer` command is used as follows:

```
appletviewer Welcome.html
```

This command causes the class loader to load the information used in the `Welcome` applet. The `appletviewer` is a minimal browser—it knows only how to interpret references to applets and ignores all other HTML in a document.

Programs might not work on the first try. Each of the preceding phases can fail because of various errors that we will discuss in this text. For example, an executing program might attempt to divide by zero (an illegal operation for whole number arithmetic in Java). This would cause the Java program to print an error message. The programmer would have to return to the edit phase, make the necessary corrections and proceed through the remaining phases again to determine that the corrections work properly.

Common Programming Error 1.1

Errors like division-by-zero occur as a program runs, so these errors are called run-time errors *or* execution-time errors. Fatal runtime errors *cause programs to terminate immediately without having successfully performed their jobs.* Nonfatal runtime errors *allow programs to run to completion, often producing incorrect results.*

Most programs in Java input or output data. When we say that a program prints a result, we normally mean that the program displays that result on the computer screen. Data may be output to other devices, such as disks and hardcopy printers.

1.14 General Notes about Java and This Book

Java is a powerful programming language. Experienced programmers sometimes take pride in being able to create weird, contorted, convoluted usage of a language. This is a poor programming practice. It makes programs more difficult to read, more likely to behave strangely, more difficult to test and debug, and more difficult to adapt to changing requirements.

This book is also geared for novice programmers, so we stress *clarity.* The following is our first "good programming practice."

Good Programming Practice 1.1

Write your Java programs in a simple and straightforward manner. This is sometimes referred to as KIS ("keep it simple"). Do not "stretch" the language by trying bizarre usages.

You have heard that Java is a portable language and that programs written in Java can run on many different computers. For programming in general, *portability is an elusive goal.* The ANSI C standard document[7] contains a lengthy list of portability issues, and complete books have been written that discuss portability.[8,9]

---

7. ANSI, *American National Standard for Information Systems–Programming Language C (ANSI Document ANSI/ISO 9899: 1990).* New York, NY: American National Standards Institute, 1990.
8. Jaeschke, R. *Portability and the C Language.* Indianapolis, IN: Hayden Books, 1989.
9. Rabinowitz, H., and C. Schaap. *Portable C.* Englewood Cliffs, NJ: Prentice Hall, 1990.

Portability Tip 1.2

Although it is easier to write portable programs in Java than in other programming languages, differences among compilers, interpreters and computers can make portability difficult to achieve. Simply writing programs in Java does not guarantee portability.

Error-Prevention Tip 1.1

Always test your Java programs on all systems on which you intend to run those programs, to ensure that they will work correctly for their intended audiences.

We audited our presentation against Sun's Java documentation for completeness and accuracy. However, Java is a rich language, and there are some topics we have not covered. For additional technical details on Java, we suggest that you read the most current Java documentation available at `java.sun.com`. This book contains an extensive bibliography of books and papers on Java and on object-oriented programming. A Web-based version of the Java API documentation can be found at `java.sun.com/j2se/1.4.1/docs/api/index.html`. Also, you can download this documentation to your own computer from `java.sun.com/j2se/1.4.1/download.html`.

Good Programming Practice 1.2

Read the documentation for the version of Java you are using. Refer to this documentation frequently to be sure you are aware of the rich collection of Java features and that you are using these features correctly.

Good Programming Practice 1.3

Your computer and compiler are good teachers. If, after carefully reading your Java documentation manual, you are not sure how a feature of Java works, experiment and see what happens. Study each error or warning message you get when you compile your programs (called compile-time errors*), and correct the programs to eliminate these messages.*

Good Programming Practice 1.4

The Java 2 Software Development Kit comes with the Java source code. Many programmers read the source code of the Java API classes to determine how those classes work and to learn additional programming techniques.

This book explains how Java works in its current implementations. Perhaps the most striking problem with earlier Java versions is that programs executed interpretively on the client's machine. Interpreters execute slowly compared to fully compiled machine code.

Performance Tip 1.2

Interpreters have an advantage over compilers—namely, that an interpreted program can begin execution immediately after it is downloaded to the client's machine, whereas a source program to be compiled must first suffer a potentially long delay while the program is compiled before it can be executed.

Portability Tip 1.3

Although on early Java systems only Java interpreters were available to execute bytecodes at the client's site, compilers that translate Java bytecodes (or in some cases the Java source code) into the native machine code of the client's machine have been written for most popular platforms. These compiled programs perform comparably to compiled C or C++ code. However, there are not bytecode compilers for every Java platform, so Java programs will not perform at the same level on all platforms.

Applets present some more interesting issues. Remember, an applet could be coming from virtually any Web server in the world. So the applet will have to be able to run on any possible Java platform.

Performance Tip 1.3

An intermediate step between interpreters and compilers is a just-in-time (JIT) compiler, which produces compiled code for the program as the interpreter runs and executes the programs in machine language rather than reinterpreting them. JIT compilers might not produce machine language that is as efficient as that from a full optimizing compiler.

Performance Tip 1.4

For the latest information on high-speed Java program translation, you might want to read about Sun's HotSpot™ compiler, a standard component of the Java 2 Runtime Environment. Visit java.sun.com/products/hotspot.

The Java compiler, `javac`, is not a traditional compiler in that it does not convert a Java program from source code into native machine code for a particular computer platform. Instead, the Java compiler translates source code into bytecodes—the language of the Java Virtual Machine (JVM). The JVM is a program that simulates the operation of a computer and executes its own machine language (i.e., Java bytecodes).

Software Engineering Observation 1.4

For organizations wanting to do heavy-duty information systems development, Integrated Development Environments (IDEs) are available from many major software suppliers, including Sun Microsystems. The IDEs provide many tools that support the software-development process, such as editors for writing and editing programs, debuggers for locating logic errors in programs and many other features. Several popular IDEs include Borland® JBuilder® (www.borland.com/jbuilder), IntelliJ IDEA (www.intellij.com/idea) and Netbeans (www.netbeans.org).

Software Engineering Observation 1.5

Sun Microsystems, Inc.'s powerful Java IDE—Sun™ ONE Studio, Community Edition—is available on the CD that accompanies this book and is downloadable from wwws.sun.com/software/sundev/jde/index.html. Sun also provides an enterprise version of Sun ONE Studio at a charge and a free version for developing mobile applications with Java 2 Micro Edition (J2ME).

1.15 Thinking About Objects: Introduction to Object Technology and the Unified Modeling Language

Now we begin our early introduction to object orientation. Object orientation is a natural way of thinking about the world and a natural way of writing computer programs.

In the first seven chapters, we concentrate on the "conventional" methodology of structured programming, because the objects we will build will be composed in part of structured-program pieces. However, we end each of those chapters with an optional "Thinking About Objects" case study in which we present a carefully paced introduction to object orientation. Our goal in these "Thinking About Objects" sections is to help you develop an object-oriented way of thinking, so that you immediately can use the object-oriented programming techniques that we present starting in Chapter 8. The "Thinking About Objects" sections also introduce you to the *Unified Modeling Language™* (*UML™*). The UML is a graphical language that allows people who build systems (e.g., software architects, systems engineers, programmers and so on) to represent their requirements and object-oriented analyses and designs using a common notation.

In this section, we introduce basic object-oriented concepts and terminology. The optional sections throughout the book present the design and implementation of an object-oriented elevator simulator. The optional sections at the ends of Chapter 2–Chapter 7 analyze a typical problem statement that requires a system to be built, determine the objects required to implement that system, determine the attributes the objects will have, determine the behaviors these objects will exhibit and specify how the objects will interact with one another to meet the system requirements. All this occurs *before* you learn to write object-oriented Java programs! The optional sections at the ends of Chapter 8, Chapter 10–Chapter 14 and Chapter 1 modify and enhance the design presented in Chapter 2–Chapter 7. Chapter 19 presents the way to display our multimedia-rich design on the screen. In Appendix D–Appendix F, we present a complete Java implementation of the object-oriented system we design in the earlier chapters.

This case study will help prepare you for the more substantial projects you are likely to encounter in industry. If you are a student and your instructor does not plan to include this case study in your course, you might want to cover it on your own time. The case-study sections reinforce the material covered in the corresponding chapters. You will experience a solid introduction to object-oriented design with the UML. Also, you will sharpen your code-reading skills by touring a carefully written and well-documented 3,320-line Java program that completely solves the problem presented in the case study.

We begin our introduction to object orientation with some key terminology. Everywhere you look in the real world you see *objects*: People, animals, plants, cars, planes, buildings, computers and so on. Humans think in terms of objects. We possess the marvelous ability of *abstraction*, which enables us to view digital images of people, planes, trees and mountains as objects, rather than as individual dots of color. We can, if we wish, think in terms of beaches rather than grains of sand, forests rather than trees and houses rather than bricks.

We might be inclined to divide objects into two categories: animate objects and inanimate objects. Animate objects are "alive" in some sense; they move around and do things. Inanimate objects, on the other hand, seem not to do much at all. They do not move on their own. All these objects, however, do have some things in common. They all have *attributes* like size, shape, color and weight, and they all exhibit *behaviors* (e.g., a ball rolls, bounces, inflates and deflates; a baby cries, sleeps, crawls, walks and blinks; a car accelerates, brakes and turns; a towel absorbs water).

Humans learn about objects by studying their attributes and observing their behaviors. Different objects can have similar attributes and can exhibit similar behaviors. Comparisons can be made, for example, between babies and adults and between humans and chimpanzees. Cars, trucks, little red wagons and roller skates have much in common.

Object-oriented design models software in terms similar to those people use to describe real-world objects. It takes advantage of *class* relationships, where objects of a certain class—such as a class of vehicles—have the same characteristics. It takes advantage of *inheritance* relationships, and even *multiple-inheritance*[10] relationships, where new classes

---

10. We will learn later that although Java, unlike C++, does not support multiple inheritance, it does offer most of the key benefits of this technology by supporting multiple "interfaces" per class.

of objects are derived by absorbing characteristics of existing classes and adding unique characteristics of their own. An object of class "convertible" certainly has the characteristics of the more general class "automobile," plus a convertible's roof goes up and down.

Object-oriented design (OOD) provides a more natural and intuitive way to view the design process—namely, by *modeling* software components just as we describe real-world objects—by their attributes and behaviors. OOD also models communication between objects. Just as people send messages to one another (e.g., a sergeant commanding a soldier to stand at attention), objects also communicate via messages.

OOD *encapsulates* attributes and *operations* (behavior) into *objects;* the attributes and operations of an object are intimately tied together. Objects have the property of *information hiding*. This means that, although objects may know how to communicate with one another across well-defined *interfaces,* objects normally are not allowed to know how other objects are implemented—implementation details are hidden within the objects themselves. Surely, it is possible to drive a car effectively without knowing the details of how engines, transmissions and exhaust systems work internally. We will see why information hiding is so crucial to good software engineering.

Languages such as Java are *object oriented*. Programming in such a language is called *object-oriented programming* (*OOP*) and allows designers to implement an object-oriented design as a working system. Languages such as C, on the other hand, are *procedural,* so programming tends to be *action oriented*. In C, the unit of programming is the *function*. In Java, the unit of programming is the *class* from which objects are eventually *instantiated* (created). Java classes contain *methods* (which implement operations) and *fields* (which implement attributes).

C programmers concentrate on writing functions. Groups of actions that perform some common task are formed into functions, and functions are grouped to form programs. Data is certainly important in C, but data exists primarily in support of the actions that functions perform.

Java programmers concentrate on creating *programmer-defined types* called *classes* and *interfaces*. Each class contains fields and the set of methods that manipulate those fields and provide services to clients. The programmer uses pre-defined types as the "building blocks" for constructing new classes. The focus in Java is on classes (out of which we make objects) rather than on functions.

Classes are to objects as blueprints are to houses. We can build many houses from one blueprint, and we can *instantiate* many objects from one class. Classes can also have relationships with other classes. For example, in an object-oriented design of a bank, the "bankteller" class needs to relate to the "customer" class. These relationships are called *associations*.

When software is packaged as classes, these classes can be reused in future software systems. Groups of related classes are often packaged as reusable *components*. Just as real-estate brokers tell their clients that the three most important factors affecting the price of real estate are "location, location and location," many people in the software community believe that the three most important factors affecting the future of software development are "reuse, reuse and reuse." Reusing existing classes when building new classes and programs saves time and effort. Reuse also helps programmers build more reliable systems, since existing classes and components often have gone through extensive testing and debugging.

Indeed, with object technology, we can build much of the software we will need by combining classes, which are "interchangeable parts." Each new class you create will have the potential to become a valuable software asset that you and other programmers can use to speed and enhance the quality of future software-development efforts.

Introduction to Object-Oriented Analysis and Design (OOA/D)

You soon will be writing programs in Java. How will you create the code for your programs? If you are like many beginning programmers, you will simply turn on your computer and start typing. This approach may work for small projects, but what would you do if you were asked to create a software system to control the automated teller machines for a major bank? Such a project is too large and complex for you to sit down and simply start typing.

To create the best solutions, you should follow a detailed process for obtaining an *analysis* of your project's requirements and developing a *design* that satisfies those requirements. Ideally, you would go through this process and review the design before writing any code for your project. If this process involves analyzing and designing your system from an object-oriented point of view, we call it an *object-oriented analysis and design (OOA/D) process.* Experienced programmers know that, no matter how simple a problem appears, analysis and design can save innumerable hours that might be lost from abandoning an ill-planned system-development approach part of the way through its implementation.

OOA/D is the generic term for the process of analyzing a problem and developing an approach for solving it. Small problems like the ones discussed in these first few chapters do not require an exhaustive process. It may be sufficient to write *pseudocode* before we begin writing code. Pseudocode is an informal means of expressing program code. It is not actually a programming language, but we can use it as a kind of "outline" to guide us as we write our code. We introduce pseudocode in Chapter 4.

Pseudocode can suffice for small problems, but as problems and the groups of people solving these problems increase in size, the methods of OOA/D become more necessary. Ideally, a group should agree on a strictly defined process for solving its problem and on a uniform way of communicating the results of that process to one another. Although many different OOA/D processes exist, a single graphical language for communicating the results of any OOA/D process has become widely used. This language is known as the *Unified Modeling Language (UML)*. The UML was developed in the mid-1990s under the initial direction of three software methodologists: Grady Booch, James Rumbaugh and Ivar Jacobson.

History of the UML

In the 1980s, increasing numbers of organizations began using OOP to program their applications, and a need developed for an established process with which to approach OOAD. Many methodologists—including Booch, Rumbaugh and Jacobson—individually produced and promoted separate processes to satisfy this need. Each of these processes had its own notation, or "language" (in the form of graphical diagrams), to convey the results of analysis and design.

By the early 1990s, different companies, and even different divisions within the same company, were using different processes and notations. Additionally, these companies wanted to use software tools that would support their particular processes. With so many processes, software vendors found it difficult to provide such tools. Clearly, a standard notation and standard processes were needed.

In 1994, James Rumbaugh joined Grady Booch at Rational Software Corporation, and the two began working to unify their popular processes. They were soon joined by Ivar Jacobson. In 1996, the group released early versions of the UML to the software engineering community and requested feedback. Around the same time, an organization known as the *Object Management Group™ (OMG™)* invited submissions for a common modeling language. The OMG is a not-for-profit organization that promotes the use of object-oriented technology by issuing guidelines and specifications for object-oriented technologies. Several corporations—among them HP, IBM, Microsoft, Oracle and Rational Software—had already recognized the need for a common modeling language. These companies formed the *UML Partners* in response to the OMG's request for proposals. This consortium developed the UML version 1.1 and submitted it to the OMG. The OMG accepted the proposal and, in 1997, assumed responsibility for the continuing maintenance and revision of the UML. In 2001, the OMG released the UML version 1.4 (the current version at the time this book was written) and is working on version 2.0 (scheduled tentatively for release in 2003).

What Is the UML?

The Unified Modeling Language is now the most widely used graphical representation scheme for modeling object-oriented systems. It has indeed unified the various popular notational schemes. Those who design systems use the language (in the form of diagrams) to model their systems.

An attractive feature of the UML is its flexibility. The UML is extensible and is independent of the many OOAD processes. UML modelers are free to design systems by using various processes, but all developers can now express those designs with one standard set of notations.

The UML is a complex, feature-rich graphical language. In our "Thinking About Objects" sections, we present a concise, simplified subset of these features. We then use this subset to guide the reader through a first design experience with the UML intended for the novice object-oriented designer/programmer. For a more complete discussion of the UML, refer to the Object Management Group's Web site (www.omg.org) and to the official UML 1.4 specification document (www.omg.org/uml). In addition, many books on the UML have been published. Rational Software Corporation provides a recommended-reading list for UML books at rational.com/uml/reading/index.jsp. The books are divided into basic, intermediate and advanced levels. Several books of interest include *The Unified Modeling Language User Guide* (ISBN# 0201571684), by Grady Booch, Ivar Jacobson and James Rumbaugh; *UML Distilled: A Brief Guide to the Standard Object Modeling Language* (2nd Edition, ISBN# 020165783X), by Martin Fowler and Kendall Scott; *UML and the Unified Process: Practical Object-Oriented Analysis and Design* (ISBN# 0201770601), by Jim Arlow and Ila Neustadt; *The Unified Process for Practitioners: Object Oriented Design, UML and Java* (ISBN# 1852332751), by John Hunt. For additional books on the UML, visit www.amazon.com and search for UML.

1.16 Discovering Design Patterns: Introduction

This section begins our treatment of design patterns, entitled "Discovering Design Patterns." Most of the examples provided in this book are relatively small. These examples do not require an extensive design process, because they use only a few classes and illustrate introductory programming concepts. However, some programs, such as our optional elevator-simulation case study, are more complex—they can require thousands of lines of code or even more, contain many interactions among objects and involve many user interactions. Larger systems, such as automated teller machines or air-traffic control systems, could contain millions of lines of code. Effective design is crucial to the proper construction of such complex systems.

Over the past decade, the software-engineering industry has made significant progress in the field of *design patterns*—proven architectures for constructing flexible and maintainable object-oriented software.[11] Using design patterns can substantially reduce the complexity of the design process. Designing an ATM system will be a somewhat less formidable task if developers use design patterns. Design patterns benefit system developers by

- helping to construct reliable software using proven architectures and accumulated industry expertise,

- promoting design reuse in future systems,

- helping to identify common mistakes and pitfalls that occur when building systems,

- helping to design systems independently of the language in which they will ultimately be implemented,

- establishing a common design vocabulary among developers, and

- shortening the design phase in a software-development process.

The notion of using design patterns to construct software systems originated in the field of architecture. Architects use a set of established architectural design elements, such as arches and columns, when designing buildings. Designing with arches and columns is a proven strategy for constructing sound buildings—these elements may be viewed as architectural design patterns.

In software, design patterns are neither classes nor objects. Rather, designers use design patterns to construct sets of classes and objects. To use design patterns effectively, designers must familiarize themselves with the most popular and effective patterns used in the software-engineering industry. In this book, we discuss fundamental object-oriented design patterns and architectures, as well as their importance in constructing well-engineered software.

Throughout the book, we present several design patterns in Java, but these design patterns can be implemented in any object-oriented language, such as C++ or Visual Basic. We describe several design patterns used by Sun Microsystems in the Java API. We use design patterns in many programs in this book, which we will identify throughout our discussion. These programs provide examples of the use of design patterns to construct reliable, robust object-oriented software.

History of Object-Oriented Design Patterns
During 1991–1994, Erich Gamma, Richard Helm, Ralph Johnson, and John Vlissides—collectively known as the "Gang of Four"—used their combined expertise to write the book

---

11. Gamma, E., R. Helm, R. Johnson, and J. Vlissides. *Design Patterns: Elements of Reusable Object-Oriented Software*. Reading, MA: Addison-Wesley, 1995.

Design Patterns: Elements of Reusable Object-Oriented Software. This book describes 23 design patterns, each providing a solution to a common software design problem in industry. The book groups design patterns into three categories—*creational design patterns*, *structural design patterns* and *behavioral design patterns*. Creational design patterns describe techniques to instantiate objects (or groups of objects). Structural design patterns allow designers to organize classes and objects into larger structures. Behavioral design patterns assign responsibilities to objects.

The gang-of-four book showed that design patterns evolved naturally through years of industry experience. In his article *Seven Habits of Successful Pattern Writers*,[12] John Vlissides states that "the single most important activity in pattern writing is reflection." This statement implies that, to create patterns, developers must reflect on, and document, their successes (and mistakes). Developers use design patterns to capture and employ this collective industry experience, which ultimately helps them avoid making the same mistakes twice. New design patterns are being created all the time and are introduced rapidly to designers worldwide via the Internet.

Our treatment of design patterns begins here and continues with five optional "Discovering Design Patterns" sections at the ends of Chapters 10, 14, 16, 18 and 22. Each of these sections is placed at the end of the chapter that introduces the necessary Java technologies. If you are a student and your instructor does not plan to include this material in your course, we encourage you to read this material on your own.

SUMMARY

- The various devices that comprise a computer system (such as the keyboard, screen, disks, memory and processing units) are referred to as hardware.
- The computer programs that run on a computer are referred to as software.
- Java is one of today's most popular software-development languages. Java is a fully object-oriented language with strong support for proper software-engineering techniques.
- Java was developed by Sun Microsystems. Sun provides an implementation of the Java 2 Platform, Standard Edition called the Java 2 Software Development Kit (J2SDK), version 1.4.1 that includes the minimum set of tools you need to write software in Java.
- A computer is a device capable of performing computations and making logical decisions at speeds millions, even billions, of times faster than human beings can.
- Computers process data under the control of sets of instructions called computer programs. Computer programs guide the computer through sets of actions specified by computer programmers.
- The input unit is the "receiving" section of the computer. It obtains information from input devices and places this information at the disposal of other units for processing.
- The output unit is the "shipping" section of the computer. It takes information processed by the computer and places it on output devices to make it available for use outside the computer.
- The memory unit is the rapid access, relatively low-capacity "warehouse" section of the computer. It retains information that has been entered through the input unit so that the information may be made immediately available for processing when it is needed and retains information that has already been processed until that information can be placed on output devices by the output unit.
- The arithmetic and logic unit (ALU) is the "manufacturing" section of the computer. It is responsible for performing calculations and for making decisions.

---

12. Vlissides, J. *Pattern Hatching: Design Patterns Applied*. Reading, MA: Addison-Wesley, 1998.

- The central processing unit (CPU) is the "administrative" section of the computer. It is the computer's coordinator and is responsible for supervising the operation of the other sections.

- The secondary storage unit is the long-term, high-capacity "warehousing" section of the computer. Programs or data not being used by the other units are normally placed on secondary storage devices (such as disks) until they are needed, possibly hours, days, months or even years later.

- Software systems called operating systems were developed to help make it more convenient to use computers. Early operating systems managed the smooth transition between jobs and minimized the time it took for computer operators to switch between jobs.

- Multiprogramming involves the "simultaneous" operation of many jobs on the computer—the computer shares its resources among the jobs competing for its attention.

- Timesharing is a special case of multiprogramming in which dozens or even hundreds of users share a computer through terminals. The computer runs a small portion of one user's job, then moves on to service the next user. The computer does this so quickly that it might provide service to each user several times per second, so programs appear to run simultaneously.

- In 1977, Apple Computer popularized the phenomenon of personal computing. In 1981, IBM introduced the IBM Personal Computer, immediately legitimizing personal computing in business, industry and government organizations.

- With distributed computing, an organization's computing is distributed over networks to the sites at which the real work of the organization is performed. Today, information is shared easily across computer networks where file servers offer a common store of programs and data that may be used by client computers distributed throughout the network—hence the term client/server computing.

- Java has become the language of choice for developing Internet-based applications (and for many other purposes).

- Computer languages may be divided into three general types: machine languages, assembly languages and high-level languages.

- Any computer can directly understand only its own machine language. Machine languages generally consist of strings of numbers (ultimately reduced to 1s and 0s) that instruct computers to perform their most elementary operations one at a time. Machine languages are machine dependent.

- English-like abbreviations form the basis of assembly languages. Translator programs called assemblers convert assembly-language programs to machine language.

- Compilers translate high-level language programs into machine-language programs. High-level languages (like Java) contain English words and conventional mathematical notations.

- Interpreter programs directly execute high-level language programs without the need for compiling those programs into machine language.

- Objects are essentially reusable software components that are modeled in terms like those we use to describe things in the real world.

- Java originated at Sun Microsystems as a project for intelligent consumer-electronic devices. Java is now used to create Web pages with dynamic and interactive content, to develop large-scale enterprise applications, to enhance the functionality of Web servers, to provide applications for consumer devices and so on.

- Java programs consist of pieces called classes. Classes consist of pieces called methods that perform tasks and return information when they complete their tasks. Most Java programmers use the rich collections of existing classes in Java class libraries.

- C++, an extension of C, was developed by Bjarne Stroustrup in the early 1980s at Bell Laboratories. C++ provides a number of features that "spruce up" the C language, but more importantly, it provides capabilities for object-oriented programming.

- FORTRAN (FORmula TRANslator) was developed by IBM Corporation in the 1950s for scientific and engineering applications that require complex mathematical computations.

- COBOL (COmmon Business Oriented Language) was developed in 1959 by a group of computer manufacturers and government and industrial computer users. COBOL is used primarily for commercial applications that require precise and efficient manipulation of large amounts of data.

- Pascal was designed at about the same time as C. It was created by Professor Niklaus Wirth and was intended for academic use.

- Basic was developed in 1965 at Dartmouth College as a simple language to help novices become comfortable with programming.

- Ada was developed under the sponsorship of the United States Department of Defense (DOD) during the 1970s and early 1980s. One important capability of Ada is called multitasking; this allows programmers to specify that many activities are to occur in parallel.

- The BASIC (Beginner's All-Purpose Symbolic Instruction Code) programming language was developed in the mid-1960s by Professors John Kemeny and Thomas Kurtz of Dartmouth College as a language for writing simple programs. BASIC's primary purpose was to familiarize novices with programming techniques. Visual Basic was introduced in 1991 to simplify the process of developing Microsoft Windows applications.

- Comparably, to Java, the .NET platform enables Web-based applications to be distributed to many devices (even cell phones) and to desktop computers.

- Visual Basic .NET is designed for Microsoft's .NET programming platform. Visual Basic .NET offers enhanced object orientation over earlier versions of Visual Basic and makes use of .NET's powerful library of reusable software components called the Framework Class Library (FCL).

- Visual C++ is a Microsoft implementation of C++ that includes Microsoft's own extensions to the language. Early graphics and GUI programming in Visual C++ was implemented using the Microsoft Foundation Classes (MFC). Now, with the introduction of .NET, the FCL is shared among Visual Basic, Visual C++, C# (Microsoft's new language) and many other languages that Microsoft and other software vendors are making available for .NET.

- The C# programming language, developed at Microsoft by a team led by Anders Hejlsberg and Scott Wiltamuth, was designed specifically for the .NET platform as a language that would enable programmers to migrate easily to .NET.

- Java, through a technique called multithreading, enables programmers to write programs with parallel activities.

- The Internet was developed more than four decades ago with funding supplied by the Department of Defense. Today, the Internet is accessible by hundreds of millions of computers worldwide.

- The Web allows computer users to view multimedia-intensive documents over the Internet.

- Java source-code file names end with the .java extension.

- The Java compiler (javac) translates a Java program into bytecodes—the language understood by the Java interpreter. If a program compiles correctly, the compiler produces a file with the .class extension. This is the file containing the bytecodes that are interpreted during the execution phase.

- A Java program must first be placed in memory before it can execute. This is done by the class loader, which takes the .class file (or files) containing the bytecodes and transfers it to memory. The .class file can be loaded from a disk on your system or over a network.

- An application is a program that is normally stored and executed on the user's local computer. Applications are loaded into memory, then executed by the java interpreter.

- An applet is a program that is normally stored on a remote computer that users connect to via a Web browser. Applets are loaded from a remote computer into the browser to execute.

- Browsers are used to view HTML documents on the World Wide Web. When a browser encounters an applet in an HTML document, the browser launches the Java class loader to load the applet. Browsers that support Java have built-in Java interpreters. Once the applet is loaded, the Java interpreter in the browser begins executing the applet.

- Applets can also be executed from the command line using the `appletviewer` command provided with the Java 2 Software Development Kit (J2SDK). The `appletviewer` is commonly referred to as the minimum browser—it knows only how to interpret applets.

- Before the bytecodes in an applet are executed by the Java interpreter built into a browser or the `appletviewer`, they are verified by the bytecode verifier to ensure that the bytecodes for downloaded classes are valid and that they do not violate Java's security restrictions.

- An intermediate step between interpreters and compilers is a just-in-time (JIT) compiler that, as the interpreter runs, produces compiled code for the programs and executes the programs in machine language rather than reinterpreting them. JIT compilers do not produce machine language that is as efficient as a full compiler.

- For organizations wanting to do heavy-duty information-systems development, Integrated Development Environments (IDEs) are available from the major software suppliers. The IDEs provide many tools for supporting the software-development process.

- Object orientation is a natural way of thinking about the world and of writing computer programs.

- The Unified Modeling Language (UML) is a graphical language that allows people who build systems to represent their object-oriented designs in a common notation.

- Humans think in terms of objects. Abstraction enables us to view screen images as people, planes, trees and mountains rather than as individual dots of color (called pixels—for "picture elements"). Humans learn about objects by studying their attributes and observing their behaviors. Different objects can have similar attributes and can exhibit similar behaviors.

- Object-oriented design (OOD) models software components in terms of real-world objects. It takes advantage of class relationships, where objects of a certain class have the same characteristics. It takes advantage of inheritance relationships, and even multiple-inheritance relationships, where newly created classes of objects are derived by absorbing characteristics of existing classes and adding unique characteristics of their own. OOD encapsulates data (attributes) and functions (behavior) into objects; the data and functions of an object are intimately tied together.

- Objects have the property of information hiding—although objects may know how to communicate with one another across well-defined interfaces, objects normally are not allowed to know how other objects are implemented.

- Object-oriented programming (OOP) allows programmers to implement object-oriented designs as working systems.

- In Java, the unit of programming is the class from which objects are eventually instantiated. Java programmers concentrate on creating their classes. Each class contains data and functions that manipulate that data. Data components are called fields. Function components are called methods.

- An instance of a class is called an object.

- Classes can have relationships with other classes. These relationships are called associations.

- With object technology, we can build much of the software we will need by combining "standardized, interchangeable parts" called classes.

- The process of analyzing and designing a system from an object-oriented point of view is called object-oriented analysis and design (OOAD).

- The Unified Modeling Language (the UML) is now the most widely used graphical representation scheme for modeling object-oriented systems. Those who design systems use the language (in the form of graphical diagrams) to model their systems.

- Over the past decade, the software-engineering industry has made significant progress in the field of design patterns—proven architectures for constructing flexible and maintainable object-oriented software. Using design patterns can substantially reduce the complexity of the design process.

- Design patterns benefit system developers by helping to construct reliable software using proven architectures and accumulated industry expertise, promoting design reuse in future systems, identifying common mistakes and pitfalls that occur when building systems, helping to design systems independently of the language in which they will be implemented, establishing a common design vocabulary among developers and shortening the design phase in a software-development process.

- Designers use design patterns to construct sets of classes and objects.

- Creational design patterns describe techniques to instantiate objects (or groups of objects).

- Structural design patterns allow designers to organize classes and objects into larger structures.

- Behavioral design patterns assign responsibilities to objects.

TERMINOLOGY

abstraction
Ada
ALU (arithmetic and logic unit)
ANSI C
applet
`appletviewer` command
application
arithmetic and logic unit (ALU)
assembly language
attribute
Basic
behavior
behavioral design pattern
bytecode
bytecode verifier
C
C#
C++
central processing unit (CPU)
class
`.class` file
class libraries
class loader
client/server computing
COBOL
compile phase
compiler
compile-time error
computer
computer program
computer programmer
CPU (central processing unit)
creational design pattern
design pattern
disk

distributed computing
dynamic content
edit phase
editor
encapsulation
execute phase
execution-time error
fatal runtime error
file server
FORTRAN
hardware
high-level language
HotSpot™ compiler
HTML (Hypertext Markup Language)
IDE (Integrated Development Environment)
information hiding
inheritance
input device
input unit
input/output (I/O)
Internet
interpreter
Java
`.java` file-name extension
Java 2 Software Development Kit (J2SDK)
`java` interpreter
Java Virtual Machine (JVM)
`javac` compiler
JIT (just-in-time) compiler
KIS (keep it simple)
legacy systems
LIVE-CODE™ approach
load phase
machine dependent
machine independent

machine language   portability
memory unit   primary memory
method   problem statement
Microsoft Internet Explorer Web browser   procedural programming
modeling   requirements document
multiprocessor   reusable componentry
multitasking   runtime error
multithreading   secondary storage unit
.NET   software
Netscape Web browser   software reuse
nonfatal run-time error   structural design pattern
object   Sun Microsystems
object-oriented analysis and design (OOA/D)   timesharing
object-oriented design (OOD)   translator program
object-oriented programming (OOP)   Unified Modeling Language (UML)
output device   verify phase
output unit   Visual Basic .NET
Pascal   Visual C++ .NET
personal computing   World Wide Web
platform

SELF-REVIEW EXERCISES

1.1   Fill in the blanks in each of the following statements:
  a) The company that popularized personal computing was _____.
  b) The computer that made personal computing legitimate in business and industry was the _____.
  c) Computers process data under the control of sets of instructions called _____.
  d) The six key logical units of the computer are the _____, _____, _____, _____, _____ and _____.
  e) The three classes of languages discussed in the chapter are _____, _____ and _____.
  f) The programs that translate high-level language programs into machine language are called _____.
  g) The _____ allows computer users to locate and view multimedia-based documents on almost any subject over the Internet.
  h) Java _____ typically are stored on your computer and are designed to execute independent of World Wide Web browsers.
  i) _____ allows an applet or application to perform multiple activities in parallel.

1.2   Fill in the blanks in each of the following sentences about the Java environment:
  a) The _____ command from the Java 2 Software Development Kit executes an applet.
  b) The _____ command from the Java 2 Software Development Kit executes an application.
  c) The _____ command from the Java 2 Software Development Kit compiles a Java program.
  d) A(n) _____ document is required to invoke a Java applet.
  e) A Java program file must end with the _____ file extension.
  f) When a Java program is compiled, the file produced by the compiler ends with the _____ file extension.
  g) The file produced by the Java compiler contains _____ that are interpreted to execute a Java applet or application.

1.3 Fill in the blanks in each of the following statements (based on Section 1.15 and Section 1.16):

    a) Over the past decade, the software-engineering industry has made significant progress in the field of _____—proven architectures for constructing flexible and maintainable object-oriented software.

    b) Objects have the property of _____—although objects may know how to communicate with one another across well-defined interfaces, objects normally are not allowed to know how other objects are implemented.

    c) Java programmers concentrate on creating their own user-defined types, called _____.

    d) Classes can have relationships with other classes. These relationships are called _____.

    e) The process of analyzing and designing a system from an object-oriented point of view is called _____.

ANSWERS TO SELF-REVIEW EXERCISES

1.1 a) Apple. b) IBM Personal Computer. c) programs. d) input unit, output unit, memory unit, arithmetic and logic unit, central processing unit, secondary storage unit. e) machine languages, assembly languages, high-level languages. f) compilers. g) World Wide Web. h) applications. i) Multithreading.

1.2 a) `appletviewer`. b) `java`. c) `javac`. d) HTML. e) `.java`. f) `.class`. g) bytecodes.

1.3 a) design patterns. b) information hiding. c) classes. d) associations. e) object-oriented analysis and design (OOAD).

EXERCISES

1.4 Categorize each of the following items as either hardware or software:

    a) CPU
    b) Java compiler
    c) Java interpreter
    d) input unit
    e) editor

1.5 Fill in the blanks in each of the following statements:

    a) The logical unit of the computer that receives information from outside the computer for use by the computer is the _____.

    b) The process of instructing the computer to solve specific problems is called _____.

    c) _____ is a type of computer language that uses English-like abbreviations for machine language instructions.

    d) _____ is a logical unit of the computer that sends information which has already been processed by the computer to various devices so that the information may be used outside the computer.

    e) _____ is a logical unit of the computer that retains information.

    f) _____ is a logical unit of the computer that performs calculations.

    g) _____ is a logical unit of the computer that makes logical decisions.

    h) _____ languages are most convenient to the programmer for writing programs quickly and easily.

    i) The only language that a computer can directly understand is called that computer's _____.

    j) _____ is a logical unit of the computer coordinates the activities of all the other logical units.

1.6   Distinguish between the terms fatal error and nonfatal error. Why might you prefer to experience a fatal error rather than a nonfatal error?

1.7   Use your Web browser to visit the following Web sites and familiarize yourself with the Java resources available to you on the World Wide Web:
   a) `java.sun.com`
   b) `java.sun.com/applets`
   c) `developer.java.sun.com/developer` [*Note:* You may need to register to access this site. However, registration is free.]
   d) `www.javalobby.org`
   e) `www.jguru.com`
   f) `www.javaworld.com`
   g) `www.fawcette.com/javapro`

1.8   Fill in the blanks in each of the following statements (based on Section 1.15 and Section 1.16):
   a) _____ design patterns describe techniques to instantiate objects (or groups of objects).
   b) The _____ is now the most widely used graphical representation scheme for modeling object-oriented systems.
   c) Java classes contain _____ (which implement class behaviors) and _____ (which implement class data).
   d) _____ design patterns allow designers to organize classes and objects into larger structures.
   e) _____ design patterns assign responsibilities to objects.
   f) Objects are instantiated from _____.

1.9   Why is it valuable to study design patterns?

Introduction to Java Applications

Objectives

- To be able to write simple Java applications.
- To be able to use input and output statements.
- To become familiar with primitive types.
- To understand basic memory concepts.
- To be able to use arithmetic operators.
- To understand arithmetic-operator precedence.
- To be able to write decision-making statements.
- To be able to use relational and equality operators.

Comment is free, but facts are sacred.
C. P. Scott

The creditor hath a better memory than the debtor.
James Howell

When faced with a decision, I always ask, "What would be the most fun?"
Peggy Walker

He has left his body to science—
and science is contesting the will.
David Frost

Equality, in a social sense, may be divided into that of condition and that of rights.
James Fenimore Cooper

2.1 Introduction

We now introduce Java programming and present examples that illustrate several important features of Java. We analyze each example one line at a time. This chapter and Chapter 3 present two types of Java programs—*applications* and *applets*. In Chapter 4 and Chapter 5, we present a detailed treatment of *program development* and *program control* in Java.

2.2 A First Program in Java: Printing a Line of Text

Every time you use a computer, you execute various applications that perform tasks for you. For example, your e-mail application helps you send and receive e-mail, and your Web browser enables you to view Web pages from Web sites around the world. Computer programmers create such applications by writing computer programs that enable computer users to perform their everyday tasks.

Let us consider a simple *application* that displays a line of text. A Java application is a program that executes using the `java` interpreter. (Later in this section we discuss how to compile and run a program.) The program and its output are shown in Fig. 2.1. The program illustrates several important Java language features. Java uses notations that may appear strange to nonprogrammers. In addition, each program we present in this book has line numbers included for your convenience; line numbers are not part of actual Java programs. We will soon see that line 9 does the "real work" of the program—namely, displaying the phrase `Welcome to Java Programming!` on the screen. We now consider each line of the program in order.

Line 1

```
// Fig. 2.1: Welcome1.java
```

begins with `//`, indicating that the remainder of the line is a *comment*. Programmers insert comments to *document* programs and improve program readability. Comments also help other people read and understand a program. The Java compiler ignores comments, so they

```
1   // Fig. 2.1: Welcome1.java
2   // Text-printing program.
3
4   public class Welcome1 {
5
6       // main method begins execution of Java application
7       public static void main( String args[] )
8       {
9           System.out.println( "Welcome to Java Programming!" );
10
11      } // end method main
12
13  } // end class Welcome1
```

```
Welcome to Java Programming!
```

Fig. 2.1   Text-printing program.

do not cause the computer to perform any action when the program is run. We begin every program with a comment indicating the figure number and file name.

A comment that begins with // is called an *end-of-line* (or *single-line*) *comment*, because the comment terminates at the end of the line on which it appears. A // comment can begin in the middle of a line and continue until the end of that line.

Traditional comments (also called *Multiple-line comments*), such as

```
/* This is a traditional
   comment. It can be
   split over many lines */
```

are spread over several lines. This type of comment begins with the delimiter /* and ends with */. All text between the delimiters of the comment is ignored by the compiler. A similar form of comment called a *Javadoc™ comment* is delimited by /** and */.[1]

 Common Programming Error 2.1

Forgetting one of the delimiters of a traditional or Javadoc comment is a syntax error. A syntax error occurs when the compiler does not recognize a line of program code. The compiler normally issues an error message to help the programmer identify and fix the incorrect line of code. Syntax errors are violations of the language rules. Syntax errors are also called compiler errors, compile-time errors *or* compilation errors, *because the compiler detects them during the compilation phase. You will be unable to execute your program until you correct all the syntax errors in it.*

---

1. Java incorporated comments delimited with /* and */ from the C programming language and end-of-line comments delimited with // from the C++ programming language. In this book, we use C++-style end-of-line comments. Comments delimited by /** and */ are special cases of traditional comments. These comments enable programmers to embed program documentation directly in the programs. Such comments are the preferred Java commenting format in industry. The *javadoc* utility program (provided by Sun Microsystems with the Java 2 Software Development Kit) reads those comments and uses them to prepare your program's documentation in HTML format. There are subtleties in using Javadoc-style comments properly. We do not use Javadoc-style comments in the programs presented in this book due to space constraints. For complete information on using javadoc, visit the javadoc Tool Home Page at java.sun.com/j2se/javadoc.

Line 2

```
// Text-printing program.
```

is an end-of-line comment that describes the purpose of the program.

 Good Programming Practice 2.1

Every program should begin with a comment that explains the purpose of the program, author, date and time.[2]

Line 3 is simply a blank line. Programmers use blank lines and space characters to make programs easier to read. Together, blank lines, space characters and tab characters are known as *white space*. (Space characters and tabs are known specifically as *white-space characters*.) White space is ignored by the compiler. In this chapter and the next several chapters, we discuss conventions for using white space to enhance program readability.

 Good Programming Practice 2.2

Use blank lines and space characters to enhance program readability.

Line 4

```
public class Welcome1 {
```

begins a *class declaration*[3] for class `Welcome1`. Every program in Java consists of at least one class declaration that is defined by you—the programmer. These classes are known as *programmer-defined classes* or *user-defined classes*. The `class` *keyword* introduces a class declaration in Java and is immediately followed by the *class name* (`Welcome1`). Keywords[4] (sometimes called *reserved words*) are reserved for use by Java (we discuss the various keywords throughout the text) and are always spelled with all lowercase letters.

By convention, all class names in Java begin with a capital letter and have a capital letter for every word in the class name (e.g., `SampleClassName`). The name of the class is called an *identifier*, which is a series of characters consisting of letters, digits, underscores (_) and dollar signs ($) that does not begin with a digit and does not contain spaces. Some valid identifiers are `Welcome1`, `$value`, `_value`, `m_inputField1` and `button7`. The name `7button` is not a valid identifier, because it begins with a digit, and the name `input field` is not a valid identifier, because it contains a space. Java is *case sensitive*—that is, uppercase and lowercase letters are distinct, so `a1` and `A1` are different (but both valid) identifiers.

 Good Programming Practice 2.3

By convention, always begin a class name with a capital letter and start each subsequent word in the class name with a capital letter.

 Good Programming Practice 2.4

When reading a Java program, look for identifiers in which the first letter of the identifier is capitalized. Such identifiers normally represent Java classes.

---

2. We are not showing the author, date and time in this book's programs because this information would be redundant.
3. Many programmers refer to this as a *class definition*. However, the *Java Language Specification* (`java.sun.com/docs/books/jls`) uses the term "class declaration."
4. The complete list of Java keywords is shown in Fig. 4.2.

Software Engineering Observation 2.1

Avoid using identifiers that contain dollar signs ($). The compiler often uses dollar signs to create identifier names.

Common Programming Error 2.2

Java is case sensitive. Not using the proper uppercase and lowercase letters for an identifier normally causes a compilation error.

In Chapter 2 through Chapter 7, every class we define begins with the `public` keyword. For now, we will simply require this keyword. Keyword `public` is discussed in detail in Chapter 8 along with classes that do not begin with keyword `public`.[5]

When you save your `public` class declaration in a file, the file name must be the class name followed by the ".java" file-name extension. For our application, the file name is `Welcome1.java`. All Java class declarations are stored in files ending with the file-name extension ".java."

Common Programming Error 2.3

It is an error for a `public` class to have a file name that is not identical to the class name (plus the .java extension) in terms of both spelling and capitalization. Therefore, it is also an error for a file to contain two or more `public` classes.

Common Programming Error 2.4

It is an error not to end a file name with the .java extension for a file containing a class declaration. If that extension is missing, the Java compiler will not be able to compile the class declaration.

A *left brace* (at the end of line 4), {, begins the *body* of every class declaration. A corresponding *right brace* (at line 13 in this program), }, must end each class declaration. Notice that lines 6–11 are indented. This indentation is one of the spacing conventions mentioned earlier. We define each spacing convention as a *Good Programming Practice*.

Good Programming Practice 2.5

Whenever you type an opening left brace, {, in your program, immediately type the closing right brace, }, then reposition the cursor between the braces and indent to begin typing the body. This practice helps prevent errors due to missing braces.

Good Programming Practice 2.6

Indent the entire body of each class declaration one "level" of indentation between the left brace, {, and the right brace, }, that delimit the body of the class. This format emphasizes the structure of the class declaration and helps make the class declaration easier to read.

Good Programming Practice 2.7

Set a convention for the indent size you prefer, and then uniformly apply that convention. The Tab key may be used to create indents, but tab stops may vary among text editors. We recommend using three spaces to form a level of indent.

---

5.   Several times early in this text, we ask you to mimic in your own programs certain Java features we introduce. We specifically do this when it is not yet important for you to know all of the details of a feature in order for you to use that feature in Java. All programmers initially learn how to program by mimicking what other programmers have done before them. For each detail that we ask you to mimic, we indicate where the full discussion will be presented later in the text.

Common Programming Error 2.5

It is a syntax error if braces do not occur in matching pairs.

Line 5 is a blank line, inserted for program readability. Line 6

```
// main method begins execution of Java application
```

is an end-of-line comment indicating the purpose of lines 7–11 of the program.
Line 7

```
public static void main( String args[] )
```

is the starting point of every Java application. The parentheses after `main` indicate that `main` is a program building block called a *method*. Java class declarations normally contain one or more methods. For a Java application, exactly one of those methods must be called `main` and must be defined as shown on line 7; otherwise, the `java` interpreter will not execute the application. Methods are able to perform tasks and return information when they complete their tasks. Keyword **void** indicates that this method will perform a task (displaying a line of text, in this program), but will not return any information when it completes its task. Later, we will see that many methods return information when they complete their task. Methods are explained in detail in Chapter 6. For now, simply mimic `main`'s first line in your Java applications.[6]

The left brace, {, on line 8 begins the *body of the method declaration.*[7] A corresponding right brace, }, must end the method declaration's body (line 11 of the program). Notice that line 9 in the body of the method is indented between the braces.

Good Programming Practice 2.8

Indent the entire body of each method declaration one "level" of indentation between the left brace, {, and the right brace, }, that define the body of the method. This format makes the structure of the method stand out and helps make the method declaration easier to read.

Line 9

```
System.out.println( "Welcome to Java Programming!" );
```

instructs the computer to *perform an action*—namely, to print the *string* of characters contained between the double quotation marks. A string is sometimes called a *character string*, a *message* or a *string literal*. We refer to characters between double quotation marks generically as *strings*. White-space characters in strings are not ignored by the compiler.

Common Programming Error 2.6

It is a syntax error if a string does not appear between double quote characters on one line in a program.

`System.out` is known as the *standard output object*. `System.out` allows Java applications to display sets of characters in the *command window* from which the Java application executes. In Microsoft Windows 95/98/ME, the command window is the *MS-DOS*

---

6. In Line 7, the `String args[]` in parentheses is a required part of the method `main`'s declaration. We discuss this in Chapter 7, Arrays.
7. Many programmers refer to this as a *method definition*. However, the *Java Language Specification* (`java.sun.com/docs/books/jls`) uses the term "method declaration."

prompt. In Microsoft Windows NT/2000/XP, the command window is the *Command Prompt*. In UNIX/Linux/Mac OS X, the command window is called a *terminal window* or a *shell*.

Method `System.out.println` *displays* (or *prints*) *a line* of text in the command window. The string in the parentheses on line 9 is the *argument* to the method. Method `System.out.println` performs its task by outputting its argument in the command window. When `System.out.println` completes its task, it positions the *output cursor* (the location where the next character will be displayed in the command window) to the beginning of the next line in the command window. (This move of the cursor is similar to a user pressing the *Enter* key when typing in a text editor—the cursor appears at the beginning of the next line in your file.)

The entire line 9, including `System.out.println`, the argument `"Welcome to Java Programming!"` in the parentheses and the *semicolon* (`;`), is called a *statement*. Most statements end with a semicolon. When the statement on line 9 of our program executes, it displays the message `Welcome to Java Programming!` in the command window. Typically, a method is composed of one or more statements that perform the method's task, as we will see in subsequent programs.

Common Programming Error 2.7

Omitting the semicolon at the end of a statement is a syntax error.

Error-Prevention Tip 2.1

When learning how to program, sometimes it is helpful to "break" a working program so you can familiarize yourself with the compiler's syntax error messages. These messages do not always state the exact problem in the code. When you encounter such syntax-error messages in the future, you will have an idea of what caused the error. Try removing a semicolon or brace from the program of Fig. 2.1, then recompile the program to see the error messages generated by the omission.

Error-Prevention Tip 2.2

When the compiler reports a syntax error, the error may not be on the line number indicated by the error message. First, check the line for which the error was reported. If that line does not contain syntax errors, check the preceding several lines in the program.

Some programmers find it difficult when reading or writing a program to match the left and right braces (`{` and `}`) that delimit the body of a class declaration or a method declaration. For this reason, some programmers include an end-of-line comment after a closing right brace (`}`) that ends a method declaration and after a closing right brace that ends a class declaration. For example, line 11

```
} // end method main
```

specifies the closing right brace (`}`) of method `main`, and line 13

```
} // end class Welcome1
```

specifies the closing right brace (`}`) of class `Welcome1`. Each comment indicates the method or class that the right brace terminates. We use such comments to help beginning programmers determine where each program component terminates. After Chapter 6, we use such comments when pairs of braces contain many statements, which makes the closing braces difficult to identify.

Good Programming Practice 2.9

Following the closing right brace (}) of a method body or class declaration with an end-of-line comment indicating the method or class declaration to which the brace belongs improves program readability.

Compiling and Executing Your First Java Application[8]

We are now ready to compile and execute our program. To compile the program, open a command window, change to the directory where the program is stored and type

```
javac Welcome1.java
```

If the program contains no syntax errors, the preceding command creates a new file called `Welcome1.class` (known as the *class file* for `Welcome1`) containing the Java bytecodes that represent our application. These bytecodes will be interpreted by the `java` interpreter when we tell it to execute the program.

Error-Prevention Tip 2.3

When attempting to compile a program, if you receive a message such as "bad command or filename," "javac: command not found" or "'javac' is not recognized as an internal or external command, operable program or batch file," then your Java software installation was not completed properly. With the Java 2 Software Development Kit, this indicates that the system's PATH environment variable was not set properly. Please review the Java 2 Software Development Kit installation instructions carefully. On some systems, after correcting the PATH, you may need to reboot your computer or open a new command window for these settings to take effect.

Error-Prevention Tip 2.4

The Java compiler generates syntax error messages when the syntax of a program is incorrect. Each error message contains the file name and line number where the error occurred. For example, Welcome1.java:6 indicates that an error occurred in the file Welcome1.java at line 6. The remainder of the error message provides information about the syntax error.

Figure 2.2 shows the program of Fig. 2.1 executing in a Microsoft® Windows® XP command-prompt window. To execute the program, we typed `java Welcome1`, which launches the `java` interpreter and indicates that it should load the ".`class`" file for class `Welcome1`. Note that the ".`class`" file-name extension is omitted from the preceding command; otherwise, the interpreter will not execute the program. The interpreter calls method `main`. Next, the statement at line 9 of `main` displays "`Welcome to Java Programming!`"

---

8. On our Web site at `www.deitel.com/books/downloads.html`, we provide *DEITEL™ DIVE IN-TO™ Series* publications to help you begin using several popular Java™ development tools, including the Sun™ Microsystems Java™ 2 Software Development Kit version 1.4, Sun Microsystems SunOne Studio 4 Community Edition and Borland® JBuilder™ 7 Personal. We will make other *DIVE INTO™ Series* publications available as instructors request them.

Fig. 2.2   Executing `Welcome1` in a Microsoft Windows 2000 **Command Prompt** window.

 Error-Prevention Tip 2.5

When attempting to run a Java program, if you receive a message such as "`Exception in thread "main" java.lang.NoClassDefFoundError: Welcome1`," your CLASSPATH environment variable has not been set properly. Please review the Java 2 Software Development Kit installation instructions carefully. On some systems, you may need to reboot your computer or open a new command window for these settings to take effect.

2.3 Modifying Our First Java Program

This section continues our introduction to Java programming with two examples that modify the example in Fig. 2.1 to print text on one line by using multiple statements and to print text on several lines by using a single statement.

Displaying a Single Line of Text with Multiple Statements
`Welcome to Java Programming!` can be displayed several ways. Class `Welcome2`, shown in Fig. 2.3,[9] uses two statements to produce the same output as that shown in Fig. 2.1.

```
1   // Fig. 2.3: Welcome2.java
2   // Printing a line of text with multiple statements.
3
4   public class Welcome2 {
5
6      // main method begins execution of Java application
7      public static void main( String args[] )
8      {
9         System.out.print( "Welcome to " );
10        System.out.println( "Java Programming!" );
11
12     } // end method main
13
14  } // end class Welcome2
```

```
Welcome to Java Programming!
```

Fig. 2.3   Printing a line of text with multiple statements.

9.   From this point forward, we highlight in bold yellow the new and key features in each program.

The program is almost identical to Fig. 2.1, so we discuss only the changes here. Line 2

```
// Printing a line of text with multiple statements.
```

is an end-of-line comment stating the purpose of this program. Line 4 begins the `Welcome2` class declaration.

Lines 9–10 of method `main`

```
System.out.print( "Welcome to " );
System.out.println( "Java Programming!" );
```

display one line of text in the command window. The first statement uses `System.out`'s method `print` to display a string. Unlike `println`, after displaying its argument, `print` does not position the output cursor at the beginning of the next line in the command window; the next character the program displays in the command window will appear immediately after the last character that `print` displays. Thus, line 10 positions the first character in its argument, "J," immediately after the last character that line 9 displays (the space character before the closing double quote character of the string on line 9). Each `print` or `println` statement resumes displaying characters from where the last `print` or `println` statement stopped displaying characters.

Displaying Multiple Lines of Text with a Single Statement

A single statement can display multiple lines by using *newline characters*. Newline characters are special characters that indicate to `System.out`'s `print` and `println` methods when they should position the output cursor at the beginning of the next line in the command window. Like blank lines, space characters and tab characters, newline characters are white-space characters. Figure 2.4 outputs four lines of text, using newline characters to determine when to begin each new line.

```
1   // Fig. 2.4: Welcome3.java
2   // Printing multiple lines of text with a single statement.
3
4   public class Welcome3 {
5
6      // main method begins execution of Java application
7      public static void main( String args[] )
8      {
9         System.out.println( "Welcome\nto\nJava\nProgramming!" );
10
11     } // end method main
12
13  } // end class Welcome3
```

```
Welcome
to
Java
Programming!
```

Fig. 2.4   Printing multiple lines of text with a single statement.

Most of the program is identical to those of Fig. 2.1 and Fig. 2.3, so we discuss only the changes here. Line 2

```
// Printing multiple lines of text with a single statement.
```

is an end-of-line comment stating the purpose of this program. Line 4 begins the `Welcome3` class declaration.

Line 9

```
System.out.println( "Welcome\nto\nJava\nProgramming!" );
```

displays four separate lines of text in the command window. Normally, the characters in a string are displayed exactly as they appear in the double quotes. Notice, however, that the two characters \ and n (repeated three times in the statement) do not appear on the screen. The *backslash* (\) is called an *escape character*. It indicates to `System.out`'s `print` and `println` methods that a "special character" is to be output. When a backslash appears in a string of characters, Java combines the next character with the backslash to form an *escape sequence*. The escape sequence \n represents the newline character. When a newline character appears in a string being output with `System.out`, the newline character causes the screen's output cursor to move to the beginning of the next line in the command window. Several common escape sequences are listed in Fig. 2.5 with descriptions of how they affect the display of characters in the command window.

2.4 Displaying Text in a Dialog Box

Although the first several programs presented in this chapter display output in the command window, many Java applications use windows or *dialog boxes* (also called *dialogs*) to display output. For example, World Wide Web browsers such as Netscape or Microsoft Internet Explorer display Web pages in their own windows. E-mail programs allow you to

Escape sequence	Description
\n	Newline. Position the screen cursor at the beginning of the next line.
\t	Horizontal tab. Move the screen cursor to the next tab stop.
\r	Carriage return. Position the screen cursor at the beginning of the current line; do not advance to the next line. Any characters output after the carriage return overwrite the characters previously output on that line.
\\	Backslash. Used to print a backslash character.
\"	Double quote. Used to print a double-quote character. For example,

```
System.out.println( "\"in quotes\"" );
```

displays

```
"in quotes"
```

Fig. 2.5   Some common escape sequences.

type and read messages in a window provided by the e-mail program. Typically, dialog boxes are windows in which programs display important messages to the user of the program. Java's class *JOptionPane* provides prepackaged dialog boxes that enable programs to display windows containing messages to users. Figure 2.6 displays the same string as in Fig. 2.4 in a predefined dialog box known as a *message dialog*.

One of the great strengths of Java is its rich set of predefined classes that programmers can reuse rather than "reinventing the wheel." We use many of these classes throughout the book. Java's numerous predefined classes are grouped into categories of related classes called *packages*. A package is a named collection of classes. The packages are referred to collectively as the *Java class library*, or the *Java Application Programming Interface* (*Java API*). The packages of the Java API are split into *core packages* and *optional packages*. The names of most Java API packages begin with either "java" (core packages) or "javax" (optional packages).[10] Many of the core and optional packages are included as part of the Java 2 Software Development Kit. We overview these included packages in Chapter 6. As Java continues to evolve, most new packages are developed as optional packages. These often can be downloaded from java.sun.com and used to enhance Java's capabilities. In this example, we use Java's predefined class JOptionPane, which is in package *javax.swing*.

```java
1   // Fig. 2.6: Welcome4.java
2   // Printing multiple lines in a dialog box.
3
4   // Java packages
5   import javax.swing.JOptionPane;  // program uses JOptionPane
6
7   public class Welcome4 {
8
9      // main method begins execution of Java application
10     public static void main( String args[] )
11     {
12        JOptionPane.showMessageDialog(
13           null, "Welcome\nto\nJava\nProgramming!" );
14
15        System.exit( 0 );  // terminate application with window
16
17     } // end method main
18
19  } // end class Welcome4
```

Fig. 2.6   Displaying multiple lines in a dialog box.

---

10. Some package names in the Java API begin with org.

Line 5

```
import javax.swing.JOptionPane;  // import class JOptionPane
```

is an *import* declaration. Programmers use `import` declarations to identify the predefined classes used in a Java program. The compiler attempts to ensure that you use classes from the Java API correctly. The `import` declarations help the compiler locate the classes you intend to use.[11] For each new class we use from the Java API, we indicate the package in which you can find that class. This package information is important. It helps you locate descriptions of each package and class in the *Java API documentation*. A Web-based version of this documentation can be found at

```
java.sun.com/j2se/1.4/docs/api/index.html
```

Also, you can download this documentation to your own computer from

```
java.sun.com/docs
```

We provide an overview of the use of this documentation with the downloads and resources for *Java How to Program, Fifth Edition* on our Web site, `www.deitel.com`. Packages are discussed in detail in Chapter 8, Object-Based Programming.

Common Programming Error 2.8

All `import` declarations must appear before the class declaration. Placing an `import` declaration inside a class declaration's body or after a class declaration is a syntax error.

Line 5 tells the compiler that our program uses class *JOptionPane* from package *javax.swing*. This package contains many classes that help Java programmers create *graphical user interfaces* (*GUIs*) for applications. *GUI components* facilitate data entry by a program's user and formatting or presentation of data outputs to that user. For example, Fig. 2.7 shows a Netscape 7 window. In the window, there is a bar containing *menus* (**File**, **Edit**, **View**, etc.), called a *menu bar*. Below the menu bar is a set of *buttons* that each specify a task for Netscape to perform if you click them. To the right of the buttons, there is a *text field* in which you can type the name of a Web site to visit. The menus, buttons and text fields are part of Netscape's GUI. They enable you to interact with Netscape. Java contains classes that implement the GUI components described here and others that will be described in Chapter 13 and Chapter 14, Graphical User Interface Components: Parts 1 and 2.

Error-Prevention Tip 2.6

Forgetting to include an `import` declaration for a class used in your program typically results in a compilation error containing the message, "`cannot resolve symbol.`" When this occurs, check that you provided the proper `import` declarations and that the names in the `import` declarations are spelled correctly, including proper use of uppercase and lowercase letters.

---

11. Line 4 of Fig. 2.6 is an end-of-line comment indicating the section of the program in which we specify `import` declarations for classes in Java's packages. We separate the `import` declarations into the following groups: Java packages (for package names starting with `java` or `javax`) and Deitel packages (for our own packages defined later in the book).

buttons   menu   menu bar   text field

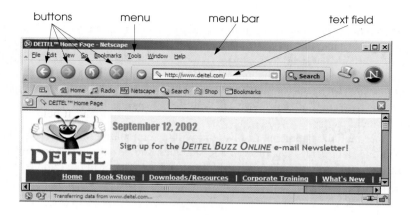

Fig. 2.7   Netscape 7 window with GUI components.

In method `main` of Fig. 2.6, lines 12–13

```
JOptionPane.showMessageDialog(
    null, "Welcome\nto\nJava\nProgramming!" );
```

call method *showMessageDialog* of class `JOptionPane` to display a dialog box containing a message. The method requires two arguments. When a method requires multiple arguments, the arguments are separated with *commas* (,). Until we discuss `JOptionPane` in detail in Chapter 14, the first argument will always be the keyword **null**. The second argument is the string to display in the dialog box. The first argument helps the Java application determine where to position the dialog box. When the first argument is `null`, the dialog box appears in the center of the computer screen.[12]

Good Programming Practice 2.10

Place a space after each comma (,) in an argument list, to make programs more readable.

Method `JOptionPane.showMessageDialog` is a special method of class `JOptionPane` called a *static method*. Such methods often define frequently used tasks, so that programmers are not required to define those tasks themselves. For example, many programs display messages to users in dialog boxes. Rather than require programmers to create code that performs this task, the designers of Java's `JOptionPane` class defined a `static` method for this purpose. Now, with a simple method call, all programmers can make a program display a dialog box containing a message. Static methods typically are called by using their class name followed by a dot (.) and the method name, as in

---

12. Most applications you use on your computer execute in their own window (e.g., e-mail programs, Web browsers and word processors). When such an application displays a dialog box, it normally appears in the center of the application window, which is not necessarily the center of the screen. Later in this book, you will see more elaborate applications in which the first argument to method `showMessageDialog` will cause the dialog box to appear in the center of the application window, rather than the center of the screen.

ClassName . *methodName* (*arguments*)

Many of the predefined methods we introduce early in this book are **static** methods.[13]

Executing the statement at lines 12–13 displays the dialog box in Fig. 2.8. The *title bar* of the dialog contains the string **Message**, to indicate that the dialog is presenting a message to the user. The dialog box includes an **OK** button that the user can press to *dismiss* (*hide*) *the dialog*. This is accomplished by positioning the *mouse cursor* (also called the *mouse pointer*) over the **OK** button and clicking the left mouse button (or the only mouse button on a Macintosh).

Remember that all statements in Java end with a semicolon (;). Therefore, lines 12–13 represent one statement. Java allows large statements to be split over many lines. However, you cannot split a statement in the middle of an identifier or in the middle of a string.

Common Programming Error 2.9

Splitting a statement in the middle of an identifier or a string is a syntax error.

Line 15

```
System.exit( 0 );  // terminate application with window
```

uses static method *exit* of class **System** to terminate the application. This is required to terminate any application that displays a graphical user interface. Notice once again the syntax used to call the method—the class name (**System**), a dot (**.**) and the method name (**exit**). Recall from Section 2.2 that identifiers starting with capital letters normally represent class names. So, you can assume that **System** is a class. Class **System** is part of package *java.lang*. Notice that class **System** is not imported with an **import** declaration at the beginning of the program. By default, package **java.lang** is imported in every Java program; thus, **java.lang** is the only package in the Java API that does not require an **import** declaration.

The argument 0 to method **exit** indicates successful program termination. (A nonzero value normally indicates that an error has occurred.) This value is passed to the command window that executed the program. The argument is useful if the program is executed from a *batch file* (on Windows systems) or a *shell script* (on UNIX/Linux/Mac OS X systems). Batch files and shell scripts often execute several programs in sequence. When the first program ends, the next program begins execution. It is possible to use the argument to method

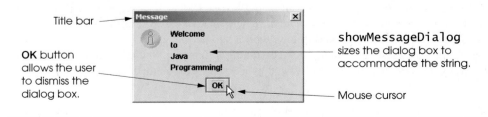

Fig. 2.8 Message dialog box.

---

13. We ask you to mimic our use of **static** methods until we discuss alternatives in Chapter 8, Object-Based Programming.

exit in a batch file or shell script to determine whether other programs should execute. For more information on batch files or shell scripts, see your operating system's documentation.

 Common Programming Error 2.10

Forgetting to call System.exit *in an application that displays a graphical user interface prevents the program from terminating properly. This omission normally results in the command window preventing you from typing any other commands. Chapter 15 discusses in more detail the reason that* System.exit *is required in GUI-based applications.*

2.5 Another Java Application: Adding Integers

Our next application reads (or inputs) two *integers* (whole numbers, like –22, 7 and 1024) typed by a user at the keyboard, computes the sum of the values and displays the result. This program uses another predefined dialog box from class JOptionPane called an *input dialog* that allows the user to input a value for use in the program. The program displays a message dialog containing the sum of the integers. An important concept in this program is that the program must keep track of the numbers supplied by the user for the calculation later in the program. Programs keep track of numbers and other data in the computer's memory and access that data through program elements called *variables*. The program of Fig. 2.9 demonstrates these concepts.

```java
1   // Fig. 2.9: Addition.java
2   // Addition program that displays the sum of two numbers.
3
4   // Java packages
5   import javax.swing.JOptionPane;  // program uses JOptionPane
6
7   public class Addition {
8
9      // main method begins execution of Java application
10     public static void main( String args[] )
11     {
12        String firstNumber;    // first string entered by user
13        String secondNumber;   // second string entered by user
14
15        int number1;           // first number to add
16        int number2;           // second number to add
17        int sum;               // sum of number1 and number2
18
19        // read in first number from user as a String
20        firstNumber = JOptionPane.showInputDialog( "Enter first integer" );
21
22        // read in second number from user as a String
23        secondNumber =
24           JOptionPane.showInputDialog( "Enter second integer" );
25
26        // convert numbers from type String to type int
27        number1 = Integer.parseInt( firstNumber );
28        number2 = Integer.parseInt( secondNumber );
29
```

Fig. 2.9   Addition program that displays the sum of two numbers. (Part 1 of 2.)

```
30        // add numbers
31        sum = number1 + number2;
32
33        // display result
34        JOptionPane.showMessageDialog( null, "The sum is " + sum,
35           "Results", JOptionPane.PLAIN_MESSAGE );
36
37        System.exit( 0 );    // terminate application with window
38
39     } // end method main
40
41  } // end class Addition
```

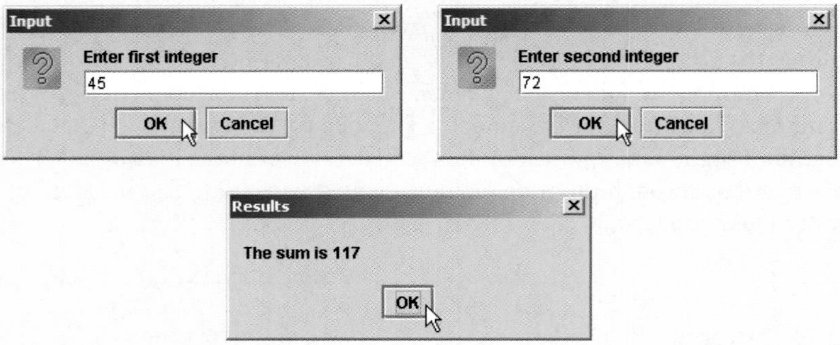

Fig. 2.9   Addition program that displays the sum of two numbers. (Part 2 of 2.)

Lines 1 and 2

```
// Fig. 2.9: Addition.java
// Addition program that displays the sum of two numbers.
```

are end-of-line comments stating the figure number, file name and purpose of the program.
Lines 4–5

```
// Java packages
import javax.swing.JOptionPane;   // import class JOptionPane
```

indicate that the program uses class `JOptionPane` of package `javax.swing`.

As stated in Section 2.2, every Java program consists of at least one class declaration.
Line 7

```
public class Addition {
```

begins the declaration of class `Addition`. The file name for this `public` class must be
`Addition.java`.

Remember that the body of each class declaration starts with an opening left brace (at
the end of line 7), {, and ends with a closing right brace (line 43), }.

As stated in Section 2.2 also, every application begins execution with method `main`
(lines 10–41). The left brace (line 11) marks the beginning of `main`'s body, and the corresponding right brace (line 41) marks the end of `main`'s body. Notice that the entire decla-

ration of `main` is indented one level in the body of class `Addition` and that the code in the body of `main` is indented another level for readability.

Lines 12–13

```
String firstNumber;   // first string entered by user
String secondNumber;  // second string entered by user
```

are *variable declaration statements* (also called *declarations*) that specify the names and types of *variables* that are used in this program. A variable is a location in the computer's memory where a value can be stored for use by a program. All variables must be declared with a *name* and a *type* before they can be used. A variable's name enables the programmer to access the value of the variable in memory. A variable name can be any valid identifier. (See Section 2.2 for identifier naming requirements.) A variable's type specifies what kind of information is stored at that location in memory. The declarations in lines 12–13 specify that the variables named `firstNumber` and `secondNumber` are data of type *String*—i.e., these variables will hold sequences of characters. Class `String` is defined in package `java.lang`.[14] As we will see, Java has many predefined types. Like statements, declarations end with a semicolon (`;`). Notice the end-of-line comments at the end of each line. This use and placement of the comments is a common programming practice that indicates the purpose of each variable in the program.

Good Programming Practice 2.11

Choosing meaningful variable names helps a program to be self-documenting *(i.e., it becomes easier to understand the program simply by reading it rather than by reading manuals or viewing an excessive number of comments).*

Good Programming Practice 2.12

By convention, variable-name identifiers begin with a lowercase letter. As with class names, every word in the name after the first word should begin with a capital letter. For example, identifier `firstNumber` *has a capital* N *in its second word,* Number.

Good Programming Practice 2.13

Declare each variable on a separate line. This format allows for easy insertion of a descriptive comment next to each declaration.

Declarations can be split over several lines, with each variable in the declaration separated by a comma (i.e., a *comma-separated list* of variable names). Several variables of the same type may be declared in one declaration or in multiple declarations. For example, lines 12–13 can also be written as follows:

```
String firstNumber,   // first string entered by user
       secondNumber;  // second string entered by user
```

Lines 15–17

```
int number1;   // first number to add
int number2;   // second number to add
int sum;       // sum of number1 and number2
```

---

14. Remember that Java imports classes from package `java.lang` for you, so `import` declarations are not required for classes in this package.

declare that variables `number1`, `number2` and `sum` are data of type *int*, which means that these variables will hold *integer* values (whole numbers such as 7, –11, 0 and 31,914).[15]

Line 19 is an end-of-line comment indicating that the next statement reads the first number from the user. Line 20

```
firstNumber = JOptionPane.showInputDialog( "Enter first integer" );
```

uses method `JOptionPane` method `showInputDialog` to display the input dialog in Fig. 2.10. The argument to `showInputDialog` indicates what the user should type in the text field. This message is called a *prompt*, because it directs the user to take a specific action. The user types characters in the text field, then clicks the **OK** button or presses the *Enter* key to return the string to the program.[16] Unfortunately, Java's simple form of input that is analogous to displaying output in the command window with `System.out` methods `print` and `println` has limited capabilities. For this reason, we normally receive input from a user through a GUI component (an input dialog box in this program).

Technically, the user can type anything in the text field of the input dialog. Our program assumes that the user follows directions and enters a valid integer value. In this program, if the user either types a noninteger value or clicks the **Cancel** button in the input dialog, a runtime logic error will occur and the program will not operate correctly. Chapter 15, Exception Handling, discusses how to make your programs more robust by enabling them to handle such errors. This is also known as making your program *fault tolerant.*

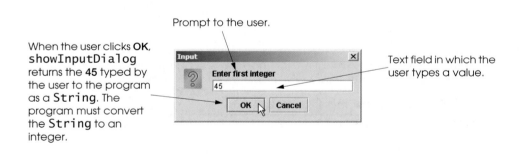

When the user clicks **OK**, `showInputDialog` returns the **45** typed by the user to the program as a `String`. The program must convert the `String` to an integer.

Prompt to the user.

Text field in which the user types a value.

Fig. 2.10 Input dialog box.

15. We will soon discuss types `float` and `double`, for specifying real numbers (numbers with decimal points, such as `3.4`, `0.0` and `-11.19`), and variables of type `char`, for specifying character data. A `char` variable may hold only a single lowercase letter, a single uppercase letter, a single digit or a single special character (e.g., x, A, 7 or *) and escape sequences (such as the newline character, \n). Types such as `int`, `double` and `char` are often called *primitive types*, or *built-in types*. Primitive-type names are keywords; thus, they must appear in all lowercase letters. Chapter 4 summarizes the characteristics of the eight primitive types (`boolean`, `char`, `byte`, `short`, `int`, `long`, `float` and `double`).

16. When you run this program, if you type and nothing appears in the text field, position the mouse pointer in the text field and click the left mouse button—or the only mouse button on a Macintosh—to activate the text field.

The result of `JOptionPane` method `showInputDialog` (a `String` containing the characters typed by the user) is given to variable `firstNumber` by using the *assignment operator*, `=`. The statement (line 20) is read as "`firstNumber` *gets* the value of `JOptionPane.showInputDialog( "Enter first integer" )`." Operator `=` is called a *binary operator*, because it has two *operands*: `firstNumber` and the result of the method call `JOptionPane.showInputDialog( "Enter first integer" )`. This whole statement is called an *assignment statement*, because it is a statement that assigns a value to a variable. Everything to the right side of the assignment operator, `=`, is always evaluated first. Lines 23–24

```
secondNumber =
    JOptionPane.showInputDialog( "Enter second integer" );
```

display an input dialog in which the user types a `String` representing the second of the two integers to add.

Lines 27–28

```
number1 = Integer.parseInt( firstNumber );
number2 = Integer.parseInt( secondNumber );
```

convert the two `String` values input by the user to `int` values that the program can use in a calculation. Static method *parseInt* of class `Integer` converts its `String` argument to an integer. Class `Integer` is in package `java.lang`. Line 27 assigns the `int` (integer) value that `parseInt` returns to variable `number1`. Line 28 assigns the `int` (integer) value that `parseInt` returns to variable `number2`.

Line 31

```
sum = number1 + number2;
```

is an assignment statement that calculates the sum of the variables `number1` and `number2` and assigns the result to variable `sum` by using the assignment operator, `=`. The statement is read as "`sum` *gets* the value of `number1 + number2`." Most calculations are performed in assignment statements. When the program encounters the addition operation, it uses the values stored in the variables `number1` and `number2` to perform the calculation. In the preceding statement, the addition operator is a binary operator—its two operands are `number1` and `number2`.[17]

Good Programming Practice 2.14

Place spaces on either side of a binary operator to make the operator stand out and make the program more readable.

After the calculation has been performed, lines 34–35

```
JOptionPane.showMessageDialog( null, "The sum is " + sum,
    "Results", JOptionPane.PLAIN_MESSAGE );
```

---

17. Portions of statements that contain calculations are called *expressions*. In fact, an expression is any portion of a statement that has a value associated with it. For example, the value of the expression `number1 + number2` is the sum of the numbers. Similarly, the value of the expression in line 21 is the string the user enters in the input dialog.

use static method `showMessageDialog` of class `JOptionPane` to display the result of the addition. This new version of `JOptionPane` method `showMessageDialog` requires four arguments. As in Fig. 2.6, the `null` first argument indicates that the message dialog will appear in the center of the screen. The second argument is the message to display. The third argument of method `showMessageDialog` in Fig. 2.9—`"Results"`— represents the string that should appear in the dialog box's *title bar*. The fourth argument—`JOption-Pane.PLAIN_MESSAGE`—is the *dialog box type*, a value indicating the type of message dialog to display. This type of message dialog does not display an icon to the left of the message. Figure 2.11 illustrates the second and third arguments and shows that there is no icon in the window (below the title bar).

In lines 34–35, the second argument is the expression

```
"The sum is " + sum
```

which uses the operator + to "add" a string (`"The sum is "`) and the value of variable `sum` (the `int` variable containing the addition result from line 31). Java has a version of + for *string concatenation*—combining two strings to form a bigger string. In this context, operator + concatenates a `String` and a value of another type (possibly another `String`); the result of this operation is a new (and normally longer) `String` in which the left operand of + is at the beginning of the string and the right operand is at the end of the string. If we assume that `sum` contains the integer value `117`, the expression evaluates as follows:

1. Java determines that the two operands of the + operator (the string `"The sum is "` and the integer `sum`) are of different types and one of them is a `String`.

2. Java converts `sum` to a `String`—in this case, `"117"`.

3. Java appends the `String` representation of `sum` to the end of `"The sum is "` (notice the space at the end of the string), resulting in the string `"The sum is 117"`.

Next, method `showMessageDialog` displays the resulting string in the dialog box. Note that the automatic conversion of integer `sum` occurs only because the addition operation concatenates the string `"The sum is "` and `sum`. Also, note that the space between `is` and `117` is part of the string `"The sum is "`.

The message dialog types are shown in Fig. 2.12. All message dialog types except `PLAIN_MESSAGE` dialogs display an icon to the user indicating the type of message. Note that a `QUESTION_MESSAGE` icon is displayed on an input dialog box (see Fig. 2.10).

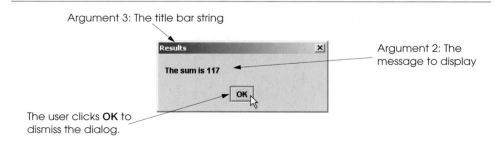

Argument 3: The title bar string

Argument 2: The message to display

The user clicks **OK** to dismiss the dialog.

Fig. 2.11   Message dialog box customized with the four-argument version of method `showMessageDialog`.

Message dialog type	Icon	Description
JOptionPane.ERROR_MESSAGE	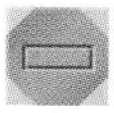	Displays a dialog that indicates an error to the user.
JOptionPane.INFORMATION_MESSAGE		Displays a dialog with an informational message to the user. The user can simply dismiss the dialog.
JOptionPane.WARNING_MESSAGE		Displays a dialog that warns the user of a potential problem.
JOptionPane.QUESTION_MESSAGE		Displays a dialog that poses a question to the user. This dialog normally requires a response, such as clicking on a **Yes** or a **No** button.
JOptionPane.PLAIN_MESSAGE	no icon	Displays a dialog that simply contains a message, with no icon.

Fig. 2.12   JOptionPane constants for message dialogs.

Common Programming Error 2.11

Confusing the + operator used for string concatenation with the + operator used for addition can lead to strange results. For example, if integer variable y has the value 5, the expression "y + 2 = " + y + 2 results in the string "y + 2 = 52", not "y + 2 = 7", because first the value of y is concatenated with the string "y + 2 = ", then the value 2 is concatenated with the new larger string "y + 2 = 5". The expression "y + 2 = " + (y + 2) produces the desired result "y + 2 = 7".

2.6 Memory Concepts

Variable names such as number1, number2 and sum actually correspond to *locations* in the computer's memory. Every variable has a *name*, a *type*, a *size* and a *value*.

In the addition program of Fig. 2.9, when the statement

```
number1 = Integer.parseInt( firstNumber );
```

executes, the string previously typed by the user in the input dialog and stored in firstNumber is converted to an int and placed into a memory location to which the name number1 has been assigned by the compiler. Suppose that the user enters the string 45 as the value for firstNumber. The program converts firstNumber to an int, and the computer places that integer value, 45, into location number1, as shown in Fig. 2.13.

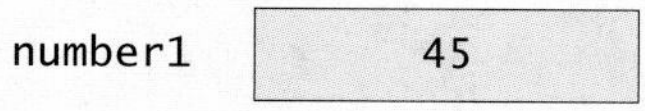

number1   45

Fig. 2.13   Memory location showing the name and value of variable number1.

Whenever a value is placed in a memory location, the value replaces the previous value in that location. The previous value is lost.

When the statement

```
number2 = Integer.parseInt( secondNumber );
```

executes, suppose that the user enters the string 72 as the value for secondNumber. The program converts secondNumber to an int, and the computer places that integer value, 72, into location number2. The memory now appears as shown in Fig. 2.14.

After the program of Fig. 2.9 obtains values for number1 and number2, it adds the values and places the sum into variable sum. The statement

```
sum = number1 + number2;
```

performs the addition and also replaces sum's previous value. After sum has been calculated, memory appears as shown in Fig. 2.15. Note that the values of number1 and number2 appear exactly as they did before they were used in the calculation of sum. These values were used, but not destroyed, as the computer performed the calculation. Thus, when a value is read from a memory location, the process is nondestructive.

2.7 Arithmetic

Most programs perform arithmetic calculations. The *arithmetic operators* are summarized in Fig. 2.16. Note the use of various special symbols not used in algebra. The *asterisk (*)* indicates multiplication, and the *percent sign (%)* is the *remainder operator* (called *modulus* in some languages), which we will discuss shortly. The arithmetic operators in Fig. 2.16 are binary operators, because they each operate on two operands. For example, the expression sum + value contains the binary operator + and the two operands sum and value.

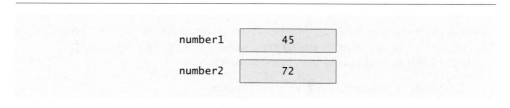

Fig. 2.14 Memory locations after storing values for number1 and number2.

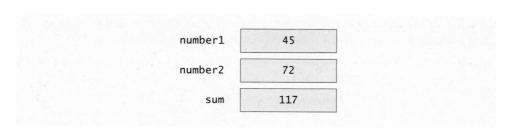

Fig. 2.15 Memory locations after calculating the sum of number1 and number2.

Java operation	Arithmetic operator	Algebraic expression	Java expression
Addition	+	$f + 7$	f + 7
Subtraction	−	$p - c$	p - c
Multiplication	*	bm	b * m
Division	/	$x / y \ or \ \dfrac{x}{y} \ or \ x \div y$	x / y
Remainder	%	$r \ mod \ s$	r % s

Fig. 2.16 Arithmetic operators.

Integer division yields an integer quotient; for example, the expression 7 / 4 evaluates to 1, and the expression 17 / 5 evaluates to 3. Any fractional part in integer division is simply discarded (i.e., truncated)—no rounding occurs. Java provides the remainder operator, %, which yields the remainder after division. The expression x % y yields the remainder after x is divided by y. Thus, 7 % 4 yields 3, and 17 % 5 yields 2. This operator is most commonly used with integer operands, but also can be used with other arithmetic types. In later chapters, we consider many interesting applications of the remainder operator, such as determining whether one number is a multiple of another. There is no arithmetic operator for exponentiation in Java.[18]

Arithmetic expressions in Java must be written in *straight-line form* to facilitate entering programs into the computer. Thus, expressions such as "a divided by b" must be written as a / b, so that all constants, variables and operators appear in a straight line. The following algebraic notation is generally not acceptable to compilers:

$$\frac{a}{b}$$

Parentheses are used to group terms in Java expressions in the same manner as in algebraic expressions. For example, to multiply a times the quantity b + c, we write

```
a * ( b + c )
```

Java applies the operators in arithmetic expressions in a precise sequence determined by the following *rules of operator precedence*, which are generally the same as those followed in algebra:

1. Multiplication, division and remainder operations are applied first. If an expression contains several multiplication, division or remainder operations, the operators are applied from left to right. Multiplication, division and remainder operators have the same level of precedence.

2. Addition and subtraction operations are applied next. If an expression contains several addition and subtraction operations, the operators are applied from left to right. Addition and subtraction operators have the same level of precedence.

---

18. Chapter 5 shows how to perform exponentiation in Java.

The rules of operator precedence enable Java to apply operators in the correct order. When we say that operators are applied from left to right, we are referring to the *associativity* of the operators. We will see that some operators associate from right to left. Figure 2.17 summarizes these rules of operator precedence. This table will be expanded as additional Java operators are introduced. A complete precedence chart is included in Appendix A.

Now, let us consider several expressions in light of the rules of operator precedence. Each example lists an algebraic expression and its Java equivalent. The following is an example of an arithmetic mean (average) of five terms:

Algebra: $m = \dfrac{a + b + c + d + e}{5}$

Java: m = (a + b + c + d + e) / 5;

The parentheses are required, because division has higher precedence than addition. The entire quantity (a + b + c + d + e) is to be divided by 5. If the parentheses are erroneously omitted, we obtain a + b + c + d + e / 5, which evaluates as

$$a + b + c + d + \frac{e}{5}$$

The following is an example of the equation of a straight line:

Algebra: $y = mx + b$

Java: y = m * x + b;

No parentheses are required. The multiplication operator is applied first, because multiplication has a higher precedence than that of addition. The assignment occurs last, because it has a lower precedence than that of multiplication or addition.

The following example contains remainder (%), multiplication, division, addition and subtraction operations:

Algebra: $z = pr\%q + w/x - y$

Java: z = p * r % q + w / x - y;
                  ⑥   ①   ②   ④   ③   ⑤

Operator(s)	Operation(s)	Order of evaluation (precedence)
* / %	Multiplication Division Remainder	Evaluated first. If there are several of this type of operator, they are evaluated from left to right.
+ -	Addition Subtraction	Evaluated next. If there are several of this type of operator, they are evaluated from left to right.

Fig. 2.17   Precedence of arithmetic operators.

The circled numbers under the statement indicate the order in which Java applies the operators. The multiplication, remainder and division operations are evaluated first in left-to-right order (i.e., they associate from left to right), because they have higher precedence than addition and subtraction. The addition and subtraction operations are evaluated next. These operations are also applied from left to right.

To develop a better understanding of the rules of operator precedence, consider the evaluation of a second-degree polynomial ($y = ax^2 + bx + c$):

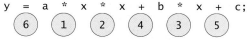

The circled numbers indicate the order in which Java applies the operators. The multiplication operations are evaluated first in left-to-right order (i.e., they associate from left to right), because they have higher precedence than addition. The addition operations are evaluated next. These operations are also applied from left to right. There is no arithmetic operator for exponentiation in Java, so x^2 is represented as x * x.

Suppose that a, b, c and x in the preceding second-degree polynomial are initialized (given values) as follows: a = 2, b = 3, c = 7 and x = 5. Figure 2.18 illustrates the order in which the operators are applied.

Step 1.   y = 2 * 5 * 5 + 3 * 5 + 7;   (Leftmost multiplication)

          2 * 5 is 10

Step 2.   y = 10 * 5 + 3 * 5 + 7;   (Leftmost multiplication)

          10 * 5 is 50

Step 3.   y = 50 + 3 * 5 + 7;   (Multiplication before addition)

          3 * 5 is 15

Step 4.   y = 50 + 15 + 7;   (Leftmost addition)

          50 + 15 is 65

Step 5.   y = 65 + 7;   (Last addition)

          65 + 7 is 72

Step 6.   y = 72;   (Last operation—place 72 in y)

Fig. 2.18   Order in which a second-degree polynomial is evaluated.

As in algebra, it is acceptable to place unnecessary parentheses in an expression to make the expression clearer. Such unnecessary parentheses are called *redundant parentheses*. For example, the preceding assignment statement might be parenthesized as follows:

```
y = ( a * x * x ) + ( b * x ) + c;
```

Good Programming Practice 2.15

Using parentheses for complex arithmetic expressions, even when the parentheses are not necessary, can make the arithmetic expressions easier to read.

2.8 Decision Making: Equality and Relational Operators

This section introduces a simple version of Java's *if statement* that allows a program to make a decision based on whether a *condition* is *true* or *false*. For example, the condition "grade is greater than or equal to 60" determines whether a student passed a test. If the condition in an if statement is *true*, the body of the if statement executes. If the condition is *false*, the body does not execute. We will see an example shortly.

Conditions in if statements can be formed by using the *equality operators* and *relational operators* summarized in Fig. 2.19. Both equality operators have the same level of precedence, which is lower than the precedence of the relational operators. The equality operators associate from left to right. The relational operators all have the same level of precedence and also associate from left to right.

Common Programming Error 2.12

Confusing the equality operator, ==, with the assignment operator, =, can cause a logic error or a syntax error. The equality operator should be read as "is equal to," and the assignment operator should be read as "gets" or "gets the value of." Some people read the equality operator as "double equals" or "equals equals."

Common Programming Error 2.13

It is a syntax error if the operators ==, !=, >= and <= contain spaces between their symbols, as in = =, ! =, > = and < =, respectively.

Standard algebraic equality or relational operator	Java equality or relational operator	Example of Java condition	Meaning of Java condition
Equality operators			
=	==	x == y	x is equal to y
≠	!=	x != y	x is not equal to y
Relational operators			
>	>	x > y	x is greater than y
<	<	x < y	x is less than y
≥	>=	x >= y	x is greater than or equal to y
≤	<=	x <= y	x is less than or equal to y

Fig. 2.19   Equality and relational operators.

Common Programming Error 2.14

Reversing the operators !=, >= and <=, as in =!, => and =<, is a syntax error.

The next example uses six if statements to compare two numbers input by the user. If the condition in any of these if statements is true, the assignment statement associated with that if statement executes. The user inputs two values through input dialogs. Next, the program converts the input values to integers and stores them in variables number1 and number2. Then, the program compares the numbers and displays the results of the comparisons in an information dialog. The program and sample outputs are shown in Fig. 2.20.

```
1   // Fig. 2.20: Comparison.java
2   // Compare integers using if statements, relational operators
3   // and equality operators.
4
5   // Java packages
6   import javax.swing.JOptionPane;
7
8   public class Comparison {
9
10     // main method begins execution of Java application
11     public static void main( String args[] )
12     {
13        String firstNumber;    // first string entered by user
14        String secondNumber;   // second string entered by user
15        String result;         // a string containing the output
16
17        int number1;           // first number to compare
18        int number2;           // second number to compare
19
20        // read first number from user as a string
21        firstNumber = JOptionPane.showInputDialog( "Enter first integer:" );
22
23        // read second number from user as a string
24        secondNumber =
25           JOptionPane.showInputDialog( "Enter second integer:" );
26
27        // convert numbers from type String to type int
28        number1 = Integer.parseInt( firstNumber );
29        number2 = Integer.parseInt( secondNumber );
30
31        // initialize result to empty String
32        result = "";
33
34        if ( number1 == number2 )
35           result = result + number1 + " == " + number2;
36
37        if ( number1 != number2 )
38           result = result + number1 + " != " + number2;
39
40        if ( number1 < number2 )
41           result = result + "\n" + number1 + " < " + number2;
```

Fig. 2.20   Equality and relational operators. (Part 1 of 3.)

```
42
43            if ( number1 > number2 )
44               result = result + "\n" + number1 + " > " + number2;
45
46            if ( number1 <= number2 )
47               result = result + "\n" + number1 + " <= " + number2;
48
49            if ( number1 >= number2 )
50               result = result + "\n" + number1 + " >= " + number2;
51
52            // Display results
53            JOptionPane.showMessageDialog( null, result, "Comparison Results",
54               JOptionPane.INFORMATION_MESSAGE );
55
56            System.exit( 0 );  // terminate application
57
58         } // end method main
59
60   } // end class Comparison
```

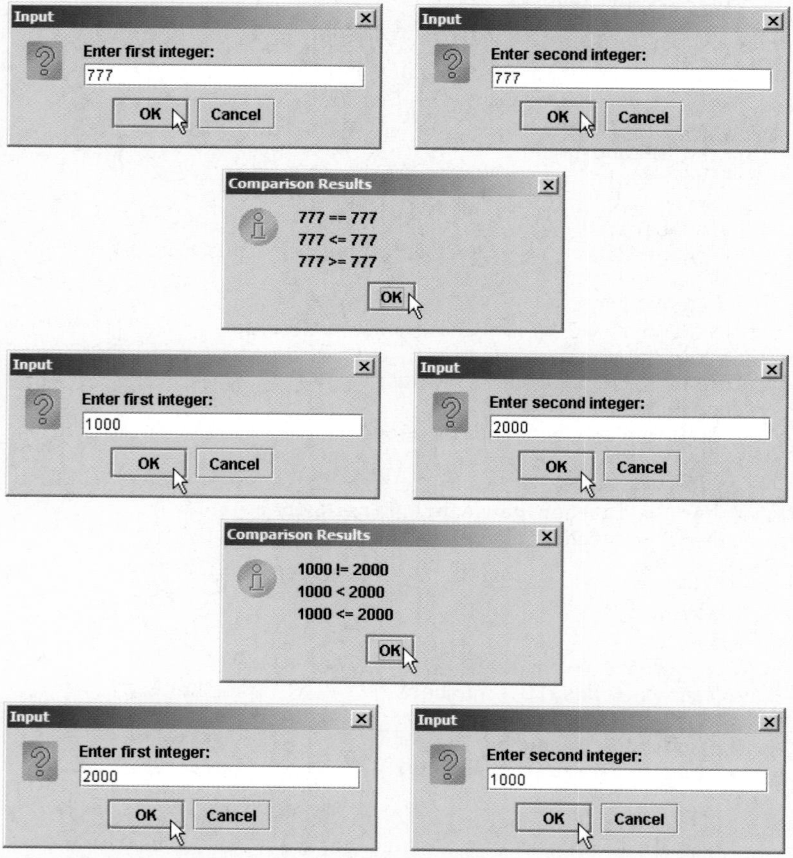

Fig. 2.20   Equality and relational operators. (Part 2 of 3.)

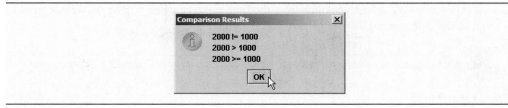

Fig. 2.20   Equality and relational operators. (Part 3 of 3.)

The declaration of class `Comparison` begins at line 8

```
public class Comparison {
```

As discussed in Section 2.2, method `main` (lines 11–58) begins the execution of every Java application.

Lines 13–18

```
String firstNumber;     // first string entered by user
String secondNumber;    // second string entered by user
String result;          // a string containing the output

int number1;            // first number to compare
int number2;            // second number to compare
```

declare the variables used in method `main`. Note that there are three variables of type `String` and two variables of type `int`. Recall from Section 2.5 that variables of the same type may be declared in one declaration or in multiple declarations. Once again, notice the comment at the end of each declaration in lines 13–18, indicating the purpose of each variable in the program.

Line 21

```
firstNumber = JOptionPane.showInputDialog( "Enter first integer:" );
```

use an input dialog to allow the user to enter the first integer value as a string and store it in `firstNumber`. Lines 24–25

```
secondNumber =
    JOptionPane.showInputDialog( "Enter second integer:" );
```

use an input dialog to allow the user to enter the second integer value as a string and store it in `secondNumber`.

Lines 28–29

```
number1 = Integer.parseInt( firstNumber );
number2 = Integer.parseInt( secondNumber );
```

convert each string input by the user in the input dialogs to type `int` and assign the values to `int` variables `number1` and `number2`.

Line 32

```
result = "";
```

assigns to `result` the *empty string*—a string containing no characters. Every variable declared in a method (such as `main`) must be initialized (given a value) before it can be used

in an expression. We do not yet know what the final `result` string will be, so we assign to
`result` the empty string as a temporary initial value.

 Common Programming Error 2.15

Not initializing a variable defined in a method before that variable is used is a syntax error.

Lines 34–35

```
if ( number1 == number2 )
    result = result + number1 + " == " + number2;
```

define an *if statement* that compares the values of the variables `number1` and `number2` to
determine whether they are equal. An `if` statement always begins with keyword `if`, followed by a condition in parentheses. An `if` statement expects one statement in its body. The
indentation shown here is not required, but it improves the readability of the program by emphasizing that the statement in line 35 is part of the `if` statement that begins on line 34.

 Common Programming Error 2.16

*Forgetting the left and right parentheses for the condition in an if statement is a syntax er-
ror. The parentheses are required.*

 Good Programming Practice 2.16

*Indent the statement in the body of an if statement to make the body stand out and to en-
hance program readability.*

Good Programming Practice 2.17

Place only one statement per line in a program. This format enhances program readability.

In the preceding `if` statement, if the values of variables `number1` and `number2` are
equal, line 35 assigns to `result` the value of `result + number1 + " == " + number2`. As
discussed in Fig. 2.9, the + operator in this expression performs string concatenation. For
this discussion, we assume that variables `number1` and `number2` have the value `123`. First,
the expression converts `number1`'s value to a string and appends it to `result` (which currently contains the empty string) to produce the string `"123"`. Next, the expression appends
`" == "` to `"123"` to produce the string `"123 == "`. Finally, the expression appends
`number2`'s string value to `"123 == "` to produce the string `"123 == 123"`. The string
`result` becomes longer as the program proceeds through the `if` statements and performs
more concatenations. For example, given the value `123` for both `number1` and `number2` in
this discussion, the `if` conditions at lines 46 (<=) and 49 (>=) are also true. So, the program
displays the `result`

```
123 == 123
123 <= 123
123 >= 123
```

in a message dialog.

Notice that there is no semicolon (`;`) at the end of the first line of each `if` statement.
Such a semicolon would result in a logic error at execution time. For example,

```
if ( number1 == number2 );  // logic error
    result = result + number1 + " == " + number2;
```

would actually be interpreted by Java as

```
if ( number1 == number2 )
    ;

result = result + number1 + " == " + number2;
```

where the semicolon on the line by itself—called the *empty statement*—is the statement to execute if the condition in the if statement is true. When the empty statement executes, no task is performed in the program. The program then continues with the assignment statement, which executes whether the condition is true or false.

Common Programming Error 2.17

Placing a semicolon immediately after the right parenthesis of the condition in an if state-ment is normally a logic error.

Notice the use of white space in Fig. 2.20. Recall from Section 2.3 that white-space characters, such as tabs, newlines and spaces, are normally ignored by the compiler. So, statements may be split over several lines and may be spaced according to the programmer's preferences without affecting the meaning of a program. It is incorrect to split identifiers and strings. Ideally, statements should be kept small, but it is not always possible to do so.

Good Programming Practice 2.18

A lengthy statement can be spread over several lines. If a single statement must be split across lines, choose breaking points that make sense, such as after a comma in a comma-separated list, or after an operator in a lengthy expression. If a statement is split across two or more lines, indent all subsequent lines until the end of the statement.

Figure 2.21 shows the precedence of the operators introduced in this chapter. The operators are shown from top to bottom in decreasing order of precedence. Notice that all of these operators, with the exception of the assignment operator, =, associate from left to right. Addition is left associative, so an expression like x + y + z is evaluated as if it had been written as (x + y) + z. The assignment operator, =, associates from right to left, so an expression like x = y = 0 is evaluated as if it had been written as x = (y = 0), which, as we will soon see, first assigns the value 0 to variable y and then assigns the result of that assignment, 0, to x.

Operators	Associativity	Type
* / %	left to right	multiplicative
+ -	left to right	additive
< <= > >=	left to right	relational
== !=	left to right	equality
=	right to left	assignment

Fig. 2.21 Precedence and associativity of the operators discussed so far.

Good Programming Practice 2.19

Refer to the operator precedence chart (see the complete chart in Appendix A) when writing expressions containing many operators. Confirm that the operations in the expression are performed in the order you expect. If you are uncertain about the order of evaluation in a complex expression, use parentheses to force the order, exactly as you would do in algebraic expressions. Observe that some operators, such as assignment, =, associate from right to left rather than from left to right.

We have introduced many important features of Java in this chapter, including displaying data on the screen in both a command prompt and in a dialog box, inputting data from the keyboard, performing calculations and making decisions. The applications presented here are meant to introduce you to basic programming concepts. As you will see in later chapters, more substantial Java applications contain just a few lines of code in method main—those statements normally create the objects that perform the work of the application. In Chapter 3, we demonstrate many similar techniques as we introduce Java applet programming. In Chapter 4, we build on the techniques of Chapter 2 and Chapter 3 as we introduce *structured programming.* You will become more familiar with indentation techniques. We will study how to specify and vary the order in which statements are executed; this order is called *flow of control.*

2.9 (Optional Case Study) Thinking About Objects: Examining the Problem Statement

Now we begin our optional object-oriented design and implementation case study. The "Thinking About Objects" sections at the ends of this and the next several chapters will ease you into object orientation by examining an elevator simulation case study. This case study will provide you with a substantial, carefully paced, complete design and implementation experience. In Chapter 3–Chapter 14, Chapter 16 and Chapter 19, we will perform the various steps of an object-oriented design (OOD) process using the UML while relating to the object-oriented concepts discussed in the chapters. In Appendix D, Appendix E and Appendix F, we will implement the elevator simulator using the techniques of object-oriented programming (OOP) in Java. We present the complete case-study solution. This is not an exercise; rather, it is an end-to-end learning experience that concludes with a detailed walkthrough of the actual Java code that we implement based on our design. We have provided this case study so that you can become accustomed to the kinds of substantial problems encountered in industry. We hope you enjoy this learning experience.

Problem Statement

A company intends to build a two-floor office building and equip it with an elevator. The company wants you to develop an object-oriented *software-simulator application* that models the operation of the elevator to determine whether the elevator will meet the company's needs. The company wants the simulation to contain an elevator system consisting of an elevator shaft and an elevator car.

In our simulation, we model people who ride the elevator car (referred to as "the elevator") to travel between the floors in the elevator shaft, as shown in Fig. 2.22–Fig. 2.24.

The elevator contains a door (called the "elevator door") that opens upon the elevator's arrival at a floor and closes upon the elevator's departure from that floor. The elevator door is closed during the trips between floors to prevent the passenger from being injured by brushing against the wall of the elevator shaft. In addition, the elevator shaft connects to a door on each floor (referred to as the two "floor doors") that closes, so people cannot fall down the shaft when the elevator is not at a floor. [*Note*: We do not display the floor doors in the figures, because they would obscure the inside of the elevator. We use a mesh door to represent the elevator door because mesh allows us to see inside the elevator.] The elevator door has a mechanism that pulls the floor doors open and pushes the floor doors closed when the elevator arrives and departs, so it appears as if both doors open at the same time. A person sees only one door, depending on that person's location. A person inside the elevator sees the elevator door and can exit the elevator when this door opens; a person outside the elevator sees the floor door and can enter the elevator when that door opens.[19]

The elevator starts on the first floor with all the doors closed. To conserve energy, the elevator moves only when necessary. For simplicity, the elevator and floors each have a capacity of only one person.[20]

The user of our application should, at any time, be able to create a unique person in the simulation and situate that person on either the first or second floor (Fig. 2.22).[21] When created, the person walks across the floor to the elevator. If the floor door is not already open, the person then presses a button on the floor next to the elevator shaft (referred to as a "floor button"). When pressed, the floor button illuminates, then requests the elevator. When summoned, the elevator travels to the person's floor. If the elevator is already on that person's floor, the elevator does not travel. Upon arrival, the elevator resets the button inside the elevator (called the "elevator button"), sounds the bell inside the elevator, then opens the elevator door (which opens the floor door on that floor). The elevator then signals the elevator shaft of the arrival. The elevator shaft, upon receiving this message, resets the floor button and illuminates the light on that floor.

Occasionally, a person requests the elevator when it is moving. If the request was generated at the floor from which the elevator just departed, the elevator must "remember" to revisit that floor after carrying the current passenger to the other floor.

When the floor door opens, the person who was waiting for the elevator to arrive enters the elevator after the elevator passenger (if there is one) exits. If a person neither enters nor requests the elevator, the elevator closes its door and remains on that floor until the next person presses a floor button to summon the elevator. When a person enters the elevator, that person presses the elevator button, which also illuminates when pressed. The elevator closes its door (which also closes the floor door on that floor) and travels to the opposite floor. The elevator takes five seconds to travel between floors. When the elevator arrives at the destination floor, the elevator door opens (along with the floor door on that floor), and the person exits the elevator.

---

19. Most people think of one "elevator door," when in reality, there is a door in the elevator and a separate door on the floor, and these doors open and close in tandem.
20. After you have studied this simulation, you may want to modify it to allow more than one person to ride the elevator at once and more than one person to wait on each floor at once.
21. To create portions of the graphics for the elevator simulation, we used images that Microsoft provides free for download at `msdn.microsoft.com/downloads/default.asp`. We created other graphics with Paint Shop Pro™ from Jasc® Software (`www.jasc.com`).

The application user introduces a person onto the first or second floor by pressing the **First Floor** button or the **Second Floor** button. When the user presses the **First Floor** button, a person should be created (by the elevator simulation) and positioned on the first floor of the building. When the user presses the **Second Floor** button, a person should be created and positioned on the second floor. Over time, the user can create any number of people in the simulation, but the user cannot create a new person on a floor where there is another person waiting for the elevator. For example, Fig. 2.22 shows that the **First Floor** button is disabled to prevent the user from creating more than one person on the first floor. Figure 2.23 shows that this button is reenabled when the person enters the elevator.

The company requests that we display the execution of the simulation graphically, as shown in Fig. 2.22, Fig. 2.23 and Fig. 2.24. At appropriate points in time, the screen should display a person walking to the elevator, pressing a button, and entering, riding and exiting the elevator. The display should also show the elevator moving, the doors opening, the lights turning on and off, the buttons illuminating when they are pressed and the buttons darkening when they are reset.

The company requests that audio be integrated into the simulation. For example, as a person walks, the application user should hear the footsteps. Each time a floor or elevator button is pressed or reset, the user should hear a click. The bell should ring upon the elevator's arrival, and doors should creak when they open or close. Lastly, "elevator music" should play as the elevator travels between floors.

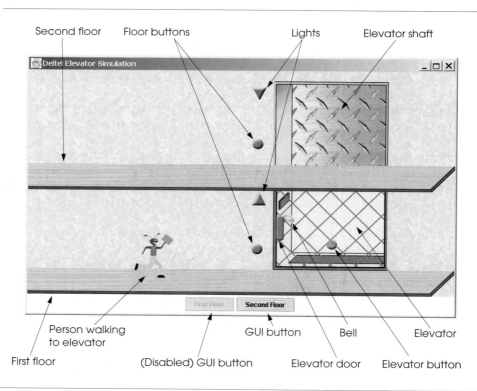

Fig. 2.22   Person moving towards elevator on the first floor.

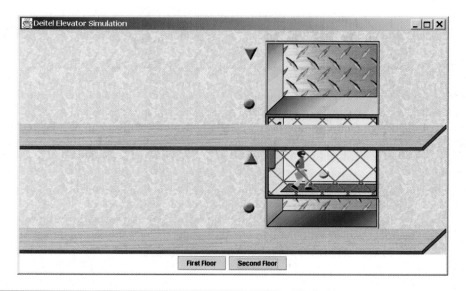

Fig. 2.23   Person riding the elevator to the second floor.

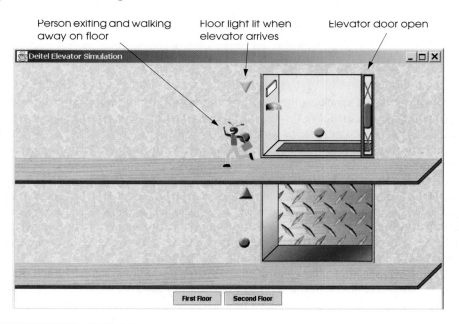

Fig. 2.24   Person walking away from elevator.

Analyzing and Designing the Elevator System

The preceding problem statement we provided for this case study is a simplified example of a *requirements document*—the problem statement specifies the overall purpose of the system and the conditions it must satisfy to solve the company's problem. A requirements document typically is the result of a detailed process of *requirements gathering*, which might include interviews with the users of the system and specialists in particular fields. For example, a consultant who is hired to design software for a bank might interview finance specialists to gain a better understanding of how the software must function.

Software architects must analyze the requirements document and design the system before beginning the program implementation. An analysis of the requirements document should produce a high-level design that describes *what* is needed to solve the problem. The output of the design phase should specify clearly *how* the system should be constructed to satisfy the requirements document. In the next several "Thinking About Objects" sections, we perform the steps of an object-oriented design (OOD) process on the elevator system. The UML is designed for use with any OOD process—many such processes exist. One popular method is the Rational Unified Process™ developed by Rational Software Corporation. For this case study, we present our own simplified design process.

We now begin the design phase of our elevator system. A system is a set of components that interact to solve a problem. In our case study, the elevator-simulator application represents the system. A system may contain "subsystems," which are "systems within a system." Subsystems simplify the design process by managing subsets of system responsibilities. System designers may allocate system responsibilities among the subsystems, design the subsystems, then integrate the subsystems with the overall system. We have decided to divide our elevator-simulation system into three subsystems:

1. the simulator logic (which represents the operation of the elevator system),

2. the display of the simulator on screen (so that the user may view it graphically), and

3. the graphical user interface (which allows the user to control the simulation).

We develop the simulator logic gradually through Chapter 16 and present the implementation in Appendix E. We discuss the GUI components that allow the user to control the model and how the subsystems work together to form the system in Chapter 14. Finally, we introduce the display of the simulator in Chapter 19 and conclude the display in Appendix F.

System *structure* describes the system's objects and their relationships. System *behavior* describes how the system changes as its objects interact with one another. Every system has both structure and behavior—we must design both. However, there are several distinct *types* of system structures and behaviors. For example, the interactions among objects in the system differ from the interactions between the user and the system, yet both are interactions that constitute a portion of the system behavior.

The UML specifies nine types of diagrams for modeling systems.[22] Each diagram models a distinct characteristic of a system's structure or behavior—the first four diagrams relate to system structure; the remaining five diagrams relate to system behavior:

1. *Class diagrams*, which we explain in Section 3.7, model the classes, or "building blocks," used in a system. Each entity in the problem statement is a candidate to be a class in the system (e.g., `Person`, `Elevator`, `Floor`, etc.).

---

22. The UML defines three additional diagram types for managing the nine diagram types that constitute the model. We do not discuss these "model management diagrams"—the *Packages*, *Subsystems* and *Models* diagrams—in this case study.

2. *Object diagrams* model a "snapshot" of the system by modeling a system's objects and their relationships at a specific point in time. Each object represents an instance of a class from the class diagram (e.g., the elevator object is an instance of class `Elevator`), and there may be several objects created from one class (e.g., both the first floor button object and the second floor button object are created from class `FloorButton`). The design for our elevator simulation does not benefit from an object diagram, so we do not include one in this case study.

3. *Component diagrams*, which we present in Section 14.13, model the *artifacts* and *components*—resources (which include graphics, audio and source files) and *packages* (which are groups of classes)—that make up the system.

4. *Deployment diagrams* model the runtime requirements of the system (such as the computer or computers on which the system will reside), memory requirements for the system, or other devices the system requires during execution. We do not present deployment diagrams in this case study, because we are not designing a "hardware-specific" system—our simulation requires only one computer containing the Java 2 runtime environment on which to run.

5. *Statechart diagrams*, which we introduce in Section 5.11, model *how* an object changes *state* (i.e., the condition of an object at a specific time). When an object changes state, that object may behave differently in the system.

6. *Activity diagrams*, which we also introduce in Section 5.11, model an object's *activity*—the object's workflow during program execution. An activity diagram is a flowchart that models the actions the object will perform and in what order.

7. *Collaboration diagrams* model the interactions among objects in a system with an emphasis on what interactions occur. We introduce these diagrams in Section 7.10.

8. *Sequence diagrams* also model the interactions among the objects in a system, but unlike collaboration diagrams, they emphasize when interactions occur. We present these diagrams in Section 16.11.

9. *Use Case diagrams* represent the interaction between the user and our system (i.e., all actions the user may perform on the system). We introduce use-case diagrams in Section 13.17.

In Section 3.7, we continue designing our elevator system by identifying the classes in the problem statement. We accomplish this by extracting all the nouns and noun clauses from the problem statement.[23] Using these classes, we develop a class diagram that models the structure of our elevator simulation system.

Internet and World-Wide-Web Resources

The following URLs provide information on object-oriented design with the UML. You may find these references helpful as you study the remaining sections of our case-study presentation.

---

23. This "noun analysis" of the problem statement is part of our simplified object-oriented analysis (OOA) phase. As mentioned previously, industry software architects typically use a more formal OOA process, such as that prescribed by the Rational Unified Process (RUP).

www.omg.com/technology/uml
This is the UML resource page from the Object Management Group (OMG), which provides specifications for various object-oriented technologies, such as the UML.

www.smartdraw.com/resources/centers/uml
This site shows how to draw UML diagrams without the use of modeling tools.

www.rational.com/uml
This is the UML resource page for Rational Software Corporation—the company that created the UML.

microgold.com/Stage/UML_FAQ.html
This site provides the UML FAQ maintained by Rational Software.

www.softdocwiz.com/Dictionary.htm
This site hosts the Unified Modeling Language Dictionary, which lists and defines all terms used in the UML.

www.embarcadero.com
This site provides a free 30-day license to download a trial-version of Describe™—a UML modeling tool from Embarcadero Technologies®.

www.togethersoft.com
This site provides a free 30-day license to download a trial-version of Together® ControlCenter™—a software-development tool that supports the UML.

www.ics.uci.edu/pub/arch/uml/uml_books_and_tools.html
This site lists books on the UML and software tools that use the UML, such as Rational Rose™ and Embarcadero Describe™.

www.ootips.org/ood-principles.html
This site provides answers to the question "what makes a good OOD?"

wdvl.internet.com/Authoring/Scripting/Tutorial/oo_design.html
This site introduces OOD and provides OOD resources.

Recommended Readings

The following books provide information on object-oriented design with the UML. You may find these references helpful as you study the remaining sections of our case-study presentation.

Booch, G. *Object-Oriented Analysis and Design with Applications*. Reading, MA: Addison-Wesley, 1994.

Fowler, M. and K. Scott. *UML Distilled Second Edition: A Brief Guide to the Standard Object Modeling Language*. Reading, MA: Addison-Wesley, 1999.

Larman, C. *Applying UML and Patterns: An Introduction to Object-Oriented Analysis and Design*. Upper Saddle River, NJ: Prentice Hall, 1998.

Page-Jones, M. *Fundamentals of Object-Oriented Design in UML*. Reading, MA: Addison-Wesley, 1999.

Rumbaugh, J., I. Jacobson and G. Booch. The *Unified Modeling Language Reference Manual*. Reading, MA: Addison-Wesley, 1999.

Rumbaugh, J., I. Jacobson and G. Booch. *The Unified Modeling Language User Guide*. Reading, MA: Addison-Wesley, 1999.

Rumbaugh, J., I. Jacobson and G. Booch. *The Complete UML Training Course*. Upper Saddle River, NJ: Prentice Hall, 2000.

Rumbaugh, J., I. Jacobson and G. Booch. *The Unified Software Development Process*. Reading, MA: Addison-Wesley, 1999.

Rosenburg, D. and K. Scott. *Applying Use Case Driven Object Modeling with UML: An Annotated e-Commerce Example*. Reading, MA: Addison-Wesley, 2001.

Schach, S. *Object-Oriented and Classical Software Engineering*. New York, NY: McGraw Hill, 2001.

Schneider, G. and J. Winters. *Applying Use Cases*. Reading, MA: Addison-Wesley, 1998.

Scott, K. *UML Explained*. Reading, MA: Addison-Wesley, 2001.

Stevens, P. and R. J. Pooley. *Using UML: Software Engineering with Objects and Components Revised Edition*. Reading, MA: Addison-Wesley, 2000.

SUMMARY

- A Java application is a standalone program that executes using the `java` interpreter.

- Programmers insert comments to document programs and improve program readability. A comment that begins with `//` is an end-of-line comment. A comment that starts with `/*` and ends with `*/` is a traditional comment that can span multiple lines.

- A string of characters contained between double quotation marks is called a string, a character string, a message or a string literal.

- Blank lines, space characters, newline characters and tab characters are white-space characters, which, when outside strings, are ignored by the compiler.

- Keywords are reserved for use by Java. Keywords must appear in all lowercase letters.

- Keyword `class` introduces a class declaration and is immediately followed by the class name, which, by convention begins with a capital letter. If a class name contains more than one word, the first letter of each word should be capitalized.

- An identifier is a series of characters consisting of letters, digits, underscores (_) and dollar signs ($) that does not begin with a digit, does not contain any spaces and is not a keyword.

- Java is case sensitive—that is, uppercase and lowercase letters are distinct.

- A left brace, {, and a right brace, }, delimit the body of a class declaration.

- Methods are able to perform tasks and return information when they complete their tasks.

- Java applications begin executing at method `main`. The first line of method `main` must be

```
public static void main( String args[] )
```

- A left brace, {, and a right brace, }, delimit the body of a method declaration.

- `System.out` is the standard output object. `System.out` allows Java applications to display strings in the command window from which the Java application executes.

- Methods `print` and `println` of the `System.out` object display information in the command window. Method `print` does not position the output cursor to the beginning of the next line in the command window when it finishes displaying its argument. The next character displayed in the command window appears immediately after the last character displayed with `print`. When `println` completes its task, it positions the output cursor to the beginning of the next line in the command window.

- The escape sequence `\n` indicates a newline character. Other escape sequences include `\t` (tab), `\r` (carriage return), `\\` (backslash) and `\"` (double quote).

- Every statement must end with a semicolon (the statement terminator).

- Java contains many predefined classes that are grouped into packages—categories of related classes. Collectively, these packages make up the Java class library or the Java API.

- The `javax.swing` package contains many classes for creating the graphical user interface (GUI) of an application. GUI components facilitate user input and program output.
- Class `JOptionPane` is defined in package `javax.swing`. Class `JOptionPane` contains methods that display dialog boxes.
- Programmers use `import` declarations to specify the classes required to compile a program.
- `JOptionPane` method `showMessageDialog` displays a dialog box containing a message.
- A `static` method is called by following its class name with a dot (`.`) and the method's name.
- `System` method `exit` terminates an application. Class `System` is in package `java.lang`, which all Java programs import by default.
- A variable is a location in the computer's memory where a value can be stored for use by a program. Every variable has a name, a type, a size and a value. The name of a variable can be any valid identifier. All variables must be declared with a name and a type before they can be used in a program.
- Declarations end with a semicolon (`;`) and can be split over several lines, with each variable in the declaration separated by a comma (forming a comma-separated list of variable names).
- Variables of type `int` hold integer values.
- Types such as `int`, `float`, `double` and `char` are primitive types. Names of primitive types are keywords of the Java programming language.
- A prompt directs the user to take a specific action.
- A variable is assigned a value by an assignment statement, which uses the assignment operator, `=`. The `=` operator is called a binary operator, because it has two operands.
- When a value is placed in a memory location, the value replaces the value previously in that location. When a value is read out of a memory location, the variable's value remains unchanged.
- `Integer` method `parseInt` converts its `String` argument to an `int` value.
- Java uses operator `+` for string concatenation to enable a string and a value of another type (possibly another string) to be concatenated.
- The arithmetic operators are binary operators, because each operates on two operands.
- Integer division yields an integer result—any fractional part of the result is discarded.
- Arithmetic expressions in Java must be written in straight-line form.
- Operators in arithmetic expressions are applied in a precise sequence determined by the rules of operator precedence. Parentheses may be used to group expressions.
- Some operators associate from left to right; others associate from right to left.
- Java's `if` statement allows a program to make a decision based on whether a condition is true or false. If the condition is true, the body of the `if` statement executes. If the condition is false, the body does not execute.
- Conditions in `if` statements can be formed by using the equality operators and relational operators.
- An empty string is a string containing no characters.
- Every variable declared in a method must be initialized before it can be used.

TERMINOLOGY

addition operator (+)	assignment operator (=)
application	assignment statement
argument to a method	associativity of operators
arithmetic operators (*, /, %, + and -)	backslash (\) escape character

binary operator
body of a class declaration
body of a method declaration
braces ({ and })
case sensitive
character string
class
class declaration
.class file extension
class keyword
class name
comma-separated list
comment
compilation error
compiler
compiler error
compile-time error
condition
decision
declaration
dialog box
division operator (/)
document a program
documentation comment (/** */)
empty string ("")
end-of-line comment (//)
equality operators
     == "is equal to"
     != "is not equal to"
escape sequence
exit method of class System
false
graphical user interface (GUI)
identifier
if statement
import declaration
input dialog
int (integer) primitive type
Integer class
integer division
interpreter
Java Application Programming Interface (API)
Java class library
.java file extension
java interpreter
java.lang package
Javadoc comment
javax.swing package
JOptionPane class
JOptionPane.ERROR_MESSAGE

JOptionPane.INFORMATION_MESSAGE
JOptionPane.PLAIN_MESSAGE
JOptionPane.QUESTION_MESSAGE
JOptionPane.WARNING_MESSAGE
literal
main method
memory
memory location
message
message dialog
method
mouse cursor
mouse pointer
multiplication operator (*)
nested parentheses
newline character (\n)
object
operand
operator
package
parentheses ()
parseInt method of class Integer
precedence
primitive type
programmer-defined class
prompt
relational operators
     < "is less than"
     <= "is less than or equal to"
     > "is greater than"
     >= "is greater than or equal to"
remainder operator (%)
reserved words
right-to-left associativity
rules of operator precedence
semicolon (;) statement terminator
showInputDialog method of JOptionPane
showMessageDialog method of JOptionPane
standard output object
statement
statement terminator (;)
static method
straight-line form
string
String class
string concatenation
string concatenation operator (+)
subtraction operator (-)
syntax error
System class

System.out object
System.out.print method
System.out.println method
terminal window
title bar of a dialog
traditional comment (/* */)
true
type

user-defined class
variable
variable declaration
variable name
variable value
void keyword
white space

SELF-REVIEW EXERCISES

2.1 Fill in the blanks in each of the following statements:
a) A _____ begins the body of every method, and a _____ ends the body of every method.
b) Every statement ends with a _____.
c) The _____ statement (presented in this chapter) is used to make decisions.
d) _____ begins an end-of-line comment.
e) _____, _____, _____ and _____ are called white space.
f) Class _____ contains methods that display message dialogs and input dialogs.
g) _____ are reserved for use by Java.
h) Java applications begin execution at method _____.
i) Methods _____ and _____ display information in the command window.
j) A _____ method is called by using its class name followed by a dot (.) and its method name.

2.2 State whether each of the following is *true* or *false*. If *false*, explain why.
a) Comments cause the computer to print the text after the // on the screen when the program executes.
b) All variables must be given a type when they are declared.
c) Java considers the variables number and NuMbEr to be identical.
d) The remainder operator (%) can be used only with integer operands.
e) The arithmetic operators *, /, %, + and - all have the same level of precedence.
f) Method Integer.parseInt converts an integer to a String.

2.3 Write declarations or Java statements to accomplish each of the following tasks:
a) Declare variables c, thisIsAVariable, q76354 and number to be of type int.
b) Display a dialog asking the user to enter an integer and assign the result to String variable value.
c) Convert the String in part (b) to an integer, and store the converted value in integer variable age.
d) If the variable number is not equal to 7, display "The variable number is not equal to 7" in a message dialog. Use the version of the message dialog that requires two arguments.
e) Print "This is a Java program" on one line in the command window.
f) Print "This is a Java program" on two lines in the command window; the first line should end with Java. Use only one statement.

2.4 Identify and correct the errors in each of the following statements:
a) if (c < 7);
        JOptionPane.showMessageDialog(null, "c is less than 7");
b) if (c => 7)
        JOptionPane.showMessageDialog(null,
            "c is equal to or greater than 7");

2.5 Write declarations, statements or comments that accomplish each of the following tasks:

    a) State that a program will calculate the product of three integers.

    b) Declare the variables x, y, z and `result` to be of type `int`.

    c) Declare the variables xVal, yVal and zVal to be of type `String`.

    d) Prompt the user to enter the first value, read the value from the user and store it in the variable xVal.

    e) Prompt the user to enter the second value, read the value from the user and store it in the variable yVal.

    f) Prompt the user to enter the third value, read the value from the user and store it in the variable zVal.

    g) Convert xVal to an `int`, and store the result in the variable x.

    h) Convert yVal to an `int`, and store the result in the variable y.

    i) Convert zVal to an `int`, and store the result in the variable z.

    j) Compute the product of the three integers contained in variables x, y and z, and assign the result to the variable `result`.

    k) Display a dialog containing the message "The product is " followed by the value of the variable `result`.

    l) Terminate the program and indicate successful termination.

2.6 Using the statements you wrote in Exercise 2.5, write a complete program that calculates and prints the product of three integers.

ANSWERS TO SELF-REVIEW EXERCISES

2.1 a) left brace ({), right brace (}). b) semicolon (;). c) `if`. d) `//`. e) Blank lines, space characters, newline characters and tab characters. f) `JOptionPane`. g) Keywords. h) `main`. i) `System.out.print` and `System.out.println`. j) `static`.

2.2 a) False. Comments do not cause any action to be performed when the program executes. They are used to document programs and improve their readability.

    b) True.

    c) False. Java is case sensitive, so these variables are distinct.

    d) False. The remainder operator can also be used with noninteger operands in Java.

    e) False. The operators *, / and % are on the same level of precedence, and the operators + and – are on a lower level of precedence.

    f) False. `Integer.parseInt` method converts a `String` to an integer (`int`) value.

2.3 a)
```
int c, thisIsAVariable, q76354, number;
```
    or
```
int c;
int thisIsAVariable;
int q76354;
int number;
```
    b)
```
String value = JOptionPane.showInputDialog( "Enter an integer" );
```
    c)
```
int age = Integer.parseInt( value );
```
    d)
```
if ( number != 7 )
    JOptionPane.showMessageDialog( null,
        "The variable number is not equal to 7" );
```
    e)
```
System.out.println( "This is a Java program" );
```
    f)
```
System.out.println( "This is a Java\nprogram" );
```

2.4   The solutions to Self-Review Exercise 2.4 are as follows:

    a)   Error: Semicolon after the right parenthesis of the condition (c < 7) in the if.
       Correction: Remove the semicolon after the right parenthesis. [*Note*: As a result, the output statement will execute regardless of whether the condition in the if is true.]

    b)   Error: The relational operator => is incorrect.
       Correction: Change => to >=.

2.5   a) `// Calculate the product of three integers`

    b) `int x, y, z, result;`
       or
       `int x;`
       `int y;`
       `int z;`
       `int result;`

    c) `String xVal, yVal, zVal;`
       or
       `String xVal;`
       `String yVal;`
       `String zVal;`

    d) `xVal = JOptionPane.showInputDialog( "Enter first integer:" );`
    e) `yVal = JOptionPane.showInputDialog( "Enter second integer:" );`
    f) `zVal = JOptionPane.showInputDialog( "Enter third integer:" );`
    g) `x = Integer.parseInt( xVal );`
    h) `y = Integer.parseInt( yVal );`
    i) `z = Integer.parseInt( zVal );`
    j) `result = x * y * z;`
    k) `JOptionPane.showMessageDialog( null, "The product is " + result );`
    l) `System.exit( 0 );`

2.6   The solution to Exercise 2.6 is as follows:

```
1    // Ex. 2.6: Product.java
2    // Calculate the product of three integers.
3
4    // Java packages
5    import javax.swing.JOptionPane;
6
7    public class Product {
8
9        public static void main( String args[] )
10       {
11           int x;          // first number
12           int y;          // second number
13           int z;          // third number
14           int result;     // product of numbers
15
16           String xVal;    // first string input by user
17           String yVal;    // second string input by user
18           String zVal;    // third string input by user
19
20           xVal = JOptionPane.showInputDialog( "Enter first integer:" );
21           yVal = JOptionPane.showInputDialog( "Enter second integer:" );
22           zVal = JOptionPane.showInputDialog( "Enter third integer:" );
23
24           x = Integer.parseInt( xVal );
25           y = Integer.parseInt( yVal );
```

```
26          z = Integer.parseInt( zVal );
27
28          result = x * y * z;
29
30          JOptionPane.showMessageDialog( null, "The product is " + result );
31
32          System.exit( 0 );
33
34       } // end method main
35
36    } // end class Product
```

Input ✕

Enter first integer:

`3`

OK   Cancel

Input ✕

Enter second integer:

`4`

OK   Cancel

Input ✕

Enter third integer:

`5`

OK   Cancel

Message ✕

The product is 60

OK

EXERCISES

2.7   Fill in the blanks in each of the following statements:
   a) _____ are used to document a program and improve its readability.
   b) An input dialog capable of receiving input from the user is displayed with method _____ of class _____.
   c) A decision can be made in a Java program with an _____.
   d) Calculations are normally performed by _____ statements.
   e) A dialog capable of displaying a message to the user is displayed with method _____ of class _____.

2.8   Write Java statements that accomplish each of the following tasks:
   a) Display the message "Enter two numbers", using class JOptionPane.
   b) Assign the product of variables b and c to variable a.
   c) State that a program performs a sample payroll calculation (i.e., use text that helps to document a program).

2.9   State whether each of the following is *true* or *false*. If *false*, explain why.
   a) Java operators are evaluated from left to right.
   b) The following are all valid variable names: _under_bar_, m928134, t5, j7, her_sales$, his_$account_total, a, b$, c, z and z2.
   c) A valid Java arithmetic expression with no parentheses is evaluated from left to right.
   d) The following are all invalid variable names: 3g, 87, 67h2, h22 and 2h.

2.10 Fill in the blanks in each of the following statements:
   a) The arithmetic operations that have the same precedence as multiplication are the _____.
   b) When parentheses in an arithmetic expression are nested, the _____ set of parentheses is evaluated first?
   c) A location in the computer's memory that may contain different values at various times throughout the execution of a program is called a _____.

2.11   What displays in the message dialog when each of the given Java statements is performed? Assume that x = 2 and y = 3.

      a) `JOptionPane.showMessageDialog( null, "x = " + x );`
      b) `JOptionPane.showMessageDialog( null,`
          `"The value of x + x is " + ( x + x ) );`
      c) `JOptionPane.showMessageDialog( null, "x =" );`
      d) `JOptionPane.showMessageDialog( null,`
          `( x + y ) + " = " + ( y + x ) );`

2.12   Which of the following Java statements contain variables whose values are changed or replaced?

      a) `p = i + j + k + 7;`
      b) `JOptionPane.showMessageDialog( null,`
          `"variables whose values are destroyed" );`
      c) `JOptionPane.showMessageDialog( null, "a = 5" );`
      d) `stringVal = JOptionPane.showInputDialog( "Enter string:" );`

2.13   Given that $y = ax^3 + 7$, which of the following are correct Java statements for this equation?

      a) `y = a * x * x * x + 7;`
      b) `y = a * x * x * ( x + 7 );`
      c) `y = ( a * x ) * x * ( x + 7 );`
      d) `y = ( a * x ) * x * x + 7;`
      e) `y = a * ( x * x * x ) + 7;`
      f) `y = a * x * ( x * x + 7 );`

2.14   State the order of evaluation of the operators in each of the following Java statements, and show the value of x after each statement is performed:

      a) `x = 7 + 3 * 6 / 2 - 1;`
      b) `x = 2 % 2 + 2 * 2 - 2 / 2;`
      c) `x = ( 3 * 9 * ( 3 + ( 9 * 3 / ( 3 ) ) ) );`

2.15   Write an application that displays the numbers 1 to 4 on the same line, with each pair of adjacent numbers separated by one space. Write the program using the following techniques;

      a) using one `System.out` statement.
      b) using four `System.out` statements.

2.16   Write an application that asks the user to enter two numbers, obtains the numbers from the user and prints the sum, product, difference and quotient (division) of the numbers. Use the techniques shown in Fig. 2.9.

2.17   Write an application that asks the user to enter two integers, obtains the numbers from the user and displays the larger number followed by the words "is larger" in an information message dialog. If the numbers are equal, print the message "These numbers are equal." Use the techniques shown in Fig. 2.20.

2.18   Write an application that inputs three integers from the user and displays the sum, average, product, smallest and largest of the numbers in an information message dialog. Use the GUI techniques shown in Fig. 2.20. [*Note*: The calculation of the average in this exercise should result in an integer representation of the average. So, if the sum of the values is 7, the average should be 2, not 2.3333....]

2.19   Write an application that inputs from the user the radius of a circle as an integer and prints the circle's diameter, circumference and area. Use the value 3.14159 for π. Use the GUI techniques shown in Fig. 2.9. [*Note*: You may also use the predefined constant `Math.PI` for the value of π. This constant is more precise than the value 3.14159. Class `Math` is defined in the `java.lang` package, so you do not need to `import` it.] Use the following formulas (r is the radius):

$$diameter = 2r$$
$$circumference = 2\pi r$$
$$area = \pi r^2$$

Do not store the results of each calculation in a variable. Rather, add the result of each directly to a string that will be used to display the results.

2.20   Write an application that displays in the command window a box, an oval, an arrow and a diamond using asterisks (*), as follows:

2.21   Modify the program you created in Exercise 2.20 to display the shapes in a `JOption-Pane.PLAIN_MESSAGE` dialog. Does the program display the shapes exactly as in Exercise 2.20?

2.22   What does the following code print?

```
System.out.println( "*\n**\n***\n****\n*****" );
```

2.23   What does the following code print?

```
System.out.println( "*" );
System.out.println( "***" );
System.out.println( "*****" );
System.out.println( "****" );
System.out.println( "**" );
```

2.24   What does the following code print?

```
System.out.print( "*" );
System.out.print( "***" );
System.out.print( "*****" );
System.out.print( "****" );
System.out.println( "**" );
```

2.25   What does the following code print?

```
System.out.print( "*" );
System.out.println( "***" );
System.out.println( "*****" );
System.out.print( "****" );
System.out.println( "**" );
```

2.26   Write an application that reads five integers and determines and prints the largest and the smallest integers in the group. Use only the programming techniques you learned in this chapter.

2.27   Write an application that reads an integer and determines and prints whether it is odd or even. [*Hint*: Use the remainder operator. An even number is a multiple of 2. Any multiple of 2 leaves a remainder of 0 when divided by 2.]

2.28   Write an application that reads two integers and determines whether the first is a multiple of the second and prints the result. [*Hint*: Use the remainder operator.]

2.29   Write an application that displays in the command window a checkerboard pattern as follows:

```
* * * * * * * *
 * * * * * * * *
* * * * * * * *
 * * * * * * * *
* * * * * * * *
 * * * * * * * *
* * * * * * * *
 * * * * * * * *
```

2.30   Modify the program you wrote in Exercise 2.29 to display the checkerboard pattern in a JOptionPane.PLAIN_MESSAGE dialog. Does the program display the shapes exactly as in Exercise 2.29?

2.31   Here's a peek ahead. In this chapter, you have learned about integers and the type int. Java can also represent uppercase letters, lowercase letters and a considerable variety of special symbols. Every character has a corresponding integer representation. The set of characters a computer uses and the corresponding integer representations for those characters is called that computer's *character set*. You can indicate a character value in a program simply by enclosing that character in single quotes, as in 'A'.

You can determine the integer equivalent of a character by preceding that character with (int), as in

```
(int) 'A'
```

This form is called a *cast operator*. (We will say more about these in Chapter 4.) The following statement outputs a character and its integer equivalent:

```
System.out.println( "The character " + 'A' +
    " has the value " + ( int ) 'A' );
```

When the preceding statement executes, it displays the character A and the value 65 (from the so-called Unicode character set) as part of the string.

Using statements similar to the one shown earlier in this exercise, write an application that displays the integer equivalents of some uppercase letters, lowercase letters, digits and special symbols. Display the integer equivalents of the following: A B C a b c 0 1 2 $ * + / and the blank character.

2.32   Write an application that inputs one number consisting of five digits from the user, separates the number into its individual digits and prints the digits separated from one another by three spaces each. For example, if the user types in the number 42339, the program should print

```
4   2   3   3   9
```

[*Hint*: It is possible to do this exercise with the techniques you learned in this chapter. You will need to use both division and remainder operations to "pick off" each digit.]

Assume that the user enters the correct number of digits. What happens when you execute the program and type a number with more than five digits? What happens when you execute the program and type a number with fewer than five digits?

2.33 Using only the programming techniques you learned in this chapter, write an application that calculates the squares and cubes of the numbers from 0 to 10 and prints the resulting values in table format as shown below. [*Note*: This program does not require any input from the user.]

```
number   square   cube
0        0        0
1        1        1
2        4        8
3        9        27
4        16       64
5        25       125
6        36       216
7        49       343
8        64       512
9        81       729
10       100      1000
```

2.34 Write a program that reads a first name and a last name from the user as two separate inputs and concatenates the first name and last name, separating them by a space. Display the concatenated name in a message dialog.

2.35 Write a program that inputs five numbers and determines and prints the number of negative numbers input, the number of positive numbers input and the number of zeros input.

Introduction to Java Applets

Objectives

- To differentiate between applets and applications.
- To observe some of Java's exciting capabilities through the Java 2 Software Development Kit's demonstration applets.
- To be able to write simple Java applets.
- To be able to write a simple HyperText Markup Language (HTML) document to load an applet into the `appletviewer` or a Web browser and execute the applet.
- To understand the difference between variables and references.

He would answer to "Hi!" or to any loud cry,
Such as "Fry me!" or "Fritter my wig!"
To "What-you-may-call-um!" or "What-was-his-name!"
But especially "Thing-um-a-jig!"
Lewis Carroll

Painting is only a bridge linking the painter's mind with that of the viewer.
Eugène Delacroix

My method is to take the utmost trouble to find the right thing to say, and then to say it with the utmost levity.
George Bernard Shaw

Though this be madness, yet there is method in 't.
William Shakespeare

Outline

3.1 Introduction

In Chapter 2, we introduced Java application programming and several important aspects of Java applications. We also demonstrated how to execute a Java application by using the java interpreter. This chapter introduces another type of Java program, called a Java *applet*— a Java program that can be embedded in a *HyperText Markup Language (HTML) document (i.e.,* a Web page). When a browser loads a Web page containing an applet, the applet downloads into the Web browser and begins execution. This enables us to create programs that anyone can execute simply by loading the appropriate Web page in their Web browser.

The browser that executes an applet is generically known as the *applet container.* The Java 2 Software Development Kit (J2SDK) 1.4.1 includes the *appletviewer* applet container for testing applets before you embed them in a Web page. We normally demonstrate our applets using the appletviewer. Some Web browsers in use today do not support Java 2 directly. One browser that does support Java 2 is Netscape 7.[1] Executing applets in other Web browsers, such as Microsoft Internet Explorer or earlier versions of Netscape, requires the *Java Plug-in,* which is installed as part of the J2SDK 1.4.1.

For positive reinforcement of previous concepts, this chapter revisits several topics presented in Chapter 2. This chapter also begins using the object-oriented programming terminology introduced in Section 1.15.

As in Chapter 2, there are a few cases where we do not as yet provide all the details necessary to create complex applications and applets in Java. It is important to build your knowledge of fundamental programming concepts first. In Chapter 4 and Chapter 5, we present a detailed treatment of *program development* and *program control* in Java. As we proceed through the text, we present many substantial applications and applets.

3.2 Sample Applets from the Java 2 Software Development Kit

We begin by considering several sample applets provided with the Java 2 Software Development Kit (J2SDK) version 1.4. The applets demonstrate a small portion of Java's powerful capabilities. Each J2SDK sample program also comes with its Java *source code*—the .java files containing the Java applet programs. This source code will be helpful as you

---

1.   Netscape 7 is available at channels.netscape.com/ns/browsers/download.jsp.

enhance your Java knowledge—you can read the source code provided to learn new and exciting features of Java. Remember, all programmers initially learn new programming concepts by mimicking the use of those concepts in existing programs. The J2SDK comes with many such programs and there are a tremendous number of Java resources on the Internet and World Wide Web that include Java source code.

The demonstration programs provided with the J2SDK are located in your J2SDK install directory in a subdirectory called demo. For the Java 2 Software Development Kit version 1.4, the default location of the demo directory on Windows is

```
c:\j2sdk1.4.1\demo
```

On UNIX/Linux/Mac OS X, it is the directory in which you install the J2SDK followed by j2sdk1.4.1/demo—for example,

```
/usr/local/j2sdk1.4.1/demo
```

For other platforms, there will be a similar directory (or folder) structure. This chapter assumes that the J2SDK is installed in c:\j2sdk1.4.1 on Windows and in your home directory in ~/j2sdk1.4.1 on UNIX/Linux/Max OS X.[2]

If you are using a Java development tool that does not come with the Sun Java demos, you can download the J2SDK (with the demos) from the Sun Microsystems Java Web site

```
java.sun.com/j2se/1.4.1/
```

TicTacToe Applet

The TicTacToe demonstration applet allows you to play Tic-Tac-Toe against the computer. To execute this applet, open a command window (MS-DOS Prompt on Windows 95/98/ME, Command Prompt on Windows NT/2000/XP or a terminal window/shell on UNIX/Linux/Max OS X) and change directories to the J2SDK's demo directory. Each operating system mentioned here uses the command *cd* to *change directories*. For example,

```
cd c:\j2sdk1.4.1\demo
```

changes to the demo directory on Windows and

```
cd ~/j2sdk1.4.1/demo
```

changes to the demo directory on UNIX/Linux/Max OS X.

The demo directory contains several subdirectories. You can list these directories by issuing in the command window the dir command on Windows or the ls command on UNIX/Linux/Max OS X. We discuss the directories *applets* and *jfc*. The applets directory contains many demonstration applets. The *jfc* (Java Foundation Classes) directory contains many examples of Java's graphics and GUI features (some of these examples are also applets). Change directories to the applets directory by issuing the command

```
cd applets
```

on either Windows or UNIX/Linux/Max OS X.

List the contents of the applets directory to see the directory names for the demonstration applets. Figure 3.1 provides a brief description of each example.

---

2. You may need to update these locations to reflect your chosen installation directory and disk drive, or a different version of the J2SDK.

Example	Description
Animator	Performs one of four separate animations.
ArcTest	Demonstrates drawing arcs. You can interact with the applet to change attributes of the arc that is displayed.
BarChart	Draws a simple bar chart.
Blink	Displays blinking text in different colors.
CardTest	Demonstrates several GUI components and a variety of ways in which GUI components can be arranged on the screen. (The arrangement of GUI components is also known as the *layout* of the GUI components.)
Clock	Draws a clock with rotating "hands," the current date and the current time. The clock is updated once per second.
DitherTest	Demonstrates drawing with a graphics technique known as dithering that allows gradual transformation from one color to another.
DrawTest	Allows the user to drag the mouse to draw lines and points on the applet in different colors.
Fractal	Draws a fractal. Fractals typically require complex calculations to determine how they are displayed.
GraphicsTest	Draws a variety of shapes to illustrate graphics capabilities.
GraphLayout	Draws a graph consisting of many nodes (represented as rectangles) connected by lines. Drag a node to see the other nodes in the graph adjust on the screen and demonstrate complex graphical interactions.
ImageMap	Demonstrates an image with *hot spots*. Positioning the mouse pointer over certain areas of the image highlights the area and a message is displayed in the lower-left corner of the `appletviewer` window. Position over the mouth in the image to hear the applet say "hi."
JumpingBox	Moves a rectangle randomly around the screen. Try to catch it by clicking it with the mouse!
MoleculeViewer	Presents a three-dimensional view of several different chemical molecules. Drag the mouse to view the molecule from different angles.
NervousText	Draws text that jumps around the screen.
SimpleGraph	Draws a complex curve.
SortDemo	Compares three sorting techniques. Sorting (described in Chapter 7) arranges information in order—like alphabetizing words. When you execute the applet, three `appletviewer` windows appear. Click in each one to start the sort. Notice that the sorts all operate at different speeds.
SpreadSheet	Demonstrates a simple spreadsheet of rows and columns.
SymbolTest	Draws characters from the Java character set.
TicTacToe	Allows the user to play Tic-Tac-Toe against the computer.
WireFrame	Draws a three-dimensional shape as a wire frame. Drag the mouse to view the shape from different angles.

Fig. 3.1   The examples from the `applets` directory.

Change directories to subdirectory `TicTacToe`. In that directory, you will find the HTML document `example1.html` that is used to execute the applet. In the command window, type the command

```
appletviewer example1.html
```

and press the *Enter* key. This executes the `appletviewer` applet container, which loads the HTML document `example1.html` specified as its *command-line argument*, determines from the file which applet to load[3] and begins executing the applet. Figure 3.2 shows several screen captures of playing Tic-Tac-Toe with this applet.

Error-Prevention Tip 3.1

If the `appletviewer` command does not work or you receive a message indicating that the command `appletviewer` cannot be found, the PATH environment variable may not be defined properly on your computer. Review the installation directions for the Java 2 Software Development Kit to ensure that the PATH environment variable is defined correctly for your system. You may need to restart your computer after modifying the PATH.

You are player **X**. To interact with the applet, point the mouse at the square where you want to place an **X** and click the mouse button. The applet plays a sound (assuming that your computer supports audio playback) and places an **X** in the square if the square is open. If the square is occupied, this is an invalid move and the applet plays a different sound indicating that you cannot make the specified move. After you make a valid move, the applet responds by making its own move.

To play again, click the `appletviewer`'s **Applet** *menu* and select the **Reload** *menu item* (Fig. 3.3). To terminate the `appletviewer`, click the `appletviewer`'s **Applet** menu and select the **Quit** *menu item*.

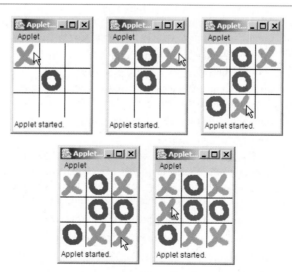

Fig. 3.2   Sample execution of applet `TicTacToe`.

---

3.   We discuss the details of this in Section 3.3.

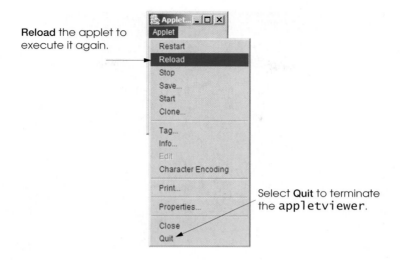

Reload the applet to
execute it again.

Select **Quit** to terminate
the appletviewer.

Fig. 3.3   Applet menu in the appletviewer.

DrawTest Applet

Demonstration applet DrawTest allows you to draw lines and points in different colors. In the command window, change directories to directory applets, then to subdirectory DrawTest. You can move up the directory tree incrementally toward demo using the command "cd .." in both Windows and UNIX/Linux/Mac OS X. In the DrawTest directory is the example1.html document that is used to execute the applet. In the command window, type the command

```
appletviewer example1.html
```

and press the *Enter* key. This executes the appletviewer. The appletviewer loads the HTML document specified as its command-line argument (example1.html again), determines from the file which applet to load and begins execution of the applet. Figure 3.4 shows a screen capture of this applet after drawing some lines and points.

The default shape to draw is a line and the default color is black, so you can draw black lines immediately by *dragging the mouse* across the applet. To drag the mouse, press and hold the mouse button and move the mouse. Notice that the line follows the mouse pointer around the applet. The line is not permanent until you release the mouse button. You can then start a new line by repeating the process.

Select a color by clicking the circle inside one of the colored rectangles at the bottom of the applet. You can select from red, green, blue, pink, orange and black. The GUI components used to present these options are commonly known as *radio buttons*. If you think of a car radio, only one radio station can be selected at a time. Similarly, only one drawing color can be selected at a time.

Change the shape to draw from **Lines** to **Points** by clicking the down arrow to the right of the word **Lines** at the bottom of the applet. A list drops down from the GUI component containing the two choices—**Lines** and **Points**. To select **Points**, click the word **Points** in the list. The GUI component closes the list and the current shape type is now **Points**. This GUI component is called a *combo box*, *choice* or *drop-down list*.

Drag the mouse pointer in the white area to draw.

Select the drawing color by clicking the circle for the color you want. These GUI components are commonly known as *radio buttons*.

Select the shape to draw by clicking the down arrow, then clicking **Lines** or **Points**. This GUI component is commonly known as a *combo box*, *choice* or *drop-down list*.

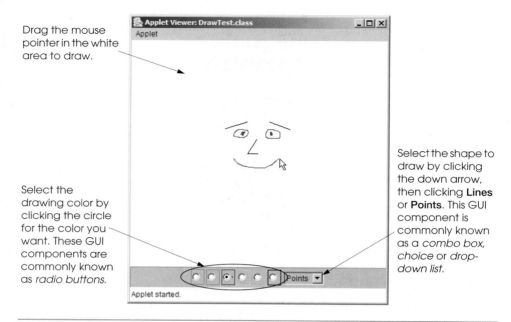

Fig. 3.4   Sample execution of applet `DrawTest`.

To start a new drawing, select **Reload** from the `appletviewer`'s **Applet** menu. To terminate the applet, select **Quit** from the `appletviewer`'s **Applet** menu.

Java2D Applet

Applet Java2D demonstrates the *Java2D API*—Java's capabilities for drawing and manipulating complex, two-dimensional graphics. Change directories to the `jfc` directory in the J2SDK's `demo` directory, then change to the `Java2D` directory. In that directory is the HTML document `Java2Demo.html` that is used to load and execute the applet. In the command window, type the command

```
appletviewer Java2Demo.html
```

to load the HTML document `Java2Demo.html` and begin executing the applet. This demo takes some time to load as it is quite large. Figure 3.5 shows a screen capture of one of this applet's many demonstrations of Java's two-dimensional graphics capabilities.

At the top of the applet are tabs that look like file folders in a filing cabinet. This demo provides 12 tabs with several features on each tab. To change to a different part of the demo, simply click one of the tabs. Also, try changing the options in the upper-right corner of the applet. Some of these affect the speed with which the applet draws the graphics. For example, click the small box with a check in it (a GUI component known as a *checkbox*) to the left of the word **Anti-Aliasing** to turn off anti-aliasing (a graphics technique for producing smoother on-screen graphics in which the edges of the graphic are blurred). When this feature is turned off (i.e., its *checkbox* is unchecked), the animation speed increases for the animated shapes at the bottom of the demo shown in Fig. 3.5. This occurs because an animated shape displayed with anti-aliasing takes longer to draw than an animated shape without anti-aliasing.

Click a tab to select a two-dimensional graphics demo.

Try changing the options to see their effect on the demonstration.

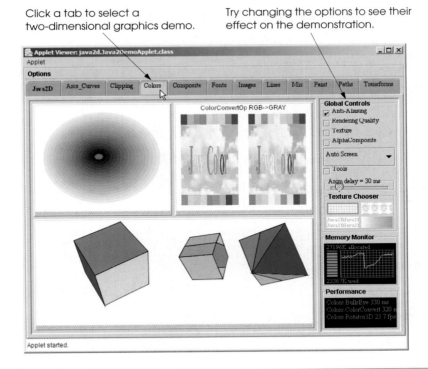

Fig. 3.5   Sample execution of applet `Java2D`.

3.3 Simple Java Applet: Drawing a String

Now, let's build some applets of our own. Remember, we are just getting started—we have many more topics to learn before we can write applets similar to those demonstrated in Section 3.2. However, we will cover many of the same techniques in this book.

We begin with a simple applet that draws `"Welcome to Java Programming!"` on the applet. The applet and its screen output are shown in Fig. 3.6. The screen outputs show this applet executing in three applet containers: The `appletviewer`, the Netscape Web browser and the Microsoft Internet Explorer Web browser. At the end of this section, we explain how to execute the applet in a Web browser.

```
1   // Fig. 3.6: WelcomeApplet.java
2   // A first applet in Java.
3
4   // Java packages
5   import java.awt.Graphics;      // import class Graphics
6   import javax.swing.JApplet;    // import class JApplet
7
```

Fig. 3.6   Applet that draws a string. (Part 1 of 2.)

```
8   public class WelcomeApplet extends JApplet {
9
10      // draw text on applet's background
11      public void paint( Graphics g )
12      {
13         // call superclass version of method paint
14         super.paint( g );
15
16         // draw a String at x-coordinate 25 and y-coordinate 25
17         g.drawString( "Welcome to Java Programming!", 25, 25 );
18
19      } // end method paint
20
21   } // end class WelcomeApplet
```

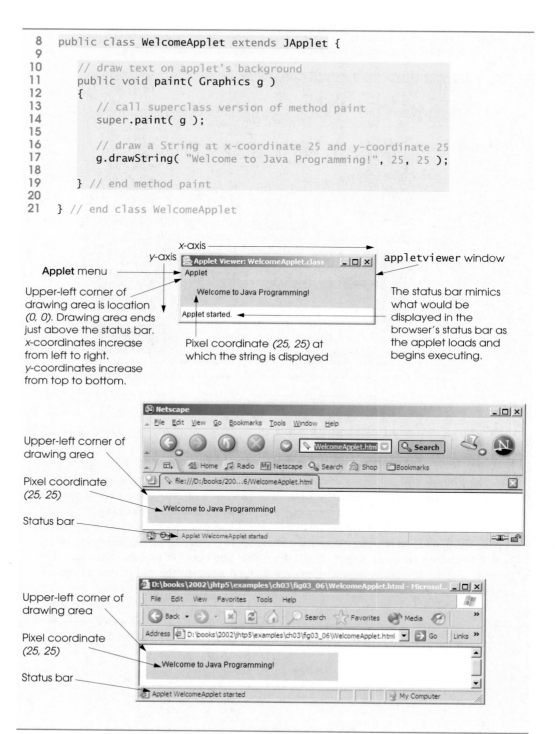

Fig. 3.6   Applet that draws a string. (Part 2 of 2.)

This program illustrates several important Java features. We consider each line of the program in detail. Line 17 does the "real work" of the program—namely, drawing the string `Welcome to Java Programming!` on the screen. But let us consider each line of the program in order. Lines 1–2

```
// Fig. 3.6: WelcomeApplet.java
// A first applet in Java.
```

are comments. Line 1 indicates the figure number and file name for the applet source code. Line 2 simply describes the purpose of the program.

Recall from Chapter 2 that Java contains many predefined entities called classes that are grouped into packages (named collections of classes) in the Java API. Line 5

```
import java.awt.Graphics;      // import class Graphics
```

is an `import` declaration, which indicates that the applet uses class *Graphics* from package *java.awt*. Class `Graphics` enables a Java applet to draw graphics such as lines, rectangles, ovals and strings of characters.[4]

Line 6

```
import javax.swing.JApplet;    // import class JApplet
```

is an `import` declaration, which indicates that the applet uses class *JApplet* from package `javax.swing`. When you create an applet in Java 2, you import class `JApplet`.[5]

As with applications, every Java applet contains at least one public class declaration. A key feature of class declarations is that programmers rarely create class declarations "from scratch." In fact, when you create a class declaration, you normally use pieces of an existing class declaration. Java uses *inheritance* (introduced in Section 1.15 and discussed in detail in Chapter 9, Object-Oriented Programming) to create new classes from existing class declarations. Line 8

```
public class WelcomeApplet extends JApplet {
```

begins a `class` declaration for class `WelcomeApplet`. The class's body is delimited by the left brace, {, at line 8 and the corresponding right brace, }, at line 21. Keyword `class` introduces the class declaration. `WelcomeApplet` is the class name. Keyword *extends* indicates that class `WelcomeApplet` *inherits* existing members (data and methods) from another class. The class from which `WelcomeApplet` inherits, `JApplet`, appears to the right of keyword `extends`. In this inheritance relationship, `JApplet` is called the *superclass* and `WelcomeApplet` is called the *subclass*.[6] Using inheritance here results in a `WelcomeApplet` class that has the attributes (data) and behaviors (methods) of class `JApplet` as well as the new features we are adding in our `WelcomeApplet` class declaration (specifically, the ability to draw `Welcome to Java Programming!` on the applet).

---

4. Chapter 12 demonstrates how to draw in an application.
5. There is an older class called `Applet` (from package `java.applet`) that is not compatible with Java's GUI components from package `javax.swing`. All applet classes in this book extend class `JApplet`.
6. In some languages, superclasses and subclasses are called *base classes* and *derived classes*.

We extend class JApplet because someone else previously defined "what it means to be an applet." Applet containers expect every Java applet to have certain behaviors (methods). Class JApplet already provides all those behaviors. In fact, an applet container expects each applet the container executes to have over 200 different methods. In our programs to this point, we defined one method in each program. If we had to define over 200 methods just to display Welcome to Java Programming!, we would never create an applet, because it would take too long to create one! Using extends to inherit from class JApplet enables us to create new applets quickly by defining only what is new and different about our applets.

The inheritance mechanism is easy to use; the programmer does not need to know every detail of class JApplet or any other superclass from which a new class inherits. The programmer needs to know only that class JApplet defines the capabilities required to create the minimum applet. However, to make the best use of any class, programmers should study all the capabilities of the superclass.

Good Programming Practice 3.1

Investigate the capabilities of a class in the Java API documentation (java.sun.com/j2se/ 1.4/docs/api/index.html) carefully before extending the class to create a subclass. This helps ensure that you do not unintentionally redefine a capability that the superclass already provides.

Classes are used as "templates" or "blueprints" to *instantiate* (or create) *objects* for use in a program. An object (or *instance* or *class instance*)[7] resides in the computer's memory and contains information used by the program. The term *object* normally implies that attributes (data) and behaviors (methods) are associated with the object. The object's methods use the attributes of the object to provide useful services to the *client of the object* (i.e., the code in a program that calls the methods).

When an applet container loads class WelcomeApplet, the container creates an object of type WelcomeApplet that implements the applet's attributes and behaviors. The applet container is the client of the WelcomeApplet object—i.e., the applet container will call WelcomeApplet's methods. Applet containers can create only objects of classes that are public and extend JApplet.[8] Thus, applet containers require applet class declarations to begin with the keyword public[9] (line 8). Otherwise, the applet container cannot load and execute the applet.

Recall from Chapter 2 that when you save a public class in a file, the file name must be the class name followed by the .java file-name extension. For our applet, the file name must be WelcomeApplet.java. For reinforcement, we repeat two Common Programming Errors from Chapter 2.

Common Programming Error 3.1

It is an error for a public class if the file name is not identical to the class name (plus the .java extension) in both spelling and capitalization. Therefore, it is also an error for a file to contain two or more public classes.

---

7. The terms instance, class instance and object are often used interchangeably.
8. Actually, applet containers also can create objects of classes that extend class Applet from older versions of Java.
9. Chapter 8, Object-Based Programming, discusses keyword public and related keywords (such as private and protected) in detail. For now, begin all class declarations with public.

Common Programming Error 3.2

It is an error not to end a file name with the `.java` extension for a file containing a class declaration. The Java compiler will not be able to compile the class declaration.

Error-Prevention Tip 3.2

The compiler error message "`Public class ClassName must be defined in a file called ClassName.java`" indicates that the file name does not exactly match the name of the `public` class in the file or that you typed the class name incorrectly when compiling the class.

Line 11

```
public void paint( Graphics g )
```

begins the declaration of the applet's *paint method*, which is one of three applet methods (sometimes called behaviors) that the applet container calls when it begins executing the applet. In order, these methods are: `init` (discussed later in this chapter), `start` (discussed in Chapter 6) and `paint`.[10] Your applet class gets a "free" version of each of these methods from class `JApplet` when you specify `extends JApplet` in the first line of the class declaration. If you do not declare these methods in your applet, the applet container calls the inherited versions. The superclass methods `init` and `start` have empty bodies (i.e., their bodies do not contain statements, so they do not perform a task) and the superclass method `paint` does not draw anything on the applet.

To enable our applet to draw, class `WelcomeApplet` *overrides* (*redefines*) the superclass version of `paint` by placing statements in the body of `paint` that draw a message on the screen. When the applet container tells the applet to "draw itself" on the screen by calling method `paint`, our message `Welcome to Java Programming!` appears rather than a blank screen.

Lines 11–19 declare method `paint`, which draws graphics (such as lines, ovals and strings of characters) on an applet. Keyword `void` (line 11) indicates that this method does not return any results when it completes its task. The set of parentheses after `paint` defines the method's *parameter list*, which specifies the data that the method requires to perform its task. Normally, programmers pass data to a method through a method call (also known as *invoking a method* or *sending a message*). In Chapter 2, we passed data, such as the message to display, to `JOptionPane`'s `showMessageDialog` method, and we passed data to `System.out.println` to display in the command window. When writing applets, programmers do not call method `paint` explicitly. Rather, the applet container calls `paint` to tell the applet to draw, and the applet container passes an argument to `paint`—namely, a `Graphics` object (called g)—that `paint` requires to perform its task. It is the applet container's responsibility to create the `Graphics` object to which g refers. Method `paint` uses the reference (g) to the `Graphics` object to draw graphics on the applet. The `public` keyword at the beginning of line 11 is required so the applet container can call your `paint` method. For now, all method declarations (like class declarations) should begin with keyword `public`.[11]

Method `paint`'s body is delimited by the left brace, {, on line 12. The corresponding right brace, }, on line 19 ends `paint`'s body.

---

10. Chapter 6, Methods, discusses several other methods that an applet container calls during an applet's execution.
11. We introduce other alternatives in Chapter 8.

Line 14

```
super.paint( g );
```

calls the version of method `paint` from superclass `JApplet`.[12] For now this should be the first statement in every `paint` method declaration.

Line 17

```
g.drawString( "Welcome to Java Programming!", 25, 25 );
```

instructs the computer to perform an action (or task)—namely, to draw the characters of the string `Welcome to Java Programming!` on the applet. This statement uses method `draw-String` of class `Graphics`, which provides drawing capabilities such as drawing strings of characters, lines, rectangles and ovals. The statement calls `drawString` using the reference g from `paint`'s parameter list followed by a *dot separator* (`.`) followed by the method name `drawString`. The method name is followed by a set of parentheses containing the arguments `drawString` needs to perform its task. The "`g.`" at the beginning of the statement indicates that `paint` should use the `Graphics` object that the applet container passes to `paint`.

The first argument to `drawString` is a string to draw. The last two arguments in the list—`25` and `25`—are the *x-y coordinates* (or *position*) at which the bottom-left corner of the string should appear. Drawing methods from class `Graphics` require coordinates to specify where to draw.[13] Figure 3.7 shows the Java coordinate system. Coordinates are measured from the upper-left corner of the applet in *pixels*. A pixel ("picture element") is a unit of display for your computer's screen. Each pixel has a *coordinate pair* that describes the pixel's position on the screen. In a coordinate pair, the first coordinate is the *x-coordinate* (the number of pixels from the left side of the applet), and the second coordinate is the *y-coordinate* (the number of pixels from the top of the applet). In the `appletviewer`, the *(0, 0)* coordinate of the applet appears just below the **Applet** menu. In a Web browser, the *(0, 0)* coordinate of the applet appears in the upper-left corner of the rectangular area of in which the applet executes (see Fig. 3.6).

On a computer screen, a pixel appears as one colored dot on the screen. Many personal computers have 800 pixels for the width of the screen and 600 pixels for the height of the screen, for a total of 800 times 600 or 480,000 displayable pixels. Most computers are capable of higher screen resolutions—i.e., they have more pixels for the width and height of the screen. The size of an applet on the screen depends on the size and resolution of the screen. For screens with the same size, the applet will appear smaller on the screen with the higher resolution due to the greater number of pixels on the screen.

When line 17 executes, it draws `Welcome to Java Programming!` on the applet at the coordinates `25` and `25`. Note that the quotation marks enclosing the string are *not* displayed on the screen.

---

12. For reasons that will become clear later in the text, this statement should be the first statement in every applet's `paint` method. Although the early examples of applets will work without this statement, omitting this statement causes subtle errors in more elaborate applets that combine drawing and GUI components. Including this statement now will get you in the habit of using it and will save time and effort as you build more substantial applets later. We explain the "`super.`" syntax in Chapter 9.

13. We demonstrate drawing in applications in Chapter 12.

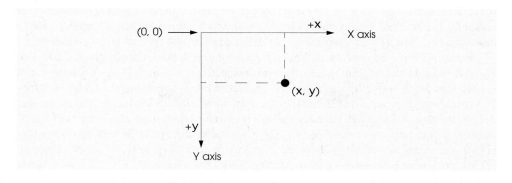

Fig. 3.7   Java coordinate system. Units are measured in pixels.

As an aside, why would you want copies of methods `init`, `start` and `paint` if they do not perform a task? The predefined start-up sequence of method calls made by the applet container for every applet is always `init`, `start` and `paint`—this guarantees that these methods will be called as every applet begins execution. Every applet does not need all three of these methods. However, the applet container does not know that. Thus, it expects each of these methods to be defined so it can provide a consistent start-up sequence for each applet. This is similar to applications always starting execution with `main`. Inheriting the "default" versions of these methods guarantees that the applet container can treat each applet uniformly by calling `init`, `start` and `paint` as applet execution begins. Also, the programmer can concentrate on defining only the methods required for a particular applet.

Compiling and Executing `WelcomeApplet`[14]

As with application classes, you must compile an applet class before it can execute. After creating class `WelcomeApplet` and saving it in `WelcomeApplet.java`, open a command window, change to the directory in which you saved the applet class declaration and type the command

```
javac WelcomeApplet.java
```

to compile class `WelcomeApplet`. If there are no syntax errors, the resulting bytecodes are stored in the file `WelcomeApplet.class` (the class file for `WelcomeApplet`).

Recall that applets are embedded in Web pages for execution in an applet container (`appletviewer` or a browser). Before you can execute the applet, you must create an *HTML (HyperText Markup Language)* document to load the applet into the applet container. Typically, an HTML document ends with an ".*html*" or ".*htm*" file-name extension. Browsers display the contents of documents that contain text (also known as *text*

---

14. On our Web site at `www.deitel.com/books/downloads.html`, we provide *DEITEL™ DIVE IN-TO™ Series* publications to help you begin using several popular Java™ development tools, including the Sun™ Microsystems Java™ 2 Software Development Kit version 1.4, Sun Microsystems Sun One Studio 4 Community Edition and Borland® JBuilder™ 7 Personal. We will make other *DIVE INTO™ Series* publications available as instructors request them.

files). To execute a Java applet, an HTML document must indicate which applet the applet container should load and execute. Figure 3.8 shows a simple HTML document—`WelcomeApplet.html`—that loads the applet defined in Fig. 3.6 into an applet container.

Many HTML elements are delimited by pairs of *tags*. For example, lines 1 and 4 of Fig. 3.8 indicate the beginning and the end, respectively, of the HTML document. All HTML tags begin with a *left angle bracket, <,* and end with a *right angle bracket, >.* Lines 2–3 specify an *applet element* that tells the applet container to load a specific applet and defines the size of the applet's display area (its *width* and *height* in pixels) in the applet container (i.e., the `appletviewer` or browser). Normally, the applet and its corresponding HTML document are stored in the same directory on disk. Typically, a browser loads an HTML document from a computer (other than your own) connected to the Internet. However, HTML documents also can reside on your computer (as we demonstrated in Section 3.2). When an applet container encounters an HTML document that specifies an applet to execute, the applet container automatically loads the applet's `.class` file (or files) from the same directory on the computer in which the HTML document resides.

The `applet` element has several *attributes*. The first attribute on line 2, `code = "WelcomeApplet.class"`, indicates that the file `WelcomeApplet.class` contains the compiled applet class. Recall that when you compile your Java programs, every class is compiled into a separate file that has the same name as the class and ends with the `.class` extension. The second and third attributes on line 2 indicate the *width* and the *height* of the applet in pixels. The upper-left corner of the applet's display area always has *x*-coordinate 0 and *y*-coordinate 0. The width of this applet is 300 pixels and its height is 45 pixels. You may want (or need) to use larger `width` and `height` values to define a larger area for your applets. The `</applet>` tag (line 3) terminates the `applet` element that began on line 2. The `</html>` tag (line 4) specifies the end of the HTML document.

Look-and-Feel Observation 3.1

To ensure that an applet can be viewed properly on most people's computer screens, each applet should generally be less than 800 pixels wide and 600 pixels tall—dimensions supported by most computer screens.

Common Programming Error 3.3

Forgetting the ending `</applet>` tag prevents the applet from loading into the `appletviewer` or browser properly.

Error-Prevention Tip 3.3

If you receive a `MissingResourceException` error message when loading an applet into the `appletviewer` or a browser, check the `<applet>` tag in the HTML document carefully for syntax errors, such as commas (,) between the attributes.

```
1    <html>
2    <applet code = "WelcomeApplet.class" width = "300" height = "45">
3    </applet>
4    </html>
```

Fig. 3.8   `WelcomeApplet.html` loads class `WelcomeApplet` of Fig. 3.6 into the `appletviewer`.

The `appletviewer` understands only the `<applet>` and `</applet>` HTML tags, so it is sometimes referred to as the "minimal browser." (It ignores all other HTML tags.) The `appletviewer` is an ideal place to test an applet and ensure that it executes properly. Once the applet's execution is verified, you can add the applet's HTML tags to an HTML document that will be viewed by people browsing the Internet.

To execute `WelcomeApplet` in the `appletviewer`, open a command window, change to the directory containing your applet and HTML document, then type

```
appletviewer WelcomeApplet.html
```

The `appletviewer` uses an HTML document to load an applet. This is different from the `java` interpreter for applications, which requires only the class name of the application class. Also, the preceding command must be issued from the directory in which the HTML document and the applet's `.class` file are located.

Error-Prevention Tip 3.4

Test your applets in the `appletviewer` applet container before executing them in a Web browser. This enables you to see error messages that may occur. Also, once an applet is executing in a browser, it is sometimes difficult to reload the applet after making changes to the applet's class declaration. Browsers often save a copy of an applet in memory until the current browsing session terminates (i.e., all browser windows are closed). Thus, if you change an applet, recompile the applet, then reload the applet in the browser, you may not see the changes because the browser may still be executing the original version of the applet. Close all your browser windows to remove the old version of the applet from memory. Open a new browser window and load the applet to see your changes.

Error-Prevention Tip 3.5

Test your applets in every Web browser (including multiple versions of the same Web browser) in which the applets will execute to ensure that they operate correctly in each browser.

Running an Applet in a Web Browser

The sample program executions in Fig. 3.6 demonstrate `WelcomeApplet` executing in the appletviewer and in the Netscape and Microsoft Internet Explorer Web browsers. To execute an applet in Netscape, perform the following steps:

1. Select **Open File...** from the **File** menu.

2. In the dialog box that appears, locate the directory containing the `.class` file and HTML document for the applet you wish to execute.

3. Select the HTML document.

4. Click the **Open** button.

To execute an applet in Microsoft Internet Explorer, perform the following steps:

1. Select **Open...** from the **File** menu.

2. In the dialog box that appears, click the **Browse...** button.

3. In the dialog box that appears, locate the directory containing the `.class` file and HTML document for the applet you wish to execute.

4. Select the HTML document.

5. Click the **Open** button.

If your applet executes in the `appletviewer`, but does not execute in Netscape or Internet Explorer, the Java Plug-in might not be installed. In this case, visit the Web site `java.sun.com/getjava`. This site provides Java Plug-in installation instructions for several platforms. If you are using Internet Explorer, you can simply click the **Free Download** button at the top of the page to install the Java Plug-in for Internet Explorer.[15]

3.4 Drawing Strings and Lines

Let us consider another applet. An applet can draw `Welcome to Java Programming!` several ways. For example, an applet can call method `drawString` twice in method `paint` to display multiple lines of text as in Fig. 3.9. The HTML document to load this applet into an applet container is shown in Fig. 3.10.

```
1   // Fig. 3.9: WelcomeApplet2.java
2   // Displaying multiple strings in an applet.
3
4   // Java packages
5   import java.awt.Graphics;     // import class Graphics
6   import javax.swing.JApplet;   // import class JApplet
7
8   public class WelcomeApplet2 extends JApplet {
9
10      // draw text on applet's background
11      public void paint( Graphics g )
12      {
13         // call superclass version of method paint
14         super.paint( g );
15
16         // draw two Strings at different locations
17         g.drawString( "Welcome to", 25, 25 );
18         g.drawString( "Java Programming!", 25, 40 );
19
20      } // end method paint
21
22   } // end class WelcomeApplet2
```

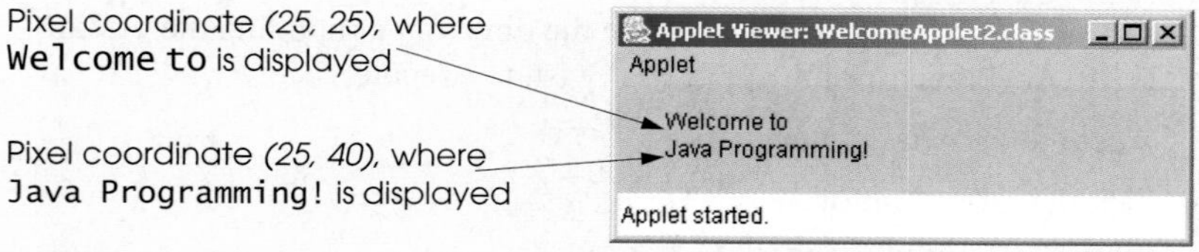

Pixel coordinate *(25, 25),* where
Welcome to is displayed

Pixel coordinate *(25, 40),* where
Java Programming! is displayed

Applet Viewer: WelcomeApplet2.class
Applet

Welcome to
Java Programming!

Applet started.

Fig. 3.9   Drawing strings on an applet.

15. If after installing the Java Plug-in, applets still do not execute in Internet Explorer, click the **Tools** menu and select **Internet Options…**, then click the **Advanced** tab in the window that appears. Locate the option "**Use Java 2 v1.4.1 for <applet> (requires restart)**" and ensure that it is checked, then click **OK**. Close all your browser windows before attempting to load another applet.

```
1  <html>
2  <applet code = "WelcomeApplet2.class" width = "300" height = "60">
3  </applet>
4  </html>
```

Fig. 3.10   `WelcomeApplet2.html` loads class `WelcomeApplet2` of Fig. 3.9 into the `appletviewer`.

Each call to **drawString** can draw at any pixel location on the applet. The reason the two lines of text are left aligned in Fig. 3.9 is that both use the same *x*-coordinate (25). Also, each **drawString** method call uses a different *y*-coordinate (25 on line 17 and 40 on line 18), so the strings appear at different vertical locations on the applet. If we reverse lines 17 and 18 in the program, the output window will still appear as shown because the order of drawing statements does not affect the pixel coordinates specified in each drawing statement. When drawing graphics, lines of text are not separated by newline characters (as was the case with **System.out**'s method **println** and **JOptionPane**'s method **showMessageDialog** in Chapter 2). In fact, if you try to output a string containing a newline character (\n), you will simply see a small black box at the newline's position in the string, which indicates that **drawString** does not understand the character.

To make drawing more interesting, the applet of Fig. 3.11 draws two lines and a string. The HTML document to load the applet into an applet container is shown in Fig. 3.12.

```
1   // Fig. 3.11: WelcomeLines.java
2   // Displaying text and lines
3
4   // Java packages
5   import java.awt.Graphics;    // import class Graphics
6   import javax.swing.JApplet;  // import class JApplet
7
8   public class WelcomeLines extends JApplet {
9
10     // draw lines and a string on applet's background
11     public void paint( Graphics g )
12     {
13        // call superclass version of method paint
14        super.paint( g );
15
16        // draw horizontal line from (15, 10) to (210, 10)
17        g.drawLine( 15, 10, 210, 10 );
18
19        // draw horizontal line from (15, 30) to (210, 30)
20        g.drawLine( 15, 30, 210, 30 );
21
22        // draw String between lines at location (25, 25)
23        g.drawString( "Welcome to Java Programming!", 25, 25 );
24
25     } // end method paint
26
27  } // end class WelcomeLines
```

Fig. 3.11   Drawing strings and lines. (Part 1 of 2.)

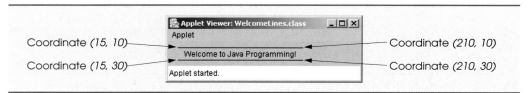

Coordinate *(15, 10)*
Coordinate *(15, 30)*
Coordinate *(210, 10)*
Coordinate *(210, 30)*

Fig. 3.11   Drawing strings and lines. (Part 2 of 2.)

```
1   <html>
2   <applet code = "WelcomeLines.class" width = "300" height = "40">
3   </applet>
4   </html>
```

Fig. 3.12   The `WelcomeLines.html` document, which loads class `WelcomeLines` of Fig. 3.11 into the `appletviewer`.

Lines 17 and 20 of method `paint`

```
g.drawLine( 15, 10, 210, 10 );
g.drawLine( 15, 30, 210, 30 );
```

use *method drawLine* of class `Graphics` to indicate that the `Graphics` object that g refers to should draw lines. Method `drawLine` requires four arguments that represent the two end points of the line on the applet—the *x*-coordinate and *y*-coordinate of the first end point of the line and the *x*-coordinate and *y*-coordinate of the second end point of the line. All coordinate values are specified with respect to the upper-left corner *(0, 0)* coordinate of the applet. Method `drawLine` draws a straight line between the two end points. In this example, we experimented with various sets of coordinates to determine the location and length of the lines.

3.5 Adding Floating-Point Numbers

Our next applet (Fig. 3.13) mimics the application of Fig. 2.9 for adding two integers. However, this applet requests that the user enter two *floating-point numbers* (i.e., numbers with a decimal point, such as 7.33, 0.0975 and 1000.12345). To store floating-point numbers in memory, we introduce primitive type *double*, which represents *double-precision floating-point* numbers. There is also primitive type *float* for *storing single-precision floating-point* numbers. A `double` requires more memory to store a floating-point value, but stores it with approximately twice the precision of a `float` (15 significant digits for `double` vs. seven significant digits for `float`).

```
1   // Fig. 3.13: AdditionApplet.java
2   // Adding two floating-point numbers.
3
4   // Java packages
5   import java.awt.Graphics;    // import class Graphics
6   import javax.swing.*;        // import package javax.swing
7
```

Fig. 3.13   Adding `double` values. (Part 1 of 3.)

```
 8   public class AdditionApplet extends JApplet {
 9      double sum;   // sum of values entered by user
10
11      // initialize applet by obtaining values from user
12      public void init()
13      {
14         String firstNumber;   // first string entered by user
15         String secondNumber;  // second string entered by user
16
17         double number1;       // first number to add
18         double number2;       // second number to add
19
20         // obtain first number from user
21         firstNumber = JOptionPane.showInputDialog(
22            "Enter first floating-point value" );
23
24         // obtain second number from user
25         secondNumber = JOptionPane.showInputDialog(
26            "Enter second floating-point value" );
27
28         // convert numbers from type String to type double
29         number1 = Double.parseDouble( firstNumber );
30         number2 = Double.parseDouble( secondNumber );
31
32         // add numbers
33         sum = number1 + number2;
34
35      } // end method init
36
37      // draw results in a rectangle on applet's background
38      public void paint( Graphics g )
39      {
40         // call superclass version of method paint
41         super.paint( g );
42
43         // draw rectangle starting from (15, 10) that is 270
44         // pixels wide and 20 pixels tall
45         g.drawRect( 15, 10, 270, 20 );
46
47         // draw results as a String at (25, 25)
48         g.drawString( "The sum is " + sum, 25, 25 );
49
50      } // end method paint
51
52   } // end class AdditionApplet
```

Fig. 3.13   Adding `double` values. (Part 2 of 3.)

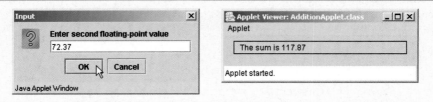

Fig. 3.13   Adding **double** values. (Part 3 of 3.)

Once again, we use **JOptionPane.showInputDialog** to request input from the user. The applet computes the sum of the input values and displays the result by drawing a string inside a rectangle on the applet. The HTML document to load this applet into the **appletviewer** is shown in Fig. 3.14.

Line 5 of Fig. 3.13

```
import java.awt.Graphics;   // import class Graphics
```

imports class **Graphics** (from package **java.awt**) for use in this applet. Actually, the **import** declaration at line 5 is not required if we always use the complete name of class **Graphics**—*java.awt.Graphics*—which includes the full package name and class name. For example, the first line of method **paint** could be written as

```
public void paint( java.awt.Graphics g )
```

Software Engineering Observation 3.1

The Java compiler does not require import *declarations in a Java source code file if the complete class name (also called the* fully qualified class name) *is specified every time a class name is used in the source code. For example, the fully qualified class name for class* Graphics *is* java.awt.Graphics.

Line 6

```
import javax.swing.*;        // import package javax.swing
```

specifies to the compiler that all classes from package **javax.swing** are available to this applet. The asterisk (*) indicates that all classes in the **javax.swing** package (such as **JApplet** and **JOptionPane**) should be available to the compiler. However, this does not cause all classes in that package to be loaded into memory when the program begins execution—only those used in the program will be loaded. This allows you to use the *simple name* (the class name by itself) of any class from the **javax.swing** package in the program. Our last two programs imported only class **JApplet** from package **javax.swing**. In this program, we use classes **JApplet** and **JOptionPane** from that package.

```
1   <html>
2   <applet code = "AdditionApplet.class" width = "300" height = "65">
3   </applet>
4   </html>
```

Fig. 3.14   AdditionApplet.html loads class AdditionApplet of Fig. 3.13 into the appletviewer.

Many packages have subpackages. For example, the `java.awt` package has subpackage `java.awt.event`. When the compiler encounters an `import` declaration that uses the `*` notation (e.g., `java.awt.*`) to indicate that a program might use multiple classes from a package, the compiler does not load classes from any of `java.awt`'s subpackages. Thus, you cannot define an `import` of `java.*` to search for classes from all Java core packages.

Common Programming Error 3.4

Assuming that an `import` declaration for an entire package also imports classes from subpackages of that package results in syntax errors for the classes from the subpackages.

Recall from Section 3.3 that applets inherit from the `JApplet` class, so they have all the methods that an applet container requires to execute the applet. Line 8

```
public class AdditionApplet extends JApplet {
```

begins class `AdditionApplet`'s declaration and indicates that it inherits from `JApplet`. The body of the class is delimited by braces at lines 8 and 52.

Line 9

```
double sum;  // sum of values entered by user
```

declares that `sum` is a variable of primitive type `double`. Because the variable is declared in the body of the class declaration, but outside the bodies of all the class's method declarations, this is a *variable declaration statement* for a *field* (sometimes called an *instance variable* in other programming languages). Every instance of the class contains one copy of each field. For example, if there are 10 `AdditionApplet` objects, each object has its own copy of `sum`. Thus, there would be 10 copies of `sum` (one per applet). [*Note:* We use the Java term "field," rather than the term "instance variable" throughout this book.]

A benefit of fields is that all the methods of the class can use the fields. Until now, we declared all variables in an application's `main` method. Variables declared in the body of a particular method are known as *local variables* and can be used only in the body of that method. Another distinction between fields and local variables is that fields have *default values* and local variables do not. The default value for a field of type `double` (`sum` in this example) is 0.0.

Good Programming Practice 3.2

Explicitly initializing fields rather than relying on automatic initialization improves program readability.

The applet of Fig. 3.13 contains two methods—`init` (lines 12–35) and `paint` (lines 38–50). When an applet container loads an applet, the container creates an instance of the applet class and calls its `init` method. The applet container calls method `init` only once during an applet's execution. Method `init` normally *initializes* the applet's fields (if they need to be initialized to values other than their defaults) and performs tasks that should occur only once when the applet begins execution. As we will see in later chapters, the applet's `init` method typically creates the applet's graphical user interface.

The order in which methods are declared in a class does not determine when those methods are called at execution time. However, conventions for the order in which methods are declared improve program readability and maintainability.

The first line of the `init` method always appears as

```
public void init()
```

indicating that `init` is a `public` method that receives no arguments (empty parentheses after `init`) to perform its task and returns no information (`void`) when it completes. Method `init`'s body is delimited by the pair of braces at lines 13 and 35.

Lines 14–15

```
String firstNumber;    // first string entered by user
String secondNumber;   // second string entered by user
```

declare `String` variables `firstNumber` and `secondNumber`, in which the applet stores the strings input by the user. These are declared in the body of method `init`, so they are local variables of method `init`.

Lines 17–18

```
double number1;    // first number to add
double number2;    // second number to add
```

declare variables `number1` and `number2` of primitive type `double`—these variables hold floating-point values. Unlike field `sum`, local variables `number1` and `number2` are not initialized to 0.0.

Let us distinguish further between the `String` declarations in lines 14–15 and the `double` declarations in lines 17–18. Types in Java are divided into two categories—*primitive types* and *reference types* (sometimes called *nonprimitive types*). The primitive types are `boolean`, `char`, `byte`, `short`, `int`, `long`, `float` and `double`. Variables of these types can each store exactly one value of their declared type. For example, variable `number1` can store exactly one `double` (floating-point) value at a time. All nonprimitive types are reference types, so all classes[16] are reference types. Programs use variables of reference types (normally called *references*) to *refer to objects* in the program. Such references contain the location in the computer's memory of an object, which might contain many pieces of data and might have many methods. A `String` is an object and the variables `firstNumber` and `secondNumber` (lines 14–15) are actually references to `String` objects.

A primitive-type variable cannot be used to invoke a method. However, an important use of a reference is to invoke methods of a particular object. In our preceding applets, method `paint` receives a reference called `g` that refers to a `Graphics` object. Statements in method `paint` use that reference to send messages to the `Graphics` object. These messages are calls to methods (like `drawString` and `drawLine`) that enable the program to draw. For example, the statement

```
g.drawString( "Welcome to Java Programming!", 25, 25 );
```

uses `g` to send the `drawString` message to (i.e., call method `drawString` of) the `Graphics` object. As part of the message (method call), we provide the information (arguments) that `drawString` requires to perform its task. The `Graphics` object uses this information to draw the string at the specified location.

---

16. In Chapter 9, we discuss interfaces, which also are reference types.

Software Engineering Observation 3.4

A hint to help you determine whether a variable is a primitive or reference type is the name of the variable's declared type. By convention, all class names in Java start with a capital letter. Therefore, if the type starts with a capital letter, normally you can assume that the variable is a reference to an object of the declared type (e.g., Graphics g indicates that g is a reference to a Graphics object).

Lines 21–22

```
firstNumber = JOptionPane.showInputDialog(
   "Enter first floating-point value" );
```

read the first floating-point number entered by the user. JOptionPane method show-InputDialog displays an input dialog that prompts the user to enter a value. The user types a value in the input dialog's text field, then clicks the **OK** button to return the string the user typed. If you type and nothing appears in the text field, position the mouse pointer in the text field and click the mouse to make the text field active. Variable firstNumber is assigned the result of the call to showInputDialog.

In lines 21–22, notice the method-call syntax. At this point, we have seen two different ways to call methods. This statement uses the static method-call syntax introduced in Chapter 2. Recall that static methods are called with the syntax

ClassName.*methodName*(*arguments*)

Also in this chapter, we have called methods of class Graphics with a similar syntax that started with a reference to a Graphics object. Generically, this syntax is

referenceName.*methodName*(*arguments*)

The latter syntax is used for most method calls in Java. In fact, the applet container uses this syntax to call methods init, start and paint on your applets.

Lines 25–26

```
secondNumber = JOptionPane.showInputDialog(
   "Enter second floating-point value" );
```

read the second floating-point entered by from the user by displaying an input dialog.

Lines 29–30

```
number1 = Double.parseDouble( firstNumber );
number2 = Double.parseDouble( secondNumber );
```

convert the two strings input by the user to double values for use in a calculation. Method *Double.parseDouble* (a static method of class Double) converts its String argument to a double floating-point value. Class Double is in package java.lang.

Software Engineering Observation 3.5

Each primitive type (such as double) has a corresponding class (such as Double) in package java.lang. These classes (called type-wrapper classes) provide methods for processing primitive-type values (such as converting a string to a primitive-type value or vice versa). Primitive types do not have methods, so methods related to a primitive type are located in the corresponding type-wrapper class (e.g., method parseDouble, which converts a String to a double value is located in class Double). See the API documentation for the complete details of the methods in the type-wrapper classes.

The assignment statement at line 33

```
sum = number1 + number2;
```

calculates the sum of the values stored in variables number1 and number2 and assigns the result to variable sum using the assignment operator =. The statement is read as "sum *gets* the value of number1 + number2." Notice that field sum is used in method init even though sum was not defined in method init. We can use sum in init (and all other methods of the class), because sum is a field.

At this point, the applet's init method returns and the applet container calls the applet's start method. We did not declare start in this applet, so the one inherited from class JApplet is called here. Normally, the start method is used with an advanced concept called multithreading.[17]

Next, the applet container calls the applet's paint method. In this example, method paint draws a rectangle in which the result of the addition will appear. Line 45

```
g.drawRect( 15, 10, 270, 20 );
```

calls method drawRect of class Graphics using the reference g. Method drawRect draws a rectangle based on its four arguments. The first two integer values represent the *upper-left x-coordinate* and *upper-left y-coordinate* where the Graphics object begins drawing the rectangle. The third and fourth arguments are non-negative integers that represent the width of the rectangle in pixels and the height of the rectangle in pixels, respectively. This particular statement draws a rectangle starting at coordinate *(15, 10)* that is 270 pixels wide and 20 pixels tall. Note that we experimented with these arguments until we found values that placed the rectangle neatly around the string on the applet.

Common Programming Error 3.5

It is a logic error to supply two points (i.e., pairs of x- and y-coordinates) as the arguments to Graphics method drawRect. The third argument must be the width in pixels, and the fourth argument must be the height in pixels of the rectangle to draw.

Common Programming Error 3.6

It is a logic error to supply a negative width or negative height as an argument to Graphics method drawRect. The rectangle will not be displayed and no error will be indicated.

Common Programming Error 3,7

It is normally a logic error to supply arguments to Graphics method drawRect that cause the rectangle to draw outside the applet's viewable area (i.e., the width and height of the applet as specified in the HTML document that references the applet). Either increase the applet's width and height in the HTML document or use arguments for method drawRect that cause the rectangle to draw inside the applet's viewable area.

Line 48

```
g.drawString( "The sum is " + sum, 25, 25 );
```

calls the Graphics object's drawString method. The expression

```
"The sum is " + sum
```

---

17. We will see typical uses of method start in Chapter 16 and Chapter 19.

uses the string concatenation operator + to concatenate the string "The sum is " and sum (converted to a string) to create the string drawString displays. Notice again that the statement uses the field sum even though method paint does not define sum as a local variable.

The benefit of declaring sum as a field is that we were able to assign sum a value in init and use sum's value in the paint method later in the program. All methods of a class are capable of using the fields of the class.[18]

Software Engineering Observation 3.6

The only statements that should be placed in an applet's init method are those that are directly related to the one-time initialization of an applet's fields. The applet's results should be displayed from other methods of the applet class.

Software Engineering Observation 3.7

The only statements that should be placed in an applet's paint method are those that are directly related to drawing (i.e., calls to methods of class Graphics) and the logic of drawing. Generally, dialog boxes should not be displayed from an applet's paint method.

In this chapter and Chapter 2, we introduced and reinforced many important Java concepts, such as applications, applets, displaying data on the screen, inputting data from the keyboard, performing calculations and making decisions. In Chapter 4, we build on these techniques as we introduce *structured programming*. We also study how to specify and vary the order in which a program executes statements—this order is called *flow of control*.

3.6 Java Applet Internet and World Wide Web Resources

If you have access to the Internet and the World Wide Web, there are a large number of Java applet resources available to you. The best place to start is at the source—the Sun Microsystems, Inc. Java Web site java.sun.com. The Web page

        java.sun.com/applets

contains several Java applet resources, including free applets you can use on your own World Wide Web site, the demonstration applets from the J2SDK and other applets (many of which can be downloaded and used on your own computer). There is also a section entitled "Applets at Work" where you can read about uses of applets in industry.

If you do not have the Java Plug-in on your computer, you can visit

        java.sun.com/getjava

to download and install the plug-in. Instructions are provided for various versions of Windows, Linux, Solaris and Mac OS.

On the Sun Microsystems Java Web site, visit the *Java Developer Services* site

        developer.java.sun.com

This free site includes technical support, discussion forums, technical articles, resources, announcements of new Java features and early access to new Java technologies.

For various on-line training courses and tutorials, visit the site

        developer.java.sun.com/developer/onlineTraining

---

18. In Chapter 8, we will see an exception to this statement.

Another useful Web site is *JARS*—originally called the *Java Applet Rating Service*. The JARS site

```
www.jars.com
```

originally was a large Java repository for applets. Its benefit was that it rated every applet registered at the site as top 1%, top 5% or top 25%, so you could view the best applets on the Web. Early in the development of the Java language, having your applet rated here was a great way to demonstrate your Java programming abilities. JARS is now an all-around resource for Java programmers.

The resources listed in this section provide hyperlinks to many other Java-related Web sites. If you have Internet access, spend some time browsing these sites, executing applets and reading the source code for the applets when it is available. This will help you rapidly expand your Java expertise. We provide many other Web-based Java resources with the resources for *Java How to Program, Fifth Edition*, at www.deitel.com.

3.7 (Optional Case Study) Thinking About Objects: Identifying the Classes in a Problem Statement

Now we begin the substantial task of designing the elevator simulator that we introduced in Chapter 2. We begin with the design of the elevator itself, and will design the user interaction and display of this model in Section 14.13 and Section 19.7, respectively.

Identifying the Classes in a System

The first step of our OOD process is to identify the objects from the problem statement and group them into classes. We will eventually describe these classes in a formal way and implement them in Java. First, we review the problem statement of Section 2.9 and identify key *nouns*; it is likely that some of these nouns will identify objects that comprise the elevator simulation.[19] Figure 3.15 lists these nouns (and noun phrases).

Nouns (and noun phrases) in the problem statement		
company	elevator system	graphical user interface (GUI)
office building	elevator shaft	person
elevator	floor door	floor (first floor; second floor)
software-simulator application	bell inside the elevator	**First Floor** GUI button
passenger	light on that floor	**Second Floor** GUI button
user of our application	energy	audio
floor button	capacity	elevator music
elevator button	elevator car	display

Fig. 3.15   Nouns (and noun phrases) in problem statement .

---

19. Noun analysis is a simple means by which we can determine the objects required by the problem statement. As we mentioned in Chapter 1, more complex processes often are used in industry.

We choose only the nouns that have significance in the elevator simulation. For this reason we omit several nouns. We do not need to model "company" as a class, because the company is not part of the simulation; the company simply wants us to build the elevator simulation. We do not model "office building," the elevator's location, because the building is outside the scope of our elevator simulation. The phrases "display," "audio" and "elevator music" pertain to the display of the simulation, but do not pertain to the simulation itself. (We use these phrases when we construct the display in Section 19.7 and Appendix F.) The phrases "graphical user interface (GUI)," "user of our application," "**First Floor** GUI button" and **Second Floor** GUI button" pertain to how the user controls the simulator. (We use these phrases when we construct the user interface in Section 14.13.) Although we'll be saving energy with the policy of not moving the elevator until requested, we do not model "energy." Lastly, "capacity" is a property of the elevator and of the floor—not a separate entity itself.

We determine the classes for our system by grouping the remaining nouns. We discard "elevator system" for the time being—we focus on designing only the simulator and disregard how this simulator relates to the system as a whole. (We discuss the system as a whole in Section 14.13.) We combine "elevator" and "elevator car" into "elevator," because the problem statement uses the two words interchangeably. Each remaining noun from Fig. 3.15 refers to one or more of the following:

- elevator shaft

- elevator

- person

- floor (first floor, second floor)

- elevator door

- floor door

- elevator button

- floor button

- bell

- light

The elements of this list are likely to be classes we will need to implement our system. Notice that we list the buttons on the floors and the button on the elevator separately. The two types of buttons perform different duties in our simulation—the buttons on the floors summon the elevator, and the button in the elevator instructs the elevator to move to the other floor.

We can now model the classes in our system based on the list we created. By convention, we capitalize class names in the design process (as we will do when we write the actual Java code that implements our design). If the name of a class contains more than one word, we run the words together and capitalize each word (e.g., `MultipleWordName`). Using this convention, we create classes `ElevatorShaft`, `Elevator`, `Person`, `Floor`, `ElevatorDoor`, `FloorDoor`, `ElevatorButton`, `FloorButton`, `Bell` and `Light`. We construct our system using all of these classes as building blocks. Before we begin building the system, however, we must gain a better understanding of how the classes relate to one another.

Modeling Classes

The UML enables us to model, via the *class diagram*, the classes in the elevator system and their relationships. Class diagrams model the structure of a system by depicting the classes, or "building blocks," of the system. Figure 3.16 represents class Elevator. In the UML, each class is modeled as a rectangle with three compartments. The top compartment contains the name of the class. The middle compartment contains the class's *attributes*. (We discuss attributes in Section 4.14 and Section 5.11.) The bottom compartment contains the class's *operations* (discussed in Section 6.15).

Figure 3.17 shows how our classes ElevatorShaft, Elevator and FloorButton relate to one another. Notice that the rectangles in this diagram are not subdivided into compartments. The UML allows the suppression of class attributes and operations in this manner to create more readable diagrams. Such a diagram is said to be an *elided diagram*: a diagram in which some information, such as the contents of the second and third compartments, is not modeled. We will place information in these compartments in Section 4.14 and Section 6.15, respectively.

In Fig. 3.17, a solid line that connects classes represents an *association*. An association is a relationship between classes. The numbers near the lines express *multiplicity* values, which indicate how many objects of a class participate in the association. From the diagram, we see that two objects of class FloorButton participate in an association with one object of class ElevatorShaft, because the two FloorButtons are located on the ElevatorShaft. Therefore, class FloorButton has a *two-to-one* relationship with class ElevatorShaft; class ElevatorShaft has a *one-to-two* relationship with class FloorButton. We also see that class ElevatorShaft has a *one-to-one* relationship with class Elevator and vice versa. Using the UML, we can model many types of multiplicity. Figure 3.18 shows the multiplicity types and how to represent them.

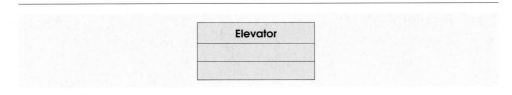

Fig. 3.16   Representing a class in the UML.

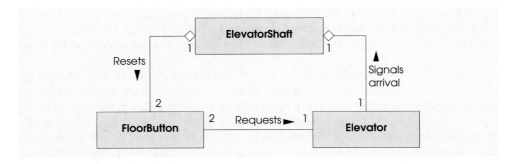

Fig. 3.17   Class diagram showing associations among classes.

Symbol	Meaning
0	None
1	One
m	An integer value
0..1	Zero or one
m, n	*m* or *n*
m..n	At least *m*, but not more than *n*
*	Zero or more
0..*	Zero or more
1..*	One or more

Fig. 3.18   Multiplicity types.

An association can be named. For example, the word `Requests` above the line connecting classes `FloorButton` and `Elevator` indicates the name of that association—the arrow shows the direction of the association name. This part of the diagram reads "two objects of class `FloorButton` request one object of class `Elevator`." Note that association names are directional with the direction indicated by the arrowhead next to the association name—so it would be improper, for example, to read the preceding association as "one object of class `Elevator` requests two objects of class `FloorButton`." In addition, the word `Resets` indicates that "one object of class `ElevatorShaft` resets two objects of class `FloorButton`." Lastly, the phrase `Signals arrival` indicates that "one object of class `Elevator` signals the `Elevator` object's arrival to one object of class `ElevatorShaft`."

In addition to indicating simple relationships, associations can specify more complex relationships in which objects of one class are composed of objects of other classes. Consider a real-world elevator. What "pieces" does a manufacturer put together to build a working elevator? The company who has asked us to build this simulator tells us that this complete elevator system is composed of an elevator shaft, two floor buttons, two lights, two floor doors and an elevator car. The elevator car itself is composed of several pieces, including an elevator button, an elevator door and a bell. From this description, we see that a working elevator is a complex thing, built from many pieces.

The *diamonds*[20] on the association lines of Fig. 3.17 indicate that the `ElevatorShaft` is built from other pieces. The relationship this association denotes is called *aggregation*—an `ElevatorShaft` is built by aggregating, or gathering together, several other objects to produce one whole `ElevatorShaft`. Aggregation implies a whole/part relationship. The class that has the aggregation symbol on its end of an association line is the whole (in this case, `ElevatorShaft`), and the class on the other end of the association line is the part (in this case, classes `FloorButton` and `Elevator`). In this diagram, the aggregation indicates that an object of class `ElevatorShaft` is formed from two objects of class `FloorButton` and one object of class `Elevator`. The elevator shaft "has an" elevator and two floor but-

---

20. The hollow diamonds in these class diagrams indicate simple aggregation. Solid diamonds would indicate a strong form of aggregation known as composition, or composite aggregation. We discuss composition and contrast it with simple aggregation in Chapter 8.

tons. The "has a" relationship defines aggregation. (We will see in Section 10.11 that the "is a" relationship defines inheritance.)

Figure 3.19 shows the complete class diagram for the elevator model based on the relationships among objects described in the problem statement. We model all classes that we identified, as well as the associations between these classes. [*Note*: In Chapter 10, we expand our class diagram by using the object-oriented concept of inheritance.]

The `ElevatorShaft` class is an aggregation of one object of class `Elevator` and two objects each of classes `Light`, `FloorDoor` and `FloorButton`. (Notice the two-to-one relationships between each of these classes and `ElevatorShaft`.) Class `Elevator` is an aggregation of classes `ElevatorDoor`, `ElevatorButton` and `Bell`. Class `Person` has associations with both `FloorButton` and `ElevatorButton` (and other classes, as we will soon see). The association name `Presses` and the name-direction arrowheads indicate that the object of class `Person` presses these buttons. The object of class `Person` also rides the object of class `Elevator` and walks across the object of class `Floor`. The association name `Requests` indicates that an object of class `FloorButton` requests an object of class `Elevator`. The association name `Signals to move` indicates that the object of class `ElevatorButton` signals the object of class `Elevator` to move to the other floor. The diagram indicates many other associations as well.

Notice the word `passenger` on the association line between `Person` and `Elevator`. This is a *role name*, which identifies the role the `Person` object plays in its relationship with the `Elevator`. A role name adds meaning to an association between classes. In this case, the role name `passenger` indicates that when a `Person` rides the `Elevator`, that person is a passenger of the `Elevator`. For many associations in this class diagram, explicit role names are not necessary, since the meanings of the associations are clear without them.

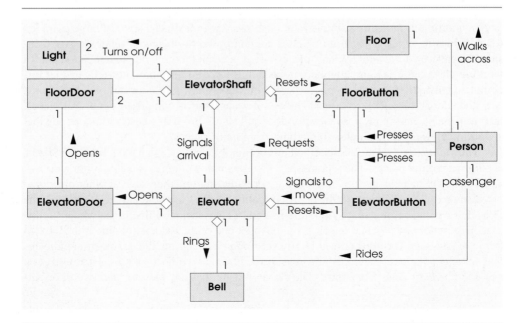

Fig. 3.19   Class diagram for the elevator model.

Now we have identified the classes for our system (although we may discover others in later phases of the design process). In Section 4.14, we determine the attributes for each of these classes, and in Section 5.11, we use these attributes to examine how the system changes over time and to introduce its behavioral aspects. As we expand our knowledge, we will discover new information that will enable us to describe our classes more completely.

Questions

1. Why might it be more complicated to implement a three-story (or taller) building?

2. It is common for large buildings to have many elevators. We will see in Chapter 10 that once we have created one elevator object, it is easy to create as many as we like. What problems or opportunities do you foresee in having several elevators, each of which may pick up and discharge passengers at every floor in a large building?

3. For simplicity, we have given our elevator and each floor a capacity of one passenger. What problems and opportunities do you foresee in having to increase these capacities?

SUMMARY

- Applets are Java programs that can be embedded in HyperText Markup Language (HTML) documents (i.e., Web pages). When a browser loads a Web page containing an applet, the applet downloads into the Web browser and begins execution.

- In the `appletviewer`, you can execute an applet again by clicking the `appletviewer`'s **Applet** menu and selecting the **Reload** menu item. To terminate an applet, select the **Quit** menu item.

- Class `Graphics` is in package `java.awt`.

- Class `JApplet` is in package `javax.swing`. Applet containers that support applets expect every Java applet to have certain behaviors, which class `JApplet` already provides.

- Inheritance is used to create new classes from existing class declarations. Keyword `extends` followed by a class name indicates the superclass from which a new class inherits. The new class is the subclass. Inheritance results in a subclass that has the attributes and behaviors of the superclass as well as the new features added in the subclass declaration.

- Classes are used as "templates" or "blueprints" to instantiate objects in memory for use in a program. The term object normally implies that attributes and behaviors are associated with the object and that those behaviors perform operations on the attributes.

- Method `paint` is one of three methods that an applet container calls when any applet begins execution. Those methods are `init`, `start` and `paint`, and are called in that order.

- Methods declare the data required to complete their tasks via their parameter lists. Normally, data is passed by programmers when calling methods. For method `paint`, the applet container calls the method and passes the `Graphics` argument.

- `Graphics` method `drawString` draws a string at a specified location. Its first argument is the string to draw. The last two arguments are the coordinates off the string's bottom left corner. Coordinates are measured in pixels from an applet's upper-left *(0, 0)* coordinate.

- You must create an HTML document to load an applet into an applet container. Normally, the applet and its corresponding HTML document are stored in the same directory.

- Many HTML elements have pairs of tags. Each tag is enclosed in angle brackets (< and >).

- The first component of the `<applet>` tag indicates the file containing the compiled applet class. The second and third components of the `<applet>` tag indicate the `width` and the `height` of the applet in pixels. The `appletviewer` only understands the `<applet>` and `</applet>` HTML tags, so it is sometimes referred to as the "minimal browser."

- `import` declarations are not required if you always use a class's fully qualified name, which includes the package name and class name (e.g., `java.awt.Graphics`).

- The asterisk (*) notation after a package name in an `import` declaration indicates that multiple classes from that package might be used in the program. This allows programmers to use the simple name (the class name by itself) of any class from the package in the program.

- Every object (instance of a class) contains one copy of each of that class's fields. Fields are declared in the body of a class declaration, but not in the body of any method. Fields can be used in all methods of the class.

- Variables declared in the body of a method are local variables; they can be used only in the body of the method in which they are declared.

- Fields are always assigned a default value, and local variables are not.

- Method `init` normally initializes an applet's fields and performs any tasks that should occur only once when the applet begins execution.

- Types in Java are divided into two categories—primitive types and reference types (sometimes called nonprimitive types). The primitive types are `boolean`, `char`, `byte`, `short`, `int`, `long`, `float` and `double`. Variables of these types can each store exactly one value of their declared type. A primitive-type variable cannot be used as a reference to invoke a method.

- All nonprimitive types are reference types, so all classes are reference types. Programs use variables of reference types (normally called references) to refer to objects in the program. Such references contain the location of an object in the computer's memory and an object might contain many pieces of data and might have many methods. An important use of a reference is to invoke methods of a particular object.

- Primitive type `double` stores double-precision floating-point numbers. Primitive type `float` stores single-precision floating-point numbers. A `double` requires more memory to store a floating-point value, but stores it with approximately twice the precision of a `float`.

- Method `Double.parseDouble` (a `static` method of class `Double`) converts its `String` argument to a `double` floating-point value. Class `Double` is part of the package `java.lang`.

- Method `drawLine` of class `Graphics` draws lines. The method requires four arguments representing the two end points of the line on the applet—the x-coordinate and y-coordinate of the first end point in the line and the x-coordinate and y-coordinate of the second end point in the line. All coordinate values are specified with respect to the upper-left corner *(0, 0)* coordinate of the applet.

- Method `drawRect` draws a rectangle based on its four arguments. The first two integer values represent the upper-left x-coordinate and upper-left y-coordinate where the `Graphics` object begins drawing the rectangle. The third and fourth arguments are non-negative integers that represent the width of the rectangle in pixels and the height of the rectangle in pixels, respectively.

- To use the features of Java 2 in an applet, Sun provides the Java Plug-in to bypass a browser's Java support and use a complete version of the Java 2 Runtime Environment (J2RE) that is installed on the user's local computer.

TERMINOLOGY

applet
applet container
`applet` HTML element
`<applet>` tag

Applet menu in `appletviewer`
`appletviewer`
`boolean` primitive type
browser

byte primitive type
char primitive type
command-line argument
coordinate
create an object
derived class
double primitive type
Double class
drawLine method of Graphics
drawRect method of Graphics
drawString method of Graphics
extends keyword
field (instance variable)
float primitive type
floating-point number
Graphics class
height of an applet
HTML element
HyperText Markup Language (HTML)
init method of JApplet
instantiate an object
int primitive type
invoke a method
JApplet class
java.awt package
Java Plug-in

Java 2 Runtime Environment (J2RE)
javax.swing package
local variable
long primitive type
message
method call
Microsoft Internet Explorer
Netscape
object
paint method of JApplet
parameter list
parseDouble method of Double
pixel (picture element)
primitive type
Quit menu item in appletviewer
reference
reference type
Reload menu item in appletviewer
short primitive type
source code
start method of JApplet
subclass
superclass
text file
variable
width of an applet

SELF-REVIEW EXERCISES

3.1   Fill in the blanks in each of the following:
a) Class _____ provides methods for drawing.
b) Java applets begin execution with a series of three method calls: _____, _____ and _____.
c) Methods _____ and _____ display lines and rectangles, respectively.
d) Keyword _____ indicates that a new class is a subclass of an existing class.
e) Every Java 2 applet should extend class _____.
f) Java's eight primitive types are _____, _____, _____, _____, _____, _____, _____ and _____.

3.2   State whether each of the following is *true* or *false*. If *false*, explain why.
a) To draw a rectangle, method drawRect requires four arguments that specify two points on the applet.
b) Method drawLine requires four arguments that specify two points on the applet to draw a line.
c) Type Double is a primitive type.
d) Type int is used to declare a floating-point number.
e) Method Double.parseDouble converts a String to a primitive double value.

3.3   Write Java statements to accomplish each of the following:
a) Display a dialog asking the user to enter a floating-point number.
b) Convert a string to a floating-point number and store the converted value in double variable age. Assume that the string is stored in stringValue.

    c) Draw the message "This is a Java program" on one line at position *(10, 10)* on an applet (assume you are defining this statement in the applet's paint method).

    d) Draw the message "This is a Java program" on two lines starting at position *(10, 10)* on an applet (assume these statements are defined in applet method paint). Have the first line end with Java. Make the two lines start at the same *x*-coordinate.

3.4   What is the difference between a local variable and a field?

ANSWERS TO SELF-REVIEW EXERCISES

3.1   a) Graphics.   b) init, start, paint.   c) drawLine, drawRect.   d) extends. e) JApplet. f) char, byte, short, int, long, float, double, boolean.

3.2   a) False. Method drawRect requires four arguments—two that specify the upper-left corner of the rectangle and two that specify the width and height of the rectangle. b) True. c) False. Type Double is a class in the java.lang package; double is a primitive date type. Remember that names that start with a capital letter are normally class names. d) False. Type double or type float can be used to declare a floating-point number. Type int is used to declare integers. e) True.

3.3   a) stringValue = JOptionPane.showInputDialog(
            "Enter a floating-point number");
    b) age = Double.parseDouble(stringValue);
    c) g.drawString("This is a Java program", 10, 10);
    d) g.drawString("This is a Java", 10, 10);
       g.drawString("program", 10, 25);

3.4   A local variable is declared in the body of a method and can be used only from the point at which it is declared through the end of the method declaration. A field is declared in a class, but not in the body of any of that class's methods. Every object (instance) of a class has a separate copy of that class's fields. Also, the fields are accessible to all methods of the class. (We will see an exception to this in Chapter 8.)

EXERCISES

3.5   Fill in the blanks in each of the following:

    a) Type _____ declares a single-precision floating-point variable.

    b) If class Double provides method parseDouble to convert a string to a double and class Integer provides method parseInt to convert a string to an int, then class Float probably provides method _____ to convert a string to a float.

    c) Type _____ is used to declare double-precision, floating-point variables.

    d) The _____ or a browser can be used to execute a Java applet.

    e) To load an applet into a browser, you must first define a(n) _____ file.

    f) The _____ and _____ HTML tags specify that an applet should be loaded into an applet container and executed.

3.6   State whether each of the following is *true* or *false*. If *false*, explain why.

    a) The application that executes an applet is generically referred to as an applet container.

    b) When using an import declaration of the form javax.swing.*, all classes in the package are imported.

    c) You do not need import declarations if the full package name and class name are specified each time you refer to a class in a program.

3.7   Write an applet that asks the user to enter two floating-point numbers, obtains the two numbers from the user and draws the sum, product (multiplication), difference and quotient (division) of the two numbers. Use the techniques shown in Fig. 3.13.

3.8 Write an applet that asks the user to enter two floating-point numbers, obtains the numbers from the user and displays the larger number followed by the words "is larger" as a string on the applet. If the numbers are equal, print the message "These numbers are equal." Use the techniques shown in Fig. 3.13.

3.9 Write an applet that inputs three floating-point numbers from the user and displays the sum, average, product, smallest and largest of these numbers as strings on the applet. Use the techniques shown in Fig. 3.13.

3.10 Write an applet that asks the user to input the radius of a circle as a floating-point number and draws the circle's diameter, circumference and area. Use the value 3.14159 for π. Use the techniques shown in Fig. 3.13. [*Note:* You may also use the predefined constant Math.PI for the value of π. This constant is more precise than the value 3.14159. Class Math is defined in the java.lang package, so you do not need to import it.] Use the following formulas (*r* is the radius):

$$diameter = 2r$$
$$circumference = 2\pi r$$
$$area = \pi r^2$$

3.11 Write an applet that reads five integers and determines and prints the largest and smallest integers in the group. Use only the programming techniques you learned in this chapter and Chapter 2. Draw the results on the applet.

3.12 What does the following code print?

```
g.drawString( "*", 25, 25 );
g.drawString( "***", 25, 55 );
g.drawString( "*****", 25, 85 );
g.drawString( "****", 25, 70 );
g.drawString( "**", 25, 40 );
```

3.13 Write an applet that draws a checkerboard pattern as follows:

```
*  *  *  *  *  *  *  *
  *  *  *  *  *  *  *  *
*  *  *  *  *  *  *  *
  *  *  *  *  *  *  *  *
*  *  *  *  *  *  *  *
  *  *  *  *  *  *  *  *
*  *  *  *  *  *  *  *
  *  *  *  *  *  *  *  *
```

3.14 Write an applet that draws rectangles of different sizes and locations.

3.15 Write an applet that allows the user to input values for the arguments required by method drawRect, then draws a rectangle using the four input values.

3.16 Class Graphics contains method drawOval, which takes as arguments the same four arguments as method drawRect. The arguments for method drawOval specify the "bounding box" for the oval—the sides of the bounding box are the boundaries of the oval. Write a Java applet that draws an oval and a rectangle with the same four arguments. The oval will touch the rectangle at the center of each side.

3.17 Modify the solution to Exercise 3.16 to output ovals of different shapes and sizes.

3.18 Write an applet that allows the user to input the four arguments required by method drawOval, then draws an oval using the four input values.

3.19   Using only programming techniques from this chapter and Chapter 2, write an applet that calculates the squares and cubes of the numbers from 0 to 10 and draws the resulting values in table format as shown below. [*Note*: This program does not require any input from the user.]

number	square	cube
0	0	0
1	1	1
2	4	8
3	9	27
4	16	64
5	25	125
6	36	216
7	49	343
8	64	512
9	81	729
10	100	1000

Control Statements:
Part 1

Objectives

- To understand basic problem-solving techniques.
- To be able to develop algorithms through the process of top-down, stepwise refinement.
- To be able to use the `if` and `if...else` selection statements to choose among alternative actions.
- To be able to use the `while` repetition statement to execute statements in a program repeatedly.
- To understand counter-controlled repetition and sentinel-controlled repetition.
- To be able to use the assignment, increment and decrement operators.

Let's all move one place on.
Lewis Carroll

The wheel is come full circle.
William Shakespeare

How many apples fell on Newton's head before he took the hint!
Robert Frost

Outline

4.1 Introduction

Before writing a program to solve a problem, it is essential to have a thorough understanding of the problem and a carefully planned approach to solving the problem. When writing a program, it is equally essential to understand the types of building blocks that are available and to employ proven program-construction principles. In this chapter and in Chapter 5, we discuss these issues in our presentation of the theory and principles of structured programming. The techniques you learn here are applicable to Java as well as most other high-level languages. When we study object-based programming in more depth in Chapter 8, we will see that concepts presented here are helpful in building classes and manipulating objects.

4.2 Algorithms

Any computing problem can be solved by executing a series of actions in a specific order. A *procedure* for solving a problem in terms of

1. the *actions* to execute and
2. the *order* in which these actions execute

is called an *algorithm*. The following example demonstrates that correctly specifying the order in which the actions execute is important.

Consider the "rise-and-shine algorithm" followed by one junior executive for getting out of bed and going to work: (1) Get out of bed; (2) take off pajamas; (3) take a shower; (4) get dressed; (5) eat breakfast; (6) carpool to work. This routine gets the junior executive to work well prepared to make critical decisions. Suppose that the same steps are performed in a slightly different order: (1) Get out of bed; (2) take off pajamas; (3) get dressed; (4) take a shower; (5) eat breakfast; (6) carpool to work. In this case, our junior executive shows up for work soaking wet.

Specifying the order in which statements (actions) execute in a program is called *program control*. This chapter investigates Java's *control structures* for program control.

4.3 Pseudocode

Pseudocode is an informal language that helps programmers develop algorithms without having to worry about the strict details of Java language syntax. The pseudocode we present is particularly useful for developing algorithms that will be converted to structured portions of Java programs. Pseudocode is similar to everyday English; it is convenient and user friendly, although it is not an actual computer programming language.

Pseudocode does not execute on computers. Rather, pseudocode helps the programmer "think out" a program before attempting to write it in a programming language, such as Java. This chapter provides several examples of how to use pseudocode effectively in developing Java programs.

The style of pseudocode we present consists purely of characters, so programmers can type pseudocode conveniently, using any editor program. A carefully prepared pseudocode program can easily be converted to a corresponding Java program. In many cases, this requires simply replacing pseudocode statements with Java equivalents.

Pseudocode normally describes only *executable statements*—the actions that occur after a programmer converts a program from pseudocode to Java and the program is run on a computer. Declarations are not executable statements. For example, the declaration

```
int integerValue;
```

tells the compiler variable `integerValue`'s type and instructs Java to reserve space in memory for the variable. When the program executes, this declaration does not cause any action to occur, such as input, output or a calculation. So, the declaration need not appear in the pseudocode. However, some programmers choose to list variables and mention their purposes at the beginning of their pseudocode.

4.4 Control Structures[1]

Normally, statements in a program are executed one after the other in the order in which they are written. This process is called *sequential execution*. Various Java statements, which we will soon discuss, enable the programmer to specify that the next statement to execute may not be the next one in sequence. This is called *transfer of control*.

During the 1960s, it became clear that the indiscriminate use of transfers of control was the root of much difficulty experienced by software development groups. The finger of

---

1. The term "control structures" comes from the field of computer science. When we introduce Java's implementations of control structures, we refer to them with the terminology of the Java Language Specification, which refers to them as "statements."

blame was pointed at the *goto statement* (used in several programming languages, including C and Basic), which allows the programmer to specify a transfer of control to one of a very wide range of possible destinations in a program. The notion of so-called *structured programming* became almost synonymous with "goto elimination."[2]

The research of Bohm and Jacopini[3] had demonstrated that programs could be written without any goto statements. The challenge of the era for programmers was to shift their styles to "goto-less programming." It was not until the 1970s that programmers started taking structured programming seriously. The results were impressive, as software development groups reported reduced development times, more frequent on-time delivery of systems and more frequent within-budget completion of software projects. The key to these successes was that structured programs were clearer, easier to debug and modify and more likely to be bug free in the first place.

Bohm and Jacopini's work demonstrated that all programs could be written in terms of only three control structures—the *sequence structure*, the *selection structure* and the *repetition structure*. The sequence structure is built into Java. Unless directed otherwise, the computer executes Java statements one after the other in the order in which they are written. The *activity diagram* of Fig. 4.1 illustrates a typical sequence structure in which two calculations are performed in order. Java allows us to have as many actions as we want in a sequence structure. As we will soon see, anywhere a single action may be placed, we may place several actions in sequence.

Activity diagrams are part of the *Unified Modeling Language (UML)*—an industry standard for modeling software systems.[4] An activity diagram models the *workflow* (also called the *activity*) of a portion of a software system. Such workflows may include a portion of an algorithm, such as the sequence structure in Fig. 4.1. Activity diagrams are composed of special-purpose symbols, such as *action-state symbols* (a rectangle with its left and right sides replaced with arcs curving outward), *diamonds* and *small circles*; these symbols are connected by *transition arrows*, which represent the flow of the activity.

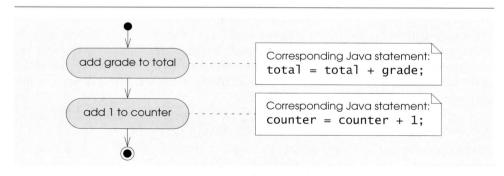

Fig. 4.1   Sequence structure activity diagram.

2. Java does not have a goto statement; however, goto is reserved by Java and should not be used as an identifier in programs.
3. Bohm, C., and G. Jacopini, "Flow Diagrams, Turing Machines, and Languages with Only Two Formation Rules," *Communications of the ACM*, Vol. 9, No. 5, May 1966, pp. 336–371.
4. For more information on the UML, see our optional case study, which appears at the ends of Chapters 1–8, 10–14, 16 and 19, or visit www.uml.org.

Like pseudocode, activity diagrams help programmers develop and represent algorithms, although many programmers prefer pseudocode. Activity diagrams clearly show how control structures operate.

Consider the activity diagram for the sequence structure in Fig. 4.1. The activity diagram contains two *action states* that represent actions to perform. Each action state contains an *action expression*—for example, "add grade to total" or "add 1 to counter"—that specifies a particular action to perform. Other actions might include calculations or input/output operations. The arrows in the activity diagram are called transition arrows. These arrows represent *transitions*, which indicate the order in which the actions represented by the action states occur—the program that implements the activities illustrated by the activity diagram in Fig. 4.1 first adds `grade` to `total`, then adds `1` to `counter`.

The *solid circle* located at the top of the activity diagram represents the activity's *initial state*—the beginning of the workflow before the program performs the modeled activities. The solid circle surrounded by a hollow circle that appears at the bottom of the activity diagram represents the *final state*—the end of the workflow after the program performs its activities.

Figure 4.1 also includes rectangles with the upper-right corners folded over. These are UML *notes*—explanatory remarks that describe the purpose of symbols in the diagram. Figure 4.1 uses UML notes to show the Java code associated with each action state in the activity diagram. A *dotted line* connects each note with the element that the note describes. Activity diagrams normally do not show the Java code that implements the activity. We use notes for this purpose here to illustrate how the diagram relates to Java code.

Java has three types of selection structures (discussed in this chapter and Chapter 5). The `if` statement either performs (selects) an action, if a condition is true, or skips the action, if the condition is false. The `if...else` statement performs an action if a condition is true and performs a different action if the condition is false. The `switch` statement (Chapter 5) performs one of many different actions, depending on the value of an expression.

The `if` statement is a *single-selection structure*, because it selects or ignores a single action (or, as we will soon see, a single group of actions). The `if...else` statement is called a *double-selection structure*, because it selects between two different actions (or groups of actions). The `switch` statement is called a *multiple-selection structure*, because it selects among many different actions (or groups of actions).

Java provides three repetition structures (also called *looping structures*) that enable programs to perform statements repeatedly as long as a condition (called the *loop-continuation condition*) remains true. The repetition structures are implemented with the `while`, `do...while` and `for` statements.[5] The `while` and `for` statements perform the action (or group of actions) in their bodies zero or more times—if the loop continuation condition is initially false, the action (or group of actions) will not execute. The `do...while` statement performs the action (or group of actions) in its body one or more times.

The words `if`, `else`, `switch`, `while`, `do` and `for` are Java *keywords*. These words are used to implement various Java features, such as control structures in Java. Keywords cannot be used as identifiers, such as for variable names. A complete list of Java keywords is shown in Fig. 4.2. In addition to the keywords, Java also contains *reserved words* `true`, `false` and `null` that represent special values. These also cannot be used as identifiers.

---

5. Chapter 5 presents the `do...while` and `for` repetition structures.

Java Keywords				
abstract	assert	boolean	break	byte
case	catch	char	class	continue
default	do	double	else	extends
final	finally	float	for	if
implements	import	instanceof	int	interface
long	native	new	package	private
protected	public	return	short	static
strictfp	super	switch	synchronized	this
throw	throws	transient	try	void
volatile	while			

Keywords that are reserved, but not currently used

const	goto

Fig. 4.2   Java keywords.

Common Programming Error 4.1

Using a keyword as an identifier is a syntax error.

Common Programming Error 4.2

Placing a space character in a keyword (e.g., `instance of`) is a syntax error.

So, Java has only three control structures: The sequence structure, selection structure (three types) and repetition structure (three types). Each program is formed by combining as many sequence, selection and repetition structures as is appropriate for the algorithm the program implements. As with the sequence structure of Fig. 4.1, we can model each control structure as an activity diagram. Each diagram contains an initial state and a final state that represent a control structure's entry point and exit point, respectively. *Single-entry/single-exit control structures* make it easy to build programs; the control structures are attached to one another by connecting the exit point of one control structure to the entry point of the next. This procedure is similar to the way in which a child stacks building blocks, so we call it *control-structure stacking*. We will learn that there is only one other way in which control structures may be connected—*control-structure nesting*—in which a control structure appears inside another control structure. Thus, algorithms in Java programs are constructed from only three major types of control structures, combined in only two ways.

4.5 if Single-Selection Statement

Programs use selection structures to choose among alternative courses of action. For example, suppose that the passing grade on an exam is 60. The pseudocode statement

> *If student's grade is greater than or equal to 60*
>   *Print "Passed"*

determines whether the condition "student's grade is greater than or equal to 60" is true or false. If the condition is true, "Passed" is printed, and the next pseudocode statement in order is "performed." (Remember that pseudocode is not a real programming language.) If the condition is false, the Print statement is ignored, and the next pseudocode statement in order would be performed. The indentation of the second line of this selection structure is optional, but recommended, because it emphasizes the inherent structure of structured programs.

The preceding pseudocode *If* statement may be written in Java as

```
if ( studentGrade >= 60 )
    System.out.println( "Passed" );
```

Notice that the Java code corresponds closely to the pseudocode. This is one of the properties of pseudocode that makes it such a useful program development tool.

Figure 4.3 illustrates the single-selection `if` statement. This activity diagram contains what is perhaps the most important symbol in an activity diagram—the diamond or *decision symbol*, which indicates that a decision is to be made. A decision symbol indicates that the workflow will continue along a path determined by the symbol's associated *guard conditions* that can be true or false.[6] Each transition arrow emerging from a decision symbol has a guard condition (specified in square brackets above or next to the transition arrow). If a guard condition is true, the workflow enters the action state to which that transition arrow points. In Fig. 4.3, if the grade is greater than or equal to 60, the program prints "Passed," then transitions to the final state of this activity. If the grade is less than 60, the program immediately transitions to the final state without displaying a message.

The `if` statement is a single-entry/single-exit control structure. We will see that the activity diagrams for the remaining control structures also contain initial states, transition arrows, action states that indicate actions to perform, decision symbols (with associated guard conditions) that indicate decisions to be made and final states. This is consistent with the *action/decision model of programming* we have been emphasizing.

Envision seven bins, each containing only one of Java's control statements. These control statements are empty. Your task is to assemble a program from as many of each type of control statement as the algorithm demands, combining those control statements in only two possible ways (stacking or nesting), then filling in the action states and decisions with action expressions and guard conditions in a manner appropriate for the algorithm. We will discuss the variety of ways in which actions and decisions can be written.

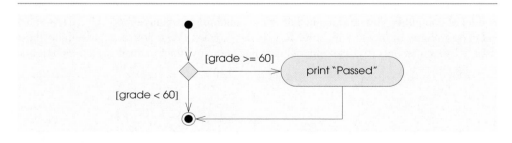

Fig. 4.3   `if` single-selection statement activity diagram.

---

6. We learned in Chapter 2 that decisions can be based on conditions containing relational or equality operators. Actually, a decision can be made on any expression that evaluates to a value of Java's `boolean` type (i.e., any expression that evaluates to `true` or `false`).

4.6 if...else Selection Statement

The `if` single-selection statement performs an indicated action only when the condition is `true`; otherwise, the action is skipped. The `if...else` double-selection statement allows the programmer to specify an action to perform when the condition is true and a different action to perform when the condition is false. For example, the pseudocode statement

> *If student's grade is greater than or equal to 60*
> > *Print "Passed"*
>
> *Else*
> > *Print "Failed"*

prints "Passed" if the student's grade is greater than or equal to 60, but prints "Failed" if the student's grade is less than 60. In either case, after printing occurs, the next pseudocode statement in sequence is "performed."

The preceding pseudocode *If...Else* can be written in Java as

```java
if ( grade >= 60 )
   System.out.println( "Passed" );
else
   System.out.println( "Failed" );
```

Note that the body of the `else` is also indented. Whatever indentation convention you choose should be applied consistently throughout your programs. It is difficult to read programs that do not obey uniform spacing conventions.

Good Programming Practice 4.1

Indent both body statements of an `if...else` *statement.*

Good Programming Practice 4.2

If there are several levels of indentation, each level should be indented the same additional amount of space.

Figure 4.4 illustrates the flow of control in the `if...else` statement. Once again, (besides the initial state, transition arrows and final state) the symbols in the activity diagram represent action states and decisions. We continue to emphasize this action/decision model of computing. Imagine again a deep bin containing as many empty `if...else` statements as might be needed to build any Java program. Your job is to assemble these `if...else` statements (by stacking and nesting) with any other control structures required

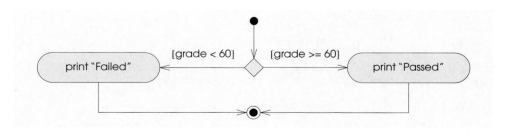

Fig. 4.4   `if...else` double-selection statement activity diagram.

by the algorithm. You fill in the action states and decision symbols with action expressions and guard conditions appropriate to the algorithm.

Conditional Operator (?:)

Java provides the *conditional operator* (?:) that sometimes can be used in place of an if...else statement. This is Java's only *ternary operator*—i.e., it takes three operands. Together, the operands and ?: form a *conditional expression*. The first operand (to the left of the ?) is a boolean expression (i.e., a condition), the second operand (between the ? and :) is the value of the conditional expression if the boolean expression is true and the third operand (to the right of the :) is the value of the conditional expression if the boolean expression evaluates to false. For example, the statement

```
System.out.println( studentGrade >= 60 ? "Passed" : "Failed" );
```

prints the value of println's argument, which is a conditional expression. The conditional expression in this statement evaluates to the string "Passed" if the boolean expression studentGrade >= 60 is true and evaluates to the string "Failed" if the boolean expression is false. Thus, this statement with the conditional operator performs essentially the same function as the if...else statement shown earlier in this section. The precedence of the conditional operator is low, so the entire conditional expression is normally placed in parentheses. We will see that conditional expressions can be used in some situations where if...else statements cannot.

Good Programming Practice 4.3

In general, conditional expressions are more difficult to read than if...else statements. In most cases, conditional expressions should be used to replace only simple if...else statements that choose between two values.

Nested if...else Statements

A program can test multiple cases by placing if...else statements inside other if...else statement to create *nested if...else statements*. For example, the following pseudocode represents a nested if...else that prints A for exam grades greater than or equal to 90, B for grades in the range 80 to 89, C for grades in the range 70 to 79, D for grades in the range 60 to 69 and F for all other grades:

> *If student's grade is greater than or equal to 90*
> > *Print "A"*
> *else*
> > *If student's grade is greater than or equal to 80*
> > > *Print "B"*
> > *else*
> > > *If student's grade is greater than or equal to 70*
> > > > *Print "C"*
> > > *else*
> > > > *If student's grade is greater than or equal to 60*
> > > > > *Print "D"*
> > > > *else*
> > > > > *Print "F"*

This pseudocode may be written in Java as

```java
if ( studentGrade >= 90 )
   System.out.println( "A" );
else
   if ( studentGrade >= 80 )
      System.out.println( "B" );
   else
      if ( studentGrade >= 70 )
         System.out.println( "C" );
      else
         if ( studentGrade >= 60 )
            System.out.println( "D" );
         else
            System.out.println( "F" );
```

If `studentGrade` is greater than or equal to 90, the first four conditions will be true, but only the statement in the `if` part of the first `if...else` statement will execute. After that statement executes, the `else` part of the "outermost" `if...else` statement is skipped. Most Java programmers prefer to write the preceding `if...else` as

```java
if ( studentGrade >= 90 )
   System.out.println( "A" );
else if ( studentGrade >= 80 )
   System.out.println( "B" );
else if ( studentGrade >= 70 )
   System.out.println( "C" );
else if ( studentGrade >= 60 )
   System.out.println( "D" );
else
   System.out.println( "F" );
```

The two forms are identical except for the spacing and indentation, which the compiler ignores. The latter form is popular because it avoids deep indentation of the code to the right. Such indentation often leaves little room on a line of code, forcing lines to be split and decreasing program readability.

Dangling-*else* Problem

The Java compiler always associates an `else` with the immediately preceding `if` unless told to do otherwise by the placement of braces ({}). This behavior can lead to what is referred to as the *dangling-else problem*. For example,

```java
if ( x > 5 )
   if ( y > 5 )
      System.out.println( "x and y are > 5" );
else
   System.out.println( "x is <= 5" );
```

appears to indicate that if x is greater than 5, the nested `if` statement determines whether y is also greater than 5. If so, the string `"x and y are > 5"` is output. Otherwise, it *appears* that if x is not greater than 5, the `else` part of the `if...else` outputs the string `"x is <= 5"`.

Beware! This nested if...else statement does not execute as it appears. The compiler actually interprets the statement as

```
if ( x > 5 )
   if ( y > 5 )
      System.out.println( "x and y are > 5" );
   else
      System.out.println( "x is <= 5" );
```

in which the body of the first if is a nested if...else. This statement tests whether x is greater than 5. If so, execution continues by testing whether y is also greater than 5. If the second condition is true, the proper string—"x and y are > 5"—is displayed. However, if the second condition is false, the string "x is <= 5" is displayed, even though we know that x is greater than 5.

To force the nested if...else statement to execute as it was originally intended, it must be written as follows:

```
if ( x > 5 ) {
   if ( y > 5 )
      System.out.println( "x and y are > 5" );
}
else
   System.out.println( "x is <= 5" );
```

The braces ({}) indicate to the compiler that the second if statement is in the body of the first if and that the else is associated with the first if. Exercise 4.21 and Exercise 4.22 investigate the dangling-else problem further.

Blocks

The if statement normally expects only one statement in its body. To include several statements in the body of an if (or the body of else for an if...else statement), enclose the statements in braces ({ and }). A set of statements contained within a pair of braces is called a *block*.

 Software Engineering Observation 4.1

A block can be placed anywhere in a program that a single statement can be placed.

The following example includes a block in the else part of an if...else statement:

```
if ( grade >= 60 )
   System.out.println( "Passed" );
else {
   System.out.println( "Failed" );
   System.out.println( "You must take this course again." );
}
```

In this case, if grade is less than 60, the program executes both statements in the body of the else and prints

```
Failed.
You must take this course again.
```

Notice the braces surrounding the two statements in the else clause. These braces are important. Without the braces, the statement

```
System.out.println( "You must take this course again." );
```

would be outside the body of the else part of the if...else statement and would execute regardless of whether the grade is less than 60.

Syntax errors (such as when one brace in a block is left out of the program) are caught by the compiler. A *logic error* (such as when both braces in a block are left out of the program) has its effect at execution time. A *fatal logic error* causes a program to fail and terminate prematurely. A *nonfatal logic error* allows a program to continue executing, but the program produces incorrect results.

Common Programming Error 4.3

Forgetting one or both of the braces that delimit a block can lead to syntax errors or logic errors in a program.

Good Programming Practice 4.4

Always using braces in an if...else (or other) statement helps prevent their accidental omission, especially when adding statements to an if or else at a later time. To avoid omitting one or both of the braces, some programmers type the beginning and ending braces of blocks before typing the individual statements within the braces.

Just as a block can be placed anywhere a single statement can be placed, it is also possible to have no statement at all—called an *empty statement* (or a *null statement* in some languages). The empty statement is represented by placing a semicolon (;) where a statement would normally be.

Common Programming Error 4.4

Placing a semicolon after the condition in an if or if...else statement leads to a logic error in single-selection if statements and a syntax error in double-selection if...else statements (when the if part contains an actual body statement).

4.7 while Repetition Statement

A *repetition structure* (also called a *looping structure* or a *loop*) allows the programmer to specify that a program should repeat an action while some condition remains true. The pseudocode statement

> *While there are more items on my shopping list*
> *Purchase next item and cross it off my list*

describes the repetition that occurs during a shopping trip. The condition "there are more items on my shopping list" may be true or false. If it is true, then the action "Purchase next item and cross it off my list" is performed. This action will be performed repeatedly while the condition remains true. The statement(s) contained in the *while* repetition structure constitute the body of the *while* repetition structure, which may be a single statement or a block. Eventually, the condition will become false (when the last item on the shopping list has been purchased and crossed off the list). At this point, the repetition terminates, and the first statement after the repetition structure executes.

As an example of Java's `while` statement, consider a program segment designed to find the first power of 2 larger than 1000. Suppose that the `int` variable `product` is initialized to 2. When the following `while` statement finishes executing, `product` contains the result:

```
int product = 2;

while ( product <= 1000 )
    product = 2 * product;
```

When this `while` statement begins execution, the value of variable `product` is 2. Each iteration of the `while` statement multiplies `product` by 2, so `product` takes on the values 4, 8, 16, 32, 64, 128, 256, 512 and 1024 successively. When variable `product` becomes 1024, the `while`-statement condition—`product <= 1000`—becomes false. This terminates the repetition, so the final value of `product` is 1024. At this point, program execution would continue with the next statement after the `while` statement.

Common Programming Error 4.5

Not providing, in the body of a `while` statement, an action that eventually causes the condition in the `while` to become false normally results in a logic error called an infinite loop, *in which the loop never terminates.*

The activity diagram of Fig. 4.5 illustrates the flow of control that corresponds to the preceding `while` statement. Once again, (besides the initial state, transition arrows, a final state and two notes) the symbols in the diagram represent an action state and a decision. This diagram also introduces the UML's *merge symbol*. The UML represents both the merge symbol and the decision symbol as diamonds. The merge symbol joins two flows of activity into one flow of activity. In this diagram, the merge symbol joins the transitions from the initial state and from the action state, so they both flow into the decision that determines whether the loop should begin (or continue) executing. Although the UML represents decision and merge symbols with the diamond shape, the symbols can be distinguished by the number of "incoming" and "outgoing" transition arrows. A decision symbol has one transition arrow pointing to the diamond and two or more transition arrows pointing out from the diamond to indicate possible transitions from that point. In addition, each transition arrow pointing out of a decision symbol has a guard condition next to it. A merge symbol has two or more transition arrows pointing to the diamond and only one transition arrow pointing from the diamond, to indicate multiple activity flows merging to continue the activity. Note that, unlike the decision symbol, the merge symbol does not have a counterpart in Java code.

Imagine a bin of empty `while` statements that can be stacked and nested with other control structures to form a structured implementation of an algorithm's flow of control. You fill in the action states and decision symbols with action expressions and guard conditions appropriate to the algorithm. The diagram clearly shows the repetition of the `while` statement shown earlier in this section. The transition arrow emerging from the action state points to the merge. From the merge, program flow transitions back to the decision that is tested at the beginning of each iteration of the loop. The loop continues to execute until the guard condition `product > 1000` becomes true. Then, the `while` statement exits (reaches its final state) and control passes to the next statement in sequence in the program.

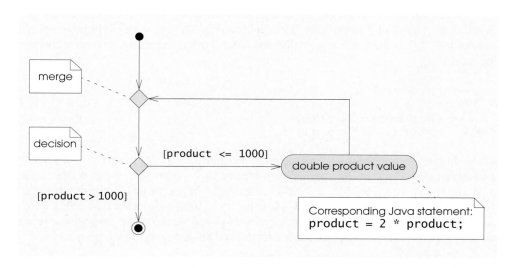

Fig. 4.5   while repetition statement activity diagram.

4.8 Formulating Algorithms: Case Study 1 (Counter-Controlled Repetition)

To illustrate how algorithms are developed, we solve two variations of a problem that averages student grades. Consider the following problem statement:

> *A class of ten students took a quiz. The grades (integers in the range 0 to 100) for this quiz are available to you. Determine the class average on the quiz.*

The class average is equal to the sum of the grades divided by the number of students. The algorithm for solving this problem on a computer must input each grade, keep track of the total of all grades input, perform the averaging calculation and print the result.

Let us use pseudocode to list the actions to execute and specify the order in which these actions should execute. We use *counter-controlled repetition* to input the grades one at a time. This technique uses a variable called a *counter* (or *control variable*) to control the number of times a set of statements will execute. Counter-controlled repetition is often called *definite repetition*, because the number of repetitions is known before the loop begins executing. In this example, repetition terminates when the counter exceeds 10. This section presents a fully developed pseudocode algorithm (Fig. 4.6) and the corresponding Java program (Fig. 4.7). Section 4.9 shows how to use pseudocode to develop an algorithm.

Software Engineering Observation 4.2

Experience has shown that the most difficult part of solving a problem on a computer is developing the algorithm for the solution. Once a correct algorithm has been specified, the process of producing a working Java program from the algorithm is normally straightforward.

Note the references in the algorithm to a total and a counter. A *total* is a variable used to accumulate the sum of several values. A *counter* is a variable used to count—in this case, to count the number of grades entered. Variables used to store totals normally are initialized to zero before being used in a program.

Set total to zero
Set grade counter to one

While grade counter is less than or equal to ten
    Input the next grade
    Add the grade into the total
    Add one to the grade counter

Set the class average to the total divided by ten
Print the class average

Fig. 4.6   Pseudocode algorithm that uses counter-controlled repetition to solve the class-average problem.

```
1   // Fig. 4.7: Average1.java
2   // Class-average program with counter-controlled repetition.
3   import javax.swing.JOptionPane;
4
5   public class Average1 {
6
7      public static void main( String args[] )
8      {
9         int total;          // sum of grades input by user
10        int gradeCounter;   // number of grade to be entered next
11        int grade;          // grade value
12        int average;        // average of grades
13
14        String gradeString; // grade typed by user
15
16        // initialization phase
17        total = 0;          // initialize total
18        gradeCounter = 1;   // initialize loop counter
19
20        // processing phase
21        while ( gradeCounter <= 10 ) {  // loop 10 times
22
23           // prompt for input and read grade from user
24           gradeString = JOptionPane.showInputDialog(
25              "Enter integer grade: " );
26
27           // convert gradeString to int
28           grade = Integer.parseInt( gradeString );
29
30           total = total + grade;              // add grade to total
31           gradeCounter = gradeCounter + 1;    // increment counter
32
33        } // end while
34
35        // termination phase
36        average = total / 10;  // integer division
```

Fig. 4.7   Counter-controlled repetition: Class-average problem. (Part 1 of 2.)

```
37
38        // display average of exam grades
39        JOptionPane.showMessageDialog( null, "Class average is " + average,
40           "Class Average", JOptionPane.INFORMATION_MESSAGE );
41
42        System.exit( 0 );  // terminate the program
43
44     } // end main
45
46  } // end class Average1
```

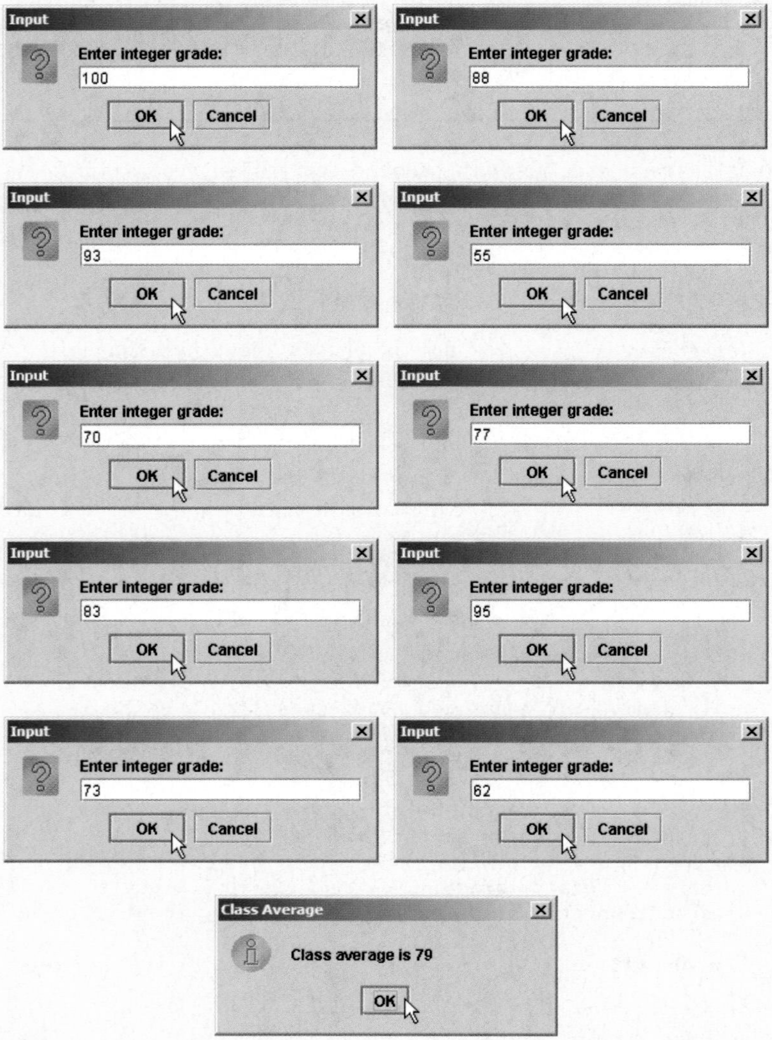

Fig. 4.7   Counter-controlled repetition: Class-average problem. (Part 2 of 2.)

Line 3 imports class `JOptionPane` so the program can use the input dialogs and message dialogs presented in Chapter 2. Line 5 begins the declaration of application class `Average1`. Recall from Section 2.2 that the declaration of an application class must contain a `main` method (lines 7–44) where the application begins execution.

Lines 9–14 declare variables `total`, `gradeCounter`, `grade` and `average` to be of type `int` and variable `gradeString` to be of type `String`. Variable `gradeString` stores the string the user types in the input dialog. Variable `grade` stores the integer value of `gradeString` after the program converts it to an `int`.

Notice that the declarations (in lines 9–14) appear in the body of method `main`. Recall from Section 3.5 that variables declared in a method body are *local variables* and can be used only from the line of their declaration in the method to the closing right brace (`}`) of the method declaration. A local variable's declaration must appear before the variable is used in that method. For example, lines 9–14 must appear before lines 17–40 in Fig. 4.7. A local variable cannot be accessed outside the method in which it is declared.

Good Programming Practice 4.5

If you prefer to place declarations at the beginning of a method, separate the declarations from the executable statements in that method with one blank line, to highlight where the declarations end and the executable statements begin.

Good Programming Practice 4.6

Declare each variable on a separate line to make programs more readable.

Good Programming Practice 4.7

Always place a blank line before a declaration that appears between executable statements to make the declaration stand out in the program. This contributes to program clarity.

The assignments (in lines 17–18) initialize `total` to `0` and `gradeCounter` to `1`. Note that these initializations occur before they are used in calculations.

Common Programming Error 4.6

Attempting to use a local variable before initializing the variable results in a compile error indicating that the variable may not have been initialized. The value of a local variable cannot be used in an expression until the variable is initialized. The program will not compile properly until the variable receives an initial value.

Error-Prevention Tip 4.1

Initialize counters and totals.

Line 21 indicates that the `while` statement should continue iterating (also called *looping*) as long as the value of `gradeCounter` is less than or equal to 10. While this condition remains true, the `while` statement executes the statements between the braces that delimit its body (lines 21–33)

The statement at lines 24–25, which displays an input dialog with the prompt "Enter integer grade:," corresponds to the pseudocode statement "*Input the next grade.*"

After the user enters a `gradeString`, the program converts it to an `int` at line 28. Recall from Section 2.5 that class `Integer` is from package `java.lang`, which every Java program implicitly imports. The pseudocode for the class-average problem does not reflect the statement at line 28. The pseudocode statement "*Input the next grade*" requires the programmer to implement the code that obtains the value from the user and converts it to a type that can be used in the average calculation. As you learn to program, you will find that you require fewer pseudocode statements to help you implement a program.

Next, line 30 updates the `total` with the new `grade` entered by the user. Line 30 adds `grade` to the previous value of `total` and assigns the result to `total`.

Line 31 adds `1` to `gradeCounter` to indicate that the program has processed a grade and is ready to input the next grade from the user. Incrementing `gradeCounter` eventually causes `gradeCounter` to exceed 10, which enables the condition in the `while` loop to become false and the loop to terminate.

When the loop terminates, line 36 assigns the variable `average` result of the average calculation. Lines 39–40 display an information message dialog containing `"Class average is  "` followed by the value of variable `average`. The string `"Class Average"` (the third argument) is the title of the message dialog. Line 43 terminates the application.

After compiling the class declaration with `javac`, execute the application from the command window with the command

```
java Average1
```

which invokes the Java interpreter and tells it that the `main` method for this application is declared in class `Average1`.

The averaging calculation in the program of Fig. 4.7 produced an integer result. Actually, the sum of the grade-point values in the sample execution is 796, which, when divided by 10, should yield the floating-point number 79.6. We will see how to use integers in a floating-point calculation in the next section.

4.9 Formulating Algorithms with Top-Down, Stepwise Refinement: Case Study 2 (Sentinel-Controlled Repetition)

Let us generalize Section 4.8's class-average problem. Consider the following problem:

> *Develop a class-averaging program that processes grades for an arbitrary number of students each time the program is run.*

In the previous class-average example, the problem statement specified the number of students, so the number of grades (10) was known in advance. In this example, no indication is given of how many grades the user will enter during the program's execution. The program must process an arbitrary number of grades. How can the program determine when to stop the input of grades? How will it know when to calculate and print the class average?

One way to solve this problem is to use a special value called a *sentinel value* (also called a *signal value*, a *dummy value* or a *flag value*) to indicate "end of data entry." The user enters grades until all legitimate grades have been entered. The user then types the sentinel value to indicate that no more grades will be entered. Sentinel-controlled repetition is often called *indefinite repetition* because the number of repetitions is not known before the loop begins executing.

Clearly, the sentinel value must be chosen so that it cannot be confused with an acceptable input value. Grades on a quiz are nonnegative integers, so –1 is an acceptable sentinel value for this problem. Thus, a run of the class-average program might process a stream of inputs such as 95, 96, 75, 74, 89 and –1. The program would then compute and print the class average for the grades 95, 96, 75, 74 and 89. Note that –1 is the sentinel value, so it should not enter into the averaging calculation.

Common Programming Error 4.7

Choosing a sentinel value that is also a legitimate data value is a logic error.

Top-Down, Stepwise Refinement

We approach the class-average program with a technique called *top-down, stepwise refinement*, which is essential to the development of well-structured programs. We begin with a pseudocode representation of the *top*—a single statement that conveys the overall function of the program:

> *Determine the class average for the quiz*

The *top* is, in effect, a complete representation of a program. Unfortunately, the *top* rarely conveys sufficient detail from which to write a Java program. So we now begin the refinement process. We divide the top into a series of smaller tasks and list these in the order in which they will be performed. This results in the following *first refinement*:

> *Initialize variables*
> *Input, sum and count the quiz grades*
> *Calculate and print the class average*

This refinement uses only the sequence structure—the steps listed should execute in order, one after the other.

Software Engineering Observation 4.3

Each refinement, as well as the top itself, is a complete specification of the algorithm; only the level of detail varies.

Software Engineering Observation 4.4

Many programs can be divided logically into three phases: An initialization phase that initializes the variables; a processing phase that inputs data values and adjusts program variables accordingly; and a termination phase that calculates and outputs the final results.

Software Engineering Observation 4.4 is often all you need for the first refinement in the top-down process. To proceed to the next level of refinement, i.e., the *second refinement*, we commit to specific variables. In this example, we need a running total of the numbers, a count of how many numbers have been processed, a variable to receive the value of each grade as it is input by the user and a variable to hold the calculated average. The pseudocode statement

> *Initialize variables*

can be refined as follows:

> *Initialize total to zero*
> *Initialize counter to zero*

Only the variables *total* and *counter* need to be initialized before they are used; the variables *average* and *grade* (for the calculated average and the user input, respectively) need not be initialized, because their values will be replaced as they are calculated or input.

The pseudocode statement

> *Input, sum and count the quiz grades*

requires a repetition structure (i.e., a loop) that successively inputs each grade. We do not know in advance how many grades are to be processed, so we will use sentinel-controlled repetition. The user enters legitimate grades one at a time. After entering the last legitimate grade, the user enters the sentinel value. The program tests for the sentinel value after each grade is input and terminates the loop when the user enters the sentinel value. The second refinement of the preceding pseudocode statement is then

> *Input the first grade (possibly the sentinel)*
> *While the user has not yet entered the sentinel*
>   *Add this grade into the running total*
>   *Add one to the grade counter*
>   *Input the next grade (possibly the sentinel)*

In pseudocode, we do not use braces around the set of statements that form the body of the *While* structure. We simply indent the statements under the *While* to show that they belong to the *While*. Again, pseudocode is only an informal program-development aid.

The pseudocode statement

> *Calculate and print the class average*

can be refined as follows:

> *If the counter is not equal to zero*
>   *Set the average to the total divided by the counter*
>   *Print the average*
> *else*
>   *Print "No grades were entered"*

We are careful here to test for the possibility of division by zero—normally a logic error that, if undetected, would cause the program to fail or produce invalid output. The complete second refinement of the pseudocode for the class-average problem is shown in Fig. 4.8.

Initialize total to zero
Initialize counter to zero

Input the first grade (possibly the sentinel)
While the user has not yet entered the sentinel
     Add this grade into the running total
     Add one to the grade counter
     Input the next grade (possibly the sentinel)

If the counter is not equal to zero
     Set the average to the total divided by the counter
     Print the average
else
     Print "No grades were entered"

Fig. 4.8   Class-average problem pseudocode algorithm with sentinel-controlled repetition.

Error-Prevention Tip 4.2

When performing division by an expression whose value could be zero, explicitly test for this possibility and handle it appropriately in your program (such as by printing an error message) rather than allowing the error to occur.

In Fig. 4.6 and Fig. 4.8, we include some completely blank lines and indentation in the pseudocode to make the pseudocode more readable. The blank lines separate the pseudocode algorithms into their various phases and the indentation emphasizes the bodies of the control structures.

The pseudocode algorithm in Fig. 4.8 solves the more general class-averaging problem. This algorithm was developed after only two refinements. Sometimes more refinements are necessary.

Software Engineering Observation 4.5

Terminate the top-down, stepwise refinement process when the pseudocode algorithm is specified in sufficient detail to be able to convert the pseudocode to Java. Normally, implementing the Java program is then straightforward.

Software Engineering Observation 4.6

Some experienced programmers write programs without ever using program-development tools like pseudocode. These programmers feel that their ultimate goal is to solve the problem on a computer and that writing pseudocode merely delays the production of final outputs. Although this method may work for simple and familiar problems, it can lead to serious errors and delays in large, complex projects.

Figure 4.9 shows the Java application that implements the pseudocode algorithm of Fig. 4.8. Although each grade is an integer, the averaging calculation is likely to produce a number with a decimal point (i.e., a real number). The type `int` cannot represent real numbers, so this program uses type `double` to handle floating-point numbers (as in Section 3.5). The program introduces a special operator called a *cast operator* to convert the `int` values to type `double` for use in the averaging calculation.

In this example, we see that control structures may be stacked on top of one another (in sequence) just as a child stacks building blocks. The `while` statement (lines 31–42) is followed by an `if...else` statement (lines 48–62) in sequence. Much of the code in this program is identical to the code in Fig. 4.7, so we concentrate in the program discussion on the new features and issues.

```
1   // Fig. 4.9: Average2.java
2   // Class-average program with sentinel-controlled repetition.
3   import java.text.DecimalFormat;   // class to format numbers
4   import javax.swing.JOptionPane;
5
6   public class Average2 {
7
8       public static void main( String args[] )
9       {
10          int total;              // sum of grades
```

Fig. 4.9   Sentinel-controlled repetition: Class-average program. (Part 1 of 3.)

```
11      int gradeCounter;     // number of grades entered
12      int grade;            // grade value
13
14      double average;   // number with decimal point for average
15
16      String gradeString;   // grade typed by user
17
18      // initialization phase
19      total = 0;            // initialize total
20      gradeCounter = 0;  // initialize loop counter
21
22      // processing phase
23      // get first grade from user
24      gradeString = JOptionPane.showInputDialog(
25         "Enter Integer Grade or -1 to Quit:" );
26
27      // convert gradeString to int
28      grade = Integer.parseInt( gradeString );
29
30      // loop until sentinel value read from user
31      while ( grade != -1 ) {
32         total = total + grade;            // add grade to total
33         gradeCounter = gradeCounter + 1;  // increment counter
34
35         // get next grade from user
36         gradeString = JOptionPane.showInputDialog(
37            "Enter Integer Grade or -1 to Quit:" );
38
39         // convert gradeString to int
40         grade = Integer.parseInt( gradeString );
41
42      } // end while
43
44      // termination phase
45      DecimalFormat twoDigits = new DecimalFormat( "0.00" );
46
47      // if user entered at least one grade...
48      if ( gradeCounter != 0 ) {
49
50         // calculate average of all grades entered
51         average = (double) total / gradeCounter;
52
53         // display average with two digits of precision
54         JOptionPane.showMessageDialog( null,
55            "Class average is " + twoDigits.format( average ),
56            "Class Average", JOptionPane.INFORMATION_MESSAGE );
57
58      } // end if part of if...else
59
60      else // if no grades entered, output appropriate message
61         JOptionPane.showMessageDialog( null, "No grades were entered",
62            "Class Average", JOptionPane.INFORMATION_MESSAGE );
63
```

Fig. 4.9   Sentinel-controlled repetition: Class-average program. (Part 2 of 3.)

```
64          System.exit( 0 );   // terminate application
65
66      } // end main
67
68  } // end class Average2
```

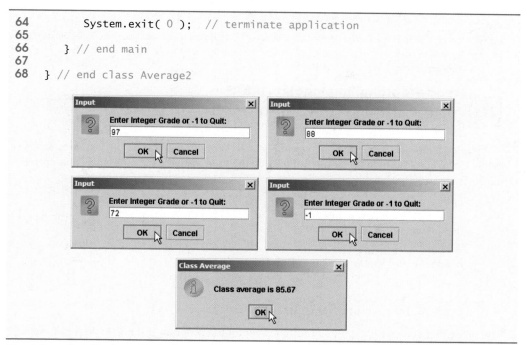

Fig. 4.9   Sentinel-controlled repetition: Class-average program. (Part 3 of 3.)

Line 14 declares **double** variable **average**. This variable allows us to store the class average as a floating-point number. Line 20 initializes **gradeCounter** to 0, because no grades have been entered yet. Remember that this program uses sentinel-controlled repetition. To keep an accurate record of the number of grades entered, the program increments **gradeCounter** only when the user inputs a valid grade value.

Compare the program logic for sentinel-controlled repetition with that for counter-controlled repetition in Fig. 4.7. In counter-controlled repetition, each iteration of the **while** statement (lines 21–33 of Fig. 4.7) reads a value from the user, for the specified number of iterations. In sentinel-controlled repetition, the program reads and converts one value (lines 24–28 of Fig. 4.9) before reaching the **while**. This value determines whether the program's flow of control should enter the body of the **while**. If the condition of the **while** is false, the user entered the sentinel value, so the body of the **while** does not execute (i.e., no grades were entered). If, on the other hand, the condition is true, the body begins execution, and the loop adds the value input by the user to the **total**. After the value has been processed, lines 36–40 in the loop's body input the next value from the user before program control reaches the end of the block. As program control reaches the closing right brace (**}**) of the body at line 42, execution continues with the next test of the condition of the **while** (line 31). The condition uses the new value just input by the user to determine whether the **while** statement's body should execute again. Notice that the next value always is input from the user immediately before the program tests the condition of the **while**. This allows the program to determine whether the value just input by the user is the sentinel value *before* the program processes that value (i.e., adds it to the **total**). If the value input is the sentinel value, the **while** terminates, and the program does not add –1 to the **total**.

Common Programming Error 4.8

Forgetting to read the first data value before a `while` *statement that uses sentinel-controlled repetition results in logic errors that might cause the loop to be skipped entirely or might treat the sentinel value as a valid data value.*

Good Programming Practice 4.8

In a sentinel-controlled loop, the prompts requesting data entry should explicitly remind the user of the value that represents the sentinel.

Notice the block in the `while` loop in Fig. 4.9. Without the braces, the last three statements in the body of the loop would fall outside the loop, causing the computer to interpret the code incorrectly as follows:

```
while ( grade != -1 )
   total = total + grade;          // add grade to total
gradeCounter = gradeCounter + 1;   // increment counter

// get next grade from user
gradeString = JOptionPane.showInputDialog(
   "Enter Integer Grade or -1 to Quit:" );

// convert gradeString to int
grade = Integer.parseInt( gradeString );
```

The preceding code would cause an infinite loop in the program if the user does not input the sentinel -1 as the input value at lines 24–25 (before the `while` statement) in the program.

Common Programming Error 4.9

Omitting the braces that delimit a block can lead to logic errors such as infinite loops. To prevent this problem, some programmers enclose the body of every control statement in braces.

Line 45 declares `twoDigits` as a reference to an object of class *DecimalFormat* (package *java.text*). `DecimalFormat` objects format numbers. In this example, we decided to output the class average with two digits to the right of the decimal point (i.e., rounded to the nearest hundredth). Line 45 creates a `DecimalFormat` object that is initialized with the pattern `"0.00"`. Each 0 specifies a required digit position in the formatted floating-point number. This particular format indicates that every number formatted with `twoDigits` will have at least one digit to the left of the decimal point and exactly two digits to the right of the decimal point. If the number does not meet the formatting requirements, 0s are inserted in the formatted number at the required positions. The *new* keyword begins a *class instance creation expression* that creates an object of the type specified to the right of `new`. The process of creating new objects is also known as *creating an instance*, or *instantiating an object*. The value in parentheses after the type in a class instance creation expression is used to *initialize* (i.e., give a value to) the new object. Reference `twoDigits` is assigned the value of the `new` operation, which is a reference the new object. The statement in line 45 is read as "`twoDigits` *gets* the value of `new` `DecimalFormat( "0.00" )`."

Software Engineering Observation 4.7

Normally, objects are created with `new`. *One exception to this is a string literal that is contained in quotes, such as* `"hello"`. *String literals are references to objects of class* `String` *that are implicitly created whenever Java encounters a string literal.*

Averages do not always evaluate to integer values. Often, an average is a value that contains a fractional part, such as 3.333 or 2.7. These values are referred to as *floating-point numbers* and are represented by the type `double` (see Section 3.5). In line 14, variable `average` is declared to be of type `double` to capture the fractional result of our calculation. However, the result of the calculation `total / gradeCounter` (line 51) is an integer, because `total` and `gradeCounter` are both integer variables. Dividing two integers results in *integer division*—any fractional part of the calculation is lost (i.e., *truncated*). The fractional part is lost before the result can be assigned to `average`, because the calculation is performed before the assignment occurs.

Common Programming Error 4.10

Assuming that integer division rounds (rather than truncates) can lead to incorrect results.

To perform a floating-point calculation with integer values, we must create temporary values that are floating-point numbers for the calculation. Java provides the *unary cast operator* to accomplish this task. Line 51 uses the unary cast operator `(double)` to create a temporary floating-point copy of its operand—`total` (which appears to the right of the operator). Using a cast operator in this manner is called *explicit conversion*. The value stored in `total` is still an integer. The calculation now consists of a floating-point value (the temporary `double` version of `total`) divided by the integer `gradeCounter`. Java knows how to evaluate only arithmetic expressions in which the operands' types are identical. To ensure that the operands are of the same type, Java performs an operation called *promotion* (or *implicit conversion*) on selected operands. For example, in an expression containing values of the types `int` and `double`, the `int` values are *promoted* to `double` values for use in the expression. In this example, Java promotes the value of `grade-Counter` to type `double`, then the program performs the calculation and assigns the result of the floating-point division to `average`. Later in this chapter, we discuss all of the standard types and their promotion rules.

Common Programming Error 4.11

The cast operator can be used to convert between primitive numeric types and to convert between related reference types (as we discuss in Chapter 9). Casting to the wrong type may cause compilation errors or runtime errors.

Good Programming Practice 4.9

Do not compare floating-point values for equality or inequality. Rather, determine whether the absolute value of the difference between the numbers is less than a specified small value.

Cast operators are available for any type. The cast operator is formed by placing parentheses around the name of a type. The operator is a *unary operator* (i.e., an operator that takes only one operand). In Chapter 2, we studied the binary arithmetic operators. Java also supports unary versions of the plus (+) and minus (-) operators, so the programmer can write expressions like -7 or +5. Cast operators associate from right to left and have the same precedence as other unary operators, such as unary + and unary -. This precedence is one level higher than that of the *multiplicative operators* *, / and % and one level lower than that of parentheses. (See the operator precedence chart in Appendix A.) We indicate the cast operator with the notation *(type)* in our precedence charts, to indicate that any type name can be used to form a cast operator.

Although floating-point numbers are not always 100% precise, they have numerous applications. For example, when we speak of a "normal" body temperature of 98.6, we do not need to be precise to a large number of digits. When we read the temperature on a thermometer as 98.6, it may actually be 98.5999473210643. Calling this number simply 98.6 is fine for most applications.

Another way in which floating-point numbers occur is through division. When we divide 10 by 3, the result is 3.3333333…, with the sequence of 3s repeating infinitely. The computer allocates only a fixed amount of space to hold such a value, so clearly the stored floating-point value can be only an approximation.

Common Programming Error 4.12

Using floating-point numbers in a manner that assumes they are represented precisely can lead to inaccurate results.

4.10 Formulating Algorithms with Top-Down, Stepwise Refinement: Case Study 3 (Nested Control Structures)

For the next example, we will once again formulate the algorithm by using pseudocode and top-down, stepwise refinement, and write a corresponding Java program. We have seen that control statements can be stacked on top of one another (in sequence) just as a child stacks building blocks. In this case study, we examine the only other structured way control statements can be connected, namely, by *nesting* of one control statement within another.

Consider the following problem statement:

> *A college offers a course that prepares students for the state licensing exam for real estate brokers. Last year, ten of the students who completed this course took the exam. The college wants to know how well its students did on the exam. You have been asked to write a program to summarize the results. You have been given a list of these 10 students. Next to each name is written a 1 if the student passed the exam or a 2 if the student failed.*
>
> *Your program should analyze the results of the exam as follows:*
>
> 1. *Input each test result (i.e., a 1 or a 2). Display the message "Enter result" on the screen each time the program requests another test result.*
>
> 2. *Count the number of test results of each type.*
>
> 3. *Display a summary of the test results indicating the number of students who passed and the number of students who failed.*
>
> 4. *If more than eight students passed the exam, print the message "Raise tuition."*

After reading the problem statement carefully, we make the following observations:

1. The program must process test results for 10 students. A counter-controlled loop can be used because the number of test results is known in advance.

2. Each test result has a numeric value—either a 1 or a 2. Each time the program reads a test result, the program must determine whether the number is a 1 or a 2. We test for a 1 in our algorithm. If the number is not a 1, we assume that it is a 2. (Exercise 4.18 considers the consequences of this assumption.)

3. Two counters are used to keep track of the exam results—one to count the number of students who passed the exam and one to count the number of students who failed the exam.

4. After the program has processed all the results, it must decide whether more than eight students passed the exam.

Let us proceed with top-down, stepwise refinement. We begin with a pseudocode representation of the top:

> *Analyze exam results and decide whether tuition should be raised*

Once again, the top is a complete representation of the program, but several refinements are likely to be needed before the pseudocode can evolve naturally into a Java program.

Our first refinement is

> *Initialize variables*
> *Input the 10 quiz grades, and count passes and failures*
> *Print a summary of the exam results and decide whether tuition should be raised*

Here, too, even though we have a complete representation of the entire program, further refinement is necessary. We now commit to specific variables. Counters are needed to record the passes and failures, a counter will be used to control the looping process and a variable is needed to store the user input. The variable in which the user input will be stored is not initialized, because its value is read from the user during each iteration of the loop.

The pseudocode statement

> *Initialize variables*

can be refined as follows:

> *Initialize passes to zero*
> *Initialize failures to zero*
> *Initialize student counter to one*

Notice that only the counters are initialized.

The pseudocode statement

> *Input the 10 quiz grades, and count passes and failures*

requires a loop that successively inputs the result of each exam. We know in advance that there are precisely 10 exam results, so counter-controlled looping is appropriate. Inside the loop (i.e., *nested* within the loop), a double-selection structure will determine whether each exam result is a pass or a failure and will increment the appropriate counter. The refinement of the preceding pseudocode statement is then

> *While student counter is less than or equal to 10*
> >   *Input the next exam result*
>
> >   *If the student passed*
> > >   *Add one to passes*
> >   *Else*
> > >   *Add one to failures*
>
> >   *Add one to student counter*

We use blank lines to isolate the *If...Else* control structure, which improves readability.

The pseudocode statement

> *Print a summary of the exam results and decide whether tuition should be raised*

can be refined as follows:

> *Print the number of passes*
> *Print the number of failures*
>
> *If more than eight students passed*
>   *Print "Raise tuition"*

The complete second refinement appears in Fig. 4.10. Notice that blank lines are also used to set off the *While* structure for program readability. This pseudocode is now sufficiently refined for conversion to Java. The Java program and a sample execution are shown in Fig. 4.11.

Initialize passes to zero
Initialize failures to zero
Initialize student counter to one

While student counter is less than or equal to 10
    Input the next exam result

    If the student passed
        Add one to passes
    Else
        Add one to failures

    Add one to student counter

Print the number of passes
Print the number of failures

If more than eight students passed
    Print "Raise tuition"

Fig. 4.10   Pseudocode for examination-results problem.

```
1   // Fig. 4.11: Analysis.java
2   // Analysis of examination results.
3   import javax.swing.JOptionPane;
4
5   public class Analysis {
6
7      public static void main( String args[] )
8      {
9         // initializing variables in declarations
10        int passes = 0;          // number of passes
11        int failures = 0;        // number of failures
12        int studentCounter = 1;  // student counter
13        int result;              // one exam result
14
```

Fig. 4.11   Nested-control structures: Examination-results problem. (Part 1 of 3.)

```
15      String input;              // user-entered value
16      String output;             // output string
17
18      // process 10 students using counter-controlled loop
19      while ( studentCounter <= 10 ) {
20
21         // prompt user for input and obtain value from user
22         input = JOptionPane.showInputDialog(
23            "Enter result (1 = pass, 2 = fail)" );
24
25         // convert result to int
26         result = Integer.parseInt( input );
27
28         // if result 1, increment passes; if...else nested in while
29         if ( result == 1 )
30            passes = passes + 1;
31
32         else // if result not 1, increment failures
33            failures = failures + 1;
34
35         // increment studentCounter so loop eventually terminates
36         studentCounter = studentCounter + 1;
37
38      } // end while
39
40      // termination phase; prepare and display results
41      output = "Passed: " + passes + "\nFailed: " + failures;
42
43      // determine whether more than 8 students passed
44      if ( passes > 8 )
45         output = output + "\nRaise Tuition";
46
47      JOptionPane.showMessageDialog( null, output,
48         "Analysis of Examination Results",
49         JOptionPane.INFORMATION_MESSAGE );
50
51      System.exit( 0 );  // terminate application
52
53   } // end main
54
55 } // end class Analysis
```

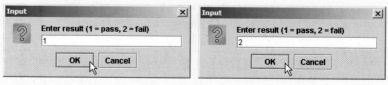

Fig. 4.11   Nested-control structures: Examination-results problem. (Part 2 of 3.)

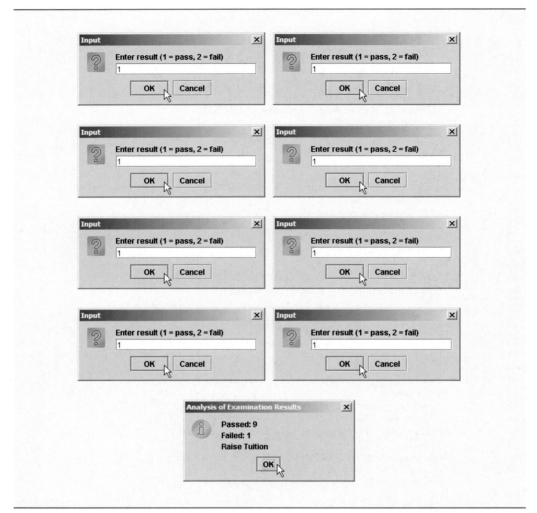

Fig. 4.11   Nested-control structures: Examination-results problem. (Part 3 of 3.)

Lines 10–16 declare the variables used in main to process the examination results. Several of these declarations use Java's ability to incorporate variable initialization into declarations (passes is assigned 0, failures is assigned 0 and student is assigned 1). Looping programs may require initialization at the beginning of each repetition; such reinitialization would normally be performed by assignment statements.

Good Programming Practice 4.10

Initializing local variables when they are declared helps the programmer avoid compiler messages warning of uninitialized data.

Notice that the if...else statement at lines 29–33 is nested in the while statement (lines 19–38). Also, notice the use of String reference output in lines 41 and 45 to build the string that lines 47–49 display in a message dialog.

4.11 Compound Assignment Operators

Java provides several compound assignment operators for abbreviating assignment expressions. Any statement of the form

   variable = variable   operator   expression;

where *operator* is one of the binary operators +, -, *, / or % (or others we discuss later in the text), can be written in the form

   variable   operator=   expression;

For example, you can abbreviate the statement

   c = c + 3;

with the *addition compound assignment operator*, +=, as

   c += 3;

The += operator adds the value of the expression on the right of the operator to the value of the variable on the left of the operator and stores the result in the variable on the left of the operator. Thus, the assignment expression c += 3 adds 3 to c. Figure 4.12 shows the arithmetic compound assignment operators, sample expressions using the operators and explanations of what the operators do.

4.12 Increment and Decrement Operators

Java provides two unary operators for adding 1 to or subtracting 1 from the value of a numeric variable. These operators are the unary *increment operator*, ++, and the unary *decrement operator*, --, which are summarized in Fig. 4.13. A program can increment by 1 the value of a variable called c using the increment operator, ++, rather than the expression c = c + 1 or c += 1. An increment or decrement operator that is prefixed to (is placed before) a variable is referred to as the *preincrement* or *predecrement operator*, respectively. An increment or decrement operator that is postfixed to (is placed after) a variable is referred to as the *postincrement* or *postdecrement operator*, respectively.[7]

Assignment operator	Sample expression	Explanation	Assigns
Assume: int c = 3, d = 5, e = 4, f = 6, g = 12;			
+=	c += 7	c = c + 7	10 to c
-=	d -= 4	d = d - 4	1 to d
*=	e *= 5	e = e * 5	20 to e
/=	f /= 3	f = f / 3	2 to f
%=	g %= 9	g = g % 9	3 to g

Fig. 4.12   Arithmetic assignment operators.

---

7.   The *Java Language Specification* uses the terms *prefix increment operator, postfix increment operator, prefix decrement operator* and *postfix decrement operator* to describe these operators.

Operator	Called	Sample expression	Explanation
++	preincrement	++a	Increment a by 1, then use the new value of a in the expression in which a resides.
++	postincrement	a++	Use the current value of a in the expression in which a resides, then increment a by 1.
--	predecrement	--b	Decrement b by 1, then use the new value of b in the expression in which b resides.
--	postdecrement	b--	Use the current value of b in the expression in which b resides, then decrement b by 1.

Fig. 4.13   The increment and decrement operators .

Preincrementing (or predecrementing) a variable causes the variable to be incremented (decremented) by 1, and then the new value of the variable is used in the expression in which it appears. Postincrementing (or postdecrementing) the variable causes the current value of the variable to be used in the expression in which it appears, and then the variable value is incremented (decremented) by 1.

Good Programming Practice 4.11

Unlike binary operators, unary operators should be placed next to their operands, with no intervening spaces.

The application in Fig. 4.14 demonstrates the difference between the preincrementing version and the postincrementing version of the ++ increment operator. Postincrementing the variable c causes it to be incremented after it is used in the System.out.println method call (line 13). Preincrementing the variable c causes it to be incremented before it is used in the System.out.println method call (line 21).

```java
1   // Fig. 4.14: Increment.java
2   // Preincrementing and postincrementing operators.
3
4   public class Increment {
5
6      public static void main( String args[] )
7      {
8         int c;
9
10        // demonstrate postincrement
11        c = 5;                        // assign 5 to c
12        System.out.println( c );     // print 5
13        System.out.println( c++ );   // print 5 then postincrement
14        System.out.println( c );     // print 6
15
16        System.out.println();        // skip a line
17
```

Fig. 4.14   Preincrementing and postincrementing. (Part 1 of 2.)

```
18          // demonstrate preincrement
19          c = 5;                        // assign 5 to c
20          System.out.println( c );      // print 5
21          System.out.println( ++c );    // preincrement then print 6
22          System.out.println( c );      // print 6
23
24       } // end main
25
26    } // end class Increment
```

```
5
5
6

5
6
6
```

Fig. 4.14   Preincrementing and postincrementing. (Part 2 of 2.)

The program displays the value of c before and after the ++ operator is used. The decrement operator (--) works similarly.

Line 16 uses System.out.println to output a blank line. If println receives no arguments, it simply outputs a newline character.

The arithmetic compound assignment operators and the increment and decrement operators can be used to simplify program statements. For example, the three assignment statements in Fig. 4.11 (lines 30, 32 and 36)

```
passes = passes + 1;
failures = failures + 1;
studentCounter = studentCounter + 1;
```

can be written more concisely with assignment operators as

```
passes += 1;
failures += 1;
studentCounter += 1;
```

with preincrement operators as

```
++passes;
++failures;
++studentCounter;
```

or with postincrement operators as

```
passes++;
failures++;
studentCounter++;
```

It is important to note that when incrementing or decrementing a variable in a statement by itself, the preincrement and postincrement forms have the same effect, and the predecrement and postdecrement forms have the same effect. It is only when a variable appears in the context of a larger expression that preincrementing and postincrementing the variable have different effects (and similarly for predecrementing and postdecrementing).

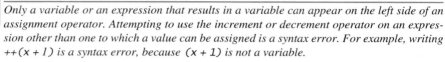

Common Programming Error 4.13

Only a variable or an expression that results in a variable can appear on the left side of an assignment operator. Attempting to use the increment or decrement operator on an expression other than one to which a value can be assigned is a syntax error. For example, writing ++(x + 1) is a syntax error, because (x + 1) is not a variable.

Figure 4.15 shows the precedence and associativity of the operators that have been introduced up to this point. The operators are shown from top to bottom in decreasing order of precedence. The second column describes the associativity of the operators at each level of precedence. Notice that the conditional operator (?:); the unary operators increment (++), decrement (--), plus (+) and minus (-); the cast operators and the assignment operators =, +=, -=, *=, /= and %= associate from right to left. All other operators in the operator precedence chart in Fig. 4.15 associate from left to right. The third column names the groups of operators.

4.13 Primitive Types

The table in Fig. 4.16 lists the eight primitive types in Java. Like its predecessor languages C and C++, Java requires all variables to have a type. For this reason, Java is referred to as a *strongly typed language*.

In C and C++ programs, programmers frequently had to write separate versions of programs to support different computer platforms, because the primitive types were not guaranteed to be identical from computer to computer. For example, an int value on one machine might be represented by 16 bits (2 bytes) of memory, while an int value on another machine might be represented by 32 bits (4 bytes) of memory. In Java, int values are always 32 bits (4 bytes).

Operators					Associativity	Type
++	--				right to left	unary postfix
++	--	+	-	(*type*)	right to left	unary
*	/	%			left to right	multiplicative
+	-				left to right	additive
<	<=	>	>=		left to right	relational
==	!=				left to right	equality
?:					right to left	conditional
=	+=	-=	*=	/= %=	right to left	assignment

Fig. 4.15 Precedence and associativity of the operators discussed so far.

Type	Size in bits	Values	Standard
boolean		true or false [*Note:* The representation of a boolean is specific to the Java Virtual Machine on each computer platform.]	
char	16	'\u0000' to '\uFFFF' (0 to 65535)	(ISO Unicode character set)
byte	8	−128 to +127 (-2^7 to $2^7 - 1$)	
short	16	−32,768 to +32,767 (-2^{15} to $2^{15} - 1$)	
int	32	−2,147,483,648 to +2,147,483,647 (-2^{31} to $2^{31} - 1$)	
long	64	−9,223,372,036,854,775,808 to +9,223,372,036,854,775,807 (-2^{63} to $2^{63} - 1$)	
float	32	*Negative range:* −3.4028234663852886E+38 to −1.40129846432481707e−45 *Positive range:* 1.40129846432481707e−45 to 3.4028234663852886E+38	(IEEE 754 floating point)
double	64	*Negative range:* −1.7976931348623157E+308 to −4.94065645841246544e−324 *Positive range:* 4.94065645841246544e−324 to 1.7976931348623157E+308	(IEEE 754 floating point)

Fig. 4.16   The Java primitive types.

Portability Tip 4.1

Unlike C and C++, the primitive types in Java are portable across all computer platforms that support Java. This and many other portability features of Java enable programmers to write programs once, without knowing on which computer platform the program will execute. This attribute is sometimes referred to as WORA (Write Once, Run Anywhere).

Each type in Fig. 4.16 is listed with its size in bits (there are eight bits to a byte) and its range of values. Because the designers of Java want it to be maximally portable, they use internationally recognized standards for both character formats (Unicode) and floating-point numbers (IEEE 754).

When variables of the primitive types are declared outside of a method, they are automatically assigned default values unless explicitly initialized. Variables of types char, byte, short, int, long, float and double are all given the value 0 by default. Variables of type boolean are given the value false by default.

4.14 (Optional Case Study) Thinking About Objects: Identifying Class Attributes

In Section 3.7, we began the first phase of an object-oriented design (OOD) for our elevator simulator—analyzing the problem statement and identifying the classes needed to implement the simulator. We listed the nouns in the problem statement and identified a separate class for each category of noun and noun phrase with significance for the elevator simulation. We then modeled the classes and their relationships in a UML class diagram (Fig. 3.19). Classes have attributes (data) and operations (behaviors). Class attributes are implemented in Java programs as fields; class behaviors are implemented as methods. In this section, we determine many of the attributes needed in the elevator simulator. In Chapter 5, we will examine how these attributes represent an object's *state*, or condition. In Chapter 6, we will determine class behavior.

Consider the attributes of some real-world objects: A person's attributes include height and weight. A radio's attributes include its station setting, its volume setting and its AM or FM setting. A car's attributes include its speedometer and odometer readings, the amount of gas in its tank, what gear it is in, etc. A personal computer's attributes include its manufacturer (e.g., Dell, Sun, Apple, IBM, etc.), type of screen (e.g., flat panel or CRT), main memory size (in megabytes), hard disk size (in gigabytes), etc.

We can identify the attributes of the classes in our system by looking for descriptive words and phrases in the problem statement. For each descriptive word or phrase we find, we create an attribute and assign that attribute to one of the classes identified in Section 3.7. We also create attributes to represent any additional data that a class may need (as the need for this data becomes clear throughout the design process).

We begin examining the problem statement to discover attributes distinct to each class. Figure 4.17 lists the words or phrases from the problem statement that describe each class.

Class	Descriptive words and phrases
ElevatorShaft	[no descriptive words or phrases]
Elevator	moving summoned current floor destination floor capacity of only one person five seconds to travel between floors
Person	unique waiting / moving current floor
Floor	first or second; capacity for only one person
FloorButton	pressed / reset
ElevatorButton	pressed / reset
FloorDoor	door closed / door open

Fig. 4.17   Descriptive words and phrases from problem statement. (Part 1 of 2.)

Class	Descriptive words and phrases
ElevatorDoor	door closed / door open
Bell	[no descriptive words or phrases]
Light	turned on / turned off

Fig. 4.17   Descriptive words and phrases from problem statement. (Part 2 of 2.)

Class Elevator has several attributes. The phrases "is moving" and "is summoned" describe possible states of Elevator (we introduce states in the next "Thinking About Objects" section), so we include moving and summoned as boolean attributes. Elevator also arrives at a "destination floor," so we include the attribute destinationFloor, representing the Floor to which the Elevator will travel. Although the problem statement does not mention explicitly that the Elevator leaves from a current Floor, we may infer another attribute called currentFloor representing the Floor on which the Elevator is resting. The problem statement specifies that "the elevator and floors each have a capacity of only one person," so we include the capacity attribute for class Elevator (and class Floor) and set the value to 1. Lastly, the problem statement specifies that the elevator "takes five seconds to travel between floors," so we introduce the travelTime attribute and set the value to 5.

Class Person has several attributes. The user must be able to "create a unique person," which implies that each Person object should have a unique identifier. We assign integer attribute ID to the Person object. The ID attribute helps to identify that Person object. In addition, the problem statement specifies that the Person can be "waiting for the elevator to arrive." Therefore, "waiting" is a state that Person object may enter. Though not mentioned explicitly, if the Person is not waiting for the Elevator, the Person is moving to (or away from) the Elevator. We assign the boolean attribute moving to class Person. When this attribute is set to false, the Person is "waiting." Lastly, the phrase "on that floor" implies that the Person occupies a floor. We cannot assign a Floor reference to class Person, because we are interested only in attributes. However, we want to include the location of the Person object in the model, so we include the currentFloor attribute, which may have a value of either 1 or 2.

Class Floor has a capacity attribute. The problem statement specified that the user could situate the person on either "the first or second floor"—therefore, a Floor object requires a value that distinguishes that Floor object as the first or second floor, so we include the floorNumber attribute.

According to the problem statement, the ElevatorButton and FloorButton are "pressed" by a Person. The buttons may be "reset" as well. The state of each button is either "pressed" or "reset." We include the boolean attribute pressed in both button classes. When pressed is true, the button object is pressed; when pressed is false, the button object is reset. Both the elevator door and the floor door are either "open" or "closed," so we include the Boolean attribute open in classes ElevatorDoor and FloorDoor. Class Light also falls into this category—the light is either "turned on" or "turned off," so we include the boolean attribute on in class Light. Note that although the problem statement mentions that the bell rings, there is no mention of when the bell "is ringing," so we do not include a separate `ring` attribute for class `Bell`. As we progress through this case study, we will continue to add, modify and delete information about the classes in our system.

The class diagram of Fig. 4.18 lists some of the attributes for each class in our system—the descriptive words and phrases in Fig. 4.17 help us generate these attributes. Note that, for simplicity, Fig. 4.18 does not show the associations among objects—we showed these associations in Fig. 3.19. Recall from Section 3.7 that in the UML, a class's attributes are placed in the middle compartment of the class's rectangle.

Consider the `open` attribute of class `ElevatorDoor`:

    open : Boolean = false

This listing contains three pieces of information about the attribute. The *attribute name* is `open`. The *attribute type* is `Boolean`.[8] The type depends on the language used to implement the software system. In Java, for example, an attribute can be represented by a *primitive type*, such as `boolean` or `float`, or a reference type like a class—we begin our study of classes in Chapter 8, where we will see that each new class is a new reference type.

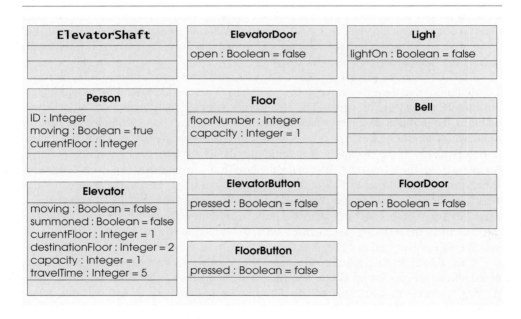

Fig. 4.18   Classes with attributes.

---

8. Note that the attribute types in Fig. 4.18 are in UML notation. We will associate the attribute types `Boolean` and `Integer` in the UML diagram with the attribute types `boolean` and `int` in Java, respectively. We described in Chapter 3 that Java provides a "type-wrapper class" for each primitive type. The Java type-wrapper classes have the same notation as the UML notation for attribute types; however, when we implement our design in Java starting in Chapter 8, we use primitive types for simplicity. Deciding whether to use primitive types or type-wrapper classes is an implementation-specific issue that should not be mentioned in the UML.

We can also indicate an initial value for each attribute. The `open` attribute in class `ElevatorDoor` has an initial value of `false`. This indicates that the elevator door is closed initially. If a particular attribute has no initial value specified, only its name and type (separated by a colon) are shown. For example, the `ID` attribute of class `Person` is an integer—in Java, the `ID` attribute is of type `int`. Here we show no initial value, because the value of this attribute is a number that we do not yet know; this number will be determined at execution time. Integer attribute `currentFloor` for class `Person` is not determined until program execution as well—this attribute is determined when the simulation user decides on which `Floor` to place the `Person`.

Note that Fig. 4.18 does not include attributes for class `ElevatorShaft`. Actually, class `ElevatorShaft` has seven attributes that we can determine from associations modeled in the class diagram of Fig. 3.19—references to the `Elevator` object, the two `FloorButton` objects, the two `FloorDoor` objects and the two `Light` objects. Class `Elevator` also contains three programmer-defined attributes—references to the `ElevatorButton` object, the `ElevatorDoor` object and the `Bell` object. To save space, we will not show these additional attributes in our class diagrams—we will, however, include them in the code in the appendices.

The class diagram of Fig. 4.18 provides a basis for the structure of our model, but the diagram is not complete. For example, the attribute `currentFloor` in class `Person` represents the floor on which a person is currently located. However, on what floor is the person when that person rides the elevator? These attributes do not yet sufficiently represent the structure of the model. As we present more of the UML and object-oriented design, we will continue to strengthen the structure of our model.

SUMMARY

- An algorithm is a procedure for solving a problem in terms of the actions to be executed and the order in which the actions should be executed.

- Specifying the order in which statements execute in a computer program is called program control.

- Pseudocode helps a programmer "think out" a program before attempting to write it in a programming language.

- Activity diagrams are part of the Unified Modeling Language (UML)—an industry standard for modeling software systems.

- An activity diagram models the workflow (also called the activity) of a software system.

- Activity diagrams are composed of special-purpose symbols, such as action-state symbols, diamonds and small circles; these symbols are connected by transition arrows that represent the flow of the activity.

- Like pseudocode, activity diagrams help programmers develop and represent algorithms, although many programmers prefer pseudocode.

- An action state is represented as parallel horizontal lines connected at each end with convex arcs. The action expression appears inside the action state.

- The arrows in the activity diagram are called transition arrows. These arrows model transitions, which indicate the order in which the action states are performed.

- The solid circle located at the top of the activity diagram represents the initial state—the beginning of the workflow before the program performs the modeled activity.

- The solid circle surrounded by a hollow circle that appears at the bottom of the activity diagram represents the final state—the end of the workflow after the program performs the activity.

- Rectangles with the upper-right corners folded over are called notes in the UML. Notes are explanatory remarks that describe the purpose of symbols in the diagram. A dotted line connects each note with the element that the note describes.

- The diamond or decision symbol indicates that a decision is to be made. A decision symbol indicates that the workflow will continue along a path determined by the associated guard conditions that can be true or false. Each transition arrow emerging from a decision symbol has a guard condition (specified in square brackets above or next to the transition arrow). If a particular guard condition is true, the workflow enters the action state to which that transition arrow points.

- The diamond also represents the merge symbol, which joins two flows of activity into one flow of activity. A merge symbol has two or more transition arrows pointing to the diamond and only one transition arrow pointing from the diamond, to indicate multiple activity flows merging to continue the activity. The merge symbol does not have a counterpart in Java code.

- Top-down, stepwise refinement is a process for refining pseudocode by maintaining a complete representation of the program during each refinement.

- Declarations are messages to the compiler telling it the names and attributes of variables and telling it to reserve space for variables.

- There are three types of control structures—sequence, selection and repetition.

- The sequence structure is built into Java—by default, statements execute in the order they appear.

- A selection structure chooses among alternative courses of action.

- The if statement executes an indicated action only when the condition is true.

- The if...else statement specifies separate actions to execute when the condition is true and when the condition is false.

- When more than one statement should execute where normally only a single statement appears, the statements must be enclosed in braces, forming a block. A block can be placed anywhere a single statement can be placed.

- An empty statement, indicating that no action is to be taken, is indicated by a semicolon (;).

- A repetition structure specifies that an action is to be repeated while some condition remains true.

- The format for the while statement is

```
while ( condition )
    statement
```

- Counter-controlled repetition is used when the number of iterations is known in advance.

- A floating-point number (a value that contains a fractional part) is represented by the type float or double.

- The unary cast operator (double) creates a temporary floating-point copy of its operand.

- Sentinel-controlled repetition is used when the number of iterations is not known in advance.

- A nested control structure appears in the body of another control structure.

- Java provides the arithmetic compound assignment operators +=, -=, *=, /= and %=, which help abbreviate certain common types of expressions.

- The increment operator, ++, and the decrement operator, --, increment or decrement a variable by 1, respectively. If the operator is prefixed to the variable, the variable is incremented or decremented by 1 first, then used in its expression. If the operator is postfixed to the variable, the variable is used in its expression and incremented or decremented by 1.

- The primitive types (boolean, char, byte, short, int, long, float and double) are portable across all computer platforms that support Java.
- Java is a strongly typed language—it requires all variables to have a type.
- Local variables are declared inside methods and are not assigned default values.
- Variables declared outside of methods are assigned default values. Variables of types char, byte, short, int, long, float and double are all given the value 0 by default. Variables of type boolean are given the value false by default.

TERMINOLOGY

-- operator	initial state
?: operator	initialization
++ operator	integer division
action	logic error
action/decision model	loop counter
action expression	loop-continuation condition
action state	merge symbol
action-state symbol	nested control structures
activity	note
algorithm	postdecrement operator
arithmetic compound assignment operators:	postincrement operator
+=, -=, *=, /= and %=	predecrement operator
block	preincrement operator
body of a loop	primitive types
cast operator, (*type*)	promotion
class instance creation expression	pseudocode
conditional expression	repetition
conditional operator (?:)	repetition structure
control structure	selection structure
control statement	sentinel-controlled repetition
counter-controlled repetition	sentinel value
decision	sequence structure
decrement operator (--)	sequential execution
definite repetition	single-entry/single-exit control structures
double	single-selection structure
double-selection structure	stacked control structure
empty statement (;)	structured programming
final state	syntax error
if statement	top-down, stepwise refinement
if...else statement	transition arrow
implicit conversion	unary operator
increment operator (++)	Unified Modeling Language (UML)
indefinite repetition	while statement
infinite loop	

SELF-REVIEW EXERCISES

4.1   Fill in the blanks in each of the following statements:

a) All programs can be written in terms of three types of control structures: _____, _____ and _____.

    b) The _____ statement is used to execute one action when a condition is true and another action when that condition is false.

    c) Repeating a set of instructions a specific number of times is called _____ repetition.

    d) When it is not known in advance how many times a set of statements will be repeated, a _____ value can be used to terminate the repetition.

4.2   Write four different Java statements that each add 1 to integer variable x.

4.3   Write Java statements to accomplish each of the following tasks:

    a) Assign the sum of x and y to z, and increment x by 1 after the calculation. Use only one statement.

    b) Test whether variable count is greater than 10. If it is, print "Count is greater than 10".

    c) Decrement the variable x by 1, then subtract it from the variable total. Use only one statement.

    d) Calculate the remainder after q is divided by divisor, and assign the result to q. Write this statement in two different ways.

4.4   Write a Java statement to accomplish each of the following tasks:

    a) Declare variables sum and x to be of type int.

    b) Assign 1 to variable x.

    c) Assign 0 to variable sum.

    d) Add variable x to variable sum, and assign the result to variable sum.

    e) Print "The sum is: ", followed by the value of variable sum.

4.5   Combine the statements that you wrote in Exercise 4.4 into a Java application that calculates and prints the sum of the integers from 1 to 10. Use a while statement to loop through the calculation and increment statements. The loop should terminate when the value of x becomes 11.

4.6   Determine the value of each of the following variables after the calculation is performed. Assume that when each statement begins executing, all variables are type int and have the value 5.

    a) `product *= x++;`

    b) `quotient /= ++x;`

4.7   Identify and correct the errors in each of the following sets of code:

    a)
```
while ( c <= 5 ) {
   product *= c;
   ++c;
```

    b)
```
if ( gender == 1 )
   System.out.println( "Woman" );
else;
   System.out.println( "Man" );
```

4.8   What is wrong with the following while statement?

```
while ( z >= 0 )
   sum += z;
```

ANSWERS TO SELF-REVIEW EXERCISES

4.1   a) sequence, selection, repetition. b) if...else. c) counter-controlled (or definite). d) sentinel, signal, flag or dummy.

4.2
```
x = x + 1;
x += 1;
++x;
x++;
```

4.3 a) `z = x++ + y;`
b) `if ( count > 10 )`
         `System.out.println( "Count is greater than 10" );`
c) `total -= --x;`
d) `q %= divisor;`
    `q = q % divisor;`

4.4 a) `int sum, x;`
b) `x = 1;`
c) `sum = 0;`
d) `sum += x;` or `sum = sum + x;`
e) `System.out.println( "The sum is: " + sum );`

4.5   The program is as follows:

```
1    // Calculate the sum of the integers from 1 to 10
2    public class Calculate {
3
4       public static void main( String args[] )
5       {
6          int sum, x;
7
8          x = 1;
9          sum = 0;
10
11         while ( x <= 10 ) {
12            sum += x;
13            ++x;
14         }
15
16         System.out.println( "The sum is: " + sum );
17
18      } // end main
19
20   } // end class Calculate
```

4.6 a) `product = 25, x = 6`
b) `quotient = 0, x = 6`

4.7 a) Error: The closing right brace of the `while` statement's body is missing.
        Correction: Add a closing right brace after the statement `++c;`.
b) Error: Semicolon after `else` results in a logic error. The second output statement will always be executed.
        Correction: Remove the semicolon after `else`.

4.8   The value of the variable `z` is never changed in the `while` statement. Therefore, if the loop-continuation condition (`z >= 0`) is true, an infinite loop is created. To prevent an infinite loop from occurring, `z` must be decremented so that it eventually becomes less than 0.

EXERCISES

4.9   Identify and correct the errors in each of the following pieces of code. [*Note*: There may be more than one error in each piece of code.]

a) `if ( age >= 65 );`
        `System.out.println( "Age greater than or equal to 65" );`
    `else`
        `System.out.println( "Age is less than 65 )";`

b) `int x = 1, total;`
    `while ( x <= 10 ) {`
        `total += x;`
        `++x;`
    `}`

c) `While ( x <= 100 )`
        `total += x;`
        `++x;`

d) `while ( y > 0 ) {`
        `System.out.println( y );`
        `++y;`

4.10   What does the following program print?

```
1   public class Mystery {
2
3       public static void main( String args[] )
4       {
5           int y, x = 1, total = 0;
6
7           while ( x <= 10 ) {
8               y = x * x;
9               System.out.println( y );
10              total += y;
11              ++x;
12          }
13
14          System.out.println( "Total is " + total );
15
16      } // end main
17
18  } // end class Mystery
```

For Exercise 4.11 through Exercise 4.14, perform each of the following steps:
   a) Read the problem statement.
   b) Formulate the algorithm using pseudocode and top-down, stepwise refinement.
   c) Write a Java program.
   d) Test, debug and execute the Java program.
   e) Process three complete sets of data.

4.11   Drivers are concerned with the mileage their automobiles get. One driver has kept track of several tankfuls of gasoline by recording miles driven and gallons used for each tankful. Develop a Java application that will input the miles driven and gallons used (both as integers) for each tankful. The program should calculate and display the miles per gallon obtained for each tankful and print the combined miles per gallon obtained for all tankfuls up to this point. All averaging calculations should produce floating-point results. Use input dialogs to obtain the data from the user.

4.12   Develop a Java application that will determine whether a department-store customer has exceeded the credit limit on a charge account. For each customer, the following facts are available:

a) account number,
b) balance at the beginning of the month,
c) total of all items charged by the customer this month,
d) total of all credits applied to the customer's account this month and
e) allowed credit limit.

The program should input each of these facts from input dialogs as integers, calculate the new balance (= *beginning balance + charges – credits*), display the new balance and determine whether the new balance exceeds the customer's credit limit. For those customers whose credit limit is exceeded, the program should display the message "Credit limit exceeded."

4.13   A large company pays its salespeople on a commission basis. The salespeople receive $200 per week, plus 9% of their gross sales for that week. For example, a salesperson who sells $5000 worth of merchandise in a week receives $200 plus 9% of $5000, or a total of $650. You have been supplied with a list of items sold by each salesperson. The values of these items are as follows:

Item	Value
1	239.99
2	129.75
3	99.95
4	350.89

Develop a Java application that inputs one salesperson's items sold for last week and calculates and displays that salesperson's earnings. There is no limit to the number of items that can be sold by a salesperson.

4.14   Develop a Java application that will determine the gross pay for each of three employees. The company pays "straight time" for the first 40 hours worked by each employee and pays "time and a half" for all hours worked in excess of 40 hours. You are given a list of the employees of the company, the number of hours each employee worked last week and the hourly rate of each employee. Your program should input this information for each employee and should determine and display the employee's gross pay. Use input dialogs to input the data.

4.15   The process of finding the largest value (i.e., the maximum of a group of values) is used frequently in computer applications. For example, a program that determines the winner of a sales contest would input the number of units sold by each salesperson. The salesperson who sells the most units wins the contest. Write a pseudocode program and then a Java application that inputs a series of 10 single-digit numbers as characters and determines and prints the largest of the numbers. Your program should use at least the following three variables:
  a) counter: A counter to count to 10 (i.e., to keep track of how many numbers have been input and to determine when all 10 numbers have been processed);
  b) number: The current digit input to the program;
  c) largest: The largest number found so far.

4.16   Write a Java application that uses looping to print the following table of values:

N	10*N	100*N	1000*N
1	10	100	1000
2	20	200	2000
3	30	300	3000
4	40	400	4000
5	50	500	5000

4.17 Using an approach similar to that for Exercise 4.15, find the *two* largest values of the 10 digits entered. [*Note*: You may input each number only once.]

4.18 Modify the program in Fig. 4.11 to validate its inputs. For any input, if the value entered is other than 1 or 2, keep looping until the user enters a correct value.

4.19 What does the following program print?

```java
public class Mystery2 {

    public static void main( String args[] )
    {
        int count = 1;

        while ( count <= 10 ) {
            System.out.println( count % 2 == 1 ? "****" : "++++++++" );

            ++count;
        }

    } // end main

} // end class Mystery2
```

4.20 What does the following program print?

```java
public class Mystery3 {

    public static void main( String args[] )
    {
        int row = 10, column;

        while ( row >= 1 ) {
            column = 1;

            while ( column <= 10 ) {
                System.out.print( row % 2 == 1 ? "<" : ">" );
                ++column;
            }

            --row;
            System.out.println();
        }

    } // end main

} // end class Mystery3
```

4.21 (*Dangling-else Problem*) Determine the output for each of the given sets of code when x is 9 and y is 11 and when x is 11 and y is 9. Note that the compiler ignores the indentation in a Java program. Also, the Java compiler always associates an else with the immediately preceding if unless told to do otherwise by the placement of braces ({}). On first glance, the programmer may not be sure which if an else matches; this situation is referred to as the "dangling-else problem." We have eliminated the indentation from the following code to make the problem more challenging. [*Hint*: Apply indentation conventions you have learned.]

a)
```
if ( x < 10 )
if ( y > 10 )
System.out.println( "*****" );
else
System.out.println( "#####" );
System.out.println( "$$$$$" );
```

b)
```
if ( x < 10 ) {
if ( y > 10 )
System.out.println( "*****" );
}
else {
System.out.println( "#####" );
System.out.println( "$$$$$" );
}
```

4.22 (*Another Dangling-else Problem*) Modify the given code to produce the output shown in each part of the problem. Use proper indentation techniques. Make no changes other than inserting braces and changing the indentation of the code. The compiler ignores indentation in a Java program. We have eliminated the indentation from the given code to make the problem more challenging. [*Note*: It is possible that no modification is necessary for some of the parts.]

```
if ( y == 8 )
if ( x == 5 )
System.out.println( "@@@@@" );
else
System.out.println( "#####" );
System.out.println( "$$$$$" );
System.out.println( "&&&&&" );
```

a) Assuming that x = 5 and y = 8, the following output is produced:

```
@@@@@
$$$$$
&&&&&
```

b) Assuming that x = 5 and y = 8, the following output is produced:

```
@@@@@
```

c) Assuming that x = 5 and y = 8, the following output is produced:

```
@@@@@
&&&&&
```

d) Assuming that x = 5 and y = 7, the following output is produced. [*Note*: The last three output statements after the **else** are all part of a block.]

```
#####
$$$$$
&&&&&
```

4.23 Write an applet that reads in the size of the side of a square and displays a hollow square of that size out of asterisks, by using the **drawString** method inside your applet's **paint** method. Use an input dialog to read the size from the user. Your program should work for squares of all side lengths between 1 and 20.

4.24   A palindrome is a sequence of characters that reads the same backward as forward. For example, each of the following five-digit integers is a palindrome: 12321, 55555, 45554 and 11611. Write an application that reads in a five-digit integer and determines whether it is a palindrome. If the number is not five digits long, display an error message dialog indicating the problem to the user. When the user dismisses the error dialog, allow the user to enter a new value.

4.25   Write an application that inputs an integer containing only 0s and 1s (i.e., a "binary" integer) and prints its decimal equivalent. [*Hint*: Use the remainder and division operators to pick off the "binary number's" digits one at a time, from right to left. In the decimal number system, the rightmost digit has a positional value of 1 and the next digit to the left has a positional value of 10, then 100, then 1000, etc. The decimal number 234 can be interpreted as 4 * 1 + 3 * 10 + 2 * 100. In the binary number system, the rightmost digit has a positional value of 1, the next digit to the left has a positional value of 2, then 4, then 8, etc. The decimal equivalent of binary 1101 is 1 * 1 + 0 * 2 + 1 * 4 + 1 * 8, or 1 + 0 + 4 + 8 or, 13.]

4.26   Write an application that uses only the output statements

```
System.out.print( "* " );
System.out.print( " " );
System.out.println();
```

to display the checkerboard pattern that follows. Note that a `System.out.println` method call with no arguments causes the program to output a single newline character. [*Hint*: Repetition structures are required.]

```
* * * * * * * *
 * * * * * * * *
* * * * * * * *
 * * * * * * * *
* * * * * * * *
 * * * * * * * *
* * * * * * * *
 * * * * * * * *
```

4.27   Write an application that keeps displaying in the command window the multiples of the integer 2—namely, 2, 4, 8, 16, 32, 64, etc. Your loop should not terminate (i.e., create an infinite loop). What happens when you run this program?

4.28   What is wrong with the following statement? Provide the correct statement to add one to the sum of x and y.

```
System.out.println( ++(x + y) );
```

4.29   Write an application that reads three nonzero values entered by the user in input dialogs and determines whether and prints they could represent the sides of a triangle.

4.30   Write an application that reads three nonzero integers and determines whether and prints if they could represent the sides of a right triangle.

4.31   A company wants to transmit data over the telephone, but is concerned that its phones may be tapped. It has asked you to write a program that will encrypt its data so that the data may be transmitted more securely. All of its data is transmitted as four-digit integers. Your application should read a four-digit integer entered by the user in an input dialog and encrypt it as follows: Replace each digit with the result of adding 7 to the digit and getting the remainder after dividing the new value by 10.

Then swap the first digit with the third, and swap the second digit with the fourth. Then print the encrypted integer. Write a separate application that inputs an encrypted four-digit integer and decrypts it to form the original number.

4.32 The factorial of a nonnegative integer n is written as $n!$ (pronounced "n factorial") and is defined as follows:

$n! = n \cdot (n - 1) \cdot (n - 2) \cdot \ldots \cdot 1$ (for values of n greater than or equal to 1)

and

$n! = 1$ (for $n = 0$).

For example, $5! = 5 \cdot 4 \cdot 3 \cdot 2 \cdot 1$, which is 120.

     a)   Write an application that reads a nonnegative integer from an input dialog and computes and prints its factorial.

     b)   Write an application that estimates the value of the mathematical constant e by using the formula

$$e = 1 + \frac{1}{1!} + \frac{1}{2!} + \frac{1}{3!} + \ldots$$

     c)   Write an application that computes the value of e^x by using the formula

$$e^x = 1 + \frac{x}{1!} + \frac{x^2}{2!} + \frac{x^3}{3!} + \ldots$$

Control Statements: Part 2

Objectives

- To be able to use the `for` and `do...while` repetition statements to execute statements in a program repeatedly.
- To understand multiple selection using the `switch` selection statement.
- To be able to use the `break` and `continue` program control statements.
- To be able to use the logical operators.

Who can control his fate?
William Shakespeare

The used key is always bright.
Benjamin Franklin

Man is a tool-making animal.
Benjamin Franklin

Intelligence ... is the faculty of making artificial objects, especially tools to make tools.
Henri Bergson

Outline

5.1 Introduction

Chapter 4 began our introduction to the types of building blocks that are available for problem solving. We used those building blocks to employ proven program construction principles. In this chapter, we continue our presentation of the theory and principles of structured programming by introducing Java's remaining control statements. As in Chapter 4, the Java techniques you learn here are applicable to most high-level languages. When we begin our formal treatment of object-based programming in Java in Chapter 8, we will see that the control statements we study in this chapter and Chapter 4 are helpful in building and manipulating objects.

5.2 Essentials of Counter-Controlled Repetition

This section uses the while repetition statement introduced in Chapter 4 to formalize the elements required to perform counter-controlled repetition. Counter-controlled repetition requires

1. a *control variable* (or loop counter),

2. the *initial value* of the control variable,

3. the amount of *increment* (or *decrement*) by which the control variable is modified each time through the loop (also known as *each iteration of the loop*) and

4. the *condition* that tests for the *final value* of the control variable (i.e., whether looping should continue).

To see these elements of counter-controlled repetition, consider the applet shown in Fig. 5.1, which draws 10 lines from the applet's paint method. Recall from Chapter 3 that an applet requires a separate HTML document to load the applet into an applet container. The HTML document that accompanies this applet (on CD) contains an applet element with a width of 275 pixels and a height of 110 pixels.[1]

```
1   // Fig. 5.1: WhileCounter.java
2   // Counter-controlled repetition.
3   import java.awt.Graphics;
4
5   import javax.swing.JApplet;
6
7   public class WhileCounter extends JApplet {
8
9      // draw lines on applet's background
10     public void paint( Graphics g )
11     {
12        super.paint( g );   // call paint method inherited from JApplet
13
14        int counter = 1;    // initialization
15
16        while ( counter <= 10 ) {  // repetition condition
17           g.drawLine( 10, 10, 250, counter * 10 );
18           ++counter;  // increment
19
20        } // end while
21
22     } // end method paint
23
24  } // end class WhileCounter
```

Fig. 5.1   Counter-controlled repetition with the `while` repetition statement.

Recall from Chapter 3 that the applet container loads the applet class, creates one object of the applet class and calls that applet object's `init`, `start` and `paint` methods. In `paint` (lines 10–22), the elements of counter-controlled repetition are defined in lines 14–20. Line 14 declares the *control variable* (`counter`) as an integer, reserves space for it in memory and sets its *initial value* to 1. Recall from Section 4.10 that a variable declaration can specify the initial value of the variable. The declaration and initialization of `counter` could also have been accomplished with the following local-variable declaration and assignment statements:

```
int counter;   // declare counter
counter = 1;   // assign 1 to counter
```

We use both techniques to initialize variables throughout this book.

---

1. We do not show the HTML document for each applet for the remainder of the book unless the document presents a new feature. However, we do provide on the CD that accompanies this book an HTML document with each applet that you can use to test the applet in an applet container.

Line 17 in the `while` statement uses `Graphics` reference g, which refers to the applet's `Graphics` object, to send the `drawLine` message to the `Graphics` object, asking it to draw a line. Remember that "sending a message to an object" actually means calling a method to perform a task. So, we can also say that line 17 uses g to call method `drawLine` of the `Graphics` object. Method `drawLine` requires four arguments, representing the line's first *x*-coordinate, first *y*-coordinate, second *x*-coordinate and second *y*-coordinate. In this example, the second *y*-coordinate changes value during each iteration of the loop with the calculation `counter * 10`. This change causes the second point (the endpoint of the line) in each call to `drawLine` to move 10 pixels down the applet's display area.

Line 18 in the `while` statement *increments* the control variable by 1 for each iteration of the loop. The loop-continuation *condition* in the `while` tests whether the value of the control variable is less than or equal to 10 (the *final value* for which the condition is `true`). Note that the program performs the body of this `while` even when the control variable is 10. The loop terminates when the control variable exceeds 10 (i.e., `counter` becomes `11`).

Common Programming Error 5.1

Because floating-point values may be approximate, controlling loops with floating-point variables may result in imprecise counter values and inaccurate tests for termination. For this reason, programs should control counting loops with integers.

Good Programming Practice 5.1

Place blank lines above and below control statements and indent the bodies of control statements within the control statements' headers (first lines) to give programs a two-dimensional appearance that enhances readability.

The program in Fig. 5.1 can be made more concise by initializing `counter` to 0 and preincrementing `counter` in the `while` condition as follows:

```
while ( ++counter <= 10 )       // repetition condition
    g.drawLine( 10, 10, 250, counter * 10 );
```

This code saves a statement (and eliminates the need for braces around the loop's body), because the `while` condition performs the increment before testing the condition. (Recall from Section 4.12 that the precedence of ++ is higher than that of <=.) Coding in such a condensed fashion takes practice and makes code more difficult to read, debug, modify and maintain. In general, it is best to avoid coding in this manner. However, sometimes you will encounter code like this and you should be able to understand how it works.

5.3 for Repetition Statement

Section 5.2 presented the four components required for counter-controlled repetition. The `while` statement can be used to implement any counter-controlled loop. However, Java also provides the `for` repetition statement, which specifies the counter-controlled-repetition details in a single line of code. To illustrate the power of the `for` statement, we reimplement the applet of Fig. 5.1. The new applet appears in Fig. 5.2. The HTML document for testing this applet defines a width of 275 pixels and a height of 110 pixels.

The applet's `paint` method operates as follows: When the `for` statement (lines 16–17) begins executing, the control variable `counter` is declared and initialized to `1`. (Recall from Section 5.2 that the first two elements of counter-controlled repetition are the *control variable* and its *initial value*.) Next, the program checks the loop-continuation *condition*,

```
1   // Fig. 5.2: ForCounter.java
2   // Counter-controlled repetition with the for statement.
3   import java.awt.Graphics;
4
5   import javax.swing.JApplet;
6
7   public class ForCounter extends JApplet {
8
9      // draw lines on applet's background
10     public void paint( Graphics g )
11     {
12        super.paint( g );  // call paint method inherited from JApplet
13
14        // for statement header includes initialization,
15        // repetition condition and increment
16        for ( int counter = 1; counter <= 10; counter++ )
17           g.drawLine( 10, 10, 250, counter * 10 );
18
19     } // end method paint
20
21  } // end class ForCounter
```

![Applet Viewer: ForCounter.class showing lines drawn on the applet background]

Fig. 5.2   Counter-controlled repetition with the `for` repetition statement.

counter <= 10. The condition contains the *final value* (10) of the control variable. Because the initial value of counter is 1, the condition initially is true. Therefore, the body statement (line 17) draws a line. After executing the body of the loop, the program *increments* variable counter in the expression counter++. Then, the program performs the loop-continuation test again to determine whether the program should continue with the next iteration of the loop. At this point, the control variable value is 2, so the condition is true (the final value is not exceeded); thus, the program performs the body statement again (i.e., the next iteration of the loop). This process continues until the counter's value becomes 11, causing the loop-continuation test to fail and repetition to terminate. Then, the program performs the first statement after the for. (In this case, method paint terminates, because the program reaches the end of paint.)

Notice that Fig. 5.2 uses the loop-continuation condition counter <= 10. If the programmer incorrectly specified counter < 10 as the condition, the loop would be executed only nine times. This mistake is a common logic error called an *off-by-one error*.

Common Programming Error 5.2

Using an incorrect relational operator or using an incorrect final value of a loop counter in the condition of a repetition statement can cause an off-by-one error.

Good Programming Practice 5.2

Using the final value in the condition of a while *or* for *statement and using the* <= *relational operator helps avoid off-by-one errors. For a loop that prints the values 1 to 10, the loop-continuation condition should be* counter <= 10 *rather than* counter < 10 *(which causes an off-by-one error) or* counter < 11 *(which is correct). Many programmers prefer so-called zero-based counting, in which to count 10 times,* counter *would be initialized to zero and the loop-continuation test would be* counter < 10.

Figure 5.3 takes a closer look at the for statement of Fig. 5.2. The for's first line (including the keyword for and everything in parentheses after for)—line 16 in Fig. 5.2—is sometimes called the *for statement header*, or simply the *for header*. Notice that the for statement "does it all": It specifies each of the items needed for counter-controlled repetition with a control variable. If there is more than one statement in the body of the for, braces ({ and }) are required to define the body of the loop.

The general format of the for statement is

> for (*initialization*; *loopContinuationCondition*; *increment*)
>   *statement*

where the *initialization* expression names the loop's control variable and provides its initial value, *loopContinuationCondition* is the condition that determines whether the loop should continue executing (this condition contains the final value for which the condition is true), and *increment* modifies the control variable's value, so that the loop-continuation condition eventually becomes false. In most cases, the for statement can be represented with an equivalent while statement[2] as follows:

> *initialization*;
>
> while (*loopContinuationCondition*) {
>   *statement*
>   *increment*;
> }

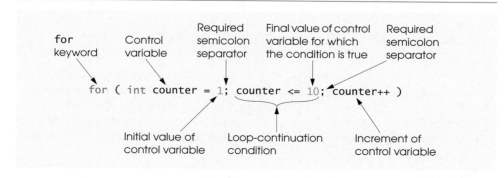

Fig. 5.3   for statement header components.

---

2.   In Section 5.7, we show a case in which a for statement cannot be represented with an equivalent while statement.

Typically, `for` statements are used for counter-controlled repetition and `while` statement are used for sentinel-controlled repetition. However, `while` and `for` can be used for either repetition type.

If the *initialization* expression in the `for` header declares the control variable (i.e., the control variable's type is specified before the variable name, as in Fig. 5.3), the control variable can be used only in that `for` statement—the control variable will not exist outside the `for` statement. This restricted use of the name of the control variable is known as the variable's *scope*. The scope of a variable defines where it can be used in a program. For example, a local variable can be used only in the method that declares the variable. Scope is discussed in detail in Chapter 6, Methods.

Common Programming Error 5.3

When a `for` statement's control variable is declared in the initialization section of the `for`'s header, using the control variable after the `for`'s body is a syntax error.

As we discuss in Section 5.4, the *initialization* and *increment* expressions can be comma-separated lists of expressions that enable the programmer to use multiple initialization expressions or multiple increment expressions. For example, there may be several control variables in a single `for` that must be initialized and incremented.

Good Programming Practice 5.3

Place only expressions involving the control variables in the initialization and increment sections of a `for` statement. Manipulations of other variables should appear either before the loop (if they execute only once, like initialization statements) or in the body of the loop (if they execute once per iteration of the loop, like increment or decrement statements).

All three expressions in a `for` header are optional. If the *loopContinuationCondition* is omitted, Java assumes that the loop-continuation condition is true, thus creating an infinite loop. You might omit the *initialization* expression if the program initializes the control variable before the loop. You might omit the *increment* expression if the program calculates the increment with statements in the loop's body or if no increment is needed. The increment expression in a `for` acts as a stand-alone statement at the end of the `for`'s body. Therefore, the expressions

```
counter = counter + 1
counter += 1
++counter
counter++
```

are equivalent increment expressions in a `for` statement. Many programmers prefer `counter++`, because a `for` loop evaluates its increment expression after its body executes. Therefore, the postincrementing form seems more natural. In this case, the variable being incremented does not appear in a larger expression, so both preincrementing and postincrementing actually have the same effect. The two semicolons in the `for` header are required.

Common Programming Error 5.4

Using commas instead of the two required semicolons in a `for` header is a syntax error.

Common Programming Error 5.5

Placing a semicolon immediately to the right of the right parenthesis of a `for` header makes that `for`'s body an empty statement. This is normally a logic error.

Common Programming Error 5.6

Infinite loops occur when the loop-continuation condition in a repetition statement never becomes false. *To prevent this situation, make sure that there is not a semicolon immediately after the header of a* while *or* for. *In a counter-controlled loop, ensure that the control variable is incremented (or decremented) during each iteration of the loop. In a sentinel-controlled loop, ensure that the sentinel value is eventually input.*

The initialization, loop-continuation condition and increment portions of a for statement can contain arithmetic expressions. For example, assume that x = 2 and y = 10. If x and y are not modified in the body of the loop, the statement

```
for ( int j = x; j <= 4 * x * y; j += y / x )
```

is equivalent to the statement

```
for ( int j = 2; j <= 80; j += 5 )
```

The increment of a for statement may also be negative, in which case it is really a decrement, and the loop counts downward.

If the loop-continuation condition is initially false, the program does not execute the for statement's body. Instead, execution proceeds with the statement following the for.

Programs frequently display the control variable value or use it in calculations in the loop body. However, this use is not required. It is common to use the control variable for controlling repetition while never mentioning it in the body of the for.

Error-Prevention Tip 5.1

Although the value of the control variable can be changed in the body of a for *loop, avoid doing so, because this practice can lead to subtle errors.*

The for statement's activity diagram is similar to that of the while statement's (Fig. 4.5). Figure 5.4 shows the activity diagram of the for statement in Fig. 5.2. The dia-

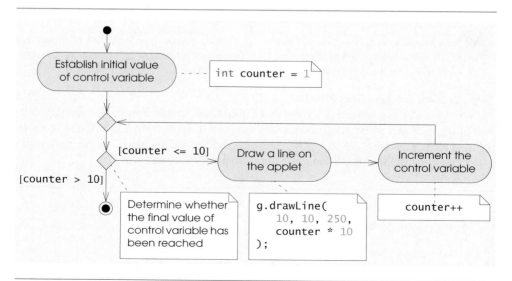

Fig. 5.4   for statement activity diagram.

gram makes it clear that initialization occurs once before the loop-continuation test is evaluated the first time, and that incrementing occurs *after* the body statement executes.

5.4 Examples Using the for Statement

The examples given next show techniques for varying the control variable in a for statement. In each case, we write the appropriate for header. Note the change in the relational operator for loops that decrement the control variable.

a) Vary the control variable from 1 to 100 in increments of 1.

```
for ( int i = 1; i <= 100; i++ )
```

b) Vary the control variable from 100 to 1 in increments of –1 (i.e., decrements of 1).

```
for ( int i = 100; i >= 1; i-- )
```

c) Vary the control variable from 7 to 77 in increments of 7.

```
for ( int i = 7; i <= 77; i += 7 )
```

d) Vary the control variable from 20 to 2 in increments of –2.

```
for ( int i = 20; i >= 2; i -= 2 )
```

e) Vary the control variable over the following sequence of values: 2, 5, 8, 11, 14, 17, 20.

```
for ( int j = 2; j <= 20; j += 3 )
```

f) Vary the control variable over the following sequence of values: 99, 88, 77, 66, 55, 44, 33, 22, 11, 0.

```
for ( int j = 99; j >= 0; j -= 11 )
```

 Common Programming Error 5.7

Not using the proper relational operator in the loop-continuation condition of a loop that counts downward (such as using i <= 1 in a loop counting down to 1) is usually a logic error and will yield incorrect results when the program runs.

Sum the Even Integers from 2 to 100

We now consider two sample programs that demonstrate simple uses of for. The application in Fig. 5.5 uses a for statement to sum the even integers from 2 to 100 and store the result in an int variable called total. This program is an application, so the java interpreter must be used to execute the application from the command window.

```
1   // Fig. 5.5: Sum.java
2   // Summing integers with the for statement.
3   import javax.swing.JOptionPane;
4
5   public class Sum {
6
```

Fig. 5.5   Summation with the for statement. (Part 1 of 2.)

```
7     public static void main( String args[] )
8     {
9        int total = 0;  // initialize sum
10
11       // total even integers from 2 through 100
12       for ( int number = 2; number <= 100; number += 2 )
13          total += number;
14
15       // display results
16       JOptionPane.showMessageDialog( null, "The sum is " + total,
17          "Total Even Integers from 2 to 100",
18          JOptionPane.INFORMATION_MESSAGE );
19
20       System.exit( 0 );   // terminate application
21
22    } // end main
23
24 } // end class Sum
```

```
Total Even Integers from 2 to 100          [X]

    (i)    The sum is 2550

              [ OK ]
```

Fig. 5.5   Summation with the `for` statement. (Part 2 of 2.)

The body of the `for` statement in lines 12–13 of Fig. 5.5 could be merged into the rightmost portion of the `for` header by using a comma as follows:

```
for ( int number = 2; number <= 100; total += number, number += 2 )
   ;  // empty statement
```

Similarly, the initialization `total` = 0 could be merged into the initialization section of the `for` statement.

Good Programming Practice 5.4

Limit the size of control statement headers to a single line if possible.

Compound Interest Calculations

The next example uses the `for` statement to compute compound interest. Consider the following problem:

A person invests $1000.00 in a savings account yielding 5% interest. Assuming that all interest is left on deposit, calculate and print the amount of money in the account at the end of each year for 10 years. Use the following formula to determine the amounts:

$$a = p (1 + r)^n$$

where

> *p is the original amount invested (i.e., the principal)*
> *r is the annual interest rate*
> *n is the number of years*
> *a is the amount on deposit at the end of the nth year.*

This problem involves a loop that performs the indicated calculation for each of the 10 years the money remains on deposit. The solution is the application shown in Fig. 5.6.

Lines 13–15 in method main declare double variables amount, principal and rate, and initialize principal to 1000.0 and rate to 0.05. Java treats floating-point

```java
1   // Fig. 5.6: Interest.java
2   // Calculating compound interest.
3   import java.text.NumberFormat;  // class for numeric formatting
4   import java.util.Locale;  // class for country-specific information
5
6   import javax.swing.JOptionPane;
7   import javax.swing.JTextArea;
8
9   public class Interest {
10
11     public static void main( String args[] )
12     {
13       double amount;          // amount on deposit at end of each year
14       double principal = 1000.0;  // initial amount before interest
15       double rate = 0.05;         // interest rate
16
17       // create NumberFormat for currency in US dollar format
18       NumberFormat moneyFormat =
19         NumberFormat.getCurrencyInstance( Locale.US );
20
21       // create JTextArea to display output
22       JTextArea outputTextArea = new JTextArea();
23
24       // set first line of text in outputTextArea
25       outputTextArea.setText( "Year\tAmount on deposit\n" );
26
27       // calculate amount on deposit for each of ten years
28       for ( int year = 1; year <= 10; year++ ) {
29
30         // calculate new amount for specified year
31         amount = principal * Math.pow( 1.0 + rate, year );
32
33         // append one line of text to outputTextArea
34         outputTextArea.append( year + "\t" +
35           moneyFormat.format( amount ) + "\n" );
36
37       } // end for
38
39       // display results
40       JOptionPane.showMessageDialog( null, outputTextArea,
41         "Compound Interest", JOptionPane.INFORMATION_MESSAGE );
42
43       System.exit( 0 );  // terminate the application
44
45     } // end main
46
47   } // end class Interest
```

Fig. 5.6   Compound-interest calculations with for. (Part 1 of 2.)

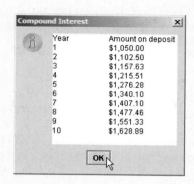

Fig. 5.6   Compound-interest calculations with `for`. (Part 2 of 2.)

constants, like `1000.0` and `0.05`, as type `double`. Similarly, Java treats whole number constants, like `7` and `-22`, as type `int`. Lines 18–19 declare *NumberFormat* reference money-Format and initialize it by calling `NumberFormat` static method *getCurrencyInstance*. This method returns a `NumberFormat` object that can format numeric values as currency (e.g., in the United States, currency values normally are preceded with a dollar sign, $). The argument to the method—`Locale.US`—indicates that the currency values should be displayed as U.S. dollars—start with a dollar sign ($), use a decimal point to separate dollars and cents and use a comma to delineate thousands (e.g., $1,234.56). Class `Locale` provides constants that can be used to customize this program to represent currency values for other countries, so that currency formats are displayed properly for each *locale* (i.e., each country's local-currency format). Class `NumberFormat` (imported at line 3) is in package `java.text`, and class `Locale` (imported at line 4) is in package *java.util*.

Line 22 declares `JTextArea` reference `outputTextArea` and initializes it with a new object of class `JTextArea` (from package `javax.swing`). A `JTextArea` is a GUI component that can display many lines of text. The message dialog that displays the `JTextArea` determines the width and height of the `JTextArea`, based on the string it contains. We introduce this GUI component now because we will see many examples throughout the text in which the program outputs contain too many lines to display on the screen. As we will see later in this chapter, a `JTextArea` (when combined with another component called a `JScrollPane`) allows us to scroll through the lines of text so that we can see all the program output. The methods for placing text in a `JTextArea` include *setText* and *append*.

Line 25 uses `JTextArea` method `setText` to place a string in the `JTextArea` to which `outputTextArea` refers. Initially, a `JTextArea` contains an empty string (i.e., a string with no characters in it). The preceding statement replaces the empty string with one containing the column heads for our two columns of output—"`Year`" and "`Amount on Deposit`." The column heads are separated with a tab character (escape sequence `\t`). Also, the string contains the newline character (escape sequence `\n`), indicating that any additional text appended to the `JTextArea` should begin on the next line.

The `for` statement (lines 28–37) executes its body 10 times, varying control-variable `year` from 1 to 10 in increments of 1. This loop terminates when control-variable `year` becomes 11. (Note that `year` represents *n* in the problem statement.) Java does not include

an exponentiation operator. Instead, we use static method pow of class Math for this purpose. Math.pow(x, y) calculates the value of x raised to the yth power. Method pow takes
two arguments of type double and returns a double value. Line 31 performs the calculation from the statement of the problem,

$$a = p \, (1 + r)^n$$

where a is amount, p is principal, r is rate and n is year.

Lines 34–35 append more text to the end of the outputTextArea. The text includes
the current value of year, a tab character (to position to the second column), the result of
the method call moneyFormat.format(amount)—which formats the amount as U.S.
currency—and a newline character (to position the cursor in the JTextArea at the beginning of the next line).

Lines 40–41 display the results of the calculations in a message dialog. Until now, the
message displayed has always been a string. In this example, the second argument is
outputTextArea—a GUI component. An interesting feature of class JOptionPane is
that the message it displays with showMessageDialog can be a string or a GUI component, such as a JTextArea. In this example, the message dialog sizes itself to accommodate the JTextArea.

We declared variables amount, principal and rate to be of type double in this
example. We are dealing with fractional parts of dollars and thus need a type that allows
decimal points in its values. Unfortunately, this setting can cause trouble. Here is a simple
explanation of what can go wrong when using double (or float) to represent dollar
amounts (assuming that dollar amounts are displayed with two digits to the right of the decimal point): Two double dollar amounts stored in the machine could be 14.234 (which
would normally be rounded to 14.23 for display purposes) and 18.673 (which would normally be rounded to 18.67 for display purposes). When these amounts are added, they produce the internal sum 32.907, which would normally be rounded to 32.91 for display
purposes. Thus, your output could appear as

```
   14.23
 + 18.67
 -------
   32.91
```

but a person adding the individual numbers as displayed would expect the sum to be 32.90.
You have been warned!

Good Programming Practice 5.5

*Do not use variables of type double (or float) to perform precise monetary calculations.
The imprecision of floating-point numbers can cause errors that will result in incorrect monetary values. In the exercises, we explore the use of integers to perform monetary calculations. [Note: Some third-party vendors provide for-sale class libraries that perform precise
monetary calculations. In addition, the Java API provides class java.math.BigDecimal
for performing calculations with arbitrary precision floating-point values.]*

Note that the body of the for statement contains the calculation 1.0 + rate, which
appears as an argument to the Math.pow method. In fact, this calculation produces the
same result each time through the loop, so repeating the calculation every iteration of the
loop is wasteful.

Performance Tip 5.1

In loops, avoid calculations for which the result never changes. [Note: Many of today's sophisticated optimizing compilers will place such calculations outside loops in the compiled code.]

5.5 do...while Repetition Statement

The do...while statement is similar to the while statement. In the while statement, the program tests the loop-continuation condition at the beginning of the loop, before performing the body of the loop. If the condition is false, the while loop's body never executes. The do...while repetition structure tests the loop-continuation condition *after* performing the body of the loop; therefore, *the loop body always executes at least once.* When a do...while repetition structure terminates, execution continues with the statement after the while clause. It is not necessary to use braces in the do...while repetition structure if there is only one statement in the body. However, most programmers include the braces, to avoid confusion between the while and do...while statements. For example,

```
while ( condition )
```

normally is the first line of a while statement. A do...while statement with no braces around a single-statement body appears as

```
do
    statement
while ( condition );
```

which can be confusing. A reader may misinterpret the last line—while(*condition*);—as a while statement containing an empty statement (the semicolon by itself). Thus, to avoid confusion, the do...while statement with one statement usually is written as follows:

```
do {
    statement
} while ( condition );
```

Good Programming Practice 5.6

Always include braces in a do...while statement, even if the braces are not necessary. This helps eliminate ambiguity between the while statement and the do...while statement containing only one statement.

The applet in Fig. 5.7 uses a do...while statement to draw 10 nested circles, with Graphics method drawOval.

```
1   // Fig. 5.7: DoWhileTest.java
2   // Using the do...while statement.
3   import java.awt.Graphics;
4
5   import javax.swing.JApplet;
6
```

Fig. 5.7   do...while statement. (Part 1 of 2.)

```
 7   public class DoWhileTest extends JApplet {
 8
 9       // draw lines on applet
10       public void paint( Graphics g )
11       {
12           super.paint( g );   // call paint method inherited from JApplet
13
14           int counter = 1;    // initialize counter
15
16           do {
17               g.drawOval( 110 - counter * 10, 110 - counter * 10,
18                   counter * 20, counter * 20 );
19               ++counter;
20           } while ( counter <= 10 );   // end do...while
21
22       } // end method paint
23
24   } // end class DoWhileTest
```

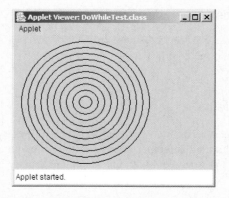

Fig. 5.7   do...while statement. (Part 2 of 2.)

In method paint (lines 10–22), line 14 declares control variable counter and initializes it to 1. Upon entering the do...while statement, lines 17–18 call the Graphics object's drawOval method. The four arguments that represent the upper left x-coordinate, upper left y-coordinate, width and height of the oval's *bounding box* (an imaginary rectangle in which the oval touches the center of all four sides of the rectangle) are calculated based on the value of counter. The program draws the innermost circle first. The bounding box's upper left corner for each subsequent circle moves closer to the upper left corner of the applet. At the same time, the width and height of the bounding box are increased, to ensure that each new circle contains all the previous circles. Line 19 increments counter. Then, the program evaluates the loop-continuation test at the bottom of the loop.

Figure 5.8 contains the activity diagram for the do...while statement. This diagram makes it clear that the loop-continuation condition does not evaluate until after the loop performs the action state at least once. Compare this activity diagram with that of the while statement (Fig. 4.5).

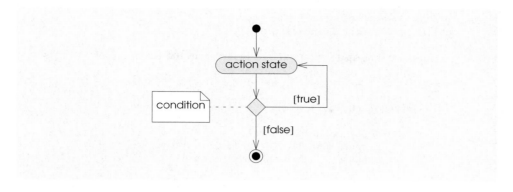

Fig. 5.8　do...while repetition statement activity diagram.

5.6 switch Multiple-Selection Statement

We discussed the if single-selection statement and the if...else double-selection statement in Chapter 4. Java provides the switch multiple-selection statement to perform different actions based on the possible values of an integer variable or expression. Each action is associated with a constant integral value (i.e., a value of type byte, short, int or char, but not long) that the variable or expression may assume. The applet of Fig. 5.9 uses a switch statement in a paint method that draws lines, rectangles or ovals, based on an integer the user inputs via an input dialog.

```
1   // Fig. 5.9: SwitchTest.java
2   // Drawing lines, rectangles or ovals based on user input.
3   import java.awt.Graphics;
4
5   import javax.swing.*;
6
7   public class SwitchTest extends JApplet {
8      int choice;  // user's choice of which shape to draw
9
10     // initialize applet by obtaining user's choice
11     public void init()
12     {
13        String input;  // user's input
14
15        // obtain user's choice
16        input = JOptionPane.showInputDialog(
17           "Enter 1 to draw lines\n" +
18           "Enter 2 to draw rectangles\n" +
19           "Enter 3 to draw ovals\n" );
20
21        choice = Integer.parseInt( input );  // convert input to int
22
23     } // end method init
24
```

Fig. 5.9　switch statement testing multiple input values. (Part 1 of 3.)

```
25     // draw shapes on applet's background
26     public void paint( Graphics g )
27     {
28        super.paint( g );  // call paint method inherited from JApplet
29
30        for ( int i = 0; i < 10; i++ ) {  // loop 10 times (0-9)
31
32           switch ( choice ) {  // determine shape to draw
33
34              case 1:  // draw a line
35                 g.drawLine( 10, 10, 250, 10 + i * 10 );
36                 break;  // done processing case
37
38              case 2:  // draw a rectangle
39                 g.drawRect( 10 + i * 10, 10 + i * 10,
40                    50 + i * 10, 50 + i * 10 );
41                 break;  // done processing case
42
43              case 3:  // draw an oval
44                 g.drawOval( 10 + i * 10, 10 + i * 10,
45                    50 + i * 10, 50 + i * 10 );
46                 break;  // done processing case
47
48              default: // draw string indicating invalid value entered
49                 g.drawString( "Invalid value entered",
50                    10, 20 + i * 15 );
51
52           } // end switch
53
54        } // end for
55
56     } // end method paint
57
58  } // end class SwitchTest
```

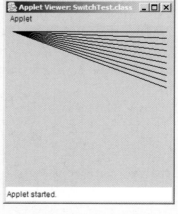

Fig. 5.9   switch statement testing multiple input values. (Part 2 of 3.)

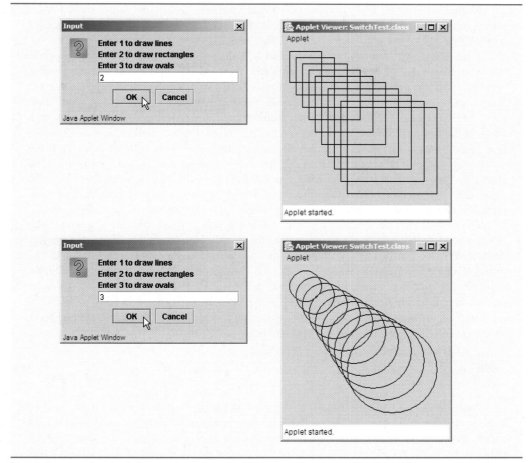

Fig. 5.9   `switch` statement testing multiple input values. (Part 3 of 3.)

Line 8 in applet `SwitchTest` declares field `choice` of type `int`. This variable stores the user's input that determines which shape to draw in `paint`.

Method `init` (lines 11–23) declares local variable `input` of type `String` in line 13. This variable stores the string the user types in the input dialog. Lines 16–19 display the input dialog with `JOptionPane` static method `showInputDialog` and prompt the user to enter 1 to draw lines, 2 to draw rectangles or 3 to draw ovals. Line 21 converts `input` to an `int` and assigns the result to field `choice`. Because it is a field of the class, variable `choice` can be used in method `init` and in method `paint` in this example.

Method `paint` (lines 26–56) contains a `for` (lines 30–54) that loops 10 times. In this example, the `for` header, in line 30, uses zero-based counting. The values of `i` for the 10 iterations of the loop are 0, 1, 2, 3, 4, 5, 6, 7, 8 and 9, and the loop terminates when `i`'s value becomes 10. [*Note*: As we discussed in Section 3.3, the applet container calls method `paint` after methods `init` and `start`. The applet container also calls method `paint` whenever the applet's screen area must be refreshed—e.g., after another window that covered the applet's area is moved to a different location on the screen.]

Nested in the for's body is a switch statement (lines 32–52) that draws shapes based on the integer value input by the user in method init. The switch statement consists of a block that contains a sequence of *case labels* and an optional *default case*.

When the flow of control reaches the switch, the program evaluates the expression in the parentheses (choice) following keyword switch. This is called the *controlling expression* of the switch. The program compares the value of the controlling expression (which must evaluate to an integral value of type byte, char, short or int) with each case label. For example, if the user enters the integer 2, the program compares 2 with each case in the switch. If a match occurs (case 2:), the program executes the statements for that case. For the integer 2, lines 39–40 draw a rectangle, using four arguments, representing the upper left *x*-coordinate, upper left *y*-coordinate, width and height of the rectangle, and the switch statement exits immediately with the break statement (line 41). Then, the program increments the counter variable in the for and reevaluates the loop-continuation condition to determine whether to perform another iteration of the loop.

The break statement causes program control to proceed with the first statement after the switch. (In this case, we reach the end of the for's body, so control flows to increment expression in the for header.) Without break, the cases in a switch statement would "fall through" to the statements in subsequent cases. Thus, each time a match would occur in the switch, the statements for all the remaining cases would execute. (This feature is perfect for programming the iterative song "The Twelve Days of Christmas" in Exercise 5.25.) If no match occurs between the controlling expression's value and a case label, the default case (lines 48–50) executes, and the program draws an error message on the applet.

Common Programming Error 5.8

Forgetting a break statement when one is needed in a switch is a logic error.

Each case can have multiple statements. The switch statement differs from other control statements in that it does not require braces around multiple statements in each case. Figure 5.10 shows the activity diagram for the general switch statement. A majority of switch statements use a break in each case to terminate the switch statement after processing the case. Figure 5.10 emphasizes this by including break statements in the activity diagram. Without the break statement, control would not transition to the end of the switch statement after a case is processed. Instead, control would transition to the next case's actions. The diagram makes it clear that the break statement at the end of a case causes control to exit the switch statement immediately.

The break statement is not required for the switch's last case (or the default case, when it appears last), because execution continues with the next statement after the switch.

Good Programming Practice 5.7

Provide a default case in switch statements. In a switch statement without a default case, cases that are not explicitly matched are ignored. Including a default case focuses you on the need to process exceptional conditions. There are situations in which no default processing is needed.

Good Programming Practice 5.8

Although each case and the default case in a switch can occur in any order, place the default case last. When the default case is listed last, the break for that case is not required. Some programmers include this break for clarity and symmetry with other cases.

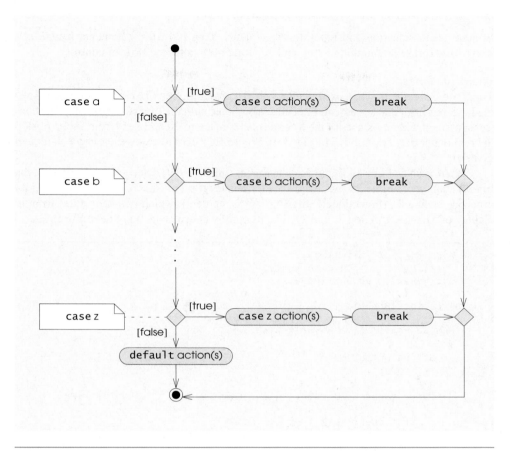

Fig. 5.10   `switch` multiple-selection statement activity diagram with `break` statements.

Note that listing `case` labels together (such as `case 1: case 2: case 3:` with no statements between the cases) indicates that the same set of actions should be performed for each case.

When using the `switch` statement, remember that the expression after each `case` can be only a *constant integral expression* (i.e., any combination of character constants and integer constants that evaluates to a constant integer value). A character constant is represented as the specific character in single quotes, such as `'A'` or `'$'`. An integer constant is simply an integer value. The expression in each `case` also can be a *constant variable*—i.e., a variable that contains a value which does not change for the entire program. Such a variable is declared with keyword *`final`* (discussed in Chapter 6). When we discuss object-oriented programming in Chapter 9, Object-Oriented Programming: Inheritance, we present a more elegant way to implement `switch` logic. We use a technique called *polymorphism* to create programs that are often clearer, easier to maintain and easier to extend than programs using `switch` logic.

5.7 break and continue Statements

In addition to selection and repetition statements, Java provides statements *break* and *continue* (presented in this section and Section 5.8) to alter the flow of control.

break *Statement*

The break statement, when executed in a while, for, do...while or switch, causes immediate exit from that statement. Execution continues with the first statement after the control statement. Common uses of the break statement are to escape early from a loop or skip the remainder of a switch (as in Fig. 5.9). Figure 5.11 demonstrates the break statement in a for.

When the if at line 14 in the for statement (lines 12–19) detects that count is 5, the break statement at line 15 executes. This terminates the for statement, and the program proceeds to line 21 (immediately after the for statement), which completes the string to display in a message dialog at line 22. The loop fully executes its body only four times.

```java
1   // Fig. 5.11: BreakTest.java
2   // Terminating a loop with break.
3   import javax.swing.JOptionPane;
4
5   public class BreakTest {
6
7      public static void main( String args[] )
8      {
9         String output = "";
10        int count;
11
12        for ( count = 1; count <= 10; count++ ) {  // loop 10 times
13
14           if ( count == 5 )  // if count is 5,
15              break;          // terminate loop
16
17           output += count + " ";
18
19        } // end for
20
21        output += "\nBroke out of loop at count = " + count;
22        JOptionPane.showMessageDialog( null, output );
23
24        System.exit( 0 );  // terminate application
25
26     } // end main
27
28  } // end class BreakTest
```

Fig. 5.11   break statement exiting a for statement.

***continue* Statement**

The continue statement, when executed in a while, for or do...while, skips the remaining statements in the loop body and proceeds with the next iteration of the loop. In while and do...while statements, the program evaluates the loop-continuation test immediately after the continue statement executes. In a for statement, the increment expression executes, then the program evaluates the loop-continuation test. In Section 5.3, we stated that while could be used in most cases in place of for. The one exception occurs when the increment expression in the while follows a continue statement. In this case, the increment does not execute before the program evaluates the repetition-continuation condition, so the while does not execute in the same manner as does the for. Figure 5.12 uses the continue statement in a for to skip the string concatenation statement (line 16) when the if (line 13) determines that the value of count is 5. When the continue statement executes, program control continues with the increment of the control variable in the for statement.

```
1   // Fig. 5.12: ContinueTest.java
2   // Continuing with the next iteration of a loop.
3   import javax.swing.JOptionPane;
4
5   public class ContinueTest {
6
7      public static void main( String args[] )
8      {
9         String output = "";
10
11        for ( int count = 1; count <= 10; count++ ) {  // loop 10 times
12
13           if ( count == 5 )  // if count is 5,
14              continue;        // skip remaining code in loop
15
16           output += count + " ";
17
18        } // end for
19
20        output += "\nUsed continue to skip printing 5";
21        JOptionPane.showMessageDialog( null, output );
22
23        System.exit( 0 );  // terminate application
24
25     } // end main
26
27  } // end class ContinueTest
```

Fig. 5.12   continue statement terminating a single iteration of a for statement.

Performance Tip 5.2

The break *and* continue *statements, when used properly, may perform faster than the corresponding structured techniques. Some programmers feel that* break *and* continue *violate structured programming. Because the effects of these statements are achievable with structured programming techniques, these programmers do not use* break *or* continue.

Software Engineering Observation 5.1

There is a tension between achieving quality software engineering and achieving the best performing software. Often, one of these goals is achieved at the expense of the other. For all but the most performance-intensive situations, apply the following rule of thumb: First, make your code simple and correct; then make it fast and small, but only if necessary.

5.8 Labeled break and continue Statements

Java provides the labeled break and continue statements for cases in which a program needs to alter the flow of control in nested control statements.

Labeled *break* Statement

The break statement presented in Section 5.7 enables a program to break out of the while, for, do...while or switch in which the break statement appears. Sometimes these control statements are nested in other repetition statements. A program might need to exit the entire nested control statement in one operation, rather than wait for the nested control statement to complete execution normally. To break out of such nested control statements, you can use the *labeled break statement*. This statement, when executed in a while, for, do...while or switch, causes immediate exit from that control statement and any number of enclosing statements. Program execution resumes with the first statement after the enclosing *labeled statement*. The statement that follows the label can be either a repetition statement or a block in which a repetition statement appears. Figure 5.13 demonstrates the labeled break statement in a nested for statement.

The block (lines 11–33 in Fig. 5.13) begins with a *label* (an identifier followed by a colon) at line 11; here we use the label "stop:." The block is enclosed in braces (lines 11 and 33) and includes the nested for (lines 14–28) and the string-concatenation statement at line 31. When the if at line 19 detects that row is equal to 5, the break statement at line 20 executes. This statement terminates both the for at lines 17–24 and its enclosing for at lines 14–28. Then the program proceeds immediately to line 35—the first statement after the labeled block. The outer for fully executes its body only four times. The string-concatenation statement at line 31 never executes, because it is in the labeled block's body, and the outer for never completes.

Good Programming Practice 5.9

Too many levels of nested control statements can make a program difficult to read. As a general rule, try to avoid using more than three levels of nesting.

```
1   // Fig. 5.13: BreakLabelTest.java
2   // Labeled break statement.
3   import javax.swing.JOptionPane;
```

Fig. 5.13   Labeled break statement exiting a nested for statement. (Part 1 of 2.)

```
4
5    public class BreakLabelTest {
6
7       public static void main( String args[] )
8       {
9          String output = "";
10
11         stop: {  // labeled block
12
13            // count 10 rows
14            for ( int row = 1; row <= 10; row++ ) {
15
16               // count 5 columns
17               for ( int column = 1; column <= 5 ; column++ ) {
18
19                  if ( row == 5 )  // if row is 5,
20                     break stop;   // jump to end of stop block
21
22                  output += "*   ";
23
24               } // end inner for
25
26               output += "\n";
27
28            } // end outer for
29
30            // following line is skipped
31            output += "\nLoops terminated normally";
32
33         } // end labeled block
34
35         JOptionPane.showMessageDialog( null, output,
36            "Testing break with a label",
37            JOptionPane.INFORMATION_MESSAGE );
38
39         System.exit( 0 );  // terminate application
40
41      } // end main
42
43   } // end class BreakLabelTest
```

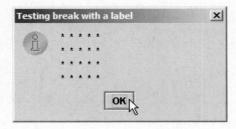

Fig. 5.13 Labeled **break** statement exiting a nested **for** statement. (Part 2 of 2.)

Labeled *continue* Statement

The continue statement proceeds with the next iteration (repetition) of the immediately enclosing while, for or do...while. The *labeled continue statement* skips the remaining statements in that statement's body and any number of enclosing repetition statements and proceeds with the next iteration of the enclosing *labeled repetition statement* (i.e., a for, while or do...while preceded by a label). In labeled while and do...while statements, the program evaluates the loop-continuation test of the labeled loop immediately after the continue statement executes. In a labeled for, the increment expression is executed and the loop-continuation test is evaluated. Figure 5.14 uses a labeled continue statement in a nested for to enable execution to continue with the next iteration of the outer for.

```java
1   // Fig. 5.14: ContinueLabelTest.java
2   // Labeled continue statement.
3   import javax.swing.JOptionPane;
4
5   public class ContinueLabelTest {
6
7      public static void main( String args[] )
8      {
9         String output = "";
10
11        nextRow:  // target label of continue statement
12
13           // count 5 rows
14           for ( int row = 1; row <= 5; row++ ) {
15              output += "\n";
16
17              // count 10 columns per row
18              for ( int column = 1; column <= 10; column++ ) {
19
20                 // if column greater than row, start next row
21                 if ( column > row )
22                    continue nextRow; // next iteration of labeled loop
23
24                 output += "* ";
25
26              } // end inner for
27
28           } // end outer for
29
30        JOptionPane.showMessageDialog( null, output,
31           "Testing continue with a label",
32           JOptionPane.INFORMATION_MESSAGE );
33
34        System.exit( 0 );  // terminate application
35
36     } // end main
37
38  } // end class ContinueLabelTest
```

Fig. 5.14   Labeled continue statement terminating a nested for statement. (Part 1 of 2.)

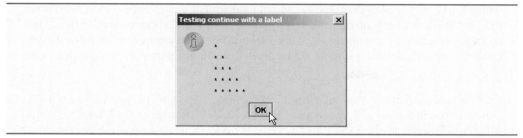

Fig. 5.14 Labeled `continue` statement terminating a nested `for` statement. (Part 2 of 2.)

The labeled `for` (lines 11–28) actually starts at the `nextRow` label. When the `if` at line 21 in the inner `for` (lines 18–26) detects that `column` is greater than `row`, the `continue` statement at line 22 executes, and program control continues with the increment of the control variable of the outer `for` loop. Even though the inner `for` counts from 1 to 10, the number of `*` characters output on a row never exceeds the value of `row`.

Performance Tip 5.3

The program in Fig. 5.14 can be made simpler and more efficient by replacing the condition in the `for` *at line 18 with* `column <= row` *and removing the* `if` *statement at lines 21–22.*

5.9 Logical Operators

The `if`, `if…else`, `while`, `do…while` and `for` statements each require a condition to determine how to continue a program's flow of control. So far, we have studied only *simple conditions*, such as `count <= 10`, `number != sentinelValue` and `total > 1000`. Simple conditions are expressed in terms of the relational operators `>`, `<`, `>=` and `<=` and the equality operators `==` and `!=`, and each decision tests one condition. To test multiple conditions in the process of making a decision, we performed these tests in separate statements or in nested `if` or `if…else` statements. Sometimes, control statements require more complex conditions to determine a program's flow of control.

Java provides *logical operators* to enable programmers to form more complex conditions by combining simple conditions. The logical operators are `&&` (*conditional AND*), `||` (*conditional OR*), `&` (*boolean logical AND*), `|` (*boolean logical inclusive OR*), `^` (*boolean logical exclusive OR*) and `!` (*logical NOT*, also called *logical negation*).

Conditional AND (&&) Operator

Suppose that we wish to ensure at some point in a program that two conditions are *both* true before we choose a certain path of execution. In this case, we can use the `&&` (conditional AND) operator, as follows:

```
if ( gender == FEMALE && age >= 65 )
    ++seniorFemales;
```

This `if` statement contains two simple conditions. The condition `gender == FEMALE` might be evaluated, for example, to determine whether a person is a female. The condition `age >= 65` is evaluated to determine whether a person is a senior citizen. The `if` statement considers the combined condition

```
gender == FEMALE && age >= 65
```

which is true *if and only if* both simple conditions are true. If the combined condition is true, the `if` statement's body increments `seniorFemales` by `1`. If either or both of the simple conditions are false, the program skips the increment. Some programmers find that the preceding combined condition is more readable when redundant parentheses are added as in:

```
( gender == FEMALE ) && ( age >= 65 )
```

The table in Fig. 5.15 summarizes the **&&** operator. The table shows all four possible combinations of `false` and `true` values for *expression1* and *expression2*. Such tables are called *truth tables.* Java evaluates to `false` or `true` all expressions that include relational operators, equality operators or logical operators.

Conditional OR (||) Operator

Now suppose that we wish to ensure that either *or* both of two conditions are true before we choose a certain path of execution. In this case, we use the **||** (conditional OR) operator, as in the following program segment:

```
if ( semesterAverage >= 90 || finalExam >= 90 )
    System.out.println ( "Student grade is A" );
```

This statement also contains two simple conditions. The condition `semesterAverage >= 90` evaluates to determine whether the student deserves an "A" in the course because of a solid performance throughout the semester. The condition `finalExam >= 90` evaluates to determine whether the student deserves an "A" in the course because of an outstanding performance on the final exam. The `if` statement then considers the combined condition

```
semesterAverage >= 90 || finalExam >= 90
```

and awards the student an "A" if either or both of the simple conditions are true. The only time the message "`Student grade is A`" is *not* printed is when both of the simple conditions are false. Figure 5.16 is a truth table for operator conditional OR (**||**). Operator **&&** has a higher precedence than operator **||**. Both operators associate from left to right.

expression1	expression2	expression1 && expression2
false	false	false
false	true	false
true	false	false
true	true	true

Fig. 5.15   && (conditional AND) operator truth table.

expression1	expression2	expression1 || expression2
false	false	false
false	true	true

Fig. 5.16 || (conditional OR) operator truth table. (Part 1 of 2.)

expression1	expression2	expression1 || expression2
true	false	true
true	true	true

Fig. 5.16 | \|\| (conditional OR) operator truth table. (Part 2 of 2.)

Short-Circuit Evaluation of Complex Conditions

The parts of an expression containing && or \|\| operators is evaluated only until it is known whether the condition is true or false. Thus, evaluation of the expression

```
gender == FEMALE && age >= 65
```

stops immediately if gender is not equal to FEMALE (i.e., the entire expression is false) and continues if gender is equal to FEMALE (i.e., the entire expression could still be true if the condition age >= 65 is true). This feature of conditional AND and conditional OR expressions is called *short-circuit evaluation*.

 Common Programming Error 5.9

*In expressions using operator **&&**, it is possible that a condition—we will call this the dependent condition—may require another condition to be true for it to be meaningful to evaluate the dependent condition. In this case, the dependent condition should be placed after the other condition, or an error might occur.*

Boolean Logical AND (&) and Boolean Logical OR (|) Operators

The *boolean logical AND* (&) and *boolean logical inclusive OR* (|) operators work identically to the && (conditional AND) and \|\| (conditional OR) operators, with one exception: The boolean logical operators always evaluate both of their operands (i.e., they do not perform short-circuit evaluation). Therefore, the expression

```
gender == 1 & age >= 65
```

evaluates age >= 65 regardless of whether gender is equal to 1. This is useful if the right operand of the boolean logical AND or boolean logical inclusive OR operator has a required *side effect*—a modification of a variable's value. For example, the expression

```
birthday == true | ++age >= 65
```

guarantees that the condition ++age >= 65 will be evaluated. Thus, the variable age is incremented in the preceding expression, regardless of whether the overall expression is true or false.

 Good Programming Practice 5.10

For clarity, avoid expressions with side effects in conditions. The side effects may look clever, but they are often more trouble than they are worth.

Boolean Logical Exclusive OR (^)

A condition containing the *boolean logical exclusive OR* (^) operator is true *if and only if one of its operands is* true *and the other is* false. If both operands are true or both are false, the entire condition is false. Figure 5.17 is a truth table for the boolean logical exclusive OR operator (^). This operator is also guaranteed to evaluate both of its operands.

expression1	expression2	expression1 ∧ expression2
false	false	false
false	true	true
true	false	true
true	true	false

Fig. 5.17   ∧ (boolean logical exclusive OR) operator truth table.

Logical Negation (!) Operator
Java provides the ! (logical negation) operator to enable a programmer to "reverse" the meaning of a condition. Unlike the logical operators &&, ||, &, | and ∧, which are binary operators that combine two conditions, the logical negation operator is a unary operator that has only a single condition as an operand. The logical negation operator is placed before a condition to choose a path of execution if the original condition (without the logical negation operator) is false, such as in the program segment

```
if ( ! ( grade == sentinelValue ) )
    System.out.println( "The next grade is " + grade );
```

which executes the println statement only if grade is not equal to sentinelValue. The parentheses around the condition grade == sentinelValue are needed, because the logical negation operator has a higher precedence than the equality operator.

In most cases, the programmer can avoid using logical negation by expressing the condition differently with an appropriate relational or equality operator. For example, the previous statement may also be written as follows:

```
if ( grade != sentinelValue )
    System.out.println( "The next grade is " + grade );
```

This flexibility can help a programmer express a condition in a more convenient manner. Figure 5.18 is a truth table for the logical negation operator.

Logical Operators Example
The application in Fig. 5.19 demonstrates all of the logical operators and boolean logical operators by producing their truth tables. The program uses string concatenation to create the string that is displayed in a JTextArea.

expression	!expression
false	true
true	false

Fig. 5.18   ! (logical negation, or logical NOT) operator truth table.

```java
1   // Fig. 5.19: LogicalOperators.java
2   // Logical operators.
3   import javax.swing.*;
4
5   public class LogicalOperators
6   {
7      public static void main( String args[] )
8      {
9         // create JTextArea to display results
10        JTextArea outputArea = new JTextArea( 17, 20 );
11
12        // attach JTextArea to a JScrollPane so user can scroll results
13        JScrollPane scroller = new JScrollPane( outputArea );
14
15        // create truth table for && (logical AND) operator
16        String output = "Logical AND (&&)" +
17           "\nfalse && false: " + ( false && false ) +
18           "\nfalse && true: " + ( false && true ) +
19           "\ntrue && false: " + ( true && false ) +
20           "\ntrue && true: " + ( true && true );
21
22        // create truth table for || (logical OR) operator
23        output += "\n\nLogical OR (||)" +
24           "\nfalse || false: " + ( false || false ) +
25           "\nfalse || true: " + ( false || true ) +
26           "\ntrue || false: " + ( true || false ) +
27           "\ntrue || true: " + ( true || true );
28
29        // create truth table for & (boolean logical AND) operator
30        output += "\n\nBoolean logical AND (&)" +
31           "\nfalse & false: " + ( false & false ) +
32           "\nfalse & true: " + ( false & true ) +
33           "\ntrue & false: " + ( true & false ) +
34           "\ntrue & true: " + ( true & true );
35
36        // create truth table for | (boolean logical inclusive OR) operator
37        output += "\n\nBoolean logical inclusive OR (|)" +
38           "\nfalse | false: " + ( false | false ) +
39           "\nfalse | true: " + ( false | true ) +
40           "\ntrue | false: " + ( true | false ) +
41           "\ntrue | true: " + ( true | true );
42
43        // create truth table for ^ (boolean logical exclusive OR) operator
44        output += "\n\nBoolean logical exclusive OR (^)" +
45           "\nfalse ^ false: " + ( false ^ false ) +
46           "\nfalse ^ true: " + ( false ^ true ) +
47           "\ntrue ^ false: " + ( true ^ false ) +
48           "\ntrue ^ true: " + ( true ^ true );
49
50        // create truth table for ! (logical negation) operator
51        output += "\n\nLogical NOT (!)" +
52           "\n!false: " + ( !false ) +
53           "\n!true: " + ( !true );
```

Fig. 5.19   Logical operators. (Part 1 of 2.)

```
54
55              outputArea.setText( output );   // place results in JTextArea
56
57              JOptionPane.showMessageDialog( null, scroller,
58                 "Truth Tables", JOptionPane.INFORMATION_MESSAGE );
59
60              System.exit( 0 );   // terminate application
61
62        } // end main
63
64     } // end class LogicalOperators
```

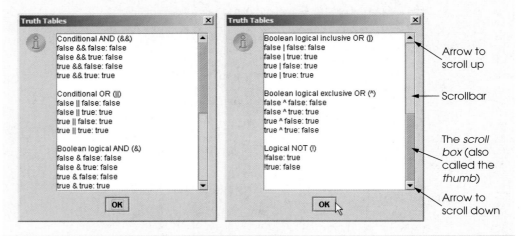

Fig. 5.19   Logical operators. (Part 2 of 2.)

In the output of Fig. 5.19, the strings "true" and "false" indicate true and false for the operands in each condition. The result of the condition is shown as true or false. Note that when you concatenate a boolean value with a string, Java automatically adds the string "false" or "true," based on the boolean value.

Line 10 in main creates a JTextArea. The numbers in the parentheses indicate that the JTextArea has 17 rows and 20 columns.[3] Line 13 declares JScrollPane reference scroller and initializes it with a new JScrollPane object. Class JScrollPane (from package javax.swing) provides scrolling for a GUI component. A JScrollPane object is initialized with the GUI component for which it will provide scrolling functionality (outputArea in this example). This initialization attaches the GUI component to the JScrollPane. When you execute this application, notice the *scrollbar* on the right side of the JTextArea. You can click the *arrows* at the top or bottom of the scrollbar to scroll up or down, respectively, through the text in the JTextArea one line at a time. You can also drag the *scroll box* (also called the *thumb*) up or down to scroll through the text rapidly.

Lines 16–53 build the output string that is displayed in the outputArea. Line 55 uses method setText to replace the text in outputArea with the output string. Lines

---

3. The width, in pixels, of the JTextArea is determined by multiplying the number of columns specified by the number of pixels for the width of a capital letter M in the JTextArea's default font.

57–58 display a message dialog. The second argument, `scroller`, indicates that the `scroller` (and the `outputArea` attached to it) should be displayed as the message in the message dialog, which sizes itself to accommodate the `JTextArea`.

Figure 5.20 shows the precedence and associativity of the Java operators introduced so far. The operators are shown from top to bottom in decreasing order of precedence.

5.10 Structured Programming Summary

Just as architects design buildings by employing the collective wisdom of their profession, so should programmers design programs. Our field is younger than architecture is, and our collective wisdom is considerably sparser. We have learned that structured programming produces programs that are easier than unstructured programs to understand, test, debug, modify, and even prove correct in a mathematical sense.

Figure 5.21 uses activity diagrams to summarize Java's control statements. The initial and final states indicate the single entry point and the single exit point of each control statement. Arbitrarily connecting individual symbols in an activity diagram can lead to unstructured programs. Therefore, the programming profession has chosen a limited set of control structures that can be combined in only two simple ways to build structured programs.

For simplicity, only single-entry/single-exit control statements are used—there is only one way to enter and only one way to exit each control statement. Connecting control statements in sequence to form structured programs is simple—the final state of one control statement is connected to the initial state of the next control statement—that is, the control statements are placed one after another in a program in sequence. We have called this "control-structure stacking." The rules for forming structured programs also allow for control structures to be nested.

Operators						Associativity	Type
++	--					right to left	unary postfix
++	--	+	-	!	(type)	right to left	unary
*	/	%				left to right	multiplicative
+	-					left to right	additive
<	<=	>	>=			left to right	relational
==	!=					left to right	equality
&						left to right	boolean logical AND
^						left to right	boolean logical exclusive OR
|						left to right	boolean logical inclusive OR
&&						left to right	conditional AND
||						left to right	conditional OR
?:						right to left	conditional
=	+=	-=	*=	/=	%=	right to left	assignment

Fig. 5.20   Precedence/associativity of the operators discussed so far.

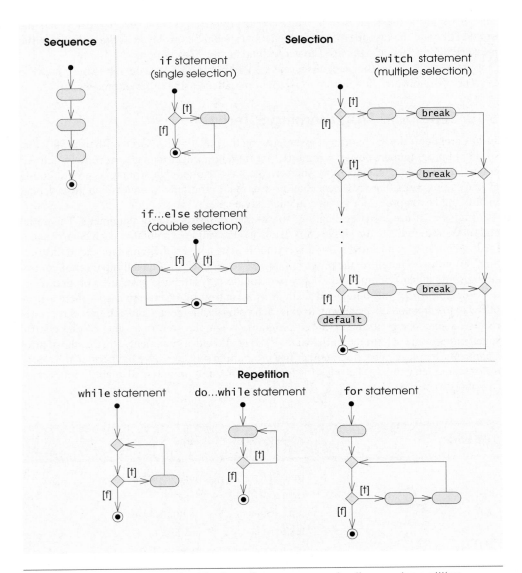

Fig. 5.21   Java's single-entry/single-exit sequence, selection and repetition statements.

Figure 5.22 shows the rules for forming structured programs. The rules assume that action states may be used to indicate any action. The rules also assume that we begin with the simplest activity diagram (Fig. 5.23) consisting of only an initial state, an action state, a final state and transition arrows.

Applying the rules of Fig. 5.22 always results in an activity diagram with a neat, building-block appearance. For example, repeatedly applying rule 2 to the simplest activity diagram results in an activity diagram containing many action states in sequence

(Fig. 5.24). Rule 2 generates a stack of control structures, so let us call rule 2 the *stacking rule*. [*Note:* The vertical dashed lines in Fig. 5.24 are not part of the UML. We use them to separate the four activity diagrams that demonstrate rule 2 of Fig. 5.22 being applied.]

Rules for Forming Structured Programs

1) Begin with the "simplest activity diagram" (Fig. 5.23).

2) Any action state can be replaced by two action states in sequence.

3) Any action state can be replaced by any control statement (sequence, `if`, `if...else`, `switch`, `while`, `do...while` or `for`).

4) Rules 2 and 3 can be applied as often as you like and in any order.

Fig. 5.22   Rules for forming structured programs.

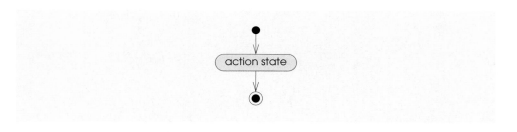

Fig. 5.23   Simplest activity diagram.

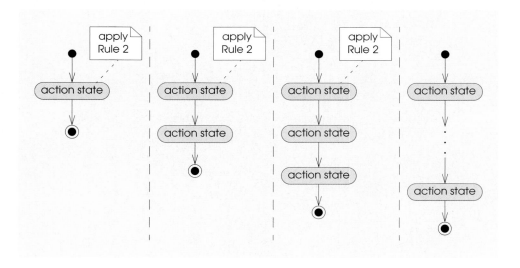

Fig. 5.24   Repeatedly applying rule 2 of Fig. 5.22 to the simplest activity diagram.

Rule 3 is called the *nesting rule*. Repeatedly applying rule 3 to the simplest activity diagram results in an activity diagram with neatly nested control statements. For example, in Fig. 5.25, the action state in the simplest activity diagram is replaced with a double-selection (if...else) statement. Then rule 3 is applied again to the action states in the double-selection statement, replacing each of these action states with a double-selection statement. The dashed action-state symbols around each of the double-selection statements represent the action state that was replaced in the original simplest activity diagram. [*Note:* The

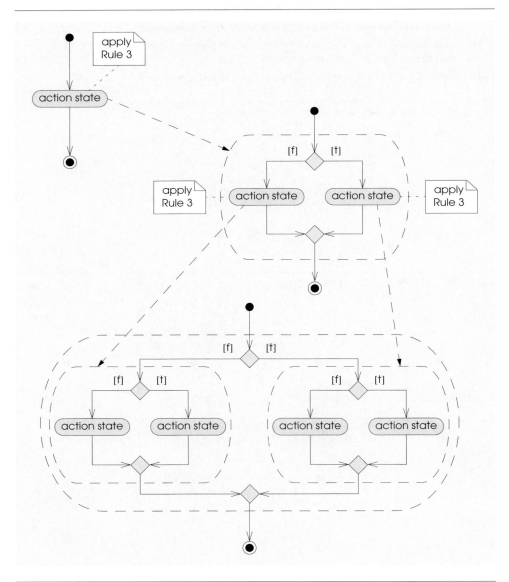

Fig. 5.25 Applying rule 3 of Fig. 5.22 to the simplest activity diagram.

dashed arrows and dashed action state symbols shown in Fig. 5.25 are not part of the UML. They are used here as pedagogic devices to illustrate that any action state can be replaced with a control statement.]

Rule 4 generates larger, more involved and more deeply nested statements. The diagrams that emerge from applying the rules in Fig. 5.22 constitute the set of all possible activity diagrams and hence the set of all possible structured programs. The beauty of the structured approach is that we use only seven simple single-entry/single-exit control statements and assemble them in only two simple ways.

If the rules in Fig. 5.22 are followed, an activity diagram with illegal syntax (such as that in Fig. 5.26) cannot be created. If you are uncertain about whether a particular diagram is legal, apply the rules of Fig. 5.22 in reverse to reduce the diagram to the simplest activity diagram. If the diagram is reducible to the simplest activity diagram, the original diagram is structured; otherwise, it is not.

Structured programming promotes simplicity. Bohm and Jacopini have given us the result that only three forms of control are needed to implement an algorithm:

- Sequence
- Selection
- Repetition

The sequence structure is trivial. Simply list the statements to execute in the order in which they should execute.

Selection is implemented in one of three ways:

- `if` statement (single selection)
- `if...else` statement (double selection)
- `switch` statement (multiple selection)

In fact, it is straightforward to prove that the simple `if` statement is sufficient to provide any form of selection—everything that can be done with the `if...else` statement and the `switch` statement can be implemented by combining `if` statements (although perhaps not as clearly and efficiently).

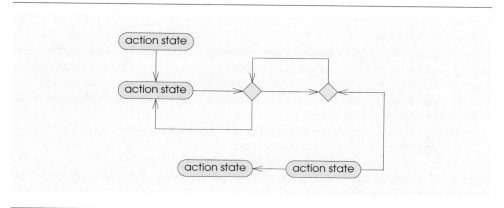

Fig. 5.26   Activity diagram with illegal syntax.

Repetition is implemented in one of three ways:

- `while` statement
- `do...while` statement
- `for` statement

It is straightforward to prove that the `while` statement is sufficient to provide any form of repetition. Everything that can be done with the `do...while` statement and the `for` statement can be done with the `while` statement (although perhaps not as smoothly).

Combining these results illustrates that any form of control ever needed in a C++ program can be expressed in terms of

- sequence,
- `if` statement (selection) and
- `while` statement (repetition)

and that these can be combined in only two ways—stacking and nesting. Indeed, structured programming promotes simplicity.

In this chapter, we discussed how to compose programs from control statements containing actions and decisions. In Chapter 6, we introduce another program structuring unit, called the *method*. We will learn to compose large programs by combining methods that, in turn, are composed of control statements. We will also discuss how methods promote software reusability. In Chapter 8, we discuss in more detail Java's other program-structuring unit, called the *class*. We will then create objects from classes and proceed with our treatment of object-oriented programming.

5.11 (Optional Case Study) Thinking About Objects: Identifying Objects' States and Activities

In Section 4.14, we identified many of the class attributes needed to implement the elevator simulator and added them to the class diagram of Fig. 4.18. In this section, we show how these attributes, in addition to an object's relationships, represent an object's *state*, or condition. We identify the set of possible states that our objects may occupy and discuss how these objects change state in response to *events*. We also discuss the workflow, or the *activities*, that an object performs in our elevator simulation.

Statechart Diagrams
Each object in a system goes through a series of *states*. A state is the condition of an object at a given time. *Statechart diagrams* (also called *state transition diagrams*) give designers a way to express how, and under what conditions, the objects in a system change state. Unlike the class diagrams presented in earlier case-study sections, statechart diagrams model some of the behavior of the system.

Figure 5.27 is a simple statechart diagram that models the states of an object either of class `FloorButton` or class `ElevatorButton`. The UML represents each state in a statechart diagram as a *rounded rectangle* with the name of the state placed inside the rectangle. A *solid circle* with an attached arrowhead designates the initial state. Notice that we modeled this state information as the `Boolean` attribute `pressed` in the class diagram of Fig. 4.18. This attribute is initialized to `false`, or the "Not Pressed" state, according to the statechart diagram.

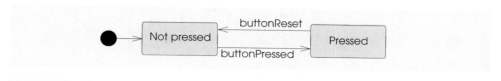

Fig. 5.27   Statechart diagram for `FloorButton` and `ElevatorButton` objects.

The arrows indicate *transitions* between states. An object can transition from one state to another in response to *events* and messages. For example, the `FloorButton` and `ElevatorButton` objects change from the "Not pressed" state to the "Pressed" state in response to a `buttonPressed` event, and the `pressed` attribute changes to a value of `true`. The name of the event that causes a transition is written near the line that corresponds to that transition. (We explain events further in Section 7.10 and Section 11.9.)

We model the state transitions of other classes, such as `Light`, `Elevator` and `Person`, with similar statechart diagrams. Class `Light` has an "on" state and an "off" state—transitions between these states occur as a result of "turn on" and "turn off" messages, respectively. Class `Elevator` and class `Person` each have a "moving" state and a "waiting" state—transitions between these states occur as a result of "start moving" and "stop moving" messages, respectively.

Activity Diagrams

Like a statechart diagram, an *activity diagram* models aspects of system behavior. Unlike a statechart diagram, an activity diagram models an object's *workflow* (sequence of activities) during program execution. An activity diagram is a flowchart that models the *actions* the object will perform and in what order. The activity diagram in Fig. 5.28 models the activities of a person. The diagram begins with the person moving toward the floor button. If the floor door is open, the person waits for the current passenger (if one exists) to exit, then enters the elevator.[4] If the floor door is closed, the person presses the floor button and waits for the elevator to open the door. When the door opens, the person waits for the elevator passenger to exit (if one exists) then enters the elevator. The person presses the elevator button, which causes the elevator to move to the other floor. The person then waits for the doors to re-open and exits the elevator after the doors open.

The UML represents activities as ovals in activity diagrams. The name of the activity is placed inside the oval. An arrow connects two activities, indicating the order in which the activities are performed. The solid circle indicates the starting activity. In this case, the person first transitions to the "moving toward floor button" state. The activity flow arrives at a *branch* (a fork indicated by the *small diamond symbol*) after the person moves to the floor button. This point determines the next activity based on the associated *guard condition* (in square brackets next to the transition), which states that the transition occurs if this condition is met. For example, in Fig. 5.28, if the floor door is closed, the person presses the floor button, waits for the door to open, waits for the passenger (if there is one) to exit the elevator, then enters the elevator. However, if the floor door is already open, the person waits for the passenger (if there is one) to exit the elevator, then enters the elevator. Regardless of whether the floor door was open or closed at the last small diamond symbol, the

---

4.   We will use *multithreading* and `synchronized` *methods* in Section 16.11 to guarantee that the passenger exits before the person waiting enters.

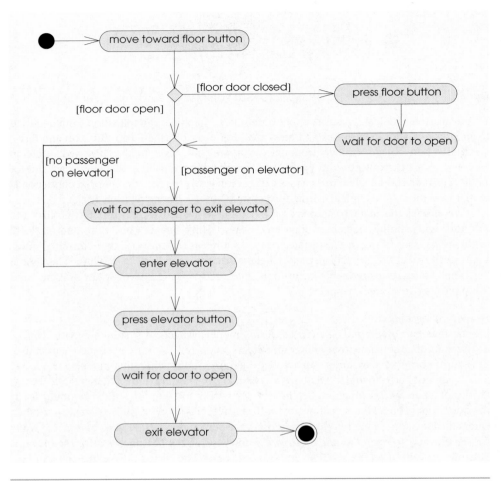

Fig. 5.28   Activity diagram for a **Person** object.

person now presses the elevator button (which causes the doors to close and the elevator to move to the other floor) and waits for the elevator door to open—when this door opens, the person exits the elevator. The solid circle enclosed in an open circle indicates the end of activity. We used activity diagrams to demonstrate the flow of control for the control statements presented in Chapter 4 and Chapter 5.

Figure 5.29 shows an activity diagram for the elevator. After the starting activity, the diagram begins when a button is pressed. If the button is an elevator button, the elevator sets **summoned** to false (a **Boolean** variable originally modeled in Fig. 4.18), so that the elevator will not return to that floor unless the button is pressed again. The elevator then closes the elevator door, moves to the other floor, resets the elevator button, rings the bell and opens the elevator door. If the button is a floor button, the branch determines the next transition based on whether the elevator is moving. If the elevator is idle, the next branch determines which floor button generated the request. If the request originated from the floor on which

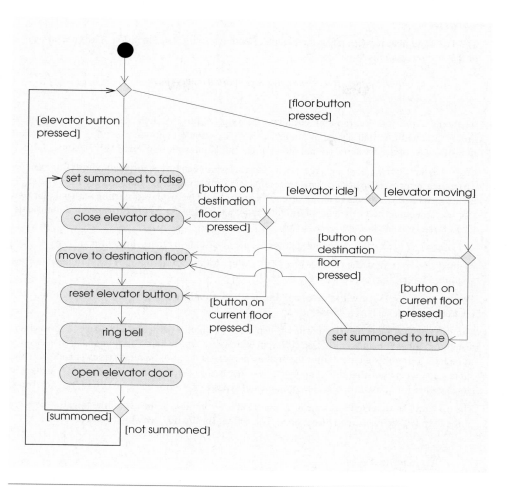

Fig. 5.29   Activity diagram for the `Elevator` object.

the elevator currently is located, the elevator resets its button, rings the bell and opens its door. If the request originated from the opposite floor, the elevator closes the door and moves to the opposite (destination) floor, where the elevator resets its button, rings the bell and opens its door. Now consider the activity if the elevator is moving. A separate branch determines which floor button generated the request. If the request originated from the destination floor, the elevator continues traveling to that floor. If the request originated from the floor from which the elevator departed, the elevator continues traveling to the destination floor, but must remember to return to the requesting floor. The `summoned` attribute is set to `true` so that the elevator knows to return to the other floor after the elevator opens its door.

We have taken the first steps in modeling the behavior of the system and have shown how the attributes of an object participate in that object's activity. In Section 6.15, we investigate the behaviors for all classes to give a more accurate interpretation of the system behavior by "filling in" the third compartment for the classes in our class diagram.

SUMMARY

- The `for` statement handles all of the details of counter-controlled repetition. The general format of the `for` statement is

      for (*initialization*; *loopContinuationCondition*; *increment*)
          statement

  where the *initialization* expression initializes the loop's control variable, *loopContinuationCondition* is the condition that determines whether the loop should continue executing and *increment* modifies the control variable, so that the loop-continuation condition eventually becomes false.

- Class `NumberFormat` is in package `java.text`. `NumberFormat` static method `getCurrencyInstance` returns a `NumberFormat` object that can format numeric values as currency. The argument `Locale.US` indicates that the currency values should be displayed starting with a dollar sign ($), use a decimal point to separate dollars and cents and use a comma to delineate thousands. Class `Locale` is in package `java.util`.

- A `JTextArea` is a GUI component that is capable of displaying many lines of text.

- Method `setText` replaces the text in a `JTextArea`. Method `append` adds text to the end of the text in a `JTextArea`.

- The message displayed with `JOptionPane` method `showMessageDialog` can be a string or a GUI component, such as a `JTextArea`.

- The `switch` statement handles a series of decisions in which a particular variable or expression is tested for values it may assume, and different actions are taken. In most programs, it is necessary to include a `break` statement after the statements for each `case`. Several `cases` can execute the same statements by listing the `case` labels together before the statements. The `switch` statement can test only for constant-integral expressions of types `byte`, `short`, `int` or `char`, but not `long`.

- The `do...while` statement tests the loop-continuation condition at the end of the loop, so the body of the loop will be executed at least once. The format for the `do...while` statement is

      do {
          statement
      } while (*condition*);

- The `break` statement, when executed in one of the repetition statements, causes immediate exit from the repetition statement.

- The `continue` statement, when executed in one of the repetition statements, skips any remaining statements in the body of the repetition statement and proceeds with the next iteration of the loop.

- To break out of a nested set of control statements, use the labeled `break` statement. This statement, when executed in a `while`, `for`, `do...while` or `switch` statement, causes immediate exit from that statement and any number of enclosing statements. Program execution resumes with the first statement after the enclosing labeled block.

- The labeled `continue` statement skips the remaining statements in a repetition statement's body and any number of enclosing repetition statements and proceeds with the next iteration of the enclosing labeled repetition statement.

- Logical operators can be used to form complex conditions by combining conditions. The logical operators are `&&` (conditional AND), `||` (conditional OR), `&` (boolean logical AND), `|` (boolean logical inclusive OR), `^` (boolean logical exclusive OR) and `!` (logical negation).

- Class `JScrollPane` provides a GUI component with scrolling functionality.

TERMINOLOGY

! operator
& operator
&& operator
| operator
|| operator
^ operator
append method of JTextArea
boolean logical AND (&)
boolean logical exclusive OR (^)
boolean logical inclusive OR (|)
break
case label
conditional AND (&&)
conditional OR (||)
continue
counter-controlled repetition
default case in switch
definite repetition
do…while repetition statement
for repetition statement
format method of class NumberFormat
getCurrencyInstance method of
    NumberFormat
java.text package

java.util package
JScrollPane class
JTextArea class
labeled break statement
labeled statement
labeled continue statement
labeled repetition statement
Locale class
Locale.US
logical negation (!)
logical operators
loop-continuation condition
multiple selection
nested control statements
NumberFormat class
off-by-one error
repetition statement
scroll box
scrollbar
short-circuit evaluation
single-entry/single-exit control statements
stacked control structures
switch selection statement
thumb of a scrollbar

SELF-REVIEW EXERCISES

5.1 State whether each of the following is true or false. If false, explain why.
a) The default case is required in the switch selection statement.
b) The break statement is required in the last case of a switch selection statement.
c) The expression (x > y && a < b) is true if either x > y is true or a < b is true.
d) An expression containing the || operator is true if either or both of its operands is true.

5.2 Write a Java statement or a set of Java statements to accomplish each of the following tasks:
a) Sum the odd integers between 1 and 99, using a for statement. Assume that the integer variables sum and count have been declared.
b) Calculate the value of 2.5 raised to the power of 3, using the pow method.
c) Print the integers from 1 to 20, using a while loop and the counter variable i. Assume that the variable i has been declared, but not initialized. Print only five integers per line. [*Hint*: Use the calculation i % 5. When the value of this expression is 0, print a newline character; otherwise, print a tab character. Assume that this code is an application; use the System.out.println() method to output the newline character, and use the System.out.print('\t') method to output the tab character.]
d) Repeat Exercise 5.2 (c), using a for statement.

5.3 Find the error in each of the following code segments, and explain how to correct it:
a) i = 1;

```
while ( i <= 10 );
    i++;
}
```

```
b) for ( k = 0.1; k != 1.0; k += 0.1 )
      System.out.println( k );
c) switch ( n ) {
      case 1:
         System.out.println( "The number is 1" );
      case 2:
         System.out.println( "The number is 2" );
         break;
      default:
         System.out.println( "The number is not 1 or 2" );
         break;
   }
```

d) The following code should print the values 1 to 10:

```
n = 1;

while ( n < 10 )
   System.out.println( n++ );
```

ANSWERS TO SELF-REVIEW EXERCISES

5.1 a) False. The `default` case is optional. If no default action is needed, then there is no need for a `default` case. b) False. The `break` statement is used to exit the `switch` statement. The `break` statement is not required for the last case in a `switch` statement. c) False. Both of the relational expressions must be true for the entire expression to be true when using the **&&** operator. d) True.

5.2
```
a) sum = 0;
   for ( count = 1; count <= 99; count += 2 )
      sum += count;
b) Math.pow( 2.5, 3 )
c) i = 1;

   while ( i <= 20 ) {
      System.out.print( i );

      if ( i % 5 == 0 )
         System.out.println();
      else
         System.out.print( '\t' );

      ++i;
   }
d) for ( i = 1; i <= 20; i++ ) {
      System.out.print( i );

      if ( i % 5 == 0 )
         System.out.println();
      else
         System.out.print( '\t' );
   }
```

or

```
for ( i = 1; i <= 20; i++ )

    if ( i % 5 == 0 )
        System.out.println( i );
    else
        System.out.print( i + "\t" );
```

5.3 a) Error: The semicolon after the `while` header causes an infinite loop, and there is a missing left brace.
Correction: Replace the semicolon by a {, or remove both the ; and the }.

b) Error: Using a floating-point number to control a `for` statement may not work, because floating-point numbers are represented only approximately by most computers.
Correction: Use an integer, and perform the proper calculation in order to get the values you desire:

```
for ( k = 1; k != 10; k++ )
    System.out.println( ( float ) k / 10 );
```

c) Error: The missing code is the `break` statement in the statements for the first `case`.
Correction: Add a `break` statement at the end of the statements for the first `case`. Note that this omission is not necessarily an error if the programmer wants the statement of `case 2:` to execute every time the `case 1:` statement executes.

d) Error: An improper relational operator is used in the `while` repetition-continuation condition.
Correction: Use <= rather than <, or change 10 to 11.

EXERCISES

5.4 Find the error(s) in each of the following segments of code:

a)
```
For ( i = 100, i >= 1, i++ )
    System.out.println( i );
```

b) The following code should print whether integer `value` is odd or even:

```
switch ( value % 2 ) {

    case 0:
        System.out.println( "Even integer" );

    case 1:
        System.out.println( "Odd integer" );
}
```

c) The following code should output the odd integers from 19 to 1:

```
for ( i = 19; i >= 1; i += 2 )
    System.out.println( i );
```

d) The following code should output the even integers from 2 to 100:

```
counter = 2;

do {
    System.out.println( counter );
    counter += 2;
} While ( counter < 100 );
```

5.5   What does the following program do?

```
1   public class Printing {
2
3      public static void main( String args[] )
4      {
5         for ( int i = 1; i <= 10; i++ ) {
6
7            for ( int j = 1; j <= 5; j++ )
8               System.out.print( '@' );
9
10           System.out.println();
11
12        } // end outer for
13
14     } // end main
15
16  } // end class Printing
```

5.6   Write an application that finds the smallest of several integers. Assume that the first value read specifies the number of values to input from the user.

5.7   Write an application that calculates the product of the odd integers from 1 to 15 and displays the results in a message dialog.

5.8   *Factorials* are used frequently in probability problems. The factorial of a positive integer *n* (written *n!* and pronounced "*n* factorial") is equal to the product of the positive integers from 1 to *n*. Write an application that evaluates the factorials of the integers from 1 to 5. Display the results in tabular format in a JTextArea that is displayed on a message dialog. What difficulty might prevent you from calculating the factorial of 20?

5.9   Modify the compound-interest application of Fig. 5.6 to repeat its steps for interest rates of 5, 6, 7, 8, 9 and 10%. Use a for loop to vary the interest rate. Add scrolling functionality to the JTextArea, so you can scroll through all the output.

5.10   Write an application that displays the following patterns separately, one below the other. Use for loops to generate the patterns. All asterisks (*) should be printed by a single statement of the form System.out.print('*'); which causes the asterisks to print side by side. A statement of the form System.out.println(); can be used to position to the next line. A statement of the form System.out.print(' '); can be used to display a space for the last two patterns. There should be no other output statements in the program. [*Hint*: The last two patterns require that each line begin with an appropriate number of blank spaces.]

(a)	(b)	(c)	(d)
*	**********	**********	*
**	**********	*********	**
***	*********	********	***
****	********	*******	****
*****	*******	******	*****
******	******	*****	******
*******	*****	****	*******
********	****	***	********
*********	***	**	*********
**********	**	*	**********

5.11   One interesting application of computers is drawing graphs and bar charts (sometimes called "histograms"). Write an applet that reads five numbers, each between 1 and 30. For each number read, your program should draw that number of adjacent asterisks. For example, if your program reads the number 7, it should display *******. [*Hint:* All asterisks on one line should be drawn with the same *y*-coordinate.]

5.12   A mail-order house sells five products whose retail prices are as follows: Product 1, $2.98; product 2, $4.50; product 3, $9.98; product 4, $4.49 and product 5, $6.87. Write an application that reads a series of pairs of numbers as follows:

      a) product number;
      b) quantity sold.

Your program should use a `switch` statement to determine the retail price for each product. It should calculate and display the total retail value of all products sold. Use a sentinel-controlled loop to determine when the program should stop looping and display the final results.

5.13   Modify the application in Fig. 5.6 to use only integers to calculate the compound interest. [*Hint:* Treat all monetary amounts as integral numbers of pennies. Then "break" the result into its dollar portion and cents portion by using the division and remainder operations, respectively. Insert a period between the dollar and the cents portions.]

5.14   Assume that i = 1, j = 2, k = 3 and m = 2. What does each of the following statements print?

      a) `System.out.println( i == 1 );`
      b) `System.out.println( j == 3 );`
      c) `System.out.println( i >= 1 && j < 4 );`
      d) `System.out.println( m <= 99 & k < m );`
      e) `System.out.println( j >= i || k == m );`
      f) `System.out.println( k + m < j | 3 - j >= k );`
      g) `System.out.println( !( k > m ) );`

5.15   Write an application that prints a table of the binary, octal, and hexadecimal equivalents of the decimal numbers in the range 1 through 256. If you are not familiar with these number systems, read Appendix C first. Place the results in a `JTextArea` with scrolling functionality. Display the `JTextArea` in a message dialog.

5.16   Calculate the value of π from the infinite series

$$\pi = 4 - \frac{4}{3} + \frac{4}{5} - \frac{4}{7} + \frac{4}{9} - \frac{4}{11} + \cdots$$

Print a table that shows the value of π approximated by computing one term of this series, by two terms, by three terms, etc. How many terms of this series do you have to use before you first get 3.14? 3.141? 3.1415? 3.14159?

5.17   (*Pythagorean Triples*) A right triangle can have sides whose lengths are all integers. The set of three integer values for the lengths of the sides of a right triangle is called a Pythagorean triple. The lengths of the three sides must satisfy the relationship that the sum of the squares of two of the sides is equal to the square of the hypotenuse. Write an application to find all Pythagorean triples for `side1`, `side2` and the `hypotenuse`, all no larger than 500. Use a triple-nested `for` loop that tries all possibilities. This method is an example of "brute force" computing. You will learn in more advanced computer science courses that there are large numbers of interesting problems for which there is no known algorithmic approach other than using sheer brute force.

5.18   Modify Exercise 5.10 to combine your code from the four separate triangles of asterisks such that all four patterns print side by side. Make clever use of nested `for` loops.

```
*               **********    **********              *
**              **********    **********             **
***             *********      *********            ***
****            ********        ********           ****
*****           *******          *******          *****
******          *****            *****          ******
*******         ****              ****         *******
********        ***                ***        ********
*********       **                  **       *********
**********      *                    *      **********
```

5.19 (*De Morgan's Laws*) In this chapter, we have discussed the logical operators &&, &, | |, |, ^ and !. De Morgan's Laws can sometimes make it more convenient for us to express a logical expression. These laws state that the expression !(*condition1* && *condition2*) is logically equivalent to the expression (!*condition1* | | !*condition2*). Also, the expression !(*condition1* | | *condition2*) is logically equivalent to the expression (!*condition1* && !*condition2*). Use De Morgan's Laws to write equivalent expressions for each of the following, then write an application to show that both the original expression and the new expression in each case produce the same value:

    a) !(x < 5) && !(y >= 7)
    b) !(a == b) || !(g != 5)
    c) !((x <= 8) && (y > 4))
    d) !((i > 4) || (j <= 6))

5.20 Write an application that prints the following diamond shape. You may use output statements that print a single asterisk (*), a single space or a single newline character. Maximize your use of repetition (with nested for statements), and minimize the number of output statements.

```
      *
     ***
    *****
   *******
  *********
   *******
    *****
     ***
      *
```

5.21 Modify the application you wrote in Exercise 5.20 to read an odd number in the range 1 to 19 to specify the number of rows in the diamond. Your program should then display a diamond of the appropriate size.

5.22 A criticism of the break statement and the continue statement is that each is unstructured. Actually, break statements and continue statements can always be replaced by structured statements, although doing so can be awkward. Describe in general how you would remove any break statement from a loop in a program and replace that statement with some structured equivalent. [*Hint*: The break statement exits a loop from the body of the loop. The other way to exit is by failing the loop-continuation test. Consider using in the loop-continuation test a second test that indicates "early exit because of a 'break' condition."] Use the technique you developed here to remove the break statement from the application in Fig. 5.11.

5.23   What does the following program segment do?

```
for ( i = 1; i <= 5; i++ ) {

    for ( j = 1; j <= 3; j++ ) {

        for ( k = 1; k <= 4; k++ )
            System.out.print( '*' );

        System.out.println();

    } // end inner for

    System.out.println();

} // end outer for
```

5.24   Describe in general how you would remove any `continue` statement from a loop in a program and replace that statement with some structured equivalent. Use the technique you developed here to remove the `continue` statement from the program in Fig. 5.12.

5.25   (*"The Twelve Days of Christmas" Song*) Write an application that uses repetition and `switch` statements to print the song "The Twelve Days of Christmas." One `switch` statement should be used to print the day (i.e., "First," "Second," etc.). A separate `switch` statement should be used to print the remainder of each verse. Visit the Web site `www.12days.com/library/carols/12daysofxmas.htm` for the complete lyrics to the song.

6

Methods

Objectives

- To understand how to construct programs modularly from small pieces called *methods*.
- To introduce the common math methods available in the Java API.
- To be able to create new methods.
- To understand the mechanisms for passing information between methods.
- To introduce simulation techniques that use random-number generation.
- To understand how the visibility of declarations is limited to specific regions of programs.
- To understand how to write and use methods that call themselves.

Form ever follows function.
Louis Henri Sullivan

E pluribus unum.
(One composed of many.)
Virgil (Publius Vergilius Maro)

O! call back yesterday, bid time return.
William Shakespeare

Call me Ishmael.
Herman Melville

When you call me that, smile.
Owen Wister

Outline

6.1 Introduction

Most computer programs that solve real-world problems are much larger than the programs presented in the first few chapters of this book. Experience has shown that the best way to develop and maintain a large program is to construct it from small, simple pieces, or *modules*. This technique is called *divide and conquer.* This chapter describes how to declare and use methods to facilitate the design, implementation, operation and maintenance of large programs.

6.2 Program Modules in Java

There are two kinds of modules in Java—*methods* and *classes.* Java programs are written by combining new methods and classes that the programmer writes with "prepackaged" methods and classes available in the *Java Application Programming Interface* (also referred to as the *Java API* or *Java class library*) and in various other class libraries. The Java API provides a rich collection of classes that contain methods for performing common mathematical calculations, string manipulations, character manipulations, input/output operations, error checking and many other useful operations. This set of classes makes writing programs easier, because the Java API provides many of the capabilities programmers need. The Java API classes are part of the Java 2 Software Development Kit (J2SDK), which contains thousands of prepackaged classes.

Good Programming Practice 6.1

Familiarize yourself with the rich collection of classes and methods provided by the Java API (`java.sun.com/j2se/1.4.1/docs/api/index.html`) and with the rich collections of classes available in various class libraries.

Software Engineering Observation 6.1

Avoid reinventing the wheel. When possible, use Java API classes and methods instead of writing new classes and methods. This reduces program development time and avoids introducing programming errors.

Performance Tip 6.1

Do not try to rewrite existing Java API classes and methods to make them more efficient. You usually will not be able to increase their performance.

Methods (sometimes called *functions* or *procedures* in other programming languages) allow the programmer to modularize a program by separating its tasks into self-contained units are sometimes referred to as *programmer-declared methods.* The actual statements implementing the methods are written only once and are hidden from other methods.

There are several motivations for modularizing a program by means of methods. One motivation is that of the divide-and-conquer approach makes program development more manageable. Another is *software reusability*—using existing methods as building blocks to create new programs. Often, you can create programs from standardized methods rather than by building customized code. For example, in earlier programs, we did not have to define how to convert strings to integers and floating-point numbers; Java provides these capabilities in class `Integer` (static method `parseInt`) and class `Double` (static method `parseDouble`), respectively. A third motivation is to avoid repeating code within the program. Packaging code as a method allows a program to execute that code from several locations in a program simply by calling the method. Also, methods make programs easier to debug and maintain.

Software Engineering Observation 6.2

To promote software reusability, each method should be limited to performing a single, well-defined task, and the name of the method should express that task effectively. Such methods make programs easier to write, debug, maintain and modify.

Error-Prevention Tip 6.1

Small methods that perform one task are easier to test and debug than larger methods that perform many tasks.

Software Engineering Observation 6.3

If you cannot choose a concise name that expresses a method's task, your method might be attempting to perform too many diverse tasks. It is usually best to break such a method into several smaller method declarations.

Software Engineering Observation 6.4

A method should usually be no longer than one printed page. Better yet, a method should usually be no longer than half a printed page. Regardless of how long a method is, it should perform one task well. Small methods promote software reusability.

A method is *invoked* or *called* (i.e., made to perform its designated task) by a *method call.* The method call specifies the name of the method and provides information (as *argu-*

ments) that the called method requires to perform its task. When the method call completes, the method either returns a result to the *calling method* (or *caller*) or simply returns control to the calling method. An analogy to this program structure is the hierarchical form of management. A boss (the caller) asks a worker (the *called method*) to perform a task and report back (i.e., *return*) the results after completing the task. The boss method does not know *how* the worker method performs its designated tasks. The worker may also call other worker methods, unbeknownst to the boss. This "hiding" of implementation details promotes good software engineering. Figure 6.1 shows the boss method communicating with several worker methods in a hierarchical manner. The boss method divides the responsibilities among the various worker methods. Note that worker1 acts as a "boss method" to worker4 and worker5. Relationships among methods may also be different from the hierarchical structure shown in this figure.

6.3 Math-Class Methods

Class Math provides a collection of methods that enable you to perform common mathematical calculations. We use various Math-class methods here to introduce the concept of methods. Throughout the book, we discuss many other methods from the Java API classes.

Methods are called by writing the name of the method, followed by a left parenthesis, followed by the *argument* (or a comma-separated list of arguments) of the method, followed by a right parenthesis. For example, a programmer desiring to calculate the square root of 900.0 might write

```
Math.sqrt( 900.0 )
```

When this statement executes, it calls the static Math method sqrt[1] to calculate the square root of the number contained in the parentheses (900.0). The number 900.0 is method sqrt's argument. The preceding expression evaluates to 30.0. Method sqrt takes an argument of type double and returns a result of type double. To output the value of the preceding method call in the command window, you might write

```
System.out.println( Math.sqrt( 900.0 ) );
```

In this statement, the value that sqrt returns becomes the argument to method println.

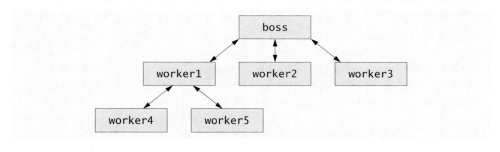

Fig. 6.1   Hierarchical boss-method/worker-method relationship.

1.   All Math class methods are static; therefore, they are called by preceding the name of the method with the class name Math and a dot (.).

Software Engineering Observation 6.5

It is not necessary to import class Math to use its methods. Math is part of the java.lang package, which is automatically imported by the compiler.

Common Programming Error 6.1

Forgetting to call a Math class method by preceding the name of the method with the class name Math and a dot (.) results in a syntax error.

Method arguments may be constants, variables or expressions. If c = 13.0, d = 3.0 and f = 4.0, then the statement

```
System.out.println( Math.sqrt( c + d * f ) );
```

calculates and prints the square root of 13.0 + 3.0 * 4.0 = 25.0—namely, 5.0.

Figure 6.2 summarizes several Math-class methods. In the figure, the variables x and y are of type double. Class Math also declares two commonly used mathematical constants: Math.PI and Math.E. The constant Math.PI (3.14159265358979323846) of class Math is the ratio of a circle's circumference to its diameter. The constant Math.E (2.7182818284590452354) is the base value for natural logarithms (calculated with static Math method log).

Method	Description	Example
abs(x)	absolute value of *x* (this method also has float, int and long versions)	abs(23.7) is 23.7 abs(0.0) is 0.0 abs(-23.7) is 23.7
ceil(x)	rounds *x* to the smallest integer not less than *x*	ceil(9.2) is 10.0 ceil(-9.8) is -9.0
cos(x)	trigonometric cosine of *x* (*x* is in radians)	cos(0.0) is 1.0
exp(x)	exponential method e^x	exp(1.0) is 2.71828 exp(2.0) is 7.38906
floor(x)	rounds *x* to the largest integer not greater than *x*	floor(9.2) is 9.0 floor(-9.8) is -10.0
log(x)	natural logarithm of *x* (base *e*)	log(Math.E) is 1.0 log(Math.E * Math.E) is 2.0
max(x, y)	larger value of *x* and *y* (this method also has float, int and long versions)	max(2.3, 12.7) is 12.7 max(-2.3, -12.7) is -2.3
min(x, y)	smaller value of *x* and *y* (this method also has float, int and long versions)	min(2.3, 12.7) is 2.3 min(-2.3, -12.7) is -12.7
pow(x, y)	*x* raised to the power *y* (x^y)	pow(2.0, 7.0) is 128.0 pow(9.0, 0.5) is 3.0
sin(x)	trigonometric sine of *x* (*x* is in radians)	sin(0.0) is 0.0
sqrt(x)	square root of *x*	sqrt(900.0) is 30.0 sqrt(9.0) is 3.0
tan(x)	trigonometric tangent of *x* (*x* is in radians)	tan(0.0) is 0.0

Fig. 6.2   Math-class methods.

6.4 Method Declarations

The programs presented up to this point each consisted of a class declaration containing at least one method declaration that called Java API methods to accomplish its tasks. We now consider how programmers write their own customized methods.[2]

Consider an applet (Fig. 6.3) that uses a method **square** to calculate the squares of the integers from 1 to 10. When the applet begins execution, the applet container (the **applet-viewer** or a Web browser) calls the applet's **init** method (declared at lines 10–35). Line 13 declares a **JTextArea** reference called **outputArea** and initializes it with a new **JTextArea** object. This **JTextArea** will display the program's results.

```
1    // Fig. 6.3: SquareIntegers.java
2    // Creating and using a programmer-defined method.
3    import java.awt.Container;
4
5    import javax.swing.*;
6
7    public class SquareIntegers extends JApplet {
8
9        // set up GUI and calculate squares of integers from 1 to 10
10       public void init()
11       {
12           // JTextArea to display results
13           JTextArea outputArea = new JTextArea();
14
15           // get applet's content pane (GUI component display area)
16           Container container = getContentPane();
17
18           // attach outputArea to container
19           container.add( outputArea );
20
21           int result;           // store result of call to method square
22           String output = "";    // String containing results
23
24           // loop 10 times
25           for ( int counter = 1; counter <= 10; counter++ ) {
26               result = square( counter );  // method call
27
28               // append result to String output
29               output += "The square of " + counter + " is " + result + "\n";
30
31           } // end for
32
33           outputArea.setText( output );  // place results in JTextArea
34
35       } // end method init
```

Fig. 6.3   Programmer-defined method **square**. (Part 1 of 2.)

2. We have seen several applet examples in which multiple methods (**init**, **start** and **paint**) were declared. We will continue to use applets for programs with multiple method declarations until we discuss the details of class declarations in Chapter 8–Chapter 10. At that point, we will use more elaborate applications for many examples.

```
36
37      // square method declaration
38      public int square( int y )
39      {
40         return y * y;  // return square of y
41
42      } // end method square
43
44   } // end class SquareIntegers
```

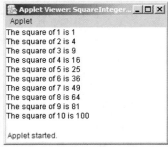

Fig. 6.3   Programmer-defined method `square`. (Part 2 of 2.)

This program is the first in which we display a graphical user interface (GUI) component on an applet. The on-screen display area for an object of class `JApplet` has a *content pane*—an object of class `Container` from the *java.awt package*—to which the GUI components must be attached so that they can be displayed at execution time. This object is provided by the applet, so our program does not need to create a `Container` object. Class `Container` was imported on line 3 for use in the applet. Line 16 declares `Container` reference `container` and assigns to it the result of a call to method *getContentPane*—one of the many methods that our class `SquareIntegers` inherits from class `JApplet`. This method returns a reference to the applet's content pane object. The program uses that reference to attach GUI components, like a `JTextArea`, to the applet's user interface.

When the applet executes, all GUI components attached to the applet's content pane are displayed. So line 19 attaches the `JTextArea` object to which `outputArea` refers to applet's content pane by using reference `container` to call `Container` method `add`. For the moment, we can attach only one GUI component to the applet's content pane, and that GUI component will occupy the applet's entire drawing area on the screen (as defined by the `width` and `height` of the applet in the applet's HTML document). In Section 6.8, we will discuss how to attach many GUI components to an applet by changing the applet's *layout*, which controls how the applet positions GUI components in its area on the screen.

Line 21 declares `int` variable `result` to store the result of each square calculation. Line 22 declares `String` reference `output` and initializes it with the empty string. This string will contain the results of squaring the values from 1 to 10. Lines 25–31 define a `for` statement. During each iteration of this loop, line 26 calculates the `square` of the current value of control variable `counter` and stores the value in `result`, and line 29 concatenates `result` to the end of string `output`.

The applet calls its `square` method on line 26 with the statement

```
result = square( counter );
```

The parentheses to the right of `square` indicate a method call and enclose the method's argument list. At this point, the program makes a copy of the value of `counter` (the argument to the method call) and transfers program control to the first line of method `square` (declared at lines 38–42). Line 38 of method `square`'s declaration shows that `square` expects an integer argument as specified by method `square`'s parameter list. Method `square` uses *parameter*[3] y to manipulate the value `square` receives as an argument. Keyword `int` preceding the name of the method indicates that `square` returns an integer result. Method `square` receives the copy of the value of `counter` in the parameter y. Then, `square` calculates y * y (line 40). Method `square` uses a *return* statement to return (i.e., give back) the result of the calculation to the statement in method `init` that called `square`. Note that the entire method declaration (lines 38–42) appears between the braces of class `Square-Integers`. All methods must be declared inside a class declaration.

Good Programming Practice 6.2

Place a blank line between method declarations to separate the methods and enhance program readability.

Common Programming Error 6.2

Declaring a method outside the braces of a class declaration is a syntax error.

In method `init`, the return value is assigned to variable `result`. Line 29 concatenates "The `square` of ", the value of `counter`, " is ", the value of `result` and a newline character to the end of string `output`. This process repeats for each iteration of the `for` statement. Line 33 uses reference `outputArea` to call the `JTextArea` object's `setText` method, which sets the text (`output`) to display in the text area.

We declared references `outputArea`, `container` and `output`, and variable `result` as local variables in `init`, because they are used only in that method. Variables should be declared as fields only if they are required for use in more than one method of the class or if the program should save their values between calls to the class's methods.

Note that method `init` calls method `square` directly, without qualifying the method name with a class name and a dot (.) or a reference name and a dot. Each method in a class is able to call the class's other methods directly.[4]

General Format of a Method Declaration
The first line of the method declaration is called the *method header*. Following the method header, *declarations and statements* in braces form the *method body,* which is a block. Variables can be declared in any block, and blocks can be nested. A method cannot be declared inside another method.

---

3. Parameters are sometimes called *formal parameters*.
4. There is an exception to this rule: A class's `static` methods can call only other `static` methods of the class directly. Chapter 8 discusses `static` methods in detail.

The basic format of a method declaration is

return-value-type *method-name*(*parameter1* , *parameter2* , ... , *parameterN*)
{
    declarations and statements
}

The *method-name* is any valid identifier. The *return-value-type* is the type of the result returned by the method to the caller. The *return-value-type* `void` indicates that a method does
not return a value. Methods can return at most one value.

Common Programming Error 6.3
Omitting the return-value-type *in a method declaration is a syntax error.*

Common Programming Error 6.4
*Forgetting to return a value from a method that should return a value is a syntax error. If a
return value type other than* `void` *is specified, the method must contain a* `return` *statement
that returns a value of the method's* return-value-type. *Similarly, returning a value from a
method whose return type has been declared* `void` *is a syntax error.*

The *parameters* are declared in a comma-separated list enclosed in parentheses that
declares each parameter's type and name. There must be one argument in the method call
for each parameter in the method declaration. Also, each argument must be compatible with
the type of the corresponding parameter. For example, a parameter of type `double` can
receive values of 7.35, 22 or –0.03546, but not `"hello"` (because a string cannot be implicitly converted to a `double` variable). If a method does not accept any arguments, the parameter list is empty (i.e., the name of the method is followed by an empty set of parentheses).

Common Programming Error 6.5
Declaring method parameters of the same type as `float x, y` *(which is variable declaration
syntax) instead of* `float x, float y` *is a syntax error, because a type is required for each
parameter in the parameter list.*

Common Programming Error 6.6
*Placing a semicolon after the right parenthesis enclosing the parameter list of a method dec-
laration is a syntax error.*

Common Programming Error 6.7
Redeclaring a method parameter as a local variable in the method's body is a syntax error.

Common Programming Error 6.8
*Passing an argument that is not compatible with the corresponding parameter's type in the
method's parameter list is a syntax error (e.g., passing a* `String` *when an* `int` *is expected).*

Good Programming Practice 6.3
*Choosing meaningful method names and meaningful parameter names makes programs
more readable and helps avoid excessive use of comments.*

Software Engineering Observation 6.6
*The method header and method calls must agree in the number, type and order of parameters
and arguments.*

Software Engineering Observation 6.7

A method that has a many parameters may be performing too many tasks. Consider dividing the method into smaller methods that perform the separate tasks. The method header should fit on one line if possible.

There are three ways to return control to the statement that calls a method. If the method does not return a result, control returns when the program flow reaches the method-ending right brace or when the statement

```
return;
```

is executed. If the method returns a result, the statement

```
return expression;
```

evaluates the *expression*, then returns the resulting value to the caller. When a `return` statement executes, control returns immediately to the statement that called the method.

Notes on Method-Call Syntax

Figure 6.3 contains two method declarations: `init` (lines 10–35) and `square` (lines 38–42). Recall from Section 3.5 that the applet container calls method `init` to initialize the applet. In this example, method `init` repeatedly calls method `square` to perform a calculation; then it places the results in the `JTextArea` that is attached to the applet's content pane. When the applet appears on the screen, the results are displayed in the textarea.

Notice the syntax used to call method `square`—we use just the name of the method, followed by the arguments to the method in parentheses. Methods in a class declaration are allowed to call other methods in the same class declaration by using this syntax.[5] Methods in the same class declaration include both the methods declared in that class and methods inherited into that class—i.e., the methods from the class that the current class `extends` (`JApplet` in Fig. 6.3; see line 7). We have now seen three ways to call a method:

1. method name by itself—such as, `square( counter )` in line 26 of Fig. 6.3

2. reference to an object, followed by a dot (`.`) and the method name—such as, `g.drawLine( 15, 10, 210, 10 )` in line 17 of Fig. 3.11

3. class name qualifying a method name—such as, `Integer.parseInt( first-Number )` in line 28 of Fig. 2.9.

The last syntax is only for `static` class methods (discussed in detail in Chapter 8).

Programmer-Defined Method Maximum

The applet in Fig. 6.4 uses a programmer-defined method called `maximum` to determine and return the largest of three floating-point values.

Lines 13–18 of method `init` use input dialogs to read three floating-point values from the user. Lines 21–23 use method `Double.parseDouble` to convert the strings input by the user to `double` values. Line 25 calls method `maximum` (declared on lines 44–48) to determine the largest `double` value of the three `double` values passed as arguments to the method. Method `maximum` returns the result to method `init`, using a `return` statement. The program assigns the result to variable `max` on line 25. Lines 31–32 use `String` con-

---

5.   There is an exception to this rule, discussed in Chapter 8.

catenation to form a string containing the three `double` values input by the user and the `max` value and place the result in the textarea `outputArea`.

```
1   // Fig. 6.4: MaximumTest.java
2   // Finding the maximum of three floating-point numbers.
3   import java.awt.Container;
4
5   import javax.swing.*;
6
7   public class MaximumTest extends JApplet {
8
9      // initialize applet by obtaining user input and creating GUI
10     public void init()
11     {
12        // obtain user input
13        String s1 = JOptionPane.showInputDialog(
14           "Enter first floating-point value" );
15        String s2 = JOptionPane.showInputDialog(
16           "Enter second floating-point value" );
17        String s3 = JOptionPane.showInputDialog(
18           "Enter third floating-point value" );
19
20        // convert user input to double values
21        double number1 = Double.parseDouble( s1 );
22        double number2 = Double.parseDouble( s2 );
23        double number3 = Double.parseDouble( s3 );
24
25        double max = maximum( number1, number2, number3 ); // method call
26
27        // create JTextArea to display results
28        JTextArea outputArea = new JTextArea();
29
30        // display numbers and maximum value
31        outputArea.setText( "number1: " + number1 + "\nnumber2: " +
32           number2 + "\nnumber3: " + number3 + "\nmaximum is: " + max );
33
34        // get applet's GUI component display area
35        Container container = getContentPane();
36
37        // attach outputArea to Container c
38        container.add( outputArea );
39
40     } // end method init
41
42     // maximum method uses Math class method max to help
43     // determine maximum value
44     public double maximum( double x, double y, double z )
45     {
46        return Math.max( x, Math.max( y, z ) );
47
48     } // end method maximum
49
50  } // end class Maximum
```

Fig. 6.4   Programmer-defined method `maximum`. (Part 1 of 2.)

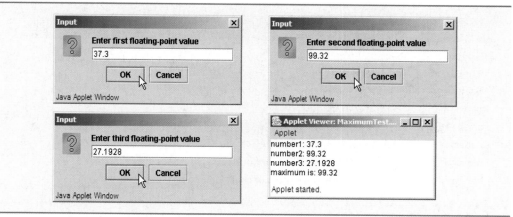

Fig. 6.4   Programmer-defined method `maximum`. (Part 2 of 2.)

Consider the declaration of method `maximum` (lines 44–48). Line 44 indicates that the method returns a `double` floating-point value, that the method's name is `maximum` and that the method requires three `double` parameters (x, y and z) to accomplish its task. Line 46 returns the largest of the three floating-point values, using two calls to the `Math.max` method. First, the statement calls method `Math.max` with the values of variables y and z to determine the larger of the two values. Next, the statement passes the value of variable x and the result of the first call to `Math.max` as arguments to method `Math.max`. Finally, the statement returns the result of the second call to `Math.max` to line 25 (the point at which method `init` called method `maximum`).

6.5 Argument Promotion

Another important feature of method calls is *argument promotion* (or *coercion of arguments*)—i.e., the forcing of arguments to the appropriate type to pass to a method. For example, a program can call `Math` method `sqrt` with an integer argument, even though the method expects to receive a `double` argument. For example, the statement

```
System.out.println( Math.sqrt( 4 ) );
```

correctly evaluates `Math.sqrt( 4 )` and prints the value 2. The method declaration's parameter list causes Java to convert the integer value 4 to the `double` value 4.0 before passing the value to `sqrt`. In some cases, attempting these conversions leads to compiler errors if Java's *promotion rules* are not satisfied. The promotion rules specify how to convert types to other types without losing data. In the `sqrt` example above, an `int` is converted to a `double` without changing its value. However, converting a `double` to an `int` truncates the fractional part of the `double` value; thus, part of the value is lost. Converting large integer types to small integer types (e.g., `long` to `int`) may also result in changed values.

The promotion rules apply to expressions containing values of two or more primitive types (also referred to as *mixed-type expressions*) and to primitive-type values passed as arguments to methods. The type of each value in a mixed-type expression is promoted to the "highest" type in the expression. (Actually, the expression uses a temporary copy of each value; the original values remain unchanged.) Figure 6.5 lists the primitive types and

Type	Valid promotions
double	None
float	double
long	float or double
int	long, float or double
char	int, long, float or double
short	int, long, float or double
byte	short, int, long, float or double
boolean	None (boolean values are not considered to be numbers in Java)

Fig. 6.5   Allowed promotions for primitive types.

the types to which each can be promoted. Notice that the valid promotions for a given type are all types "higher" in the table. For example, an int can be promoted to the higher types long, float and double.

Converting values to types lower in the table of Fig. 6.5 can result in different values. Therefore, in cases where information may be lost due to conversion, the Java compiler requires the programmer to use a cast operator (see Section 4.9) to explicitly force the conversion to occur. Our square method (of Fig. 6.3) uses an integer parameter. To call square with a double variable, named counter, we would be required to write the method call as square((int) counter). This method call explicitly casts (converts) the value of y to an integer for use in method square. Thus, if y's value is 4.5, method square returns 16, not 20.25.

Common Programming Error 6.9

Converting a primitive-type value to another primitive type may change the value if the new type is not a valid promotion. For example, converting a floating-point value to an integral value may introduce truncation errors (loss of the factional part) into the result.

6.6 Java API Packages

As we have seen, Java contains many predefined classes that are grouped into categories of related classes called *packages*. Together, we refer to these packages as the *Java Application Programming Interface* (*Java API*), or the *Java class library*.

Throughout the text, import declarations specify the classes required to compile a Java program. For example, a program includes the declaration

```
import javax.swing.JApplet;
```

to specify that the program uses class JApplet from the javax.swing package. This allows programmers to use the class name JApplet, rather than the fully qualified class name javax.swing.JApplet, in the code. One of the great strengths of Java is the large number of classes in the packages of the Java API that programmers can reuse. We exercise a large number of these classes in this book. Figure 6.6 provides a brief description of a subset of the packages in the Java API. We use classes from these packages and others through-

Package	Description
java.applet	The *Java Applet Package* contains the Applet class and several interfaces that enable applet/browser interaction and the playing of audio clips. In Java 2, class javax.swing.JApplet is used to define an applet that uses the Swing GUI components.
java.awt	The *Java Abstract Window Toolkit Package* contains the classes and interfaces required to create and manipulate GUIs in Java 1.0 and 1.1. In Java 2, the Swing GUI components of the javax.swing packages are often used instead.
java.awt.event	The *Java Abstract Window Toolkit Event Package* contains classes and interfaces that enable event handling for GUI components in both the java.awt and javax.swing packages.
java.io	The *Java Input/Output Package* contains classes that enable programs to input and output data (see Chapter 17, Files and Streams).
java.lang	The *Java Language Package* contains classes and interfaces (discussed throughout this text) that are required by many Java programs. This package is imported by the compiler into all programs.
java.net	The *Java Networking Package* contains classes that enable programs to communicate via networks (see Chapter 18, Networking).
java.text	The *Java Text Package* contains classes and interfaces that enable a Java program to manipulate numbers, dates, characters and strings. The package provides many of Java's internationalization capabilities that enable a program to be customized to a specific locale (e.g., an applet may display strings in different languages, based on the user's country).
java.util	The *Java Utilities Package* contains utility classes and interfaces, such as date and time manipulations, random-number processing capabilities with class Random, storing and processing large amounts of data and breaking strings into smaller pieces called *tokens* with class String-Tokenizer (see Chapter 20; Data Structures, Chapter 21, Java Utilities Package and Bit Manipulation; and Chapter 22, Collections).
javax.swing	The *Java Swing GUI Components Package* contains classes and interfaces for Java's Swing GUI components that provide support for portable GUIs.
javax.swing.event	The *Java Swing Event Package* contains classes and interfaces that enable event handling for GUI components in package javax.swing.

Fig. 6.6   Java API packages (a subset).

out this book. We provide this listing to begin introducing you to the variety of reusable components available in the Java API. When learning Java, spend a portion of your time browsing the descriptions of the packages and classes in the Java API documentation (java.sun.com/j2se/1.4.1/docs/api).

The set of packages available in the Java 2 Software Development Kit (J2SDK) is quite large. In addition to the packages summarized in Fig. 6.6, the J2SDK includes packages for complex graphics, advanced graphical user interfaces, printing, advanced networking, security, database processing, multimedia, accessibility (for people with disabilities) and many other functions. For an overview of the packages in the J2SDK version 1.4.1, visit

> `java.sun.com/j2se/1.4.1/docs/api/overview-summary.html`

Also, many other packages are available for download at `java.sun.com`.

6.7 Random-Number Generation

We now take a brief and, hopefully, entertaining diversion into a popular programming application—simulation and game playing. In this and the next section, we develop a nicely structured game-playing program with multiple methods. The program uses most of the control statements presented to this point in the book and introduces several new concepts.

There is something in the air of a gambling casino that invigorates people—from the high rollers at the plush mahogany-and-felt craps tables to the quarter poppers at the one-armed bandits. It is the *element of chance*, the possibility that luck will convert a pocketful of money into a mountain of wealth. The element of chance can be introduced through the *random* method from the `Math` class.[6]

Consider the following statement:

> `double randomValue = Math.random();`

`Math` method `random` generates a random `double` value in the range from 0.0 up to, but not including, 1.0. If method `random` truly produces values at random, then every value from 0.0 up to, but not including, 1.0 should have an equal *chance* (or *probability*) of being chosen each time method `random` is called. The values returned by `random` are actually *pseudorandom numbers*—a sequence of values produced by a complex mathematical calculation. That calculation uses the current time of day to *seed* the random-number generator such that each execution of a program yields a different sequence of random values.

The range of values produced directly by method `random` often is different from the range of values required in a particular Java application. For example, a program that simulates coin tossing might require only 0 for "heads" and 1 for "tails." A program that simulates the rolling of a six-sided die would require random integers in the range 1–6. A program that randomly predicts the next type of spaceship (out of four possibilities) that will fly across the horizon in a video game would require random integers in the range 1–4.

To demonstrate method `random`, let us develop a program that simulates 20 rolls of a six-sided die and displays the value of each roll. We use the multiplication operator (*) in conjunction with method `random` as follows to produce integers in the range from 0 to 5:

> `( int ) ( Math.random() * 6 )`

This manipulation is called *scaling* the range of values produced by `Math` method `random`. The number 6 in the expression is called the *scaling factor*. The integer cast operator truncates the floating-point part (the part after the decimal point) of each value produced by the expression. Next, we *shift* the range of numbers produced by adding a *shifting value*—in this case 1—to our previous result, as in

> `1 + ( int ) ( Math.random() * 6 )`

---

6. Java also provides class `Random` in package `java.util` for producing random values. An object of this class can produce random `int`, `long`, `float` or `double` values.

The shifting value specifies the first value in the desired set of random integers. Figure 6.7 confirms that the results of the preceding calculation are integers in the range from 1 to 6. Line 16 in the application's main method executes 20 times in a loop, and the results are displayed in a message dialog.

```java
1   // Fig. 6.7: RandomIntegers.java
2   // Shifted, scaled random integers.
3   import javax.swing.JOptionPane;
4
5   public class RandomIntegers {
6
7      public static void main( String args[] )
8      {
9         int value;
10        String output = "";
11
12        // loop 20 times
13        for ( int counter = 1; counter <= 20; counter++ ) {
14
15           // pick random integer between 1 and 6
16           value = 1 + ( int ) ( Math.random() * 6 );
17
18           output += value + "   ";   // append value to output
19
20           // if counter divisible by 5, append newline to String output
21           if ( counter % 5 == 0 )
22              output += "\n";
23
24        } // end for
25
26        JOptionPane.showMessageDialog( null, output,
27           "20 Random Numbers from 1 to 6",
28           JOptionPane.INFORMATION_MESSAGE );
29
30        System.exit( 0 );   // terminate application
31
32     } // end main
33
34  } // end class RandomIntegers
```

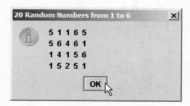

Fig. 6.7   Shifted and scaled random integers.

To show that these numbers occur with approximately equal likelihood, let us simulate 6000 rolls of a die with the application in Fig. 6.8. Each integer from 1 to 6 should appear approximately 1000 times.

```java
1   // Fig. 6.8: RollDie.java
2   // Roll a six-sided die 6000 times.
3   import javax.swing.*;
4
5   public class RollDie {
6
7      public static void main( String args[] )
8      {
9         int frequency1 = 0, frequency2 = 0, frequency3 = 0,
10           frequency4 = 0, frequency5 = 0, frequency6 = 0, face;
11
12        // summarize results
13        for ( int roll = 1; roll <= 6000; roll++ ) {
14           face = 1 + ( int ) ( Math.random() * 6 );
15
16           // determine roll value and increment appropriate counter
17           switch ( face ) {
18
19              case 1:
20                 ++frequency1;
21                 break;
22
23              case 2:
24                 ++frequency2;
25                 break;
26
27              case 3:
28                 ++frequency3;
29                 break;
30
31              case 4:
32                 ++frequency4;
33                 break;
34
35              case 5:
36                 ++frequency5;
37                 break;
38
39              case 6:
40                 ++frequency6;
41                 break;
42
43           } // end switch
44
45        } // end for
46
47        JTextArea outputArea = new JTextArea();
48
```

Fig. 6.8   Rolling a six-sided die 6000 times. (Part 1 of 2.)

```
49      outputArea.setText( "Face\tFrequency" + "\n1\t" + frequency1 +
50         "\n2\t" + frequency2 + "\n3\t" + frequency3 +
51         "\n4\t" + frequency4 + "\n5\t" + frequency5 +
52         "\n6\t" + frequency6 );
53
54      JOptionPane.showMessageDialog( null, outputArea,
55         "Rolling a Die 6000 Times", JOptionPane.INFORMATION_MESSAGE );
56
57      System.exit( 0 );   // terminate application
58
59   } // end main
60
61 } // end class RollDie
```

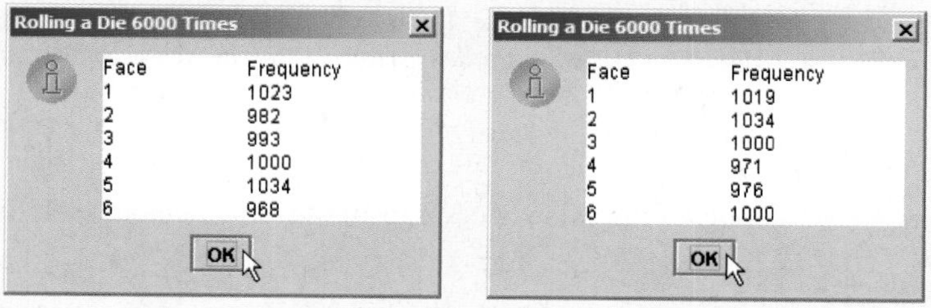

Fig. 6.8   Rolling a six-sided die 6000 times. (Part 2 of 2.)

As the two sample outputs show, scaling and shifting the values produced by method random enables the program to realistically simulate the rolling of a six-sided die. Nested control statements are used in the program to determine the number of times each side of the die occurred. The for statement at lines 13–45 iterates 6000 times. During each iteration, line 14 produces a value from 1 to 6. The face value that was randomly chosen is used as the controlling expression of the nested switch statement (lines 17–43). Based on the face value, the switch statement increments one of the six counter variables during each iteration of the loop.[7] Note that the switch statement has no default case, because we have a case for every possible die value. Run the program several times, and observe the results. Each time you execute this program, notice that it produces different results.

Previously, we demonstrated the statement

```
face = 1 + ( int ) ( Math.random() * 6 );
```

which simulates the rolling of a six-sided die. This statement always assigns to variable face an integer in the range $1 \leq face \leq 6$. The width of this range (i.e., the number of consecutive integers in the range) is 6, and the starting number in the range is 1. Referring to the preceding statement, we see that the width of the range is determined by the number 6 used to scale random with the multiplication operator, and the starting number of the range is equal to the number 1 added to (int) (Math.random() * 6). We can generalize this result as

```
number = shiftingValue + ( int ) ( Math.random() * scalingFactor );
```

---

7. When we study arrays in Chapter 7, we will show how to replace the entire switch statement in this program with a single statement.

where *shiftingValue* is equal to the first number in the desired range of consecutive integers and *scalingFactor* is equal to the width of that range. In the exercises, we will see that it is possible to choose integers at random from sets of values other than ranges of consecutive integers.

6.8 Example: A Game of Chance

One of the most popular games of chance is a dice game known as "craps," which is played in casinos and back alleys throughout the world. The rules of the game are straightforward:

> *A player rolls two dice. Each die has six faces, which contain one, two, three, four, five and six spots, respectively. After the dice have come to rest, the sum of the spots on the two upward faces is calculated. If the sum is 7 or 11 on the first throw, the player wins. If the sum is 2, 3 or 12 on the first throw (called "craps"), the player loses (i.e., the "house" wins). If the sum is 4, 5, 6, 8, 9 or 10 on the first throw, that sum becomes the player's "point." To win, the player must continue rolling the dice until you "make your point" (i.e., roll that same point value). The player loses by rolling a 7 before making the point.*

The applet in Fig. 6.9 simulates the game of craps, using several methods to define the logic of the game.

```
1   // Fig. 6.9: Craps.java
2   // Craps.
3   import java.awt.*;          // Container, FlowLayout
4   import java.awt.event.*;    // ActionEvent, ActionListener
5
6   import javax.swing.*;       // JApplet, JButton, JLabel, JTextField
7
8   public class Craps extends JApplet implements ActionListener {
9
10      // constant variables for game status
11      final int WON = 0, LOST = 1, CONTINUE = 2;
12
13      boolean firstRoll = true;  // true if first roll of dice
14      int sumOfDice = 0;         // sum of the dice
15      int myPoint = 0;           // point if no win or loss on first roll
16      int gameStatus = CONTINUE; // game not over yet
17
18      // graphical user interface components
19      JLabel die1Label, die2Label, sumLabel, pointLabel;
20      JTextField die1Field, die2Field, sumField, pointField;
21      JButton rollButton;
22
23      // set up GUI components
24      public void init()
25      {
26          // obtain content pane and change its layout to FlowLayout
27          Container container = getContentPane();
28          container.setLayout( new FlowLayout() );
29
```

Fig. 6.9   Craps simulation. (Part 1 of 4.)

```
30          // create label and text field for die 1
31          die1Label = new JLabel( "Die 1" );
32          container.add( die1Label );
33          die1Field = new JTextField( 10 );
34          die1Field.setEditable( false );
35          container.add( die1Field );
36
37          // create label and text field for die 2
38          die2Label = new JLabel( "Die 2" );
39          container.add( die2Label );
40          die2Field = new JTextField( 10 );
41          die2Field.setEditable( false );
42          container.add( die2Field );
43
44          // create label and text field for sum
45          sumLabel = new JLabel( "Sum is" );
46          container.add( sumLabel );
47          sumField = new JTextField( 10 );
48          sumField.setEditable( false );
49          container.add( sumField );
50
51          // create label and text field for point
52          pointLabel = new JLabel( "Point is" );
53          container.add( pointLabel );
54          pointField = new JTextField( 10 );
55          pointField.setEditable( false );
56          container.add( pointField );
57
58          // create button user clicks to roll dice
59          rollButton = new JButton( "Roll Dice" );
60          rollButton.addActionListener( this );
61          container.add( rollButton );
62
63    } // end method init
64
65    // process one roll of dice
66    public void actionPerformed( ActionEvent actionEvent )
67    {
68        sumOfDice = rollDice();   // roll dice
69
70        // first roll of dice
71        if ( firstRoll ) {
72
73            switch ( sumOfDice ) {
74
75                // win on first roll
76                case 7:
77                case 11:
78                    gameStatus = WON;
79                    pointField.setText( "" );   // clear point field
80                    break;
81
```

Fig. 6.9   Craps simulation. (Part 2 of 4.)

```
82                   // lose on first roll
83                   case 2:
84                   case 3:
85                   case 12:
86                      gameStatus = LOST;
87                      pointField.setText( "" );   // clear point field
88                      break;
89
90                   // remember point
91                   default:
92                      gameStatus = CONTINUE;
93                      myPoint = sumOfDice;
94                      pointField.setText( Integer.toString( myPoint ) );
95                      firstRoll = false;
96                      break;
97
98               } // end switch
99
100         } // end if part of if...else
101
102         else { // subsequent roll of dice
103
104            // determine game status
105            if ( sumOfDice == myPoint )  // win by making point
106               gameStatus = WON;
107            else
108               if ( sumOfDice == 7 )       // lose by rolling 7
109                  gameStatus = LOST;
110
111         } // end else part of if...else
112
113         displayMessage();   // display message indicating game status
114
115      } // end method actionPerformed
116
117      // roll dice, calculate sum and display results
118      public int rollDice()
119      {
120         // pick random die values
121         int die1 = 1 + ( int ) ( Math.random() * 6 );
122         int die2 = 1 + ( int ) ( Math.random() * 6 );
123
124         int sum = die1 + die2;    // sum die values
125
126         // display results in textfields
127         die1Field.setText( Integer.toString( die1 ) );
128         die2Field.setText( Integer.toString( die2 ) );
129         sumField.setText( Integer.toString( sum ) );
130
131         return sum;   // return sum of dice
132
133      } // end method rollDice
134
```

Fig. 6.9   Craps simulation. (Part 3 of 4.)

```
135     // determine game status; display appropriate message in status bar
136     public void displayMessage()
137     {
138        // game should continue
139        if ( gameStatus == CONTINUE )
140           showStatus( "Roll again." );
141
142        else { // game won or lost
143
144           if ( gameStatus == WON )
145              showStatus( "Player wins. Click Roll Dice to play again." );
146           else
147              showStatus( "Player loses. Click Roll Dice to play again." );
148
149           firstRoll = true;  // next roll is first roll of new game
150
151        } // end else part of if...else
152
153     } // end method displayMessage
154
155  } // end class Craps
```

Win on first roll   Lose on first roll

A JLabel object   A JButton object   A JTextfield object

Win by making the point

Lose by rolling 7 before making the point

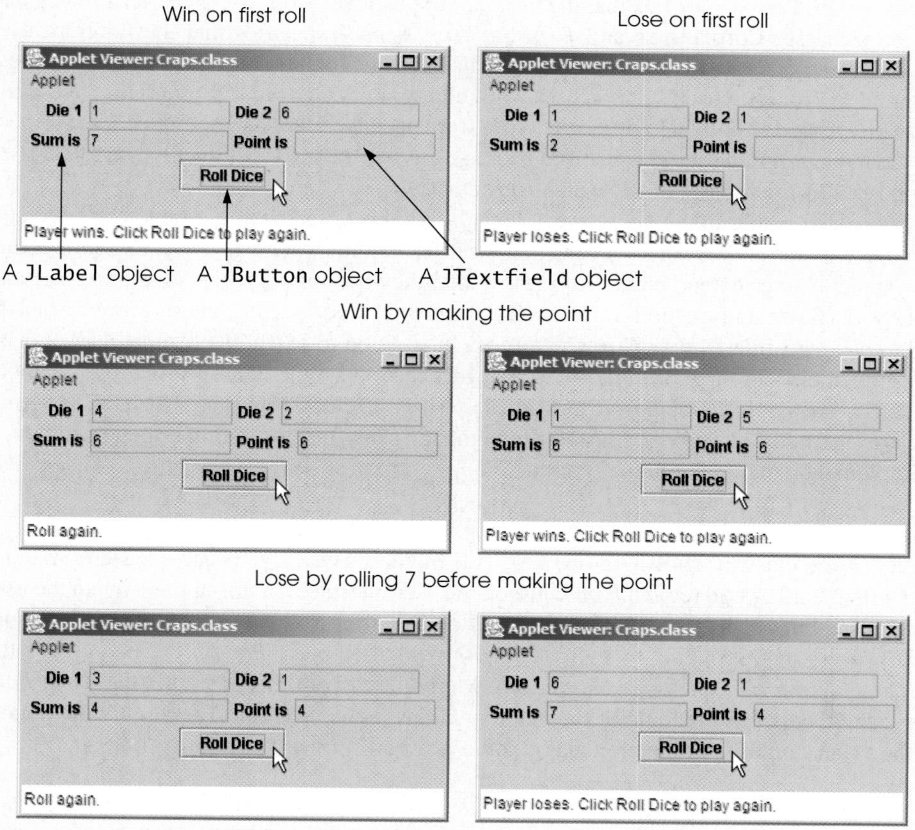

Fig. 6.9   Craps simulation. (Part 4 of 4.)

The player must roll two dice on all rolls. When you execute the applet, click the **Roll Dice** button to play the game. The status bar at the bottom of the `appletviewer` window displays the result of each roll. The screen captures show four separate executions of the applet (a win on the first roll, a loss on the first roll, a win by making the point and a loss by rolling a 7 before making the point).

Until now, most user interactions in our programs have been through either an input dialog (in which the user could type an input value for the program) or a message dialog (in which a message was displayed to the user and the user could click **OK** to dismiss the dialog). Although these dialogs are valid ways to receive input from a user and display output in a Java program, their capabilities are fairly limited—an input dialog can obtain only one value at a time from the user, and a message dialog can display only one message. It is much more common to receive multiple inputs from the user at once (such as the user entering name and address information) or to display many pieces of data at once (such as the values of the dice, the sum of the dice and the point, in this example). To begin our introduction to more elaborate user interfaces, our program illustrates two new graphical user interface concepts: attaching several GUI components to an applet and GUI *event handling*. We discuss each of the new issues as they are encountered in the program.

The `import` declarations in lines 3–6 indicate the packages from which classes are used in this applet. Line 3 specifies that the program uses classes from package `java.awt` (specifically, classes `Container` and `FlowLayout`). Line 4 specifies that the program uses classes from package *java.awt.event*. This package contains many types that enable a program to process a user's interactions with a program's GUI. In our program, we use the *ActionListener* and *ActionEvent* types from package `java.awt.event`. Line 6 specifies that the program uses classes from package `javax.swing` (specifically, we use classes `JApplet, JLabel, JTextField` and `JButton`).

As stated earlier in the book, every Java program is based on at least one class declaration that extends and enhances an existing class declaration via inheritance. Remember that new applet classes extend class `JApplet` so that they can inherit its existing attributes and behaviors (fields and methods). Line 8 indicates that class `Craps` inherits from `JApplet` and *implements* interface *ActionListener*. In addition to extending a superclass, a class can implement one or more *interfaces*. An interface is a type that specifies one or more methods (behaviors), which you must declare in your class. Interface `ActionListener` declares method `actionPerformed`. Implementing interface `ActionListener` forces us to implement a method with the first line

```
public void actionPerformed( ActionEvent actionEvent )
```

in our `Craps` class (as shown on line 66). This method's task is to process a user's interaction with the `JButton` (called **Roll Dice** on the user interface) in this applet. When the user presses the button, `actionPerformed` will be called in response to the user interaction. This process of responding to user interactions is called *event handling*. The *event* is the user interaction (i.e., pressing the button). Method `actionPerformed` is the *event handler*, which contains the logic of the game of Craps in the program. We discuss the details of the event-handling interaction and method `actionPerformed` shortly.[8]

---

8. Chapter 9, Object-Oriented Programming, discusses interfaces in detail. For now, as you develop your own applets that have graphical user interfaces, mimic the features that support event handling of the GUI components we present.

The game of craps is reasonably involved. The player may win or lose on the first roll or may win or lose on any subsequent roll. Line 11 creates and initializes variables that specify the three states of a game of craps: Game won (WON), game lost (LOST) or continue rolling the dice (CONTINUE). Keyword *final* at the beginning of the declaration indicates that these are *constant variables*—variables whose values cannot be changed. When a program declares a final variable, the program must initialize the variable before using it and cannot change its value thereafter. If the variable is a field, this initialization normally occurs in the variable's declaration.[9] Programmers often refer to constant variables as *constants, named constants* or *read-only variables*.

Common Programming Error 6.10

Using the value of an uninitialized final variable or attempting to modify a final variable after it is initialized results in a compilation error.

Good Programming Practice 6.4

By convention, use only uppercase letters (with underscores between words) in the names of final variables. This format makes constants stand out in a program.

Good Programming Practice 6.5

Using meaningfully named final variables rather than literals (such as 2) makes programs more readable and easier to modify.

Lines 13–16 declare several fields that are used throughout the Craps applet's methods. Variable firstRoll is a boolean variable that indicates whether the next roll of the dice is the first roll in the current game (true when the applet begins execution and when each new game begins). Variable sumOfDice maintains the sum of the dice for the last roll. Variable myPoint stores the "point" if the player does not win or lose on the first roll. Variable gameStatus keeps track of the current state of the game (WON, LOST or CONTINUE).

Lines 19–21 declare references to the GUI components used in this applet's graphical user interface. References die1Label, die2Label, sumLabel and pointLabel each will refer to an object of class *JLabel*—a GUI component that contains a string of characters to be displayed on the screen. Normally, a JLabel indicates the purpose of another GUI component on the screen. In the screen captures of Fig. 6.9, the JLabel objects are the text to the left of each rectangle in the first two rows of the user interface. References die1Field, die2Field, sumField and pointField each will refer to an object of class *JTextField*—a GUI component that is used to get a string of information from the user at the keyboard or to display information on the screen. The JTextField objects are the rectangles to the right of each JLabel in the first two rows of the user interface. Reference rollButton will refer to an object of class *JButton*. When the user presses a JButton, the program normally responds by performing a task (rolling the dice, in this example). The JButton object is the rectangle containing the words **Roll Dice** at the bottom of the user interface shown in Fig. 6.9. We have seen JButtons in previous programs: Every message dialog and every input dialog contained an **OK** button to dismiss the message dialog or send the user's input to the program. We also have seen JTextFields in previous programs: Every input dialog contains a JTextField in which the user types an input value.

---

9. The initialization also can occur in the class's *constructor* (discussed in Chapter 8), which is similar to a method. We provide more details on keyword final in Chapter 7 and Chapter 8.

Method `init` (lines 24–63) creates the GUI component objects and attaches them to the applet's content pane (as in Fig. 6.3). Line 27 initializes `Container` reference `container` with the result of calling the applet's inherited `getContentPane` method. Recall from Section 6.4 that method `getContentPane` returns a reference to the applet's content pane that can be used to attach GUI components to the applet's user interface.

Line 28 uses `Container` method *setLayout* to specify the *layout manager* for the applet's user interface. A layout manager arranges GUI components on a `Container` for presentation purposes. The layout manager determines the position and size of every GUI component attached to the container, thereby processing most of the layout details and enabling the programmer to concentrate on the basic look and feel of the programs.

`FlowLayout` is the simplest layout manager. GUI components are placed from left to right in the order in which they are attached to the `Container` (the applet's content pane in this example) with method `add`. When the layout manager reaches the edge of the container, it begins a new row of components and continues laying out the components on that row. Line 28 creates a new object of class `FlowLayout` and passes it as the argument to method `setLayout`. Normally, the layout is set before any GUI components are added to a `Container`.[10] When you execute this applet in `appletviewer`, resize the `appletviewer` window to see how the `FlowLayout` works for different-size applet areas. We chose a width and height for this applet that enabled the `FlowLayout` to position the GUI components as shown in Fig. 6.9.

Common Programming Error 6.11

If a `Container` is not large enough to display the GUI components attached to it, some or all of the GUI components simply will not display.

Lines 31–35, 38–42, 45–49 and 52–56 each create a `JLabel` and `JTextField` pair and attach them to the user interface. Because these sets of lines are all quite similar, we concentrate on lines 31–35. Line 31 creates a new `JLabel` object, initializes it with the string `"Die 1"` and assigns the object to reference `die1Label`. This label precedes the corresponding `JTextField` (named `die1Field`) in the user interface, so the user can determine the purpose of the value displayed in the textfield. Line 32 attaches `die1Label` to the applet's content pane. Line 33 creates a new `JTextField` object, initializes it to be 10 characters wide and assigns the object to reference `die1Field`. This `JTextField` displays the value of the first die after each roll of the dice. Line 34 uses `JTextField` method `setEditable` with the argument `false` to indicate that the user should not be able to type in the `JTextField` (also called making the `JTextField` *uneditable*). Uneditable textfields are displayed with a gray background by default. An *editable* `JTextField` has a white background (as seen in input dialogs). Line 35 attaches `die1Field` to the applet's content pane. Lines 38–56 perform identical tasks for the other labels and textfields.

Line 59 creates a new `JButton` object, initializes it with the string `"Roll Dice"` (which will appear on the button) and assigns that object to reference `rollButton`.

---

10. Each `Container` can have only one layout manager at a time. Separate `Container` objects in the same program can have different layout managers. Most Java programming environments provide GUI design tools that help a programmer graphically design a GUI; then the tools write Java code to create the GUI. Chapter 13 and Chapter 14 discuss several layout managers that allow more precise control over the layout of the GUI components.

Line 60 specifies that *this* applet should *listen* for events from the `rollButton`. Keyword `this` enables the applet to refer to itself. (We discuss `this` in detail in Chapter 8.) When the user interacts with a GUI component, an event is sent to the applet. GUI events are messages indicating that the user of the program has interacted with one of the program's GUI components. For example, when you press the `JButton` object on this program's user interface, a message indicating the event that occurred is sent to the applet to notify it that you pressed the button. For a `JButton`, the message indicates to the applet that *an action was performed* by the user on the `JButton`, which results in a call to method `actionPerformed` to process the user's interaction.

This programming style is known as *event-driven programming*—the user interacts with a GUI component, and the program is notified of the event and processes it. The user's interaction with the GUI "drives" the program. The methods that are called when an event occurs are known as *event-handling methods*, or simply *event handlers*. When a GUI event occurs in a program, the event-handling mechanism creates an object containing information about the event that occurred and calls an appropriate event-handling method (`actionPerformed` for a `JButton`). Before any event can be processed, each GUI component must know which object in the program has the event-handling method that will be called when an event occurs. In line 60, `JButton` method *addActionListener* is used to tell `rollButton` that the applet (`this`) can listen for *action events* and contains method `actionPerformed`. This procedure is called *registering the event handler* with the GUI component. (We also like to call it the *start-listening line*, because the applet is now listening for events from the button.) To respond to an action event, we must declare a class that implements `ActionListener` (this requires that the class also declare method `actionPerformed`), and we must register the event handler with the GUI component. Finally, line 61 of `init` attaches the `JButton` to which `roll` refers to the applet's content pane, thus completing the user interface.

Method `actionPerformed` (lines 66–115) processes interactions between the user and the `JButton` in this applet's GUI.[11] The first line of the method indicates that `actionPerformed` is a public method that returns nothing (`void`) when it completes its task. Method `actionPerformed` receives one argument—an `ActionEvent`—when it is called in response to an action performed on a GUI component by the user (in this case, pressing the `JButton`). The `ActionEvent` argument contains information about the action that occurred. This object is passed to `actionPerformed` by Java's event-handling mechanism. Method `actionPerformed` is yet another method that Java calls for you.

We declare method `rollDice` (lines 118–133) to roll the dice and compute and display their sum. Method `rollDice` takes no arguments, so it has an empty parameter list. Method `rollDice` returns the sum of the two dice, so a return type of `int` is indicated in the method's header.

The user clicks the **Roll Dice** button to roll the dice. This action calls method `actionPerformed` of the applet. Line 68 in `actionPerformed` calls `rollDice`, which picks two random values from 1 to 6, displays the value of the first die, the value of the second die and the sum of the dice in the first three `JTextField`s, respectively, and returns the sum of the dice. The integer values are converted to strings (lines 127–129) with `Integer` static method *toString*, because `JTextField`s can display only strings. Method `actionPer-`

---

11. We will see that there are many event-handling methods for different GUI components. We discuss several of these GUI components and event-handling methods in Chapter 13 and Chapter 14.

formed next checks the boolean variable firstRoll (line 71) to determine whether it is true. If so, this is the first roll of the game. The nested switch statement at lines 73–98 determines whether the game has been won or lost or whether it should continue with another roll. After the first roll, if the game is not over, sumOfDice is saved in myPoint (line 93) and displayed in the textfield pointField (line 94).

Line 113 calls method displayMessage (declared at lines 136–153) to display the current status of the game. The method calls applet method *showStatus* to display a string in the applet container's status bar. Line 140 displays

    Roll again.

if gameStatus is equal to CONTINUE. Line 145 displays

    Player wins. Click Roll Dice to play again.

if gameStatus is equal to WON. Line 147 displays

    Player loses. Click Roll Dice to play again.

if gameStatus is equal to LOST. If the game is over, line 149 sets firstRoll to true to indicate that the next roll of the dice is the first roll of the next game.

The program then waits for the user to click the **Roll Dice** button again. Each time the user presses that button, method actionPerformed calls method rollDice to produce a new sumOfDice. If the current roll is a continuation of an incomplete game, the code in lines 102–111 executes. In line 105, if sumOfDice matches myPoint, line 106 sets gameStatus to WON, and the game is complete. In line 108, if sumOfDice is equal to 7, line 109 sets gameStatus to LOST, and the game is complete. When the game completes, displayMessage displays an appropriate message, and the user can click the **Roll Dice** button to begin a new game. Throughout the program, the textfields die1Field, die2Field and sumField are updated with the new values of the dice and the sum on each roll, and the pointField is updated each time a new game begins.

Note the use of the various program control mechanisms we have discussed. The craps program uses four methods—init, actionPerformed, rollDice and displayMessage—and the switch, if...else and nested if statements. Note also the use of multiple case labels in the switch statement to execute the same statements for sums of 7 and 11 (lines 76–80) and for sums of 2, 3 and 12 (lines 83–88). The event-handling mechanism also acts as a form of program control. In this program, event handling enables user-controlled repetition: Each time the user clicks **Roll Dice**, the program rolls the dice again. In Exercise 6.46, we investigate various interesting characteristics of the game of craps.

6.9 Scope of Declarations

Throughout the examples, you have seen declarations of various Java entities such as classes, methods, variables and parameters. Declarations introduce names that can be used to refer to such Java entities. The *scope* of a declaration is the portion of the program that can refer to an entity by its name. Such a declaration is *in scope* for that portion of the program. This section provides an introduction to several important scope issues.[12]

---

12. See the *Java Language Specification, Section 6.3: Scope of a Declaration* (java.sun.com/docs/books/jls/second_edition/html/names.doc.html#103228), for complete details of Java scopes.

The basic scope rules are as follows:

1. The scope of a parameter declaration is the body of the method in which the declaration appears. (In Chapter 8, we discuss constructors, which are similar to methods. The scope of a constructor parameter declaration is the body of that constructor.)

2. The scope of a local-variable declaration is from the point at which the declaration appears in the block to the end of that block.

3. The scope of a label in a labeled `break` or `continue` statement (introduced in Section 5.8) is the statement enclosed by the labeled statement (i.e., the body of the labeled statement).

4. The scope of a local-variable declaration that appears in the initialization section of a `for` statement's header is the body of the `for` statement and the other expressions in the header.

5. The scope of a method or field of a class is the entire body of the class. This enables methods of a class to use simple names to call other methods declared in the class or inherited by that class (such as the methods inherited by our applets from class `JApplet`) and to access fields declared in the class.[13]

Any block may contain variable or reference declarations. When blocks are nested in a method's body and an identifier declared in an outer block has the same name as an identifier declared in an inner block, the compiler generates a syntax error stating that the variable is already declared. If a local variable or parameter in a method has the same name as a field, the field is "hidden" until the block terminates execution. Java calls this *shadowing*. In Chapter 8, we discuss how to access shadowed fields.

Common Programming Error 6.12

Declaring an entity in an inner block with the same name as an entity in an outer block of the same method results in a syntax error.

Good Programming Practice 6.6

Avoid using the same names for fields and local variables. Different names help readers of your program distinguish variables used in different parts of a class declaration.

The applet of Fig. 6.10 demonstrates scoping issues with fields and local variables. This is our first example of an applet that implements the `start` method (lines 24–37). Recall from Section 3.3 that when an applet container loads an applet, the container first creates an instance of the applet class. It then calls the applet's `init`, `start` and `paint` methods (`paint` is not used in this example). Method `start` is always declared with the header shown on line 24.

---

13. In Chapter 8, we will see that `static` methods are an exception to this rule. This is the reason we use applets to create programs that contain multiple method declarations. Once the complete details of classes are presented in Chapter 8–Chapter 10, we use primarily applications to implement the examples in the remainder of the book.

```
1   // Fig. 6.10: Scoping.java
2   // A scoping example.
3   import java.awt.Container;
4
5   import javax.swing.*;
6
7   public class Scoping extends JApplet {
8      JTextArea outputArea;
9
10     // field that is accessible to all methods of this class
11     int x = 1;
12
13     // create applet's GUI
14     public void init()
15     {
16        outputArea = new JTextArea();
17        Container container = getContentPane();
18        container.add( outputArea );
19
20     } // end method init
21
22     // method start called after init completes; start calls
23     // methods useLocal and useField
24     public void start()
25     {
26        int x = 5;    // local variable in method start that shadows field x
27
28        outputArea.append( "local x in start is " + x );
29
30        useLocal();   // useLocal has local x
31        useField();   // useField uses Scoping's field x
32        useLocal();   // useLocal reinitializes local x
33        useField();   // Scoping's field x retains its value
34
35        outputArea.append( "\n\nlocal x in start is " + x );
36
37     } // end method start
38
39     // useLocal creates and initializes local variable x during each call
40     public void useLocal()
41     {
42        int x = 25;   // initialized each time useLocal is called
43
44        outputArea.append( "\n\nlocal x in useLocal is " + x +
45           " after entering useLocal" );
46        ++x;
47        outputArea.append( "\nlocal x in useLocal is " + x +
48           " before exiting useLocal" );
49
50     } // end method useLocal
51
```

Fig. 6.10   Scoping example. (Part 1 of 2.)

```
52        // useField modifies Scoping's field x during each call
53        public void useField()
54        {
55            outputArea.append( "\n\nfield x is " + x +
56                " on entering useField" );
57            x *= 10;
58            outputArea.append( "\nfield x is " + x +
59                " on exiting useField" );
60
61        } // end method useField
62
63   } // end class Scoping
```

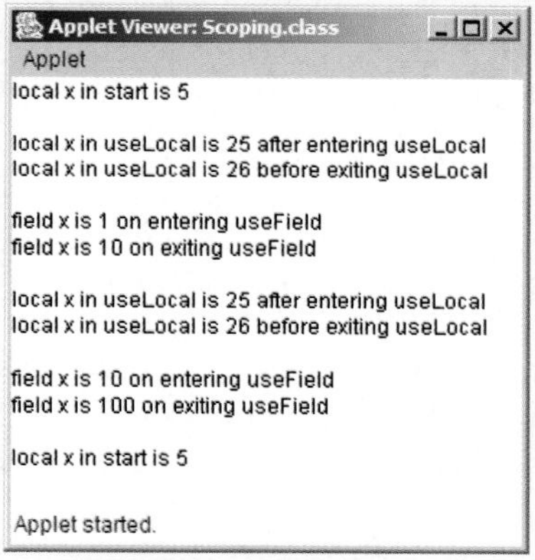

Fig. 6.10   Scoping example. (Part 2 of 2.)

Line 11 declares and initializes the field x to 1. This field is shadowed (hidden) in any block (or method) that declares a variable named x. Method start declares a local variable x (line 26) and initializes it to 5. This variable's value is appended to textarea outputArea to show that the field x is shadowed in start. The program declares two other methods— useLocal (lines 40–50) and useField (lines 53–61)—that each take no arguments and do not return results. Method start calls each method twice (lines 30–33). Method useLocal declares local variable x (line 42). When useLocal is first called (line 30), it creates local variable x and initializes it to 25 (line 42), appends the value of x to outputArea (lines 44–45), increments x (line 46) and appends the value of x to outputArea again (line 47). When useILocal is called a second time (line 32), it re-creates local variable x and initializes x to 25, so the output of each useLocal call is identical.

Method useField does not declare any variables. Therefore, when it refers to variable x, the field x (line 11) is used. When method useField is first called (line 31), it appends the value of field x to outputArea (lines 55–56), multiplies the field x by 10 (line 57) and appends the value of field x to outputArea again (line 58) before returning. The next time method useField is called (line 33), the field has its modified value, 10. Finally, in method start, the program appends the value of local variable x to outputArea again (line 35) to show that none of the method calls modified start's local variable x, because the methods all referred to variables in other scopes.

6.10 Methods of Class JApplet

We have written many applets to this point, but we have not yet discussed the key methods of class JApplet that the applet container calls during the execution of an applet. Figure 6.11 lists the key methods of class JApplet, specifies when they get called and explains the purpose of each. With the exception of method paint, these JApplet methods are declared by the Java API such that they do nothing unless you provide a declaration in your applet class. The original method paint ensures that graphics and GUI components display correctly. If you would like to redefine one of these methods in an applet, you *must* use the appropriate method header, as shown in Fig. 6.11. Otherwise, the applet container will not call your version of the method during the applet's execution. Declaring the methods as discussed here is known as *overriding* the original method—the new method declaration replaces the inherited one. The applet container will call the overridden version of a method for your applet before it attempts to call the default versions inherited from JApplet. Overriding is discussed in detail in Chapter 9.

Common Programming Error 6.13

Providing a declaration for one of the JApplet methods init, start, paint, stop or destroy that does not match the corresponding method header shown in Figure 6.11 results in a method that will not be called automatically during execution of the applet.

Method	When the method is called and its purpose
public void init()	This method is called once by the applet container when an applet is loaded for execution. It performs initialization of an applet. Typical actions performed here are initializing fields, creating GUI components, loading sounds to play, loading images to display (see Chapter 19, Multimedia) and creating threads (see Chapter 16, Multithreading).
public void start()	This method is called after the init method completes execution. In addition, if the browser user visits another Web site and later returns to the HTML page on which the applet resides, method start is called again. The method performs any tasks that must be completed when the applet is loaded for the first time and that must be performed every time the HTML page on which the applet resides is revisited. Typical actions performed here include starting an animation (see Chapter 19) and starting other threads of execution (see Chapter 16).
public void paint(Graphics g)	This drawing method is called after the init method completes execution and the start method has started. It is also called every time the applet needs to be repainted. For example, if the user covers the applet with another open window on the screen and later uncovers the applet, the paint method is called. Typical actions performed here involve drawing with the Graphics object g that is passed to the paint method by the applet container.

Fig. 6.11   JApplet methods that the applet container calls during an applet's execution. (Part 1 of 2.)

Method	When the method is called and its purpose

`public void` stop()

> This method is called when the applet should stop executing—normally, when the user of the browser leaves the HTML page on which the applet resides. The method performs any tasks that are required to suspend the applet's execution. Typical actions performed here are to stop execution of animations and threads.

`public void` destroy()

> This method is called when the applet is being removed from memory—normally, when the user of the browser exits the browsing session (i.e., closes all browser windows). The method performs any tasks that are required to destroy resources allocated to the applet.

Fig. 6.11   JApplet methods that the applet container calls during an applet's execution. (Part 2 of 2.)

Method *repaint* is also of interest to many applet programmers. The applet's paint method normally is called by the applet container. What if you would like to change the appearance of the applet in response to the user's interactions with the applet? In such situations, you might want to call paint directly. However, to call paint, we must pass it the Graphics parameter it expects. We do not have a Graphics object at our disposal to pass to paint (nor do we know how to create one). For this reason, class JApplet provides method repaint. The statement

```
repaint();
```

obtains the Graphics object for you and calls another method, named *update*, which in turn calls method paint and passes to it the Graphics object. The repaint method is discussed in detail in Chapter 19, Multimedia.

6.11 Method Overloading

Java allows several methods of the same name to be declared in the same class, as long as the methods have different sets of parameters (determined by the number and the types of the parameters). This technique is called *method overloading*. When an overloaded method is called, the Java compiler selects the proper method by examining the number and types of the arguments in the call. Method overloading is commonly used to create several methods with the same name that perform similar tasks, but on different types. Figure 6.12 uses overloaded method square to calculate the square of an int and the square of a double.

Good Programming Practice 6.7

> *Overloading methods that perform closely related, but not identical, tasks can make programs more readable and understandable.*

Overloaded methods are distinguished by their *signature*—a combination of the method's name and the number and types of its parameters. If the Java compiler looked only at method names during compilation, the code in Fig. 6.12 would be ambiguous—the

```
1    // Fig. 6.12: MethodOverload.java
2    // Using overloaded methods
3    import java.awt.Container;
4
5    import javax.swing.*;
6
7    public class MethodOverload extends JApplet {
8
9       // create GUI and call each square method
10      public void init()
11      {
12         JTextArea outputArea = new JTextArea();
13         Container container = getContentPane();
14         container.add( outputArea );
15
16         outputArea.setText( "The square of integer 7 is " + square( 7 ) +
17            "\nThe square of double 7.5 is " + square( 7.5 ) );
18
19      } // end method init
20
21      // square method with int argument
22      public int square( int intValue )
23      {
24         System.out.println( "Called square with int argument: " +
25            intValue );
26
27         return intValue * intValue;
28
29      } // end method square with int argument
30
31      // square method with double argument
32      public double square( double doubleValue )
33      {
34         System.out.println( "Called square with double argument: " +
35            doubleValue );
36
37         return doubleValue * doubleValue;
38
39      } // end method square with double argument
40
41   } // end class MethodOverload
```

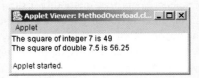

```
Called square with int argument: 7
Called square with double argument: 7.5
```

Fig. 6.12   Overloaded method declarations.

compiler would not know how to distinguish between the two `square` methods (lines 22–29 and 32–39). The compiler uses longer "mangled" or "decorated" names that include the original method name, the types of each parameter and the exact order of the parameters, to determine whether the methods in a class are unique in that class.

For example, in Fig. 6.12, the compiler might use the logical name "square of int" for the `square` method that specifies an `int` parameter and "square of double" for the `square` method that specifies a `double` parameter. If `method1`'s declaration begins as

```
void method1( int a, float b )
```

then the compiler might use the logical name "method1 of int and float." If the parameters are specified as

```
void method1( float a, int b )
```

then the compiler might use the logical name "method1 of float and int." Note that the order of the parameter types is important to the compiler. The preceding two `method1` headers are considered to be distinct by the compiler.

Note that in discussing the logical names of methods used by the compiler, we did not mention the return types of the methods, because methods cannot be distinguished by return type. The program in Fig. 6.13 illustrates the compiler errors generated when two methods have the same signature and different return types. Overloaded methods can have different return types, but must have different parameter lists. Also, overloaded methods need not have the same number of parameters.

Common Programming Error 6.14

Declaring overloaded methods with identical parameter lists is a syntax error.

```
1   // Fig. 6.13: MethodOverload.java
2   // Overloaded methods with identical signatures.
3   import javax.swing.JApplet;
4
5   public class MethodOverload extends JApplet {
6
7      //  declaration of method square with int argument
8      public int square( int x )
9      {
10         return x * x;
11     }
12
13     // second declaration of method square
14     // with int argument causes syntax error
15     public double square( int y )
16     {
17        return y * y;
18     }
19
20  } // end class MethodOverload
```

Fig. 6.13   Overloaded method declarations with identical parameter lists cause compilation errors. (Part 1 of 2.)

```
MethodOverload.java:15: square(int) is already defined in MethodOverload
    public double square( int y )
                  ^
1 error
```

Fig. 6.13   Overloaded method declarations with identical parameter lists cause compilation errors. (Part 2 of 2.)

6.12 Recursion

The programs we have discussed thus far are generally structured as methods that call one another in a disciplined, hierarchical manner. For some problems, however, it is useful to have a method call itself. A *recursive method* is a method that calls itself either directly, or indirectly through another method. Recursion is an important topic discussed at length in upper-level computer science courses. In this section and the next, simple examples of recursion are presented. This book contains an extensive recursion treatment. Figure 6.18 (at the end of Section 6.14) summarizes the recursion examples and exercises in the book.

We consider recursion conceptually first. Then we examine several programs containing recursive methods. Recursive problem-solving approaches have a number of elements in common. When a recursive method is called to solve a problem, the method actually is capable of solving only the simplest case(s), or *base case(s)*. If the method is called with a base case, the method returns a result. If the method is called with a more complex problem, the method divides the problem into two conceptual pieces: a piece that the method knows how to do (the base case) and a piece that the method does not know how to do. To make recursion feasible, the latter piece must resemble the original problem, but be a slightly simpler or slightly smaller version of it. Because this new problem looks like the original problem, the method calls a fresh copy of itself to work on the smaller problem; this procedure is referred to as a *recursive call* and is also called the *recursion step*. The recursion step normally includes a `return` statement, because its result will be combined with the portion of the problem the method knew how to solve to form a result that will be passed back to the original caller.

The recursion step executes while the original call to the method is still active (i.e., while it has not finished executing). The recursion step can result in many more recursive calls, as the method divides each new subproblem into two conceptual pieces. For the recursion to terminate eventually, each time the method calls itself with a slightly simpler version of the original problem, the sequence of smaller and smaller problems must converge on the base case. At that point, the method recognizes the base case and returns a result to the previous copy of the method. A sequence of returns ensues until the original method call returns the final result to the caller. This process sounds complex compared with the conventional problem solving we have performed to this point.

Recursive Factorial Calculations

As an example of recursion concepts at work, let us write a recursive program to perform a popular mathematical calculation. Consider the factorial of a nonnegative integer n, written $n!$ (and pronounced "n factorial"), which is the product

$$n \cdot (n-1) \cdot (n-2) \cdot \ldots \cdot 1$$

1! is equal to 1 and 0! is defined to be 1. For example, 5! is the product $5 \cdot 4 \cdot 3 \cdot 2 \cdot 1$, which is equal to 120.

The factorial of an integer, `number`, greater than or equal to 0, can be calculated *iteratively* (nonrecursively) using the `for` statement as follows:

```
factorial = 1;

for ( int counter = number; counter >= 1; counter-- )
    factorial *= counter;
```

A recursive declaration of the factorial method is arrived at by observing the following relationship:

$$n! = n \cdot (n - 1)!$$

For example, 5! is clearly equal to $5 \cdot 4!$, as is shown by the following equations:

$$5! = 5 \cdot 4 \cdot 3 \cdot 2 \cdot 1$$
$$5! = 5 \cdot (4 \cdot 3 \cdot 2 \cdot 1)$$
$$5! = 5 \cdot (4!)$$

The evaluation of 5! would proceed as shown in Fig. 6.14. Figure 6.14(a) shows how the succession of recursive calls proceeds until 1! is evaluated to be 1, which terminates the recursion. Figure 6.14(b) shows the values returned from each recursive call to its caller until the final value is calculated and returned.

Figure 6.15 uses recursion to calculate and print the factorials of the integers from 0 to 10. The recursive method `factorial` (lines 26–36) first tests to determine whether a terminating condition (line 29) is `true`. If `number` is less than or equal to 1 (the base case), `factorial` returns 1, no further recursion is necessary and the method returns. If `number` is greater than 1, line 34 expresses the problem as the product of `number` and a recursive call to `factorial` evaluating the factorial of `number - 1`, which is a slightly simpler problem than the original calculation, `factorial( number )`.

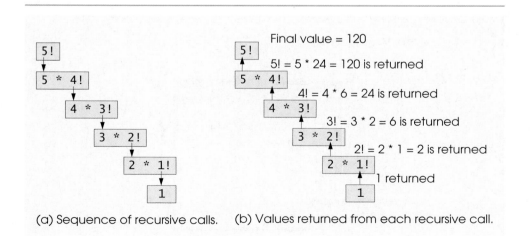

(a) Sequence of recursive calls.   (b) Values returned from each recursive call.

Fig. 6.14   Recursive evaluation of 5!.

```
1   // Fig. 6.15: FactorialTest.java
2   // Recursive factorial method.
3   import java.awt.*;
4
5   import javax.swing.*;
6
7   public class FactorialTest extends JApplet {
8      JTextArea outputArea;
9
10     // create GUI and calculate factorials of 0-10
11     public void init()
12     {
13        outputArea = new JTextArea();
14
15        Container container = getContentPane();
16        container.add( outputArea );
17
18        // calculate the factorials of 0 through 10
19        for ( long counter = 0; counter <= 10; counter++ )
20           outputArea.append( counter + "! = " +
21              factorial( counter ) + "\n" );
22
23     } // end method init
24
25     // recursive declaration of method factorial
26     public long factorial( long number )
27     {
28        // base case
29        if ( number <= 1 )
30           return 1;
31
32        // recursive step
33        else
34           return number * factorial( number - 1 );
35
36     } // end method factorial
37
38  } // end class FactorialTest
```

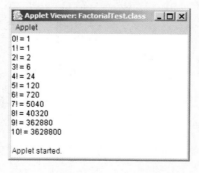

Fig. 6.15   Factorial calculations with a recursive method.

Method `factorial` (lines 26–36) receives a parameter of type `long` and returns a result of type `long`. As can be seen in Fig. 6.15, factorial values become large quickly. We chose type `long` (which can represent relatively large integers) so the program could calculate factorials greater than 20!. Unfortunately, the `factorial` method produces large values so quickly that factorial values soon exceed the maximum value that can be stored in a `long` variable. Due to the restrictions on the integral types, variables of type `float` and `double` might ultimately be needed to calculate factorials of larger numbers. This situation points to a weakness in most programming languages—namely, that the languages are not easily extended to handle the unique requirements of various applications. As we will see in Chapter 9 Java is an extensible language that allows us to create arbitrarily large integers if we wish. In fact, package `java.math` provides class `BigInteger` and class `BigDecimal` explicitly for mathematical calculations of arbitrary precision that cannot be represented with Java's primitive types.

Common Programming Error 6.15

Either omitting the base case or writing the recursion step incorrectly so that it does not converge on the base case will cause infinite recursion, eventually exhausting memory. This error is analogous to the problem of an infinite loop in an iterative (nonrecursive) solution.

6.13 Example Using Recursion: The Fibonacci Series

The Fibonacci series,

> *0, 1, 1, 2, 3, 5, 8, 13, 21, ...*

begins with 0 and 1 and has the property that each subsequent Fibonacci number is the sum of the previous two Fibonacci numbers. This series occurs in nature and, in particular, describes a form of spiral. The ratio of successive Fibonacci numbers converges on a constant value of 1.618..., a number that has been called the *golden ratio* or the *golden mean.* Humans tend to find the golden mean aesthetically pleasing. Architects often design windows, rooms and buildings whose length and width are in the ratio of the golden mean. Postcards are often designed with a golden-mean length-to-width ratio.

The Fibonacci series may be defined recursively as follows:

> *fibonacci(0) = 0*
> *fibonacci(1) = 1*
> *fibonacci(n) = fibonacci(n – 1) + fibonacci(n – 2)*

Note that there are two base cases for the Fibonacci calculation: fibonacci(0) is defined to be 0, and fibonacci(1) is defined to be 1. The applet of Fig. 6.16 calculates the ith Fibonacci number recursively, using method `fibonacci` (lines 62–72). The applet enables the user to input an integer in a textfield. The value that is input indicates the ith Fibonacci number to calculate. When the user presses the *Enter* key, method `actionPerformed` (lines 43–59) executes in response to the user interface event and calls method `fibonacci` to calculate the specified Fibonacci number. Fibonacci numbers tend to become large quickly. Therefore, we use type `long` as the parameter type and the return type of `fibonacci`. In Fig. 6.16, the screen captures show the results of calculating several Fibonacci numbers.

Once again, method `init` (lines 13–40) creates the GUI components and attaches them to the applet's content pane. The layout manager for the content pane is set to `FlowLayout` at line 17.

```
1   // Fig. 6.16: FibonacciTest.java
2   // Recursive fibonacci method.
3   import java.awt.*;
4   import java.awt.event.*;
5
6   import javax.swing.*;
7
8   public class FibonacciTest extends JApplet implements ActionListener {
9      JLabel numberLabel, resultLabel;
10     JTextField numberField, resultField;
11
12     // set up applet's GUI
13     public void init()
14     {
15        // obtain content pane and set its layout to FlowLayout
16        Container container = getContentPane();
17        container.setLayout( new FlowLayout() );
18
19        // create numberLabel and attach it to content pane
20        numberLabel = new JLabel( "Enter an integer and press Enter" );
21        container.add( numberLabel );
22
23        // create numberField and attach it to content pane
24        numberField = new JTextField( 10 );
25        container.add( numberField );
26
27        // register this applet as numberField's ActionListener
28        numberField.addActionListener( this );
29
30        // create resultLabel and attach it to content pane
31        resultLabel = new JLabel( "Fibonacci value is" );
32        container.add( resultLabel );
33
34        // create numberField, make it uneditable
35        // and attach it to content pane
36        resultField = new JTextField( 15 );
37        resultField.setEditable( false );
38        container.add( resultField );
39
40     } // end method init
41
42     // obtain user input and call method fibonacci
43     public void actionPerformed( ActionEvent event )
44     {
45        long number, fibonacciValue;
46
47        // obtain user's input and convert to long
48        number = Long.parseLong( numberField.getText() );
49
50        showStatus( "Calculating ..." );
51
52        // calculate fibonacci value for number user input
53        fibonacciValue = fibonacci( number );
```

Fig. 6.16 Fibonacci numbers generated with a recursive method. (Part 1 of 3.)

```
54
55          // indicate processing complete and display result
56          showStatus( "Done." );
57          resultField.setText( Long.toString( fibonacciValue ) );
58
59       } // end method actionPerformed
60
61       // recursive declaration of method fibonacci
62       public long fibonacci( long n )
63       {
64          // base case
65          if ( n == 0 || n == 1 )
66             return n;
67
68          // recursive step
69          else
70             return fibonacci( n - 1 ) + fibonacci( n - 2 );
71
72       } // end method fibonacci
73
74    } // end class FibonacciTest
```

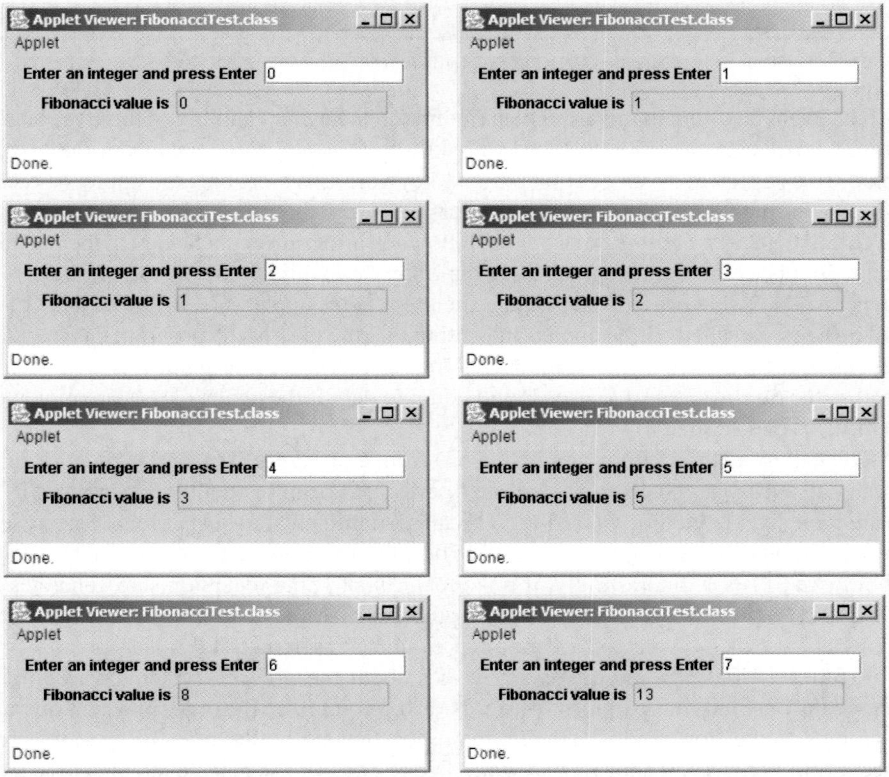

Fig. 6.16   Fibonacci numbers generated with a recursive method. (Part 2 of 3.)

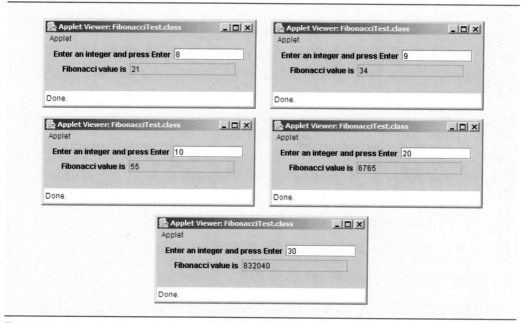

Fig. 6.16   Fibonacci numbers generated with a recursive method. (Part 3 of 3.)

The event handling in this example is similar to the event handling of the `Craps` applet in Fig. 6.9. Line 28 specifies that `this` applet should listen for events from the textfield `numberField`. Recall from Section 6.8 that keyword `this` enables the applet to refer to itself. So, in line 28, the applet is telling `numberField` that the applet should be notified (with a call to its `actionPerformed` method) when an action event occurs in the `number-Field`. In this example, the user presses the *Enter* key while typing in the `numberField` to generate the action event. A message is then sent to the applet (i.e., a method—`action-Performed`—is called on the applet) indicating that the user of the program has interacted with one of the program's GUI components (`numberField`). The statement to register the applet as the `numberField`'s listener will compile only if the applet class also implements `ActionListener` (line 8).

The call to method `fibonacci` (line 53) from `actionPerformed` is not a recursive call, but all subsequent calls to `fibonacci` performed from the body of `fibonacci` (line 70) are recursive. Each time `fibonacci` is called, it immediately tests for the base cases—n equal to 0 or 1. If this condition is true, `fibonacci` returns n: `fibonacci(0)` is 0, and `fibonacci(1)` is 1. Interestingly, if n is greater than 1, the recursion step generates *two* recursive calls, each for a slightly simpler problem than the original call to `fibonacci`. Figure 6.17 shows how method `fibonacci` evaluates `fibonacci( 3 )`.

Figure 6.17 raises some interesting issues about the order in which Java compilers evaluate the operands of operators. This order is different from the order in which operators are applied to their operands—namely, the order dictated by the rules of operator precedence. From Fig. 6.17, it appears that while `fibonacci(3)` is being evaluated, two recursive calls will be made: `fibonacci( 2 )` and `fibonacci(1)`. But in what order will these calls be made? Most programmers assume that the operands will be evaluated from left to

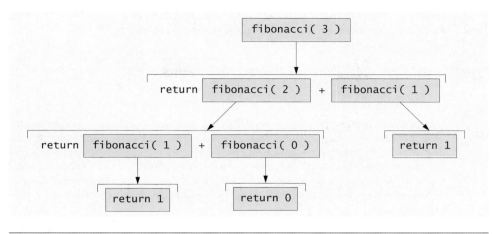

Fig. 6.17   Set of recursive calls for `fibonacci( 3 )`.

right. In Java, this assumption is true.[14] The Java language specifies that the order of evaluation of the operands is from left to right. Thus, the method calls are in fact `fibonacci( 2 )` first and `fibonacci( 1 )` second.

Good Programming Practice 6.8

Do not write expressions that depend on the order of evaluation of the operands of an operator. The use of such expressions often results in programs that are difficult to read, debug, modify and maintain.

A word of caution is in order about recursive programs like the one we use here to generate Fibonacci numbers. Each invocation of the `fibonacci` method that does not match one of the base cases (0 or 1) results in two more recursive calls to the `fibonacci` method. Hence, this set of recursive calls rapidly gets out of hand. Calculating the Fibonacci value of 20 with the program in Fig. 6.16 requires 21,891 calls to the `fibonacci` method; calculating the Fibonacci value of 30 requires 2,692,537 calls to the method. As you try to calculate larger Fibonacci values, you will notice that each consecutive Fibonacci number you ask the applet to calculate results in a substantial increase in calculation time and in the number of calls to the `fibonacci` method. For example, the Fibonacci value of 31 requires 4,356,617 calls, and the Fibonacci value of 32 requires 7,049,155 calls. As you can see, the number of calls to `fibonacci` is increasing quickly—1,664,080 additional calls between Fibonacci values of 30 and 31 and 2,692,538 additional calls between Fibonacci values of 31 and 32. The difference in the number of calls made between Fibonacci values of 31 and

---

14. The C and C++ languages (on which many of Java's features are based) do not specify the order in which the operands of most operators are evaluated. In those languages, programmers cannot assume any information about the order in which the calls in this example execute. The calls could, in fact, execute `fibonacci( 2 )` first and `fibonacci( 1 )` second, or the calls could be executed in the reverse order—`fibonacci( 1 )`, followed by `fibonacci( 2 )`. In this program and in most other programs, the final result would be the same in either case. But in some programs, the evaluation of an operand may have side effects that could affect the final result of the expression.

32 is more than 1.5 times the number of calls for Fibonacci values between 30 and 31. Problems of this nature humble even the world's most powerful computers.[15]

Performance Tip 6.2

Avoid Fibonacci-style recursive programs, which result in an exponential "explosion" of method calls.

Error-Prevention Tip 6.2

Try enhancing the Fibonacci program of Fig. 6.16 such that it calculates the approximate amount of time required to perform the calculation. For this purpose, call static System *method* currentTimeMillis, *which takes no arguments and returns the computer's current time in milliseconds. Call this method twice—once before the call to* fibonacci *and once after the call to* fibonacci. *Save each of these values and calculate the difference in the times to determine how many milliseconds were required to perform the calculation. Display your result.*

6.14 Recursion vs. Iteration

In the previous sections, we studied methods factorial and fibonacci, which can easily be implemented either recursively or iteratively. In this section, we compare the two approaches and discuss why the programmer might choose one approach over the other in a particular situation.

Both iteration and recursion are based on a control statement: Iteration uses a repetition statement (such as for, while or do...while); recursion uses a selection statement (such as if, if...else or switch). Both iteration and recursion involve repetition: Iteration explicitly uses a repetition statement; recursion achieves repetition through repeated method calls. Iteration and recursion each involve a termination test: Iteration terminates when the loop-continuation condition fails; recursion terminates when a base case is recognized. Iteration with counter-controlled repetition and recursion each gradually approach termination: Iteration keeps modifying a counter until the counter assumes a value that makes the loop-continuation condition fail; recursion keeps producing simpler versions of the original problem until the base case is reached. Both iteration and recursion can occur infinitely: An infinite loop occurs with iteration if the loop-continuation test never becomes false; infinite recursion occurs if the recursion step does not reduce the problem each time in a manner that converges on the base case.

Recursion has many negatives. It repeatedly invokes the mechanism, and consequently the overhead, of method calls. This repetition can be expensive in terms of both processor time and memory space. Each recursive call causes another copy of the method (actually, only the method's variables) to be created; this set of copies can consume considerable memory space. Iteration occurs within a method, so repeated method calls and extra memory assignment are avoided. So why choose recursion?

---

15. In the field of complexity theory, computer scientists study how hard algorithms work to complete their tasks. Complexity issues are discussed in detail in the upper-level computer science curriculum course generally called "Algorithms."

Software Engineering Observation 6.8

Any problem that can be solved recursively can also be solved iteratively (nonrecursively). A recursive approach is normally preferred over an iterative approach when the recursive approach more naturally mirrors the problem and results in a program that is easier to understand and debug. Often, a recursive approach can be implemented with few lines of code, but a corresponding iterative approach might take large amounts of code. Another reason to choose a recursive solution is that an iterative solution might not be apparent.

Performance Tip 6.3

Avoid using recursion in situations requiring performance. Recursive calls take time and consume additional memory.

Common Programming Error 6.16

Accidentally having a nonrecursive method call itself either directly or indirectly through another method can cause infinite recursion.

Most programming textbooks introduce recursion much later than we have done here. We feel that recursion is a sufficiently rich and complex topic that it is better to introduce it earlier and spread examples of it over the remainder of the text. Figure 6.18 summarizes the recursion examples and exercises in this text.

Let us consider again some observations we make repeatedly throughout this book. Good software engineering is important. In many cases, high performance is important. Unfortunately, these goals are often at odds with one another. Good software engineering is key to managing the task of developing larger and more complex software systems. High performance in these systems is key to realizing the systems of the future, which will place ever greater computing demands on hardware. Where do methods fit in here?

Chapter	Recursion examples and exercises
6	Factorial method (Fig. 6.15), Fibonacci method (Fig. 6.16), Raising an integer to an integer power (Exercise 6.36), Towers of Hanoi (Exercise 6.37), Visualizing recursion (Exercise 6.39), Greatest common divisor (Exercise 6.40), What does this method do?(Exercise 6.43), Find the error in the recursive method (Exercise 6.45)
7	What does this program do? (Exercise 7.16), What does this program do? (Exercise 7.19), Determine whether a string is a palindrome (Exercise 7.32), Linear search (Exercise 7.33), Binary search (Exercise 7.34), Eight Queens (Exercise 7.35) Print an array (Exercise 7.36), Print an array backward (Exercise 7.37), Minimum value in an array (Exercise 7.38), Quicksort (Exercise 7.39), Maze traversal (Exercise 7.40)
20	Binary-tree insert (Fig. 20.17), Preorder traversal of a binary tree (Fig. 20.17), Inorder traversal of a binary tree (Fig. 20.17), Postorder traversal of a binary tree (Fig. 20.17), Print a linked list backward (Exercise 20.20), Search a linked list (Exercise 20.21)

Fig. 6.18   Summary of recursion examples and exercises in this text.

Software Engineering Observation 6.9

Modularizing programs in a neat, hierarchical manner promotes good software engineering, but it has a price.

Performance Tip 6.4

A heavily modularized program makes potentially large numbers of method calls, which consume execution time and space on a computer's processor(s). Today's Java virtual machines are capable of eliminating much of the overhead generated by additional method calls from heavily modularized programs.

Modularize your programs judiciously, always keeping in mind the delicate balance between performance and good software engineering.

6.15 (Optional Case Study) Thinking About Objects: Identifying Class Operations

In the "Thinking About Objects" sections at the ends of Chapters 3, 4 and 5, we performed the first few steps in the object-oriented design for our elevator simulator. In Chapter 3, we identified the classes we need to implement and created our first class diagram. In Chapter 4, we modeled the attributes of our classes. In Chapter 5, we examined objects' states and modeled objects' activities and state transitions. In this section, we concentrate on determining the *operations* (or *behaviors*) needed to implement the elevator simulator.

An operation is a service that objects of the class provide to "clients" (users) of those objects. Consider the operations of some real-world objects. A radio's operations include setting its station and volume (typically invoked by a person adjusting the radio's controls). A car's operations include accelerating (invoked by the driver pressing the accelerator pedal), decelerating (invoked by the driver pressing the brake pedal or releasing the gas pedal), turning and shifting gears.

We can derive many of the operations of each class directly from the problem statement. To do so, we examine the verbs and verb phrases in the problem statement. We then relate each of these to particular classes in our system (Fig. 6.19). Many of the verb phrases in Fig. 6.19 help us determine the operations of our classes.[16]

To create operations, we examine the verb phrases listed with each class. The phrase "moves to other floor" listed with class `Elevator` refers to the activity in which the elevator moves between floors. Should "moves" be an operation of class `Elevator`? The elevator decides to move in response to a button press. A button *signals* the elevator to move, but a button does not actually *move* the elevator—therefore, "moves to other floor" does not correspond to an operation. (We include the operations for instructing the elevator to move to the other floor later in the discussion, when we discuss the verb phrases associated with the buttons.) The "arrives at a floor" phrase is also not an operation, because the elevator itself decides when to arrive on the floor after five seconds of travel.

The "resets elevator button" phrase associated with class `Elevator` implies that the elevator instructs the elevator button to reset. Therefore, class `ElevatorButton` needs an

---

16. Verb analysis is a simple means of identifying behaviors. In industry, it is common to use more rigorous methods, such as those prescribed by the Rational Unified Process (RUP).

Class	Verb phrases
Elevator	moves to other floor, arrives at a floor, resets elevator button, rings elevator bell, signals its arrival, opens its door, closes its door
ElevatorShaft	turns off light, turns on light, resets floor button
Person	walks on floor, presses floor button, presses elevator button, rides elevator, enters elevator, exits elevator
Floor	[none in the problem statement]
FloorButton	requests elevator
ElevatorButton	closes elevator door, signals elevator to move to opposite floor
FloorDoor	signals person to enter elevator (by opening)
ElevatorDoor	signals person to exit elevator (by opening), opens floor door, closes floor door
Bell	[none in the problem statement]
Light	[none in the problem statement]

Fig. 6.19　Verb phrases for each class in simulator.

operation to provide this service to the elevator. We place this operation (resetButton) in the third compartment of class ElevatorButton in our class diagram (Fig. 6.20).

We represent operations by listing the operation name, followed by a comma-separated list of parameters in parentheses, then a colon followed by the return type:

name(*parameter1*, *parameter2*, …, *parameterN*) : *return type*

For the moment, most of our operations have no parameters. We do not yet know the return types for many of the methods, so we omit them from the diagram. As our design and implementation processes proceed, we will add the appropriate parameter lists and return types.

From the "ring the elevator bell" phrase listed with class Elevator, we conclude that class Bell should have an operation that provides a service—namely, ringing. We list the ringBell operation under class Bell.

When arriving at a floor, the elevator "signals its arrival" to the doors. The elevator door responds by opening. Therefore, class ElevatorDoor needs an operation for opening. We place the openDoor operation in the third compartment of this class. The phrase "closes [the elevator's] door" indicates that class ElevatorDoor needs an operation for closing, so we place the closeDoor operation in the same compartment.

Class ElevatorShaft has "turns off light" and "turns on light" in its verb-phrases column, so we create the turnOffLight and turnOnLight operations and list them under class Light. The "resets floor button" phrase implies that the elevator instructs a floor button to reset. Therefore, class FloorButton needs a resetButton operation.

The phrase "walks on floor" listed by class Person is not an operation, because a person decides to walk across the floor in response to that person's creation. However, the phrases "presses floor button" and "presses elevator button" are operations pertaining to the button classes. We therefore place the pressButton operation under classes FloorButton and ElevatorButton in our class diagram (Fig. 6.20). The phrase "rides elevator"

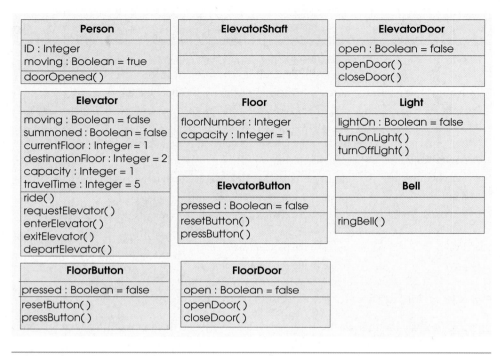

Fig. 6.20 Classes with attributes and operations.

implies that `Elevator` needs an operation that allows a person to ride the elevator, so we place operation `ride` in the bottom compartment of `Elevator`. The "enters elevator" and "exits elevator" phrases listed with class `Person` suggest that class `Elevator` needs operations that correspond to these actions.[17] We place operations `enterElevator` and `exitElevator` in the bottom compartment of class `Elevator`.

The "requests elevator" phrase listed under class `FloorButton` implies that class `Elevator` needs a `requestElevator` operation. The phrase "signals elevator to move to opposite floor" listed with class `ElevatorButton` implies that `ElevatorButton` instructs `Elevator` to depart. Therefore, the `Elevator` needs to provide a "departure" service; we place a `departElevator` operation in the bottom compartment of `Elevator`.

The phrases listed with classes `FloorDoor` and `ElevatorDoor` mention that the doors—by opening—signal a `Person` object to enter or exit the elevator. Specifically, a door informs a person that the door has opened. (The person then enters or exits the elevator, accordingly.) We place the `doorOpened` operation in the bottom compartment for class `Person`. In addition, the `ElevatorDoor` opens and closes the `FloorDoor`, so we assign `openDoor` and `closeDoor` to the bottom compartment of class `FloorDoor`.

For now, we do not concern ourselves with operation parameters or return types; we attempt to gain only a basic understanding of the operations of each class. As we continue

---

17. At this point, we can only guess what these operations do. For example, perhaps these operations model real-world elevators, some of which have sensors that detect when passengers enter and exit. For now, we simply list these operations. We will discover what, if any, actions these operations perform as we continue our design process.

our design process, the number of operations belonging to each class may vary—we might find that new operations are needed or that some current operations are unnecessary—and we might determine that some of our class operations need particular return types.

SUMMARY

- The best way to develop and maintain a large program is to divide it into several smaller modules. Modules are written in Java as classes and methods.

- A method is an executable unit invoked by a method call. The method call mentions the method by name and provides arguments in parentheses that the called method requires to perform its task. If the method is being called on an object, the call must be preceded by a reference name and a dot. If the method is `static`, it must be preceded by a class name and a dot.

- Each argument of a method may be a constant, a variable or an expression.

- A local variable is known only in the method that declares the variable. Methods are not allowed to know the implementation details of any other method.

- The on-screen display area for an object of class `JApplet` has a content pane to which the GUI components must be attached so that they can be displayed at execution time. The content pane is an object of class `Container` from the `java.awt` package. `JApplet` method `getContentPane` returns a reference to the applet's content pane.

- The basic format for a method declaration is

      return-value-type   method-name(*parameter1* ,   *parameter2* ,   ... ,   *parameterN*)
      {
          declarations and statements
      }

  The *return-value-type* states the type of the value returned to the caller. If a method does not return a value, the *return-value-type* is `void`. The *method-name* is any valid identifier. The *parameters* are declared in a comma-separated list (the parameter list) enclosed in parentheses that declares each parameter's type and name. If a method does not accept any values, parameter list is empty. The method body is a block of *declarations and statements* that constitute the method.

- The arguments passed to a method should match in number, type and order with the parameters in the method declaration.

- When a program encounters a method call, control transfers from the point of invocation to the called method, the method executes and control returns to the caller. A called method can return control to the caller in one of three ways. If a method has a `void` return type, control returns at the method-ending right brace or by executing the statement

      return;

  If the method does return a value, the statement

      return *expression*;

  returns the value of *expression*.

- There are three ways to call a method—the method name by itself; a reference to an object, followed by a dot (.) and the method name; and a class name, followed by a dot (.) and a method name. The last syntax is for `static` methods.

- In many cases, argument values that do not correspond precisely to the parameter types in the method declaration are converted to the proper type before the method is called. This can lead to compiler errors if Java's promotion rules are violated.

- Method `Math.random` generates a double value from 0.0 up to, but not including, 1.0. Values produced by `Math.random` can be scaled and shifted to produce values in a range.

- The general equation for scaling and shifting a random number is

  n = *shiftingValue* + (`int`) (`Math.random()` * *scalingFactor*);

- A class can inherit existing attributes and behaviors (fields and methods) from another class specified to the right of keyword `extends` in the class declaration. In addition, a class can implement one or more interfaces. An interface specifies one or more methods that you must declare in the implementing class.

- The interface `ActionListener` specifies that a class must implement a method with the first line

  ```
  public void actionPerformed( ActionEvent actionEvent )
  ```

- Method `actionPerformed` processes a user's interaction with a GUI component that generates an action event. The method is called in response to the user interaction. The process is called event handling. The `actionPerformed` method is an event handler. This style of programming is called event-driven programming.

- Keyword `final` declares constant variables, which must be initialized once before they are used in a program. Constant variables are often called constants, named constants or read-only variables.

- An object of class `JLabel` contains a string of characters to be displayed on the screen. Normally, a `JLabel` indicates the purpose of another GUI element on the screen.

- Objects of class `JTextField` get information from the user or display information on the screen.

- When the user presses a `JButton`, the program normally responds by performing a task.

- `Container` method `setLayout` specifies the layout manager for the applet's user interface. Layout managers are provided to arrange GUI components on a `Container` for presentation purposes. In a `FlowLayout`, GUI components are placed on a `Container` from left to right in the order in which they are attached to the `Container` with method `add`. When the edge of the container is reached, components are continued on the next line.

- Before any event can be processed, each GUI component must know which object in the program contains the event-handling method that will be called when an event occurs. Method `addActionListener` is used to register an event for a `JButton` or `JTextField`. To respond to an action event, a class must implement `ActionListener` and method `actionPerformed`.

- Method `showStatus` displays a string in the applet container's status bar.

- The scope of a declaration is the portion of a program that can refer to the entity in the declaration by name.

- The scope of a parameter declaration is the body of the method in which the declaration appears.

- The scope of a local-variable declaration is from the point at which the declaration appears in the block to the end of that block.

- The scope of a label in a labeled **break** or **continue** statement is the statement enclosed by the labeled statement (i.e., the body of the labeled statement).

- The scope of a local-variable declaration that appears in the initialization section of a **for** statement's header is the body of the **for** statement and the other expressions in the header.

- The scope of a method or field of a class is the entire body of the class. This enables methods of a class to use simple names to call other methods declared in the class or inherited by that class and to access fields declared in the class.

- A recursive method is a method that calls itself, either directly or indirectly.

- If a recursive method is called with a base case, the method immediately returns a result. If the method is called with a more complex problem, the method divides the problem into two or more conceptual pieces: a piece that the method knows how to do and a slightly smaller version of the original problem. Because this new problem looks like the original problem, the method makes a recursive call to work on the smaller problem.

- For recursion to terminate, the sequence of smaller and smaller problems must converge to the base case. When the method recognizes the base case, the result is returned to the previous method call, and a sequence of returns ensues all the way up the line, until the original call of the method returns the final result.

- The applet's `init` method is called once by the applet container when an applet is loaded for execution. It performs initialization of an applet. The applet's `start` method is called after the `init` method completes execution and every time the user of the browser returns to the HTML page on which the applet resides (after browsing another HTML page).

- The applet's `paint` method is called after method `start` has started executing to draw on the applet. It is also called every time the applet needs to be repainted.

- The applet's `stop` method is called when the applet should suspend execution—normally, when the user of the browser leaves the HTML page on which the applet resides.

- The applet's `destroy` method is called when the applet is being removed from memory—normally, when the user of the browser exits the browsing session.

- Method `repaint` can be called in an applet to cause a fresh call to `paint`. Method `repaint` calls another method, named `update`, and passes it the `Graphics` object. Method `update` calls the `paint` method and passes it the `Graphics` object.

- Method overloading occurs when methods have the same name, but different parameter lists. When an overloaded method is called, the compiler selects the proper method by examining the arguments in the call. Overloaded methods must have different parameter lists.

TERMINOLOGY

`ActionEvent` class
`ActionListener` interface
`actionPerformed` method of `ActionListener`
argument in a method call
base case in recursion
block
call a method
called method
calling method (caller)
class
coercion of arguments
constant
constant variable
copy of a value
`destroy` method of class `JApplet`
divide and conquer
element of chance
event-driven programming
factorial method
`final`
`FlowLayout` class

`init` method of class `JApplet`
interface
invoke a method
iteration
Java API (Java class library)
`JButton` class
`JLabel` class
`JTextField`
local variable
`Math` class
`Math.E`
`Math.PI`
`Math.random` method
method
method call
method declaration
method overloading
method signature
mixed-type expression
modular program
named constant

paint method of class JApplet   scaling
parameter in a method declaration   scope
programmer-defined method   setLayout method of class JApplet
promotion rules   shifting
random-number generation   showStatus method of class JApplet
read-only variable   signature
recursion   simulation
recursion step   software engineering
recursive call   software reusability
recursive method   start method of class JApplet
reference types   stop method of class JApplet
repaint method of class JApplet   this
return   update method of class JApplet
return-value type   void

SELF-REVIEW EXERCISES

6.1   Fill in the blanks in each of the following statements:
   a) A method is invoked with a(n) _____.
   b) A variable known only within the method in which it is declared is called a(n) _____.
   c) The _____ statement in a called method can be used to pass the value of an expression back to the calling method.
   d) The keyword _____ indicates that a method does not return a value.
   e) The _____ of a declaration is the portion of a program that can refer to the entity in the declaration by name.
   f) The three ways to return control from a called method to a caller are _____, _____ and _____.
   g) The _____ method is called once when an applet begins execution.
   h) The _____ method produces random numbers.
   i) The _____ method is called each time the user of a browser revisits the HTML page on which an applet resides.
   j) The _____ method is invoked to draw on an applet.
   k) The _____ method invokes the applet's update method, which in turn invokes the applet's paint method.
   l) The _____ method is invoked for an applet each time the user of a browser leaves an HTML page on which the applet resides.
   m) A method that calls itself either directly or indirectly is a(n) _____ method.
   n) A recursive method typically has two components: one that provides a means for the recursion to terminate by testing for a(n) _____ case and one that expresses the problem as a recursive call for a slightly simpler problem than does the original call.
   o) In Java, it is possible to have various methods with the same name that each operate on different types or numbers of arguments. This feature is called method _____.
   p) The _____ modifier is used to declare constant variables.

6.2   For the following program, state the scope of each of the following entities:
   a) the variable x.
   b) the variable y.
   c) the method cube.
   d) the method paint.
   e) the variable yPos.

```
1   public class CubeTest extends JApplet {
2      int x;
3
4      public void paint( Graphics g )
5      {
6         int yPos = 25;
7
8         for ( x = 1; x <= 10; x++ ) {
9            g.drawString( cube( x ), 25, yPos );
10           yPos += 15;
11        }
12     }
13
14     public int cube( int y )
15     {
16        return y * y * y;
17     }
18  }
```

6.3   Write an application that tests whether the examples of the math-library method calls shown in Fig. 6.2 actually produce the indicated results.

6.4   Give the method header for each of the following methods:
   a) Method hypotenuse, which takes two double-precision, floating-point arguments side1 and side2 and returns a double-precision, floating-point result.
   b) Method smallest, which takes three integers x, y and z and returns an integer.
   c) Method instructions, which does not take any arguments and does not return a value. [*Note*: Such methods are commonly used to display instructions to a user.]
   d) Method intToFloat, which takes an integer argument number and returns a floating-point result.

6.5   Find the error in each of the following program segments. Explain how to correct the error.
   a) ```
      int g() {
          System.out.println("Inside method g");
          int h() {
              System.out.println("Inside method h");
          }
      }
      ```
   b) ```
      int sum( int x, int y ) {
          int result;
          result = x + y;
      }
      ```
   c) ```
      int sum(int n) {
          if (n == 0)
              return 0;
          else
              n + sum(n - 1);
      }
      ```
   d) ```
      void f( float a ); {
          float a;
          System.out.println( a );
      }
      ```

```
e) void product() {
     int a = 6, b = 5, c = 4, result;
     result = a * b * c;
     System.out.println( "Result is " + result );
     return result;
}
```

6.6   Write a complete Java applet to prompt the user for the double radius of a sphere, and call method sphereVolume to calculate and display the volume of that sphere, using the assignment

volume = (4.0 / 3.0) * Math.PI * Math.pow(radius, 3)

The user should input the radius through a JTextField.

ANSWERS TO SELF-REVIEW EXERCISES

6.1   a) method call. b) local variable. c) return. d) void. e) scope. f) return; or return *expression*; or encountering the closing right brace of a method. g) init. h) Math.random. i) start. j) paint. k) repaint. l) stop. m) recursive. n) base. o) overloading. p) final.

6.2   a) class body. b) block that defines method cube's body. c) class body. d) class body. e) block that defines method paint's body.

6.3   The following solution demonstrates the Math class methods in Fig. 6.2:

```
1   // Exercise 6.3: MathTest.java
2   // Testing the Math class methods.
3
4   public class MathTest {
5
6      public static void main( String args[] )
7      {
8         System.out.println( "Math.abs( 23.7 ) = " + Math.abs( 23.7 ) );
9         System.out.println( "Math.abs( 0.0 ) = " + Math.abs( 0.0 ) );
10        System.out.println( "Math.abs( -23.7 ) = " + Math.abs( -23.7 ) );
11        System.out.println( "Math.ceil( 9.2 ) = " + Math.ceil( 9.2 ) );
12        System.out.println( "Math.ceil( -9.8 ) = " + Math.ceil( -9.8 ) );
13        System.out.println( "Math.cos( 0.0 ) = " + Math.cos( 0.0 ) );
14        System.out.println( "Math.exp( 1.0 ) = " + Math.exp( 1.0 ) );
15        System.out.println( "Math.exp( 2.0 ) = " + Math.exp( 2.0 ) );
16        System.out.println( "Math.floor( 9.2 ) = " + Math.floor( 9.2 ) );
17        System.out.println( "Math.floor( -9.8 ) = " + Math.floor( -9.8 ) );
18        System.out.println( "Math.log( Math.E ) = " +
19           Math.log( Math.E ) );
20        System.out.println( "Math.log( Math.E * Math.E ) = " +
21           Math.log( Math.E * Math.E ) );
22        System.out.println( "Math.max( 2.3, 12.7 ) = " +
23           Math.max( 2.3, 12.7 ) );
24        System.out.println( "Math.max( -2.3, -12.7 ) = " +
25           Math.max( -2.3, -12.7 ) );
26        System.out.println( "Math.min( 2.3, 12.7 ) = " +
27           Math.min( 2.3, 12.7 ) );
28        System.out.println( "Math.min( -2.3, -12.7 ) = " +
29           Math.min( -2.3, -12.7 ) );
30        System.out.println( "Math.pow( 2.0, 7.0 ) = " +
31           Math.pow( 2.0, 7.0 ) );
32        System.out.println( "Math.pow( 9.0, 0.5 ) = " +
33           Math.pow( 9.0, 0.5 ) );
34        System.out.println( "M''ath.sin( 0.0 ) = " + Math.sin( 0.0 ) );
```

```
35      System.out.println( "Math.sqrt( 900.0 ) = " + Math.sqrt( 900.0 ) );
36      System.out.println( "Math.sqrt( 9.0 ) = " + Math.sqrt( 9.0 ) );
37      System.out.println( "Math.tan( 0.0 ) = " + Math.tan( 0.0 ) );
38
39    } // end main
40
41  } // end class MathTest
```

```
Math.abs( 23.7 ) = 23.7
Math.abs( 0.0 ) = 0.0
Math.abs( -23.7 ) = 23.7
Math.ceil( 9.2 ) = 10.0
Math.ceil( -9.8 ) = -9.0
Math.cos( 0.0 ) = 1.0
Math.exp( 1.0 ) = 2.7182818284590455
Math.exp( 2.0 ) = 7.38905609893065
Math.floor( 9.2 ) = 9.0
Math.floor( -9.8 ) = -10.0
Math.log( Math.E ) = 1.0
Math.log( Math.E * Math.E ) = 2.0
Math.max( 2.3, 12.7 ) = 12.7
Math.max( -2.3, -12.7 ) = -2.3
Math.min( 2.3, 12.7 ) = 2.3
Math.min( -2.3, -12.7 ) = -12.7
Math.pow( 2.0, 7.0 ) = 128.0
Math.pow( 9.0, 0.5 ) = 3.0
Math.sin( 0.0 ) = 0.0
Math.sqrt( 900.0 ) = 30.0
Math.sqrt( 9.0 ) = 3.0
Math.tan( 0.0 ) = 0.0
```

6.4   a)   `double hypotenuse( double side1, double side2 )`
          b)   `int smallest( int x, int y, int z )`
          c)   `void instructions()`
          d)   `float intToFloat( int number )`

6.5   a)   Error: Method h is declared within method g.
            Correction: Move the declaration of h outside the declaration of g.
          b)   Error: The method is supposed to return an integer, but does not.
            Correction: Delete the variable `result`, and place the statement
              `return x + y;`
            in the method, or add the following statement at the end of the method body:
              `return result;`
          c)   Error: The result of `n + sum( n - 1 )` is not returned by this recursive method, resulting
            in a syntax error.
            Correction: Rewrite the statement in the `else` clause as
              `return n + sum( n - 1 );`
          d)   Error: Both the semicolon after the right parenthesis of the parameter list is incorrect and
            the parameter a should not be redeclared in the method.
            Correction: Delete the semicolon after the right parenthesis of the parameter list, and de-
            lete the declaration `float a;`.
          e)   Error: The method returns a value when it is not supposed to.
            Correction: Change the return type from `void` to `int`.

6.6   The following solution calculates the volume of a sphere, using the radius entered by the user:

```java
// Exercise 6.6: SphereTest.java
// Calculate the volume of a sphere.
import java.awt.*;
import java.awt.event.*;

import javax.swing.*;

public class SphereTest extends JApplet implements ActionListener {
    JLabel promptLabel;
    JTextField inputField;

    // create GUI
    public void init()
    {
        Container container = getContentPane();
        container.setLayout( new FlowLayout() );

        promptLabel = new JLabel( "Enter sphere radius: " );
        inputField = new JTextField( 10 );
        inputField.addActionListener( this );
        container.add( promptLabel );
        container.add( inputField );

    } // end method init

    // calculate sphere volume when user presses Enter in inputField
    public void actionPerformed( ActionEvent actionEvent )
    {
        double radius =
            Double.parseDouble( actionEvent.getActionCommand() );

        showStatus( "Volume is " + sphereVolume( radius ) );

    } // end method actionPerformed

    // calculate and return sphere volume
    public double sphereVolume( double radius )
    {
        double volume = ( 4.0 / 3.0 ) * Math.PI * Math.pow( radius, 3 );

        return volume;

    } // end method sphereVolume

} // end class SphereTest
```

Applet Viewer: SphereTest.class

Applet

Enter sphere radius: 4

Volume is 268.082573106329

EXERCISES

6.7   What is the value of x after each of the following statements is executed?

a) x = Math.abs(7.5);

b) x = Math.floor(7.5);
c) x = Math.abs(0.0);
d) x = Math.ceil(0.0);
e) x = Math.abs(-6.4);
f) x = Math.ceil(-6.4);
g) x = Math.ceil(-Math.abs(-8 + Math.floor(-5.5)));

6.8   A parking garage charges a $2.00 minimum fee to park for up to three hours. The garage charges an additional $0.50 per hour for each hour *or part thereof* in excess of three hours. The maximum charge for any given 24-hour period is $10.00. Assume that no car parks for longer than 24 hours at a time. Write an applet that calculates and displays the parking charges for each customer who parked in the garage yesterday. You should enter in a JTextField the hours parked for each customer. The program should display the charge for the current customer and should calculate and display the running total of yesterday's receipts. The program should use the method calculate-Charges to determine the charge for each customer.

6.9   An application of method Math.floor is rounding a value to the nearest integer. The statement

    y = Math.floor(x + 0.5);

will round the number x to the nearest integer and assign the result to y. Write an applet that reads double values and uses the preceding statement to round each of the numbers to the nearest integer. For each number processed, display both the original number and the rounded number.

6.10   Math.floor may be used to round a number to a specific decimal place. The statement

    y = Math.floor(x * 10 + 0.5) / 10;

rounds x to the tenths position (i.e., the first position to the right of the decimal point). The statement

    y = Math.floor(x * 100 + 0.5) / 100;

rounds x to the hundredths position (i.e., the second position to the right of the decimal point). Write an applet that defines four methods for rounding a number x in various ways:
a) roundToInteger(number)
b) roundToTenths(number)
c) roundToHundredths(number)
d) roundToThousandths(number)

For each value read, your program should display the original value, the number rounded to the nearest integer, the number rounded to the nearest tenth, the number rounded to the nearest hundredth and the number rounded to the nearest thousandth.

6.11   Answer each of the following questions:
a) What does it mean to choose numbers "at random?"
b) Why is the Math.random method useful for simulating games of chance?
c) Why is it often necessary to scale or shift the values produced by Math.random?
d) Why is computerized simulation of real-world situations a useful technique?

6.12   Write statements that assign random integers to the variable n in the following ranges:
a) $1 \leq n \leq 2$
b) $1 \leq n \leq 100$
c) $0 \leq n \leq 9$
d) $1000 \leq n \leq 1112$
e) $-1 \leq n \leq 1$
f) $-3 \leq n \leq 11$

6.13   For each of the following sets of integers, write a single statement that will print a number at random from the set:

 a) 2, 4, 6, 8, 10.
 b) 3, 5, 7, 9, 11.
 c) 6, 10, 14, 18, 22.

6.14   Write a method integerPower(base, exponent) that returns the value of

$$base^{\ exponent}$$

For example, integerPower(3, 4) calculates 3^4 (or 3 * 3 * 3 * 3). Assume that exponent is a positive, nonzero integer and that base is an integer. Method integerPower should use a for or while loop to control the calculation. Do not use any math-library methods. Incorporate this method into an applet that reads integer values for base and exponent from JTextField objects and performs the calculation with the integerPower method. [*Note*: Register for event handling on only the second JTextField. The user should interact with the program by typing numbers in both JTextFields, but pressing *Enter* only in the second JTextField.]

6.15   Define a method hypotenuse that calculates the length of the hypotenuse of a right triangle when the lengths of the other two sides are given. (Use the sample data in Fig. 6.21.) The method should take two arguments of type double and return the hypotenuse as a double. Incorporate this method into an applet that reads values for side1 and side2 from JTextField objects and performs the calculation with the hypotenuse method. Determine the length of the hypotenuse for each of the triangles in Fig. 6.21. [*Note*: Register for event handling on only the second JTextField. The user should interact with the program by typing numbers in both JTextFields, but pressing *Enter* only in the second JTextField.]

6.16   Write a method multiple that determines, for a pair of integers, whether the second integer is a multiple of the first. The method should take two integer arguments and return true if the second is a multiple of the first and false otherwise. Incorporate this method into an applet that inputs a series of pairs of integers (one pair at a time, using JTextFields). [*Note:* Register for event handling on only the second JTextField. The user should interact with the program by typing numbers in both JTextFields, but pressing *Enter* only in the second JTextField.]

6.17   Write a method isEven that uses the remainder operator (%) to determine whether an integer is even. The method should take an integer argument and return true if the integer is even and false otherwise. Incorporate this method into an applet that inputs a sequence of integers (one at a time, using a JTextField).

6.18   Write a method squareOfAsterisks that displays a solid square (the same number of rows and columns) of asterisks whose side is specified in integer parameter side. For example, if side is 4, the method displays the pattern of asterisks at the top of the next page.

Triangle	Side 1	Side 2
1	3.0	4.0
2	5.0	12.0
3	8.0	15.0

Fig. 6.21   Values for the sides of triangles in Exercise 6.15.

```
****
****
****
****
```

Incorporate this method into an applet that reads an integer value for side from the user and performs the drawing with the squareOfAsterisks method. Note that this method should be called from the applet's paint method and should be passed the Graphics object from paint.

6.19   Modify the method created in Exercise 6.18 to form the square out of whatever character is contained in character parameter fillCharacter. Thus, if side is 5 and fillCharacter is "#", the method should print

```
#####
#####
#####
#####
#####
```

6.20   Write an applet that uses a method circleArea to prompt the user for the radius of a circle and to calculate and print the area of that circle.

6.21   Modify the program of Exercise 6.18 to draw a solid square with the fillRect method of the Graphics class. Method fillRect requires four arguments: x-coordinate, y-coordinate, width and height. Allow the user to input the coordinates at which the square should appear and the length of the side.

6.22   Write program segments that accomplish each of the following tasks:
   a) Calculate the integer part of the quotient when integer a is divided by integer b.
   b) Calculate the integer remainder when integer a is divided by integer b.
   c) Use the program pieces developed in parts (a) and (b) to write a method displayDigits that receives an integer between 1 and 99999 and displays it as a sequence of digits, separating each pair of digits by two spaces. For example, the integer 4562 should appear as

```
4   5   6   2
```

   d) Incorporate the method developed in part (c) into an applet that inputs an integer from a textfield and calls displayDigits by passing the method the integer entered. Display the results in a second textfield.

6.23   Implement the following integer methods:
   a) Method celsius returns the Celsius equivalent of a Fahrenheit temperature, using the calculation

```
C = 5.0 / 9.0 * ( F - 32 );
```

   b) Method fahrenheit returns the Fahrenheit equivalent of a Celsius temperature, using the calculation

```
F = 9.0 / 5.0 * C + 32;
```

   c) Use the methods from parts (a) and (b) to write an applet that enables the user either to enter a Fahrenheit temperature and display the Celsius equivalent or to enter a Celsius temperature and display the Fahrenheit equivalent.

[*Note*: This applet will require two JTextField objects that have registered action events. When actionPerformed is called, the ActionEvent parameter has method getSource() to determine the GUI component with which the user interacted. Your `actionPerformed` method should contain an `if...else` statement of the form

```
if ( actionEvent.getSource() == input1 ) {
    // process input1 interaction here
}
else {  // e.getSource() == input2
    // process input2 interaction here
}
```

where `input1` and `input2` are `JTextField` references.]

6.24   Write a method `minimum3` that returns the smallest of three floating-point numbers. Use the `Math.min` method to implement `minimum3`. Incorporate the method into an applet that reads three values from the user and determines the smallest value. Display the result in the status bar.

6.25   An integer number is said to be a *perfect number* if its factors, including 1 (but not the number itself), sum to the number. For example, 6 is a perfect number, because 6 = 1 + 2 + 3. Write a method `perfect` that determines whether parameter `number` is a perfect number. Use this method in an applet that determines and displays all the perfect numbers between 1 and 1000. Print the factors of each perfect number to confirm that the number is indeed perfect. Challenge the computing power of your computer by testing numbers much larger than 1000. Display the results in a `JTextArea` that has scrolling functionality.

6.26   An integer is said to be *prime* if it is divisible only by 1 and itself. For example, 2, 3, 5 and 7 are prime, but 4, 6, 8 and 9 are not.
   a) Write a method that determines whether a number is prime.
   b) Use this method in an applet that determines and prints all the prime numbers less than 10,000. How many numbers up to 10,000 do you have to test to ensure that you have found all the primes? Display the results in a `JTextArea` that has scrolling functionality.
   c) Initially, you might think that $n/2$ is the upper limit for which you must test to see whether a number is prime, but you need only go as high as the square root of n. Why? Rewrite the program, and run it both ways. Estimate the performance improvement.

6.27   Write a method that takes an integer value and returns the number with its digits reversed. For example, given the number 7631, the method should return 1367. Incorporate the method into an applet that reads a value from the user. Display the result of the method in the status bar.

6.28   The *greatest common divisor* (GCD) of two integers is the largest integer that evenly divides each of the two numbers. Write a method `gcd` that returns the greatest common divisor of two integers. Incorporate the method into an applet that reads two values from the user. Display the result of the method in the status bar.

6.29   Write a method `qualityPoints` that inputs a student's average and returns 4 if the student's average is 90–100, 3 if the average is 80–89, 2 if the average is 70–79, 1 if the average is 60–69 and 0 if the average is lower than 60. Incorporate the method into an applet that reads a value from the user. Display the result of the method in the status bar.

6.30   Write an applet that simulates coin tossing. Let the program toss a coin each time the user presses the "`Toss`" button. Count the number of times each side of the coin appears. Display the results. The program should call a separate method `flip` that takes no arguments and returns `false` for tails and `true` for heads. [*Note*: If the program realistically simulates coin tossing, each side of the coin should appear approximately half the time.]

6.31   Computers are playing an increasing role in education. Write a program that will help an elementary school student learn multiplication. Use `Math.random` to produce two positive one-digit integers. The program should then display a question in the status bar, such as

```
How much is 6 times 7?
```

The student then types the answer into a `JTextField`. Next, the program checks the student's answer. If it is correct, draw the string "`Very good!`" on the applet and ask another multiplication question. If the answer is wrong, draw the string "`No. Please try again.`" on the applet and let the student try the same question repeatedly until the student finally gets it right. A separate method should be used to generate each new question. This method should be called once when the applet begins execution and each time the user answers the question correctly. All drawing on the applet should be performed by the `paint` method.

6.32　The use of computers in education is referred to as *computer-assisted instruction (CAI)*. One problem that develops in CAI environments is student fatigue. This problem can be eliminated by varying the computer's dialogue to hold the student's attention. Modify the program of Exercise 6.31 so that the various comments are printed for each correct answer and each incorrect answer as follows:

Responses to a correct answer:

```
Very good!
Excellent!
Nice work!
Keep up the good work!
```

Responses to an incorrect answer:

```
No. Please try again.
Wrong. Try once more.
Don't give up!
No. Keep trying.
```

Use random-number generation to choose a number from 1 to 4 that will be used to select an appropriate response to each answer. Use a `switch` statement in the `paint` method to issue the responses.

6.33　More sophisticated computer-assisted instruction systems monitor the student's performance over a period of time. The decision to begin a new topic is often based on the student's success with previous topics. Modify the program of Exercise 6.32 to count the number of correct and incorrect responses typed by the student. After the student types 10 answers, your program should calculate the percentage of correct responses. If the percentage is lower than 75%, print `Please ask your instructor for extra help` and reset the program so another student can try it.

6.34　Write an applet that plays "guess the number" as follows: Your program chooses the number to be guessed by selecting a random integer in the range 1 to 1000. The applet displays the prompt `Guess a number between 1 and 1000` next to a `JTextField`. The player types a first guess into the `JTextField` and presses the *Enter* key. If the player's guess is incorrect, your program should display `Too high. Try again.` or `Too low. Try again.` in the status bar to help the player "zero in" on the correct answer. The program should clear the `JTextField` so the user can enter the next guess. When the user enters the correct answer, display `Congratulations. You guessed the number!` in the status bar, and clear the `JTextField` so the user can play again. [*Note*: The guessing technique employed in this problem is similar to a *binary search*.]

6.35　Modify the program of Exercise 6.34 to count the number of guesses the player makes. If the number is 10 or fewer, print `Either you know the secret or you got lucky!` If the player guesses the number in 10 tries, print `Aha! You know the secret!` If the player makes more than 10 guesses, print `You should be able to do better!` Why should it take no more than 10 guesses? Well, with each "good guess," the player should be able to eliminate half of the numbers. Now show why any number from 1 to 1000 can be guessed in 10 or fewer tries.

6.36   Write a recursive method power(base, exponent) that, when called, returns

$$base^{\,exponent}$$

For example, power(3, 4) = 3 * 3 * 3 * 3. Assume that exponent is an integer greater than or equal to 1. (*Hint*: The recursion step should use the relationship

$$base^{\,exponent} = base \cdot base^{\,exponent-1}$$

and the terminating condition occurs when exponent is equal to 1, because

$$base^1 = base$$

Incorporate this method into an applet that enables the user to enter the base and exponent.)

6.37   (*Towers of Hanoi*) Every budding computer scientist must grapple with certain classic problems, and the *Towers of Hanoi* (see Fig. 6.22) is one of the most famous. Legend has it that in a temple in the Far East, priests are attempting to move a stack of disks from one peg to another. The initial stack has 64 disks threaded onto one peg and arranged from bottom to top by decreasing size. The priests are attempting to move the stack from this peg to a second peg under the constraints that exactly one disk is moved at a time and at no time may a larger disk be placed above a smaller disk. A third peg is available for temporarily holding disks. Supposedly, the world will end when the priests complete their task, so there is little incentive for us to facilitate their efforts.

Let us assume that the priests are attempting to move the disks from peg 1 to peg 3. We wish to develop an algorithm that will print the precise sequence of peg-to-peg disk transfers.

If we were to approach this problem with conventional methods, we would rapidly find ourselves hopelessly knotted up in managing the disks. Instead, if we attack the problem with recursion in mind, it immediately becomes tractable. Moving *n* disks can be viewed in terms of moving only *n* – 1 disks (hence the recursion) as follows:

a)   Move *n* – 1 disks from peg 1 to peg 2, using peg 3 as a temporary holding area.

b)   Move the last disk (the largest) from peg 1 to peg 3.

c)   Move the *n* – 1 disks from peg 2 to peg 3, using peg 1 as a temporary holding area.

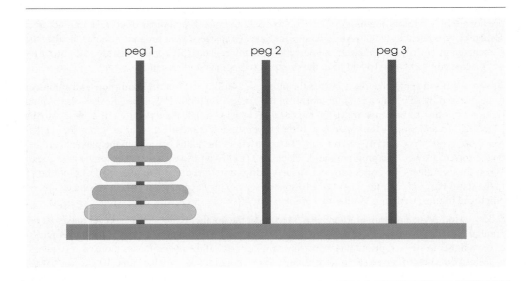

Fig. 6.22   The Towers of Hanoi for the case with four disks.

The process ends when the last task involves moving $n = 1$ disk (i.e., the base case). This task is accomplished by simply moving the disk, without the need for a temporary holding area.

Write an applet to solve the Towers of Hanoi problem. Allow the user to enter the number of disks in a JTextField. Use a recursive tower method with four parameters:

a) the number of disks to be moved,
b) the peg on which these disks are initially threaded,
c) the peg to which this stack of disks is to be moved, and
d) the peg to be used as a temporary holding area.

Your program should display in a JTextArea with scrolling functionality the precise instructions it will take to move the disks from the starting peg to the destination peg. For example, to move a stack of three disks from peg 1 to peg 3, your program should print the following series of moves:

```
1  →  3  (This notation means "Move one disk from peg 1 to peg 3.")
1  →  2
3  →  2
1  →  3
2  →  1
2  →  3
1  →  3
```

6.38   Any program that can be implemented recursively can be implemented iteratively, although sometimes with more difficulty and less clarity. Try writing an iterative version of the Towers of Hanoi. If you succeed, compare your iterative version with the recursive version you developed in Exercise 6.37. Investigate issues of performance, clarity and your ability to demonstrate the correctness of the programs.

6.39   (*Visualizing Recursion*) It is interesting to watch recursion "in action." Modify the factorial method of Fig. 6.15 to print its local variable and recursive-call parameter. For each recursive call, display the outputs on a separate line, and add a level of indentation. Do your utmost to make the outputs clear, interesting and meaningful. Your goal here is to design and implement an output format that helps a person understand recursion better. You may want to add such display capabilities to the many other recursion examples and exercises throughout the text.

6.40   The greatest common divisor of integers x and y is the largest integer that evenly divides into both x and y. Write a recursive method gcd that returns the greatest common divisor of x and y. The gcd of x and y is defined recursively as follows: If y is equal to 0, then gcd(x, y) is x; otherwise, gcd(x, y) is gcd(y, x % y), where % is the remainder operator. Use this method to replace the one you wrote in the applet of Exercise 6.28.

6.41   Exercise 6.31 through Exercise 6.33 developed a computer-assisted instruction program to teach an elementary school student multiplication. Perform the following enhancements:

a) Modify the program to allow the user to enter a school grade-level capability. A grade level of 1 means that the program should use only single-digit numbers in the problems, a grade level of 2 means that the program should use numbers as large as two digits, etc.
b) Modify the program to allow the user to pick the type of arithmetic problems he or she wishes to study. An option of 1 means addition problems only, 2 means subtraction problems only, 3 means multiplication problems only, 4 means division problems only and 5 means a random mixture of problems of all these types.

6.42   Write method distance, to calculate the distance between two points $(x1, y1)$ and $(x2, y2)$. All numbers and return values should be of type double. Incorporate this method into an applet that enables the user to enter the coordinates of the points.

6.43   What does the following method do?

```
// Parameter b must be a positive
// integer to prevent infinite recursion
public int mystery( int a, int b )
{
   if ( b == 1 )
      return a;
   else
      return a + mystery( a, b - 1 );
}
```

6.44   After you determine what the program in Exercise 6.43 does, modify the method to operate properly following the removal of the restriction that the second argument must be nonnegative. Also, incorporate the method into an applet that enables the user to enter two integers. Test the method.

6.45   Find the error in the following recursive method, and explain how to correct it:

```
public int sum( int n )
{
   if ( n == 0 )
      return 0;
   else
      return n + sum( n );
}
```

6.46   Modify the craps program of Fig. 6.9 to allow wagering. Initialize variable bankBalance to 1000 dollars. Prompt the player to enter a wager. Check that wager is less than or equal to bankBalance, and if not, have the user reenter wager until a valid wager is entered. After a correct wager is entered, run one game of craps. If the player wins, increase bankBalance by wager and print the new bankBalance. If the player loses, decrease bankBalance by wager, print the new bankBalance, check whether bankBalance has become zero and, if so, print the message "Sorry. You busted!" As the game progresses, print various messages to create some "chatter," such as "Oh, you're going for broke, huh?" or "Aw c'mon, take a chance!" or "You're up big. Now's the time to cash in your chips!". Implement the "chatter" as a separate method that randomly chooses the string to display.

7

Arrays

Objectives

- To introduce the array data structure.
- To understand the use of arrays to store, sort and search lists and tables of values.
- To understand how to declare an array, initialize an array and refer to individual elements of an array.
- To be able to pass arrays to methods.
- To be able to declare and manipulate multidimensional arrays.

With sobs and tears he sorted out
Those of the largest size …
Lewis Carroll

Attempt the end, and never stand to doubt;
Nothing's so hard, but search will find it out.
Robert Herrick

Now go, write it before them in a table,
and note it in a book.
Isaiah 30:8

'Tis in my memory lock'd,
And you yourself shall keep the key of it.
William Shakespeare

7.1 Introduction

This chapter introduces the important topic of *data structures*—collections of related data items. *Arrays* are data structures consisting of related data items of the same type. Arrays are fixed-length entities—they remain the same length once they are created, although an array reference may be reassigned to a new array of a different length. Chapter 20, Data Structures, introduces dynamic data structures, such as lists, queues, stacks and trees, that can grow and shrink as programs execute. Chapter 21, Java Utilities Package and Bit Manipulation, discusses class `Vector`, which is an array-like class whose objects can grow and shrink in response to a Java program's changing storage requirements. Chapter 22, Collections, introduces Java's predefined data structures that enable the programmer to use existing data structures for lists, queues, stacks and trees. The Collections API also provides class `Arrays`, which provides a set of utility methods for array manipulation.

7.2 Arrays

In Java, an array is a group of variables (called *elements* or *components*) containing values that all have the same type. Recall from Section 3.5 that types in Java are divided into two categories—*primitive types* and *reference types*. Java arrays are objects, so they are considered reference types. The elements of a Java array can be either primitive types or reference types (including arrays, as we will see in Section 7.9). To refer to a particular element in an array, we specify the name of the reference to the array and the position number of the element in the array. The position number of the element is formally called the element's *index* or *subscript*.

Figure 7.1 presents a logical representation of an integer array called c. This array contains 12 elements (i.e., variables). A program refers to any one of these elements with an *array-access expression* that includes the name of the array followed by the index of the particular element in *square brackets* (`[]`). The first element in every array has *index zero*

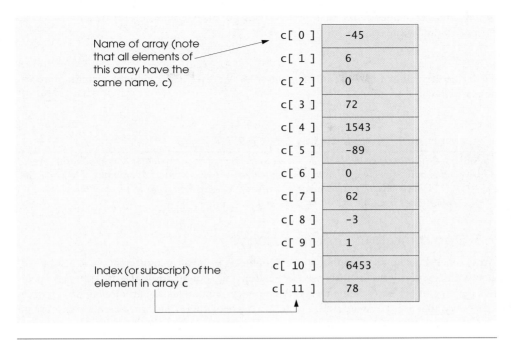

Fig. 7.1   A 12-element array.

(sometimes called the *zeroth element*). Thus, the first element of array c is c[0], the second element of array c is c[1], the seventh element of array c is c[6] and, in general, the *i*th element of array c is c[i - 1]. Array names follow the same conventions as do other variable names.

An index must be a positive integer or an integer expression that can be promoted to an int. If a program uses an expression as an index, the program evaluates the expression to determine the index. For example, if we assume that variable a is 5 and that variable b is 6, then the statement

```
c[ a + b ] += 2;
```

adds 2 to array element c[11]. Note that an indexed array name is an array-access expression. Such expressions can be used on the left side of an assignment to place a new value into an array element.

 Common Programming Error 7.1

Using a value of type long as an array index results in a compilation error.

Let us examine array c in Fig. 7.1 more closely. The *name* of the reference to the array is c. Every array object in Java *knows* its own length and maintains this information in a field of the array object called *length*. The expression c.length accesses array c's length field to determine the length of the array. This array's 12 elements are referred to as c[0], c[1], c[2], ..., c[11]. The *value* of c[0] is -45, the value of c[1] is 6, the value of c[2] is 0, the value of c[7] is 62 and the value of c[11] is 78. To calculate the sum

of the values contained in the first three elements of array c and store the result in variable
sum, we would write

    sum = c[0] + c[1] + c[2];

To divide the value of the seventh element of array c by 2 and assign the result to the variable x, we would write

    x = c[6] / 2;

Common Programming Error 7.2

*Note the difference between the "seventh element of the array" and "array element seven."
Array indices begin at 0, so the "seventh element of the array" has an index of 6, while "array element seven" has an index of 7 and is actually the eighth element of the array. This
confusion is a source of "off-by-one" errors.*

7.3 Declaring and Creating Arrays

Array objects occupy space in memory. All objects in Java (including arrays) must be created with keyword new (as discussed in Section 4.9). For an array, the programmer specifies the type of the array elements and the number of elements as part of an *array-creation
expression* that uses keyword new. The following declaration and array-creation expression
create 12 elements for the integer array c in Fig. 7.1:

    int c[] = new int[12];

This task also can be performed in two steps as follows:

    int c[];   // declares the array variable
    c = new int[12];   // creates the array

When creating an array, each element of the array receives a default value—zero for the
numeric primitive-type elements, false for boolean elements and null for references
(any nonprimitive type).

Common Programming Error 7.3

*Unlike array declarations in several other programming languages (such as C and C++),
Java array declarations do not specify the number of array elements in the square brackets
after the array name (e.g., int c[12];); otherwise, a syntax error occurs.*

A program can create several arrays in a single declaration. The following String
array declaration reserves 100 elements for b and 27 elements for x:

    String b[] = new String[100], x[] = new String[27];

When declaring an array, the type of the array and the square brackets can be combined
at the beginning of the declaration to indicate that all identifiers in the declaration are array
references. For example,

    double[] array1, array2;

declares array1 and array2 as references to arrays of double values. As shown previously, the declaration and creation of the array can be combined in the declaration. The following declaration reserves 10 elements for array1 and 20 elements for array2:

```
double[] array1 = new double[ 10 ], array2 = new double[ 20 ];
```

A program can declare arrays of any type. Every element of a primitive-type array is a variable of the array's declared type. For example, every element of an `int` array is an `int` variable. In an array of a reference type, every element of the array is a reference to an object of the array's declared type. For example, every element of a `String` array is a reference to a `String` object.

7.4 Examples Using Arrays

This section presents several examples that demonstrate declaring arrays, creating arrays, initializing arrays and manipulating array elements. For simplicity, the examples in this section use arrays that contain elements of type `int`. Please remember that programs can create arrays of any type.

Creating and Initializing an Array

The application of Fig. 7.2 uses keyword `new` to create an array of 10 `int` elements, which are initially zero (the default for `int` variables). The program displays the array elements in tabular format in an object of class `JTextArea`.

```java
1   // Fig. 7.2: InitArray.java
2   // Creating an array.
3   import javax.swing.*;
4
5   public class InitArray {
6
7      public static void main( String args[] )
8      {
9         int array[];              // declare reference to an array
10
11        array = new int[ 10 ];  // create array
12
13        String output = "Index\tValue\n";
14
15        // append each array element's value to String output
16        for ( int counter = 0; counter < array.length; counter++ )
17           output += counter + "\t" + array[ counter ] + "\n";
18
19        JTextArea outputArea = new JTextArea();
20        outputArea.setText( output );
21
22        JOptionPane.showMessageDialog( null, outputArea,
23           "Initializing an Array of int Values",
24           JOptionPane.INFORMATION_MESSAGE );
25
26        System.exit( 0 );
27
28     } // end main
29
30  } // end class InitArray
```

Fig. 7.2   Initializing the elements of an array to zero. (Part 1 of 2.)

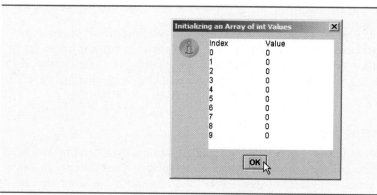

Fig. 7.2   Initializing the elements of an array to zero. (Part 2 of 2.)

Line 9 declares `array`—a reference capable of referring to an array of `int` elements. Line 11 creates the array and assigns a reference to the resulting array object to reference `array`. The program builds its output in the `String` called `output` that will be displayed in a `JTextArea` on a message dialog. Line 13 assigns `output` the headings for the columns displayed by the program. The first column represents the index for each array element, and the second column represents the value of each array element.

Lines 16–17 use a `for` statement to append the index number (represented by `counter`) and value of each array element (represented by `array[ counter ]`) to `output`. Note that the loop uses zero-based counting (remember, index values start at 0), so that the loop can access every array element. Also, in the `for`'s condition, note the use of the expression `array.length` to determine the length of the array. In this example, the length of the array is 10, so the loop continues executing as long as the value of control variable `counter` is less than 10. For a 10-element array, the index values are 0 through 9, so using the less-than operator guarantees that the loop does not attempt to access an element beyond the end of the array.

Using an Array Initializer

As an alternative to an array-creation expression, a program can create an array and initialize its elements with an *array initializer*, which is a comma-separated list of expressions (sometimes called an *initializer list*) enclosed in braces ({ and }). In this case, the array length is determined by the number of elements in the initializer list. For example, the declaration

```
int n[] = { 10, 20, 30, 40, 50 };
```

creates a five-element array with index values 0, 1, 2, 3 and 4. This declaration does not require `new` to create the array object. When the compiler encounters an array declaration that includes an initializer list, the compiler counts the number of initializers in the list to determine the appropriate number of array elements.

The application of Fig. 7.3 initializes an integer array with 10 values (line 11) and displays the array in tabular format in a `JTextArea` on a message dialog. The code for displaying the array elements (lines 13–24) is identical to that of Fig. 7.2.

```
1    // Fig. 7.3: InitArray.java
2    // Initializing an array with a declaration.
3    import javax.swing.*;
4
5    public class InitArray {
6
7       public static void main( String args[] )
8       {
9          // array initializer specifies number of elements and
10         // value for each element
11         int array[] = { 32, 27, 64, 18, 95, 14, 90, 70, 60, 37 };
12
13         String output = "Index\tValue\n";
14
15         // append each array element's value to String output
16         for ( int counter = 0; counter < array.length; counter++ )
17            output += counter + "\t" + array[ counter ] + "\n";
18
19         JTextArea outputArea = new JTextArea();
20         outputArea.setText( output );
21
22         JOptionPane.showMessageDialog( null, outputArea,
23            "Initializing an Array with a Declaration",
24            JOptionPane.INFORMATION_MESSAGE );
25
26         System.exit( 0 );
27
28      } // end main
29
30   } // end class InitArray
```

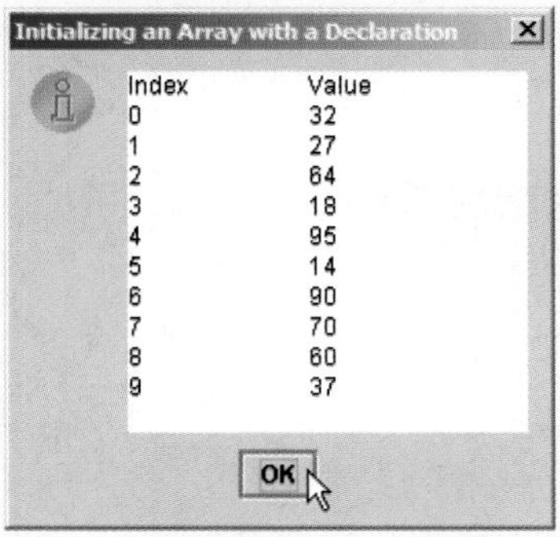

Fig. 7.3   Initializing the elements of an array with a declaration.

Calculating the Value to Store in Each Array Element

Some programs calculate the value stored in each array element. The application of Fig. 7.4 creates a 10-element array and assigns each element on of the even integers from 2 to 20 (2, 4, 6, ..., 20). Then the program displays the array in tabular format. The for statement at lines 15–16 generates an array element's value by multiplying the current value of the for loop's control variable counter by 2 and adding 2.

```
1   // Fig. 7.4: InitArray.java
2   // Initialize array with the even integers from 2 to 20.
3   import javax.swing.*;
4
5   public class InitArray {
6
7      public static void main( String args[] )
8      {
9         final int ARRAY_LENGTH = 10;     // constant
10        int array[];                     // reference to int array
11
12        array = new int[ ARRAY_LENGTH ];  // create array
13
14        // calculate value for each array element
15        for ( int counter = 0; counter < array.length; counter++ )
16           array[ counter ] = 2 + 2 * counter;
17
18        String output = "Index\tValue\n";
19
20        for ( int counter = 0; counter < array.length; counter++ )
21           output += counter + "\t" + array[ counter ] + "\n";
22
23        JTextArea outputArea = new JTextArea();
24        outputArea.setText( output );
25
26        JOptionPane.showMessageDialog( null, outputArea,
27           "Initializing to Even Numbers from 2 to 20",
28           JOptionPane.INFORMATION_MESSAGE );
29
30        System.exit( 0 );
31
32     } // end main
33
34  } // end class InitArray
```

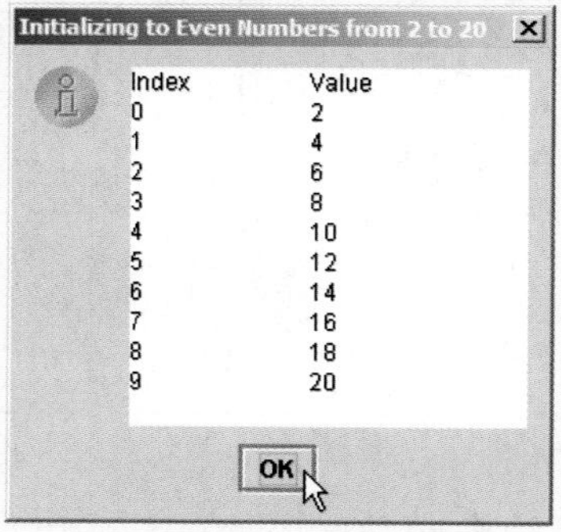

Initializing to Even Numbers from 2 to 20	
Index	Value
0	2
1	4
2	6
3	8
4	10
5	12
6	14
7	16
8	18
9	20

Fig. 7.4   Generating values to be placed into elements of an array.

Line 9 uses the final qualifier to declare constant ARRAY_LENGTH, whose value is 10. Recall from Section 6.8 that constants must be initialized before they are used and cannot be modified thereafter. If an attempt is made to modify a `final` variable after it is declared as shown on line 11, the compiler issues a message like

    cannot assign a value to final variable *variableName*

If an attempt is made to use a `final` variable before it is initialized, the compiler issues the error message

    Variable *variableName* may not have been initialized

Constants also are called *named constants* or *read-only variables*. Such variables often can make programs more readable.

 Common Programming Error 7.4

Assigning a value to a constant after the variable has been initialized results in a compilation error.

Summing the Elements of an Array

Often, the elements of an array represent a series of values to be used in a calculation. For example, if the elements of an array represent the grades for an exam, the professor may wish to total the elements of the array and use that sum to calculate the class average for the exam.

The application of Fig. 7.5 sums the values contained in the 10-element integer array. The program declares, creates and initializes the array at line 9. The `for` statement at lines 13–14 performs the calculations. [*Note:* The values supplied as array initializers normally are read into a program, rather than specified in an initializer list. For example, an applet user could enter the values through a `JTextField`, or, in an application, the values could be read from a file on disk (as discussed in Chapter 17). Reading the data into a program makes the program more flexible, because it can be used with different sets of data.]

```
1   // Fig. 7.5: SumArray.java
2   // Total the values of the elements of an array.
3   import javax.swing.*;
4
5   public class SumArray {
6
7      public static void main( String args[] )
8      {
9         int array[] = { 1, 2, 3, 4, 5, 6, 7, 8, 9, 10 };
10        int total = 0;
11
12        // add each element's value to total
13        for ( int counter = 0; counter < array.length; counter++ )
14           total += array[ counter ];
15
16        JOptionPane.showMessageDialog( null,
17           "Total of array elements: " + total,
18           "Sum the Elements of an Array",
19           JOptionPane.INFORMATION_MESSAGE );
20
```

Fig. 7.5   Computing the sum of the elements of an array. (Part 1 of 2.)

```
21            System.exit( 0 );
22
23      } // end main
24
25  } // end class SumArray
```

Sum the Elements of an Array   [x]

   ⓘ   **Total of array elements: 55**

           OK

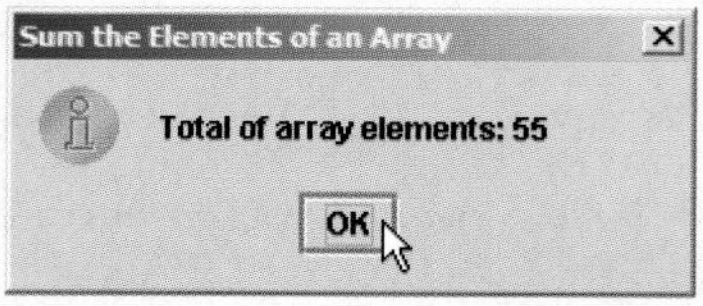

Fig. 7.5   Computing the sum of the elements of an array. (Part 2 of 2.)

Using Histograms to Display Array Data Graphically

Many programs present data to users in a graphical manner. For example, numeric values are often displayed as bars in a bar chart, or *histogram*. In such a chart, longer bars represent larger numeric values. One simple way to display numeric data graphically is with a histogram that shows each numeric value as a bar of asterisks (*).

Our next application (Fig. 7.6) reads numbers from an array and graphs the information in the form of a histogram. The program displays each value followed by a bar consisting of that many asterisks. The nested `for` statements (lines 14–21) append the bars to the string `output` that will be displayed in textarea `outputArea` on a message dialog. Note the condition of the `for` statement at line 18 (`stars < array[ counter ]`). Each time the program reaches that inner `for` statement (lines 18–19), the loop counts from 0 up to `array[ counter ]`, thus using a value in `array` to determine the final value of the control variable `stars` and the number of asterisks to display.

```java
1  // Fig. 7.6: Histogram.java
2  // Histogram printing program.
3  import javax.swing.*;
4
5  public class Histogram {
6
7     public static void main( String args[] )
8     {
9        int array[] = { 19, 3, 15, 7, 11, 9, 13, 5, 17, 1 };
10
11       String output = "Element\tValue\tHistogram";
12
13       // for each array element, output a bar in histogram
14       for ( int counter = 0; counter < array.length; counter++ ) {
15          output += "\n" + counter + "\t" + array[ counter ] + "\t";
16
17          // print bar of asterisks
18          for ( int stars = 0; stars < array[ counter ]; stars++ )
19             output += "*";
20
21       } // end outer for
```

Fig. 7.6   A program that prints histograms. (Part 1 of 2.)

```
22
23          JTextArea outputArea = new JTextArea();
24          outputArea.setText( output );
25
26          JOptionPane.showMessageDialog( null, outputArea,
27             "Histogram Printing Program", JOptionPane.INFORMATION_MESSAGE );
28
29          System.exit( 0 );
30
31       } // end main
32
33    } // end class Histogram
```

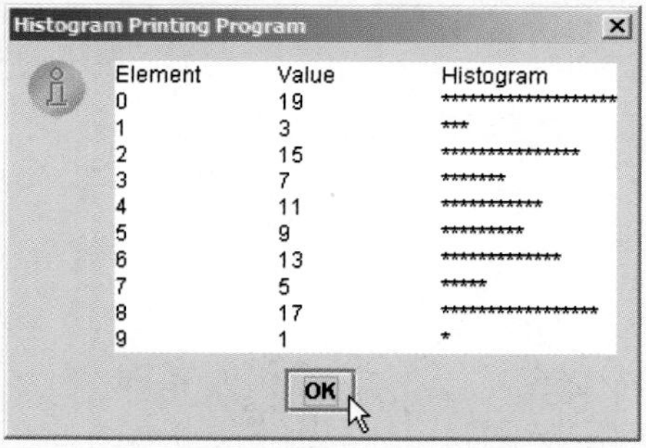

Fig. 7.6   A program that prints histograms. (Part 2 of 2.)

Using the Elements of an Array as Counters

Sometimes, programs use a series of counter variables to summarize data, such as the results of a survey. In Fig. 6.8, we used a series of counters in our die-rolling program to track the number of occurrences of each side on a six-sided die as the program rolled the die 6000 times. We also indicated that there is a more elegant technique for summarizing the die values. An array version of the application in Fig. 6.8 is shown in Fig. 7.7.

```
1   // Fig. 7.7: RollDie.java
2   // Roll a six-sided die 6000 times.
3   import javax.swing.*;
4
5   public class RollDie {
6
7      public static void main( String args[] )
8      {
9         int frequency[] = new int[ 7 ];
10
11        // roll die 6000 times; use die value as frequency index
12        for ( int roll = 1; roll <= 6000; roll++ )
13           ++frequency[ 1 + ( int ) ( Math.random() * 6 ) ];
14
15        String output = "Face\tFrequency";
16
```

Fig. 7.7   Die-rolling program using arrays instead of `switch`. (Part 1 of 2.)

```
17          // append frequencies to String output
18          for ( int face = 1; face < frequency.length; face++ )
19             output += "\n" + face + "\t" + frequency[ face ];
20
21          JTextArea outputArea = new JTextArea();
22          outputArea.setText( output );
23
24          JOptionPane.showMessageDialog( null, outputArea,
25             "Rolling a Die 6000 Times", JOptionPane.INFORMATION_MESSAGE );
26
27          System.exit( 0 );
28
29       } // end main
30
31    } // end class RollDie
```

Rolling a Die 6000 Times		
Face	Frequency	
1	973	
2	990	
3	1011	
4	993	
5	1008	
6	1025	

Fig. 7.7 Die-rolling program using arrays instead of `switch`. (Part 2 of 2.)

The program uses the seven-element array `frequency` (line 9) to count the occurrences of each side of the die. Line 13 of this program replaces lines 17–43 of Fig. 6.8. Line 13 uses the random value as the index for array `frequency` to determine which element the program should increment during each iteration of the loop. The random-number calculation on line 13 produces numbers from 1 to 6 (the values for a six-sided die), so the `frequency` array must be large enough to store six counters. However, in this program, we chose to use a seven-element array. We ignore the first array element, `frequency[ 0 ]`, because it is more logical to have the face value 1 increment `frequency[ 1 ]` than `frequency[ 0 ]`. This allows us to use each face value directly as an index for array `frequency`.

Good Programming Practice 7.1

Strive for program clarity. It is sometimes worthwhile to trade off the most efficient use of memory or processor time in favor of writing clearer programs.

Also, lines 18–19 of this program replace lines 49–52 from Fig. 6.8. We can loop through array `frequency`, so we do not have to enumerate each line of text to display in the `JTextArea` as we did in Fig. 6.8.

Using Arrays to Analyze Survey Results

Our next example uses arrays to summarize the results of data collected in a survey. Consider the following problem:

Forty students were asked to rate the quality of the food in the student cafeteria on a scale of 1 to 10 (where 1 means awful and 10 means excellent). Place the 40 responses in an integer array, and summarize the results of the poll.

The solution to this problem is a typical array-processing application (see Fig. 7.8). We wish to summarize the number of responses of each type (i.e., 1 through 10). The array responses is a 40-element integer array of the students' responses to the survey. We use an 11-element array frequency to count the number of occurrences of each response. As in Fig. 7.7, we ignore the first element (frequency[0]), because it is more logical to have the response 1 increment frequency[1] than frequency[0]. This allows us to use each response directly as the frequency array index. Each element of the array is used as a counter for one of the survey responses.

The for loop at lines 16–17 takes the responses one at a time from array responses and increments one of the 10 counters in the frequency array (frequency[1] to frequency[10]). The key statement in the loop is line 17, which increments the appropriate frequency counter, depending on the value of responses[answer].

```java
1   // Fig. 7.8: StudentPoll.java
2   // Student poll program.
3   import javax.swing.*;
4
5   public class StudentPoll {
6
7      public static void main( String args[] )
8      {
9         int responses[] = { 1, 2, 6, 4, 8, 5, 9, 7, 8, 10, 1, 6, 3, 8, 6,
10           10, 3, 8, 2, 7, 6, 5, 7, 6, 8, 6, 7, 5, 6, 6, 5, 6, 7, 5, 6,
11           4, 8, 6, 8, 10 };
12        int frequency[] = new int[ 11 ];
13
14        // for each answer, select responses element and use that value
15        // as frequency index to determine element to increment
16        for ( int answer = 0; answer < responses.length; answer++ )
17           ++frequency[ responses[ answer ] ];
18
19        String output = "Rating\tFrequency\n";
20
21        // append frequencies to String output
22        for ( int rating = 1; rating < frequency.length; rating++ )
23           output += rating + "\t" + frequency[ rating ] + "\n";
24
25        JTextArea outputArea = new JTextArea();
26        outputArea.setText( output );
27
28        JOptionPane.showMessageDialog( null, outputArea,
29           "Student Poll Program", JOptionPane.INFORMATION_MESSAGE );
30
31        System.exit( 0 );
32
33     } // end main
34
35  } // end class StudentPoll
```

Fig. 7.8   A simple student-poll analysis program. (Part 1 of 2.)

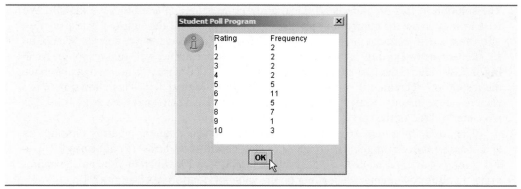

Fig. 7.8   A simple student-poll analysis program. (Part 2 of 2.)

Let's consider several iterations of the `for` loop. When control variable `answer` is 0, the value of `responses[ answer ]` is the value of the first element of array `responses` (i.e., 1), so the program interprets `++frequency[ responses[ answer ] ];` as

    `++frequency[ 1 ];`

which increments the value in array element one. To evaluate the expression, start with the value in the innermost set of square brackets (`answer`). Once you know `answer`'s value, plug that value into the expression and evaluate the next outer set of square brackets (i.e., `responses[ answer ]`). Then, use the resulting value as the index for the `frequency` array to determine which counter to increment.

When `answer` is 1, `responses[ answer ]` is the value of `responses`'s second element (2), so the program interprets `++frequency[ responses[ answer ] ];` as

    `++frequency[ 2 ];`

which increments array element two (the third element of the array).

When `answer` is 2, `responses[ answer ]` is the value of `responses`'s third element (6), so the program interprets `++frequency[ responses[ answer ] ];` as

    `++frequency[ 6 ];`

which increments array element six (the seventh element of the array), and so on. Regardless of the number of responses processed in the survey, the program requires only an 11-element array (ignoring element zero) to summarize the results, because all the response values are between 1 and 10 and the index values for an 11-element array are 0 through 10. Also, note that the summarized results are correct, because the elements of array `frequency` were initialized to zero when the array was created with `new`.

If the data had contained invalid values, such as 13, the program would have attempted to add 1 to `frequency[ 13 ]`. This element is outside the bounds of the array. In the C and C++ programming languages, such a reference would be allowed by the compiler and at execution time. The program would "walk" past the end of the array to where element number 13 would have been located had it existed and add 1 to whatever happens to be at that location in memory. This operation could potentially modify another variable in the program or even result in premature program termination. Java prevents accessing elements outside the array bounds.

Error-Prevention Tip 7.1

When a Java program executes, the Java interpreter checks array indices to ensure that they are valid (i.e., all array indices must be greater than or equal to 0 and less than the length of the array). If there is an invalid index, Java generates an exception.

Error-Prevention Tip 7.2

Exceptions indicate that an error occurred in a program. A programmer can write code to recover from an exception and continue program execution, rather than abnormally terminating the program. When a program attempts to access an element outside the array bounds, Java generates an `ArrayIndexOutOfBoundsException`.[1]

Error-Prevention Tip 7.3

When looping through an array, the array index should never go below 0 and should always be less than the length of the array. The loop-terminating condition should prevent the accessing of elements outside this range.

7.5 References and Reference Parameters

Section 7.5 demonstrates how to pass arrays and array elements as arguments to methods. First, we introduce the mechanisms used to pass arguments to methods. Two ways to pass arguments to methods in many programming languages (like C and C++) are *pass-by-value* and *pass-by-reference* (also called *call-by-value* and *call-by-reference*). When an argument is passed by value, a *copy* of the argument's value is made and passed to the called method.

Error-Prevention Tip 7.4

With pass-by-value, changes to the called method's copy do not affect the original variable's value in the caller. This prevents the accidental side effects that greatly hinder the development of correct and reliable software systems.

When an argument is passed by reference, the caller gives the called method the ability to access the caller's data directly and possibly modify that data. Pass-by-reference also improves performance by eliminating the overhead of copying large amounts of data.

Software Engineering Observation 7.1

Unlike other languages, Java does not allow the programmer to choose whether to pass each argument by value or by reference. Primitive-type variables are always passed by value. Objects are not passed to methods; rather, references to objects are passed. The references themselves are passed by value—that is, a copy of a reference is passed to a method. With a reference to an object, the method can manipulate the object directly.

Software Engineering Observation 7.2

When returning information from a method via a `return` *statement, primitive types are always returned by value (i.e., a copy is returned) and objects are always returned by reference (i.e., a reference to the object is returned).*

---

1. Exception handling is discussed in Chapter 15.

To pass a reference to an object to a method, simply specify the reference name in the method call. The corresponding method-parameter name actually refers to the original object in memory, and the original object can thus be accessed directly in the called method.

Recall from Section 7.2 that arrays are objects in Java; therefore, arrays are passed to methods by reference—a called method can access the elements of the caller's original arrays. The name of an array variable is actually a reference to an object that contains the array elements and the `length` field, a constant that indicates the number of elements in the array. In the next section, we demonstrate pass-by-value and pass-by-reference as used with arrays.

Performance Tip 7.1

Passing arrays by reference makes sense for performance reasons. If arrays were passed by value, a copy of each element would be passed. For large, frequently passed arrays, this would waste time and would consume a considerable amount of storage for the copies of the arrays.

7.6 Passing Arrays to Methods

To pass an array argument to a method, specify the name of the array without any brackets. For example, if array `hourlyTemperatures` is declared as

```
int hourlyTemperatures[] = new int[ 24 ];
```

then the method call

```
modifyArray( hourlyTemperatures );
```

passes a reference to array `hourlyTemperatures` to method `modifyArray`. In Java, every array object "knows" its own length (via the `length` field). Thus, when we pass an array object into a method, we are not required to pass the length of the array as an additional argument.

Although entire arrays and objects referred to by individual elements of reference-type arrays are passed by reference, individual array elements of primitive types are passed by value exactly as simple variables are. Such primitive values are called *scalars* or *scalar quantities.* To pass an array element to a method, use the indexed name of the array as an argument in the method call.

For a method to receive an array through a method call, the method's parameter list must specify an array parameter (or several if more than one array is to be received). For example, the method header for method `modifyArray` might be written as

```
void modifyArray( int b[] )
```

indicating that `modifyArray` expects to receive an integer array in parameter b. Since arrays are passed by reference, when the called method uses the array name b, it refers to the actual array (`hourlyTemperatures` in the preceding call) in the calling method.

The applet of Fig. 7.9 demonstrates the difference between passing an entire array and passing a primitive-type array element. Once again, we use an applet here because we have not yet defined an application that contains methods other than `main`. We are still taking advantage of some applet features, such as the automatic creation of an applet object and the calls to `init`, `start` and `paint` by the applet container. In Chapter 9, Object-Oriented Programming, we will introduce applications that execute in their own windows. At that point, we will begin to see application classes that contain several methods.

```java
1   // Fig. 7.9: PassArray.java
2   // Passing arrays and individual array elements to methods.
3   import java.awt.Container;
4   import javax.swing.*;
5
6   public class PassArray extends JApplet {
7
8      // initialize applet
9      public void init()
10     {
11        JTextArea outputArea = new JTextArea();
12        Container container = getContentPane();
13        container.add( outputArea );
14
15        int array[] = { 1, 2, 3, 4, 5 };
16
17        String output = "Effects of passing entire array by reference:\n" +
18           "The values of the original array are:\n";
19
20        // append original array elements to String output
21        for ( int counter = 0; counter < array.length; counter++ )
22           output += "   " + array[ counter ];
23
24        modifyArray( array );   // array passed by reference
25
26        output += "\n\nThe values of the modified array are:\n";
27
28        // append modified array elements to String output
29        for ( int counter = 0; counter < array.length; counter++ )
30           output += "   " + array[ counter ];
31
32        output += "\n\nEffects of passing array element by value:\n" +
33           "array[3] before modifyElement: " + array[ 3 ];
34
35        modifyElement( array[ 3 ] );  // attempt to modify array[ 3 ]
36
37        output += "\narray[3] after modifyElement: " + array[ 3 ];
38        outputArea.setText( output );
39
40     } // end method init
41
42     // multiply each element of an array by 2
43     public void modifyArray( int array2[] )
44     {
45        for ( int counter = 0; counter < array2.length; counter++ )
46           array2[ counter ] *= 2;
47     }
48
```

Fig. 7.9   Passing arrays and individual array elements to methods. (Part 1 of 2.)

```
49        // multiply argument by 2
50        public void modifyElement( int element )
51        {
52            element *= 2;
53        }
54
55    } // end class PassArray
```

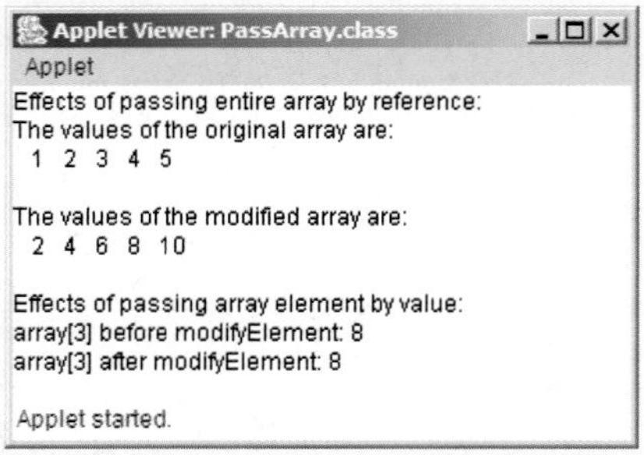

Fig. 7.9   Passing arrays and individual array elements to methods. (Part 2 of 2.)

Lines 11–13 in method `init` create the `JTextArea` called `outputArea` and attach it to the applet's content pane. The `for` statement at lines 21–22 appends the five elements of `array` (an array of `int` values) to the `String` called `output`. Line 24 invokes method `modifyArray`, passing `array` as an argument. Method `modifyArray` (lines 43–47) multiplies each element by two. To illustrate that `array`'s elements were modified, the `for` statement at lines 29–30 appends the five elements of `array` to `output` again. As the screen capture shows, method `modifyArray` did change the value of each element.

Next, the program demonstrates that individual elements of primitive-type arrays are passed to methods by value. To show the value of `array[ 3 ]` before calling method `modifyElement`, lines 32–33 append the value of `array[ 3 ]` (the fourth element with the value 8) to `output`. Line 35 invokes method `modifyElement` and passes `array[ 3 ]` as an argument. Remember that `array[ 3 ]` is actually one `int` value (8) in `array`. Also, remember that values of primitive types are passed to methods by value. Therefore, the program passes a copy of `array[ 3 ]`. Method `modifyElement` multiplies its argument by two and stores the result (16) in its parameter `element`. Method parameters, like local variables, cease to exist when the method in which they are declared completes execution. So, when method `modifyElement` terminates, the method parameter `element` is destroyed. Thus, when the program returns control to `init`, line 37 appends the unmodified value of `array[ 3 ]` (i.e., 8) to `output`. Line 38 displays the results in the `JTextArea`.

7.7 Sorting Arrays

Sorting data (i.e., placing the data into some particular order, such as ascending or descending) is one of the most important computing applications. A bank sorts all checks by account number so that it can prepare individual bank statements at the end of each month. Telephone companies sort their lists of accounts by last name and, further, by first name to make it easy to find phone numbers. Virtually every organization must sort some data and, in many cases, massive amounts of data. Sorting data is an intriguing problem that has attracted some of the most intense research efforts in the field of computer science. In this chapter, we discuss one of the simplest sorting schemes. In the exercises in this chapter, Chapter 20 and Chapter 22, we investigate more complex schemes that yield superior performance.

Figure 7.10 sorts the values of array (a 10-element array of int variables) into ascending order. The technique we use is called the *bubble sort* or the *sinking sort*, because the smaller values gradually "bubble" their way to the top of the array (i.e., toward the first element) like air bubbles rising in water, while the larger values sink to the bottom (end) of the array. The technique uses nested loops to make several passes through the array. Each pass compares successive pairs of elements. If a pair is in increasing order (or the values are equal), the bubble sort leaves the values as they are. If a pair is in decreasing order, the bubble sort swaps their values in the array. The applet contains methods init, bubble-Sort and swap. Method init (lines 9–33) initializes the applet. Method bubbleSort (lines 36–55) is called from init to sort the elements of array. Method bubbleSort calls method swap (lines 58–65) as necessary to exchange two elements of the array.

```java
1    // Fig. 7.10: BubbleSort.java
2    // Sort an array's values into ascending order.
3    import java.awt.*;
4    import javax.swing.*;
5
6    public class BubbleSort extends JApplet {
7
8       // initialize applet
9       public void init()
10      {
11         JTextArea outputArea = new JTextArea();
12         Container container = getContentPane();
13         container.add( outputArea );
14
15         int array[] = { 2, 6, 4, 8, 10, 12, 89, 68, 45, 37 };
16
17         String output = "Data items in original order\n";
18
19         // append original array values to String output
20         for ( int counter = 0; counter < array.length; counter++ )
21            output += "   " + array[ counter ];
22
23         bubbleSort( array );   // sort array
24
25         output += "\n\nData items in ascending order\n";
26
27         // append sorted\ array values to String output
28         for ( int counter = 0; counter < array.length; counter++ )
29            output += "   " + array[ counter ];
30
31         outputArea.setText( output );
32
33      } // end method init
34
```

Fig. 7.10   Sorting an array with bubble sort. (Part 1 of 2.)

```
35      // sort elements of array with bubble sort
36      public void bubbleSort( int array2[] )
37      {
38         // loop to control number of passes
39         for ( int pass = 1; pass < array2.length; pass++ ) {
40
41            // loop to control number of comparisons
42            for ( int element = 0;
43                  element < array2.length - 1;
44                  element++ ) {
45
46               // compare side-by-side elements and swap them if
47               // first element is greater than second element
48               if ( array2[ element ] > array2[ element + 1 ] )
49                  swap( array2, element, element + 1 );
50
51            } // end loop to control comparisons
52
53         } // end loop to control passes
54
55      } // end method bubbleSort
56
57      // swap two elements of an array
58      public void swap( int array3[], int first, int second )
59      {
60         int hold;  // temporary holding area for swap
61
62         hold = array3[ first ];
63         array3[ first ] = array3[ second ];
64         array3[ second ] = hold;
65      }
66
67   } // end class BubbleSort
```

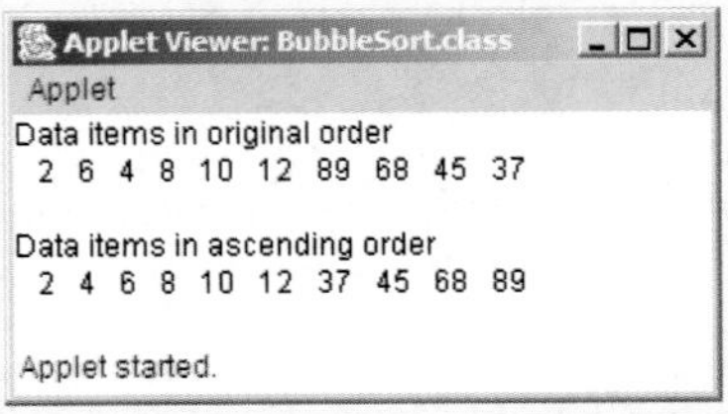

```
Applet Viewer: BubbleSort.class         _ □ ×
Applet
Data items in original order
  2  6  4  8  10  12  89  68  45  37

Data items in ascending order
  2  4  6  8  10  12  37  45  68  89

Applet started.
```

Fig. 7.10   Sorting an array with bubble sort. (Part 2 of 2.)

Lines 20–21 append the original values of array to the String called output. Line 23 invokes method bubbleSort and passes array as the array to sort. The method receives the array as parameter array2. The nested for statement at lines 39–53 performs the sort. The outer loop controls the number of passes of the array. The inner loop controls the comparisons and swapping (if necessary) of the elements during each pass. Method bubbleSort compares array2[0] to array2[1], then array2[1] to array2[2], then array2[2] to array2[3] and so on until it completes the pass by comparing array2[8] to array2[9]. Although there are 10 elements, the comparison loop performs only nine comparisons. During each pass, a large value might move down the array (sink) many positions. However, a small value can move up (bubble) only one position per pass. On the first pass, the largest value is guaranteed to sink to the bottom element of the array, `array2[ 9 ]`. On the second pass, the second largest value is guaranteed to sink to `array2[ 8 ]`. On the ninth pass, the ninth largest value sinks to `array2[ 1 ]`, leaving the smallest value in `array2[ 0 ]`. So, only nine passes are required to sort a 10-element array.

If a comparison reveals that the two elements are in descending order, line 49 of `bubbleSort` calls method `swap` to exchange the two elements so they will be in ascending order in the array. Method `swap` receives a reference to the array (which it calls `array3`) and two integers representing the indices of the two elements of the array to exchange. The exchange is performed by the three assignments in lines 62–64. The extra variable `hold` temporarily stores one of the two values being swapped. The swap cannot be performed with only the two assignments

```
array3[ first ] = array3[ second ];
array3[ second ] = array3[ first ];
```

If `array3[ first ]` is 7 and `array3[ second ]` is 5, after the first assignment both array elements contain 5 and the value 7 is lost—hence, the extra variable `hold` is needed.

The chief virtue of the bubble sort is that it is easy to program. However, the bubble sort runs slowly. This becomes apparent when sorting large arrays. In Exercise 7.11, we ask you to develop more efficient versions of the bubble sort. Other exercises investigate some sorting algorithms that are far more efficient than the bubble sort.[2]

Performance Tip 7.2

Sometimes, the simplest algorithms perform poorly. Their virtue is that they are easy to program, test and debug. Sometimes, more complex algorithms are required to realize maximum performance.

7.8 Searching Arrays: Linear Search and Binary Search

Often, programmers work with large amounts of data stored in arrays. It may be necessary to determine whether an array contains a value that matches a certain *key value*. The process of locating a key value in an array is called *searching*. In this section, we discuss two searching techniques—the simple *linear search* and the more efficient *binary search*.[3]

Searching an Array with Linear Search

In the applet of Fig. 7.11, method `linearSearch` (declared at lines 47–58) uses a `for` statement (lines 50–54) containing an `if` statement to iterate over the elements of an array and compare each element with a *search key*—the value to locate in the array. If the search key is found, the method returns the index of the element, thereby indicating the exact position of the search key in the array. If the search key is not found, the method returns the value –1. We return –1 because it is not a valid index. If the array being searched is not in any particular order, it is just as likely that the search key will be found in the first element

---

2. More advanced courses (often titled "Data Structures," "Algorithms" or "Computational Complexity") investigate sorting and searching in greater depth.

3. Exercise 7.33 and Exercise 7.34 ask you to implement recursive versions of the linear search and the binary search, respectively.

as the last. On average, therefore, the program will have to compare the search key with half the elements of the array.

Figure 7.11 contains a 100-element array filled with the even integers from 0 to 198. The user types the search key in a `JTextField` and presses *Enter* to start the search. We pass a reference to the array to method `linearSearch` even though the array can be accessed in that method directly via the field `array` of class `LinearSearch`. We do this because a reference to an array normally is passed to a method of another class to search the corresponding array. For example, class `Arrays` (see Chapter 22) contains a variety of `static` methods for sorting arrays; searching arrays; comparing the contents of arrays; and filling arrays of primitive types, arrays of `Object`s and arrays of `String`s.

```java
1   // Fig. 7.11: LinearSearch.java
2   // Linear search of an array.
3   import java.awt.*;
4   import java.awt.event.*;
5   import javax.swing.*;
6
7   public class LinearSearch extends JApplet implements ActionListener {
8
9       JLabel enterLabel, resultLabel;
10      JTextField enterField, resultField;
11      int array[];
12
13      // set up applet's GUI
14      public void init()
15      {
16          // get content pane and set its layout to FlowLayout
17          Container container = getContentPane();
18          container.setLayout( new FlowLayout() );
19
20          // set up JLabel and JTextField for user input
21          enterLabel = new JLabel( "Enter integer search key" );
22          container.add( enterLabel );
23
24          enterField = new JTextField( 10 );
25          container.add( enterField );
26
27          // register this applet as enterField's action listener
28          enterField.addActionListener( this );
29
30          // set up JLabel and JTextField for displaying results
31          resultLabel = new JLabel( "Result" );
32          container.add( resultLabel );
33
34          resultField = new JTextField( 20 );
35          resultField.setEditable( false );
36          container.add( resultField );
37
38          // create array and populate with even integers 0 to 198
39          array = new int[ 100 ];
40
```

Fig. 7.11 Linear search of an array. (Part 1 of 2.)

```
41          for ( int counter = 0; counter < array.length; counter++ )
42              array[ counter ] = 2 * counter;
43
44      } // end method init
45
46      // search array for specified key value
47      public int linearSearch( int array2[], int key )
48      {
49          // loop through array elements
50          for ( int counter = 0; counter < array2.length; counter++ )
51
52              // if array element equals key value, return location
53              if ( array2[ counter ] == key )
54                  return counter;
55
56          return -1;  // key not found
57
58      } // end method linearSearch
59
60      // obtain user input and call method linearSearch
61      public void actionPerformed( ActionEvent actionEvent )
62      {
63          // input also can be obtained with enterField.getText()
64          String searchKey = actionEvent.getActionCommand();
65
66          // pass array reference to linearSearch; normally, a reference to an
67          // array is passed to a method to search corresponding array object
68          int element = linearSearch( array, Integer.parseInt( searchKey ) );
69
70          // display search result
71          if ( element != -1 )
72              resultField.setText( "Found value in element " + element );
73          else
74              resultField.setText( "Value not found" );
75
76      } // method actionPerformed
77
78  } // end class LinearSearch
```

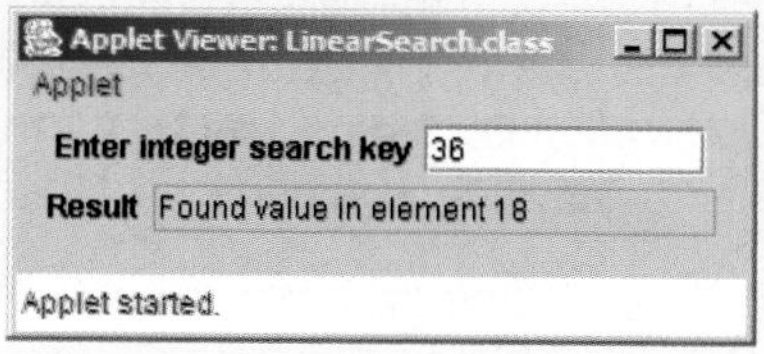

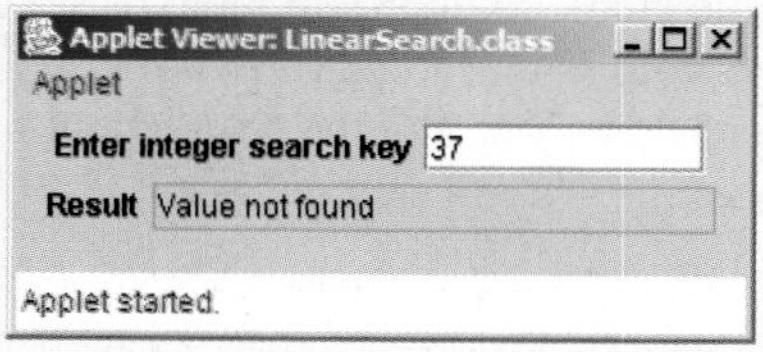

Fig. 7.11   Linear search of an array. (Part 2 of 2.)

Searching a Sorted Array with Binary Search

The linear-search method works well for small arrays or for unsorted arrays. However, for large arrays, linear searching is inefficient. If the array is sorted, the high-speed binary-search technique can be used.

As we saw in the previous example, the linear-search algorithm compares the search key with an average of half the elements in the array. However, the binary-search algorithm eliminates half of the elements in the array being searched after each comparison. The algorithm locates the middle array element and compares it with the search key. If they are equal, the search key has been found, and the binary search returns the index of that element. Otherwise, the binary search reduces the problem to searching half of the sorted array. If the search key is less than the middle array element, the first half of the array will be searched; otherwise, the second half of the array will be searched.[4] If the search key is not the middle element in the specified subarray (i.e., part of the original array), the algorithm repeats on one quarter of the original array. The search continues until the search key is equal to the middle element of a subarray or until the subarray consists of one element that is not equal to the search key (i.e., the search key is not found).

In the worst-case scenario, searching a sorted array of 1023 elements will take only 10 comparisons when using a binary search. Repeatedly dividing 1024 by 2 (because after each comparison, we are able to eliminate half of the array) yields the values 512, 256, 128, 64, 32, 16, 8, 4, 2 and 1. The number 1024 (2^{10}) is divided by 2 only 10 times to get the value 1. Dividing by 2 is equivalent to one comparison in the binary-search algorithm. Thus, an array of 1,048,576 (2^{20}) elements takes a maximum of 20 comparisons to find the key, and an array of one billion elements takes a maximum of 30 comparisons to find the key. This is a tremendous increase in performance over the linear search. For a one-billion-element array, this is a difference between an average of 500 million comparisons and a maximum of 30 comparisons! The maximum number of comparisons needed for the binary search of any sorted array is the exponent of the first power of 2 greater than the number of elements in the array.

Figure 7.12 presents an iterative `binarySearch` method (lines 78–108) that receives as arguments an integer array called `array2` (the array to search) and an integer `key` (the search key). The program passes a reference to the array to method `binarySearch`. Once again, we do this because a reference to an array normally is passed to a method of another class to search the corresponding array. In `binarySearch`, if `key` matches the `middle` element of a subarray, `binarySearch` returns `middle` (the index of the current element) to indicate that the value was found and the search is complete. If `key` does not match the `middle` element of a subarray, `binarySearch` adjusts the `low` index or `high` index (both declared in the method), to continue the search, using a smaller subarray. If `key` is less than the middle element, the `high` index is set to `middle - 1`, and the search continues on the elements from `low` to `middle - 1`. If `key` is greater than the middle element, the `low` index is set to `middle + 1`, and the search continues on the elements from `middle + 1` to `high`. The nested `if…else` statement at lines 93–102 performs these comparisons.

```
1   // Fig. 7.12: BinarySearch.java
2   // Binary search of an array.
3   import java.awt.*;
4   import java.awt.event.*;
5   import java.text.*;
```

Fig. 7.12   Binary search of a sorted array. (Part 1 of 5.)

---

4.   This example assumes that the array is sorted in ascending order.

```
6
7   import javax.swing.*;
8
9   public class BinarySearch extends JApplet implements ActionListener {
10      JLabel enterLabel, resultLabel;
11      JTextField enterField, resultField;
12      JTextArea output;
13
14      int array[];
15      String display = "";
16
17      // set up applet's GUI
18      public void init()
19      {
20          // get content pane and set its layout to FlowLayout
21          Container container = getContentPane();
22          container.setLayout( new FlowLayout() );
23
24          // set up JLabel and JTextField for user input
25          enterLabel = new JLabel( "Enter integer search key" );
26          container.add( enterLabel );
27
28          enterField = new JTextField( 10 );
29          container.add( enterField );
30
31          // register this applet as enterField's action listener
32          enterField.addActionListener( this );
33
34          // set up JLabel and JTextField for displaying results
35          resultLabel = new JLabel( "Result" );
36          container.add( resultLabel );
37
38          resultField = new JTextField( 20 );
39          resultField.setEditable( false );
40          container.add( resultField );
41
42          // set up JTextArea for displaying comparison data
43          output = new JTextArea( 6, 60 );
44          output.setFont( new Font( "Monospaced", Font.PLAIN, 12 ) );
45          container.add( output );
46
47          // create array and fill with even integers 0 to 28
48          array = new int[ 15 ];
49
50          for ( int counter = 0; counter < array.length; counter++ )
51              array[ counter ] = 2 * counter;
52
53      } // end method init
54
55      // obtain user input and call method binarySearch
56      public void actionPerformed( ActionEvent actionEvent )
57      {
```

Fig. 7.12   Binary search of a sorted array. (Part 2 of 5.)

```
58          // input also can be obtained with enterField.getText()
59          String searchKey = actionEvent.getActionCommand();
60
61          // initialize display string for new search
62          display = "Portions of array searched\n";
63
64          // perform binary search
65          int element = binarySearch( array, Integer.parseInt( searchKey ) );
66
67          output.setText( display );
68
69          // display search result
70          if ( element != -1 )
71             resultField.setText( "Found value in element " + element );
72          else
73             resultField.setText( "Value not found" );
74
75      } // end method actionPerformed
76
77      // method to perform binary search of an array
78      public int binarySearch( int array2[], int key )
79      {
80         int low = 0;                        // low element index
81         int high = array2.length - 1;   // high element index
82         int middle;                        // middle element index
83
84         // loop until low index is greater than high index
85         while ( low <= high ) {
86            middle = ( low + high ) / 2;   // determine middle index
87
88            // display subset of array elements used in this
89            // iteration of binary search loop
90            buildOutput( array2, low, middle, high );
91
92            // if key matches middle element, return middle location
93            if ( key == array[ middle ] )
94               return middle;
95
96            // if key less than middle element, set new high element
97            else if ( key < array[ middle ] )
98               high = middle - 1;
99
100           // key greater than middle element, set new low element
101           else
102              low = middle + 1;
103
104        } // end while
105
106        return -1;   // key not found
107
108     } // end method binarySearch
109
```

Fig. 7.12   Binary search of a sorted array. (Part 3 of 5.)

```
110      // build row of output showing subset of array elements
111      // currently being processed
112      void buildOutput( int array3[], int low, int middle, int high )
113      {
114         // create 2-digit integer number format
115         DecimalFormat twoDigits = new DecimalFormat( "00" );
116
117         // loop through array elements
118         for ( int counter = 0; counter < array3.length; counter++ ) {
119
120            // if counter outside current array subset, append
121            // padding spaces to String display
122            if ( counter < low || counter > high )
123               display += "    ";
124
125            // if middle element, append element to String display
126            // followed by asterisk (*) to indicate middle element
127            else if ( counter == middle )
128               display += twoDigits.format( array3[ counter ] ) + "* ";
129
130            else // append element to String display
131               display += twoDigits.format( array3[ counter ] ) + "  ";
132
133         } // end for
134
135         display += "\n";
136
137      } // end method buildOutput
138
139   } // end class BinarySearch
```

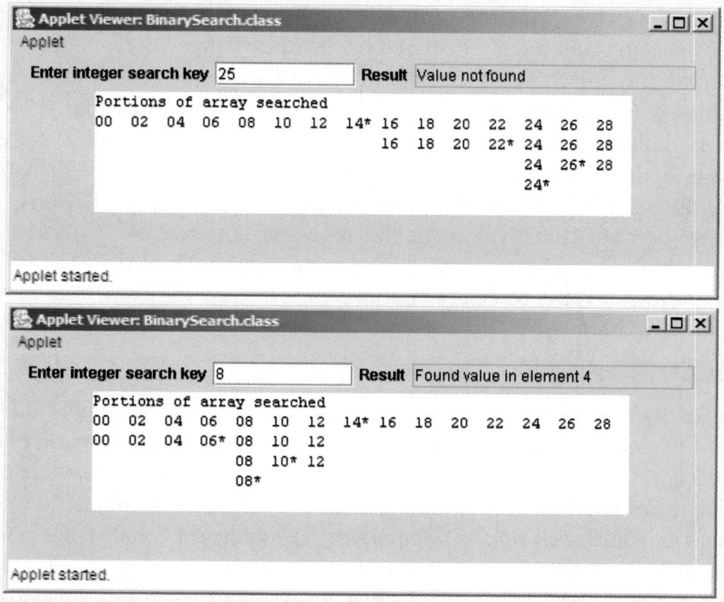

Fig. 7.12   Binary search of a sorted array. (Part 4 of 5.)

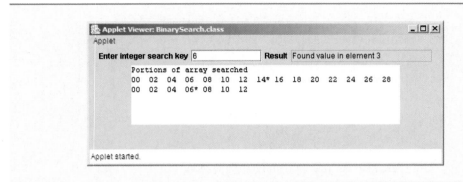

Fig. 7.12   Binary search of a sorted array. (Part 5 of 5.)

This program uses a 15-element array. The first power of 2 greater than the number of elements is 16 (2^4), so binarySearch requires at most four comparisons to find the key. To illustrate this, line 90 calls method buildOutput (declared at lines 112–137) to output each subarray during the binary-search process. Method buildOutput marks the middle element in each subarray with an asterisk (*) to indicate the element with which the key is compared. No matter what search key is entered, each search in this example results in a maximum of four lines of output—one per comparison.

Textarea output uses *Monospaced* font (a *fixed-width font*—i.e., all characters are the same width) to help align the displayed text in each line of output. Line 44 uses method setFont to change the font displayed in output. Method setFont can change the font of text displayed on most GUI components. The method requires a **_Font_** (package java.awt) object as its argument. A Font object is initialized with three arguments—the String name of the font ("Monospaced"), an int representing the style of the font (Font.PLAIN is a constant integer declared in class Font that indicates plain font) and an int representing the point size of the font (12). Java provides generic names for several fonts available on every Java platform. *Monospaced* font is also called *Courier*. Other common fonts include *Serif* (also called *TimesRoman*) and *SansSerif* (also called *Helvetica*). Java provides access to all fonts on your system via methods of class *Graphics-Environment* (package java.awt). The style can also be Font.BOLD, Font.ITALIC or Font.BOLD + Font.ITALIC. The point size represents the size of the font. There are 72 points to an inch. The actual size of the text as it appears on the screen may vary based on the size of the screen and the screen resolution.

7.9 Multidimensional Arrays

Multidimensional arrays with two dimensions are often used to represent *tables* of values consisting of information arranged in *rows* and *columns*. To identify a particular table element, we must specify two indices. By convention, the first identifies the element's row and the second identifies the element's column. Arrays that require two indices to identify a particular element are called *two-dimensional arrays*. (Multidimensional arrays can have more than two dimensions.) Java does not support multidimensional arrays directly, but does allow the programmer to specify one-dimensional arrays whose elements are also one-dimensional arrays, thus achieving the same effect. Figure 7.13 illustrates a two-dimensional array

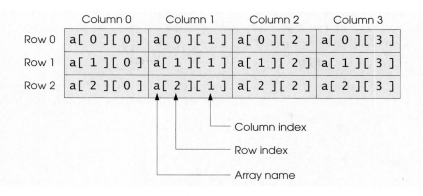

Fig. 7.13 Two-dimensional array with three rows and four columns.

a that contains three rows and four columns (i.e., a three-by-four array). In general, an array with *m* rows and *n* columns is called an *m-by-n array*.

Every element in array a is identified in Fig. 7.13 by an array-access expression of the form a[row][column]; a is the name of the array reference, and row and column are the indices that uniquely identify each element in array a by row and column number. Notice that the names of the elements in the first row all have a first index of 0; the names of the elements in the fourth column all have a second index of 3.

Arrays of One-Dimensional Arrays

Like one-dimensional arrays, multidimensional arrays can be initialized with array initializers in declarations. A two-dimensional array b with two rows and two columns could be declared and initialized with *nested array initializers* as follows:

```
int b[][] = { { 1, 2 }, { 3, 4 } };
```

The initializer values are grouped by row in braces. So, 1 and 2 initialize b[0][0] and b[0][1], and 3 and 4 initialize b[1][0] and b[1][1]. The compiler determines the number of rows by counting the number of nested array initializers (represented by sets of braces within the outer braces) in the array initializer. The compiler determines the number of columns in a row by counting the initializer values in the array initializer for that row.

In Java, multidimensional arrays are maintained as arrays of one-dimensional arrays. So, the array b in the preceding declaration is actually composed of three separate one-dimensional arrays. The array b itself is a one-dimensional array containing two elements. Each element is a reference to a one-dimensional array of int variables.

Two-Dimensional Arrays with Rows of Different Lengths

The manner in which Java represents multidimensional arrays makes them quite flexible. In fact, the lengths of the rows in array b are not required to be the same. For example,

```
int b[][] = { { 1, 2 }, { 3, 4, 5 } };
```

creates integer array b with two elements (determined by the number of nested array initializers) that represent the rows of the two-dimensional array. Each element of b is a reference to a one-dimensional array of int variables. The int array for row 0 is a one-dimensional array with two elements (1 and 2) and the int array for row 1 is a one-dimensional array with three elements (3, 4 and 5).

Creating Two-Dimensional Arrays with Array-Creation Expressions
A multidimensional array with the same number of columns in every row can be created with an array-creation expression. For example, the following lines declare array b and assign it a reference to a three-by-four array:

```
int b[][];
b = new int[ 3 ][ 4 ];
```

In this case, we use the literal values 3 and 4 to specify the number of rows and number of columns, respectively, but this is not required. Programs also can use variables to specify array dimensions. As with one-dimensional arrays, the elements of a multidimensional array are initialized when the array object is created.

A multidimensional array in which each row has a different number of columns can be created as follows:

```
int b[][];
b = new int[ 2 ][ ];    // create 2 rows
b[ 0 ] = new int[ 5 ]; // create 5 columns for row 0
b[ 1 ] = new int[ 3 ]; // create 3 columns for row 1
```

The preceding statements create a two-dimensional array with two rows. Row 0 has five columns, and row 1 has three columns.

Two-Dimensional Array Example: Displaying Element Values
The applet of Fig. 7.14 demonstrates initializing two-dimensional arrays with array initializers and using nested for loops (lines 31–38) to *traverse* the arrays (i.e., manipulate every element of each array).

```
1   // Fig. 7.14: InitArray.java
2   // Initializing two-dimensional arrays.
3   import java.awt.Container;
4   import javax.swing.*;
5
6   public class InitArray extends JApplet {
7      JTextArea outputArea;
8
9      // set up GUI and initialize applet
10     public void init()
11     {
12        outputArea = new JTextArea();
13        Container container = getContentPane();
14        container.add( outputArea );
15
16        int array1[][] = { { 1, 2, 3 }, { 4, 5, 6 } };
17        int array2[][] = { { 1, 2 }, { 3 }, { 4, 5, 6 } };
```

Fig. 7.14   Initializing two-dimensional arrays. (Part 1 of 2.)

```
18
19          outputArea.setText( "Values in array1 by row are\n" );
20          buildOutput( array1 );
21
22          outputArea.append( "\nValues in array2 by row are\n" );
23          buildOutput( array2 );
24
25    } // end method init
26
27    // append rows and columns of an array to outputArea
28    public void buildOutput( int array[][] )
29    {
30        // loop through array's rows
31        for ( int row = 0; row < array.length; row++ ) {
32
33            // loop through columns of current row
34            for ( int column = 0; column < array[ row ].length; column++ )
35                outputArea.append( array[ row ][ column ] + "   " );
36
37            outputArea.append( "\n" );
38        }
39
40    } // end method buildOutput
41
42  } // end class InitArray
```

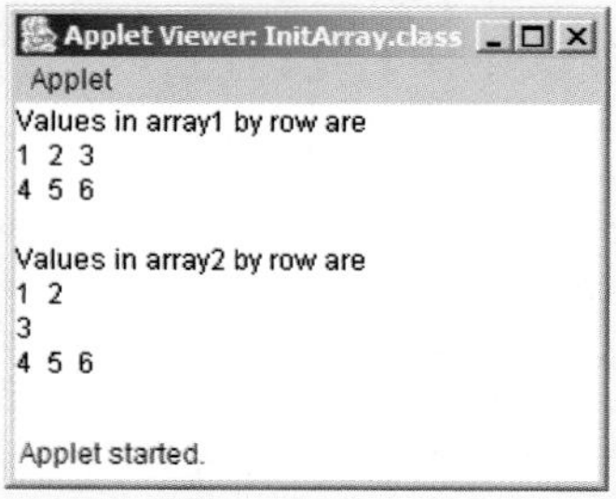

Fig. 7.14   Initializing two-dimensional arrays. (Part 2 of 2.)

The program declares two arrays in method `init`. The declaration of `array1` (line 16) uses nested array initializers to initialize the first row of the array to the values 1, 2 and 3, and the second row of the array to the values 4, 5 and 6. The declaration of `array2` (line 17) uses nested initializers of different lengths. In this case, the first row is initialized to have two elements with values 1 and 2, respectively. The second row is initialized to have one element with value 3. The third row is initialize to have three elements with the values 4, 5 and 6, respectively.

Line 20 of method `init` calls method `buildOutput` (declared in lines 28–40) to append each array's elements to textarea `outputArea`. Method `buildOutput` specifies the array parameter as `int array[][]` to indicate that the method receives a two-dimensional array as an argument. The nested `for` statement (lines 31–38) outputs the rows of a two-dimensional array. In the outer `for` statement, the expression `array.length` determines the number of rows in the array. In the inner `for` statement, the expression `array[ row ].length` determines the number of columns in the current row of the array. This condition enables the loop to determine the exact number of columns in each row.

Common Multidimensional-Array Manipulations Performed with for Statements
Many common array manipulations use `for` statements. As an example, the following `for` statement sets all the elements in the third row of array a in Fig. 7.13 to zero:

```
for ( int column = 0; column < a[ 2 ].length; column++)
    a[ 2 ][ column ] = 0;
```

We specified the *third* row; therefore, we know that the first index is always 2 (0 is the first row, and 1 is the second row). This `for` loop varies only the second index (i.e., the column index). The preceding `for` statement is equivalent to the assignment statements

```
a[ 2 ][ 0 ] = 0;
a[ 2 ][ 1 ] = 0;
a[ 2 ][ 2 ] = 0;
a[ 2 ][ 3 ] = 0;
```

The following nested `for` statement totals the values of all the elements in array a:

```
int total = 0;

for ( int row = 0; row < a.length; row++ )

    for ( int column = 0; column < a[ row ].length; column++ )

        total += a[ row ][ column ];
```

This `for` statement totals the array elements one row at a time. The outer `for` statement begins by setting the `row` index to 0 so that the elements of the first row may be totaled by the inner `for` statement. The outer `for` statement then increments `row` to 1 so that the second row can be totaled. Then, the outer `for` statement increments `row` to 2 so that the third row can be totaled. The result can be displayed when the nested `for` statement terminates.

Two-Dimensional Array Example: Summarizing Student's Exam Grades
The applet of Fig. 7.15 performs several other common array manipulations on the three-by-four array `grades`. Each row of the array represents a student, and each column represents a grade on one of the four exams the students took during the semester. Four methods perform the array manipulations. Method `minimum` (lines 48–65) determines the lowest grade of any student for the semester. Method `maximum` (lines 68–85) determines the highest grade of any student for the semester. Method `average` (lines 88–99) determines a particular student's semester average. Method `buildString` (lines 102–118) appends the two-dimensional array to string `output` in a tabular format.

Methods `minimum`, `maximum` and `buildString` each use array `grades` and the variables `students` (number of rows in the array) and `exams` (number of columns in the array). Each method loops through array `grades` by using nested `for` statements—for example, the nested `for` statement from the declaration of method `minimum` (lines 54–61). The outer `for` statement sets `row` (the row index) to 0 so that the elements of the first row can be compared with variable `lowGrade` in the body of the inner `for` statement. The inner

```
1    // Fig. 7.15: DoubleArray.java
2    // Two-dimensional array example.
3    import java.awt.*;
4    import javax.swing.*;
5
6    public class DoubleArray extends JApplet {
7       int grades[][] = { { 77, 68, 86, 73 },
8                          { 96, 87, 89, 81 },
9                          { 70, 90, 86, 81 } };
10
11      int students, exams;
12      String output;
13      JTextArea outputArea;
14
15      // initialize fields
16      public void init()
17      {
18         students = grades.length;      // number of students
19         exams = grades[ 0 ].length;    // number of exams
20
21         // create JTextArea and attach to applet
22         outputArea = new JTextArea();
23         Container container = getContentPane();
24         container.add( outputArea );
25
26         // build output string
27         output = "The array is:\n";
28         buildString();
29
30         // call methods minimum and maximum
31         output += "\n\nLowest grade: " + minimum() +
32            "\nHighest grade: " + maximum() + "\n";
33
34         // call method average to calculate each student's average
35         for ( int counter = 0; counter < students; counter++ )
36            output += "\nAverage for student " + counter + " is " +
37               average( grades[ counter ] );  // pass one row of array grades
38
39         // change outputArea's display font
40         outputArea.setFont( new Font( "Monospaced", Font.PLAIN, 12 ) );
41
42         // place output string in outputArea
43         outputArea.setText( output );
44
45      } // end method init
46
47      // find minimum grade
48      public int minimum()
49      {
50         // assume first element of grades array is smallest
51         int lowGrade = grades[ 0 ][ 0 ];
52
```

Fig. 7.15   Two-dimensional arrays. (Part 1 of 3.)

```
53          // loop through rows of grades array
54          for ( int row = 0; row < students; row++ )
55
56              // loop through columns of current row
57              for ( int column = 0; column < exams; column++ )
58
59                  // if grade is less than lowGrade, assign it to lowGrade
60                  if ( grades[ row ][ column ] < lowGrade )
61                      lowGrade = grades[ row ][ column ];
62
63          return lowGrade;   // return lowest grade
64
65      } // end method minimum
66
67      // find maximum grade
68      public int maximum()
69      {
70          // assume first element of grades array is largest
71          int highGrade = grades[ 0 ][ 0 ];
72
73          // loop through rows of grades array
74          for ( int row = 0; row < students; row++ )
75
76              // loop through columns of current row
77              for ( int column = 0; column < exams; column++ )
78
79                  // if grade is greater than highGrade, assign it to highGrade
80                  if ( grades[ row ][ column ] > highGrade )
81                      highGrade = grades[ row ][ column ];
82
83          return highGrade;   // return highest grade
84
85      } // end method maximum
86
87      // determine average grade for particular student (or set of grades)
88      public double average( int setOfGrades[] )
89      {
90          int total = 0;   // initialize total
91
92          // sum grades for one student
93          for ( int count = 0; count < setOfGrades.length; count++ )
94              total += setOfGrades[ count ];
95
96          // return average of grades
97          return ( double ) total / setOfGrades.length;
98
99      } // end method average
100
101     // build output string
102     public void buildString()
103     {
104         output += "                ";  // used to align column heads
105
```

Fig. 7.15   Two-dimensional arrays. (Part 2 of 3.)

```
106        // create column heads
107        for ( int counter = 0; counter < exams; counter++ )
108           output += "[" + counter + "]   ";
109
110        // create rows/columns of text representing array grades
111        for ( int row = 0; row < students; row++ ) {
112           output += "\ngrades[" + row + "]    ";
113
114           for ( int column = 0; column < exams; column++ )
115              output += grades[ row ][ column ] + "    ";
116        }
117
118     } // end method buildString
119
120 } // end class DoubleArray
```

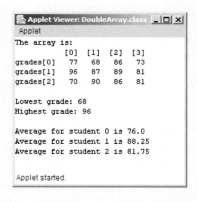

Fig. 7.15   Two-dimensional arrays. (Part 3 of 3.)

for statement loops through the four grades of a particular row and compares each grade with lowGrade. If a grade is less than lowGrade, lowGrade is set to that grade. The outer for statement then increments the row index by 1, and the elements of the second row are compared with variable lowGrade. The outer for statement then increments the row index to 2, and the elements of the third row are compared with variable lowGrade. When execution of the nested statement is complete, lowGrade contains the smallest grade in the two-dimensional array. Method maximum works similarly to method minimum.

Method average takes one argument—a one-dimensional array of test results for a particular student. When line 37 calls average, the argument is grades[counter], which specifies that a particular row of the two-dimensional array grades should be passed to average. For example, the argument grades[1] represents the four values (a one-dimensional array of grades) stored in the second row of the two-dimensional array grades. Remember that, in Java, a two-dimensional array is an array with elements that are one-dimensional arrays. Method average calculates the sum of the array elements, divides the total by the number of test results and returns the floating-point result as a double value (line 97).

7.10 (Optional Case Study) Thinking About Objects: Collaboration Among Objects

In this section, we concentrate on the collaborations (interactions) among objects. When two objects communicate with each other to accomplish a task, they are said to *collaborate*—objects do this by invoking one another's operations. We say that objects send *messages* to other objects. A *collaboration* consists of an object of one class sending a particular message to an object of another class. We will explain how messages are sent and received in Java in Section 11.9.

The message sent by the first object invokes an operation of the second object. In Section 6.15, we determined many of the operations of the classes in our system. In this section, we concentrate on the messages that invoke these operations. Figure 7.16 is the table of classes and verb phrases from Section 6.15. We have removed all the verb phrases in classes Elevator and Person that do not correspond to operations. The remaining phrases are our first estimate of the collaborations in our system. As we proceed through this and the remaining "Thinking About Objects" sections, we will discover additional collaborations.

We examine the list of verb phrases to determine the collaborations in our system. For example, class Elevator lists the phrase "resets elevator button." To accomplish this task, an object of class Elevator sends the resetButton message to an object of class ElevatorButton (invoking the resetButton operation of ElevatorButton). Figure 7.17 lists all the collaborations that can be gleaned from our table of verb phrases. According to Fig. 7.16, the Elevator[5] rings the Bell and opens (and closes) the ElevatorDoor, so we include a ringBell, openDoor and closeDoor message in Fig. 7.17. However, we must consider how the FloorDoors open and close. According to the class diagram of Fig. 3.19, ElevatorShaft associates with FloorDoor. The Elevator signals its arrival

Class	Verb phrases
Elevator	resets elevator button, rings elevator bell, signals its arrival, signals its departure, opens its door, closes its door
ElevatorShaft	turns off light, turns on light, resets floor button
Person	presses floor button, presses elevator button, rides elevator, enters elevator, exits elevator
FloorButton	summons (requests) elevator
ElevatorButton	signals elevator to move to opposite floor
FloorDoor	signals person to enter elevator (by opening)
ElevatorDoor	signals person to exit elevator (by opening), opens floor door, closes floor door

Fig. 7.16   Verb phrases for each class exhibiting behaviors in simulation.

5. We refer to an object by using that object's class name preceded by an article ("a," "an" or "the")—for example, the Elevator refers to an object of class Elevator. Our syntax is a more concise informality—we avoid repeating the phrase "an object of class...."

An object of class...	Sends the message...	To an object of class...
Elevator	resetButton	ElevatorButton
	ringBell	Bell
	elevatorArrived	ElevatorShaft
	elevatorDeparted	ElevatorShaft
	openDoor	ElevatorDoor
	closeDoor	ElevatorDoor
ElevatorShaft	resetButton	FloorButton
	turnOnLight	Light
	turnOffLight	Light
Person	pressButton	FloorButton, ElevatorButton
	enterElevator	Elevator
	exitElevator	Elevator
FloorButton	requestElevator	Elevator
ElevatorButton	moveElevator	Elevator
FloorDoor	doorOpened	Person
	doorClosed	Person
ElevatorDoor	doorOpened	Person
	doorClosed	Person
	openDoor	FloorDoor
	closeDoor	FloorDoor

Fig. 7.17   Collaborations in the elevator system.

(to the ElevatorShaft, we assume) by sending an elevatorArrived message. The ElevatorShaft responds to this message by resetting the appropriate FloorButton and turning on the appropriate Light—the ElevatorShaft sends resetButton and turnOnLight messages. At this point in the design, we may assume that the Elevator also signals its departure—that is, the Elevator sends an elevatorDeparted message to the ElevatorShaft, which then turns off the appropriate Light by sending it a turnOffLight message.

A Person may press either a FloorButton or the ElevatorButton. A Person may enter or exit the Elevator. Therefore, a Person may send pressButton, enterElevator and exitElevator messages. A FloorButton requests, or summons, the Elevator, so a FloorButton may send a requestElevator message. The ElevatorButton signals the Elevator to begin moving to the other floor, so the ElevatorButton may send a moveElevator message.

Both a FloorDoor and the ElevatorDoor inform a Person that the doors have opened or closed, so both objects send doorOpened and doorClosed messages.[6] Lastly, the ElevatorDoor must send openDoor and closeDoor messages to a FloorDoor to guarantee that these doors open and close together.

---

6. Note that most of the messages perform some specific action on the receiving object; for example, the Elevator resets the ElevatorButton. However, other messages inform receiving objects of *events* that have already happened; for example, the FloorDoor informs the Person that the FloorDoor has opened. In Section 11.9, we will elaborate on the topic of events—for now, however, we proceed as if the two types of messages are indistinguishable.

Collaboration Diagrams

Now let us consider the objects that must interact so people in our simulation can enter and exit the elevator when it arrives on a floor. The UML provides the *collaboration diagram* to model such interactions. Collaboration diagrams are a type of *interaction diagram*; they model the behavioral aspects of a system by providing information about how objects interact. Collaboration diagrams emphasize which objects participate in the interactions. (The other type of interaction diagram is the *sequence diagram*, which we will present in Chapter 16.) Figure 7.18 shows a collaboration diagram that models a person who is pressing a floor button. Objects are modeled with names in the form `objectName : ClassName`. In this example, we disregard the object name, because we care only about the object type. Collaborating objects are connected with solid lines, and messages are passed between objects along these lines in the direction shown by arrows. The name of the message, which appears next to the arrow, is the name of a method belonging to the receiving object—think of the name as a "service" that the receiving object provides for its sending objects (its "clients").

The arrow in Fig. 7.18 represents a message in the UML and a method call—or *synchronous call*—in Java. This arrow indicates that the flow of control is from the sending object (a `Person`) to the receiving object (a `FloorButton`). Since this is a synchronous call, the sending object may not send another message until the receiving object processes the message and returns control to the sending object. For example, in Fig. 7.18, a `Person` calls method `pressButton` of a `FloorButton` and may not send another message to an object until `pressButton` has finished and returns control to that `Person`. If our program contains a `FloorButton` object called `firstFloorButton`, and we assume that the `Person` manages the flow of control, the Java code implementation in class `Person` that represents this collaboration diagram is

```
firstFloorButton.pressButton();
```

Figure 7.19 shows a collaboration diagram that models the interactions among objects in the system while objects of class `Person` enter and exit the elevator. The collaboration begins when the `Elevator` arrives on a `Floor`. The number to the left of the message name indicates the order in which the message is passed. The *sequence of messages* in a collaboration diagram progresses in numerical order from least to greatest. In this diagram, the numbering starts with message `1` and ends with message `4.2`. The sequence of passing messages follows a nested structure—for example, message `3.1` is the first message nested in message `3`, and message `3.2` is the second message nested in message `3`. Message `3.2.1` is the first message nested in message `3.2`. A message may be passed only when all nested messages from the previous message have been passed. For example, in Fig. 7.19, the `Elevator` passes message 4 after messages 3, `3.1`, `3.1.1`, `3.1.1.1`, `3.2` and `3.2.1` have been passed, in that order.

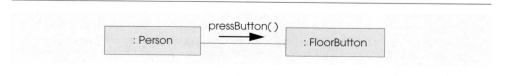

Fig. 7.18   Collaboration diagram of a person pressing a floor button.

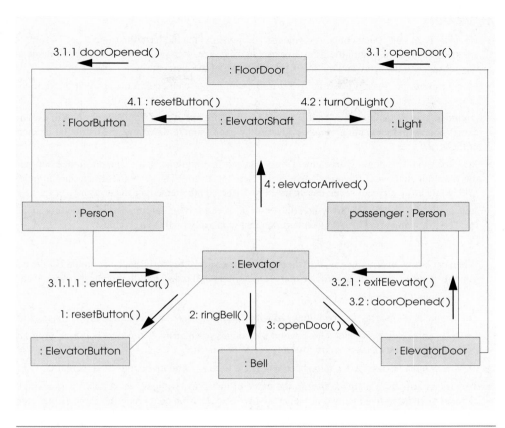

Fig. 7.19 Collaboration diagram for passengers exiting and entering the elevator.

The Elevator sends the resetButton message (message 1) to the Elevator-Button to reset the ElevatorButton. Next, the Elevator sends the ringBell message (message 2) to the Bell, then opens the ElevatorDoor by passing the openDoor message (message 3). The ElevatorDoor then opens the FloorDoor by sending an open-Door message (message 3.1, at the top of the diagram) to that FloorDoor. The FloorDoor informs the waiting Person that the FloorDoor has opened (message 3.1.1), and the waiting Person enters the Elevator (message 3.1.1.1). The Eleva-torDoor then informs the passenger that the ElevatorDoor has opened (message 3.2), so that the passenger may exit the Elevator (message 3.2.1). Lastly, the Ele-vator informs the ElevatorShaft of the arrival (message 4), so that the Elevator-Shaft can reset the FloorButton (message 4.1) and turn on the Light (message 4.2).

Unfortunately, this design creates a problem. According to the diagram, the waiting Person enters the Elevator (message 3.1.1.1) before the passenger (message 3.2.1) exits. We will modify this diagram in Section 11.9 to indicate more accurately the message passing when we discuss *event handling*. In Section 16.11, we refine this diagram further and apply multithreading, synchronization and active classes in our system to force the waiting Person to wait for the passenger to exit the Elevator.

SUMMARY

- An array is an object that contains elements (components) that all have the same type. To refer to a particular element within the array, we use an array-access expression containing the name of the reference to the array and the index (or subscript) of the element.

- Each array has a `length` field that is set to the number of elements in the array at the time the program creates the array object.

- An index may be an integer or an integer expression (but not of type `long`). If a program uses an expression as an index, the program evaluates the expression to determine the particular element of the array.

- Java arrays always begin with element zero. Thus, it is important to note the difference between the "seventh element of the array" and "array element seven." The seventh element has an index of 6, while array element seven has an index of 7 (the eighth element of the array).

- Java arrays are objects. An array-creation expression or array initializer reserves space for an array. The following array-creation expression creates an array of 100 `int` values:

      int b[] = new int[100];

- When declaring an array, the type of the array and the square brackets can be combined at the beginning of the declaration to indicate that all identifiers in the declaration represent arrays, as in

      double[] array1, array2;

- The elements of an array can be initialized with initializer lists in a declaration or by assignment.

- Java prevents referencing elements beyond the bounds of an array. If this occurs during program execution, an `ArrayIndexOutOfBoundsException` occurs.

- Constants must be assigned a value before they are used and cannot be modified thereafter.

- To pass an array to a method, specify the name of the array, without brackets. To pass a single element of an array to a method, use an array-access expression containing the name of the reference to the array an the appropriate index (or indices).

- Arrays are passed to methods as references; therefore, the called methods can modify the element values in the caller's original arrays. Single elements of primitive-type arrays are passed to methods by value.

- To accept an array argument in a method, the method's parameter list must declare an array parameter.

- An array can be sorted by using the bubble-sort technique. Several passes through the array are made. On each pass, successive pairs of elements are compared. If a pair is in order (or the values are identical), it is left as is. If a pair is out of order, the values are swapped.

- A linear search compares each element of the array with a search key. If the array is not in any particular order, it is just as likely that the value will be found in the first element as the last. On average, therefore, the program will have to compare the search key with half the elements of the array. Linear search works well for small arrays and is acceptable even for large unsorted arrays.

- For sorted arrays, the binary search eliminates from consideration half the elements in the array after each comparison. The algorithm locates the middle element of the array and compares it with the search key. If they are equal, the search key is found, and the array index of that element is returned. Otherwise, the problem is reduced to searching half the array that is still under consideration.

- Most GUI components have method `setFont` to change the font of the text on the GUI component. The method requires a `Font` (package `java.awt`) object as its argument.

- A `Font` object is initialized with three arguments—a `String` representing the name of the font, an `int` representing the style of the font and an `int` representing the point size of the font. The style can be Font.PLAIN, Font.BOLD, Font.ITALIC or Font.BOLD + Font.ITALIC. The point size represents the size of the font. There are 72 points to an inch. The actual size of the text on the screen may vary based on the screen size and the screen resolution.

- Arrays may be used to represent tables of values consisting of information arranged in rows and columns. To identify a particular element of a table, two indices are specified: The first identifies the row in which the element is contained, and the second identifies the column in which the element is contained. Tables or arrays that require two indices to identify a particular element are called two-dimensional arrays.

- Multidimensional arrays in Java are maintained as arrays of arrays.

- A two-dimensional array can be initialized with an array initializer of the form

    arrayType arrayName[][] = { { *row1 initializer* }, { *row2 initializer* }, ... };

- To create an array with a fixed number of rows and columns, use

    arrayType arrayName[][] = new *arrayType*[*numRows*][*numColumns*];

- To pass one row of a two-dimensional array to a method that receives a one-dimensional array, simply pass the name of the reference to the array followed by only the row index.

TERMINOLOGY

a[i]	name of an array
a[i][j]	named constant
array	off-by-one error
array-access expression	one-dimensional array
array-creation expression	pass of a bubble sort
array initializer	pass-by-reference
binary search of an array	pass-by-value
bounds checking	passing arrays to methods
bubble sort	position number
column index	row index
component of an array	search key
constant	searching an array
declare an array	setFont method
element of an array	sinking sort
final	sorting
Font class from java.awt	sorting an array
Font.BOLD	square brackets, []
Font.ITALIC	subscript
Font.PLAIN	table of values
index	tabular format
initialize an array	temporary area for exchange of values
linear search of an array	two-dimensional array
m-by-*n* array	value of an element
multidimensional array	zeroth element

SELF-REVIEW EXERCISES

7.1   Fill in the blank(s) in each of the following statements:
   a) Lists and tables of values can be stored in _____.
   b) The elements of an array are related by the fact that they have the same _____ and _____.

c) The number used to refer to a particular element of an array is called the element's
_____.

d) The process of placing the elements of an array in order is called _____ the array.

e) Determining whether an array contains a certain key value is called _____ the array.

f) An array that uses two indices is referred to as a(n) _____ array.

7.2 Determine whether each of the following is *true* or *false*. If *false*, explain why.
   a) An array can store many different types of values.
   b) An array index should normally be of type `float`.
   c) An individual array element that is passed to a method and modified in that method will contain the modified value when the called method completes execution.

7.3 Perform the following tasks for an array called `fractions`:
   a) Declare a constant ARRAY_SIZE that is initialized to 10.
   b) Declare an array with ARRAY_SIZE elements of type `float`, and initialize the elements to 0.
   c) Name the fourth element of the array.
   d) Refer to array element four.
   e) Assign the value `1.667` to array element nine.
   f) Assign the value `3.333` to the seventh element of the array.
   g) Sum all the elements of the array, using a `for` statement. Declare the integer variable x as a control variable for the loop.

7.4 Perform the following tasks for an array called `table`:
   a) Declare and create the array as an integer array that has three rows and three columns. Assume that the constant ARRAY_SIZE has been declared to be 3.
   b) How many elements does the array contain?
   c) Use a `for` statement to initialize each element of the array to the sum of its indices. Assume that the integer variables x and y are declared as control variables.

7.5 Find and correct the error in each of the following program segments:
   a) `final int ARRAY_SIZE = 5;`
      `ARRAY_SIZE = 10;`
   b) `Assume int b[] = new int[ 10 ];`
      `for ( int i = 0; i <= b.length; i++ )`
      `    b[ i ] = 1;`
   c) `Assume int a[][] = { { 1, 2 }, { 3, 4 } };`
      `    a[ 1, 1 ] = 5;`

ANSWERS TO SELF-REVIEW EXERCISES

7.1   a) arrays. b) name, type. c) index (or subscript or position number). d) sorting. e) searching. f) two-dimensional.

7.2   a) False. An array can store only values of the same type.
   b) False. An array index must be an integer or an integer expression.
   c) For individual primitive-type elements of an array: False. Such elements are passed by value. If a reference to an array is passed, then modifications to the array elements are reflected in the original. For individual elements of a nonprimitive type: True. Such elements are passed by reference, and changes to the object will be reflected in the original array element.

7.3   a) `final int ARRAY_SIZE = 10;`
   b) `float fractions[] = new float[ ARRAY_SIZE ];`

c) `fractions[ 3 ]`
d) `fractions[ 4 ]`
e) `fractions[ 9 ] = 1.667;`
f) `fractions[ 6 ] = 3.333;`
g) `float total = 0.0;`
   `for ( int x = 0; x < fractions.length; x++ )`
   `  total += fractions[ x ];`

7.4   a) `int table[][] = new int[ ARRAY_SIZE ][ ARRAY_SIZE ];`
      b) Nine.
      c) `for ( int x = 0; x < table.length; x++ )`
         `  for ( int y = 0; y < table[ x ].length; y++ )`
         `    table[ x ][ y ] = x + y;`

7.5   a) Error: Assigning a value to a constant after it has been initialized.
         Correction: Assign the correct value to the constant in a `final int ARRAY_SIZE` decla-
         ration or create another variable.
      b) Error: Referencing an array element outside the bounds of the array (`b[10]`).
         Correction: Change the `<=` operator to `<`.
      c) Error: Array indexing is performed incorrectly.
         Correction: Change the statement to `a[ 1 ][ 1 ] = 5;`.

EXERCISES

7.6   Fill in the blanks in each of the following statements:
      a) Java stores lists of values in _____.
      b) The elements of an array are related by the fact that they _____.
      c) When referring to an array element, the position number contained within brackets is
         called a(n) _____.
      d) The names of the four elements of one-dimensional array p are _____, _____,
         _____ and _____.
      e) Naming an array, stating its type and specifying the number of dimensions in the array is
         called _____ the array.
      f) The process of placing the elements of an array into either ascending or descending order
         is called _____.
      g) In a two-dimensional array, the first index identifies the _____ of an element and
         the second index identifies the _____ of an element.
      h) An *m*-by-*n* array contains _____ rows, _____ columns and _____ ele-
         ments.
      i) The name of the element in row 3 and column 5 of array d is _____.

7.7   Determine whether each of the following is *true* or *false*. If *false*, explain why.
      a) To refer to a particular location or element within an array, we specify the name of the
         array and the value of the particular element.
      b) An array declaration reserves space for the array.
      c) To indicate that 100 locations should be reserved for integer array p, the programmer
         writes the declaration
         `   p[ 100 ];`
      d) A Java program that initializes the elements of a 15-element array to zero must contain
         at least one `for` statement.
      e) A Java program that totals the elements of a two-dimensional array must contain nested
         `for` statements.

7.8   Write Java statements to accomplish each of the following tasks:
a) Display the value of the seventh element of character array f.
b) Initialize each of the five elements of one-dimensional integer array g to 8.
c) Total the 100 elements of floating-point array c.
d) Copy 11-element array a into the first portion of array b, which contains 34 elements.
e) Determine and print the smallest and largest values contained in 99-element floating-point array w.

7.9   Consider a two-by-three integer array t.
a) Write a statement that declares and creates t.
b) How many rows does t have?
c) How many columns does t have?
d) How many elements does t have?
e) Write the names of all the elements in the second row of t.
f) Write the names of all the elements in the third column of t.
g) Write a single statement that sets the element of t in row 1 and column 2 to zero.
h) Write a series of statements that initializes each element of t to zero. Do not use a repetition statement.
i) Write a nested for statement that initializes each element of t to zero.
j) Write a nested for statement that inputs the values for the elements of t from the user.
k) Write a series of statements that determines and prints the smallest value in t.
l) Write a statement that displays the elements of the first row of t.
m) Write a statement that totals the elements of the third column of t.
n) Write a series of statements that prints the contents of t in neat, tabular format. List the column indices as headings across the top, and list the row indices at the left of each row.

7.10   Use a one-dimensional array to solve the following problem: A company pays its salespeople on a commission basis. The salespeople receive $200 per week plus 9% of their gross sales for that week. For example, a salesperson who grosses $5000 in sales in a week receives $200 plus 9% of $5000, or a total of $650. Write an applet (using an array of counters) that determines how many of the salespeople earned salaries in each of the following ranges (assume that each salesperson's salary is truncated to an integer amount):
a) $200–299
b) $300–399
c) $400–499
d) $500–599
e) $600–699
f) $700–799
g) $800–899
h) $900–999
i) $1000 and over

The applet should use the GUI techniques introduced in Chapter 6. Display the results in a JTextArea. Use JTextArea method setText to update the results after each value is input by the user.

7.11   The bubble sort presented in Fig. 7.10 is inefficient for large arrays. Make the following simple modifications to improve the performance of the bubble sort:
a) After the first pass, the largest number is guaranteed to be in the highest-numbered element of the array; after the second pass, the two highest numbers are "in place"; etc. Instead of making nine comparisons on every pass, modify the bubble sort to make eight comparisons on the second pass, seven on the third pass, etc.
b) The data in the array may already be in the proper order or near-proper order, so why make nine passes if fewer will suffice? Modify the sort to check at the end of each pass

if any swaps have been made. If none have been made, the data must already be in the proper order, so the program should terminate. If swaps have been made, at least one more pass is needed.

7.12   Write statements that perform the following one-dimensional-array operations:
   a) Set the 10 elements of integer array `counts` to zero.
   b) Add one to each of the 15 elements of integer array `bonus`.
   c) Print the five values of integer array `bestScores` in column format.

7.13   Use a one-dimensional array to solve the following problem: Write an applet that inputs 5 numbers, each of which is between 10 and 100, inclusive. As each number is read, display it only if it is not a duplicate of a number already read. Provide for the "worst case," in which all 5 numbers are different. Use the smallest possible array to solve this problem. The applet should use the GUI techniques introduced in Chapter 6. Display the results in a `JTextArea`. Use `JTextArea` method `setText` to update the results after each value is input by the user.

7.14   Label the elements of three-by-five two-dimensional array `sales` to indicate the order in which they are set to zero by the following program segment:

```
for ( int row = 0; row < sales.length; row++ )

    for ( int col = 0; col < sales[ row ].length; col++ )

        sales[ row ][ col ] = 0;
```

7.15   Write an applet to simulate the rolling of two dice. The program should use `Math.random` once to roll the first die and again to roll the second die. The sum of the two values should then be calculated. Each die can show an integer value from 1 to 6, so the sum of the values will vary from 2 to 12, with 7 being the most frequent sum and 2 and 12 being the least frequent sums. Figure 7.20 shows the 36 possible combinations of the two dice. Your program should roll the dice 36,000 times. Use a one-dimensional array to tally the numbers of times each possible sum appears. Display the results in a `JTextArea` in tabular format. Also, determine whether the totals are reasonable (i.e., there are six ways to roll a 7, so approximately one-sixth of the rolls should be 7). The applet should use the GUI techniques introduced in Chapter 6. Provide a `JButton` to allow the user of the applet to roll the dice another 36,000 times. The applet should reset the elements of the one-dimensional array to zero before rolling the dice again.

	1	2	3	4	5	6
1	2	3	4	5	6	7
2	3	4	5	6	7	8
3	4	5	6	7	8	9
4	5	6	7	8	9	10
5	6	7	8	9	10	11
6	7	8	9	10	11	12

Fig. 7.20   The 36 possible sums of two dice.

7.16   What does the program of Fig. 7.21 do?

7.17   Write a program that runs 1000 games of craps (Fig. 6.9) and answers the following questions:

    a) How many games are won on the first roll, second roll, ..., twentieth roll and after the twentieth roll?

    b) How many games are lost on the first roll, second roll, ..., twentieth roll and after the twentieth roll?

    c) What are the chances of winning at craps? [*Note*: You should discover that craps is one of the fairest casino games. What do you suppose this means?]

    d) What is the average length of a game of craps?

    e) Do the chances of winning improve with the length of the game?

7.18   (*Airline Reservations System*) A small airline has just purchased a computer for its new automated reservations system. You have been asked to program the new system. You are to write an applet to assign seats on each flight of the airline's only plane (capacity: 10 seats).

    Your program should display the following alternatives: Please type 1 for First Class and Please type 2 for Economy. If the user types 1, your program should assign a seat in the first-class section (seats 1–5). If the person types 2, your program should assign a seat in the economy section (seats 6–10). Your program should then print a boarding pass indicating the person's seat number and whether it is in the first-class or economy section of the plane.

    Use a one-dimensional array of primitive type boolean to represent the seating chart of the plane. Initialize all the elements of the array to false to indicate that all seats are empty. As each seat is assigned, set the corresponding elements of the array to true to indicate that the seat is no longer available.

```
1   // Exercise 7.16: WhatDoesThisDo.java
2   import java.awt.*;
3   import javax.swing.*;
4
5   public class WhatDoesThisDo extends JApplet {
6      int result;
7
8      public void init()
9      {
10         int array[] = { 1, 2, 3, 4, 5, 6, 7, 8, 9, 10 };
11
12         result = whatIsThis( array, array.length );
13
14         Container container = getContentPane();
15         JTextArea output = new JTextArea();
16         output.setText( "Result is: " + result );
17         container.add( output );
18      }
19
20      public int whatIsThis( int array2[], int length )
21      {
22         if ( length == 1 )
23            return array2[ 0 ];
24         else
25            return array2[ length - 1 ] + whatIsThis( array2, length - 1 );
26      }
27   }
```

Fig. 7.21   What does this program do?

Your program should never assign a seat that has already been assigned. When the economy section is full, your program should ask the person if it is acceptable to be placed in the first-class section (and vice versa). If yes, make the appropriate seat assignment. If no, print the message "Next flight leaves in 3 hours."

7.19   What does the program of Fig. 7.22 do?

7.20   Use a two-dimensional array to solve the following problem: A company has four salespeople (1 to 4) who sell five different products (1 to 5). Once a day, each salesperson passes in a slip for each type of product sold. Each slip contains the following:
  a)   The salesperson number
  b)   The product number
  c)   The total dollar value of that product sold that day

Thus, each salesperson passes in between 0 and 5 sales slips per day. Assume that the information from all of the slips for last month is available. Write an applet that will read all this information for last month's sales and summarize the total sales by salesperson by product. All totals should be stored in the two-dimensional array `sales`. After processing all the information for last month, display the results in tabular format, with each column representing a particular salesperson and each row representing a particular product. Cross-total each row to get the total sales of each product for last month; cross-total each column to get the total sales by salesperson for last month. Your tabular printout should include these cross-totals to the right of the totaled rows and to the bottom of the totaled columns. Display the results in a `JTextArea`.

7.21   (*Turtle Graphics*) The Logo language made the concept of *turtle graphics* famous. Imagine a mechanical turtle that walks around the room under the control of a Java program. The turtle holds a pen in one of two positions, up or down. While the pen is down, the turtle traces out shapes as it moves; while the pen is up, the turtle moves about freely without writing anything. In this problem, you will simulate the operation of the turtle and create a computerized sketchpad.

```
1  // Exercise 7.19: WhatDoesThisDo2.java
2  import java.awt.*;
3  import javax.swing.*;
4
5  public class WhatDoesThisDo2 extends JApplet {
6
7     public void init()
8     {
9        int array[] = { 1, 2, 3, 4, 5, 6, 7, 8, 9, 10 };
10       JTextArea outputArea = new JTextArea();
11
12       someFunction( array, 0, outputArea );
13
14       Container container = getContentPane();
15       container.add( outputArea );
16    }
17
18    public void someFunction( int array2[], int x, JTextArea out )
19    {
20       if ( x < array2.length ) {
21          someFunction( array2, x + 1, out );
22          out.append( array2[ x ] + "  " );
23       }
24    }
25 }
```

Fig. 7.22   What does this program do?

Use a 20-by-20 array `floor` that is initialized to zeros. Read commands from an array that contains them. Keep track of the current position of the turtle at all times and whether the pen is currently up or down. Assume that the turtle always starts at position (0, 0) of the floor with its pen up. The set of turtle commands your program must process are shown in Fig. 7.23.

Suppose that the turtle is somewhere near the center of the floor. The following "program" would draw and print a 12-by-12 square, leaving the pen in the up position:

```
2
5,12
3
5,12
3
5,12
3
5,12
1
6
9
```

As the turtle moves with the pen down, set the appropriate elements of array `floor` to 1s. When the 6 command (print) is given, wherever there is a 1 in the array, display an asterisk or any character you choose. Wherever there is a 0, display a blank.

Write a Java applet to implement the turtle graphics capabilities discussed here. The applet should display the turtle graphics in a `JTextArea`, using Monospaced font. Write several turtle graphics programs to draw interesting shapes. Add other commands to increase the power of your turtle graphics language.

7.22   (*Knight's Tour*) One of the more interesting puzzlers for chess buffs is the Knight's Tour problem, originally proposed by the mathematician Euler. Can the chess piece called the knight move around an empty chessboard and touch each of the 64 squares once and only once? We study this intriguing problem in depth here.

The knight makes only L-shaped moves (two spaces in one direction and one space in a perpendicular direction). Thus, as shown in Fig. 7.24, from a square near the middle of an empty chessboard, the knight (labeled K) can make eight different moves (numbered 0 through 7).

a) Draw an eight-by-eight chessboard on a sheet of paper, and attempt a Knight's Tour by hand. Put a 1 in the starting square, a 2 in the second square, a 3 in the third, etc. Before starting the tour, estimate how far you think you will get, remembering that a full tour consists of 64 moves. How far did you get? Was this close to your estimate?

Command	Meaning
1	Pen up
2	Pen down
3	Turn right
4	Turn left
5,10	Move forward 10 spaces (replace 10 for a different number of spaces)
6	Print the 20-by-20 array
9	End of data (sentinel)

Fig. 7.23   Turtle graphics commands.

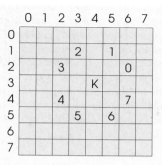

Fig. 7.24   The eight possible moves of the knight.

b) Now let us develop an applet that will move the knight around a chessboard. The board is represented by an eight-by-eight two-dimensional array board. Each square is initialized to zero. We describe each of the eight possible moves in terms of both their horizontal and vertical components. For example, a move of type 0 as shown in Fig. 7.24 consists of moving two squares horizontally to the right and one square vertically upward. A move of type 2 consists of moving one square horizontally to the left and two squares vertically upward. Horizontal moves to the left and vertical moves upward are indicated with negative numbers. The eight moves may be described by two one-dimensional arrays horizontal and vertical as follows:

```
horizontal[ 0 ] = 2          vertical[ 0 ] = -1
horizontal[ 1 ] = 1          vertical[ 1 ] = -2
horizontal[ 2 ] = -1         vertical[ 2 ] = -2
horizontal[ 3 ] = -2         vertical[ 3 ] = -1
horizontal[ 4 ] = -2         vertical[ 4 ] = 1
horizontal[ 5 ] = -1         vertical[ 5 ] = 2
horizontal[ 6 ] = 1          vertical[ 6 ] = 2
horizontal[ 7 ] = 2          vertical[ 7 ] = 1
```

Let the variables currentRow and currentColumn indicate the row and column; respectively, of the knight's current position. To make a move of type moveNumber, where moveNumber is between 0 and 7, your program should use the statements

```
currentRow += vertical[ moveNumber ];
currentColumn += horizontal[ moveNumber ];
```

Write a program to move the knight around the chessboard. Keep a counter that varies from 1 to 64. Record the latest count in each square the knight moves to. Test each potential move to see if the knight already visited that square. Test every potential move to ensure that the knight does not land off the chessboard. Run the program. How many moves did the knight make?

c) After attempting to write and run a Knight's Tour program, you have probably developed some valuable insights. We will use these insights to develop a *heuristic* (or "rule of thumb") for moving the knight. Heuristics do not guarantee success, but a carefully developed heuristic greatly improves the chance of success. You may have observed that the outer squares are more troublesome than the squares nearer the center of the board. In fact, the most troublesome or inaccessible squares are the four corners.

Intuition may suggest that you should attempt to move the knight to the most troublesome squares first and leave open those that are easiest to get to, so that when the board gets congested near the end of the tour, there will be a greater chance of success.

We could develop an "accessibility heuristic" by classifying each of the squares according to how accessible it is and always moving the knight (using the knight's L-shaped moves) to the most inaccessible square. We label a two-dimensional array `accessibility` with numbers indicating from how many squares each particular square is accessible. On a blank chessboard, each of the 16 squares nearest the center is rated as 8; each corner square is rated as 2; and the other squares have accessibility numbers of 3, 4 or 6 as follows:

```
2   3   4   4   4   4   3   2
3   4   6   6   6   6   4   3
4   6   8   8   8   8   6   4
4   6   8   8   8   8   6   4
4   6   8   8   8   8   6   4
4   6   8   8   8   8   6   4
3   4   6   6   6   6   4   3
2   3   4   4   4   4   3   2
```

Write a new version of the Knight's Tour, using the accessibility heuristic. The knight should always move to the square with the lowest accessibility number. In case of a tie, the knight may move to any of the tied squares. Therefore, the tour may begin in any of the four corners. [*Note*: As the knight moves around the chessboard, your program should reduce the accessibility numbers as more squares become occupied. In this way, at any given time during the tour, each available square's accessibility number will remain equal to precisely the number of squares from which that square may be reached.] Run this version of your program. Did you get a full tour? Modify the program to run 64 tours, one starting from each square of the chessboard. How many full tours did you get?

d) Write a version of the Knight's Tour program that, when encountering a tie between two or more squares, decides what square to choose by looking ahead to those squares reachable from the "tied" squares. Your program should move to the tied square for which the next move would arrive at a square with the lowest accessibility number.

7.23 (*Knight's Tour: Brute-Force Approaches*) In part (c) of Exercise 7.22, we developed a solution to the Knight's Tour problem. The approach used, called the "accessibility heuristic," generates many solutions and executes efficiently.

As computers continue to increase in power, we will be able to solve more problems with sheer computer power and relatively unsophisticated algorithms. Let us call this approach "brute-force" problem solving.

a) Use random-number generation to enable the knight to walk around the chessboard (in its legitimate L-shaped moves) at random. Your program should run one tour and print the final chessboard. How far did the knight get?

b) Most likely, the program in part (a) produced a relatively short tour. Now modify your program to attempt 1000 tours. Use a one-dimensional array to keep track of the number of tours of each length. When your program finishes attempting the 1000 tours, it should print this information in neat tabular format. What was the best result?

c) Most likely, the program in part (b) gave you some "respectable" tours, but no full tours. Now let your program run until it produces a full tour. (*Caution*: This version of the program could run for hours on a powerful computer.) Once again, keep a table of the number of tours of each length, and print this table when the first full tour is found. How many tours did your program attempt before producing a full tour? How much time did it take?

d) Compare the brute-force version of the Knight's Tour with the accessibility-heuristic version. Which required a more careful study of the problem? Which algorithm was more difficult to develop? Which required more computer power? Could we be certain (in advance) of obtaining a full tour with the accessibility-heuristic approach? Could we be certain (in advance) of obtaining a full tour with the brute-force approach? Argue the pros and cons of brute-force problem solving in general.

7.24 (*Eight Queens*) Another puzzler for chess buffs is the Eight Queens problem, which asks the following: Is it possible to place eight queens on an empty chessboard so that no queen is "attacking" any other (i.e., no two queens are in the same row, in the same column or along the same diagonal)? Use the thinking developed in Exercise 7.22 to formulate a heuristic for solving the Eight Queens problem. Run your program. (*Hint*: It is possible to assign a value to each square of the chessboard to indicate how many squares of an empty chessboard are "eliminated" if a queen is placed in that square. Each of the corners would be assigned the value 22, as demonstrated by Fig. 7.25. Once these "elimination numbers" are placed in all 64 squares, an appropriate heuristic might be as follows: Place the next queen in the square with the smallest elimination number. Why is this strategy intuitively appealing?

7.25 (*Eight Queens: Brute-Force Approaches*) In this exercise, you will develop several brute-force approaches to solving the Eight Queens problem introduced in Exercise 7.24.
a) Use the random brute-force technique developed in Exercise 7.23 to solve the Eight Queens problem.
b) Use an exhaustive technique (i.e., try all possible combinations of eight queens on the chessboard) to solve the Eight Queens problem.
c) Why might the exhaustive brute-force approach not be appropriate for solving the Knight's Tour problem?
d) Compare and contrast the random brute-force and exhaustive brute-force approaches.

7.26 (*Knight's Tour: Closed-Tour Test*) In the Knight's Tour (Exercise 7.22), a full tour occurs when the knight makes 64 moves, touching each square of the chessboard once and only once. A closed tour occurs when the 64th move is one move away from the square in which the knight started the tour. Modify the program you wrote in Exercise 7.22 to test for a closed tour if a full tour has occurred.

7.27 (*The Sieve of Eratosthenes*) A prime number is any integer that is evenly divisible only by itself and one. The Sieve of Eratosthenes is a method of finding prime numbers. It operates as follows:
a) Create a primitive type boolean array with all elements initialized to true. Array elements with prime indices will remain true. All other array elements will eventually be set to false.

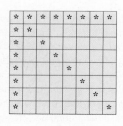

Fig. 7.25   The 22 squares eliminated by placing a queen in the upper left corner.

b) Starting with array index 2, determine whether a given element is true. If so, loop through the remainder of the array and set to false every element whose index is a multiple of the index for the element with value true. Then continue the process with the next element with value true. For array index 2, all elements beyond element 2 in the array that have indices which are multiples of 2 (indices 4, 6, 8, 10, etc.) will be set to false; for array index 3, all elements beyond element 3 in the array that have indices which are multiples of 3 (indices 6, 9, 12, 15, etc.) will be set to false; and so on.

When this process is complete, the array elements that are still true indicate that the index is a prime number. These indices can be displayed. Write a program that uses an array of 1000 elements to determine and print the prime numbers between 2 and 999. Ignore elements 0 and 1 of the array.

7.28 (*Bucket Sort*) A bucket sort begins with a one-dimensional array of positive integers to be sorted and a two-dimensional array of integers with rows indexed from 0 to 9 and columns indexed from 0 to $n - 1$, where n is the number of values to be sorted. Each row of the two-dimensional array is referred to as a bucket. Write an applet containing a method called bucketSort that takes an integer array as an argument and performs as follows:

a) Place each value of the one-dimensional array into a row of the bucket array, based on the value's "ones" digit. For example, 97 is placed in row 7, 3 is placed in row 3 and 100 is placed in row 0. This procedure is called a "distribution pass."

b) Loop through the bucket array row by row, and copy the values back to the original array. This procedure is called a "gathering pass." The new order of the preceding values in the one-dimensional array is 100, 3 and 97.

c) Repeat this process for each subsequent digit position (tens, hundreds, thousands, etc.).

On the second (tens digit) pass, 100 is placed in row 0, 3 is placed in row 0 (because 3 has no tens digit) and 97 is placed in row 9. After the gathering pass, the order of the values in the one-dimensional array is 100, 3 and 97. On the third (hundreds digit) pass, 100 is placed in row 1, 3 is placed in row 0 and 97 is placed in row 0 (after the 3). After this last gathering pass, the original array is in sorted order.

Note that the two-dimensional array of buckets is 10 times the length of the integer array being sorted. This sorting technique provides better performance than a bubble sort, but requires much more memory; the bubble sort requires space for only one additional element of data. This comparison is an example of the space–time trade-off: The bucket sort uses more memory than the bubble sort, but performs better. This version of the bucket sort requires copying all the data back to the original array on each pass. Another possibility is to create a second two-dimensional bucket array and repeatedly swap the data between the two bucket arrays.

7.29 (*Simulation: The Tortoise and the Hare*) In this problem, you will re-create the classic race of the tortoise and the hare. You will use random-number generation to develop a simulation of this memorable event.

Our contenders begin the race at "square 1" of 70 squares. Each square represents a possible position along the race course. The finish line is at square 70. The first contender to reach or pass square 70 is rewarded with a pail of fresh carrots and lettuce. The course weaves its way up the side of a slippery mountain, so occasionally the contenders lose ground.

A clock ticks once per second. With each tick of the clock, your applet should adjust the position of the animals according to the rules in Fig. 7.26. Use variables to keep track of the positions of the animals (i.e., position numbers are 1–70). Start each animal at position 1 (the "starting gate"). If an animal slips left before square 1, move the animal back to square 1.

Generate the percentages in Fig. 7.26 by producing a random integer i in the range $1 \le i \le 10$. For the tortoise, perform a "fast plod" when $1 \le i \le 5$, a "slip" when $6 \le i \le 7$ or a "slow plod" when $8 \le i \le 10$. Use a similar technique to move the hare.

Animal	Move type	Percentage of the time	Actual move
Tortoise	Fast plod	50%	3 squares to the right
	Slip	20%	6 squares to the left
	Slow plod	30%	1 square to the right
Hare	Sleep	20%	No move at all
	Big hop	20%	9 squares to the right
	Big slip	10%	12 squares to the left
	Small hop	30%	1 square to the right
	Small slip	20%	2 squares to the left

Fig. 7.26   Rules for adjusting the positions of the tortoise and the hare.

Begin the race by printing

```
BANG !!!!!
AND THEY'RE OFF !!!!!
```

Then, for each tick of the clock (i.e., each repetition of a loop), print a 70-position line showing the letter T in the position of the tortoise and the letter H in the position of the hare. Occasionally, the contenders will land on the same square. In this case, the tortoise bites the hare, and your program should print OUCH!!! beginning at that position. All print positions other than the T, the H or the OUCH!!! (in case of a tie) should be blank.

After each line is printed, test for whether either animal has reached or passed square 70. If so, print the winner and terminate the simulation. If the tortoise wins, print TORTOISE WINS!!! YAY!!! If the hare wins, print Hare wins. Yuch. If both animals win on the same tick of the clock, you may want to favor the tortoise (the "underdog"), or you may want to print It's a tie. If neither animal wins, perform the loop again to simulate the next tick of the clock. When you are ready to run your program, assemble a group of fans to watch the race. You'll be amazed at how involved your audience gets!

Later in the book, we introduce a number of Java capabilities, such as graphics, images, animation, sound and multithreading. As you study those features, you might enjoy enhancing your tortoise-and-hare contest simulation.

7.30   The Fibonacci series

0, 1, 1, 2, 3, 5, 8, 13, 21, ...

begins with the terms 0 and 1 and has the property that each succeeding term is the sum of the two preceding terms.

a) Write a *nonrecursive* method fibonacci(n) that calculates the *n*th Fibonacci number. Incorporate this method into an applet that enables the user to enter the value of n.
b) Determine the largest Fibonacci number that can be printed on your system.
c) Modify the program you wrote in part (a) to use double instead of int to calculate and return Fibonacci numbers, and use this modified program to repeat part (b).

RECURSION EXERCISES

7.31   (*Selection Sort*) A selection sort searches an array for the smallest element in the array, and swaps that element with the first element of the array. The process is repeated for the subarray beginning with the second element. Each pass of the array places one element in its proper location. For an array of *n* elements, *n* − 1 passes must be made, and for each subarray, *n* − 1 comparisons must be made to find the smallest value. When the subarray being processed contains one element, the array is sorted. Write recursive method `selectionSort` to perform this algorithm.

7.32   (*Palindromes*) A palindrome is a string that is spelled the same way forward and backward. Some examples of palindromes are "radar," "able was i ere i saw elba" and (if blanks are ignored) "a man a plan a canal panama." Write a recursive method `testPalindrome` that returns `boolean` value `true` if the string stored in the array is a palindrome and `false` otherwise. The method should ignore spaces and punctuation in the string. [*Hint:* Use `String` method `toCharArray`, which takes no arguments, to get a `char` array containing the characters in the `String`. Then pass the array to method `testPalindrome`.]

7.33   (*Linear Search*) Modify Fig. 7.11 to use recursive method `linearSearch` to perform a linear search of the array. The method should receive an integer array, the array's length and the search key as arguments. If the search key is found, return its index in the array; otherwise, return −1.

7.34   (*Binary Search*) Modify Fig. 7.12 to use recursive method `binarySearch` to perform a binary search of the array. The method should receive an integer array, the starting index and the ending index as arguments. If the search key is found, return its index in the array; otherwise, return −1.

7.35   (*Eight Queens*) Modify the Eight Queens program you created in Exercise 7.24 to solve the problem recursively.

7.36   (*Print an array*) Write a recursive method `printArray` that takes an array of `int` values and the length of the array as arguments and returns nothing. The method should stop processing and return when it receives an array of length zero.

7.37   (*Print an array backward*) Write a recursive method `stringReverse` that takes a character array containing a string as an argument, prints the string backward and returns nothing. [*Hint:* Use `String` method `toCharArray`, which takes no arguments, to get a `char` array containing the characters in the `String`. Then, pass the array to method `testPalindrome`.]

7.38   (*Find the minimum value in an array*) Write a recursive method `recursiveMinimum` that takes an integer array and the array's length as arguments and returns the smallest element of the array. The method should stop processing and return when it receives an array of one element.

7.39   (*Quicksort*) The recursive sorting technique called *Quicksort* uses the following basic algorithm for a one-dimensional array of values:

  a) *Partitioning Step*: Take the first element of the unsorted array and determine its final location in the sorted array (i.e., all values to the left of the element in the array are less than the element, and all values to the right of the element in the array are greater than the element). We now have one element in its proper location and two unsorted subarrays.

  b) *Recursive Step*: Perform step 1 on each unsorted subarray.

Each time step 1 is performed on a subarray, another element is placed in its final location of the sorted array, and two unsorted subarrays are created. When a subarray consists of one element, that element is in its final location (because a one-element array already is sorted).

The basic algorithm seems simple enough, but how do we determine the final position of the first element of each subarray? As an example, consider the following set of values (the element in bold is the partitioning element; it will be placed in its final location in the sorted array):

37 2 6 4 89 8 10 12 68 45

a) Starting from the rightmost element of the array, compare each element with **37** until an element less than **37** is found; then swap **37** and that element. The first element less than **37** is 12, so **37** and 12 are swapped. The new array is

12 2 6 4 89 8 10 *37* 68 45

Element 12 is in italics to indicate that it was just swapped with **37**.

b) Starting from the left of the array, but beginning with the element after 12, compare each element with **37** until an element greater than **37** is found; then swap **37** and that element. The first element greater than **37** is 89, so **37** and 89 are swapped. The new array is

12 2 6 4 *37* 8 10 *89* 68 45

c) Starting from the right, but beginning with the element before 89, compare each element with **37** until an element less than **37** is found; then swap **37** and that element. The first element less than **37** is 10, so **37** and 10 are swapped. The new array is

12 2 6 4 *10* 8 *37* 89 68 45

d) Starting from the left, but beginning with the element after 10, compare each element with **37** until an element greater than **37** is found; then swap **37** and that element. There are no more elements greater than **37**, so when we compare **37** with itself we know that **37** has been placed in its final location of the sorted array.

Once the partition has been applied on the previous array, there are two unsorted subarrays. The subarray with values less than 37 contains 12, 2, 6, 4, 10 and 8. The subarray with values greater than 37 contains 89, 68 and 45. The sort continues with both subarrays being partitioned in the same manner as the original array.

Based on the preceding discussion, write recursive method `quickSort` to sort a one-dimensional integer array. The method should receive as arguments an integer array, a starting index and an ending index. Method `partition` should be called by `quickSort` to perform the partitioning step.

7.40 (*Maze Traversal*) The following grid of #s and dots (.) is a two-dimensional array representation of a maze. The #s represent the walls of the maze, and the dots represent squares in the possible paths through the maze. Moves can be made only to a location in the array that contains a dot.

```
# # # # # # # # # # # #
# . . . # . . . . . #
. . # . # . # # # # . #
# # # . # . . . . # . #
# . . . . # # # . # . .
# # # # . # . # . # . #
# . . # . # . # . # . #
# # . # . # . # . # . #
# . . . . . . . # . #
# # # # # # . # # # . #
# . . . . . . # . . . #
# # # # # # # # # # # #
```

There is a simple algorithm for walking through a maze that guarantees finding the exit (assuming there is an exit). If there is not an exit, you will arrive at the starting location again. Place your right hand on the wall to your right and begin walking forward. Never remove your hand from the wall. If the maze turns to the right, follow the wall to the right. As long as you do not remove your hand from the wall, eventually you will arrive at the exit of the maze. There may be a shorter path than the one you have taken, but you are guaranteed to get out of the maze if you follow the algorithm.

Write recursive method `mazeTraverse` to walk through this maze. The method should receive as arguments a 12-by-12 character array representing the maze and the starting location of the maze.

As `mazeTraverse` attempts to locate the exit, it should place the character X in each square in the path. The method should display the maze after each move so the user can watch as the maze is solved.

7.41 (*Generating Mazes Randomly*) Write a method `mazeGenerator` that takes as an argument a two-dimensional 12-by-12 character array and randomly produces a maze. The method should also provide the starting and ending locations of the maze. Try your method `mazeTraverse` from Exercise 7.40, using several randomly generated mazes.

7.42 (*Mazes of Any Size*) Generalize methods `mazeTraverse` and `mazeGenerator` of Exercise 7.40 and Exercise 7.41 to process mazes of any width and height.

SPECIAL SECTION: BUILDING YOUR OWN COMPUTER

In the next several problems, we take a temporary diversion from the world of high-level language programming. To "peel open" a computer and look at its internal structure. We introduce machine-language programming and write several machine-language programs. To make this an especially valuable experience, we then build a computer (through the technique of software-based *simulation*) on which you can execute your machine-language programs!

7.43 (*Machine-Language Programming*) Let us create a computer called the Simpletron. As its name implies, it is a simple, but powerful, machine. The Simpletron runs programs written in the only language it directly understands: Simpletron Machine Language, or SML for short.

The Simpletron contains an *accumulator*—a "special register" in which information is put before the Simpletron uses that information in calculations or examines it in various ways. All information in the Simpletron is handled in terms of *words*. A word is a signed four-digit decimal number such as +3364, -1293, +0007 and -0001. The Simpletron is equipped with a 100-word memory, and these words are referenced by their location numbers 00, 01, ..., 99.

Before running an SML program, we must *load*, or place, the program into memory. The first instruction (or statement) of every SML program is always placed in location 00. The simulator will start executing at this location.

Each instruction written in SML occupies one word of the Simpletron's memory (and hence instructions are signed four-digit decimal numbers). We shall assume that the sign of an SML instruction is always plus, but the sign of a data word may be either plus or minus. Each location in the Simpletron's memory may contain an instruction, a data value used by a program or an unused (and hence undefined) area of memory. The first two digits of each SML instruction are the *operation code* specifying the operation to be performed. SML operation codes are summarized in Fig. 7.27.

The last two digits of an SML instruction are the *operand*—the address of the memory location containing the word to which the operation applies. Let's consider several simple SML programs.

Operation code	Meaning
Input/output operations:	
`final int READ = 10;`	Read a word from the keyboard into a specific location in memory.
`final int WRITE = 11;`	Write a word from a specific location in memory to the screen.

Fig. 7.27 Simpletron Machine Language (SML) operation codes. (Part 1 of 2.)

Operation code	Meaning

Load/store operations:

`final int LOAD = 20;` — Load a word from a specific location in memory into the accumulator.

`final int STORE = 21;` — Store a word from the accumulator into a specific location in memory.

Arithmetic operations:

`final int ADD = 30;` — Add a word from a specific location in memory to the word in the accumulator (leave the result in the accumulator).

`final int SUBTRACT = 31;` — Subtract a word from a specific location in memory from the word in the accumulator (leave the result in the accumulator).

`final int DIVIDE = 32;` — Divide a word from a specific location in memory into the word in the accumulator (leave result in the accumulator).

`final int MULTIPLY = 33;` — Multiply a word from a specific location in memory by the word in the accumulator (leave the result in the accumulator).

Transfer of control operations:

`final int BRANCH = 40;` — Branch to a specific location in memory.

`final int BRANCHNEG = 41;` — Branch to a specific location in memory if the accumulator is negative.

`final int BRANCHZERO = 42;` — Branch to a specific location in memory if the accumulator is zero.

`final int HALT = 43;` — Halt. The program has completed its task.

Fig. 7.27 Simpletron Machine Language (SML) operation codes. (Part 2 of 2.)

The first SML program (Fig. 7.28) reads two numbers from the keyboard and computes and prints their sum. The instruction +1007 reads the first number from the keyboard and places it into location 07 (which has been initialized to 0). Then instruction +1008 reads the next number into location 08. The *load* instruction, +2007, puts the first number into the accumulator, and the *add* instruction, +3008, adds the second number to the number in the accumulator. *All SML arithmetic instructions leave their results in the accumulator.* The *store* instruction, +2109, places the result back into memory location 09, from which the *write* instruction, +1109, takes the number and prints it (as a signed four-digit decimal number). The *halt* instruction, +4300, terminates execution.

Location	Number	Instruction
00	+1007	(Read A)
01	+1008	(Read B)
02	+2007	(Load A)

Fig. 7.28 SML program that reads two integers and computes their sum. (Part 1 of 2.)

Location	Number	Instruction
03	+3008	(Add B)
04	+2109	(Store C)
05	+1109	(Write C)
06	+4300	(Halt)
07	+0000	(Variable A)
08	+0000	(Variable B)
09	+0000	(Result C)

Fig. 7.28   SML program that reads two integers and computes their sum. (Part 2 of 2.)

The second SML program (Fig. 7.29) reads two numbers from the keyboard and determines and prints the larger value. Note the use of the instruction +4107 as a conditional transfer of control, much the same as Java's if statement.

Now write SML programs to accomplish each of the following tasks:
a) Use a sentinel-controlled loop to read 10 positive numbers. Compute and print their sum.
b) Use a counter-controlled loop to read seven numbers, some positive and some negative, and compute and print their average.
c) Read a series of numbers, and determine and print the largest number. The first number read indicates how many numbers should be processed.

7.44   (*A Computer Simulator*) In this problem, you are going to build your own computer. No, you will not be soldering components together. Rather, you will use the powerful technique of *software-based simulation* to create an object-oriented *software model* of the Simpletron of Exercise 7.43. Your

Location	Number	Instruction
00	+1009	(Read A)
01	+1010	(Read B)
02	+2009	(Load A)
03	+3110	(Subtract B)
04	+4107	(Branch negative to 07)
05	+1109	(Write A)
06	+4300	(Halt)
07	+1110	(Write B)
08	+4300	(Halt)
09	+0000	(Variable A)
10	+0000	(Variable B)

Fig. 7.29   SML program that reads two integers and determines which is larger.

Simpletron simulator will turn the computer you are using into a Simpletron, and you will actually be able to run, test and debug the SML programs you wrote in Exercise 7.43. Your Simpletron will be an event-driven applet: You will click a button to execute each SML instruction, and you will be able to see the instruction "in action."

When you run your Simpletron simulator, it should begin by displaying:

```
*** Welcome to Simpletron! ***
*** Please enter your program one instruction  ***
*** (or data word) at a time into the input    ***
*** text field. I will display the location    ***
*** number and a question mark (?). You then    ***
*** type the word for that location. Press the ***
*** Done button to stop entering your program. ***
```

The program should display an input JTextField in which the user will type each instruction one at a time and a Done button for the user to click when the complete SML program has been entered. Simulate the memory of the Simpletron with a one-dimensional array memory that has 100 elements. Now assume that the simulator is running, and let us examine the dialog as we enter the program of Fig. 7.29 (Exercise 7.43):

```
00 ? +1009
01 ? +1010
02 ? +2009
03 ? +3110
04 ? +4107
05 ? +1109
06 ? +4300
07 ? +1110
08 ? +4300
09 ? +0000
10 ? +0000
```

Your program should use a JTextField to display the memory location followed by a question mark. Each of the values to the right of a question mark is typed by the user into the input JText-Field. When the Done button is clicked, the program should display the following:

```
*** Program loading completed ***
*** Program execution begins   ***
```

The SML program has now been placed (or loaded) in array memory. The Simpletron should provide an "Execute next instruction" button the user can click to execute each instruction in the SML program. Execution begins with the instruction in location 00 and, as in Java, continues sequentially, unless directed to some other part of the program by a transfer of control.

Use the variable accumulator to represent the accumulator register. Use the variable instructionCounter to keep track of the location in memory that contains the instruction being performed. Use the variable operationCode to indicate the operation currently being performed (i.e., the left two digits of the instruction word). Use the variable operand to indicate the memory location on which the current instruction operates. Thus, operand is the rightmost two digits of the instruction currently being performed. Do not execute instructions directly from memory. Rather, transfer the next instruction to be performed from memory to a variable called instructionReg-ister. Then "pick off" the left two digits and place them in operationCode, and "pick off" the right two digits and place them in operand. Each of the preceding registers should have a corresponding JTextField in which its current value is displayed at all times. When the Simpletron begins execution, the special registers are all initialized to zero.

Now, let us "walk through" execution of the first SML instruction, +1009 in memory location 00. This procedure is called an *instruction execution cycle.*

The instructionCounter tells us the location of the next instruction to be performed. We *fetch* the contents of that location from memory by using the Java statement

```
instructionRegister = memory[ instructionCounter ];
```

The operation code and the operand are extracted from the instruction register by the statements

```
operationCode = instructionRegister / 100;
operand = instructionRegister % 100;
```

Now the Simpletron must determine that the operation code is actually a *read* (versus a *write*, a *load*, etc.). A switch differentiates among the 12 operations of SML. In the switch statement, the behavior of various SML instructions is simulated as shown in Fig. 7.30. We discuss branch instructions shortly and leave the others to you.

When the SML program completes execution, the name and contents of each register as well as the complete contents of memory should be displayed. Such a printout is often called a *computer dump* (no, a computer dump is not a place where old computers go). To help you program your dump method, a sample dump format is shown in Fig. 7.31. Note that a dump after executing a Simpletron program would show the actual values of instructions and data values at the moment execution terminated. The sample dump assumes that the output will be sent to the display screen with a series of System.out.print and System.out.println method calls. However, we encourage you to experiment with a version that can be displayed on the applet using a JTextArea or an array of JTextField objects.

Let us proceed with the execution of our program's first instruction—namely, the +1009 in location 00. As we have indicated, the switch statement simulates this task by prompting the user to enter a value into the input dialog, reading the value, converting the value to an integer and storing it in memory location memory[operand]. Since your Simpletron is event driven, it waits for the user to type a value into the input JTextField and press the *Enter* key. The value is then read into location 09.

At this point, simulation of the first instruction is completed. All that remains is to prepare the Simpletron to execute the next instruction. Since the instruction just performed was not a transfer of control, we need merely increment the instruction-counter register as follows:

```
++instructionCounter;
```

This action completes the simulated execution of the first instruction. When the user clicks the Execute next instruction button, the entire process (i.e., the instruction execution cycle) begins again with the fetch of the next instruction to be executed.

Instruction	Description
read:	Display an input dialog with the prompt "Enter an integer." Convert the input value to an integer and store it in location memory[operand].
load:	accumulator = memory[operand];
add:	accumulator += memory[operand];

Fig. 7.30   Behavior of several SML instructions in the Simpletron.

```
REGISTERS:
accumulator              +0000
instructionCounter          00
instructionRegister      +0000
operationCode               00
operand                     00

MEMORY:
        0     1     2     3     4     5     6     7     8     9
 0  +0000 +0000 +0000 +0000 +0000 +0000 +0000 +0000 +0000 +0000
10  +0000 +0000 +0000 +0000 +0000 +0000 +0000 +0000 +0000 +0000
20  +0000 +0000 +0000 +0000 +0000 +0000 +0000 +0000 +0000 +0000
30  +0000 +0000 +0000 +0000 +0000 +0000 +0000 +0000 +0000 +0000
40  +0000 +0000 +0000 +0000 +0000 +0000 +0000 +0000 +0000 +0000
50  +0000 +0000 +0000 +0000 +0000 +0000 +0000 +0000 +0000 +0000
60  +0000 +0000 +0000 +0000 +0000 +0000 +0000 +0000 +0000 +0000
70  +0000 +0000 +0000 +0000 +0000 +0000 +0000 +0000 +0000 +0000
80  +0000 +0000 +0000 +0000 +0000 +0000 +0000 +0000 +0000 +0000
90  +0000 +0000 +0000 +0000 +0000 +0000 +0000 +0000 +0000 +0000
```

Fig. 7.31   A sample dump.

Now let us consider how the branching instructions—the transfers of control—are simulated. All we need to do is adjust the value in the instruction counter appropriately. Therefore, the unconditional branch instruction (40) is simulated within the `switch` as

```
instructionCounter = operand;
```

The conditional "branch if accumulator is zero" instruction is simulated as

```
if ( accumulator == 0 )
    instructionCounter = operand;
```

At this point, you should implement your Simpletron simulator and run each of the SML programs you wrote in Exercise 7.43. If you desire, you may embellish SML with additional features and provide for these features in your simulator.

Your simulator should check for various types of errors. During the program-loading phase, for example, each number the user types into the Simpletron's `memory` must be in the range –9999 to +9999. Your simulator should test that each number entered is in this range and, if not, keep prompting the user to reenter the number until the user enters a correct number.

During the execution phase, your simulator should check for various serious errors, such as attempts to divide by zero, attempts to execute invalid operation codes, and accumulator overflows (i.e., arithmetic operations resulting in values larger than +9999 or smaller than –9999). Such serious errors are called *fatal errors*. When a fatal error is detected, your simulator should print an error message such as

```
*** Attempt to divide by zero ***
*** Simpletron execution abnormally terminated ***
```

and should print a full computer dump in the format we discussed previously. This treatment will help the user locate the error in the program.

7.45   (*Modifications to the Simpletron Simulator*) In Exercise 7.44, you wrote a software simulation of a computer that executes programs written in Simpletron Machine Language (SML). In this exercise, we propose several modifications and enhancements to the Simpletron Simulator. In Exercise 20.26 and Exercise 20.27, we propose building a compiler that converts programs written in a high-level programming language (a variation of Basic) to Simpletron Machine Language. Some of the following modifications and enhancements may be required to execute the programs produced by the compiler:

a) Extend the Simpletron Simulator's memory to contain 1000 memory locations to enable the Simpletron to handle larger programs.

b) Allow the simulator to perform remainder calculations. This modification requires an additional Simpletron Machine Language instruction.

c) Allow the simulator to perform exponentiation calculations. This modification requires an additional Simpletron Machine Language instruction.

d) Modify the simulator to use hexadecimal values rather than integer values to represent Simpletron Machine Language instructions.

e) Modify the simulator to allow output of a newline. This modification requires an additional Simpletron Machine Language instruction.

f) Modify the simulator to process floating-point values in addition to integer values.

g) Modify the simulator to handle string input. [*Hint*: Each Simpletron word can be divided into two groups, each holding a two-digit integer. Each two-digit integer represents the ASCII decimal equivalent of a character. Add a machine-language instruction that will input a string and store the string, beginning at a specific Simpletron memory location. The first half of the word at that location will be a count of the number of characters in the string (i.e., the length of the string). Each succeeding half-word contains one ASCII character expressed as two decimal digits. The machine-language instruction converts each character into its ASCII equivalent and assigns it to a half-word.]

h) Modify the simulator to handle output of strings stored in the format of part (g). [*Hint*: Add a machine-language instruction that will print a string, beginning at a certain Simpletron memory location. The first half of the word at that location is a count of the number of characters in the string (i.e., the length of the string). Each succeeding half-word contains one ASCII character expressed as two decimal digits. The machine-language instruction checks the length and prints the string by translating each two-digit number into its equivalent character.]

Object-Based Programming

Objectives

- To understand encapsulation and data hiding.
- To understand the notions of data abstraction and abstract data types (ADTs).
- To create Java ADTs—namely, classes.
- To be able to create and use objects.
- To be able to control access to instance variables and methods.
- To understand the use of the `this` reference.
- To be able to use class variables and methods.
- To appreciate the value of object orientation.

My object all sublime
I shall achieve in time.
W. S. Gilbert

Is it a world to hide virtues in?
William Shakespeare

Your public servants serve you right.
Adlai Stevenson

But what, to serve our private ends,
Forbids the cheating of our friends?
Charles Churchill

This above all: to thine own self be true.
William Shakespeare

Have no friends not equal to yourself.
Confucius

Outline

8.1 Introduction

In this chapter, we investigate object orientation in Java. Some readers might ask, why have we deferred this topic until now? There are several reasons. First, the objects we build in this chapter partially are composed of structured program pieces. To explain the organization of objects, we needed to establish a basis in structured programming with control structures. We also wanted to study methods in detail before introducing object orientation. Finally, we wanted to familiarize you with arrays, which are Java objects.

In our discussions of object-oriented programs in prior chapters, we introduced many basic concepts (i.e., "object think") and terminology (i.e., "object speak") that relate to Java object-oriented programming (OOP). We also discussed our program-development methodology: We analyzed typical problems that required applets or applications to be built and determined what classes from the Java API were needed to implement each program. We then selected appropriate variables and methods for each program and specified the manner in which an object of our class collaborated with objects of classes from the Java API to accomplish the program's overall goals.

Let us briefly review some key concepts and terminology of object orientation. Object orientation uses classes to *encapsulate* (i.e., wrap together) data (attributes) and methods (behaviors). For example, a car stereo encapsulates all the attributes and behaviors that enable the driver of the car to select a radio station, or play tapes or CDs. The companies that build cars do not build the car stereos; rather, they purchase the stereos and simply plug one into the dashboard of each car. The components of the radio are encapsulated in the radio's box.

Encapsulation enables objects to hide their implementation from other objects—a principle called *information hiding*. Although objects can communicate with one another across well-defined *interfaces* (just like the driver's interface to a car includes a steering wheel, accelerator pedal, brake pedal and gear shift), objects are unaware of how other objects are implemented—just as the driver may be unaware of how the steering, engine, brake and transmission mechanisms are implemented. Normally, implementation details are hidden within the objects themselves. Surely, it is possible to drive a car effectively without knowing the details of how engines, transmissions and exhaust systems work. Similarly, it is possible to select a radio station on a car stereo without knowing how the radio works. Later, we will see why information hiding is so crucial to good software engineering.

In *procedural programming languages* (like C), programming tends to be *action oriented*. Java programming, however, is *object oriented*. In procedural programming languages, the unit of programming is the *function* (functions are called *methods* in Java). In Java, the unit of programming is the *class*. Objects eventually are *instantiated* (i.e., created) from these classes, and attributes and behaviors are encapsulated within the "boundaries" of classes as fields and methods.

Procedural programmers concentrate on writing functions. They group actions that perform some task into a function and then group functions to form a program. Data is certainly important in procedural programs, but it exists primarily to support the actions that functions perform. The *verbs* in a system-requirements document describing the requirements for a new application help a procedural programmer determine the set of functions that will work together to implement the system.

In contrast, Java programmers concentrate on creating their own reference types, called *classes*. Each class contains as its *members* a set of fields (variables) and methods that manipulate those fields. (The fields of a class are sometimes called *data members*[1] in other programming languages.) The *nouns* in a system-requirements document help the Java programmer determine an initial set of classes with which to begin the design process. Programmers use these classes to instantiate objects that work together to implement the system.

This chapter explains how to create and use classes and objects, a subject known as *object-based programming (OBP)*. Chapter 9 and Chapter 10 introduce *inheritance* and *polymorphism*, respectively—key technologies that enable object-oriented programming. Although we do not discuss inheritance in detail until Chapter 9, it is part of several class declarations in this chapter and has been used in several examples previously. For example, every applet class defined to this point inherited from class `JApplet`.

8.2 Implementing a Time Abstract Data Type with a Class

Classes in Java facilitate the creation of *abstract data types (ADT)*, which hide their implementation from clients (or users of the class). A problem in procedural programming lan-

---

1. We sometimes use informal terminology that is familiar to programmers in other languages, such as "data members," rather than Java-specific terminology, such as "fields." For a listing of Java-specific terminology, please see the *Java Language Specification*, which can be downloaded from the Web site `java.sun.com/docs/books/jls/index.html`.

guages is that client code often is dependent on implementation details of the data used in the code. This dependency might necessitate rewriting the client code if the data implementation changes. ADTs eliminate this problem by providing implementation-independent *interfaces* (sets of methods offered by classes) to their clients. It is possible for the creator of a class to change the internal implementation of that class without affecting the clients of that class.

Software Engineering Observation 8.1

It is important to write programs that are understandable and easy to maintain. Change is the rule, rather than the exception. Programmers should anticipate that their code will be modified. As we will see, classes facilitate program modifiability.

Time1 Class Declaration

The next example consists of two classes—Time1 (Fig. 8.1) and TimeTest1 (Fig. 8.2). Class Time1 (declared in file Time1.java) is used to create objects that represent the time. Class TimeTest1 (declared in a separate file called TimeTest1.java) is an application class in which the main method will create an object of class Time1 and invoke its methods. These classes *must* be declared in separate files, because they are both public classes. In fact, each class declaration that begins with keyword public must be stored in a file that has exactly the same name as the class and ends with the .java file-name extension. [*Note:* The output of this program appears in Fig. 8.2.]

Common Programming Error 8.1

Declaring more than one public class in the same file is a syntax error.

```
1    // Fig. 8.1: Time1.java
2    // Time1 class declaration maintains the time in 24-hour format.
3    import java.text.DecimalFormat;
4
5    public class Time1 extends Object {
6        private int hour;      // 0 - 23
7        private int minute;    // 0 - 59
8        private int second;    // 0 - 59
9
10       // Time1 constructor initializes each instance variable to zero;
11       // ensures that each Time1 object starts in a consistent state
12       public Time1()
13       {
14           setTime( 0, 0, 0 );
15       }
16
17       // set a new time value using universal time; perform
18       // validity checks on the data; set invalid values to zero
19       public void setTime( int h, int m, int s )
20       {
21           hour = ( ( h >= 0 && h < 24 ) ? h : 0 );
22           minute = ( ( m >= 0 && m < 60 ) ? m : 0 );
23           second = ( ( s >= 0 && s < 60 ) ? s : 0 );
24       }
```

Fig. 8.1   Time1 abstract data type implementation as a class. (Part 1 of 2.)

```
25
26      // convert to String in universal-time format
27      public String toUniversalString()
28      {
29         DecimalFormat twoDigits = new DecimalFormat( "00" );
30
31         return twoDigits.format( hour ) + ":" +
32            twoDigits.format( minute ) + ":" + twoDigits.format( second );
33      }
34
35      // convert to String in standard-time format
36      public String toStandardString()
37      {
38         DecimalFormat twoDigits = new DecimalFormat( "00" );
39
40         return ( (hour == 12 || hour == 0) ? 12 : hour % 12 ) + ":" +
41            twoDigits.format( minute ) + ":" + twoDigits.format( second ) +
42            ( hour < 12 ? " AM" : " PM" );
43      }
44
45   } // end class Time1
```

Fig. 8.1   Time1 abstract data type implementation as a class. (Part 2 of 2.)

In Fig. 8.1, line 5 begins the Time1 class declaration, which indicates that class Time1 *extends* class *Object* (from package java.lang). Java programmers use *inheritance* to create classes from existing classes. In fact, every class in Java (except Object) *extends* (inherits from) an existing class. On line 5, the extends keyword followed by class name Object indicates that class Time1 inherits existing attributes and behaviors of class Object. If a class declaration does not specify extends and a class name to the right of the new class name, the new class implicitly extends class Object. In fact, every Java class contains the 11 methods declared in class Object. It is not necessary to understand inheritance to learn the concepts and programs in this chapter. We explore inheritance and class Object in detail in Chapter 9.

The *body* of the class declaration is delimited with left and right braces ({ and }) on lines 5 and 45. Any information that we place in the body is said to be encapsulated (i.e., wrapped) in the class. For example, class Time1 contains three integer variables—hour, minute and second—that represent the time in *universal-time* format (*24-hour clock* format). Previously, we referred to variables declared in a class declaration, but not inside a method declaration, as fields. An field that is not declared static is called an *instance variable*—each instance (object) of the class contains its own separate copy of the class's instance variables. (We discuss static fields in Section 8.11.)

Keywords *public* and *private* are *access modifiers*. Variables or methods declared public are accessible wherever the program has a reference to an object of the class. Variables or methods declared with access modifier private are accessible *only* to methods of the class in which they are declared.

Good Programming Practice 8.1

Precede every field and method declaration with an access modifier. As a rule of thumb, fields should be declared private and methods should be declared public.

The three integer instance variables `hour`, `minute` and `second` are each declared (lines 6–8) with access modifier `private`, indicating that these instance variables are accessible only to methods of the class—this is known as *data hiding*. When a program creates (instantiates) an object of class `Time1`, such variables are encapsulated in the object and can be accessed only through methods of that object's class (normally through the class's `public` methods). Typically, fields are declared `private`, and methods are declared `public`. It is possible to have `private` methods and `public` fields, as we will see later. The `private` methods are known as *utility methods* or *helper methods* because they can be called only by other methods of that class and are used to support the operation of those methods. Using `public` fields is uncommon and is a dangerous programming practice.

Good Programming Practice 8.2

We prefer to list the `private` fields of a class first, so that, as you read the code, you see the names and types of the variables before they are used in the methods of the class.

Software Engineering Observation 8.2

Make a class member `private` if there is no reason for that member to be accessed outside of the class declaration.

Classes often include accessor methods that can read or return data. Another common use for accessor methods is to test whether a condition is true or false—such methods are often called *predicate methods*. An example of a predicate method would be an `isEmpty` method for a *container class*—a class capable of holding many objects, such as a linked list, a stack or a queue. (These data structures are discussed in depth in Chapter 20, Chapter 21 and Chapter 22.) A program might test `isEmpty` before attempting to read another item from a container object. A program might test `isFull` before attempting to insert another item into a container object.

Class `Time1` contains constructor `Time1` (lines 12–15) and methods `setTime` (lines 19–24), `toUniversalString` (lines 27–33) and `toStandardString` (lines 36–43). These are the `public` methods (also called the *public services* or the *public interface*) of the class. *Clients* of class `Time1`, such as class `TimeTest1` (Fig. 8.2), use `Time1`'s `public` methods to manipulate the data stored in `Time1` objects or to cause class `Time1` to perform some service. The clients of a class use references to interact with an object of the class. For example, an applet's `paint` method is a client of class `Graphics`. Method `paint` uses its argument—a reference to a `Graphics` object (such as g)—to draw on the applet by calling methods that are `public` services of class `Graphics` (such as `drawString`, `drawLine`, `drawOval` and `drawRect`). As we will see in Fig. 8.2, a `Time1` reference will be used to interact with a `Time1` object.

Lines 12–15 declare the *constructor* of class `Time1`. A constructor initializes objects of a class. When a program creates an object of class `Time1`, `new` allocates memory for the object and calls the constructor to initialize the object. Class `Time1`'s constructor calls method `setTime` (lines 19–24) to initialize instance variables `hour`, `minute` and `second` to 0 (representing midnight). Constructors can take arguments, but cannot return values. An important difference between constructors and methods is that constructors *cannot specify a return type* (not even `void`). The constructor name must be the same as the class name. Normally, constructors are declared `public`.

Common Programming Error 8.2

Attempting to declare a return type for a constructor or attempting to return a value from a constructor is an error. Java allows other methods of the class to have the same name as the class and to specify return types. Such methods are not constructors and will not be called when an object of the class is instantiated. Java determines which methods are constructors by locating the methods that have the same name as the class and do not specify a return type.

Method setTime (lines 19–24) is a public method that declares three int parameters and uses them to set the time. A conditional expression tests each argument to determine whether the value is in a specified range. For example, the hour value must be greater than or equal to 0 and less than 24 (line 21), because universal-time format represents hours as integers from 0 to 23. Similarly, both minute and second values must be greater than or equal to 0 and less than 60 (lines 22 and 23). Any values outside these ranges are invalid values and are set to zero by default to ensure that a Time1 object always contains valid data. (In this example, zero is a valid value for hour, minute and second.) This is also known as *keeping the object in a consistent state* or *maintaining the object's integrity*. When setTime receives invalid data values, the program might want to indicate that the time was invalid. In Chapter 15, we discuss exception handling, which can be used to indicate invalid initialization values.

Good Programming Practice 8.3

Include constructors in a class declaration to ensure that the class's instance variables contain valid values when objects of the class are created.

Method toUniversalString (lines 27–33) takes no arguments and returns a string in universal-time format, consisting of six digits—two for the hour, two for the minute and two for the second. For example, if the time were 1:30:07 PM, method toUniversalString would return 13:30:07. Line 29 creates an instance of class DecimalFormat (imported at line 3 from package java.text) to format the universal time. Reference twoDigits is assigned a reference to an object of class DecimalFormat that is initialized with the pattern "00". This indicates that a formatted number should consist of two digits—each 0 is a placeholder for a digit. If the number being formatted is a single digit, it is automatically preceded by a leading 0 (i.e., 8 is formatted as 08). The return statement at lines 31–32 uses twoDigits to invoke DecimalFormat method format (which returns a string containing the formatted number) to format the hour, minute and second values into two-digit strings. Those strings are concatenated with the + operator (separated by colons), and the resulting string is returned by method toUniversalString.

Method toStandardString (lines 36–43) takes no arguments and returns a String in standard-time format, consisting of the hour, minute and second values separated by colons and followed by an AM or a PM indicator (e.g., 1:27:06 PM). Like method toUniversalString, method toStandardString uses DecimalFormat method format to format the minute and second as two-digit values with leading zeros if necessary. Line 40 determines the value for hour in the string—if the hour is 0 or 12 (AM or PM), the hour appears as 12; otherwise, the hour appears as a value from 1–11.

Using Class Time1

After declaring the class, we can use it as a type in declarations such as

```
Time1 sunset;  // reference to a Time1 object
```

The class name (Time1) is a type name. A class can yield many objects, just as a primitive type, such as int, can yield many variables. Programmers can declare new class types as needed; this is one reason why Java is known as an *extensible language*.

The TimeTest1 application class of Fig. 8.2 uses class Time1. Method main of class TimeTest1 declares and creates an instance of class Time1 called time in line 9. When the object is instantiated, new allocates the memory in which the Time1 object will be stored, then calls the Time1 constructor to initialize the instance variables of the new Time1 object. The constructor invokes method setTime to initialize each instance variable explicitly to 0. Then new returns a reference to the new object, and that reference is assigned to time. Similarly, lines 29 and 38 in class Time1 (Fig. 8.1) use new to create DecimalFormat objects, and pass the argument "00" to each object's constructor to indicate the patter used for formatting.

Software Engineering Observation 8.3

Every time new creates an object of a class, that class's constructor is called to initialize the instance variables of the new object.

```java
1   // Fig. 8.2: TimeTest1.java
2   // Class TimeTest1 to exercise class Time1.
3   import javax.swing.JOptionPane;
4
5   public class TimeTest1 {
6
7      public static void main( String args[] )
8      {
9         Time1 time = new Time1();   // calls Time1 constructor
10
11        // append String version of time to String output
12        String output = "The initial universal time is: " +
13           time.toUniversalString() + "\nThe initial standard time is: " +
14           time.toStandardString();
15
16        // change time and append updated time to output
17        time.setTime( 13, 27, 6 );
18        output += "\n\nUniversal time after setTime is: " +
19           time.toUniversalString() +
20           "\nStandard time after setTime is: " + time.toStandardString();
21
22        // set time with invalid values; append updated time to output
23        time.setTime( 99, 99, 99 );
24        output += "\n\nAfter attempting invalid settings: " +
25           "\nUniversal time: " + time.toUniversalString() +
26           "\nStandard time: " + time.toStandardString();
27
28        JOptionPane.showMessageDialog( null, output,
29           "Testing Class Time1", JOptionPane.INFORMATION_MESSAGE );
30
31        System.exit( 0 );
32
33     } // end main
```

Fig. 8.2   Time1 object used in a program. (Part 1 of 2.)

```
34
35   } // end class TimeTest1
```

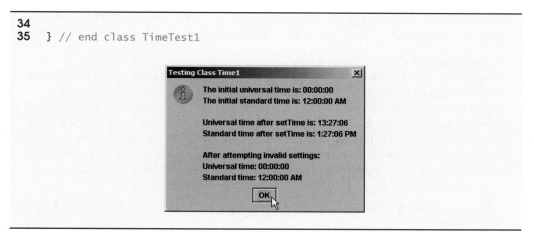

Fig. 8.2   Time1 object used in a program. (Part 2 of 2.)

Note that the TimeTest1.java file does not import class Time1. If a class is in the same package as the class that uses it, the import declaration is not required. Every class in Java is part of a package. If a programmer does not specify a package for a class, the class is placed in an unnamed *default package*, which includes all compiled classes in the current directory that were not placed explicitly in a package. We must specify import declarations for classes from the Java API, because they are declared outside the package of each new class we create. (Section 8.13 illustrates how to declare your own packages.) Note that import declarations are not required if the program fully qualifies the name of each class by preceding the class name with its package name and a dot (.). For example, a program can invoke class JOptionPane's showMessageDialog method as follows:

```
javax.swing.JOptionPane.showMessageDialog( "Your message here" );
```

However, such lengthy names can be cumbersome.

Lines 12–14 declare String reference output, which represents a string that will be displayed in a message box. Initially, the program assigns to output the time in universal-time format (by invoking time's toUniversalString method) and standard-time format (by invoking time's toStandardString method) to confirm that the Time1 object was initialized properly. Note the syntax of the method call in each case—the reference time is followed by a dot (.) and the method name. The reference refers to the object that will receive the method call (i.e., the object to which the message will be sent).

Line 17 uses time to invoke method setTime and change the time. Then lines 18–20 append the time to output again in both formats to confirm that the time was set correctly.

To illustrate that method setTime validates the values passed to it, line 23 calls method setTime and attempts to set the instance variables to invalid values of 99. Then lines 24–26 append the time to output again in both formats to confirm that setTime validated the data. Lines 28–29 display a message box with the results of our program. The last two lines of the output window show that the time is reset to midnight—the default value of a Time1 object—after attempting to set the time with three invalid values.

Class Time1 is our first example of a class that is not an applet and does not contain a main method. Class TimeTest1 declares method main, so class TimeTest1 can be used to begin program execution. Method `main` is known as the *entry point* into the program. A class containing main is known as an *application class* or *executable class*.

Notes on the `Time1` Class Declaration

Consider several issues of class design with respect to class `Time1`. The instance variables `hour`, `minute` and `second` are each declared `private`, so they are not directly accessible outside the class in which they are declared. The actual data representation used within the class is of no concern to the class's clients. For example, it would be perfectly reasonable for the class to represent the time internally as the number of seconds since midnight. Clients could use the same `public` methods and get the same results without being aware of this.[2] In this sense, implementation of a class is said to be *hidden* from its clients.

Software Engineering Observation 8.4

Information hiding promotes program modifiability and simplifies the client's perception of a class.

In Fig. 8.1, the `Time1` constructor initializes the instance variables to 0 (i.e., the universal-time equivalent of 12 AM). This ensures that the object is created in a consistent state (i.e., all instance variable values are valid). Invalid values cannot be stored in the instance variables of a `Time1` object, because the constructor is called when the `Time1` object is created and subsequent attempts by a client to modify the instance variables are scrutinized by the method `setTime`.

The instance variables of a class are initialized in that class's constructor, but they also can be initialized when they are declared in the class body. If you do not initialize instance variables explicitly, the compiler implicitly initializes them—primitive numeric variables are set to zero, `boolean` values are set to `false` and references are set to `null`.

It is interesting that the `toUniversalString` and `toStandardString` methods take no arguments. These methods belong to the same class as the instance variables `hour`, `minute` and `second`. Therefore, these methods implicitly have access to the instance variables of the particular `Time1` object on which these methods are invoked. This makes method calls more concise than conventional function calls in procedural programming. It also reduces the likelihood of passing the wrong arguments, the wrong types of arguments or the wrong number of arguments, as often happens in C function calls.

Software Engineering Observation 8.5

Using an object-oriented programming approach often simplifies method calls by reducing the number of arguments that must be passed. This benefit of object-oriented programming derives from the encapsulation of instance variables and methods within an object.

Classes simplify programming, because the client need be concerned only with the `public` methods exposed by the class. Usually, such methods are designed to be client oriented, rather than implementation oriented. Clients are neither aware of, nor involved in, a class's implementation. Interfaces change less frequently than do implementations. When an implementation changes, implementation-dependent code must change accordingly. By hiding the implementation, we reduce the possibility that other program parts will become dependent on class-implementation details.

---

2. Exercise 8.18 asks you to make precisely this modification to the `Time1` class of Figure 8.1 and show that there is no change visible to the clients of the class.

8.3 Class Scope

Recall from Section 6.9 that a class's variables and methods belong to that *class's scope*. Within a class's scope, class members are accessible to all of that class's methods and can be referenced directly by name.[3] Outside a class's scope, class members cannot be referenced directly by name. Those class members (such as `public` members) that are visible can be accessed only through a "handle"—a reference to an object of the class or the class name itself for `static` members. Members can be referred to by *objectReference-Name*. *objectMemberName*. For example, a program can determine the number of elements in array `grades` by accessing the array's `public` member `length` through the reference `grade` as in `grades.length`.

Variables declared in a method are known only to that method (i.e., they are local variables to that method). If a method declares a local variable with the same name as a variable declared in the method's enclosing class, the variable declared in the class's scope is shadowed (hidden) by the local variable. A hidden instance variable can be accessed in the method by preceding its name with the keyword `this` and a dot (`.`), as in `this.variableName`. Keyword `this` is discussed in more detail Section 8.5.

8.4 Controlling Access to Members

The access modifiers `public` and `private` control access to a class's variables and methods.[4] As we stated in Section 8.2, the primary purpose of `public` methods is to present to the class's clients a view of the *services* the class provides (the class's public interface). Clients of the class need not be concerned with how the class accomplishes its tasks. For this reason, the `private` variables and `private` methods of a class (i.e., the class's implementation details) are not directly accessible to the clients of a class. Restricting access to class members via keyword `private` is called information hiding.

Figure 8.3 demonstrates that `private` class members are not directly accessible outside the class. Line 10 attempts to access directly the `private` instance variable `hour` of the `Time1` object to which `time` refers. When this program is compiled, the compiler generates error messages stating that `private` members `hour`, `minute` and `second` are not accessible. [*Note:* This program assumes that the `Time1` class from Fig. 8.1 is used.]

Common Programming Error 8.3

An attempt by a method that is not a member of a particular class to access a `private` member of that class is a syntax error.

```
1   // Fig. 8.3: TimeTest2.java
2   // Errors resulting from attempts to access private members of Time1.
3   public class TimeTest2 {
4
5      public static void main( String args[] )
6      {
7         Time1 time = new Time1();
```

Fig. 8.3   Private members of class `Time1` are not accessible. (Part 1 of 2.)

3. In Section 8.11, we will see that `static` methods are an exception to this rule.
4. In Chapter 9, we will introduce the additional access modifier `protected`.

```
 8
 9         time.hour = 7;     // error: hour is a private instance variable
10         time.minute = 15; // error: minute is a private instance variable
11         time.second = 30; // error: second is a private instance variable
12      }
13
14   } // end class TimeTest2
```

```
TimeTest2.java:9: hour has private access in Time1
     time.hour = 7;     // error: hour is a private instance variable
          ^
TimeTest2.java:10: minute has private access in Time1
     time.minute = 15; // error: minute is a private instance variable
          ^
TimeTest2.java:11: second has private access in Time1
     time.second = 30; // error: second is a private instance variable
          ^
3 errors
```

Fig. 8.3   Private members of class Time1 are not accessible. (Part 2 of 2.)

8.5 Referring to the Current Object's Members with this

Every object can access a reference to itself, with keyword *this* (sometimes called the *this reference*). In a method, the this reference can be used implicitly and explicitly to refer to the instance variables and other methods of the object on which the method was called.

We now demonstrate implicit and explicit use of the this reference to enable the main method of class ThisTest to display the private data of a SimpleTime object (Fig. 8.4). Class SimpleTime (lines 22–55) declares three private instance variables—hour, minute and second (lines 23–25). The constructor (lines 29–34) receives three int arguments to initialize a SimpleTime object. Note that, for this example, we have made the parameter names for the constructor (line 29) identical to the instance variable names for the class (lines 23–25). We did this to illustrate explicit use of this. If a method contains a local variable with the same name as a field of that class, that method will refer to the local variable, rather than the field. In this case, the local variable shadows the field in that method scope. However, the method can use this to refer to the shadowed field explicitly, as shown in lines 31–33 for the shadowed instance variables of class SimpleTime.

```
1    // Fig. 8.4: ThisTest.java
2    // Using the this reference to refer to instance variables and methods.
3    import javax.swing.*;
4    import java.text.DecimalFormat;
5
6    public class ThisTest {
7
8       public static void main( String args[] )
9       {
```

Fig. 8.4   this used implicitly and explicitly to refer to members of an object. (Part 1 of 2.)

```
10            SimpleTime time = new SimpleTime( 12, 30, 19 );
11
12            JOptionPane.showMessageDialog( null, time.buildString(),
13               "Demonstrating the \"this\" Reference",
14               JOptionPane.INFORMATION_MESSAGE );
15
16            System.exit( 0 );
17         }
18
19  } // end class ThisTest
20
21  // class SimpleTime demonstrates the "this" reference
22  class SimpleTime {
23     private int hour;
24     private int minute;
25     private int second;
26
27     // constructor uses parameter names identical to instance variable
28     // names; "this" reference required to distinguish between names
29     public SimpleTime( int hour, int minute, int second )
30     {
31        this.hour = hour;       // set "this" object's hour
32        this.minute = minute;   // set "this" object's minute
33        this.second = second;   // set "this" object's second
34     }
35
36     // use explicit and implicit "this" to call toStandardString
37     public String buildString()
38     {
39        return "this.toStandardString(): " + this.toStandardString() +
40           "\ntoStandardString(): " + toStandardString();
41     }
42
43     // return String representation of SimpleTime
44     public String toStandardString()
45     {
46        DecimalFormat twoDigits = new DecimalFormat( "00" );
47
48        // "this" is not required here, because method does not
49        // have local variables with same names as instance variables
50        return twoDigits.format( this.hour ) + ":" +
51           twoDigits.format( this.minute ) + ":" +
52           twoDigits.format( this.second );
53     }
54
55  } // end class SimpleTime
```

Demonstrating the "this" Reference ☒

　　　this.toStandardString(): 12:30:19
　　　toStandardString(): 12:30:19

[OK]

Fig. 8.4   this used implicitly and explicitly to refer to members of an object. (Part 2 of 2.)

Method `buildString` (lines 37–41) returns a `String` created by a statement that uses the `this` reference explicitly and implicitly. Line 39 uses `this` explicitly to call method `toStandardString`. However, line 40 uses `this` implicitly to call the same method. Note that both lines perform the same task. Therefore, programmers usually do not use the `this` reference explicitly to reference methods within the current object.

Common Programming Error 8.4

For a method in which a parameter or local variable has the same name as a field of the class, use reference `this` if you wish to access the field of the class; otherwise, the method parameter or local variable will be referenced.

Error-Prevention Tip 8.1

Avoid method-parameter names or local variable names that conflict with field names. This helps prevent subtle, hard-to-locate bugs.

Good Programming Practice 8.4

The explicit use of the `this` reference can increase program clarity in some contexts where `this` is optional.

Class `ThisTest` (lines 6–19) runs the application that demonstrates explicit use of `this`. Line 10 creates an instance of class `SimpleTime` and invokes its constructor. Lines 12–14 invoke method `buildString` of the `SimpleTime` object, then display the results to the user in a message dialog. Subsequent examples in this and later chapters will demonstrate how the `this` reference can be used to pass a reference to the current object into a method of another object for processing.

Performance Tip 8.1

Java conserves storage by maintaining only one copy of each method per class; this method is invoked by every object of that class. Each object, on the other hand, has its own copy of the class's instance variables. Each method of the class uses `this` to determine the specific object of the class to manipulate.

When you compile this program, the compiler produces two separate files—a class file for class `SimpleTime` and a class file for class `ThisTest`. Every `public` Java class has its own class file with a `.class` extension. These two class files are placed in the same directory by the compiler.

8.6 Initializing Class Objects: Constructors

Recall from Section 8.2 that a *constructor* initializes the instance variables of a class. When an object of a class is created, `new` calls the class's *constructor* to perform the initialization. A constructor must have the same name as its class (including the same uppercase and lowercase letters). A constructor cannot specify a return type or a return value. A class can contain *overloaded constructors* that enable objects of that class to be initialized different ways.

When a program instantiates an object of a class, the program can supply *initializers* (arguments) in parentheses to the right of the class name. These initializers are passed as arguments to the class's constructor. This technique will be demonstrated in Fig. 8.6. We have also seen this technique several times previously as we created new objects of classes like `DecimalFormat`, `JLabel`, `JTextField`, `JTextArea` and `JButton`. For each of these classes, we have seen class-instance creation expressions of the form new *ClassName*(*argument1*, *argument2*, …, *argumentN*)

where **new** indicates that a new object is being created, *ClassName* indicates the type of the new object, the arguments specify the values used by the class's constructor to initialize the object and the entire expression returns a reference to the new object.

It is required that every class have at least one constructor. Therefore, if no constructors are declared for a class, the compiler creates a *default constructor* that takes no arguments. The default constructor for a class calls the no-argument constructor for its superclass (the class it extends), then proceeds to initialize the instance variables to the initial values specified in their declarations or to their default values (zero for primitive numeric types, **false** for **boolean** values and **null** for references). If the class that this class extends does not have a no-argument constructor, the compiler issues an error message. It is also possible for the programmer to provide a no-argument constructor. In fact, the constructor for class **Time1** in Fig. 8.1 is a no-argument constructor. If a programmer declares any constructors for a class, Java will not create a default constructor for that class.

Good Programming Practice 8.5

When appropriate (almost always), provide a constructor to ensure that every object's instance variables are properly initialized with meaningful values.

Common Programming Error 8.5

*If a class has constructors, but none of the **public** constructors are no-argument constructors, and a program attempts to call a no-argument constructor to initialize an object of the class, a compilation error occurs. A constructor can be called with no arguments only if there are no constructors for the class (the default constructor is called) or if there is a **public** no-argument constructor.*

8.7 Using Overloaded Constructors

As we stated in Section 8.6, constructors of a class can be *overloaded*. Overloaded constructors enable objects of a class to be initialized different ways. To overload constructors, simply provide multiple constructor declarations with different parameter lists. Recall from Section 6.11 that overloaded methods *must* have different parameter lists.

Common Programming Error 8.6

Attempting to overload a constructor with another constructor that has the exact same signature (name and parameters) is a syntax error.

The **Time1** constructor in lines 12–15 of Fig. 8.1 initialized **hour**, **minute** and **second** to 0 (which is midnight in universal time) by calling the class's **setTime** method. However, this constructor did not enable the class's clients to initialize the time with specific values. Class **Time2** (Fig. 8.5) contains five overloaded constructors that provide convenient ways to initialize objects of the new class **Time2**. Each constructor guarantees that every object the constructor initializes begins in a consistent state. In this program, four of the constructors invoke a fifth constructor, which, in turn, calls method **setTime** to ensure that the value supplied for **hour** is in the range 0 to 23 and that the values for **minute** and **second** are each in the range 0 to 59. If a value is out of range, it is set to zero by **setTime** (once again ensuring that each instance variable remains in a consistent state). The appropriate constructor is invoked by matching the number and types of the arguments specified in the constructor call with the number and types of the parameters specified in each con-

structor declaration. This is also known as *matching the signatures*. Figure 8.6 uses class
Time2 to demonstrate its constructors.

```java
1   // Fig. 8.5: Time2.java
2   // Time2 class declaration with overloaded constructors.
3   import java.text.DecimalFormat;
4
5   public class Time2 {
6      private int hour;     // 0 - 23
7      private int minute;   // 0 - 59
8      private int second;   // 0 - 59
9
10     // Time2 constructor initializes each instance variable to zero;
11     // ensures that Time object starts in a consistent state
12     public Time2()
13     {
14        this( 0, 0, 0 ); // invoke Time2 constructor with three arguments
15     }
16
17     // Time2 constructor: hour supplied, minute and second defaulted to 0
18     public Time2( int h )
19     {
20        this( h, 0, 0 ); // invoke Time2 constructor with three arguments
21     }
22
23     // Time2 constructor: hour and minute supplied, second defaulted to 0
24     public Time2( int h, int m )
25     {
26        this( h, m, 0 ); // invoke Time2 constructor with three arguments
27     }
28
29     // Time2 constructor: hour, minute and second supplied
30     public Time2( int h, int m, int s )
31     {
32        setTime( h, m, s ); // invoke setTime to validate time
33     }
34
35     // Time2 constructor: another Time2 object supplied
36     public Time2( Time2 time )
37     {
38        // invoke Time2 constructor with three arguments
39        this( time.hour, time.minute, time.second );
40     }
41
42     // set a new time value using universal time; perform
43     // validity checks on data; set invalid values to zero
44     public void setTime( int h, int m, int s )
45     {
46        hour = ( ( h >= 0 && h < 24 ) ? h : 0 );
47        minute = ( ( m >= 0 && m < 60 ) ? m : 0 );
48        second = ( ( s >= 0 && s < 60 ) ? s : 0 );
49     }
```

Fig. 8.5   Time2 class with overloaded constructors. (Part 1 of 2.)

```
50
51      // convert to String in universal-time format
52      public String toUniversalString()
53      {
54         DecimalFormat twoDigits = new DecimalFormat( "00" );
55
56         return twoDigits.format( hour ) + ":" +
57            twoDigits.format( minute ) + ":" + twoDigits.format( second );
58      }
59
60      // convert to String in standard-time format
61      public String toStandardString()
62      {
63         DecimalFormat twoDigits = new DecimalFormat( "00" );
64
65         return ( (hour == 12 || hour == 0) ? 12 : hour % 12 ) + ":" +
66            twoDigits.format( minute ) + ":" + twoDigits.format( second ) +
67            ( hour < 12 ? " AM" : " PM" );
68      }
69
70   } // end class Time2
```

Fig. 8.5   Time2 class with overloaded constructors. (Part 2 of 2.)

Most of the code in class Time2 is identical to that in class Time1, so we concentrate on the new constructors. Lines 12–15 declare the no-argument (default) constructor and introduce a special use of the this reference that is allowed only as the first statement in the body of a constructor. Line 14 uses this in method-call syntax to invoke the Time2 constructor that takes three arguments (declared at lines 30–33). The no-argument constructor passes values of 0 for the hour, minute and second. Using reference this as shown here enables us to reuse initialization code provided by another constructor, rather than defining similar or identical code in the body of the no-argument constructor.

Common Programming Error 8.7

It is a syntax error, when the this reference is used in a constructor's body to call another constructor of the same class and that statement is not the first statement in the constructor. It is also a syntax error when a non-constructor method attempts to invoke a constructor directly via the this reference.

Lines 18–21 declare a Time2 constructor that receives a single int argument representing the hour, which is passed with 0 for the minute and second to the constructor at lines 30–33. Lines 24–27 declare a Time2 constructor that receives two int arguments representing the hour and minute, which are passed with 0 for the second to the constructor at lines 30–33. Lines 30–33 declare the Time2 constructor that receives three int arguments representing the hour, minute and second. This constructor calls setTime to perform the initialization of the instance variables.

Common Programming Error 8.8

A constructor can call other methods of the class. Be aware that the instance variables might not yet be in a consistent state, because the constructor is in the process of initializing the object. Using instance variables before they have been initialized properly is a logic error.

Lines 36–40 declare a Time2 constructor that receives a Time2 reference to another Time2 object.[5] In this case, the values from the Time2 argument are passed to the constructor at lines 30–33 to initialize the hour, minute and second. Notice that this constructor directly accesses the hour, minute and second values of its argument time. Even though we know that hour, minute and second are declared as private variables of class Time2, we are able to access these values with the expressions time.hour, time.minute and time.second (line 39). This is due to a special relationship between objects of the same class.

Software Engineering Observation 8.6

When one object of a class has a reference to another object of the same class, the first object can access all the second object's data and methods (including those that are private).

None of the constructors specifies a return type. (Remember, this is not allowed for constructors.) Also, all the constructors receive different numbers of arguments and/or different types of arguments. Even though only two of the constructors receive values for the hour, minute and second, all the constructors specify values for hour, minute and second by substituting zeros for the missing values.

Class TimeTest3 (Fig. 8.6) creates six Time2 objects (lines 9–14) to demonstrate how to invoke the different Time2 constructors. Line 9 shows that the no-argument constructor is invoked by placing an empty set of parentheses after the class name when allocating a Time2 object with new. Lines 10–14 of the program demonstrate passing arguments to the Time2 constructors. The appropriate constructor is invoked by matching the number and types of the arguments specified in the constructor call with the number and types of the parameters specified in each constructor declaration. So line 10 invokes the constructor at lines 18–21 of Fig. 8.5. Line 11 invokes the constructor at lines 24–27 of Fig. 8.5. Lines 12–13 invoke the constructor at lines 30–33 of Fig. 8.5. Line 14 invokes the constructor at lines 36–40 of Fig. 8.5. The remainder of the application creates a string containing the string representations of each initialized Time2 object.

```
1   // Fig. 8.6: TimeTest3.java
2   // Overloaded constructors used to initialize Time2 objects.
3   import javax.swing.*;
4
5   public class TimeTest3 {
6
7      public static void main( String args[] )
8      {
9         Time2 t1 = new Time2();              // 00:00:00
10        Time2 t2 = new Time2( 2 );           // 02:00:00
11        Time2 t3 = new Time2( 21, 34 );      // 21:34:00
12        Time2 t4 = new Time2( 12, 25, 42 );  // 12:25:42
13        Time2 t5 = new Time2( 27, 74, 99 );  // 00:00:00
14        Time2 t6 = new Time2( t4 );          // 12:25:42
15
16        String output = "Constructed with: " +
```

Fig. 8.6   Overloaded constructors used to initialize Time2 objects. (Part 1 of 2.)

---

5.   In some languages, such a constructor is called a copy constructor.

```
17                  "\nt1: all arguments defaulted" +
18                  "\n          "  + t1.toUniversalString() +
19                  "\n          "  + t1.toStandardString();
20
21         output += "\nt2: hour specified; minute and second defaulted" +
22                  "\n          "  + t2.toUniversalString() +
23                  "\n          "  + t2.toStandardString();
24
25         output += "\nt3: hour and minute specified; second defaulted" +
26                  "\n          "  + t3.toUniversalString() +
27                  "\n          "  + t3.toStandardString();
28
29         output += "\nt4: hour, minute and second specified" +
30                  "\n          "  + t4.toUniversalString() +
31                  "\n          "  + t4.toStandardString();
32
33         output += "\nt5: all invalid values specified" +
34                  "\n          "  + t5.toUniversalString() +
35                  "\n          "  + t5.toStandardString();
36
37         output += "\nt6: Time2 object t4 specified" +
38                  "\n          "  + t6.toUniversalString() +
39                  "\n          "  + t6.toStandardString();
40
41         JOptionPane.showMessageDialog( null, output,
42            "Overloaded Constructors", JOptionPane.INFORMATION_MESSAGE );
43
44         System.exit( 0 );
45
46      } // end main
47
48   } // end class TimeTest3
```

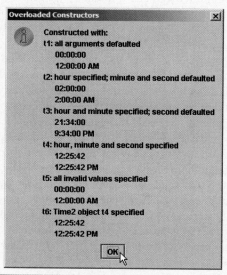

Fig. 8.6   Overloaded constructors used to initialize `Time2` objects. (Part 2 of 2.)

Each `Time2` constructor in Fig. 8.5 could be written to include a copy of the appropriate statements from method `setTime`. This could be slightly more efficient, because the extra constructor call and the call to `setTime` are eliminated. However, consider changing the representation of the time from three `int` values (requiring 12 bytes of memory) to a single `int` value representing the total number of seconds that have elapsed in the day (requiring 4 bytes of memory). Coding the `Time2` constructors and method `setTime` identically makes such a change in this class declaration more difficult. If the implementation of method `setTime` changes, the implementation of the `Time2` constructors would need to change accordingly. Having the `Time2` constructors call the constructor with three arguments (or even call `setTime` directly) requires any changes to the implementation of `setTime` to be made only once. This reduces the likelihood of a programming error when altering the implementation.

Software Engineering Observation 8.7

If a method of a class provides functionality required by a constructor (or other method) of the class, call that method from the constructor (or other method). This simplifies the maintenance of the code and reduces the likelihood of introducing errors into the code.

8.8 Using *Set* and *Get* Methods

Private fields can be manipulated only by methods of the class in which the fields are declared. A typical manipulation might be the adjustment of a customer's bank balance (e.g., a `private` instance variable of a class `BankAccount`) by a method `computeInterest`. Classes often provide `public` methods to allow clients of the class to *set* (i.e., assign values to) or *get* (i.e., obtain the values of) `private` instance variables. These methods need not be called *set* and *get*, but they often are.

As a naming example, a method that sets instance variable `interestRate` would typically be named `setInterestRate` and a method that gets the `interestRate` would typically be called `getInterestRate`. *Set* methods are also commonly called *mutator methods* (because they typically change a value). *Get* methods are also commonly called *accessor methods* or *query methods*.

It would seem that providing *set* and *get* capabilities is essentially the same as making the instance variables public. This is a subtlety of Java that makes the language so desirable for software engineering. If an instance variable is declared `public`, the instance variable can be read or written at will by any method that has a reference to an object of the class in which the instance variable is declared. If an instance variable is declared `private`, a `public` *get* method certainly seems to allow other methods to access the variable; however, the *get* method controls how the client can access the variable. For example, if we represent the time as the total number of seconds in a day, a `getHour` method would calculate the current hour and return that value. The client code does not need to know that there is not an `hour` instance variable in the object. The client simply cares about the service(s) the object provides. A public *set* method can—and should—carefully scrutinize attempts to modify the variable's value. This ensures that the new value is appropriate for that data item. For example, an attempt to *set* the day of the month for a date to 37 would be rejected, an attempt to *set* a person's weight to a negative value would be rejected, and so on. So, although *set* and *get* methods could provide access to private data, the access is restricted by the programmer's implementation of the methods.

The benefits of data integrity are not automatic simply because instance variables are declared `private`—the programmer must provide validity checking. Java enables programmers to design better programs in a convenient manner. A class's *set* methods can return values indicating that attempts were made to assign invalid data to objects of the class. This enables clients of the class to test the return values of *set* methods to determine whether the objects they are manipulating are valid and to take appropriate action if the objects are not valid. In Chapter 15, Exception Handling, we illustrate a more robust way in which clients of a class can be notified if an object is not valid.

Software Engineering Observation 8.8

Methods that set the values of `private` variables should verify that the intended new values are proper; if they are not, the set methods should place the `private` variables into an appropriate consistent state.

Software Engineering Observation 8.9

Keep all the instance variables of a class `private`. When necessary, provide `public` methods to change the values of `private` instance variables and to retrieve the values of `private` instance variables. This architecture helps hide the implementation of a class from its clients, which improves program modifiability.

Software Engineering Observation 8.10

Class designers need not provide set or get methods for each private field; these capabilities should be provided only when it makes sense.

Error-Prevention Tip 8.2

Making the instance variables of a class `private` and the methods of the class `public` facilitates debugging because problems with data manipulation are localized to the class's methods.

The applet of Fig. 8.7 (class `Time3`) and Fig. 8.8 (class `TimeTest4`) enhances our `Time` class (now called `Time3`) to include *get* and *set* methods for the private instance variables `hour`, `minute` and `second`. The *set* methods strictly control the setting of the instance variables to valid values. Attempts to set any instance variable to an incorrect value cause the instance variable to be set to zero (thus leaving the instance variable in a consistent state). Each *get* method returns the appropriate instance variable's value. This applet also introduces enhanced GUI event-handling techniques to enable you to test the new *set* and *get* methods of class `Time3` interactively.

```
1  // Fig. 8.7: Time3.java
2  // Time3 class declaration with set and get methods.
3  import java.text.DecimalFormat;
4
5  public class Time3 {
6     private int hour;      // 0 - 23
7     private int minute;    // 0 - 59
8     private int second;    // 0 - 59
9
```

Fig. 8.7　Time3 class with *set* and *get* methods. (Part 1 of 3.)

```
10      // Time3 constructor initializes each instance variable to zero;
11      // ensures that Time object starts in a consistent state
12      public Time3()
13      {
14         this( 0, 0, 0 ); // invoke Time3 constructor with three arguments
15      }
16
17      // Time3 constructor: hour supplied, minute and second defaulted to 0
18      public Time3( int h )
19      {
20         this( h, 0, 0 ); // invoke Time3 constructor with three arguments
21      }
22
23      // Time3 constructor: hour and minute supplied, second defaulted to 0
24      public Time3( int h, int m )
25      {
26         this( h, m, 0 ); // invoke Time3 constructor with three arguments
27      }
28
29      // Time3 constructor: hour, minute and second supplied
30      public Time3( int h, int m, int s )
31      {
32         setTime( h, m, s );
33      }
34
35      // Time3 constructor: another Time3 object supplied
36      public Time3( Time3 time )
37      {
38         // invoke Time3 constructor with three arguments
39         this( time.getHour(), time.getMinute(), time.getSecond() );
40      }
41
42      // Set Methods
43      // set a new time value using universal time; perform
44      // validity checks on data; set invalid values to zero
45      public void setTime( int h, int m, int s )
46      {
47         setHour( h );   // set the hour
48         setMinute( m ); // set the minute
49         setSecond( s ); // set the second
50      }
51
52      // validate and set hour
53      public void setHour( int h )
54      {
55         hour = ( ( h >= 0 && h < 24 ) ? h : 0 );
56      }
57
58      // validate and set minute
59      public void setMinute( int m )
60      {
61         minute = ( ( m >= 0 && m < 60 ) ? m : 0 );
62      }
```

Fig. 8.7   Time3 class with *set* and *get* methods. (Part 2 of 3.)

```
63
64     // validate and set second
65     public void setSecond( int s )
66     {
67        second = ( ( s >= 0 && s < 60 ) ? s : 0 );
68     }
69
70     // Get Methods
71     // get hour value
72     public int getHour()
73     {
74        return hour;
75     }
76
77     // get minute value
78     public int getMinute()
79     {
80        return minute;
81     }
82
83     // get second value
84     public int getSecond()
85     {
86        return second;
87     }
88
89     // convert to String in universal-time format
90     public String toUniversalString()
91     {
92        DecimalFormat twoDigits = new DecimalFormat( "00" );
93
94        return twoDigits.format( getHour() ) + ":" +
95           twoDigits.format( getMinute() ) + ":" +
96           twoDigits.format( getSecond() );
97     }
98
99     // convert to String in standard-time format
100    public String toStandardString()
101    {
102       DecimalFormat twoDigits = new DecimalFormat( "00" );
103
104       return ( ( getHour() == 12 || getHour() == 0 ) ?
105          12 : getHour() % 12 ) + ":" + twoDigits.format( getMinute() ) +
106          ":" + twoDigits.format( getSecond() ) +
107          ( getHour() < 12 ? " AM" : " PM" );
108    }
109
110  } // end class Time3
```

Fig. 8.7   Time3 class with *set* and *get* methods. (Part 3 of 3.)

The new *set* methods of class Time3 are declared in Fig. 8.7 at lines 53–56, 59–62 and 65–68. Each method performs the same conditional statement that was previously in method setTime for setting the hour, minute or second. These new methods enabled us to redefine the body of method `setTime` for better software engineering. Remember, if a method of a class already provides all or part of the functionality required by another method of the class, call that method. Method `setTime` (lines 45–50) now calls methods `setHour`, `setMinute` and `setSecond`—each of which performs part of `setTime`'s task.

The new *get* methods of the class are declared at lines 72–75, 78–81 and 84–87. Each method returns the `hour`, `minute` or `second` value. A copy of each value is returned, because these are all primitive-type variables. Using these new methods, we modified the bodies of methods `toUniversalString` (lines 90–97) and `toStandardString` (lines 100–108). In both cases, every use of instance variables `hour`, `minute` or `second` is replaced with a call to `getHour`, `getMinute` or `getSecond`.

Set and *get* methods have an important software-engineering advantage—flexibility. When we use *set* and *get* methods throughout the constructors and other methods of class `Time3`, we minimize the changes that we must make to the class declaration in the event that we alter the data representation. For example, we could change the data representation from `hour`, `minute` and `second` to another representation, such as a single integer that represents the total elapsed seconds in the day. When such changes are made, we must change every part of the class that accessed hour, minute or second directly. If we use the class's *set* and *get* methods to access the `hour`, `minute` and `second` throughout the class, then we would only need to provide new *set* and *get* method logic. Using this technique also enables programmers to change the implementation of a class without affecting the clients of that class (as long as all the `public` methods of the class still are called in the same way).

Software Engineering Observation 8.11

Accessing `private` data through set and get accessors not only protects the instance variables from receiving invalid values, but also hides the internal representation of the instance variables from that class's clients. Thus, if representation of the data changes (typically, to reduce the amount of required storage or to improve performance), only the method implementations need to change—the client implementations need not change, as long as the interface provided by the methods is preserved.

The `TimeTest4` applet (Fig. 8.8) provides a graphical user interface that enables the user to test class `Time3`'s method. The user can set the hour, minute or second value by typing a value in the appropriate `JTextField` and pressing the *Enter* key. The user can also click the **Add 1 to Second** button to increment the time by one second. The event handling demonstrated in this example is similar to that shown in Fig. 6.9 and Fig. 6.16. The `JTextField` and `JButton` events in this applet are all processed in method `actionPerformed` (lines 64–90). Notice that lines 54–57 all call `addActionListener` to indicate that the applet should start listening for events from the `JTextField`s `hourField`, `minuteField` and `secondField` and the `JButton` `tickButton`. All four calls use `this` as the argument, indicating that our `TimeTest4` applet object's `actionPerformed` method should be invoked for each user interaction with these four GUI components. In prior GUI examples, only one GUI component generated events. This raises an interesting question—how do we determine the GUI component with which the user interacted?

In `actionPerformed`, `event.getSource()` (lines 67, 71, 77 and 83) determines which GUI component generated the event. For example, line 67 determines whether `tickButton` was clicked by the user. If so, the body of the `if` statement executes. Otherwise, the program tests the condition in the `if` statement at line 71, and so on. Every event has a *source*—the GUI component with which the user interacted to signal the program to do a task. The `ActionEvent` parameter contains a reference to the source of the event. The condition in line 67 asks, "Is the *event source* the `tickButton`?" This condition compares the references on either side of the == operator to determine whether they refer to the same object. In this case, if they both refer to the `JButton tickButton`, then the program knows that the user pressed that button. Recall from Section 6.8 that the source of the event calls `actionPerformed` in response to the user interaction.

```
1   // Fig. 8.8: TimeTest4.java
2   // Demonstrating the Time3 class set and get methods.
3   import java.awt.*;
4   import java.awt.event.*;
5   import javax.swing.*;
6
7   public class TimeTest4 extends JApplet implements ActionListener {
8       private Time3 time;
9
10      private JLabel hourLabel, minuteLabel, secondLabel;
11      private JTextField hourField, minuteField, secondField, displayField;
12      private JButton tickButton;
13
14      // create Time3 object and set up GUI
15      public void init()
16      {
17          time = new Time3();  // create Time3 object
18
19          // get applet's content pane and change its layout to FlowLayout
20          Container container = getContentPane();
21          container.setLayout( new FlowLayout() );
22
23          // set up hourLabel and hourField
24          hourLabel = new JLabel( "Set Hour" );
25          hourField = new JTextField( 10 );
26          container.add( hourLabel );
27          container.add( hourField );
28
29          // set up minuteLabel and minuteField
30          minuteLabel = new JLabel( "Set Minute" );
31          minuteField = new JTextField( 10 );
32          container.add( minuteLabel );
33          container.add( minuteField );
34
35          // set up secondLabel and secondField
36          secondLabel = new JLabel( "Set Second" );
37          secondField = new JTextField( 10 );
38          container.add( secondLabel );
39          container.add( secondField );
40
41          // set up displayField
42          displayField = new JTextField( 30 );
43          displayField.setEditable( false );
44          container.add( displayField );
45
```

Fig. 8.8   *Set* and *get* methods used to manipulate a `Time3` object. (Part 1 of 4.)

```
46        // set up tickButton
47        tickButton = new JButton( "Add 1 to Second" );
48        container.add( tickButton );
49
50        // register event handlers; this applet is the ActionListener,
51        // which contains method actionPerformed that will be called to
52        // handle action events generated by hourField, minuteField,
53        // secondField and tickButton
54        hourField.addActionListener( this );
55        minuteField.addActionListener( this );
56        secondField.addActionListener( this );
57        tickButton.addActionListener( this );
58
59        displayTime(); // update text in displayField and status bar
60
61     } // end method init
62
63     // event handler for button and textfield events
64     public void actionPerformed( ActionEvent event )
65     {
66        // process tickButton event
67        if ( event.getSource() == tickButton )
68           tick();
69
70        // process hourField event
71        else if ( event.getSource() == hourField ) {
72           time.setHour( Integer.parseInt( event.getActionCommand() ) );
73           hourField.setText( "" );
74        }
75
76        // process minuteField event
77        else if ( event.getSource() == minuteField ) {
78           time.setMinute( Integer.parseInt( event.getActionCommand() ) );
79           minuteField.setText( "" );
80        }
81
82        // process secondField event
83        else if ( event.getSource() == secondField ) {
84           time.setSecond( Integer.parseInt( event.getActionCommand() ) );
85           secondField.setText( "" );
86        }
87
88        displayTime(); // update text in displayField and status bar
89
90     } // end method actionPerformed
91
92     // update displayField and applet container's status bar
93     public void displayTime()
94     {
95        displayField.setText( "Hour: " + time.getHour() + "; Minute: " +
96           time.getMinute() + "; Second: " + time.getSecond() );
97
```

Fig. 8.8 *Set* and *get* methods used to manipulate a Time3 object. (Part 2 of 4.)

```
98              showStatus( "Standard time is: " + time.toStandardString() +
99                 "; Universal time is: " + time.toUniversalString() );
100
101       } // end method displayTime
102
103       // add one to second and update hour/minute if necessary
104       public void tick()
105       {
106          time.setSecond( ( time.getSecond() + 1 ) % 60 );
107
108          if ( time.getSecond() == 0 ) {
109             time.setMinute( ( time.getMinute() + 1 ) % 60 );
110
111             if ( time.getMinute() == 0 )
112                time.setHour( ( time.getHour() + 1 ) % 24 );
113          }
114
115       } // end method tick
116
117 } // end class TimeTest4
```

Before and after setting the hour

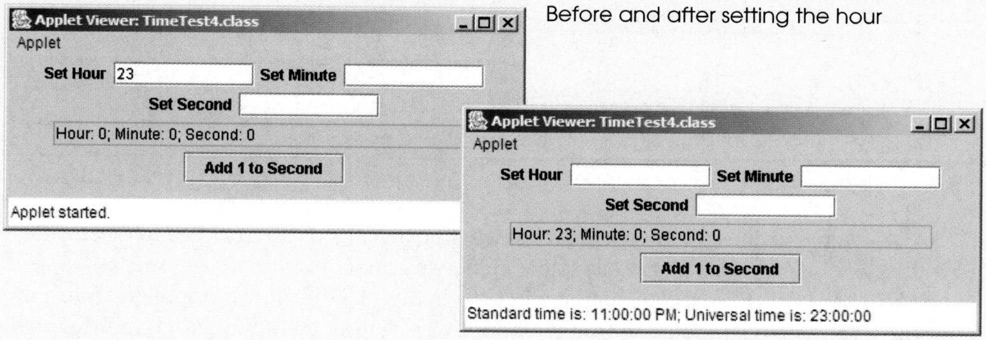

Before and after setting the minute

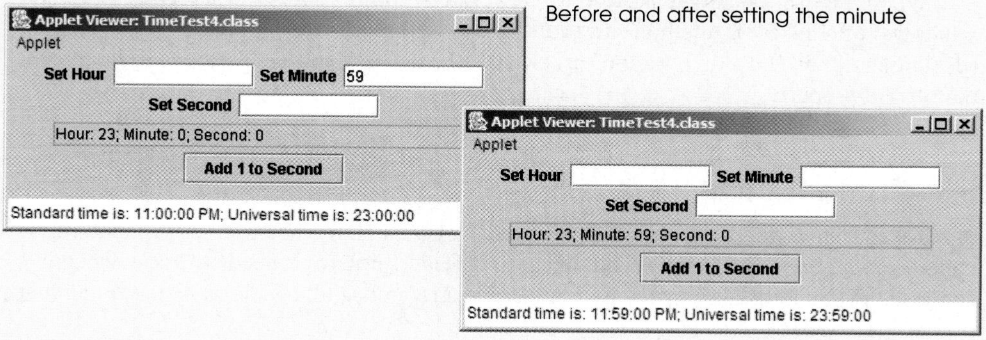

Fig. 8.8   *Set* and *get* methods used to manipulate a Time3 object. (Part 3 of 4.)

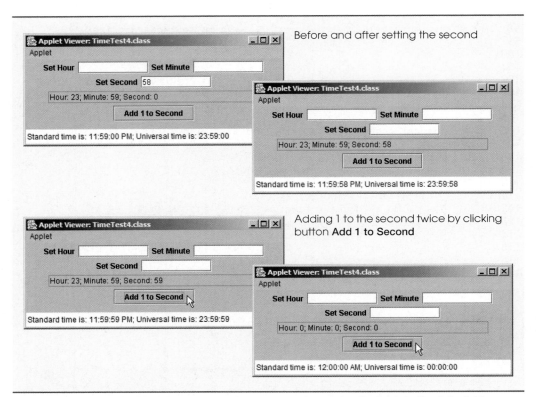

Fig. 8.8   *Set* and *get* methods used to manipulate a Time3 object. (Part 4 of 4.)

After each user interface event is processed, line 88 calls displayTime to display the new time as a string in the status bar of the applet and the hour, minute and second values in textfield displayField. The output windows in Fig. 8.8 illustrate the applet before and after the following operations: setting the hour to 23, setting the minute to 59, setting the second to 58 and incrementing the second value twice with the **Add 1 to Second** button.

When the user clicks the **Add 1 to Second** button (as shown in the last two output windows of Fig. 8.8), method actionPerformed calls the applet's tick method (declared at lines 104–115). Method tick uses the new *set* and *get* methods to increment the second properly.

8.9 Composition

A class can have references to objects of other classes as members. Such a capability is called *composition*. For example, an object of class AlarmClock needs to know when it is supposed to sound its alarm, so why not include a reference to a Time object as a member of the AlarmClock object?

Software Engineering Observation 8.12

One form of software reuse is composition, in which a class has references to objects of other classes as members.

The next program contains three classes—Date (Fig. 8.9), Employee (Fig. 8.10) and EmployeeTest (Fig. 8.11). Class Employee has instance variables firstName, last-Name, birthDate and hireDate. Members birthDate and hireDate (lines 7–8 of Fig. 8.10) are references to Date objects that have instance variables month, day and year. This demonstrates that a class can have references to objects of other classes. Note that class Employee does not import class Date because both classes are in the same default package.

Class EmployeeTest instantiates an Employee and initializes and displays the values of its instance variables. The Employee constructor (Fig. 8.10, lines 11–18) takes four arguments—first, last, dateOfBirth and dateOfHire. The objects referenced by these parameters are assigned to the Employee object's corresponding instance variables.

```
1   // Fig. 8.9: Date.java
2   // Date class declaration.
3
4   public class Date {
5      private int month;  // 1-12
6      private int day;    // 1-31 based on month
7      private int year;   // any year
8
9      // constructor: call checkMonth to confirm proper value for month;
10     // call checkDay to confirm proper value for day
11     public Date( int theMonth, int theDay, int theYear )
12     {
13        month = checkMonth( theMonth ); // validate month
14        year = theYear;                 // could validate year
15        day = checkDay( theDay );       // validate day
16
17        System.out.println( "Date object constructor for date " +
18           toDateString() );
19
20     } // end Date constructor
21
22     // utility method to confirm proper month value
23     private int checkMonth( int testMonth )
24     {
25        if ( testMonth > 0 && testMonth <= 12 )  // validate month
26           return testMonth;
27
28        else { // month is invalid
29           System.out.println( "Invalid month (" + testMonth +
30              ") set to 1." );
31           return 1;  // maintain object in consistent state
32        }
33
34     } // end method checkMonth
35
36     // utility method to confirm proper day value based on month and year
37     private int checkDay( int testDay )
38     {
```

Fig. 8.9   Date class. (Part 1 of 2.)

```
39          int daysPerMonth[] =
40              { 0, 31, 28, 31, 30, 31, 30, 31, 31, 30, 31, 30, 31 };
41
42          // check if day in range for month
43          if ( testDay > 0 && testDay <= daysPerMonth[ month ] )
44              return testDay;
45
46          // check for leap year
47          if ( month == 2 && testDay == 29 && ( year % 400 == 0 ||
48              ( year % 4 == 0 && year % 100 != 0 ) ) )
49              return testDay;
50
51          System.out.println( "Invalid day (" + testDay + ") set to 1." );
52
53          return 1;  // maintain object in consistent state
54
55      } // end method checkDay
56
57      // return a String of the form month/day/year
58      public String toDateString()
59      {
60          return month + "/" + day + "/" + year;
61      }
62
63  } // end class Date
```

Fig. 8.9   Date class. (Part 2 of 2.)

```
1   // Fig. 8.10: Employee.java
2   // Employee class declaration.
3
4   public class Employee {
5       private String firstName;
6       private String lastName;
7       private Date birthDate;
8       private Date hireDate;
9
10      // constructor to initialize name, birth date and hire date
11      public Employee( String first, String last, Date dateOfBirth,
12          Date dateOfHire )
13      {
14          firstName = first;
15          lastName = last;
16          birthDate = dateOfBirth;
17          hireDate = dateOfHire;
18      }
19
20      // convert Employee to String format
21      public String toEmployeeString()
22      {
23          return lastName + ", " + firstName +
24              "  Hired: " + hireDate.toDateString() +
```

Fig. 8.10   Employee class with member object references. (Part 1 of 2.)

```
25                   "  Birthday: " + birthDate.toDateString();
26       }
27
28   } // end class Employee
```

Fig. 8.10   Employee class with member object references. (Part 2 of 2.)

```
1    // Fig. 8.11: EmployeeTest.java
2    // Demonstrating an object with a member object.
3    import javax.swing.JOptionPane;
4
5    public class EmployeeTest {
6
7       public static void main( String args[] )
8       {
9          Date birth = new Date( 7, 24, 1949 );
10         Date hire = new Date( 3, 12, 1988 );
11         Employee employee = new Employee( "Bob", "Jones", birth, hire );
12
13         JOptionPane.showMessageDialog( null, employee.toEmployeeString(),
14            "Testing Class Employee", JOptionPane.INFORMATION_MESSAGE );
15
16         System.exit( 0 );
17      }
18
19   } // end class EmployeeTest
```

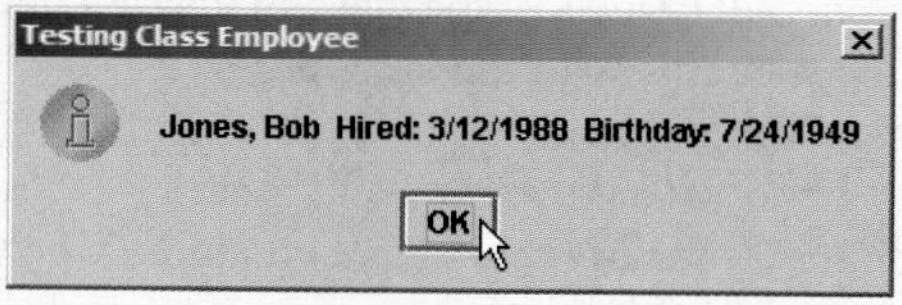

```
Date object constructor for date 7/24/1949
Date object constructor for date 3/12/1988
```

Fig. 8.11   Member object demonstration.

8.10 Garbage Collection

We have seen that constructors are capable of initializing an object's instance variables when the object is created. Constructors acquire various system resources, such as memory. We need a disciplined way to give resources back to the system when they are no longer needed to avoid "resource leaks." Java performs automatic *garbage collection* to help return the memory occupied by objects that are no longer in use back to the system. When an there are no more references to an object, the object is *marked for garbage collection*. The memory for such an object can be reclaimed when the *garbage collector* executes. Therefore, memory leaks that are common in other languages like C and C++ (because memory is not automatically reclaimed in those languages) are less likely to happen in Java. However, other resource leaks can occur.

Every class in Java has a *finalizer method* that returns resources to the system. The finalizer method is called to perform *termination housekeeping* on an object just before the garbage collector reclaims that object's memory. A class's finalizer always has the name `finalize`, does not take parameters and has return type `void`. This method cannot be overloaded. Method `finalize` is declared in class `Object` as a placeholder that does nothing. Recall from Section 8.2 that all classes in Java inherit the methods of class `Object`. This guarantees that every class has a `finalize` method for the garbage collector to call.

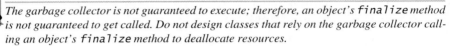

Software Engineering Observation 8.13

The garbage collector is not guaranteed to execute; therefore, an object's `finalize` method is not guaranteed to get called. Do not design classes that rely on the garbage collector calling an object's `finalize` method to deallocate resources.

Finalizers are rarely used in real-world Java applications. Primarily, `finalize` is used in classes that invoke *native code*—programs or libraries not written in Java and specific to the operating system of the computer on which the Java program executes. Native code is beyond the scope of this book. Declaring a `finalize` method for a class is generally discouraged. However, we use a `finalize` method in Section 8.11 for demonstration purposes to show when the garbage collector executes.

8.11 Static Class Members

Each object has its own copy of all the instance variables of the class. In certain cases, only one copy of a particular variable should be shared by all objects of a class. A *static field*—called a *class variable*—is used in such cases, among others. A class variable represents *class-wide information*—all objects of the class share the same piece of data. The declaration of a `static` member begins with the keyword `static`.

Let us motivate the need for `static` class-wide data with a video game example. Suppose that we have a video game with `Martian`s and other space creatures. Each `Martian` tends to be brave and willing to attack other space creatures when the `Martian` is aware that there are at least four other `Martian`s present. If fewer than five `Martian`s are present, each `Martian` becomes cowardly, so each `Martian` needs to know the `martianCount`. We could endow class `Martian` with `martianCount` as instance data. If we do this, then every `Martian` will have a separate copy of the instance data, and every time we create a new `Martian`, we will have to update the instance variable `martianCount` in every `Martian`. This wastes space with the redundant copies, wastes time in updating the separate copies and is error prone. Instead, we declare `martianCount` to be `static`. This makes `martianCount` class-wide data. Every `Martian` can see the `martianCount` as if it were instance data of class `Martian`, but only one copy of the static `martianCount` is maintained by Java. This saves space. We save time by having the `Martian` constructor increment the static `martianCount`. Because there is only one copy, we do not have to increment separate copies of `martianCount` for each `Martian` object.

Software Engineering Observation 8.14

Use a class variable when all objects of a class should be required to use the same copy of the variable.

Although class variables may seem like global variables, class variables have class scope. A class's `public static` members can be accessed through a reference to any object of that class, or they can be accessed by qualifying the member name with the class name and a dot (.), as in Math.random(). A class's private static class members can be accessed only through methods of that class. Actually, static class members exist even when no objects of that class exist—they are available as soon as the class is loaded into memory at execution time. To access a public static member when no objects of the class exist, prefix the class name and a dot (.) to the class member. To access a private static member when no objects of the class exist, a public static method must be provided and the method must be called by qualifying its name with the class name and a dot.

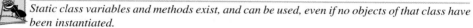

Software Engineering Observation 8.15

Static class variables and methods exist, and can be used, even if no objects of that class have been instantiated.

Our next program declares two classes—Employee (Fig. 8.12) and EmployeeTest (Fig. 8.13). Class Employee declares private static variable count (Fig. 8.12, line 6), and public static method getCount (Fig. 8.12, lines 43–46). The class variable count is initialized to zero in line 6. If a static class variable is not initialized, the compiler assigns the variable its default value. Class variable count maintains a count of the number of objects of class Employee that currently reside in memory. This includes objects that have already been marked for garbage collection, but have not yet been reclaimed.

```
1   // Fig. 8.12: Employee.java
2   // Employee class declaration.
3   public class Employee {
4       private String firstName;
5       private String lastName;
6       private static int count = 0;   // number of objects in memory
7
8       // initialize employee, add 1 to static count and
9       // output String indicating that constructor was called
10      public Employee( String first, String last )
11      {
12          firstName = first;
13          lastName = last;
14
15          ++count;   // increment static count of employees
16          System.out.println( "Employee constructor: " +
17              firstName + " " + lastName );
18      }
19
20      // subtract 1 from static count when garbage collector
21      // calls finalize to clean up object and output String
22      // indicating that finalize was called
23      protected void finalize()
24      {
25          --count;   // decrement static count of employees
26          System.out.println( "Employee finalizer: " +
27              firstName + " " + lastName + "; count = " + count );
28      }
```

Fig. 8.12   static variable used to maintain a count of the number of Employee objects in memory. (Part 1 of 2.)

```
29
30      // get first name
31      public String getFirstName()
32      {
33          return firstName;
34      }
35
36      // get last name
37      public String getLastName()
38      {
39          return lastName;
40      }
41
42      // static method to get static count value
43      public static int getCount()
44      {
45          return count;
46      }
47
48   } // end class Employee
```

Fig. 8.12   `static` variable used to maintain a count of the number of `Employee` objects in memory. (Part 2 of 2.)

When `Employee` objects exist, member `count` can be used in any method of an `Employee` object—this example increments `count` in the constructor (line 15) and decrements it in the finalizer (line 25). When no objects of class `Employee` exist, member `count` can still be referenced, but only through a call to `public static` method `getCount` (lines 43–46), as in `Employee.getCount()`, which returns the number of `Employee` objects currently in memory. However, when there are objects instantiated, method `getCount` can also be called through a reference to one of the objects, as in the call `e1.getCount()`.

Good Programming Practice 8.6

Always invoke `static` methods by using the class name and a dot (.). This emphasizes to other programmers reading your code that the method being called is a `static` method.

Notice that the `Employee` class has a `finalize` method (lines 23–28). This method is included only to show when the garbage collector executes in this program. Method `finalize` normally is declared *protected*, so it is not part of the `public` services of a class. We will discuss the **protected** member access modifier in detail in Chapter 9.

`EmployeeTest` method `main` (Fig. 8.13) instantiates two `Employee` objects (lines 15–16). When each `Employee` object's constructor is invoked, lines 12–13 of Fig. 8.12 store references to that `Employee`'s first name and last name `String` objects.[6]

---

6. These two statements *do not* make copies of the original `String` arguments. Actually, `String` objects in Java are immutable—they cannot be modified after they are created. Because a reference cannot be used to modify a `String`, it is safe to have many references to one `String` object. This is not normally the case for most other classes in Java. If `String` objects are immutable, why are we able to use the + and += operators to concatenate `String` objects? As we will discuss in Chapter 11, Strings and Characters, `String` concatenation operations actually result in a new `String` object containing the concatenated values. The original `String` objects are not modified.

When `main` has finished using the two `Employee` objects, the references `e1` and `e2` are set to `null` at lines 32–33. At this point, references `e1` and `e2` no longer refer to the objects that were instantiated on lines 15–16. This "marks the objects for garbage collection" because there are no more references to the objects in the program.

```java
1   // Fig. 8.13: EmployeeTest.java
2   // Test Employee class with static class variable,
3   // static class method, and dynamic memory.
4   import javax.swing.*;
5
6   public class EmployeeTest {
7
8      public static void main( String args[] )
9      {
10        // prove that count is 0 before creating Employees
11        String output = "Employees before instantiation: " +
12           Employee.getCount();
13
14        // create two Employees; count should be 2
15        Employee e1 = new Employee( "Susan", "Baker" );
16        Employee e2 = new Employee( "Bob", "Jones" );
17
18        // prove that count is 2 after creating two Employees
19        output += "\n\nEmployees after instantiation: " +
20           "\nvia e1.getCount(): " + e1.getCount() +
21           "\nvia e2.getCount(): " + e2.getCount() +
22           "\nvia Employee.getCount(): " + Employee.getCount();
23
24        // get names of Employees
25        output += "\n\nEmployee 1: " + e1.getFirstName() +
26           " " + e1.getLastName() + "\nEmployee 2: " +
27           e2.getFirstName() + " " + e2.getLastName();
28
29        // decrement reference count for each Employee object; in this
30        // example, there is only one reference to each Employee, so these
31        // statements mark each Employee object for garbage collection
32        e1 = null;
33        e2 = null;
34
35        System.gc(); // suggest call to garbage collector
36
37        // show Employee count after calling garbage collector; count
38        // displayed may be 0, 1 or 2 based on whether garbage collector
39        // executes immediately and number of Employee objects collected
40        output += "\n\nEmployees after System.gc(): " +
41           Employee.getCount();
42
43        JOptionPane.showMessageDialog( null, output,
44           "Static Members", JOptionPane.INFORMATION_MESSAGE );
45
46        System.exit( 0 );
47     }
```

Fig. 8.13   `static` member demonstration. (Part 1 of 2.)

```
48
49  } // end class EmployeeTest
```

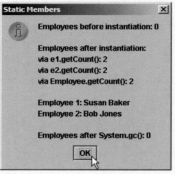

```
Employee constructor: Susan Baker
Employee constructor: Bob Jones
Employee finalizer: Susan Baker; count = 1
Employee finalizer: Bob Jones; count = 0
```

Fig. 8.13   `static` member demonstration. (Part 2 of 2.)

Eventually, the garbage collector might reclaim the memory for these objects (or the operating system reclaims the memory when the program terminates). It is not guaranteed when the garbage collector will execute (or if it will even execute), so this program makes an explicit call to the garbage collector in line 35 using `static` method *gc* from class `System` (package `java.lang`) to indicate that the garbage collector should immediately make a best effort attempt to reclaim objects that are eligible for garbage collection. However, this is just a best effort—it is possible that no objects or a subset of the garbage objects will be collected. In our example, the garbage collector did execute before lines 43–44 displayed the results of the program. The last line of the output indicates that the number of `Employee` objects in memory is 0 after the call to `System.gc()`. Also, the last two lines of the command window output show that the `Employee` object for **Susan Baker** was finalized before the `Employee` object for **Bob Jones**. Remember, the garbage collector is not guaranteed to execute when `System.gc()` is invoked, nor is it guaranteed to collect objects in a specific order, so it is possible that the output of this program on your system may differ.

[*Note*: A method declared `static` cannot access non-`static` class members. Unlike non-`static` methods, a `static` method has no `this` reference because `static` variables and `static` methods exist independent of any objects of a class and whether or not any objects of the class have been instantiated.]

Common Programming Error 8.9

It is a syntax error for a `static` method to call an instance method directly or to access an instance variable directly. However, a `static` method can call an instance method or access an instance variable through a reference to an object if such a reference is available in the method.

Common Programming Error 8.10

Referring to the `this` *reference in a* `static` *method is a syntax error—there is no object of the class to reference.*

8.12 Final Instance Variables

The *principle of least privilege* is one of the most fundamental principles of good software engineering. Let us see one way in which this principle applies to instance variables.

Some instance variables need to be modifiable and some do not. The programmer can use the keyword `final` to specify that a variable is not modifiable (i.e., it is a constant) and that any attempt to modify the variable is an error. For example,

```
private final int INCREMENT = 5;
```

declares a `final` (constant) instance variable `INCREMENT` of type `int` and initializes it to 5. Constants are not required to be initialized when they are declared. They can also be initialized by each of the class's constructors.

Software Engineering Observation 8.16

Declaring an instance variable as `final` *helps enforce the principle of least privilege. If an instance variable should not be modified, declare it to be* `final` *to prevent modification.*

Common Programming Error 8.11

Attempting to modify a `final` *instance variable after it is initialized is a compilation error.*

Error-Prevention Tip 8.3

Accidental attempts to modify a `final` *instance variable are caught at compilation time rather than causing execution-time errors. It is always preferable to get bugs out at compilation time, if possible, rather than allowing them to slip through to execution time (where studies have found that the cost of repair is often as much as ten times more expensive).*

Figure 8.14 contains two classes—applet class `IncrementTest` (lines 7–30) and class `Increment` (lines 33–57). Class `Increment` contains a `final` instance variable `INCREMENT` of type `int` (line 36). The final variable is not initialized in its declaration, so it must be initialized by a constructor of the class. The constructor at lines 39–42 receives int parameter `incrementValue`, which is assigned to `INCREMENT` at line 41. A `final` variable cannot be modified by assignment after it is initialized. Applet `IncrementTest` creates an object of class `Increment` at line 14 and provides as the argument to the constructor the value 5 to be assigned to the constant `INCREMENT`.

Common Programming Error 8.12

Not initializing a `final` *instance variable in its declaration or in every constructor of the class is a syntax error.*

```
1   // Fig. 8.14: IncrementTest.java
2   // Initializing a final variable.
3   import java.awt.*;
4   import java.awt.event.*;
```

Fig. 8.14   `final` variable initialized with constructor argument. (Part 1 of 3.)

```
5    import javax.swing.*;
6
7    public class IncrementTest extends JApplet implements ActionListener {
8       private Increment incrementObject;
9       private JButton button;
10
11      // set up GUI
12      public void init()
13      {
14         incrementObject = new Increment( 5 );
15
16         Container container = getContentPane();
17
18         button = new JButton( "Click to increment" );
19         button.addActionListener( this );
20         container.add( button );
21      }
22
23      // add INCREMENT to total when user clicks button
24      public void actionPerformed( ActionEvent actionEvent )
25      {
26         incrementObject.increment();
27         showStatus( incrementObject.toIncrementString() );
28      }
29
30   } // end class Increment
31
32   // class containing constant variable
33   class Increment {
34      private int count = 0;      // number of increments
35      private int total = 0;      // total of all increments
36      private final int INCREMENT; // constant variable
37
38      // initialize constant INCREMENT
39      public Increment( int incrementValue )
40      {
41         INCREMENT = incrementValue; // intialize constant variable (once)
42      }
43
44      // add INCREMENT to total and add 1 to count
45      public void increment()
46      {
47         total += INCREMENT;
48         ++count;
49      }
50
51      // return String representation of an Increment object's data
52      public String toIncrementString()
53      {
54         return "After increment " + count + ": total = " + total;
55      }
56
57   } // end class IncrementTest
```

Fig. 8.14   final variable initialized with constructor argument. (Part 2 of 3.)

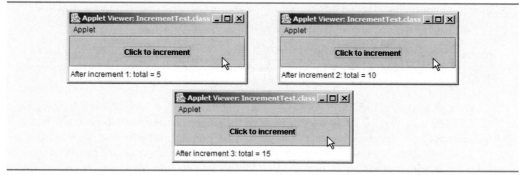

Fig. 8.14   `final` variable initialized with constructor argument. (Part 3 of 3.)

If a final variable is not initialized, a compilation error occurs. To demonstrate this, we placed line 41 of Fig. 8.14 in a comment and recompiled the program. Figure 8.15 shows the error message produced by the compiler in this case.

```
IncrementTest.java:40: variable INCREMENT might not have been initialized
   {
   ^
1 error
```

Fig. 8.15   `final` variable INCREMENT must be initialized.

8.13 Creating Packages

We have seen in almost every example in the text that classes and interfaces[7] from preexisting libraries, such as the Java API, can be imported into a Java program. Each class and interface in the Java API belongs to a package that contains a group of related classes and interfaces. As applications become more complex, packages help programmers manage the complexity of application components. Packages also facilitate software reuse by enabling programs to import classes from other packages (as we have done in most examples). Another benefit of packages is that they provide a convention for *unique class names*. With hundreds of thousands of Java programmers around the world, there is a good chance that the names you choose for classes will conflict with the names that other programmers choose for their classes. This section introduces how to create your own packages.

The application of Fig. 8.16 and Fig. 8.17 illustrates how to create your own package and use a class from that package in a program. The steps for creating a reusable class are:

1. Declare a `public` class. If the class is not `public`, it can be used only by other classes in the same package.

2. Choose a package name, and add a *`package` declaration* to the source code file for the reusable class declaration. There can be only one `package` declaration in a Java source code file and it must precede all other declarations and statements in the file.

---

7.   Interfaces were first introduced in Section 6.8 and are discussed in detail in Chapter 10.

3. Compile the class so it is placed in the appropriate package directory structure.

4. Import the reusable class into a program, and use the class.

 Common Programming Error 8.13

A syntax error occurs if any declaration or statement appears in a Java source file before the ***package*** *declaration (if there is one) in the file.*

We chose to demonstrate *Step 1* by modifying the `public` class `Time1` declared in Fig. 8.1. The new version is shown in Fig. 8.16. No modifications have been made to the implementation of the class, so we will not discuss its implementation details again here.

To satisfy *Step 2*, we added a `package` declaration at the beginning of the file. Line 3 uses a `package` declaration to declare a `package` named `com.deitel.jhtp5.ch08`. Placing a `package` declaration at the beginning of a Java source file indicates that the class (or classes) declared in the file is part of the specified package. Only `package` declarations, `import` declarations and comments can appear outside the braces of a class declaration. A Java source-code file has the following order: A `package` declaration (if any), `import` declarations (if any), then class declarations. Only one of the class declarations in a particular file can be public. Other classes in the file are also placed in the package, but are reusable only from other classes in that package—they cannot be imported into classes in another package. They are in the package to support the reusable class in the file.

```
1   // Fig. 8.16: Time1.java
2   // Time1 class declaration maintains the time in 24-hour format.
3   package com.deitel.jhtp5.ch08;
4
5   import java.text.DecimalFormat;
6
7   public class Time1 extends Object {
8      private int hour;      // 0 - 23
9      private int minute;    // 0 - 59
10     private int second;    // 0 - 59
11
12     // Time1 constructor initializes each instance variable to zero;
13     // ensures that each Time1 object starts in a consistent state
14     public Time1()
15     {
16        setTime( 0, 0, 0 );
17     }
18
19     // set a new time value using universal time; perform
20     // validity checks on the data; set invalid values to zero
21     public void setTime( int h, int m, int s )
22     {
23        hour = ( ( h >= 0 && h < 24 ) ? h : 0 );
24        minute = ( ( m >= 0 && m < 60 ) ? m : 0 );
25        second = ( ( s >= 0 && s < 60 ) ? s : 0 );
26     }
27
```

Fig. 8.16   Packaging class `Time1` for reuse. (Part 1 of 2.)

```
28      // convert to String in universal-time format
29      public String toUniversalString()
30      {
31         DecimalFormat twoDigits = new DecimalFormat( "00" );
32
33         return twoDigits.format( hour ) + ":" +
34            twoDigits.format( minute ) + ":" + twoDigits.format( second );
35      }
36
37      // convert to String in standard-time format
38      public String toStandardString()
39      {
40         DecimalFormat twoDigits = new DecimalFormat( "00" );
41
42         return ( (hour == 12 || hour == 0) ? 12 : hour % 12 ) + ":" +
43            twoDigits.format( minute ) + ":" + twoDigits.format( second ) +
44            ( hour < 12 ? " AM" : " PM" );
45      }
46
47   } // end class Time1
```

Fig. 8.16   Packaging class Time1 for reuse. (Part 2 of 2.)

In an effort to provide unique names for every package, Sun Microsystems specifies a convention for package naming that all Java programmers should follow. Every package name should start with your Internet domain name in reverse order. For example, for the Internet domain name deitel.com, the package name should begin with com.deitel. For the domain name *yourcollege*.edu, the package name should begin with edu.*yourcollege*. After the domain name is reversed, you can choose any other names you want for your package. If you are part of a company with many divisions or a university with many schools, you may want to use the name of your division or school as the next name in the package. We chose to use jhtp5 as the next name in our package name to indicate that this class is from *Java How to Program: Fifth Edition*. The last name in our package name specifies that this package is for Chapter 8 (ch08).[8]

Step 3 is to compile the class so it is stored in the appropriate package. When a Java file containing a package declaration is compiled, the resulting class file is placed in the directory structure specified by the package declaration. The package declaration of Fig. 8.16 indicates that class Time1 should be placed in the directory ch08. The other names—com, deitel and jhtp5—are also directories. The directory names in the package declaration specify the exact location of the classes in the package. If these directories do not exist before the class is compiled, the compiler can create them.

When compiling a class in a package, the (*-d*) command-line option causes the javac compiler to create appropriate directories based on the class's package declaration. The option also specifies where to create (or locate) the directories. For example, in a command window, we used the compilation command

---

8.   We use our own packages several times throughout the book. You can determine the chapter in which one of our reusable classes is declared by looking at the last part of the package name in the import declaration. This appears before the name of the class being imported or before the * if a particular class is not specified.

```
javac -d . Time1.java
```

to specify that the first directory in our package name should be placed in the current directory. The . after -d in the preceding command represents the current directory on the Windows, UNIX and Linux operating systems (and several others as well). After executing the
compilation command, the current directory contains a directory called com, com contains
a directory called deitel, deitel contains a directory called jhtp5 and jhtp5 contains
a directory called ch08. In the ch08 directory, you can find the file Time1.class. [*Note:*
If you do not use the -d option, then you must copy or move the class file to the appropriate
package directory after compiling it.]

The package name is part of the class name. The class name in this example is actually com.deitel.jhtp5.ch08.Time1. You can use this *fully qualified* name in your
programs, or you can import the class and use its simple name (Time1) in the program. If
another package also contains a Time1 class, the fully qualified class names can be used to
distinguish between the classes in the program and prevent a *name conflict* (also called a
name collision).

Once the class is compiled and stored in its package, the class can be imported into programs (*Step 4*). In the TimeTest1 application of Fig. 8.17, line 8 specifies that class Time1
should be imported for use in class TimeTest1. [*Note:* Classes in a package never need to
import other classes from the same package.]

```
1    // Fig. 8.17: TimeTest1.java
2    // Class TimeTest1 to exercise class Time1.
3
4    // Java packages
5    import javax.swing.JOptionPane;
6
7    // Deitel packages
8    import com.deitel.jhtp5.ch08.Time1;   // import Time1 class
9
10   public class TimeTest1 {
11
12      public static void main( String args[] )
13      {
14         Time1 time = new Time1();   // calls Time1 constructor
15
16         // append String version of time to String output
17         String output = "The initial universal time is: " +
18            time.toUniversalString() + "\nThe initial standard time is: " +
19            time.toStandardString();
20
21         // change time and append updated time to output
22         time.setTime( 13, 27, 6 );
23         output += "\n\nUniversal time after setTime is: " +
24            time.toUniversalString() +
25            "\nStandard time after setTime is: " + time.toStandardString();
26
27         // set time with invalid values; append updated time to output
28         time.setTime( 99, 99, 99 );
```

Fig. 8.17   Importing your own class from a package. (Part 1 of 2.)

```
29          output += "\n\nAfter attempting invalid settings: " +
30             "\nUniversal time: " + time.toUniversalString() +
31             "\nStandard time: " + time.toStandardString();
32
33          JOptionPane.showMessageDialog( null, output,
34             "Testing Class Time1", JOptionPane.INFORMATION_MESSAGE );
35
36          System.exit( 0 );
37
38       } // end main
39
40    } // end class TimeTest1
```

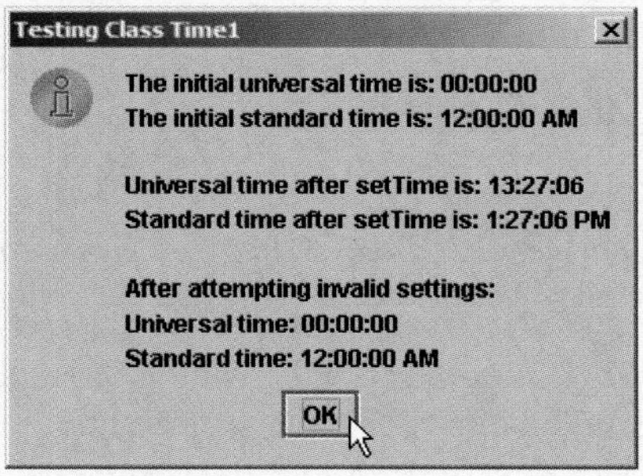

Fig. 8.17   Importing your own class from a package. (Part 2 of 2.)

When compiling `TimeTest1`, `javac` must locate the `.class` file for `Time1` to ensure that class `TimeTest1` uses class `Time1` correctly. The compiler uses a special object called a *class loader* to locate the classes it needs. The class loader begins by searching the standard Java classes that are bundled with the J2SDK. Then it searches for *optional packages*. Java 2 provides an *extension mechanism* that enables new (optional) packages to be added to Java for development and execution purposes.[9] If the class is not found in the standard Java classes or in the extension classes, the class loader searches the *classpath*, which contains a list of locations in which classes are stored. The classpath consists of a list of directories or *archive files*, each separated by a *directory separator*—a semicolon (`;`) on Windows or a colon (`:`) on UNIX/Linux/Mac OS X. Archive files are individual files that contain directories of other files, typically in a compressed format. For example, the standard classes of Java are contained in the archive file `rt.jar`, which is installed with the J2SDK. Archive files normally end with the `.jar` or `.zip` file-name extensions. The directories and archive files specified in the classpath contain the classes you wish to make available to the Java compiler and virtual machine.

By default, the classpath consists only of the current directory. However, the classpath can be modified[10] by

---

9. The extension mechanism is beyond the scope of this book. For more information, visit `java.sun.com/j2se/1.4.1/docs/guide/extensions`.
10. For more information on the classpath, visit `java.sun.com/j2se/1.4.1/docs/tooldocs/windows/classpath.html` for Windows or `java.sun.com/j2se/1.4.1/docs/tooldocs/solaris/classpath.html` for Solaris/Linux.

1. providing the *-classpath* option to the javac compiler or

2. setting the *CLASSPATH* environment variable (a special variable that you define and the operating system maintains so that applications can search for classes in the specified locations).

Common Programming Error 8.14

Specifying an explicit classpath eliminates the current directory from the classpath. This prevents classes in the current directory (including packages in the current directory) from loading properly. If classes must be loaded from the current directory, include the current directory (.) in the explicit classpath.

Software Engineering Observation 8.17

In general, it is a better practice to use the -classpath option of the compiler, rather than the CLASSPATH environment variable, to specify the classpath for a program. This enables each application to have its own classpath.

Error-Prevention Tip 8.4

Specifying the classpath with the CLASSPATH environment variable can cause subtle and difficult-to-locate errors in programs that use different versions of the same package.

For the example of Fig. 8.16 and Fig. 8.17, we did not specify an explicit classpath. Thus, to locate the classes in the com.deitel.jhtp5.ch08 package from this example, the class loader looks in the current directory for the first name in the package—com. Next, the class loader navigates the directory structure. Directory com contains the subdirectory deitel. Directory deitel contains the subdirectory jhtp5. Finally, directory jhtp5 contains subdirectory ch08. In the ch08 directory is the file Time1.class, which is loaded by the class loader to ensure that the class is used properly in our program.

Locating the classes to execute the program is similar to locating the classes to compile the program. Like the compiler, the java interpreter uses a class loader that searches the standard classes and extension classes first, then searches the classpath (the current directory by default). The classpath for the interpreter can be specified explicitly by using either of the techniques discussed for the compiler. As with the compiler, it is better to specify an individual program's classpath via command-line options to the interpreter. You can specify the classpath to the java interpreter via the -classpath or -cp command-line options followed by a list of directories or archive files separated by semicolons (;) on Windows or colons (:) on UNIX/Linux/Mac OS X.

8.14 Package Access

If no access modifier (public, protected or private) is specified for a method or variable when it is declared in a class, the method or variable is considered to have *package access*. In a program that consists of one class declaration, this has no specific effect on the program. However, if a program uses multiple classes from the same package (i.e., a group of related classes), these classes can access each other's package-access methods and fields directly through references to objects of the appropriate classes.

Let us consider a mechanical example of package access. The application of Fig. 8.18 contains two classes—the PackageDataTest application class (lines 6–30) and the PackageData class (lines 33–50). In the PackageData class declaration, lines 34–35 declare the instance variables `number` and `string` with no access modifiers; therefore, these are package-access instance variables. The `PackageDataTest` application's `main` method creates an instance of the `PackageData` class (line 10) to demonstrate the ability to modify the `PackageData` instance variables directly (as shown on lines 17–18). The results of the modification can be seen in the output window.

```
1  // Fig. 8.18: PackageDataTest.java
2  // Classes in the same package (i.e., the same directory) can
3  // use package access data of other classes in the same package.
4  import javax.swing.JOptionPane;
5
6  public class PackageDataTest {
7
8     public static void main( String args[] )
9     {
10       PackageData packageData = new PackageData();
11
12       // append String representation of packageData to output
13       String output = "After instantiation:\n" +
14          packageData.toPackageDataString();
15
16       // change package access data in packageData object
17       packageData.number = 77;
18       packageData.string = "Goodbye";
19
20       // append String representation of packageData to output
21       output += "\nAfter changing values:\n" +
22          packageData.toPackageDataString();
23
24       JOptionPane.showMessageDialog( null, output, "Package Access",
25          JOptionPane.INFORMATION_MESSAGE );
26
27       System.exit( 0 );
28    }
29
30 } // end class PackageDataTest
31
32 // class with package access instance variables
33 class PackageData {
34    int number;      // package-access instance variable
35    String string;   // package-access instance variable
36
37    // constructor
38    public PackageData()
39    {
40       number = 0;
41       string = "Hello";
42    }
43
```

Fig. 8.18 Package-access members of a class are accessible by other classes in the same package. (Part 1 of 2.)

```
44         // return PackageData object String representation
45         public String toPackageDataString()
46         {
47            return "number: " + number + "    string: " + string;
48         }
49
50     } // end class PackageData
```

Package Access   [×]

　　After instantiation:
　　number: 0   string: Hello
　　After changing values:
　　number: 77   string: Goodbye

　　　　　　　　[OK]

Fig. 8.18   Package-access members of a class are accessible by other classes in the same package. (Part 2 of 2.)

When you compile this program, the compiler produces two separate files—a class file for class `PackageDataTest` and a class file for class `PackageData`. Recall from Section 8.5 that every Java class has its own class file with a `.class` extension. The compiler places the two classes in Fig. 8.18 in the same directory, so they are considered to be part of the same package. (They are certainly related by the fact that they are in the same `.java` file.) Because they are part of the same package, class `PackageDataTest` is allowed to modify the package access data of objects of class `PackageData`.

Software Engineering Observation 8.18

Some people in the OOP community feel that package access corrupts information hiding and weakens the value of the object-oriented design approach, because the programmer must assume responsibility for error checking and data validation in any code that manipulates the package-access data members.

8.15 Software Reusability

Java programmers concentrate on crafting new classes and reusing existing classes. Many *class libraries* exist, and others are being developed worldwide. Software is then constructed from existing, well-defined, carefully tested, well-documented, portable, widely available components. This kind of software reusability speeds the development of powerful, high-quality software. *Rapid application development (RAD)* is of great interest today.

Java programmers now have thousands of classes in the Java API from which to choose to help them implement Java programs. Indeed, Java is not just a programming language. It is a framework in which Java developers can work to achieve true reusability and rapid application development. Java programmers can focus on the task at hand when developing their programs and leave the lower-level details to the classes of the Java API. For example, to write a program that draws graphics, a Java programmer does not require knowledge of graphics on every computer platform where the program will execute. Instead, a Java programmer can concentrate on learning Java's graphics capabilities (which are quite substantial and growing) and write a Java program that draws the graphics, using Java's API classes such as `Graphics`. When the program executes on a given computer, it is the job of the interpreter to translate Java commands into commands that the local computer can understand.

The Java API classes enable Java programmers to bring new applications to market faster by using preexisting, tested components. Not only does this reduce development time, it also improves programmers' ability to debug and maintain applications. To take advantage of Java's many capabilities, it is essential that programmers familiarize themselves with the variety of packages and classes in the Java API. There are many Web-based resources at `java.sun.com` to help you with this task. The primary resource for learning about the Java API is the *Java API documentation*,[11] which can be found at

```
java.sun.com/j2se/1.4.1/docs/api/index.html
```

In addition, `java.sun.com` provides many other resources, including tutorials, articles and sites specific to individual Java topics.

 Good Programming Practice 8.7

Avoid reinventing the wheel. Study the capabilities of the Java API. If the API contains a class that meets your program's requirements, use that class rather than creating your own.

To realize the full potential of software reusability, we need to improve cataloging schemes, licensing schemes, protection mechanisms that ensure master copies of classes are not corrupted, description schemes that system designers use to determine whether existing objects meet their needs, browsing mechanisms that determine what classes are available and how closely they meet software developer requirements and the like. Many interesting research and development problems have been solved and many more need to be solved; these problems will be solved because the potential value of software reuse is enormous.

8.16 Data Abstraction and Encapsulation

As we pointed out at the beginning of this chapter, classes normally hide the details of their implementation from their clients. This is called *information hiding.* As an example of information hiding, let us consider a data structure called a *stack.* Students can think of a stack as analogous to a pile of dishes. When a dish is placed on the pile, it is always placed at the top (referred to as *pushing* the dish onto the stack). Similarly, when a dish is removed from the pile, it is always removed from the top (referred to as *popping* the dish off the stack). Stacks are known as *last-in, first-out (LIFO) data structures*—the last item pushed (inserted) on the stack is the first item popped (removed) from the stack.

Stacks can be implemented with arrays and with other data structures, such as linked lists. (We discuss stacks and linked lists in Chapter 20, Data Structures.) A client of a stack class need not be concerned with the stack's implementation. The client knows only that when data items are placed in the stack, these items will be recalled in last-in, first-out order. The client cares about *what* functionality a stack offers, but not about *how* that func-

---

11. You can download this documentation from `java.sun.com/j2se/1.4.1/download.html`.

tionality is implemented. This concept is referred to as *data abstraction*. Although programmers might know the details of a class's implementation, they should not write code that depends on these details. This enables a particular class (such as one that implements a stack and its operations, *push* and *pop*) to be replaced with another version without affecting the rest of the system. As long as the `public` services of the class do not change (i.e., every original method still has the same name, return type and parameter list in the new class declaration), the rest of the system is not affected.

Most programming languages emphasize actions. In these languages, data exists to support the actions that programs must take. Data is "less interesting" than actions. Data is "crude." Only a few primitive types exist, and it is difficult for programmers to create their own types. Java and the object-oriented style of programming elevate the importance of data. The primary activities of object-oriented programming in Java are the creation of types (e.g., classes) and the expression of the interactions among objects of those types. To create languages that emphasize data, the programming-languages community needed to formalize some notions about data. The formalization we consider here is the notion of *abstract data types (ADTs)*. ADTs receive as much attention today as structured programming did decades earlier. ADTs, however, do not replace structured programming. Rather, they provide an additional formalization to improve the program-development process.

Consider primitive type `int`, which most people would associate with an integer in mathematics. Rather, an `int` is an abstract representation of an integer. Unlike mathematical integers, computer `int`s are fixed in size. For example, type `int` in Java is limited approximately to the range –2 billion to +2 billion. If the result of a calculation falls outside this range, an error occurs, and the computer responds in some machine-dependent manner. It might, for example, "quietly" produce an incorrect result, such as a value too large to fit in an `int` variable (commonly called *arithmetic overflow*). Mathematical integers do not have this problem. Therefore, the notion of a computer `int` is only an approximation of the notion of a real-world integer. The same is true of `float` and other built-in types.

We have taken the notion of `int` for granted until this point, but we now consider it from a new perspective. Types like `int`, `float`, `char` and others are all examples of abstract data types. These types are representations of real-world notions to some satisfactory level of precision within a computer system.

An ADT actually captures two notions: A *data representation* and the *operations* that can be performed on that data. For example, in Java, an `int` contains an integer value (data) and provides addition, subtraction, multiplication, division and remainder operations; however, division by zero is undefined. Java programmers use classes to implement abstract data types.

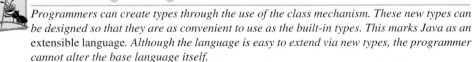

Software Engineering Observation 8.19

Programmers can create types through the use of the class mechanism. These new types can be designed so that they are as convenient to use as the built-in types. This marks Java as an extensible language. *Although the language is easy to extend via new types, the programmer cannot alter the base language itself.*

Another abstract data type we discuss is a *queue*, which is similar to a "waiting line." Computer systems use many queues internally. A queue offers well-understood behavior to its clients: Clients place items in a queue one at a time via an *enqueue* operation, then get those items back one at a time via a *dequeue* operation. A queue returns items in *first-in, first-out (FIFO)* order, which means that the first item inserted in a queue is the first item removed from the queue. Conceptually, a queue can become infinitely long, but real queues are finite.

The queue hides an internal data representation that keeps track of the items currently waiting in line, and it offers a set of operations to its clients (*enqueue* and *dequeue*). The clients are not concerned about the implementation of the queue—clients simply depend upon the queue to operate "as advertised." When a client enqueues an item, the queue should accept that item and place it in some kind of internal FIFO data structure. Similarly, when the client wants the next item from the front of the queue, the queue should remove the item from its internal representation and deliver the item in FIFO order (i.e., the item that has been in the queue the longest should be the next one returned by the next dequeue operation).

The queue ADT guarantees the integrity of its internal data structure. Clients cannot manipulate this data structure directly—only the queue ADT has access to its internal data. Clients are able to perform only allowable operations on the data representation; the ADT rejects operations that its public interface does not provide.

8.17 (Optional Case Study) Thinking About Objects: Starting to Program the Classes for the Elevator Simulation

In the "Thinking About Objects" sections in Chapter 1–Chapter 7, we introduced the fundamentals of object orientation and developed an object-oriented design for our elevator simulation. Earlier in Chapter 8, we introduced the details of programming with Java classes. We now begin implementing our object-oriented design in Java. At the end of this section, we show how to generate code in Java, working from class diagrams. This process is referred to as *forward engineering*.[12]

Visibility

We now apply *access modifiers* (see Section 8.2) to the members of our classes. In Section 8.2, we introduced access modifiers `public` and `private`. These determine the *visibilities* or accessibilities of an object's attributes and methods to other objects. Before we create class files, we consider which attributes and methods of our classes should be `public` and which should be `private`.

In Section 8.2, we discussed how attributes generally should be `private` and that methods, which are operations invoked by clients of a given class, normally should be `public`. The UML employs *visibility markers* for modeling the visibility of attributes and operations. Public visibility is indicated by placing a plus sign (+) before a particular operation or attribute; a minus sign (-) indicates private visibility. Figure 8.19 shows our updated class diagram with visibility notations included.

---

12. Booch, G. *The Unified Modeling Language User Guide*. Reading, MA: Addison Wesley Longman, Inc., 1999: 16. [Once code exists, the process of going backward from the code to reproduce the design is called *reverse engineering*.]

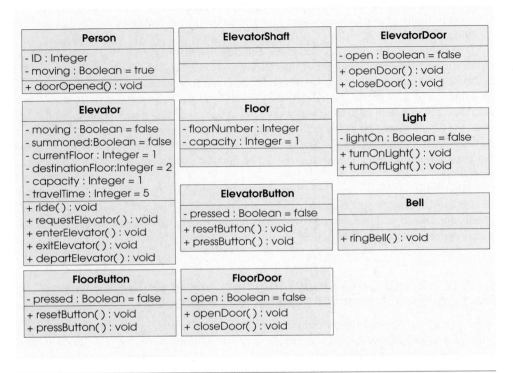

Fig. 8.19   Class diagram with visibility notations.

Navigability

Before we begin implementing our design in Java, we introduce an additional piece of UML notation. The class diagram of Fig. 8.20 further refines the relationships among classes in the elevator simulation by adding *navigability* arrows to the association lines. Navigability arrows indicate in which direction an association can be navigated. For example, we can navigate from class `Elevator` to class `Bell`, which enables the `Elevator` to ring the `Bell`. However, because the navigability arrow points from class `Elevator` to class `Bell`, the `Bell` cannot access the `Elevator`. Note that associations in this diagram that do not have navigability arrows indicate bidirectional navigability—navigation can proceed in either direction across the association.[13] When implementing a system designed using the UML, navigability helps programmers determine which objects need references to other objects.

---

13. The UML specification version 1.4 states that the absence of navigability arrows on an association indicates either bidirectional navigability or unknown navigability. In earlier chapters, we had not yet introduced the concept of navigability, so we omitted the arrows to indicate unknown navigability. Now that we have introduced navigability, we omit the arrows to indicate bidirectional navigability.

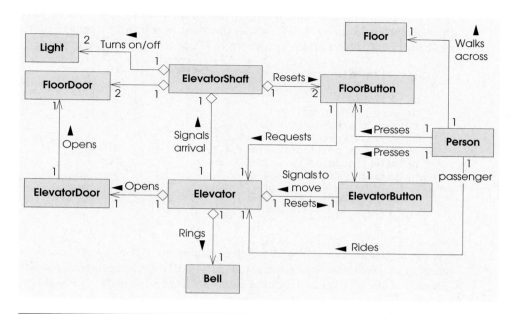

Fig. 8.20   Class diagram with navigability.

Implementation: Forward Engineering

Forward engineering is the process of transforming a design, such as that in a UML model, into code of a specific programming language, such as Java. Now that we have discussed programming Java classes, we forward engineer the classes in the diagram of Fig. 8.19 and Fig. 8.20 into the Java code for our simulator. The generated code will represent the "skeleton," or the structure, of the simulator.[14] In Chapter 10 and Chapter 11, we will modify the code to incorporate inheritance and interfaces, respectively. In Appendix D, Appendix E and Appendix F, we will present the complete, working Java code for our model.

As an example, we forward engineer our design of class Elevator from Fig. 8.19. We use this figure to determine the attributes and operations of that class. We use the UML model as shown in Fig. 3.19 to determine associations among classes. We adhere to the following four guidelines for each class:

1. Use the name located in the first compartment to declare the class as a public class with an empty constructor. For example, class Elevator yields

```
public class Elevator {

   public Elevator() {}
}
```

---

14. So far, we have presented only about half of the case-study material—we have not yet discussed inheritance, event handling, multithreading or animation. The standard development process recommends finishing the design process before starting the coding process. Technically, we will not have finished designing our system until we have discussed these additional topics, so our current code implementation might seem premature. We present only a partial implementation illustrating the topics covered in Chapter 8.

2. Use the attributes located in the second compartment to declare the instance variables. For example, the `private` attributes moving, summoned, currentFloor, destinationFloor, capacity and travelTime of class Elevator yield

```
public class Elevator {

   // attributes
   private boolean moving;
   private boolean summoned;
   private int currentFloor = 1;
   private int destinationFloor = 2;
   private int capacity = 1;
   private int travelTime = 5;

   // constructor
   public Elevator() {}
}
```

3. Use the associations described in the class diagram to declare the references to other objects. For example, according to Fig. 3.19, Elevator aggregates one object each of classes ElevatorDoor, ElevatorButton and Bell. This yields

```
public class Elevator {

   // attributes
   private boolean moving;
   private boolean summoned;
   private int currentFloor = 1;
   private int destinationFloor = 2;
   private int capacity = 1;
   private int travelTime = 5;

   // associated objects
   private ElevatorDoor elevatorDoor;
   private ElevatorButton elevatorButton;
   private Bell bell;

   // constructor
   public Elevator() {}
}
```

4. Use the operations located in the third compartment of Fig. 8.19 to declare the methods. For example, the `public` operations ride, requestElevator, enterElevator, exitElevator and departElevator in class Elevator yield

```
public class Elevator {

   // attributes
   private boolean moving;
   private boolean summoned;
   private int currentFloor = 1;
   private int destinationFloor = 2;
   private int capacity = 1;
   private int travelTime = 5;
```

```
    // associated objects
    private ElevatorDoor elevatorDoor;
    private ElevatorButton elevatorButton;
    private Bell bell;

    // constructor
    public Elevator() {}

    // operations
    public void ride() {}
    public void requestElevator() {}
    public void enterElevator() {}
    public void exitElevator() {}
    public void departElevator() {}
}
```

This concludes the basics of forward engineering.

SUMMARY

- Object-oriented programming (OOP) encapsulates data (attributes) and methods (behaviors) into objects; the data and methods of an object are intimately tied together. Object-based programming (OBP) deals with the creation and use of objects.

- Objects have the property of information hiding. Objects might know how to communicate with one another across well-defined interfaces, but they normally are not allowed to know how other objects are implemented.

- Java programmers create their own types called classes.

- The non-static fields of a class are called instance variables. The static fields of a class are called class variables.

- Java uses inheritance to create new classes from existing class declarations.

- Every class in Java is a subclass of Object. Thus, every new class has the attributes and behaviors of class Object.

- Keywords public and private are access modifiers.

- Fields and methods declared with access modifier public are accessible wherever the program has a reference to an object of the class in which they are declared.

- Fields and methods declared with access modifier private are accessible only to methods of the class in which they are declared.

- Instance variables are normally declared private and methods are normally declared public.

- The public methods (or public services) of a class are used by clients of the class to manipulate the data stored in objects of the class.

- A constructor has same name as its class and initializes the instance variables of an object of the class when the object is instantiated. Constructors can be overloaded. Constructors can take arguments, but cannot specify a return type.

- Constructors and other methods that change instance variable values should always maintain data in a consistent state.

- When an object is created, new allocates the memory for the object, then calls the constructor for the class to initialize the instance variables of the object.

- Within a class's scope, class members are accessible to all of that class's methods and can be referenced by name. Outside a class's scope, class members can only be accessed off a handle—a reference for non-static members or the class name for static members.

- Each object has access to a reference to itself—called `this`—that can be used inside the methods of the class to refer to the object's fields and methods explicitly.
- If no constructors are declared for a class, the compiler creates a default constructor.
- When one object of a class has a reference to another object of the same class, the first object can access all of the second object's fields and methods, even if they are `private`.
- Classes often provide `public` methods to allow clients of the class to *set* or *get* `private` instance variables. *Set* methods are also commonly called mutator methods. *Get* methods are also commonly called accessor methods or query methods.
- Every event has a source—the GUI component with which the user interacted to signal the program to do a task.
- With composition, an object has references to objects of other classes as members.
- If a method declares a variable with the same name as a field of the class, the field is shadowed (hidden) by the variable in the method. A shadowed instance variable can be accessed in the method by preceding its name with the keyword `this` and a dot (`.`).
- Any time you have a reference in a program (even as the result of a method call), the reference can be followed by a dot and a call to one of the methods for the reference type.
- Java performs automatic garbage collection of memory. When there are no more references to an object, the object is marked for garbage collection.
- Every class in Java has a `finalize` method that has no parameters and returns no value. This method is called by the garbage collector before an object is removed from memory.
- A `static` class variable represents class-wide information—all objects of the class share the same piece of data. A class's `public static` members can be accessed through a reference to any object of that class, or they can be accessed through the class name using a dot.
- `public static` method `gc` from class `System` suggests that the garbage collector immediately make a best effort attempt to collect garbage objects. The garbage collector is not guaranteed to collect objects in a specific order (or at all).
- A method declared `static` cannot access non-`static` class members. Unlike non-`static` methods, a `static` method has no `this` reference, because `static` variables and `static` methods exist independent of any objects of a class.
- `static` members exist even when no objects of that class exist—they are available as soon as the class is loaded into memory at execution time.
- Use keyword `final` to specify that a variable is a constant (not modifiable) and that any attempt to modify the variable is an error. A `final` variable cannot be modified after it is first assigned a value. Such a variable must be initialized in its declaration or in every constructor of the class.
- If the `.class` files for the classes used in a program are in the same directory as the class that uses them, `import` declarations are not required.
- Each class and interface in the Java API belongs to a specific package that contains a group of related classes and interfaces. Packages are directory structures used to organize classes and interfaces. Packages provide a mechanism for software reuse and a convention for unique class names.
- Creating a reusable class requires declaring a `public` class, adding a `package` declaration to the class declaration file and compiling the class into the appropriate package directory structure. Then the class can be imported into a program.
- When compiling a class in a package, use the compiler command-line option `-d` to specify where to create all the directories in the `package` declaration and enable the compiler to place the class in the proper directory structure.

- The `package` directory names become part of the class name when the class is compiled. Use this fully qualified name in programs or `import` the class and use its simple name (the name of the class by itself) in the program.

- When no access modifier is provided for a method or variable when it is declared in a class, the method or variable is considered to have package access.

- If a program uses multiple classes from the same package, these classes can access each other's package-access methods and fields through a reference to an object.

TERMINOLOGY

abstract data type (ADT)
access modifier
accessor method
attribute
behavior
class
class declaration
class-instance creation expression
class library
class method (`static`)
class scope
class variable (`static`)
client of a class
composition
consistent state for an instance variable
constructor
container class
`-d` compiler option
default constructor
dot (`.`) for member access
encapsulation
`extends`
extensibility
field
`finalize` method
get method
helper method
implementation of a class
information hiding
initialize a class object

instance method
instance of a class
instance variable
instantiate an object of a class
interface to a class
member-access control
message
mutator method
`new`
no-argument constructor
`Object`
object-based programming (OBP)
object-oriented programming (OOP)
overloaded constructors
package access
`package` declaration
predicate method
principle of least privilege
`private`
`public`
`public` interface of a class
rapid application development (RAD)
reusable code
services of a class
set method
software reusability
`static` variable
`static` method
`this` reference
utility method

SELF-REVIEW EXERCISES

8.1　Fill in the blanks in each of the following statements:

a) Members of a class specified as _____ are accessible only to methods of the class.

b) A(n) _____ is used to initialize the instance variables of a class.

c) A(n) _____ method is used to assign values to `private` instance variables of a class.

d) Methods of a class are normally made _____, and instance variables of a class are normally made _____.

e) A(n) _____ method is used to retrieve values of `private` data of a class.

f) The keyword _____ introduces a class declaration.

g) Members of a class specified as _____ are accessible anywhere an object of the class is in scope.

h) A(n) _____ creates an object of a specified type and returns a _____ to that object.

i) A(n) _____ variable represents class-wide information.

j) The keyword _____ specifies that a variable is not modifiable after it is initialized.

k) A method declared `static` cannot access _____ class members directly.

ANSWERS TO SELF-REVIEW EXERCISES

8.1   a) `private`. b) constructor. c) *set* (or mutator). d) `public, private`. e) *get* (or accessor). f) `class`. g) `public`. h) class-instance creation expression, reference. i) `static` (or class). j) `final`. k) non-`static`.

EXERCISES

8.2   Create a class called `Complex` for performing arithmetic with complex numbers. Complex numbers have the form

$$realPart + imaginaryPart * i$$

where *i* is

$$\sqrt{-1}$$

Write a program to test your class. Use floating-point variables to represent the `private` data of the class. Provide a constructor that enables an object of this class to be initialized when it is declared. Provide a no-argument constructor with default values in case no initializers are provided. Provide `public` methods that perform the following operations:

a) Add two `Complex` numbers: The real parts are added together and the imaginary parts are added together.

b) Subtract two `Complex` numbers: The real part of the right operand is subtracted from the real part of the left operand, and the imaginary part of the right operand is subtracted from the imaginary part of the left operand.

c) Print `Complex` numbers in the form (a, b), where a is the real part and b is the imaginary part.

8.3   Create a class called `Rational` for performing arithmetic with fractions. Write a program to test your class. Use integer variables to represent the `private` instance variables of the class—the `numerator` and the `denominator`. Provide a constructor that enables an object of this class to be initialized when it is declared. The constructor should store the fraction in reduced form—the fraction

2/4

is equivalent to 1/2 and would be stored in the object as 1 in the `numerator` and 2 in the `denominator`. Provide a no-argument constructor with default values in case no initializers are provided. Provide `public` methods that perform each of the following operations:

a) Add two `Rational` numbers: The result of the addition should be stored in reduced form.

b) Subtract two `Rational` numbers: The result of the subtraction should be stored in reduced form.

c) Multiply two `Rational` numbers: The result of the multiplication should be stored in reduced form.

d) Divide of two `Rational` numbers: The result of the division should be stored in reduced form.

e) Print Rational numbers in the form a/b, where a is the numerator and b is the denominator.

f) Print Rational numbers in floating-point format. (Consider providing formatting capabilities that enable the user of the class to specify the number of digits of precision to the right of the decimal point.)

8.4   Modify class Time3 of Fig. 8.7 to include the tick method that increments the time stored in a Time3 object by one second. Also provide method incrementMinute to increment the minute and method incrementHour to increment the hour. The Time3 object should always remain in a consistent state. Write a program that tests the tick method, the incrementMinute method and the incrementHour method to ensure that they work correctly. Be sure to test the following cases:

a) incrementing into the next minute,

b) incrementing into the next hour and

c) incrementing into the next day (i.e., 11:59:59 PM to 12:00:00 AM).

8.5   Modify class Date of Fig. 8.9 to perform error-checking on the initializer values for instance variables month, day and year (currently it validates only the month and day). Also, provide a method nextDay to increment the day by one. The Date object should always remain in a consistent state. Write a program that tests the nextDay method in a loop that prints the date during each iteration of the loop to illustrate that the nextDay method works correctly. Test the following cases:

a) incrementing into the next month and

b) incrementing into the next year.

8.6   Create class DateAndTime that combines the modified Time3 class of Exercise 8.4 and the modified Date class of Exercise 8.5. Modify method incrementHour to call method nextDay if the time is incremented into the next day. Modify methods toStandardString and toUniversal-String to output the date in addition to the time. Write a program to test the new class DateAndTime. Specifically, test incrementing the time to the next day.

8.7   Modify the *set* methods in class Time3 of Fig. 8.7 to return appropriate error values if an attempt is made to set one of the instance variables hour, minute or second of an object of class Time to an invalid value. (*Hint:* Use boolean return types on each method.) Write a program that tests these new *set* methods and outputs error messages when incorrect values are supplied.

8.8   Create a class Rectangle. The class has attributes length and width, each of which defaults to 1. It has methods that calculate the perimeter and the area of the rectangle. It has *set* and *get* methods for both length and width. The *set* methods should verify that length and width are each floating-point numbers larger than 0.0 and less than 20.0. Write a program to test class Rectangle.

8.9   Create a more sophisticated Rectangle class than the one you created in Exercise 8.8. This class stores only the Cartesian coordinates of the four corners of the rectangle. The constructor calls a *set* method that accepts four sets of coordinates and verifies that each of these is in the first quadrant with no single x- or y-coordinate larger than 20.0. The *set* method also verifies that the supplied coordinates specify a rectangle. Provide methods to calculate the length, width, perimeter and area. The length is the larger of the two dimensions. Include a predicate method isSquare which determines whether the rectangle is a square. Write a program to test class Rectangle.

8.10   Create a class HugeInteger which uses a 40-element array of digits to store integers as large as 40 digits each. Provide methods input, output, add and subtract. For comparing HugeInteger objects, provide the following methods: isEqualTo, isNotEqualTo, isGreaterThan, isLessThan, isGreaterThanOrEqualTo and isLessThanOrEqualTo. Each of these is a predicate method that returns true if the relationship holds between the two HugeInteger objects and returns false if the relationship does not hold. Provide a predicate method isZero. If you feel ambitious, also provide methods multiply, divide and remainder.

8.11   Create a class `TicTacToe` that will enable you to write a complete program to play the game of Tic-Tac-Toe. The class contains a private 3-by-3 two-dimensional array of integers. The constructor should initialize the empty board to all zeros. Allow two human players. Wherever the first player moves, place a 1 in the specified square; place a 2 wherever the second player moves. Each move must be to an empty square. After each move determine whether the game has been won and whether the game is a draw. If you feel ambitious, modify your program so that the computer makes the moves for one of the players. Also, allow the player to specify whether he or she wants to go first or second. If you feel exceptionally ambitious, develop a program that will play three-dimensional Tic-Tac-Toe on a 4-by-4-by-4 board [*Note:* This is a challenging project that could take many weeks of effort!].

8.12   Explain the notion of package access in Java. Explain the negative aspects of package access.

8.13   What happens when a return type, even `void`, is specified for a constructor?

8.14   Create class `Date` with the following capabilities:
a) Output the date in multiple formats such as

```
MM/DD/YYYY
June 14, 1992
DDD YYYY
```

b) Use overloaded constructors to create `Date` objects initialized with dates of the formats in part (a). In the first case, constructor should receive three integer values. In the second case the constructor should receive a `String` and two integer values. In the third case the constructor should receive two integer values, the first of which represents the day number in the year. [*Hint:* To convert the string representation of the month to a numeric value, compare strings using the `equals` method. For example, if `s1` and `s2` are strings, the method call `s1.equals( s2 )` returns `true` of the strings are identical; otherwise, the method call returns `false`.]

8.15   Create class `SavingsAccount`. Use a `static` variable `annualInterestRate` to store the annual interest rate for all account holders. Each object of the class contains a `private` instance variable `savingsBalance` indicating the amount the saver currently has on deposit. Provide method `calculateMonthlyInterest` to calculate the monthly interest by multiplying the `savingsBalance` by `annualInterestRate` divided by 12; this interest should be added to `savingsBalance`. Provide a `static` method `modifyInterestRate` that sets the `annualInterestRate` to a new value. Write a program to test class `SavingsAccount`. Instantiate two `savingsAccount` objects, `saver1` and `saver2`, with balances of $2000.00 and $3000.00, respectively. Set `annualInterestRate` to 4%, then calculate the monthly interest and print the new balances for both savers. Then set the `annualInterestRate` to 5%, calculate the next month's interest and print the new balances for both savers.

8.16   Create class `IntegerSet`. Each `IntegerSet` object can hold integers in the range 0–100. The set is represented by an array of `boolean`s. Array element `a[i]` is `true` if integer *i* is in the set. Array element `a[j]` is `false` if integer *j* is not in the set. The no-argument constructor initializes the Java array to the "empty set" (i.e., a set whose array representation contains all `false` values).

Provide the following methods: Method `union` creates a third set that is the set-theoretic union of two existing sets (i.e., an element of the third set's array is set to `true` if that element is `true` in either or both of the existing sets; otherwise, the element of the third set is set to `false`). Method `intersection` creates a third set which is the set-theoretic intersection of two existing sets (i.e., an element of the third set's array is set to `false` if that element is `false` in either or both of the existing sets; otherwise, the element of the third set is set to `true`). Method `insertElement` inserts a new integer *k* into a set (by setting `a[k]` to `true`). Method `deleteElement` deletes integer *m* (by setting `a[m]` to `false`). Method `toSetString` returns a string containing a set as a list of numbers separated by spaces. Include only those elements that are present in the set. Use `---` to represent an empty set. Method isEqualTo determines whether two sets are equal. Write a program to test class IntegerSet. Instantiate several IntegerSet objects. Test that all your methods work properly.

8.17   It would be perfectly reasonable for the Time3 class of Fig. 8.7 to represent the time internally as the number of seconds since midnight rather than the three integer values hour, minute and second. Clients could use the same public methods and get the same results. Modify the Time3 class of Fig. 8.7 to implement the Time3 as the number of seconds since midnight and show that there is no change visible to the clients of the class.

8.18   *(Drawing Program)* Create a drawing applet that randomly draws lines, rectangles and ovals. For this purpose, create a set of "smart" shape classes where objects of these classes know how to draw themselves if provided with a Graphics object that tells them where to draw (i.e., the applet's Graphics object allows a shape to draw on the applet's background). The class names should be MyLine, MyRectangle and MyOval.

The data for class MyLine should include *x1*, *y1*, *x2* and *y2* coordinates. Method drawLine of class Graphics will connect the two points supplied with a line. The data for classes MyRectangle and MyOval should include an upper-left *x*-coordinate value, an upper-left *y*-coordinate value, a *width* (must be nonnegative) and a *height* (must be nonnegative). All data in each class must be private.

In addition to the data, each class should declare at least the following public methods:

a) A constructor with no arguments that sets the coordinates to 0.

b) A constructor with arguments that sets the coordinates to the supplied values.

c) *Set* methods for each individual piece of data that allow the programmer to set any piece of data in a shape independently (e.g., if you have an instance variable x1, you should have a method setX1).

d) *Get* methods for each individual piece of data that allow the programmer to retrieve any piece of data in a shape independently (e.g., if you have an instance variable x1, you should have a method getX1).

e) A draw method with the first line

```
public void draw( Graphics g )
```

that will be called from the applet's paint method to draw a shape onto the screen.

If you would like to provide more methods for flexibility, please do so.

Begin by declaring class MyLine and an applet to test your classes. The applet should have a MyLine instance variable line that can refer to one MyLine object (created in the applet's init method with random coordinates). The applet's paint method should draw the shape with a statement like

```
line.draw( g );
```

where line is the MyLine reference and g is the Graphics object that the shape will use to draw itself on the applet.

Next, change the single MyLine reference into an array of MyLine references and hard code several MyLine objects into the program for drawing. The applet's paint method should walk through the array of MyLine objects and draw every one.

After the preceding part is working, you should declare the MyOval and MyRectangle classes and add objects of these classes into the MyRectangle and MyOval arrays. The applet's paint method should walk through each array and draw every shape. Create five shapes of each type.

Once the applet is running, select **Reload** from the appletviewer's **Applet** menu to reload the applet. This will cause the applet to choose new random numbers for the shapes and draw the shapes again.[15]

---

15. In Chapter 10, we will modify this exercise to take advantage of the similarities between the classes and to avoid reinventing the wheel.

Object-Oriented Programming: Inheritance

Objectives

- To understand how inheritance promotes software reusability.
- To understand the notions of superclasses and subclasses.
- To understand access modifier `protected`.
- To be able to access superclass members with `super`.
- To understand the use of constructors and finalizers in inheritance hierarchies.
- To present a case study that demonstrates the mechanics of inheritance.

Say not you know another entirely, till you have divided an inheritance with him.
Johann Kasper Lavater

This method is to define as the number of a class the class of all classes similar to the given class.
Bertrand Russell

Good as it is to inherit a library, it is better to collect one.
Augustine Birrell

Outline

9.1 Introduction

This chapter begins our discussion of object-oriented programming (OOP) by introducing one of its primary features—*inheritance*, which is a form of software reuse in which classes are created by absorbing an existing class's data (attributes) and methods (behaviors) and embellishing them with new or modified capabilities. Software reusability saves time during program development. It also encourages the reuse of proven and debugged high-quality software, which increases the likelihood that a system will be implemented effectively.

When creating a class, rather than declaring completely new members (variables and methods), the programmer can designate that the new class should *inherit* the members from an existing class. This existing class is called the *superclass*, and the new class is called the *subclass*. (Other programming languages, such as C++, refer to the superclass as the *base class* and the subclass as the *derived class*.) Once created, each subclass can become the superclass for future subclasses. A subclass normally adds its own variables and methods. Therefore, a subclass is more specific than its superclass and represents a more specialized group of objects. Typically, the subclass exhibits the behaviors of its superclass and additional behaviors that are specific to the subclass. The *direct superclass* is the superclass from which the subclass explicitly inherits. An *indirect superclass* is inherited from two or more levels up the *class hierarchy*, which defines the inheritance relationships between classes. In Java, the class hierarchy begins with class `Object` (in package `java.lang`), from which every class in Java directly or indirectly inherits. In the case of *single inheritance,* a class is derived from one superclass. Java, unlike C++, does not support *multiple inheritance* (which occurs when a class is derived from more than one direct superclass).[1]

Experience in building software systems indicates that significant amounts of code deal with closely related special cases. When programmers are preoccupied with special cases, the details can obscure the "big picture." With object-oriented programming, programmers focus on the commonalities among objects in the system, rather than on the special cases. This process is called *abstraction*.

We distinguish between the *"is-a" relationship* and the *"has-a" relationship*. "Is-a" represents inheritance. In an "is-a" relationship, an object of a subclass also can be treated

---

1. In Chapter 10, we explain how Java can use interfaces to realize many of the benefits of multiple inheritance while avoiding the associated problems.

as an object of its superclasses. For example, a car *is a* vehicle. By contrast, "has-a" identifies composition (see Chapter 8). In a "has-a" relationship, an object contains one or more object references as members. For example, a car *has a* steering wheel.

New classes can inherit from classes in abundant *class libraries*. Organizations develop their own class libraries and can take advantage of other libraries available worldwide. Someday, the vast majority of new software likely will be constructed from *standardized reusable components*, as most hardware is constructed today. This will facilitate the development of more powerful and abundant software.

9.2 Superclasses and Subclasses

Often, an object of one class "is an" object of another class as well. For example, in geometry, a rectangle *is a* quadrilateral (as are squares, parallelograms and trapezoids). Thus, in Java, class `Rectangle` can be said to *inherit* from class `Quadrilateral`. In this context, class `Quadrilateral` is a superclass, and class `Rectangle` is a subclass. A rectangle *is a* specific type of quadrilateral, but it is incorrect to claim that every quadrilateral *is a* rectangle—the quadrilateral could be a parallelogram or some other shape. Figure 9.1 lists several simple examples of superclasses and subclasses.

Because every subclass object "is an" object of its superclass, and one superclass can have many subclasses, the set of objects represented by a superclass typically is larger than the set of objects represented by any of its subclasses. For example, the superclass `Vehicle` represents all vehicles, including cars, trucks, boats, bicycles and so on. By contrast, subclass `Car` represents a smaller, more specific subset of all vehicles.

Inheritance relationships form tree-like hierarchical structures. A superclass exists in a hierarchical relationship with its subclasses. Although classes can exist independently, when they participate in inheritance relationships, they become affiliated with other classes. A class becomes either a superclass, supplying data and behaviors to other classes, or a subclass, inheriting its data and behaviors from other classes.

Let us develop a simple class hierarchy (also called an *inheritance hierarchy*). A university community has thousands of members, consisting of employees, students and alumni. Employees are either faculty members or staff members. Faculty members are either administrators (such as deans and department chairpersons) or teachers. This organizational structure yields the inheritance hierarchy depicted in Fig. 9.2. Note that this inheritance hierarchy could contain many other classes. For example, students can be graduate or undergraduate students. Undergraduate students can be freshmen, sophomores, juniors

Superclass	Subclasses
Student	`GraduateStudent, UndergraduateStudent`
Shape	`Circle, Triangle, Rectangle`
Loan	`CarLoan, HomeImprovementLoan, MortgageLoan`
Employee	`Faculty, Staff`
BankAccount	`CheckingAccount, SavingsAccount`

Fig. 9.1   Inheritance examples.

or seniors. Each arrow in the hierarchy represents an "is-a" relationship. For instance, as we follow the arrows in this class hierarchy, we can state, "an Employee *is a* CommunityMember" and "a Teacher *is a* Faculty member." CommunityMember is the *direct superclass* of Employee, Student and Alumnus, and is an *indirect superclass* of all the other classes in the diagram. Starting from the bottom of the diagram, the reader can follow the arrows and apply the *is-a* relationship up to the topmost superclass. For example, an Administrator *is a* Faculty member, *is an* Employee and *is a* CommunityMember.

Another inheritance hierarchy is the Shape hierarchy of Fig. 9.3. To specify that class TwoDimensionalShape extends (or inherits from) class Shape, class TwoDimensionalShape could be declared in Java as follows:

```
public class TwoDimensionalShape extends Shape
```

Inheritance is not appropriate for every class relationship. In Chapter 8, we discussed the *has-a* relationship, in which classes have members that refer to objects of other classes.

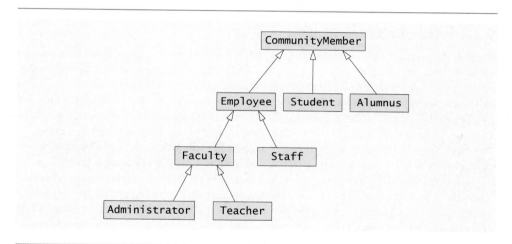

Fig. 9.2   Inheritance hierarchy for university CommunityMembers.

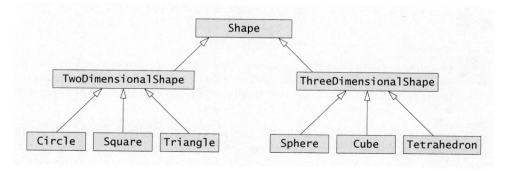

Fig. 9.3   Inheritance hierarchy for Shapes.

Such relationships create classes by composition of existing classes. For example, given the classes Employee, BirthDate and TelephoneNumber, it is improper to say that an Employee *is a* BirthDate or that an Employee *is a* TelephoneNumber. However, an Employee *has a* BirthDate, and an Employee *has a* TelephoneNumber.

It is possible to treat superclass objects and subclass objects similarly—their commonalities are expressed in the members of the superclass. Objects of all classes that extend a common superclass can be treated as objects of that superclass (i.e., such objects have an "is-a" relationship with the superclass). However, superclass objects cannot be treated as objects of their subclasses. For example, all cars are vehicles, but not all vehicles are cars. In later sections, we consider many examples that take advantage of this relationship.

One problem with inheritance is that a subclass can inherit methods it does not need or should not have. Even when a superclass method is appropriate for a subclass, that subclass often requires the method to perform its task in a manner specific to the subclass. In such cases, the subclass can *override* (redefine) the superclass method with an appropriate implementation.

9.3 protected Members

Chapter 8 discussed access modifiers public and private. A class's public members are accessible anywhere that the program has a reference to an object of that class or one of its subclasses. A class's private members are accessible only in the class's methods. These private superclass members are not inherited. In this section, we introduce access modifier *protected*. Using protected access offers an intermediate level of access between public and private. A superclass's protected members can be accessed by members of that superclass, by members of any classes derived from that superclass and by members of other classes in the same package (protected members also have package access).

All public and protected superclass members retain their original access modifier when they become members of the subclass (e.g., public members of the superclass become public members of the subclass, and, as we will soon see, protected members of the superclass become protected members of the subclass). A subclass can effect state changes in private superclass members, but only through non-private methods provided in the superclass and inherited by the subclass.

Software Engineering Observation 9.1

Methods of a subclass cannot access private members of their superclass.

Software Engineering Observation 9.2

Declaring private data helps programmers test, debug and correctly modify systems. If a subclass could access its superclass's private data, classes that inherit from that subclass could access data as well. This would propagate access to what should be private data, and the benefits of information hiding would be lost.

Subclass methods can refer to public and protected members inherited from the superclass simply by using the member names. When a subclass method overrides a superclass method, the superclass method can be accessed from the subclass by preceding the superclass method name with keyword *super* and a dot (.). We discuss accessing overridden members of the superclass in Section 9.4.

9.4 Relationship between Superclasses and Subclasses

In this section, we use a point–circle[2] inheritance hierarchy to discuss the relationship between a superclass and a subclass. We divide our discussion of the point–circle relationship into several parts. First, we declare class `Point`, which directly inherits from class `Object` and declares as `private` data an *x-y* coordinate pair. Then, we declare class `Circle`, which directly inherits from class `Object` and declares as `private` data an *x-y* coordinate pair (representing the location of the center of the circle) and a radius. We do not extend class `Point` to create class `Circle`; rather, we construct the class by writing every line of code the class requires. Next, we declare a separate `Circle2` class that extends class `Point` (i.e., a `Circle2` *is a* `Point` that also has a radius) and attempts to access class `Point`'s `private` members—this results in compilation errors, because the subclass does not have access to the superclass's `private` data. We then show that if `Point`'s data is declared as `protected`, a `Circle3` class that extends class `Point2` can access that data. For this purpose, we declare class `Point2` with `protected` data. Both the `Circle` classes contain identical functionality, but we show how the class `Circle3` is easier to create and manage. After discussing the convenience of using `protected` data, we set the `Point` data back to `private` in class `Point3` (to enforce good software engineering). Then we show how a separate `Circle4` class, which extends class `Point3`, can use `Point3` methods to manipulate `Point3`'s `private` data.

Creating and Using a Point Class

Let us first examine `Point`'s class declaration (Fig. 9.4). Recall from Section 8.2 that every class in Java (except `Object`) extends an existing class. Class `Point` does not specify the class that it extends, so the class implicitly extends class `Object` (package `java.lang`). The `public` services of class `Point` include two constructors (lines 9–12 and lines 15–20) and methods `setX` (lines 23–26), `getX` (lines 29–32), `setY` (lines 35–38), `getY` (lines 41–44) and `toString` (lines 47–50). Class `Point` specifies instance variables x and y as `private` (lines 5–6), so objects of other classes cannot access x and y directly. Technically, even if `Point`'s instance variables x and y were public, `Point` could never maintain an invalid state—a `Point` object's x and y instance variables cannot contain invalid values, because the *x-y* coordinate plane is infinite in both directions. In general, however, declaring instance variables as `private` and providing *get* and *set* methods to manipulate and validate the instance variables enforces good software engineering.

Software Engineering Observation 9.3

The Java compiler sets the superclass of a class to `Object` *when the program does not specify a superclass explicitly.*

```
1   // Fig. 9.4: Point.java
2   // Point class declaration represents an x-y coordinate pair.
3
```

Fig. 9.4   `Point` class represents an x-y coordinate pair. (Part 1 of 2.)

---

2. The point–circle relationship may seem unnatural when we say that a circle "is a" point. This example teaches what is sometimes called *structural inheritance* and focuses on the "mechanics" of inheritance and how a superclass and a subclass relate to one another. In the exercises and later sections, we present more natural inheritance examples.

```
 4   public class Point {
 5      private int x; // x part of coordinate pair
 6      private int y; // y part of coordinate pair
 7
 8      // no-argument constructor
 9      public Point()
10      {
11         // implicit call to Object constructor occurs here
12      }
13
14      // constructor
15      public Point( int xValue, int yValue )
16      {
17         // implicit call to Object constructor occurs here
18         x = xValue;  // no need for validation
19         y = yValue;  // no need for validation
20      }
21
22      // set x in coordinate pair
23      public void setX( int xValue )
24      {
25         x = xValue;  // no need for validation
26      }
27
28      // return x from coordinate pair
29      public int getX()
30      {
31         return x;
32      }
33
34      // set y in coordinate pair
35      public void setY( int yValue )
36      {
37         y = yValue;  // no need for validation
38      }
39
40      // return y from coordinate pair
41      public int getY()
42      {
43         return y;
44      }
45
46      // return String representation of Point object
47      public String toString()
48      {
49         return "[" + x + ", " + y + "]";
50      }
51
52   } // end class Point
```

Fig. 9.4   Point class represents an x-y coordinate pair. (Part 2 of 2.)

Constructors are not inherited. Therefore, Class Point does not inherit class Object's constructor. However, class Point's constructors call class Object's constructor implicitly. In fact, the first task of any subclass constructor is to call its direct superclass's constructor, either implicitly or explicitly. (The syntax for calling a superclass constructor explicitly is discussed later in this section.) If the code does not include an explicit call to the superclass constructor, Java implicitly calls the superclass's default or no-argument constructor. The comments in lines 11 and 17 indicate where the implicit calls to the superclass `Object`'s default constructor occur.

Method `toString` (lines 47–50) is special. Every class in Java (such as class `Point`) inherits either directly or indirectly from class `Object`, which is the root of the Java class hierarchy. As we mentioned previously, this means that every class inherits the methods of class `Object`. One such method is `toString`, which returns a `String` representation of an object. Sometimes this method is called implicitly by the program, such as when an object is concatenated to a string. The original `toString` method of class `Object` is a generic version, used mainly as a placeholder that can be overridden by a subclass (as we do in applets with methods `init`, `start` and `paint` from class `JApplet`). Method `toString` of class `Point` overrides method `toString` of class `Object`—when invoked, method `toString` of class `Point` returns a `String` containing an ordered pair of the values x and y (line 49). To override a superclass method, a subclass must declare a method with the same signature (name and parameters) as the method in the superclass.

Common Programming Error 9.1

It is a syntax error to override a method with a more restricted access modifier. A `public` method of the superclass cannot become a `protected` or `private` method in the subclass.

Figure 9.5 tests class `Point`. Line 9 instantiates `Point` object `point` and passes 72 as the x-coordinate value and 115 as the y-coordinate value to the constructor. Lines 12–13 use `point`'s `getX` and `getY` methods to retrieve these values, and append the values to the string `output`. Lines 15–16 invoke `point`'s methods `setX` and `setY` to change the values of `point`'s x and y instance variables. Line 19 concatenates `point` to a string, which implicitly calls `point`'s `toString` method to get the string representation of the object. Concatenating a string with any object results in an implicit call to the object's `toString` method to obtain a string representation of the object; then the strings are concatenated. Line 21 displays the `output` string by calling `JOptionPane`'s method `showMessageDialog`.

```
1    // Fig. 9.5: PointTest.java
2    // Testing class Point.
3    import javax.swing.JOptionPane;
4
5    public class PointTest {
6
7       public static void main( String[] args )
8       {
9          Point point = new Point( 72, 115 );  // create Point object
10
11          // get point coordinates
12          String output = "X coordinate is " + point.getX() +
13             "\nY coordinate is " + point.getY();
```

Fig. 9.5   `Point` class test program. (Part 1 of 2.)

```
14
15        point.setX( 10 );   // set x-coordinate
16        point.setY( 20 );   // set y-coordinate
17
18        // get String representation of new point value
19        output += "\n\nThe new location of point is " + point;
20
21        JOptionPane.showMessageDialog( null, output ); // display output
22
23        System.exit( 0 );
24
25     } // end main
26
27  } // end class PointTest
```

```
Message                                    [x]
   ⓘ    X coordinate is 72
        Y coordinate is 115

        The new location of point is [10, 20]

              OK
```

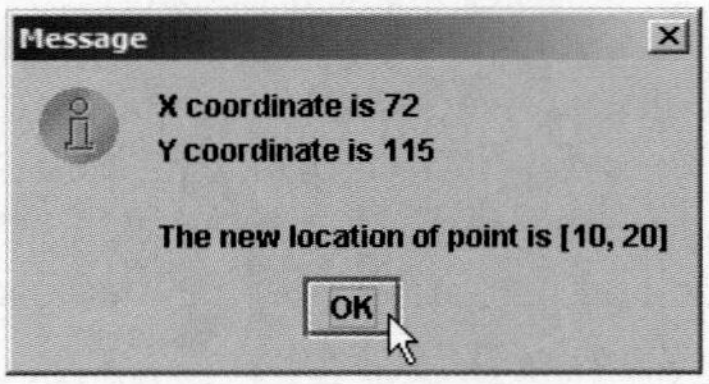

Fig. 9.5   `Point` class test program. (Part 2 of 2.)

Creating a Circle Class without Using Inheritance

We now discuss the second part of our introduction to inheritance by declaring and testing (a completely new) class `Circle` (Fig. 9.6), which contains an *x-y* coordinate pair (indicating the center of the circle) and a radius. Class `Circle`'s public services include the two `Circle` constructors (lines 10–13 and lines 16–22) and methods `setX` (lines 25–28), `getX` (lines 31–34), `setY` (lines 37–40), `getY` (lines 43–46), `setRadius` (lines 49–52), `getRadius` (lines 55–58), `getDiameter` (lines 61–64), `getCircumference` (lines 67–70), `getArea` (lines 73–76) and `toString` (lines 79–82). Lines 5–7 declare variables x, y and `radius` as `private` instance variables. These variables and methods encapsulate all necessary features (i.e., the "analytic geometry") of a circle. In Section 9.5, we show how this encapsulation enables us to reuse and extend this class.

```
1   // Fig. 9.6: Circle.java
2   // Circle class contains x-y coordinate pair and radius.
3
4   public class Circle {
5      private int x;         // x-coordinate of Circle's center
6      private int y;         // y-coordinate of Circle's center
7      private double radius; // Circle's radius
8
9      // no-argument constructor
10     public Circle()
11     {
12        // implicit call to Object constructor occurs here
13     }
```

Fig. 9.6   `Circle` class contains an *x-y* coordinate and a radius. (Part 1 of 3.)

```
14
15      // constructor
16      public Circle( int xValue, int yValue, double radiusValue )
17      {
18          // implicit call to Object constructor occurs here
19          x = xValue;  // no need for validation
20          y = yValue;  // no need for validation
21          setRadius( radiusValue );
22      }
23
24      // set x in coordinate pair
25      public void setX( int xValue )
26      {
27          x = xValue;  // no need for validation
28      }
29
30      // return x from coordinate pair
31      public int getX()
32      {
33          return x;
34      }
35
36      // set y in coordinate pair
37      public void setY( int yValue )
38      {
39          y = yValue;  // no need for validation
40      }
41
42      // return y from coordinate pair
43      public int getY()
44      {
45          return y;
46      }
47
48      // set radius
49      public void setRadius( double radiusValue )
50      {
51          radius = ( radiusValue < 0.0 ? 0.0 : radiusValue );
52      }
53
54      // return radius
55      public double getRadius()
56      {
57          return radius;
58      }
59
60      // calculate and return diameter
61      public double getDiameter()
62      {
63          return 2 * radius;
64      }
65
```

Fig. 9.6   Circle class contains an *x-y* coordinate and a radius. (Part 2 of 3.)

```
66        // calculate and return circumference
67        public double getCircumference()
68        {
69            return Math.PI * getDiameter();
70        }
71
72        // calculate and return area
73        public double getArea()
74        {
75            return Math.PI * radius * radius;
76        }
77
78        // return String representation of Circle object
79        public String toString()
80        {
81            return "Center = [" + x + ", " + y + "]; Radius = " + radius;
82        }
83
84    } // end class Circle
```

Fig. 9.6   Circle class contains an *x-y* coordinate and a radius. (Part 3 of 3.)

Figure 9.7 tests class Circle. Line 10 instantiates a Circle, passing 37 as the *x*-coordinate value, 43 as the *y*-coordinate value and 2.5 as the radius value to the constructor, then assigns the object's reference to circle. Lines 13–15 use methods getX, getY and getRadius to retrieve circle's values, and append the values to the string output. Lines 17–19 invoke circle's setX, setY and setRadius methods to change the *x-y* coordinates and the radius, respectively. Method setRadius (Fig. 9.6, lines 49–52) ensures that instance variable radius cannot be assigned a negative value (i.e., a circle cannot have a negative radius). Lines 22–23 of Fig. 9.7 calls circle's toString method explicitly to get the string representation of the new circle object. Lines 29–37 call circle's getDiameter, getCircumference and getArea methods to get circle's diameter, circumference and area, respectively. Line 39 displays the output string.

```
1    // Fig. 9.7: CircleTest.java
2    // Testing class Circle.
3    import java.text.DecimalFormat;
4    import javax.swing.JOptionPane;
5
6    public class CircleTest {
7
8        public static void main( String[] args )
9        {
10           Circle circle = new Circle( 37, 43, 2.5 ); // create Circle object
11
12           // get Circle's initial x-y coordinates and radius
13           String output = "X coordinate is " + circle.getX() +
14               "\nY coordinate is " + circle.getY() +
15               "\nRadius is " + circle.getRadius();
16
```

Fig. 9.7   Circle class test program. (Part 1 of 2.)

```
17        circle.setX( 35 );            // set new x-coordinate
18        circle.setY( 20 );            // set new y-coordinate
19        circle.setRadius( 4.25 );     // set new radius
20
21        // get String representation of new circle value
22        output += "\n\nThe new location and radius of circle are\n" +
23           circle.toString();
24
25        // format floating-point values with 2 digits of precision
26        DecimalFormat twoDigits = new DecimalFormat( "0.00" );
27
28        // get Circle's diameter
29        output += "\nDiameter is " +
30           twoDigits.format( circle.getDiameter() );
31
32        // get Circle's circumference
33        output += "\nCircumference is " +
34           twoDigits.format( circle.getCircumference() );
35
36        // get Circle's area
37        output += "\nArea is " + twoDigits.format( circle.getArea() );
38
39        JOptionPane.showMessageDialog( null, output ); // display output
40
41        System.exit( 0 );
42
43     } // end main
44
45  } // end class CircleTest
```

Message

X coordinate is 37
Y coordinate is 43
Radius is 2.5

The new location and radius of circle are
Center = [35, 20]; Radius = 4.25
Diameter is 8.50
Circumference is 26.70
Area is 56.75

OK

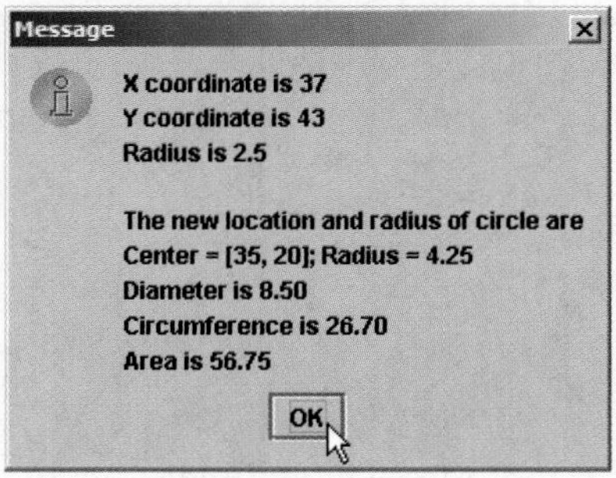

Fig. 9.7 Circle class test program. (Part 2 of 2.)

Note that much of the code for class Circle (Fig. 9.6) is similar, if not identical, to the code for class Point (Fig. 9.4). For example, in class Circle, private instance variables x and y and methods setX, getX, setY and getY are identical to those of class Point. In addition, the Circle constructors are almost identical to those of class Point, except that they also manipulate the radius. The other additions to class Circle are private instance variable radius and methods setRadius, getRadius, getDiameter, getCircumference and getArea.

It appears that we literally copied code from class `Point` and pasted this code into class `Circle`. Then we modified class `Circle` to include a radius and methods that manipulate the radius. This "copy-and-paste" approach is often error prone and time consuming. Worse yet, it can result in many physical copies of the same code existing throughout a system, creating a code-maintenance nightmare. Is there a way to "absorb" the attributes and behaviors of one class in a way that makes them part of other classes without duplicating code? In the next several examples, we answer that question, using a more elegant class construction approach emphasizing the benefits of inheritance.

Point–Circle Hierarchy Using Inheritance

Now we declare and test class `Circle2` (Fig. 9.8), which inherits instance variables `x` and `y` and methods `setX`, `getX`, `setY` and `getY` from class `Point` (Fig. 9.4). An object of class `Circle2` "is a" `Point` (because inheritance passes on the capabilities of class `Point`), but, as evidenced by the class `Circle2`, also has instance variable `radius` (Fig. 9.8, line 5). Keyword `extends` in line 4 of the class declaration indicates inheritance. As a subclass, `Circle2` inherits the `public` and `protected` instance variables and methods of class `Point`. The constructors of class `Point` are not inherited. Thus, the public services of `Circle2` include the two `Circle2` constructors (lines 8–20)—each class provides its own constructors that are specific to the class—the `public` methods inherited from class `Point`; methods `setRadius` and `getRadius` (lines 23–32); and methods `getDiameter`, `getCircumference`, `getArea` and `toString` (lines 35–57).

```
1   // Fig. 9.8: Circle2.java
2   // Circle2 class inherits from Point.
3
4   public class Circle2 extends Point {
5      private double radius;   // Circle2's radius
6
7      // no-argument constructor
8      public Circle2()
9      {
10        // implicit call to Point constructor occurs here
11     }
12
13     // constructor
14     public Circle2( int xValue, int yValue, double radiusValue )
15     {
16        // implicit call to Point constructor occurs here
17        x = xValue;   // not allowed: x private in Point
18        y = yValue;   // not allowed: y private in Point
19        setRadius( radiusValue );
20     }
21
22     // set radius
23     public void setRadius( double radiusValue )
24     {
25        radius = ( radiusValue < 0.0 ? 0.0 : radiusValue );
26     }
27
```

Fig. 9.8   `private` superclass members cannot be accessed in subclass. (Part 1 of 2.)

```
28      // return radius
29      public double getRadius()
30      {
31          return radius;
32      }
33
34      // calculate and return diameter
35      public double getDiameter()
36      {
37          return 2 * radius;
38      }
39
40      // calculate and return circumference
41      public double getCircumference()
42      {
43          return Math.PI * getDiameter();
44      }
45
46      // calculate and return area
47      public double getArea()
48      {
49          return Math.PI * radius * radius;
50      }
51
52      // return String representation of Circle object
53      public String toString()
54      {
55          // use of x and y not allowed: x and y private in Point
56          return "Center = [" + x + ", " + y + "]; Radius = " + radius;
57      }
58
59  } // end class Circle2
```

```
Circle2.java:17: x has private access in Point
       x = xValue;  // not allowed: x private in Point
       ^
Circle2.java:18: y has private access in Point
       y = yValue;  // not allowed: y private in Point
       ^
Circle2.java:56: x has private access in Point
       return "Center = [" + x + ", " + y + "]; Radius = " + radius;
                             ^
Circle2.java:56: y has private access in Point
       return "Center = [" + x + ", " + y + "]; Radius = " + radius;
                                        ^
4 errors
```

Fig. 9.8　`private` superclass members cannot be accessed in subclass. (Part 2 of 2.)

The no-argument constructor (lines 8–11) implicitly calls class `Point`'s no-argument constructor; then Java implicitly sets the x-y coordinates to 0. The other constructor (lines 14–20) implicitly calls class `Point`'s no-argument constructor, then sets the *x-y* coordinate to a specific value. The compiler generates syntax errors for lines 17 and 18 (and line 56, where Circle2's toString method attempts to use the values of x and y directly), because the subclass Circle2 has not inherited, and therefore is not allowed to access, superclass Point's private instance variables x and y.

Point–Circle Hierarchy Using protected Data

To enable class Circle2 to access superclass instance variables x and y, we can declare those members as protected in the superclass. As we discussed in Section 9.3, a superclass's protected members are inherited by any subclasses of that superclass. Class Point2 (Fig. 9.9) is a modification of class Point (Fig. 9.4) that declares instance variables x and y as protected (Fig. 9.9, lines 5–6) rather than private. Other than the change in the class name (and, hence, the change in the constructor name) to Point2, the rest of the class declaration in Fig. 9.9 is identical to Fig. 9.4.

```java
1   // Fig. 9.9: Point2.java
2   // Point2 class declaration represents an x-y coordinate pair.
3
4   public class Point2 {
5      protected int x;  // x part of coordinate pair
6      protected int y;  // y part of coordinate pair
7
8      // no-argument constructor
9      public Point2()
10     {
11        // implicit call to Object constructor occurs here
12     }
13
14     // constructor
15     public Point2( int xValue, int yValue )
16     {
17        // implicit call to Object constructor occurs here
18        x = xValue;  // no need for validation
19        y = yValue;  // no need for validation
20     }
21
22     // set x in coordinate pair
23     public void setX( int xValue )
24     {
25        x = xValue;  // no need for validation
26     }
27
28     // return x from coordinate pair
29     public int getX()
30     {
31        return x;
32     }
33
```

Fig. 9.9   Point2 class represents an *x-y* coordinate pair as protected data. (Part 1 of 2.)

```
34      // set y in coordinate pair
35      public void setY( int yValue )
36      {
37         y = yValue;   // no need for validation
38      }
39
40      // return y from coordinate pair
41      public int getY()
42      {
43         return y;
44      }
45
46      // return String representation of Point2 object
47      public String toString()
48      {
49         return "[" + x + ", " + y + "]";
50      }
51
52   } // end class Point2
```

Fig. 9.9   Point2 class represents an *x-y* coordinate pair as **protected** data. (Part 2 of 2.)

Class Circle3 (Fig. 9.10) is a modification of class Circle2 (Fig. 9.8) that extends class Point2 rather than class Point. Because class Circle3 extends class Point2 (line 5), objects of class Circle3 inherit instance variables that were declared **protected** in class Point2 (i.e., variables x and y). As a result, the compiler does not generate errors when compiling the Circle3 constructor at lines 15–21 and method toString at lines 54–57, because x and y are now members of class Circle3. Objects of a subclass also inherit **protected** members from any of that subclass's indirect superclasses.

```
1    // Fig. 9.10: Circle3.java
2    // Circle3 class inherits from Point2 and has access to Point2
3    // protected members x and y.
4
5    public class Circle3 extends Point2 {
6       private double radius;   // Circle3's radius
7
8       // no-argument constructor
9       public Circle3()
10      {
11         // implicit call to Point2 constructor occurs here
12      }
13
14      // constructor
15      public Circle3( int xValue, int yValue, double radiusValue )
16      {
17         // implicit call to Point2 constructor occurs here
18         x = xValue;   // no need for validation
```

Fig. 9.10   Circle3 class that inherits Point2's **protected** data. (Part 1 of 2.)

```
19          y = yValue;   // no need for validation
20          setRadius( radiusValue );
21      }
22
23      // set radius
24      public void setRadius( double radiusValue )
25      {
26          radius = ( radiusValue < 0.0 ? 0.0 : radiusValue );
27      }
28
29      // return radius
30      public double getRadius()
31      {
32          return radius;
33      }
34
35      // calculate and return diameter
36      public double getDiameter()
37      {
38          return 2 * radius;
39      }
40
41      // calculate and return circumference
42      public double getCircumference()
43      {
44          return Math.PI * getDiameter();
45      }
46
47      // calculate and return area
48      public double getArea()
49      {
50          return Math.PI * radius * radius;
51      }
52
53      // return String representation of Circle3 object
54      public String toString()
55      {
56          return "Center = [" + x + ", " + y + "]; Radius = " + radius;
57      }
58
59   } // end class Circle3
```

Fig. 9.10   Circle3 class that inherits Point2's protected data. (Part 2 of 2.)

Class Circle3 does not inherit class Point2's constructors. However, class Circle3's no-argument constructor (lines 9–12) calls class Point2's no-argument constructor implicitly. Recall that the first task of any subclass constructor is to call its direct superclass's constructor, either implicitly or explicitly. If the code does not include an explicit call to the superclass constructor, an implicit call is made to the superclass' no-argument constructor. The constructor at lines 9–12 first calls the Point2 no-argument constructor, then Java initializes inherited variables and sets radius to their default zero values.

Figure 9.11 performs identical tests on class `Circle3` as those which Fig. 9.7 performed on `Circle` (Fig. 9.6). Note that the outputs of the two programs are identical. Although we declared class `Circle` without using inheritance and declared class `Circle3` using inheritance, both classes provide the same functionality. The source code for class `Circle3`, which is 59 lines, is considerably shorter than the source code for class `Circle`, which is 84 lines, because class `Circle3` inherits part of its functionality from `Point2`, whereas class `Circle` does not inherit any functionality. Also, there is now only one copy of the point functionality mentioned in class `Point2`. This makes the code easier to debug, maintain and modify, because the point-related code exists only in the file of Fig. 9.9.

```java
1   // Fig. 9.11: CircleTest3.java
2   // Testing class Circle3.
3   import java.text.DecimalFormat;
4   import javax.swing.JOptionPane;
5
6   public class CircleTest3 {
7
8      public static void main( String[] args )
9      {
10        // instantiate Circle object
11        Circle3 circle = new Circle3( 37, 43, 2.5 );
12
13        // get Circle3's initial x-y coordinates and radius
14        String output = "X coordinate is " + circle.getX() +
15           "\nY coordinate is " + circle.getY() +
16           "\nRadius is " + circle.getRadius();
17
18        circle.setX( 35 );           // set new x-coordinate
19        circle.setY( 20 );           // set new y-coordinate
20        circle.setRadius( 4.25 );    // set new radius
21
22        // get String representation of new circle value
23        output += "\n\nThe new location and radius of circle are\n" +
24           circle.toString();
25
26        // format floating-point values with 2 digits of precision
27        DecimalFormat twoDigits = new DecimalFormat( "0.00" );
28
29        // get Circle's diameter
30        output += "\nDiameter is " +
31           twoDigits.format( circle.getDiameter() );
32
33        // get Circle's circumference
34        output += "\nCircumference is " +
35           twoDigits.format( circle.getCircumference() );
36
37        // get Circle's area
38        output += "\nArea is " + twoDigits.format( circle.getArea() );
39
40        JOptionPane.showMessageDialog( null, output ); // display output
41
```

Fig. 9.11   `protected` superclass members inherited into subclass `Circle3`. (Part 1 of 2.)

```
42          System.exit( 0 );
43
44     } // end method main
45
46   } // end class CircleTest3
```

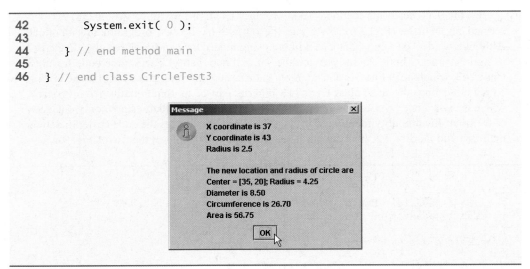

Fig. 9.11   `protected` superclass members inherited into subclass `Circle3`. (Part 2 of 2.)

In this example, we declared superclass instance variables as `protected`, so that subclasses could inherit them. The inheritance of protected instance variables allows for a slight increase in performance, because we avoid incurring the overhead of a call to a *set* or *get* method. However, such performance increases are often negligible compared to the optimizations compilers can perform. It is better to use `private` data to encourage proper software engineering. Your code will be easier to maintain, modify and debug.

Using `protected` instance variables creates two problems. First, the subclass object does not have to use a method to set the value of the variable. Therefore, a subclass object can assign an invalid value to the variable, thus leaving the object in an invalid state. For example, if we were to declare `Circle3`'s instance variable `radius` as `protected`, a subclass object (e.g., `Cylinder`) could then assign a negative value to `radius`. The second problem with using `protected` instance variables is that subclass methods are more likely to be written so that they depend on the superclass implementation. In practice, subclasses should depend only on the superclass services (i.e., non-`private` methods) and not on the superclass implementation. With `protected` instance variables in the superclass, if the superclass implementation changes, we may need to modify all subclasses of that superclass. For example, if, for some reason, we were to change the names of instance variables `x` and `y` to `xCoordinate` and `yCoordinate`, then we would have to do so for all occurrences in which a subclass references these superclass instance variables directly. In such a case, the software is said to be *fragile* or *brittle*, because a small change in the superclass can "break" subclass implementation. The programmer should be able to change the superclass implementation freely, while still providing the same services to subclasses. (Of course, if the superclass services change, we must reimplement our subclasses, but good object-oriented design attempts to prevent this.)

Good Programming Practice 9.1

Use the `protected` access modifier when a superclass should provide a service (i.e., a method) only to its subclasses and should not provide the service to other clients.

Good Programming Practice 9.2

Declare superclass instance variables `private` (as opposed to `protected`) so that the superclass implementation can change without affecting subclass implementations.

Error-Prevention Tip 9.1

When possible, avoid including `protected` instance variables in a superclass. Rather, include non-`private` methods that access `private` instance variables, ensuring that the object maintains a consistent state.

Point–Circle Hierarchy Using *private* Data

We now reexamine our point–circle hierarchy example once more, this time attempting to use the best software-engineering practices. Class `Point3` (Fig. 9.12) declares instance variables x and y as `private` (lines 5–6) and exposes methods setX, getX, setY, getY and toString for manipulating these values. Subclass `Circle4` (Fig. 9.13) inherits these non-`private` superclass methods (setX, getX, setY and getY) and can access the `private` superclass members with these methods.

```
1    // Fig. 9.12: Point3.java
2    // Point class declaration represents an x-y coordinate pair.
3
4    public class Point3 {
5       private int x;   // x part of coordinate pair
6       private int y;   // y part of coordinate pair
7
8       // no-argument constructor
9       public Point3()
10      {
11          // implicit call to Object constructor occurs here
12      }
13
14      // constructor
15      public Point3( int xValue, int yValue )
16      {
17          // implicit call to Object constructor occurs here
18          x = xValue;  // no need for validation
19          y = yValue;  // no need for validation
20      }
21
22      // set x in coordinate pair
23      public void setX( int xValue )
24      {
25          x = xValue;  // no need for validation
26      }
27
28      // return x from coordinate pair
29      public int getX()
30      {
31          return x;
32      }
33
```

Fig. 9.12   Point3 class uses methods to manipulate its `private` data. (Part 1 of 2.)

```
34        // set y in coordinate pair
35        public void setY( int yValue )
36        {
37           y = yValue;  // no need for validation
38        }
39
40        // return y from coordinate pair
41        public int getY()
42        {
43           return y;
44        }
45
46        // return String representation of Point3 object
47        public String toString()
48        {
49           return "[" + getX() + ", " + getY() + "]";
50        }
51
52     } // end class Point3
```

Fig. 9.12   Point3 class uses methods to manipulate its private data. (Part 2 of 2.)

Class Circle4 (Fig. 9.13) has several changes to its method implementations that distinguish it from class Circle3 (Fig. 9.10). Class Circle4's constructor (lines 16–20) invokes a Point3 constructor to initialize the superclass portion of a Circle4 object (i.e., variables x and y inherited from Point3). Java actually requires a subclass constructor to call its superclass constructor to initialize the superclass instance variables that are inherited by the subclass. The no-argument constructor at lines 10–13 does not call a Point3 constructor explicitly, so Java automatically calls class Point3's no-argument constructor (declared at lines 9–12 of Fig. 9.12).

```
1    // Fig. 9.13: Circle4.java
2    // Circle4 class inherits from Point3 and accesses Point3's
3    // private x and y via Point3's public methods.
4
5    public class Circle4 extends Point3 {
6
7       private double radius;   // Circle4's radius
8
9       // no-argument constructor
10      public Circle4()
11      {
12         // implicit call to Point3 constructor occurs here
13      }
14
15      // constructor
16      public Circle4( int xValue, int yValue, double radiusValue )
17      {
18         super( xValue, yValue );  // call Point3 constructor explicitly
```

Fig. 9.13   Circle4 class that extends Point3, which does not provide protected data. (Part 1 of 2.)

```
19          setRadius( radiusValue );
20       }
21
22       // set radius
23       public void setRadius( double radiusValue )
24       {
25          radius = ( radiusValue < 0.0 ? 0.0 : radiusValue );
26       }
27
28       // return radius
29       public double getRadius()
30       {
31          return radius;
32       }
33
34       // calculate and return diameter
35       public double getDiameter()
36       {
37          return 2 * getRadius();
38       }
39
40       // calculate and return circumference
41       public double getCircumference()
42       {
43          return Math.PI * getDiameter();
44       }
45
46       // calculate and return area
47       public double getArea()
48       {
49          return Math.PI * getRadius() * getRadius();
50       }
51
52       // return String representation of Circle4 object
53       public String toString()
54       {
55          return "Center = " + super.toString() + "; Radius = " + getRadius();
56       }
57
58    } // end class Circle4
```

Fig. 9.13   Circle4 class that extends Point3, which does not provide protected data. (Part 2 of 2.)

Line 18 in Circle4's second constructor invokes the Point3 constructor (declared at lines 15–20 of Fig. 9.12) by using the *superclass constructor call syntax*—keyword *super*, followed by a set of parentheses containing the superclass constructor arguments. The arguments are xValue and yValue, which are used to initialize superclass members x and y. If Circle4's constructor did not invoke Point3's constructor explicitly, Point3's no-argument constructor would be invoked implicitly and Java would set x and y to their default 0 values. If class Point3 did not provide a no-argument constructor, the compiler would issue an error. The superclass constructor call must be the first statement in the subclass constructor's body. Use super() to call the superclass no-argument constructor explicitly.

Common Programming Error 9.2

A compilation error occurs if a subclass constructor calls one of its superclass constructors with arguments that do not match exactly the number and types of parameters specified in one of the superclass constructor declarations.

Note that methods `getDiameter` (Fig. 9.13, lines 35–38), `getArea` (lines 47–50) and `toString` (lines 53–56) each invoke method `getRadius` to obtain the radius value, rather than accessing `radius` directly. If we decide to rename instance variable `radius`, only the bodies of method `setRadius` and `getRadius` will need to change.

Class `Circle4`'s `toString` method (Fig. 9.13, lines 53–56) overrides class `Point3`'s `toString` method (Fig. 9.12, lines 47–50). The new version displays the values of class `Point3`'s `private` instance variables x and y by calling `Point3`'s `toString` method with the expression `super.toString()` (Fig. 9.13, line 55). Note the syntax used to invoke an overridden superclass method from a subclass—place the keyword `super` and a dot (.) before the superclass method name. This method invocation is a good software-engineering practice: Recall that if a method performs all or some of the actions needed by another method, call that method rather than duplicating its code. By having `Circle4`'s `toString` method invoke `Point3`'s `toString` method to perform part of the task of returning the string representation of a `Circle4` object (i.e., to display the *x*- and *y*-coordinate values), we avoid duplicating code and reduce code-maintenance problems.

Common Programming Error 9.3

When a superclass method is overridden in a subclass, the subclass version often calls the superclass version to do additional work. Failure to prefix the superclass method name with the keyword super and a dot (.) when referencing the superclass's method causes infinite recursion, because the subclass method would then call itself.

Common Programming Error 9.4

Declaring a superclass public or protected method with a different parameter list in the subclass hides the superclass version of the method. Attempts to call the superclass version result in compilation errors.

Figure 9.14 performs identical manipulations on a `Circle4` object as did Fig. 9.7 and Fig. 9.11 on objects of classes `Circle` and `Circle3`, respectively. Although each "circle" class behaves identically, class `Circle4` is the best engineered. Using inheritance, we have efficiently and effectively constructed a well-engineered class.

```
1   // Fig. 9.14: CircleTest4.java
2   // Testing class Circle4.
3   import java.text.DecimalFormat;
4   import javax.swing.JOptionPane;
5
6   public class CircleTest4 {
7
8      public static void main( String[] args )
9      {
10         // instantiate Circle object
11         Circle4 circle = new Circle4( 37, 43, 2.5 );
```

Fig. 9.14   Superclass `private` data is accessible to a subclass via `public` or `protected` methods inherited by the subclass. (Part 1 of 2.)

```
12
13        // get Circle4's initial x-y coordinates and radius
14        String output = "X coordinate is " + circle.getX() +
15           "\nY coordinate is " + circle.getY() +
16           "\nRadius is " + circle.getRadius();
17
18        circle.setX( 35 );        // set new x-coordinate
19        circle.setY( 20 );        // set new y-coordinate
20        circle.setRadius( 4.25 ); // set new radius
21
22        // get String representation of new circle value
23        output += "\n\nThe new location and radius of circle are\n" +
24           circle.toString();
25
26        // format floating-point values with 2 digits of precision
27        DecimalFormat twoDigits = new DecimalFormat( "0.00" );
28
29        // get Circle's diameter
30        output += "\nDiameter is " +
31           twoDigits.format( circle.getDiameter() );
32
33        // get Circle's circumference
34        output += "\nCircumference is " +
35           twoDigits.format( circle.getCircumference() );
36
37        // get Circle's area
38        output += "\nArea is " + twoDigits.format( circle.getArea() );
39
40        JOptionPane.showMessageDialog( null, output ); // display output
41
42        System.exit( 0 );
43
44     } // end main
45
46  } // end class CircleTest4
```

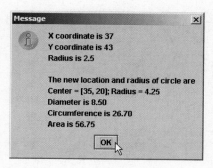

Fig. 9.14   Superclass `private` data is accessible to a subclass via `public` or `protected` methods inherited by the subclass. (Part 2 of 2.)

9.5 Case Study: Three-Level Inheritance Hierarchy

Let us consider a more substantial inheritance example involving a three-level point–circle–cylinder hierarchy. In Section 9.4, we developed classes Point3 (Fig. 9.12) and Circle4 (Fig. 9.13). Now we present an example in which we derive class Cylinder from class Circle4.

The first class that we use in our case study is class Point3 (Fig. 9.12). We declared Point3's instance variables as private. Class Point3 also contains methods setX, getX, setY and getY for accessing x and y, and method toString for returning the string representation of a Point3 object.

We also use class Circle4 (Fig. 9.13), which extends class Point3. Class Circle4 contains functionality from class Point3 and provides method setRadius (to ensure that the radius instance variable cannot hold a negative value) and methods getRadius, getDiameter, getCircumference, getArea and toString. Subclasses of Circle4 (such as class Cylinder, which we introduce momentarily) should override these methods as necessary to provide implementations specific to the subclass. For example, a circle has an area that is calculated by the formula πr^2, in which r represents the circle's radius. However, a cylinder has a surface area that is calculated by the formula $(2\pi r^2) + (2\pi r h)$, in which r represents the cylinder's radius and h represents the cylinder's height. Therefore, class Cylinder should override method getArea to reflect this calculation.

Figure 9.15 presents class Cylinder, which inherits from class Circle4. Class Cylinder specifies that a Cylinder has a height (line 5). Class Cylinder's public services include inherited Circle4 methods setRadius, getRadius, getDiameter, getCircumference, getArea and toString; indirectly inherited Point3 methods setX, getX, setY and getY; the Cylinder constructors (lines 8–19); and Cylinder methods setHeight, getHeight, getArea, getVolume and toString (lines 22–49). Methods getArea and toString override the methods with the same names that are inherited from class Circle4.

```
1   // Fig. 9.15: Cylinder.java
2   // Cylinder class inherits from Circle4.
3
4   public class Cylinder extends Circle4 {
5      private double height;  // Cylinder's height
6
7      // no-argument constructor
8      public Cylinder()
9      {
10        // implicit call to Circle4 constructor occurs here
11     }
12
13     // constructor
14     public Cylinder( int xValue, int yValue, double radiusValue,
15        double heightValue )
16     {
17        super( xValue, yValue, radiusValue ); // call Circle4 constructor
```

Fig. 9.15   Cylinder class inherits from Circle4 and overrides method getArea. (Part 1 of 2.)

```
18          setHeight( heightValue );
19       }
20
21       // set Cylinder's height
22       public void setHeight( double heightValue )
23       {
24          height = ( heightValue < 0.0 ? 0.0 : heightValue );
25       }
26
27       // get Cylinder's height
28       public double getHeight()
29       {
30          return height;
31       }
32
33       // override Circle4 method getArea to calculate Cylinder area
34       public double getArea()
35       {
36          return 2 * super.getArea() + getCircumference() * getHeight();
37       }
38
39       // calculate Cylinder volume
40       public double getVolume()
41       {
42          return super.getArea() * getHeight();
43       }
44
45       // return String representation of Cylinder object
46       public String toString()
47       {
48          return super.toString() + "; Height = " + getHeight();
49       }
50
51    } // end class Cylinder
```

Fig. 9.15   Cylinder class inherits from Circle4 and overrides method getArea. (Part 2 of 2.)

Method getArea (lines 34–37) overrides Circle4's method getArea to calculate the cylinder's surface area. Method toString (lines 46–49) overrides method toString of class Circle4 to return the String representation of the cylinder. Class Cylinder also declares method getVolume (lines 40–43) to calculate the cylinder's volume.

Figure 9.16 is a CylinderTest application that tests class Cylinder. Line 11 instantiates a Cylinder object called cylinder. Lines 14–16 use cylinder's methods getX, getY, getRadius and getHeight to obtain information about cylinder, because CylinderTest cannot access the private instance variables of class Cylinder directly. Lines 18–21 use methods setX, setY, setRadius and setHeight to reset cylinder's x-y coordinates (we assume that the cylinder's x-y coordinates specify the position of the center of its bottom on the x-y plane), radius and height. Class Cylinder can use class Point3's setX, getX, setY and getY methods, because class Cylinder inherits them indirectly from class Point3. (Class Cylinder inherits methods setX, getX, setY and getY directly from class Circle4, which inherited them directly from class Point3.)

Lines 24–26 invoke `cylinder`'s `toString` method to get the `String` representation of object `cylinder`. Lines 32–33 and 36–37 invoke methods `getDiameter` and `getCircumference`, respectively, of the `cylinder` object—because class `Cylinder` inherits the methods from class `Circle4`, these methods, exactly as declared in `Circle4`, are invoked. Lines 40 and 43 invoke methods `getArea` and `getVolume`, respectively, to obtain the surface area and volume of `cylinder`. Line 45 displays the output string.

```java
1   // Fig. 9.16: CylinderTest.java
2   // Testing class Cylinder.
3   import java.text.DecimalFormat;
4   import javax.swing.JOptionPane;
5
6   public class CylinderTest {
7
8      public static void main( String[] args )
9      {
10        // create Cylinder object
11        Cylinder cylinder = new Cylinder( 12, 23, 2.5, 5.7 );
12
13        // get Cylinder's initial x-y coordinates, radius and height
14        String output = "X coordinate is " + cylinder.getX() +
15           "\nY coordinate is " + cylinder.getY() + "\nRadius is " +
16           cylinder.getRadius() + "\nHeight is " + cylinder.getHeight();
17
18        cylinder.setX( 35 );          // set new x-coordinate
19        cylinder.setY( 20 );          // set new y-coordinate
20        cylinder.setRadius( 4.25 );   // set new radius
21        cylinder.setHeight( 10.75 );  // set new height
22
23        // get String representation of new cylinder value
24        output +=
25           "\n\nThe new location, radius and height of cylinder are\n" +
26           cylinder.toString();
27
28        // format floating-point values with 2 digits of precision
29        DecimalFormat twoDigits = new DecimalFormat( "0.00" );
30
31        // get Cylinder's diameter
32        output += "\n\nDiameter is " +
33           twoDigits.format( cylinder.getDiameter() );
34
35        // get Cylinder's circumference
36        output += "\nCircumference is " +
37           twoDigits.format( cylinder.getCircumference() );
38
39        // get Cylinder's area
40        output += "\nArea is " + twoDigits.format( cylinder.getArea() );
41
42        // get Cylinder's volume
43        output += "\nVolume is " + twoDigits.format( cylinder.getVolume() );
44
```

Fig. 9.16   `Point-Circle-Cylinder` hierarchy test program. (Part 1 of 2.)

```
45              JOptionPane.showMessageDialog( null, output ); // display output
46
47              System.exit( 0 );
48
49        } // end main
50
51    } // end class CylinderTest
```

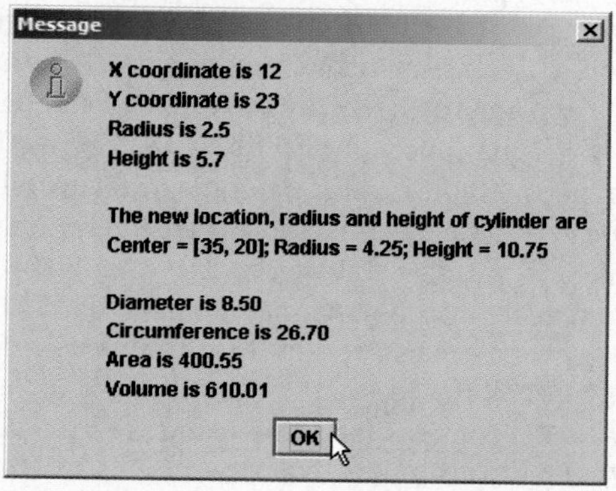

Fig. 9.16   Point-Circle-Cylinder hierarchy test program. (Part 2 of 2.)

Using the point–circle–cylinder example, we have shown the use and benefits of inheritance. We were able to develop classes Circle4 and Cylinder much more quickly by using inheritance than if we had developed those classes "from scratch." Inheritance avoids duplicating code and the associated code-maintenance problems.

9.6 Constructors and Finalizers in Subclasses

As we explained in the previous section, instantiating a subclass object begins a chain of constructor calls in which the subclass constructor, before performing its own tasks, invokes its direct superclass's constructor either explicitly (via the super reference) or implicitly (calling the superclass's default constructor or no-argument constructor). Similarly, if the superclass was derived from another class, the superclass constructor would be required to invoke the constructor of the next class up in the hierarchy, and so on. The last constructor called in the chain is always the constructor for class Object. The original subclass constructor's body finishes executing last. Each superclass's constructor manipulates the superclass instance variables that the subclass object inherits. For example, consider again the Point3–Circle4–Cylinder hierarchy from Fig. 9.12, Fig. 9.13 and Fig. 9.15. When a program creates a Cylinder object, the Cylinder constructor is called. That constructor calls Circle4's constructor, which in turn calls Point3's constructor. Point3's constructor calls Object's constructor. Class Object's constructor has an empty body, so it immediately returns control to Point3's constructor, which then manipulates the *x-y* coordinates of the Cylinder object. When Point3's constructor completes execution, it returns control to Circle4's constructor, which manipulates the Cylinder object's radius. When Circle4's constructor completes execution, it returns control to Cylinder's constructor, which manipulates the Cylinder object's height.

Software Engineering Observation 9.4

When a program creates a subclass object, the subclass constructor immediately calls the superclass constructor (explicitly, via super, *or implicitly). The superclass constructor's body executes to manipulate the superclass's instance variables, and the subclass constructor's body executes to manipulate the subclass's instance variables. Java ensures that all instance variables are initialized with their default values. Thus, even if a constructor does not assign a value to an instance variable, the variable is still initialized.*

If the classes in your class hierarchy declare their own `finalize` methods, subclass method `finalize` should invoke superclass method `finalize` as its last action, to ensure that all parts of an object are finalized properly if the garbage collector reclaims the memory for the object. When a subclass object's `finalize` method is called, it performs its task, then should invoke method `finalize` of the next superclass in the hierarchy. This process should be repeated until the finalizer of superclass `Object` is called. Then the memory becomes available for use by new objects.

Our next example revisits the point–circle hierarchy by declaring a new `Point` class (Fig. 9.17) and a new `Circle` class (Fig. 9.18). Each class declares constructors and `finalize` methods that each print messages when they are invoked.[3]

Class `Point` (Fig. 9.17) contains the same features as the version of the class shown in Fig. 9.4. We modified the constructors (lines 9–13 and 16–23) and added a `finalize` method (lines 26–29). Each outputs a line of text at the command line upon its invocation. Note the concatenation of `this` to a string in lines 12, 22 and 28, which implicitly invokes the object's `toString` method to obtain the object's string representation.

```
1   // Fig. 9.17: Point.java
2   // Point class declaration represents an x-y coordinate pair.
3
4   public class Point {
5      private int x;   // x part of coordinate pair
6      private int y;   // y part of coordinate pair
7
8      // no-argument constructor
9      public Point()
10     {
11        // implicit call to Object constructor occurs here
12        System.out.println( "Point no-argument constructor: " + this );
13     }
14
15     // constructor
16     public Point( int xValue, int yValue )
17     {
18        // implicit call to Object constructor occurs here
19        x = xValue;   // no need for validation
20        y = yValue;   // no need for validation
21
```

Fig. 9.17   `Point` superclass contains two constructors and a finalizer. (Part 1 of 2.)

---

3. As in Section 8.11, we use method `finalize` in this example only to show when the garbage collector is removing an object from memory. Using `finalize` is generally discouraged.

```
22          System.out.println( "Point constructor: " + this );
23      }
24
25      // finalizer
26      protected void finalize()
27      {
28          System.out.println( "Point finalizer: " + this );
29      }
30
31      // set x in coordinate pair
32      public void setX( int xValue )
33      {
34          x = xValue;   // no need for validation
35      }
36
37      // return x from coordinate pair
38      public int getX()
39      {
40          return x;
41      }
42
43      // set y in coordinate pair
44      public void setY( int yValue )
45      {
46          y = yValue;   // no need for validation
47      }
48
49      // return y from coordinate pair
50      public int getY()
51      {
52          return y;
53      }
54
55      // return String representation of Point4 object
56      public String toString()
57      {
58          return "[" + getX() + ", " + getY() + "]";
59      }
60
61  } // end class Point
```

Fig. 9.17   Point superclass contains two constructors and a finalizer. (Part 2 of 2.)

Class Circle (Fig. 9.18) contains features from class Circle4 (Fig. 9.13). We modified the constructors (lines 9–13 and 16–22 of Fig. 9.18) and added a finalize method (Fig. 9.18, lines 25–30). Each outputs a line of text at the command line upon its invocation. Again, note the concatenation of this to a string in lines 12, 21 and 27 to obtain the object's string representation.

```
1   // Fig. 9.18: Circle.java
2   // Circle5 class declaration.
```

Fig. 9.18   Circle class extends Point. (Part 1 of 3.)

```
3
4    public class Circle extends Point {
5
6        private double radius;   // Circle's radius
7
8        // no-argument constructor
9        public Circle()
10       {
11           // implicit call to Point constructor occurs here
12           System.out.println( "Circle no-argument constructor: " + this );
13       }
14
15       // constructor
16       public Circle( int xValue, int yValue, double radiusValue )
17       {
18           super( xValue, yValue );   // call Point constructor
19           setRadius( radiusValue );
20
21           System.out.println( "Circle constructor: " + this );
22       }
23
24       // finalizer
25       protected void finalize()
26       {
27           System.out.println( "Circle finalizer: " + this );
28
29           super.finalize();   // call superclass finalize method
30       }
31
32       // set radius
33       public void setRadius( double radiusValue )
34       {
35           radius = ( radiusValue < 0.0 ? 0.0 : radiusValue );
36       }
37
38       // return radius
39       public double getRadius()
40       {
41           return radius;
42       }
43
44       // calculate and return diameter
45       public double getDiameter()
46       {
47           return 2 * getRadius();
48       }
49
50       // calculate and return circumference
51       public double getCircumference()
52       {
53           return Math.PI * getDiameter();
54       }
55
```

Fig. 9.18   Circle class extends Point. (Part 2 of 3.)

```
56          // calculate and return area
57          public double getArea()
58          {
59              return Math.PI * getRadius() * getRadius();
60          }
61
62          // return String representation of Circle5 object
63          public String toString()
64          {
65              return "Center = " + super.toString() + "; Radius = " + getRadius();
66          }
67
68      } // end class Circle
```

Fig. 9.18   Circle class extends Point. (Part 3 of 3.)

Figure 9.19 demonstrates the order in which constructors and finalizers are called for objects of classes that are part of an inheritance hierarchy. Method main (lines 7–28) begins by instantiating a Point object (line 12). Next, line 15 instantiates Circle object circle1. This invokes the Point constructor to perform output with values passed from the Circle constructor, then performs the output specified in the Circle constructor. Line 18 then instantiates Circle object circle2. Again, the Point and Circle constructors are both called. Note that, in each case, the body of the Point constructor is executed before the body of the Circle constructor executes.

```
1   // Fig. 9.19: ConstructorFinalizerTest.java
2   // Display order in which superclass and subclass
3   // constructors and finalizers are called.
4
5   public class ConstructorFinalizerTest {
6
7      public static void main( String args[] )
8      {
9          Point point;
10         Circle circle1, circle2;
11
12         point = new Point( 11, 22 );
13
14         System.out.println();
15         circle1 = new Circle( 72, 29, 4.5 );
16
17         System.out.println();
18         circle2 = new Circle( 5, 7, 10.67 );
19
20         point = null;      // mark for garbage collection
21         circle1 = null;    // mark for garbage collection
22         circle2 = null;    // mark for garbage collection
23
24         System.out.println();
25
```

Fig. 9.19   Constructor and finalizer call order. (Part 1 of 2.)

```
26              System.gc();   // call the garbage collector
27
28        } // end main
29
30    } // end class ConstructorFinalizerTest
```

```
Point constructor: [11, 22]

Point constructor: Center = [72, 29]; Radius = 0.0
Circle constructor: Center = [72, 29]; Radius = 4.5

Point constructor: Center = [5, 7]; Radius = 0.0
Circle constructor: Center = [5, 7]; Radius = 10.67

Point finalizer: [11, 22]
Circle finalizer: Center = [72, 29]; Radius = 4.5
Point finalizer: Center = [72, 29]; Radius = 4.5
Circle finalizer: Center = [5, 7]; Radius = 10.67
Point finalizer: Center = [5, 7]; Radius = 10.67
```

Fig. 9.19   Constructor and finalizer call order. (Part 2 of 2.)

Lines 20–22 set point, circle1 and circle2 to null. The objects referenced by these variables are no longer needed in the program, so Java marks the objects for garbage collection. Java guarantees that, before the garbage collector runs to reclaim the space for each of these objects, the finalize methods for each object will be called. Recall, however, from Section 8.10 that it is not guaranteed when the garbage collector actually will execute. For this reason, we invoke class System's static method gc in line 26. Java does not guarantee the order in which objects will be garbage collected; therefore, it cannot guarantee which object's finalizer will execute first. When method System.gc is called, the finalizers are called for objects point, circle1 and circle2. The Circle finalizer and Point finalizer are called (in that order) for object circle1, and the Circle and Point finalizers are called (in that order) for object circle2. [Note: Class Object's finalize method does nothing, so we did not call it from class Point's finalize.]

9.7 Software Engineering with Inheritance

This section discusses customizing existing software with inheritance. When a new class extends an existing class, the new class inherits the non-private members of the existing class. We can customize the new class to meet our needs by including additional members and by overriding superclass members. This is done in Java without the subclass programmer changing the superclass's source code. Java simply requires access to the superclass's .class file so it can compile and execute any program that uses or extends the superclass. This powerful capability is attractive to independent software vendors (ISVs), which can develop proprietary classes for sale or license and make those classes available to users in object-code format. Users then can derive new classes from these library classes rapidly and without accessing the ISVs' proprietary source code.

Sometimes, it is difficult for students to appreciate the scope of problems faced by designers who work on large-scale software projects in industry. People experienced with such projects say that effective software reuse improves the software-development process. Object-oriented programming facilitates software reuse, thus shortening development time.

The availability of substantial and useful class libraries delivers the maximum benefits of software reuse through inheritance. Interest in class libraries is growing exponentially. Just as shrink-wrapped software produced by ISVs became an explosive-growth industry with the arrival of the personal computer, so, too, is the creation and sale of class libraries. Application designers build their applications with these libraries, and library designers are being rewarded by having their libraries included with the applications. The standard Java class libraries that are shipped with J2SE 1.4.0 tend to be rather general purpose. However, there is massive worldwide commitment to the development of class libraries for a huge variety of applications.

Software Engineering Observation 9.5

At the design stage in an object-oriented system, the designer often finds that certain classes are closely related. The designer should "factor out" common attributes and behaviors and place these in a superclass. Then, the designer should use inheritance to develop subclasses, endowing them with capabilities beyond those inherited from the superclass.

Software Engineering Observation 9.6

Declaring a subclass does not affect its superclass's source code. Inheritance preserves the integrity of a superclass.

Software Engineering Observation 9.7

Just as designers of non-object-oriented systems should avoid a proliferation of methods, designers of object-oriented systems should avoid the proliferation of classes. Proliferation of classes creates management problems and can hinder software reusability, because it becomes difficult for a client to locate the most appropriate class in a huge class library. The alternative is to create fewer classes that provide more substantial functionality, but such classes might provide too much functionality.

Performance Tip 9.1

If subclasses are larger than they need to be (i.e., contain too much functionality), memory and processing resources might be wasted. Extend the class with the functionality that is "closest" to what is needed.

Reading subclass declarations can be confusing, because inherited members are not declared explicitly in the subclasses, but nevertheless are members of them. A similar problem exists in documenting subclass members.

In earlier sections, we introduced inheritance—the ability to create classes by absorbing an existing class's members, and embellishing them with new capabilities. In Chapter 10, we build upon our discussion of inheritance by introducing *polymorphism*—an object-oriented concept that enables us to write programs that handle, in a more general manner, a wide variety of classes related by inheritance. After studying Chapter 10, you will be familiar with classes, encapsulation, inheritance and polymorphism—the most crucial aspects of object-oriented programming.

SUMMARY

- Software reuse reduces program-development time.
- The direct superclass of a subclass is the superclass from which the subclass inherits (specified by the keyword `extends` in the first line of a class declaration). An indirect superclass of a subclass is two or more levels up the class hierarchy from that subclass.

- In single inheritance, a class is derived from one direct superclass. In multiple inheritance, a class is derived from more than one direct superclass. Java does not support multiple inheritance.
- A subclass can declare its own members (instance variables and methods), so a subclass is often larger than its superclass.
- A subclass is more specific than its superclass and represents a smaller group of objects.
- Every object of a subclass is also an object of that class's superclass. However, a superclass object is not an object of its class's subclasses.
- An "is-a" relationship represents inheritance. In an "is-a" relationship, an object of a subclass also can be treated as an object of its superclass.
- A "has-a" relationship represents composition. In a "has-a" relationship, a class object contains references to objects of other classes.
- A subclass cannot access or inherit the `private` members of its superclass; allowing this would violate the encapsulation of the superclass. A subclass can, however, inherit the `public` and `protected` members of its superclass.
- When a superclass method is inappropriate for a subclass, that method can be overridden in the subclass with an appropriate implementation.
- Single-inheritance relationships form tree-like hierarchical structures—a superclass exists in a hierarchical relationship with its subclasses.
- A superclass's `public` members are accessible anywhere that the program has a reference to an object of that superclass or to an object of one of that superclass's subclasses.
- A superclass's `private` members are accessible only within the declaration of that superclass.
- A superclass's `protected` members have an intermediate level of protection between `public` and `private` access. A superclass's `protected` members can be accessed by members of that superclass and inherited by members of any classes derived from that superclass.
- When a subclass method overrides a superclass method, the superclass method can be accessed from the subclass by preceding the superclass method name with the keyword `super` and a dot (.).
- Declaring instance variables `private`, while providing non-`private` methods to manipulate and perform validation checking, enforces good software engineering.
- Method `toString` takes no arguments and returns a `String`. The original `toString` method of class `Object` is a placeholder that is normally overridden by a subclass.
- Concatenating a string and any object results in an implicit call to the object's `toString` method to obtain a string representation of an object, then the strings are concatenated.

TERMINOLOGY

abstraction	information hiding
access control	inheritance
class hierarchy	inheritance hierarchy
class library	inherited instance variable
composition	inherited member
direct superclass	inherited method
extends	independent software vendor (ISV)
garbage collection	invoke a superclass constructor
has-a relationship	invoke a superclass overridden method
hierarchical relationship	*is-a* relationship
hierarchy diagram	multiple inheritance
indirect superclass	Object class

object of a subclass
object of a superclass
object-oriented programming (OOP)
overloaded constructor
override a superclass method
`private` superclass member
`protected` keyword
`protected` superclass member
`public` superclass member
reference to a superclass object
reference to a subclass object

single inheritance
software reusability
subclass
subclass constructor
subclass finalizer
`super`
superclass
superclass constructor
superclass finalizer
superclass no-argument constructor
`toString` method of class `Object`

SELF-REVIEW EXERCISES

9.1   Fill in the blanks in each of the following statements:

a) _____ is a form of software reusability in which new classes acquire the data and behaviors of existing classes and embellish those classes with new capabilities.

b) A superclass's _____ members can be accessed only in the superclass declaration or in inherited by subclasses.

c) In a(n) _____ relationship, an object of a subclass also can be treated as an object of its superclass.

d) In a(n) _____ relationship, a class object has references to objects of other classes as members.

e) In single inheritance, a class exists in a(n) _____ relationship with its subclasses.

f) A superclass's _____ members are accessible anywhere that the program has a reference to an object of that superclass or to an object of one of its subclasses.

g) A superclass's `protected` access members have a level of protection between those of _____ and _____ access.

h) When an object of a subclass is instantiated, a superclass _____ is called implicitly or explicitly.

i) Subclass constructors can call superclass constructors via the _____ keyword.

9.2   State whether each of the following is *true* or *false*. If a statement is *false*, explain why.

a) It is possible to treat superclass objects and subclass objects similarly.

b) Superclass constructors are not inherited by subclasses.

c) A "has-a" relationship is implemented via inheritance.

d) A Car class has an "is a" relationship with its `SteeringWheel` and `Brakes`.

e) Inheritance encourages the reuse of proven high-quality software.

f) When a subclass redefines a superclass method by using the same signature, the subclass is said to overload that superclass method.

ANSWERS TO SELF-REVIEW EXERCISES

9.1   a) Inheritance. b) `protected`. c) "is-a" or inheritance. d) "has-a" or composition or aggregation. e) hierarchical. f) `public`. g) `public`, `private`. h) constructor. i) `super`.

9.2   a) True. b) True. c) False. A "has-a" relationship is implemented via composition. An "is-a" relationship is implemented via inheritance. d) False. This is an example of a "has–a" relationship. Class Car has an "is–a" relationship with class `Vehicle`. e) True. f) False. This is known as overriding, not overloading.

EXERCISES

9.3   Many programs written with inheritance could be written with composition instead, and vice versa. Rewrite classes Circle4 (Fig. 9.13) and Cylinder (Fig. 9.15) of the Point3/Circle4/Cylinder hierarchy to use composition rather than inheritance. After you do this, assess the relative merits of the two approaches for the Point3, Circle4, and Cylinder problems, as well as for object-oriented programs in general. Which approach is more natural? Why?

9.4   Some programmers prefer not to use protected access, because they believe it breaks the encapsulation of the superclass. Discuss the relative merits of using protected access vs. using private access in superclasses.

9.5   Rewrite the case study of Section 9.5 as a Point–Square–Cube hierarchy. Do this two ways—once via inheritance and once via composition.

9.6   Write an inheritance hierarchy for class Quadrilateral, Trapezoid, Parallelogram, Rectangle and Square. Use Quadrilateral as the superclass of the hierarchy. Make the hierarchy as deep (i.e., as many levels) as possible. Specify the instance variables and methods for each class. The private data of Quadrilateral should be the *x-y* coordinate pairs for the four endpoints of the Quadrilateral. Write a program that instantiates objects of your classes and outputs each object's area (except Quadrilateral).

9.7   Write down all the shapes you can think of—both two-dimensional and three-dimensional—and form those shapes into a shape hierarchy. Your hierarchy should have class Shape at the top. Class TwoDimensionalShape and class ThreeDimensionalShape should extend Shape. Once you have developed the hierarchy, declare each of the classes in it. We will use this hierarchy in the exercises to process all shapes as objects of superclass Shape.

9.8   Create the classes in the inheritance hierarchy of Fig. 9.20. An Employee should have a first name, last name and social-security number. In addition, a SalariedEmployee should have a weekly salary; an HourlyEmployee should have a wage and a number of hours worked; a CommissionEmployee should have a commission rate and gross sales; and a BasePlusCommissionEmployee should have a base salary. Each class should have appropriate constructors, *set* methods and *get* methods. Write a program that instantiates objects of each of these classes and outputs all the information associated with each object (including the inherited information).

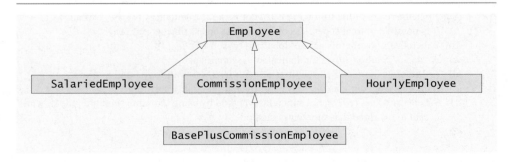

Fig. 9.20   Employee inheritance hierarchy.

10

Object-Oriented Programming: Polymorphism

Objectives

- To understand the concept of polymorphism.
- To understand how to use overridden methods to effect polymorphism.
- To distinguish between abstract and concrete classes.
- To learn how to declare `abstract` methods to create abstract classes.
- To appreciate how polymorphism makes systems extensible and maintainable.
- To be able to determine an object's type at execution time.

One Ring to rule them all, One Ring to find them,
One Ring to bring them all and in the darkness bind them.
John Ronald Reuel Tolkien

General propositions do not decide concrete cases.
Oliver Wendell Holmes

A philosopher of imposing stature doesn't think in a vacuum.
Even his most abstract ideas are, to some extent, conditioned
by what is or is not known in the time when he lives.
Alfred North Whitehead

10.1 Introduction

Chapter 8 discussed object-based programming and its component technologies—classes, objects, encapsulation and data abstraction. Chapter 9 focused on a key object-oriented programming (OOP) technology—inheritance. We now continue our study of OOP by explaining and demonstrating *polymorphism* with inheritance hierarchies. Polymorphism enables us to "program in the general" rather than "program in the specific." In particular, polymorphism enables us to write programs that process objects of classes that are part of the same class hierarchy as if they are all objects of their superclasses. As we will soon see, polymorphism works off superclass references.

This chapter has several key parts. We begin with a sequence of small, focused examples that demonstrate the relationships between classes in a hierarchy. The initial example provides our first introduction to polymorphism and demonstrates the allowed ways to assign superclass and subclass objects to superclass and subclass references. The other examples in this sequence show the errors that occur when a program attempts assignments that are not allowed. We then present a case study that revisits the `Point3-Circle4-Cylinder` hierarchy of Section 9.5. In the case study, we declare a common "interface" (i.e., set of functionality) for all the classes in the hierarchy. This common functionality among shapes is declared in a so-called *abstract class*, `Shape`, from which class `Point` inherits directly and classes `Circle` and `Cylinder` inherit indirectly.

We then present a more "natural" `Employee` class hierarchy. We develop a simple payroll system for this hierarchy in which every employee has an earnings method that calculates the employee's weekly pay. These earnings methods vary by employee type—a `SalariedEmployee` is paid a fixed weekly salary regardless of the number of hours worked, an `HourlyEmployee` is paid by the hour and receives overtime pay, a `CommissionEmployee` receives a percentage of its sales and a `BasePlusCommissionEmployee` receives a base salary plus a percentage of its sales. We show how to process each employee "in the general" by invoking its `earnings` method off a superclass reference.

Occasionally, when performing polymorphic processing, it is necessary to program "in the specific." Our `Employee` case study demonstrates that a program can determine the type of an object at execution time and act on that object accordingly. In the case study, we use these capabilities to determine whether a particular employee object *is a* `BasePlusCommissionEmployee`; if so, we give that employee a 10% bonus on its base salary.

With polymorphism, it is possible to design and implement systems that are easily extensible. New classes can be added with little or no modification to the generic portions of the program, as long as those classes are part of the inheritance hierarchy that the program processes generically. The only parts of a program that must be altered to accommodate new classes are those program components that require direct knowledge of the new classes that the programmer adds to the hierarchy.

The chapter continues with an introduction to Java interfaces. An interface describes a set of methods that can be called on an object. Programmers can declare classes that *implement* one or more interfaces. Each interface method must be declared in the class that implements the interface. Once a class implements an interface, all objects of that class have the *is-a* relationship with the interface type, and all objects of the class are guaranteed to provide the functionality described by the interface. As we will see, this enables polymorphic capabilities similar to those demonstrated with inheritance early in the chapter.

After introducing interfaces, we discuss more of the details of event handling, which uses interfaces to enable GUI components to interact with event-handler objects. We demonstrate these concepts in the context of our first applications that execute in their own windows. We also demonstrate a new form of class called an *inner class* in these examples. Inner classes are declared completely inside other classes.

10.2　Relationships Among Objects in an Inheritance Hierarchy

Section 9.4 created a point-circle class hierarchy, in which class `Circle` inherited from class `Point`. The examples in that section manipulated `Point` and `Circle` objects by using references to those objects to invoke their methods. We now examine the relationships among classes in a hierarchy. The next several examples demonstrate how superclass and subclass variables can be assigned references to superclass and subclass objects and how those references can be used to invoke methods that manipulate those objects.

In Section 10.2.1, we aim a superclass reference at a subclass object. Then we show how invoking a method via the superclass reference invokes the subclass functionality—the type of the referenced object determines which method is called. In Section 10.2.2, we aim a subclass reference at a superclass object, which results in a compilation error. We discuss the error message and investigate why the compiler does not allow such an assignment. In Section 10.2.3, we aim a superclass reference at a subclass object to show that a superclass reference can be used to invoke only the superclass functionality—when we attempt to invoke subclass methods through the superclass reference, compilation errors occur.

A key concept that these examples demonstrate is that an object of a subclass can be treated as an object of its superclass. This enables various interesting manipulations. For example, a program can create an array of superclass references that refer to objects of many subclass types. This is allowed despite the fact that the subclass objects are of different types, because each subclass object *is an* object of its superclass. However, a superclass object is not an object of any of its subclasses. For example, a Point is not a Circle in the hierarchy shown in Section 9.4—a Point does not have a radius instance variable and does not have methods setRadius, getRadius and getArea. The *is–a* relationship applies only from a subclass to its direct and indirect superclasses.

10.2.1 Invoking Superclass Methods from Subclass Objects

The example in Fig. 10.1 demonstrates three ways to use superclass- and subclass-type variables to store references to superclass and subclass objects. The first two are straightforward—we assign a superclass reference to a superclass-type variable, and we assign a subclass reference to a subclass-type variable. Then, we demonstrate the relationship between subclasses and superclasses (i.e., the *is–a* relationship) by assigning a subclass reference to a superclass variable. [*Note*: This program uses classes Point3 and Circle4 of Fig. 9.12 and Fig. 9.13.]

```
1   // Fig. 10.1: HierarchyRelationshipTest1.java
2   // Assigning superclass and subclass references to superclass- and
3   // subclass-type variables.
4   import javax.swing.JOptionPane;
5
6   public class HierarchyRelationshipTest1 {
7
8      public static void main( String[] args )
9      {
10         // assign superclass reference to superclass-type variable
11         Point3 point = new Point3( 30, 50 );
12
13         // assign subclass reference to subclass-type variable
14         Circle4 circle = new Circle4( 120, 89, 2.7 );
15
16         // invoke toString on superclass object using superclass variable
17         String output = "Call Point3's toString with superclass" +
18            " reference to superclass object: \n" + point.toString();
19
20         // invoke toString on subclass object using subclass variable
21         output += "\n\nCall Circle4's toString with subclass" +
22            " reference to subclass object: \n" + circle.toString();
```

Fig. 10.1   Aiming superclass and subclass references at superclass and subclass objects. (Part 1 of 2.)

```
23
24          // invoke toString on subclass object using superclass variable
25          Point3 pointRef = circle;
26          output += "\n\nCall Circle4's toString with superclass" +
27             " reference to subclass object: \n" + pointRef.toString();
28
29          JOptionPane.showMessageDialog( null, output );  // display output
30
31          System.exit( 0 );
32
33       } // end main
34
35    } // end class HierarchyRelationshipTest1
```

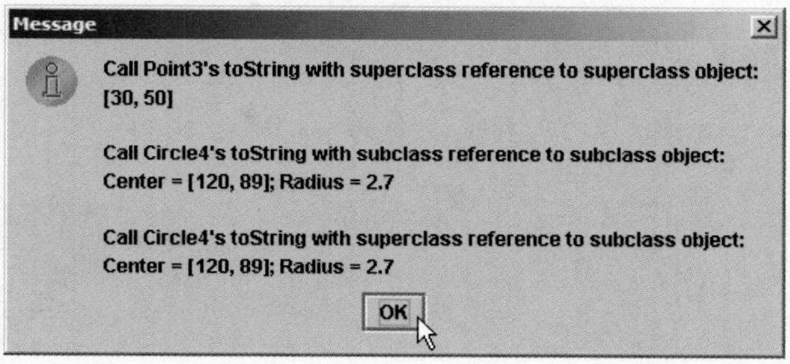

Message

Call Point3's toString with superclass reference to superclass object:
[30, 50]

Call Circle4's toString with subclass reference to subclass object:
Center = [120, 89]; Radius = 2.7

Call Circle4's toString with superclass reference to subclass object:
Center = [120, 89]; Radius = 2.7

OK

Fig. 10.1   Aiming superclass and subclass references at superclass and subclass objects. (Part 2 of 2.)

In the figure, line 11 creates a Point3 object and assigns its reference to Point3 variable point. Line 14 creates a Circle4 object and assigns its reference to Circle4 variable circle. Lines 17–18 use reference point to invoke toString on the Point3 object, which calls superclass Point3's version of toString. Similarly, lines 21–22 use circle to invoke toString on the Circle4 object. This invokes subclass Circle4's version of toString. Line 25 then assigns the reference of subclass object circle to superclass-type variable pointRef, which lines 26–27 use to invoke method toString. A superclass-type variable that contains a reference to a subclass object calls the subclass method; hence, pointRef.toString() actually calls class Circle4's toString method. The Java compiler allows this "crossover" because an object of a subclass *is an* object of its superclass. For any non-static method call, the type of the variable used to call the method determines which methods can be called. The type of the object to which the variable refers determines the actual methods used to respond to the method call.

10.2.2 Using Superclass References with Subclass-Type Variables

In Section 10.2.1, we assigned the reference of a subclass object to a superclass-type variable and explained that the Java compiler allows this assignment, because a subclass object *is a* superclass object. Now we take the opposite approach in Fig. 10.2, attempt to assign a superclass object's reference to a a subclass-type variable. [*Note*: This program uses classes Point3 and Circle4 of Fig. 9.12–Fig. 9.13.] Line 8 creates a Point3 object, and line 9 declares a Circle4 variable. Line 12 attempts to assign the reference of superclass object point to circle, but the Java compiler generates an error. The compiler prevents this

```
1   // Fig. 10.2: HierarchyRelationshipTest2.java
2   // Attempt to assign a superclass reference to a subclass-type variable.
3
4   public class HierarchyRelationshipTest2 {
5
6      public static void main( String[] args )
7      {
8         Point3 point = new Point3( 30, 50 );
9         Circle4 circle;  // subclass-type variable
10
11        // assign superclass reference to subclass-type variable
12        circle = point;  // Error: a Point3 is not a Circle4
13     }
14
15  } // end class HierarchyRelationshipTest2
```

```
HierarchyRelationshipTest2.java:12: incompatible types
found   : Point3
required: Circle4
      circle = point;  // Error: a Point3 is not a Circle4
             ^
1 error
```

Fig. 10.2   Aiming a subclass reference at a superclass object.

assignment, because a `Point3` is not a `Circle4`—the is-a relationship applies only between the subclass and its superclasses.

It turns out that the Java compiler does allow this assignment if we explicitly cast the superclass reference to the subclass type—a technique we discuss in greater detail in Section 10.7. You may wonder why you ever would want to perform that assignment. In programs that process superclass and subclass objects by using superclass references, only methods of the superclass can be invoked via the superclass references. Casting superclass references to subclass references (also known as *downcasting*) enables a program to invoke subclass functionality to perform subclass-specific operations on subclass objects.

Common Programming Error 10.1

Assigning the reference of a superclass object to a subclass-type variable (without an explicit cast) is a compiler error.

Software Engineering Observation 10.1

If the reference of a subclass object has been assigned to a variable of one of its direct or indirect superclasses, it is acceptable to cast that superclass reference back to a reference of the subclass type. In fact, this must be done to invoke subclass methods that do not appear in the superclass.

10.2.3 Subclass Method Calls via Superclass-Type Variables

From a subclass reference, the compiler allows us to invoke all subclass methods. Thus, if a subclass reference could be aimed at a superclass object, and an attempt were made to access a subclass-only method, errors almost certainly would occur. So we saw in Section 10.2.2 that trying to use a subclass variable to refer to a superclass object is a compiler error.

Figure 10.3 attempts to call a subclass method with a superclass reference. [*Note*: This example uses classes Point3 and Circle4 of Fig. 9.12–Fig. 9.13.] Line 9 declares Point3 variable point. Line 10 declares Circle4 variable circle and creates a Circle4 object. Line 12 assigns the subclass Circle4 object's reference to superclass Point3 variable point. Recall from Section 10.2.1 that the Java compiler allows this, because a Circle4 *is a* Point3. Lines 16–20 invoke superclass methods getX, getY, setX, setY and toString off the superclass reference. We know that point contains a reference to a Circle4 object, so in lines 24–28 we attempt to invoke Circle4 methods getRadius, setRadius, getDiameter, getCircumference and getArea. The Java compiler generates errors on each of these lines, because these are not methods of superclass Point3. Although the actual method that is called depends on the object's type at execution time, a variable can be used to invoke only those methods that are members of that variables's type, which the compiler can check at compilation time. (In this case, using a Point3 variable, we can invoke only Point3 methods getX, getY, setX, setY and toString.)

```java
1    // Fig. 10.3: HierarchyRelationshipTest3.java
2    // Attempting to invoke subclass-only member methods through
3    // a superclass reference.
4
5    public class HierarchyRelationshipTest3 {
6
7       public static void main( String[] args )
8       {
9          Point3 point;
10         Circle4 circle = new Circle4( 120, 89, 2.7 );
11
12         point = circle;   // aim superclass reference at subclass object
13
14         // invoke superclass (Point3) methods on subclass
15         // (Circle4) object through superclass reference
16         int x = point.getX();
17         int y = point.getY();
18         point.setX( 10 );
19         point.setY( 20 );
20         point.toString();
21
22         // attempt to invoke subclass-only (Circle4) methods on
23         // subclass object through superclass (Point3) reference
24         double radius = point.getRadius();
25         point.setRadius( 33.33 );
26         double diameter = point.getDiameter();
27         double circumference = point.getCircumference();
28         double area = point.getArea();
29
30      } // end main
31
32   } // end class HierarchyRelationshipTest3
```

Fig. 10.3   Attempting to invoke subclass-only methods via a superclass reference. (Part 1 of 2.)

```
HierarchyRelationshipTest3.java:24: cannot resolve symbol
symbol  : method getRadius ()
location: class Point3
      double radius = point.getRadius();
                           ^
HierarchyRelationshipTest3.java:25: cannot resolve symbol
symbol  : method setRadius (double)
location: class Point3
      point.setRadius( 33.33 );
           ^
HierarchyRelationshipTest3.java:26: cannot resolve symbol
symbol  : method getDiameter ()
location: class Point3
      double diameter = point.getDiameter();
                             ^
HierarchyRelationshipTest3.java:27: cannot resolve symbol
symbol  : method getCircumference ()
location: class Point3
      double circumference = point.getCircumference();
                                  ^
HierarchyRelationshipTest3.java:28: cannot resolve symbol
symbol  : method getArea ()
location: class Point3
      double area = point.getArea();
                         ^
5 errors
```

Fig. 10.3   Attempting to invoke subclass-only methods via a superclass reference. (Part 2 of 2.)

Summary of the Allowed Assignments Between Superclass and Subclass Variables
Despite the fact that a subclass object also *is a* superclass object, the subclass and superclass objects are indeed different. As we have discussed previously, subclass objects can be treated as if they were superclass objects. This is a logical relationship, because the subclass contains all the members of the superclass, but the subclass can have additional subclass-only members. For this reason, assigning a superclass reference to a subclass-type variable is not allowed without an explicit cast; such an assignment would leave the subclass-only members undefined for the superclass object.

We have discussed four ways to assign superclass and subclass references to variables of superclass and subclass types:

1. Assigning a superclass reference to a superclass-type variable is straightforward.

2. Assigning a subclass reference to a subclass-type variable is straightforward.

3. Assigning a subclass object's reference to a superclass-type variable is safe, because the subclass object *is an* object of its superclass. However, this reference can be used to invoke only superclass methods. If this code refers to subclass-only members through the superclass variable, the compiler reports errors.

4. Attempting to assign a superclass object's reference to a subclass-type variable is a compilation error. To avoid this error, the superclass reference must be cast to a subclass type explicitly. At execution time, if the object to which the reference re-

fers is not a subclass object, an exception will occur. Section 10.7 demonstrates how to ensure that such a cast is performed only if the object is a subclass object.

Common Programming Error 10.2

After aiming a superclass reference at a subclass object, attempting to reference subclass-only members with the superclass reference is a compilation error.

10.3 Polymorphism Examples

Consider the following example of polymorphism. If class `Rectangle` is derived from class `Quadrilateral`, then a `Rectangle` object is a more specific version of a `Quadrilateral` object. Any operation (e.g., calculating the perimeter or the area) that can be performed on a `Quadrilateral` object also can be performed on a `Rectangle` object. These operations also can be performed on other `Quadrilaterals`, such as `Squares`, `Parallelograms` and `Trapezoids`. When a program invokes a method through a superclass variable, Java polymorphically chooses the correct subclass version of the method to call based on the type of the reference stored in the superclass variable.

As another example, suppose we design a video game that manipulates objects of many different types, including objects of classes `Martian`, `Venusian`, `Plutonian`, `SpaceShip` and `LaserBeam`. Also, imagine that each of these classes inherits from the common superclass called `SpaceObject`, which contains method `draw`. Each subclass implements this method. A screen-manager program would maintain a collection (such as a `SpaceObject` array) of references to objects of the various classes. To refresh the screen, the screen manager would periodically send each object the same message—namely, `draw`. However, each object responds in a unique way. For example, a `Martian` object might draw itself in red with the appropriate number of antennae. A `SpaceShip` object might draw itself as a bright silver flying saucer. A `LaserBeam` object might draw itself as a bright red beam across the screen. Again, the same message (in this case, `draw`) sent to a variety of objects would have "many forms" of results—hence, the term *polymorphism*.

A polymorphic screen manager might use polymorphism to facilitate adding new classes to a system with minimal modifications to the system's code. Suppose that we want to add `Mercurian` objects to our video game. To do so, we must build a class `Mercurian` that extends `SpaceObject`, but provides its own implementation of method `draw`. Then, when objects of class `Mercurian` appear in the container, the programmer does not need to modify the code for the screen manager. The screen manager invokes method `draw` on every object in the container, regardless of the object's type, so the new `Mercurian` objects simply "plug right in." Thus, without modifying the system (other than to build the classes themselves and to modify the code that creates new objects), programmers can use polymorphism to include additional types that were not envisioned when the system was created.

With polymorphism, the same method name and signature can be used to cause different actions to occur, depending on the type of the object on which the method is invoked. This gives the programmer tremendous expressive capability.

Software Engineering Observation 10.2

Polymorphism enables programmers to deal in generalities and let the execution-time environment handle the specifics. Programmers can command objects to behave in manners appropriate to those objects, without knowing the types of the objects (as long as the objects belong to the same inheritance hierarchy).

Software Engineering Observation 10.3

Polymorphism promotes extensibility: Software that invokes polymorphic behavior is independent of the object types to which messages are sent. New object types that can respond to existing method calls can be incorporated into a system without modifying the base system. Only client code that instantiates new objects must be modified to accommodate new types.

10.4 Abstract Classes and Methods

When we think of a class type, we assume that programs will create objects of that type. However, there are cases in which it is useful to declare classes for which the programmer never intends to instantiate objects. Such classes are called *abstract classes*. Because abstract classes are used only as superclasses in inheritance hierarchies, we refer to those classes as *abstract superclasses*. These classes cannot be used to instantiate objects, because, as we will soon see, abstract classes are incomplete. Subclasses must declare the "missing pieces." We build programs with abstract classes in Section 10.5 and Section 10.7.

The purpose of an abstract class is to provide an appropriate superclass from which other classes can inherit. Classes that can be used to instantiate objects are called *concrete classes*. Such classes provide implementations of every method they declare. We could have an abstract superclass TwoDimensionalShape and derive such concrete classes as Square, Circle and Triangle. We could also have an abstract superclass ThreeDimensionalShape and derive such concrete classes as Cube, Sphere and Cylinder. Abstract superclasses are too generic to create real objects—they specify only what is common among subclasses. We need to be more specific before we can create objects. For example, if someone tells you to "draw the shape," what shape would you draw? Concrete classes provide the specifics that make it reasonable to instantiate objects.

An inheritance hierarchy is not required to contain abstract classes. However, class hierarchies headed by abstract superclasses often are used to reduce client code's dependencies on specific subclass types. Abstract classes sometimes constitute several levels of the hierarchy. For example consider the shape hierarchy in Fig. 9.3, which begins with abstract class Shape. On the next level of the hierarchy, we have two more abstract classes, namely, TwoDimensionalShape and ThreeDimensionalShape. The next level of the hierarchy declares concrete classes for two-dimensional shapes (namely, Circle, Square and Triangle) and for three-dimensional shapes (namely, Sphere, Cube and Tetrahedron).

A class is made abstract by declaring it with keyword abstract. An abstract class normally contains one or more *abstract methods* (static methods cannot be abstract). An abstract method is a method with keyword abstract in its declaration, as in

```
public abstract void draw();  // abstract method
```

Abstract methods do not provide implementations. A class that contains abstract methods must be declared as an abstract class. Each concrete subclass of an abstract superclass must provide concrete implementations of the superclass's abstract methods. Constructors are not inherited, so they cannot be declared abstract.

Software Engineering Observation 10.4

An abstract class declares common attributes and behaviors of the various classes in a class hierarchy. An abstract class typically contains one or more abstract methods that subclasses must override. The instance variables and concrete methods of an abstract class are subject to the normal rules of inheritance.

Common Programming Error 10.3

Attempting to instantiate an object of an abstract class causes a compilation error.

Common Programming Error 10.4

Failure to implement a superclass's abstract method in a subclass is a compilation error, unless the subclass also is declared `abstract`.

Although we cannot instantiate objects of abstract superclasses, we *can* use abstract superclasses to declare variables that can hold references to objects of any concrete class derived from those abstract classes. Programs typically use such variables to manipulate subclass objects polymorphically. We also can use abstract superclass names to invoke `static` methods declared in those abstract superclasses.

Consider another application of polymorphism. A drawing program needs to display many shapes, including new shape types that the programmer will add to the system after writing the drawing program. The drawing program might need to display shapes, such as `Circles`, `Triangles`, `Rectangles` or others, that derive from abstract superclass `Shape`. The drawing program uses `Shape` variables to manage the objects that are displayed. To draw any object (regardless of the level at which that object's class appears in the inheritance hierarchy), the drawing program uses a superclass `Shape` variable containing a reference to the subclass object to invoke the object's `draw` method. This method is declared `abstract` in superclass `Shape`; therefore, each subclass must implement method `draw` in a manner specific to that shape. Each object in the `Shape` inheritance hierarchy knows how to draw itself. The drawing program does not have to worry about the type of each object or whether the drawing program has ever encountered objects of that type.

Polymorphism is particularly effective for implementing layered software systems. In operating systems, for example, each type of physical device could operate quite differently from the others. Even so, commands to *read* or *write* data from and to devices may have a certain uniformity. The write message sent to a device-driver object needs to be interpreted specifically in the context of that device driver and how it manipulates devices of a specific type. However, the write call itself really is no different from the write to any other device in the system: Place some number of bytes from memory onto that device. An object-oriented operating system might use an abstract superclass to provide an interface appropriate for all device drivers. Then, through inheritance from that abstract superclass, subclasses are formed that all operate similarly. The device driver methods are declared as abstract methods in the abstract superclass. The implementations of these abstract methods are provided in the subclasses that correspond to the specific types of device drivers.

It is common in object-oriented programming to declare an *iterator class* that can traverse all the objects in a container, such as an array (Chapter 7) or an `ArrayList` (Chapter 22). For example, a program can print an `ArrayList` of objects by creating an iterator object, then using the iterator to obtain the next list element each time the iterator is called. Iterators often are used in polymorphic programming to traverse a collection that contains references to objects from various levels of a hierarchy. (Chapter 22, Collections, presents a thorough treatment of `ArrayList` and iterators.) A list of objects of class `TwoDimensionalShape` could contain objects from subclasses `Square`, `Circle`, `Triangle` and so on. Calling method `draw` for each `TwoDimensionalShape` object would polymorphically draw each object correctly on the screen.

10.5 Case Study: Inheriting Interface and Implementation

This section reexamines the `Point-Circle-Cylinder` hierarchy that we explored in Section 9.5. In our next example, the hierarchy begins with abstract superclass `Shape`, which declares the "interface" to the hierarchy—i.e., the set of methods that a program can invoke on all `Shape` objects. The class diagram of Fig. 10.4 begins with abstract class *Shape*. Note that an abstract class's name appears in italics in a class diagram.

Class `Shape` provides three methods—`getArea`, `getVolume` and `getName`. In addition, class `Shape` extends `Object`. So, class `Shape` also contains the 11 methods of class `Object`—one of which is `toString`. The diagram of Fig. 10.5 shows each of the four classes in the hierarchy down the left side and shows the three methods of class `Shape` and method `toString` across the top. For each class, the diagram shows the desired results of each method. Note that class `Shape` declares method `getName` as `abstract`, because a default implementation does not make sense for method `getName`—there is not enough information to determine what string `getName` should return. Each subclass overrides this method to provide appropriate implementations. Methods `getArea` and `getVolume` each have default implementations that return `0.0`. Class `Point` inherits these implementations—`Point`s indeed have an area of `0.0` and a volume of `0.0`. Class `Circle` inherits the default implementation of `getVolume`—`Circle`s indeed have a volume of `0.0`—and overrides method `getArea` to calculate the true area of a circle. Finally, class `Cylinder` overrides both `getArea` and `getVolume` to perform calculations appropriate for a cylinder.

Software Engineering Observation 10.5

A subclass can inherit "interface" or "implementation" from a superclass. Hierarchies designed for implementation inheritance *tend to have their functionality high in the hierarchy—each new subclass inherits one or more methods that were declared in a superclass, and the subclass uses the superclass declarations. Hierarchies designed for* interface inheritance *tend to have their functionality lower in the hierarchy—a superclass specifies one or more abstract methods that must be declared for each class in the hierarchy, and the individual subclasses override these methods to provide subclass-specific implementations.*

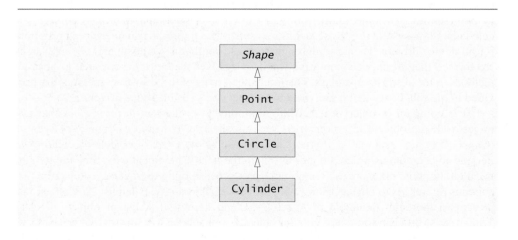

Fig. 10.4   Shape hierarchy class diagram.

	getArea	getVolume	getName	toString
Shape	0.0	0.0	abstract	default `Object` implementation
Point	0.0	0.0	"Point"	[x,y]
Circle	πr^2	0.0	"Circle"	center=[x,y]; radius=r
Cylinder	$2\pi r^2 + 2\pi rh$	$\pi r^2 h$	"Cylinder"	center=[x,y]; radius=r; height=h

Fig. 10.5   Polymorphic interface for the **Shape** hierarchy classes.

   The hierarchy in this example mechanically demonstrates the power of polymorphism. The exercises explore a more substantial shape hierarchy. Abstract class **Shape** (Fig. 10.6) declares methods **getArea** (lines 7–10) and **getVolume** (lines 13–16), each of which has an implementation that returns zero by default, and abstract method **getName** (line 19). **Shape** contains abstract method **getName**, so **Shape** must be declared an abstract class (line 4). All shapes have an area and a volume in this example, so methods **getArea** and **getVolume** have concrete declarations in the **Shape** class. The volume of two-dimensional shapes is always zero, whereas three-dimensional shapes have a positive, nonzero volume. Programmers can override methods **getArea** and **getVolume** in derived concrete subclasses with appropriate implementations (see Fig. 10.5). We declare method **getName** as an abstract method, so subclasses that inherit directly from **Shape** must implement **getName** to be concrete classes.

```
1   // Fig. 10.6: Shape.java
2   // Shape abstract-superclass declaration.
3
4   public abstract class Shape extends Object {
5
6      // return area of shape; 0.0 by default
7      public double getArea()
8      {
9         return 0.0;
10     }
11
12     // return volume of shape; 0.0 by default
13     public double getVolume()
14     {
15        return 0.0;
16     }
17
```

Fig. 10.6   Abstract class **Shape**. (Part 1 of 2.)

```
18        // abstract method, overridden by subclasses
19        public abstract String getName();
20
21    } // end abstract class Shape
```

Fig. 10.6   Abstract class Shape. (Part 2 of 2.)

Class Point (Fig. 10.7) extends abstract superclass Shape (line 4) and overrides abstract method getName (lines 47–50), which makes Point a concrete class. A point's area and volume are zero, so class Point does not override superclass methods getArea and getVolume, thus inheriting Shape's implementations of these methods. Lines 47–50 implement method getName to return the string "Point". If we do not implement get-Name, class Point must be declared abstract; otherwise, a compilation error occurs.

```
1    // Fig. 10.7: Point.java
2    // Point class declaration inherits from Shape.
3
4    public class Point extends Shape {
5        private int x;  // x part of coordinate pair
6        private int y;  // y part of coordinate pair
7
8        // no-argument constructor; x and y default to 0
9        public Point()
10        {
11           // implicit call to Object constructor occurs here
12        }
13
14        // constructor
15        public Point( int xValue, int yValue )
16        {
17           // implicit call to Object constructor occurs here
18           x = xValue;  // no need for validation
19           y = yValue;  // no need for validation
20        }
21
22        // set x in coordinate pair
23        public void setX( int xValue )
24        {
25           x = xValue;  // no need for validation
26        }
27
28        // return x from coordinate pair
29        public int getX()
30        {
31           return x;
32        }
33
34        // set y in coordinate pair
35        public void setY( int yValue )
36        {
```

Fig. 10.7   Point class that extends Shape. (Part 1 of 2.)

```
37            y = yValue;  // no need for validation
38        }
39
40        // return y from coordinate pair
41        public int getY()
42        {
43            return y;
44        }
45
46        // override abstract method getName to return "Point"
47        public String getName()
48        {
49            return "Point";
50        }
51
52        // override toString to return String representation of Point
53        public String toString()
54        {
55            return "[" + getX() + ", " + getY() + "]";
56        }
57
58    } // end class Point
```

Fig. 10.7   Point class that extends Shape. (Part 2 of 2.)

Class Circle (Fig. 10.8) extends Point (line 4) and declares methods setRadius (lines 21–24) and getRadius (lines 27–30) to access a circle's radius. Class Circle also adds methods getDiameter (lines 33–36) and getCircumference (lines 39–42) to obtain the circle's diameter and circumference, respectively. Note that, because a circle has a volume of zero, Circle does not override superclass method getVolume. Rather, Circle inherits this method from Point, which, in turn, inherited it from Shape. However, a circle does require its own area calculation (i.e., πr^2), so Circle overrides Point method getArea (lines 45–48). Method getName (lines 51–54) of class Circle overrides Point method getName. If class Circle did not override method getName, Circle would have inherited the Point version of getName. In that case, Circle's getName method would have erroneously returned "Point". For the same reason, Circle method toString (lines 57–60) overrides Point method toString to return information specific to a circle. Note that line 59 of method toString invokes Point's toString method to perform part of the work of Circle's toString method; this is a nice example of code reuse.

```
1    // Fig. 10.8: Circle.java
2    // Circle class inherits from Point.
3
4    public class Circle extends Point {
5        private double radius;  // Circle's radius
6
7        // no-argument constructor; radius defaults to 0.0
8        public Circle()
9        {
```

Fig. 10.8   Circle class that extends Point. (Part 1 of 2.)

```
10          // implicit call to Point constructor occurs here
11       }
12
13       // constructor
14       public Circle( int x, int y, double radiusValue )
15       {
16          super( x, y );   // call Point constructor
17          setRadius( radiusValue );
18       }
19
20       // set radius
21       public void setRadius( double radiusValue )
22       {
23          radius = ( radiusValue < 0.0 ? 0.0 : radiusValue );
24       }
25
26       // return radius
27       public double getRadius()
28       {
29          return radius;
30       }
31
32       // calculate and return diameter
33       public double getDiameter()
34       {
35          return 2 * getRadius();
36       }
37
38       // calculate and return circumference
39       public double getCircumference()
40       {
41          return Math.PI * getDiameter();
42       }
43
44       // override method getArea to return Circle area
45       public double getArea()
46       {
47          return Math.PI * getRadius() * getRadius();
48       }
49
50       // override method getName to return "Circle"
51       public String getName()
52       {
53          return "Circle";
54       }
55
56       // override toString to return String representation of Circle
57       public String toString()
58       {
59          return "Center = " + super.toString() + "; Radius = " + getRadius();
60       }
61
62    } // end class Circle
```

Fig. 10.8   Circle class that extends Point. (Part 2 of 2.)

Class `Cylinder` (Fig. 10.9) extends `Circle` (line 4) and overrides all three methods originally declared in class `Shape` to provide `Cylinder`-specific functionality. A cylinder has different area and volume calculations from those of a circle, so `Cylinder` overrides method `getArea` (lines 33–36) to calculate the cylinder's surface area (i.e., $2\pi r^2 + 2\pi rh$) and overrides method `getVolume` (lines 39–42) to calculate the cylinder's volume ($\pi r^2 h$). Note that `Cylinder` method `getArea` invokes `Circle`'s `getArea` (line 35) to perform part of the area calculation; this is another nice example of code reuse. Method `getName` (lines 45–48) overrides `Circle` method `getName`. If class `Cylinder` did not override this method, the class would have inherited `Circle` method `getName`, which would have erroneously returned `"Circle"`. Similarly, `Cylinder` method `toString` (lines 51–54) overrides `Circle` method `toString` to output information specific to a cylinder. Once again, note that `Cylinder`'s `toString` method invokes `Circle`'s `toString` (line 53) to get the `Circle` part of the `Cylinder`; yet another example of code reuse.

```java
1   // Fig. 10.9: Cylinder.java
2   // Cylinder class inherits from Circle.
3
4   public class Cylinder extends Circle {
5      private double height;  // Cylinder's height
6
7      // no-argument constructor; height defaults to 0.0
8      public Cylinder()
9      {
10        // implicit call to Circle constructor occurs here
11     }
12
13     // constructor
14     public Cylinder( int x, int y, double radius, double heightValue )
15     {
16        super( x, y, radius );  // call Circle constructor
17        setHeight( heightValue );
18     }
19
20     // set Cylinder's height
21     public void setHeight( double heightValue )
22     {
23        height = ( heightValue < 0.0 ? 0.0 : heightValue );
24     }
25
26     // get Cylinder's height
27     public double getHeight()
28     {
29        return height;
30     }
31
32     // override abstract method getArea to return Cylinder area
33     public double getArea()
34     {
35        return 2 * super.getArea() + getCircumference() * getHeight();
36     }
```

Fig. 10.9   `Cylinder` class that extends `Circle`. (Part 1 of 2.)

```
37
38        // override abstract method getVolume to return Cylinder volume
39        public double getVolume()
40        {
41           return super.getArea() * getHeight();
42        }
43
44        // override abstract method getName to return "Cylinder"
45        public String getName()
46        {
47           return "Cylinder";
48        }
49
50        // override toString to return String representation of Cylinder
51        public String toString()
52        {
53           return super.toString() + "; Height = " + getHeight();
54        }
55
56     } // end class Cylinder
```

Fig. 10.9   Cylinder class that extends `Circle`. (Part 2 of 2.)

The program of Fig. 10.10 creates an object of each of the three concrete classes
`Point`, `Circle` and `Cylinder`. The program manipulates those objects, first via variables
of each object's own type (lines 19–22), then polymorphically, using an array of `Shape`
variables. Lines 14–16 create a `Point`, a `Circle` and a `Cylinder` object and assign their
references to variables `point`, `circle` and `cylinder`, respectively. Lines 19–22 then
invoke methods `getName` and `toString` for the objects to get a string representation of
each object's name and data (i.e., *x*–*y* coordinate pair, radius and height, depending on each
object's type).

```
1     // Fig. 10.10: AbstractInheritanceTest.java
2     // Driver for shape, point, circle, cylinder hierarchy.
3     import java.text.DecimalFormat;
4     import javax.swing.JOptionPane;
5
6     public class AbstractInheritanceTest {
7
8        public static void main( String args[] )
9        {
10          // set floating-point number format
11          DecimalFormat twoDigits = new DecimalFormat( "0.00" );
12
13          // create Point, Circle and Cylinder objects
14          Point point = new Point( 7, 11 );
15          Circle circle = new Circle( 22, 8, 3.5 );
16          Cylinder cylinder = new Cylinder( 20, 30, 3.3, 10.75 );
17
```

Fig. 10.10   Polymorphism via an inheritance hierarchy headed by an abstract
superclass. (Part 1 of 2.)

```
18        // obtain name and string representation of each object
19        String output = point.getName() + ": " + point + "\n" +
20           circle.getName() + ": " + circle + "\n" +
21           cylinder.getName() + ": " + cylinder + "\n";
22
23        Shape arrayOfShapes[] = new Shape[ 3 ];  // create Shape array
24
25        // aim arrayOfShapes[ 0 ] at subclass Point object
26        arrayOfShapes[ 0 ] = point;
27
28        // aim arrayOfShapes[ 1 ] at subclass Circle object
29        arrayOfShapes[ 1 ] = circle;
30
31        // aim arrayOfShapes[ 2 ] at subclass Cylinder object
32        arrayOfShapes[ 2 ] = cylinder;
33
34        // loop through arrayOfShapes to get name, string
35        // representation, area and volume of every Shape in array
36        for ( int i = 0; i < arrayOfShapes.length; i++ ) {
37           output += "\n\n" + arrayOfShapes[ i ].getName() + ": " +
38              arrayOfShapes[ i ].toString() + "\nArea = " +
39              twoDigits.format( arrayOfShapes[ i ].getArea() ) +
40              "\nVolume = " +
41              twoDigits.format( arrayOfShapes[ i ].getVolume() );
42        }
43
44        JOptionPane.showMessageDialog( null, output );  // display output
45
46        System.exit( 0 );
47
48     } // end main
49
50  } // end class AbstractInheritanceTest
```

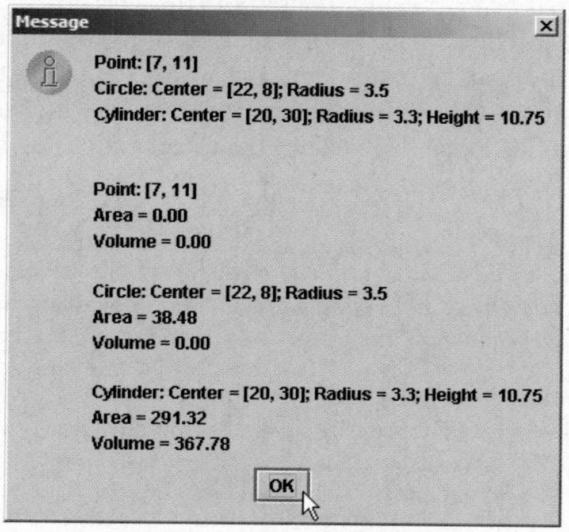

Message

Point: [7, 11]
Circle: Center = [22, 8]; Radius = 3.5
Cylinder: Center = [20, 30]; Radius = 3.3; Height = 10.75

Point: [7, 11]
Area = 0.00
Volume = 0.00

Circle: Center = [22, 8]; Radius = 3.5
Area = 38.48
Volume = 0.00

Cylinder: Center = [20, 30]; Radius = 3.3; Height = 10.75
Area = 291.32
Volume = 367.78

OK

Fig. 10.10 Polymorphism via an inheritance hierarchy headed by an abstract superclass. (Part 2 of 2.)

Line 23 declares arrayOfShapes and assigns it an array of three Shape variables. Line 26 assigns element arrayOfShapes[0] the reference to the Point object stored in point. Line 29 assigns element arrayOfShapes[1] the reference to the Circle object stored in circle. Line 32 assigns element arrayOfShapes[2] the reference to the Cylinder object stored in cylinder. Each assignment is allowed, because a Point *is a* Shape, a Circle *is a* Shape and a Cylinder *is a* Shape. Therefore, we can assign the references of Point, Circle and Cylinder objects to superclass Shape variables, even though Shape is an abstract class.

Next, lines 36–42 iterate through arrayOfShapes and invoke methods getName, toString, getArea and getVolume with arrayOfShapes[i], which contains the reference to one Shape. The output illustrates that the appropriate methods for each class are indeed invoked. First, the string "Point" and the coordinates of the Point are output; the area and volume are both output as 0.00. Next, the string "Circle", the coordinates of the center of the Circle and the radius of Circle are output; the area of the Circle is calculated and the volume is returned as 0.00. Finally, the string "Cylinder", the coordinates of the center of the base of the Cylinder, the radius of the Cylinder and the height of the Cylinder are output; the area and volume of the Cylinder are calculated. All method calls to getName, toString, getArea and getVolume are resolved at execution time, based on the type of the object to which element arrayOfShapes[i] currently refers. This process is known as *dynamic binding* or *late binding*. In Section 10.8, we revisit this Shape/Point/Circle/Cylinder example using the Java interface construct and show that polymorphism also can be achieved with interfaces.

10.6 final Methods and Classes

We saw in Section 6.8 that variables can be declared final to indicate that they cannot be modified after they are declared and that they must be initialized when they are declared. It is also possible to declare methods and classes with the final modifier.

A method that is declared final in a superclass cannot be overridden in a subclass. Methods that are declared private are implicitly final, because it is impossible to override them in a subclass. Methods that are declared static are implicitly final, because only non-static methods can be overridden. Because a final method's declaration can never change, the compiler can optimize the program by removing calls to final methods and replacing them with the expanded code of their declarations at each method call location—a technique known as *inlining the code*.

Performance Tip 10.1

The compiler can decide to inline a final method call and will do so for small, simple final methods. Inlining does not violate encapsulation or information hiding (but does improve performance because it eliminates the overhead of making a method call).

A class that is declared final cannot be a superclass (i.e., a class cannot extend a final class). All methods in a final class are implicitly final.

Software Engineering Observation 10.6

In the Java API, the vast majority of classes are not declared final. This enables inheritance and polymorphism—the fundamental capabilities of object-oriented programming. However, in some cases it is important to declare classes final—typically for security or object-oriented design reasons.

Class `String` is an example of a final class. This class cannot be extended, so programs that use strings can rely on the functionality of `String` objects as specified in the Java API. Making the class `final` also prevents programmers from creating subclasses that might bypass security restrictions. For more information on `final` classes and methods, visit `java.sun.com/docs/books/tutorial/java/javaOO/final.html`.

10.7 Case Study: Payroll System Using Polymorphism

Now we use abstract methods and polymorphism to perform payroll calculations based on the type of an employee. Consider the following problem:

> *A company pays its employees on a weekly basis. The company has four types of employees:*
> *salaried employees, who are paid a fixed weekly salary regardless of the number of hours*
> *worked; hourly employees, who are paid by the hour and receive overtime pay; commission*
> *employees, who are paid a percentage of their sales; and salaried-commission employees,*
> *who receive a base salary plus a percentage of their sales. For the current pay period, the*
> *company has decided to reward salaried-commission employees by adding 10% to their sal-*
> *aries. The company wants to implement a Java application that performs its payroll calcula-*
> *tions polymorphically.*

We use class `Employee` to represent a "generic" employee. The classes that extend `Employee` are `SalariedEmployee`, `CommissionEmployee` and `HourlyEmployee`. Class `BasePlusCommissionEmployee`—which extends `CommissionEmployee`—represents the last employee type. The class diagram of Fig. 10.11 shows the inheritance hierarchy for our employee-payroll application. Note that abstract class *Employee* is italicized, as per the convention of the UML.

An `earnings` method certainly applies generically to all employees. But each employee's earnings calculation depends on the employee's class. So we declare `earnings` as an abstract method in superclass `Employee` (because in this class no specific implementation is appropriate), and each subclass overrides `earnings` with an appropriate implementation. To calculate an employee's earnings, the program assigns a reference to that employee's object to a superclass variable, then invokes the employee's `earnings` method. We maintain an array of `Employee` variables that hold references to each `Employee` object. The program iterates through the array and calls method `earnings` for each employee object. Java processes these method calls polymorphically.

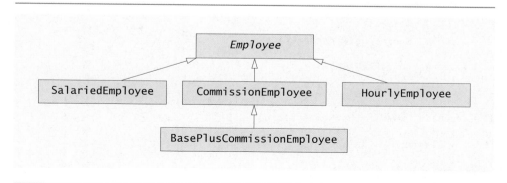

Fig. 10.11 Class hierarchy for the polymorphic employee-payroll application.

Let us consider class **Employee**'s declaration (Fig. 10.12). The class includes a constructor that takes the first name, last name and social security number as arguments (lines 10–15); *get* methods that return the first name, last name and social security number (lines 24–27, 36–39 and 48–51); *set* methods that set the first name, last name and social security number (lines 18–21, 30–33 and 42–45); method **toString** (lines 54–58), which returns the **String** representation of **Employee**; and abstract method **earnings** (line 61), which will be implemented by subclasses. Why did we decide to declare method **earnings** as an abstract method? The answer is that it does not make sense to provide an implementation of this method in class **Employee**. We cannot calculate the earnings for a generic employee. We first must know the specific **Employee** type to determine the appropriate earnings calculation. By declaring this method **abstract**, we indicate that each concrete subclass will provide an appropriate **earnings** implementation and that the program will be able to use superclass **Employee** variables to invoke method **earnings** for any type of employee. Note that the **Employee** constructor does not validate the social security number in this example. Normally, such validation should be provided.

```java
1   // Fig. 10.12: Employee.java
2   // Employee abstract superclass.
3
4   public abstract class Employee {
5      private String firstName;
6      private String lastName;
7      private String socialSecurityNumber;
8
9      // constructor
10     public Employee( String first, String last, String ssn )
11     {
12        firstName = first;
13        lastName = last;
14        socialSecurityNumber = ssn;
15     }
16
17     // set first name
18     public void setFirstName( String first )
19     {
20        firstName = first;
21     }
22
23     // return first name
24     public String getFirstName()
25     {
26        return firstName;
27     }
28
29     // set last name
30     public void setLastName( String last )
31     {
32        lastName = last;
33     }
34
```

Fig. 10.12 Employee abstract superclass. (Part 1 of 2.)

```
35      // return last name
36      public String getLastName()
37      {
38          return lastName;
39      }
40
41      // set social security number
42      public void setSocialSecurityNumber( String number )
43      {
44          socialSecurityNumber = number;   // should validate
45      }
46
47      // return social security number
48      public String getSocialSecurityNumber()
49      {
50          return socialSecurityNumber;
51      }
52
53      // return String representation of Employee object
54      public String toString()
55      {
56          return getFirstName() + " " + getLastName() +
57              "\nsocial security number: " + getSocialSecurityNumber();
58      }
59
60      // abstract method overridden by subclasses
61      public abstract double earnings();
62
63  } // end abstract class Employee
```

Fig. 10.12 Employee abstract superclass. (Part 2 of 2.)

Class SalariedEmployee (Fig. 10.13) extends class Employee (line 4). The class includes a constructor (lines 8–13) that takes a first name, a last name, a social security number and a weekly salary as arguments; a *set* method to assign a new value to instance variable weeklySalary (lines 16–19); a *get* method to return weeklySalary's value (lines 22–25); a method earnings (lines 29–32), which calculates a SalariedEmployee's earnings; and a method toString (lines 35–38), which returns the employee's type, namely, "salaried employee: ". Class SalariedEmployee's constructor passes the first name, last name and social security number to the Employee constructor to initialize the fields inherited from the superclass (line 11). Method toString calls the superclass toString method (line 37) to obtain the superclass Employee-specific information (i.e., first name, last name and social security number).

```
1   // Fig. 10.13: SalariedEmployee.java
2   // SalariedEmployee class extends Employee.
3
4   public class SalariedEmployee extends Employee {
5       private double weeklySalary;
```

Fig. 10.13 SalariedEmployee class extends Employee. (Part 1 of 2.)

```
6
7      // constructor
8      public SalariedEmployee( String first, String last,
9         String socialSecurityNumber, double salary )
10     {
11        super( first, last, socialSecurityNumber );
12        setWeeklySalary( salary );
13     }
14
15     // set salaried employee's salary
16     public void setWeeklySalary( double salary )
17     {
18        weeklySalary = salary < 0.0 ? 0.0 : salary;
19     }
20
21     // return salaried employee's salary
22     public double getWeeklySalary()
23     {
24        return weeklySalary;
25     }
26
27     // calculate salaried employee's pay;
28     // override abstract method earnings in Employee
29     public double earnings()
30     {
31        return getWeeklySalary();
32     }
33
34     // return String representation of SalariedEmployee object
35     public String toString()
36     {
37        return "\nsalaried employee: " + super.toString();
38     }
39
40  } // end class SalariedEmployee
```

Fig. 10.13   SalariedEmployee class extends Employee. (Part 2 of 2.)

Class HourlyEmployee (Fig. 10.14) also extends class Employee (line 4). The class includes a constructor (lines 9–15) that takes a first name, a last name, a social security number, an hourly wage and the number of hours worked as arguments; *set* methods (lines 18–21 and 30–34) to assign new values to instance variables wage and hours; *get* methods (lines 24–27 and 37–40) to return the values of wage and hours; a method earnings (lines 44–50), which calculates an HourlyEmployee's earnings; and a method toString (lines 53–56), which returns the employee's type, namely, "hourly employee: " and employee-specific information. Note that, like the SalariedEmployee constructor, the HourlyEmployee constructor also passes the first name, last name and social security number to the Employee constructor to initialize the inherited fields (line 12). In addition, method toString calls superclass method toString (line 55) to obtain the Employee-specific information (i.e., first name, last name and social security number).

```java
1    // Fig. 10.14: HourlyEmployee.java
2    // HourlyEmployee class extends Employee.
3
4    public class HourlyEmployee extends Employee {
5       private double wage;   // wage per hour
6       private double hours;  // hours worked for week
7
8       // constructor
9       public HourlyEmployee( String first, String last,
10         String socialSecurityNumber, double hourlyWage, double hoursWorked )
11      {
12         super( first, last, socialSecurityNumber );
13         setWage( hourlyWage );
14         setHours( hoursWorked );
15      }
16
17      // set hourly employee's wage
18      public void setWage( double wageAmount )
19      {
20         wage = wageAmount < 0.0 ? 0.0 : wageAmount;
21      }
22
23      // return wage
24      public double getWage()
25      {
26         return wage;
27      }
28
29      // set hourly employee's hours worked
30      public void setHours( double hoursWorked )
31      {
32         hours = ( hoursWorked >= 0.0 && hoursWorked <= 168.0 ) ?
33            hoursWorked : 0.0;
34      }
35
36      // return hours worked
37      public double getHours()
38      {
39         return hours;
40      }
41
42      // calculate hourly employee's pay;
43      // override abstract method earnings in Employee
44      public double earnings()
45      {
46         if ( hours <= 40 )  // no overtime
47            return wage * hours;
48         else
49            return 40 * wage + ( hours - 40 ) * wage * 1.5;
50      }
51
```

Fig. 10.14 HourlyEmployee class extends Employee. (Part 1 of 2.)

```
52        // return String representation of HourlyEmployee object
53        public String toString()
54        {
55           return "\nhourly employee: " + super.toString();
56        }
57
58     } // end class HourlyEmployee
```

Fig. 10.14 HourlyEmployee class extends Employee. (Part 2 of 2.)

Class CommissionEmployee (Fig. 10.15) extends class Employee (line 4). The class includes a constructor (lines 9–16) that takes a first name, a last name, a social security number, a sales amount and a commission rate; *set* methods (lines 19–22 and 31–34) to assign new values to instance variables commissionRate and grossSales, respectively; *get* methods (lines 25–28 and 37–40) that retrieve the values of these instance variables; method earnings (lines 44–47), which calculates a CommissionEmployee's earnings; and method toString (lines 50–53), which returns the employee's type, namely, "commission employee: " and employee-specific information. The CommissionEmployee's constructor also passes the first name, last name and social security number to the Employee constructor to initialize the inherited fields (line 13). Method toString calls superclass method toString (line 52) to obtain the Employee-specific information (i.e., first name, last name and social security number).

```
1     // Fig. 10.15: CommissionEmployee.java
2     // CommissionEmployee class extends Employee.
3
4     public class CommissionEmployee extends Employee {
5        private double grossSales;      // gross weekly sales
6        private double commissionRate;  // commission percentage
7
8        // constructor
9        public CommissionEmployee( String first, String last,
10          String socialSecurityNumber,
11          double grossWeeklySales, double percent )
12       {
13          super( first, last, socialSecurityNumber );
14          setGrossSales( grossWeeklySales );
15          setCommissionRate( percent );
16       }
17
18       // set commission employee's rate
19       public void setCommissionRate( double rate )
20       {
21          commissionRate = ( rate > 0.0 && rate < 1.0 ) ? rate : 0.0;
22       }
23
```

Fig. 10.15 CommissionEmployee class extends Employee. (Part 1 of 2.)

```
24       // return commission employee's rate
25       public double getCommissionRate()
26       {
27          return commissionRate;
28       }
29
30       // set commission employee's weekly base salary
31       public void setGrossSales( double sales )
32       {
33          grossSales = sales < 0.0 ? 0.0 : sales;
34       }
35
36       // return commission employee's gross sales amount
37       public double getGrossSales()
38       {
39          return grossSales;
40       }
41
42       // calculate commission employee's pay;
43       // override abstract method earnings in Employee
44       public double earnings()
45       {
46          return getCommissionRate() * getGrossSales();
47       }
48
49       // return String representation of CommissionEmployee object
50       public String toString()
51       {
52          return "\ncommission employee: " + super.toString();
53       }
54
55    } // end class CommissionEmployee
```

Fig. 10.15 CommissionEmployee class extends Employee. (Part 2 of 2.)

Class BasePlusCommissionEmployee (Fig. 10.16) extends class CommissionEmployee (line 4) and therefore also is an indirect subclass of class Employee. Class BasePlusCommissionEmployee has a constructor (lines 8–14) that takes as arguments a first name, a last name, a social security number, a base salary, a sales amount and a commission rate; a *set* method (lines 17–20) to assign a new value to instance variable baseSalary; a *get* method (lines 23–26) to return baseSalary's value; method earnings (lines 30–33), which calculates a BasePlusCommissionEmployee's earnings; and method toString (lines 36–41), which returns the employee's type, namely, "base-salaried commission employee: " and uses class Employee's methods to obtain the worker's name and social-security number. BasePlusCommissionEmployee's constructor passes the first name, last name, social security number, sales amount and commission rate to the CommissionEmployee constructor to initialize the inherited members (line 12). Notice that line 32 of method earnings calls superclass CommissionEmployee's earnings method to calculate the commission-based portion of the earnings. This is a nice example of code reuse.

```
1   // Fig. 10.16: BasePlusCommissionEmployee.java
2   // BasePlusCommissionEmployee class extends CommissionEmployee.
3
4   public class BasePlusCommissionEmployee extends CommissionEmployee {
5      private double baseSalary;  // base salary per week
6
7      // constructor
8      public BasePlusCommissionEmployee( String first, String last,
9         String socialSecurityNumber, double grossSalesAmount,
10        double rate, double baseSalaryAmount )
11     {
12        super( first, last, socialSecurityNumber, grossSalesAmount, rate );
13        setBaseSalary( baseSalaryAmount );
14     }
15
16     // set base-salaried commission employee's base salary
17     public void setBaseSalary( double salary )
18     {
19        baseSalary = salary < 0.0 ? 0.0 : salary;
20     }
21
22     // return base-salaried commission employee's base salary
23     public double getBaseSalary()
24     {
25        return baseSalary;
26     }
27
28     // calculate base-salaried commission employee's earnings;
29     // override method earnings in CommissionEmployee
30     public double earnings()
31     {
32        return getBaseSalary() + super.earnings();
33     }
34
35     // return String representation of BasePlusCommissionEmployee
36     public String toString()
37     {
38        return "\nbase-salaried commission employee: " +
39           super.getFirstName() + " " + super.getLastName() +
40           "\nsocial security number: " + super.getSocialSecurityNumber();
41     }
42
43  } // end class BasePlusCommissionEmployee
```

Fig. 10.16 BasePlusCommissionEmployee class extends CommissionEmployee.

The program of Fig. 10.17 tests our Employee hierarchy and increases the base salary of each BasePlusCommissionEmployee by 10%. Line 13 creates four-element Employee array employees that stores references to Employee objects. Lines 16–22 populate the array with references to objects of classes SalariedEmployee, CommissionEmployee, BasePlusCommissionEmployee and HourlyEmployee. The for loop (lines 28–50) iterates through array employees and displays each employee's name, social security number and earnings. Line 29 invokes method `toString` of the object to which `employees[ i ]` refers. This method call is another example of dynamic binding.

In this example, we want to perform special processing on `BasePlusCommission-Employee` objects; as we encounter these objects, we wish to increase their base salary by 10%. We process the employees polymorphically; therefore, we cannot be certain as to which type of `Employee` is being manipulated at any given time. This creates a problem, because `BasePlusCommissionEmployee` employees must be identified so they can be paid properly. Line 32 uses operator *instanceof* to determine whether each object's type is compatible with type `BasePlusCommissionEmployee`. The condition on line 32 is true if the object referenced by `employees[ i ]` *is a* `BasePlusCommissionEmployee`. This would also be true for any object of a `BasePlusCommissionEmployee` subclass. Lines 36–37 downcast `employees[ i ]` from type `Employee` to type `BasePlusCommissionEmployee`. This cast is allowed only if the object has an *is-a* relationship with `BasePlusCommissionEmployee`. The condition at line 32 ensures this is the case.

```java
1   // Fig. 10.17: PayrollSystemTest.java
2   // Employee hierarchy test program.
3   import java.text.DecimalFormat;
4   import javax.swing.JOptionPane;
5
6   public class PayrollSystemTest {
7
8      public static void main( String[] args )
9      {
10         DecimalFormat twoDigits = new DecimalFormat( "0.00" );
11
12         // create Employee array
13         Employee employees[] = new Employee[ 4 ];
14
15         // initialize array with Employees
16         employees[ 0 ] = new SalariedEmployee( "John", "Smith",
17            "111-11-1111", 800.00 );
18         employees[ 1 ] = new CommissionEmployee( "Sue", "Jones",
19            "222-22-2222", 10000, .06 );
20         employees[ 2 ] = new BasePlusCommissionEmployee( "Bob", "Lewis",
21            "333-33-3333", 5000, .04, 300 );
22         employees[ 3 ] = new HourlyEmployee( "Karen", "Price",
23            "444-44-4444", 16.75, 40 );
24
25         String output = "";
26
27         // generically process each element in array employees
28         for ( int i = 0; i < employees.length; i++ ) {
29            output += employees[ i ].toString();
30
31            // determine whether element is a BasePlusCommissionEmployee
32            if ( employees[ i ] instanceof BasePlusCommissionEmployee ) {
33
```

Fig. 10.17 `Employee` class hierarchy test program. (Part 1 of 2.)

```
34                // downcast Employee reference to
35                // BasePlusCommissionEmployee reference
36                BasePlusCommissionEmployee currentEmployee =
37                   ( BasePlusCommissionEmployee ) employees[ i ];
38
39                double oldBaseSalary = currentEmployee.getBaseSalary();
40                output += "\nold base salary: $" + oldBaseSalary;
41
42                currentEmployee.setBaseSalary( 1.10 * oldBaseSalary );
43                output += "\nnew base salary with 10% increase is: $" +
44                   currentEmployee.getBaseSalary();
45
46             } // end if
47
48             output += "\nearned $" + employees[ i ].earnings() + "\n";
49
50          } // end for
51
52          // get type name of each object in employees array
53          for ( int j = 0; j < employees.length; j++ )
54             output += "\nEmployee " + j + " is a " +
55                employees[ j ].getClass().getName();
56
57          JOptionPane.showMessageDialog( null, output );  // display output
58          System.exit( 0 );
59
60       } // end main
61
62    } // end class PayrollSystemTest
```

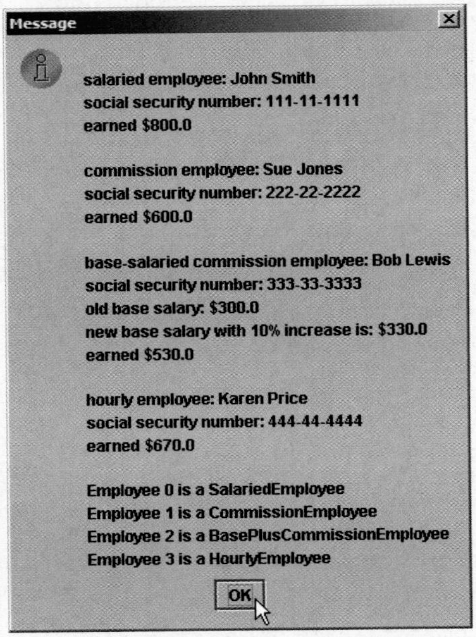

Fig. 10.17 Employee class hierarchy test program. (Part 2 of 2.)

Common Programming Error 10.5

In a downcast operation, if the type of the object does not have an is-a relationship with the type specified in the cast operator, a `ClassCastException` occurs. An object can be cast only to its own type or to the type of one of its superclasses.

If the value returned by the `instanceof` in line 32 is `true`, the `if` statement (lines 32–46) performs the special processing required for the `BasePlusCommissionEmployee` object. Lines 39 and 42 invoke `BasePlusCommissionEmployee` methods `getBase-Salary` and `setBaseSalary` to retrieve and update the employee's salary. Line 48 invokes method `earnings` on `employees[i]`, which calls the subclass object's `earnings` method, using dynamic binding.

The `for` loop (lines 53–55) displays each employee's type as a string. Every object in Java knows its own class and can access this information through method *getClass*, which all classes inherit from class `Object`. Method `getClass` returns an object of type `Class` (package `java.lang`), which contains information about the object's type, including its class name. Line 55 invokes method `getClass` on the object to get the runtime class (`Class` object) of that object. Then method *getName* is invoked on the object returned by `getClass` to get the name of the class. Line 57 displays the output string by invoking method `showMessageDialog` of class `JOptionPane`.

Software Engineering Observation 10.7

Java provides mechanisms for loading classes into a program dynamically to enhance the functionality of an executing program. In particular, static method forName of class `Class` (package `java.lang`) can be used to load a class and create new objects of that class for use in a program. (This concept is beyond the scope of the text. For more information, see the online API documentation for `Class`).

10.8 Case Study: Creating and Using Interfaces

Our next example (Fig. 10.18–Fig. 10.20) reexamines the `Point-Circle-Cylinder` hierarchy one last time, replacing abstract superclass `Shape` with the interface `Shape` (Fig. 10.18). An interface declaration begins with the keyword *interface* and contains a set of `public abstract` methods. Interfaces may also contain `public static final` data. To use an interface, a class must specify that it `implements` the interface and must declare each method in the interface with the signature specified in the interface declaration. If the class does not implement any method of the interface, the class is an abstract class and must be declared `abstract`. Implementing an interface is like signing a contract with the compiler that states, "I will declare all the methods specified by the interface."

Common Programming Error 10.6

Failing to implement any method of an interface in a class that `implements` the interface results in a compile error indicating that the class must be declared `abstract`.

We started using interfaces when we introduced GUI event handling in Chapter 6, Methods. Recall that our `Craps` applet class in Fig. 6.9 included `implements Action-Listener` (an interface in package `java.awt.event`). We were required to implement `actionPerformed` in the applets with event handling to fulfill the contract of interface `ActionListener`, which specifies that `actionPerformed` must be implemented. Interfaces are an important part of GUI event handling, as we will see in the next section.

An interface is typically used in place of an abstract class when there is no default implementation to inherit—i.e., no instance variables and no default method implementations. Like `public abstract` classes, interfaces are typically `public` types, so they are normally declared in files by themselves with the same name as the interface and the `.java` file-name extension.

The declaration of interface `Shape` begins in Fig. 10.18 at line 4. Interface `Shape` has public abstract methods `getArea`, `getVolume` and `getName`. All methods in an interface are required to be `public` and `abstract`, so they do not need to be declared as such. By coincidence, these three methods take no arguments. However, this is not a requirement of methods in an interface. (In fact, method `actionPerformed` of interface `ActionListener` requires an argument.)

In Fig. 10.19, line 4 indicates that class `Point` extends class `Object` and implements interface `Shape`. Java does not allow subclasses to inherit from more than one superclass, but it does allow a class to inherit from a superclass and implement interfaces. Class `Point` implements all three methods in the interface. Method `getArea` is declared at lines 47–50. Method `volume` is declared at lines 53–56. Method `getName` is declared at lines 59–62. These three methods satisfy the implementation requirement for the three methods in the interface. Therefore, we have fulfilled our contract with the compiler.

```
1  // Fig. 10.18: Shape.java
2  // Shape interface declaration.
3
4  public interface Shape {
5     public double getArea();      // calculate area
6     public double getVolume();    // calculate volume
7     public String getName();      // return shape name
8
9  } // end interface Shape
```

Fig. 10.18 `Shape` interface declaration.

```
1  // Fig. 10.19: Point.java
2  // Point class declaration implements interface Shape.
3
4  public class Point extends Object implements Shape {
5     private int x;  // x part of coordinate pair
6     private int y;  // y part of coordinate pair
7
8     // no-argument constructor; x and y default to 0
9     public Point()
10    {
11       // implicit call to Object constructor occurs here
12    }
13
```

Fig. 10.19 `Point` implementation of interface `Shape`. (Part 1 of 3.)

```
14      // constructor
15      public Point( int xValue, int yValue )
16      {
17          // implicit call to Object constructor occurs here
18          x = xValue;  // no need for validation
19          y = yValue;  // no need for validation
20      }
21
22      // set x in coordinate pair
23      public void setX( int xValue )
24      {
25          x = xValue;  // no need for validation
26      }
27
28      // return x from coordinate pair
29      public int getX()
30      {
31          return x;
32      }
33
34      // set y in coordinate pair
35      public void setY( int yValue )
36      {
37          y = yValue;  // no need for validation
38      }
39
40      // return y from coordinate pair
41      public int getY()
42      {
43          return y;
44      }
45
46      // declare abstract method getArea
47      public double getArea()
48      {
49          return 0.0;
50      }
51
52      // declare abstract method getVolume
53      public double getVolume()
54      {
55          return 0.0;
56      }
57
58      // override abstract method getName to return "Point"
59      public String getName()
60      {
61          return "Point";
62      }
63
64      // override toString to return String representation of Point
65      public String toString()
66      {
```

Fig. 10.19   Point implementation of interface Shape. (Part 2 of 3.)

```
67          return "[" + getX() + ", " + getY() + "]";
68       }
69
70  } // end class Point
```

Fig. 10.19 `Point` implementation of interface `Shape`. (Part 3 of 3.)

When a class implements an interface, the same *is-a* relationship provided by inheritance applies. For example, class `Point` implements `Shape`. Therefore, a `Point` object *is a* `Shape`. In fact, objects of any class that extends `Point` are also `Shape` objects. Using this relationship, we have maintained the original declarations of class `Circle` and class `Cylinder` from Section 10.5. To illustrate that an interface can be used instead of an abstract class to process `Shape`s polymorphically, class `InterfaceTest` (Fig. 10.20) used a `main` method identical to that of class `AbstractInheritanceTest` (Fig. 10.10). Notice that the output of the program in Fig. 10.20 is identical to that of Fig. 10.10. Also, notice that line 38 invokes method `toString` through a `Shape` interface reference, even though `toString` is not declared in interface `Shape`.

Software Engineering Observation 10.8

*All methods of class **Object** can be called by using a reference of an interface type. A reference refers to an object, and all objects inherit the methods of class **Object**.*

```
1   // Fig. 10.20: InterfaceTest.java
2   // Test Point, Circle, Cylinder hierarchy with interface Shape.
3   import java.text.DecimalFormat;
4   import javax.swing.JOptionPane;
5
6   public class InterfaceTest {
7
8      public static void main( String args[] )
9      {
10         // set floating-point number format
11         DecimalFormat twoDigits = new DecimalFormat( "0.00" );
12
13         // create Point, Circle and Cylinder objects
14         Point point = new Point( 7, 11 );
15         Circle circle = new Circle( 22, 8, 3.5 );
16         Cylinder cylinder = new Cylinder( 20, 30, 3.3, 10.75 );
17
18         // obtain name and string representation of each object
19         String output = point.getName() + ": " + point + "\n" +
20            circle.getName() + ": " + circle + "\n" +
21            cylinder.getName() + ": " + cylinder + "\n";
22
23         Shape arrayOfShapes[] = new Shape[ 3 ];   // create Shape array
24
25         // aim arrayOfShapes[ 0 ] at subclass Point object
26         arrayOfShapes[ 0 ] = point;
27
```

Fig. 10.20 `Point-Circle-Cylinder` hierarchy with `Shape` interface. (Part 1 of 2.)

```
28          // aim arrayOfShapes[ 1 ] at subclass Circle object
29          arrayOfShapes[ 1 ] = circle;
30
31          // aim arrayOfShapes[ 2 ] at subclass Cylinder object
32          arrayOfShapes[ 2 ] = cylinder;
33
34          // loop through arrayOfShapes to get name, string
35          // representation, area and volume of every Shape in array
36          for ( int i = 0; i < arrayOfShapes.length; i++ ) {
37             output += "\n\n" + arrayOfShapes[ i ].getName() + ": " +
38                arrayOfShapes[ i ].toString() + "\nArea = " +
39                twoDigits.format( arrayOfShapes[ i ].getArea() ) +
40                "\nVolume = " +
41                twoDigits.format( arrayOfShapes[ i ].getVolume() );
42          }
43
44          JOptionPane.showMessageDialog( null, output );   // display output
45
46          System.exit( 0 );
47
48       } // end main
49
50    } // end class Test
```

Message

Point: [7, 11]
Circle: Center = [22, 8]; Radius = 3.5
Cylinder: Center = [20, 30]; Radius = 3.3; Height = 10.75

Point: [7, 11]
Area = 0.00
Volume = 0.00

Circle: Center = [22, 8]; Radius = 3.5
Area = 38.48
Volume = 0.00

Cylinder: Center = [20, 30]; Radius = 3.3; Height = 10.75
Area = 291.32
Volume = 367.78

OK

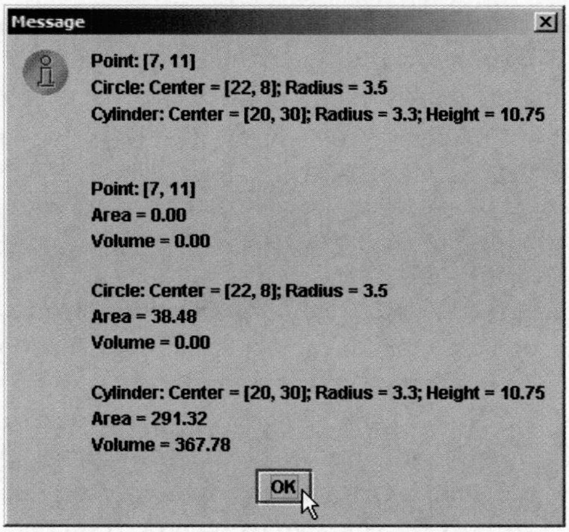

Fig. 10.20   Point-Circle-Cylinder hierarchy with Shape interface. (Part 2 of 2.)

Implementing Multiple Interfaces

One benefit of using interfaces is that a class can implement as many interfaces as it needs, in addition to extending a class. To implement more than one interface, simply provide a comma-separated list of interface names after keyword implements in the class declaration. This is particularly useful in the GUI event-handling mechanism. A class that implements more than one event-listener interface (such as ActionListener in earlier examples) can process different types of GUI events, as we will see in Chapter 13 and Chapter 14.

Declaring Constants with Interfaces

Another use of interfaces is to declare a set of constants that can be used in many class declarations. Consider interface `Constants`

```
public interface Constants {
    public static final int ONE = 1;
    public static final int TWO = 2;
    public static final int THREE = 3;
}
```

Classes that implement interface `Constants` can use ONE, TWO and THREE anywhere in the class declaration. A class can even use these constants by importing the interface, then referring to each constant as `Constants.ONE`, `Constants.TWO` and `Constants.THREE`. There are no methods declared in this interface, so a class that implements the interface is not required to implement any methods.

10.9 Nested Classes

All the classes discussed so far were *top-level classes*—i.e., not declared inside a class or a method. For example, if a file contained two classes, one was not *nested* in the body of the other. Java allows called *nested classes*—classes that are declared inside other classes. Nested classes can be `static`. Nested classes that are not static are called *inner classes*. Inner classes are used primarily in event handling. However, they have other benefits. For example, the implementation of the queue abstract data type discussed in Section 8.16 might use an inner class to represent the objects that store each item currently in the queue. Only the queue data structure requires knowledge of how the objects are stored internally, so the implementation can be hidden by declaring an inner class as part of class `Queue`.

The next example not only demonstrates nested-class declarations with inner classes, but also demonstrates an application that executes in its own window. After you complete this example, you will be able to use in your applications the GUI techniques shown only in applets so far.

Recall the applet of Fig. 8.7 and Fig. 8.8 in which we created and used an object of class `Time3` to maintain the time that the applet's user could manipulate through the GUI provided by the applet. We now reimplement the program as an application that runs in its own window. We modified class `Time3` and created a new class called `Time` (Fig. 10.21) with minor differences. Class `Time` renames `toStandardString` as `toString`, so the standard time format is the default string representation of a `Time` object. Also, in class `Time3`, methods `toUniversalString` and `toStandardString` each created a `DecimalFormat` object each time they were called. Class `Time` declares one `DecimalFormat` variable at line 11 as a static field of the class. Methods `toUniversalString` and `toString` both use this object for formatting. [*Note:* We do not discuss class `Time` here, because all its features were discussed in Chapter 8.]

```
1   // Fig. 10.21: Time.java
2   // Time class declaration with set and get methods.
3   import java.text.DecimalFormat;
4
```

Fig. 10.21 Time class declaration. (Part 1 of 3.)

```
5   public class Time {
6      private int hour;      // 0 - 23
7      private int minute;    // 0 - 59
8      private int second;    // 0 - 59
9
10     // one formatting object to share in toString and toUniversalString
11     private static DecimalFormat twoDigits = new DecimalFormat( "00" );
12
13     // Time constructor initializes each instance variable to zero;
14     // ensures that Time object starts in a consistent state
15     public Time()
16     {
17        this( 0, 0, 0 ); // invoke Time constructor with three arguments
18     }
19
20     // Time constructor: hour supplied, minute and second defaulted to 0
21     public Time( int h )
22     {
23        this( h, 0, 0 ); // invoke Time constructor with three arguments
24     }
25
26     // Time constructor: hour and minute supplied, second defaulted to 0
27     public Time( int h, int m )
28     {
29        this( h, m, 0 ); // invoke Time constructor with three arguments
30     }
31
32     // Time constructor: hour, minute and second supplied
33     public Time( int h, int m, int s )
34     {
35        setTime( h, m, s );
36     }
37
38     // Time constructor: another Time3 object supplied
39     public Time( Time time )
40     {
41        // invoke Time constructor with three arguments
42        this( time.getHour(), time.getMinute(), time.getSecond() );
43     }
44
45     // Set Methods
46     // set a new time value using universal time; perform
47     // validity checks on data; set invalid values to zero
48     public void setTime( int h, int m, int s )
49     {
50        setHour( h );   // set the hour
51        setMinute( m ); // set the minute
52        setSecond( s ); // set the second
53     }
54
55     // validate and set hour
56     public void setHour( int h )
57     {
```

Fig. 10.21 Time class declaration. (Part 2 of 3.)

```
58          hour = ( ( h >= 0 && h < 24 ) ? h : 0 );
59       }
60
61       // validate and set minute
62       public void setMinute( int m )
63       {
64          minute = ( ( m >= 0 && m < 60 ) ? m : 0 );
65       }
66
67       // validate and set second
68       public void setSecond( int s )
69       {
70          second = ( ( s >= 0 && s < 60 ) ? s : 0 );
71       }
72
73       // Get Methods
74       // get hour value
75       public int getHour()
76       {
77          return hour;
78       }
79
80       // get minute value
81       public int getMinute()
82       {
83          return minute;
84       }
85
86       // get second value
87       public int getSecond()
88       {
89          return second;
90       }
91
92       // convert to String in universal-time format
93       public String toUniversalString()
94       {
95          return twoDigits.format( getHour() ) + ":" +
96             twoDigits.format( getMinute() ) + ":" +
97             twoDigits.format( getSecond() );
98       }
99
100      // convert to String in standard-time format
101      public String toString()
102      {
103         return ( ( getHour() == 12 || getHour() == 0 ) ?
104            12 : getHour() % 12 ) + ":" + twoDigits.format( getMinute() ) +
105            ":" + twoDigits.format( getSecond() ) +
106            ( getHour() < 12 ? " AM" : " PM" );
107      }
108
109   } // end class Time
```

Fig. 10.21 Time class declaration. (Part 3 of 3.)

Figure 10.22 declares class `TimeTestWindow` as an application. The application executes in its own window and provides a GUI that enables the user to change the time. The example uses an inner class to implement the event handlers for the windows's various GUI components.

```java
1   // Fig. 10.22: TimeTestWindow.java
2   // Inner class declarations used to create event handlers.
3   import java.awt.*;
4   import java.awt.event.*;
5   import javax.swing.*;
6
7   public class TimeTestWindow extends JFrame {
8      private Time time;
9      private JLabel hourLabel, minuteLabel, secondLabel;
10     private JTextField hourField, minuteField, secondField, displayField;
11     private JButton exitButton;
12
13     // set up GUI
14     public TimeTestWindow()
15     {
16        // call JFrame constructor to set title bar string
17        super( "Inner Class Demonstration" );
18
19        time = new Time();  // create Time object
20
21        // use inherited method getContentPane to get window's content pane
22        Container container = getContentPane();
23        container.setLayout( new FlowLayout() );  // change layout
24
25        // set up hourLabel and hourField
26        hourLabel = new JLabel( "Set Hour" );
27        hourField = new JTextField( 10 );
28        container.add( hourLabel );
29        container.add( hourField );
30
31        // set up minuteLabel and minuteField
32        minuteLabel = new JLabel( "Set Minute" );
33        minuteField = new JTextField( 10 );
34        container.add( minuteLabel );
35        container.add( minuteField );
36
37        // set up secondLabel and secondField
38        secondLabel = new JLabel( "Set Second" );
39        secondField = new JTextField( 10 );
40        container.add( secondLabel );
41        container.add( secondField );
42
43        // set up displayField
44        displayField = new JTextField( 30 );
45        displayField.setEditable( false );
46        container.add( displayField );
47
```

Fig. 10.22 Inner class used for event handling in a windowed application. (Part 1 of 3.)

```
48          // set up exitButton
49          exitButton = new JButton( "Exit" );
50          container.add( exitButton );
51
52          // create an instance of inner class ActionEventHandler
53          ActionEventHandler handler = new ActionEventHandler();
54
55          // register event handlers; the object referenced by handler
56          // is the ActionListener, which contains method actionPerformed
57          // that will be called to handle action events generated by
58          // hourField, minuteField, secondField and exitButton
59          hourField.addActionListener( handler );
60          minuteField.addActionListener( handler );
61          secondField.addActionListener( handler );
62          exitButton.addActionListener( handler );
63
64       } // end constructor
65
66       // display time in displayField
67       public void displayTime()
68       {
69          displayField.setText( "The time is: " + time );
70       }
71
72       // launch application: create, size and display TimeTestWindow;
73       // when main terminates, program continues execution because a
74       // window is displayed by the statements in main
75       public static void main( String args[] )
76       {
77          TimeTestWindow window = new TimeTestWindow();
78
79          window.setSize( 400, 140 );
80          window.setVisible( true );
81
82       } // end main
83
84       // inner class declaration for handling JTextField and JButton events
85       private class ActionEventHandler implements ActionListener {
86
87          // method to handle action events
88          public void actionPerformed( ActionEvent event )
89          {
90             // user pressed exitButton
91             if ( event.getSource() == exitButton )
92                System.exit( 0 );    // terminate the application
93
94             // user pressed Enter key in hourField
95             else if ( event.getSource() == hourField ) {
96                time.setHour( Integer.parseInt(
97                   event.getActionCommand() ) );
98                hourField.setText( "" );
99             }
100
```

Fig. 10.22 Inner class used for event handling in a windowed application. (Part 2 of 3.)

```
101            // user pressed Enter key in minuteField
102            else if ( event.getSource() == minuteField ) {
103               time.setMinute( Integer.parseInt(
104                  event.getActionCommand() ) );
105               minuteField.setText( "" );
106            }
107
108            // user pressed Enter key in secondField
109            else if ( event.getSource() == secondField ) {
110               time.setSecond( Integer.parseInt(
111                  event.getActionCommand() ) );
112               secondField.setText( "" );
113            }
114
115            displayTime();  // call outer class's method
116
117         } // end method actionPerformed
118
119      } // end inner class ActionEventHandler
120
121   } // end class TimeTestWindow
```

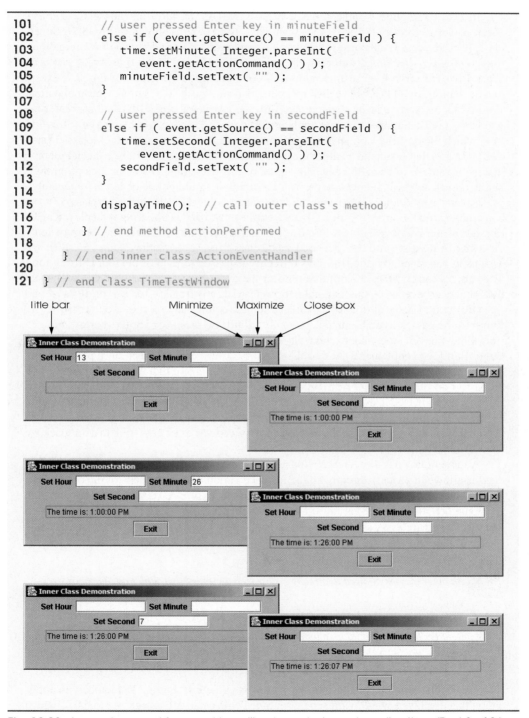

Fig. 10.22 Inner class used for event handling in a windowed application. (Part 3 of 3.)

In Fig. 10.22, line 7 indicates that class `TimeTestWindow` extends class *JFrame* (from package `javax.swing`) rather than class `JApplet` (as shown in Fig. 8.7). Superclass `JFrame` provides the basic attributes and behaviors of a window—a *title bar* and buttons to *minimize, maximize* and *close* the window (all labeled in the first screen capture). Class `TimeTestWindow` uses the same GUI components as the applet of Fig. 8.7, except that the button (line 11) is now called `exitButton` and is used to terminate the application.

Applet method `init` has been replaced by a constructor (lines 14–64) that creates the window's GUI components as the application begins executing. Method `main` (lines 75–82), which begins the application's execution, creates a new object of class `Time-TestWindow` that results in a call to the constructor. Remember, `init` is a special method that is guaranteed to be called when an applet begins execution. However, this program is not an applet, so if we did declare the `init` method, it would not be called automatically.

Several new features appear in the constructor. Line 17 calls the superclass `JFrame` constructor with the string `"Inner Class Demonstration"`. This string is displayed in the title bar of the window by class `JFrame`'s constructor. Line 53 creates an object of inner class `ActionEventHandler` (declared inside class `TimeTestWindow` at lines 85–119) and assigns its reference to `handler`. This reference is passed to each of the four calls to `add-ActionListener` (lines 59–62) that register the event handlers for each GUI component that generates events in this example (`hourField`, `minuteField`, `secondField` and `exitButton`). Each call to `addActionListener` requires an object of type `ActionListener` to be passed as an argument. Actually, `handler` *is an* `ActionListener`. Line 85 (the first line of the inner class declaration) indicates that inner class `Action-EventHandler` implements `ActionListener`. Thus, every object of type `Action-EventHandler` *is an* `ActionListener`, and the requirement that `addActionListener` be passed an object of type `ActionListener` is satisfied! The *is-a* relationship is used extensively in the GUI event-handling mechanism, as you will see over the next several chapters. The inner class is declared as `private` because it will be used only in this class declaration. Inner classes can be declared `private`, `protected`, `public` or package access (the default).

An inner class has a special relationship with the outer class that declares it. The inner class is allowed to access directly all the instance variables and methods of the outer class. Method `actionPerformed` (line 88–117) of class `ActionEventHandler` does just that. In the method, the instance variables `time`, `exitButton`, `hourField`, `minuteField` and `secondField` are used, as is method `displayTime`. Notice that none of these needs a reference to the outer class object.

Software Engineering Observation 10.9

An inner class is allowed to directly access its outer class's variables and methods.

Software Engineering Observation 10.10

Reference `this` used in an inner class refers to the current inner-class object being manipulated. An inner-class method can use its outer-class object's `this` reference by preceding `this` with the outer-class name and a dot, as in OuterClassName.`this`.

This application must be terminated by pressing the **Exit** button. Remember, an application that displays a window must be terminated with a call to `System.exit( 0 )`, which is exactly what the event handler does for `exitButton` (lines 91–92). Also, note that a window in Java is 0 pixels wide, 0 pixels tall and not displayed by default. Lines 79–80 use methods `setSize` and `setVisible` to size the window and display it on the screen. These methods are declared in class `java.awt.Component`, inherited by class `JFrame` and inherited again by `TimeTestWindow`.

Anonymous Inner Classes

An inner class can also be declared inside a method of a class. Such an inner class has access to its outer class's members. However, it has limited access to the local variables of the method in which it is declared.

Software Engineering Observation 10.11

An inner class declared in a method can access the instance variables and methods of the outer class object that declared it, as well as the method's `final` local variables.

Figure 10.23 modifies class `TimeTestWindow` of Fig. 10.22 to use *anonymous inner classes*. An anonymous inner class has no name, so one object of the anonymous inner class is created at the point where the class is declared in the program. We demonstrate anonymous inner classes two ways in this example. First, we use *separate anonymous inner classes that implement an interface* (`ActionListener`) to create event handlers for each of `JTextField`—`hourField`, `minuteField` and `secondField`. We also demonstrate how to terminate an application when the user clicks the window's **Close**. In this case, the event handler is declared as an *anonymous inner class that extends a class* (`Window-Adapter`). Class `Time` (Fig. 10.21) is used again here. Also, we removed the **Exit** button from this example. The `TimeTestWindow2` constructor invokes method `createGUI` (lines 24–48) to build the GUI; then it invokes method `registerEventHandlers` (lines 51–103) to register the event handler for `hourField`, `minuteField` and `secondField`.

```
1   // Fig. 10.23: TimeTestWindow2.java
2   // Demonstrating the Time class set and get methods
3   import java.awt.*;
4   import java.awt.event.*;
5   import javax.swing.*;
6
7   public class TimeTestWindow2 extends JFrame {
8      private Time time;
9      private JLabel hourLabel, minuteLabel, secondLabel;
10     private JTextField hourField, minuteField, secondField, displayField;
11
12     // constructor
13     public TimeTestWindow2()
14     {
15        // call JFrame constructor to set title bar string
16        super( "Anonymous Inner Class Demonstration" );
17
18        time = new Time();          // create Time object
19        createGUI();                // set up GUI
20        registerEventHandlers();    // set up event handling
21     }
```

Fig. 10.23 Anonymous inner classes. (Part 1 of 4.)

```
22
23      // create GUI components and attach to content pane
24      private void createGUI()
25      {
26         Container container = getContentPane();
27         container.setLayout( new FlowLayout() );
28
29         hourLabel = new JLabel( "Set Hour" );
30         hourField = new JTextField( 10 );
31         container.add( hourLabel );
32         container.add( hourField );
33
34         minuteLabel = new JLabel( "Set minute" );
35         minuteField = new JTextField( 10 );
36         container.add( minuteLabel );
37         container.add( minuteField );
38
39         secondLabel = new JLabel( "Set Second" );
40         secondField = new JTextField( 10 );
41         container.add( secondLabel );
42         container.add( secondField );
43
44         displayField = new JTextField( 30 );
45         displayField.setEditable( false );
46         container.add( displayField );
47
48      } // end method createGUI
49
50      // register event handlers for hourField, minuteField and secondField
51      private void registerEventHandlers()
52      {
53         // register hourField event handler
54         hourField.addActionListener(
55
56            new ActionListener() {  // anonymous inner class
57
58               public void actionPerformed( ActionEvent event )
59               {
60                  time.setHour( Integer.parseInt(
61                     event.getActionCommand() ) );
62                  hourField.setText( "" );
63                  displayTime();
64               }
65
66            } // end anonymous inner class
67
68         ); // end call to addActionListener for hourField
69
70         // register minuteField event handler
71         minuteField.addActionListener(
72
73            new ActionListener() {  // anonymous inner class
74
```

Fig. 10.23 Anonymous inner classes. (Part 2 of 4.)

```
75                  public void actionPerformed( ActionEvent event )
76                  {
77                      time.setMinute( Integer.parseInt(
78                          event.getActionCommand() ) );
79                      minuteField.setText( "" );
80                      displayTime();
81                  }
82
83              } // end anonymous inner class
84
85          ); // end call to addActionListener for minuteField
86
87          secondField.addActionListener(
88
89              new ActionListener() {  // anonymous inner class
90
91                  public void actionPerformed( ActionEvent event )
92                  {
93                      time.setSecond( Integer.parseInt(
94                          event.getActionCommand() ) );
95                      secondField.setText( "" );
96                      displayTime();
97                  }
98
99              } // end anonymous inner class
100
101         ); // end call to addActionListener for secondField
102
103     } // end method registerEventHandlers
104
105     // display time in displayField
106     public void displayTime()
107     {
108         displayField.setText( "The time is: " + time );
109     }
110
111     // create TimeTestWindow2 object, register for its window events
112     // and display it to begin application's execution
113     public static void main( String args[] )
114     {
115         TimeTestWindow2 window = new TimeTestWindow2();
116
117         // register listener for windowClosing event
118         window.addWindowListener(
119
120             // anonymous inner class for windowClosing event
121             new WindowAdapter() {
122
123                 // terminate application when user closes window
124                 public void windowClosing( WindowEvent event )
125                 {
126                     System.exit( 0 );
127                 }
```

Fig. 10.23 Anonymous inner classes. (Part 3 of 4.)

```
128
129          } // end anonymous inner class
130
131       ); // end call to addWindowListener for window
132
133       window.setSize( 400, 105 );
134       window.setVisible( true );
135
136    } // end main
137
138 } // end class TimeTestWindow2
```

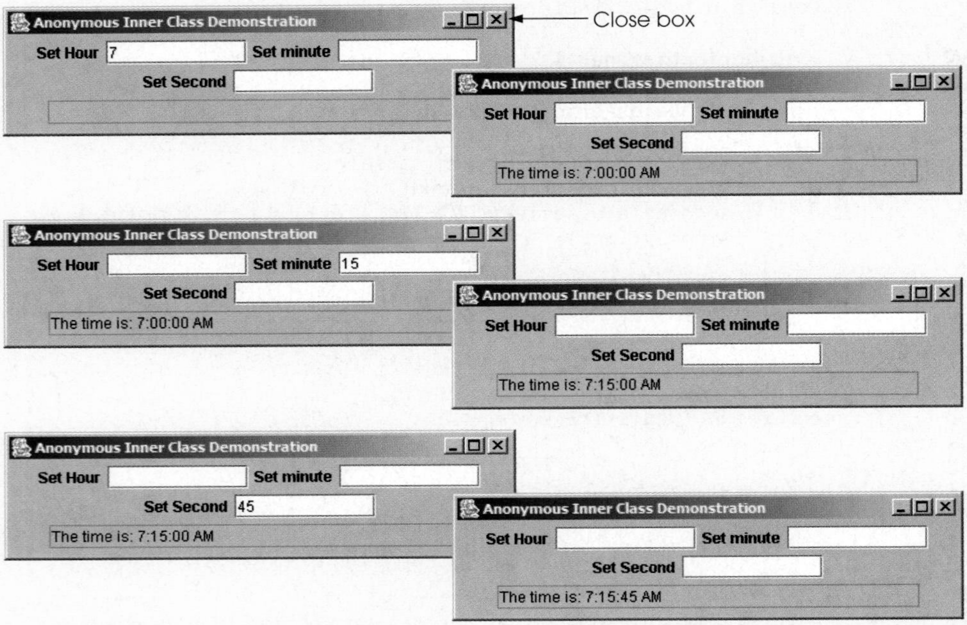

Fig. 10.23 Anonymous inner classes. (Part 4 of 4.)

Each JTextField that generates events in this program has a similar anonymous inner class to handle its events, so we discuss only the anonymous inner class for hour-Field here. Lines 54–68 are a call to hourField's addActionListener method. The argument to this method must be an object that *is an* ActionListener (i.e., any object of a class that implements ActionListener). Lines 56–66 are a class-instance creation expression that both declares an anonymous inner class and creates one object of that class that is passed as the argument to addActionListener. The syntax ActionListener() after new begins the declaration of an anonymous inner class that implements interface ActionListener. This is similar to beginning a class declaration with

```
public class MyHandler implements ActionListener {
```

The parentheses after ActionListener indicate a call to the default constructor of the anonymous inner class.

The opening left brace ({) at 56 and the closing right brace (}) at line 66 delimit the body of the class. Lines 58–64 declare method `actionPerformed`, which is required in any class that implements `ActionListener`. Method `actionPerformed` is called when the user presses *Enter* while typing in `hourField`. Notice that no `if...else` logic is required in `actionPerformed` to determine which GUI component was the event source. This event handler is specific to `hourField` and will be called only in response to an action event on the `hourField`. Separate event handlers are declared and registered for `minute-Field` and `secondField` at lines 71–85 and 87–101, respectively.[1]

 Software Engineering Observation 10.12

When an anonymous inner class implements an interface, the class must implement every method in the interface.

Method `main` (lines 113–136) creates one instance of class `TimeTestWindow` (line 115), sizes the window (line 133) and displays the window (line 134).

Windows generate a variety of events that are discussed in Chapter 14. For this example, we discuss the one event—a *window-closing event*—generated when the user clicks the window's close box. Lines 118–131 enable the user to terminate the application by clicking the window's close box (labeled in the first screen capture). Method *addWindowListener* (inherited from `JFrame`) registers a window-event listener. The argument to `addWindowListener` must be a reference to an object that *is a WindowListener* (an interface in package `java.awt.event`)—i.e., any object of a class that implements `WindowListener`. However, there are seven different methods that must be declared in every class that implements `WindowListener`, and we need only one of them in this example—*windowClosing*. For event-handling interfaces with more than one method, Java provides a corresponding class (called an *adapter class*) that already implements all the methods in the interface for you and provides an empty body for each method. All you need to do is extend the adapter class and override the methods you require in your program.

 Common Programming Error 10.7

Extending an adapter class and misspelling the name of the method you are overriding is a logic error. Your method simply becomes another method in the class that would not be called as an event-handling method.

Lines 121–129 declare an anonymous inner class and create one object of that class, which is passed as the argument to `addWindowListener`. After `new`, the syntax `Window-Adapter()` begins the declaration of an anonymous inner class that *extends* class `Window-Adapter`. This is similar to beginning a class declaration with

```
public class MyHandler extends WindowAdapter {
```

The compiler knows to extend, rather than implement, `WindowAdapter` because `Window-Adapter` is a class. The parentheses after `WindowAdapter` indicate a call to the default constructor of the anonymous inner class. Class `WindowAdapter` implements interface `WindowListener`, so every `WindowAdapter` object *is a* `WindowListener`—the exact type required for the argument to `addWindowListener`. Of course, any object of a class

---

1. The syntax shown here for creating event handlers is similar to the code that would be generated by a Java integrated development environment (IDE). Typically, an IDE enables the programmer to design a GUI visually; then the IDE generates code that implements the GUI. The programmer simply inserts statements in the event-handling methods that declare how to handle each event.

that extends `WindowAdapter` *is a* `WindowAdapter`, which implies that the object also *is a* `WindowListener`.

The opening left brace (`{`) at line 121 and the closing right brace (`}`) at line 129 delimit the body of the class. Lines 124–127 override the `windowClosing` method of `Window-Adapter` that is called when the user clicks the window's close box. In this example, `windowClosing` terminates the application. Because the event handling shown here is common for application windows, class `JFrame` provides a shorthand technique for registering the event handler for a window-closing event. The statement

```
window.setDefaultCloseOperation( JFrame.EXIT_ON_CLOSE );
```

performs the same tasks as lines 118–131. In this case, we specify as the argument the constant `JFrame.EXIT_ON_CLOSE` to indicate that the program should terminate when the user clicks the close box. Other options are `DO_NOTHING_ON_CLOSE` (to ignore the window-closing event), `HIDE_ON_CLOSE` (to hide the window, such that it can be redisplayed later) and `DISPOSE_ON_CLOSE` (to dispose of the window, such that it cannot be redisplayed later). From this point forward, we implement our own `WindowListener` only if the program should perform additional tasks when the user clicks the window's close box. Otherwise, we use method `setDefaultCloseOperation` to specify that the program should terminate when the user clicks the close box.

In the last two examples, we have seen that inner classes can be used to create event handlers and that separate anonymous inner classes can be declared to handle events individually for each GUI component. In Chapter 13 and Chapter 14, we revisit this concept as we discuss the event-handling mechanism in detail.

Notes on Nested Classes

There are several items of interest to programmers regarding the declaration and use of nested classes:

1. Compiling a class that contains nested classes results in a separate `.class` file for every class. Nested classes with names have a file name of the form *OuterClassName*$*InnerClassName*`.class`. Anonymous inner classes have the file name *OuterClassName*$*#*`.class`, where *#* starts at 1 and is incremented for each anonymous inner class encountered during compilation.

2. Inner classes with names can be declared as `public`, `protected`, package access or `private` and are subject to the same usage restrictions as other class members.

3. An inner class can access its outer class's `this` reference with an expression of the form *OuterClassName*`.this`.

4. The outer class is responsible for creating objects of its inner classes. To create an object of another class's inner class, first create an object of the outer class and assign its reference to a variable of the outer class type (we will call it `ref`). Then use a statement of the following form to create an inner-class object:

   OuterClassName`.`*InnerClassName* `innerRef = ref.new` *InnerClassName*`();`

5. A `static` nested class does not require an object of its outer class to be created (whereas an inner class does). A static nested class does not have access to its outer class's non-`static` members.

10.10 Type-Wrapper Classes for Primitive Types

As we saw in Section 3.5, each of the primitive types has a corresponding *type-wrapper class* (in package `java.lang`). These classes are called `Character`, `Byte`, `Short`, `Integer`, `Long`, `Float`, `Double` and `Boolean`. Each type-wrapper class enables you to manipulate primitive-type values as objects. Therefore, values of the primitive types can be processed polymorphically if they are maintained as objects of the type-wrapper classes. Many of the classes we will develop or reuse manipulate and share `Object`s. These classes cannot polymorphically manipulate variables of primitive types, but they can polymorphically manipulate objects of the type-wrapper classes, because every class ultimately is derived from class `Object`.

Each of the numeric type-wrapper classes—`Byte`, `Short`, `Integer`, `Long`, `Float` and `Double`—extends class `Number`. Each of the type wrappers is declared `final`, so their methods are implicitly `final` and may not be overridden. Note that many of the methods that process primitive types are declared as `static` methods of the type-wrapper classes. If you need to manipulate a primitive value in your program, first refer to the documentation for the type-wrapper classes—the method you need might already be declared. We will use the type-wrapper classes polymorphically in our study of data structures in Chapter 20–Chapter 22.

10.11 (Optional Case Study) Thinking About Objects: Incorporating Inheritance into the Elevator Simulation

We now revisit our elevator-simulator design to see how it might benefit from inheritance. To apply inheritance, we first look for commonality among classes in the simulation. We begin by examining the similarities between classes `FloorButton` and `ElevatorButton`. Figure 10.24 shows the attributes and operations of each class. Both classes have their attribute (`pressed`) and operations (`pressButton` and `resetButton`) in common.

We might be tempted to use inheritance in this situation—i.e., to extract the commonality between classes `FloorButton` and `ElevatorButton`, place this commonality into a common superclass `Button`, then derive subclasses `FloorButton` and `ElevatorButton` from class `Button`. However, if the `FloorButton` and `ElevatorButton` objects have the exact same behavior, then we cannot justify using inheritance. In fact, we cannot even justify using two separate classes for these objects! The `FloorButton` signals the `Elevator` to move to the `Floor` of the request. The `ElevatorButton` signals the `Elevator` to move to the opposite `Floor`. As shown in the activity diagram of Fig. 5.29, the `FloorButton` and the `ElevatorButton` signal the `Elevator` to move to a `Floor`. The `Elevator` moves in response to a `FloorButton`'s signal only if the `Elevator` is on the opposite

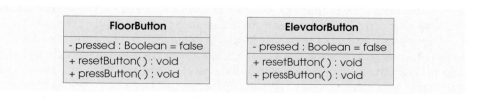

Fig. 10.24   Attributes and operations of classes `FloorButton` and `ElevatorButton`.

Floor of the request and the Elevator is idle. The Elevator moves in response to a signal from the ElevatorButton only if the Elevator is idle. However, neither the FloorButton nor the ElevatorButton orders the Elevator to move to the other Floor. Rather, the Elevator responds to a button signal depending on the Elevator's current state. Each button has only one behavior—to signal the Elevator to move. The FloorButton and ElevatorButton objects are really just different objects of the same class, so we combine classes FloorButton and ElevatorButton into class Button and discard classes FloorButton and ElevatorButton from our case study.

Software Engineering Observation 10.13

If several objects have the same attributes and exhibit identical behaviors, they are probably objects of the same class. Before using inheritance in your programs, make sure that each class has distinct attributes and/or exhibits distinct behaviors, but still "is an" object of its superclass.

Now we begin looking for classes that exhibit similar (but not identical) behaviors. In Section 4.14, we encountered the problem of representing the location of the Person—on what Floor is the Person located when riding in the Elevator? Using inheritance, we can now model a solution. Both the Elevator and the two Floors are locations at which the Person exists in the simulator. In other words, the Elevator and the Floors are *types of* locations, but an Elevator is certainly not a Floor.

We modify classes Elevator and Floor to inherit from a new superclass called Location. The UML specifies a relationship called a *generalization* to model inheritance. Figure 10.25 is the class diagram that models the generalization of superclass Location and subclasses Elevator and Floor. The arrows with empty arrowheads indicate that classes Elevator and Floor inherit from class Location. Class Location contains the private attribute locationName, which contains a String value of "firstFloor", "secondFloor" or "elevator". We include method setLocationName so each subclass can set the appropriate String value. Note that method setLocationName has an access modifier that we have not yet seen—the pound sign (#), indicating that method setLocationName is protected, so only subclasses Elevator and Floor can use this method to set their locationNames. In addition, we include the public method getLocationName, so any object can obtain the name of the Location.

We search for more similarities between classes Floor and Elevator. According to the class diagram of Fig. 6.20, both classes share integer attribute capacity (which equals 1). Now, class Location contains private attribute capacity, which represents the maximum number of Persons that can occupy that location. In our simulation, this attribute will not change in execution, so class Location declares attribute capacity as a constant by using the term {frozen} next to attribute capacity. Class Location also contains public method getCapacity, which returns the capacity value. Class Location does not require method setCapacity, because attribute capacity cannot be changed. Subclasses Floor and Elevator inherit attribute capacity and method getCapacity.

We continue searching for similarities. According to Fig. 3.19, class Elevator contains references to its Button and its Door. Class Floor contains references to its Button and its Door through the Floor's association with class ElevatorShaft—class ElevatorModel aggregates classes Floor and ElevatorShaft and can pass an ElevatorShaft reference to class Floor's constructor. Using this association, class Floor can reference the ElevatorShaft's Button and Door. Therefore, in our simulation, the

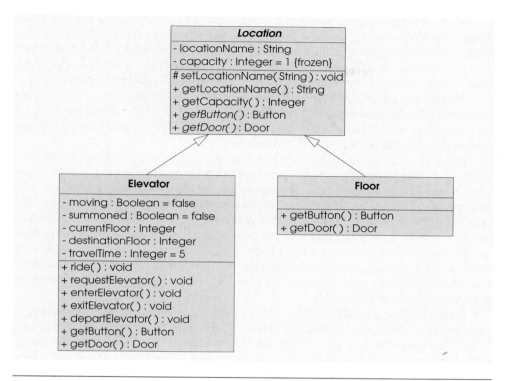

Fig. 10.25   Class diagram modeling generalization of superclass `Location` and subclasses `Elevator` and `Floor`.

`Location` class will contain `public` methods `getButton` and `getDoor` that return `Button` and `Door` references, respectively. Class `Floor` overrides these methods to return the `Button` and `Door` references of that `Floor`, and class `Elevator` overrides these methods to return the `Button` and `Door` references of the `Elevator`.[2] We declare class `Location` as `abstract` to require subclasses `Floor` and `Elevator` to implement methods `getButton` and `getDoor`. The UML recommends that we place abstract class names (and abstract methods) in italics, so we place class `Location` and its methods `getButton` and `getDoor` in italics in Fig. 10.25. However, methods `getButton` and `getDoor` are not italicized in subclasses `Floor` and `Elevator`—these methods are concrete because they override and implement the abstract methods. Each concrete method has a distinct implementation here (i.e., class `Elevator` implements methods `getButton` and `getDoor` differently than does class `Floor`). Note that classes `Elevator` and `Floor` provide operations `getButton` and `getDoor` in their third compartment, because each class has different implementations of the overridden method.

---

2.   Most methods introduced in this chapter—such as method `getRadius` (Fig. 10.8) or `getHeight` (Fig. 10.9)—return primitive values, whereas methods `getButton` and `getDoor` of classes `Elevator` and `Floor` return references to a `Button` and `Door` object, respectively.

In this simulation, using inheritance seems appropriate for designing `Elevator` and `Floor`. Each class represents a `Location` that the `Person` can occupy. However, class `Elevator` contains additional attributes and methods that distinguish it from class `Floor`.

We introduce an association between class `Person` and class `Location` that represents whether the `Person` is on the first or second `Floor`, or inside the `Elevator`.

We now turn our attention to classes `ElevatorDoor` and `FloorDoor`. Once again, we consider whether to use inheritance with these classes. Fig. 10.26 shows that the attributes and operations of each class are identical to each other—both classes possess attribute `open` and operations `openDoor` and `closeDoor`.

However, based on the problem statement, we know that `ElevatorDoor` and `FloorDoor` have different behavior. When the `ElevatorDoor` opens, it must open the `FloorDoor` to ensure that the doors open in tandem. Class `FloorDoor` has the basic attributes and operations needed for all doors, so we rename class `FloorDoor` to class `Door`. This new Door class represents a generalization of the doors in our case study. Class `ElevatorDoor` represents a "special case" of the more general Door class—an `ElevatorDoor` has the responsibility of opening another `Door` when the `ElevatorDoor` opens. Therefore, we establish a generalization relationship between class `ElevatorDoor` and class `Door`. Class `ElevatorDoor` overrides methods `openDoor` and `closeDoor` to implement the specialized behavior (Fig. 10.27).

Figure 10.28 is an updated class diagram of our model that reflects these changes, incorporates inheritance, eliminates classes `FloorButton`, `ElevatorButton` and `FloorDoor` and introduces classes `Button`, `Door` and `Location`. We remove the association between `Person` and `Elevator` and the association between `Person` and `Floor` from the class diagram, because the `Person`'s `Location` reference can act as either an `Elevator` or a `Floor` reference. A `Person` sets its `Location` reference to the `Elevator` when that `Person` enters the `Elevator`. A `Person` sets its `Location` reference to a `Floor` when the `Person` walks onto that particular `Floor`. Lastly, we assign class `Elevator` two `Location` references, representing the `Elevator`'s current `Floor` and the destination `Floor`. (We originally used integers to describe these references in Fig. 4.18.)

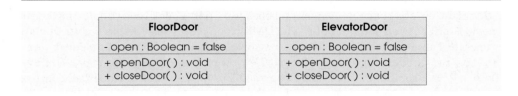

Fig. 10.26 Attributes and operations of classes `FloorDoor` and `ElevatorDoor`.

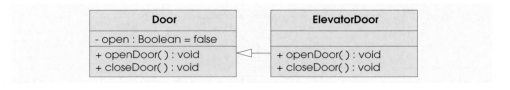

Fig. 10.27 Generalization of superclass `Door` and subclass `ElevatorDoor`.

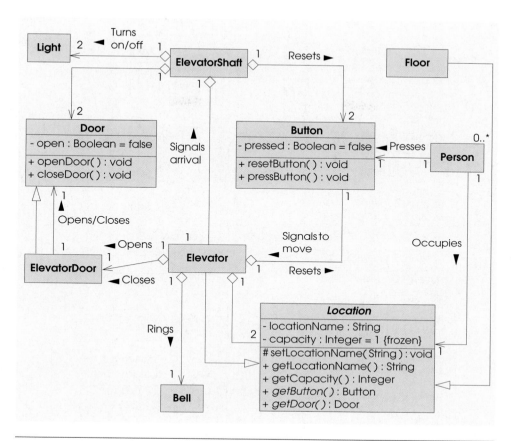

Fig. 10.28   Class diagram of our simulator (incorporating inheritance).

We allow a `Person` occupying a `Location` to interact with several of the objects (accessible from that `Location`) in the simulator. For example, a `Person` can press a `Button` from that `Person`'s specific `Location`. A `Person` can occupy only one `Location` at a time, so that `Person` should be restricted to interacting with only the objects known to that `Location`. Using its `Location` reference, a `Person` cannot perform an illegal action, such as pressing the first `Floor`'s `Button` while riding the `Elevator`. This restriction mimics a real-world situation in that a person cannot press a button on a floor when riding an elevator, and cannot press a button inside the elevator when walking on a floor.

We presented the class attributes and operations with access modifiers in the class diagram of Fig. 8.19. Now, we present a modified class diagram incorporating inheritance in Fig. 10.29. This abbreviated diagram does not show inheritance relationships, but instead shows the attributes and methods after we have employed inheritance in our system. This diagram does not include those attributes shown by aggregations in Fig. 10.28 for classes `ElevatorShaft` and `Elevator`. As we did in Fig. 4.18, we chose to save space in Fig. 10.29 by not showing these additional attributes—we will, however, include them in the Java implementation in the appendices.

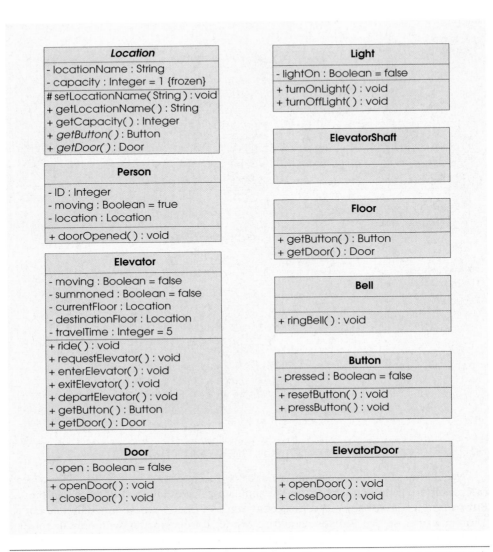

Fig. 10.29   Class diagram with attributes and operations (incorporating inheritance).

Software Engineering Observation 10.14

A complete class diagram shows all associations among classes and all attributes and oper-ations for each class. When the number of class attributes, methods and associations is sub-stantial (as in Fig. 10.28 and Fig. 10.29), common practice is to divide this information between two class diagrams: One focusing on associations, the other focusing on attributes and methods. Creating two class diagrams in this manner promotes readability.

Class Person now contains a reference to a Location object—location—that indicates whether Person is on a Floor or in the Elevator.

Implementation: Forward Engineering (Incorporating Inheritance)
In Section 8.17, we used the UML to express the Java class structure for our simulation. We continue our implementation while incorporating inheritance, using class `Elevator` as an example.

1. If a class B is a generalization of class A, then class A extends class B in the class declaration. For example, abstract superclass `Location` is a generalization of class `Elevator`, so the class declaration should read

    ```
    public class Elevator extends Location {

        // constructor
        public Elevator() {}
    }
    ```

2. If class B is an abstract class and class A is a subclass of class B, then class A must implement the abstract methods of class B (if class A is to be a concrete class). For example, class `Location` contains abstract methods `getButton` and `getDoor`, so class `Elevator` must implement these methods, because we want to instantiate an `Elevator` object. Figure 10.30 is the Java code for class `Elevator` from Fig. 10.28 and Fig. 10.29. Note that method `getButton` (lines 26–29) returns a reference to the `Elevator`'s `Button` object, and method `getDoor` (lines 32–35) returns a reference to the `Elevator`'s `Door` object—`Elevator` has associations with both objects, according to the class diagram of Fig. 10.28. Class `Elevator` inherits fields `capacity` and `locationName`, and nonabstract methods `get-Capacity`, `setLocationName` and `getLocationName` from superclass `Location`, so we do not need to declare these fields and methods in class `Elevator`. Figure 10.29 specifies attributes `moving`, `summoned`, `currentFloor`, `destinationFloor` and `travelTime` and operations `ride`, `requestElevator`, `enterElevator`, `exitElevator` and `departElevator` for class `Elevator`. Lines 6–10 of Fig. 10.30 declare fields for these attributes, and lines 19–23 declare methods for these operations. The `elevatorButton`, `elevatorDoor` and `bell` references (lines 11–13) are fields specified from `Elevator`'s aggregations in Fig. 10.28.

```
1   // Elevator.java
2   // Generated using class diagrams 10.28 and 10.29
3   public class Elevator extends Location {
4
5       // attributes
6       private boolean moving;
7       private boolean summoned;
8       private Location currentFloor;
9       private Location destinationFloor;
10      private int travelTime = 5;
11      private Button elevatorButton;
12      private Door elevatorDoor;
13      private Bell bell;
```

Fig. 10.30 Class `Elevator` is generated by Fig. 10.28 and Fig. 10.29. (Part 1 of 2.)

```
14
15        // constructor
16        public Elevator() {}
17
18        // operations
19        public void ride() {}
20        public void requestElevator() {}
21        public void enterElevator() {}
22        public void exitElevator() {}
23        public void departElevator() {}
24
25        // method overriding getButton
26        public Button getButton()
27        {
28            return elevatorButton;
29        }
30
31        // method overriding getDoor
32        public Door getDoor()
33        {
34            return elevatorDoor;
35        }
36    }
```

Fig. 10.30   Class `Elevator` is generated by Fig. 10.28 and Fig. 10.29. (Part 2 of 2.)

Error-Prevention Tip 10.1

Using UML modeling tools to generate code automatically helps reduce the amount of programming errors programmers tend to introduce when writing code manually.

Software Engineering Observation 10.15

Several UML modeling tools convert UML-based designs into Java. These tools can speed the implementation process considerably.[3]

We have provided a sound beginning for implementing UML-based designs in Java. In Section 11.9, we will return to interactions, focusing on how objects generate and handle the messages passed in collaborations, and we will forward engineer more class diagrams into Java code. We present completely implemented Java code for our simulator in Appendix D, Appendix E and Appendix F.

10.12 (Optional) Discovering Design Patterns: Introducing Creational, Structural and Behavioral Design Patterns

Now that we have introduced object-oriented programming, we begin our deeper presentation of design patterns. In Section 1.16, we mentioned that the "Gang of Four" described 23 design patterns using three categories—creational, structural and behavioral. In this and the remaining "Discovering Design Patterns" sections, we discuss the design patterns in each category and their importance, and how each pattern relates to the Java material in the

---

3. For more information on these tools, refer to the Internet and World Wide Web Resources listed at the end of Section 2.9.

book. For example, several Java Swing components that we introduce in Chapter 13 and Chapter 14 use the Composite design pattern, so we introduce the Composite design pattern in Section 10.12. Figure 10.31 identifies the 18 Gang of Four design patterns discussed in this book.

Figure 10.31 lists 18 of the most widely used patterns in the software-engineering industry. There are many popular patterns that have been documented since the Gang of Four book—these include the *concurrent design patterns*, which are especially helpful in the design of multithreaded systems. Section 16.12 discusses some of these patterns used in industry. Architectural patterns, as we discuss in Section 18.12, specify how subsystems interact with each other. Figure 10.32 lists the concurrency patterns and architectural patterns that we discuss in this book.

10.12.1 Creational Design Patterns

Creational design patterns address issues related to the creation of objects, such as preventing a system from creating more than one object of a class (the Singleton creational design pattern) or deferring until execution time the decision as to what types of objects are going to be created (the purpose of the other creational design patterns discussed here). For example, suppose we are designing a 3-D drawing program, in which the user can create several 3-D geometric objects, such as cylinders, spheres, cubes, tetrahedrons, etc. Further

Section	Creational design patterns	Structural design patterns	Behavioral design patterns
10.12	Singleton	Proxy	Memento, State
14.14	Factory Method	Adapter, Bridge, Composite	Chain of Responsibility, Command, Observer, Strategy, Template Method
18.12	Abstract Factory	Decorator, Facade	
22.12	Prototype		Iterator

Fig. 10.31   18 Gang of Four design patterns discussed in *Java How to Program 5/e.*

Section	Concurrent design patterns	Architectural patterns
16.12	Single-Threaded Execution, Guarded Suspension, Balking, Read/Write Lock, Two-Phase Termination	
18.12		Model-View-Controller, Layers

Fig. 10.32   Concurrent design patterns and architectural patterns discussed in *Java How to Program, 5/e.*

suppose that each shape in the drawing program is represented by an object. At compile time, the program does not know what shapes the user will choose to draw. Based on user input, this program should be able to determine the class from which to instantiate an appropriate object for the shape the user selected. If the user creates a cylinder in the GUI, our program should "know" to instantiate an object of class Cylinder. When the user decides what geometric object to draw, the program should determine the specific subclass from which to instantiate that object.

The Gang of Four book describes five creational patterns (four of which we discuss in this book):

- Abstract Factory (Section 18.12)
- Builder (not discussed)
- Factory Method (Section 14.14)
- Prototype (Section 22.12)
- Singleton (Section 10.12)

Singleton

Occasionally, a system should contain exactly one object of a class—that is, once the program instantiates that object, the program should not be allowed to create additional objects of that class. For example, some systems connect to a database using only one object that manages database connections, which ensures that other objects cannot initialize unnecessary connections that would slow the system. The *Singleton design pattern* guarantees that a system instantiates a maximum of one object of a class.

Figure 10.33 demonstrates Java code using the Singleton design pattern. Line 4 declares class Singleton as final, so subclasses cannot be created that could provide multiple instantiations. Lines 10–13 declare a private constructor—only class Singleton can instantiate a Singleton object using this constructor. Line 7 declares a static reference to a Singleton object and invokes the private constructor. This creates the one instance of class Singleton that will be provided to clients. When invoked, static method getSingletonInstance (lines 16–19) simply returns a copy of this reference.

```
1   // Singleton.java
2   // Demonstrates Singleton design pattern
3
4   public final class Singleton {
5
6       // Singleton object to be returned by getSingletonInstance
7       private static final Singleton singleton = new Singleton();
8
9       // private constructor prevents instantiation by clients
10      private Singleton()
11      {
12          System.err.println( "Singleton object created." );
13      }
```

Fig. 10.33 Class Singleton ensures that only one object of its class is created (Part 1 of 2.).

```
14
15        // return static Singleton object
16        public static Singleton getInstance()
17        {
18            return singleton;
19        }
20    }
```

Fig. 10.33 Class Singleton ensures that only one object of its class is created (Part 2 of 2.).

Lines 9–10 of class SingletonTest (Fig. 10.34) declare two references to Singleton objects—firstSingleton and secondSingleton. Lines 13–14 call method getSingletonInstance and assign Singleton references to firstSingleton and secondSingleton, respectively. Line 17 tests whether these references both refer to the same Singleton object. Figure 10.34 shows that firstSingleton and secondSingleton indeed are both references to the same Singleton object, because each time method getSingletonInstance is called, it returns a reference to the same Singleton object.

```
1     // SingletonTest.java
2     // Attempt to create two Singleton objects
3
4     public class SingletonTest {
5
6         // run SingletonExample
7         public static void main( String args[] )
8         {
9             Singleton firstSingleton;
10            Singleton secondSingleton;
11
12            // create Singleton objects
13            firstSingleton = Singleton.getInstance();
14            secondSingleton = Singleton.getInstance();
15
16            // the "two" Singletons should refer to same Singleton
17            if ( firstSingleton == secondSingleton )
18                System.err.println( "firstSingleton and secondSingleton " +
19                    "refer to the same Singleton object" );
20        }
21    }
```

```
Singleton object created.
firstSingleton and secondSingleton refer to the same Singleton object
```

Fig. 10.34 Class SingletonTest attempts to create Singleton object more than once.

10.12.2 Structural Design Patterns

Structural design patterns describe common ways to organize classes and objects in a system. The Gang of Four book describes seven structural design patterns (six of which we discuss in this book):

- Adapter (Section 14.14)
- Bridge (Section 14.14)
- Composite (Section 14.14)
- Decorator (Section 18.12)
- Facade (Section 18.12)
- Flyweight (not discussed)
- Proxy (Section 10.12)

Proxy

An applet should always display something while images load to provide positive feedback to users, so they know the applet is working. Whether that "something" is a smaller image or a string of text informing the user that the images are loading, the *Proxy design pattern* can be applied to achieve this effect. This pattern allows one object to act as a replacement for another. Consider loading several large images (several megabytes) in a Java applet. Ideally, we would like to see these images instantaneously—however, loading large images into memory can take time to complete (especially across a network). The Proxy design pattern allows the system to use one object—called a *proxy object*—in place of another. In our example, the proxy object could be a gauge that informs the user of what percentage of a large image has been loaded. When this image finishes loading, the proxy object is no longer needed—the applet can then display an image instead of the proxy. Class `javax.swing.JProgressBar` can be used to create such proxy objects.

10.12.3 Behavioral Design Patterns

There are many examples of *behavioral design patterns*, which provide proven strategies to model how objects collaborate with one another in a system and offer special behaviors appropriate for a wide variety of applications. Let us consider the Observer behavioral design pattern—a classic example of a design pattern illustrating collaborations between objects. For example, GUI components collaborate with their listeners to respond to user interactions. GUI components use this pattern to process user interface events. A listener observes state changes in a particular GUI component by registering to handle that GUI component's events. When the user interacts with that GUI component, the component notifies its listeners (also known as its observers) that the GUI component's state has changed (e.g., a button has been pressed).

We also consider the Memento behavioral design pattern—an example of offering special behavior for many applications. The Memento pattern enables a system to save an object's state, so that state can be restored at a later time. For example, many applications provide an "undo" capability that allows users to revert to previous versions of their work.

The Gang of Four book describes 11 behavioral design patterns (eight of which we discuss in this book):

- Chain of Responsibility (Section 14.14)
- Command (Section 14.14)
- Interpreter (not discussed)
- Iterator (Section 22.12)
- Mediator (not discussed)
- Memento (Section 10.12)
- Observer (Section 14.14)
- State (Section 10.12)
- Strategy (Section 14.14)
- Template Method (Section 14.14)
- Visitor (not discussed)

Memento

Consider a painting program. This type of program allows a user to create graphics. Occasionally the user may position a graphic improperly in the drawing area. Painting programs offer an "undo" feature that allows the user to unwind such an error. Specifically, the program restores the drawing area's state to that before the user placed the graphic. More sophisticated painting programs offer a *history*, which stores several states in a list, so the user can restore the program to any state in the history. The *Memento design pattern* allows an object to save its state, so that—if necessary—the object can be restored to its former state.

The Memento design pattern requires three types of objects. The *originator object* occupies some *state*—the set of attribute values at a specific time in program execution. In our painting-program example, the drawing area acts as the originator, because it contains attribute information describing its state—when the program first executes, the area contains no elements. The *memento object* stores a copy of necessary attributes associated with the originator's state (i.e., the memento saves the drawing area's state). The memento is stored as the first item in the history list, which acts as the *caretaker object*—the object that contains references to all memento objects associated with the originator.   Now, suppose that the user draws a circle in the drawing area. The area contains different information describing its state—a circle object centered at specified *x–y* coordinates. The drawing area then uses another memento to store this information. This memento becomes the second item in the history list. The history list displays all mementos on screen, so the user can select which state to restore. Suppose that the user wishes to remove the circle—if the user selects the first memento from the list, the drawing area uses the first memento to restore the blank drawing area.

State

In certain designs, we must convey an object's state information or represent the various states that an object can occupy. Our optional elevator simulation case study in the "Thinking About Objects" sections uses the *State design pattern*. Our simulation includes an elevator that moves between floors in a two-story building. A person walks across a floor and rides the elevator to the other floor. Originally, we used an integer value to represent on which floor the person is walking. However, we encountered a problem when we tried to answer the question "on what floor is the person when riding the elevator?" Actually, the person is located on neither floor—rather the person is located inside the elevator. We also realized that the elevator and the floors are locations that the person can occupy in our simulation. We created an abstract superclass called `Location` to represent a "location." Subclasses `Elevator` and `Floor` inherit from superclass `Location`. Class `Person` contains a reference to a `Location` object, which represents the current location—elevator, first floor or second floor—of that person. Because a superclass reference can hold a subclass reference, the person's `Location` attribute references the appropriate `Floor` object when that person is on a floor and references the `Elevator` object when that person is inside the elevator.

The elevator and floors contain buttons. (The elevator's button signals the elevator to move to the other floor, and the floors' buttons summon the elevator to the floor of the request.) Because all locations in our simulation contain buttons, class `Location` provides abstract method `getButton`. Class `Elevator` implements method `getButton` to return a reference to the `Button` object inside the elevator, and class `Floor` implements method `getButton` to return a reference to the `Button` object on the floor. Using its `Location` reference, the person is able to press the correct button (i.e., the person will not press a floor's button when inside the elevator and will not press the elevator's button when on a floor).

The State design pattern uses an abstract superclass—called the *State class*—which contains methods that describe behaviors for states that an object (called the *context object*) can occupy. In our elevator simulation, the State class is superclass `Location`, and the context object is the object of class `Person`. Note that class `Location` does not describe all states of class `Person` (e.g., whether that person is walking or waiting for the elevator)—class `Location` describes only the location of the `Person` and contains method `getButton` so the `Person` can access the `Button` object at various locations.

A *State subclass*, which extends the State class, represents an individual state that the context can occupy. The State subclasses in our simulation are `Elevator` and `Floor`. Each State subclass contains methods that implement the State class's abstract methods. For example, both classes `Elevator` and `Floor` implement method `getButton`.

The context contains exactly one reference to an object of the State class—this object is called the *state object*. In the simulation, the state object is the object of class `Location`. When the context changes state, the state object references the State subclass object associated with that new state. For example, when the person walks from the floor into the elevator, the `Person` object's `Location` is changed from referencing one of the `Floor` objects to referencing the `Elevator` object. When the person walks onto the floor from the elevator, the `Person` object's `Location` references the appropriate `Floor` object.

10.12.4 Conclusion

In "Discovering Design Patterns," Section 10.12, we listed the three types of design patterns introduced in the Gang of Four book, we identified 18 of these design patterns that we discuss in this book and we discussed specific design patterns, including Singleton, Proxy, Memento and State. In "Discovering Design Patterns," Section 14.14, we introduce some design patterns associated with AWT and Swing GUI components. After reading this section, you should understand better how Java GUI components take advantage of design patterns.

10.12.5 Internet and World-Wide-Web Resources

The following URLs provide further information on the nature, importance and applications of design patterns.

Design Patterns

www.hillside.net/patterns
This page displays links to information on design patterns and languages.

www.hillside.net/patterns/books/
This site lists books on design patterns.

www.netobjectives.com/design.htm
This site introduces the importance of design patterns.

umbc7.umbc.edu/~tarr/dp/dp.html
This site links to design patterns Web sites, tutorials and papers.

www.c2.com/ppr/
This site discusses recent advances in design patterns and ideas for future projects.

Design Patterns in Java

www.enteract.com/~bradapp/javapats.html
This site discusses Java design patterns and presents design patterns in distributed computing.

Design Patterns in C++ & Visual Basic

mspress.microsoft.com/prod/books/sampchap/2322.htm
This site overviews the book, *Microsoft Visual Basic Design Patterns* (Microsoft Press: 2000).

Architectural Patterns

www.javaworld.com/javaworld/jw-04-1998/jw-04-howto.html
This site contains an article discussing how Swing components use Model-View-Controller architecture.

www.ootips.org/mvc-pattern.html
This site provides information and tips on using MVC.

www.ftech.co.uk/~honeyg/articles/pda.htm
This site contains an article on the importance of architectural patterns in software.

www.tml.hut.fi/Opinnot/Tik-109.450/1998/niska/sld001.htm
This site provides information on architectural patterns, design pattern, and idioms (patterns targeting a specific language).

SUMMARY

- With polymorphism, it becomes possible to design and implement systems that are more easily extensible. Programs can be written to process objects of types that might not exist when the program is under development.

- There are many situations in which it is useful to declare abstract classes for which the programmer never intends to create objects. Because these are used only as superclasses, we refer to them as abstract superclasses. No objects of an abstract class may be created.

- Classes from which objects can be created are called concrete classes.

- A class must be declared abstract if one or more of its methods abstract. An abstract method is a method with keyword abstract in its declaration.

- If a class extends a class with an `abstract` method and does not implement that `abstract` method, then that method remains `abstract` in the subclass. Consequently, the subclass is also an `abstract` class and must be declared `abstract`.

- Java enables polymorphism—the ability for objects of different classes related by inheritance or interface implementation to respond differently to the same method call.

- When a request is made through a superclass reference to use an `abstract` method, Java chooses the correct overridden method in the object's subclass.

- Although we cannot instantiate objects of `abstract` classes, we can declare variables of abstract-class types. Such variables can be used to reference subclass objects.

- New kinds of classes are regularly added to systems. New classes are accommodated by dynamic binding (also called late binding). The type of an object need not be known at compile time for a method call to be compiled. At execution time, the appropriate method will be called on the object to which the reference refers.

- Operator `instanceof` checks the type of the object to which its left operand refers and determines whether this type has an *is-a* relationship with the type specified as its right operand. If the two have an *is-a* relationship, `instanceof` returns `true`. If not, `instanceof` returns `false`.

- Every object in Java knows its own class and can access this information through method `getClass`, which all classes inherit from class `Object`. Method `getClass` returns an object of type `Class` (package `java.lang`), which contains information about the object's type, including its class name. `Class` method `getName` returns the name of the class.

- An interface declaration begins with the keyword `interface` and contains a set of `public abstract` methods. Interfaces may also contain `public static final` fields.

- To use an interface, a class must specify that it `implements` the interface and must declare every method in the interface with the signatures specified in the interface declaration.

- An interface is typically used in place of an `abstract` class when there is no default implementation to inherit.

- When a class implements an interface, it establishes an "is a" relationship with the interface type.

- To implement more than one interface, simply provide a comma-separated list of interface names after keyword `implements` in the class declaration.

- Nested classes are declared inside other classes.

- An inner-class has access to all the variables and methods of its outer class.

- An inner class can be declared inside a method. Such an inner class has access to its outer class's members and to the `final` local variables for the method in which it is declared.

- Inner classes are used mainly in event handling.

- An anonymous inner class has no name and is declared at the point in the program where an object of the class is created.

- An anonymous inner class can implement an interface or extend a class.

- Compiling a class that contains nested classes results in a separate `.class` file for every declared class.

- Inner classes can be declared as `public`, `protected`, package access or `private` and are subject to the same usage restrictions as other members of a class.

- To access the outer class's `this` reference in an inner class, use *OuterClassName*`.this`.

- An inner class is a nested class that is not declared `static`.

- Class `JFrame` provides the basic attributes and behaviors of a window—a title bar and buttons to minimize, maximize and close the window.

- The event generated when the user clicks the window's close box is a window-closing event.
- Method addWindowListener registers a window event listener. The argument to addWindow-Listener must be a reference to an object that *is a* WindowListener.
- For event-handling interfaces with more than one method, Java provides a corresponding adapter class that already implements all the methods in the interface for you. Class WindowAdapter implements interface WindowListener, so every WindowAdapter object *is a* WindowListener.

TERMINOLOGY

abstract class
abstract keyword
abstract method
abstract superclass
anonymous inner class
Boolean class
Byte class
Character class
Class class
class hierarchy
concrete class
constant in an interface
Double class
downcasting
dynamic method binding
extensibility
final class
final instance variable
final method
Float class
getClass method of Object
getName method of Class
implements keyword
implementation inheritance
implement an interface
inner class
instanceof operator
Integer class

interface
interface inheritance
interface keyword
JFrame class
late binding
Long class
nested class
Number class
override an abstract method
polymorphism
programming "in the general"
programming "in the specific"
reference
reference to an abstract class
reference type
setDefaultCloseOperation method
　　of JFrame
setSize method of class Component
setVisible method of class Component
Short class
static binding
superclass abstract method
type-wrapper class
variable of a superclass type
WindowAdapter class
windowClosing method of WindowListener
WindowEvent class
WindowListener interface

SELF-REVIEW EXERCISES

10.1   Fill in the blanks in each of the following statements:
 a) Treating a superclass object as a(n) _____ can cause errors.
 b) Polymorphism helps eliminate _____ logic.
 c) If a class contains at least one abstract method, it is a(n) _____ class.
 d) Classes from which objects can be instantiated are called _____ classes.
 e) _____ involves using a superclass variable to invoke methods on superclass and subclass objects.
 f) Abstract methods are declared using keyword _____.
 g) Casting a superclass object to a subclass object is called _____.

10.2   State whether each of the statements that follows is *true* or *false*. If *false*, explain why.
 a) It is possible to treat superclass objects and subclass objects similarly.

b) All methods in an abstract class must be declared as abstract methods.
c) Referring to a subclass object with a superclass variable is dangerous.
d) A class is made abstract by declaring it abstract.
e) If a superclass declares an abstract method, a subclass must implement that method to become a concrete class.
f) Inner classes are not allowed to access the members of the enclosing class.

ANSWERS TO SELF-REVIEW EXERCISES

10.1   a) subclass object. b) switch. c) abstract. d) concrete. e) Polymorphism. f) abstract. g) downcasting.

10.2   a) True. b) False. An abstract class can include methods with implementations. c) False. Referring to a superclass object with a subclass variable is dangerous. d) True. e) True. f) False. Inner classes have access to all members of the enclosing class declaration.

EXERCISES

10.3   How is it that polymorphism enables you to program "in the general" rather than "in the specific"? Discuss the key advantages of programming "in the general."

10.4   Distinguish between inheriting interface and inheriting implementation. How do inheritance hierarchies designed for inheriting interface differ from those designed for inheriting implementation?

10.5   What are abstract methods? Describe a circumstance in which abstract methods would be appropriate.

10.6   How does polymorphism promote extensibility?

10.7   Modify the payroll system of Fig. 10.12–Fig. 10.17 to include private instance variable birthDate (use class Date) in class Employee. Assume that payroll is processed once per month. Create an array of Employee variables to store references to the various employee objects. In a loop, calculate the payroll for each Employee (polymorphically), and add a $100.00 bonus to the person's payroll amount if the current month is the month in which the Employee's birthday occurs.

10.8   Implement the Shape hierarchy shown in Fig. 9.3. Each TwoDimensionalShape should contain method getArea to calculate the area of the two-dimensional shape. Each ThreeDimensionalShape should have methods getArea and getVolume to calculate the surface area and volume, respectively, of the three-dimensional shape, respectively. Create a program that uses an array of Shape references to objects of each concrete class in the hierarchy. The program should print the object to which each array element refers. Also, in the loop that processes all the shapes in the array, determine whether each shape is a TwoDimensionalShape or a ThreeDimensionalShape. If a shape is a TwoDimensionalShape, display its area. If a shape is a ThreeDimensionalShape, display its area and volume.

10.9   (Drawing Application) Modify the drawing program of Exercise 8.18 to create an application that draws random lines, rectangles and ovals. [Note: Like an applet, a JFrame has a paint method that you can override to draw on the background of the JFrame.]
    For this exercise, modify the MyLine, MyOval and MyRectangle classes of Exercise 8.18 to create the class hierarchy in Fig. 10.35. The classes of the MyShape hierarchy should be "smart" shape classes such that objects of these classes know how to draw themselves (if provided with a Graphics object that tells them where to draw). The only switch or if...else logic in your program should be to determine the type of shape object to create. (Use random numbers to pick the shape type and the coordinates of each shape.) Once an object from this hierarchy is created, it will be manipulated for the rest of its lifetime as a superclass MyShape reference.

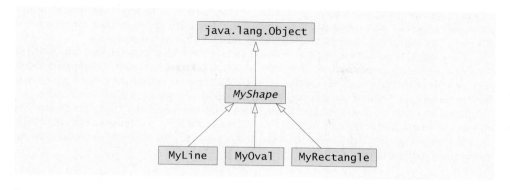

Fig. 10.35 MyShape hierarchy.

Class MyShape in Fig. 10.35 *must* be abstract. The only data representing the coordinates of the shapes in the hierarchy should be declared in class MyShape. Lines, rectangles and ovals can all be drawn if you know two points in space. Lines require *x1*, *y1*, *x2* and *y2* coordinates. The drawLine method of the Graphics class will connect the two points supplied with a line. If you have the same four coordinate values (*x1*, *y1*, *x2* and *y2*) for ovals and rectangles, you can calculate the four arguments needed to draw them. Each requires an upper-left *x*-coordinate value (the minimum of the two *x*-coordinate values), an upper-left *y*-coordinate value (minimum of the two *y* coordinate values), a *width* (the absolute value of the difference between the two *x*-coordinate values and a *height* (the absolute value of difference between the two *y*-coordinate values). [*Note*: In Chapter 13, each *x,y* pair will be captured by using mouse events from mouse interactions between the user and the program's background. These coordinates will be stored in an appropriate shape object selected by the user. As you begin the exercise, you will use random coordinate values as arguments to the constructor.]

In addition to the common data, class MyShape should declare at least the following methods:

a) A constructor with no arguments that sets the coordinates to 0.

b) A constructor with arguments that sets the coordinates to the values supplied.

c) Set methods, for each individual piece of data, that allow the programmer to set any piece of data independently for a shape in the hierarchy (e.g., if you have an instance variable x1, you should have a method setX1).

d) Get methods, for each individual piece of data, that allow the programmer to retrieve any piece of data independently for a shape in the hierarchy (e.g., if you have an instance variable x1, you should have a method getX1).

e) The abstract method
```
public abstract void draw( Graphics g );
```
which will be called from the program's paint method to draw a shape on the screen.

The preceding methods are required. If you would like to provide more methods for flexibility, please do so. However, be sure that any method you declare in this class is a method that would be used by *all* shapes in the hierarchy.

All data *must* be private to class MyShape. This forces you to use proper encapsulation of the data and provide proper *set/get* methods to manipulate the data. You are not allowed to declare new data that can be derived from existing information. As explained previously, the upper-left *x*, upper-left *y*, *width* and *height* needed to draw an oval or a rectangle can be calculated if you already know two points in space. All subclasses of MyShape should provide two constructors that mimic those provided by class MyShape.

Objects of the MyOval and MyRectangle classes should not calculate their upper-left *x*-coordinate, upper-left *y*-coordinate, *width* or *height* until they are about to draw. Never modify the *x1*, *y1*, *x2* and *y2* coordinates of a MyOval or MyRectangle object to prepare to draw them. Instead, use the temporary results of the calculations described above. This will help us enhance the program in Chapter 13 by allowing the user to select each shape's coordinates with the mouse.

There should be no MyLine, MyOval or MyRectangle variables in the program—only MyShape variables that contain references to MyLine, MyOval and MyRectangle objects. The program should keep an array of MyShape variables containing all shapes. The program's paint method should walk through the array of MyShape variables and draw every shape (i.e., call every shape's draw method).

Begin by declaring class MyShape, class MyLine and an application to test your classes. The application should have a MyShape instance variable that can refer to one MyLine object (created in the application's constructor). The paint method (for your subclass of JFrame) should draw the shape with a statement like

```
currentShape.draw( g );
```

where currentShape is the MyShape reference and g is the Graphics object that the shape will use to draw itself on the background of the window.

Next, change the single MyShape reference into an array of MyShape references, and hard code several MyLine objects into the program for drawing. The application's paint method should walk through the array of shapes and draw every shape.

After the preceding part is working, you should declare the MyOval and MyRectangle classes and add objects of these classes into the existing array. For now, all the shape objects should be created in the constructor for your subclass of JFrame. In Chapter 13, we will create the objects when the user chooses a shape and begins drawing it with the mouse.

10.10   In Exercise 10.9, you created a MyShape hierarchy in which classes MyLine, MyOval and MyRectangle extend MyShape directly. If the hierarchy was properly designed, you should be able to see the tremendous similarities between the MyOval and MyRectangle classes. Redesign and re-implement the code for the MyOval and MyRectangle classes to "factor out" the common features into the abstract class MyBoundedShape to produce the hierarchy in Fig. 10.36.

Class MyBoundedShape should declare two constructors that mimic the constructors of class MyShape and should also declare methods that calculate the upper-left *x*-coordinate, upper-left *y*-coordinate, *width* and *height*. No new data pertaining to the dimensions of the shapes should be declared in this class. Remember, the values needed to draw an oval or a rectangle can be calculated from two *(x,y)* coordinates. If designed properly, the new MyOval and MyRectangle classes should each have two constructors and a draw method.

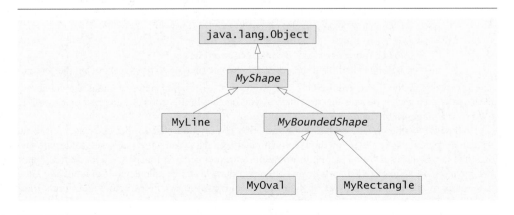

Fig. 10.36   MyShape hierarchy with MyBoundedShape.

11

Strings and Characters

Objectives

- To be able to create and manipulate nonmodifiable character string objects of class `String`.
- To be able to create and manipulate modifiable character string objects of class `StringBuffer`.
- To be able to create and manipulate objects of class `Character`.
- To be able to use a `StringTokenizer` object to break a `String` object into tokens.

The chief defect of Henry King
Was chewing little bits of string.
Hilaire Belloc

Vigorous writing is concise. A sentence should contain no unnecessary words, a paragraph no unnecessary sentences.
William Strunk, Jr.

I have made this letter longer than usual, because I lack the time to make it short.
Blaise Pascal

The difference between the almost-right word & the right word is really a large matter—it's the difference between the lightning bug and the lightning.
Mark Twain

Mum's the word.
Miguel de Cervantes

Outline

11.1 Introduction

This chapter introduces Java's string- and character-processing capabilities. The techniques discussed here are appropriate for validating program input, displaying information to users and other text-based manipulations. The techniques also are appropriate for developing text editors, word processors, page-layout software, computerized typesetting systems and other kinds of text-processing software. We have already presented several string-processing capabilities in earlier chapters. This chapter discusses in detail the capabilities of class *String*, class *StringBuffer* and class *Character* from the java.lang package and class *StringTokenizer* from the java.util package. These classes provide the foundation for string and character manipulation in Java.

11.2 Fundamentals of Characters and Strings

Characters are the fundamental building blocks of Java source programs. Every program is composed of a sequence of characters that—when grouped together meaningfully—is interpreted by the computer as a series of instructions used to accomplish a task. A program might contain *character literals.* A character literal is an integer value represented as a character in single quotes. For example, `'z'` represents the integer value of z, and `'\n'` represents the integer value of newline. The value of a character literal is the integer value of the character in the *Unicode character set.*[1]

Recall from Section 2.2 that a string is a sequence of characters treated as a single unit. A string may include letters, digits and various *special characters,* such as +, -, *, / and $. A string is an object of class `String`. *String literals* (stored in memory as *anonymous* `String` *objects*) are written as a sequence of characters in double quotation marks as in:

```
"John Q. Doe"              (a name)
"9999 Main Street"         (a street address)
"Waltham, Massachusetts"   (a city and state)
"(201) 555-1212"           (a telephone number)
```

A string may be assigned in a declaration to a `String` reference. The declaration

```
String color = "blue";
```

initializes `String` reference `color` to refer to an anonymous `String` object that contains the string `"blue"`.

Performance Tip 11.1

Java treats all string literals with the same contents as one anonymous `String` *object that has many references. This conserves memory.*

11.3 Class `String`

Class `String` is used to represent strings in Java. The next several subsections cover many of class `String`'s capabilities.

11.3.1 String Constructors

Class `String` provides nine constructors for initializing `String` objects several ways. Six of the constructors are demonstrated in the `main` method of Fig. 11.1.

Line 17 instantiates a new `String` object using class `String`'s default constructor and assigns its reference to s1. The new `String` object contains no characters (the *empty string*) and has a length of 0.

Line 18 instantiates a new `String` object using class `String`'s constructor that takes a String object as an argument and assigns its reference to s2. The new `String` object contains the same sequence of characters as the `String` object s that is passed as an argument to the constructor.

---

1. Appendix B presents the integer equivalents of the characters in the ASCII character set, which is a subset of Unicode. Appendix G discusses the Unicode character set. For detailed information on Unicode, visit `www.unicode.org`.

```java
1   // Fig. 11.1: StringConstructors.java
2   // String class constructors.
3   import javax.swing.*;
4
5   public class StringConstructors {
6
7      public static void main( String args[] )
8      {
9         char charArray[] = { 'b', 'i', 'r', 't', 'h', ' ', 'd', 'a', 'y' };
10        byte byteArray[] = { ( byte ) 'n', ( byte ) 'e',
11           ( byte ) 'w', ( byte ) ' ', ( byte ) 'y',
12           ( byte ) 'e', ( byte ) 'a', ( byte ) 'r' };
13
14        String s = new String( "hello" );
15
16        // use String constructors
17        String s1 = new String();
18        String s2 = new String( s );
19        String s3 = new String( charArray );
20        String s4 = new String( charArray, 6, 3 );
21        String s5 = new String( byteArray, 4, 4 );
22        String s6 = new String( byteArray );
23
24        // append Strings to output
25        String output = "s1 = " + s1 + "\ns2 = " + s2 + "\ns3 = " + s3 +
26           "\ns4 = " + s4 + "\ns5 = " + s5 + "\ns6 = " + s6;
27
28        JOptionPane.showMessageDialog( null, output,
29           "String Class Constructors", JOptionPane.INFORMATION_MESSAGE );
30
31        System.exit( 0 );
32     }
33
34  } // end class StringConstructors
```

String Class Constructors

s1 =
s2 = hello
s3 = birth day
s4 = day
s5 = year
s6 = new year

[OK]

Fig. 11.1   String class constructors.

Software Engineering Observation 11.1

It is not necessary to copy an existing String object. String objects are immutable—their character contents cannot be changed after they are created. If there are one or more references to a String object (or any object for that matter), the object cannot be reclaimed by the garbage collector. Thus, a String reference cannot be used to modify a String or to delete a String from memory as in other programming languages, such as C or C++.

Line 19 instantiates a new `String` object and assigns its reference to s3 using class `String`'s constructor that takes a character array as an argument. The new `String` object contains a copy of the characters in the array.

Line 20 instantiates a new `String` object and assigns its reference to s4 using class `String`'s constructor that takes a `char` array and two integers as arguments. The second argument specifies the starting position (the *offset*) from which characters in the array are accessed. Remember that the first character is at position 0. The third argument specifies the number of characters (the *count*) to access in the array. The new `String` object contains a string formed from the accessed characters. If the `offset` or the `count` specified as arguments result in accessing an element outside the bounds of the character array, a `StringIndexOutOfBoundsException` is thrown. We discuss exceptions in detail in Chapter 15.

Common Programming Error 11.1

Attempting to access a character that is outside the bounds of a string (i.e., an index less than 0 or an index greater than or equal to the string's length) results in a `StringIndexOutOfBoundsException`.

Line 21 instantiates a new `String` object and assigns its reference to s5 using class `String`'s constructor that takes a `byte` array and two integers as arguments. The second and third arguments specify the `offset` and `count`, respectively. The new `String` object contains copies of the specified bytes. If the `offset` or the `count` specified as arguments result in accessing an element outside the bounds of the array, a `StringIndexOutOfBoundsException` is thrown.

Line 22 instantiates a new `String` object and assigns it to reference s6 using class `String`'s constructor that takes a `byte` array as an argument. The new `String` object contains copies of the bytes in the array.

11.3.2 String Methods `length`, `charAt` and `getChars`

`String` methods *length*, *charAt* and *getChars* determine the length of a string, obtain the character at a specific location in a string and retrieve the entire set of characters in a string, respectively. The application of Fig. 11.2 demonstrates each of these methods.

```
1   // Fig. 11.2: StringMiscellaneous.java
2   // This program demonstrates the length, charAt and getChars
3   // methods of the String class.
4   import javax.swing.*;
5
6   public class StringMiscellaneous {
7
8      public static void main( String args[] )
9      {
10        String s1 = "hello there";
11        char charArray[] = new char[ 5 ];
12
13        String output = "s1: " + s1;
14
15        // test length method
16        output += "\nLength of s1: " + s1.length();
```

Fig. 11.2   `String` class character-manipulation methods. (Part 1 of 2.)

```
17
18        // loop through characters in s1 and display reversed
19        output += "\nThe string reversed is: ";
20
21        for ( int count = s1.length() - 1; count >= 0; count-- )
22            output += s1.charAt( count ) + " ";
23
24        // copy characters from string into charArray
25        s1.getChars( 0, 5, charArray, 0 );
26        output += "\nThe character array is: ";
27
28        for ( int count = 0; count < charArray.length; count++ )
29            output += charArray[ count ];
30
31        JOptionPane.showMessageDialog( null, output,
32            "String class character manipulation methods",
33            JOptionPane.INFORMATION_MESSAGE );
34
35        System.exit( 0 );
36    }
37
38 } // end class StringMiscellaneous
```

Fig. 11.2   String class character-manipulation methods. (Part 2 of 2.)

Line 16 uses String method length to determine the number of characters in string s1. Like arrays, strings always know their own length. However, unlike arrays, strings do not have a length field that holds the number of elements in a string.

The for statement at lines 21–22 appends to string output the characters of the string s1 in reverse order (and separated by spaces). String method charAt (line 22) returns the character at a specific position in the string. Method charAt receives an integer argument that is used as the *index* and returns the character at that position. Like arrays, the first element of a string is considered to be at position 0.

Error-Prevention Tip 11.1

In general, String methods that take starting and ending indices as arguments treat the starting index as inclusive and treat the ending index as exclusive.

Line 25 uses String method getChars to copy the characters of a string into a character array. The first argument is the starting index in the string from which characters are to be copied. The second argument is the index that is one past the last character to be copied from the string. The third argument is the character array into which the characters are to be copied. The last argument is the starting index where the copied characters are placed in the character array. Next, the `char` array contents are appended one character at a time to string `output` with the `for` statement at lines 28–29 for display.

11.3.3 Comparing Strings

Chapter 7 discussed sorting and searching arrays. Frequently, the information being sorted or searched consists of strings that must be compared to determine sorting order or to determine whether a string appears in an array (or other collection). Class `String` provides several methods for comparing strings; these are demonstrated in the next two examples.

To understand what it means for one string to be "greater than" or "less than" another string, consider the process of alphabetizing a series of last names. You would, no doubt, place "Jones" before "Smith" because the first letter of "Jones" comes before the first letter of "Smith" in the alphabet. But the alphabet is more than just a list of 26 letters—it is an ordered set of characters. Each letter occurs in a specific position within the set. "Z" is more than just a letter of the alphabet; "Z" is specifically the twenty-sixth letter of the alphabet.

How does the computer know that one letter comes before another? All characters are represented in the computer as numeric codes (see Appendix B). When the computer compares two strings, it actually compares the numeric codes of the characters in the strings.

Figure 11.3 demonstrates `String` methods *equals*, *equalsIgnoreCase*, *compareTo* and *regionMatches* and demonstrates using the equality operator == to compare `String` objects.

```
1   // Fig. 11.3: StringCompare.java
2   // String methods equals, equalsIgnoreCase, compareTo and regionMatches.
3   import javax.swing.JOptionPane;
4
5   public class StringCompare {
6
7      public static void main( String args[] )
8      {
9         String s1 = new String( "hello" );  // s1 is a copy of "hello"
10        String s2 = "goodbye";
11        String s3 = "Happy Birthday";
12        String s4 = "happy birthday";
13
14        String output = "s1 = " + s1 + "\ns2 = " + s2 + "\ns3 = " + s3 +
15           "\ns4 = " + s4 + "\n\n";
16
17        // test for equality
18        if ( s1.equals( "hello" ) )  // true
19           output += "s1 equals \"hello\"\n";
20        else
21           output += "s1 does not equal \"hello\"\n";
22
23        // test for equality with ==
24        if ( s1 == "hello" )  // false; they are not the same object
25           output += "s1 equals \"hello\"\n";
26        else
27           output += "s1 does not equal \"hello\"\n";
28
```

Fig. 11.3   String comparisons. (Part 1 of 2.)

```
29        // test for equality (ignore case)
30        if ( s3.equalsIgnoreCase( s4 ) )   // true
31           output += "s3 equals s4\n";
32        else
33           output += "s3 does not equal s4\n";
34
35        // test compareTo
36        output += "\ns1.compareTo( s2 ) is " + s1.compareTo( s2 ) +
37           "\ns2.compareTo( s1 ) is " + s2.compareTo( s1 ) +
38           "\ns1.compareTo( s1 ) is " + s1.compareTo( s1 ) +
39           "\ns3.compareTo( s4 ) is " + s3.compareTo( s4 ) +
40           "\ns4.compareTo( s3 ) is " + s4.compareTo( s3 ) + "\n\n";
41
42        // test regionMatches (case sensitive)
43        if ( s3.regionMatches( 0, s4, 0, 5 ) )
44           output += "First 5 characters of s3 and s4 match\n";
45        else
46           output += "First 5 characters of s3 and s4 do not match\n";
47
48        // test regionMatches (ignore case)
49        if ( s3.regionMatches( true, 0, s4, 0, 5 ) )
50           output += "First 5 characters of s3 and s4 match";
51        else
52           output += "First 5 characters of s3 and s4 do not match";
53
54        JOptionPane.showMessageDialog( null, output,
55           "String comparisons", JOptionPane.INFORMATION_MESSAGE );
56
57        System.exit( 0 );
58     }
59
60  } // end class StringCompare
```

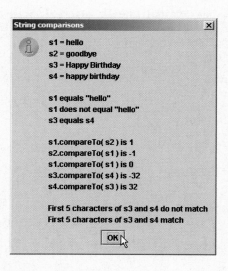

Fig. 11.3   String comparisons. (Part 2 of 2.)

The condition in the `if...else` statement at line 18 uses method `equals` to compare string `s1` and the string literal `"hello"` for equality. Method `equals` (a method of class `Object` overridden in `String`) tests any two objects for equality—the strings contained in the two objects are identical. The method returns `true` if the objects are equal and `false` otherwise. The preceding condition is `true` because string `s1` was initialized with the string literal `"hello"`. Method `equals` uses a *lexicographical comparison*—the integer Unicode values that represent each character in each string are compared. Thus, if the string `"hello"` is compared with the string `"HELLO"`, the result is `false`, because the integer representation of a lowercase letter is different from that of the corresponding uppercase letter.

The condition in the `if...else` statement at line 24 uses the equality operator `==` to compare string `s1` for equality with the string literal `"hello"`. *Operator `==` has different functionality when it is used to compare references than when it is used to compare values of primitive types.* When primitive-type values are compared with `==`, the result is `true` if both values are identical. When references are compared with `==`, the result is `true` if both references *refer to the same object in memory*. To compare the actual contents (or state information) of objects for equality, methods (such as `equals`) must be invoked. The preceding condition evaluates to `false` at line 24 because the reference `s1` was initialized with the statement

```
s1 = new String( "hello" );
```

which creates a new `String` object with a copy of string literal `"hello"` and assigns the new object to variable `s1`. If `s1` had been initialized with the statement

```
s1 = "hello";
```

which directly assigns the string literal `"hello"` to variable `s1`, the condition would be `true`. Remember that Java treats all string literal objects with the same contents as one anonymous `String` object that has many references. Thus, lines 9, 18 and 24 all refer to the same anonymous `String` object `"hello"` in memory.

Common Programming Error 11.2

Comparing references with `==` can lead to logic errors, because `==` compares the references to determine whether they refer to the same object, not whether two objects have the same contents. When two identical (but separate) objects are compared with `==`, the result will be `false`. When comparing objects to determine whether they have the same contents, use method `equals`.

If you are sorting `String`s, you may compare them for equality with method `equalsIgnoreCase`, which ignores the case of the letters in each string when performing the comparison. Thus, the string `"hello"` and the string `"HELLO"` compare as equal. The `if...else` statement at line 30 uses `String` method `equalsIgnoreCase` to compare string `s3`—Happy Birthday—for equality with string `s4`—happy birthday. The result of this comparison is `true`, because the comparison ignores case sensitivity.

Lines 36–40 use `String` method `compareTo` to compare strings. For example, line 36 compares string `s1` to string `s2`. Method `compareTo` returns 0 if the strings are equal, a negative number if the string that invokes `compareTo` is less than the string that is passed as an argument and a positive number if the string that invokes `compareTo` is greater than the string that is passed as an argument. Method `compareTo` uses a lexicographical comparison—it compares the numeric values of corresponding characters in each string.

The condition in the `if...else` statement at line 43 uses `String` method `region-Matches` to compare portions of two strings for equality. The first argument is the starting index in the string that invokes the method. The second argument is a comparison string. The third argument is the starting index in the comparison string. The last argument is the number of characters to compare between the two strings. The method returns `true` only if the specified number of characters are lexicographically equal.

Finally, the condition in the `if...else` statement at line 49 uses a second version of `String` method `regionMatches` to compare portions of two strings for equality. When the first argument is `true`, the method ignores the case of the characters being compared. The remaining arguments are identical to those described for the four-argument `region-Matches` method.

The second example of this section (Fig. 11.4) demonstrates `String` methods *startsWith* and *endsWith*. Method `main` creates array `strings` containing the strings `"started"`, `"starting"`, `"ended"` and `"ending"`. The remainder of method `main` consists of three `for` statements that test the elements of the array to determine whether they start with or end with a particular set of characters.

```java
1   // Fig. 11.4: StringStartEnd.java
2   // String methods startsWith and endsWith.
3   import javax.swing.*;
4
5   public class StringStartEnd {
6
7      public static void main( String args[] )
8      {
9         String strings[] = { "started", "starting", "ended", "ending" };
10        String output = "";
11
12        // test method startsWith
13        for ( int count = 0; count < strings.length; count++ )
14
15           if ( strings[ count ].startsWith( "st" ) )
16              output += "\"" + strings[ count ] + "\" starts with \"st\"\n";
17
18        output += "\n";
19
20        // test method startsWith starting from position
21        // 2 of the string
22        for ( int count = 0; count < strings.length; count++ )
23
24           if ( strings[ count ].startsWith( "art", 2 ) )
25              output += "\"" + strings[ count ] +
26                 "\" starts with \"art\" at position 2\n";
27
28        output += "\n";
29
```

Fig. 11.4 String class `startsWith` and `endsWith` methods. (Part 1 of 2.)

```
30              // test method endsWith
31              for ( int count = 0; count < strings.length; count++ )
32
33                  if ( strings[ count ].endsWith( "ed" ) )
34                      output += "\"" + strings[ count ] + "\" ends with \"ed\"\n";
35
36              JOptionPane.showMessageDialog( null, output,
37                  "String Class Comparisons", JOptionPane.INFORMATION_MESSAGE );
38
39              System.exit( 0 );
40          }
41
42      } // end class StringStartEnd
```

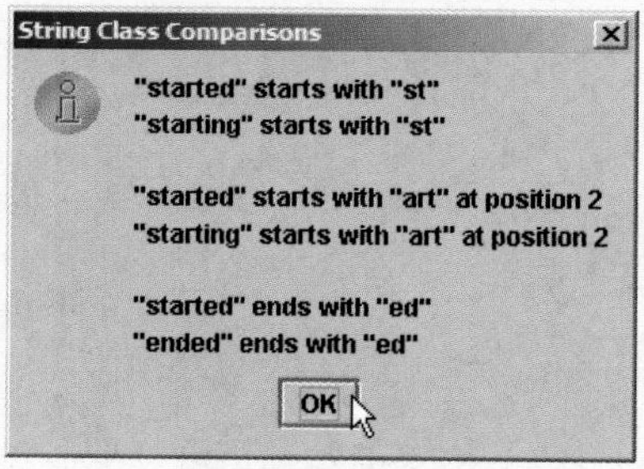

String Class Comparisons

"started" starts with "st"
"starting" starts with "st"

"started" starts with "art" at position 2
"starting" starts with "art" at position 2

"started" ends with "ed"
"ended" ends with "ed"

OK

Fig. 11.4   String class startsWith and endsWith methods. (Part 2 of 2.)

The first for statement (lines 13–16) uses the version of method startsWith that takes a String argument. The condition in the if statement (line 15) determines whether the string at location count of the array starts with the characters "st". If so, the method returns true and the program appends strings[count] to output for display. Otherwise, the method returns false and nothing is appended.

The second for statement (lines 22–26) uses the version of method startsWith that takes a String and an integer as arguments. The integer argument specifies the index at which the comparison should begin in the string. The condition in the if statement (line 24) determines whether the string at location count of the array has the characters "art" beginning with the third character in each string. If so, the method returns true and the program appends strings[count] to output for display purposes.

The third for statement (lines 31–34) uses method endsWith, which takes a String argument. The condition in the if statement (line 33) determines whether the string at location count of the array ends with the characters "ed". If so, the method returns true and the program appends strings[count] to output for display purposes.

11.3.4 Locating Characters and Substrings in Strings

Often it is useful to search for a character or set of characters in a string. For example, if you are creating your own word processor, you might want to provide a capability for searching through documents. Figure 11.5 demonstrates the many versions of String methods *indexOf* and *lastIndexOf* that search for a specified character or substring in a string. All the searches in this example are performed on the string letters (initialized with "abcdefghijklmabcdefghijklm") in method main.

```java
1   // Fig. 11.5: StringIndexMethods.java
2   // String searching methods indexOf and lastIndexOf.
3   import javax.swing.*;
4
5   public class StringIndexMethods {
6
7       public static void main( String args[] )
8       {
9           String letters = "abcdefghijklmabcdefghijklm";
10
11          // test indexOf to locate a character in a string
12          String output = "'c' is located at index " + letters.indexOf( 'c' );
13
14          output += "\n'a' is located at index " + letters.indexOf( 'a', 1 );
15
16          output += "\n'$' is located at index " + letters.indexOf( '$' );
17
18          // test lastIndexOf to find a character in a string
19          output += "\n\nLast 'c' is located at index " +
20              letters.lastIndexOf( 'c' );
21
22          output += "\nLast 'a' is located at index " +
23              letters.lastIndexOf( 'a', 25 );
24
25          output += "\nLast '$' is located at index " +
26              letters.lastIndexOf( '$' );
27
28          // test indexOf to locate a substring in a string
29          output += "\n\n\"def\" is located at index " +
30              letters.indexOf( "def" );
31
32          output += "\n\"def\" is located at index " +
33              letters.indexOf( "def", 7 );
34
35          output += "\n\"hello\" is located at index " +
36              letters.indexOf( "hello" );
37
38          // test lastIndexOf to find a substring in a string
39          output += "\n\nLast \"def\" is located at index " +
40              letters.lastIndexOf( "def" );
41
42          output += "\nLast \"def\" is located at index " +
43              letters.lastIndexOf( "def", 25 );
44
45          output += "\nLast \"hello\" is located at index " +
46              letters.lastIndexOf( "hello" );
47
48          JOptionPane.showMessageDialog( null, output,
49              "String searching methods", JOptionPane.INFORMATION_MESSAGE );
```

Fig. 11.5   String class searching methods. (Part 1 of 2.)

```
50
51              System.exit( 0 );
52         }
53
54    }  // end class StringIndexMethods
```

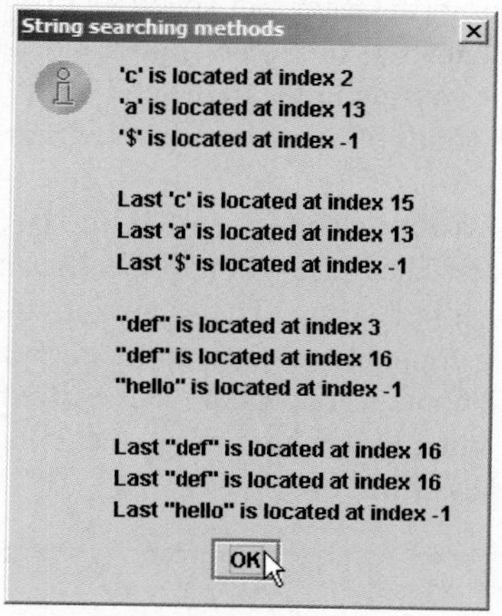

Fig. 11.5 `String` class searching methods. (Part 2 of 2.)

Lines 12–16 use method `indexOf` to locate the first occurrence of a character in a string. If `indexOf` finds the character, it returns the index of that character in the string; otherwise, `indexOf` returns –1. There are two versions of `indexOf` that search for characters in a string. The expression on line 12 uses method `indexOf` that takes one integer argument, which is the integer representation of a character. Recall from Section 11.2 that a character literal in single quotes is of type `char` and specifies the integer representation of the character in the Unicode character set. The expression at line 14 uses the second version of method `indexOf`, which takes two integer arguments—the integer representation of a character and the starting index at which the search of the string should begin.

The statements at lines 19–26 use method `lastIndexOf` to locate the last occurrence of a character in a string. Method `lastIndexOf` performs the search from the end of the string toward the beginning of the string. If method `lastIndexOf` finds the character, `lastIndexOf` returns the index of that character in the string; otherwise, `lastIndexOf` returns –1. There are two versions of `lastIndexOf` that search for characters in a string. The expression at line 20 uses the version of method `lastIndexOf` that takes one integer argument that is the integer representation of a character. The expression at line 23 uses the version of method `lastIndexOf` that takes two integer arguments—the integer representation of a character and the index from which to begin searching backward for the character.

Lines 29–46 demonstrate versions of methods `indexOf` and `lastIndexOf` that each take a `String` as the first argument. These versions of the methods perform identically to those described earlier except that they search for sequences of characters (or substrings) that are specified by their `String` arguments. If the substring is found, these methods return the index in the string of the first character in the substring.

11.3.5 Extracting Substrings from Strings

Class `String` provides two *substring* methods to enable a new `String` object to be created by copying part of an existing `String` object. Each method returns a new `String` object. Both methods are demonstrated in Fig. 11.6.

The expression `letters.substring( 20 )` at line 13 uses the `substring` method that takes one integer argument. The argument specifies the starting index in the original string `letters` from which characters are to be copied. The substring returned contains a copy of the characters from the starting index to the end of the string. If the index specified as an argument is outside the bounds of the string, the program generates a `StringIndex-OutOfBoundsException`.

The expression `letters.substring( 3, 6 )` at line 16 uses the `substring` method that takes two integer arguments. The first argument specifies the starting index from which characters are copied in the original string. The second argument specifies the index one beyond the last character to be copied (i.e., copy up to, but not including, that index in the string). The substring returned contains copies of the specified characters from the original string. If the arguments are outside the bounds of the string, the program generates a `StringIndexOutOfBoundsException`.

```
1   // Fig. 11.6: SubString.java
2   // String class substring methods.
3   import javax.swing.*;
4
5   public class SubString {
6
7      public static void main( String args[] )
8      {
9         String letters = "abcdefghijklmabcdefghijklm";
10
11        // test substring methods
12        String output = "Substring from index 20 to end is " +
13           "\"" + letters.substring( 20 ) + "\"\n";
14
15        output += "Substring from index 3 up to 6 is " +
16           "\"" + letters.substring( 3, 6 ) + "\"";
17
18        JOptionPane.showMessageDialog( null, output,
19           "String substring methods", JOptionPane.INFORMATION_MESSAGE );
20
21        System.exit( 0 );
22     }
23
24   } // end class SubString
```

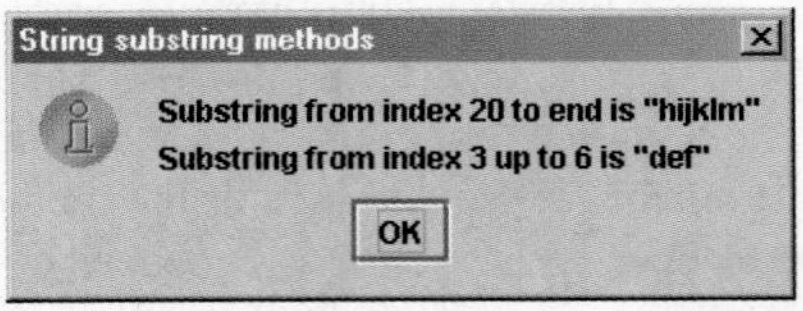

String substring methods

> Substring from index 20 to end is "hijklm"
> Substring from index 3 up to 6 is "def"
>
> OK

Fig. 11.6   `String` class `substring` methods.

11.3.6 Concatenating Strings

String method concat (Fig. 11.7) concatenates two String objects and returns a new String object containing the characters from both original strings. If the argument String has no characters in it, the original string is returned. The expression s1.concat(s2) at line 14 forms a string by appending the characters in string s2 to the characters in string s1. The original Strings to which s1 and s2 refer are not modified.

Performance Tip 11.2

In programs that frequently perform string concatenation, or other string modifications, it is more efficient to implement those modifications with class StringBuffer (covered in Section 11.4).

11.3.7 Miscellaneous String Methods

Class String provides several methods that return modified copies of strings or that return character arrays. These methods are demonstrated in the application of Fig. 11.8.

```
1  // Fig. 11.7: StringConcatenation.java
2  // String concat method.
3  import javax.swing.*;
4
5  public class StringConcatenation {
6
7     public static void main( String args[] )
8     {
9        String s1 = new String( "Happy " );
10       String s2 = new String( "Birthday" );
11
12       String output = "s1 = " + s1 + "\ns2 = " + s2;
13
14       output += "\n\nResult of s1.concat( s2 ) = " + s1.concat( s2 );
15       output += "\ns1 after concatenation = " + s1;
16
17       JOptionPane.showMessageDialog( null, output,
18          "String method concat", JOptionPane.INFORMATION_MESSAGE );
19
20       System.exit( 0 );
21    }
22
23 } // end class StringConcatenation
```

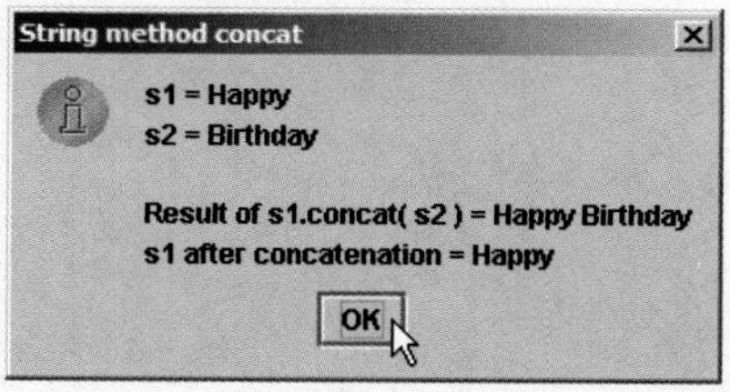

Fig. 11.7   String method concat.

Line 17 uses `String` method `replace` to return a new `String` object in which the every occurrence in string `s1` of character `'l'` (el) is replaced with character `'L'`. Method `replace` leaves the original string unchanged. If there are no occurrences of the first argument in the string, Method `replace` returns the original string.

Line 20 uses `String` method `toUpperCase` to generate a new `String` object with uppercase letters where corresponding lowercase letters exist in `s1`. The method returns a new `String` object containing the converted string and leaves the original string unchanged. If there are no characters to convert, method `toUpperCase` returns the original string.

Line 21 uses `String` method `toLowerCase` to return a new `String` object with lowercase letters where corresponding uppercase letters exist in `s2`. The original string remains

```java
1   // Fig. 11.8: StringMiscellaneous2.java
2   // String methods replace, toLowerCase, toUpperCase, trim and toCharArray.
3   import javax.swing.*;
4
5   public class StringMiscellaneous2 {
6
7      public static void main( String args[] )
8      {
9         String s1 = new String( "hello" );
10        String s2 = new String( "GOODBYE" );
11        String s3 = new String( "   spaces   " );
12
13        String output = "s1 = " + s1 + "\ns2 = " + s2 + "\ns3 = " + s3;
14
15        // test method replace
16        output += "\n\nReplace 'l' with 'L' in s1: " +
17           s1.replace( 'l', 'L' );
18
19        // test toLowerCase and toUpperCase
20        output += "\n\ns1.toUpperCase() = " + s1.toUpperCase() +
21           "\ns2.toLowerCase() = " + s2.toLowerCase();
22
23        // test trim method
24        output += "\n\ns3 after trim = \"" + s3.trim() + "\"";
25
26        // test toCharArray method
27        char charArray[] = s1.toCharArray();
28        output += "\n\ns1 as a character array = ";
29
30        for ( int count = 0; count < charArray.length; ++count )
31           output += charArray[ count ];
32
33        JOptionPane.showMessageDialog( null, output,
34           "Additional String methods", JOptionPane.INFORMATION_MESSAGE );
35
36        System.exit( 0 );
37     }
38
39  } // end class StringMiscellaneous2
```

Fig. 11.8 String methods `replace`, `toLowerCase`, `toUpperCase`, `trim`, `toString` and `toCharArray`. (Part 1 of 2.)

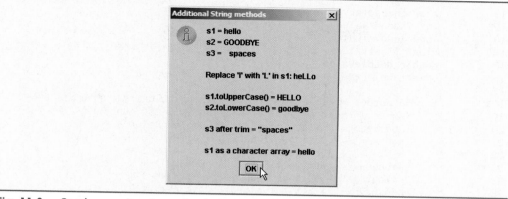

Fig. 11.8 String methods replace, toLowerCase, toUpperCase, trim, toString and toCharArray. (Part 2 of 2.)

unchanged. If there are no characters in the original string to convert, toLowerCase returns the original string.

Line 24 uses String method trim to generate a new String object that removes all white-space characters that appear at the beginning or end of the string on which trim operates. The method returns a new String object containing the string without leading or trailing white space. The original string remains unchanged.

 Error-Prevention Tip 11.2

Invoke String method trim on user input strings to ensure that any extra spaces the user accidentally typed at the beginning or end of the input are removed before processing.

Line 27 creates a new character array containing a copy of the characters in string s1 and assigns a reference to variable charArray.

11.3.8 String Method valueOf

As we have seen, every object in Java has a toString method that enables a program to obtain the object's string representation. Unfortunately, this technique cannot be used with primitive types because they do not have methods. Class String provides static methods that take an argument of any type and convert the argument to a String object. Class StringValueOf (Fig. 11.9) demonstrates the String class *valueOf* methods.

```
1   // Fig. 11.9: StringValueOf.java
2   // String valueOf methods.
3   import javax.swing.*;
4
5   public class StringValueOf {
6
7      public static void main( String args[] )
8      {
9         char charArray[] = { 'a', 'b', 'c', 'd', 'e', 'f' };
10        boolean booleanValue = true;
```

Fig. 11.9 String class valueOf methods. (Part 1 of 2.)

```
11        char characterValue = 'Z';
12        int integerValue = 7;
13        long longValue = 10000000L;
14        float floatValue = 2.5f; // f suffix indicates that 2.5 is a float
15        double doubleValue = 33.333;
16        Object objectRef = "hello"; // assign string to an Object reference
17
18        String output = "char array = " + String.valueOf( charArray ) +
19           "\npart of char array = " + String.valueOf( charArray, 3, 3 ) +
20           "\nboolean = " + String.valueOf( booleanValue ) +
21           "\nchar = " + String.valueOf( characterValue ) +
22           "\nint = " + String.valueOf( integerValue ) +
23           "\nlong = " + String.valueOf( longValue ) +
24           "\nfloat = " + String.valueOf( floatValue ) +
25           "\ndouble = " + String.valueOf( doubleValue ) +
26           "\nObject = " + String.valueOf( objectRef );
27
28        JOptionPane.showMessageDialog( null, output,
29           "String valueOf methods", JOptionPane.INFORMATION_MESSAGE );
30
31        System.exit( 0 );
32     }
33
34  } // end class StringValueOf
```

String valueOf methods

char array = abcdef
part of char array = def
boolean = true
char = Z
int = 7
long = 10000000
float = 2.5
double = 33.333
Object = hello

OK

Fig. 11.9   String class valueOf methods. (Part 2 of 2.)

The expression String.valueOf(charArray) at line 18 uses the character array charArray to create a new String object. The expression String.valueOf(charArray, 3, 3) at line 19 uses a portion of the character array charArray to create a new String object. The second argument specifies the starting index from which the characters are used. The third argument specifies the number of characters to be used.

There are seven other versions of method valueOf, which take arguments of type boolean, char, int, long, float, double and Object, respectively. These are demonstrated in lines 20–26. Note that the version of valueOf that takes an Object as an argument can do so because all Objects can be converted to Strings with method toString.

[*Note:* Lines 13–14 use literal values 10000000L and 2.5f as the initial values of long variable longValue and float variable floatValue, respectively. By default, Java treats integer literals as type int and floating-point literals as type double. Appending the letter L to the literal 10000000 and appending letter f to the literal 2.5 indicates to the compiler that 10000000 should be treated as a long and that 2.5 should be treated as a float.]

11.4 Class `StringBuffer`

Class `String` provides many capabilities for processing strings. However, once a `String` object is created, its contents can never change. We now discuss the features of class `StringBuffer` for creating and manipulating dynamic string information—that is, modifiable strings. Every `StringBuffer` is capable of storing a number of characters specified by its capacity. If the capacity of a `StringBuffer` is exceeded, the capacity is automatically expanded to accommodate the additional characters. As we will see, class `String-Buffer` is also used to implement operators + and += for string concatenation.

Performance Tip 11.3

String objects are constant strings, whereas StringBuffer objects are modifiable strings. Java distinguishes constant strings from modifiable strings for optimization purposes; in particular, Java can perform certain optimizations involving String objects (such as sharing one String object among multiple references) because it knows these objects will not change.

Performance Tip 11.4

When given the choice between using a String object to represent a string versus a StringBuffer object to represent that string, always use a String object if the string will not change; this improves performance.

11.4.1 StringBuffer Constructors

Class `StringBuffer` provides three constructors (demonstrated in Fig. 11.10). Line 9 uses the default `StringBuffer` constructor to create a `StringBuffer` with no characters in it and an initial capacity of 16 characters (the default for a `StringBuffer`). Line 10 uses the `StringBuffer` constructor that takes an integer argument to create a `StringBuffer` with no characters in it and the initial capacity specified by the integer argument (i.e., 10). Line 11 uses the `StringBuffer` constructor that takes a `String` argument (in this case, a string literal) to create a `StringBuffer` containing the characters in the `String` argument. The initial capacity is the number of characters in the `String` argument plus 16.

```
1   // Fig. 11.10: StringBufferConstructors.java
2   // StringBuffer constructors.
3   import javax.swing.*;
4
5   public class StringBufferConstructors {
6
7      public static void main( String args[] )
8      {
9         StringBuffer buffer1 = new StringBuffer();
10        StringBuffer buffer2 = new StringBuffer( 10 );
11        StringBuffer buffer3 = new StringBuffer( "hello" );
12
13        String output = "buffer1 = \"" + buffer1.toString() + "\"" +
14           "\nbuffer2 = \"" + buffer2.toString() + "\"" +
15           "\nbuffer3 = \"" + buffer3.toString() + "\"";
16
```

Fig. 11.10 `StringBuffer` class constructors. (Part 1 of 2.)

```
17          JOptionPane.showMessageDialog( null, output,
18              "StringBuffer constructors", JOptionPane.INFORMATION_MESSAGE );
19
20          System.exit( 0 );
21      }
22
23  } // end class StringBufferConstructors
```

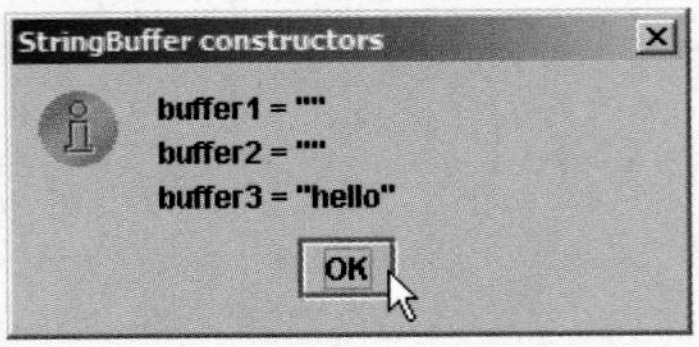

Fig. 11.10 StringBuffer class constructors. (Part 2 of 2.)

The statement on lines 13–15 uses StringBuffer method toString to convert the StringBuffers into String objects that can be displayed with drawString. Note the use of operator + to concatenate strings for output. In Section 11.4.4, we discuss how Java uses StringBuffer objects to implement the + and += operators for string concatenation.

11.4.2 StringBuffer Methods length, capacity, setLength and ensureCapacity

Class StringBuffer provides the length and capacity methods to return the number of characters currently in a StringBuffer and the number of characters that can be stored in a StringBuffer without allocating more memory, respectively. Method ensureCapacity allows the programmer to guarantee that a StringBuffer has at least the specified capacity. Method setLength enables the programmer to increase or decrease the length of a StringBuffer. The program of Fig. 11.11 demonstrates these methods.

```
1   // Fig. 11.11: StringBufferCapLen.java
2   // StringBuffer length, setLength, capacity and ensureCapacity methods.
3   import javax.swing.*;
4
5   public class StringBufferCapLen {
6
7       public static void main( String args[] )
8       {
9           StringBuffer buffer = new StringBuffer( "Hello, how are you?" );
10
11          String output = "buffer = " + buffer.toString() + "\nlength = " +
12              buffer.length() + "\ncapacity = " + buffer.capacity();
13
14          buffer.ensureCapacity( 75 );
15          output += "\n\nNew capacity = " + buffer.capacity();
16
17          buffer.setLength( 10 );
```

Fig. 11.11 StringBuffer method length and capacity. (Part 1 of 2.)

```
18          output += "\n\nNew length = " + buffer.length() +
19             "\nbuf = " + buffer.toString();
20
21          JOptionPane.showMessageDialog( null, output,
22             "StringBuffer length and capacity Methods",
23             JOptionPane.INFORMATION_MESSAGE );
24
25          System.exit( 0 );
26       }
27
28    } // end class StringBufferCapLen
```

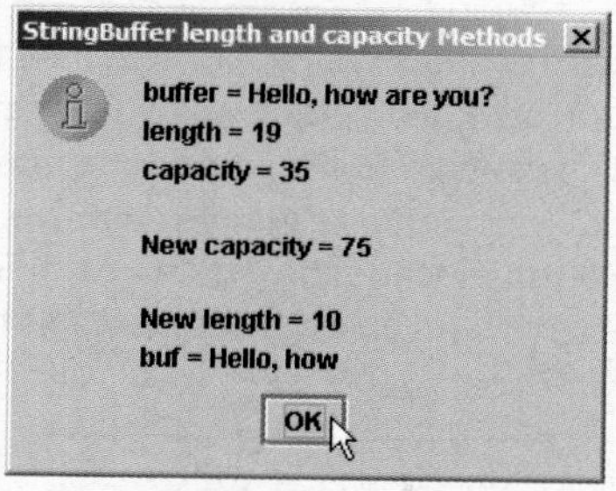

Fig. 11.11   StringBuffer method `length` and `capacity`. (Part 2 of 2.)

The program contains one `StringBuffer` called `buffer`. Line 9 uses the `String-Buffer` constructor that takes a `String` argument to initialize the `StringBuffer` with `"Hello, how are you?"`. Lines 11–12 assign to `output` the contents, the length and the capacity of the `StringBuffer`. Notice in the output window that the capacity of the `StringBuffer` is initially 35. Recall from Section 11.4.1 that the `StringBuffer` constructor that takes a `String` argument initializes the capacity to the length of the string passed as an argument plus 16.

Line 14 uses method `ensureCapacity` to expand the capacity of the `StringBuffer` to a minimum of 75 characters. Actually, if the original capacity is less than the argument, the method ensures a capacity that is the greater of the number specified as an argument or twice the original capacity plus 2. If the `StringBuffer`'s current capacity is more than the specified capacity, the `StringBuffer`'s capacity remains unchanged.

Line 17 uses method `setLength` to set the length of the `StringBuffer` to 10. If the specified length is less than the current number of characters in the `StringBuffer`, the buffer is truncated to the specified length (i.e., the characters in the `StringBuffer` after the specified length are discarded). If the specified length is greater than the number of characters currently in the `StringBuffer`, null characters (characters with the numeric representation 0) are appended to the `StringBuffer` until the total number of characters in the `StringBuffer` is equal to the specified length.

11.4.3 StringBuffer Methods charAt, setCharAt, getChars and reverse

Class `StringBuffer` provides the `charAt`, `setCharAt`, `getChars` and `reverse` methods to manipulate the characters in a `StringBuffer`. Each of these methods is demonstrated in Fig. 11.12. Method `charAt` takes an integer argument and returns the character in the `StringBuffer` at that index. Method `setCharAt` takes an integer and a character argument and sets the character at the specified position in the `StringBuffer` to the character argument. The index specified in the `charAt` and `setCharAt` methods must be greater than or equal to 0 and less than the `StringBuffer` length; otherwise, a `StringIndexOutOfBoundsException` occurs.

Common Programming Error 11.3

Attempting to access a character that is outside the bounds of a StringBuffer (i.e., with an index less than 0 or greater than or equal to the StringBuffer's length) results in a StringIndexOutOfBoundsException.

Method `getChars` (line 16) copies characters from a `StringBuffer` into the character array passed as an argument. This method takes four arguments—the starting index from which characters should be copied in the `StringBuffer`, the index one past the last character to be copied from the `StringBuffer`, the character array into which the characters are to be copied and the starting location in the character array where the first character should be placed. Method `reverse` reverses the contents of the `StringBuffer`.

```
1   // Fig. 11.12: StringBufferChars.java
2   // StringBuffer methods charAt, setCharAt, getChars and reverse.
3   import javax.swing.*;
4
5   public class StringBufferChars {
6
7      public static void main( String args[] )
8      {
9         StringBuffer buffer = new StringBuffer( "hello there" );
10
11        String output = "buffer = " + buffer.toString() +
12           "\nCharacter at 0: " + buffer.charAt( 0 ) +
13           "\nCharacter at 4: " + buffer.charAt( 4 );
14
15        char charArray[] = new char[ buffer.length() ];
16        buffer.getChars( 0, buffer.length(), charArray, 0 );
17        output += "\n\nThe characters are: ";
18
19        for ( int count = 0; count < charArray.length; ++count )
20           output += charArray[ count ];
21
22        buffer.setCharAt( 0, 'H' );
23        buffer.setCharAt( 6, 'T' );
24        output += "\n\nbuf = " + buffer.toString();
25
26        buffer.reverse();
27        output += "\n\nbuf = " + buffer.toString();
28
29        JOptionPane.showMessageDialog( null, output,
30           "StringBuffer character methods",
31           JOptionPane.INFORMATION_MESSAGE );
```

Fig. 11.12 `StringBuffer` class character-manipulation methods. (Part 1 of 2.)

```
32
33          System.exit( 0 );
34      }
35
36  } // end class StringBufferChars
```

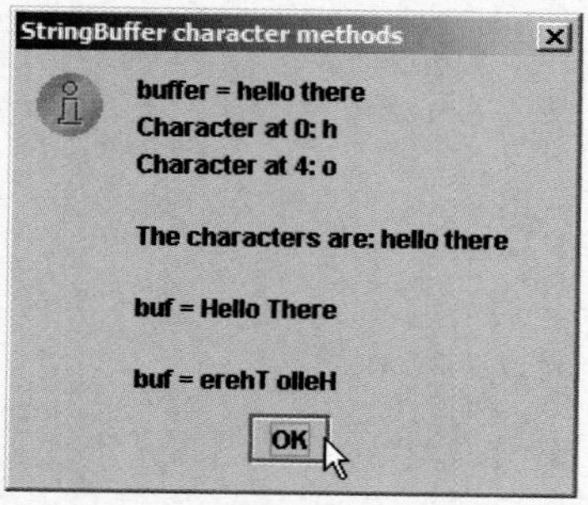

StringBuffer character methods

buffer = hello there
Character at 0: h
Character at 4: o

The characters are: hello there

buf = Hello There

buf = erehT olleH

OK

Fig. 11.12 StringBuffer class character-manipulation methods. (Part 2 of 2.)

11.4.4 StringBuffer append Methods

Class StringBuffer provides 11 overloaded append methods to allow values of various types to be added to the end of a StringBuffer. Versions are provided for each of the primitive types and for character arrays, Strings, Objects and StringBuffer. (Remember that method toString produces a string representation of any Object.) Each of the methods takes its argument, converts it to a string and appends it to the StringBuffer. The append methods are demonstrated in Fig. 11.13.

```
1   // Fig. 11.13: StringBufferAppend.java
2   // StringBuffer append methods.
3   import javax.swing.*;
4
5   public class StringBufferAppend {
6
7      public static void main( String args[] )
8      {
9         Object objectRef = "hello";
10        String string = "goodbye";
11        char charArray[] = { 'a', 'b', 'c', 'd', 'e', 'f' };
12        boolean booleanValue = true;
13        char characterValue = 'Z';
14        int integerValue = 7;
15        long longValue = 10000000;
16        float floatValue = 2.5f; // f suffix indicates 2.5 is a float
17        double doubleValue = 33.333;
18        StringBuffer lastBuffer = new StringBuffer( "last StringBuffer" );
19        StringBuffer buffer = new StringBuffer();
20
```

Fig. 11.13 StringBuffer class append methods. (Part 1 of 2.)

```
21          buffer.append( objectRef );
22          buffer.append( "  " );     // each of these contains two spaces
23          buffer.append( string );
24          buffer.append( "  " );
25          buffer.append( charArray );
26          buffer.append( "  " );
27          buffer.append( charArray, 0, 3 );
28          buffer.append( "  " );
29          buffer.append( booleanValue );
30          buffer.append( "  " );
31          buffer.append( characterValue );
32          buffer.append( "  " );
33          buffer.append( integerValue );
34          buffer.append( "  " );
35          buffer.append( longValue );
36          buffer.append( "  " );
37          buffer.append( floatValue );
38          buffer.append( "  " );
39          buffer.append( doubleValue );
40          buffer.append( "  " );
41          buffer.append( lastBuffer );
42
43          JOptionPane.showMessageDialog( null,
44             "buffer = " + buffer.toString(), "StringBuffer append Methods",
45             JOptionPane.INFORMATION_MESSAGE );
46
47          System.exit( 0 );
48       }
49
50    } // end StringBufferAppend
```

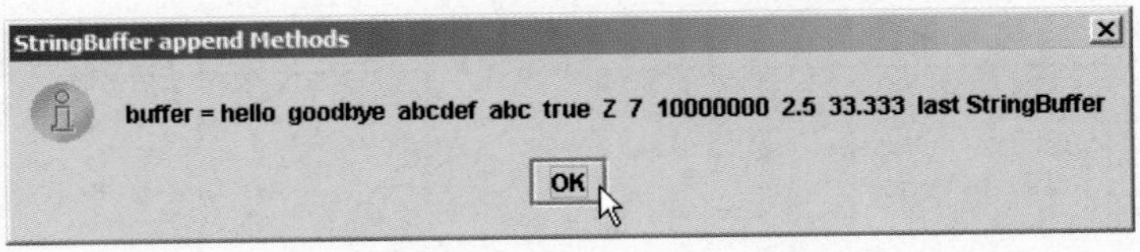

StringBuffer append Methods

buffer = hello goodbye abcdef abc true Z 7 10000000 2.5 33.333 last StringBuffer

OK

Fig. 11.13 StringBuffer class append methods. (Part 2 of 2.)

Actually, StringBuffers and the append methods are used by the compiler to implement the + and += operators for concatenating Strings. For example, assuming the declarations

```
String string1 = "hello";
String string2 = "BC"
int value = 22;
```

the statement

```
String s = string1 + string2 + value;
```

concatenates "hello", "BC" and 22. The concatenation is performed as follows:

```
new StringBuffer().append( "hello" ).append( "BC" ).append(
   22 ).toString();
```

First, Java creates an empty `StringBuffer`, then appends to the `StringBuffer` the string `"hello"`, the string `"BC"` and the integer 22. Next, `StringBuffer`'s method `toString` converts the `StringBuffer` to a string representation and the result is assigned to `String` s. The statement

```
s += "!";
```

is performed as follows:

```
s = new StringBuffer().append( s ).append( "!" ).toString()
```

First, Java creates an empty `StringBuffer`, then appends to the `StringBuffer` the current contents of s followed by `"!"`. Next, `StringBuffer`'s method `toString` converts the `StringBuffer` to a string representation and the result is assigned to s.

11.4.5 StringBuffer Insertion and Deletion Methods

Class `StringBuffer` provides ten overloaded `insert` methods to allow values of various types to be inserted at any position in a `StringBuffer`. Versions are provided for each of the primitive types and for character arrays, `String`s and `Object`s. Each of the methods takes its second argument, converts it to a string and inserts it preceding the index specified by the first argument. The index specified by the first argument must be greater than or equal to 0 and less than the length of the `StringBuffer`; otherwise, a `StringIndex-OutOfBoundsException` occurs. Class `StringBuffer` also provides methods *delete* and *deleteCharAt* for deleting characters at any position in a `StringBuffer`. Method `delete` takes two arguments—the starting index and the index one past the end of the characters to delete. All characters beginning at the starting index up to, but not including the ending index are deleted. Method `deleteCharAt` takes one argument—the index of the character to delete. Invalid indices cause both methods to throw a `StringIndexOutOf-BoundsException`. The `insert` and `delete` methods are demonstrated in Fig. 11.14.

```
1   // Fig. 11.14: StringBufferInsert.java
2   // StringBuffer methods insert and delete.
3   import javax.swing.*;
4
5   public class StringBufferInsert {
6
7      public static void main( String args[] )
8      {
9         Object objectRef = "hello";
10        String string = "goodbye";
11        char charArray[] = { 'a', 'b', 'c', 'd', 'e', 'f' };
12        boolean booleanValue = true;
13        char characterValue = 'K';
14        int integerValue = 7;
15        long longValue = 10000000;
16        float floatValue = 2.5f;   // f suffix indicates that 2.5 is a float
17        double doubleValue = 33.333;
18        StringBuffer buffer = new StringBuffer();
```

Fig. 11.14 StringBuffer methods `insert` and `delete`. (Part 1 of 2.)

```
19
20          buffer.insert( 0, objectRef );
21          buffer.insert( 0, "  " );  // each of these contains two spaces
22          buffer.insert( 0, string );
23          buffer.insert( 0, "  " );
24          buffer.insert( 0, charArray );
25          buffer.insert( 0, "  " );
26          buffer.insert( 0, charArray, 3, 3 );
27          buffer.insert( 0, "  " );
28          buffer.insert( 0, booleanValue );
29          buffer.insert( 0, "  " );
30          buffer.insert( 0, characterValue );
31          buffer.insert( 0, "  " );
32          buffer.insert( 0, integerValue );
33          buffer.insert( 0, "  " );
34          buffer.insert( 0, longValue );
35          buffer.insert( 0, "  " );
36          buffer.insert( 0, floatValue );
37          buffer.insert( 0, "  " );
38          buffer.insert( 0, doubleValue );
39
40          String output = "buffer after inserts:\n" + buffer.toString();
41
42          buffer.deleteCharAt( 10 );   // delete 5 in 2.5
43          buffer.delete( 2, 6 );       // delete .333 in 33.333
44
45          output += "\n\nbuffer after deletes:\n" + buffer.toString();
46
47          JOptionPane.showMessageDialog( null, output,
48             "StringBuffer insert/delete", JOptionPane.INFORMATION_MESSAGE );
49
50          System.exit( 0 );
51       }
52
53    } // end class StringBufferInsert
```

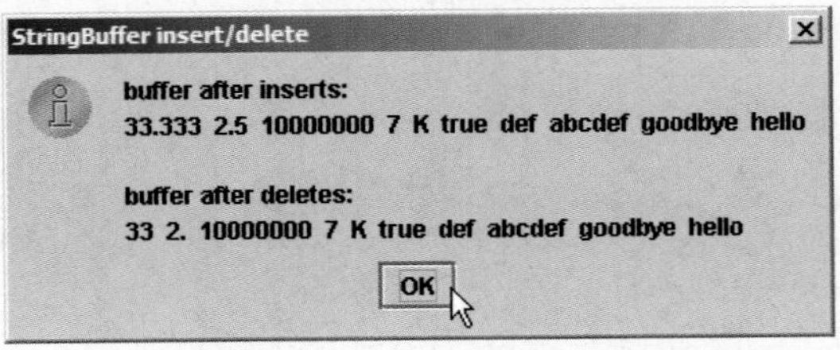

Fig. 11.14 StringBuffer methods insert and delete. (Part 2 of 2.)

11.5 Class Character

Recall from Section 10.10 that Java provides eight type-wrapper classes—Boolean, Character, Double, Float, Byte, Short, Integer and Long—that enable primitive-type values to be treated as objects. In this section, we present class Character—the type-wrapper class for characters.

Most `Character` methods are `static`, take at least a character argument and perform either a test or a manipulation of the character. This class also contains a constructor that receives a `char` argument to initialize a `Character` object. Most of the methods of class `Character` are presented in the next three examples. For more information on class `Character` (and all the type-wrapper classes), see the `java.lang` package in the Java API documentation.

Figure 11.15 demonstrates some `static` methods that test characters to determine whether they are a specific character type and the `static` methods that perform case conversions on characters. Each method is used in method `buildOutput` (lines 51–65) of class `StaticCharMethods`. You can enter any character and apply the preceding methods to the character. Note the use of anonymous inner classes for the event handling as demonstrated in Chapter 9.

Line 53 uses `Character` method `isDefined` to determine whether character c is defined in the Unicode character set. If so, the method returns `true`; otherwise, it returns `false`.

Line 54 uses `Character` method `isDigit` to determine whether character c is a defined Unicode digit. If so, the method returns `true`; otherwise, it returns `false`.

Line 56 uses `Character` method `isJavaIdentifierStart` to determine whether c is a character that can be the first character of an identifier in Java—i.e., a letter, an underscore (_) or a dollar sign ($). If so, the method returns `true`; otherwise, it returns `false`. Line 58 uses `Character` method `isJavaIdentifierPart` to determine whether character c is a character that can be used in an identifier in Java—i.e., a digit, a letter, an underscore (_) or a dollar sign ($). If so, the method returns `true`; otherwise, it returns `false`.

```
1   // Fig. 11.15: StaticCharMethods.java
2   // Static Character testing methods and case conversion methods.
3   import java.awt.*;
4   import java.awt.event.*;
5   import javax.swing.*;
6
7   public class StaticCharMethods extends JFrame {
8       private char c;
9       private JLabel promptLabel;
10      private JTextField inputField;
11      private JTextArea outputArea;
12
13      // constructor builds GUI
14      public StaticCharMethods()
15      {
16          super( "Static Character Methods" );
17
18          Container container = getContentPane();
19          container.setLayout( new FlowLayout() );
20
21          promptLabel = new JLabel( "Enter a character and press Enter" );
22          container.add( promptLabel );
23          inputField = new JTextField( 5 );
```

Fig. 11.15 `Character` class static methods for testing characters and converting character case. (Part 1 of 3.)

```
24
25          inputField.addActionListener(
26
27             new ActionListener() {  // anonymous inner class
28
29                // handle textfield event
30                public void actionPerformed( ActionEvent event )
31                {
32                   String s = event.getActionCommand();
33                   c = s.charAt( 0 );
34                   buildOutput();
35                }
36
37             } // end anonymous inner class
38
39          ); // end call to addActionListener
40
41          container.add( inputField );
42          outputArea = new JTextArea( 10, 20 );
43          container.add( outputArea );
44
45          setSize( 300, 220 );  // set the window size
46          setVisible( true );   // show the window
47
48       } // end constructor
49
50       // display character info in outputArea
51       private void buildOutput()
52       {
53          outputArea.setText( "is defined: " + Character.isDefined( c ) +
54             "\nis digit: " + Character.isDigit( c ) +
55             "\nis first character in a Java identifier: " +
56             Character.isJavaIdentifierStart( c ) +
57             "\nis part of a Java identifier: " +
58             Character.isJavaIdentifierPart( c ) +
59             "\nis letter: " + Character.isLetter( c ) +
60             "\nis letter or digit: " + Character.isLetterOrDigit( c ) +
61             "\nis lower case: " + Character.isLowerCase( c ) +
62             "\nis upper case: " + Character.isUpperCase( c ) +
63             "\nto upper case: " + Character.toUpperCase( c ) +
64             "\nto lower case: " + Character.toLowerCase( c ) );
65       }
66
67       // create StaticCharMethods object to begin execution
68       public static void main( String args[] )
69       {
70          StaticCharMethods application = new StaticCharMethods();
71          application.setDefaultCloseOperation( JFrame.EXIT_ON_CLOSE );
72       }
73
74    } // end class StaticCharMethods
```

Fig. 11.15 Character class static methods for testing characters and converting character case. (Part 2 of 3.)

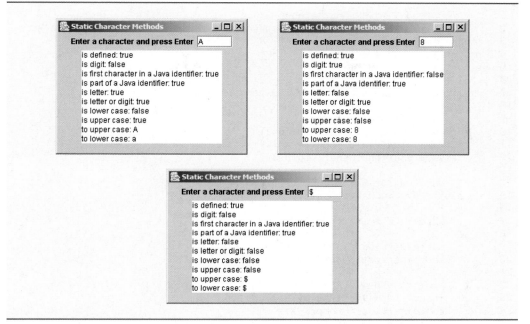

Fig. 11.15 Character class static methods for testing characters and converting character case. (Part 3 of 3.)

Line 59 uses Character method isLetter to determine whether character c is a letter. If so, the method returns true; otherwise, it returns false. Line 60 uses Character method isLetterOrDigit to determine whether character c is a letter or a digit. If so, the method returns true; otherwise, it returns false.

Line 61 uses Character method isLowerCase to determine whether character c is a lowercase letter. If so, the method returns true; otherwise, it returns false. Line 62 uses Character method isUpperCase to determine whether character c is an uppercase letter. If so, the method returns true; otherwise, it returns false.

Line 63 uses Character method toUpperCase to convert the character c to its uppercase equivalent. The method returns the converted character if the character has an uppercase equivalent; otherwise, the method returns its original argument. Line 64 uses Character method toLowerCase to convert the character c to its lowercase equivalent. The method returns the converted character if the character has a lowercase equivalent; otherwise, the method returns its original argument.

Figure 11.16 demonstrates static Character methods digit and forDigit, which convert characters to digits and digits to characters, respectively, in different number systems. Common number systems include decimal (base 10), octal (base 8), hexadecimal (base 16) and binary (base 2). The base of a number is also known as its *radix*. For more information on conversions between number systems, see Appendix C.

Line 44 uses method forDigit to convert the integer digit into a character in the number system specified by the integer radix (the base of the number). For example, the decimal integer 13 in base 16 (the radix) has the character value 'd'. Note that the lowercase and uppercase letters are equivalent in number systems.

```
1   // Fig. 11.15: StaticCharMethods2.java
2   // Static Character conversion methods.
3   import java.awt.*;
4   import java.awt.event.*;
5   import javax.swing.*;
6
7   public class StaticCharMethods2 extends JFrame {
8      private char c;
9      private int digit, radix;
10     private JLabel prompt1, prompt2;
11     private JTextField input, radixField;
12     private JButton toChar, toInt;
13
14     // constructor builds GUI
15     public StaticCharMethods2()
16     {
17        super( "Character Conversion Methods" );
18
19        Container container = getContentPane();
20        container.setLayout( new FlowLayout() );
21
22        prompt1 = new JLabel( "Enter a digit or character " );
23        input = new JTextField( 5 );
24        container.add( prompt1 );
25        container.add( input );
26
27        prompt2 = new JLabel( "Enter a radix " );
28        radixField = new JTextField( 5 );
29        container.add( prompt2 );
30        container.add( radixField );
31
32        toChar = new JButton( "Convert digit to character" );
33        toChar.addActionListener(
34
35           new ActionListener() { // anonymous inner class
36
37              // handle toChar JButton event
38              public void actionPerformed( ActionEvent actionEvent )
39              {
40                 digit = Integer.parseInt( input.getText() );
41                 radix = Integer.parseInt( radixField.getText() );
42                 JOptionPane.showMessageDialog( null,
43                    "Convert digit to character: " +
44                    Character.forDigit( digit, radix ) );
45              }
46
47           } // end anonymous inner class
48
49        ); // end call to addActionListener
50
51        toInt = new JButton( "Convert character to digit" );
52        toInt.addActionListener(
53
```

Fig. 11.16 Character class static conversion methods. (Part 1 of 2.)

```
54                new ActionListener() {  // anonymous inner class
55
56                    // handle toInt JButton event
57                    public void actionPerformed( ActionEvent actionEvent )
58                    {
59                        String s = input.getText();
60                        c = s.charAt( 0 );
61                        radix = Integer.parseInt( radixField.getText() );
62                        JOptionPane.showMessageDialog( null,
63                            "Convert character to digit: " +
64                            Character.digit( c, radix ) );
65                    }
66
67                } // end anonymous inner class
68
69            ); // end call to addActionListener
70
71        container.add( toChar );
72        container.add( toInt );
73        setSize( 275, 150 );  // set the window size
74        setVisible( true );   // show the window
75    }
76
77    // create StaticCharMethods2 object execute application
78    public static void main( String args[] )
79    {
80        StaticCharMethods2 application = new StaticCharMethods2();
81        application.setDefaultCloseOperation( JFrame.EXIT_ON_CLOSE );
82    }
83
84 } // end class StaticCharMethods2
```

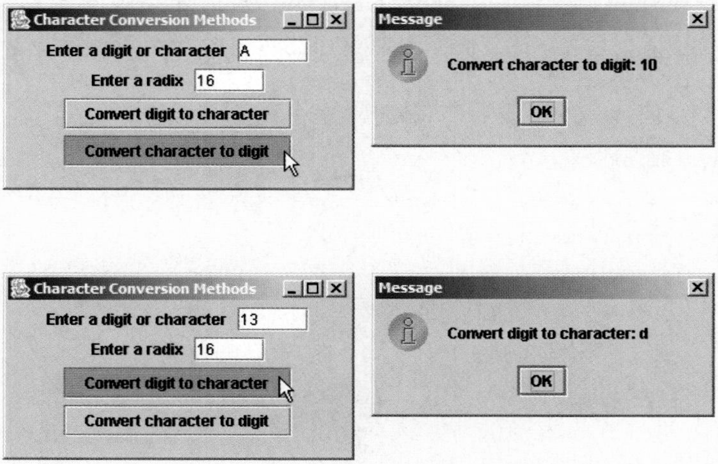

Fig. 11.16 *Character* class static conversion methods. (Part 2 of 2.)

Line 64 uses method `digit` to convert the character `c` into an integer in the number system specified by the integer `radix` (the base of the number). For example, the character `'A'` in base 16 (the `radix`) has the integer value 10.

The program in Fig. 11.17 demonstrates the constructor and several non-`static` methods of class `Character`—`charValue`, `toString` and `equals`.

Lines 9–10 instantiate two `Character` objects and pass character literals to the constructor to initialize those objects.

Line 12 uses `Character` method `charValue` to return the `char` value stored in `Character` object `c1`. Line 13 returns a string representation of `Character` object `c2` using method `toString`.

The condition in the `if...else` statement at lines 15–18 uses method `equals` to determine whether the object `c1` has the same contents as the object `c2` (i.e., the characters inside each object are equal).

```
1   // Fig. 11.17: OtherCharMethods.java
2   // Non-static Character methods.
3   import javax.swing.*;
4
5   public class OtherCharMethods {
6
7      public static void main( String args[] )
8      {
9         Character c1 = new Character( 'A' );
10        Character c2 = new Character( 'a' );
11
12        String output = "c1 = " + c1.charValue() +
13           "\nc2 = " + c2.toString();
14
15        if ( c1.equals( c2 ) )
16           output += "\n\nc1 and c2 are equal";
17        else
18           output += "\n\nc1 and c2 are not equal";
19
20        JOptionPane.showMessageDialog( null, output,
21           "Non-static Character methods",
22           JOptionPane.INFORMATION_MESSAGE );
23
24        System.exit( 0 );
25     }
26
27   } // end class OtherCharMethods
```

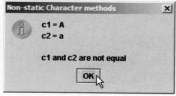

Fig. 11.17 `Character` class non-static methods.

11.6 Class StringTokenizer

When you read a sentence, your mind breaks the sentence into *tokens*—individual words and punctuation, each of which conveys meaning to you. Compilers also perform tokenization. They break up statements into individual pieces like keywords, identifiers, operators and other elements of a programming language. In this section, we study Java's StringTokenizer class (from package java.util), which breaks a string into its component tokens. Tokens are separated from one another by *delimiters*, typically white-space characters such as space, tab, newline and carriage return. Other characters can also be used as delimiters to separate tokens. The program in Fig. 11.18 demonstrates class StringTokenizer. The window for class TokenTest displays a JTextField where the user types a sentence to tokenize. Output in this program is displayed in a JTextArea.

```java
1   // Fig. 11.18: TokenTest.java
2   // StringTokenizer class.
3   import java.util.*;
4   import java.awt.*;
5   import java.awt.event.*;
6   import javax.swing.*;
7
8   public class TokenTest extends JFrame {
9      private JLabel promptLabel;
10     private JTextField inputField;
11     private JTextArea outputArea;
12
13     // set up GUI and event handling
14     public TokenTest()
15     {
16        super( "Testing Class StringTokenizer" );
17
18        Container container = getContentPane();
19        container.setLayout( new FlowLayout() );
20
21        promptLabel = new JLabel( "Enter a sentence and press Enter" );
22        container.add( promptLabel );
23
24        inputField = new JTextField( 20 );
25        inputField.addActionListener(
26
27           new ActionListener() {  // anonymous inner class
28
29              // handle text field event
30              public void actionPerformed( ActionEvent event )
31              {
32                 StringTokenizer tokens =
33                    new StringTokenizer( event.getActionCommand() );
34
35                 outputArea.setText( "Number of elements: " +
36                    tokens.countTokens() + "\nThe tokens are:\n" );
37
```

Fig. 11.18 StringTokenizer object used to tokenize strings. (Part 1 of 2.)

```
38              while ( tokens.hasMoreTokens() )
39                 outputArea.append( tokens.nextToken() + "\n" );
40           }
41
42        } // end anonymous inner class
43
44     ); // end call to addActionListener
45
46     container.add( inputField );
47
48     outputArea = new JTextArea( 10, 20 );
49     outputArea.setEditable( false );
50     container.add( new JScrollPane( outputArea ) );
51     setSize( 275, 240 );   // set the window size
52     setVisible( true );    // show the window
53   }
54
55   // execute application
56   public static void main( String args[] )
57   {
58     TokenTest application = new TokenTest();
59     application.setDefaultCloseOperation( JFrame.EXIT_ON_CLOSE );
60   }
61
62 } // end class TokenTest
```

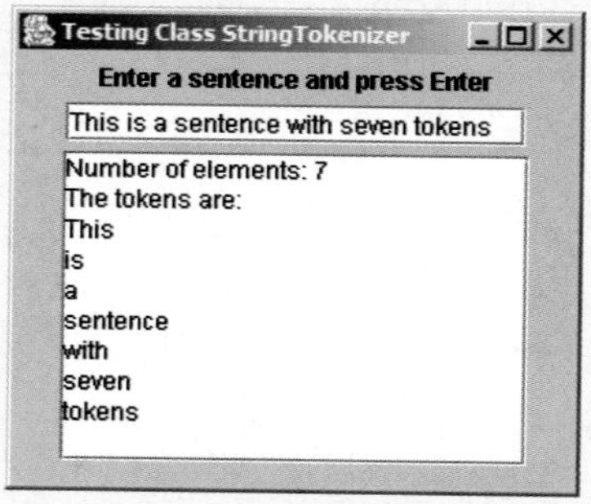

Fig. 11.18 `StringTokenizer` object used to tokenize strings. (Part 2 of 2.)

When the user presses the *Enter* key in the `JTextField`, method `actionPerformed` (lines 30–40) is invoked. Lines 32–33 create an instance of class `StringTokenizer` using the string in the textfield (`event.getActionCommand()`) as an argument. This `String-Tokenizer` constructor takes a string argument and creates a `StringTokenizer` for that string and will use the default delimiter string " \t\n\r\f" consisting of a space, a newline, a tab and a carriage return for tokenization. There are two other constructors for class `StringTokenizer`. In the version that takes two `String` arguments, the second `String` is the delimiter string. In the version that takes three arguments, the second `String` is the delimiter string and the third argument (a `boolean`) determines whether the delimiters are also returned as tokens (only if the argument is `true`). This is useful if you need to know what the delimiters are.

The statement at lines 38–39 uses `StringTokenizer` method `countTokens` to determine the number of tokens in the string to be tokenized.

The condition in the `while` statement at lines 33–34 uses `StringTokenizer` method `hasMoreTokens` to determine whether there are more tokens in the string being tokenized. If so, the `append` method is invoked for the `JTextArea` `outputArea` to append the next token to the string in the `JTextArea`. The next token is obtained with a call to `StringTokenizer` method `nextToken` (line 39) that returns a `String`. The token is output followed by a newline character, so subsequent tokens appear on separate lines.

If you would like to change the delimiter string while tokenizing a string, you may do so by specifying a new delimiter string in a `nextToken` call as follows:

```
tokens.nextToken( newDelimiterString );
```

This feature is not demonstrated in Fig. 11.18.

11.7 Card Shuffling and Dealing Simulation

In this section, we use random number generation to develop a card shuffling and dealing simulation program. This program can then be used to implement programs that play specific card games.

We develop application `DeckOfCards` (Fig. 11.19), which creates a deck of 52 playing cards using `Card` objects, then enables the user to deal each card by clicking on a "`Deal card`" button. Each card dealt is displayed in a `JTextField`. The user can also shuffle the deck at any time by clicking on a "`Shuffle cards`" button.

```
1   // Fig. 11.19: DeckOfCards.java
2   // Card shuffling and dealing program.
3   import java.awt.*;
4   import java.awt.event.*;
5   import javax.swing.*;
6
7   public class DeckOfCards extends JFrame {
8      private Card deck[];
9      private int currentCard;
10     private JButton dealButton, shuffleButton;
11     private JTextField displayField;
12     private JLabel statusLabel;
13
14     // set up deck of cards and GUI
15     public DeckOfCards()
16     {
17        super( "Card Dealing Program" );
18
19        String faces[] = { "Ace", "Deuce", "Three", "Four", "Five", "Six",
20           "Seven", "Eight", "Nine", "Ten", "Jack", "Queen", "King" };
21        String suits[] = { "Hearts", "Diamonds", "Clubs", "Spades" };
22
23        deck = new Card[ 52 ];
24        currentCard = -1;
25
```

Fig. 11.19 Card shuffling and dealing simulation. (Part 1 of 4.)

```
26          // populate deck with Card objects
27          for ( int count = 0; count < deck.length; count++ )
28             deck[ count ] = new Card( faces[ count % 13 ],
29                suits[ count / 13 ] );
30
31          // set up GUI and event handling
32          Container container = getContentPane();
33          container.setLayout( new FlowLayout() );
34
35          dealButton = new JButton( "Deal card" );
36          dealButton.addActionListener(
37
38             new ActionListener() {  // anonymous inner class
39
40                // deal one card
41                public void actionPerformed( ActionEvent actionEvent )
42                {
43                   Card dealt = dealCard();
44
45                   if ( dealt != null ) {
46                      displayField.setText( dealt.toString() );
47                      statusLabel.setText( "Card #: " + currentCard );
48                   }
49                   else {
50                      displayField.setText( "NO MORE CARDS TO DEAL" );
51                      statusLabel.setText( "Shuffle cards to continue" );
52                   }
53                }
54
55             } // end anonymous inner class
56
57          ); // end call to addActionListener
58
59          container.add( dealButton );
60
61          shuffleButton = new JButton( "Shuffle cards" );
62          shuffleButton.addActionListener(
63
64             new ActionListener() {  // anonymous inner class
65
66                // shuffle deck
67                public void actionPerformed( ActionEvent actionEvent )
68                {
69                   displayField.setText( "SHUFFLING ..." );
70                   shuffle();
71                   displayField.setText( "DECK IS SHUFFLED" );
72                }
73
74             } // end anonymous inner class
75
76          ); // end call to addActionListener
77
78          container.add( shuffleButton );
```

Fig. 11.19 Card shuffling and dealing simulation. (Part 2 of 4.)

```
79
80        displayField = new JTextField( 20 );
81        displayField.setEditable( false );
82        container.add( displayField );
83
84        statusLabel = new JLabel();
85        container.add( statusLabel );
86
87        setSize( 275, 120 );   // set window size
88        setVisible( true );    // show window
89     }
90
91     // shuffle deck of cards with one-pass algorithm
92     private void shuffle()
93     {
94        currentCard = -1;
95
96        // for each card, pick another random card and swap them
97        for ( int first = 0; first < deck.length; first++ ) {
98           int second = ( int ) ( Math.random() * 52 );
99           Card temp = deck[ first ];
100          deck[ first ] = deck[ second ];
101          deck[ second ] = temp;
102       }
103
104       dealButton.setEnabled( true );
105    }
106
107    // deal one card
108    private Card dealCard()
109    {
110       if ( ++currentCard < deck.length )
111          return deck[ currentCard ];
112       else {
113          dealButton.setEnabled( false );
114          return null;
115       }
116    }
117
118    // execute application
119    public static void main( String args[] )
120    {
121       DeckOfCards application = new DeckOfCards();
122
123       application.setDefaultCloseOperation( JFrame.EXIT_ON_CLOSE );
124    }
125
126 } // end class DeckOfCards
127
128 // class to represent a card
129 class Card {
130    private String face;
131    private String suit;
```

Fig. 11.19 Card shuffling and dealing simulation. (Part 3 of 4.)

```
132
133        // constructor to initialize a card
134        public Card( String cardFace, String cardSuit )
135        {
136            face = cardFace;
137            suit = cardSuit;
138        }
139
140        // return String represenation of Card
141        public String toString()
142        {
143            return face + " of " + suit;
144        }
145
146    } // end class Card
```

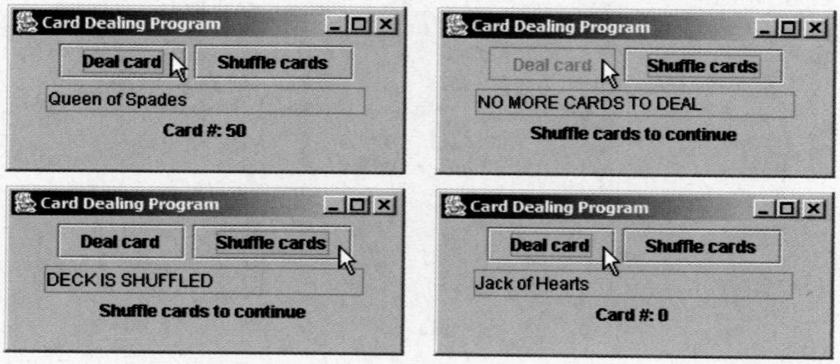

Fig. 11.19   Card shuffling and dealing simulation. (Part 4 of 4.)

Class `Card` (lines 129–146) contains two `String` instance variables—`face` and `suit`—that are used to store references to the face name and suit name for a specific `Card`. The constructor for the class (lines 134–138) receives two `String`s that it uses to initialize `face` and `suit`. Method `toString` (lines 141–144) is provided to create a `String` consisting of the `face` of the card, the string `" of "` and the `suit` of the card.

Class `DeckOfCards` (lines 7–126) consists of an array `deck` of 52 `Card` references, an integer `currentCard` representing the most recently dealt card in the deck array (–1 if no cards have been dealt yet) and the GUI components used to manipulate the deck of cards. The constructor method of the application instantiates the `deck` array (line 23) and uses the `for` statement at lines 27–29 to fill the `deck` array with `Card`s. Each `Card` is instantiated and initialized with two strings—one from the `faces` array (strings `"Ace"` through `"King"`) and one from the `suits` array (`"Hearts"`, `"Diamonds"`, `"Clubs"` and `"Spades"`). The calculation `count % 13` always results in a value from 0 to 12 (the thirteen indices of the `faces` array), and the calculation `count / 13` always results in a value from 0 to 3 (the four indices in the `suits` array). When the `deck` array is initialized, it contains the cards with faces ace through king in order for each suit.

When the user clicks the **Deal card** button, method `actionPerformed` at lines 41–53 invokes method `dealCard` (declared at lines 108–116) to get the next card in the array. If the `deck` is not empty, a `Card` object reference is returned; otherwise, `null` is returned. If the reference is not `null`, lines 46–47 display the `Card` in textfield `displayField` and display the card number in label `statusLabel`. If the reference returned by `dealCard` was `null`, the string "NO MORE CARDS TO DEAL" is displayed in the textfield and the string "`Shuffle cards to continue`" is displayed in the label.

When the user clicks the **Shuffle cards** button, its `actionPerformed` method at lines 67–72 invokes method `shuffle` (declared on lines 92–105) to shuffle the cards. The method loops through all 52 cards (array indices 0 to 51). For each card, a number between 0 and 51 is picked randomly. Next, the current `Card` object and the randomly selected `Card` object are swapped in the array. A total of only 52 swaps are made in a single pass of the entire array, and the array of `Card` objects is shuffled! When the shuffling is complete, the string "DECK IS SHUFFLED" is displayed in the `JTextField`.

Lines 104 and 113 use method `setEnabled` to activate and deactivate `dealButton`. Method `setEnabled` can be used on many GUI components. When it is called with a `false` argument, the GUI component for which it is called is disabled so the user cannot interact with it. To reactivate the button, call `setEnabled` with a `true` argument.

11.8 Regular Expressions, Class `Pattern` and Class `Matcher`

Regular expressions are sequence of characters and symbols that define a set of strings. They are useful for validating input and ensuring that data is in a particular format. For example, a ZIP code must consist of five digits, and a last name must start with a capital letter. One application of regular expressions is to facilitate the construction of a compiler. Often, a large and complex regular expression is used to validate the syntax of a program. If the program code does not match the regular expression, the compiler knows that there is a syntax error within the code. Regular expressions are part of Java's New I/O API, which is part of the Java 2 Platform, Standard Edition version 1.4. We discuss additional features of the New I/O API in Chapter 17 and Chapter 18.

Class `String` provides several methods for performing regular expression operations, the simplest of which is the matching operation. `String` method *matches* receives a string that specifies the regular expression and matches the contents of the `String` object on which it is called to the regular expression. The method returns a `boolean` indicating whether the match succeeded.

A regular expression consists of literal characters and special symbols. The table in Fig. 11.20 specifies some *predefined character classes* that can be used with regular expressions. A character class is an escape sequence that represents a group of characters. A *word character* is any alphanumeric character or underscore. A *white-space* character is a space, a tab, a carriage return, a newline or a form feed. A *digit* is any numeric character. Each character class matches a single character in the string we are attempting to match with the regular expression.

Character	Matches	Character	Matches
\d	any digit	\D	any non-digit
\w	any word character	\W	any non-word character
\s	any white space	\S	any non-white space

Fig. 11.20 Predefined character classes.

Regular expressions are not limited to these predefined character classes, however. The expressions employ various operators and other forms of notation to search for complex patterns. We examine several of these techniques in the application in Fig. 11.21 which validates user input via regular expressions.

When a user clicks **OK**, the program checks for empty fields (lines 98–104). If one or more fields are empty, the program informs the user that all fields must be filled before the program can validate the input (line 106). If there are no empty fields, the user input is validated. Line 109 validates the **first name**. To match a set of characters that does not have a predefined character class, use square brackets, []. For example, the pattern "[aeiou]" can be used to match a single vowel. Ranges of characters can be represented by placing a dash (-) between two characters. In the example, "[A-Z]" matches a single uppercase letter. If the first character in the brackets is the "^", the expression accepts any character other than those indicated. However, it is important to note that "[^Z]" is not the same as "[A-Y]", which matches uppercase letters A–Y; "[^Z]" matches any non-uppercase character (such as 'a' or the newline character), in addition to the uppercase letters other than Z. Ranges in character classes are determined by the letters' integer values. In this example, "[A-Za-z]" matches all uppercase and lowercase letters. The range "[A-z]" matches all letters and also matches those characters with an integer value between uppercase Z and lowercase a (such as % and 6). Like predefined character classes, character classes delimited by square brackets match a single character in the search object.

In line 109, the asterisk after the second character class indicates that any number of letters can be matched. In general, when the regular expression operator "*" appears in a regular expression, the program attempts to match zero or more occurrences of the subexpression immediately preceding the "*". Operator "+" attempts to match one or more occurrences of the subexpression immediately preceding "+". So, both "A*" and "A+" will match "A", but only "A*" will match an empty string.

```
1   // Fig. 11.21: ValidateFrame.java
2   // Validate user information using regular expressions.
3   import java.awt.*;
4   import java.awt.event.*;
5   import javax.swing.*;
6
7   public class ValidateFrame extends JFrame {
8       private JTextField phoneTextField, zipTextField, stateTextField,
9          cityTextField, addressTextField, firstTextField, lastTextField;
10
11      public ValidateFrame()
12      {
13          super( "Validate" );
14
15          // create the GUI components
16          JLabel phoneLabel = new JLabel( "Phone" );
17          JLabel zipLabel = new JLabel( "Zip" );
18          JLabel stateLabel = new JLabel( "State" );
19          JLabel cityLabel = new JLabel( "City" );
20          JLabel addressLabel = new JLabel( "Address" );
21          JLabel firstLabel = new JLabel( "First Name" );
```

Fig. 11.21 Validating user information using regular expressions. (Part 1 of 4.)

```
22          JLabel lastLabel = new JLabel( "Last Name" );
23
24          JButton okButton = new JButton( "OK" );
25          okButton.addActionListener(
26
27             new ActionListener() { // inner class
28
29                public void actionPerformed( ActionEvent event ) {
30                   validateDate();
31                }
32
33             } // end inner class
34
35          ); // end call to addActionListener
36
37          phoneTextField = new JTextField( 15 );
38          zipTextField = new JTextField( 5 );
39          stateTextField = new JTextField( 2 );
40          cityTextField = new JTextField( 12 );
41          addressTextField = new JTextField( 20 );
42          firstTextField = new JTextField( 20 );
43          lastTextField = new JTextField( 20 );
44
45          JPanel firstName = new JPanel();
46          firstName.add( firstLabel );
47          firstName.add( firstTextField );
48
49          JPanel lastName = new JPanel();
50          lastName.add( lastLabel );
51          lastName.add( lastTextField );
52
53          JPanel address1 = new JPanel();
54          address1.add( addressLabel );
55          address1.add( addressTextField );
56
57          JPanel address2 = new JPanel();
58          address2.add( cityLabel );
59          address2.add( cityTextField );
60          address2.add( stateLabel );
61          address2.add( stateTextField );
62          address2.add( zipLabel );
63          address2.add( zipTextField );
64
65          JPanel phone = new JPanel();
66          phone.add( phoneLabel );
67          phone.add( phoneTextField );
68
69          JPanel ok = new JPanel();
70          ok.add( okButton );
71
72          // add the components to the application
73          Container container = getContentPane();
74          container.setLayout( new GridLayout( 6, 1 ) );
```

Fig. 11.21   Validating user information using regular expressions. (Part 2 of 4.)

```
75
76          container.add( firstName );
77          container.add( lastName );
78          container.add( address1 );
79          container.add( address2 );
80          container.add( phone );
81          container.add( ok );
82
83          setSize( 325, 225 );
84          setVisible( true );
85
86       } // end ValidateFrame constructor
87
88       public static void main( String args[] )
89       {
90          ValidateFrame application = new ValidateFrame();
91          application.setDefaultCloseOperation( JFrame.EXIT_ON_CLOSE );
92       }
93
94       // handles okButton action event
95       private void validateDate()
96       {
97          // ensure that no textboxes are empty
98          if ( lastTextField.getText().equals( "" ) ||
99             firstTextField.getText().equals( "" ) ||
100            addressTextField.getText().equals( "" ) ||
101            cityTextField.getText().equals( "" ) ||
102            stateTextField.getText().equals( "" ) ||
103            zipTextField.getText().equals( "" ) ||
104            phoneTextField.getText().equals( "" ) ) // end condition
105
106            JOptionPane.showMessageDialog( this, "Please fill all fields" );
107
108         // if first name format invalid show message
109         else if ( !firstTextField.getText().matches( "[A-Z][a-zA-Z]*" ) )
110            JOptionPane.showMessageDialog( this, "Invalid first name" );
111
112         // if last name format invalid show message
113         else if ( !lastTextField.getText().matches( "[A-Z][a-zA-Z]*" ) )
114            JOptionPane.showMessageDialog( this, "Invalid last name" );
115
116         // if address format invalid show message
117         else if ( !addressTextField.getText().matches(
118               "\\d+\\s+([a-zA-Z]+|[a-zA-Z]+\\s[a-zA-Z]+)" ) )
119            JOptionPane.showMessageDialog( this, "Invalid address" );
120
121         // if city format invalid show message
122         else if ( !cityTextField.getText().matches(
123               "([a-zA-Z]+|[a-zA-Z]+\\s[a-zA-Z]+)" ) )
124            JOptionPane.showMessageDialog( this, "Invalid city" );
125
126         // if state format invalid show message
127         else if ( !stateTextField.getText().matches(
```

Fig. 11.21   Validating user information using regular expressions. (Part 3 of 4.)

```
128                     "([a-zA-Z]+|[a-zA-Z]+\\s[a-zA-Z]+)" ) )
129         JOptionPane.showMessageDialog( this, "Invalid state" );
130
131     // if zip code format invalid show message
132     else if ( !zipTextField.getText().matches( "\\d{5}" ) )
133         JOptionPane.showMessageDialog( this, "Invalid zip code" );
134
135     // if phone number format invalid show message
136     else if ( !phoneTextField.getText().matches(
137             "[1-9]\\d{2}-[1-9]\\d{2}-\\d{4}" ) )
138         JOptionPane.showMessageDialog( this, "Invalid phone number" );
139
140     else // information is valid, signal user
141         JOptionPane.showMessageDialog( this, "Thank you" );
142
143   } // end method validateDate
144
145 } // end class ValidateFrame
```

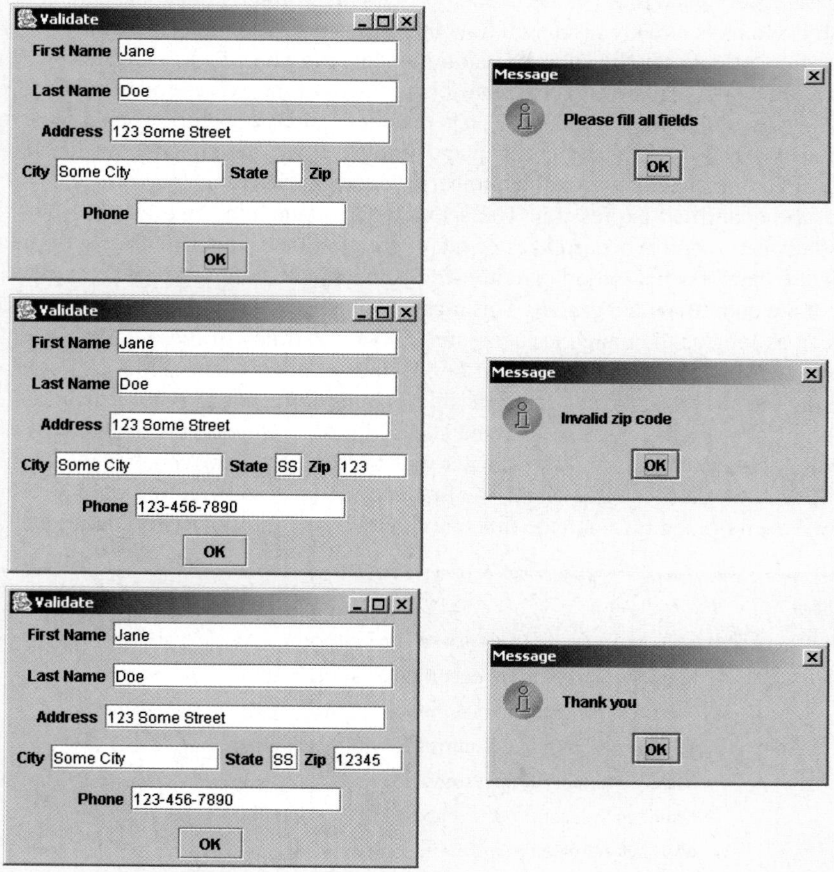

Fig. 11.21 Validating user information using regular expressions. (Part 4 of 4.)

If method `matches` returns `true` (line 109), the program attempts to validate the **last name** (line 113). The regular expression to validate the last name is identical to the one used to validate the first name. Again, this regular expression will match any word that begins with a capital letter.

Lines 117–118 validate the address. The first character class matches any digit one or more times (\\d+). Note that two \ characters are used because \ normally starts an escape sequences in a string. So, \\d in a Java string represents the regular expression pattern \d. Then we match one or more white-space characters (\\s+). The character "|" matches the expression to its left or to its right. For example, Hi (John|Jane) matches both Hi John and Hi Jane. The parentheses are used to group parts of the regular expression. In this example, the left side of | matches a single word and the right side matches two words separated by any amount of white space. So the address must contain a number followed by one or two words. Therefore, "10 Broadway" and "10 Main Street" are both valid addresses in this example. The **city** (line 122) and **state** (line 127) fields also match any word of at least one character or, alternatively, any two words of at least one character if the words are separated by a single space. This means both Waltham and West Newton would match.

The asterisk (*) and plus (+) are formally called *quantifiers*. Figure 11.22 lists various quantifiers. We have already discussed how the asterisk (*) and plus (+) quantifiers work. All quantifiers affect only the subexpression immediately preceding the quantifier. Quantifier question mark (?) matches zero or one occurrences of the expression that it quantifies. A set of braces containing one number ({n}) matches exactly n occurrences of the expression it quantifies. We demonstrate this quantifier to validate the zip code in Fig. 11.21 at line 132. Including a comma after the number enclosed in braces matches at least n occurrences of the quantified expression. The set of braces containing two numbers ({n,m}), matches between n and m occurrences of the expression that it qualifies. Quantifiers may be applied to patterns enclosed in parentheses to create more complex regular expressions.

All of the quantifiers are *greedy*. This means that they will match as many occurrences as they can as long as the match is successful. However, if any of these quantifiers is followed by a question mark (?), the quantifier becomes *reluctant* (sometimes called *lazy*). It then will match as few occurrences as possible as long as the match is successful.

The zip code (Fig. 11.21, line 132) matches a digit five times. This regular expression uses the digit character class and a quantifier with the digit five between braces. The phone number (line 136) matches three digits (the first one cannot be zero) followed by a dash followed by three more digits (again the first one cannot be zero) followed by four more digits.

Quantifier	Matches
*	Matches zero or more occurrences of the pattern.
+	Matches one or more occurrences of the pattern.
?	Matches zero or one occurrences of the pattern.
{n}	Matches exactly n occurrences.
{n,}	Matches at least n occurrences.
{n,m}	Matches between n and m (inclusive) occurrences.

Fig. 11.22   Quantifiers used in regular expressions.

Method `matches` checks whether an entire string conforms to a regular expression. For example, we want to accept `"Smith"` as a last name, but not `"9@Smith#"`. Method `matches` determines whether the entire string matches the regular expression. If only a substring matches the regular expression, method matches returns false.

Replacing Substrings and Splitting Strings

Sometimes it is useful to replace parts of a string, or split a string into pieces. For this purpose, class `String` provides methods *replaceAll*, *replaceFirst* and *split*. These methods are demonstrated in Fig. 11.23.

```
1   // Fig. 11.23: RegexSubstitution.java
2   // Using methods replaceFirst, replaceAll and split.
3   import javax.swing.*;
4
5   public class RegexSubstitution
6   {
7      public static void main( String args[] )
8      {
9         String firstString = "This sentence ends in 5 stars *****";
10        String secondString = "1, 2, 3, 4, 5, 6, 7, 8";
11
12        String output = "Original String 1: " + firstString;
13
14        // replace '*' with '^'
15        firstString = firstString.replaceAll( "\\*", "^" );
16
17        output += "\n^ substituted for *: " + firstString;
18
19        // replace 'stars' with 'carets'
20        firstString = firstString.replaceAll( "stars", "carets" );
21
22        output += "\n\"carets\" substituted for \"stars\": " + firstString;
23
24        // replace words with 'word'
25        output += "\nEvery word replaced by \"word\": " +
26           firstString.replaceAll( "\\w+", "word" );
27
28        output += "\n\nOriginal String 2: " + secondString;
29
30        // replace first three digits with 'digit'
31        for ( int i = 0; i < 3; i++ )
32           secondString = secondString.replaceFirst( "\\d", "digit" );
33
34        output += "\nFirst 3 digits replaced by \"digit\" : " +
35           secondString;
36        output += "\nString split at commas: [";
37
38        String[] results = secondString.split( ",\\s*" ); // split on commas
39
40        for ( int i = 0; i < results.length; i++ )
41           output += "\"" + results[ i ] + "\", "; // output results
```

Fig. 11.23 Methods `replaceFirst`, `replaceAll` and `split`. (Part 1 of 2.)

```
42
43            // remove the extra comma and add a bracket
44            output = output.substring( 0, output.length() - 2 ) + "]";
45
46            JOptionPane.showMessageDialog( null, output );
47            System.exit( 0 );
48
49       } // end method main
50
51   } // end class RegexSubstitution
```

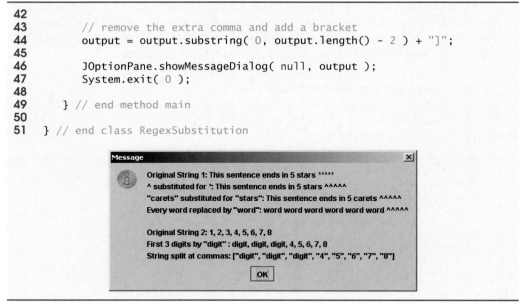

Fig. 11.23   Methods `replaceFirst`, `replaceAll` and `split`. (Part 2 of 2.)

Method `replaceAll` replaces text in a string with new text (the second argument) wherever the original string matches a regular expression (the first argument). Line 15 replaces every instance of `"*"` in `firstString` with `"^"`. Notice that the regular expression (`"\\*"`) precedes character * with two backslashes, \. Normally, * is a quantifier indicating that a regular expression should match any number of occurrences of a preceding pattern. However, in line 15, we want to find all occurrences of the literal character *; to do this, we must escape character * with character \. By escaping a special regular expression character with a \, we instruct the regular-expression matching engine to find the actual character, as opposed to what it represents in a regular expression. Because the expression is stored in a Java string and \ is a special character in Java strings, we must include an additional \. So, the Java string `"\\*"` represents the regular expression pattern `\*` which matches a single `'*'` character in the search string. In line 20, every match for the regular expression `"stars"` in `firstString` is replaced with `"carets"`.

Method `replaceFirst` (line 32) replaces the first occurrence of a pattern match. Java strings are immutable, therefore method `replaceFirst` returns a new string in which the appropriate characters have been replaced. This line takes the original string and replaces it with the string returned by `replaceFirst`. By iterating three times we replace the first three instances of a digit (`\d`) in `secondString` with the text `"digit"`.

Method `split` divides a string into several substrings. The original string is broken in any location that matches a specified regular expression. Method `split` returns an array of strings containing the substrings between matches for the regular expression. In line 38, we use method `split` to tokenize a string of comma-separated integers. The argument is the regular expression that locates the delimiter. In this case, we use the regular expression `",\\s*"` to separate the substrings wherever a comma occurs. By matching any white-space characters, we eliminate extra spaces from the resulting substrings. Notice that the commas and white space are not returned as part of the substrings. Again, note that the Java string `",\\s*"` represents the regular expression `,\s*`.

Classes *Pattern* and *Matcher*

In addition to the regular expression capabilities of class `String`, Java provides other classes in package `java.util.regex` that help developers manipulate regular expressions. Class `Pattern` represents a regular expression. Class `Matcher` contains both a regular expression pattern and a *CharSequence* in which to search for the pattern.

CharSequence is an interface that allows read access to a sequence of characters. The interface requires that the methods `charAt`, `length`, `subSequence` and `toString` be declared. Both `String` and `StringBuffer` implement interface `CharSequence`, so an instance of either of these classes can be used with class `Matcher`.

Common Programming Error 11.4

A regular expression can be tested against an object of any class that implements interface *CharSequence, but the regular expression must be a* *String*. *Attempting to create a regular expression as a* *StringBuffer is an error.*

If a regular expression will be used only once, static `Pattern` method *matches* can be used. This method takes a string that specifies the regular expression and a CharSequence on which to perform the match. This method returns a `boolean` indicating whether the search object (the second argument) matches the regular expression.

If a regular expression will be used more than once, it is more efficient to use static `Pattern` method `compile` to create a specific `Pattern` object for that regular expression. This method receives a string representing the pattern and returns a new `Pattern` object, which can then be used to call method *matcher*. This method receives a CharSequence to search and returns a `Matcher` object.

`Matcher` provides method *matches* which performs the same task as `Pattern` method `matches`, but receives no arguments—the search pattern and search object are encapsulated in the `Matcher` object. Class `Matcher` provides other methods, including `find`, `lookingAt`, `replaceFirst` and `replaceAll`.

Figure 11.24 presents a simple example that employs regular expressions. This program matches birthdays against a regular expression. The expression matches only birthdays that do not occur in April and that belong to people whose names begin with `"J"`.

```
1   // Fig. 11.24: RegexMatches.java
2   // Demonstrating Classes Pattern and Matcher.
3   import java.util.regex.*;
4   import javax.swing.*;
5
6   class RegexMatches
7   {
8      public static void main( String args[] )
9      {
10         String output = "";
11
```

Fig. 11.24 Regular expressions checking birthdays. (Part 1 of 2.)

```
12          // create regular expression
13          Pattern expression =
14             Pattern.compile( "J.*\\d[0-35-9]-\\d\\d-\\d\\d" );
15
16          String string1 = "Jane's Birthday is 05-12-75\n" +
17             "Dave's Birthday is 11-04-68\n" +
18             "John's Birthday is 04-28-73\n" +
19             "Joe's Birthday is 12-17-77";
20
21          // match regular expression to string and print matches
22          Matcher matcher = expression.matcher( string1 );
23
24          while ( matcher.find() )
25             output += matcher.group() + "\n";
26
27          JOptionPane.showMessageDialog( null, output );
28          System.exit( 0 );
29
30       } // end main
31
32    } // end class RegexMatches
```

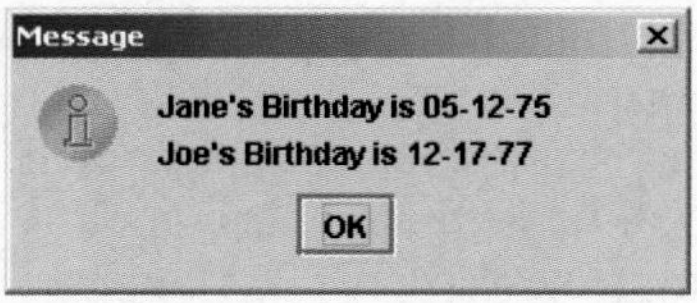

Message

> Jane's Birthday is 05-12-75
> Joe's Birthday is 12-17-77
>
> **OK**

Fig. 11.24 Regular expressions checking birthdays. (Part 2 of 2.)

Lines 13–14 create a `Pattern` by invoking static `Pattern` method `compile`. The dot character " . " in the regular expression (line 14) matches any single character except a newline character.

Line 22 creates the `Matcher` object for the compiled regular expression and the matching sequence (`string1`). Lines 24–25 use a `while` loop to iterate through the string. Line 24 uses `Matcher` method *find* to attempt to match a piece of the search object to the search pattern. Each call to this method starts at the point where the last call ended, so multiple matches can be found. `Matcher` method *lookingAt* performs the same way, except it always starts from the beginning of the search object and will always find the first match if there is one.

Common Programming Error 11.5

Method `matches` (from class `String`, `Pattern` or `Matcher`) will return `true` only if the entire search object matches the regular expression. Methods `find` and `lookingAt` (from class `Matcher`) will return `true` if a portion of the search object matches the regular expression.

Line 25 uses `Matcher` method *group*, which returns the string from the search object that matches the search pattern. The string that is returned is the one that was last matched by a call to `find` or `lookingAt`. The output in Fig. 11.24 shows the two matches that were found in `string1`.

Regular Expression Web Resources

This section presented several of Java's regular expression capabilities. The following Web sites provides more information on regular expressions.

`developer.java.sun.com/developer/technicalArticles/releases/1.4regex`
This is a thorough description of the regular expression capabilities of the Java language.

`java.sun.com/docs/books/tutorial/extra/regex/index.html`
This tutorial explains how to use the regular expression API found in Java.

`java.sun.com/j2se/1.4.1/docs/api/java/util/regex/package-summary.html`
This page is the javadoc overview of package `java.util.regex`.

11.9 (Optional Case Study) Thinking About Objects: Event Handling

Objects do not ordinarily perform their operations spontaneously. Rather, a specific operation is normally invoked when one object sends an *event*, or message, to a receiving object. In earlier sections, we mentioned that objects interact by sending and receiving messages. We began to model the behavior of our elevator system by using statechart and activity diagrams in Section 5.11 and collaboration diagrams in Section 7.10. In this section, we discuss how the objects of the elevator system interact.

Events

In Fig. 7.18, we presented an example of a person pressing a button by sending a `press-Button` message to the button—specifically, the `Person` object called method `press-Button` of the `Button` object. This message describes an action that is currently happening; in other words, the `Person` presses a `Button`. In general, the message name structure is a verb preceding a noun—e.g., the name of the `pressButton` message consists of the verb "press" followed by the noun "button."

An event is a message that notifies an object of an action that has already happened. For example, in this section, we modify our simulation so the `Elevator` sends an `elevatorArrived` event to the `Elevator`'s `Door` when the `Elevator` arrives at a `Floor`. In Section 7.10, the `Elevator` opens this `Door` directly by sending an `openDoor` message. Listening for an `elevatorArrived` event allows the `Door` to determine the appropriate actions to take when the `Elevator` has arrived, such as notifying the `Person` that the `Door` has opened. This reinforces the OOD principle of encapsulation and models the real world more closely. In reality, the door—not the elevator—"notifies" a person of a door's opening.

Notice that the event-naming structure is the inverse of the first type of message's naming structure. By convention, the event name consists of the noun preceding the verb. For instance, the `elevatorArrived` event name consists of the noun "elevator" preceding the verb "arrived."

In our simulation, we create a superclass called `ElevatorSimulationEvent` (Fig. 11.25) that represents an event in our model. `ElevatorSimulationEvent` contains a `Location` reference (line 11) that represents the location where the event was generated and an `Object` reference (line 14) to the source of the event. In our simulation, objects use instances of `ElevatorSimulationEvent` to send events to other objects. When an object receives an event, that object may use method `getLocation` (lines 31–34) and method `getSource` (lines 43–46) to determine the event's location and origin.

```
1    // ElevatorSimulationEvent.java
2    // Basic event packet holding Location object
3    package com.deitel.jhtp5.elevator.event;
4
5    // Deitel packages
6    import com.deitel.jhtp5.elevator.model.*;
7
8    public class ElevatorSimulationEvent {
9
10      // Location that generated ElevatorSimulationEvent
11      private Location location;
12
13      // source of generated ElevatorSimulationEvent
14      private Object source;
15
16      // ElevatorSimulationEvent constructor sets Location
17      public ElevatorSimulationEvent( Object source,
18         Location location )
19      {
20         setSource( source );
21         setLocation( location );
22      }
23
24      // set ElevatorSimulationEvent Location
25      public void setLocation( Location eventLocation )
26      {
27         location = eventLocation;
28      }
29
30      // get ElevatorSimulationEvent Location
31      public Location getLocation()
32      {
33         return location;
34      }
35
36      // set ElevatorSimulationEvent source
37      private void setSource( Object eventSource )
38      {
39         source = eventSource;
40      }
41
42      // get ElevatorSimulationEvent source
43      public Object getSource()
44      {
45         return source;
46      }
47   }
```

Fig. 11.25 Class `ElevatorSimulationEvent` is the superclass for all other event classes in our model .

For example, a `Door` may send an `ElevatorSimulationEvent` to a `Person` when opening or closing, and the `Elevator` may send an `ElevatorSimulationEvent` informing a person of a departure or arrival. Having different objects send the same event type to describe different actions could be confusing. To eliminate ambiguity as we discuss which events are sent by objects, we create several ElevatorSimulationEvent subclasses in Fig. 11.26, so we will have an easier time associating each event with its sender. According to Fig. 11.26, classes BellEvent, PersonMoveEvent, LightEvent, ButtonEvent, ElevatorMoveEvent and DoorEvent are subclasses of class ElevatorSimulationEvent. Using these event subclasses, a Door sends a different event (a DoorEvent) than does a Button (which sends a ButtonEvent). Figure 11.27 displays the triggering actions of the subclass events. Note that all actions in Fig. 11.27 appear in the form "noun" + "verb".

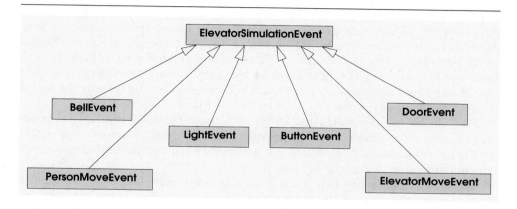

Fig. 11.26 Class diagram that models the generalization between ElevatorSimulationEvent and its subclasses.

Event	Sent when (triggering action)	Sent by object of class
BellEvent	the Bell has rung	Bell
ButtonEvent	a Button has been pressed a Button has been reset	Button Button
DoorEvent	a Door has opened a Door has closed	Door Door
LightEvent	a Light has turned on a Light has turned off	Light
PersonMoveEvent	a Person has been created a Person has arrived at the Elevator a Person has entered the Elevator a Person has exited the Elevator a Person has pressed a Button a Person has exited the simulation	Person
ElevatorMoveEvent	the Elevator has arrived at a Floor the Elevator has departed from a Floor	Elevator

Fig. 11.27 Triggering actions of the ElevatorSimulationEvent subclass events.

Event Handling
Java event handling is similar to the concept of a *collaboration* described in Section 7.10. Event handling consists of an object of one class sending a particular message (an event) to objects of other classes *listening for that type of message.*[2] The difference is that the objects receiving the message must *register* to receive the message; therefore, event handling describes *how* an object sends an event to other objects "listening" for that type of event— these objects are called *event listeners*. To send an event, the sending object invokes a particular method of the receiving object while passing the event object as a parameter. In our simulation, this event object belongs to a class that extends ElevatorSimulationEvent.

We presented a collaboration diagram in Fig. 7.19 showing interactions of two Person objects—waitingPassenger and ridingPassenger—as they enter and exit the Elevator. Figure 11.28 shows a modified diagram that incorporates event handling. There are two differences between the diagrams. First, the interactions of Fig. 11.28 occur on the first Floor. This allows us to name all Button and Door objects (firstFloor-Door and firstFloorButton) to eliminate ambiguity, because the Button and Door classes each have three objects in our simulation. The interactions that occur on the second Floor are identical to the ones that occur on the first Floor.

The second, and most substantial, difference between Fig. 11.28 and Fig. 7.19 is that the Elevator *informs* each object (via an event) of an action *that has already happened*— the Elevator *has arrived*. The objects that receive the event then perform some action in response to the type of message they receive.

According to messages 1, 2, 3 and 4, the Elevator performs only one action—it sends elevatorArrived events to objects interested in receiving those events. Specifically, the Elevator object sends an ElevatorMoveEvent using the receiving object's elevatorArrived method. Figure 11.28 begins with the Elevator sending an elevatorArrived event to the elevatorButton. The elevatorButton then *resets itself* (message 1.1). The Elevator then sends an elevatorArrived event to the Bell (message 2), and the Bell invokes its ringBell method accordingly (i.e., the Bell object sends *itself* a ringBell message in message 2.1).

Next, the Elevator sends an elevatorArrived message to the elevatorDoor (message 3). The elevatorDoor then opens itself by invoking its openDoor method (message 3.1). At this point, the elevatorDoor is open, but has not informed the ridingPassenger of opening. Before informing the ridingPassenger, the elevatorDoor opens the firstFloorDoor by sending it an openDoor message (message 3.2)—this guarantees that the ridingPassenger will not exit before the firstFloor-Door opens. The firstFloorDoor then informs the waitingPassenger that the firstFloorDoor has opened (message 3.2.1), and the waitingPassenger enters the Elevator (message 3.2.1.1). All messages nested in 3.2 have been passed, so the elevatorDoor may inform the ridingPassenger that elevatorDoor has opened by invoking method doorOpened of the ridingPassenger (message 3.3). The riding-Passenger responds by exiting the Elevator (message 3.3.1).[3]

---

2. Technically, one object sends a notification of an event—or some triggering action—to another object. However, Java parlance refers to sending this notification as "sending an event."
3. The collaboration diagram still has the problem of the waitingPassenger entering the Elevator (message 3.2.1.1) before the ridingPassenger exits (message 3.3.1). Section 16.12 shows how to solve this problem by using multithreading, synchronization and active classes.

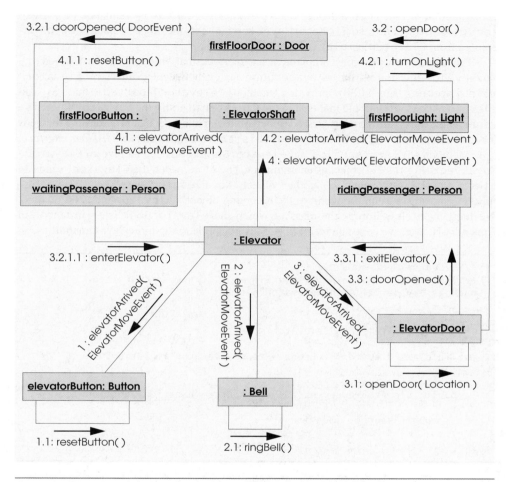

Fig. 11.28 Modified collaboration diagram for passengers entering and exiting the Elevator on the first Floor.

Lastly, the Elevator informs the ElevatorShaft of the arrival (message 4). The ElevatorShaft then informs the firstFloorButton of the arrival (message 4.1), and the firstFloorButton resets itself (message 4.1.1). The ElevatorShaft then informs the firstFloorLight of the arrival (message 4.2), and the firstFloorLight illuminates itself (message 4.2.1).

Event Listeners

We demonstrated event handling between the Elevator and object elevatorDoor using the modified collaboration diagram of Fig. 11.28—the Elevator sends an elevator-Arrived event to the elevatorDoor (message 3). We first must determine the event object that the Elevator will pass to the elevatorDoor. According to the note in the lower left-hand corner of Fig. 11.28, the Elevator passes an ElevatorMoveEvent (Fig. 11.29) object when the Elevator invokes an elevatorArrived method. The generalization class diagram of Fig. 11.26 indicates that ElevatorMoveEvent is a subclass of ElevatorSimulationEvent, so ElevatorMoveEvent inherits the Object and Location references from ElevatorSimulationEvent.[4]

The elevatorDoor must implement an interface that "listens" for an ElevatorMoveEvent—this makes the elevatorDoor an event listener. Interface ElevatorMoveListener (Fig. 11.30) provides methods elevatorDeparted (line 8) and elevatorArrived (line 11) that enable the Elevator to notify the ElevatorMoveListener when the Elevator has arrived or departed. An interface that provides the methods for an event listener, such as ElevatorMoveListener, is called an *event listener interface*.

Methods elevatorArrived and elevatorDeparted each receive an ElevatorMoveEvent (Fig. 11.29) object as an argument. Therefore, when the Elevator "sends an elevatorArrived event" to another object, the Elevator passes an ElevatorMoveEvent object as an argument to the receiving object's elevatorArrived method. We implement class Door—the class of which the elevatorDoor is an instance—in Appendix H, after we continue refining our design and learning more Java capabilities.

```java
1   // ElevatorMoveEvent.java
2   // Indicates on which Floor the Elevator arrived or departed
3   package com.deitel.jhtp5.elevator.event;
4
5   // Deitel package
6   import com.deitel.jhtp5.elevator.model.*;
7
8   public class ElevatorMoveEvent extends ElevatorSimulationEvent {
9
10      // ElevatorMoveEvent constructor
11      public ElevatorMoveEvent( Object source, Location location )
12      {
13          super( source, location );
14      }
15  }
```

Fig. 11.29 Class ElevatorMoveEvent, a subclass of ElevatorSimulationEvent, is sent when the Elevator has arrived at or departed from a Floor.

```java
1   // ElevatorMoveListener.java
2   // Methods invoked when Elevator has either departed or arrived
3   package com.deitel.jhtp5.elevator.event;
4
5   public interface ElevatorMoveListener {
6
```

Fig. 11.30 Interface ElevatorMoveListener provides the methods required to listen for Elevator departure and arrival events. (Part 1 of 2.)

---

4. In our simulation, all event classes have this structure—that is, the structure of class ElevatorMoveEvent is identical to the structure of class DoorEvent, ButtonEvent, etc. When you finish reading this section, we recommend that you view the implementation of the events in Appendix D for more details of the structure of our system events—Fig. D.1–Fig. D.7 present the code for the events, and Fig. D.8–Fig. D.14 present the code for the event listeners.

```
 7        // invoked when Elevator has departed
 8        public void elevatorDeparted( ElevatorMoveEvent moveEvent );
 9
10        // invoked when Elevator has arrived
11        public void elevatorArrived( ElevatorMoveEvent moveEvent );
12    }
```

Fig. 11.30   Interface `ElevatorMoveListener` provides the methods required to listen for `Elevator` departure and arrival events. (Part 2 of 2.)

Class Diagram Revisited

Figure 11.31 modifies the associations in the class diagram of Fig. 10.28 to include event handling. Like the collaboration diagram of Fig. 11.28, Fig. 11.31 indicates that an object informs, or *signals*, another object that some event has occurred. If an object receiving the event invokes a `private` method, the class diagram represents this method invocation as a *self association*—that is, the class contains an association with itself. The `Button`, `Door`, `Light` and `Bell` classes contain self associations; note that the association does not include an arrowhead indicating the direction of the association, because the class's association is with itself. Lastly, the diagram includes an association between class `Door` and class `Person` (the `Door` informs a `Person` that the `Door` has opened), because we established the relationship between all `Door` objects and a `Person` object.

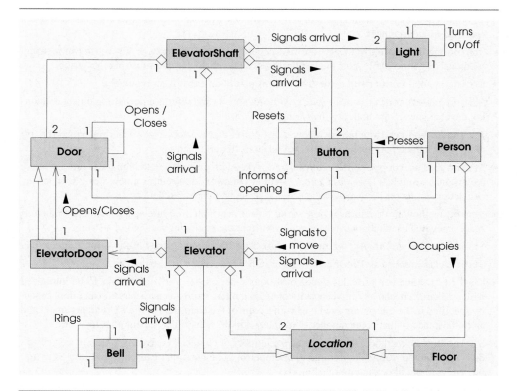

Fig. 11.31   Class diagram of our simulator (including event handling).

SUMMARY

- A character literal's value is its integer value in the Unicode character set. Strings can include letters, digits and special characters such as +, -, *, / and $. A string in Java is an object of class `String`. String literals (string constants) are often referred to as anonymous `String` objects and are written in double quotes in a program.

- `String` method `length` returns the number of characters in a `String`.

- `String` method `charAt` returns the character at a specific position.

- Method `equals` tests any two objects for equality. The method returns `true` if the objects are equal, `false` otherwise. Method `equals` uses a lexicographical comparison for `String`s.

- When primitive-type values are compared with ==, the result is `true` if both values are identical. When references are compared with ==, the result is `true` if both references refer to the same object in memory.

- Java treats all string literals with the same contents as one anonymous `String` object.

- `String` method `equalsIgnoreCase` performs a case-insensitive string comparison.

- `String` method `compareTo` uses a lexicographical comparison and returns 0 if the strings it is comparing are equal, a negative number if the string `compareTo` is invoked on is less than the `String` that is passed as an argument and a positive number if the string that `compareTo` is invoked on is greater than the string that is passed as an argument.

- `String` method `regionMatches` compares portions of two strings for equality.

- `String` method `startsWith` determines whether a string starts with the characters specified as an argument. `String` method `endsWith` determines whether a string ends with the characters specified as an argument.

- `String` method `indexOf` locates the first occurrence of a character or a substring in a string. Method `lastIndexOf` locates the last occurrence of a character or a substring in a string.

- `String` method `substring` copies and returns part of an existing string object.

- `String` method `concat` concatenates two string objects and returns a new string object containing the characters from both original strings.

- `String` method `replace` returns a new string object that replaces every occurrence in a `String` of its first character argument with its second character argument.

- `String` method `toUpperCase` returns a new string with uppercase letters in the positions where the original string had lowercase letters. Method `toLowerCase` returns a new string with lowercase letters in the positions where the original string had uppercase letters.

- `String` method `trim` returns a new string object in which all white-space characters (such as spaces, newlines and tabs) have been removed from the beginning and end of a string.

- `String` method `toCharArray` returns a `char` array containing a copy of the string's characters.

- `String` class method `valueOf` returns its argument converted to a string.

- Class `StringBuffer` provides three constructors that enable `StringBuffer`s to be initialized with no characters and an initial capacity of 16 characters; with no characters and an initial capacity specified in the integer argument; or with a copy of the characters of the `String` argument and an initial capacity that is the number of characters in the `String` argument plus 16.

- `StringBuffer` method `length` returns the number of characters currently stored in a `String-Buffer`. Method `capacity` returns the number of characters that can be stored in a `String-Buffer` without allocating more memory.

- Method `ensureCapacity` ensures that a `StringBuffer` has at least the specified capacity. Method `setLength` increases or decreases the length of a `StringBuffer`.

- `StringBuffer` method `charAt` returns the character at the specified index. Method `setCharAt` sets the character at the specified position. Method `getChars` copies characters in the `String-Buffer` into the character array passed as an argument.

- Class `StringBuffer` provides overloaded `append` methods to add primitive-type, character array, `String` and `Object` values to the end of a `StringBuffer`. `StringBuffer`s and the `append` methods are used by the Java compiler to implement the + and += concatenation operators.

- Class `StringBuffer` provides overloaded `insert` methods to insert primitive-type, character array, `String` and `Object` values at any position in a `StringBuffer`.

- Class `Character` provides a constructor that takes a character argument.

- `Character` method `isDefined` determines whether a character is defined in the Unicode character set. If so, the method returns `true`; otherwise, it returns `false`.

- `Character` method `isDigit` determines whether a character is a defined Unicode digit. If so, the method returns `true`; otherwise, it returns `false`.

- `Character` method `isJavaIdentifierStart` determines whether a character can be used as the first character of an identifier in Java [i.e., a letter, an underscore (_) or a dollar sign ($)]. If so, the method returns `true`; otherwise, it returns `false`.

- `Character` method `isJavaIdentifierPart` determines whether a character can be used in an identifier in Java [i.e., a digit, a letter, an underscore (_) or a dollar sign ($)]. Method `isLetter` determines whether a character is a letter. Method `isLetterOrDigit` determines whether a character is a letter or a digit. In each case, if so, the method returns `true`; otherwise, it returns `false`.

- `Character` method `isLowerCase` determines whether a character is a lowercase letter. `Character` method `isUpperCase` determines whether a character is an uppercase letter. In both cases, if so, the method returns `true`; otherwise, `false`.

- `Character` method `toUpperCase` converts a character to its uppercase equivalent. Method `toLowerCase` converts a character to its lowercase equivalent.

- `Character` method `digit` converts its character argument into an integer in the number system specified by its integer argument `radix`. Method `forDigit` converts its integer argument `digit` into a character in the number system specified by its integer argument `radix`.

- `Character` method `charValue` returns the `char` stored in a `Character` object. Method `toString` returns a `String` representation of a `Character`.

- `StringTokenizer`'s default constructor creates a `StringTokenizer` for its string argument that will use the default delimiter string " \t\n\r\f", consisting of a space, a newline, a tab and a carriage return for tokenization.

- `StringTokenizer` method `countTokens` returns the number of tokens in a string to be tokenized.

- `StringTokenizer` method `hasMoreTokens` determines whether there are more tokens in the string being tokenized.

- `StringTokenizer` method `nextToken` returns a `String` with the next token.

TERMINOLOGY

append method of class `StringBuffer`	character set
appending strings to other strings	`charAt` method of class `String`
array of strings	`charAt` method of class `StringBuffer`
`capacity` method of class `StringBuffer`	`charValue` method of class `Character`
`Character` class	`compareTo` method of class `String`
character code	comparing strings
character literal	`concat` method of class `String`

concatenation
countTokens method (StringTokenizer)
delimiter
digit method of class Character
empty string
endsWith method of class String
equals method of class String
equalsIgnoreCase method of String
forDigit method of class Character
getChars method of class String
getChars method of class StringBuffer
hasMoreTokens method
hexadecimal digits
indexOf method of class String
StringIndexOutOfBoundsException
insert method of class StringBuffer
isDefined method of class Character
isDigit method of class Character
isJavaIdentifierPart method
isJavaIdentifierStart method
isLetter method of class Character
isLetterOrDigit method of Character
isLowerCase method of class Character
isUpperCase method of class Character
lastIndexOf method of class String
length method of class String
length method of class StringBuffer
length of a string
literal

nextToken method of StringTokenizer
numeric code representation of a character
regionMatches method of class String
replace method of class String
search string
setCharAt method of class StringBuffer
startsWith method of class String
string
String class
string concatenation
string literal
string processing
StringBuffer class
StringTokenizer class
substring method of String class
toCharArray method of class String
token
tokenizing strings
toLowerCase method of class Character
toLowerCase method of class String
toString method of class Character
toString method of class StringBuffer
toUpperCase method of class Character
toUpperCase method of class String
trim method of class String
Unicode character set
valueOf method of class String
white-space characters

SELF-REVIEW EXERCISES

11.1 State whether each of the following is *true* or *false*. If *false*, explain why.
   a) When String objects are compared using ==, the result is true if the Strings contain the same values.
   b) A String can be modified after it is created.

11.2 For each of the following, write a single statement that performs the indicated task:
   a) Compare the string in s1 to the string in s2 for equality of contents.
   b) Append the string s2 to the string s1, using +=.
   c) Determine the length of the string in s1.

ANSWERS TO SELF-REVIEW EXERCISES

11.1 a) False. String objects that are compared using operator == are compared to determine whether they are the same object in memory.
   b) False. String objects are immutable and cannot be modified after they are created. StringBuffer objects can be modified after they are created.

11.2 a) s1.equals(s2)
   b) s1 += s2;
   c) s1.length()

EXERCISES

Exercise 11.3–Exercise 11.6 are reasonably challenging. Once you have done these problems, you ought to be able to implement most popular card games easily.

11.3   Modify the program in Fig. 11.19 so that the card-dealing method deals a five-card poker hand. Then write methods that determine whether the hand contains

     a)   a pair;

     b)   two pairs;

     c)   three of a kind (e.g., three jacks);

     d)   four of a kind (e.g., four aces);

     e)   a flush (i.e., all five cards of the same suit);

     f)   a straight (i.e., five cards of consecutive face values);

     g)   a full house (i.e., two cards of one face value and three cards of another face value).

11.4   Use the methods developed in Exercise 11.3 to write a program that deals two five-card poker hands, evaluates each hand and determines which is the better hand.

11.5   Modify the program developed in Exercise 11.4 so that it can simulate the dealer. The dealer's five-card hand is dealt "face down" so the player cannot see it. The program should then evaluate the dealer's hand and, based on the quality of the hand, the dealer should draw one, two or three more cards to replace the corresponding number of unneeded cards in the original hand. The program should then reevaluate the dealer's hand. (*Caution*: This is a difficult problem!)

11.6   Modify the program developed in Exercise 11.5 so that it can handle the dealer's hand automatically, but the player is allowed to decide which cards of the player's hand to replace. The program should then evaluate both hands and determine who wins. Now, use this new program to play 20 games against the computer. Who wins more games, you or the computer? Have a friend play 20 games against the computer. Who wins more games? Based on the results of these games, refine your poker-playing program. (This, too, is a difficult problem.) Play 20 more games. Does your modified program play a better game?

11.7   Write an application that uses `String` method `compareTo` to compare two strings input by the user. Output whether the first string is less than, equal to or greater than the second.

11.8   Write an application that uses `String` method `regionMatches` to compare two strings input by the user. The program should input the number of characters to be compared and the starting index of the comparison. The program should state whether the strings are equal. Ignore the case of the characters when performing the comparison.

11.9   Write an application that uses random number generation to create sentences. Use four arrays of strings called `article`, `noun`, `verb` and `preposition`. Create a sentence by selecting a word at random from each array in the following order: `article`, `noun`, `verb`, `preposition`, `article` and `noun`. As each word is picked, concatenate it to the previous words in the sentence. The words should be separated by spaces. When the final sentence is output, it should start with a capital letter and end with a period. The program should generate 20 sentences and output them to a text area.

     The article array should contain the articles `"the"`, `"a"`, `"one"`, `"some"` and `"any"`; the noun array should contain the nouns `"boy"`, `"girl"`, `"dog"`, `"town"` and `"car"`; the verb array should contain the verbs `"drove"`, `"jumped"`, `"ran"`, `"walked"` and `"skipped"`; the preposition array should contain the prepositions `"to"`, `"from"`, `"over"`, `"under"` and `"on"`.

     After the preceding program is written, modify the program to produce a short story consisting of several of these sentences. (How about the possibility of a random term paper writer?)

11.10   (*Limericks*) A limerick is a humorous five-line verse in which the first and second lines rhyme with the fifth, and the third line rhymes with the fourth. Using techniques similar to those developed in Exercise 11.9, write a Java program that produces random limericks. Polishing this program to produce good limericks is a challenging problem, but the result will be worth the effort!

11.11 *(Pig Latin)* Write an application that encodes English language phrases into pig Latin. Pig Latin is a form of coded language. Many variations exist in the methods used to form pig Latin phrases. For simplicity, use the following algorithm:

To form a pig Latin phrase from an English language phrase, tokenize the phrase into words with an object of class `StringTokenizer`. To translate each English word into a pig Latin word, place the first letter of the English word at the end of the word and add the letters "ay." Thus, the word "jump" becomes "umpjay," the word "the" becomes "hetay," and the word "computer" becomes "omputercay." Blanks between words remain as blanks. Assume the following: The English phrase consists of words separated by blanks, there are no punctuation marks and all words have two or more letters. Method `printLatinWord` should display each word. Each token returned from `nextToken` is passed to method `printLatinWord` to print the pig Latin word. Enable the user to input the sentence. Keep a running display of all the converted sentences in a text area.

11.12 Write an application that inputs a telephone number as a string in the form (555) 555-5555. The program should use an object of class `StringTokenizer` to extract the area code as a token, the first three digits of the phone number as a token and the last four digits of the phone number as a token. The seven digits of the phone number should be concatenated into one string. The program should convert the area code string to `int` (remember `parseInt`!) and convert the phone number string to `long`. Both the area code and the phone number should be printed. Remember that you will have to change delimiter characters during the tokenization process.

11.13 Write an application that inputs a line of text, tokenizes the line with an object of class `StringTokenizer` and outputs the tokens in reverse order. Use space characters as delimiters.

11.14 Use the string-comparison methods discussed in this chapter and the techniques for sorting arrays developed in Chapter 7 to write a program that alphabetizes a list of strings. Allow the user to enter the strings in a text field. Display the results in a text area.

11.15 Write an application that inputs a line of text and outputs the text twice—once in all uppercase letters and once in all lowercase letters.

11.16 Write an application that inputs several lines of text and a search character and uses `String` method `indexOf` to determine the number of occurrences of the character in the text.

11.17 Write an application based on the program in Exercise 11.16 that inputs several lines of text and uses `String` method `indexOf` to determine the total number of occurrences of each letter of the alphabet in the text. Uppercase and lowercase letters should be counted together. Store the totals for each letter in an array, and print the values in tabular format after the totals have been determined.

11.18 Write an application that reads a line of text, tokenizes the line using space characters as delimiters and outputs only those words beginning with the letter "b." The results should appear in a text area.

11.19 Write an application that reads a line of text, tokenizes it using space characters as delimiters and outputs only those words ending with the letters "ED." The results should appear in a text area.

11.20 Write an application that inputs an integer code for a character and displays the corresponding character. Modify this program so that it generates all possible three-digit codes in the range from 000 to 255 and attempts to print the corresponding characters. Display the results in a text area.

11.21 Write your own versions of `String` search methods `indexOf` and `lastIndexOf`.

11.22 Write a program that reads a five-letter word from the user and produces all possible three-letter words that can be derived from the letters of the five-letter word. For example, the three-letter words produced from the word "bathe" include "ate," "bat," "bet," "tab," "hat," "the" and "tea."

SPECIAL SECTION: ADVANCED STRING-MANIPULATION EXERCISES

The preceding exercises are keyed to the text and designed to test your understanding of fundamental string-manipulation concepts. This section includes a collection of intermediate and advanced string-manipulation exercises. You should find these problems challenging, yet entertaining. The problems vary considerably in difficulty. Some require an hour or two of program writing and implementation. Others are useful for lab assignments that might require two or three weeks of study and implementation. Some are challenging term projects.

11.23 *(Text Analysis)* The availability of computers with string-manipulation capabilities has resulted in some rather interesting approaches to analyzing the writings of great authors. Much attention has been focused on whether William Shakespeare ever lived. Some scholars believe there is substantial evidence indicating that Christopher Marlowe or other authors actually penned the masterpieces attributed to Shakespeare. Researchers have used computers to find similarities in the writings of these two authors. This exercise examines three methods for analyzing texts with a computer.

   a) Write an application that reads several lines of text from the keyboard and prints a table indicating the number of occurrences of each letter of the alphabet in the text. For example, the phrase

         To be, or not to be: that is the question:

   contains one "a," two "b's," no "c's," etc.

   b) Write an application that reads several lines of text and prints a table indicating the number of one-letter words, two-letter words, three-letter words, etc., appearing in the text. For example, Fig. 11.32 shows the counts for the phrase

         Whether 'tis nobler in the mind to suffer

   c) Write an application that reads several lines of text and prints a table indicating the number of occurrences of each different word in the text. The first version of your program should include the words in the table in the same order in which they appear in the text. For example, the lines

         To be, or not to be: that is the question:
         Whether 'tis nobler in the mind to suffer

   contain the word "to" three times, the word "be" two times, the word "or" once, etc. A more interesting (and useful) printout should then be attempted in which the words are sorted alphabetically.

Word length	Occurrences
1	0
2	2
3	1
4	2 (including 'tis)
5	0
6	2
7	1

Fig. 11.32 Word-length counts for the string "Whether 'tis nobler in the mind to suffer".

11.24 *(Printing Dates in Various Formats)* Dates are printed in several common formats. Two of the more common formats are

04/25/1955 and April 25, 1955

Write an application that reads a date in the first format and prints that date in the second format.

11.25 *(Check Protection)* Computers are frequently employed in check-writing systems such as payroll and accounts payable applications. Many strange stories circulate regarding weekly paychecks being printed (by mistake) for amounts in excess of $1 million. Incorrect amounts are printed by computerized check-writing systems because of human error or machine failure. Systems designers build controls into their systems to prevent such erroneous checks from being issued.

Another serious problem is the intentional alteration of a check amount by someone who plans to cash a check fraudulently. To prevent a dollar amount from being altered, most computerized check-writing systems employ a technique called *check protection*. Checks designed for imprinting by computer contain a fixed number of spaces in which the computer may print an amount. Suppose a paycheck contains eight blank spaces in which the computer is supposed to print the amount of a weekly paycheck. If the amount is large, then all eight of those spaces will be filled. For example,

1,230.60 *(check amount)*

12345678 *(position numbers)*

On the other hand, if the amount is less than $1000, then several of the spaces would ordinarily be left blank. For example,

99.87

12345678

contains three blank spaces. If a check is printed with blank spaces, it is easier for someone to alter the amount of the check. To prevent a check from being altered, many check-writing systems insert *leading asterisks* to protect the amount as follows:

***99.87

12345678

Write an application that inputs a dollar amount to be printed on a check, then prints the amount in check-protected format with leading asterisks if necessary. Assume that nine spaces are available for printing the amount.

11.26 *(Writing the Word Equivalent of a Check Amount)* Continuing the discussion of Exercise 11.25, we reiterate the importance of designing check-writing systems to prevent alteration of check amounts. One common security method requires that the check amount be written in numbers and "spelled out" in words as well. Even if someone is able to alter the numerical amount of the check, it is extremely difficult to change the amount in words.

a) Many computerized check-writing systems do not print the check amount in words. Perhaps the main reason for this omission is that most high-level languages used in commercial applications do not contain adequate string-manipulation features. Another reason is that the logic for writing word equivalents of check amounts is somewhat involved.

b) Write an application that inputs a numeric check amount and writes the word equivalent of the amount. For example, the amount 112.43 should be written as

ONE HUNDRED TWELVE and 43/100

11.27 *(Morse Code)* Perhaps the most famous of all coding schemes is the Morse code, developed by Samuel Morse in 1832 for use with the telegraph system. The Morse code assigns a series of dots and dashes to each letter of the alphabet, each digit, and a few special characters (such as period, comma, colon and semicolon). In sound-oriented systems, the dot represents a short sound and the dash represents a long sound. Other representations of dots and dashes are used with light-oriented systems and signal-flag systems. Separation between words is indicated by a space or, simply, the absence of a dot or dash. In a sound-oriented system, a space is indicated by a short time during which no sound is transmitted. The international version of the Morse code appears in Fig. 11.33.

Write an application that reads an English language phrase and encodes the phrase into Morse code. Also write a program that reads a phrase in Morse code and converts the phrase into the English language equivalent. Use one blank between each Morse-coded letter and three blanks between each Morse-coded word.

11.28 *(Metric Conversion Program)* Write an application that will assist the user with metric conversions. Your program should allow the user to specify the names of the units as strings (i.e., centimeters, liters, grams, etc., for the metric system and inches, quarts, pounds, etc., for the English system) and should respond to simple questions such as

```
"How many inches are in 2 meters?"
"How many liters are in 10 quarts?"
```

Your program should recognize invalid conversions. For example, the question

```
"How many feet are in 5 kilograms?"
```

is not meaningful because `"feet"` is a unit of length while `"kilograms"` is a unit of mass.

Character	Code	Character	Code
A	. –	T	–
B	– . . .	U	. . –
C	– . – .	V	. . . –
D	– . .	W	. – –
E	.	X	– . . –
F	. . – .	Y	– . – –
G	– – .	Z	– – . .
H	. . . .		
I	. .	*Digits*	
J	. – – –	1	. – – – –
K	– . –	2	. . – – –
L	. – . .	3	. . . – –
M	– –	4	. . . . –
N	– .	5	. . . . .
O	– – –	6	– . . . .
P	. – – .	7	– – . . .
Q	– – . –	8	– – – . .
R	. – .	9	– – – – .
S	. . .	0	– – – – –

Fig. 11.33 The letters of the alphabet as expressed in international Morse code.

SPECIAL SECTION: CHALLENGING STRING-MANIPULATION PROJECTS

11.29 *(Project: A Spelling Checker)* Many popular word processing software packages have built-in spell checkers. In this project, you are asked to develop your own spell-checker utility. We make suggestions to help get you started. You should then consider adding more capabilities. Use a computerized dictionary (if you have access to one) as a source of words.

Why do we type so many words with incorrect spellings? In some cases, it is because we simply do not know the correct spelling, so we make a best guess. In some cases, it is because we transpose two letters (e.g., "defualt" instead of "default"). Sometimes we double-type a letter accidentally (e.g., "hanndy" instead of "handy"). Sometimes we type a nearby key instead of the one we intended (e.g., "biryhday" instead of "birthday"), and so on.

Design and implement a spell-checker application in Java. Your program should maintain an array `wordList` of strings. Enable the user to enter these strings. [*Note*: In Chapter 17, we will introduce file processing. Once you have this capability, you can obtain the words for the spell checker from a computerized dictionary stored in a file.]

Your program should ask a user to enter a word. The program should then look up that word in the `wordList` array. If the word is in the array, your program should print "Word is spelled correctly." If the word is not in the array, your program should print "Word is not spelled correctly." Then your program should try to locate other words in `wordList` that might be the word the user intended to type. For example, you can try all possible single transpositions of adjacent letters to discover that the word "default" is a direct match to a word in `wordList`. Of course, this implies that your program will check all other single transpositions, such as "edfault," "dfeault," "deafult," "defalut" and "defautl." When you find a new word that matches one in `wordList`, print that word in a message, such as "Did you mean "default?"."

Implement other tests, such as replacing each double letter with a single letter and any other tests you can develop to improve the value of your spell checker.

11.30 *(Project: A Crossword Puzzle Generator)* Most people have worked a crossword puzzle, but few have ever attempted to generate one. Generating a crossword puzzle is suggested here as a string-manipulation project requiring substantial sophistication and effort.

There are many issues the programmer must resolve to get even the simplest crossword puzzle-generator program working. For example, how do you represent the grid of a crossword puzzle inside the computer? Should you use a series of strings or two-dimensional arrays?

The programmer needs a source of words (i.e., a computerized dictionary) that can be directly referenced by the program. In what form should these words be stored to facilitate the complex manipulations required by the program?

If you are really ambitious, you will want to generate the "clues" portion of the puzzle, in which the brief hints for each "across" word and each "down" word are printed. Merely printing a version of the blank puzzle itself is not a simple problem.

12

Graphics and Java2D

Objectives

- To understand graphics contexts and graphics objects.
- To understand and be able to manipulate colors.
- To understand and be able to manipulate fonts.
- To use `Graphics` methods to draw lines, rectangles, rectangles with rounded corners, three-dimensional rectangles, ovals, arcs and polygons.
- To use methods of class `Graphics2D` from the Java2D API to draw lines, rectangles, rectangles with rounded corners, ellipses, arcs and general paths.
- To be able to specify `Paint` and `Stroke` characteristics of shapes displayed with `Graphics2D`.

One picture is worth ten thousand words.
Chinese proverb

Treat nature in terms of the cylinder, the sphere, the cone, all in perspective.
Paul Cezanne

Nothing ever becomes real till it is experienced—even a proverb is no proverb to you till your life has illustrated it.
John Keats

A picture shows me at a glance what it takes dozens of pages of a book to expound.
Ivan Sergeyevich Turgenev

12.1 Introduction

In this chapter, we overview several of Java's capabilities for drawing two-dimensional shapes, controlling colors and controlling fonts. One of Java's initial appeals was its support for graphics that enabled Java programmers to visually enhance their applets and applications. Java now contains many more sophisticated drawing capabilities as part of the *Java2D API*. This chapter begins with an introduction to many of the original drawing capabilities of Java. Next, we present several of the new and more powerful Java2D capabilities, such as controlling the style of lines used to draw shapes and controlling how shapes are filled with color and patterns.

Figure 12.1 shows a portion of the Java class hierarchy that includes several of the basic graphics classes and Java2D API classes and interfaces covered in this chapter. Class `Color` contains methods and constants for manipulating colors. Class `Font` contains methods and constants for manipulating fonts. Class `FontMetrics` contains methods for obtaining font information. Class `Polygon` contains methods for creating polygons. Class `Graphics` contains methods for drawing strings, lines, rectangles and other shapes. The bottom half of the figure lists several classes and interfaces from the Java2D API. Class `BasicStroke` helps specify the drawing characteristics of lines. Classes `GradientPaint` and `TexturePaint` help specify the characteristics for filling shapes with colors or patterns. Classes `GeneralPath`, `Arc2D`, `Ellipse2D`, `Line2D`, `Rectangle2D` and `RoundRectangle2D` represent several Java2D shapes.

To begin drawing in Java, we must first understand Java's *coordinate system* (Fig. 12.2), which is a scheme for identifying every possible point on the screen. By default, the upper-left corner of a GUI component (such as an applet or a window) has the coordinates (0, 0). A coordinate pair is composed of an *x-coordinate* (the *horizontal coordinate*) and a *y-coordinate* (the *vertical coordinate*). The *x*-coordinate is the horizontal distance moving right from the upper-left corner. The *y*-coordinate is the vertical distance moving down from the upper-left corner. The *x-axis* describes every horizontal coordinate, and the *y-axis* describes every vertical coordinate.

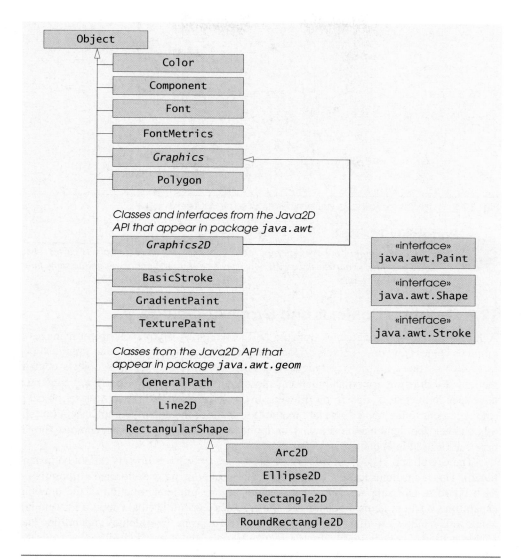

Fig. 12.1   Classes and interfaces used in this chapter from Java's original graphics capabilities and from the Java2D API. (*Note:* Class `Object` appears here because it is the superclass of the Java class hierarchy.)

Text and shapes are displayed on the screen by specifying coordinates. Coordinate units are measured in *pixels*. A pixel is a display monitor's smallest unit of resolution.

The upper-left coordinate (0, 0) of a window is *behind* the title bar of the window. For this reason, drawing coordinates should be adjusted to draw inside the borders of the window. Class *Container* (a superclass of all windows in Java) has method *getInsets*, which returns an *Insets* object (package *java.awt*) for this purpose. An *Insets* object has four *public* members—*top*, *bottom*, *left* and *right*—that represent the number of pixels from each edge of the window to the drawing area for the window.

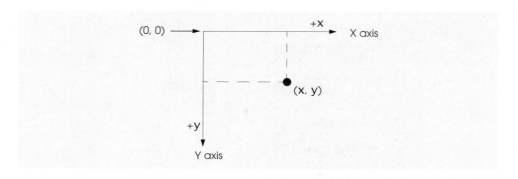

Fig. 12.2   Java coordinate system. Units are measured in pixels.

 Portability Tip 12.1

Different display monitors have different resolutions (i.e., the density of pixels varies). This can cause graphics to appear to be different sizes on different monitors or on the same monitor with different settings.

12.2 Graphics Contexts and Graphics Objects

A Java *graphics context* enables drawing on the screen. A Graphics object manages a graphics context and draws pixels on the screen that represent text and other graphical object (such as lines, ellipses, rectangles and other polygons). Graphics objects contain methods for drawing, font manipulation, color manipulation and the like. Every applet we have seen in the text that performs drawing on the screen has used the Graphics object g (the argument to the applet's paint method) to manage the applet's graphics context. In this chapter, we demonstrate drawing in applications. However, every technique shown here can be used in applets.

The Graphics class is an abstract class (i.e., Graphics objects cannot be instantiated). This contributes to Java's portability. Because drawing is performed differently on each platform that supports Java, there cannot be one implement action of the drawing capabilities on all systems. For example, the graphics capabilities that enable a PC running Microsoft Windows to draw a rectangle are different from the graphics capabilities that enable a Linux workstation to draw a rectangle—and those are both different from the graphics capabilities that enable a Macintosh to draw a rectangle. When Java is implemented on each platform, a subclass of Graphics is created that implements the drawing capabilities. This implementation is hidden from us by class Graphics, which supplies the interface that enables us to use graphics in a platform-independent manner.

Class Component is the superclass for many of the classes in the java.awt package. (We discuss class Component in Chapter 13.) Component method paint takes a Graphics object as an argument. This object is passed to the paint method by the system when a paint operation is required for a Component. The header for the paint method is

```
public void paint( Graphics g )
```

Graphics reference g receives a reference to an instance of the system-specific subclass that Graphics extends. The preceding method header should look familiar to you—it is the same one we have been using in our applet classes. Actually, class Component is an indirect superclass of JApplet—the superclass of every applet in this book. Many capabilities of class JApplet are inherited from class Component.

Method paint is seldom called directly by the programmer because drawing graphics is an *event-driven process*. When an applet executes, the applet container calls method paint (after calls to the methods init and start). For paint to be called again, an *event* must occur (such as covering and uncovering the applet with another window). Similarly, when any Component is displayed, that Component's paint method is called.

If the programmer needs to call paint, a call is made to Component method repaint. This method requests a call to the Component class update method as soon as possible to clear the Component's background of any previous drawing, then update calls paint directly. Method repaint is frequently called by the programmer to force a paint operation. Method repaint should not be overridden, because it performs some system-dependent tasks. The headers for repaint and update are

```
public void repaint()
public void update( Graphics g )
```

Method update takes a Graphics object as an argument, which is supplied automatically by the system when update is called.

In this chapter, we focus on method paint. In the next chapter, we discuss the event-driven nature of graphics and methods repaint and update in more detail. We also discuss in that chapter class JComponent—a superclass of many GUI components in package javax.swing. Subclasses of JComponent typically paint from their paintComponent methods.

12.3 Color Control

Colors enhance the appearance of a program and help convey meaning. For example, a traffic light has three different color lights—red indicates stop, yellow indicates caution and green indicates go.

Class *Color* declares methods and constants for manipulating colors in a Java program. The predeclared color constants are summarized in Fig. 12.3,[1] and several color methods and constructors are summarized in Fig. 12.4. Note that two of the methods in Fig. 12.4 are Graphics methods that are specific to colors.

Color constant	Color	RGB value
public final static Color ORANGE	orange	255, 200, 0
public final static Color PINK	pink	255, 175, 175
public final static Color CYAN	cyan	0, 255, 255

Fig. 12.3   Color constants and their RGB values. (Part 1 of 2.)

---

1.   In prior versions of Java, the Color constants had names consisting of lowercase and uppercase letters. Although those names are still available, the names shown in Fig. 12.3 are preferred because they conform to the naming conventions for constants.

Color constant	Color	RGB value
public final static Color MAGENTA	magenta	255, 0, 255
public final static Color YELLOW	yellow	255, 255, 0
public final static Color BLACK	black	0, 0, 0
public final static Color WHITE	white	255, 255, 255
public final static Color GRAY	gray	128, 128, 128
public final static Color LIGHT_GRAY	light gray	192, 192, 192
public final static Color DARK_GRAY	dark gray	64, 64, 64
public final static Color RED	red	255, 0, 0
public final static Color GREEN	green	0, 255, 0
public final static Color BLUE	blue	0, 0, 255

Fig. 12.3   Color constants and their RGB values. (Part 2 of 2.)

Method	Description

Color constructors and methods

public Color(int r, int g, int b)

> Creates a color based on red, green and blue components expressed as integers from 0 to 255.

public Color(float r, float g, float b)

> Creates a color based on red, green and blue components expressed as floating-point values from 0.0 to 1.0.

public int getRed()

> Returns a value between 0 and 255 representing the red content.

public int getGreen()

> Returns a value between 0 and 255 representing the green content.

public int getBlue()

> Returns a value between 0 and 255 representing the blue content.

Graphics methods for manipulating Colors

public Color getColor()

> Returns a Color object representing the current color for the graphics context.

public void setColor(Color c)

> Sets the current color for drawing with the graphics context.

Fig. 12.4   Color methods and color-related Graphics methods .

Every color is created from a red, a green and a blue component. Together these components are called *RGB values*. All three RGB components can be integers in the range from 0 to 255, or they can be floating-point values in the range 0.0 to 1.0. The first RGB component specifies the amount of red, the second specifies the amount of green and the third specifies the amount of blue. The larger the RGB value, the greater the amount of that particular color. Java enables the programmer to choose from $256 \times 256 \times 256$ (or approximately 16.7 million) colors. However, not all computers are capable of displaying all these colors. If this is the case, the computer will display the closest color it can.

Two `Color` constructors are shown in Fig. 12.4—one that takes three `int` arguments and one that takes three `float` arguments, with each argument specifying the amount of red, green and blue. The `int` values must be in the range 0–255 and the `float` values must be in the range 0.0–1.0. The new `Color` object will have the specified amounts of red, green and blue. `Color` methods `getRed`, `getGreen` and `getBlue` return integer values from 0 to 255 representing the amount of red, green and blue, respectively. `Graphics` method `getColor` returns a `Color` object representing the current drawing color. `Graphics` method `setColor` sets the current drawing color.

The application of Fig. 12.5 demonstrates several methods from Fig. 12.4 by drawing filled rectangles and strings in several different colors.

```
1   // Fig. 12.5: ShowColors.java
2   // Demonstrating Colors.
3   import java.awt.*;
4   import javax.swing.*;
5
6   public class ShowColors extends JFrame {
7
8       // constructor sets window's title bar string and dimensions
9       public ShowColors()
10      {
11          super( "Using colors" );
12
13          setSize( 400, 130 );
14          setVisible( true );
15      }
16
17      // draw rectangles and Strings in different colors
18      public void paint( Graphics g )
19      {
20          // call superclass's paint method
21          super.paint( g );
22
23          // set new drawing color using integers
24          g.setColor( new Color( 255, 0, 0 ) );
25          g.fillRect( 25, 25, 100, 20 );
26          g.drawString( "Current RGB: " + g.getColor(), 130, 40 );
27
28          // set new drawing color using floats
29          g.setColor( new Color( 0.0f, 1.0f, 0.0f ) );
30          g.fillRect( 25, 50, 100, 20 );
31          g.drawString( "Current RGB: " + g.getColor(), 130, 65 );
32
```

Fig. 12.5 `Color` changed for drawing. (Part 1 of 2.)

```
33          // set new drawing color using static Color objects
34          g.setColor( Color.BLUE );
35          g.fillRect( 25, 75, 100, 20 );
36          g.drawString( "Current RGB: " + g.getColor(), 130, 90 );
37
38          // display individual RGB values
39          Color color = Color.MAGENTA;
40          g.setColor( color );
41          g.fillRect( 25, 100, 100, 20 );
42          g.drawString( "RGB values: " + color.getRed() + ", " +
43             color.getGreen() + ", " + color.getBlue(), 130, 115 );
44
45       } // end method paint
46
47       // execute application
48       public static void main( String args[] )
49       {
50          ShowColors application = new ShowColors();
51          application.setDefaultCloseOperation( JFrame.EXIT_ON_CLOSE );
52       }
53
54    } // end class ShowColors
```

Fig. 12.5   Color changed for drawing. (Part 2 of 2.)

When the application begins execution, class ShowColors's paint method (lines 18–45) is called to paint the window. Line 24 uses Graphics method setColor to set the current drawing color. Method setColor receives a Color object. The expression new Color(255, 0, 0) creates a new Color object that represents red (red value 255, and 0 for the green and blue values). Line 25 uses Graphics method fillRect to draw a filled rectangle in the current color. Method fillRect receives the same parameters as method drawRect (discussed in Chapter 3). Line 26 uses Graphics method drawString to draw a String in the current color. The expression g.getColor() retrieves the current color from the Graphics object. The returned Color object is concatenated with string "Current RGB: ", resulting in an implicit call to class Color's toString method. Notice that the String representation of the Color object contains the class name and package (java.awt.Color), and the red, green and blue values.

Lines 29–31 and lines 34–36 perform the same tasks again. Line 29 uses the Color constructor with three float arguments to create the color green (0.0f for red, 1.0f for green and 0.0f for blue). Note the syntax of the values. The letter f appended to a floating-point literal indicates that the literal should be treated as type float. By default, floating-point literals are treated as type double.

Line 34 sets the current drawing color to one of the predeclared `Color` constants (`Color.BLUE`). Note that `new` is not needed to create the constant. The `Color` constants are `static`, so they are created when class `Color` is loaded into memory at execution time.

The statement at lines 42–43 demonstrates `Color` methods `getRed`, `getGreen` and `getBlue` on the predeclared `Color.MAGENTA` object.

Software Engineering Observation 12.1

To change the color, you must create a new `Color` object (or use one of the predeclared `Color` constants). `Color` objects are not modifiable (also called immutable).

Package `javax.swing` provides the *JColorChooser* GUI component to enable application users to select colors. Figure 12.6 enables you to press a button to display a `JColorChooser` dialog. When you select a color and press the dialog's **OK** button, the background color of the application window changes colors.

```java
1   // Fig. 12.6: ShowColors2.java
2   // Choosing colors with JColorChooser.
3   import java.awt.*;
4   import java.awt.event.*;
5   import javax.swing.*;
6
7   public class ShowColors2 extends JFrame {
8      private JButton changeColorButton;
9      private Color color = Color.LIGHT_GRAY;
10     private Container container;
11
12     // set up GUI
13     public ShowColors2()
14     {
15        super( "Using JColorChooser" );
16
17        container = getContentPane();
18        container.setLayout( new FlowLayout() );
19
20        // set up changeColorButton and register its event handler
21        changeColorButton = new JButton( "Change Color" );
22        changeColorButton.addActionListener(
23
24           new ActionListener() {  // anonymous inner class
25
26              // display JColorChooser when user clicks button
27              public void actionPerformed( ActionEvent event )
28              {
29                 color = JColorChooser.showDialog(
30                    ShowColors2.this, "Choose a color", color );
31
32                 // set default color, if no color is returned
33                 if ( color == null )
34                    color = Color.LIGHT_GRAY;
35
```

Fig. 12.6   JColorChooser dialog. (Part 1 of 2.)

```
36                    // change content pane's background color
37                    container.setBackground( color );
38                 }
39
40           } // end anonymous inner class
41
42        ); // end call to addActionListener
43
44        container.add( changeColorButton );
45
46        setSize( 400, 130 );
47        setVisible( true );
48
49     } // end ShowColor2 constructor
50
51     // execute application
52     public static void main( String args[] )
53     {
54        ShowColors2 application = new ShowColors2();
55        application.setDefaultCloseOperation( JFrame.EXIT_ON_CLOSE );
56     }
57
58  } // end class ShowColors2
```

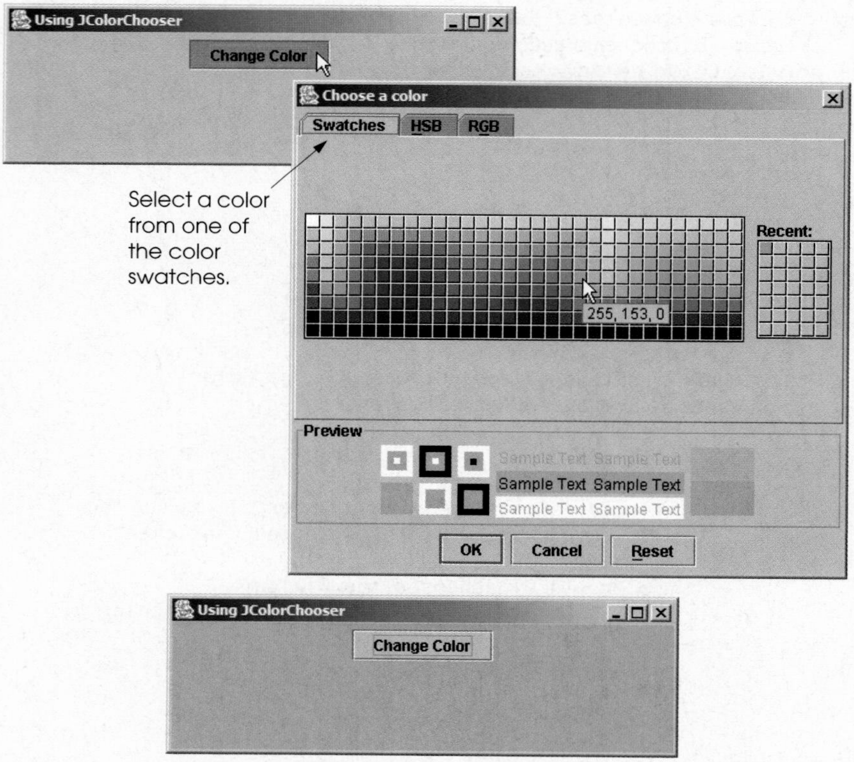

Fig. 12.6   JColorChooser dialog. (Part 2 of 2.)

Lines 29–30 in `actionPerformed` use `JColorChooser` static method *showDialog* to display the color chooser dialog. This method returns the selected `Color` object, or `null` if the user presses **Cancel** or closes the dialog without pressing **OK**. The method takes three arguments—a reference to its parent `Component`, a `String` to display in the title bar of the dialog and the initial selected `Color` for the dialog. The parent component is a reference to the window from which the dialog is displayed. The dialog will be centered on the parent. If the parent is `null`, the dialog is centered on the screen. While the color chooser dialog is on the screen, the user cannot interact with the parent component. This type of dialog is called a *modal dialog* (discussed in Chapter 14). Notice the special syntax `ShowColors2.this` used in line 30. Recall from Section 10.9 that you can access the outer class object's `this` reference by qualifying `this` with the name of the outer class and a dot (.).

After the user selects a color, lines 33–34 determine whether `color` is `null`, and, if so, sets `color` to the default `Color.LIGHT_GRAY`. Line 37 uses method `setBackground` to change the background color of the content pane (represented by `container` in this program). Method `setBackground` is one of the many `Component` methods that can be used on most GUI components.

The second screen capture of Fig. 12.6 demonstrates the default `JColorChooser` dialog that allows the user to select a color from a variety of *color swatches*. Notice that there are actually three tabs across the top of the dialog—**Swatches**, **HSB** and **RGB**. These represent three different ways to select a color. The **HSB** tab allows you to select a color based on *hue*, *saturation* and *brightness*. The **RGB** tab allows you to select a color by using sliders to select the red, green and blue components of the color. The **HSB** and **RGB** tabs are shown in Fig. 12.7.

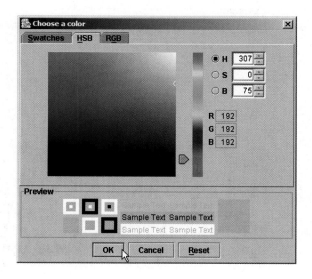

Fig. 12.7   **HSB** and **RGB** tabs of the `JColorChooser` dialog. (Part 1 of 2.)

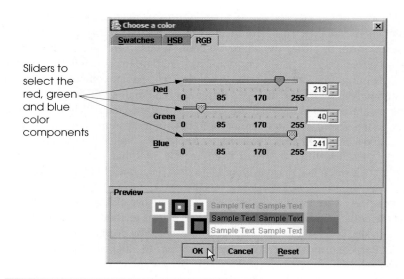

Fig. 12.7   HSB and **RGB** tabs of the JColorChooser dialog. (Part 2 of 2.)

12.4 Font Control

This section introduces methods and constants for font control. Most font methods and font constants are part of class Font. Some methods of class Font and class Graphics are summarized in Fig. 12.8.

Method or constant	Description

Font constants, constructors and methods for drawing polygons

public final static int PLAIN

A constant representing a plain font style.

public final static int BOLD

A constant representing a bold font style.

public final static int ITALIC

A constant representing an italic font style.

public Font(String name, int style, int size)

Creates a Font object with the specified font, style and size.

public int getStyle()

Returns an integer value indicating the current font style.

public int getSize()

Returns an integer value indicating the current font size.

public String getName()

Returns the current font name as a string.

Fig. 12.8   Font-related methods and constants. (Part 1 of 2.)

Method or constant	Description

`public String getFamily()`

> Returns the font's family name as a string.

`public boolean isPlain()`

> Tests a font for a plain font style. Returns `true` if the font is plain.

`public boolean isBold()`

> Tests a font for a bold font style. Returns `true` if the font is bold.

`public boolean isItalic()`

> Tests a font for an italic font style. Returns `true` if the font is italic.

Graphics methods for manipulating Fonts

`public Font getFont()`

> Returns a `Font` object reference representing the current font.

`public void setFont( Font f )`

> Sets the current font to the font, style and size specified by the `Font` object reference `f`.

Fig. 12.8   Font-related methods and constants. (Part 2 of 2.)

Class `Font`'s constructor takes three arguments—the *font name, font style* and *font size*. The font name is any font currently supported by the system in which the program is running, such as standard Java fonts `Monospaced`, `SansSerif` and `Serif`. The font style is `Font.PLAIN`, `Font.ITALIC` or `Font.BOLD` (each is a `static` field of class `Font`). Font styles can be used in combination (e.g., `Font.ITALIC + Font.BOLD`). The font size is measured in points. A *point* is 1/72 of an inch. `Graphics` method `setFont` sets the current drawing font—the font in which text will be displayed—to its `Font` argument.

Portability Tip 12.2

The number of fonts varies greatly across systems. Java guarantees that the fonts `Serif`, `Monospaced`, `SansSerif`, `Dialog` and `DialogInput` will be available.

Common Programming Error 12.1

Specifying a font that is not available on a system is a logic error. Java will substitute that system's default font—typically `Serif`.

Figure 12.9 displays text in four different fonts, with each font in a different size. The program uses the `Font` constructor to initialize `Font` objects (at lines 24, 28, 32 and 37)

```
1   // Fig. 12.9: Fonts.java
2   // Using fonts.
3   import java.awt.*;
4   import javax.swing.*;
5
6   public class Fonts extends JFrame {
7
```

Fig. 12.9   `Graphics` method `setFont` changes the drawing font. (Part 1 of 2.)

```
 8      // set window's title bar and dimensions
 9      public Fonts()
10      {
11         super( "Using fonts" );
12
13         setSize( 420, 125 );
14         setVisible( true );
15      }
16
17      // display Strings in different fonts and colors
18      public void paint( Graphics g )
19      {
20         // call superclass's paint method
21         super.paint( g );
22
23         // set font to Serif (Times), bold, 12pt and draw a string
24         g.setFont( new Font( "Serif", Font.BOLD, 12 ) );
25         g.drawString( "Serif 12 point bold.", 20, 50 );
26
27         // set font to Monospaced (Courier), italic, 24pt and draw a string
28         g.setFont( new Font( "Monospaced", Font.ITALIC, 24 ) );
29         g.drawString( "Monospaced 24 point italic.", 20, 70 );
30
31         // set font to SansSerif (Helvetica), plain, 14pt and draw a string
32         g.setFont( new Font( "SansSerif", Font.PLAIN, 14 ) );
33         g.drawString( "SansSerif 14 point plain.", 20, 90 );
34
35         // set font to Serif (Times), bold/italic, 18pt and draw a string
36         g.setColor( Color.RED );
37         g.setFont( new Font( "Serif", Font.BOLD + Font.ITALIC, 18 ) );
38         g.drawString( g.getFont().getName() + " " + g.getFont().getSize() +
39            " point bold italic.", 20, 110 );
40
41      } // end method paint
42
43      // execute application
44      public static void main( String args[] )
45      {
46         Fonts application = new Fonts();
47         application.setDefaultCloseOperation( JFrame.EXIT_ON_CLOSE );
48      }
49
50   } // end class Fonts
```

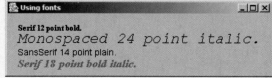

Fig. 12.9   Graphics method setFont changes the drawing font. (Part 2 of 2.)

passed to `Graphics` method `setFont` to change the drawing font. Each call to the `Font` constructor passes a font name (`Serif`, `Monospaced` or `SansSerif`) as a string, a font style (`Font.PLAIN`, `Font.ITALIC` or `Font.BOLD`) and a font size. Once `Graphics` method `setFont` is invoked, all text displayed following the call will appear in the new font until the font is changed. Note that line 36 changes the drawing color to red, so the next string displayed appears in red.

Software Engineering Observation 12.2

To change the font, you must create a new `Font` object. `Font` objects are immutable—`Font` has no `set` methods to change the characteristics of the current font.

Font Metrics

Sometimes, it is necessary to get information about the current drawing font, such as the font name, the font style and the font size. Several `Font` methods used to get font information are summarized in Fig. 12.8. Method `getStyle` returns an integer value representing the current style. The integer value returned is either `Font.PLAIN`, `Font.ITALIC`, `Font.BOLD` or the combination of `Font.ITALIC` and `Font.BOLD`.

Method `getSize` returns the font size in points. Method `getName` returns the current font name as a string. Method `getFamily` returns the name of the font family to which the current font belongs. The name of the font family is platform specific.

`Font` methods are also available to test the style of the current font and are summarized in Fig. 12.8. Methods *isPlain, isBold* and *isItalic* return `true` if the current font style is plain, bold or italic, respectively.

Sometimes precise information about a font's metrics must be known—such as *height*, *descent* (the amount a character dips below the baseline), *ascent* (the amount a character rises above the baseline) and *leading* (the difference between the descent of one line of text and the ascent of the line of text below it—i.e., the interline spacing). Figure 12.10 illustrates some of the common *font metrics*. Note that the coordinate passed to `drawString` corresponds to the lower-left corner of the baseline of the font.

Class *FontMetrics* declares several methods for obtaining font metrics. These methods and `Graphics` method *getFontMetrics* are summarized in Fig. 12.11. Figure 12.12 uses the methods of Fig. 12.11 to obtain font metric information for two fonts.

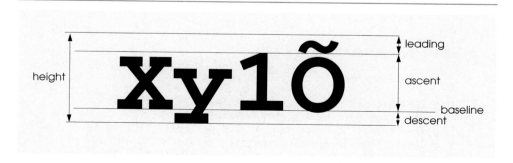

Fig. 12.10   Font metrics.

Method	Description

FontMetrics methods

```
public int getAscent()
```
> Returns a value representing the ascent of a font in points.

```
public int getDescent()
```
> Returns a value representing the descent of a font in points.

```
public int getLeading()
```
> Returns a value representing the leading of a font in points.

```
public int getHeight()
```
> Returns a value representing the height of a font in points.

Graphics methods for getting a Font's FontMetrics

```
public FontMetrics getFontMetrics()
```
> Returns the FontMetrics object for the current drawing Font.

```
public FontMetrics getFontMetrics( Font f )
```
> Returns the FontMetrics object for the specified Font argument.

Fig. 12.11 FontMetrics and Graphics methods for obtaining font metrics.

```
1   // Fig. 12.12: Metrics.java
2   // FontMetrics and Graphics methods useful for obtaining font metrics.
3   import java.awt.*;
4   import javax.swing.*;
5
6   public class Metrics extends JFrame {
7
8      // set window's title bar String and dimensions
9      public Metrics()
10     {
11        super( "Demonstrating FontMetrics" );
12
13        setSize( 510, 210 );
14        setVisible( true );
15     }
16
17     // display font metrics
18     public void paint( Graphics g )
19     {
20        super.paint( g );   // call superclass's paint method
21
22        g.setFont( new Font( "SansSerif", Font.BOLD, 12 ) );
23        FontMetrics metrics = g.getFontMetrics();
24        g.drawString( "Current font: " + g.getFont(), 10, 40 );
25        g.drawString( "Ascent: " + metrics.getAscent(), 10, 55 );
26        g.drawString( "Descent: " + metrics.getDescent(), 10, 70 );
```

Fig. 12.12 Font metrics. (Part 1 of 2.)

```
27            g.drawString( "Height: " + metrics.getHeight(), 10, 85 );
28            g.drawString( "Leading: " + metrics.getLeading(), 10, 100 );
29
30            Font font = new Font( "Serif", Font.ITALIC, 14 );
31            metrics = g.getFontMetrics( font );
32            g.setFont( font );
33            g.drawString( "Current font: " + font, 10, 130 );
34            g.drawString( "Ascent: " + metrics.getAscent(), 10, 145 );
35            g.drawString( "Descent: " + metrics.getDescent(), 10, 160 );
36            g.drawString( "Height: " + metrics.getHeight(), 10, 175 );
37            g.drawString( "Leading: " + metrics.getLeading(), 10, 190 );
38
39         } // end method paint
40
41         // execute application
42         public static void main( String args[] )
43         {
44            Metrics application = new Metrics();
45            application.setDefaultCloseOperation( JFrame.EXIT_ON_CLOSE );
46         }
47
48      } // end class Metrics
```

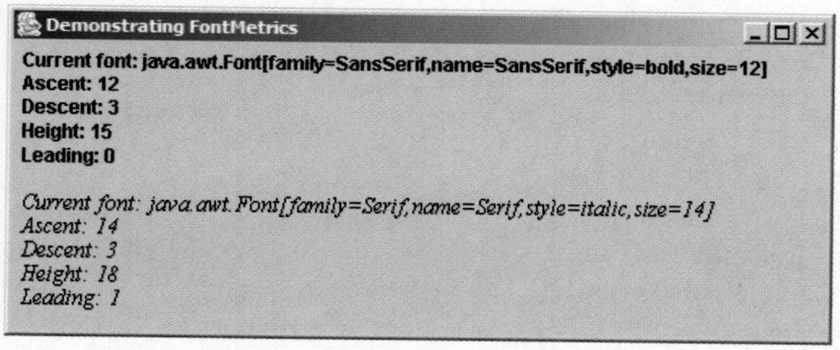

Demonstrating FontMetrics

Current font: java.awt.Font[family=SansSerif,name=SansSerif,style=bold,size=12]
Ascent: 12
Descent: 3
Height: 15
Leading: 0

Current font: java.awt.Font[family=Serif,name=Serif,style=italic,size=14]
Ascent: 14
Descent: 3
Height: 18
Leading: 1

Fig. 12.12 Font metrics. (Part 2 of 2.)

Line 22 creates and sets the current drawing font to a SansSerif, bold, 12-point font. Line 23 uses Graphics method getFontMetrics to obtain the FontMetrics object for the current font. Line 24 uses an implicit call to class Font's toString method to output the string representation of the font. Lines 25–28 use FontMetric methods to obtain the ascent, descent, height and leading for the font.

Line 30 creates a new Serif, italic, 14-point font. Line 31 uses a second version of Graphics method getFontMetrics, which receives a Font argument and returns a corresponding FontMetrics object. Lines 34–37 obtain the ascent, descent, height and leading for the font. Notice that the font metrics are slightly different for the two fonts.

12.5 Drawing Lines, Rectangles and Ovals

This section presents several Graphics methods for drawing lines, rectangles and ovals. The methods and their parameters are summarized in Fig. 12.13. For each drawing method that requires a width and height parameter, the width and height must be nonnegative values. Otherwise, the shape will not display. Figure 12.14 demonstrates drawing a variety of lines, rectangles, three-dimensional rectangles, rounded rectangles and ovals.

Method	Description

`public void drawLine( int x1, int y1, int x2, int y2 )`

Draws a line between the point (x1, y1) and the point (x2, y2).

`public void drawRect( int x, int y, int width, int height )`

Draws a rectangle of the specified width and height. The top-left corner of the rectangle has the coordinates (x, y).

`public void fillRect( int x, int y, int width, int height )`

Draws a solid rectangle with the specified width and height. The top-left corner of the rectangle has the coordinate (x, y).

`public void clearRect( int x, int y, int width, int height )`

Draws a solid rectangle with the specified width and height in the current background color. The top-left corner of the rectangle has the coordinate (x, y).

`public void drawRoundRect( int x, int y, int width, int height,`
`    int arcWidth, int arcHeight )`

Draws a rectangle with rounded corners in the current color with the specified width and height. The arcWidth and arcHeight determine the rounding of the corners (see Fig. 12.15).

`public void fillRoundRect( int x, int y, int width, int height,`
`    int arcWidth, int arcHeight )`

Draws a solid rectangle with rounded corners in the current color with the specified width and height. The arcWidth and arcHeight determine the rounding of the corners (see Fig. 12.15).

`public void draw3DRect( int x, int y, int width, int height, boolean b )`

Draws a three-dimensional rectangle in the current color with the specified width and height. The top-left corner of the rectangle has the coordinates (x, y). The rectangle appears raised when b is true and lowered when b is false.

`public void fill3DRect( int x, int y, int width, int height, boolean b )`

Draws a filled three-dimensional rectangle in the current color with the specified width and height. The top-left corner of the rectangle has the coordinates (x, y). The rectangle appears raised when b is true and lowered when b is false.

`public void drawOval( int x, int y, int width, int height )`

Draws an oval in the current color with the specified width and height. The bounding rectangle's top-left corner is at the coordinates (x, y). The oval touches all four sides of the bounding rectangle at the center of each side (see Fig. 12.16).

`public void fillOval( int x, int y, int width, int height )`

Draws a filled oval in the current color with the specified width and height. The bounding rectangle's top-left corner is at the coordinates (x, y). The oval touches all four sides of the bounding rectangle at the center of each side (see Fig. 12.16).

Fig. 12.13 Graphics methods that draw lines, rectangles and ovals.

```java
1    // Fig. 12.14: LinesRectsOvals.java
2    // Drawing lines, rectangles and ovals.
3    import java.awt.*;
4    import javax.swing.*;
5
6    public class LinesRectsOvals extends JFrame {
7
8       // set window's title bar String and dimensions
9       public LinesRectsOvals()
10      {
11         super( "Drawing lines, rectangles and ovals" );
12
13         setSize( 400, 165 );
14         setVisible( true );
15      }
16
17      // display various lines, rectangles and ovals
18      public void paint( Graphics g )
19      {
20         super.paint( g );   // call superclass's paint method
21
22         g.setColor( Color.RED );
23         g.drawLine( 5, 30, 350, 30 );
24
25         g.setColor( Color.BLUE );
26         g.drawRect( 5, 40, 90, 55 );
27         g.fillRect( 100, 40, 90, 55 );
28
29         g.setColor( Color.CYAN );
30         g.fillRoundRect( 195, 40, 90, 55, 50, 50 );
31         g.drawRoundRect( 290, 40, 90, 55, 20, 20 );
32
33         g.setColor( Color.YELLOW );
34         g.draw3DRect( 5, 100, 90, 55, true );
35         g.fill3DRect( 100, 100, 90, 55, false );
36
37         g.setColor( Color.MAGENTA );
38         g.drawOval( 195, 100, 90, 55 );
39         g.fillOval( 290, 100, 90, 55 );
40
41      } // end method paint
42
43      // execute application
44      public static void main( String args[] )
45      {
46         LinesRectsOvals application = new LinesRectsOvals();
47         application.setDefaultCloseOperation( JFrame.EXIT_ON_CLOSE );
48      }
49
50   } // end class LinesRectsOvals
```

Fig. 12.14 Drawing lines, rectangles and ovals. (Part 1 of 2.)

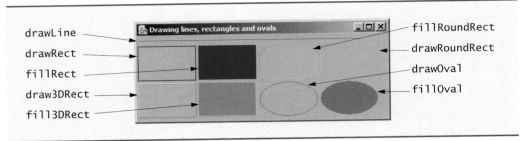

drawLine
drawRect
fillRect
draw3DRect
fill3DRect

fillRoundRect
drawRoundRect
drawOval
fillOval

Fig. 12.14 Drawing lines, rectangles and ovals. (Part 2 of 2.)

Methods fillRoundRect (line 30) and drawRoundRect (line 31) draw rectangles with rounded corners. Their first two arguments specify the coordinates of the upper-left corner of the *bounding rectangle*—the area in which the rounded rectangle will be drawn. Note that the upper-left corner coordinates are not the edge of the rounded rectangle, but the coordinates where the edge would be if the rectangle had square corners. The third and fourth arguments specify the width and height of the rectangle. Their last two arguments—arcWidth and arcHeight—determine the horizontal and vertical diameters of the arcs used to represent the corners.

Figure 12.15 labels the arc width, arc height, width and height of a rounded rectangle. Using the same value for arcWidth and arcHeight produces a quarter circle at each corner. When width, height, arcWidth and arcHeight have the same values, the result is a circle. If the values for width and height are the same and the values of arcWidth and arcHeight are 0, the result is a square.

Methods draw3DRect (line 34 of Fig. 12.14) and fill3DRect (line 35) take the same arguments. The first two arguments specify the top-left corner of the rectangle. The next two arguments specify the width and height of the rectangle, respectively. The last argument determines whether the rectangle is *raised* (true) or *lowered* (false). The three-dimensional effect of draw3DRect appears as two edges of the rectangle in the original color and two edges in a slightly darker color. The three-dimensional effect of fill3DRect appears as two edges of the rectangle in the original drawing color and the fill and other two edges in a slightly darker color. Raised rectangles have the original

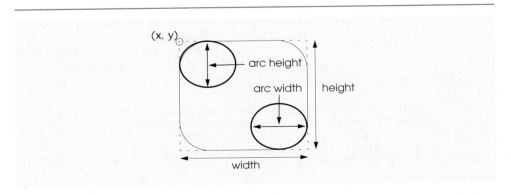

Fig. 12.15 Arc width and arc height for rounded rectangles.

drawing color edges at the top and left of the rectangle. Lowered rectangles have the original drawing color edges at the bottom and right of the rectangle. The three-dimensional effect is difficult to see in some colors.

The `drawOval` and `fillOval` methods (lines 38–39) take the same four arguments. The first two arguments specify the top-left coordinate of the bounding rectangle that contains the oval. The last two arguments specify the `width` and `height` of the bounding rectangle, respectively. Figure 12.16 shows an oval bounded by a rectangle. Note that the oval touches the center of all four sides of the bounding rectangle. (The bounding rectangle is not displayed on the screen.)

12.6 Drawing Arcs

An *arc* is drawn as a portion of an oval. Arc angles are measured in degrees. Arcs *sweep* from a *starting angle* by the number of degrees specified by their *arc angle*. The starting angle indicates in degrees where the arc begins. The arc angle specifies the total number of degrees through which the arc sweeps. Figure 12.17 illustrates two arcs. The left set of axes shows an arc sweeping from zero degrees to approximately 110 degrees. Arcs that sweep in a counterclockwise direction are measured in *positive degrees*. The right set of axes shows an arc sweeping from zero degrees to approximately –110 degrees. Arcs that sweep in a clockwise direction are measured in *negative degrees*. Notice the dashed boxes around the arcs in Fig. 12.17. When drawing an arc, we specify a bounding rectangle for an oval. The arc will sweep along part of the oval. `Graphics` methods *drawArc* and *fillArc* for drawing arcs are summarized in Fig. 12.18.

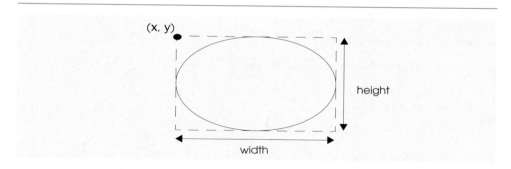

Fig. 12.16 Oval bounded by a rectangle.

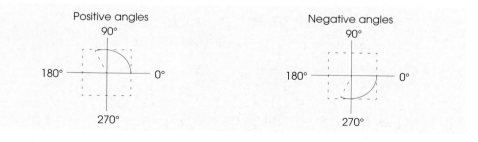

Fig. 12.17 Positive and negative arc angles.

Method	Description

`public void drawArc( int x, int y, int width, int height, int startAngle, int arcAngle )`

>Draws an arc relative to the bounding rectangle's top-left coordinates *(x, y)* with the specified width and height. The arc segment is drawn starting at startAngle and sweeps arcAngle degrees.

`public void fillArc( int x, int y, int width, int height, int startAngle, int arcAngle )`

>Draws a solid arc (i.e., a sector) relative to the bounding rectangle's top-left coordinates *(x, y)* with the specified width and height. The arc segment is drawn starting at startAngle and sweeps arcAngle degrees.

Fig. 12.18 Graphics methods for drawing arcs.

Figure 12.19 demonstrates the arc methods of Fig. 12.18. The program draws six arcs (three unfilled and three filled). To illustrate the bounding rectangle that helps determine where the arc appears, the first three arcs are displayed inside a yellow rectangle that has the same x, y, width and height arguments as the arcs.

```
1   // Fig. 12.19: DrawArcs.java
2   // Drawing arcs.
3   import java.awt.*;
4   import javax.swing.*;
5
6   public class DrawArcs extends JFrame {
7
8       // set window's title bar String and dimensions
9       public DrawArcs()
10      {
11          super( "Drawing Arcs" );
12
13          setSize( 300, 170 );
14          setVisible( true );
15      }
16
17      // draw rectangles and arcs
18      public void paint( Graphics g )
19      {
20          super.paint( g );   // call superclass's paint method
21
22          // start at 0 and sweep 360 degrees
23          g.setColor( Color.YELLOW );
24          g.drawRect( 15, 35, 80, 80 );
25          g.setColor( Color.BLACK );
26          g.drawArc( 15, 35, 80, 80, 0, 360 );
27
```

Fig. 12.19 Arcs displayed with drawArc and fillArc. (Part 1 of 2.)

```
28          // start at 0 and sweep 110 degrees
29          g.setColor( Color.YELLOW );
30          g.drawRect( 100, 35, 80, 80 );
31          g.setColor( Color.BLACK );
32          g.drawArc( 100, 35, 80, 80, 0, 110 );
33
34          // start at 0 and sweep -270 degrees
35          g.setColor( Color.YELLOW );
36          g.drawRect( 185, 35, 80, 80 );
37          g.setColor( Color.BLACK );
38          g.drawArc( 185, 35, 80, 80, 0, -270 );
39
40          // start at 0 and sweep 360 degrees
41          g.fillArc( 15, 120, 80, 40, 0, 360 );
42
43          // start at 270 and sweep -90 degrees
44          g.fillArc( 100, 120, 80, 40, 270, -90 );
45
46          // start at 0 and sweep -270 degrees
47          g.fillArc( 185, 120, 80, 40, 0, -270 );
48
49    } // end method paint
50
51    // execute application
52    public static void main( String args[] )
53    {
54          DrawArcs application = new DrawArcs();
55          application.setDefaultCloseOperation( JFrame.EXIT_ON_CLOSE );
56    }
57
58 } // end class DrawArcs
```

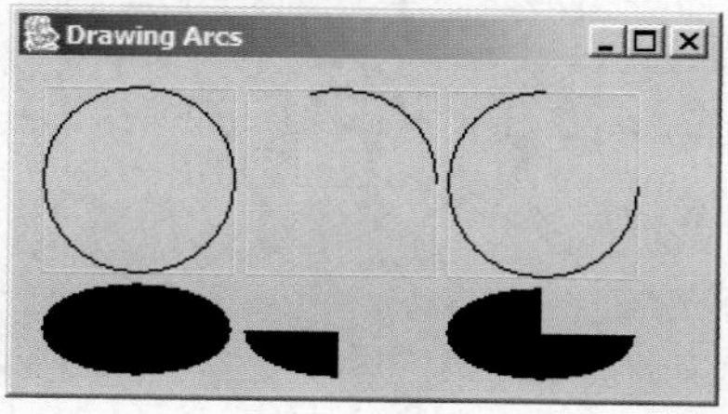

Fig. 12.19 Arcs displayed with drawArc and fillArc. (Part 2 of 2.)

12.7 Drawing Polygons and Polylines

Polygons are closed multisided shapes composed of straight line segments. *Polylines* are a sequence of connected points. Graphics methods for drawing polygons and polylines are discussed in Fig. 12.20. Note that some methods require a *Polygon* object (package java.awt). Class Polygon's constructors are also described in Fig. 12.20. Figure 12.21 draws polygons and polylines, using the methods and constructors in Fig. 12.20.

Method	Description

Graphics methods for drawing polygons

`public void` `drawPolygon( int xPoints[], int yPoints[], int points )`

Draws a polygon. The *x*-coordinate of each point is specified in the xPoints array and the *y*-coordinate of each point is specified in the yPoints array. The last argument specifies the number of points. This method draws a closed polygon. If the last point is different from the first point, the polygon is closed by a line that connects the last point to the first point.

`public void` `drawPolyline( int xPoints[], int yPoints[], int points )`

Draws a sequence of connected lines. The *x*-coordinate of each point is specified in the xPoints array and the *y*-coordinate of each point is specified in the yPoints array. The last argument specifies the number of points. If the last point is different from the first point, the polyline is not closed.

`public void` `drawPolygon( Polygon p )`

Draws the specified polygon.

`public void` `fillPolygon( int xPoints[], int yPoints[], int points )`

Draws a solid polygon. The *x*-coordinate of each point is specified in the xPoints array and the *y*-coordinate of each point is specified in the yPoints array. The last argument specifies the number of points. This method draws a closed polygon. If the last point is different from the first point, the polygon is closed by a line that connects the last point to the first point.

`public void` `fillPolygon( Polygon p )`

Draws the specified solid polygon. The polygon is closed.

Polygon constructors and methods

`public Polygon()`

Constructs a new polygon object. The polygon does not contain any points.

`public Polygon( int xValues[], int yValues[], int numberOfPoints )`

Constructs a new polygon object. The polygon has numberOfPoints sides, with each point consisting of an *x*-coordinate from xValues and a *y*-coordinate from yValues.

`public void` `addPoint( int x, int y )`

Adds pairs of *x*- and *y*-coordinates to the Polygon.

Fig. 12.20 Graphics methods for drawing polygons and class Polygon methods.

```
1   // Fig. 12.21: DrawPolygons.java
2   // Drawing polygons.
3   import java.awt.*;
4   import javax.swing.*;
```

Fig. 12.21 Polygons displayed with drawPolygon and fillPolygon. (Part 1 of 3.)

```
5
6     public class DrawPolygons extends JFrame {
7
8        // set window's title bar String and dimensions
9        public DrawPolygons()
10       {
11          super( "Drawing Polygons" );
12
13          setSize( 275, 230 );
14          setVisible( true );
15       }
16
17       // draw polygons and polylines
18       public void paint( Graphics g )
19       {
20          super.paint( g );   // call superclass's paint method
21
22          int xValues[] = { 20, 40, 50, 30, 20, 15 };
23          int yValues[] = { 50, 50, 60, 80, 80, 60 };
24          Polygon polygon1 = new Polygon( xValues, yValues, 6 );
25
26          g.drawPolygon( polygon1 );
27
28          int xValues2[] = { 70, 90, 100, 80, 70, 65, 60 };
29          int yValues2[] = { 100, 100, 110, 110, 130, 110, 90 };
30
31          g.drawPolyline( xValues2, yValues2, 7 );
32
33          int xValues3[] = { 120, 140, 150, 190 };
34          int yValues3[] = { 40, 70, 80, 60 };
35
36          g.fillPolygon( xValues3, yValues3, 4 );
37
38          Polygon polygon2 = new Polygon();
39          polygon2.addPoint( 165, 135 );
40          polygon2.addPoint( 175, 150 );
41          polygon2.addPoint( 270, 200 );
42          polygon2.addPoint( 200, 220 );
43          polygon2.addPoint( 130, 180 );
44
45          g.fillPolygon( polygon2 );
46
47       } // end method paint
48
49       // execute application
50       public static void main( String args[] )
51       {
52          DrawPolygons application = new DrawPolygons();
53          application.setDefaultCloseOperation( JFrame.EXIT_ON_CLOSE );
54       }
55
56    } // end class DrawPolygons
```

Fig. 12.21 Polygons displayed with drawPolygon and fillPolygon. (Part 2 of 3.)

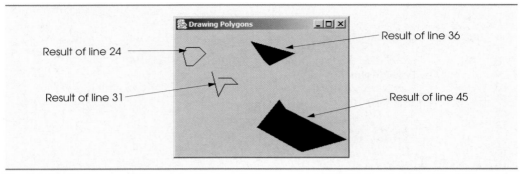

Fig. 12.21 Polygons displayed with `drawPolygon` and `fillPolygon`. (Part 3 of 3.)

Lines 22–23 create two `int` arrays and use them to specify the points for `Polygon` polygon1. The `Polygon` constructor call at line 24 receives array `xValues`, which contains the *x*-coordinate of each point; array `yValues`, which contains the *y*-coordinate of each point and 6 (the number of points in the polygon). Line 26 displays polygon1 by passing it as an argument to `Graphics` method `drawPolygon`.

Lines 28–29 create two `int` arrays and use them to specify the points for a series of connected lines. Array `xValues2` contains the *x*-coordinate of each point and array `yValues2` contains the *y*-coordinate of each point. Line 31 uses `Graphics` method `drawPolyline` to display the series of connected lines specified with the arguments `xValues2`, `yValues2` and 7 (the number of points).

Lines 33–34 create two `int` arrays and use them to specify the points of a polygon. Array `xValues3` contains the *x*-coordinate of each point and array `yValues3` contains the *y*-coordinate of each point. Line 36 displays a polygon by passing to `Graphics` method `fillPolygon` the two arrays (`xValues3` and `yValues3`) and the number of points to draw (4).

Common Programming Error 12.2

An `ArrayIndexOutOfBoundsException` is thrown if the number of points specified in the third argument to method `drawPolygon` or method `fillPolygon` is greater than the number of elements in the arrays of coordinates that specify the polygon to display.

Line 38 creates `Polygon` polygon2 with no points. Lines 39–43 use `Polygon` method *addPoint* to add pairs of *x*- and *y*-coordinates to the `Polygon`. Line 45 displays `Polygon` polygon2 by passing it to `Graphics` method `fillPolygon`.

12.8 Java2D API

The new *Java2D API* provides advanced two-dimensional graphics capabilities for programmers who require detailed and complex graphical manipulations. The API includes features for processing line art, text and images in packages `java.awt`, `java.awt.image`, `java.awt.color`, `java.awt.font`, `java.awt.geom`, `java.awt.print` and `java.awt.image.renderable`. The capabilities of the API are far too broad to cover in this textbook. For an overview of the capabilities, see the Java2D demo (demonstrated in Chapter 3) or visit `java.sun.com/products/java-media/2D/index.html`. In this section, we overview several Java2D capabilities.

Drawing with the Java2D API is accomplished with an instance of *Graphics2D* (package `java.awt`), which is an abstract subclass of class `Graphics`, so it has all the graphics capabilities demonstrated earlier in this chapter. In fact, the actual object used to draw in every `paint` method is an instance of a subclass of `Graphics2D` that is passed to method `paint` and accessed via the superclass `Graphics g`. To access `Graphics2D` capabilities, we must cast the `Graphics` reference passed to `paint` into a `Graphics2D` reference with a statement such as

```
Graphics2D g2d = ( Graphics2D ) g;
```

The next two examples use this technique.

Lines, Rectangles, Round Rectangles, Arcs and Ellipses

The next example demonstrates several Java2D shapes from package `java.awt.geom`, including *Line2D.Double*, *Rectangle2D.Double*, *RoundRectangle2D.Double*, *Arc2D.Double* and *Ellipse2D.Double*. Note the syntax of each class name. Each of these classes represents a shape with dimensions specified as double-precision floating-point values. There is a separate version of each represented with single-precision floating-point values (such as *Ellipse2D.Float*). In each case, `Double` is a `static` nested class of the class specified to the left of the dot (e.g., `Ellipse2D`). To use the `static` nested class, we simply qualify its name with the outer class name.

Figure 12.22 shows how to draw Java2D shapes and modify their drawing characteristics, such as changing line thickness, filling shapes with patterns and drawing dashed lines. These are just a few of the many capabilities provided by Java2D.

```
1   // Fig. 12.22: Shapes.java
2   // Demonstrating some Java2D shapes.
3   import java.awt.*;
4   import java.awt.geom.*;
5   import java.awt.image.*;
6   import javax.swing.*;
7
8   public class Shapes extends JFrame {
9
10      // set window's title bar String and dimensions
11      public Shapes()
12      {
13         super( "Drawing 2D shapes" );
14
15         setSize( 425, 160 );
16         setVisible( true );
17      }
18
19      // draw shapes with Java2D API
20      public void paint( Graphics g )
21      {
22         super.paint( g );  // call superclass's paint method
23
```

Fig. 12.22 Java2D shapes. (Part 1 of 3.)

```
24        Graphics2D g2d = ( Graphics2D ) g;   // cast g to Graphics2D
25
26        // draw 2D ellipse filled with a blue-yellow gradient
27        g2d.setPaint( new GradientPaint( 5, 30, Color.BLUE, 35, 100,
28           Color.YELLOW, true ) );
29        g2d.fill( new Ellipse2D.Double( 5, 30, 65, 100 ) );
30
31        // draw 2D rectangle in red
32        g2d.setPaint( Color.RED );
33        g2d.setStroke( new BasicStroke( 10.0f ) );
34        g2d.draw( new Rectangle2D.Double( 80, 30, 65, 100 ) );
35
36        // draw 2D rounded rectangle with a buffered background
37        BufferedImage buffImage = new BufferedImage( 10, 10,
38           BufferedImage.TYPE_INT_RGB );
39
40        Graphics2D gg = buffImage.createGraphics();
41        gg.setColor( Color.YELLOW ); // draw in yellow
42        gg.fillRect( 0, 0, 10, 10 ); // draw a filled rectangle
43        gg.setColor( Color.BLACK );  // draw in black
44        gg.drawRect( 1, 1, 6, 6 );   // draw a rectangle
45        gg.setColor( Color.BLUE );   // draw in blue
46        gg.fillRect( 1, 1, 3, 3 );   // draw a filled rectangle
47        gg.setColor( Color.RED );    // draw in red
48        gg.fillRect( 4, 4, 3, 3 );   // draw a filled rectangle
49
50        // paint buffImage onto the JFrame
51        g2d.setPaint( new TexturePaint( buffImage,
52           new Rectangle( 10, 10 ) ) );
53        g2d.fill( new RoundRectangle2D.Double( 155, 30, 75, 100, 50, 50 ) );
54
55        // draw 2D pie-shaped arc in white
56        g2d.setPaint( Color.WHITE );
57        g2d.setStroke( new BasicStroke( 6.0f ) );
58        g2d.draw( new Arc2D.Double( 240, 30, 75, 100, 0, 270, Arc2D.PIE ) );
59
60        // draw 2D lines in green and yellow
61        g2d.setPaint( Color.GREEN );
62        g2d.draw( new Line2D.Double( 395, 30, 320, 150 ) );
63
64        float dashes[] = { 10 };
65
66        g2d.setPaint( Color.YELLOW );
67        g2d.setStroke( new BasicStroke( 4, BasicStroke.CAP_ROUND,
68           BasicStroke.JOIN_ROUND, 10, dashes, 0 ) );
69        g2d.draw( new Line2D.Double( 320, 30, 395, 150 ) );
70
71    } // end method paint
72
73    // execute application
74    public static void main( String args[] )
75    {
76        Shapes application = new Shapes();
```

Fig. 12.22 Java2D shapes. (Part 2 of 3.)

```
77              application.setDefaultCloseOperation( JFrame.EXIT_ON_CLOSE );
78          }
79
80      } // end class Shapes
```

Fig. 12.22   Java2D shapes. (Part 3 of 3.)

Line 24 casts the Graphics reference received by paint to a Graphics2D reference and assigns it to g2d to allow access to the Java2D features.

The first shape we draw is an oval filled with gradually changing colors. Lines 27–28 invoke Graphics2D method *setPaint* to set the *Paint* object that determines the color for the shape to display. A Paint object is an object of any class that implements interface java.awt.Paint. The Paint object can be something as simple as one of the predeclared Color objects introduced in Section 12.3 (class Color implements Paint), or the Paint object can be an instance of the Java2D API's *GradientPaint, SystemColor* or *TexturePaint* classes. In this case, we use a GradientPaint object.

Class GradientPaint helps draw a shape in gradually changing colors—called a *gradient*. The GradientPaint constructor used here requires seven arguments. The first two arguments specify the starting coordinate for the gradient. The third argument specifies the starting Color for the gradient. The fourth and fifth arguments specify the ending coordinate for the gradient. The sixth argument specifies the ending Color for the gradient. The last argument specifies whether the gradient is cyclic (true) or acyclic (false). The two sets of coordinates determine the direction of the gradient. Because the second coordinate *(35, 100)* is down and to the right of the first coordinate *(5, 30)*, the gradient goes down and to the right at an angle. Because this gradient is cyclic (true), the color starts with blue, gradually becomes yellow, then gradually returns to blue. If the gradient is acyclic, the color transitions from the first color specified (e.g., blue) to the second color (e.g., yellow).

Line 29 uses Graphics2D method *fill* to draw a filled *Shape* object—an instance of any class that implements interface Shape (package java.awt). In this case, we display an instance of class Ellipse2D.Double. The Ellipse2D.Double constructor receives four arguments specifying the bounding rectangle for the ellipse to display.

Next we draw a red rectangle with a thick border. Line 32 uses setPaint to set the Paint object to Color.RED. Line 33 uses Graphics2D method *setStroke* to set the characteristics of the rectangle's border (or the lines for any other shape). Method setStroke requires as its argument a *Stroke* object, which is an instance of any class that implements interface Stroke (package java.awt). In this case, we use an instance of class *BasicStroke*. Class BasicStroke provides several constructors to specify the width of the line, how the line ends (called the *end caps*), how lines join together (called *line joins*) and the dash attributes of the line (if it is a dashed line). The constructor here specifies that the line should be 10 pixels wide.

Line 34 uses `Graphics2D` method *draw* to draw a `Shape` object—in this case, an instance of class `Rectangle2D.Double`. The `Rectangle2D.Double` constructor receives four arguments specifying the upper-left *x*-coordinate, upper-left *y*-coordinate, width and height of the rectangle.

Next we draw a rounded rectangle filled with a pattern created in a *BufferedImage* (package `java.awt.image`) object. Lines 37–38 create the `BufferedImage` object. Class `BufferedImage` can be used to produce images in color and gray scale. This particular `BufferedImage` is 10 pixels wide and 10 pixels tall. The third constructor argument `BufferedImage.TYPE_INT_RGB` indicates that the image is stored in color using the RGB color scheme.

To create the fill pattern for the rounded rectangle, we must first draw into the `BufferedImage`. Line 40 creates a `Graphics2D` object (with a call to `BufferedImage` method *createGraphics*) that can be used to draw into the `BufferedImage`. Lines 41–48 use methods `setColor`, `fillRect` and `drawRect` (discussed earlier in this chapter) to create the pattern.

Lines 51–52 set the `Paint` object to a new *TexturePaint* (package `java.awt`) object. A `TexturePaint` object uses the image stored in its associated `BufferedImage` (the first constructor argument) as the fill texture for a filled-in shape. The second argument specifies the `Rectangle` area from the `BufferedImage` that will be replicated through the texture. In this case, the `Rectangle` is the same size as the `BufferedImage`. However, a smaller portion of the `BufferedImage` can be used.

Line 53 uses `Graphics2D` method `fill` to draw a filled `Shape` object—in this case, an instance of class *RoundRectangle2D.Double*. The constructor for class `RoundRectangle2D.Double` receives six arguments specifying the rectangle dimensions and the arc width and arc height used to determine the rounding of the corners.

Next we draw a pie-shaped arc with a thick white line. Line 56 sets the `Paint` object to `Color.WHITE`. Line 57 sets the `Stroke` object to a new `BasicStroke` for a line 6 pixels wide. Line 58 uses `Graphics2D` method `draw` to draw a `Shape` object—in this case, an `Arc2D.Double`. The `Arc2D.Double` constructor's first four arguments specifying the upper-left *x*-coordinate, upper-left *y*-coordinate, width and height of the bounding rectangle for the arc. The fifth argument specifies the start angle. The sixth argument specifies the arc angle. The last argument specifies how the arc is closed. Constant *Arc2D.PIE* indicates that the arc is closed by drawing two lines. One line from the arc's starting point to the center of the bounding rectangle and one line from the center of the bounding rectangle to the ending point. Class `Arc2D` provides two other static constants for specifying how the arc is closed. Constant *Arc2D.CHORD* draws a line from the starting point to the ending point. Constant *Arc2D.OPEN* specifies that the arc should not be closed.

Finally, we draw two lines using *Line2D* objects—one solid and one dashed. Line 61 sets the `Paint` object to `Color.GREEN`. Line 62 uses `Graphics2D` method `draw` to draw a `Shape` object—in this case, an instance of class `Line2D.Double`. The `Line2D.Double` constructor's arguments specify starting coordinates and ending coordinates of the line.

Line 64 declares a one-element `float` array containing the value 10. This array will be used to describe the dashes in the dashed line. In this case, each dash will be 10 pixels long. To create dashes of different lengths in a pattern, simply provide the lengths of each dash as an element in the array. Line 66 sets the `Paint` object to `Color.YELLOW`. Lines 67–68 set the `Stroke` object to a new `BasicStroke`. The line will be 4 pixels wide and will have rounded ends (BasicStroke.CAP_ROUND). If lines join together (as in a rectangle at the corners), the joining of the lines will be rounded (BasicStroke.JOIN_ROUND). The dashes argument specifies the dash lengths for the line. The last argument indicates the starting index in the dashes array for the first dash in the pattern. Line 69 then draws a line with the current Stroke.

General Paths

Next we present a general path—a shape constructed from straight lines and complex curves. A general path is represented with an object of class *GeneralPath* (package java.awt.geom). Figure 12.23 demonstrates drawing a general path in the shape of a five-pointed star.

```
1   // Fig. 12.23: Shapes2.java
2   // Demonstrating a general path.
3   import java.awt.*;
4   import java.awt.geom.*;
5   import javax.swing.*;
6
7   public class Shapes2 extends JFrame {
8
9      // set window's title bar String, background color and dimensions
10     public Shapes2()
11     {
12        super( "Drawing 2D Shapes" );
13
14        getContentPane().setBackground( Color.WHITE );
15        setSize( 400, 400 );
16        setVisible( true );
17     }
18
19     // draw general paths
20     public void paint( Graphics g )
21     {
22        super.paint( g );   // call superclass's paint method
23
24        int xPoints[] = { 55, 67, 109, 73, 83, 55, 27, 37, 1, 43 };
25        int yPoints[] = { 0, 36, 36, 54, 96, 72, 96, 54, 36, 36 };
26
27        Graphics2D g2d = ( Graphics2D ) g;
28        GeneralPath star = new GeneralPath();   // create GeneralPath object
29
30        // set the initial coordinate of the General Path
31        star.moveTo( xPoints[ 0 ], yPoints[ 0 ] );
32
33        // create the star--this does not draw the star
34        for ( int count = 1; count < xPoints.length; count++ )
35           star.lineTo( xPoints[ count ], yPoints[ count ] );
36
37        star.closePath();   // close the shape
38
```

Fig. 12.23 Java2D general paths. (Part 1 of 2.)

```
39          g2d.translate( 200, 200 );  // translate the origin to (200, 200)
40
41          // rotate around origin and draw stars in random colors
42          for ( int count = 1; count <= 20; count++ ) {
43             g2d.rotate( Math.PI / 10.0 );  // rotate coordinate system
44
45             // set random drawing color
46             g2d.setColor( new Color( ( int ) ( Math.random() * 256 ),
47                ( int ) ( Math.random() * 256 ),
48                ( int ) ( Math.random() * 256 ) ) );
49
50             g2d.fill( star );  // draw filled star
51          }
52
53       } // end method paint
54
55       // execute application
56       public static void main( String args[] )
57       {
58          Shapes2 application = new Shapes2();
59          application.setDefaultCloseOperation( JFrame.EXIT_ON_CLOSE );
60       }
61
62    } // end class Shapes2
```

Fig. 12.23 Java2D general paths. (Part 2 of 2.)

Lines 24–25 declare two `int` arrays representing the *x*- and *y*-coordinates of the points in the star. Line 28 creates `GeneralPath` object `star`.

Line 31 uses `GeneralPath` method *moveTo* to specify the first point in the `star`. The `for` statement at lines 34–35 uses `GeneralPath` method *lineTo* to draw a line to the next point in the `star`. Each new call to `lineTo` draws a line from the previous point to the current point. Line 37 uses `GeneralPath` method *closePath* to draw a line from the last point to the point specified in the last call to `moveTo`. This completes the general path.

Line 39 uses `Graphics2D` method *translate* to move the drawing origin to location *(200, 200)*. All drawing operations now use location *(200, 200)* as *(0, 0)*.

The `for` statement at lines 42–51 draws the `star` 20 times by rotating it around the new origin point. Line 43 uses `Graphics2D` method *rotate* to rotate the next displayed shape. The argument specifies the rotation angle in radians (with $360° = 2\pi$ radians). Line 50 uses `Graphics2D` method `fill` to draw a filled version of the `star`.

12.9 (Optional Case Study) Thinking About Objects: Designing Interfaces with the UML

In Section 11.9, we incorporated event handling into our simulation by modifying the collaboration diagram that deals with passengers entering and exiting the elevator. We included both event handling and inheritance in that diagram. The `Elevator` informs its `Door` of the `Elevator`'s arrival. This `Door` opens the arrival `Floor`'s `Door` by obtaining its handle through a `Location` object (which was included in the arrival event), and potentially two `Person` objects exit and enter the `Elevator` after both `Door`s open. We also discussed listener interfaces. In this section, we represent our listener interface with the UML.

Realizations

The UML expresses the relationship between a class and an interface through a *realization*. A class *realizes*, or implements, the behaviors of an interface. A class diagram can show a realization between classes and interfaces. Figure 12.24 models the realization between class `Person` and interface `DoorListener`. The relationship between Person and DoorListener appears similar to a generalization, except that the arrow expressing the relationship is dashed instead of solid. Note that the middle compartment in interface `DoorListener` is empty, because interfaces do not contain attributes. Lastly, note the word "JavaInterface" placed in guillemets (« ») located in the first compartment of interface `DoorListener`. This notation distinguishes interface `DoorListener` as a Java interface in our system. Items placed in guillemets are called *stereotypes* in the UML. A stereotype is an extension of the UML. In this case, the stereotype « JavaInterface » extends the UML so that we can model Java interfaces.[2]

Figure 12.25 shows the alternate way to represent the realization of class `Person` and interface `DoorListener` in the UML. Figure 12.25 is the elided diagram of Fig. 12.24. The small circle represents the interface, and the solid line represents the realization. By hiding its operations, we condense the interface, making it easier to read; however, in doing so, we sacrifice the information about its behaviors. When constructing an elided diagram, common practice is to place the information regarding any behavior in a separate diagram—for example, we place the full `DoorListener` interface in the class diagram of Fig. 12.28.

---

2. According to the UML specification version 1.4, interfaces do not have attributes. However, Java interfaces can have attributes (in the form of static final fields). Through the Java Community Process (JCP), the Java community is developing a mapping from UML to Java that includes the « JavaInterface » stereotype (Java Specification Request 26). For more information on the JCP, visit **www.jcp.org**.

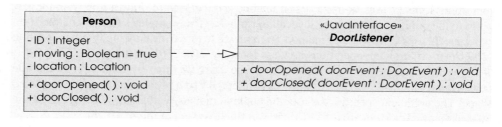

Fig. 12.24 Class diagram that models class `Person` realizing interface
`DoorListener`.

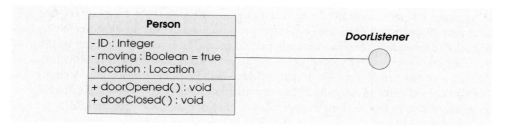

Fig. 12.25 Elided class diagram that models class `Person` realizing interface
`DoorListener`.

   Forward engineering from the UML to implemented Java code benefits from well-constructed realization diagrams. When declaring any class, specify the realization between that class and its interface—that class will "implement" the interface and override the interface's methods. For example, we use Fig. 12.24 to begin constructing `Person.java`. Figure 12.26 shows the Java implementation for Fig. 12.24. Lines 6–8 and lines 14–15 declare the attributes and operations of `Person`, including those required by interface `DoorListener`.

```
1   // Person.java
2   // Generated from Fig. 11.24
3   public class Person implements DoorListener {
4
5       // attributes
6       private int ID;
7       private boolean moving = true;
8       private Location location;
9
10      // constructor
11      public Person() {}
12
13      // methods of DoorListener
14      public void doorOpened( DoorEvent doorEvent ) {}
15      public void doorClosed( DoorEvent doorEvent ) {}
16  }
```

Fig. 12.26 Class `Person` is generated from Fig. 12.24 .

When a Door opens or closes, that Door invokes the appropriate method declared in interface DoorListener, but only if the Person has registered with that Door to receive DoorEvents. Finally, we present an elided model of the realizations in our elevator model in Fig. 12.27. The elided diagram does not contain any interface methods (making the diagram easier to read). Therefore, we model the interfaces in Fig. 12.28, which shows all interface methods. We model the realization of interface PersonMoveListener in Section 14.13. Refer to these diagrams when studying the elevator simulation implementation in Appendices D, E and F.

According to Fig. 12.27, classes Door, Light, Bell and Button implement interface ElevatorMoveListener. Class Elevator implements interfaces ButtonListener, DoorListener and BellListener. Class ElevatorShaft implements interfaces LightListener, ButtonListener and DoorListener. Lastly, class Person implements interface DoorListener. We re-examine Fig. 12.27 in Appendix E when we begin coding our model.

In this section we showed how to represent interfaces and realizations with the UML. We also presented class diagrams showing the listener interfaces and their realizations for our elevator simulation. In Section 14.13, we model how the user interacts with our simulation.

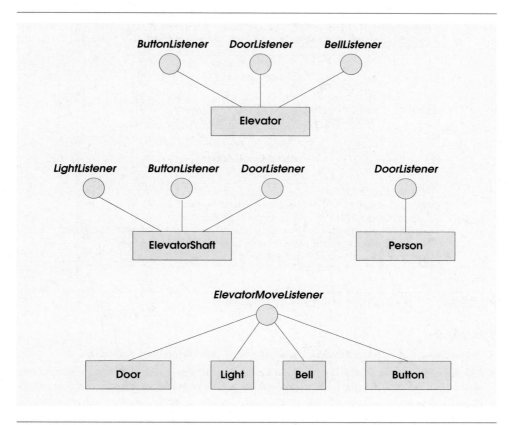

Fig. 12.27 Class diagram that models realizations in the elevator model.

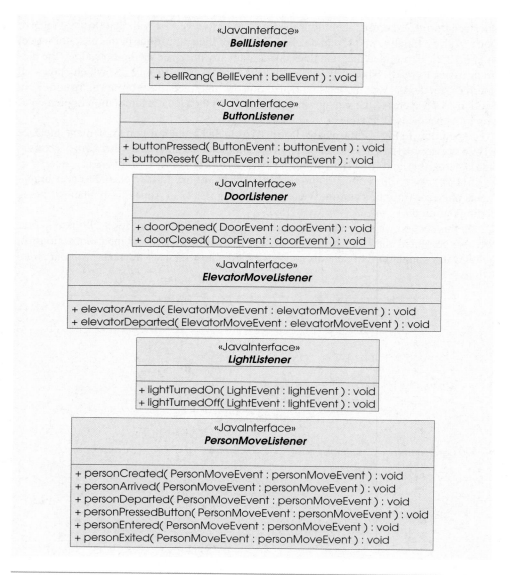

Fig. 12.28 Class diagram for listener interfaces.

SUMMARY

- A coordinate system is a scheme for identifying every possible point on the screen.
- The upper-left corner of a GUI component has the coordinates *(0, 0)*. A coordinate pair is composed of an *x*-coordinate (the horizontal coordinate) and a *y*-coordinate (the vertical coordinate).
- Coordinate units are measured in pixels. A pixel is a display monitor's smallest unit of resolution.
- A graphics context enables drawing on the screen in Java. A Graphics object manages a graphics context by controlling how pixels are displayed.

- `Graphics` objects contain methods for drawing, font manipulation, color manipulation and so on.

- Method `paint` is normally called in response to an event, such as uncovering a window.

- Method `repaint` requests a call to `Component` method `update` as soon as possible to clear the `Component`'s background of any previous drawing, then `update` calls `paint` directly.

- Class `Color` declares methods and constants for manipulating colors in a Java program.

- Java uses RGB colors in which the red, green and blue color components are integers in the range from 0 to 255 or floating-point values in the range from 0.0 to 1.0.

- `Color` methods `getRed`, `getGreen` and `getBlue` return integer values from 0 to 255 representing the amount of red, green and blue in a `Color`. Class `Color` provides 13 predeclared `Color` objects.

- `Graphics` method `getColor` returns a `Color` object representing the current drawing color. `Graphics` method setColor sets the current drawing color.

- Java provides class `JColorChooser` to display a dialog for selecting colors. `JColorChooser` method `showDialog` displays a color chooser dialog and returns the selected `Color` object.

- The default `JColorChooser` dialog allows you to select a color from a variety of color swatches. The **HSB** tab allows you to select a color based on hue, saturation and brightness. The **RGB** tab allows you to select a color by using sliders for the red, green and blue components of the color.

- `Component` method `setBackground` changes the background color of a component.

- Class `Font`'s constructor takes three arguments—the font name, the font style and the font size. The font name is any font currently supported by the system. The font style is `Font.PLAIN`, `Font.ITALIC` or `Font.BOLD`. The font size is measured in points.

- `Graphics` method `setFont` sets the drawing font.

- Class `FontMetrics` declares several methods for obtaining font metrics. `Graphics` method `get-FontMetrics` with no arguments obtains the `FontMetrics` object for the current font. `Graphics` method `getFontMetrics` with a `Font` argument returns that `Font`'s `FontMetrics` object.

- Methods `draw3DRect` and `fill3DRect` take five arguments specifying the top-left corner of the rectangle, the `width` and `height` of the rectangle and whether the rectangle is raised or lowered.

- Methods `drawRoundRect` and `fillRoundRect` draw rectangles with rounded corners. Their first two arguments specify the upper-left corner, the third and fourth arguments specify the `width` and `height`, and the last two arguments—`arcWidth` and `arcHeight`—determine the horizontal and vertical diameters of the arcs used to represent the corners.

- Methods `drawOval` and `fillOval` take the same arguments—the top-left coordinate and the `width` and the `height` of the bounding rectangle that contains the oval.

- Arcs sweep from a starting angle the number of degrees specified by their arc angle. The starting angle specifies where the arc begins and the arc angle specifies the total number of degrees through which the arc sweeps. Arcs that sweep counterclockwise are measured in positive degrees and arcs that sweep clockwise are measured in negative degrees.

- Methods `drawArc` and `fillArc` take the same arguments—the top-left coordinate, the `width` and the `height` of the bounding rectangle that contains the arc and the `startAngle` and `arcAngle` that specify the sweep of the arc.

- Polygons are closed multisided shapes composed of straight segments. Polylines are a sequence of connected points.

- One version of `Graphics` method `drawPolygon` displays a `Polygon` object. Another version receives an array containing the *x*-coordinate of each point, an array containing the *y*-coordinate of each point and the number of points in the polygon and displays the corresponding polygon.

- Graphics method drawPolyline displays a series of connected lines specified by its arguments (an array containing the *x*-coordinate of each point, an array containing the *y*-coordinate of each point and the number of points).
- Polygon method addPoint adds pairs of *x*- and *y*-coordinates to a Polygon.
- The Java2D API provides advanced two-dimensional graphics capabilities for processing line art, text and images.
- To access the Graphics2D capabilities, downcast the Graphics reference passed to paint to a Graphics2D reference.
- Graphics2D method setPaint sets the Paint object that determines the color and texture for the shape to display. The Paint object can be a Color or an instance of the Java2D API's GradientPaint, SystemColor or TexturePaint classes.
- Class GradientPaint draws a shape in a gradually changing color called a gradient.
- Graphics2D method fill draws a filled Shape object.
- The Ellipse2D.Double constructor receives four arguments specifying the bounding rectangle for the ellipse to display.
- Graphics2D method setStroke sets the characteristics of the lines used to draw a shape.
- Graphics2D method draw draws a Shape object.
- The Rectangle2D.Double constructor receives four arguments specifying the upper-left *x*-coordinate, upper-left *y*-coordinate, width and height of the rectangle.
- Class BufferedImage can be used to produce images in color and gray scale.
- A TexturePaint object uses the image stored in its associated BufferedImage as the fill texture for a filled-in shape.
- The RoundRectangle2D.Double constructor receives six arguments specifying the rectangle's dimensions and the arc width and arc height used to determine the rounding of the corners.
- The Arc2D.Double constructor's first four arguments specify the upper-left *x*-coordinate, upper-left *y*-coordinate, width and height of the bounding rectangle for the arc. The fifth argument specifies the start angle. The sixth argument specifies the end angle. The last argument specifies the type of arc (Arc2D.PIE, Arc2D.CHORD or Arc2D.OPEN).
- The Line2D.Double constructor's arguments specify starting and ending line coordinates.
- A general path is a shape constructed from straight lines and complex curves represented with an object of class GeneralPath (package java.awt.geom).
- GeneralPath method moveTo specifies the first point in a general path. GeneralPath method lineTo draws a line to the next point in the general path. Each new call to lineTo draws a line from the previous point to the current point. GeneralPath method closePath draws a line from the last point to the point specified in the last call to moveTo.
- Graphics2D method translate moves the drawing origin to a new location. All drawing operations now use that location as *(0, 0)*. Graphics2D method rotate is used to rotate the next displayed shape. Its argument specifies the rotation angle in radians (with $360° = 2\pi$ radians).

TERMINOLOGY

addPoint method of Polygon
arc
arc bounded by a rectangle
arc height
arc sweeping through an angle

arc width
Arc2D.Double class
ascent
background color
baseline

bounding rectangle
BufferedImage class
closed polygon
closePath method of GeneralPath
Color class
Component class
coordinate
coordinate system
degree
descent
draw method
draw3DRect method of Graphics
drawArc method of Graphics
drawLine method of Graphics
drawOval method of Graphics
drawPolygon method of Graphics
drawPolyline method of Graphics
drawRect method of Graphics
drawRoundRect method of Graphics
Ellipse2D.Double class
fill method of Graphics2D
fill3DRect method of Graphics
fillArc method of Graphics
filled polygon
fillOval method of Graphics
fillPolygon method of Graphics
fillRect method of Graphics
fillRoundRect method of Graphics
font
Font class
font metrics
font name
font style
FontMetrics class
GeneralPath class
getAscent method of FontMetrics
getBlue method of Color
getDescent method of FontMetrics
getFamily method of Font
getFont method of Graphics
getFontMetrics method of Graphics
getGreen method of Color
getHeight method of FontMetrics
getLeading method of FontMetrics
getName method of Font

getRed method of Color
getSize method of Font
getStyle method of Font
GradientPaint class
Graphics class
graphics context
graphics object
Graphics2D class
isBold method of Font
isItalic method of Font
isPlain method of Font
Java2D API
leading
Line2D.Double class
lineTo method of GeneralPath
Monospaced font
moveTo method of GeneralPath
negative degrees
oval
Paint interface
pixel
point
polygon
Polygon class
positive degrees
Rectangle2D.Double class
RGB value
rotate method of Graphics2D
RoundRectangle2D.Double class
SansSerif font
Serif font
setColor method of Graphics
setFont method of Graphics
setPaint method of Graphics2D
setStroke method of Graphics2D
Shape interface
Stroke interface
SystemColor class
TexturePaint class
translate method of Graphics2D
vertical component
x-axis
x-coordinate
y-axis
y-coordinate

SELF-REVIEW EXERCISES

12.1 Fill in the blanks in each of the following statements:
   a) In Java2D, method _____ of class _____ sets the characteristics of a line used to draw a shape.

b) Class _____ helps specify the fill for a shape such that the fill gradually changes from one color to another.

c) The _____ method of class Graphics draws a line between two points.

d) RGB is short for _____, _____ and _____.

e) Font sizes are measured in units called _____.

f) Class _____ helps specify the fill for a shape using a pattern drawn in a Buffered-Image.

12.2 State whether each of the following is *true* or *false*. If *false*, explain why.

a) The first two arguments of Graphics method drawOval specify the center coordinate of the oval.

b) In the Java coordinate system, *x* values increase from left to right.

c) Method fillPolygon draws a solid polygon in the current color.

d) Method drawArc allows negative angles.

e) Method getSize returns the size of the current font in centimeters.

f) Pixel coordinate *(0, 0)* is located at the exact center of the monitor.

12.3 Find the error(s) in each of the following and explain how to correct the error(s). Assume that g is a Graphics object.

```
a) g.setFont( "SansSerif" );
b) g.erase( x, y, w, h );      // clear rectangle at (x, y)
c) Font f = new Font( "Serif", Font.BOLDITALIC, 12 );
d) g.setColor( Color.Yellow );  // change color to yellow
```

ANSWERS TO SELF-REVIEW EXERCISES

12.1 a) setStroke, Graphics2D. b) GradientPaint. c) drawLine. d) red, green, blue. e) points. f) TexturePaint.

12.2 a) False. The first two arguments specify the upper-left corner of the bounding rectangle.

b) True.

c) True.

d) True.

e) False. Font sizes are measured in points.

f) False. The coordinate *(0,0)* corresponds to the upper-left corner of a GUI component on which drawing occurs.

12.3 a) The setFont method takes a Font object as an argument—not a String.

b) The Graphics class does not have an erase method. The clearRect method should be used.

c) Font.BOLDITALIC is not a valid font style. To get a bold italic font, use Font.BOLD + Font.ITALIC.

d) Yellow should be all uppercase letters as in: g.setColor(Color.YELLOW);.

EXERCISES

12.4 Fill in the blanks in each of the following statements:

a) Class _____ of the Java2D API is used to draw ovals.

b) Methods draw and fill of class Graphics2D require an object of type _____ as their argument.

c) The three constants that specify font style are _____, _____ and _____.

d) Graphics2D method _____ sets the painting color for Java2D shapes.

12.5 State whether each of the following is *true* or *false*. If *false*, explain why.
a) The `drawPolygon` method automatically connects the endpoints of the polygon.
b) The `drawLine` method draws a line between two points.
c) The `fillArc` method uses degrees to specify the angle.
d) In the Java coordinate system, *y* values increase from top to bottom.
e) The `Graphics` class inherits directly from class `Object`.
f) The `Graphics` class is an `abstract` class.
g) The `Font` class inherits directly from class `Graphics`.

12.6 Write a program that draws a series of eight concentric circles. The circles should be separated by 10 pixels. Use the `drawOval` method of class `Graphics`.

12.7 Write a program that draws a series of eight concentric circles. The circles should be separated by 10 pixels. Use the `drawArc` method.

12.8 Modify your solution to Exercise 12.6 to draw the ovals by using instances of class `Ellipse2D.Double` and method `draw` of class `Graphics2D`.

12.9 Write a program that draws lines of random lengths in random colors.

12.10 Modify your solution to Exercise 12.9 to draw random lines, in random colors and random line thicknesses. Use class `Line2D.Double` and method `draw` of class `Graphics2D` to draw the lines.

12.11 Write a program that displays randomly generated triangles in different colors. Each triangle should be filled with a different color. Use class `GeneralPath` and method `fill` of class `Graphics2D` to draw the triangles.

12.12 Write a program that randomly draws characters in different font sizes and colors.

12.13 Write a program that draws an 8-by-8 grid. Use the `drawLine` method.

12.14 Modify your solution to Exercise 12.13 to draw the grid using instances of class `Line2D.Double` and method `draw` of class `Graphics2D`.

12.15 Write a program that draws a 10-by-10 grid. Use the `drawRect` method.

12.16 Modify your solution to Exercise 12.15 to draw the grid by using instances of class `Rectangle2D.Double` and method `draw` of class `Graphics2D`.

12.17 Write a program that draws a tetrahedron (a three-dimensional shape with four triangular faces). Use class `GeneralPath` and method `draw` of class `Graphics2D`.

12.18 Write a program that draws a cube. Use class `GeneralPath` and method `draw` of class `Graphics2D`.

12.19 In Exercise 3.10, you wrote an applet that input the radius of a circle from the user and displayed the circle's diameter, circumference and area. Modify your solution to Exercise 3.10 to read a set of coordinates in addition to the radius. Then draw the circle, and display the circle's diameter, circumference and area, using an `Ellipse2D.Double` object to represent the circle and method `draw` of class `Graphics2D` to display the circle.

12.20 Write an application that simulates a screen saver. The application should randomly draw lines using method `drawLine` of class `Graphics`. After drawing 100 lines, the application should clear itself and start drawing lines again. To allow the program to draw continuously, place a call to `repaint` as the last line in method `paint`. Do you notice any problems with this on your system?

12.21 Here is a peek ahead. Package `javax.swing` contains a class called `Timer` that is capable of calling method `actionPerformed` of interface `ActionListener` at a fixed time interval (specified in milliseconds). Modify your solution to Exercise 12.20 to remove the call to `repaint` from method `paint`. Declare your class so it implements `ActionListener`. (The `actionPerformed` method should simply call `repaint`.) Declare an instance variable of type `Timer` called `timer` in your class. In the constructor for your class, write the following statements:

```
timer = new Timer( 1000, this );
timer.start();
```

This creates an instance of class `Timer` that will call `this` object's `actionPerformed` method every 1000 milliseconds (i.e., every second).

12.22 Modify your solution to Exercise 12.21 to enable the user to enter the number of random lines that should be drawn before the application clears itself and starts drawing lines again. Use a `JText-Field` to obtain the value. The user should be able to type a new number into the `JTextField` at any time during the program's execution. Use an inner class to perform event handling for the `JText-Field`.

12.23 Modify your solution to Exercise 12.21 such that it uses random number generation to choose different shapes to display. Use methods of class `Graphics`.

12.24 Modify your solution to Exercise 12.23 to use classes and drawing capabilities of the Java2D API. For shapes such as rectangles and ellipses, draw them with randomly generated gradients. Use class `GradientPaint` to generate the gradient.

12.25 Modify your solution to Exercise 7.21—*Turtle Graphics*—to add a graphical user interface using `JTextFields` and `JButtons`. Also, draw lines rather than drawing asterisks (*). When the turtle graphics program specifies a move, translate the number of positions into a number of pixels on the screen by multiplying the number of positions by 10 (or any value you choose). Implement the drawing with Java2D API features.

12.26 Produce a graphical version of the Knight's Tour problem (Exercise 7.22, Exercise 7.23 and Exercise 7.26). As each move is made, the appropriate cell of the chessboard should be updated with the proper move number. If the result of the program is a *full tour* or a *closed tour*, the program should display an appropriate message. If you would like, use class `Timer` (see Exercise 11.24) to help animate the Knight's Tour. Every second, the next move should be made.

12.27 Produce a graphical version of the *Tortoise and the Hare* simulation (Exercise 7.15). Simulate the mountain by drawing an arc that extends from the bottom-left of the window to the top-right of the window. The tortoise and the hare should race up the mountain. Implement the graphical output so the tortoise and the hare are actually printed on the arc every move. [*Note:* Extend the length of the race from 70 to 300 to allow yourself a larger graphics area.]

12.28 Write a program that uses method `drawPolyline` to draw a spiral.

12.29 Write a program that inputs four numbers and graphs the numbers as a pie chart. Use class `Arc2D.Double` and method `fill` of class `Graphics2D` to perform the drawing. Draw each piece of the pie in a separate color.

12.30 Write an applet that inputs four numbers and graphs the numbers as a bar graph. Use class `Rectangle2D.Double` and method `fill` of class `Graphics2D` to perform the drawing. Draw each bar in a different color.

13

Graphical User Interface Components: Part 1

Objectives

- To understand the design principles of graphical user interfaces (GUI).
- To be able to build graphical user interfaces.
- To understand the packages containing GUI-related components, event-handling classes and interfaces.
- To be able to create and manipulate buttons, labels, lists, text fields and panels.
- To understand mouse events and keyboard events.
- To understand and be able to use layout managers.

… the wisest prophets make sure of the event first.
Horace Walpole

Do you think I can listen all day to such stuff?
Lewis Carroll

Speak the affirmative; emphasize your choice by utter ignoring of all that you reject.
Ralph Waldo Emerson

You pays your money and you takes your choice.
Punch

Guess if you can, choose if you dare.
Pierre Corneille

All hope abandon, ye who enter here!
Dante Alighieri

Exit, pursued by a bear.
William Shakespeare

Outline

13.1 Introduction

A *graphical user interface* (*GUI*) presents a user-friendly mechanism for interacting with a program. A GUI (pronounced "GOO-EE") gives a program a distinctive "look" and "feel." Providing different programs with consistent, intuitive user interface components allows users to be somewhat familiar with a program before they ever use it. In turn, this reduces the time users require to learn a program and increases their ability to use the program in a productive manner.

 **Look-and-Feel Observation 13.1**

Consistent user interfaces enable a user to learn new applications faster.

As an example of a GUI, Fig. 13.1 contains a Netscape Web-browser window with some of its GUI components labeled. In the window is a *menu bar* containing *menus* (**File**, **Edit**, **View**, etc.). Below the menu bar is a set of *buttons*, each of which has a defined task in Netscape. To the right of the buttons is a *combo box* in which the user can type the name of a Web site to visit, or the user can click the down arrow at the right side of the combo box to select from a list of sites previously visited. The menus, buttons and combo box are

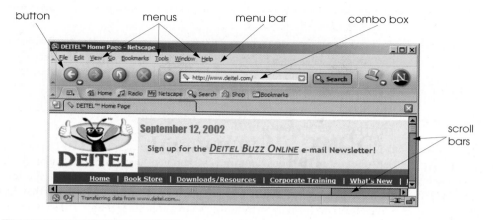

Fig. 13.1   Netscape window with GUI components.

part of Netscape's GUI. They enable you to interact with Netscape. In this chapter and the next, we demonstrate many GUI components that enable users to interact with your programs.

GUIs are built from *GUI components* (sometimes called *controls* or *widgets*—short for *window gadgets*). A GUI component is an object with which the user interacts via the mouse, the keyboard or another form of input, such as voice recognition. Several common Java GUI components are listed in Figure 13.2. In the sections that follow, we discuss each of these GUI components in detail.

13.2 Overview of Swing Components

The classes that create the GUI components listed in Fig. 13.2 are some of the *Swing GUI components* from package *javax.swing*. These GUI components became standard in Java with the release of the Java 2 platform version 1.2. Most *Swing components*, as they are commonly called, are written, manipulated and displayed completely in Java (so-called *pure Java* components). The swing components are part of the *Java Foundation Classes (JFC)*—Java's libraries for cross-platform GUI development. For complete information on the JFC, visit `java.sun.com/products/jfc`.

Component	Description
JLabel	An area where uneditable text or icons can be displayed.
JTextField	An area in which the user inputs data from the keyboard. The area can also display information.
JButton	An area that triggers an event when clicked with the mouse.
JCheckBox	A GUI component that is either selected or not selected.
JComboBox	A drop-down list of items from which the user can make a selection by clicking an item in the list or possibly by typing into the box.

Fig. 13.2   Some basic GUI components. (Part 1 of 2.)

Component	Description
JList	An area containing a list of items from which the user can make a selection by clicking on any element in the list. Multiple elements can be selected.
JPanel	A container in which components can be placed and organized.

Fig. 13.2   Some basic GUI components. (Part 2 of 2.)

The original GUI components from the *Abstract Window Toolkit* (*AWT*) package **java.awt** are tied directly to the local platform's graphical user interface capabilities. When a Java program with an AWT GUI executes on different Java platforms, the program's GUI components display differently on each platform. Consider a program that displays an object of type **Button** (package **java.awt**). On a computer running the Microsoft Windows operating system, the **Button** will have the same look and feel as the buttons in other Windows applications. Similarly, on a computer running the Apple Mac OS operating system, the **Button** will have the same look and feel as the buttons in other Macintosh applications. Sometimes, the manner in which a user can interact with a particular AWT component differs between platforms.

Together, the appearance and the way in which the user interacts with the program are known as that program's *look-and-feel*. The Swing components allow the programmer to specify a uniform look-and-feel across all platforms or to provide a custom look-and-feel for each platform. A program can even change the look-and-feel during program execution. For example, a program could enable users to choose their preferred look-and-feel.

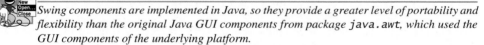

Look-and-Feel Observation 13.2

Swing components are implemented in Java, so they provide a greater level of portability and flexibility than the original Java GUI components from package **java.awt**, *which used the GUI components of the underlying platform.*

Swing components are often referred to as *lightweight components*; they are written completely in Java, so they are not "weighed down" by the complex GUI capabilities of the platform on which they are used. AWT components (many of which parallel the Swing components), which are tied to the local platform, are correspondingly called *heavyweight components*; they rely on the local platform's *windowing system* to determine their functionality and their look-and-feel. Each heavyweight component has a *peer* (from package **java.awt.peer**) that is responsible for the interactions between the component and the local platform that display and manipulate the component. Several Swing components are heavyweight components, such as subclasses of **java.awt.Window** (e.g., **JFrame**) that display windows on the screen and subclasses of **java.applet.Applet** (such as **JApplet**). These components still require direct interaction with the local windowing system. As such, the appearance and functionality of a heavyweight Swing GUI component are restricted by the local windowing system. As we will see, lightweight components provide more control over their appearance and functionality.

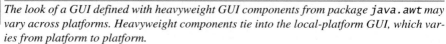

Portability Tip 13.1

The look of a GUI defined with heavyweight GUI components from package **java.awt** *may vary across platforms. Heavyweight components tie into the local-platform GUI, which varies from platform to platform.*

Figure 13.3 shows an inheritance hierarchy containing classes that declare attributes and behaviors that are common to most Swing components. Class `Object` is the superclass of the Java class hierarchy. Class *Component* (package `java.awt`) is a subclass of `Object`; class *Container* (package `java.awt`) is a subclass of `Component`; and class *JComponent* (package `javax.swing`) is a subclass of `Container`. A class that extends class `Component` *is a* `Component`. For example, class `Container` extends class `Component`, and class `Component` extends `Object`. Thus, a `Container` *is a* `Component` and *is an* `Object`, and a `Component` *is an* `Object`. A class that extends class `Container` *is a* `Container`. Thus, a `JComponent` *is a* `Container`. `Component`s can be organized by `Container`s. Because a `Container` *is a* `Component`, a GUI can be structured with `Container`s attached to other `Container`s.

Software Engineering Observation 13.1

To use GUI components effectively, the `javax.swing` and `java.awt` inheritance hierarchies must be understood—especially class `Component`, class `Container` and class `JComponent`, which declare features common to most Swing components.

Class `Component` declares the common attributes and behaviors of all subclasses of `Component`. With few exceptions, most GUI components extend class `Component` directly or indirectly. One method that originates in class `Component` and that we have used frequently in applets is `paint`. Another method discussed previously that originates in `Component` is `repaint`. It is important to understand the methods of class `Component`, because operations common to most GUI components (both Swing and AWT components) are found in class `Component`.

Good Programming Practice 13.1

Study the methods of class `Component` (`java.sun.com/j2se/1.4.1/docs/api/java/awt/Component.html`) in the Java 2 SDK on-line documentation to learn the capabilities common to most GUI components.

A `Container` manages a collection of related components. In applications with `JFrame`s and in applets, we attach components to the content pane, which is an object of class `Container`. Class `Container` declares the common attributes and behaviors for all subclasses of `Container`. One method that originates in class `Container` is method `add`, which has been used to attach components to the content pane (a `Container`). Another method that originates in class `Container` is `setLayout`, which enables a program to specify the layout manager that helps a `Container` position and size its components.

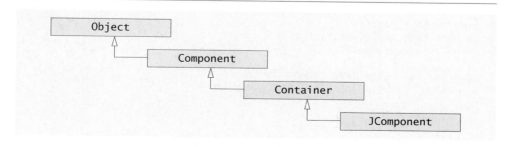

Fig. 13.3   Common superclasses of many of the Swing components.

Good Programming Practice 13.2

Study the methods of class Container *(java.sun.com/j2se/1.4.1/docs/api/java/ awt/Container.html) in the Java 2 SDK on-line documentation to learn the capabilities common to every container for GUI components.*

Class **JComponent** is the superclass of most Swing components. This class declares the common attributes and behaviors of all subclasses of **JComponent**, including:

1. a *pluggable look-and-feel* that can be used to customize the appearance of components (e.g., for use on particular platforms);

2. shortcut keys (called *mnemonics*) for direct access to GUI components through the keyboard;

3. common event-handling capabilities for cases where several GUI components initiate the same actions in a program;

4. brief descriptions of a GUI component's purpose (called *tool tips*) that are displayed when the mouse cursor is positioned over the component for a short time;

5. support for assistive technologies, such as braille screen readers for the visually impaired;

6. support for user interface *localization*—that is, customizing the user interface to display in different languages and use local cultural conventions.

These are just some of the many features of the Swing components. We discuss several of these features here and in Chapter 14.

Good Programming Practice 13.3

Study the methods of class JComponent *(java.sun.com/j2se/1.4.1/docs/api/javax/ swing/JComponent.html) in the Java 2 SDK on-line documentation to learn the capabilities common to Swing components.*

13.3 JLabel

Labels provide text instructions or information on a GUI. Labels are defined with class *JLabel*, a subclass of **JComponent**. A label displays a single line of *read-only text*, an image, or both text and an image. Programs rarely change a label's contents after creating it. The application of Figure 13.4 demonstrates several **JLabel** features.

```
1   // Fig. 13.4: LabelTest.java
2   // Demonstrating the JLabel class.
3   import java.awt.*;
4   import java.awt.event.*;
5   import javax.swing.*;
6
7   public class LabelTest extends JFrame {
8      private JLabel label1, label2, label3;
9
10     // set up GUI
11     public LabelTest()
12     {
```

Fig. 13.4   JLabels with text and icons. (Part 1 of 2.)

```
13              super( "Testing JLabel" );
14
15              // get content pane and set its layout
16              Container container = getContentPane();
17              container.setLayout( new FlowLayout() );
18
19              // JLabel constructor with a string argument
20              label1 = new JLabel( "Label with text" );
21              label1.setToolTipText( "This is label1" );
22              container.add( label1 );
23
24              // JLabel constructor with string, Icon and alignment arguments
25              Icon bug = new ImageIcon( "bug1.gif" );
26              label2 = new JLabel( "Label with text and icon", bug,
27                 SwingConstants.LEFT );
28              label2.setToolTipText( "This is label2" );
29              container.add( label2 );
30
31              // JLabel constructor no arguments
32              label3 = new JLabel();
33              label3.setText( "Label with icon and text at bottom" );
34              label3.setIcon( bug );
35              label3.setHorizontalTextPosition( SwingConstants.CENTER );
36              label3.setVerticalTextPosition( SwingConstants.BOTTOM );
37              label3.setToolTipText( "This is label3" );
38              container.add( label3 );
39
40              setSize( 275, 170 );
41              setVisible( true );
42
43           } // end constructor
44
45           public static void main( String args[] )
46           {
47              LabelTest application = new LabelTest();
48              application.setDefaultCloseOperation( JFrame.EXIT_ON_CLOSE );
49           }
50
51        } // end class LabelTest
```

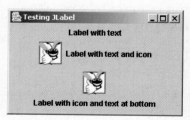
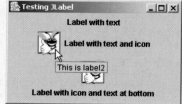

Fig. 13.4   JLabels with text and icons. (Part 2 of 2.)

Good Programming Practice 13.4

Study the methods of class `JLabel` *(*`java.sun.com/j2se/1.4.1/docs/api/javax/`
`swing/JLabel.html`*) in the Java 2 SDK on-line documentation to learn the complete capabilities of the class before using it.*

The program declares three `JLabel`s at line 8. The `JLabel` objects are instantiated in the `LabelTest` constructor (lines 11–43). Line 20 creates a `JLabel` object with the text `"Label with text"`. The label displays this text when the label appears on the screen (i.e., when the `LabelTest` window is displayed in this program).

Line 21 uses method *setToolTipText* (inherited by `JLabel` from `JComponent`) to specify the tool tip (see the second screen capture in Fig. 13.4) that is displayed when the user positions the mouse cursor over the label in the GUI. When you execute this program, try positioning the mouse over each label to see its tool tip. Line 22 adds `label1` to the content pane of the `LabelTest` window.

Look-and-Feel Observation 13.3

Use tool tips to add descriptive text to your GUI components. This text helps the user determine the GUI component's purpose in the user interface.

Several Swing components can display images with an *Icon* argument to their constructor or by using a method that is normally called *setIcon*. An `Icon` is an object of any class that implements interface *Icon* (package `javax.swing`). One such class is *ImageIcon* (package `javax.swing`), which supports several image formats, including *Graphics Interchange Format (GIF), Portable Network Graphics (PNG)* and *Joint Photographic Experts Group (JPEG)*. File names for each of these types end with `.gif`, `.png` or `.jpg` (or `.jpeg`), respectively. We discuss images in more detail in Chapter 19, Multimedia: Images, Animation and Audio. Line 25 declares an `ImageIcon` object. The file `bug1.gif` contains the image to load and store in the `ImageIcon` object. For now, we assume that the file is in the same directory as the program. (We will discuss locating the image file elsewhere in Chapter 19.) The `ImageIcon` object is assigned to `Icon` reference `bug`. Remember, class `ImageIcon` implements interface `Icon`; therefore, an `ImageIcon` *is an* `Icon`.

A `JLabel` can display an `Icon`. Lines 26–27 use another `JLabel` constructor to create a label that displays the text `"Label with text and icon"` and the `Icon` to which `bug` refers. The last constructor argument indicates that the label's contents are *left justified*, or *left aligned* (i.e., the icon and text are at the left side of the label's area on the screen). Interface *SwingConstants* (package `javax.swing`) declares a set of common integer constants (such as `SwingConstants.LEFT`) that are used with many Swing components. By default, the text appears to the right of the image when a label contains both text and an image. The horizontal and vertical alignments of a label can be set with methods *setHorizontalAlignment* and *setVerticalAlignment*, respectively. Line 28 specifies the tool-tip text for `label2`, and line 29 adds `label2` to the content pane.

Common Programming Error 13.1

If you do not explicitly add a GUI component to a container, the GUI component will not be displayed when the container appears on the screen.

Common Programming Error 13.2

A `NullPointerException` *occurs when a program invokes* `Container` *method* `add` *with a* `null` *reference as an argument.*

Class JLabel provides many methods to change a label's appearance after the label has been instantiated. Line 32 creates a JLabel and invokes its no-argument constructor. Such a label initially has no text or Icon. Line 33 uses JLabel method *setText* to set the text displayed on the label. The corresponding method *getText* retrieves the current text displayed on a label. Line 34 uses JLabel method *setIcon* to specify the Icon to display on the label. The corresponding method *getIcon* retrieves the current Icon displayed on a label. Lines 35–36 use JLabel methods *setHorizontalTextPosition* and *setVerticalTextPosition* to specify the text position in the label. In this case, the text will be centered horizontally and will appear at the bottom of the label. Thus, the Icon will appear above the text. The horizontal-position constants in SwingConstants are LEFT, CENTER and RIGHT. The vertical-positions constants in SwingConstants are TOP, CENTER and BOTTOM. Line 37 sets the tool-tip text for label3. Line 38 adds label3 to the content pane.

13.4　Event Handling

The preceding section did not discuss event handling, because users do not interact with JLabels. GUIs are *event driven* (i.e., they generate *events* when the user of the program interacts with the GUI). Some common events (interactions) are moving the mouse, clicking the mouse buttons, clicking a button, typing in a text field, selecting an item from a menu and closing a window. When a user interaction occurs, a message is sent to the program. GUI event information is stored in an object of a class that extends AWTEvent. Figure 13.5 illustrates a hierarchy containing many of the event classes from package java.awt.event. Some of these event classes are discussed throughout this chapter and Chapter 14. The event types from package *java.awt.event* are used with both AWT and Swing components. Additional Swing-specific event types are declared in package *javax.swing.event.*.

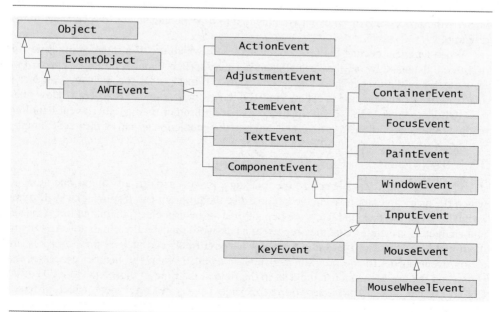

Fig. 13.5　Some event classes of package java.awt.event.

There are three parts to the event-handling mechanism—the *event source*, the *event object* and the *event listener*. The event source is the particular GUI component with which the user interacts. The event object encapsulates information about the event that occurred. This information includes a reference to the event source and any event-specific information that may be required by the event listener for it to handle the event. The event listener is an object that is notified by the event source when an event occurs; in effect, it "listens" for an event and executes in response to the event. The event listener receives an event object when it is notified of the event. It then uses the object to respond to the event. The event source is required to provide methods that enable listeners to be either registered or unregistered. The event source maintains a list of its registered listeners and notifies every registered listener when an event occurs

The programmer must perform two key tasks to process a graphical user interface event in a program—register an *event listener* for the GUI component that is expected to generate the event, and it must implement an *event-handling method* (or a set of event-handling methods). Event-handling methods are commonly called *event handlers*. An event listener for a GUI event is an object of a class that implements one or more of the event-listener interfaces from package `java.awt.event` and package `javax.swing.event`. Many of the event-listener types are common to both Swing and AWT components. Such types are declared in package `java.awt.event`, and many of them are shown in Fig. 13.6. Additional event-listener types that are specific to Swing components are declared in package `javax.swing.event`.

Each event-listener interface specifies one or more event-handling methods that *must* be declared in the class that implements the event-listener interface. Recall from Section 10.8 that any class which implements an interface must declare all the `abstract` methods of that interface; otherwise, the class is an `abstract` class and cannot be used to create objects. The use of event listeners in event handling is known as the *delegation event model*—the processing of an event is delegated to a particular object (the listener) in the program.

When an event occurs, the GUI component with which the user interacted notifies its registered listeners by calling each listener's appropriate event-handling method. For example, when the user presses the *Enter* key in a `JTextField`, the registered listener's `actionPerformed` method is called. How did the event handler get registered? How does the GUI component know to call `actionPerformed` rather than another event-handling method? We answer these questions and diagram the interaction as part of the next example.

13.5 Textfields

JTextFields and *JPasswordFields* (package `javax.swing`) are single-line areas in which the user can enter text via the keyboard or the program can display text. A `JPasswordField` shows that characters are being typed as the user enters them, but hides the actual characters, assuming that they represent a password that should remain known only to the user. When the user types data into any of these fields and presses the *Enter* key, an action event occurs. If the program registers an event listener, the listener processes the event, and the program can use the data in the field at the time of the event. Class `JTextField` extends class *JTextComponent* (package `javax.swing.text`), which provides many features common to Swing's text-based components. Class `JPasswordField` extends `JTextField` and adds several methods that are specific to processing passwords.

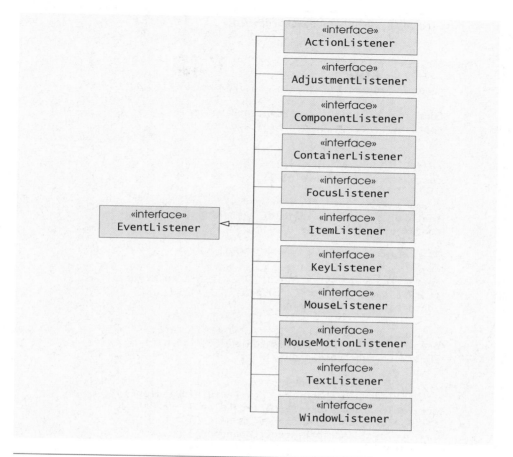

Fig. 13.6   Event-listener interfaces of package `java.awt.event`.

The application of Fig. 13.7 uses classes `JTextField` and `JPasswordField` to create and manipulate four textfields. When the user presses *Enter* in the currently active field a message dialog box containing the text in the field is displayed. The currently active field is said to be "in *focus*." One can change the focus to any component by clicking that component or by calling the component's `requestFocus` method in the program. In this example, when an event occurs in the `JPasswordField`, the password is revealed.

```
1   // Fig. 13.7: TextFieldTest.java
2   // Demonstrating the JTextField class.
3   import java.awt.*;
4   import java.awt.event.*;
5   import javax.swing.*;
6
7   public class TextFieldTest extends JFrame {
8       private JTextField textField1, textField2, textField3;
```

Fig. 13.7   `JTextField`s and `JPasswordField`s. (Part 1 of 4.)

```
9        private JPasswordField passwordField;
10
11       // set up GUI
12       public TextFieldTest()
13       {
14          super( "Testing JTextField and JPasswordField" );
15
16          Container container = getContentPane();
17          container.setLayout( new FlowLayout() );
18
19          // construct textfield with default sizing
20          textField1 = new JTextField( 10 );
21          container.add( textField1 );
22
23          // construct textfield with default text
24          textField2 = new JTextField( "Enter text here" );
25          container.add( textField2 );
26
27          // construct textfield with default text,
28          // 20 visible elements and no event handler
29          textField3 = new JTextField( "Uneditable text field", 20 );
30          textField3.setEditable( false );
31          container.add( textField3 );
32
33          // construct passwordfield with default text
34          passwordField = new JPasswordField( "Hidden text" );
35          container.add( passwordField );
36
37          // register event handlers
38          TextFieldHandler handler = new TextFieldHandler();
39          textField1.addActionListener( handler );
40          textField2.addActionListener( handler );
41          textField3.addActionListener( handler );
42          passwordField.addActionListener( handler );
43
44          setSize( 325, 100 );
45          setVisible( true );
46
47       } // end constructor TextFieldTest
48
49       public static void main( String args[] )
50       {
51          TextFieldTest application = new TextFieldTest();
52          application.setDefaultCloseOperation( JFrame.EXIT_ON_CLOSE );
53       }
54
55       // private inner class for event handling
56       private class TextFieldHandler implements ActionListener {
57
58          // process textfield events
59          public void actionPerformed( ActionEvent event )
60          {
61             String string = "";
```

Fig. 13.7   JTextFields and JPasswordFields. (Part 2 of 4.)

```
62
63          // user pressed Enter in JTextField textField1
64          if ( event.getSource() == textField1 )
65             string = "textField1: " + event.getActionCommand();
66
67          // user pressed Enter in JTextField textField2
68          else if ( event.getSource() == textField2 )
69             string = "textField2: " + event.getActionCommand();
70
71          // user pressed Enter in JTextField textField3
72          else if ( event.getSource() == textField3 )
73             string = "textField3: " + event.getActionCommand();
74
75          // user pressed Enter in JTextField passwordField
76          else if ( event.getSource() == passwordField ) {
77             string = "passwordField: " +
78                new String( passwordField.getPassword() );
79          }
80
81          JOptionPane.showMessageDialog( null, string );
82
83       } // end method actionPerformed
84
85    } // end private inner class TextFieldHandler
86
87 } // end class TextFieldTest
```

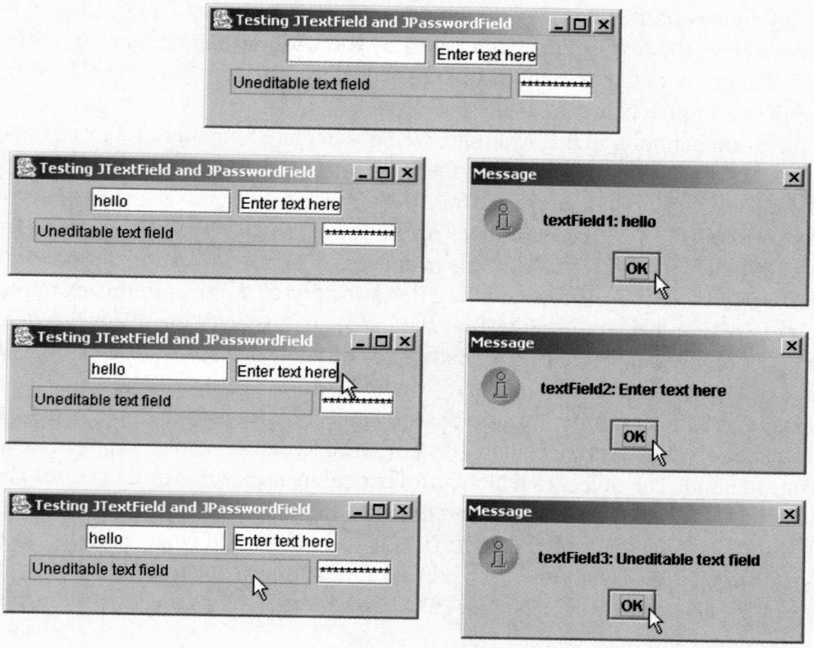

Fig. 13.7   JTextFields and JPasswordFields. (Part 3 of 4.)

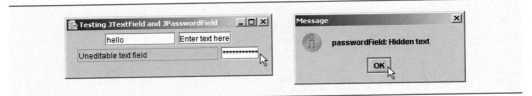

Fig. 13.7   JTextFields and JPasswordFields. (Part 4 of 4.)

Line 8 declares three JTextField variables (textField1, textField2 and textField3), and line 9 declares a JPasswordField variable (passwordField). Each of the corresponding textfields is instantiated in the constructor (lines 12–47). Line 20 creates textField1 with 10 columns of text. The pixels size of a text column is determined by the average width of a character in the textfield's current font. Line 21 adds textField1 to the content pane.

Line 24 creates textField2 with the initial text "Enter text here" to display in the text field. The width of the text field is determined by the width of the default text. Line 25 adds textField2 to the content pane.

Line 29 creates textField3 and calls the JTextField constructor with two arguments—the default text "Uneditable text field" to display and the number of columns (20). The width of the text field is determined by the number of columns specified. Line 30 uses method *setEditable* (inherited into JTextField from class JTextComponent) to make the textfield uneditable—i.e., the user cannot modify the text in the text field. Line 31 adds textField3 to the content pane.

Line 34 creates passwordField with the text "Hidden text" to display in the text field. The width of the text field is determined by the width of the default text. When you execute the program, notice that the text is displayed as a string of asterisks. Line 35 adds passwordField to the content pane.

For the event handling in this example, we have declared inner class TextFieldHandler (lines 56–85), which implements interface ActionListener. (This class TextFieldHandler is discussed shortly). Thus, every instance of class TextFieldHandler *is an* ActionListener. Line 38 creates an instance of class TextFieldHandler and assigns its reference to handler. This one instance will be used as the event-listener object for the three JTextField objects and the JPasswordField object in this example.

Lines 39–42 are the event-registration statements that specify the event-listener object for each GUI component. The program calls JTextField method addActionListener to register the event for each component. Method addActionListener receives as its argument an ActionListener object. Thus, any object of a class that implements interface ActionListener (i.e., any object that *is an* ActionListener) can be supplied as an argument to this method. The object to which handler refers *is an* ActionListener, because its class implements interface ActionListener. After these statements execute, the object to which handler refers *listens for events* (i.e., it will be notified when an event occurs) on these four objects. Now, when the user presses *Enter* in any of these four fields, method actionPerformed (line 59–83) in class TextFieldHandler is called to handle the event.

 Software Engineering Observation 13.2

 *The event listener for an event must implement the appropriate event-listener interface.*

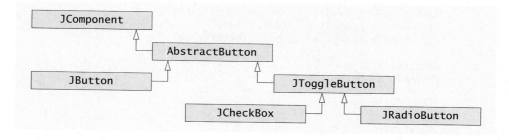

Fig. 13.9   Swing button hierarchy.

Look-and-Feel Observation 13.4

Having more than one JButton with the same label makes the JButtons ambiguous to the user. Provide a unique label for each button.

The application of Fig. 13.10 creates two JButtons and demonstrates that JButtons, like JLabels, support the display of Icons. Event handling for the buttons is performed by a single instance of inner class ButtonHandler (declared at lines 47–56).

```
1   // Fig. 13.10: ButtonTest.java
2   // Creating JButtons.
3   import java.awt.*;
4   import java.awt.event.*;
5   import javax.swing.*;
6
7   public class ButtonTest extends JFrame {
8      private JButton plainButton, fancyButton;
9
10     // set up GUI
11     public ButtonTest()
12     {
13        super( "Testing Buttons" );
14
15        // get content pane and set its layout
16        Container container = getContentPane();
17        container.setLayout( new FlowLayout() );
18
19        // create buttons
20        plainButton = new JButton( "Plain Button" );
21        container.add( plainButton );
22
23        Icon bug1 = new ImageIcon( "bug1.gif" );
24        Icon bug2 = new ImageIcon( "bug2.gif" );
25        fancyButton = new JButton( "Fancy Button", bug1 );
26        fancyButton.setRolloverIcon( bug2 );
27        container.add( fancyButton );
28
29        // create an instance of inner class ButtonHandler
30        // to use for button event handling
```

Fig. 13.10   Command buttons and action events. (Part 1 of 2.)

```
31          ButtonHandler handler = new ButtonHandler();
32          fancyButton.addActionListener( handler );
33          plainButton.addActionListener( handler );
34
35          setSize( 275, 100 );
36          setVisible( true );
37
38       } // end ButtonTest constructor
39
40       public static void main( String args[] )
41       {
42          ButtonTest application = new ButtonTest();
43          application.setDefaultCloseOperation( JFrame.EXIT_ON_CLOSE );
44       }
45
46       // inner class for button event handling
47       private class ButtonHandler implements ActionListener {
48
49          // handle button event
50          public void actionPerformed( ActionEvent event )
51          {
52             JOptionPane.showMessageDialog( ButtonTest.this,
53                "You pressed: " + event.getActionCommand() );
54          }
55
56       } // end private inner class ButtonHandler
57
58    } // end class ButtonTest
```

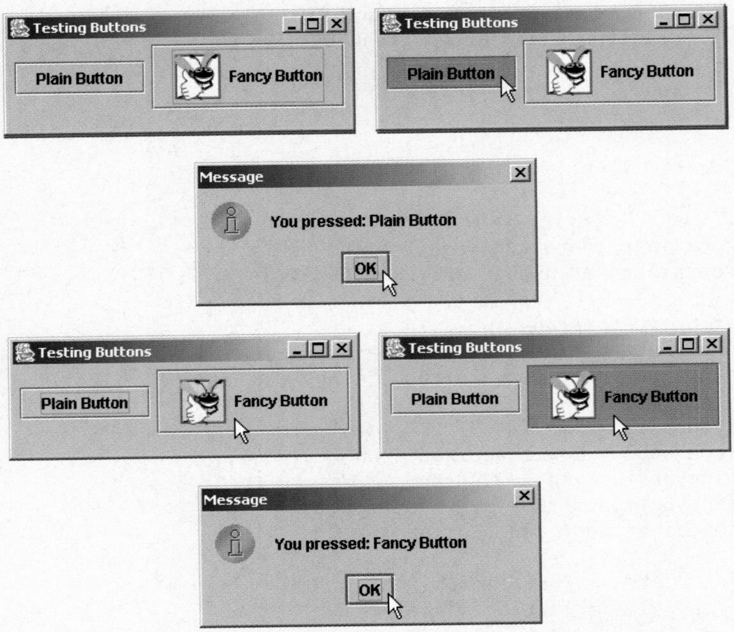

Fig. 13.10 Command buttons and action events. (Part 2 of 2.)

Line 8 declares JButton variables plainButton and fancyButton. The corresponding objects are instantiated in the constructor. Line 20 creates plainButton with the button label "Plain Button". Line 21 adds the button to the content pane.

A JButton can display an Icon. To provide the user with an extra level of visual interaction with the GUI, a JButton can also have a *rollover* Icon—an Icon that is displayed when the user positions the mouse over the button. The icon on the button changes as the mouse moves in and out of the button's area on the screen. Lines 23–24 create two ImageIcon objects that represent the default Icon and rollover Icon for the JButton created at line 25. Both statements assume that the image files are stored in the same directory as the program (which is commonly the case for applications that use images).

Line 25 creates fancyButton with the text "Fancy Button" and the icon bug1. By default, the text is displayed to the right of the icon. Line 26 uses *setRolloverIcon* (inherited from AbstractButton) to specify the image displayed on the button when the user positions the mouse over the button. Line 27 adds the button to the content pane.

Look-and-Feel Observation 13.5

Because class AbstractButton supports displaying text and images on a button, all subclasses of AbstractButton also support displaying text and images.

Look-and-Feel Observation 13.6

Using rollover icons for JButtons provides users with visual feedback indicating that when they click the mouse while the cursor is positioned over the button, an action will occur.

JButtons, like JTextFields, generate ActionEvents. As mentioned previously, an ActionEvent can be processed by any ActionListener object. Lines 31–33 create an event-listener object and register an ActionListener for each JButton. Inner class ButtonHandler (lines 47–56) declares actionPerformed to display a message dialog box containing the label for the button the user pressed. For a JButton event, ActionEvent method getActionCommand returns the label on the button.

13.8 JCheckBox and JRadioButton

The Swing GUI components contain three types of *state buttons—JToggleButton*, *JCheckBox* and *JRadioButton*—that have on/off or true/false values. Classes JCheckBox and JRadioButton are subclasses of JToggleButton (Fig. 13.9). A JRadioButton is different from a JCheckBox in that there are normally several JRadioButtons that are grouped together, and only one of the JRadioButtons in the group can be selected (true) at any time. We first discuss class JCheckBox.

JCheckBox

Figure 13.11 uses two JCheckBox objects to select the desired font style of the text displayed in a JTextField. One JCheckBox applies a bold style when selected and the other applies an italic style when selected. If both are selected, the style of the font is bold and italic. When the program initially executes, neither JCheckBox is checked (i.e., they are both false), so the font is plain.

After the JTextField is created and initialized, line 22 sets the font of the JTextField to Serif, PLAIN style and 14-point size. Next, lines 26 and 29 create two JCheckBox objects. The string passed to the JCheckBox constructor is the *checkbox label* that appears to the right of the JCheckBox by default.

```
1   // Fig. 13.11: CheckBoxTest.java
2   // Creating JCheckBox buttons.
3   import java.awt.*;
4   import java.awt.event.*;
5   import javax.swing.*;
6
7   public class CheckBoxTest extends JFrame {
8      private JTextField field;
9      private JCheckBox bold, italic;
10
11     // set up GUI
12     public CheckBoxTest()
13     {
14        super( "JCheckBox Test" );
15
16        // get content pane and set its layout
17        Container container = getContentPane();
18        container.setLayout( new FlowLayout() );
19
20        // set up JTextField and set its font
21        field = new JTextField( "Watch the font style change", 20 );
22        field.setFont( new Font( "Serif", Font.PLAIN, 14 ) );
23        container.add( field );
24
25        // create checkbox objects
26        bold = new JCheckBox( "Bold" );
27        container.add( bold );
28
29        italic = new JCheckBox( "Italic" );
30        container.add( italic );
31
32        // register listeners for JCheckBoxes
33        CheckBoxHandler handler = new CheckBoxHandler();
34        bold.addItemListener( handler );
35        italic.addItemListener( handler );
36
37        setSize( 275, 100 );
38        setVisible( true );
39
40     } // end CheckBoxText constructor
41
42     public static void main( String args[] )
43     {
44        CheckBoxTest application = new CheckBoxTest();
45        application.setDefaultCloseOperation( JFrame.EXIT_ON_CLOSE );
46     }
47
48     // private inner class for ItemListener event handling
49     private class CheckBoxHandler implements ItemListener {
50        private int valBold = Font.PLAIN;
51        private int valItalic = Font.PLAIN;
52
```

Fig. 13.11   JCheckBox buttons and item events. (Part 1 of 2.)

```
53        // respond to checkbox events
54        public void itemStateChanged( ItemEvent event )
55        {
56           // process bold checkbox events
57           if ( event.getSource() == bold )
58              valBold = bold.isSelected() ? Font.BOLD : Font.PLAIN;
59
60           // process italic checkbox events
61           if ( event.getSource() == italic )
62              valItalic = italic.isSelected() ? Font.ITALIC : Font.PLAIN;
63
64           // set text field font
65           field.setFont( new Font( "Serif", valBold + valItalic, 14 ) );
66
67        } // end method itemStateChanged
68
69     } // end private inner class CheckBoxHandler
70
71 } // end class CheckBoxTest
```

Fig. 13.11 JCheckBox buttons and item events. (Part 2 of 2.)

When the user clicks a JCheckBox, an ItemEvent occurs that can be handled by an ItemListener (any object of a class that implements interface ItemListener). An ItemListener must implement method *itemStateChanged*. In this example, the event handling is performed by an instance of inner class CheckBoxHandler (lines 49–69). Lines 33–35 create an instance of class CheckBoxHandler and register it with method *addItemListener* as the listener for both the checkboxes bold and italic.

Method itemStateChanged (lines 54–67) is called when the user clicks the bold or the italic checkbox. The method uses event.getSource() to determine which JCheckBox was clicked. If it was the bold checkbox, line 58 uses JCheckBox method *isSelected* to determine if the button is selected. If the checkbox is selected, local variable valBold is assigned Font.BOLD; otherwise, it is assigned Font.PLAIN. A similar statement executes if italic is clicked. If the italic checkbox is selected, local variable valItalic is assigned Font.ITALIC; otherwise, it is assigned Font.PLAIN. Line 65 uses the sum of valBold and valItalic as the style of the textfield's new font.

JRadioButton

Radio buttons (declared with class *JRadioButton*) are similar to check boxes in that they have two states—*selected* and *not selected* (also called *deselected*). However, radio buttons normally appear as a *group* in which only one radio button can be selected at a time. Selecting a different radio button in the group forces all other radio buttons in the group to be deselected. Radio buttons are used to represent a set of *mutually exclusive* options (i.e., multiple options in the group cannot be selected at the same time). The logical relationship between radio buttons is maintained by a *ButtonGroup* object (package `javax.swing`), which itself is not a GUI component. Therefore, a `ButtonGroup` object organizes a group of buttons and is not itself displayed in a user interface. Rather, the individual `JRadioButton` objects from the group are displayed in the GUI.

Common Programming Error 13.4

Adding a ButtonGroup *object (or an object of any other class that does not derive from* Component*) to a container results in a compilation error.*

The application of Fig. 13.12 is similar to that of Fig. 13.11. The user can alter the font style of a `JTextField`'s text. The program uses radio buttons that permit only a single font style in the group to be selected at a time.

Lines 28–38 in the constructor create four `JRadioButton` objects and add them to the application window's content pane. Each `JRadioButton` is created with a constructor call like that in line 28. This constructor initializes the label that appears to the right of the `JRadioButton` by default and the initial state of the `JRadioButton`. A `true` second argument indicates that the `JRadioButton` should appear selected when it is displayed.

```java
1   // Fig. 13.12: RadioButtonTest.java
2   // Creating radio buttons using ButtonGroup and JRadioButton.
3   import java.awt.*;
4   import java.awt.event.*;
5   import javax.swing.*;
6
7   public class RadioButtonTest extends JFrame {
8      private JTextField field;
9      private Font plainFont, boldFont, italicFont, boldItalicFont;
10     private JRadioButton plainButton, boldButton, italicButton,
11        boldItalicButton;
12     private ButtonGroup radioGroup;
13
14     // create GUI and fonts
15     public RadioButtonTest()
16     {
17        super( "RadioButton Test" );
18
19        // get content pane and set its layout
20        Container container = getContentPane();
21        container.setLayout( new FlowLayout() );
22
23        // set up JTextField
24        field = new JTextField( "Watch the font style change", 25 );
25        container.add( field );
26
27        // create radio buttons
28        plainButton = new JRadioButton( "Plain", true );
```

Fig. 13.12 JRadioButtons and ButtonGroups. (Part 1 of 3.)

```
29          container.add( plainButton );
30
31          boldButton = new JRadioButton( "Bold", false );
32          container.add( boldButton );
33
34          italicButton = new JRadioButton( "Italic", false );
35          container.add( italicButton );
36
37          boldItalicButton = new JRadioButton( "Bold/Italic", false );
38          container.add( boldItalicButton );
39
40          // create logical relationship between JRadioButtons
41          radioGroup = new ButtonGroup();
42          radioGroup.add( plainButton );
43          radioGroup.add( boldButton );
44          radioGroup.add( italicButton );
45          radioGroup.add( boldItalicButton );
46
47          // create font objects
48          plainFont = new Font( "Serif", Font.PLAIN, 14 );
49          boldFont = new Font( "Serif", Font.BOLD, 14 );
50          italicFont = new Font( "Serif", Font.ITALIC, 14 );
51          boldItalicFont = new Font( "Serif", Font.BOLD + Font.ITALIC, 14 );
52          field.setFont( plainFont );   // set initial font
53
54          // register events for JRadioButtons
55          plainButton.addItemListener( new RadioButtonHandler( plainFont ) );
56          boldButton.addItemListener( new RadioButtonHandler( boldFont ) );
57          italicButton.addItemListener(
58             new RadioButtonHandler( italicFont ) );
59          boldItalicButton.addItemListener(
60             new RadioButtonHandler( boldItalicFont ) );
61
62          setSize( 300, 100 );
63          setVisible( true );
64
65       } // end RadioButtonTest constructor
66
67       public static void main( String args[] )
68       {
69          RadioButtonTest application = new RadioButtonTest();
70          application.setDefaultCloseOperation( JFrame.EXIT_ON_CLOSE );
71       }
72
73       // private inner class to handle radio button events
74       private class RadioButtonHandler implements ItemListener {
75          private Font font;
76
77          public RadioButtonHandler( Font f )
78          {
79             font = f;
80          }
81
```

Fig. 13.12   JRadioButtons and ButtonGroups. (Part 2 of 3.)

```
82          // handle radio button events
83          public void itemStateChanged( ItemEvent event )
84          {
85              field.setFont( font );
86          }
87
88      } // end private inner class RadioButtonHandler
89
90  } // end class RadioButtonTest
```

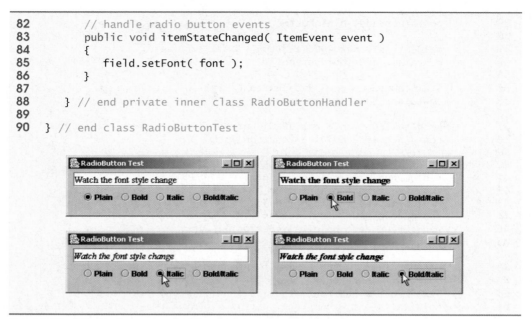

Fig. 13.12   JRadioButtons and ButtonGroups. (Part 3 of 3.)

JRadioButtons, like JCheckBoxes, generate ItemEvents when they are clicked. Lines 55–60 create instances of inner class RadioButtonHandler (declared at lines 74–88) and register each to handle an ItemEvent generated when the user clicks any one of the JRadioButtons.

Line 41 instantiates a ButtonGroup object and assigns it to reference radioGroup. This object is the "glue" that forms the logical relationship between the four JRadio-Button objects and allows only one of the four to be selected at a time. Lines 42–45 use ButtonGroup method *add* to associate each of the JRadioButtons with radioGroup. If more than one selected JRadioButton object is added to the group, the first selected JRadioButton added will be selected when the GUI is displayed.

Class RadioButtonHandler (line 74–88) implements interface ItemListener so it can handle item events generated by the JRadioButtons. Each JRadioButton in the program has a different instance of this class registered as its ItemListener. When these instances are created, a Font object is passed in each constructor call. The constructor stores this font in an instance variable (line 79) in the event-handler object. When the user clicks a JRadioButton, radioGroup turns off the previously selected JRadioButton, and method itemStateChanged (line 83–86) sets the font in the JTextField to the font stored in the event-handling object.

13.9 JComboBox

A *combo box* (sometimes called a *drop-down list*) provides a list of items from which the user can make a single selection. Combo boxes are implemented with class *JComboBox*, which extends class JComponent. JComboBoxes generate ItemEvents like JCheckBox-es and JRadioButtons.

The application of Fig. 13.13 uses a JComboBox to provide a list of four image file names. When an image file name is selected, the corresponding image is displayed as an Icon on a JLabel. The screen captures for this program show the JComboBox list after the selection was made to illustrate which image file name was selected.

Lines 13–15 declare and initialize array icons with four new ImageIcon objects. String array names (declared on lines 11–12) contains the names of the four image files that are stored in the same directory as the application.

Line 27 creates a JComboBox object, using the Strings in array names as the elements in the list. Each item in the list has an *index*. The first item is added at index 0; the next item is added at index 1; and so forth. The first item added to a JComboBox appears as the currently selected item when the JComboBox is displayed. Other items are selected by clicking the JComboBox. When clicked, the JComboBox expands into a list from which the user can make a selection.

Line 28 uses JComboBox method *setMaximumRowCount* to set the maximum number of elements that are displayed to 3 when the user clicks the JComboBox. If there are more items in the JComboBox than the maximum number of elements that are displayed, the JComboBox provides a *scrollbar* (see the first screen capture) that allows the user to scroll through all the elements in the list. The user can click the *scroll arrows* at the top and bottom of the scrollbar to move up and down through the list one element at a time, or the user can drag the *scroll box* in the middle of the scrollbar up and down to move through the list. To drag the scroll box, hold the mouse button down while the mouse cursor is on the scroll box and move the mouse.

```
1   // Fig. 13.13: ComboBoxTest.java
2   // Using a JComboBox to select an image to display.
3   import java.awt.*;
4   import java.awt.event.*;
5   import javax.swing.*;
6
7   public class ComboBoxTest extends JFrame {
8      private JComboBox imagesComboBox;
9      private JLabel label;
10
11     private String names[] =
12        { "bug1.gif", "bug2.gif",  "travelbug.gif", "buganim.gif" };
13     private Icon icons[] = { new ImageIcon( names[ 0 ] ),
14        new ImageIcon( names[ 1 ] ), new ImageIcon( names[ 2 ] ),
15        new ImageIcon( names[ 3 ] ) };
16
17     // set up GUI
18     public ComboBoxTest()
19     {
20        super( "Testing JComboBox" );
21
22        // get content pane and set its layout
23        Container container = getContentPane();
```

Fig. 13.13 JComboBox that displays a list of image names. (Part 1 of 3.)

```
24          container.setLayout( new FlowLayout() );
25
26          // set up JComboBox and register its event handler
27          imagesComboBox = new JComboBox( names );
28          imagesComboBox.setMaximumRowCount( 3 );
29          imagesComboBox.addItemListener(
30
31             new ItemListener() {  // anonymous inner class
32
33                // handle JComboBox event
34                public void itemStateChanged( ItemEvent event )
35                {
36                   // determine whether check box selected
37                   if ( event.getStateChange() == ItemEvent.SELECTED )
38                      label.setIcon( icons[
39                         imagesComboBox.getSelectedIndex() ] );
40                }
41
42             }  // end anonymous inner class
43
44          ); // end call to addItemListener
45
46          container.add( imagesComboBox );
47
48          // set up JLabel to display ImageIcons
49          label = new JLabel( icons[ 0 ] );
50          container.add( label );
51
52          setSize( 350, 100 );
53          setVisible( true );
54
55       } // end ComboBoxTest constructor
56
57       public static void main( String args[] )
58       {
59          ComboBoxTest application = new ComboBoxTest();
60          application.setDefaultCloseOperation( JFrame.EXIT_ON_CLOSE );
61       }
62
63    } // end class ComboBoxTest
```

Scrollbar to scroll through   scroll arrows   scroll box
the items in the list

Fig. 13.13 JComboBox that displays a list of image names. (Part 2 of 3.)

Fig. 13.13　JComboBox that displays a list of image names. (Part 3 of 3.)

 Look-and-Feel Observation 13.7

Set the maximum row count for a JComboBox to a number of rows that prevents the list from expanding outside the bounds of the window or applet in which it is used. This configuration will ensure that the list displays correctly when it is expanded by the user.

Lines 29–44 register an instance of an anonymous inner class that implements Item-Listener as the listener for JComboBox images. When the user makes a selection from images, method itemStateChanged (line 34–40) sets the Icon for label. The Icon is selected from array icons by determining the index of the selected item in the JComboBox with method *getSelectedIndex* in line 39. Note that line 37 changes the icon only for a selected item. Method *getStateChange* determines the state of a JToggleButton. The reason for the if statement here is that, for each item that is selected from a JComboBox, another item is deselected. Thus, two events occur for each item selected. We wish to display only the icon for the item the user just selected.

13.10 JList

A *list* displays a series of items from which the user may select one or more items. Lists are created with class JList, which directly extends class JComponent. Class JList supports *single-selection lists* (lists that allow only one item to be selected at a time) and *multiple-selection lists* (lists that allow any number of items to be selected). In this section, we discuss single-selection lists.

The application of Fig. 13.14 creates a JList containing the names of 13 colors. When a color name is clicked in the JList, a *ListSelectionEvent* occurs and the program changes the background color of the application window to the selected color.

A JList object is created at line 30 and assigned to reference colorList by the constructor. The argument to the JList constructor is the array of Objects (in this case strings) to display in the list. Line 31 uses JList method *setVisibleRowCount* to determine the number of items that are visible in the list.

```
1   // Fig. 13.14: ListTest.java
2   // Selecting colors from a JList.
3   import java.awt.*;
4   import javax.swing.*;
5   import javax.swing.event.*;
6
7   public class ListTest extends JFrame {
8      private JList colorList;
```

Fig. 13.14　JList that displays a list of colors. (Part 1 of 3.)

```
9        private Container container;
10
11       private final String colorNames[] = { "Black", "Blue", "Cyan",
12          "Dark Gray", "Gray", "Green", "Light Gray", "Magenta",
13          "Orange", "Pink", "Red", "White", "Yellow" };
14
15       private final Color colors[] = { Color.BLACK, Color.BLUE, Color.CYAN,
16          Color.DARK_GRAY, Color.GRAY, Color.GREEN, Color.LIGHT_GRAY,
17          Color.MAGENTA, Color.ORANGE, Color.PINK, Color.RED, Color.WHITE,
18          Color.YELLOW };
19
20       // set up GUI
21       public ListTest()
22       {
23          super( "List Test" );
24
25          // get content pane and set its layout
26          container = getContentPane();
27          container.setLayout( new FlowLayout() );
28
29          // create a list with items in colorNames array
30          colorList = new JList( colorNames );
31          colorList.setVisibleRowCount( 5 );
32
33          // do not allow multiple selections
34          colorList.setSelectionMode( ListSelectionModel.SINGLE_SELECTION );
35
36          // add a JScrollPane containing JList to content pane
37          container.add( new JScrollPane( colorList ) );
38          colorList.addListSelectionListener(
39
40             new ListSelectionListener() {  // anonymous inner class
41
42                // handle list selection events
43                public void valueChanged( ListSelectionEvent event )
44                {
45                   container.setBackground(
46                      colors[ colorList.getSelectedIndex() ] );
47                }
48
49             } // end anonymous inner class
50
51          ); // end call to addListSelectionListener
52
53          setSize( 350, 150 );
54          setVisible( true );
55
56       } // end ListTest constructor
57
58       public static void main( String args[] )
59       {
60          ListTest application = new ListTest();
61          application.setDefaultCloseOperation( JFrame.EXIT_ON_CLOSE );
```

Fig. 13.14   JList that displays a list of colors. (Part 2 of 3.)

```
62       }
63
64   } // end class ListTest
```

Fig. 13.14 `JList` that displays a list of colors. (Part 3 of 3.)

Line 34 uses `JList` method *setSelectionMode* to specify the list *selection mode*. Class *ListSelectionModel* (of package `javax.swing`) declares three constants that specify a `JList`'s selection mode—*SINGLE_SELECTION* (which allows only one item to be selected at a time), *SINGLE_INTERVAL_SELECTION* (for a multiple-selection list that allows selection of several contiguous items) and *MULTIPLE_INTERVAL_SELECTION* (for a multiple-selection list that does not restrict the items that can be selected).

Unlike a `JComboBox`, a `JList` *does not* provide a scrollbar if there are more items in the list than the number of visible rows. In this case, a *JScrollPane* object is used to provide the scrolling capability for the `JList`. Line 37 adds a new instance of class *JScroll-Pane* to the content pane. The `JScrollPane` constructor receives as its argument the `JComponent` that needs scrolling functionality (in this case, `colorList`). Notice in the screen captures that a scrollbar created by the `JScrollPane` appears at the right side of the `JList`. By default, the scrollbar appears only when the number of items in the `JList` exceeds the number of visible items.

Lines 38–51 use `JList` method *addListSelectionListener* to register an instance of an anonymous inner class that implements *ListSelectionListener* (in package `javax.swing.event`) as the listener for `colorList`. When the user makes a selection from `colorList`, method *valueChanged* (line 43–47) executes and sets the background color of the content pane with method *setBackground*. Recall that the content pane is a `Container`. Class `Container` inherits `setBackground` from class `Component`. The color is selected from the array `colors`, using the selected item's index. `JList` method `getSelectedIndex` returns the selected item's index. As with arrays and `JComboBoxes`, `JList` indexing is zero based.

13.11 Multiple-Selection Lists

A *multiple-selection list* enables the user to select many items from a `JList`. A `SINGLE_INTERVAL_SELECTION` list allows selection of a contiguous range of items in the list. To do so, click the first item, then press and hold the *Shift* key while clicking the last item to select in the range. A `MULTIPLE_INTERVAL_SELECTION` list allows continuous range selection as described for a `SINGLE_INTERVAL_SELECTION` list. Such a list allows miscellaneous items to be selected by pressing and holding the *Ctrl* key (sometimes called the *Control* key) while clicking each item to select. To deselect an item, press and hold the *Ctrl* key while clicking the item a second time.

The application of Fig. 13.15 uses multiple-selection lists to copy items from one JList to another. One list is a MULTIPLE_INTERVAL_SELECTION list and the other is a SINGLE_INTERVAL_SELECTION list. When you execute the program, try using the selection techniques described previously to select items in both lists.

```java
1   // Fig. 13.15: MultipleSelectionTest.java
2   // Copying items from one List to another.
3   import java.awt.*;
4   import java.awt.event.*;
5   import javax.swing.*;
6
7   public class MultipleSelectionTest extends JFrame {
8      private JList colorList, copyList;
9      private JButton copyButton;
10     private final String colorNames[] = { "Black", "Blue", "Cyan",
11        "Dark Gray", "Gray", "Green", "Light Gray", "Magenta", "Orange",
12        "Pink", "Red", "White", "Yellow" };
13
14     // set up GUI
15     public MultipleSelectionTest()
16     {
17        super( "Multiple Selection Lists" );
18
19        // get content pane and set its layout
20        Container container = getContentPane();
21        container.setLayout( new FlowLayout() );
22
23        // set up JList colorList
24        colorList = new JList( colorNames );
25        colorList.setVisibleRowCount( 5 );
26        colorList.setSelectionMode(
27           ListSelectionModel.MULTIPLE_INTERVAL_SELECTION );
28        container.add( new JScrollPane( colorList ) );
29
30        // create copy button and register its listener
31        copyButton = new JButton( "Copy >>>" );
32        copyButton.addActionListener(
33
34           new ActionListener() {  // anonymous inner class
35
36              // handle button event
37              public void actionPerformed( ActionEvent event )
38              {
39                 // place selected values in copyList
40                 copyList.setListData( colorList.getSelectedValues() );
41              }
42
43           } // end anonymous inner class
44
45        ); // end call to addActionListener
46
47        container.add( copyButton );
```

Fig. 13.15 JList that allows multiple selections. (Part 1 of 2.)

```
48
49        // set up JList copyList
50        copyList = new JList( );
51        copyList.setVisibleRowCount( 5 );
52        copyList.setFixedCellWidth( 100 );
53        copyList.setFixedCellHeight( 15 );
54        copyList.setSelectionMode(
55           ListSelectionModel.SINGLE_INTERVAL_SELECTION );
56        container.add( new JScrollPane( copyList ) );
57
58        setSize( 300, 130 );
59        setVisible( true );
60
61     } // end constructor MultipleSelectionTest
62
63     public static void main( String args[] )
64     {
65        MultipleSelectionTest application = new MultipleSelectionTest();
66        application.setDefaultCloseOperation( JFrame.EXIT_ON_CLOSE );
67     }
68
69  } // end class MultipleSelectionTest
```

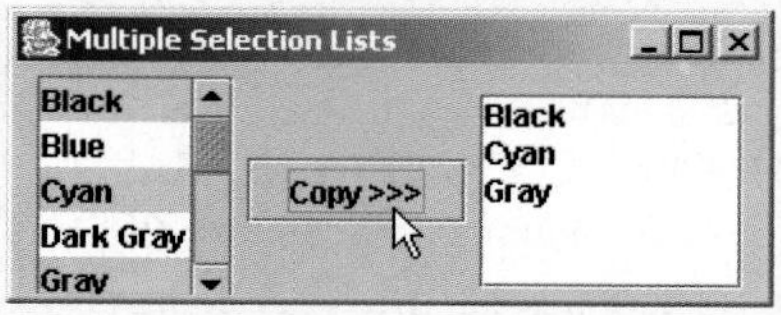

Fig. 13.15 JList that allows multiple selections. (Part 2 of 2.)

Line 24 creates JList colorList and initializes it with the strings in the array colorNames. Line 25 sets the number of visible rows in colorList to 5. Lines 26–27 specify that colorList is a MULTIPLE_INTERVAL_SELECTION list. Line 28 adds a new JScrollPane containing colorList to the content pane. Lines 50–56 perform similar tasks for copyList, which is declared as a SINGLE_INTERVAL_SELECTION list. Line 52 uses JList method *setFixedCellWidth* to set copyList's width to 100 pixels. Line 53 uses JList method *setFixedCellHeight* to set the height of each item in the JList to 15 pixels.

A multiple-selection list does not have a specific event associated with making multiple selections. Normally, an event generated by another GUI component (known as an *external event*) specifies when the multiple selections in a JList should be processed. In this example, the user clicks the JButton called copyButton to trigger the event that copies the selected items in colorList to copyList.

When the user clicks copyButton, method actionPerformed (lines 37–41) uses JList method *setListData* to set the items displayed in copyList. Line 40 calls colorList's method *getSelectedValues*, which returns an array of Objects representing the selected items in colorList. In this example, the returned array is passed as the argument to copyList's setListData method.

Many students ask how reference `copyList` can be used in line 40 even though the program does not create the object to which it refers until Line 50. Remember that method `actionPerformed` (lines 37–41) does not execute until the user presses the `copyButton`, which cannot occur until after the constructor completes execution and the program displays the GUI. At that point in the program's execution, line 40 already has initialized `copyList` with a new `JList` object. No method executes until it is called. In the case of an event handler, the method call occurs in response to an event.

13.12 Mouse Event Handling

This section presents the *MouseListener* and *MouseMotionListener* event-listener interfaces for handling *mouse events*. Mouse events can be trapped for any GUI component that derives from `java.awt.Component`. The methods of interfaces `MouseListener` and `MouseMotionListener` are summarized in Figure 13.16.[1]

`MouseListener` and `MouseMotionListener` interface methods

Methods of interface MouseListener

`public void mousePressed( MouseEvent event )`

    Called when a mouse button is pressed while the mouse cursor is on a component.

`public void mouseClicked( MouseEvent event )`

    Called when a mouse button is pressed and released while the mouse cursor remains stationary on a component.

`public void mouseReleased( MouseEvent event )`

    Called when a mouse button is released after being pressed. This event is always preceded by a `mousePressed` event.

`public void mouseEntered( MouseEvent event )`

    Called when the mouse cursor enters the bounds of a component.

`public void mouseExited( MouseEvent event )`

    Called when the mouse cursor leaves the bounds of a component.

Methods of interface MouseMotionListener

`public void mouseDragged( MouseEvent event )`

    Called when the mouse button is pressed while the mouse cursor is on a component and the mouse is moved while the mouse button remains pressed. This event is always preceded by a call to `mousePressed`. All drag events are sent to the component on which the drag began.

`public void mouseMoved( MouseEvent event )`

    Called when the mouse is moved when the mouse cursor on a component. All move events are sent to the component over which the mouse is currently positioned.

Fig. 13.16 MouseListener and MouseMotionListener interface methods.

---

1. As of Java 1.4, package `javax.swing.event` contains interface `MouseInputListener`, which extends interfaces `MouseListener` and `MouseMotionListener` to create a single interface containing all the `MouseListener` and `MouseMotionListener` methods.

Each of the mouse event-handling methods takes a *MouseEvent* object as its argument. A MouseEvent object contains information about the mouse event that occurred, including the *x*- and *y*-coordinates of the location where the event occurred. The MouseListener and MouseMotionListener methods are called when the mouse interacts with a Component if appropriate listener objects are registered for that Component. Method *mousePressed* is called when a mouse button is pressed while the mouse cursor is over a component. By using methods and constants of class *InputEvent* (the superclass of MouseEvent), a program can determine which mouse button the user clicked.

Look-and-Feel Observation 13.8

Method calls to mouseDragged are sent to the MouseMotionListener for the Component on which the drag operation started. Similarly, the mouseReleased method call at the end of a drag operation is sent to the MouseListener for the Component on which the drag operation started.

In addition to interfaces MouseListener and MouseMotionListener, Java now provides interface *MouseWheelListener* to enable programs to respond to the rotation of the wheel on a mouse with a wheel. This interface declares method *mouseWheelMoved*, which receives a *MouseWheelEvent* as its argument. Class MouseWheelEvent (a subclass of MouseEvent) contains methods that enable the event handler to obtain information about the amount of wheel rotation.

The MouseTracker application (Fig. 13.17) demonstrates the MouseListener and MouseMotionListener interface methods. The application class implements both interfaces so it can listen for its own mouse events. Note that all seven methods from these two interfaces must be declared by the programmer when a class implements both interfaces. Each mouse event in this example displays a string in JLabel statusBar at the bottom of the window.

```
1   // Fig. 13.17: MouseTracker.java
2   // Demonstrating mouse events.
3   import java.awt.*;
4   import java.awt.event.*;
5   import javax.swing.*;
6
7   public class MouseTracker extends JFrame
8      implements MouseListener, MouseMotionListener {
9
10     private JLabel statusBar;
11
12     // set up GUI and register mouse event handlers
13     public MouseTracker()
14     {
15        super( "Demonstrating Mouse Events" );
16
17        statusBar = new JLabel();
18        getContentPane().add( statusBar, BorderLayout.SOUTH );
19
20        addMouseListener( this );        // listens for own mouse and
21        addMouseMotionListener( this );  // mouse-motion events
```

Fig. 13.17 Mouse event handling. (Part 1 of 3.)

```
22
23          setSize( 275, 100 );
24          setVisible( true );
25       }
26
27       // MouseListener event handlers
28       // handle event when mouse released immediately after press
29       public void mouseClicked( MouseEvent event )
30       {
31          statusBar.setText( "Clicked at [" + event.getX() +
32             ", " + event.getY() + "]" );
33       }
34
35       // handle event when mouse pressed
36       public void mousePressed( MouseEvent event )
37       {
38          statusBar.setText( "Pressed at [" + event.getX() +
39             ", " + event.getY() + "]" );
40       }
41
42       // handle event when mouse released after dragging
43       public void mouseReleased( MouseEvent event )
44       {
45          statusBar.setText( "Released at [" + event.getX() +
46             ", " + event.getY() + "]" );
47       }
48
49       // handle event when mouse enters area
50       public void mouseEntered( MouseEvent event )
51       {
52          statusBar.setText( "Mouse entered at [" + event.getX() +
53             ", " + event.getY() + "]" );
54          getContentPane().setBackground( Color.GREEN );
55       }
56
57       // handle event when mouse exits area
58       public void mouseExited( MouseEvent event )
59       {
60          statusBar.setText( "Mouse outside window" );
61          getContentPane().setBackground( Color.WHITE );
62       }
63
64       // MouseMotionListener event handlers
65       // handle event when user drags mouse with button pressed
66       public void mouseDragged( MouseEvent event )
67       {
68          statusBar.setText( "Dragged at [" + event.getX() +
69             ", " + event.getY() + "]" );
70       }
71
72       // handle event when user moves mouse
73       public void mouseMoved( MouseEvent event )
74       {
```

Fig. 13.17 Mouse event handling. (Part 2 of 3.)

```
75          statusBar.setText( "Moved at [" + event.getX() +
76              ", " + event.getY() + "]" );
77       }
78
79       public static void main( String args[] )
80       {
81          MouseTracker application = new MouseTracker();
82          application.setDefaultCloseOperation( JFrame.EXIT_ON_CLOSE );
83       }
84
85    } // end class MouseTracker
```

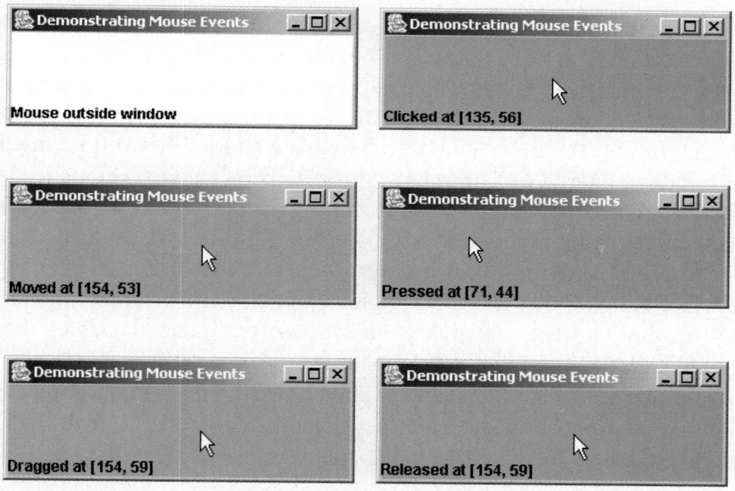

Fig. 13.17　Mouse event handling. (Part 3 of 3.)

Lines 17–18 in the constructor declare JLabel statusBar and attach it to the content pane. Until now, each time we used the content pane, method setLayout was called to set the content pane's layout manager to a FlowLayout. This allowed the content pane to display the GUI components we attached to it from left to right. If the GUI components do not fit on one line, the FlowLayout enables components to flow onto additional lines. Actually, the default layout manager is a *BorderLayout* that divides the content pane's area into five regions—north, south, east, west and center. Line 18 uses a new version of Container method add to attach statusBar to the region *BorderLayout.SOUTH*, which extends across the entire bottom of the content pane. We discuss BorderLayout and several other layout managers in detail later in Section 13.15.

Lines 20–21 in the constructor register the MouseTracker object as the listener for its own mouse events. Methods *addMouseListener* and *addMouseMotionListener* are Component methods that can be used to register mouse event listeners for an object of any class that extends Component (as does MouseTracker indirectly).

When the mouse enters or exits the application area, method mouseEntered (lines 50–55) and method mouseExited (lines 58–62) are called, respectively. Method mouse-

Entered displays a message in statusBar indicating that the mouse entered the window and changes the background color to green. Method mouseExited displays a message in statusBar indicating that the mouse is outside the application (see the first sample output window) and changes the background color to white.

When any of the other five events occur, they display a message in statusBar that includes a string containing the event that occurred and the coordinates where the mouse event occurred. The *x*- and *y*-coordinates of the mouse when the event occurred are obtained with MouseEvent methods *getX* and *getY*, respectively.

13.13 Adapter Classes

Many of the event-listener interfaces provide multiple methods; MouseListener and MouseMotionListener are examples. It is not always desirable to declare every method in an event-listener interface. For example, a program may need only the mouseClicked handler from interface MouseListener or the mouseDragged handler from MouseMotionListener. In Fig. 10.23, we demonstrated that windowClosing is called when the user closes a window. Interface WindowListener, which contains method windowClosing, actually specifies seven window event-handling methods. For many of the listener interfaces that contain multiple methods, package java.awt.event and package javax.swing.event provide event-listener *adapter classes*. An adapter class implements an interface and provides a default implementation (with an empty method body) of every method in the interface. Several java.awt.event adapter classes are shown in Fig. 13.18 along with the interfaces they implement.

The programmer can extend the adapter class to inherit the default implementation of every method and subsequently override the method(s) needed for event handling. The default implementation of each method in the adapter class has an empty body.

Software Engineering Observation 13.3

When a class implements an interface, the class has an "is a" relationship with that interface. All direct and indirect subclasses of that class inherit this interface. Thus, an object of a class that extends an event-adapter class is an object of the corresponding event-listener type (e.g., an object of a subclass of MouseAdapter is a MouseListener).

Event-adapter class	Implements interface
ComponentAdapter	ComponentListener
ContainerAdapter	ContainerListener
FocusAdapter	FocusListener
KeyAdapter	KeyListener
MouseAdapter	MouseListener
MouseMotionAdapter	MouseMotionListener
WindowAdapter	WindowListener

Fig. 13.18 Event-adapter classes and the interfaces they implement in package java.awt.event.

Extending *MouseMotionAdapter*

The `Painter` application of Fig. 13.19 uses the `mouseDragged` event handler to create a simple drawing program. The user can draw pictures with the mouse by dragging the mouse on the background of the window. This example does not use method `mouseMoved`, so our `MouseMotionListener` is declared as a subclass of `MouseMotionAdapter`. This class already declares both `mouseMoved` and `mouseDragged`, so we can simply override `mouseDragged` to provide the drawing functionality.

```
1   // Fig. 13.19: Painter.java
2   // Using class MouseMotionAdapter.
3   import java.awt.*;
4   import java.awt.event.*;
5   import javax.swing.*;
6
7   public class Painter extends JFrame {
8      private int pointCount = 0;
9
10     // array of 1000 java.awt.Point references
11     private Point points[] = new Point[ 1000 ];
12
13     // set up GUI and register mouse event handler
14     public Painter()
15     {
16        super( "A simple paint program" );
17
18        // create a label and place it in SOUTH of BorderLayout
19        getContentPane().add( new JLabel( "Drag the mouse to draw" ),
20           BorderLayout.SOUTH );
21
22        addMouseMotionListener(
23
24           new MouseMotionAdapter() {  // anonymous inner class
25
26              // store drag coordinates and repaint
27              public void mouseDragged( MouseEvent event )
28              {
29                 if ( pointCount < points.length ) {
30                    points[ pointCount ] = event.getPoint();
31                    ++pointCount;
32                    repaint();
33                 }
34              }
35
36           } // end anonymous inner class
37
38        ); // end call to addMouseMotionListener
39
40        setSize( 300, 150 );
41        setVisible( true );
42
43     } // end Painter constructor
```

Fig. 13.19 Adapter classes used to implement event handlers. (Part 1 of 2.)

```
44
45        // draw oval in a 4-by-4 bounding box at specified location on window
46        public void paint( Graphics g )
47        {
48            super.paint( g ); // clears drawing area
49
50            for ( int i = 0; i < points.length && points[ i ] != null; i++ )
51                g.fillOval( points[ i ].x, points[ i ].y, 4, 4 );
52        }
53
54        public static void main( String args[] )
55        {
56            Painter application = new Painter();
57            application.setDefaultCloseOperation( JFrame.EXIT_ON_CLOSE );
58        }
59
60    } // end class Painter
```

Fig. 13.19 Adapter classes used to implement event handlers. (Part 2 of 2.)

In this example, we use an array of 1000 *java.awt.Point* objects to store the location at which each mouse-drag event occurs. This enables method paint to draw a small oval at each location stored in the array. Lines 22–38 register a MouseMotionListener to listen for the window's mouse-motion events. Recall that, when a method is invoked using only its method name, it is actually invoked via the this reference, indicating that the method is called for the current instance of the class at execution time. Lines 24–36 declare an anonymous inner class that extends class MouseMotionAdapter (which implements MouseMotionListener). The anonymous inner class inherits a default implementation of both method mouseMoved and method mouseDragged. Thus, the anonymous inner class already satisfies the requirement that, in all methods, an interface must be implemented. However, the default methods do nothing when they are called. So, we override method mouseDragged at lines 27–34 to capture the coordinates of a mouse-dragged event and store them as an object of class Point. Line 29 ensures that we store the event's coordinates only if there are still empty elements in the array. If so, line 30 invokes the MouseEvent object's *getPoint* method to obtain the Point where the event occurred and stores it in the array at index pointCount. Line 31 increments the pointCount, and line 32 calls repaint to initiate drawing. Note that paint (lines 46–52) loops through all the Point objects in the array and draws an oval at each location. Class Point has two public instance variables—x and y—that are accessed directly in line 51 to specify the upper-left corner of the oval's bounding box. The loop terminates either when a null reference is encountered in the array or when the end of the array is reached.

Extending *MouseAdapter*

The MouseDetails application of Fig. 13.20 demonstrates how to determine the number of mouse clicks (i.e., the click count) and how to distinguish between the different mouse buttons. The event listener in this program is an object of inner class MouseClickHandler (lines 38–62) that extends MouseAdapter so we can declare just the mouseClicked method we need in this example.

```java
1   // Fig. 13.20: MouseDetails.java
2   // Demonstrating mouse clicks and distinguishing between mouse buttons.
3   import java.awt.*;
4   import java.awt.event.*;
5   import javax.swing.*;
6
7   public class MouseDetails extends JFrame {
8      private int xPos, yPos;
9
10     // set title bar String; register mouse listener; size and show window
11     public MouseDetails()
12     {
13        super( "Mouse clicks and buttons" );
14
15        addMouseListener( new MouseClickHandler() );
16
17        setSize( 350, 150 );
18        setVisible( true );
19     }
20
21     // draw String at location where mouse was clicked
22     public void paint( Graphics g )
23     {
24        // call superclass paint method
25        super.paint( g );
26
27        g.drawString( "Clicked @ [" + xPos + ", " + yPos + "]",
28           xPos, yPos );
29     }
30
31     public static void main( String args[] )
32     {
33        MouseDetails application = new MouseDetails();
34        application.setDefaultCloseOperation( JFrame.EXIT_ON_CLOSE );
35     }
36
37     // inner class to handle mouse events
38     private class MouseClickHandler extends MouseAdapter {
39
40        // handle mouse click event and determine which button was pressed
41        public void mouseClicked( MouseEvent event )
42        {
43           xPos = event.getX();
44           yPos = event.getY();
45
```

Fig. 13.20 Left, center and right mouse-button clicks. (Part 1 of 2.)

```
46                String title = "Clicked " + event.getClickCount() + " time(s)";
47
48                if ( event.isMetaDown() )   // right mouse button
49                    title += " with right mouse button";
50
51                else if ( event.isAltDown() )   // middle mouse button
52                    title += " with center mouse button";
53
54                else   // left mouse button
55                    title += " with left mouse button";
56
57                setTitle( title );   // set title bar of window
58                repaint();
59
60            } // end method mouseClicked
61
62        } // end private inner class MouseClickHandler
63
64    } // end class MouseDetails
```

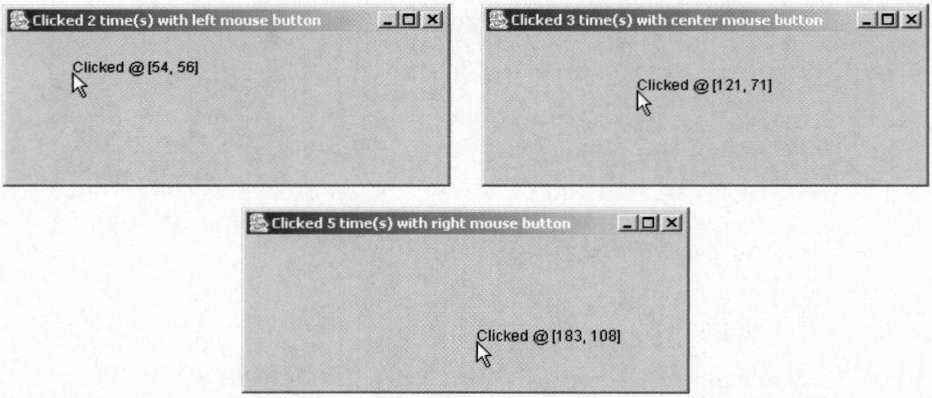

Fig. 13.20 Left, center and right mouse-button clicks. (Part 2 of 2.)

A user of a Java program may be on a system with a one-, two- or three-button mouse. Java provides a mechanism to distinguish among mouse buttons. Class MouseEvent inherits several methods from class InputEvent that can distinguish among mouse buttons on a multibutton mouse or can mimic a multibutton mouse with a combined keystroke and mouse-button click. Figure 13.21 shows the InputEvent methods used to distinguish among mouse-button clicks. Java assumes that every mouse contains a left mouse button. Thus, it is simple to test for a left-mouse-button click. However, users with a one- or two-button mouse must use a combination of keystrokes and mouse-button clicks at the same time to simulate the missing buttons on the mouse. In the case of a one- or two-button mouse, this program assumes that the center mouse button is clicked if the user holds down the *Alt* key and clicks the left mouse button on a two-button mouse or the only mouse button on a one-button mouse. In the case of a one-button mouse, this program assumes that the right mouse button is clicked if the user holds down the *Meta* key and clicks the mouse button.

`InputEvent` method	Description
`isMetaDown()`	Returns `true` when the user clicks the right mouse button on a mouse with two or three buttons. To simulate a right-mouse-button click on a one-button mouse, the user can hold down the *Meta* key on the keyboard and click the mouse button.
`isAltDown()`	Returns `true` when the user clicks the middle mouse button on a mouse with three buttons. To simulate a middle-mouse-button click on a one- or two-button mouse, the user can press the *Alt* key on the keyboard and click the only- or left-mouse button, respectively.

Fig. 13.21 `InputEvent` methods that help distinguish among left-, center- and right-mouse-button clicks.

Method `mouseClicked` (lines 41–60 of Fig. 13.20) first captures the coordinates where the event occurred and stores them in instance variables `xPos` and `yPos` of class `MouseDetails`. Line 46 creates a string containing the number of mouse clicks (as returned by `MouseEvent` method *getClickCount* at line 46). The nested `if` statement at lines 48–55 uses methods `isMetaDown` and `isAltDown` to determine which mouse button the user clicked and appends an appropriate string to `title` in each case. The resulting string is displayed in the title bar of the window, using method *setTitle* (inherited into class `JFrame` from class `Frame`) at line 57. Line 58 calls `repaint` to initiate a call to `paint` to draw a string at the location where the user clicked the mouse button.

13.14 Key Event Handling

This section presents the `KeyListener` interface for handling *key events*. Key events are generated when keys on the keyboard are pressed and released. A class that implements `KeyListener` must provide declarations for methods *keyPressed*, *keyReleased* and *keyTyped*, each of which receives a *KeyEvent* as its argument. Class `KeyEvent` is a subclass of `InputEvent`. Method `keyPressed` is called in response to pressing any key. Method `keyTyped` is called in response to pressing any key that is not an *action key*. (The actions keys are any arrow key, *Home*, *End*, *Page Up*, *Page Down*, any function key, *Num Lock*, *Print Screen*, *Scroll Lock*, *Caps Lock* and *Pause*.) Method `keyReleased` is called when the key is released after any `keyPressed` or `keyTyped` event.

Figure 13.22 demonstrates the `KeyListener` methods. Class `KeyDemo` implements the `KeyListener` interface, so all three methods are declared in the application.

```
1   // Fig. 13.22: KeyDemo.java
2   // Demonstrating keystroke events.
3   import java.awt.*;
4   import java.awt.event.*;
5   import javax.swing.*;
6
7   public class KeyDemo extends JFrame implements KeyListener {
```

Fig. 13.22 Key event handling. (Part 1 of 3.)

```
8      private String line1 = "", line2 = "", line3 = "";
9      private JTextArea textArea;
10
11     // set up GUI
12     public KeyDemo()
13     {
14        super( "Demonstrating Keystroke Events" );
15
16        // set up JTextArea
17        textArea = new JTextArea( 10, 15 );
18        textArea.setText( "Press any key on the keyboard..." );
19        textArea.setEnabled( false );
20        textArea.setDisabledTextColor( Color.BLACK );
21        getContentPane().add( textArea );
22
23        addKeyListener( this );   // allow frame to process Key events
24
25        setSize( 350, 100 );
26        setVisible( true );
27
28     } // end KeyDemo constructor
29
30     // handle press of any key
31     public void keyPressed( KeyEvent event )
32     {
33        line1 = "Key pressed: " + event.getKeyText( event.getKeyCode() );
34        setLines2and3( event );
35     }
36
37     // handle release of any key
38     public void keyReleased( KeyEvent event )
39     {
40        line1 = "Key released: " + event.getKeyText( event.getKeyCode() );
41        setLines2and3( event );
42     }
43
44     // handle press of an action key
45     public void keyTyped( KeyEvent event )
46     {
47        line1 = "Key typed: " + event.getKeyChar();
48        setLines2and3( event );
49     }
50
51     // set second and third lines of output
52     private void setLines2and3( KeyEvent event )
53     {
54        line2 = "This key is " + ( event.isActionKey() ? "" : "not " ) +
55           "an action key";
56
57        String temp = event.getKeyModifiersText( event.getModifiers() );
58
59        line3 = "Modifier keys pressed: " +
60           ( temp.equals( "" ) ? "none" : temp );
```

Fig. 13.22   Key event handling. (Part 2 of 3.)

```
61
62            textArea.setText( line1 + "\n" + line2 + "\n" + line3 + "\n" );
63         }
64
65         public static void main( String args[] )
66         {
67            KeyDemo application = new KeyDemo();
68            application.setDefaultCloseOperation( JFrame.EXIT_ON_CLOSE );
69         }
70
71      } // end class KeyDemo
```

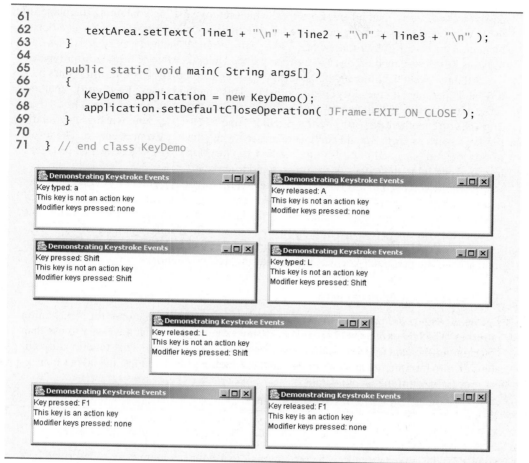

Fig. 13.22 Key event handling. (Part 3 of 3.)

The constructor (lines 12–28) registers the application to handle its own key events by using method *addKeyListener* at line 23. Method addKeyListener is declared in class Component, so every subclass of Component can notify KeyListener objects of key events for that Component.

Line 21 in the constructor adds JTextArea textArea (where the program's output is displayed) to the content pane. Notice in the screen captures that textArea occupies the entire window. This is due to the content pane's default BorderLayout (discussed in Section 13.15.2 and demonstrated in Fig. 13.25). When a single Component is added to a BorderLayout, the Component occupies the entire Container. Note that line 20 uses method setDisabledTextColor to change the color of the text in the textarea to black.

Methods keyPressed (lines 31–35) and keyReleased (lines 38–42) use KeyEvent method *getKeyCode* to get the *virtual key code* of the key that was pressed. Class KeyEvent maintains a set of constants—the virtual key-code constants—that represents every key on the keyboard. These constants can be compared with the return value of get-KeyCode to test for individual keys on the keyboard. The value returned by getKeyCode is passed to KeyEvent method *getKeyText*, which returns a string containing the name of the key that was pressed. For a complete list of virtual key constants, see the on-line documentation for class KeyEvent (package java.awt.event). Method keyTyped (lines 45–49) uses KeyEvent method *getKeyChar* to get the Unicode value of the character typed.

All three event handling methods finish by calling method setLines2and3 (lines 52–63) and passing it the KeyEvent object. This method uses KeyEvent method *isActionKey* (line 54) to determine whether the key in the event was an action key. Also, InputEvent method *getModifiers* is called (line 57) to determine whether any modifier keys (such as *Shift*, *Alt* and *Ctrl*) were pressed when the key event occurred. The result of this method is passed to KeyEvent method *getKeyModifiersText*, which produces a string containing the names of the pressed modifier keys.

[*Note:* If you need to test for a specific key on the keyboard, class KeyEvent provides a *key constant* for every key on the keyboard. These constants can be used from the key event handlers to determine whether a particular key was pressed. Also, to determine whether the *Alt*, *Ctrl*, *Meta* and *Shift* keys are pressed individually, InputEvent methods isAltDown, *isControlDown*, isMetaDown and *isShiftDown* each return a boolean indicating if the particular key was pressed during the key event.]

13.15 Layout Managers

Layout managers are provided to arrange GUI components in a container for presentation purposes. The layout managers provide basic layout capabilities that are easier to use than determining the exact position and size of every GUI component. This functionality enables the programmer to concentrate on the basic look-and-feel and lets the layout managers process most of the layout details.

Look-and-Feel Observation 13.9

Most Java programming environments provide GUI design tools that help a programmer graphically design a GUI; the design tools then write Java code to create the GUI.

Some GUI designers also allow the programmer to use the layout managers described here and in Chapter 14. Figure 13.23 summarizes the layout managers presented in this chapter. Other layout managers are discussed in Chapter 14.

Layout manager	Description
FlowLayout	Default for java.awt.Applet, java.awt.Panel and javax.swing.JPanel. Places components sequentially (left to right) in the order they were added. It is also possible to specify the order of the components by using the Container method add, which takes a Component and an integer index position as arguments.
BorderLayout	Default for the content panes of JFrames (and other windows) and JApplets. Arranges the components into five areas: NORTH, SOUTH, EAST, WEST and CENTER.
GridLayout	Arranges the components into rows and columns.

Fig. 13.23 Layout managers.

Most previous applet and application examples in which we created our own GUI used layout manager *FlowLayout*. Class FlowLayout inherits from class Object and implements interface *LayoutManager*, which declares the methods a layout manager uses to arrange and size GUI components in a container.

13.15.1 FlowLayout

FlowLayout is the simplest layout manager. GUI components are placed on a container from left to right in the order in which they are added to the container. When the edge of the container is reached, components continue to display on the next line. Class FlowLayout allows GUI components to be *left aligned*, *centered* (the default) and *right aligned*.

The application of Fig. 13.24 creates three JButton objects and adds them to the application, using a FlowLayout layout manager. The components are center aligned by default. When the user clicks **Left**, the alignment for the layout manager is changed to a left-aligned FlowLayout. When the user clicks **Right**, the alignment for the layout manager is changed to a right-aligned FlowLayout. When the user clicks **Center**, the alignment for the layout manager is changed to a center-aligned FlowLayout. Each button has its own event handler that is declared with an inner class that implements ActionListener. The sample output windows show each of the FlowLayout alignments. Also, the last sample output window shows the centered alignment after the window has been resized to a smaller width. Notice that the button **Right** flows onto a new line.

```java
1   // Fig. 13.24: FlowLayoutDemo.java
2   // Demonstrating FlowLayout alignments.
3   import java.awt.*;
4   import java.awt.event.*;
5   import javax.swing.*;
6
7   public class FlowLayoutDemo extends JFrame {
8      private JButton leftButton, centerButton, rightButton;
9      private Container container;
10     private FlowLayout layout;
11
12     // set up GUI and register button listeners
13     public FlowLayoutDemo()
14     {
15        super( "FlowLayout Demo" );
16
17        layout = new FlowLayout();
18
19        // get content pane and set its layout
20        container = getContentPane();
21        container.setLayout( layout );
22
23        // set up leftButton and register listener
24        leftButton = new JButton( "Left" );
25        container.add( leftButton );
26        leftButton.addActionListener(
27
```

Fig. 13.24 FlowLayout allows components to flow over multiple lines. (Part 1 of 3.)

```
28            new ActionListener() {  // anonymous inner class
29
30                // process leftButton event
31                public void actionPerformed( ActionEvent event )
32                {
33                    layout.setAlignment( FlowLayout.LEFT );
34
35                    // realign attached components
36                    layout.layoutContainer( container );
37                }
38
39            } // end anonymous inner class
40
41        ); // end call to addActionListener
42
43        // set up centerButton and register listener
44        centerButton = new JButton( "Center" );
45        container.add( centerButton );
46        centerButton.addActionListener(
47
48            new ActionListener() {  // anonymous inner class
49
50                // process centerButton event
51                public void actionPerformed( ActionEvent event )
52                {
53                    layout.setAlignment( FlowLayout.CENTER );
54
55                    // realign attached components
56                    layout.layoutContainer( container );
57                }
58            }
59        );
60
61        // set up rightButton and register listener
62        rightButton = new JButton( "Right" );
63        container.add( rightButton );
64        rightButton.addActionListener(
65
66            new ActionListener() {  // anonymous inner class
67
68                // process rightButton event
69                public void actionPerformed( ActionEvent event )
70                {
71                    layout.setAlignment( FlowLayout.RIGHT );
72
73                    // realign attached components
74                    layout.layoutContainer( container );
75                }
76            }
77        );
78
79        setSize( 300, 75 );
80        setVisible( true );
```

Fig. 13.24 FlowLayout allows components to flow over multiple lines. (Part 2 of 3.)

```
81
82      } // end constructor FlowLayoutDemo
83
84      public static void main( String args[] )
85      {
86         FlowLayoutDemo application = new FlowLayoutDemo();
87         application.setDefaultCloseOperation( JFrame.EXIT_ON_CLOSE );
88      }
89
90   } // end class FlowLayoutDemo
```

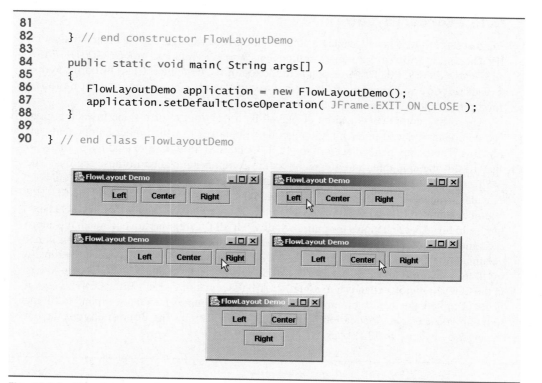

Fig. 13.24 FlowLayout allows components to flow over multiple lines. (Part 3 of 3.)

As seen previously, a container's layout is set with method *setLayout* of class Container. Line 21 sets the content pane's layout manager to the FlowLayout declared at line 17. Normally, the layout is set before any GUI components are added to a container.

Look-and-Feel Observation 13.10

Each container can have only one layout manager at a time. Separate containers in the same program can have different layout managers.

Look-and-Feel Observation 13.11

In a Container without a layout manager, the programmer must position the widgets contained in the given container and take care that, on resize events, all components are repositioned correctly.

Each button's actionPerformed event handler executes two statements. For example, line 33 in method actionPerformed for button left uses FlowLayout method *setAlignment* to change the alignment for the FlowLayout to a left-aligned (*FlowLayout.LEFT*) FlowLayout. Line 36 uses LayoutManager interface method *layoutContainer* to specify that the content pane should be rearranged based on the adjusted layout.

According to which button was clicked, the actionPerformed method for each button sets the FlowLayout's alignment to *LEFT* (line 33), *CENTER* (line 53) or *RIGHT* (line 71).

13.15.2 BorderLayout

The *BorderLayout* layout manager (the default layout manager for the content pane of a JFrame and a JApplet) arranges components into five regions: *NORTH, SOUTH, EAST, WEST* and *CENTER*. NORTH corresponds to the top of the container. Class BorderLayout extends Object and implements interface *LayoutManager2* (a subinterface of Layout-Manager that adds several methods for enhanced layout processing).

Up to five components can be displayed by a BorderLayout—one in each region. The component placed in each region can be a container to which other components are attached. The components placed in the NORTH and SOUTH regions extend horizontally to the sides of the container and are as tall as the components placed in those regions. The EAST and WEST regions expand vertically between the NORTH and SOUTH regions and are as wide as the components placed in those regions. The component placed in the CENTER region expands to fill all remaining space in the layout (which is the reason that the JTex-tArea in Fig. 13.22 occupies the entire window). If all five regions are occupied, the entire container's space is covered by GUI components. If the NORTH or SOUTH region is not occupied, the GUI components in the EAST, CENTER and WEST regions expand vertically to fill the remaining space. If the EAST or WEST region is not occupied, the GUI component in the CENTER region expands horizontally to fill the remaining space. If the CENTER region is not occupied, the area is left empty—the other GUI components do not expand to fill the remaining space. The application of Fig. 13.25 demonstrates the BorderLayout layout manager by using five JButtons.

```
1   // Fig. 13.25: BorderLayoutDemo.java
2   // Demonstrating BorderLayout.
3   import java.awt.*;
4   import java.awt.event.*;
5   import javax.swing.*;
6
7   public class BorderLayoutDemo extends JFrame implements ActionListener {
8      private JButton buttons[];
9      private final String names[] = { "Hide North", "Hide South",
10        "Hide East", "Hide West", "Hide Center" };
11     private BorderLayout layout;
12
13     // set up GUI and event handling
14     public BorderLayoutDemo()
15     {
16        super( "BorderLayout Demo" );
17
18        layout = new BorderLayout( 5, 5 ); // 5 pixel gaps
19
20        // get content pane and set its layout
21        Container container = getContentPane();
22        container.setLayout( layout );
23
24        // instantiate button objects
25        buttons = new JButton[ names.length ];
26
```

Fig. 13.25 BorderLayout containing five buttons. (Part 1 of 3.)

```
27          for ( int count = 0; count < names.length; count++ ) {
28              buttons[ count ] = new JButton( names[ count ] );
29              buttons[ count ].addActionListener( this );
30          }
31
32          // place buttons in BorderLayout; order not important
33          container.add( buttons[ 0 ], BorderLayout.NORTH );
34          container.add( buttons[ 1 ], BorderLayout.SOUTH );
35          container.add( buttons[ 2 ], BorderLayout.EAST );
36          container.add( buttons[ 3 ], BorderLayout.WEST );
37          container.add( buttons[ 4 ], BorderLayout.CENTER );
38
39          setSize( 300, 200 );
40          setVisible( true );
41
42      } // end constructor BorderLayoutDemo
43
44      // handle button events
45      public void actionPerformed( ActionEvent event )
46      {
47          for ( int count = 0; count < buttons.length; count++ )
48
49              if ( event.getSource() == buttons[ count ] )
50                  buttons[ count ].setVisible( false );
51              else
52                  buttons[ count ].setVisible( true );
53
54          // re-layout the content pane
55          layout.layoutContainer( getContentPane() );
56      }
57
58      public static void main( String args[] )
59      {
60          BorderLayoutDemo application = new BorderLayoutDemo();
61          application.setDefaultCloseOperation( JFrame.EXIT_ON_CLOSE );
62      }
63
64  } // end class BorderLayoutDemo
```

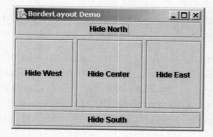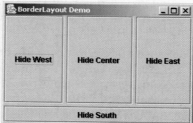

Fig. 13.25   BorderLayout containing five buttons. (Part 2 of 3.)

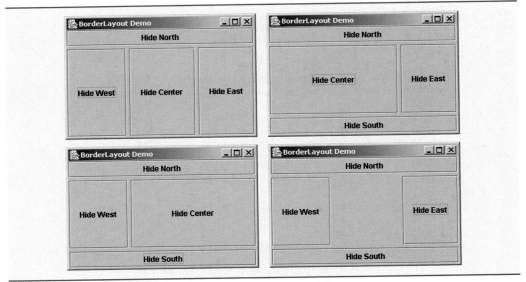

Fig. 13.25 BorderLayout containing five buttons. (Part 3 of 3.)

Line 18 creates a `BorderLayout`. The constructor arguments specify the number of pixels between components that are arranged horizontally (*horizontal gap space*) and the number of pixels between components that are arranged vertically (*vertical gap space*), respectively. The default is one pixel of gap space horizontally and vertically. Line 22 uses method `setLayout` to set the content pane's layout to `layout`.

We add `Components` to a `BorderLayout` with another version of `Container` method `add` that takes two arguments—the `Component` to add and the region in which the `Component` should appear. For example, line 33 specifies that `buttons[0]` should appear in the NORTH region. The components can be added in any order, but only one component should be added to each region.

Look-and-Feel Observation 13.12
If no region is specified when adding a Component to a BorderLayout, the layout manager assumes that the Component should be added to region BorderLayout.CENTER.

Common Programming Error 13.5
When more than one component is added to a region in a BorderLayout, only the last component added to that region will be displayed. There is no error that indicates this problem.

When the user clicks a particular `JButton` in the layout, method `actionPerformed` (lines 45–56) executes. The `for` loop at lines 47–52 uses an `if...else` to hide the particular `JButton` that generated the event. Method `setVisible` (inherited into `JButton` from class `Component`) is called with a `false` argument (line 50) to hide the `JButton`. If the current `JButton` in the array is not the one that generated the event, method `setVisible` is called with a `true` argument (line 52) to ensure that the `JButton` is displayed on the screen. Line 55 uses `LayoutManager` method `layoutContainer` to recalculate the layout of the content pane. Notice in the screen captures of Fig. 13.25 that certain regions in the `BorderLayout` change shape as `JButtons` are hidden and displayed in other regions. Try resizing the application window to see how the various regions resize based on the width and height of the window. For more complex layouts, group components in JPanels, each with a separate layout manager. Place the JPanels on the JFrame using either the default BorderLayout or some other layout.

13.15.3 GridLayout

The *GridLayout* layout manager divides the container into a grid so that components can be placed in rows and columns. Class GridLayout inherits directly from class Object and implements interface LayoutManager. Every Component in a GridLayout has the same width and height. Components are added to a GridLayout starting at the top-left cell of the grid and proceeding left to right until the row is full. Then the process continues left to right on the next row of the grid, and so on. Figure 13.26 demonstrates the GridLayout layout manager by using six JButtons.

```java
1   // Fig. 13.26: GridLayoutDemo.java
2   // Demonstrating GridLayout.
3   import java.awt.*;
4   import java.awt.event.*;
5   import javax.swing.*;
6
7   public class GridLayoutDemo extends JFrame implements ActionListener {
8      private JButton buttons[];
9      private final String names[] =
10        { "one", "two", "three", "four", "five", "six" };
11     private boolean toggle = true;
12     private Container container;
13     private GridLayout grid1, grid2;
14
15     // set up GUI
16     public GridLayoutDemo()
17     {
18        super( "GridLayout Demo" );
19
20        // set up layouts
21        grid1 = new GridLayout( 2, 3, 5, 5 );
22        grid2 = new GridLayout( 3, 2 );
23
24        // get content pane and set its layout
25        container = getContentPane();
26        container.setLayout( grid1 );
27
28        // create and add buttons
29        buttons = new JButton[ names.length ];
30
31        for ( int count = 0; count < names.length; count++ ) {
32           buttons[ count ] = new JButton( names[ count ] );
33           buttons[ count ].addActionListener( this );
34           container.add( buttons[ count ] );
35        }
```

Fig. 13.26 GridLayout containing six buttons. (Part 1 of 2.)

```
36
37          setSize( 300, 150 );
38          setVisible( true );
39
40       } // end constructor GridLayoutDemo
41
42       // handle button events by toggling between layouts
43       public void actionPerformed( ActionEvent event )
44       {
45          if ( toggle )
46             container.setLayout( grid2 );
47          else
48             container.setLayout( grid1 );
49
50          toggle = !toggle;  // set toggle to opposite value
51          container.validate();
52       }
53
54       public static void main( String args[] )
55       {
56          GridLayoutDemo application = new GridLayoutDemo();
57          application.setDefaultCloseOperation( JFrame.EXIT_ON_CLOSE );
58       }
59
60    } // end class GridLayoutDemo
```

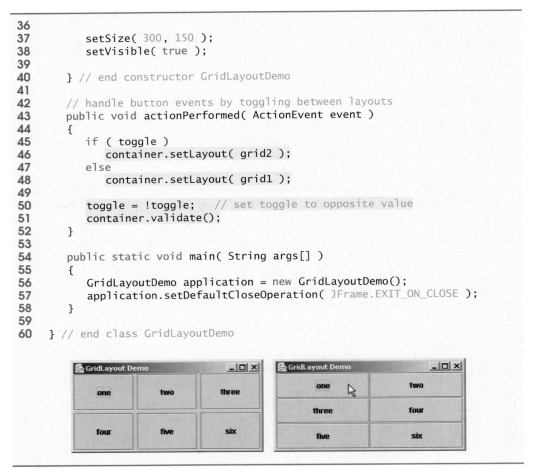

Fig. 13.26 GridLayout containing six buttons. (Part 2 of 2.)

Lines 21–22 create two GridLayout objects (variables grid1 and grid2 are declared at line 13). The GridLayout constructor used at line 21 specifies a GridLayout with 2 rows, 3 columns, 5 pixels of horizontal-gap space between Components in the grid and 5 pixels of vertical-gap space between Components in the grid. The GridLayout constructor used at line 22 specifies a GridLayout with 3 rows, 2 columns and no gap space.

The JButton objects in this example initially are arranged using grid1 (set for the content pane at line 26 with method setLayout). The first component is added to the first column of the first row. The next component is added to the second column of the first row, and so on. When a JButton is pressed, method actionPerformed (lines 43–52) is called. Every call to actionPerformed toggles the layout between grid2 and grid1, using boolean variable toggle to determine the next layout to set.

Line 51 illustrates another way to reformat a container for which the layout has changed. Container method *validate* recomputes the container's layout based on the current layout manager for the Container and the current set of displayed GUI components.

13.16 Panels

Complex GUIs (like Fig. 13.1) require that each component be placed in an exact location. They often consist of multiple *panels*, with each panel's components arranged in a specific layout. Panels are created with class JPanel, a subclass of JComponent. Class JComponent extends class java.awt.Container, so every JPanel is a Container. Thus, JPanels may have components, including other panels, added to them. The program of Fig. 13.27 demonstrates how a JPanel can be used to create a more complex layout for Components.

```java
1   // Fig. 13.27: PanelDemo.java
2   // Using a JPanel to help lay out components.
3   import java.awt.*;
4   import java.awt.event.*;
5   import javax.swing.*;
6
7   public class PanelDemo extends JFrame {
8      private JPanel buttonPanel;
9      private JButton buttons[];
10
11     // set up GUI
12     public PanelDemo()
13     {
14        super( "Panel Demo" );
15
16        // get content pane
17        Container container = getContentPane();
18
19        // create buttons array
20        buttons = new JButton[ 5 ];
21
22        // set up panel and set its layout
23        buttonPanel = new JPanel();
24        buttonPanel.setLayout( new GridLayout( 1, buttons.length ) );
25
26        // create and add buttons
27        for ( int count = 0; count < buttons.length; count++ ) {
28           buttons[ count ] = new JButton( "Button " + ( count + 1 ) );
29           buttonPanel.add( buttons[ count ] );
30        }
31
32        container.add( buttonPanel, BorderLayout.SOUTH );
33
34        setSize( 425, 150 );
35        setVisible( true );
36
37     } // end constructor PanelDemo
38
39     public static void main( String args[] )
40     {
41        PanelDemo application = new PanelDemo();
```

Fig. 13.27 JPanel with five JButtons in a GridLayout attached to the SOUTH region of a BorderLayout. (Part 1 of 2.)

```
42              application.setDefaultCloseOperation( JFrame.EXIT_ON_CLOSE );
43      }
44
45  } // end class PanelDemo
```

Fig. 13.27   JPanel with five JButtons in a GridLayout attached to the SOUTH region of a BorderLayout. (Part 2 of 2.)

After JPanel buttonPanel is declared in line 8 and created at line 23, line 24 sets buttonPanel's layout to a GridLayout of one row and five columns (there are five JButtons in array buttons). Lines 27–30 add the five JButtons in array buttons to the JPanel in the loop. Line 29 adds the buttons directly to the JPanel—class JPanel does not have a content pane, unlike a JApplet or a JFrame. Line 32 uses the content pane's default BorderLayout to add buttonPanel to the SOUTH region. Note that the SOUTH region is as tall as the buttons on buttonPanel. A JPanel is sized to the components it contains. As more components are added, the JPanel grows (according to the restrictions of its layout manager) to accommodate the components. Resize the window to see how the layout manager affects the size of the JButtons.

13.17 (Optional Case Study) Thinking About Objects: Use Cases

The previous "Thinking About Objects" sections have concentrated on the elevator simulation model. We have identified and honed the structure and behavior of our system. In this section, we model the interaction between the user and our elevator simulation through the UML use case diagram, which describes the sets of scenarios that occur between the user and the system.

Use Case Diagrams

When developers begin a project, they rarely start with as detailed a problem statement as the one we provided in Section 2.9. This document and others are the result of the requirements-gathering phase. In this phase, you meet with the people who want you to build a system and with the people who will eventually use that system. You use the information gained in these meetings to compile a list of *system requirements*. These requirements guide you and your fellow developers as you analyze and ultimately design the system. In our case study, the problem statement described the requirements of our elevator simulation in sufficient detail that you did not need to go through an extensive analysis phase. The analysis phase is enormously important—you should consult the references we provide in Section 2.9 to learn more about object-oriented analysis.

The UML provides the *use case diagram* to facilitate requirements gathering. This diagram models the interactions between the system's external clients and the *use cases* of the system. Each use case represents a different capability that the system provides to clients. For example, automated teller machines typically have several use cases, including "Deposit Money," "Withdraw Money" and "Transfer Funds."

In larger systems, use case diagrams are indispensable tools that help system designers remain focused on satisfying the users' needs. The goal of the use case diagram is to show the kinds of interactions users have with a system without providing the details of those interactions: those details are, of course, provided in other UML diagrams. Use case diagrams often are accompanied by informal text that describes the interactions in more detail.

Figure 13.28 shows the use case diagram for our elevator simulation. The stick figure represents an *actor*, which, in turn, represents a set of roles that an *external entity*—such as a person or another system—can play. Consider again our automated teller machine example. The actor is a BankCustomer who can deposit, withdraw and transfer funds from the ATM. In this sense, BankCustomer is more like a class rather than an object—it is not an actual person, but rather describes the roles that a real person—when playing the part of a BankCustomer—can perform while interacting with the ATM (deposit, withdraw and transfer funds). A person is an external entity that can play the part of a BankCustomer. In the same manner as an object is an instance of a class, a person playing the part of a BankCustomer performing one of its roles (such as making a deposit) is an *instance of actor* BankCustomer. For example, when a person named Mary plays the part of a BankCustomer making a deposit, Mary—in the role of the depositor—becomes an instance of actor BankCustomer. Later in that day, another person named Jon can be another instance of actor BankCustomer. In the course of a day, several hundred people might use the ATM machine—some are "depositors," some are "withdrawers" and some are "transferrers," but all of these people are instances of actor BankCustomer.

The problem statement in our elevator simulation supplies the actors—"The user requires the ability to create a person in the simulation and situate that person on a given floor." Therefore, the actor of in this use case is the user who controls the simulation (i.e., the user who clicks the buttons to create new Persons in the simulation). An external entity—a real person—plays the part of the user to control the simulation. In our system, the use case is "Create Person," which encompasses creating a Person object, then placing that Person on either the first or second Floor. Figure 13.28 models one actor called "User." The actor's class appears underneath the actor. The UML models each use case as an oval.

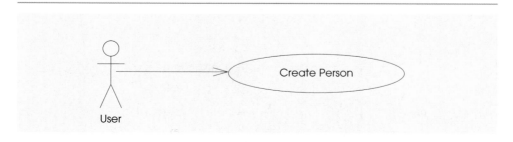

Fig. 13.28 Use case diagram for elevator simulation from user's perspective.

There is a reasonable alternate view of the use case of our elevator simulation. The problem statement from Section 2.9 mentioned that the company requested the elevator simulation to "determine whether the elevator will meet the company's needs." We are designing a simulation of a real-world scenario—the `Person` object in the simulation represents an actual human being using an actual elevator. Therefore, specifying a use case from the `Person` object's perspective helps model how a real person uses a real elevator system. We offer the use case of Fig. 13.29, titled "Relocate Person." This use case describes the `Person` moving (relocating) to the other `Floor`. (The `Person` travels to the second `Floor` if starting on the first `Floor` and to the first `Floor` if starting on the second `Floor`.) This use case encompasses all actions that the `Person` performs along his or her journey, such as walking across a `Floor` to the `Elevator`, pressing `Button`s and riding the `Elevator` to the other `Floor`.

We must ensure that our use cases do not model interactions that are too specific between the external client and the system. For example, we do not subdivide each use case into two separate use cases—such as "Create Person on first Floor" and "Create Person on second Floor," or "Relocate Person to first Floor" and "Relocate Person to second Floor"—because the functionality of such use cases is repetitive (i.e., these seemingly alternative use cases are really the same). Improper and repetitive subdivision of use cases can create problems during implementation. For example, if the designer of an automated teller machine separated its "Withdraw Money" use case into "Withdraw Specific Amounts" use cases (e.g., "Withdraw $1.00," "Withdraw $2.00," etc.), there could exist an enormous number of use cases for the system. This would make understanding the requirements tedious. (Our elevator system contains only two floors—separating the use case into two would not cause that much extra work; if our system contained 100 floors, however, creating 100 use cases would be unwieldy.)

SUMMARY

- A graphical user interface (GUI) presents a pictorial interface to a program. A GUI (pronounced "GOO-EE") gives a program a distinctive "look" and "feel."

- By providing different applications with a consistent set of intuitive user interface components, GUIs allow the user to spend more time using the program in a productive manner.

- GUIs are built from GUI components (sometimes called controls or widgets). A GUI component is a visual object with which the user interacts via the mouse, keyboard or other form of input.

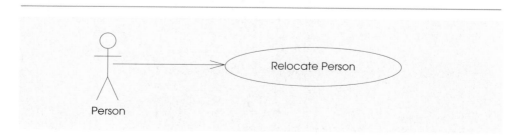

Fig. 13.29 Use case diagram from the perspective of a `Person`.

- Swing GUI components are declared in package javax.swing. Most swing components are written, manipulated and displayed completely in Java. Such components are called lightweight GUI components. Swing is a part of Java Foundation Classes.

- The original GUI components from the Abstract Windowing Toolkit package java.awt are tied directly to the local platform's graphical user interface capabilities.

- AWT components are called heavyweight components; they must rely on the local platform's windowing system to determine their functionality and their look and feel.

- Several Swing GUI components are heavyweight GUI components—in particular, subclasses of java.awt.Window (such as JFrame) that display windows on the screen. Heavyweight Swing GUI components are less flexible than lightweight components.

- Much of each Swing GUI component's functionality is inherited from classes Component, Container and JComponent (a superclass of most Swing components).

- A Container organizes a set of GUI components.

- JLabels provide text instructions or information on a GUI.

- JComponent method setToolTipText specifies the tool tip that is displayed when the user positions the mouse cursor over a JComponent in the GUI.

- Many Swing components can display images by specifying an Icon as an argument to their constructor or by using a method setIcon.

- Class ImageIcon supports several image formats, including Portable Network Graphics (PNG), Graphics Interchange Format (GIF) and Joint Photographic Experts Group (JPEG).

- Interface SwingConstants (package javax.swing) declares a set of common integer constants that are used with many Swing components.

- By default, the text of a JComponent appears to the right of the image when the JComponent contains both text and an image.

- The horizontal and vertical alignments of a JLabel can be set with methods setHorizontalAlignment and setVerticalAlignment. Method setText sets the text displayed on the label. Method getText retrieves the current text displayed on a label. Methods setHorizontalTextPosition and setVerticalTextPosition specify the text position in a label.

- JComponent method setIcon sets the Icon displayed on a JComponent. Method getIcon retrieves the current Icon displayed on a JComponent.

- GUIs generate events when the user interacts with the GUI. Information about a GUI event is stored in an object of a class that extends AWTEvent.

- To process an event, the programmer must register an event listener and implement one or more event handlers.

- The use of event listeners in event handling is known as the delegation event model—the processing of an event is delegated to a particular object in the program.

- When an event occurs, the GUI component with which the user interacted notifies its registered listeners by calling each listener's appropriate event handling method.

- JTextFields and JPasswordFields are single-line areas in which text can be entered by the user from the keyboard or text can simply be displayed. A JPasswordField shows that characters are being typed as the user enters them but hides the characters.

- When the user types data into a JTextField or JPasswordField and presses the *Enter* key, an ActionEvent occurs.

- JTextComponent method setEditable determines whether the user can modify the text in a JTextComponent.

- JPasswordField method getPassword returns the password as an array of type char.

- Every JComponent contains an object of class EventListenerList in which all registered listeners are stored.

- Every JComponent supports several different event types, including mouse events, key events and others. When an event occurs, the event is dispatched only to the registered event listeners of the appropriate type. Each event type has a corresponding event-listener interface.

- A JButton generates an ActionEvent when the user clicks the button with the mouse.

- An AbstractButton can have a rollover Icon that is displayed when the mouse cursor is positioned over the button. The icon changes as the mouse cursor moves in and out of the button's area on the screen. AbstractButton method setRolloverIcon specifies the rollover icon.

- There are three state button types—JToggleButton, JCheckBox and JRadioButton—with on/off or true/false values. JCheckBox and JRadioButton are subclasses of JToggleButton.

- When the user clicks a JCheckBox, an ItemEvent is generated that can be handled by an ItemListener. ItemListeners must declare method itemStateChanged. ItemEvent method getStateChange determines the state of a JToggleButton.

- JRadioButtons are similar to JCheckBoxes in that they have two states—selected and not selected. JRadioButtons normally appear as a group in which only one radio button can be selected at a time. JRadioButtons generate ItemEvents when they are clicked.

- The logical relationship between radio buttons is maintained by a ButtonGroup object.

- The JRadioButton constructor supplies the label that appears to the right of the JRadioButton by default, as well as the initial state of the JRadioButton. A true second argument indicates that the JRadioButton should appear selected when it is displayed.

- ButtonGroup method add associates a JRadioButton with a ButtonGroup. If more than one selected JRadioButton object is added to the group, the first selected JRadioButton added will be selected when the GUI is displayed.

- A JComboBox (sometimes called a drop-down list) provides a list of items from which the user can make a single selection. JComboBoxes generate ItemEvents. The first item is added to a JComboBox at index 0, the next item is added at index 1 and so forth. The first item added to a JComboBox appears as the currently selected item when the JComboBox is displayed. JComboBox method getSelectedIndex returns the index of the selected item.

- A JList displays a series of items from which the user may select one or more items. Class JList supports single- and multiple-selection lists. When an item is clicked in a JList, a ListSelectionEvent occurs.

- JList method setVisibleRowCount determines the number of items that are visible in the list. Method setSelectionMode specifies the selection mode for the list.

- A SINGLE_INTERVAL_SELECTION list allows selection of a contiguous range of items. To do so, click the first item, then press and hold the *Shift* key while clicking the last item to select in the range.

- A MULTIPLE_INTERVAL_SELECTION list allows continuous range selection as described for a SINGLE_INTERVAL_SELECTION list. Such a list also allows miscellaneous items to be selected by holding down the Ctrl key while clicking each item to select.

- Class JList does not provide a scrollbar if there are more items in the list than the number of visible rows. A JScrollPane object is used to provide the scrolling capability.

- JList method setFixedCellHeight specifies the height, in pixels, of each item in a JList. Method setFixedCellWidth sets the width, in pixels, of a JList.

- Normally, an event generated by another GUI component (known as an external event) specifies when the multiple selections in a JList should be processed.

- `JList` method `setListData` sets the items displayed in a `JList`. Method `getSelectedValues` returns the selected items as an array of `Objects`.
- Mouse events can be trapped for any GUI component that derives from `java.awt.Component`, using `MouseListeners` and `MouseMotionListeners`.
- Each mouse event-handling method takes as its argument a `MouseEvent` object containing information about the mouse event and the location where the event occurred.
- Methods `addMouseListener` and `addMouseMotionListener` are `Component` methods used to register mouse event listeners for an object of any class that extends `Component`.
- Many of the event-listener interfaces provide multiple methods. For each, there is a corresponding event-listener adapter class that provides a default implementation of every method in the interface. The programmer can extend the adapter class to inherit the default implementation of every method and simply override the method or methods needed for event handling in the program.
- `MouseEvent` method `getClickCount` returns the number of mouse clicks that occurred.
- `InputEvent` methods `isMetaDown` and `isAltDown` are used to determine which mouse button the user clicked.
- `KeyListeners` handle key events that are generated when keys on the keyboard are pressed and released. A `KeyListener` must provide declarations for methods `keyPressed`, `keyReleased` and `keyTyped`, each of which receives a `KeyEvent` as its argument.
- Method `keyPressed` is called in response to pressing any key. Method `keyTyped` is called in response to pressing any key that is not an action key (i.e., any arrow key, *Home*, *End*, *Page Up*, *Page Down*, any function key, *Num Lock*, *Print Screen*, *Scroll Lock*, *Caps Lock* and *Pause*). Method `keyReleased` is called when the key is released after any `keyPressed` or `keyTyped` event.
- `KeyEvent` method `getKeyCode` gets the virtual key code of the key that was pressed. Class `KeyEvent` maintains a set of virtual key-code constants that represent every key on the keyboard.
- `KeyEvent` method `getKeyText` returns a `String` containing the name of the key that corresponds to its virtual key-code argument. Method `getKeyChar` gets the Unicode value of the character typed. Method `isActionKey` determines whether the key in the event was an action key.
- `InputEvent` method `getModifiers` determines whether any modifier keys (such as *Shift*, *Alt* and *Ctrl*) were pressed when the key event occurred. `KeyEvent` method `getKeyModifiersText` produces a string containing the names of the pressed modifier keys.
- Layout managers arrange GUI components in a container for presentation purposes.
- `FlowLayout` lays out components from left to right in the order in which they are added to the container. When the right edge of the container is reached, components are continued on the next line.
- `FlowLayout` method `setAlignment` changes the alignment for the `FlowLayout` to `FlowLayout.LEFT`, `FlowLayout.CENTER` or `FlowLayout.RIGHT`.
- The `BorderLayout` layout manager arranges components into five regions: `NORTH`, `SOUTH`, `EAST`, `WEST` and `CENTER`. One component can be added to each region.
- `LayoutManager` method `layoutContainer` recalculates the layout of its `Container` argument.
- The `GridLayout` layout manager divides the container into a grid of rows and columns. Components are added to a `GridLayout` starting at the top left cell and proceeding from left to right until the row is full. Then the process continues from left to right on the next row of the grid, and so on.
- `Container` method `validate` recomputes the container's layout, based on the current layout manager for the `Container` and the current set of displayed GUI components.
- Panels are created with class `JPanel`, which extends `JComponent`. `JPanels` may have components, including other panels, added to them.

TERMINOLOGY

.gif file name extension
.jpg file name extension
.png file name extension
Abstract Window Toolkit
AbstractButton class
ActionEvent class
ActionListener interface
actionPerformed method
adapter class
add method of ButtonGroup
add method of class Container
addItemListener method
addKeyListener method
addListSelectionListener method
addMouseListener method
addMouseMotionListener method
BorderLayout class
BorderLayout.CENTER
BorderLayout.EAST
BorderLayout.NORTH
BorderLayout.SOUTH
BorderLayout.WEST
button
button label
ButtonGroup class
centered
check box
check-box label
command button
Component class
ComponentAdapter class
ComponentListener interface
Container class
ContainerAdapter class
ContainerListener interface
control
delegation event model
dispatch an event
dragging
drop-down list
event
event driven
event handler
event ID
event listener
event-listener interface
EventListenerList class
EventObject class
FlowLayout.CENTER

FlowLayout class
FlowLayout.LEFT
FlowLayout.RIGHT
focus
FocusAdapter class
FocusListener interface
Font.BOLD
Font.ITALIC
Font.PLAIN
getActionCommand method
getClickCount method
getIcon method
getKeyChar method of KeyEvent
getKeyCode method of KeyEvent
getKeyModifiersText method
getKeyText method of KeyEvent
getModifiers method of InputEvent
getPassword method of JPasswordField
getPoint method of MouseEvent
getSelectedIndex method of JComboBox
getSelectedIndex method of JList
getSelectedValues method of JList
getStateChange method of ItemEvent
getSource method of ActionEvent
getText method of JLabel
getX method of MouseEvent
getY method of MouseEvent
Graphics Interchange Format (GIF)
GridLayout class
GUI component
handle an event
heavyweight component
horizontal-gap space
Icon interface
ImageIcon class
InputEvent class
isActionKey method of KeyEvent
isAltDown method of InputEvent
isMetaDown method of InputEvent
isSelected method of JCheckBox
ItemEvent class
ItemListener interface
itemStateChanged method of ItemListener
java.awt package
java.awt.event package
Java Foundation Classes
javax.swing package
javax.swing.event package
JButton class

SELF-REVIEW EXERCISES

13.1 Fill in the blanks in each of the following statements:
a) Method _____ is called when the mouse is moved with no buttons pressed and an event listener is registered to handle the event.
b) Text that cannot be modified by the user is called _____ text.
c) A(n) _____ arranges GUI components in a `Container`.
d) The add method for attaching GUI components is a method of class _____.
e) GUI is an acronym for _____.
f) Method _____ is used to specify the layout manager for a container.
g) A mouseDragged method call is preceded by a(n) _____ method call and followed by a(n) _____ method call.

13.2 Determine whether each statement is *true* or *false*. If *false*, explain why.
a) `BorderLayout` is the default layout manager for a content pane.
b) When the mouse cursor is moved into the bounds of a GUI component, method `mouse-Over` is called.
c) A `JPanel` cannot be added to another `JPanel`.
d) In a `BorderLayout`, two buttons added to the NORTH region will be placed side by side.
e) When one is using `BorderLayout`, a maximum of five components should be displayed.

13.3 Find the error(s) in each of the following statements, and explain how to correct it (them):
a) `buttonName = JButton( "Caption" );`
b) `JLabel aLabel, JLabel;      // create references`
c) `txtField = new JTextField( 50, "Default Text" );`
d) `Container container = getContentPane();`
   `setLayout( new BorderLayout() );`
   `button1 = new JButton( "North Star" );`
   `button2 = new JButton( "South Pole" );`
   `container.add( button1 );`
   `container.add( button2 );`

ANSWERS TO SELF-REVIEW EXERCISES

13.1   a) mouseMoved. b) uneditable (read-only). c) layout manager. d) `Container`. e) graphical user interface. f) setLayout. g) mousePressed, mouseReleased.

13.2   a) True.
b) False. Method mouseEntered is called.
c) False. A `JPanel` can be added to another `JPanel`, because `JPanel` is an indirect sub-class of Component. Therefore, a `JPanel` is a Component. Any Component can be added to a `Container`.
d) False. Only the last button added will be displayed. Remember that only one component should be added to each region in a `BorderLayout`.
e) True.

13.3   a) new is needed to create an object.
b) `JLabel` is a class name and cannot be used as a variable name.
c) The arguments passed to the constructor are reversed. The `String` must be passed first.
d) `BorderLayout` has been set, and components are being added without specifying the region so both are added to the center region. Proper add statements might be

```
container.add( button1, BorderLayout.NORTH );
container.add( button2, BorderLayout.SOUTH );
```

EXERCISES

13.4 Fill in the blanks in each of the following statements:
a) The `JTextField` class directly extends class _____.
b) List three layout managers from this chapter: _____, _____ and _____.
c) `Container` method _____ attaches a GUI component to a container.
d) Method _____ is called when a mouse button is released (without moving the mouse).
e) The _____ class is used to create a group of `JRadioButtons`.

13.5 Determine whether each statement is *true* or *false*. If *false*, explain why.
a) Only one layout manager can be used per `Container`.
b) GUI components can be added to a `Container` in any order in a `BorderLayout`.
c) `JRadioButtons` provide a series of mutually exclusive options (i.e., only one can be `true` at a time).
d) `Graphics` method `setFont` is used to set the font for text fields.
e) A `JList` displays a scrollbar if there are more items in the list than can be displayed.
f) A `Mouse` object has a method called `mouseDragged`.

13.6 Determine whether each statement is *true* or *false*. If *false*, explain why.
a) A `JApplet` does not have a content pane.
b) A `JPanel` is a `JComponent`.
c) A `JPanel` is a `Component`.
d) A `JLabel` is a `Container`.
e) A `JList` is a `JPanel`.
f) An `AbstractButton` is a `JButton`.
g) A `JTextField` is an `Object`.
h) `ButtonGroup` is a subclass of `JComponent`.

13.7 Find any errors in each of the following lines of code, and explain how to correct them.
a) `import javax.swing.*`   `// include swing package`
b) `panelObject.GridLayout( 8, 8 ); // set GridLayout`
c) `container.setLayout( new FlowLayout( FlowLayout.DEFAULT ) );`
d) `container.add( eastButton, EAST );  // BorderLayout`

13.8 Create the following GUI. You do not have to provide any functionality.

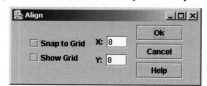

13.9 Create the following GUI. You do not have to provide any functionality.

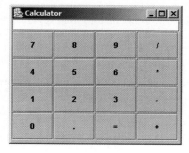

13.10   Create the following GUI. You do not have to provide any functionality.

13.11   Create the following GUI. You do not have to provide any functionality.

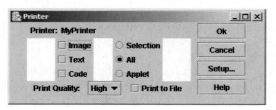

13.12   Write a temperature conversion program that converts from Fahrenheit to Celsius. The Fahrenheit temperature should be entered from the keyboard (via a JTextField). A JLabel should be used to display the converted temperature. Use the following formula for the conversion:

$$Celsius = \frac{5}{9} \times (\ Fahrenheit\ -\ 32\ )$$

13.13   Enhance the temperature conversion program of Exercise 13.12 by adding the Kelvin temperature scale. The program should also allow the user to make conversions between any two scales. Use the following formula for the conversion between Kelvin and Celsius (in addition to the formula in Exercise 13.12):

$$Kelvin\ =\ Celsius\ +\ 273.15$$

13.14   Write an application that allows the user to draw a rectangle by dragging the mouse on the application window. The upper left coordinate should be the location where the user presses the mouse button, and the lower right coordinate should be the location where the user releases the mouse button. Also display the area of the rectangle in a JLabel in the SOUTH region of a BorderLayout. Use the following formula for the area:

$$area\ =\ width\ \times\ height$$

13.15   Modify the program of Exercise 13.14 to draw different shapes. The user should be allowed to choose from an oval, an arc, a line and a rectangle with rounded corners. Also display the mouse coordinates in the status bar.

13.16   Write a program that will allow the user to draw a shape with the mouse. The shape to draw should be determined by a KeyEvent, using the following keys: *c* draws a circle, *o* draws an oval, *r* draws a rectangle and *l* draws a line. The size and placement of the shape should be determined by the mousePressed and mouseReleased events. Display the name of the current shape in a JLabel in the SOUTH region of a BorderLayout. The initial shape should default to a circle.

13.17   Create an application that enables the user to paint a picture. The user should be able to choose the shape to draw, the color in which the shape should appear and whether the shape should be filled with color. Use the graphical user interface components we discussed in this chapter, such as JComboBoxes, JRadioButtons and JCheckBoxes, to allow the user to select various options. The program should provide a JButton object that allows the user to erase the contents of the window.

13.18 Write a program that uses `System.out.println` statements to print out events as they occur. Provide a `JComboBox` with a minimum of four items. The user should be able to choose an event to monitor from the `JComboBox`. When that particular event occurs, display information about the event in a message dialog box. Use method `toString` on the event object to convert it to a string representation.

13.19 Write a program that draws a square. As the mouse moves over the drawing area, repaint the square, with the upper left corner of the square following the exact path of the mouse cursor.

13.20 Modify the program of Fig. 13.19 to incorporate colors. Allow the user to select the color with `JRadioButton` objects that represent the following six colors: red, black, magenta, blue, green and yellow. When a new color is selected, drawing should occur in the new color.

13.21 Write a program that plays "guess the number" as follows: Your program chooses the number to be guessed by selecting an integer at random in the range 1–1000. The program then displays the following in a label:

> I have a number between 1 and 1000 can you guess my number?
> Please enter your first guess.

A `JTextField` should be used to input the guess. As each guess is input, the background color should change to either red or blue. Red indicates that the user is getting "warmer," and blue indicates that the user is getting "colder." A `JLabel` should display either "Too High" or "Too Low" to help the user zero in on the correct answer. When the user gets the correct answer, "Correct!" should be displayed, and the `JTextField` used for input should be changed to be uneditable. A `JButton` should be provided to allow the user to play the game again. When the `JButton` is clicked, a new random number should be generated and the input `JTextField` changed to be editable.

13.22 It is often useful to display the events that occur during the execution of a program. This can help you understand when the events occur and how they are generated. Write a program that enables the user to generate and process every event discussed in this chapter. The program should provide methods from the `ActionListener`, `ItemListener`, `ListSelectionListener`, `MouseListener`, `MouseMotionListener` and `KeyListener` interfaces to display messages when the events occur. Use method `toString` to convert the event objects received in each event handler into a `String` that can be displayed. Method `toString` creates a `String` containing all the information in the event object.

13.23 Modify your solution to Exercise 13.17 to enable the user to select a font and a font size and type text into a `JTextField`. When the user presses *Enter*, the text should be displayed in the chosen font and size. Modify the program further to allow the user to specify the exact position at which the text should be displayed.

13.24 Write a program that allows the user to select a shape from a `JComboBox` and draws that shape 20 times with random locations and dimensions in method `paint`. The first item in the `JComboBox` should be the default shape that is displayed the first time `paint` is called.

13.25 Modify Exercise 13.24 to draw each of the 20 randomly sized shapes in a randomly selected color. Use all 13 predefined `Color` objects in an array of `Color`s.

13.26 Modify Exercise 13.25 to allow the user to select the color in which shapes should be drawn from a `JColorChooser` dialog.

13.27 Write a program using methods from interface `MouseListener`, that allows the user to press the mouse button, drag the mouse and release the mouse button. When the mouse is released, draw a rectangle with the appropriate upper-left corner, width and height. [*Hint*: The `mousePressed` method should capture the set of coordinates at which the user presses and holds the mouse button initially, and the `mouseReleased` method should capture the set of coordinates at which the user releases the mouse button. Both methods should store the appropriate coordinate values. All calculations of the width, height and upper-left corner should be performed by the `paint` method before the shape is drawn.]

13.28   Modify Exercise 13.27 to provided a "rubberbanding" effect. As the user drags the mouse, the user should be able to see the current size of the rectangle to know exactly what the rectangle will look like when the mouse button is released. [*Hint*: Method `mouseDragged` should perform the same tasks as `mouseReleased`.]

13.29   Modify Exercise 13.28 to allow the user to select which shape to draw. A `JComboBox` should provide options including at least rectangle, oval, line and rounded rectangle.

13.30   Modify Exercise 13.29 to allow the user to select the drawing color from a `JColorChooser` dialog box.

13.31   Modify Exercise 13.30 to allow the user to specify whether a shape should be filled or empty when it is drawn. The user should click a `JCheckBox` to indicate filled or empty.

14

Graphical User Interface Components: Part 2

Objectives

- To create and manipulate text areas, sliders, menus, popup menus and windows.
- To be able to create customized `JPanel` objects.
- To be able to change the look-and-feel of a GUI, using Swing's pluggable look-and-feel (PLAF).
- To be able to create a multiple-document interface with `JDesktopPane` and `JInternalFrame`.
- To be able to use additional layout managers.

I claim not to have controlled events, but confess plainly that events have controlled me.
Abraham Lincoln

A good symbol is the best argument, and is a missionary to persuade thousands.
Ralph Waldo Emerson

Capture its reality in paint!
Paul Cézanne

Outline

14.1 Introduction

In this chapter, we continue our study of GUIs. We discuss additional components and layout managers and lay the groundwork for building more complex GUIs.

We begin our discussion with another text-based GUI component—*JTextArea*—which allows multiple lines of text to be displayed or input. We continue with examples of *customizing class JPanel* in which we discuss issues that relate to painting on Swing GUI components. An important aspect of any complete GUI is a system of *menus* that enable the user to effectively perform tasks in the program, so we demonstrate how to create and use menus. The look-and-feel of a Swing GUI can be uniform across all platforms on which a Java program executes, or the GUI can be customized by using Swing's *pluggable look-and-feel (PLAF)*. We provide an example that illustrates how to change between Swing's default *metal look-and-feel*, a look-and-feel that simulates *Motif* (a popular UNIX look-and-feel) and one that simulates Microsoft's Windows look-and-feel. Many of today's applications use a *multiple-document interface (MDI)*, i.e., a main window (often called the *parent window*) containing other windows (often called *child windows*) to manage several open *documents* in parallel. For example, many e-mail programs allow you to have several e-mail windows open at the same time so you can compose or read multiple e-mail messages. We demonstrate Swing's classes for creating multiple-document interfaces. Finally, the chapter finishes with a series of examples discussing additional layout managers for organizing graphical user interfaces.

Swing is a large and complex topic. There are many more GUI components and capabilities than can be presented here. Several more Swing GUI components are introduced in the remaining chapters of this book as they are needed. Our book *Advanced Java 2 Platform How to Program* discusses other, more advanced Swing components and capabilities.

14.2 JTextArea

A *JTextArea* provides an area for manipulating multiple lines of text. Like class JText-Field, class JTextArea inherits from *JTextComponent*, which declares common methods for JTextFields, JTextAreas and several other text-based GUI components.

The application of Fig. 14.1 demonstrates JTextAreas. One JTextArea displays text that the user can select. The other JTextArea is uneditable and is used to display the text the user selected in the first JTextArea. JTextAreas do not have action events like JTextFields. As with multiple-selection JLists (Section 13.11), an external event from another GUI component indicates when to process the text in a JTextArea. For example, when typing an e-mail message, you normally click a **Send** button to send the text of the message to the recipient. Similarly, when editing a document in a word processor, you normally save the file by selecting a **Save** or **Save As...** menu item. In this program, the button **Copy >>>** generates the external event that copies the selected text in the left JTextArea and displays it in the right JTextArea.

```java
1  // Fig. 14.1: TextAreaDemo.java
2  // Copying selected text from one textarea to another.
3  import java.awt.*;
4  import java.awt.event.*;
5  import javax.swing.*;
6
7  public class TextAreaDemo extends JFrame {
8     private JTextArea textArea1, textArea2;
9     private JButton copyButton;
10
11    // set up GUI
12    public TextAreaDemo()
13    {
14       super( "TextArea Demo" );
15
16       Box box = Box.createHorizontalBox();
17
18       String string = "This is a demo string to\n" +
19          "illustrate copying text\nfrom one textarea to \n" +
20          "another textarea using an\nexternal event\n";
21
22       // set up textArea1
23       textArea1 = new JTextArea( string, 10, 15 );
24       box.add( new JScrollPane( textArea1 ) );
```

Fig. 14.1   Copying selected text from one text area to another. (Part 1 of 3.)

```
25
26          // set up copyButton
27          copyButton = new JButton( "Copy >>>" );
28          box.add( copyButton );
29          copyButton.addActionListener(
30
31             new ActionListener() {  // anonymous inner class
32
33                // set text in textArea2 to selected text from textArea1
34                public void actionPerformed( ActionEvent event )
35                {
36                   textArea2.setText( textArea1.getSelectedText() );
37                }
38
39             } // end anonymous inner class
40
41          ); // end call to addActionListener
42
43          // set up textArea2
44          textArea2 = new JTextArea( 10, 15 );
45          textArea2.setEditable( false );
46          box.add( new JScrollPane( textArea2 ) );
47
48          // add box to content pane
49          Container container = getContentPane();
50          container.add( box );    // place in BorderLayout.CENTER
51
52          setSize( 425, 200 );
53          setVisible( true );
54
55       } // end constructor TextAreaDemo
56
57       public static void main( String args[] )
58       {
59          TextAreaDemo application = new TextAreaDemo();
60          application.setDefaultCloseOperation( JFrame.EXIT_ON_CLOSE );
61       }
62
63    } // end class TextAreaDemo
```

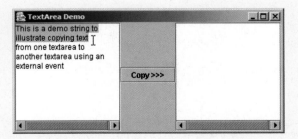

Fig. 14.1   Copying selected text from one text area to another. (Part 2 of 3.)

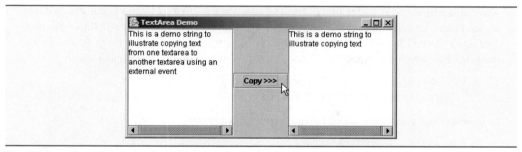

Fig. 14.1   Copying selected text from one text area to another. (Part 3 of 3.)

In the constructor (lines 12–55), line 16 creates a *Box container* (package `javax.swing`) for organizing the GUI components. Class `Box` is a subclass of `Container` that uses a *BoxLayout* layout manager to arrange the GUI components either horizontally or vertically.[1] Class `Box` provides static method *createHorizontalBox* to create a `Box` that arranges components from left to right in the order that the components are attached.

The application creates `JTextArea` objects `textArea1` (line 23) and `textArea2` (line 44). Each `JTextArea` has 10 rows and 15 columns. Line 23 specifies that `string` should be displayed as the default `JTextArea` content. A `JTextArea` does not provide scrollbars if it cannot display its complete contents. For this reason, line 24 creates a `JScrollPane` object, initializes it with `textArea1` and attaches it to container `box`. By default, horizontal and vertical scrollbars will appear as necessary.

Lines 27–41 creates `JButton` object `copyButton` with the label "Copy >>>," add `copyButton` to container `box` and register the event handler for `copyButton`'s `Action-Event`. This button provides the external event that determines when the program should copy the selected text in `textArea1` to `textArea2`. When the user clicks `copyButton`, line 36 in `actionPerformed` indicates that method *getSelectedText* (inherited into `JTextArea` from `JTextComponent`) should return the *selected text* from `textArea1`. The user selects text by dragging the mouse over the desired text to highlight it. Method `setText` changes the text in `textArea2` to the string returned by `getSelectedText`.

Lines 44–46 create `textArea2` and add it to container `box`. Lines 49–50 obtain the content pane for the window and add `box` to the content pane. Recall from Section 13.15 that the default layout of a content pane is a `BorderLayout` and that the `add` method by default attaches its argument to the `CENTER` of the `BorderLayout`.

It is sometimes desirable when text reaches the right side of a `JTextArea` to have the text wrap to the next line. This is referred to as *line-wrapping*. By default, `JTextArea` does not wrap lines.

Look-and-Feel Observation 14.1
To provide line-wrapping functionality for a JTextArea, invoke JTextArea method set-LineWrap with a true argument.

JScrollPane Scrollbar Policies
This example uses a `JScrollPane` to provide scrolling for a `JTextArea`. By default, `JScrollPane` displays scrollbars only if they are required. You can set the horizontal and

---

1.   Section 14.12 discusses `BoxLayout` in detail.

vertical *scrollbar policies* for the JScrollPane when a JScrollPane is constructed. If a program has a reference to a JScrollPane, the program can use JScrollPane methods *setHorizontalScrollBarPolicy* and *setVerticalScrollBarPolicy* to change the scrollbar policies at any time. Class JScrollPane declares the constants

```
JScrollPane.VERTICAL_SCROLLBAR_ALWAYS
JScrollPane.HORIZONTAL_SCROLLBAR_ALWAYS
```

to indicate that a scrollbar should always appear, constants

```
JScrollPane.VERTICAL_SCROLLBAR_AS_NEEDED
JScrollPane.HORIZONTAL_SCROLLBAR_AS_NEEDED
```

to indicate that a scrollbar should appear only if necessary (the defaults) and constants

```
JScrollPane.VERTICAL_SCROLLBAR_NEVER
JScrollPane.HORIZONTAL_SCROLLBAR_NEVER
```

to indicate that a scrollbar should never appear. If the horizontal scrollbar policy is set to JScrollPane.HORIZONTAL_SCROLLBAR_NEVER, a JTextArea attached to the JScrollPane will wrap lines.

14.3 Creating a Customized Subclass of JPanel

Chapter 13 demonstrated that JPanels can aggregate a set of GUI components for layout purposes. JPanels are quite flexible. Other JPanel uses include creating *dedicated drawing areas* and creating areas that receive mouse events. Programs sometimes extend class JPanel to create new GUI components. Our next example uses a JPanel to create a dedicated drawing area to separate drawing from the rest of the program's graphical user interface. This can be beneficial in Swing graphical user interfaces. If graphics and Swing GUI components are not displayed in the correct order, it is possible that the GUI components will not display correctly.

Look-and-Feel Observation 14.2

Combining graphics and Swing GUI components can lead to incorrect display of the graphics, the GUI components or both. Using JPanels for drawing can eliminate this problem by providing a dedicated graphics area.

*Painting on a Subclass of **JComponent** with Method **paintComponent***
Swing components that inherit from class JComponent contain method *paintComponent* for drawing in the context of a lightweight Swing GUI. When customizing a JPanel for use as a dedicated drawing area, the subclass should override method paintComponent and should call the superclass version of paintComponent as the first statement in the body of the overridden method. This ensures that painting occurs in the proper order and that Swing's painting mechanism paints correctly. For example, an important part of this mechanism is that subclasses of JComponent support *transparency*, which can be set with method *setOpaque* (a false argument indicates the component is transparent). To paint a component correctly, the program must determine whether the component is transparent. The code for this is in the superclass paintComponent implementation. When a component is transparent, paintComponent will not clear the component's background when the program paints the component. When a component is *opaque*, paintComponent clears

the background before continuing the painting operation. If the superclass version of `paintComponent` is not called, an opaque GUI component typically will not display correctly on the user interface. Also, if the superclass version is called after performing the customized drawing statements, the results typically will be erased.

Look-and-Feel Observation 14.3

When overriding a JComponent's `paintComponent` method, the first statement in the body should always be a call to the superclass's `paintComponent` method.

Common Programming Error 14.1

When overriding JComponent method `paintComponent`, not calling the superclass's original version of `paintComponent` might prevent the component from displaying properly.

Common Programming Error 14.2

When overriding a JComponent's `paintComponent` method, calling the superclass's `paintComponent` method after other drawing is performed erases the other drawings.

Classes JFrame and JApplet are not subclasses of JComponent; therefore, they do not contain method `paintComponent`. To draw directly on subclasses of JFrame and JApplet, override method `paint`.

Look-and-Feel Observation 14.4

Calling `repaint` for a Swing GUI component indicates that the component should be painted as soon as possible. The background of the GUI component is cleared only if the component is opaque. Most Swing components are transparent by default. JComponent method `setOpaque` can be passed a boolean argument indicating whether the component is opaque (`true`) or transparent (`false`). The AWT GUI components differ from Swing components in that `repaint` results in a call to Component method `update` (which clears the component's background) and `update` calls method `paint` (rather than `paintComponent`).

Defining the Custom Drawing Area

The program of Fig. 14.2 and Fig. 14.3 demonstrates a customized subclass of JPanel. Class CustomPanel (Fig. 14.2) has its own `paintComponent` method that draws a circle or a square, depending on the value passed to CustomPanel's `draw` method. For this purpose, line 7 declares constants that enable the program to specify the shape a CustomPanel draws on itself with each call to its `paintComponent` method. Class CustomPanelTest (Fig. 14.3) creates a CustomPanel and a GUI that enable the user to choose which shape to draw.

```
1   // Fig. 14.2: CustomPanel.java
2   // A customized JPanel class.
3   import java.awt.*;
4   import javax.swing.*;
5
6   public class CustomPanel extends JPanel {
7      public final static int CIRCLE = 1, SQUARE = 2;
8      private int shape;
9
```

Fig. 14.2　　JPanel subclass used as a custom drawing area. (Part 1 of 2.)

```
10          // use shape to draw an oval or rectangle
11          public void paintComponent( Graphics g )
12          {
13             super.paintComponent( g );
14
15             if ( shape == CIRCLE )
16                g.fillOval( 50, 10, 60, 60 );
17             else if ( shape == SQUARE )
18                g.fillRect( 50, 10, 60, 60 );
19          }
20
21          // set shape value and repaint CustomPanel
22          public void draw( int shapeToDraw )
23          {
24             shape = shapeToDraw;
25             repaint();
26          }
27
28       } // end class CustomPanel
```

Fig. 14.2   `JPanel` subclass used as a custom drawing area. (Part 2 of 2.)

Class `CustomPanel` contains one field, `shape` (line 8 of Fig. 14.2), that stores an integer representing the shape to draw. Method `paintComponent` (lines 11–19) draws a shape on the panel. If `shape` is CIRCLE, `Graphics` method `fillOval` draws a solid circle. If `shape` is SQUARE, `Graphics` method `fillRect` draws a solid square. Method `draw` (lines 22–26) sets field `shape` and calls `repaint` to refresh the `CustomPanel` object. Note that calling `repaint` for the `CustomPanel` schedules a painting operation only for the `CustomPanel`, not for the entire GUI. Method `paintComponent` will be called to repaint the `CustomPanel` and draw the appropriate shape.

The `CustomPanelTest` constructor (Fig. 14.3 lines 13–66) creates a `CustomPanel` object (line 18) and sets its background color to green (line 19), so the `CustomPanel` area is visible on the application. All `JPanel`s (`CustomPanel` extends `JPanel`) are opaque by default, so their background colors are displayed. The constructor creates `JButton` objects `squareButton` (line 22) and `circleButton` (line 37). Lines 23–35 register `square-Button`'s event handler. Lines 38–50 register `circleButton`'s event handler. Each `actionPerformed` method calls `CustomPanel` method `draw` (lines 30 and 45). In each case, the appropriate constant (`CustomPanel.SQUARE` or `CustomPanel.CIRCLE`) is passed as an argument to indicate which shape the `CustomPanel` should draw.

```
1    // Fig. 14.3: CustomPanelTest.java
2    // Using a customized Panel object.
3    import java.awt.*;
4    import java.awt.event.*;
5    import javax.swing.*;
6
7    public class CustomPanelTest extends JFrame {
8       private JPanel buttonPanel;
9       private CustomPanel myPanel;
```

Fig. 14.3   Drawing on a customized subclass of `JPanel`. (Part 1 of 3.)

```
10        private JButton circleButton, squareButton;
11
12        // set up GUI
13        public CustomPanelTest()
14        {
15           super( "CustomPanel Test" );
16
17           // create custom drawing area
18           myPanel = new CustomPanel();
19           myPanel.setBackground( Color.GREEN );
20
21           // set up squareButton
22           squareButton = new JButton( "Square" );
23           squareButton.addActionListener(
24
25              new ActionListener() {  // anonymous inner class
26
27                 // draw a square
28                 public void actionPerformed( ActionEvent event )
29                 {
30                    myPanel.draw( CustomPanel.SQUARE );
31                 }
32
33              } // end anonymous inner class
34
35           ); // end call to addActionListener
36
37           circleButton = new JButton( "Circle" );
38           circleButton.addActionListener(
39
40              new ActionListener() {  // anonymous inner class
41
42                 // draw a circle
43                 public void actionPerformed( ActionEvent event )
44                 {
45                    myPanel.draw( CustomPanel.CIRCLE );
46                 }
47
48              } // end anonymous inner class
49
50           ); // end call to addActionListener
51
52           // set up panel containing buttons
53           buttonPanel = new JPanel();
54           buttonPanel.setLayout( new GridLayout( 1, 2 ) );
55           buttonPanel.add( circleButton );
56           buttonPanel.add( squareButton );
57
58           // attach button panel & custom drawing area to content pane
59           Container container = getContentPane();
60           container.add( myPanel, BorderLayout.CENTER );
61           container.add( buttonPanel, BorderLayout.SOUTH );
62
```

Fig. 14.3   Drawing on a customized subclass of JPanel. (Part 2 of 3.)

```
63            setSize( 300, 150 );
64            setVisible( true );
65
66        } // end constructor CustomPanelTest
67
68        public static void main( String args[] )
69        {
70            CustomPanelTest application = new CustomPanelTest();
71            application.setDefaultCloseOperation( JFrame.EXIT_ON_CLOSE );
72        }
73
74    } // end class CustomPanelTest
```

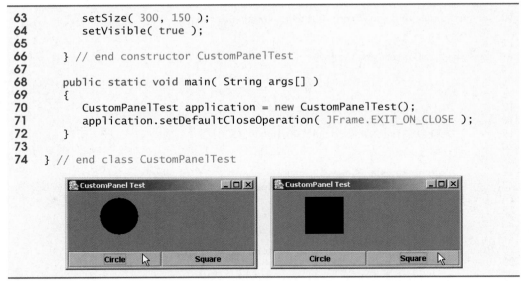

Fig. 14.3   Drawing on a customized subclass of JPanel. (Part 3 of 3.)

For layout of the buttons, CustomPanelTest creates a JPanel called buttonPanel (line 53) with a GridLayout of one row and two columns (line 54) and attaches the buttons to the panel (lines 55–56). Finally, CustomPanelTest adds myPanel to the CENTER region of the content pane (line 60) and adds buttonPanel to the SOUTH region of the content pane (line 61). Note that the BorderLayout expands myPanel to fill the center region. Resize the window to see how the position and sizes of the GUI components are managed by buttonPanel's GridLayout and CustomPanelTest's BorderLayout.

14.4 JPanel Subclass that Handles Its Own Events

JPanels do not support conventional events supported by other GUI components, such as buttons, text fields and windows. However, JPanels are capable of recognizing lower-level events, such as mouse events and key events. The program of Fig. 14.4 and Fig. 14.5 allows the user to draw an oval by dragging the mouse across a panel. Class SelfContainedPanel (Fig. 14.4) listens for its own mouse events and draws an oval on itself in response to those mouse events. The location and size of the oval are determined from the coordinates of the mouse events. The coordinates at which the user presses the mouse button specify the starting point for the oval's bounding box. As the user drags the mouse, the coordinates of the mouse pointer specify another point. Together, the program uses these points to calculate the upper-left x-y coordinate, the width and the height of the oval's bounding box. The size of the oval changes continuously while the user drags the mouse. When the user releases the mouse button, the program calculates the final bounding box for the oval and draws the oval. Line 3 of Fig. 14.4 indicates that class SelfContainedPanel is in package com.deitel.jhtp4.ch14, which enables this class to be imported into other programs. Class SelfContainedPanelTest imports SelfContainedPanel at line 8 of Fig. 14.5. See Section 8.13 for information on compiling and using packaged classes.

Class `SelfContainedPanel` (Fig. 14.4) extends class `JPanel` (line 9). Instance variables `x1` and `y1` store the initial coordinates where the `mousePressed` event occurs on the `SelfContainedPanel`. Instance variables `x2` and `y2` store the coordinates where the user drags the mouse or releases the mouse button. All the coordinates are with respect to the upper-left corner of the `SelfContainedPanel`.

```
1   // Fig. 14.4: SelfContainedPanel.java
2   // A self-contained JPanel class that handles its own mouse events.
3   package com.deitel.jhtp5.ch14;
4
5   import java.awt.*;
6   import java.awt.event.*;
7   import javax.swing.*;
8
9   public class SelfContainedPanel extends JPanel {
10     private int x1, y1, x2, y2;
11
12     // set up mouse event handling for SelfContainedPanel
13     public SelfContainedPanel()
14     {
15        // set up mouse listener
16        addMouseListener(
17
18           new MouseAdapter() {  // anonymous inner class
19
20              // handle mouse press event
21              public void mousePressed( MouseEvent event )
22              {
23                 x1 = event.getX();
24                 y1 = event.getY();
25              }
26
27              // handle mouse release event
28              public void mouseReleased( MouseEvent event )
29              {
30                 x2 = event.getX();
31                 y2 = event.getY();
32                 repaint();
33              }
34
35           } // end anonymous inner class
36
37        ); // end call to addMouseListener
38
39        // set up mouse motion listener
40        addMouseMotionListener(
41
42           new MouseMotionAdapter() {  // anonymous inner class
43
44              // handle mouse drag event
45              public void mouseDragged( MouseEvent event )
46              {
```

Fig. 14.4   `JPanel` subclass that processes mouse events. (Part 1 of 2.)

```
47                    x2 = event.getX();
48                    y2 = event.getY();
49                    repaint();
50                 }
51
52              } // end anonymous inner class
53
54        ); // end call to addMouseMotionListener
55
56     } // end constructor SelfContainedPanel
57
58     // return preferred width and height of SelfContainedPanel
59     public Dimension getPreferredSize()
60     {
61        return new Dimension( 150, 100 );
62     }
63
64     // paint an oval at the specified coordinates
65     public void paintComponent( Graphics g )
66     {
67        super.paintComponent( g );
68
69        g.drawOval( Math.min( x1, x2 ), Math.min( y1, y2 ),
70           Math.abs( x1 - x2 ), Math.abs( y1 - y2 ) );
71     }
72
73  } // end class SelfContainedPanel
```

Fig. 14.4   JPanel subclass that processes mouse events. (Part 2 of 2.)

Look-and-Feel Observation 14.5

Drawing on any GUI component is performed with coordinates that are measured from the upper-left corner (0, 0) of that GUI component.

SelfContainedPanel's constructor (lines 13–56) uses methods addMouseLis-tener and addMouseMotionListener to register inner-class objects to handle mouse events and mouse motion events for the SelfContainedPanel. Only mousePressed (lines 21–25), mouseReleased (lines 28–33) and mouseDragged (lines 45–50) are over-ridden to perform tasks. The other mouse event-handling methods are inherited by the inner classes from adapter classes MouseAdapter and MouseMotionAdapter.

By extending class JPanel, we are creating a new GUI component. Thus, we must ensure that our new component works like other components for layout purposes. Layout managers often use a GUI component's *getPreferredSize* method (inherited from class java.awt.Component) to determine the preferred width and height of the component when laying out that component as part of a GUI. If a new component has a preferred width and height, it should override method getPreferredSize (lines 59–62) to return that width and height as an object of class *Dimension* (package java.awt).

Look-and-Feel Observation 14.6

The default size of a JPanel object is 10 pixels wide and 10 pixels tall.

Look-and-Feel Observation 14.7

When subclassing `JPanel` *(or any other* `JComponent`*), override method* `getPreferred-Size` *if the new component should have a specific preferred width and height.*

Method `paintComponent` (lines 65–71) draws an oval, using the current values of instance variables `x1`, `y1`, `x2` and `y2`. The upper-left corner, width and height are determined by pressing and holding the mouse button, dragging the mouse and releasing the mouse button on the `SelfContainedPanel` object.

The initial coordinates `x1` and `y1` on the `SelfContainedPanel` drawing area are captured in `mousePressed` (lines 21–25). As the user drags the mouse, the program generates a series of calls to `mouseDragged` (lines 45–50) while the user continues to hold the mouse button and move the mouse. Each call captures in variables `x2` and `y2` the current location of the mouse with respect to the upper-left corner of the `SelfContainedPanel` and calls `repaint` to draw the current version of the oval. Drawing is strictly confined to the `SelfContainedPanel`, even if the user drags outside the `SelfContainedPanel` drawing area. Anything drawn off the `SelfContainedPanel` is *clipped*—pixels are not displayed outside the bounds of the `SelfContainedPanel`.

The calculations provided in method `paintComponent` (lines 69–70) determine the proper upper-left corner, using method `Math.min` twice to find the smaller *x*-coordinate and *y*-coordinate. The oval's width and height must be positive values or the oval is not displayed. Method `Math.abs` gets the absolute value of the calculations `x1 - x2` and `y1 - y2` that determine the width and height of the oval's bounding rectangle, respectively. When the calculations are complete, `paintComponent` draws the oval. The call to the superclass version of `paintComponent` at the beginning of the method ensures that the previous oval displayed on the `SelfContainedPanel` is erased before the new one is displayed.

Look-and-Feel Observation 14.8

Most Swing GUI components can be transparent or opaque. If a Swing GUI component is opaque, when its `paintComponent` *method is called, its background will be cleared. Otherwise, its background will not be cleared. Only opaque components can display a customized background color.*

Look-and-Feel Observation 14.9

`JPanel` objects are opaque by default.

When the user releases the mouse button, method `mouseReleased` (lines 28–33) captures in variables `x2` and `y2` the final location of the mouse and invokes `repaint` to draw the final version of the oval.

`SelfContainedPanelTest` displays a `SelfContainedPanel` object on which the user can drag the mouse to draw. The constructor (lines 14–50 of Fig. 14.5) creates a `SelfContainedPanel` (line 17) and sets its background color (line 18) to yellow so that its area is visible against the background of the application window.

We would like this program to distinguish between mouse-motion events on the `SelfContainedPanel` and mouse-motion events on the application window, so lines 25–45 register an event handler for the application window's mouse-motion events. Event handlers `mouseDragged` (lines 30–34) and `mouseMoved` (lines 37–41) use method `setTitle` (inherited indirectly from class `java.awt.Frame`) to display a string in the window's title bar that indicates the *x-y* coordinate where the mouse-motion event occurred.

```
1   // Fig. 14.5: SelfContainedPanelTest.java
2   // Creating a self-contained subclass of JPanel that processes
3   // its own mouse events.
4   import java.awt.*;
5   import java.awt.event.*;
6   import javax.swing.*;
7
8   import com.deitel.jhtp5.ch14.SelfContainedPanel;
9
10  public class SelfContainedPanelTest extends JFrame {
11     private SelfContainedPanel myPanel;
12
13     // set up GUI and mouse motion event handlers for application window
14     public SelfContainedPanelTest()
15     {
16        // set up a SelfContainedPanel
17        myPanel = new SelfContainedPanel();
18        myPanel.setBackground( Color.YELLOW );
19
20        Container container = getContentPane();
21        container.setLayout( new FlowLayout() );
22        container.add( myPanel );
23
24        // set up mouse motion event handling
25        addMouseMotionListener(
26
27           new MouseMotionListener() {  // anonymous inner class
28
29              // handle mouse drag event
30              public void mouseDragged( MouseEvent event )
31              {
32                 setTitle( "Dragging: x=" + event.getX() +
33                    "; y=" + event.getY() );
34              }
35
36              // handle mouse move event
37              public void mouseMoved( MouseEvent event )
38              {
39                 setTitle( "Moving: x=" + event.getX() +
40                    "; y=" + event.getY() );
41              }
42
43           } // end anonymous inner class
44
45        ); // end call to addMouseMotionListener
46
47        setSize( 300, 200 );
48        setVisible( true );
49
50     } // end constructor SelfContainedPanelTest
51
52     public static void main( String args[] )
53     {
```

Fig. 14.5   Capturing mouse events with a JPanel. (Part 1 of 2.)

```
54              SelfContainedPanelTest application = new SelfContainedPanelTest();
55              application.setDefaultCloseOperation( JFrame.EXIT_ON_CLOSE );
56           }
57
58        } // end class SelfContainedPanelTest
```

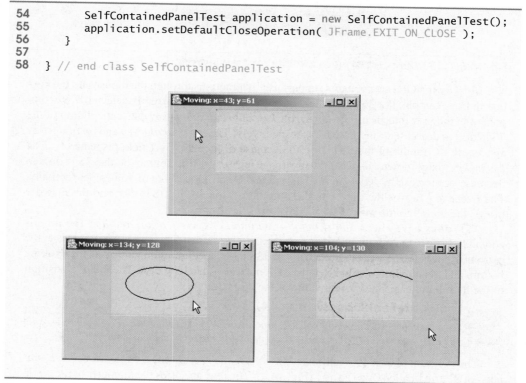

Fig. 14.5   Capturing mouse events with a JPanel. (Part 2 of 2.)

When executing this program, try dragging from the background of the application window into the SelfContainedPanel area to see that the drag events are sent to the application window rather than the SelfContainedPanel. Then, start a new drag operation in the SelfContainedPanel area and drag out to the background of the application window to see that the drag events are sent to the SelfContainedPanel rather than to the application window. Recall from Section 13.12 that mouse-drag events are sent to the component on which the drag was initiated.

 **Look-and-Feel Observation 14.10**

A mouse drag operation begins with a mouse-pressed event. All subsequent mouse drag events (until the user releases the mouse button) are sent to the GUI component that received the original mouse-pressed event.

14.5 JSlider

JSliders enable the user to select from a range of integer values. Class *JSlider* inherits from **JComponent**. Figure 14.6 shows a horizontal JSlider with *tick marks* and the *thumb* that allows the user to select a value. JSliders can be customized to display *major tick marks*, *minor tick marks* and labels for the tick marks. They also support *snap-to ticks* for which positioning the thumb between two tick marks causes the thumb to *snap* to the closest tick mark.

thumb   tick mark

Fig. 14.6   JSlider component with horizontal orientation.

Most Swing GUI components support user interactions through the mouse and the keyboard. For example, if a JSlider has the focus (i.e., it is the currently selected GUI component in the user interface), the *left arrow key* and *right arrow key* cause the thumb of the JSlider to decrease or increase by 1, respectively. The *down arrow key* and *up arrow key* also cause the thumb of the JSlider to decrease or increase by 1 tick, respectively. The *PgDn key* (page down) and *PgUp key* (page up) cause the thumb of the JSlider to decrease or increase by *block increments* of one-tenth of the range of values, respectively. The *Home key* moves the thumb to the minimum value of the JSlider and the *End key* moves the thumb to the maximum value of the JSlider.

JSliders have either a *horizontal orientation* or a *vertical orientation*. For a horizontal JSlider, the minimum value is at the extreme left and the maximum value is at the extreme right of the JSlider. For a vertical JSlider, the minimum value is at the extreme bottom and the maximum value is at the extreme top of the JSlider. The relative position of the thumb indicates the current value of the JSlider.

Look-and-Feel Observation 14.11

The minimum and maximum value positions on a JSlider can be reversed by invoking JSlider method setInverted with boolean argument true.

The program of Fig. 14.7 and Fig. 14.8 allows the user to size a circle drawn on a subclass of JPanel called OvalPanel (Fig. 14.7). The user specifies the diameter of the circle with a horizontal JSlider. Application class SliderDemo (Fig. 14.8) creates the JSlider that controls the diameter of the circle. Class OvalPanel is a subclass of JPanel that knows how to draw a circle on itself, using its own instance variable diameter to determine the diameter of the circle—the diameter is used as the width and height of the bounding box in which the circle is displayed. The diameter value is set when the user interacts with the JSlider. The event handler calls method setDiameter in class OvalPanel to set the diameter and calls repaint to draw the new circle. The repaint call results in a call to OvalPanel's paintComponent method.

Class OvalPanel (Fig. 14.7) contains a paintComponent method (lines 10–15) that draws a filled oval (a circle in this example), a setDiameter method (lines 18–23) that changes the diameter of the circle and repaints the OvalPanel, a getPreferredSize method (lines 26–29) that defaults the preferred width and height of an OvalPanel and a getMinimumSize method (lines 32–35) that defaults the minimum width and height of an OvalPanel.

Look-and-Feel Observation 14.12

If a new GUI component has a minimum width and height (i.e., smaller dimensions would render the component ineffective on the display), override method getMinimumSize to return the minimum width and height as an instance of class Dimension.

Look-and-Feel Observation 14.13

For many GUI components, method getMinimumSize is implemented to return the result of a call to that component's getPreferredSize method.

```
1    // Fig. 14.7: OvalPanel.java
2    // A customized JPanel class.
3    import java.awt.*;
4    import javax.swing.*;
5
6    public class OvalPanel extends JPanel {
7       private int diameter = 10;
8
9       // draw an oval of the specified diameter
10      public void paintComponent( Graphics g )
11      {
12         super.paintComponent( g );
13
14         g.fillOval( 10, 10, diameter, diameter );
15      }
16
17      // validate and set diameter, then repaint
18      public void setDiameter( int newDiameter )
19      {
20         // if diameter invalid, default to 10
21         diameter = ( newDiameter >= 0 ? newDiameter : 10 );
22         repaint();
23      }
24
25      // used by layout manager to determine preferred size
26      public Dimension getPreferredSize()
27      {
28         return new Dimension( 200, 200 );
29      }
30
31      // used by layout manager to determine minimum size
32      public Dimension getMinimumSize()
33      {
34         return getPreferredSize();
35      }
36
37   } // end class OvalPanel
```

Fig. 14.7   JPanel subclass for drawing circles of a specified diameter.

Class SliderDemo's constructor (lines 13–50 of Fig. 14.8) creates OvalPanel object myPanel (line 18) and sets its background color (line 19). Lines 22–23 create JSlider object diameterSlider to control the diameter of the circle drawn on the OvalPanel. The orientation of diameterSlider is HORIZONTAL (a constant in interface SwingConstants). The second and third constructor arguments to the JSlider constructor indicate the minimum and maximum integer values in the range of values for this JSlider. The last constructor argument indicates that the initial value of the JSlider (i.e., where the thumb is displayed) should be 10.

Lines 24–25 customize the appearance of the JSlider. Method *setMajorTickSpacing* indicates that each major-tick mark represents 10 values in the range of values supported by the JSlider. Method *setPaintTicks* with a true argument indicates that the tick marks should be displayed (they are not displayed by default). For other methods that are used to customize a JSlider's appearance, see the JSlider on-line documentation (java.sun.com/j2se/1.4.1/docs/api/javax/swing/JSlider.html).

```java
1   // Fig. 14.8: SliderDemo.java
2   // Using JSliders to size an oval.
3   import java.awt.*;
4   import java.awt.event.*;
5   import javax.swing.*;
6   import javax.swing.event.*;
7
8   public class SliderDemo extends JFrame {
9      private JSlider diameterSlider;
10     private OvalPanel myPanel;
11
12     // set up GUI
13     public SliderDemo()
14     {
15        super( "Slider Demo" );
16
17        // set up OvalPanel
18        myPanel = new OvalPanel();
19        myPanel.setBackground( Color.YELLOW );
20
21        // set up JSlider to control diameter value
22        diameterSlider =
23           new JSlider( SwingConstants.HORIZONTAL, 0, 200, 10 );
24        diameterSlider.setMajorTickSpacing( 10 );
25        diameterSlider.setPaintTicks( true );
26
27        // register JSlider event listener
28        diameterSlider.addChangeListener(
29
30           new ChangeListener() {  // anonymous inner class
31
32              // handle change in slider value
33              public void stateChanged( ChangeEvent e )
34              {
35                 myPanel.setDiameter( diameterSlider.getValue() );
36              }
37
38           } // end anonymous inner class
39
40        ); // end call to addChangeListener
41
42        // attach components to content pane
43        Container container = getContentPane();
44        container.add( diameterSlider, BorderLayout.SOUTH );
45        container.add( myPanel, BorderLayout.CENTER );
46
47        setSize( 220, 270 );
48        setVisible( true );
49
50     } // end constructor SliderDemo
```

Fig. 14.8   JSlider value used to determine the diameter of a circle. (Part 1 of 2.)

```
51
52      public static void main( String args[] )
53      {
54         SliderDemo application = new SliderDemo();
55         application.setDefaultCloseOperation( JFrame.EXIT_ON_CLOSE );
56      }
57
58   } // end class SliderDemo
```

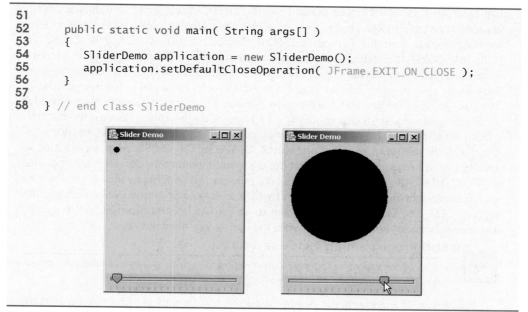

Fig. 14.8   JSlider value used to determine the diameter of a circle. (Part 2 of 2.)

JSliders generate *ChangeEvents* (package `javax.swing.event`) in response to user interactions. An object of a class that implements interface *ChangeListener* (package `javax.swing.event`) and declares method *stateChanged* can respond to ChangeEvents. Lines 28–40 register a ChangeListener to handle diameterSlider's events. When method stateChanged (lines 33–36) is called in response to a user interaction, line 35 calls myPanel's setDiameter method and passes the current value of the JSlider as an argument. JSlider method *getValue* returns the current thumb position.

14.6 Windows: Additional Notes

From Chapter 10 to this chapter, most applications have used JFrame subclasses as application windows. In this section, we discuss several important JFrame issues.

A *JFrame* is a *window* with a *title bar* and a *border*. Class JFrame is a subclass of *java.awt.Frame* (which is a subclass of `java.awt.Window`). As such, JFrame is one of the few Swing GUI components that is not a lightweight GUI component. When you display a window from a Java program, the window is provided by the local platform's windowing toolkit—the window will look like all other windows displayed on that platform. When a Java program executes on a Macintosh and displays a window, the window's title bar and borders will look like those of other Macintosh applications. When a Java program executes on Microsoft Windows and displays a window, the window's title bar and borders will look like those of other Microsoft Windows applications. And when a Java program executes on a Unix platform and displays a window, the window's title bar and borders will look like other Unix applications on that platform.

Class JFrame supports three operations when the user closes the window. By default, a window is hidden (i.e., removed from the screen) when the user closes a window. This can be controlled with JFrame method *setDefaultCloseOperation*. Interface *WindowConstants* (package javax.swing), which class JFrame implements, declares three constants for use with this method—DISPOSE_ON_CLOSE, DO_NOTHING_ON_CLOSE and HIDE_ON_CLOSE (the default). Some platforms only allow a limited number of windows to be displayed on the screen. Thus, a window is a valuable resource that should be given back to the system when it is no longer needed. Class Window (an indirect superclass of JFrame) declares method *dispose* for this purpose. When a Window is no longer needed in an application, you should explicitly dispose of the Window. This can be done by calling the Window's dispose method or by calling method setDefaultCloseOperation with the argument WindowConstants.DISPOSE_ON_CLOSE. Also, terminating an application will return window resources to the system. Setting the default close operation to DO_NOTHING_ON_CLOSE indicates that the program will determine what to do when the user indicates that the window should be closed. Recall from Section 10.9 that JFrames also support EXIT_ON_CLOSE as the argument to setDefaultCloseOperation to specify that the application should terminate when the user closes the window.

Good Programming Practice 14.1

Windows are an expensive system resource. Return them to the system when they are no longer needed.

By default, a window is not displayed on the screen until the program invokes the window's setVisible method (inherited from class java.awt.Component) with a true argument. Also, a window's size should be set with a call to method setSize (inherited from class java.awt.Component). The position of a window when it appears on the screen is specified with method *setLocation* (inherited from class java.awt.Component).

Common Programming Error 14.3

Forgetting to call method setVisible on a window is a run-time logic error; the window is not displayed.

Common Programming Error 14.4

Forgetting to call the setSize method on a window is a run-time logic error—only the title bar appears.

Windows generate *window events* when the user manipulates the window. Event listeners are registered for window events with Window method *addWindowListener*. Interface *WindowListener* provides seven window-event-handling methods—*windowActivated* (called when the user makes a window the active window), *windowClosed* (called after the window is closed), *windowClosing* (called when the user initiates closing of the window), *windowDeactivated* (called when the user makes another window the active window), *windowIconified* (called when the user minimizes a window), *windowDeiconified* (called when the user restores a window from being minimized) and *windowOpened* (called when a program first displays a window on the screen).

14.7 Using Menus with Frames

Menus are an integral part of GUIs. Menus allow the user to perform actions without unnecessarily "cluttering" a GUI with extra components. In Swing GUIs, menus can be attached only to objects of the classes that provide method set JMenuBar. Two such classes are JFrame and JApplet. The classes used to declare menus are *JMenuBar*, *JMenu*, *JMenuItem*, *JCheckBoxMenuItem* and class *JRadioButtonMenuItem*.

Look-and-Feel Observation 14.14

Menus simplify GUIs by reducing the number of components the user can see at one time.

Class JMenuBar (a subclass of JComponent) contains the methods necessary to manage a *menu bar*, which is a container for menus. Class JMenu (a subclass of javax.swing.JMenuItem) contains the methods necessary for managing *menus*. Menus contain menu items and are added to menu bars or to other menus as submenus. When a menu is clicked, the menu expands to show its list of menu items.

Class JMenuItem (a subclass of javax.swing.AbstractButton) contains the methods necessary to manage *menu items*. A menu item is a GUI component inside a menu that, when selected, causes an action event. A menu item can be used to initiate an action or it can be a *submenu* that provides more menu items from which the user can select. Submenus are useful for grouping related menu items in a menu.

Class JCheckBoxMenuItem (a subclass of javax.swing.JMenuItem) contains the methods necessary to manage menu items that can be toggled on or off. When a JCheck-BoxMenuItem is selected, a check appears to the left of the menu item. When the JCheck-BoxMenuItem is selected again, the check to the left of the menu item is removed.

Class JRadioButtonMenuItem (a subclass of javax.swing.JMenuItem) contains the methods necessary to manage menu items that can be toggled on or off like JCheck-BoxMenuItems. When multiple JRadioButtonMenuItems are maintained as part of a ButtonGroup, only one item in the group can be selected at a given time. When a JRadioButtonMenuItem is selected, a filled circle appears to the left of the menu item. When another JRadioButtonMenuItem is selected, the filled circle to the left of the previously selected menu item is removed.

The application of Fig. 14.9 demonstrates various menu items. The program also demonstrates how to specify special characters called *mnemonics* that can provide quick access to a menu or menu item from the keyboard. Mnemonics can be used with all subclasses of javax.swing.AbstractButton.

```
1   // Fig. 14.9: MenuTest.java
2   // Demonstrating menus
3   import java.awt.*;
4   import java.awt.event.*;
5   import javax.swing.*;
6
7   public class MenuTest extends JFrame {
8      private final Color colorValues[] =
9         { Color.BLACK, Color.BLUE, Color.RED, Color.GREEN };
10     private JRadioButtonMenuItem colorItems[], fonts[];
11     private JCheckBoxMenuItem styleItems[];
12     private JLabel displayLabel;
```

Fig. 14.9   JMenus and mnemonics. (Part 1 of 6.)

```
13        private ButtonGroup fontGroup, colorGroup;
14        private int style;
15
16        // set up GUI
17        public MenuTest()
18        {
19            super( "Using JMenus" );
20
21            // set up File menu and its menu items
22            JMenu fileMenu = new JMenu( "File" );
23            fileMenu.setMnemonic( 'F' );
24
25            // set up About... menu item
26            JMenuItem aboutItem = new JMenuItem( "About..." );
27            aboutItem.setMnemonic( 'A' );
28            fileMenu.add( aboutItem );
29            aboutItem.addActionListener(
30
31                new ActionListener() {  // anonymous inner class
32
33                    // display message dialog when user selects About...
34                    public void actionPerformed( ActionEvent event )
35                    {
36                        JOptionPane.showMessageDialog( MenuTest.this,
37                            "This is an example\nof using menus",
38                            "About", JOptionPane.PLAIN_MESSAGE );
39                    }
40
41                }  // end anonymous inner class
42
43            ); // end call to addActionListener
44
45            // set up Exit menu item
46            JMenuItem exitItem = new JMenuItem( "Exit" );
47            exitItem.setMnemonic( 'x' );
48            fileMenu.add( exitItem );
49            exitItem.addActionListener(
50
51                new ActionListener() {  // anonymous inner class
52
53                    // terminate application when user clicks exitItem
54                    public void actionPerformed( ActionEvent event )
55                    {
56                        System.exit( 0 );
57                    }
58
59                }  // end anonymous inner class
60
61            ); // end call to addActionListener
62
63            // create menu bar and attach it to MenuTest window
64            JMenuBar bar = new JMenuBar();
65            setJMenuBar( bar );
```

Fig. 14.9   JMenus and mnemonics. (Part 2 of 6.)

```
66          bar.add( fileMenu );
67
68          // create Format menu, its submenus and menu items
69          JMenu formatMenu = new JMenu( "Format" );
70          formatMenu.setMnemonic( 'r' );
71
72          // create Color submenu
73          String colors[] = { "Black", "Blue", "Red", "Green" };
74
75          JMenu colorMenu = new JMenu( "Color" );
76          colorMenu.setMnemonic( 'C' );
77
78          colorItems = new JRadioButtonMenuItem[ colors.length ];
79          colorGroup = new ButtonGroup();
80          ItemHandler itemHandler = new ItemHandler();
81
82          // create color radio button menu items
83          for ( int count = 0; count < colors.length; count++ ) {
84             colorItems[ count ] =
85                new JRadioButtonMenuItem( colors[ count ] );
86             colorMenu.add( colorItems[ count ] );
87             colorGroup.add( colorItems[ count ] );
88             colorItems[ count ].addActionListener( itemHandler );
89          }
90
91          // select first Color menu item
92          colorItems[ 0 ].setSelected( true );
93
94          // add format menu to menu bar
95          formatMenu.add( colorMenu );
96          formatMenu.addSeparator();
97
98          // create Font submenu
99          String fontNames[] = { "Serif", "Monospaced", "SansSerif" };
100
101         JMenu fontMenu = new JMenu( "Font" );
102         fontMenu.setMnemonic( 'n' );
103
104         fonts = new JRadioButtonMenuItem[ fontNames.length ];
105         fontGroup = new ButtonGroup();
106
107         // create Font radio button menu items
108         for ( int count = 0; count < fonts.length; count++ ) {
109            fonts[ count ] = new JRadioButtonMenuItem( fontNames[ count ] );
110            fontMenu.add( fonts[ count ] );
111            fontGroup.add( fonts[ count ] );
112            fonts[ count ].addActionListener( itemHandler );
113         }
114
115         // select first Font menu item
116         fonts[ 0 ].setSelected( true );
117
118         fontMenu.addSeparator();
```

Fig. 14.9   JMenus and mnemonics. (Part 3 of 6.)

```
119
120        // set up style menu items
121        String styleNames[] = { "Bold", "Italic" };
122
123        styleItems = new JCheckBoxMenuItem[ styleNames.length ];
124        StyleHandler styleHandler = new StyleHandler();
125
126        // create style checkbox menu items
127        for ( int count = 0; count < styleNames.length; count++ ) {
128           styleItems[ count ] =
129              new JCheckBoxMenuItem( styleNames[ count ] );
130           fontMenu.add( styleItems[ count ] );
131           styleItems[ count ].addItemListener( styleHandler );
132        }
133
134        // put Font menu in Format menu
135        formatMenu.add( fontMenu );
136
137        // add Format menu to menu bar
138        bar.add( formatMenu );
139
140        // set up label to display text
141        displayLabel = new JLabel( "Sample Text", SwingConstants.CENTER );
142        displayLabel.setForeground( colorValues[ 0 ] );
143        displayLabel.setFont( new Font( "Serif", Font.PLAIN, 72 ) );
144
145        getContentPane().setBackground( Color.CYAN );
146        getContentPane().add( displayLabel, BorderLayout.CENTER );
147
148        setSize( 500, 200 );
149        setVisible( true );
150
151     } // end constructor
152
153     public static void main( String args[] )
154     {
155        MenuTest application = new MenuTest();
156        application.setDefaultCloseOperation( JFrame.EXIT_ON_CLOSE );
157     }
158
159     // inner class to handle action events from menu items
160     private class ItemHandler implements ActionListener {
161
162        // process color and font selections
163        public void actionPerformed( ActionEvent event )
164        {
165           // process color selection
166           for ( int count = 0; count < colorItems.length; count++ )
167
168              if ( colorItems[ count ].isSelected() ) {
169                 displayLabel.setForeground( colorValues[ count ] );
170                 break;
171              }
```

Fig. 14.9   JMenus and mnemonics. (Part 4 of 6.)

```
172
173            // process font selection
174            for ( int count = 0; count < fonts.length; count++ )
175
176               if ( event.getSource() == fonts[ count ] ) {
177                  displayLabel.setFont(
178                     new Font( fonts[ count ].getText(), style, 72 ) );
179                  break;
180               }
181
182            repaint();
183
184         } // end method actionPerformed
185
186      } // end class ItemHandler
187
188      // inner class to handle item events from check box menu items
189      private class StyleHandler implements ItemListener {
190
191         // process font style selections
192         public void itemStateChanged( ItemEvent e )
193         {
194            style = 0;
195
196            // check for bold selection
197            if ( styleItems[ 0 ].isSelected() )
198               style += Font.BOLD;
199
200            // check for italic selection
201            if ( styleItems[ 1 ].isSelected() )
202               style += Font.ITALIC;
203
204            displayLabel.setFont(
205               new Font( displayLabel.getFont().getName(), style, 72 ) );
206
207            repaint();
208         }
209
210      } // end class StyleHandler
211
212   } // end class MenuTest
```

Fig. 14.9   JMenus and mnemonics. (Part 5 of 6.)

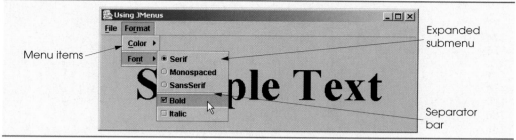

Fig. 14.9   JMenus and mnemonics. (Part 6 of 6.)

Class MenuTest (line 7) declares the GUI components and event handling for the menu items. Most of the code in this application appears in the class's constructor (lines 17–151).

Lines 22–61 set up the **File** menu and attach it to the menu bar. The **File** menu contains an **About...** menu item that displays a message dialog when the menu item is selected and an **Exit** menu item that can be selected to terminate the application.

Line 22 creates JMenu and passes to the constructor the string "File" as the name of the menu. Line 23 uses AbstractButton method *setMnemonic* (inherited into class JMenu) to indicate that F is the *mnemonic* for this menu. Pressing the *Alt* key and the letter *F* opens the menu, just as clicking the menu name with the mouse would. In the GUI, the mnemonic character in the menu's name is displayed with an underline. (See the screen captures in Fig. 14.9.)

Look-and-Feel Observation 14.15

Mnemonics provide quick access to menu commands and button commands through the keyboard.

Look-and-Feel Observation 14.16

*Different mnemonics should be used for each button or menu item. Normally, the first letter in the label on the menu item or button is used as the mnemonic. If multiple buttons or menu items start with the same letter, choose the next most prominent letter in the name (e.g., **x** is commonly chosen for a button or menu item called **Exit**).*

Lines 26–27 create JMenuItem aboutItem with the text "About..." and set its mnemonic to the letter A. This menu item is added to fileMenu at line 28 with JMenu method add. To access the **About...** item through the keyboard, press the *Alt* key and letter *F* to open the **File** menu, then press *A* to select the **About...** menu item. Lines 29–43 create an ActionListener to process aboutItem's action event. Lines 36–38 display a message dialog box. In most prior uses of showMessageDialog, the first argument has been null. The purpose of the first argument is to specify the *parent window* for the dialog box. The parent window helps determine where the dialog box will be displayed. If the parent window is specified as null, the dialog box appears in the center of the screen. If the parent window is not null, the dialog box appears centered over the specified parent window. In this example, the program specifies the parent window with MenuTest.this—the this reference of the MenuTest object. When using the this reference in an inner class, specifying this by itself refers to the inner-class object. To reference the outer-class object's this reference, qualify this with the outer-class name and a dot (.).

Dialog boxes are typically *modal*. A *modal dialog box* does not allow any other window in the application to be accessed until the dialog box is dismissed. The dialogs displayed with class `JOptionPane` are modal dialogs. Class *JDialog* can be used to create your own model or non-modal dialogs.

Lines 46–61 create menu item `exitItem`, set its mnemonic to x, add it to `fileMenu` and register an `ActionListener` that terminates the application when the user selects `exitItem`.

Lines 64–66 create the `JMenuBar`, attach it to the application window with `JFrame` method *setJMenuBar* and use `JMenuBar` method *add* to attach the `fileMenu` to the menu bar.

Common Programming Error 14.5

Forgetting to set the menu bar with `JFrame` method `setJMenuBar` results in the menu bar not being displayed on the `JFrame`.

Look-and-Feel Observation 14.17

Menus normally appear left to right in the order that they are added to a `JMenuBar`.

Lines 69–70 create menu `formatMenu` and set its mnemonic to r. (F is not used because that is the **File** menu's mnemonic.)

Lines 75–76 create menu `colorMenu` (this will be a submenu in the **Format** menu) and set its mnemonic to C. Line 78 creates `JRadioButtonMenuItem` array `colorItems` that refers to the menu items in `colorMenu`. Line 79 creates `ButtonGroup colorGroup`, which will ensure that only one of the menu items in the **Color** submenu is selected at a time. Line 80 creates an instance of inner class `ItemHandler` (declared at lines 160–186) that responds to selections from the **Color** submenu and the **Font** submenu (discussed shortly). The `for` statement at lines 83–89 creates each `JRadioButtonMenuItem` in array `colorItems`, adds each menu item to `colorMenu`, adds each menu item to `colorGroup` and registers the `ActionListener` for each menu item.

Line 92 uses `AbstractButton` method *setSelected* to select the first element in array `colorItems`. Line 95 adds `colorMenu` as a submenu of `formatMenu`. Line 96 adds a *separator* line to the menu. The separator appears as a horizontal line in the menu.

Look-and-Feel Observation 14.18

A submenu is created by adding a menu as a menu item in another menu. When the mouse is positioned over a submenu (or the submenu's mnemonic is pressed), the submenu expands to show its menu items.

Look-and-Feel Observation 14.19

Separators can be added to a menu to group menu items logically.

Look-and-Feel Observation 14.20

Any lightweight GUI component (i.e., a component that subclasses `JComponent`) can be added to a `JMenu` or to a `JMenuBar`.

Lines 101–118 create the **Font** submenu and several `JRadioButtonMenuItems` and select the first element of `JRadioButtonMenuItem` array `fonts`. Line 123 creates a `JCheckBoxMenuItem` array to represent the menu items for specifying bold and italic styles for the fonts. Line 124 creates an instance of inner class StyleHandler (declared at lines 189–210) to respond to the JCheckBoxMenuItem events. The for statement at lines 127–132 creates each JCheckBoxMenuItem, adds each menu item to fontMenu and registers the ItemListener for each menu item. Line 135 adds fontMenu as a submenu of formatMenu. Line 138 adds the formatMenu to bar (the menu bar).

Lines 141–143 create a JLabel for which the **Format** menu items control the font, font color and font style. The initial foreground color is set to the first element of array colorValues (Color.BLACK) and the initial font is set to Serif with PLAIN style and 72-point size. Line 145 sets the background color of the window's content pane to cyan, and line 146 attaches the JLabel to the CENTER of the content pane's BorderLayout.

ItemHandler method actionPerformed (lines 163–184) uses two for statements to determine which font or color menu item generated the event and sets the font or color of the JLabel displayLabel, respectively. The if condition at line 168 uses AbstractButton method *isSelected* to determine the selected JRadioButtonMenu-Item. The if condition at line 176 uses the event object's getSource method to get a reference to the JRadioButtonMenuItem that generated the event. Line 178 uses AbstractButton method getText to obtain the name of the font from the menu item.

The program calls StyleHandler method itemStateChanged (lines 192–208) if the user selects a JCheckBoxMenuItem in the fontMenu. Lines 197 and 201 determine whether either or both of the JCheckBoxMenuItems are selected and use their combined state to determine the new style of the font.

14.8 JPopupMenu

Many of today's computer applications provide so-called *context-sensitive popup menus*. In Swing, such menus are created with class JPopupMenu (a subclass of JComponent). These menus provide options that are specific to the component for which the *popup trigger event* was generated. On most systems, the popup trigger event occurs when the user presses and releases the right mouse button.

Look-and-Feel Observation 14.21

The popup trigger event is platform specific. On most platforms that use a mouse with multiple mouse buttons, the popup trigger event occurs when the user clicks the right mouse button on a component that supports a popup menu.

Figure 14.10 creates a JPopupMenu that allows the user to select one of three colors and change the background color of the window. When the user clicks the right mouse button on the PopupTest window's background, a JPopupMenu containing colors appears. If the user clicks a JRadioButtonMenuItem for a color, ItemHandler method actionPerformed changes the background color of the window's content pane.

```
1   // Fig. 14.10: PopupTest.java
2   // Demonstrating JPopupMenus
3   import java.awt.*;
4   import java.awt.event.*;
5   import javax.swing.*;
```

Fig. 14.10 JPopupMenu for selecting colors. (Part 1 of 3.)

```
6
7    public class PopupTest extends JFrame {
8       private JRadioButtonMenuItem items[];
9       private final Color colorValues[] =
10         { Color.BLUE, Color.YELLOW, Color.RED };
11      private JPopupMenu popupMenu;
12
13      // set up GUI
14      public PopupTest()
15      {
16         super( "Using JPopupMenus" );
17
18         ItemHandler handler = new ItemHandler();
19         String colors[] = { "Blue", "Yellow", "Red" };
20
21         // set up popup menu and its items
22         ButtonGroup colorGroup = new ButtonGroup();
23         popupMenu = new JPopupMenu();
24         items = new JRadioButtonMenuItem[ 3 ];
25
26         // construct each menu item and add to popup menu; also
27         // enable event handling for each menu item
28         for ( int count = 0; count < items.length; count++ ) {
29            items[ count ] = new JRadioButtonMenuItem( colors[ count ] );
30            popupMenu.add( items[ count ] );
31            colorGroup.add( items[ count ] );
32            items[ count ].addActionListener( handler );
33         }
34
35         getContentPane().setBackground( Color.WHITE );
36
37         // declare a MouseListener for the window that displays
38         // a JPopupMenu when the popup trigger event occurs
39         addMouseListener(
40
41            new MouseAdapter() {  // anonymous inner class
42
43               // handle mouse press event
44               public void mousePressed( MouseEvent event )
45               {
46                  checkForTriggerEvent( event );
47               }
48
49               // handle mouse release event
50               public void mouseReleased( MouseEvent event )
51               {
52                  checkForTriggerEvent( event );
53               }
54
55               // determine whether event should trigger popup menu
56               private void checkForTriggerEvent( MouseEvent event )
57               {
```

Fig. 14.10 JPopupMenu for selecting colors. (Part 2 of 3.)

```
58                  if ( event.isPopupTrigger() )
59                     popupMenu.show(
60                        event.getComponent(), event.getX(), event.getY() );
61               }
62
63            } // end anonymous inner clas
64
65        ); // end call to addMouseListener
66
67        setSize( 300, 200 );
68        setVisible( true );
69
70     } // end constructor PopupTest
71
72     public static void main( String args[] )
73     {
74        PopupTest application = new PopupTest();
75        application.setDefaultCloseOperation( JFrame.EXIT_ON_CLOSE );
76     }
77
78     // private inner class to handle menu item events
79     private class ItemHandler implements ActionListener {
80
81        // process menu item selections
82        public void actionPerformed( ActionEvent event )
83        {
84           // determine which menu item was selected
85           for ( int i = 0; i < items.length; i++ )
86              if ( event.getSource() == items[ i ] ) {
87                 getContentPane().setBackground( colorValues[ i ] );
88                 return;
89              }
90        }
91
92     } // end private inner class ItemHandler
93
94  } // end class PopupTest
```

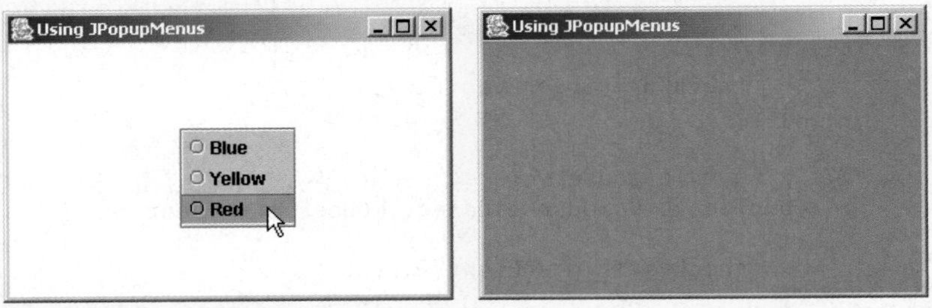

Fig. 14.10 JPopupMenu for selecting colors. (Part 3 of 3.)

Line 18 of the PopupTest constructor (lines 14–70) creates an instance of class ItemHandler (declared in lines 79–92) that will process the item events from the menu items in the popup menu. Line 23 creates the JPopupMenu. The for statement (lines 28–

33) creates a `JRadioButtonMenuItem` object (line 29), adds it to `popupMenu` (line 30), adds it to `ButtonGroup colorGroup` (line 31) to maintain one selected `JRadioButton-MenuItem` at a time and registers its `ActionListener` (line 32). Line 35 sets the initial background to white by invoking method `setBackground` of the content pane.

Lines 39–65 register a `MouseListener` to handle the mouse events of the application window. Methods `mousePressed` (lines 44–47) and `mouseReleased` (lines 50–53) check for the popup-trigger event. Each method calls private utility method `checkForTriggerEvent` (lines 56–61) to determine whether the popup-trigger event occurred. `MouseEvent` method *isPopupTrigger* returns `true` if the popup-trigger event occurred. If so, `JPopupMenu` method *show* displays the `JPopupMenu`. The first argument to method *show* specifies the *origin component,* whose position helps determine where the `JPopupMenu` will appear on the screen. The last two arguments are the *x-y* coordinate (measured from the origin component's upper-left corner) at which the `JPopupMenu` should appear.

 Look-and-Feel Observation 14.22

Displaying a `JPopupMenu` *for the popup-trigger event of multiple GUI components requires registering mouse-event handlers for each of those GUI components.*

When the user selects a menu item from the popup menu, class `ItemHandler`'s method `actionPerformed` (lines 82–90) determines which `JRadioButtonMenuItem` the user selected and sets the background color of the window's content pane.

14.9 Pluggable Look-and-Feel

A program that uses Java's Abstract Window Toolkit GUI components (package *java.awt*) takes on the look-and-feel of the platform on which the program executes. A Java program running on a Macintosh looks like other programs running on a Macintosh. A Java program running on Microsoft Windows looks like other programs running on Microsoft Windows. A Java program running on a UNIX platform looks like other programs running on that UNIX platform. This could be desirable, because it allows users of the program on each platform to use the GUI components with which they are already familiar. However, this also introduces interesting portability issues.

Portability Tip 14.1

GUI components on each platform have different looks that can require different amounts of space to display. This could change the layout and alignments of GUI components.

Portability Tip 14.2

GUI components on each platform have different default functionality (e.g., some platforms allow a button with the focus to be "pressed" with the space bar, and some do not).

Swing's lightweight GUI components eliminate many of these issues by providing uniform functionality across platforms and by defining a uniform cross-platform look-and-feel (known as the *metal* look-and-feel). Swing also provides the flexibility to customize the look-and-feel to appear as a Microsoft Windows-style look-and-feel (on Window systems), a Motif-style (UNIX) look-and-feel (across all platforms) or a Mac look-and-feel (Mac systems).

The program of Fig. 14.11 demonstrates how to change the look-and-feel of a Swing GUI. The program creates several GUI components so you can see the change in the look-

and-feel of several GUI components at the same time. The first output window shows the standard metal look-and-feel, the second output window shows the Motif look-and-feel, and the third output window shows the Windows look-and-feel.

```java
1   // Fig. 14.11: LookAndFeelDemo.java
2   // Changing the look and feel.
3   import java.awt.*;
4   import java.awt.event.*;
5   import javax.swing.*;
6
7   public class LookAndFeelDemo extends JFrame {
8      private final String strings[] = { "Metal", "Motif", "Windows" };
9      private UIManager.LookAndFeelInfo looks[];
10     private JRadioButton radio[];
11     private ButtonGroup group;
12     private JButton button;
13     private JLabel label;
14     private JComboBox comboBox;
15
16     // set up GUI
17     public LookAndFeelDemo()
18     {
19        super( "Look and Feel Demo" );
20
21        Container container = getContentPane();
22
23        // set up panel for NORTH of BorderLayout
24        JPanel northPanel = new JPanel();
25        northPanel.setLayout( new GridLayout( 3, 1, 0, 5 ) );
26
27        // set up label for NORTH panel
28        label = new JLabel( "This is a Metal look-and-feel",
29           SwingConstants.CENTER );
30        northPanel.add( label );
31
32        // set up button for NORTH panel
33        button = new JButton( "JButton" );
34        northPanel.add( button );
35
36        // set up combo box for NORTH panel
37        comboBox = new JComboBox( strings );
38        northPanel.add( comboBox );
39
40        // create array for radio buttons
41        radio = new JRadioButton[ strings.length ];
42
43        // set up panel for SOUTH of BorderLayout
44        JPanel southPanel = new JPanel();
45        southPanel.setLayout( new GridLayout( 1, radio.length ) );
46
47        // set up radio buttons for SOUTH panel
48        group = new ButtonGroup();
```

Fig. 14.11   Look-and-feel of a Swing-based GUI. (Part 1 of 3.)

```
49            ItemHandler handler = new ItemHandler();
50
51            for ( int count = 0; count < radio.length; count++ ) {
52               radio[ count ] = new JRadioButton( strings[ count ] );
53               radio[ count ].addItemListener( handler );
54               group.add( radio[ count ] );
55               southPanel.add( radio[ count ] );
56            }
57
58            // attach NORTH and SOUTH panels to content pane
59            container.add( northPanel, BorderLayout.NORTH );
60            container.add( southPanel, BorderLayout.SOUTH );
61
62            // get installed look-and-feel information
63            looks = UIManager.getInstalledLookAndFeels();
64
65            setSize( 300, 200 );
66            setVisible( true );
67
68            radio[ 0 ].setSelected( true );
69
70         } // end constructor LookAndFeelDemo
71
72         // use UIManager to change look-and-feel of GUI
73         private void changeTheLookAndFeel( int value )
74         {
75            // change look and feel
76            try {
77               UIManager.setLookAndFeel( looks[ value ].getClassName() );
78               SwingUtilities.updateComponentTreeUI( this );
79            }
80
81            // process problems changing look and feel
82            catch ( Exception exception ) {
83               exception.printStackTrace();
84            }
85         }
86
87         public static void main( String args[] )
88         {
89            LookAndFeelDemo application = new LookAndFeelDemo();
90            application.setDefaultCloseOperation( JFrame.EXIT_ON_CLOSE );
91         }
92
93         // private inner class to handle radio button events
94         private class ItemHandler implements ItemListener {
95
96            // process user's look-and-feel selection
97            public void itemStateChanged( ItemEvent event )
98            {
99               for ( int count = 0; count < radio.length; count++ )
100
101                  if ( radio[ count ].isSelected() ) {
```

Fig. 14.11 Look-and-feel of a Swing-based GUI. (Part 2 of 3.)

```
102                  label.setText( "This is a " +
103                     strings[ count ] + " look-and-feel" );
104                  comboBox.setSelectedIndex( count );
105                  changeTheLookAndFeel( count );
106               }
107           }
108
109        } // end private inner class ItemHandler
110
111  } // end class LookAndFeelDemo
```

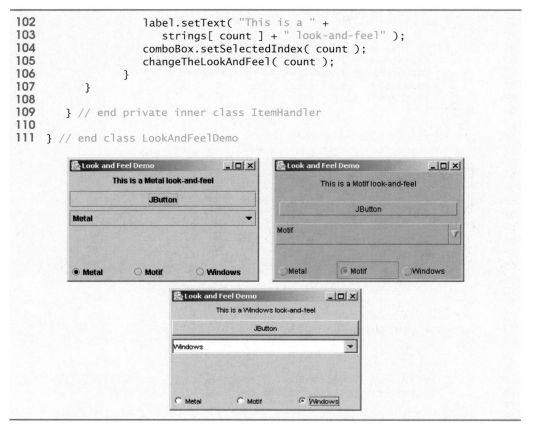

Fig. 14.11 Look-and-feel of a Swing-based GUI. (Part 3 of 3.)

All the GUI components and event handling in this example have been covered before, so we concentrate on the mechanism for changing the look-and-feel in this example. Class *UIManager* (package *javax.swing*) contains nested class *LookAndFeelInfo* (a `public static` class) that maintains information about a look-and-feel. Line 9 declares an array of type UIManager.LookAndFeelInfo (notice the syntax used to identify the inner class LookAndFeelInfo). Line 63 uses UIManager static method *getInstalled-LookAndFeels* to get the array of UIManager.LookAndFeelInfo objects that describe each look-and-feel available on your system.

Performance Tip 14.1

Each look-and-feel is represented by a Java class. UIManager method getInstalledLoo-kAndFeels does not load each class. Rather, it provides the names of the available look-and-feel classes, so a choice of look-and-feel can be made (presumably one time at program start-up). This reduces the overhead of loading additional classes that the program will not use.

Our utility method changeTheLookAndFeel (lines 73–85) is called by the event handler for the JRadioButtons at the bottom of the user interface. The event handler (declared in private inner class ItemHandler at lines 94–109) passes an integer representing the element in array looks that should be used to change the look-and-feel. Line 77 use UIManager static method *setLookAndFeel* to change the look-and-feel. Method *getClass-Name* of class UIManager.LookAndFeelInfo determines the name of the look-and-feel class that corresponds to the UIManager.LookAndFeelInfo object. If the look-and-feel class is not already loaded, it will be loaded as part of the call to setLookAndFeel. Line 78 uses *SwingUtilities* (package javax.swing) static method *updateComponent-TreeUI* to change the look-and-feel of every component attached to its argument (this instance of our application class LookAndFeelDemo) to the new look-and-feel.

Lines 77–78 appear in a special block of code called a *try block*. This code is part of the *exception-handling mechanism* discussed in detail in the next chapter. This code is required in case line 77 attempts to change the look-and-feel to a look-and-feel that does not exist. Lines 82–84 complete the exception-handling mechanism with a *catch clause* that simply processes this problem (if it occurs) by printing an error message at the command line. For now, if you need to change the look-and-feel of your GUI, mimic the code shown in lines 76–84.

14.10 JDesktopPane and JInternalFrame

Many of today's applications use a *multiple-document interface (MDI)*, i.e., a main window (often called the *parent window*) containing other windows (often called *child windows*), to manage several open *documents* that are being processed in parallel. For example, many e-mail programs allow you to have several e-mail windows open at the same time so you can compose or read multiple e-mail messages simultaneously. Similarly, many word processors allow the user to open multiple documents in separate windows so the user can switch between the documents without having to close the current document to open another document. The program of Fig. 14.12 demonstrates Swing's *JDesktopPane* and *JInternalFrame* classes for implementing multiple-document interfaces. The child windows display images in this example.

Lines 16–23 create a JMenuBar, a JMenu and a JMenuItem, add the JMenuItem to the JMenu, add the JMenu to the JMenuBar and set the JMenuBar for the application window. When the user selects the JMenuItem newFrame, the program creates and displays a new JInternalFrame object containing an image.

Line 26 assigns *JDesktopPane* (package javax.swing) reference to a variable theDesktop a new JDesktopPane object that will be used to manage the JInternal-Frame child windows. Line 27 adds the JDesktopPane to the application window's content pane. By default, the JDesktopPane is added to the center of the content pane's BorderLayout, so the JDesktopPane expands to fill the entire application window.

Lines 30–56 register an ActionListener to handle the event when the user selects the newFrame menu item. When the event occurs, method actionPerformed (lines 35–52) creates a JInternalFrame object with lines 38–39. The JInternalFrame constructor used here requires five arguments—a string for the title bar of the internal window, a boolean indicating whether the internal frame should be resizable by the user, a boolean indicating whether the internal frame should be closable by the user, a boolean indicating whether the internal frame should be maximizable by the user and a boolean indicating whether the internal frame should be minimizable by the user. For each of the boolean arguments, a true value indicates that the operation should be allowed (as is the case here).

As with JFrames and JApplets, a JInternalFrame has a content pane to which GUI components can be attached. Line 42 gets a reference to the JInternalFrame's content pane. Line 43 creates an instance of our class MyJPanel (declared at lines 72–101) that is added to the JInternalFrame's content pane at line 44.

```
1   // Fig. 14.12: DesktopTest.java
2   // Demonstrating JDesktopPane.
3   import java.awt.*;
4   import java.awt.event.*;
5   import javax.swing.*;
6
7   public class DesktopTest extends JFrame {
8      private JDesktopPane theDesktop;
9
10     // set up GUI
11     public DesktopTest()
12     {
13        super( "Using a JDesktopPane" );
14
15        // create menu bar, menu and menu item
16        JMenuBar bar = new JMenuBar();
17        JMenu addMenu = new JMenu( "Add" );
18        JMenuItem newFrame = new JMenuItem( "Internal Frame" );
19
20        addMenu.add( newFrame );
21        bar.add( addMenu );
22
23        setJMenuBar( bar );
24
25        // set up desktop
26        theDesktop = new JDesktopPane();
27        getContentPane().add( theDesktop );
28
29        // set up listener for newFrame menu item
30        newFrame.addActionListener(
31
32           new ActionListener() {  // anonymous inner class
33
34              // display new internal window
35              public void actionPerformed( ActionEvent event ) {
36
37                 // create internal frame
38                 JInternalFrame frame = new JInternalFrame(
39                    "Internal Frame", true, true, true, true );
40
41                 // attach panel to internal frame content pane
42                 Container container = frame.getContentPane();
43                 MyJPanel panel = new MyJPanel();
44                 container.add( panel, BorderLayout.CENTER );
45
46                 // set size internal frame to size of its contents
47                 frame.pack();
48
```

Fig. 14.12 Multiple-document interface. (Part 1 of 3.)

```
49                      // attach internal frame to desktop and show it
50                      theDesktop.add( frame );
51                      frame.setVisible( true );
52                  }
53
54              } // end anonymous inner class
55
56          ); // end call to addActionListener
57
58          setSize( 600, 460 );
59          setVisible( true );
60
61      } // end constructor
62
63      public static void main( String args[] )
64      {
65          DesktopTest application = new DesktopTest();
66          application.setDefaultCloseOperation( JFrame.EXIT_ON_CLOSE );
67      }
68
69  } // end class DesktopTest
70
71  // class to display an ImageIcon on a panel
72  class MyJPanel extends JPanel {
73      private ImageIcon imageIcon;
74      private String[] images = { "yellowflowers.png", "purpleflowers.png",
75          "redflowers.png", "redflowers2.png", "lavenderflowers.png" };
76
77      // load image
78      public MyJPanel()
79      {
80          int randomNumber = ( int ) ( Math.random() * 5 );
81          imageIcon = new ImageIcon( images[ randomNumber ] );
82      }
83
84      // display imageIcon on panel
85      public void paintComponent( Graphics g )
86      {
87          // call superclass paintComponent method
88          super.paintComponent( g );
89
90          // display icon
91          imageIcon.paintIcon( this, g, 0, 0 );
92      }
93
94      // return image dimensions
95      public Dimension getPreferredSize()
96      {
97          return new Dimension( imageIcon.getIconWidth(),
98              imageIcon.getIconHeight() );
99      }
100
101  } // end class MyJPanel
```

Fig. 14.12   Multiple-document interface. (Part 2 of 3.)

Fig. 14.12 Multiple-document interface. (Part 3 of 3.)

Line 47 uses `JInternalFrame` method *pack* to set the size of the child window. Method `pack` uses the preferred sizes of the components on the content pane to determine the window's size. Class `MyJPanel` declares method `getPreferredSize` (lines 95–99) to specify the panel's preferred size. Line 50 adds the `JInternalFrame` to the `JDesktopPane`, and line 51 displays the `JInternalFrame`.

Classes `JInternalFrame` and `JDesktopPane` provide many methods for managing child windows. See the `JInternalFrame` and `JDesktopPane` online API documentation for complete lists of these methods:

```
java.sun.com/j2se/1.4.1/docs/api/javax/swing/JInternalFrame.html
java.sun.com/j2se/1.4.1/docs/api/javax/swing/JDesktopPane.html
```

14.11 JTabbedPane

A *JTabbedPane* arranges GUI components into layers in which only one layer is visible at a time. Users access each layer via a tab—similar to folders in a file cabinet. When the user clicks a tab, the appropriate layer is displayed. The tabs appear at the top by default, but also can be positioned at the left, right or bottom of the `JTabbedPane`. Any component can be placed on a tab. If the component is a container, such as a panel, it can use any layout manager to layout several components on that tab. Class `JTabbedPane` is a subclass of `JComponent`. The program of Fig. 14.13 creates one tabbed pane with three tabs. Each tab displays one of the `JPanel`s—panel1, panel2 or panel3.

```java
1   // Fig. 14.13: JTabbedPaneDemo.java
2   // Demonstrating JTabbedPane.
3   import java.awt.*;
4   import javax.swing.*;
5
6   public class JTabbedPaneDemo extends JFrame {
7
8      // set up GUI
9      public JTabbedPaneDemo()
10     {
11        super( "JTabbedPane Demo " );
12
13        // create JTabbedPane
14        JTabbedPane tabbedPane = new JTabbedPane();
15
16        // set up panel1 and add it to JTabbedPane
17        JLabel label1 = new JLabel( "panel one", SwingConstants.CENTER );
18        JPanel panel1 = new JPanel();
19        panel1.add( label1 );
20        tabbedPane.addTab( "Tab One", null, panel1, "First Panel" );
21
22        // set up panel2 and add it to JTabbedPane
23        JLabel label2 = new JLabel( "panel two", SwingConstants.CENTER );
24        JPanel panel2 = new JPanel();
25        panel2.setBackground( Color.YELLOW );
26        panel2.add( label2 );
27        tabbedPane.addTab( "Tab Two", null, panel2, "Second Panel" );
```

Fig. 14.13 JTabbedPane used to organize GUI components. (Part 1 of 2.)

```
28
29        // set up panel3 and add it to JTabbedPane
30        JLabel label3 = new JLabel( "panel three" );
31        JPanel panel3 = new JPanel();
32        panel3.setLayout( new BorderLayout() );
33        panel3.add( new JButton( "North" ), BorderLayout.NORTH );
34        panel3.add( new JButton( "West" ), BorderLayout.WEST );
35        panel3.add( new JButton( "East" ), BorderLayout.EAST );
36        panel3.add( new JButton( "South" ), BorderLayout.SOUTH );
37        panel3.add( label3, BorderLayout.CENTER );
38        tabbedPane.addTab( "Tab Three", null, panel3, "Third Panel" );
39
40        // add JTabbedPane to container
41        getContentPane().add( tabbedPane );
42
43        setSize( 250, 200 );
44        setVisible( true );
45
46     } // end constructor
47
48     public static void main( String args[] )
49     {
50        JTabbedPaneDemo tabbedPaneDemo = new JTabbedPaneDemo();
51        tabbedPaneDemo.setDefaultCloseOperation( JFrame.EXIT_ON_CLOSE );
52     }
53
54  } // end class CardDeck
```

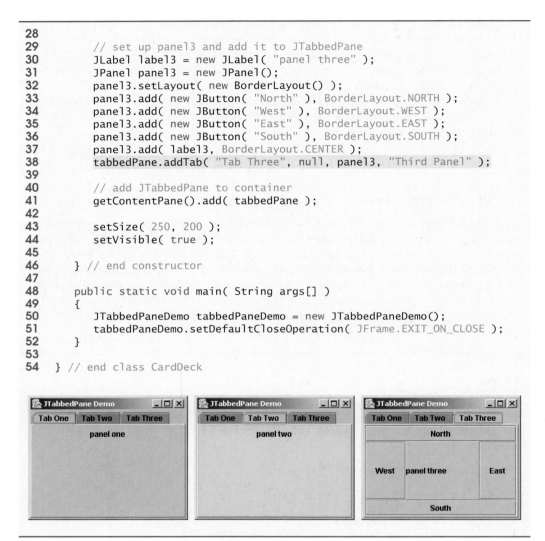

Fig. 14.13   JTabbedPane used to organize GUI components. (Part 2 of 2.)

The constructor (lines 9–46) builds the GUI. Line 14 creates an empty JTabbedPane with default settings—i.e., tabs across the top. If the tabs do not fit on one line, they will wrap to form additional lines of tabs. Next, the constructor creates the JPanels panel1, panel2 and panel3 and their GUI components. As we set up each panel, we add the panel to tabbedPane, using JTabbedPane method addTab with four arguments. The first argument is a string that specifies the title of the tab. The second argument is an Icon reference that specifies an icon to display on the tab. If the Icon is a null reference, no image is displayed. The third argument is a Component reference that represents the GUI component to display when the user clicks the tab. The last argument is a string that specifies the tool tip for the tab. For example, line 20 adds JPanel panel1 to tabbedPane with title "Tab One" and the tool tip "First Panel". JPanels panel2 and panel3 are added to tabbedPane at lines 27 and 38. To view each tab, click the tab with the mouse or use the arrow keys to cycle through the tabs.

14.12 Layout Managers: BoxLayout and GridBagLayout

In the preceding chapter, we introduced three layout managers—FlowLayout, BorderLayout and GridLayout. This section presents two additional layout managers (summarized in Figure 14.14). We discuss these layout managers in the examples that follow.

BoxLayout *Layout Manager*

The *BoxLayout layout manager* arranges GUI components horizontally along the *x*-axis or vertically along the *y*-axis of a container. The program of Fig. 14.15 demonstrates BoxLayout and the container class Box that uses BoxLayout as its default layout manager.

Layout Manager	Description
BoxLayout	A layout manager that allows GUI components to be arranged left-to-right or top-to-bottom in a container. Class *Box* declares a container with BoxLayout as its default layout manager and provides static methods to create a Box with a horizontal or vertical BoxLayout.
GridBagLayout	A layout manager similar to GridLayout. Unlike GridLayout, each component size can vary and components can be added in any order.

Fig. 14.14 Additional layout managers.

```
1   // Fig. 14.15: BoxLayoutDemo.java
2   // Demonstrating BoxLayout.
3   import java.awt.*;
4   import java.awt.event.*;
5   import javax.swing.*;
6
7   public class BoxLayoutDemo extends JFrame {
8
9      // set up GUI
10     public BoxLayoutDemo()
11     {
12        super( "Demostrating BoxLayout" );
13
14        // create Box containers with BoxLayout
15        Box horizontal1 = Box.createHorizontalBox();
16        Box vertical1 = Box.createVerticalBox();
17        Box horizontal2 = Box.createHorizontalBox();
18        Box vertical2 = Box.createVerticalBox();
19
20        final int SIZE = 3; // number of buttons on each Box
21
22        // add buttons to Box horizontal1
23        for ( int count = 0; count < SIZE; count++ )
24           horizontal1.add( new JButton( "Button " + count ) );
```

Fig. 14.15 BoxLayout layout manager. (Part 1 of 3.)

```
25
26        // create strut and add buttons to Box vertical1
27        for ( int count = 0; count < SIZE; count++ ) {
28           vertical1.add( Box.createVerticalStrut( 25 ) );
29           vertical1.add( new JButton( "Button " + count ) );
30        }
31
32        // create horizontal glue and add buttons to Box horizontal2
33        for ( int count = 0; count < SIZE; count++ ) {
34           horizontal2.add( Box.createHorizontalGlue() );
35           horizontal2.add( new JButton( "Button " + count ) );
36        }
37
38        // create rigid area and add buttons to Box vertical2
39        for ( int count = 0; count < SIZE; count++ ) {
40           vertical2.add( Box.createRigidArea( new Dimension( 12, 8 ) ) );
41           vertical2.add( new JButton( "Button " + count ) );
42        }
43
44        // create vertical glue and add buttons to panel
45        JPanel panel = new JPanel();
46        panel.setLayout( new BoxLayout( panel, BoxLayout.Y_AXIS ) );
47
48        for ( int count = 0; count < SIZE; count++ ) {
49           panel.add( Box.createGlue() );
50           panel.add( new JButton( "Button " + count ) );
51        }
52
53        // create a JTabbedPane
54        JTabbedPane tabs = new JTabbedPane(
55           JTabbedPane.TOP, JTabbedPane.SCROLL_TAB_LAYOUT );
56
57        // place each container on tabbed pane
58        tabs.addTab( "Horizontal Box", horizontal1 );
59        tabs.addTab( "Vertical Box with Struts", vertical1 );
60        tabs.addTab( "Horizontal Box with Glue", horizontal2 );
61        tabs.addTab( "Vertical Box with Rigid Areas", vertical2 );
62        tabs.addTab( "Vertical Box with Glue", panel );
63
64        getContentPane().add( tabs );   // place tabbed pane on content pane
65
66        setSize( 400, 220 );
67        setVisible( true );
68
69     } // end constructor
70
71     public static void main( String args[] )
72     {
73        BoxLayoutDemo application = new BoxLayoutDemo();
74        application.setDefaultCloseOperation( JFrame.EXIT_ON_CLOSE );
75     }
76
77  } // end class BoxLayoutDemo
```

Fig. 14.15 BoxLayout layout manager. (Part 2 of 3.)

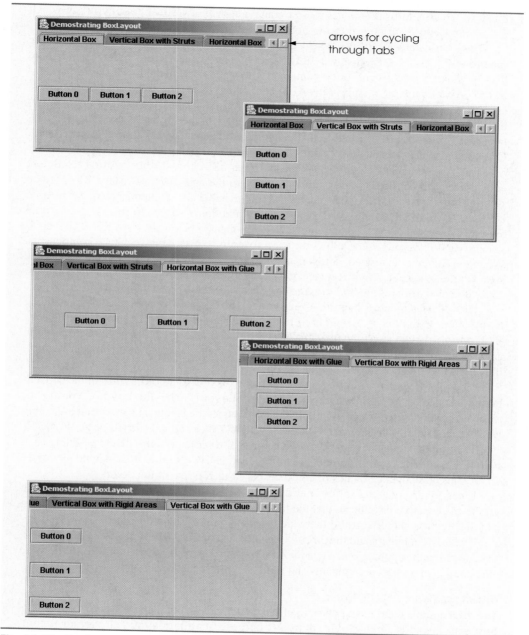

arrows for cycling through tabs

Fig. 14.15 BoxLayout layout manager. (Part 3 of 3.)

Lines 15–18 create Box containers. References horizontal1 and horizontal2 are initialized with static Box method *createHorizontalBox*, which returns a Box container with a horizontal BoxLayout in which GUI components are arranged left-to-right. Variables vertical1 and vertical2 are initialized with static Box method *createVerti-*

calBox, which returns references to Box containers with a vertical BoxLayout in which GUI components are arranged top-to-bottom.

The for statement at lines 23–24 adds three JButtons to horizontal1. The for statement at lines 27–30 adds three JButtons to vertical1. Before adding each button, line 28 adds a *vertical strut* to the container with static Box method *createVerticalStrut*. A vertical strut is an invisible GUI component that has a fixed pixel height and is used to guarantee a fixed amount of space between GUI components. The argument to method createVerticalStrut determines the height of the strut in pixels. When the container is resized, the distance between GUI components separated by struts does not change. Class Box also declares method *createHorizontalStrut* for horizontal BoxLayouts.

The for statement at lines 33–36 adds three JButtons to horizontal2. Before adding each button, line 34 adds *horizontal glue* to the container with static Box method *createHorizontalGlue*. Horizontal glue is an invisible GUI component that can be used between fixed-size GUI components to occupy additional space. Normally, extra space appears to the right of the last horizontal GUI component or below the last vertical GUI component in a BoxLayout. Glue allows the extra space to be placed between GUI components. When the container is resized, components separated by glue components remain the same size, but the glue stretches or contracts to occupy the space between the other components. Class Box also declares method *createVerticalGlue* for vertical BoxLayouts.

The for statement at lines 39–42 adds three JButtons to vertical2. Before adding each button, line 40 adds a *rigid area* to the container with static Box method *createRigidArea*. A rigid area is an invisible GUI component that always has a fixed pixel width and height. The argument to method createRigidArea is a Dimension object that specifies the width and height of the rigid area.

Lines 45–46 create a JPanel object and set its layout to a BoxLayout in the conventional manner, using Container method setLayout. The BoxLayout constructor receives a reference to the container for which it controls the layout and a constant indicating whether the layout is horizontal (*BoxLayout.X_AXIS*) or vertical (*BoxLayout.Y_AXIS*).

The for statement at lines 48–51 adds three JButtons to panel1.Before adding each button, line 49 adds a glue component to the container with static Box method *createGlue*. This component expands or contracts based on the size of the Box.

Lines 54–55 create a JTabbedPane to display the five containers in this program. The args to the constructor indicate that the tabs should appear at the top of the JTabbedPane and that the tabs should scroll if there are too many tabs to fit on one line.

The Box containers and the JPanel are attached to the JTabbedPane at lines 58–62. Try executing the application. When the window appears, resize the window to see how the glue components, strut components and rigid area affect the layout on each tab.

GridBagLayout Layout Manager

The most complex and most powerful of the predefined layout managers is *GridBagLayout*. This layout is similar to GridLayout because GridBagLayout also arranges components in a grid. However, GridBagLayout is more flexible. The components can vary in size (i.e., they can occupy multiple rows and columns) and can be added in any order.

The first step in using GridBagLayout is determining the appearance of the GUI. This step does not involve any programming; all that is needed is a piece of paper. First, draw the GUI. Next draw a grid over the GUI dividing the components into rows and columns. The initial row and column numbers should be 0 so the GridBagLayout layout manager can properly place the components in the grid. The row and column numbers will be used to place each component in an exact position in the grid. Figure 14.16 demonstrates drawing the lines for the rows and columns over a GUI.

A *GridBagConstraints* object describes how a component is placed in a GridBag-Layout. Several GridBagConstraints fields are summarized in Fig. 14.17.

Variables *gridx* and *gridy* specify the row and column can be "relative" as well where the upper-left corner of the component is placed in the grid. Variable gridx corresponds to the column and the variable gridy corresponds to the row. In Fig. 14.16, the JComboBox (displaying "Iron") has a gridx value of 1 and a gridy value of 2.

Variable *gridwidth* specifies the number of columns a component occupies. The JComboBox occupies two columns. Variable *gridheight* specifies the number of rows a component occupies. The JTextArea on the left side of the window occupies three rows.

Variable *weightx* specifies how to distribute extra horizontal space to grid slots in a GridBagLayout when the container is resized. A zero value indicates that the grid slot does not grow horizontally on its own. However, if the component spans a column con-

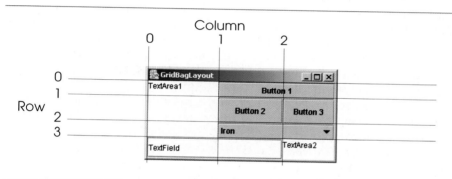

Fig. 14.16 Designing a GUI that will use GridBagLayout.

GridBagConstraints field	Description
fill	Resize the component in specified direction (NONE, HORIZONTAL, VERTICAL, BOTH) when the display area is larger than the component.
gridx	The column in which the component will be placed.
gridy	The row in which the component will be placed.
gridwidth	The number of columns the component occupies.
gridheight	The number of rows the component occupies.
weightx	The portion of extra space to allocate horizontally. The grid slot can become wider when extra space is available.
weighty	The portion of extra space to allocate vertically. The grid slot can become taller when extra space is available.

Fig. 14.17 GridBagConstraints fields.

taining a component with nonzero `weightx` value, the component with zero `weightx` value will grow horizontally in the same proportion as the other component(s) in the same column. This is because each component must be maintained in the same row and column in which it was originally placed.

Variable *weighty* specifies how to distribute extra vertical space to grid slots in a `GridBagLayout` when the container is resized. A zero value indicates that the grid slot does not grow vertically on its own. However, if the component spans a row containing a component with nonzero `weighty` value, the component with zero `weighty` value grows vertically in the same proportion as the other component(s) in the same row.

In Fig. 14.16, the effects of `weighty` and `weightx` cannot easily be seen until the container is resized and additional space becomes available. Components with larger weight values occupy more of the additional space than components with smaller weight values.

Components should be given nonzero positive weight values—otherwise the components will "huddle" together in the middle of the container. Figure 14.18 shows the GUI of Fig. 14.16 with all weights have been set to zero.

`GridBagConstraints` field `fill` defines how the component grows if the area in which the component can be displayed is larger than the component. The variable `fill` is assigned one of the following `GridBagConstraints` constants: *NONE*, *VERTICAL*, *HORIZONTAL* or *BOTH*. The default value is NONE, which indicates that the component will not grow in either direction. VERTICAL indicates that the component will grow vertically. HORIZONTAL indicates that the component will grow horizontally. BOTH indicates that the component will grow in both directions.

`GridBagConstraints` field *anchor* specifies the relative position of the component in an area when the component does not fill the entire area. The variable `anchor` is assigned one of the following `GridBagConstraints` constants: *NORTH*, *NORTHEAST*, *EAST*, *SOUTHEAST*, *SOUTH*, *SOUTHWEST*, *WEST*, *NORTHWEST* or *CENTER*. The default value is CENTER.

The program of Fig. 14.19 uses the `GridBagLayout` layout manager to arrange the components in the GUI of Fig. 14.16. The program does nothing other than demonstrate how to use `GridBagLayout`.

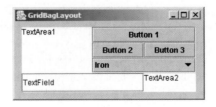

Fig. 14.18 `GridBagLayout` with the weights set to zero.

```
1    // Fig. 14.19: GridBagDemo.java
2    // Demonstrating GridBagLayout.
3    import java.awt.*;
4    import java.awt.event.*;
```

Fig. 14.19 `GridBagLayout` layout manager. (Part 1 of 4.)

```
 5   import javax.swing.*;
 6
 7   public class GridBagDemo extends JFrame {
 8      private Container container;
 9      private GridBagLayout layout;
10      private GridBagConstraints constraints;
11
12      // set up GUI
13      public GridBagDemo()
14      {
15         super( "GridBagLayout" );
16
17         container = getContentPane();
18         layout = new GridBagLayout();
19         container.setLayout( layout );
20
21         // instantiate gridbag constraints
22         constraints = new GridBagConstraints();
23
24         // create GUI components
25         JTextArea textArea1 = new JTextArea( "TextArea1", 5, 10 );
26         JTextArea textArea2 = new JTextArea( "TextArea2", 2, 2 );
27
28         String names[] = { "Iron", "Steel", "Brass" };
29         JComboBox comboBox = new JComboBox( names );
30
31         JTextField textField = new JTextField( "TextField" );
32         JButton button1 = new JButton( "Button 1" );
33         JButton button2 = new JButton( "Button 2" );
34         JButton button3 = new JButton( "Button 3" );
35
36         // weightx and weighty for textArea1 are both 0: the default
37         // anchor for all components is CENTER: the default
38         constraints.fill = GridBagConstraints.BOTH;
39         addComponent( textArea1, 0, 0, 1, 3 );
40
41         // weightx and weighty for button1 are both 0: the default
42         constraints.fill = GridBagConstraints.HORIZONTAL;
43         addComponent( button1, 0, 1, 2, 1 );
44
45         // weightx and weighty for comboBox are both 0: the default
46         // fill is HORIZONTAL
47         addComponent( comboBox, 2, 1, 2, 1 );
48
49         // button2
50         constraints.weightx = 1000;  // can grow wider
51         constraints.weighty = 1;       // can grow taller
52         constraints.fill = GridBagConstraints.BOTH;
53         addComponent( button2, 1, 1, 1, 1 );
54
55         // fill is BOTH for button3
56         constraints.weightx = 0;
57         constraints.weighty = 0;
```

Fig. 14.19 GridBagLayout layout manager. (Part 2 of 4.)

```
58              addComponent( button3, 1, 2, 1, 1 );
59
60              // weightx and weighty for textField are both 0, fill is BOTH
61              addComponent( textField, 3, 0, 2, 1 );
62
63              // weightx and weighty for textArea2 are both 0, fill is BOTH
64              addComponent( textArea2, 3, 2, 1, 1 );
65
66              setSize( 300, 150 );
67              setVisible( true );
68
69          } // end constructor GridBagDemo
70
71          // method to set constraints on
72          private void addComponent( Component component,
73              int row, int column, int width, int height )
74          {
75              // set gridx and gridy
76              constraints.gridx = column;
77              constraints.gridy = row;
78
79              // set gridwidth and gridheight
80              constraints.gridwidth = width;
81              constraints.gridheight = height;
82
83              // set constraints and add component
84              layout.setConstraints( component, constraints );
85              container.add( component );
86          }
87
88          public static void main( String args[] )
89          {
90              GridBagDemo application = new GridBagDemo();
91              application.setDefaultCloseOperation( JFrame.EXIT_ON_CLOSE );
92          }
93
94      } // end class GridBagDemo
```

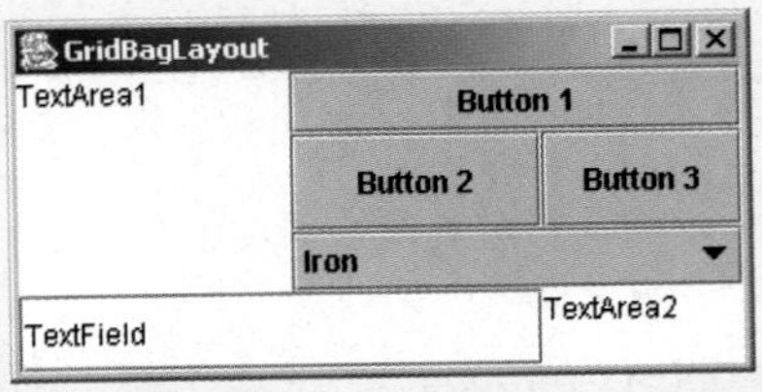

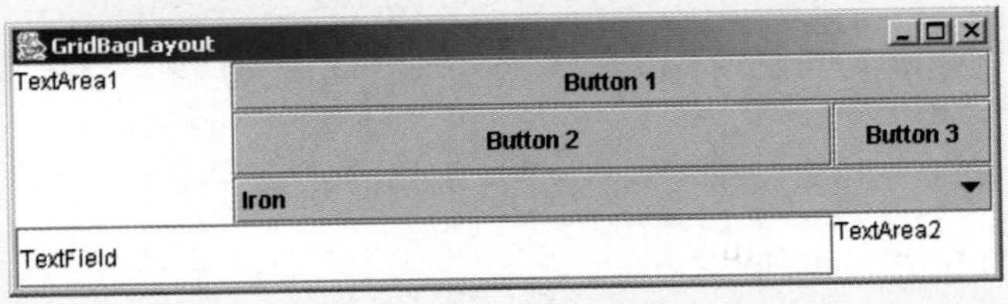

Fig. 14.19 GridBagLayout layout manager. (Part 3 of 4.)

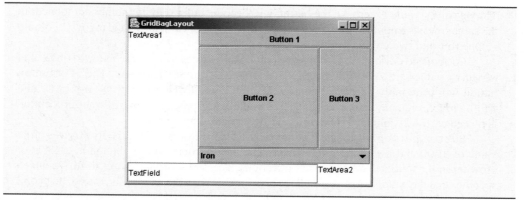

Fig. 14.19   GridBagLayout layout manager. (Part 4 of 4.)

The GUI consists of three JButtons, two JTextAreas, a JComboBox and a JText-Field. The layout manager for the content pane is GridBagLayout. Lines 18–19 create the GridBagLayout object and set the layout manager for the content pane to layout. Line 22 creates the GridBagConstraints object used to determine the location and size of each component in the grid. Lines 25–34 create each GUI component that will be added to the content pane.

Lines 38–39 configure JTextArea textArea1 and add it to the content pane. The values for weightx and weighty values are not specified in constraints, so each has the value zero by default. Thus, the JTextArea will not resize itself even if space is available. However, the JTextArea spans multiple rows, so the vertical size is subject to the weighty values of JButtons button2 and button3. When either button2 or button3 is resized vertically based on its weighty value, the JTextArea is also resized.

Line 38 sets variable fill in constraints to GridBagConstraints.BOTH, causing the JTextArea to always fill its entire allocated area in the grid. An anchor value is not specified in constraints, so the default CENTER is used. We do not use variable anchor in this program, so all components will use the default. Line 39 calls our utility method *addComponent* (declared at lines 72–86). The JTextArea object, the row, the column, the number of columns to span and the number of rows to span are passed as arguments.

Method addComponent's parameters are a Component reference component and integers row, column, width and height. Lines 76–77 set the GridBagConstraints variables gridx and gridy. The gridx variable is assigned the column in which the Component will be placed, and the gridy value is assigned the row in which the Component will be placed. Lines 80–81 set the GridBagConstraints variables gridwidth and gridheight. The gridwidth variable specifies the number of columns the Component will span in the grid and the gridheight variable specifies the number of rows the Component will span in the grid. Line 84 sets the GridBagConstraints for a component in the GridBagLayout. Method *setConstraints* of class GridBagLayout takes a Component argument and a GridBagConstraints argument. Line 85 adds the component to the content pane.

JButton button1 is the next component added (lines 42–43). The values of weightx and weighty are still zero. The fill variable is set to HORIZONTAL—the component will always fill its area in the horizontal direction. The vertical direction is not filled.

The `weighty` value is zero, so the button will become taller only if another component in the same row has a nonzero `weighty` value. `JButton button1` is located at row 0, column 1. One row and two columns are occupied.

`JComboBox comboBox` is the next component added (line 47). The `weightx` and `weighty` values are zero, and the `fill` variable is set to HORIZONTAL. The `JComboBox` button will grow only in the horizontal direction. Note that the `weightx`, `weighty` and `fill` variables remain set in `constraints` until they are changed. The `JComboBox` button is placed at row 2, column 1. One row and two columns are occupied.

`JButton button2` is the next component added (lines 50–53). It is given a `weightx` value of 1000 and a `weighty` value of 1. The area occupied by the button is capable of growing in the vertical and horizontal directions. The `fill` variable is set to BOTH, which specifies that the button will always fill the entire area. When the window is resized, `button2` will grow. The button is placed at row 1, column 1. One row and one column are occupied.

`JButton button3` is added next (lines 56–58). Both the `weightx` value and `weighty` value are set to zero, and the value of `fill` is BOTH. `JButton button3` will grow if the window is resized; it is affected by the weight values of `button2`. Note that the `weightx` value for `button2` is much larger that of than `button3`. When resizing occurs, `button2` will occupy a larger percentage of the new space. The button is placed at row 1, column 2. One row and one column are occupied.

Both the `JTextField textField` (line 61) and `JTextArea textArea2` (line 64) have a `weightx` value 0 and a `weighty` value 0. The value of `fill` is BOTH. The `JTextField` is placed at row 3, column 0, and the `JTextArea` is placed at row 3, column 2. The `JTextField` occupies one row and two columns. The `JTextArea` occupies one row and one column.

When you execute this application, try resizing the window to see how the constraints for each GUI component affect its position and size in the window.

GridBagConstraints Constants *RELATIVE and REMAINDER*

A variation of `GridBagLayout` does not use `gridx` and `gridy`. Rather, `GridBagConstraints` constants *RELATIVE* and *REMAINDER* are used in their place. RELATIVE specifies that the next-to-last component in a particular row should be placed to the right of the previous component in that row. REMAINDER specifies that a component is the last component in a row. Any component that is not the second-to-last or last component on a row must specify values for `GridbagConstraints` variables `gridwidth` and `gridheight`. Class `GridBagDemo2` in Fig. 14.20 arranges components in `GridBagLayout`, using these constants.

```
1   // Fig. 14.20: GridBagDemo2.java
2   // Demonstrating GridBagLayout constants.
3   import java.awt.*;
4   import java.awt.event.*;
5   import javax.swing.*;
6
7   public class GridBagDemo2 extends JFrame {
8      private GridBagLayout layout;
9      private GridBagConstraints constraints;
10     private Container container;
```

Fig. 14.20 `GridBagConstraints` constants RELATIVE and REMAINDER. (Part 1 of 3.)

```java
11
12      // set up GUI
13      public GridBagDemo2()
14      {
15         super( "GridBagLayout" );
16
17         container = getContentPane();
18         layout = new GridBagLayout();
19         container.setLayout( layout );
20
21         // instantiate gridbag constraints
22         constraints = new GridBagConstraints();
23
24         // create GUI components
25         String metals[] = { "Copper", "Aluminum", "Silver" };
26         JComboBox comboBox = new JComboBox( metals );
27
28         JTextField textField = new JTextField( "TextField" );
29
30         String fonts[] = { "Serif", "Monospaced" };
31         JList list = new JList( fonts );
32
33         String names[] = { "zero", "one", "two", "three", "four" };
34         JButton buttons[] = new JButton[ names.length ];
35
36         for ( int count = 0; count < buttons.length; count++ )
37            buttons[ count ] = new JButton( names[ count ] );
38
39         // define GUI component constraints for textField
40         constraints.weightx = 1;
41         constraints.weighty = 1;
42         constraints.fill = GridBagConstraints.BOTH;
43         constraints.gridwidth = GridBagConstraints.REMAINDER;
44         addComponent( textField );
45
46         // buttons[0] -- weightx and weighty are 1: fill is BOTH
47         constraints.gridwidth = 1;
48         addComponent( buttons[ 0 ] );
49
50         // buttons[1] -- weightx and weighty are 1: fill is BOTH
51         constraints.gridwidth = GridBagConstraints.RELATIVE;
52         addComponent( buttons[ 1 ] );
53
54         // buttons[2] -- weightx and weighty are 1: fill is BOTH
55         constraints.gridwidth = GridBagConstraints.REMAINDER;
56         addComponent( buttons[ 2 ] );
57
58         // comboBox -- weightx is 1: fill is BOTH
59         constraints.weighty = 0;
60         constraints.gridwidth = GridBagConstraints.REMAINDER;
61         addComponent( comboBox );
62
```

Fig. 14.20 GridBagConstraints constants RELATIVE and REMAINDER. (Part 2 of 3.)

```
63        // buttons[3] -- weightx is 1: fill is BOTH
64        constraints.weighty = 1;
65        constraints.gridwidth = GridBagConstraints.REMAINDER;
66        addComponent( buttons[ 3 ] );
67
68        // buttons[4] -- weightx and weighty are 1: fill is BOTH
69        constraints.gridwidth = GridBagConstraints.RELATIVE;
70        addComponent( buttons[ 4 ] );
71
72        // list -- weightx and weighty are 1: fill is BOTH
73        constraints.gridwidth = GridBagConstraints.REMAINDER;
74        addComponent( list );
75
76        setSize( 300, 200 );
77        setVisible( true );
78
79    }  // end constructor
80
81    // add a Component to the container
82    private void addComponent( Component component )
83    {
84        layout.setConstraints( component, constraints );
85        container.add( component );        // add component
86    }
87
88    public static void main( String args[] )
89    {
90        GridBagDemo2 application = new GridBagDemo2();
91        application.setDefaultCloseOperation( JFrame.EXIT_ON_CLOSE );
92    }
93
94  }  // end class GridBagDemo2
```

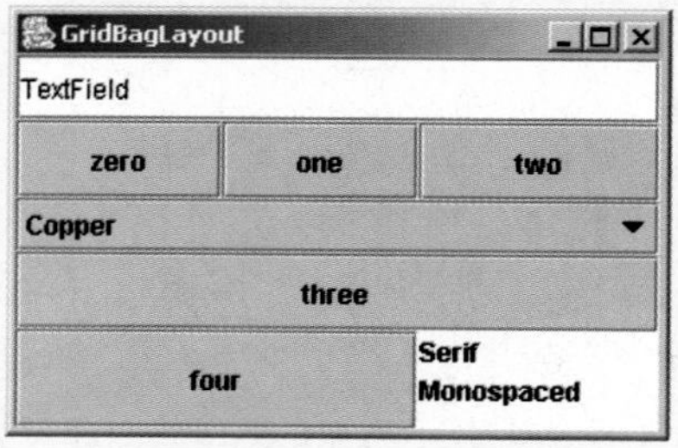

Fig. 14.20 GridBagConstraints constants RELATIVE and REMAINDER. (Part 3 of 3.)

Lines 18–19 create a GridBagLayout and use it to set the content pane's layout manager. The components that are placed in GridBagLayout are created in lines 25–37. The components are five JButtons, a JTextField, a JList and a JComboBox.

The JTextField is added first (lines 40–44). The weightx and weighty values are set to 1. The fill variable is set to BOTH. Line 43 specifies that the JTextField is the last component on the line. The JTextField is added to the content pane with a call to our utility method addComponent (declared at lines 82–86). Method addComponent takes a

Component argument and uses GridBagLayout method setConstraints to set the constraints for the Component. Method add attaches the component to the content pane.

JButton buttons[0] (lines 47–48) has weightx and weighty values of 1. The fill variable is BOTH. Because buttons[0] is not one of the last two components on the row, it is given a gridwidth of 1 so it will occupy one column. The JButton is added to the content pane with a call to utility method addComponent.

JButton buttons[1] (lines 51–52) has weightx and weighty values of 1. The fill variable is BOTH. Line 51 specifies that the JButton is to be placed relative to the previous component. The Button is added to the JFrame with a call to addComponent.

JButton buttons[2] (lines 55–56) has weightx and weighty values of 1. The fill variable is BOTH. This JButton is the last component on the line, so REMAINDER is used. The JButton is added to the content pane with a call to addComponent.

The JComboBox (lines 59–61) has a weightx of 1 and a weighty of 0. The JComboBox will not grow in the vertical direction. The JComboBox is the only component on the line, so REMAINDER is used. The JComboBox is added to the content pane with a call to addComponent.

JButton buttons[3] (lines 64–66) has weightx and weighty values of 1. The fill variable is BOTH. This JButton is the only component on the line, so REMAINDER is used. The JButton is added to the content pane with a call to addComponent.

JButton buttons[4] (lines 69–70) has weightx and weighty values of 1. The fill variable is BOTH. This JButton is the next-to-last component on the line, so RELATIVE is used. The JButton is added to the content pane with a call to addComponent.

The JList (lines 73–74) has weightx and weighty values of 1. The fill variable is BOTH. The JList is added to the content pane with a call to addComponent.

14.13 (Optional Case Study) Thinking About Objects: Model-View-Controller

Design patterns describe proven strategies for building reliable object-oriented software systems. Our case study adheres to the *Model-View-Controller* (MVC) architecture, which uses several design patterns.[2] MVC divides system responsibilities into three parts:

1. the *model*, which maintains program data and logic;

2. the *view* (or views), which provides a visual presentation of the model and

3. the *controller*, which processes user input and makes modifications to the model.

Using the controller, the user changes the data in the MVC model. The MVC model then informs the views of the change in data. The view changes its visual presentation to reflect the changes in the MVC model.

For example, in our simulation, the user adds a Person to the MVC model by pressing either the **First Floor** or **Second Floor** JButton in the controller (see Fig. 2.22–Fig. 2.24). The MVC model then notifies the view that the Person was created. The view, in response to this notification, displays a Person on a Floor. The MVC model is unaware

---

2. For those readers who seek further study in design patterns and MVC architecture, we encourage you to read our "Discovering Design Patterns" material in Sections 1.16, 9.24, 13.18, 15.13, 17.11 and 21.12

of how the view displays the Person, and the view is unaware of how or why the MVC model created the Person.

The MVC architecture helps construct reliable and easily modifiable systems. If we desire text-based output rather than graphical output for the elevator simulation, we may create an alternate view to produce text-based output, without altering the MVC model or the controller. We could also provide a three-dimensional view that uses a first-person perspective to allow the user to "take part" in the simulation; such views are commonly employed in virtual-reality-based systems.

Model-View-Controller Elevator Simulation

We now apply the MVC architecture to our elevator simulation. Each UML diagram we have provided to this point models a portion of the MVC model of our elevator system. We provide a "higher-level" UML model of the simulation in Fig. 14.21. Class ElevatorCaseStudy—a JFrame subclass—aggregates one instance each of classes ElevatorSimulation, ElevatorView and ElevatorController to create the ElevatorCaseStudy application. In the UML, a rectangle with the upper-right corner "folded over" represents a *note*. In this case, each note points to a specific class (with a dotted line) to describe that class' role in the system. Classes ElevatorSimulation, ElevatorView and ElevatorController encapsulate all objects comprising the MVC model, view and controller portions of our simulation, respectively.

Class ElevatorSimulation is an aggregation of several classes (e.g., ElevatorShaft, Elevator and Floor). To save space, we do not model this aggregation in Fig. 14.21. Class ElevatorView is also an aggregation of several classes—we expand the UML model of ElevatorView in Section 19.7 to show these additional classes. Class ElevatorController represents the simulation controller. Note that class ElevatorView implements interface ElevatorSimulationListener, which enables the ElevatorView to receive events from the MVC model.

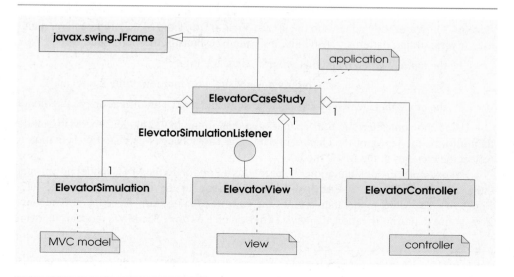

Fig. 14.21   Class diagram of the elevator simulation.

Software Engineering Observation 14.1

When appropriate, partition a UML model into several smaller diagrams, so each diagram represents a unique subsystem.

Class `ElevatorCaseStudy` contains no attributes other than its references to an `ElevatorSimulation` object, an `ElevatorView` object and an `ElevatorController` object. The only behavior for class `ElevatorCaseStudy` is to start the program—therefore, in Java, class `ElevatorCaseStudy` contains a static `main` method that instantiates an `ElevatorCaseStudy` object, which in turn instantiates the `ElevatorSimulation`, `ElevatorView` and `ElevatorController` objects. We implement class `ElevatorCaseStudy` in Java later in this section.

Artifacts

Figure 14.21 helps us design another aspect of our system—the *artifacts*. Figure 14.22 models the "pieces"—called *artifacts*—that the system needs to perform its tasks. These pieces include binary executables, compiled `.class` files, `.java` source files, images, packages, resources, etc.

In Fig. 14.22, each rectangle models an artifact. Our system contains five artifacts: `ElevatorCaseStudy.class`, `ElevatorCaseStudy.java`, `ElevatorSimulation.java`, `ElevatorView.java` and `ElevatorController.java`.

In Fig. 14.22, the graphics that resemble folders (boxes with tabs in their upper-left corners) represent *packages* in the UML (not to be confused with Java packages). We can group classes, objects, artifacts, use cases, etc., into packages. In this diagram (and in the remainder of our case study), the UML packages correspond to Java packages (introduced in Section 8.13). In our discussion, we use lower-case bold-face Courier type for package names. The packages in our system are `model` (contains classes of the MVC model), `view` (contains view-related classes) and `controller` (contains controller-related classes). Artifact `ElevatorCaseStudy.java` contains one instance each of all artifacts in these packages. Currently, each package contains only one artifact—a `.java` file. The `model` package contains `ElevatorSimulation.java`, the `view` package contains `ElevatorView.java` and the `controller` package contains `ElevatorController.java`. We add artifacts to each package in the appendices, when we implement each class from our UML model as an artifact (`.java` file).

Each dotted arrow in Fig. 14.22 indicates a *dependency* between artifacts—the direction of the arrow indicates the "depends on" relationship. A dependency describes the relationship between artifacts in which changes in one artifact affect another artifact. For example, artifact `ElevatorCaseStudy.class` depends on artifact `ElevatorCaseStudy.java`, because a change in `ElevatorCaseStudy.java` affects `ElevatorCaseStudy.class` when `ElevatorCaseStudy.java` is compiled. The `ElevatorController` object contains a reference to the `ElevatorSimulation` object (to place `Persons` on `Floors`). Therefore, `ElevatorController.java` depends on `ElevatorSimulation.java`.

According to Fig. 14.22, `ElevatorSimulation.java` and `ElevatorView.java` do not depend on each other—they communicate through interface `ElevatorSimulationListener`, which implements all interfaces in the simulation. `ElevatorView.java` realizes interface `ElevatorSimulationListener`, and `ElevatorSimulation.java` depends on interface `ElevatorSimulationListener`.

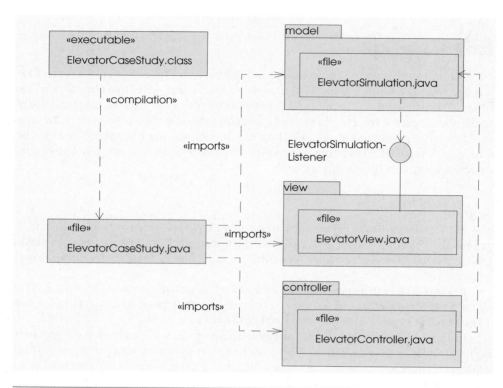

Fig. 14.22 Artifacts of the elevator simulation.

Figure 14.22 contains several stereotypes. We mentioned the «JavaInterface» stereotype in Section 12.9. The «compilation» stereotype describes the dependency between ElevatorCaseStudy.class and ElevatorCaseStudy.java—ElevatorCaseStudy.java compiles to ElevatorCaseStudy.class. The «executable» stereotype specifies that an artifact is an application, and the «file» stereotype specifies that an artifact is a file containing source code for the executable.

Implementing the Controller

Our simulation implements both the "Create Person" and "Relocate Person" use cases. We have studied the "Relocate Person" use case through the activity diagram of the Person in Fig. 5.28—we implement this use case and the activity diagram in Appendix E when we create class Person. We implement the "Create Person" use case through a graphical user interface (GUI). We implement our GUI in class ElevatorController (Fig. 14.23), which is a JPanel subclass containing two JButton objects—firstControllerButton (line 19) and secondControllerButton (line 20). Each JButton corresponds to a Floor on which to place a Person.[3] Lines 33–38 instantiate these JButtons and add them to the ElevatorController.

---

3. This approach is feasible with only two Floors. If the building had 100 Floors, we might have opted for the user to specify the desired Floor in a JTextField and press a JButton to process the request.

```
1   // ElevatorController.java
2   // Controller for Elevator Simulation
3   package com.deitel.jhtp5.elevator.controller;
4
5   import java.awt.*;
6   import java.awt.event.*;
7
8   import javax.swing.*;
9
10  // Deitel packages
11  import com.deitel.jhtp5.elevator.model.*;
12  import com.deitel.jhtp5.elevator.event.*;
13  import com.deitel.jhtp5.elevator.ElevatorConstants;
14
15  public class ElevatorController extends JPanel
16     implements ElevatorConstants {
17
18     // controller contains two JButtons
19     private JButton firstControllerButton;
20     private JButton secondControllerButton;
21
22     // reference to ElevatorSimulation
23     private ElevatorSimulation elevatorSimulation;
24
25     public ElevatorController( ElevatorSimulation simulation )
26     {
27        elevatorSimulation = simulation;
28        setBackground( Color.WHITE );
29
30        // add first button to controller
31        firstControllerButton = new JButton( "First Floor" );
32        add( firstControllerButton );
33
34        // add second button to controller
35        secondControllerButton = new JButton( "Second Floor" );
36        add( secondControllerButton );
37
38        // anonymous inner class registers to receive ActionEvents
39        // from first Controller JButton
40        firstControllerButton.addActionListener(
41           new ActionListener() {
42
43              // invoked when a JButton has been pressed
44              public void actionPerformed( ActionEvent event )
45              {
46                 // place Person on first Floor
47                 elevatorSimulation.addPerson(
48                    FIRST_FLOOR_NAME );
49
50                 // disable user input
51                 firstControllerButton.setEnabled( false );
52              }
53           } // end anonymous inner class
```

Fig. 14.23 Class ElevatorController processes user input. (Part 1 of 3.)

```
54       );
55
56       // anonymous inner class registers to receive ActionEvents
57       // from second Controller JButton
58       secondControllerButton.addActionListener(
59          new ActionListener() {
60
61             // invoked when a JButton has been pressed
62             public void actionPerformed( ActionEvent event )
63             {
64                // place Person on second Floor
65                elevatorSimulation.addPerson(
66                   SECOND_FLOOR_NAME );
67
68                // disable user input
69                secondControllerButton.setEnabled( false );
70             }
71          } // end anonymous inner class
72       );
73
74       // anonymous inner class enables user input on Floor if
75       // Person enters Elevator on that Floor
76       elevatorSimulation.addPersonMoveListener(
77          new PersonMoveListener() {
78
79             // invoked when Person has entered Elevator
80             public void personEntered(
81                PersonMoveEvent event )
82             {
83                // get Floor of departure
84                String location =
85                   event.getLocation().getLocationName();
86
87                // enable first JButton if first Floor departure
88                if ( location.equals( FIRST_FLOOR_NAME ) )
89                   firstControllerButton.setEnabled( true );
90
91                // enable second JButton if second Floor
92                else
93                   secondControllerButton.setEnabled( true );
94
95             } // end method personEntered
96
97             // other methods implementing PersonMoveListener
98             public void personCreated(
99                PersonMoveEvent event ) {}
100
101            public void personArrived(
102               PersonMoveEvent event ) {}
103
104            public void personExited(
105               PersonMoveEvent event ) {}
106
```

Fig. 14.23 Class ElevatorController processes user input. (Part 2 of 3.)

```
107                    public void personDeparted(
108                        PersonMoveEvent event ) {}
109
110                    public void personPressedButton(
111                        PersonMoveEvent event ) {}
112
113              } // end anonymous inner class
114          );
115      } // end ElevatorController constructor
116  }
```

Fig. 14.23 Class ElevatorController processes user input. (Part 3 of 3.)

Line 23 of class ElevatorController declares a reference to the ElevatorSimulation, because the ElevatorController allows the user to interact with the model. Lines 40–54 and 58–72 declare two anonymous ActionListener objects and register them with firstFloorControllerButton and secondFloorControllerButton, respectively, for ActionEvents. When the user presses either JButton, lines 47–48 and 65–66 of methods actionPerformed call the ElevatorSimulation's method addPerson, which instantiates a Person object in the ElevatorSimulation on the specified Floor. Method addPerson takes as an argument a String declared in interface ElevatorConstants (Fig. 14.24). This interface—used by such classes as ElevatorController, ElevatorSimulation, Elevator, Floor and ElevatorView—provides constants that specify the names of Locations in our simulation.

Lines 51 and 69 of methods actionPerformed disable the respective JButtons to prevent the user from creating more than one Person per Floor. Lines 76–114 of class ElevatorController declare an anonymous PersonMoveListener that registers with the ElevatorSimulation to re-enable the JButtons. Method personEntered (lines 80–95) of the PersonMoveListener re-enables the JButton associated with the Floor that the Elevator services—after the Person has entered the Elevator, the user may place another Person on the Floor.

We mentioned in Section 10.11 that classes Elevator and Floor inherited attribute capacity from superclass Location—in Appendix H, we were going to use this attribute to prevent more than one Person from occupying a Location. However, the PersonMoveListener's method personEntered in class ElevatorController prevents the user from creating more than one Person per Floor. Therefore, we have obviated the need for attribute capacity in class Location. Figure 14.25 is the modified class diagram of Fig. 10.25 removing this attribute.

```
1   // ElevatorConstants.java
2   // Constants used between ElevatorModel and ElevatorView
3   package com.deitel.jhtp5.elevator;
4
5   public interface ElevatorConstants {
6
7       public static final String FIRST_FLOOR_NAME = "firstFloor";
```

Fig. 14.24 Interface ElevatorConstants provides Location name constants. (Part 1 of 2.)

```
8    public static final String SECOND_FLOOR_NAME = "secondFloor";
9    public static final String ELEVATOR_NAME = "elevator";
10  }
```

Fig. 14.24 Interface `ElevatorConstants` provides `Location` name constants. (Part 2 of 2.)

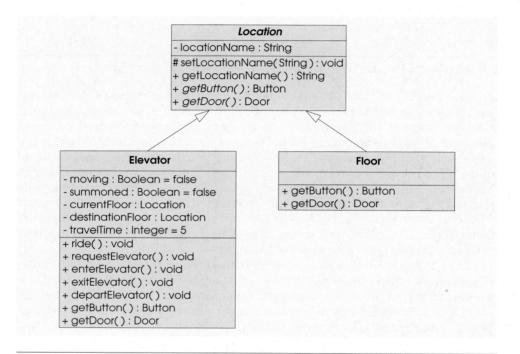

Fig. 14.25 Modified class diagram showing generalization of superclass `Location` and subclasses `Elevator` and `Floor`.

Implementation: *ElevatorCaseStudy.java*

We use the diagrams of Fig. 14.22, Fig. 14.21 and Fig. 13.28 to implement `Elevator-CaseStudy` (Fig. 14.26). Lines 12–14 import packages `model`, `view` and `controller` as specified in Fig. 14.22.

```
1    // ElevatorCaseStudy.java
2    // Application with Elevator Model, View, and Controller (MVC)
3    package com.deitel.jhtp5.elevator;
4
5    // Java core packages
6    import java.awt.*;
7
```

Fig. 14.26 Class `ElevatorCaseStudy` is the application for the elevator simulation (Part 1 of 2.).

```
8    // Java extension packages
9    import javax.swing.*;
10
11   // Deitel packages
12   import com.deitel.jhtp5.elevator.model.*;
13   import com.deitel.jhtp5.elevator.view.*;
14   import com.deitel.jhtp5.elevator.controller.*;
15
16   public class ElevatorCaseStudy extends JFrame {
17
18       // model, view and controller
19       private ElevatorSimulation model;
20       private ElevatorView view;
21       private ElevatorController controller;
22
23       // constructor instantiates model, view, and controller
24       public ElevatorCaseStudy()
25       {
26           super( "Deitel Elevator Simulation" );
27
28           // instantiate model, view and controller
29           model = new ElevatorSimulation();
30           view = new ElevatorView();
31           controller = new ElevatorController( model );
32
33           // register View for Model events
34           model.setElevatorSimulationListener( view );
35
36           // add view and controller to ElevatorCaseStudy
37           getContentPane().add( view, BorderLayout.CENTER );
38           getContentPane().add( controller, BorderLayout.SOUTH );
39
40       } // end ElevatorCaseStudy constructor
41
42       // main method starts program
43       public static void main( String args[] )
44       {
45           // instantiate ElevatorCaseStudy
46           ElevatorCaseStudy simulation = new ElevatorCaseStudy();
47           simulation.setDefaultCloseOperation( EXIT_ON_CLOSE );
48           simulation.pack();
49           simulation.setVisible( true );
50       }
51   }
```

Fig. 14.26 Class `ElevatorCaseStudy` is the application for the elevator simulation (Part 2 of 2.).

Figure 14.21 specifies that class `ElevatorCaseStudy` is a subclass of `JFrame`—line 16 declares class `ElevatorCaseStudy` as a `public` class extending class `JFrame`. Lines 19–21 implement class `ElevatorCaseStudy`'s aggregation of class `ElevatorSimulation`, the `ElevatorView` and the `ElevatorController` (shown in Fig. 14.21) by declaring one object from each class. Lines 29–31 of the `ElevatorCaseStudy` constructor initialize these objects.

Figure 14.21 and Fig. 14.22 specify that the ElevatorView is an ElevatorSimulationListener for the ElevatorSimulation. Line 34 registers the ElevatorView as a listener for ElevatorSimulationEvents, so the ElevatorView can receive events from the ElevatorSimulation and properly represent the state of the model. Lines 37–38 add the ElevatorView and the ElevatorController to the ElevatorCaseStudy. According to the stereotypes in Fig. 14.22, ElevatorCaseStudy.java compiles to ElevatorCaseStudy.class, which is executable—lines 43–50 provide method main that runs the application.

Section 16.11 concludes the design of the model by solving the interaction problems encountered in Fig. 10.26. Finally, Section 19.7 completes the design of the view and describes in greater detail how the ElevatorView receives events from the ElevatorSimulation. These last two sections will prepare you for the walkthrough of our elevator-simulation implementation in Appendix D–Appendix F.

14.14 (Optional) Discovering Design Patterns: Design Patterns Used in Packages java.awt and javax.swing

We continue our discussion from Section 1.16 on design patterns. This section introduces those design patterns associated with Java GUI components. After reading this section, you should understand better how these components take advantage of design patterns and how developers integrate design patterns with Java GUI applications.

14.14.1 Creational Design Patterns

Now, we continue our treatment of creational design patterns, which provide ways to instantiate objects in a system.

Factory Method

Suppose that we are designing a system that opens an image from a specified file. Several different image formats exist, such as GIF and JPEG. We can use method createImage of class java.awt.Component to create an Image object. For example, to create a JPEG and GIF image in an object of a Component subclass—such as a JPanel object—we pass the name of the image file to method createImage, which returns an Image object that stores the image data. We can create two Image objects, each of which contains data for two images having entirely different structures. For example, a JPEG image can hold up to 16.7 million colors, whereas a GIF image can hold up to only 256. Also, a GIF image can contain transparent pixels that are not rendered on screen, whereas a JPEG image cannot contain transparent pixels.

Class Image is an abstract class that represents an image we can display on screen. Using the parameter passed by the programmer, method createImage determines the specific Image subclass from which to instantiate the Image object. We can design systems to allow the user to specify which image to create, and method createImage will determine the subclass from which to instantiate the Image. If the parameter passed to method createImage references a JPEG file, method createImage instantiates and returns an object of an Image subclass suitable for JPEG images. If the parameter references a GIF file, createImage instantiates and returns an object of an Image subclass suitable for GIF images.

Method `createImage` is an example of the *Factory Method design pattern*. The sole purpose of this *factory method* is to create objects by allowing the system to determine which class to instantiate at run time. We can design a system that allows a user to specify what type of image to create at run time. Class `Component` might not be able to determine which `Image` subclass to instantiate until the user specifies the image to load. For more information on method `createImage`, visit

```
www.java.sun.com/j2se/1.4/docs/api/java/awt/Component.html#
    createImage(java.awt.image.ImageProducer)
```

14.14.2 Structural Design Patterns

We now discuss three more structural design patterns. The Adapter design pattern helps objects with incompatible interfaces collaborate with one another. The Bridge design pattern helps designers enhance platform independence in their systems. The Composite design pattern provides a way for designers to organize and manipulate objects.

Adapter

The *Adapter design pattern* provides an object with a new interface that *adapts* to another object's interface, allowing both objects to collaborate with one another. The adapter in this pattern is similar to an adapter for a plug on an electrical device—electrical sockets in Europe are shaped differently from those in the United States, so an adapter is needed to plug an American device into a European electrical socket and vice versa.

Java provides several classes that use the Adapter design pattern. Objects of the concrete subclasses of these classes act as adapters between objects that generate certain events and objects that handle the events. For example, a `MouseAdapter`, which we explained in Section 13.13, adapts an object that generates `MouseEvents` to an object that handles `MouseEvents`.

Bridge

Suppose that we are designing class `Button` for both the Windows and Macintosh operating systems. Class `Button` contains specific button information such as an `ActionListener` and a label. We design classes `Win32Button` and `MacButton` to extend class `Button`. Class `Win32Button` contains "look-and-feel" information on how to display a `Button` on the Windows operating system and class `MacButton` contains "look-and-feel" information on how to display a `Button` on the Macintosh operating system.

Two problems arise from this approach. First, if we create new `Button` subclasses, we must create corresponding `Win32Button` and `MacButton` subclasses. For example, if we create class `ImageButton` (a `Button` with an overlapping `Image`) that extends class `Button`, we must create additional subclasses `Win32ImageButton` and `MacImageButton`. In fact, we must create `Button` subclasses for every operating system we wish to support, which increases development time. The second problem is that when a new operating system enters the market, we must create additional `Button` subclasses specific to that operating system.

The *Bridge design pattern* avoids these problems by dividing an abstraction (e.g., a `Button`) and its implementations (e.g., `Win32Button`, `MacButton`, etc.) into separate class hierarchies. For example, the Java AWT classes use the Bridge design pattern to enable designers to create AWT `Button` subclasses without needing to create additional operating-system specific subclasses. Each AWT `Button` maintains a reference to a `But-tonPeer`, which is the superclass for platform-specific implementations, such as `Win32ButtonPeer`, `MacButtonPeer`, etc. When a programmer creates a `Button` object, class `Button` calls factory method `createButton` of class `Toolkit` to create the platform-specific `ButtonPeer` object. The `Button` object stores a reference to its `Button-Peer`—this reference is the "bridge" in the Bridge design pattern. When the programmer invokes methods on the `Button` object, the `Button` object delegates the work to the appropriate lower-level method on its `ButtonPeer` to fulfill the request. If a designer creates a `Button` subclass called `ImageButton`, the designer does not need to create a corresponding `Win32ImageButton` or `MacImageButton` with platform-specific image-drawing capabilities. An `ImageButton` "is a" `Button`. Therefore, when an `ImageButton` needs to display its image, the `ImageButton` uses its `ButtonPeer`'s `Graphics` object to render the image on each platform. This design pattern enables designers to create new cross-platform GUI components using a "bridge" to hide platform-specific details.

Portability Tip 14.3

Designers often use the Bridge design pattern to enhance the platform independence of their systems. This design pattern enables designers to create new cross-platform components using a "bridge" to hide platform-specific details.

Composite

Designers often organize components into hierarchical structures (e.g., a hierarchy of directories and files in a file system)—each node in the structure represents a component (e.g., a file or directory). Each node can contain references to other nodes. A node is called a *branch* if it contains a reference to one or more nodes (e.g., a directory containing files). A node is called a *leaf* if it does not contain a reference to another node (e.g., a file). Occasionally, a structure contains objects from several different classes (e.g., a directory can contain files and directories). When an object—called a *client*—wants to traverse the structure, the client must determine the particular class for each node. Making this determination can be time consuming, and the structure can become hard to maintain.

In the *Composite design pattern*, each component in a hierarchical structure implements the same interface or extends a common superclass. This polymorphism (introduced in Chapter 1) ensures that clients can traverse all elements—branch or leaf—uniformly in the structure. Using this pattern, a client traversing the structure does not have to determine each component type, because all components implement the same interface or extend the same superclass.

Java GUI components use the Composite design pattern. Consider the Swing component class `JPanel`, which extends class `JComponent`. Class `JComponent` extends class `java.awt.Container`, which extends class `java.awt.Component` (Fig. 14.27). Class `Container` provides method `add`, which appends a `Component` object (or `Component` subclass object) to that `Container` object. Therefore, a `JPanel` object may be added to any object of a `Component` subclass, and any object from a `Component` subclass may be added to that `JPanel` object. A `JPanel` object can contain any GUI component while remaining unaware of that component's specific type. Nearly all GUI classes are both containers and components, enabling arbitrarily complex nesting and structuring of GUIs.

A client, such as a `JPanel` object, can traverse all components uniformly in the hierarchy. For example, if the `JPanel` object calls method `repaint` of superclass `Container`,

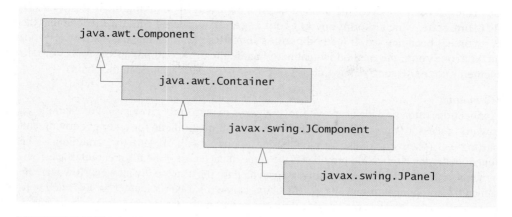

Fig. 14.27 Inheritance hierarchy for class JPanel.

method repaint displays the JPanel object and all components added to the JPanel object. Method repaint does not have to determine each component's type, because all components inherit from superclass Container, which contains method repaint.

14.14.3 Behavioral Design Patterns

This section continues our discussion on behavioral design patterns. We discuss the Chain of Responsibility, Command, Observer, Strategy and Template Method design patterns.

Chain of Responsibility

In object-oriented systems, objects interact by sending messages to one another. Often, a system needs to determine at run time the object that will handle a particular message. For example, consider the design of a three-line office phone system. When a person calls the office, the first line handles the call—if the first line is busy, the second line handles the call, and if the second line is busy, the third line handles the call. If all lines in the system are busy, an automated speaker instructs that person to wait for the next available line—when a line becomes available, that line handles the call.

The *Chain of Responsibility design pattern* enables a system to determine at run time the object that will handle a message. This pattern allows an object to send a message to several objects in a *chain* of objects. Each object in the chain either may handle the message or pass the message to the next object in the chain. For instance, the first line in the phone system is the first object in the chain of responsibility, the second line is the second object, the third line is the third object and the automated speaker is the fourth object. Note that this mechanism is not the final object in the chain—the next available line handles the message, and that line is the final object in the chain. The chain is created dynamically in response to the presence or absence of specific message handlers.

Several Java AWT GUI components use the Chain of Responsibility design pattern to handle certain events. For example, class java.awt.Button overrides method processEvent of class java.awt.Component to process AWTEvent objects. Method processEvent attempts to handle the AWTEvent upon receiving this event as an argument. If method processEvent determines that the AWTEvent is an ActionEvent (i.e., the

Button has been pressed), the method handles the event by invoking method process-ActionEvent, which informs any ActionListener registered with the Button that the Button has been pressed. If method processEvent determines that the AWTEvent is not an ActionEvent, the method is unable to handle the event and passes the AWTEvent to method processEvent of superclass Component (the next listener in the chain).

Command

Applications often provide users with several ways to perform a given task. For example, in a word processor there might be an **Edit** menu with menu items for cutting, copying and pasting text. There could also be a toolbar or a popup menu offering the same items. The functionality the application provides is the same in each case—the different interface components for invoking the functionality are provided for the user's convenience. However, the same GUI component instance (e.g., JButton) cannot be used for menus, toolbars and popup menus, so the developer must code the same functionality three times. If there were many such interface items, repeating this functionality would become tedious and error prone.

The *Command design pattern* solves this problem by enabling developers to encapsulate the desired functionality (e.g., copying text) once in a reusable object; that functionality can then be added to a menu, toolbar, popup menu or other mechanism. This design pattern is called Command because it defines a command, or instruction, to be executed. This pattern allows a designer to encapsulate a command, so that the command may be used among several objects.

Observer

Suppose that we want to design a program for viewing bank account information. This system includes class BankStatementData to store data pertaining to bank statements and classes TextDisplay, BarGraphDisplay and PieChartDisplay to display the data.[4] Figure 14.28 shows the design for our system. Class TextDisplay displays the data in text format, class BarGraphDisplay displays the data in bar-graph format and class PieChartDisplay displays the data as a pie chart. We want to design the system so that the BankStatementData object notifies the objects displaying the data of a change in the data. We also want to design the system to loosen *coupling*—the degree to which classes depend on each other in a system.

Software Engineering Observation 14.2

Loosely coupled classes are easier to reuse and modify than are tightly coupled classes, which depend heavily on each other. A modification in a class in a tightly coupled system usually results in modifying other classes in that system. A modification to one of a group of loosely coupled classes would require little or no modification to the other classes in the group.

The *Observer design pattern* is appropriate for systems like that of Fig. 14.28. This pattern promotes loose coupling between a *subject* object and *observer* objects—a subject notifies the observers when the subject changes state. When notified by the subject, the observers change in response to the change in the subject. In our example, the BankStatementData object is the subject, and the objects displaying the data are the observers. A subject can notify several observers; therefore, the subject has a one-to-many relationship with the observers.

---

4. This approach is the basis for the Model-View-Controller architecture pattern, discussed in Sections 13.17 and 17.11.

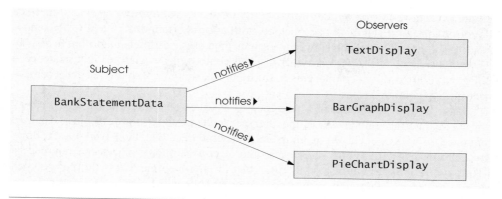

Fig. 14.28 Basis for the Observer design pattern.

The Java API contains classes that use the Observer design pattern. Class *java.util.Observable* represents a subject. Class Observable provides method addObserver, which takes a *java.util.Observer* argument. Interface Observer allows the Observable object to notify the Observer when the Observable object changes state. The Observer can be an instance of any class that implements interface Observer; because the Observable object invokes methods declared in interface Observer, the objects remain loosely coupled. If a developer changes the way in which a particular Observer responds to changes in the Observable object, the developer does not need to change the Observable object. The Observable object interacts with its Observers only through interface Observer, which enables the loose coupling.

The optional elevator simulation case study in the "Thinking About Objects" sections uses the Observer design pattern to allow the ElevatorModel object (the subject) to notify the ElevatorView object (the observer) of changes in the ElevatorModel. The simulation does not use class Observable and interface Observer from the Java library—rather, it uses a custom interface ElevatorModelListener that provides functionality similar to that of interface Observable.

The Swing GUI components use the Observer design pattern. GUI components collaborate with their listeners to respond to user interactions. For example, an ActionListener observes state changes in a JButton (the subject) by registering to handle that JButton's events. When pressed by the user, the JButton notifies its ActionListener objects (the observers) that the JButton's state has changed (i.e., the JButton has been pressed).

Strategy

The *Strategy design pattern* is similar to the State design pattern (discussed in Section 10.12). We mentioned that the State design pattern contains a state object, which encapsulates the state of a context object. The Strategy design pattern contains a *strategy object*, which is analogous to the State design pattern's state object. The key difference between a state object and a strategy object is that the strategy object encapsulates an *algorithm* rather than state information.

For example, java.awt.Container components implement the Strategy design pattern using LayoutManagers (discussed in Section 13.15) as strategy objects. In package java.awt, classes FlowLayout, BorderLayout and GridLayout implement interface LayoutManager. Each class uses method addLayoutComponent to add GUI components to a Container object. However, each method uses a different algorithm to display these GUI components: A FlowLayout displays components in a left-to-right sequence, a BorderLayout displays components in five regions and a GridLayout displays components in row-column format.

Class Container contains a reference to a LayoutManager object (the strategy object). An interface reference (i.e., the reference to the LayoutManager object) can hold references to objects of classes that implement that interface (i.e., the FlowLayout, BorderLayout or GridLayout objects), so the LayoutManager object can reference a FlowLayout, BorderLayout or GridLayout at any one time. Class Container can change this reference through method setLayout to select different layouts at run time.

Class FlowLayoutDemo (Fig. 13.24) demonstrates the application of the Strategy pattern—line 16 declares a new FlowLayout object and line 19 invokes the Container object's method setLayout to assign the FlowLayout object to the Container object. In this example, the FlowLayout provides the strategy for laying out the components.

Template Method
The *Template Method design pattern* also deals with algorithms. The Strategy design pattern allows several objects to contain distinct algorithms. However, the Template Method design pattern requires all objects to share a single algorithm defined by a superclass.

For example, consider the design of Fig. 14.28, which we mentioned in the Observer design pattern discussion. Objects of classes TextDisplay, BarGraphDisplay and PieChartDisplay use the same basic algorithm for acquiring and displaying the data—get all statements from the BankStatementData object, parse the statements, then display the statements. The Template Method design pattern allows us to create an abstract superclass called BankStatementDisplay that provides the common algorithm for displaying the data. In this example, the algorithm invokes abstract methods getData, parseData and displayData. Classes TextDisplay, BarGraphDisplay and PieChartDisplay extend class BankStatementDisplay to inherit the algorithm, so each object can use the same algorithm. Each BankStatementDisplay subclass then overrides each method in a way specific to that subclass, because each class implements the algorithm differently. For example, classes TextDisplay, BarGraphDisplay and PieChartDisplay might get and parse the data identically, but each class displays that data differently.

The Template Method design pattern allows us to extend the algorithm to other BankStatementDisplay subclasses—e.g., we could create classes, such as LineGraphDisplay or class 3DimensionalDisplay, that use the same algorithm inherited from class BankStatementDisplay and provide different implementations of the abstract methods the algorithm calls.

14.14.4 Conclusion

In this "Discovering Design Patterns" section, we discussed how Swing components take advantage of design patterns and how developers can integrate design patterns with GUI applications in Java. In "Discovering Design Patterns" Section 16.12, we discuss concurrency design patterns, which are particularly useful for developing multithreaded systems.

SUMMARY

- A JTextArea provides an area for manipulating multiple lines of text. Like class JTextField, class JTextArea extends JTextComponent. An external event normally indicates when the text in a JTextArea should be processed. Scrollbars are provided for a JTextArea by attaching it to a JScrollPane object. Method getSelectedText returns the selected text from a JTextArea. Method setText sets the text in a JTextArea.

- The horizontal and vertical scrollbar policies for a JScrollPane are set when a JScrollPane is created or with methods setHorizontalScrollBarPolicy and setVerticalScrollBar-Policy of class JScrollPane.

- To provide automatic word wrap in a JTextArea, attach it to a JScrollPane with horizontal scrollbar policy JScrollPane.HORIZONTAL_SCROLLBAR_NEVER.

- A JPanel can be used as a dedicated drawing area that can receive mouse events and is often extended to create new GUI components.

- Swing components that inherit from class JComponent contain method paintComponent, which helps them draw properly in the context of a lightweight Swing GUI. Method paintComponent should be overridden to call the superclass's paintComponent as the first statement in its body.

- Classes JFrame and JApplet are not subclasses of JComponent; therefore, they do not contain method paintComponent (they have method paint).

- Calling repaint for a Swing component indicates that it should be painted as soon as possible. The background of the GUI component is cleared only if the component is opaque. Most Swing components are transparent by default. JComponent method setOpaque can be passed a boolean argument indicating whether the component is opaque (true) or transparent (false).

- Method setTitle displays a string in a window's title bar.

- Drawing on any GUI component is performed with coordinates that are measured from the upper-left corner (0, 0) of that GUI component.

- Layout managers often use a GUI component's getPreferredSize method to determine the preferred width and height of a component when laying out that component as part of a GUI. If a new component has a preferred width and height, it should override method getPreferredSize to return that width and height as an object of class Dimension (package java.awt).

- The default size of a JPanel object is 10 pixels wide and 10 pixels tall.

- A mouse drag operation begins with a mouse-pressed event. All subsequent mouse drag events are sent to the GUI component that received the original mouse-pressed event.

- JSliders enable the user to select from a range of integer values. JSliders can display major tick marks, minor tick marks and labels for the tick marks. They also support snap-to ticks, where positioning the thumb between two tick marks causes the thumb to snap to the closest tick mark.

- If a JSlider has the focus, the left arrow key and right arrow key cause the thumb of the JSlider to decrease or increase by 1. The down arrow key and up arrow key also cause the thumb of the JSlider to decrease or increase by 1, respectively. The *PgDn key* (page down) and *PgUp key* (page up) cause the thumb of the JSlider to decrease or increase by block increments of one-tenth of the range of values, respectively. The *Home key* moves the thumb to the minimum value of the JSlider and the *End key* moves the thumb to the maximum value of the JSlider.

- JSliders have either horizontal or vertical orientation. For a horizontal JSlider, the minimum value is at the extreme left and the maximum value is at the extreme right of the JSlider. For a vertical JSlider, the minimum value is at the extreme bottom and the maximum value is at the extreme top of the JSlider. The position of the thumb indicates the current value of the JSlider. Method getValue of class JSlider returns the current thumb position.

- Method `setMajorTickSpacing` of class `JSlider` sets the spacing for tick marks on a `JSlider`. Method `setPaintTicks` with a `true` argument indicates that the tick marks should be displayed.

- `JSliders` generate `ChangeEvents` when the user interacts with a `JSlider`. A `ChangeListener` declares method `stateChanged` that can respond to `ChangeEvents`.

- A `JFrame` is a window with a title bar and a border. `JFrame` method `setDefaultCloseOperation` specifies the action to take when the user closes the window.

- A window is not displayed on the screen until its `setVisible` method is called with `true` as an argument.

- A window's size should be set with a call to method `setSize`. The position of a window when it appears on the screen is specified with method `setLocation`.

- All windows generate window events when the user manipulates the window. Interface `WindowListener` provides seven window event-handling methods—`windowActivated`, `windowClosed`, `windowClosing`, `windowDeactivated`, `windowIconified`, `windowDeiconified` and `windowOpened`.

- Menus are an integral part of GUIs. Menus allow the user to perform actions without unnecessarily "cluttering" a graphical user interface with extra GUI components. In Swing GUIs, menus can be attached only to objects of classes with method `setJMenuBar` (such as `JFrame` and `JApplet`).

- The classes used to declare menus are `JMenuBar`, `JMenuItem`, `JMenu`, `JCheckBoxMenuItem` and class `JRadioButtonMenuItem`. A `JMenuBar` is a container for menus. A `JMenuItem` is a GUI component inside a menu that, when selected, causes an action to be performed. A `JMenu` contains menu items and can be added to a `JMenuBar` or to other `JMenus` as submenus. When a menu is clicked, the menu expands to show its list of menu items. `JMenu` method `addSeparator` adds a separator line to a menu.

- When a `JCheckBoxMenuItem` is selected, a check appears to the left of the menu item. When the `JCheckBoxMenuItem` is selected again, the check to the left of the menu item is removed.

- When multiple `JRadioButtonMenuItems` are maintained as part of a `ButtonGroup`, only one item in the group can be selected at a given time. When a `JRadioButtonMenuItem` is selected, a filled circle appears to the left of the menu item. When another `JRadioButtonMenuItem` is selected, the filled circle to the left of the previously selected menu item is removed.

- `AbstractButton` method `setMnemonic` specifies the mnemonic for an `AbstractButton`. Mnemonic characters are normally displayed with an underline.

- Dialog boxes are typically modal. A modal dialog box does not allow access to any other window in the application until the dialog is dismissed. The dialogs displayed with class `JOptionPane` are modal dialogs. Class `JDialog` can be used to create your own modal or non-modal dialogs.

- Context-sensitive popup menus are created with class `JPopupMenu`. On most systems, the popup-trigger event occurs when the user presses and releases the right mouse button. `MouseEvent` method `isPopupTrigger` returns `true` if the popup-trigger event occurred.

- `JPopupMenu` method `show` displays a `JPopupMenu`. The first argument specifies the origin component, which helps determine where the `JPopupMenu` will appear. The last two arguments are the coordinates from the origin component's upper-left corner at which the `JPopupMenu` appears.

- Class `UIManager` contains nested class `LookAndFeelInfo` that maintains information about a look-and-feel. `UIManager` static method `getInstalledLookAndFeels` gets an array of `UIManager.LookAndFeelInfo` objects that describe the available look-and-feels. `UIManager` static method `setLookAndFeel` changes the look-and-feel. `SwingUtilities` static method `updateComponentTreeUI` changes the look-and-feel of every component attached to its `Component` argument to the new look-and-feel.

- Many of today's applications use a multiple-document interface (MDI) to manage several open documents that are being processed in parallel. Swing's JDesktopPane and JInternalFrame classes provide support for creating multiple-document interfaces.

- A JTabbedPane arranges GUI components into layers in which only one layer is visible at a time. Users access each layer via a tab—similar to folders in a file cabinet. When the user clicks a tab, the appropriate layer is displayed.

- BoxLayout is a layout manager that allows GUI components to be arranged left-to-right or top-to-bottom in a container. Class Box declares a container with BoxLayout as its default layout manager and provides static methods to create a Box with a horizontal or vertical BoxLayout.

- GridBagLayout is a layout manager similar to GridLayout. Unlike with GridLayout, each component size can vary, and components can be added in any order. A GridBagConstraints object specifies how a component is placed in a GridBagLayout. Method setConstraints of class GridBagLayout takes a Component argument and a GridBagConstraints argument and sets the constraints of the Component.

TERMINOLOGY

addSeparator method of class JMenu
addWindowListener method of Window
Box class
BoxLayout layout manager
ChangeEvent class
ChangeListener interface
child window
command-line arguments
context-sensitive popup menu
createHorizontalBox method of Box
createHorizontalGlue method of Box
createHorizontalStrut method of Box
createRigidArea method of Box
createVerticalBox method of Box
createVerticalGlue method of Box
createVerticalStrut method of Box
dedicated drawing area
Dimension class
dispose method of class Window
external event
first method of CardLayout
getClassName method of
    UIManager.LookAndFeelInfo
getInstalledLookAndFeels method of
    UIManager
getMinimumSize method of Component
getPreferredSize method of Component
getSelectedText method of
    JTextComponent
getValue method of class JSlider
GridBagConstraints class
GridBagLayout layout manager
isPopupTrigger method of MouseEvent

JCheckBoxMenuItem class
JDesktopPane class
JInternalFrame class
JMenu class
JMenuBar class
JMenuItem class
JPopupMenu class
JRadioButtonMenuItem class
JSlider class
JTextArea class
JTextComponent class
labels for tick marks
last method of class CardLayout
line wrapping
Mac look-and-feel
major tick mark
menu
menu bar
menu item
metal look-and-feel
method setMnemonic of AbstractButton
minor tick mark
mnemonic
modal dialog
Motif look-and-feel
multiple-document interface (MDI)
next method of class CardLayout
paintComponent method of JComponent
parent window
pluggable look-and-feel (PLAF)
previous method of class CardLayout
scrollbar policies for a JScrollPane
setConstraints method

setDefaultCloseOperation method
setHorizontalScrollBarPolicy method
setJMenuBar method
setLineWrap method
setLookAndFeel method
setMajorTickSpacing method
setOpaque method of class JComponent
setPaintTicks method of class JSlider
setSelected method of AbstractButton
setTitle method of class Frame
setVerticalScrollBarPolicy method
show method of class JPopupMenu

snap-to ticks
submenu
thumb of a JSlider
tick mark
UIManager class
UIManager.LookAndFeelInfo class
updateComponentTreeUI method
vertical strut
WindowConstants
WindowListener interface
Windows look-and-feel

SELF-REVIEW EXERCISES

14.1   Fill in the blanks in each of the following statements:
   a) The _____ class is used to create a menu object.
   b) The _____ method places a separator bar in a menu.
   c) Passing false to a TextArea's _____ method prevents its text from being modi-fied by the user.
   d) JSlider events are handled by the _____ method of interface _____.
   e) The GridBagConstraints instance variable _____ is set to CENTER by default.

14.2   State whether each of the following is *true* or *false*. If *false*, explain why.
   a) When the programmer creates a JFrame, a minimum of one menu must be created and added to the JFrame.
   b) The variable fill belongs to the GridBagLayout class.
   c) Drawing on a GUI component is performed with respect to the (0, 0) upper-left corner coordinate of the component.
   d) A JTextArea's text is always read-only.
   e) Class JTextArea is a direct subclass of class Component.
   f) The default layout for a Box is BoxLayout.

14.3   Find the error(s) in each of the following and explain how to correct the error(s).
   a) JMenubar b;
   b) mySlider = JSlider(1000, 222, 100, 450);
   c) gbc.fill = GridBagConstraints.NORTHWEST; // set fill
   d) // override to paint on a customized Swing component
```
public void paintcomponent( Graphics g )
{
    g.drawString( "HELLO", 50, 50 );
}
```
   e) // create a JFrame and display it
```
JFrame f = new JFrame( "A Window" );
f.setVisible( true );
```

ANSWERS TO SELF-REVIEW EXERCISES

14.1   a) JMenu. b) addSeparator. c) setEditable. d) stateChanged, ChangeListener. e) anchor.

14.2   a) False. A JFrame does not require any menus.
   b) False. The variable fill belongs to the GridBagConstraints class.

c) True.

d) False. JTextAreas are editable by default.

e) False. JTextArea derives from class JTextComponent.

f) True.

14.3 a) JMenubar should be JMenuBar.

b) The first argument to the constructor should be either SwingConstants.HORIZONTAL or SwingConstants.VERTICAL, and the keyword new must be used after the = operator.

c) The constant should be either BOTH, HORIZONTAL, VERTICAL or NONE.

d) paintcomponent should be paintComponent, and the method should call super.paintComponent(g) as its first statement.

e) The JFrame's setSize method must also be called to establish the size of the window.

EXERCISES

14.4 Fill in the blanks in each of the following statements:

a) A dedicated drawing area can be declared as a subclass of _____.

b) A JMenuItem that is a JMenu is called a(n) _____

c) Both JTextFields and JTextAreas directly extend class _____.

d) Method _____ attaches a JMenuBar to a JFrame.

e) Container class _____ has a default BoxLayout.

f) A(n) _____ manages a set of child windows declared with class JInternalFrame.

14.5 State whether each of the following is *true* or *false*. If *false*, explain why.

a) Menus require a JMenuBar object so they can be attached to a JFrame.

b) A JPanel object is capable of receiving mouse events.

c) BoxLayout is the default layout manager for a JFrame.

d) Method setEditable is a JTextComponent method.

e) JPanel objects are containers to which other GUI components can be attached.

f) Class JFrame directly extends class Container.

g) JApplets can contain menus.

14.6 Find the error(s) in each of the following. Explain how to correct the error(s).

```
a) x.add( new JMenuItem( "Submenu Color" ) ); // create submenu
b) container.setLayout( m = new GridbagLayout() );
c) String s = JTextArea.getText();
```

14.7 Write a program that displays a circle of random size and calculates and displays the area, radius, diameter and circumference. Use the following equations: *diameter* = 2∞ *radius*, *area* = $\pi \infty$ *radius*², *circumference* = $2 \infty \pi \infty$ *radius*. Use the constant Math.PI for pi (π). All drawing should be done on a subclass of JPanel, and the results of the calculations should be displayed in a read-only JTextArea.

14.8 Enhance the program of Exercise 14.7 by allowing the user to alter the radius with a JSlider. The program should work for all radii in the range from 100–200. As the radius changes, the diameter, area and circumference should be updated and displayed. The initial radius should be 150. Use the equations of Exercise 14.7. All drawing should be done on a subclass of JPanel, and the results of the calculations should be displayed in a read-only JTextArea.

14.9 Explore the effects of varying the weightx and weighty values of the program of Fig. 14.19. What happens when a slot has a nonzero weight, but is not allowed to fill the whole area (i.e., the fill value is not BOTH)?

14.10 Write a program that uses the paintComponent method to draw the current value of a JSlider on a subclass of JPanel. In addition, provide a JTextField where a specific value can be entered. The JTextField should display the current value of the JSlider at all times. A JLabel should be used to identify the JTextField. The JSlider methods setValue and getValue should be used. [Note: The setValue method is a public method that does not return a value and takes one integer argument—the JSlider value, which determines the position of the thumb.]

14.11 Modify the program of Fig. 14.13 by adding a minimum of two new tabs.

14.12 Declare a subclass of JPanel called MyColorChooser that provides three JSlider objects and three JTextField objects. Each JSlider represents the values from 0–255 for the red, green and blue parts of a color. Use the red, green and blue values as the arguments to the Color constructor to create a new Color object. Display the current value of each JSlider in the corresponding JTextField. When the user changes the value of the JSlider, the JTextField should be changed accordingly. Declare class MyColorChooser so it can be reused in other applications or applets. Use your new GUI component as part of an applet that displays the current Color value by drawing a filled rectangle.

14.13 Modify the MyColorChooser class of Exercise 14.12 to allow the user to enter an integer value into a JTextField to set the red, green or blue value. When the user presses *Enter* in the JTextField, the corresponding JSlider should be set to the appropriate value.

14.14 Modify the applet of Exercise 14.13 to draw the current color as a rectangle on an instance of a subclass of JPanel called DrawPanel. Class DrawPanel should provide its own paintComponent method to draw the rectangle and should provide *set* methods to set the red, green and blue values for the current color. When any *set* method is invoked for the class DrawPanel, the object should automatically repaint itself.

14.15 Modify the applet of Exercise 14.14 to allow the user to drag the mouse across the DrawPanel to draw a shape in the current color. Enable the user to choose what shape to draw.

14.16 Modify the program of Exercise 14.15 to enable the program to run as an application. The existing applet's code should be modified only by adding a main method to launch the application in its own JFrame. Provide the user with the ability to terminate the application by clicking the close box on the window that is displayed and by selecting Exit from a File menu. Use the techniques shown in Fig. 14.9.

14.17 *(Complete Drawing Application)* Using the techniques developed in Exercise 13.27–Exercise 13.31 and Exercise 14.12–Exercise 14.16, create a complete drawing program that can execute as both an applet and an application. The program should use the GUI components of Chapter 13 and Chapter 14 to enable the user to select the shape, color and fill characteristics. Each shape should be stored in an array of MyShape objects, where MyShape is the superclass in your hierarchy of shape classes (see Exercise 10.9 and Exercise 10.10). Use a JDesktopPane and JInternalFrames to allow the user to create multiple separate drawings in separate child windows. Create the user interface as a separate child window containing all the GUI components that allow the user to determine the characteristics of the shape to be drawn. The user can then click in any JInternalFrame to draw the shape.

15

Exception Handling

Objectives

- To understand exception and error handling.
- To use try, throw and catch to detect, indicate and handle exceptions, respectively.
- To use the finally clause to release resources.
- To understand the Java exception hierarchy.
- To declare new exception classes.
- To create chained exceptions.

It is common sense to take a method and try it. If it fails, admit it frankly and try another. But above all, try something.
Franklin Delano Roosevelt

O! throw away the worser part of it,
And live the purer with the other half.
William Shakespeare

If they're running and they don't look where they're going
I have to come out from somewhere and catch them.
Jerome David Salinger

And oftentimes excusing of a fault
Doth make the fault the worse by the excuse.
William Shakespeare

I never forget a face, but in your case I'll make an exception.
Groucho (Julius Henry) Marx

15.1 Introduction

In this chapter, we introduce *exception handling*. An *exception* is an indication of a problem that occurs during a program's execution. The name "exception" comes from the fact that, although a problem can occur, the problem occurs infrequently—if the "rule" is that a statement normally executes correctly, then the "exception to the rule" is that a problem occurs. Exception handling enables programmers to create applications that can resolve (or handle) exceptions. In many cases, handling an exception allows a program to continue executing as if no problem had been encountered. A more severe problem could prevent a program from continuing normal execution, instead requiring the program to notify the user of the problem before terminating in a controlled manner. The features presented in this chapter enable programmers to write robust and *fault-tolerant programs*. The style and details of Java exception handling are based in part on the work of Andrew Koenig and Bjarne Stroustrup, as presented in their paper, "Exception Handling for C++ (revised)."[1]

The chapter begins with an overview of exception-handling concepts, then demonstrates basic exception-handling techniques. We show these techniques through an example that demonstrates handling an exception that occurs when a method attempts to divide by zero. Following the example, we introduce Java's exception hierarchy including several classes that the Java packages provide for handling exceptions. We then discuss the new chained exception feature included in Java 2 Platform, Standard Edition, Version 1.4. We conclude the chapter by discussing additional exception-handling issues, such as how to handle exceptions that occur in a constructor or finalizer.

---

1.   Koenig, A. and B. Stroustrup. "Exception Handling for C++ (revised)," *Proceedings of the Usenix C++ Conference*, p. 149–176, San Francisco, April 1990.

15.2 Exception-Handling Overview

Program logic frequently tests conditions that determine how program execution should proceed. Consider the following pseudocode:

Perform a task

If the preceding task did not execute correctly
    Perform error processing

Perform next task

If the preceding task did not execute correctly
    Perform error processing

...

In this pseudocode, we begin by performing a task; then, we test whether that task executed correctly. If not, we perform error processing. Otherwise, we continue with the next task. Although this form of error handling works, intermixing program logic with error-handling logic can make the program difficult to read, modify, maintain and debug—especially in large applications. In fact, if the potential problems occur infrequently, intermixing program and error-handling logic can degrade a program's performance, because the program must test the error-handling logic to determine whether the next task can be performed.

Exception handling enables the programmer to remove error-handling code from the "main line" of the program's execution, which improves program clarity and enhances modifiability. Programmers can decide to handle any exceptions they choose—all exceptions, all exceptions of a certain type or all exceptions of a group of related types (e.g., exception types that belong to an inheritance hierarchy). Such flexibility reduces the likelihood that errors will be overlooked and thereby makes a program more robust.

Error-Prevention Tip 15.1

Exception handling helps improve a program's fault tolerance.

Software Engineering Observation 15.1

Avoid using exception handling to handle potential problems in the conventional flow of control. Handling a larger number of exception cases can be cumbersome, and programs with a large number of exception cases can be difficult to read and maintain.

Software Engineering Observation 15.2

Another reason not to use exceptions for conventional flow of control is that these "additional" exceptions can "get in the way" of genuine error-type exceptions. It becomes more difficult for the programmer to keep track of the larger number of exception cases. Exceptional situations should be rare, not commonplace.

Exception handling is designed to process *synchronous errors*, which occur when a statement executes. Common examples are out-of-range array indices, arithmetic overflow (i.e., a value outside the representable range of values), division by zero, invalid method parameters, thread interruption and unsuccessful memory allocation (due to lack of memory). Exception handling is not designed to process problems associated with *asynchronous* events (e.g., disk I/O completions, network message arrivals, mouse clicks and keystrokes), which occur in parallel with, and independent of, the program's flow of control.

Good Programming Practice 15.1

For clarity, avoid using exception handling for purposes other than handling problems that occur in a program.

With programming languages that do not support exception handling, programmers often delay writing error-processing code or sometimes forget to include it. This results in less robust software products. Java enables the programmer to deal with exception handling easily from the inception of a project. However, the programmer must incorporate an exception-handling strategy into software projects.

Software Engineering Observation 15.3

Try to incorporate an exception-handling strategy into a system from the inception of the design process. Including effective exception handling after a system has been implemented can be difficult.

Software Engineering Observation 15.4

In the past, programmers used many techniques to implement error-processing code. Exception handling provides a single, uniform technique for processing problems. This helps programmers working on large projects to understand each other's error-processing code.

The exception-handling mechanism is also useful for processing problems that occur when a program invokes methods of other classes. Rather than handling problems internally, such methods often use exceptions to notify their calling methods when problems occur. This enables programmers to implement customized error handling for each application.

Performance Tip 15.1

When no exceptions occur, exception-handling code incurs little or no performance penalty. Thus, programs that implement exception handling operate more efficiently than do programs that intermix error-handling code with program logic.

Software Engineering Observation 15.5

Methods with common error conditions should return false or null (or other appropriate values) rather than throw exceptions. A program calling such a method can check the return value to determine success or failure of the method call.

Complex applications normally consist of predefined software components and application-specific components that use the predefined components. When a predefined component encounters a problem, that component needs a mechanism to communicate the problem to the application-specific component—the predefined component cannot know in advance how each application processes a problem that occurs. Exception handling simplifies combining software components and enables them to work together effectively by enabling predefined components to communicate problems to application-specific components, which can then process the problems in an application-specific manner.

Exception handling is geared to situations in which the method that detects a problem is unable to handle it. Such a method *throws an exception*. There is no guarantee that there will be an *exception handler*—code that executes when the program detects an exception—to process that kind of exception. If there is, the exception handler *catches* and *handles* the exception. The result of an *uncaught exception* often yields adverse effects and might terminate program execution.

Common Programming Error 15.1

Aborting a program component due to an uncaught exception could leave a resource—such as a file stream or an I/O device—in a state in which other programs are unable to acquire the resource. This is known as a "resource leak."

Java provides *try statements* to enable exception handling. A `try` statement consists of keyword `try`, followed by braces (`{}`) that delimit a *try block*. The `try` block contains statements that might cause exceptions and statements that should not execute if an exception occurs. At least one *catch clause* (also called an exception handler) or a *finally* clause must immediately follow the `try` block. Each `catch` clause specifies in parentheses an *exception parameter* that identifies the exception type the handler can process. The exception parameter's name enables the `catch` clause to interact with a caught exception object. After the last `catch` handler, an optional *finally* clause provides code that always executes, whether or not an exception occurs. We will see that the `finally` clause is an ideal location for code that releases resources to prevent "resource leaks."

Common Programming Error 15.2

It is a syntax error to place code between a try block and its corresponding catch clauses.

Common Programming Error 15.3

Specifying a comma-separated list of catch parameters is a syntax error. A catch can have only a single parameter.

Common Programming Error 15.4

It is a compilation error to catch the same type in two different catch clauses associated with a particular try block.

Common Programming Error 15.5

Placing a catch for type Exception before other catch clauses that catch subclass exception types would prevent those clauses from executing, so a compilation error occurs.

The point in the program at which an exception occurs (i.e., the location where a method detects and throws an exception) is called the *throw point*. If an exception occurs in a `try` block, the `try` block terminates immediately and program control transfers to the first `catch` clause that follows the `try` block. This is known as the *termination model of exception handling*, because the `try` block that encloses a thrown exception terminates when that exception occurs.[2] As with any other block of code, when a `try` block terminates, local variables declared in the block go out of scope. Next, the program searches for the first `catch` clause that can process the type of exception that occurred. The program locates the matching `catch` by comparing the thrown exception's type with each `catch`'s exception-parameter type until the program finds a match. A match occurs if the types are identical or if the thrown exception's type is a subclass of the exception parameter's type. When a match occurs, the code contained within the matching `catch` handler executes. When a `catch` clause finishes processing, local variables declared within the `catch` clause

---

2. Some languages use the *resumption model of exception handling*, in which, after the handling of the exception, control returns to the point at which the exception was thrown and execution resumes from that point.

(including the catch parameter) go out of scope. Any remaining catch clauses that correspond to the try block are ignored and execution resumes at the first line of code after the try/catch sequence.

Software Engineering Observation 15.6

If you know that a method might throw an exception, include appropriate exception-handling code in your program. This will make your program more robust.

Good Programming Practice 15.2

Read the online API documentation for a method before using that method in a program. The documentation specifies the exceptions thrown by the method (if any) and indicates reasons why such exceptions may occur.

Good Programming Practice 15.3

Read the online API documentation for an exception class before writing exception-handling code for that type of exception. The documentation for an exception class typically contains potential reasons that such exceptions would occur during program execution.

If no exceptions occur in a try block, the program ignores the catch handler(s) for that block. Program execution resumes with the next statement after the try/catch sequence. If a finally clause appears after the last catch clause, the finally clause executes regardless of whether an exception occurs. If an exception occurs in a method and is not caught, or the statement that caused the exception is not in a try block, the method that contains the statement terminates immediately, and the program attempts to locate an enclosing try block in the calling method. This process, discussed in Section 15.7, is called *stack unwinding*).

In a method declaration, a *throws clause* specifies the exceptions the method throws. This clause appears after the parameter list and before the method body. The clause contains a comma-separated list of exceptions the method will throw if a problem occurs when the method executes. Such exceptions may be thrown by statements in the method's body, or they may be thrown by methods called in the body. A method can throw exceptions of indicated classes, or it can throw exceptions of their subclasses.

15.3 Exception-Handling Example: Divide by Zero

Consider a simple example of exception handling. The application in Fig. 15.1 uses try and catch to wrap code that might throw a "divide-by-zero" exception and to handle that exception, should one occur. The application displays two JTextFields in which the user can type integers. When the user presses the *Enter* key in the second JTextField, the program calls method actionPerformed to read the two integers from the JTextFields and pass the integers to method quotient, which calculates the quotient of the two values and returns an int result. Java does not allow division by zero in integer arithmetic. When this occurs, Java throws an ArithmeticException. In this example, if the user types 0 in the second JTextField, an ArithmeticException occurs and the program catches the exception. Also, prior examples that read numeric values from the user assumed that the user would input a proper integer value. However, users sometimes make mistakes and input noninteger values. If Integer method parseInt receives a string that does not represent a valid integer, the method throws a NumberFormatException. So, this program demonstrates how to catch NumberFormatExceptions as well.

```
1   // Fig. 15.1: DivideByZeroTest.java
2   // An exception-handling example that checks for divide-by-zero.
3   import java.awt.*;
4   import java.awt.event.*;
5   import javax.swing.*;
6
7   public class DivideByZeroTest extends JFrame
8      implements ActionListener {
9
10     private JTextField inputField1, inputField2, outputField;
11     private int number1, number2, result;
12
13     // set up GUI
14     public DivideByZeroTest()
15     {
16        super( "Demonstrating Exceptions" );
17
18        // get content pane and set its layout
19        Container container = getContentPane();
20        container.setLayout( new GridLayout( 3, 2 ) );
21
22        // set up label and inputField1
23        container.add(
24           new JLabel( "Enter numerator ", SwingConstants.RIGHT ) );
25        inputField1 = new JTextField();
26        container.add( inputField1 );
27
28        // set up label and inputField2; register listener
29        container.add( new JLabel( "Enter denominator and press Enter ",
30           SwingConstants.RIGHT ) );
31        inputField2 = new JTextField();
32        container.add( inputField2 );
33        inputField2.addActionListener( this );
34
35        // set up label and outputField
36        container.add( new JLabel( "RESULT ", SwingConstants.RIGHT ) );
37        outputField = new JTextField();
38        container.add( outputField );
39
40        setSize( 425, 100 );
41        setVisible( true );
42
43     } // end DivideByZeroTest constructor
44
45     // process GUI events
46     public void actionPerformed( ActionEvent event )
47     {
48        outputField.setText( "" );   // clear outputField
49
50        // read two numbers and calculate quotient
51        try {
52           number1 = Integer.parseInt( inputField1.getText() );
53           number2 = Integer.parseInt( inputField2.getText() );
```

Fig. 15.1   Exception-handling example with divide by zero. (Part 1 of 2.)

```
54           result = quotient( number1, number2 );
55           outputField.setText( String.valueOf( result ) );
56        }
57
58
59        // process improperly formatted input
60        catch ( NumberFormatException numberFormatException ) {
61           JOptionPane.showMessageDialog( this,
62              "You must enter two integers", "Invalid Number Format",
63              JOptionPane.ERROR_MESSAGE );
64        }
65
66        // process attempts to divide by zero
67        catch ( ArithmeticException arithmeticException ) {
68           JOptionPane.showMessageDialog( this,
69              arithmeticException.toString(), "Arithmetic Exception",
70              JOptionPane.ERROR_MESSAGE );
71        }
72
73     } // end method actionPerformed
74
75     // demonstrates throwing an exception when a divide-by-zero occurs
76     public int quotient( int numerator, int denominator )
77        throws ArithmeticException
78     {
79        return numerator / denominator;
80     }
81
82     public static void main( String args[] )
83     {
84        DivideByZeroTest application = new DivideByZeroTest();
85        application.setDefaultCloseOperation( JFrame.EXIT_ON_CLOSE );
86     }
87
88  } // end class DivideByZeroTest
```

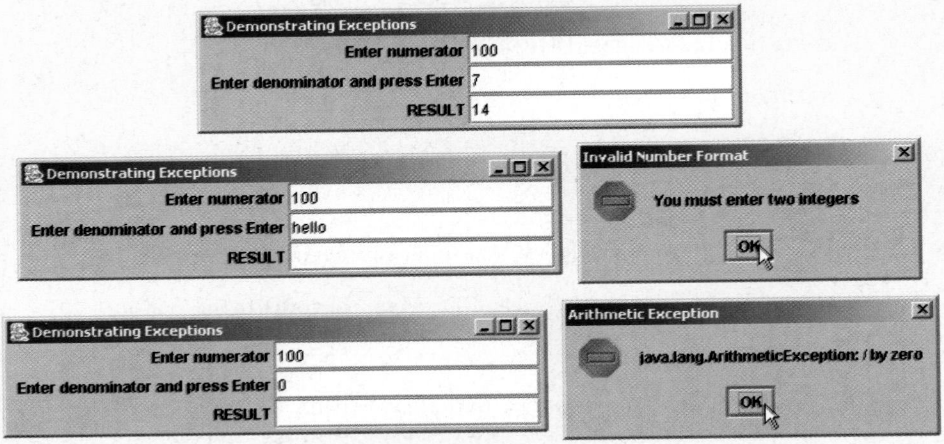

Fig. 15.1   Exception-handling example with divide by zero. (Part 2 of 2.)

In the Fig. 15.1 output, the first window shows a successful division. In the next two output windows, the user entered the string "hello" in the second JTextField. When the user presses *Enter* in the second JTextField, an error-message dialog is displayed, indicating that an integer must be entered. In the last two windows, the user entered a zero denominator. The program detected the problem, threw an exception and issued an appropriate diagnostic message.

Now consider the DivideByZeroTest application (Fig. 15.1). The application's constructor (lines 14–43) builds a graphical user interface with three JLabels (all right aligned) and three JTextFields and registers the DivideByZeroTest object as the ActionListener for JTextField inputField2 (line 33).

When the user inputs the denominator and presses the *Enter* key, the program calls method actionPerformed (lines 46–73), which begins by clearing the contents of outputField (line 48). Next, method actionPerformed proceeds with a try block (lines 51–57), which encloses the code that might throw an exception and the code that should not execute if an exception occurs. The statements that read the integers from the JTextFields (lines 52–53) each use method Integer.parseInt to convert a string to an int value. Method parseInt throws a NumberFormatException if its argument does not represent a valid integer. The division that can cause an ArithmeticException is not performed explicitly in the try block. Rather, the call to method quotient (line 55) contains the code that attempts the division. Method quotient (lines 76–80) throws the ArithmeticException object, as we will see momentarily. In general, exceptions may surface through explicitly mentioned code in a try block, through calls to other methods or even through deeply nested method calls initiated by code in a try block.

The try block in this example is followed by two catch clauses: lines 60–64 contain the catch clause for a NumberFormatException and lines 67–71 contain the catch clause for an ArithmeticException. In general, when the program detects an exception while executing a try block, the program catches the exception in a catch clause that specifies an appropriate exception type (i.e., the type in the catch matches the thrown exception type exactly or is a superclass of the thrown exception type). In Fig. 15.1, the first catch clause specifies that it will catch exception objects of type NumberFormatException (this type matches the exception object type thrown in method Integer.parseInt) and the second catch clause specifies that it will catch exception objects of type ArithmeticException. Only the matching catch clause executes when an exception occurs. Both our catch clauses simply display an error-message dialog, but catch clauses can be more elaborate than this. After executing an catch clause, this program's flow of control proceeds to the first statement after the last catch clause. In this case, control proceeds to line 72 and method actionPerformed returns to its caller.

If the code in the try block does not throw an exception, then the catch handlers following that try block are skipped and execution resumes with the first line of code after the catch handlers. (Again, method actionPerformed terminates). In Fig. 15.1, method actionPerformed simply returns, but the program could continue executing more statements after the catch clauses.

Common Programming Error 15.6

Logic errors can occur if you assume that after an exception is processed, control will return to the first statement after the throw. Program control continues with the first statement after the catch handlers.

Error-Prevention Tip 15.2

With exception handling, a program can continue executing after dealing with a problem. This helps ensure robust applications that contribute to what is called mission-critical computing or business-critical computing.

Now let us examine method `quotient` (lines 76–80). When the `denominator` is zero, Java throws an `ArithmethicException` object for the division at line 79. This object will be caught by the `catch` clause (lines 67–71) in `actionPerformed`. The `ArithmeticException` handler converts the exception to a string through `toString` and displays this string as the message in an error-message dialog.

If `denominator` is not zero, `quotient` performs the division and returns the result of the division to the point of invocation of method `quotient` in the `try` block (line 55). Line 56 displays the result of the calculation in the third JTextField. In this case, the `try` block completes successfully, so the program skips the `catch` clauses and the `action-Performed` method completes execution normally.

Note that when `quotient` throws the `ArithmeticException`, `quotient` terminates and does not return a value, where would cause any of `quotient`'s local variables to go out of scope. If `quotient` contained local variables that were references to objects, those objects would have their reference counts decremented accordingly, and the objects possibly would be marked for garbage collection. Also, when the exception occurs, the `try` block from which `quotient` was called terminates before line 56 can execute. Here, too, if there were local variables created in the `try` block prior to the exception being thrown, these variables would go out of scope.

If a `NumberFormatException` is generated by lines 52–53, the `try` block terminates, and execution continues with the `catch` clause at line 60, which displays an error message to tell the user to input integers. In this case, method `quotient` never gets called. Then the `actionPerformed` method continues with the next valid statement after the `catch` clauses (i.e., the method terminates in this example).

15.4 Java Exception Hierarchy

This section examines Java's inheritance hierarchy of exceptions. Exceptions, like almost everything in Java, are objects. Thus, programmers can create exception-class hierarchies. Figure 15.2 shows a small portion of the inheritance hierarchy for class *Throwable* (a subclass of `Object`), which is the superclass of all exceptions. Only `Throwable` objects can be used with the exception-handling mechanism. Class `Throwable` has two subclasses: *Exception* and *Error*. Class `Exception` and its subclasses (e.g., `RuntimeException` and `IOException`, each from package `java.lang`) represent exceptional situations that could occur in a Java program and be caught by the application. Class `Error` and its subclasses (e.g., `OutOfMemoryError`) represent exceptional situations that could happen in the Java runtime system, but typically should not be caught by an application.

Java distinguishes between two categories of exceptions: *checked exceptions* and *unchecked exceptions*. This distinction is important, because the Java compiler enforces a *catch-or-declare requirement* for checked exceptions. The compiler *checks* each method call and method declaration to determine whether the method throws checked exceptions. If so, the compiler ensures that the checked exception is caught or declared in a `throws` clause. To satisfy the *catch* part of the catch-or-declare requirement, the code that generates

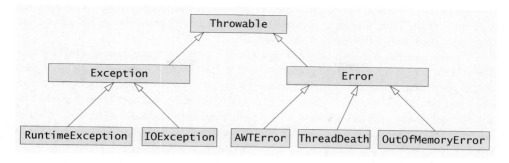

Fig. 15.2   Inheritance hierarchy for class `Throwable`.

the exception must be wrapped in a `try` block and must provide a `catch` handler for the checked-exception type (or one of its superclass types). To satisfy the *declare* part of the catch-or-declare requirement, the method containing the code that generates the exception must provide a `throws` clause containing the checked-exception type after its parameter list and before its method body. If the catch-or-declare requirement is not satisfied, the compiler will issue an error message indicating that the exception must be caught or declared.

Common Programming Error 15.7

A compilation error occurs if a method attempts to throw a checked exception that is not listed in that method's `throws` clause.

Common Programming Error 15.8

If a subclass method overrides a superclass method, it is an error for the subclass method to list more exceptions in its `throws` clause than the overridden superclass method does. However, a subclass's `throws` clause can contain a subset of a superclass's `throws` list.

Software Engineering Observation 15.7

If your method calls other methods that explicitly throw checked exceptions, those exceptions must be caught or declared in your method. If possible, a method should catch an exception rather than declare it.

The Java compiler does not check the code to determine whether an unchecked exception is caught or declared. `Error`s are considered to be unchecked by the compiler, because they typically cannot be handled by a program.

Unchecked exceptions typically can be prevented by proper coding. For example, the unchecked `ArithmeticException` (a subclass of `RuntimeException`) thrown by method `quotient` (lines 76–80) in Fig. 15.1 can be avoided if the method ensures that the denominator is not zero before attempting to perform the division. Unchecked exceptions are not required to be listed in a method's `throws` clause.

Software Engineering Observation 15.8

Although the compiler does not enforce the catch-or-declare requirement for unchecked exceptions, provide appropriate exception-handling code when it is known that such exceptions might occur. For example, a program should process NumberFormatExceptions from Integer method parseInt, even though NumberFormatExceptions are unchecked exceptions. (Class NumberFormatException is a subclass of RuntimeException.) This makes your programs more robust.

An exception's type determines whether the exception is checked or unchecked. All exception types that are direct or indirect subclasses of class `RuntimeException` (package `java.lang`) are unchecked exceptions.

Various exception classes can be derived from a common superclass. If a `catch` handler is written to catch exception objects of a superclass type, it can also catch all objects of that class's subclasses. This enables an `catch` clause to handle related errors with a concise notation and allows for polymorphic processing of related exceptions. One could certainly catch each subclass exception object individually if those exceptions require different processing. Of course, catching related exceptions in one `catch` clause makes sense only if the handling behavior would be the same for all subclasses. Otherwise, catch each subclass exception individually.

Error-Prevention Tip 15.3

Catching subclass exception objects individually is subject to error if you forget to test for one or more of the subclass types explicitly; catching the superclass guarantees that objects of all subclasses will be caught. Often, an `catch` clause for the superclass type follows all other subclass `catch` clauses to ensure that all exceptions are processed properly.

15.5 Rethrowing an Exception

It is possible that an `catch` clause, upon receiving an exception, might decide either that it cannot process that exception or that it can only partially process the exception. In such cases, the `catch` clause can defer the exception handling (or perhaps a portion of it) to another `catch` clause. In either case, the handler achieves this by *rethrowing* the exception via the statement

> `throw` *exceptionReference*;

where *exceptionReference* is the parameter name for the exception in the `catch` handler.

When a rethrow occurs, the next enclosing `try` block detects the rethrown exception, which the `catch` handler listed after that enclosing `try` block attempts to handle.

Good Programming Practice 15.4

If your method is capable of handling a given type of exception, then handle it rather than passing the exception onto other regions of your program. This makes programs clearer.

15.6 `finally` Clause

Programs that obtain certain types of resources must return those resources to the system explicitly to avoid so-called *resource leaks*. In programming languages such as C and C++, the most common kind of resource leak is a memory leak. Java performs automatic garbage collection of memory no longer used by programs, thus avoiding most memory leaks. However, other types of resource leaks can occur in Java. For example, files, database connections and network connections that are not closed properly might not be available for use in other programs, or even later in the same program's execution.

Software Engineering Observation 15.9

A `finally` clause typically contains code to release resources acquired in its corresponding `try` block; this is an effective way to eliminate resource leaks. For example, the `finally` clause should close any files opened in the `try` block.

Error-Prevention Tip 15.4

A subtle issue is that Java does not eliminate memory leaks completely. Java will not garbage collect an object until there are no more references to the object. Thus, memory leaks can occur, but only if programmers erroneously keep references to unwanted objects. Most memory leak problems are solved by Java's garbage collection.

The `finally` clause is optional. If it is present, it is placed after the last `catch` clause, as follows:

```
try {
    statements
    resource-acquisition statements
}
catch ( AKindOfException exception1 ) {
    exception-handling statements
}
catch ( AnotherKindOfException exception2 ) {
    exception-handling statements
}
finally {
    statements
    resource-release statements
}
```

Java guarantees that a `finally` clause (if one is present following a `try/catch` sequence) will execute whether or not an exception is thrown in the corresponding `try` block or any of its corresponding `catch` clauses. Java also guarantees that a `finally` clause (if one is present) will execute if a `try` block exits by using a `return`, `break` or `continue` statement.

Resource-release code typically is placed in a `finally` clause. Suppose a resource is allocated in a `try` block. If no exception occurs, the `catch` handlers are skipped and control proceeds to the `finally` clause, which frees the resource. Control proceeds to the first statement after the `finally` clause. If an exception does occur, the program skips the rest of the `try` block. If the program catches the exception in one of the `catch` handlers, the program processes the exception. Then the `finally` clause releases the resource and control proceeds to the first statement after the `finally` clause.

If an exception that occurs in the `try` block cannot be caught by one of that `try` block's the `catch` handlers, the program skips the rest of the `try` block and control proceeds to the `finally` clause, which releases the resource. Then the program passes the exception up the call chain (i.e., to the calling method), which attempts to catch it. This process can occur many times.

If a `catch` handler throws an exception, the `finally` clause still executes. Then the exception is passed to the calling method.

The Java application of Fig. 15.3 demonstrates that the `finally` clause (if one is present following a `try/catch` sequence) executes even if an exception is not thrown in the corresponding `try` block. The program contains methods `main` (lines 5–17), `throwException` (lines 20–44) and `doesNotThrowException` (lines 47–67). Methods `throwException` and `doesNotThrowException` are declared `static` so `main` (another `static` method) can call them directly.

```
1   // Fig. 15.3: UsingExceptions.java
2   // Demonstration of the try-catch-finally exception handling mechanism.
3   public class UsingExceptions {
4
5      public static void main( String args[] )
6      {
7         try {
8            throwException(); // call method throwException
9         }
10
11        // catch Exceptions thrown by method throwException
12        catch ( Exception exception ) {
13           System.err.println( "Exception handled in main" );
14        }
15
16        doesNotThrowException();
17     }
18
19     // demonstrate try/catch/finally
20     public static void throwException() throws Exception
21     {
22        // throw an exception and immediately catch it
23        try {
24           System.out.println( "Method throwException" );
25           throw new Exception();   // generate exception
26        }
27
28        // catch exception thrown in try block
29        catch ( Exception exception ) {
30           System.err.println(
31              "Exception handled in method throwException" );
32           throw exception;   // rethrow for further processing
33
34           // any code here would not be reached
35        }
36
37        // this block executes regardless of what occurs in try/catch
38        finally {
39           System.err.println( "Finally executed in throwException" );
40        }
41
42        // any code here would not be reached
43
44     } // end method throwException
45
46     // demonstrate finally when no exception occurs
47     public static void doesNotThrowException()
48     {
49        // try block does not throw an exception
50        try {
51           System.out.println( "Method doesNotThrowException" );
52        }
```

Fig. 15.3   `try-catch-finally` exception-handling mechanism. (Part 1 of 2.)

```
53
54        // catch does not execute, because no exception thrown
55        catch ( Exception exception ) {
56            System.err.println( exception );
57        }
58
59        // this clause executes regardless of what occurs in try/catch
60        finally {
61            System.err.println(
62                "Finally executed in doesNotThrowException" );
63        }
64
65        System.out.println( "End of method doesNotThrowException" );
66
67     } // end method doesNotThrowException
68
69 } // end class UsingExceptions
```

```
Method throwException
Exception handled in method throwException
Finally executed in throwException
Exception handled in main
Method doesNotThrowException
Finally executed in doesNotThrowException
End of method doesNotThrowException
```

Fig. 15.3   `try-catch-finally` exception-handling mechanism. (Part 2 of 2.)

Method `main` begins executing, enters its `try` block and immediately calls method `throwException` (line 8). Method `throwException` throws an `Exception` (line 25), catches it (line 29) and rethrows it (line 32). The rethrown exception will be handled in `main`, but first, the `finally` clause (lines 38–40) executes. Method `main` detects the rethrown exception in the `try` block in `main` (lines 7–9) and handles it by the `catch` clause (lines 12–14). Next, `main` calls method `doesNotThrowException` (line 16). No exception is thrown in `doesNotThrowException`'s `try` block (lines 50–52), so the program skips the `catch` clause (lines 55–57), but the `finally` clause (lines 60–63) nevertheless executes. Control proceeds to the statement after the `finally` clause. Then control returns to `main` and the program terminates.

Common Programming Error 15.9

If an exception has not been caught when control enters a `finally` clause and the `finally` clause throws an exception that is not caught in the `finally` clause, the first exception will be lost and the exception from the `finally` clause will be returned to the calling method.

Common Programming Error 15.10

Assuming that an exception thrown from a `catch` handler will be processed by that handler or any other handler associated with the same `try` block can lead to logic errors.

Error-Prevention Tip 15.5

Avoid placing code that can `throw` an exception in a `finally` clause. If such code is required, enclose the code in a `try/catch` within the `finally` clause.

Good Programming Practice 15.5

Java's exception-handling mechanism is intended to remove error-processing code from the main line of a program's code to improve program clarity. Do not place try/catch/final-ly *around every statement that may throw an exception. This makes programs difficult to read. Rather, place one* try *block around a significant portion of your code, follow that* try *block with* catch *clauses that handle each possible exception and follow the* catch *clauses with a single* finally *clause (if one is required).*

Performance Tip 15.2

As a rule, resources should be released as soon as it is apparent that they are no longer need-ed. This makes these resources immediately available for reuse and can improve program performance.

15.7 Stack Unwinding

When an exception is thrown but not caught in a particular scope, the method-call stack is unwound, and an attempt is made to catch the exception in the next outer try/catch statement. Unwinding the method-call stack means that the method in which the exception was not caught terminates, all local variables in that method go out of scope and control returns to the statement that originally invoked that method. If a try block encloses that statement, an attempt is made to catch the exception. If a try block does not enclose that statement, stack unwinding occurs again. If no catch handler ever catches this exception, the entire program (or a portion of it) will terminate.[3] The program of Fig. 15.4 demon-strates stack unwinding.

```
1   // Fig. 15.4: UsingExceptions.java
2   // Demonstration of stack unwinding.
3   public class UsingExceptions {
4
5       public static void main( String args[] )
6       {
7           // call throwException to demonstrate stack unwinding
8           try {
9               throwException();
10          }
11
12          // catch exception thrown in throwException
13          catch ( Exception exception ) {
14              System.err.println( "Exception handled in main" );
15          }
16      }
17
18      // throwException throws exception that is not caught in this method
19      public static void throwException() throws Exception
20      {
```

Fig. 15.4   Stack unwinding. (Part 1 of 2.)

---

3.   Chapter 16 discusses multithreading in which multiple parts of a program, called threads, run (or appear to run) in parallel. As we will see, an unhandled exception can terminate a thread of exe-cution. If that is the only remaining thread, the program will terminate.

```
21          // throw an exception and catch it in main
22          try {
23             System.out.println( "Method throwException" );
24             throw new Exception();       // generate exception
25          }
26
27          // catch is incorrect type, so Exception is not caught
28          catch ( RuntimeException runtimeException ) {
29             System.err.println(
30                "Exception handled in method throwException" );
31          }
32
33          // finally clause always executes
34          finally {
35             System.err.println( "Finally is always executed" );
36          }
37
38       } // end method throwException
39
40    } // end class UsingExceptions
```

```
Method throwException
Finally is always executed
Exception handled in main
```

Fig. 15.4   Stack unwinding. (Part 2 of 2.)

When method main executes, line 9 in the try block calls method throwException (lines 19–38). In the try block of method throwException, line 24 throws an Exception. This terminates the try block immediately and control proceeds to the catch handler at line 28. The type being caught (RuntimeException) is not an exact match with the thrown type (Exception) and is not a superclass of the thrown type, so the exception is not caught in method throwException. The exception must be handled before normal program execution can continue. Therefore, method throwException terminates (but not until its finally clause executes) and returns control to line 9—the point from which it was called in the program. Line 9 is in the enclosing try block. The exception has not yet been handled, so the try block terminates and an attempt is made to catch the exception at line 13. The type being caught (Exception) matches the thrown type. Consequently, the catch handler processes the exception and the program terminates at the end of main.

15.8 printStackTrace, getStackTrace and getMessage

Recall from Section 15.4 that exceptions derive from class Throwable. Class Throwable offers a *printStackTrace* method that prints the method-call stack. Often, this is helpful in testing and debugging. Class Throwable also provides a *getStackTrace* method that obtains stack-trace information printed by printStackTrace. Class Throwable's *getMessage* method returns the descriptive string stored in an exception. In this section, we consider an example that demonstrates these three methods.

Error-Prevention Tip 15.6

An exception that is not caught eventually causes Java's default exception handler to run. This displays the name of the exception, a message and a complete execution stack trace. The stack trace shows the method-call stack (i.e., the call chain) at the time the exception occurred, letting the programmer see the path of execution that led to the exception file-by-file (and thus class-by-class) and method-by-method. This information is helpful in debugging a program.

Error-Prevention Tip 15.7

`Throwable` method `toString` (inherited into all `Throwable` subclasses) returns a string containing the name of the class and the descriptive message that indicates the problem that occurred.

Good Programming Practice 15.6

Never ignore an exception you catch. At least use `printStackTrace` to output an error message.

Figure 15.5 demonstrates `getMessage`, `printStackTrace` and `getStackTrace`. Method `getMessage` returns the descriptive string stored in an exception. Method `printStackTrace` outputs to the standard error stream (normally, the command line or console) an error message with the class name of the exception, the descriptive string stored in the exception and a list of the methods that had not completed execution when the exception was thrown (i.e., all methods currently residing on the method-call stack). If we want to output the stack-trace information to streams other than the standard error stream, we could use `getStackTrace`.

```java
1   // Fig. 15.5: UsingExceptions.java
2   // Demonstrating getMessage and printStackTrace from class Exception.
3   public class UsingExceptions {
4
5      public static void main( String args[] )
6      {
7         try {
8            method1(); // call method1
9         }
10
11        // catch Exceptions thrown from method1
12        catch ( Exception exception ) {
13           System.err.println( exception.getMessage() + "\n" );
14           exception.printStackTrace();
15
16           // obtain the stack-trace information
17           StackTraceElement[] traceElements = exception.getStackTrace();
18
19           System.out.println( "\nStack trace from getStackTrace:" );
20           System.out.println( "Class\t\tFile\t\t\tLine\tMethod" );
21
```

Fig. 15.5   `Throwable` methods `getMessage`, `getStackTrace` and `printStackTrace`. (Part 1 of 2.)

```
22              // loop through traceElements to get exception description
23              for ( int i = 0; i < traceElements.length; i++ ) {
24                  StackTraceElement currentElement = traceElements[ i ];
25                  System.out.print( currentElement.getClassName() + "\t" );
26                  System.out.print( currentElement.getFileName() + "\t" );
27                  System.out.print( currentElement.getLineNumber() + "\t" );
28                  System.out.print( currentElement.getMethodName() + "\n" );
29
30              } // end for statement
31
32          } // end catch
33
34      } // end method main
35
36      // call method2; throw exceptions back to main
37      public static void method1() throws Exception
38      {
39          method2();
40      }
41
42      // call method3; throw exceptions back to method1
43      public static void method2() throws Exception
44      {
45          method3();
46      }
47
48      // throw Exception back to method2
49      public static void method3() throws Exception
50      {
51          throw new Exception( "Exception thrown in method3" );
52      }
53
54  } // end class Using Exceptions
```

```
Exception thrown in method3

java.lang.Exception: Exception thrown in method3
        at UsingExceptions.method3(UsingExceptions.java:51)
        at UsingExceptions.method2(UsingExceptions.java:45)
        at UsingExceptions.method1(UsingExceptions.java:39)
        at UsingExceptions.main(UsingExceptions.java:8)

Stack trace from getStackTrace:
Class              File                     Line    Method
UsingExceptions UsingExceptions.java        51      method3
UsingExceptions UsingExceptions.java        45      method2
UsingExceptions UsingExceptions.java        39      method1
UsingExceptions UsingExceptions.java        8       main
```

Fig. 15.5 Throwable methods getMessage, getStackTrace and printStackTrace.
(Part 2 of 2.)

In main, the try block (lines 7–9) calls method1 (declared at lines 37–40). Next,
method1 calls method2 (declared at lines 43–46), which in turn calls method3 (declared

at lines 49–52). Line 51 of method3 throws an Exception object. However, because no try block encloses the throw statement in line 51, stack unwinding occurs—method3 terminates at line 51, then returns control to the statement in method2 that invoked method3 (i.e., line 45). Because no try block encloses line 45, stack unwinding occurs again—method2 terminates at line 45 and returns control to the statement in method1 that invoked method2 (i.e., line 39). Because no try block encloses line 39, stack unwinding occurs one more time—method1 terminates at line 39 and returns control to the statement in main that invoked method1 (i.e., line 8). The try block of lines 7–9 encloses this statement. The exception has not been handled, so the try block terminates and the first matching catch handler (lines 12–32) catches and processes the exception.

Line 13 invokes the exception's getMessage method to get the exception description. Line 14 invokes the exception's printStackTrace method to output the stack trace that indicates where the exception occurred. Line 17 invokes the exception's getStackTrace method to obtain the stack-trace information as an array of *StackTraceElement* objects. Lines 23–30 get each StackTraceElement in the array and invoke its methods *getClassName*, *getFileName*, *getLineNumber* and *getMethodName* to get the class name, file name, line number and method name, respectively, for that StackTraceElement. Each StackTraceElement represents one method call on the method-call stack.

The output in Fig. 15.5 shows that the stack-trace information printed by printStackTrace follows the pattern: *className.methodName(fileName:lineNumber)*, where *className*, *methodName* and *fileName* indicate the names of the class, method and file in which the exception occurred, the *lineNumber* indicates where the exception occurred. Method getStackTrace enables custom processing of the exception information. Compare the output of printStackTrace with the output created from the StackTraceElements to see that both contain the same stack-trace information.

15.9 Chained Exceptions

It is relatively common for a catch handler to catch one exception type, then throw a new exception of a different type to indicate a program-specific exception that occurred. In earlier Java versions, there was no mechanism to wrap the original exception information with the new exception's information to provide a complete stack trace showing where the original problem occurred in the program. This made debugging such problems particularly difficult. The Java 2 Platform, Standard Edition, Version 1.4 provides *chained exceptions* to enable an exception object to maintain the complete stack-trace information. Figure 15.6 presents a mechanical example that demonstrates how chained exceptions work.

```
1   // Fig. 15.6: UsingChainedExceptions.java
2   // Demonstrating chained exceptions.
3   public class UsingChainedExceptions {
4
5      public static void main( String args[] )
6      {
7         try {
8            method1(); // call method1
9         }
```

Fig. 15.6   Chained exceptions. (Part 1 of 2.)

```
10
11          // catch Exceptions thrown from method1
12          catch ( Exception exception ) {
13              exception.printStackTrace();
14          }
15      }
16
17      // call method2; throw exceptions back to main
18      public static void method1() throws Exception
19      {
20          try {
21              method2(); // call method2
22          }
23
24          // catch Exception thrown from method2
25          catch ( Exception exception ) {
26              throw new Exception( "Exception thrown in method1", exception );
27          }
28      }
29
30      // call method3; throw exceptions back to method1
31      public static void method2() throws Exception
32      {
33          try {
34              method3(); // call method3
35          }
36
37          // catch Exception thrown from method3
38          catch ( Exception exception ) {
39              throw new Exception( "Exception thrown in method2", exception );
40          }
41      }
42
43      // throw Exception back to method2
44      public static void method3() throws Exception
45      {
46          throw new Exception( "Exception thrown in method3" );
47      }
48
49  } // end class Using Exceptions
```

```
java.lang.Exception: Exception thrown in method1
        at UsingChainedExceptions.method1(UsingChainedExceptions.java:26)
        at UsingChainedExceptions.main(UsingChainedExceptions.java:8)
Caused by: java.lang.Exception: Exception thrown in method2
        at UsingChainedExceptions.method2(UsingChainedExceptions.java:39)
        at UsingChainedExceptions.method1(UsingChainedExceptions.java:21)
        ... 1 more
Caused by: java.lang.Exception: Exception thrown in method3
        at UsingChainedExceptions.method3(UsingChainedExceptions.java:46)
        at UsingChainedExceptions.method2(UsingChainedExceptions.java:34)
        ... 2 more
```

Fig. 15.6   Chained exceptions. (Part 2 of 2.)

The program consists of four methods—main (lines 5–15), method1 (lines 18–28), method2 (lines 31–41) and method3 (lines 44–47). Line 8 in method main's try block calls method1. Line 21 in method1's try block calls method2. Line 34 in method2's try block calls method3. In method3, line 46 throws a new Exception. Because this statement is not in a try block, method3 terminates, and the exception is returned to the calling method (method2) at line 34. This statement is in a try block; therefore, the try block terminates and the exception is caught at lines 38–40. Line 39 in the catch handler throws a new exception. In this case, the Exception constructor with two arguments (which is new in J2SE 1.4) is called. The second argument represents the exception that was the original cause of the problem that occurred. In this program, that exception occurred in line 45. Because an exception in thrown from the catch handler, method2 terminates and returns the new exception to the calling method (method1) at line 21. Once again, this statement is in a try block, so the try block terminates and the exception is caught at lines 25–27. Line 26 in the catch handler throws a new exception and uses the exception that was caught as the second argument to the Exception constructor. Because an exception is thrown from the catch handler, method1 terminates and returns the new exception to the calling method (main) at line 8. The try block in main terminates, and the exception is caught in lines 12–14. Line 13 prints a stack trace.

Notice in the program output that the first three lines show the most recent exception that was thrown (i.e., the one from method1 at line 26). The next four lines indicate the exception that was thrown from method2 at line 39. Finally, the last four lines represent the exception that was thrown from method3 at line 46. Also, notice that as you read the output in reverse, it shows how many more chained exceptions there remain.

15.10 Declaring New Exception Types

Most Java programmers use existing classes from the Java API or from third-party vendors to build Java applications. The methods of those classes typically are declared to throw appropriate exceptions when problems occur. Programmers write code that processes those existing exceptions to make their programs more robust.

If you are a programmer who builds classes that other programmers will use in their programs, you might find it useful to declare your own exception classes that are specific to the problems that can occur when another programmer uses your reusable classes.

Software Engineering Observation 15.10

If possible, indicate exceptions from your methods by using an existing exception type, rather than creating a new class. The Java API contains many exception types that might be suitable for the type of problem your method needs to indicate.

A new exception class must extend an existing exception class to ensure that the class can be used with the exception-handling mechanism. Like any other class, an exception class can contain fields and methods. However, a typical new exception class contains only two constructors—one that takes no arguments and passes a default exception message to the superclass constructor and one that receives a customized exception message as a string and passes it to the superclass constructor.

Good Programming Practice 15.7

Associating each type of serious execution-time malfunction with an appropriately named Exception class improves program clarity.

Software Engineering Observation 15.11

When defining your own exception type, study the existing exception classes in the Java API and extend a related exception class. For example, if you are creating a new class to represent when a method attempts a division by zero, you might extend class ArithmeticException *because division by zero occurs during arithmetic. If the existing classes are not appropriate superclasses for your new exception class, decide whether your new class should be a checked or an unchecked exception class. The new exception class should be a checked exception (i.e., extend* Exception*) if the program should be required to handle the exception. The program should be able to reasonably recover from such an exception. The new class should extend* RuntimeException *if the client code should be able to ignore the exception (i.e., the exception is an unchecked exception).*

In Chapter 20, Data Structures, we provide an example of a custom exception class. We declare a reusable class called List that is capable of storing a list of references to objects. Some operations typically performed on a List are not allowed if the List is empty. For this reason, some List methods throw exceptions of exception class EmptyListException.

Good Programming Practice 15.8

By convention, all exception-class names should end with the word Exception*.*

15.11 Constructors and Exception Handling

What happens when an error is detected in a constructor? For example, how should an object's constructor respond when new fails and indicates that it was unable to allocate the required memory for storing that object's internal representation? Because the constructor cannot return a value to indicate an error, we must choose an alternative means to indicate that the object was not constructed properly. One scheme is to return the improperly constructed object and hope that anyone using the object would make appropriate tests to determine that the object exhibits an inconsistent state. Another scheme is to set some variable outside the constructor that indicates whether the object is ready for use. Perhaps the best alternative is to require the constructor to throw an exception, indicating the exact problem that occurred, thus offering an opportunity to handle the failure.

In this chapter, we demonstrated basic exception-handling concepts and constructs. The remaining chapters in the book demonstrate more advanced language features and APIs. As we will see, many of these language features and APIs generate checked exceptions when problems occur. The techniques you learned here will be important in building robust Java programs that in many cases can recover from problems that occur during program execution.

SUMMARY

- Common examples of exceptions are an out-of-bounds array index, arithmetic overflow, division by zero and invalid function parameters, as well as determining that there is insufficient memory to satisfy an allocation request by operator new.

- The spirit behind exception handling is to enable programs to catch and handle errors, rather than letting them occur and suffering the consequences.

- Exception handling is designed for dealing with synchronous errors (i.e., errors that occur as the result of a program's execution).

- Exception handling is not designed to deal with asynchronous situations, such as network message arrivals, disk I/O completions, mouse clicks and the like.

- Exception handling typically is used in situations in which the problem will be dealt with by a different part of the program (i.e., a different scope) from the one that detected the problem and threw the exception.

- Exceptions should not be used as a mechanism for specifying flow of control. Flow of control with conventional control structures generally is clearer and more efficient than with exceptions.

- Exception handling should be used to process exceptions from methods wherever it does not make sense for those methods to handle their own exceptions.

- Exception handling should be used on large projects to handle error processing in a uniform manner for the entire project.

- Java exception handling is geared to situations in which the method that detects an error is unable to deal with it. Such a method will `throw` an exception. If the exception matches the type of the parameter in one of the `catch` clauses, the code for that `catch` clause executes.

- The programmer encloses in a `try` block the code that may generate an exception and any code that should not execute if an exception occurs. The `try` block is followed by one or more `catch` clauses. Each `catch` clause is an exception handler that specifies the type of exception it can handle.

- If no exceptions are thrown in a `try` block, the `catch` clauses for that block are skipped. Then the program resumes execution after the last `catch` clause or after executing a `finally` clause (if one is provided).

- The operand of a `throw` can be of any class derived from `Throwable`. The immediate subclasses of `Throwable` are `Error` and `Exception`.

- Class `Exception` and its subclasses represent exceptional situations in a Java program and can be caught by the program.

- Class `Error` and its subclasses represent exceptional situations in the Java run-time system that typically should not be caught by a program.

- `RuntimeException`s and `Error`s are said to be "unchecked." All other exception types are said to be "checked." The checked exceptions thrown by a particular method must be specified in that method's `throws` clause.

- Exceptions are caught by the closest `catch` clause (for the `try` block from which the exception was thrown) specifying an appropriate type.

- An exception terminates the block in which the exception occurred.

- `catch( Exception exception )` catches all `Exception`s. `catch( Throwable throwable )` catches all `Exception`s and `Error`s.

- A handler may rethrow the object to an outer `try` block. Also, if no handler matches a particular thrown object, the search for a match continues in an enclosing `try` block.

- A subclass object can be caught either by a handler specifying that subclass type or by handlers specifying the types of any of its superclasses.

- A `catch` clause cannot access variables in the scope of its `try` block because, by the time the `catch` clause begins executing, the `try` block has terminated. Information the handler needs to process the exception is normally passed in the thrown object.

- Compilation errors occur if `catch` clauses for superclass types appear before `catch` clauses for subclass types.

- When an exception is caught, it is possible that resources may have been allocated, but not yet released in the `try` block. A `finally` clause should release these resources.

- It is possible that the handler that catches an exception may decide it cannot process the exception. In this case, the handler can simply rethrow the exception. A `throw` followed by the exception parameter name rethrows the exception.

- Even if a handler can process an exception, and regardless of whether it does any processing on that exception, the handler can rethrow the exception for further processing outside the handler. A rethrown exception is detected by the next enclosing `try` block (normally in a calling method) and is handled by an appropriate `catch` clause (if there is one) for that enclosing `try` block.

- A `throws` clause lists the checked exceptions that may be thrown from a method. A method may `throw` the indicated exceptions, or it may `throw` subclass types. If a checked exception not listed in the `throws` clause is thrown, a compilation error occurs.

- Chained exceptions enable a new exception object to wrap an existing exception object as part of the new exception. The stack trace will contain information about where the original exception occurred and where the new exception was thrown.

TERMINOLOGY

`ArithmeticException`
array exceptions
`ArrayIndexOutOfBoundsException`
business-critical computing
`catch ( Exception e )`
catch all exceptions
catch an exception
`catch` clause
catch-or-declare requirement
chained exception
checked exception
declare exceptions that can be thrown
default exception handler
`Error` class
error handling
exception
`Exception` class
exception handler
exception handling
exception object
fault tolerance
`finally` clause
`getMessage` method of `Throwable`

`getStackTrace` method of `Throwable`
handle an exception
`IOException`
memory exhaustion
mission-critical computing
`null` reference
`printStackTrace` method of `Throwable`
resource leak
resumption model of exception handling
rethrow an exception
`RuntimeException`
stack unwinding
`StackTraceElement`
synchronous error
termination model of exception handling
throw an exception
throw point
throw statement
`Throwable` class
`Throwable` class hierarchy
`throws` clause
`try` block
unchecked `Exception`

SELF-REVIEW EXERCISES

15.1   List five common examples of exceptions.

15.2   Give several reasons why exception-handling techniques should not be used for conventional program control.

15.3   Why are exceptions particularly appropriate for dealing with errors produced by methods of classes in the Java API?

15.4   What is a "resource leak"?

15.5   If no exceptions are thrown in a `try` block, where does control proceed to when the `try` block completes execution?

15.6   Give a key advantage of using `catch( Exception e )`.

15.7   Should a conventional applet or application catch `Error` objects?

15.8   What happens if no catch handler matches the type of a thrown object?

15.9   What happens if several handlers match the type of the thrown object?

15.10   Why would a programmer specify a superclass type as the type in a `catch` handler?

15.11   What is the key reason for using `finally` clauses?

15.12   What happens when a `catch` handler throws an `Exception`?

15.13   What does the statement `throw` *exceptionReference* do?

15.14   What happens to a local reference in a `try` block when that block throws an `Exception`?

ANSWERS TO SELF-REVIEW EXERCISES

15.1   Memory exhaustion, array index out of bounds, arithmetic overflow, division by zero, invalid method parameters.

15.2   (a) Exception handling is designed to handle infrequently occurring situations that often result in program termination, so compiler writers are not required to implement exception handling to perform optimally. (b) Flow of control with conventional control structures is generally clearer and more efficient than with exceptions. (c) Problems can occur because the stack is unwound when an exception occurs and resources allocated prior to the exception may not be freed. (d) The "additional" exceptions can get in the way of genuine error-type exceptions. It becomes more difficult for the programmer to keep track of the larger number of exception cases.

15.3   It is unlikely that methods of classes in the Java API could perform error processing that would meet the unique needs of all users.

15.4   A "resource leak" occurs when an executing program does not properly release a resource when the resource is no longer needed. If the program attempts to use the resource again in the future, the program may not be able to access the resource.

15.5   The `catch` clauses for that `try` statement are skipped, and the program resumes execution after the last `catch` clause. If there is a `finally` clause, it is executed first then the program resumes execution after the `finally` clause.

15.6   The form `catch( Exception e )` catches any type of exception thrown in a `try` statement. An advantage is that no thrown `Exception` can slip by without at least being caught. The programmer can then decide to handle the exception or possibly rethrow the exception.

15.7   `Error`s are usually serious problems with the underlying Java system; most programs will not want to catch `Error`s because the program will not be able to recover from such problems.

15.8   This causes the search for a match to continue in the next enclosing `try` statement.

15.9   The first matching `catch` clause after the `try` block is executed.

15.10   This enables a program to catch related types of exceptions and process them in a uniform manner. However, it is often useful to process the subclass types individually for more precise exception handling.

15.11   The `finally` clause is the preferred means for preventing resource leaks.

15.12 The exception will be processed by a `catch` handler (if one exists) associated with an enclosing `try` block (if one exists).

15.13 It rethrows the exception for processing by an exception handler of an enclosing `try` block.

15.14 The reference goes out of scope, and the reference count for the object is decremented. If the reference count becomes zero, the object is marked for garbage collection.

EXERCISES

15.15 List the various exceptional conditions that have occurred in programs throughout this text. List as many additional exceptional conditions as you can. For each of these, describe briefly how a program typically would handle the exception by using the exception-handling techniques discussed in this chapter. Some typical exceptions are division by zero, arithmetic overflow, array index out of bounds, etc.

15.16 Until this chapter, we have found that dealing with errors detected by constructors is a bit awkward. Explain why exception handling is an effective means for dealing with constructor failure.

15.17 Suppose a program throws an exception and the appropriate exception handler begins executing. Now suppose that the exception handler itself throws the same exception. Does this create an infinite recursion? Explain your answer.

15.18 Use inheritance to create an exception superclass and various exception subclasses. Write a program to demonstrate that the `catch` specifying the superclass catches subclass exceptions.

15.19 Write a program that demonstrates how various exceptions are caught with

```
catch ( Exception exception )
```

15.20 Write a program that shows that the order of `catch` clauses is important. If you try to catch a superclass exception type before a subclass type, the compiler should generate errors. Explain why these errors occur.

15.21 Write a program that shows a constructor passing information about constructor failure to an exception handler.

15.22 Write a program that illustrates rethrowing an exception.

15.23 Write a program that shows that a method with its own `try` block does not have to catch every possible error generated within the `try`. Some exceptions can slip through to, and be handled in, other scopes.

16

Multithreading

Objectives

- To understand multithreaded programming.
- To appreciate how multithreading can improve program performance.
- To understand the life cycle of a thread.
- To understand thread priorities and scheduling.
- To understand how to create, manage and destroy threads.
- To understand thread synchronization.
- To understand daemon threads.
- To be able to stop and suspend threads.
- To be able to display output from multiple threads in a Swing GUI.

The spider's touch, how exquisitely fine!
Feels at each thread, and lives along the line.
Alexander Pope

A person with one watch knows what time it is; a person with two watches is never sure.
Proverb

Learn to labor and to wait.
Henry Wadsworth Longfellow

The most general definition of beauty...Multeity in Unity.
Samuel Taylor Coleridge

16.1 Introduction

It would be nice if we could perform one action at a time and perform it well, but that is usually difficult to do. The human body performs a great variety of operations *in parallel*— or, as we will say throughout this chapter, *concurrently*. Respiration, blood circulation and digestion, for example, can occur concurrently. All the senses—sight, touch, smell, taste and hearing—can be employed at once. Computers, too, can perform operations concurrently.[1] It is common for desktop personal computers to compile a program, send a file to a printer and receive electronic mail messages over a network concurrently.

Most programming languages do not enable programmers to specify concurrent activities. Rather, programming languages generally provide only a simple set of control structures that enables programmers to perform one action at a time, proceeding to the next action after the previous one has finished. Historically, concurrency has been implemented as operating-system primitives available only to experienced systems programmers.

The Ada programming language, developed by the United States Department of Defense, made concurrency primitives widely available to defense contractors building military command-and-control systems. However, Ada has not been widely used in universities and commercial industry.

Java makes concurrency primitives available to the applications programmer. The programmer specifies that applications contain *threads of execution*, where each thread designates a portion of a program that may execute concurrently with other threads. This capability, called *multithreading*, gives the Java programmer powerful capabilities not available in the core C and C++ languages on which Java is based. [*Note*: On many computer platforms, C and C++ programs can perform multithreading by using platform-specific code libraries.]

---

1. Only computers that have multiple processors can execute operations concurrently. Operating systems on single-processor computers use various techniques to simulate concurrency, but on such computers only a single thread can execute at any given time.

Performance Tip 16.1

A problem with single-threaded applications is that lengthy activities must complete before other activities can begin. In a multithreaded application, threads can be distributed across multiple processors so that multiple tasks are performed concurrently. Multithreading can also increase performance on single-processor systems that simulate concurrency.

Software Engineering Observation 16.1

Unlike languages that do not have built-in multithreading capabilities (such as C and C++) and must therefore make non-portable calls to operating-system multithreading primitives, Java includes multithreading primitives as part of the language itself and as part of package `java.lang` *classes for manipulating threads in a portable manner across platforms.*

We will discuss many applications of concurrent programming. For example, when programs download large files, such as audio clips or video clips from the World Wide Web, users do not want to wait until an entire clip downloads before starting the playback. To solve this problem, we can put multiple threads to work—one thread downloads a clip, and another plays the clip. These activities, or *tasks*, proceed concurrently. To avoid choppy playback, we *synchronize* the threads so that the player thread does not begin until there is a sufficient amount of the clip in memory to keep the player thread busy.

Another example of multithreading is Java's automatic *garbage collection*. C and C++ require the programmer to reclaim dynamically allocated memory explicitly. Java provides a *garbage-collector thread* that reclaims memory which is no longer needed.

Error-Prevention Tip 16.1

When C and C++ programs do not properly reclaim dynamically allocated memory, an all-too-common error called a memory leak *occurs. Memory leaks can eventually exhaust the supply of free memory and may cause premature program termination. Java's automatic garbage collection eliminates the vast majority of memory leaks—in particular, those that are due to orphaned (unreferenced) objects.*

Writing multithreaded programs can be tricky. Although the human mind can perform functions concurrently, people find it difficult to jump between parallel trains of thought. To see why multithreading can be difficult to program and understand, try the following experiment: Open three books to page 1, and try reading the books concurrently. Read a few words from the first book, then read a few words from the second book, then read a few words from the third book, then loop back and read the next few words from the first book, etc. After this experiment, you will appreciate the challenges of multithreading—switching between books, reading briefly, remembering your place in each book, moving the book you are reading closer so you can see it, and pushing books you are not reading aside—and, amidst all this chaos, trying to comprehend the content of the books!

Although Java is perhaps the world's most portable programming language, the execution behavior of certain programs can vary across platforms. In particular, the threading mechanisms in various operating systems handle thread scheduling differently. Thread scheduling is the process by which each thread is given the processor so that the thread can perform its task. Each thread has a *priority* that helps the thread scheduler determine the order in which threads are scheduled. On some platforms, a thread of a given priority runs to completion or until a higher priority thread requires the processor. In the latter case, the processor is given to the higher priority thread, and lower-priority threads must wait. On other platforms (such as Microsoft Windows), threads are *timesliced*. In this scenario, each thread is given a limited amount of time (called a time *quantum*) to execute on a processor; when that time expires, the thread waits while another thread of equal priority gets a chance to use its quantum. This process occurs in round-robin fashion, such that all threads of equal priority get a chance to execute. Eventually, the original thread resumes execution.[2]

Portability Tip 16.1

Java thread scheduling is platform dependent. Thus, an application that uses multithreading could behave differently on various Java implementations.

16.2 Thread States: Life Cycle of a Thread

At any time, a thread is said to be in one of several *thread states* (illustrated in the UML stat-echart diagram of Fig. 16.1). A new thread begins its life cycle by transitioning to the *Born* state. The thread remains in the *Born* state until the program calls Thread method start, which transitions the thread to the *Ready* state (sometimes called the *Runnable* state). Then

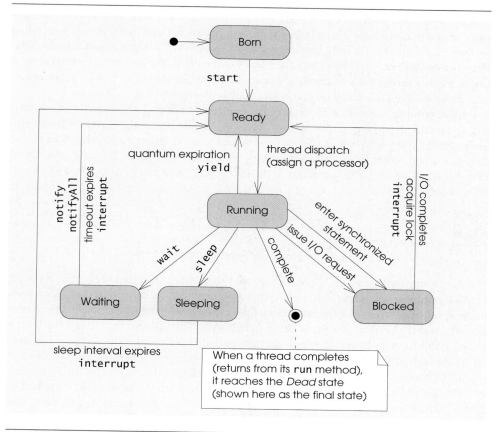

Fig. 16.1   Thread life-cycle statechart diagram.

2.   Thread priorities and thread scheduling are discussed in more detail in Section 16.3.

the thread that invoked start, the newly started thread and any other threads in the program execute concurrently. A thread in the *Ready* state transitions to the *Running* state (i.e., begins executing) when the operating system assigns a processor to the thread—also known as *dispatching the thread*.

A *Running* thread transitions to the *Dead* state when its run method completes or is terminated by an uncaught exception. In the UML statechart diagram of Fig. 16.1, the *Dead* state is represented as the UML final state (the bull's-eye symbol). When a thread is *Dead* and there are no references to the thread object, the garbage collector can remove the thread object from memory.

A thread transitions to the *Blocked* state when the thread attempts to perform a task that cannot be completed immediately and the thread must temporarily wait until that task can be completed—e.g., when a thread issues an input/output request. In this case, the operating system blocks the thread from executing until that I/O request can be completed. At that point, the thread transitions to the *Ready* state, so it can be dispatched again and resume execution. A *Blocked* thread cannot use a processor even if one is available.[3]

If a thread encounters code that it cannot execute yet (normally because the thread requires some condition to be satisfied), the thread can call Object method *wait* to transition to the *Waiting* state. Once in this state, a thread transitions to the *Ready* state when another thread invokes Object method *notify* or *notifyAll* on the object for which the thread is waiting (i.e., the object on which wait was called). Method notify transitions a single waiting thread back to the *Ready* state. Invoking method notifyAll on an object transitions all threads waiting on that object back to the *Ready* state.

If the program calls Thread method *interrupt* on a thread, the thread's *interrupted flag* is set and, depending on the thread's state, an InterruptedException is thrown. For example, if a thread is in the *Sleeping* state and method interrupt is invoked on the thread, method sleep will throw an InterruptedException. In this case, the thread exits the *Sleeping* state and transitions to the *Ready* state, so it can be dispatched again and process the exception.

 Portability Tip 16.2

Thread notification is platform dependent. On some platforms, the first thread that is waiting on an object is the first thread notified. On other implementations, an arbitrary thread waiting on an object is notified, regardless of which thread began waiting first.

A *Running* thread can call Thread method *sleep* to transition to the *Sleeping* state for a period of milliseconds specified as sleep's argument. A sleeping thread transitions back to the *Ready* state when its designated sleep time expires. Sleeping threads cannot use a processor, even if one is available. If the program calls Thread method interrupt on a sleeping thread, that thread throws an InterruptedException, exits the *Sleeping* state and transitions to the *Ready* state, so it can be dispatched again.

If a thread cannot continue executing (we will call this the dependent thread) unless another thread terminates, the dependent thread calls the other thread's *join* method to "join" the two threads. When two threads are "joined," the dependent thread leaves the *Waiting* state when the other thread finishes execution (enters the *Dead* state).

---

3. In Section 16.7, we will see another case in which a thread enters the *Blocked* state.

16.3 Thread Priorities and Thread Scheduling

Java programs can be multithreaded. Every Java thread has a priority in the range between Thread.MIN_PRIORITY (a constant of 1) and Thread.MAX_PRIORITY (a constant of 10). Informally, threads with higher priority are more important to a program and should be allocated processor time before lower priority threads. However, thread priorities cannot guarantee the order in which threads execute. By default, each thread is given priority Thread.NORM_PRIORITY (a constant of 5). Each new thread inherits the priority of the thread that creates it.

Most Java platforms support a concept called *timeslicing*, which enables threads of equal priority to share a processor. Without timeslicing, each thread in a set of equal-priority threads runs to completion (unless the thread leaves the *Running* state and enters the *Waiting*, *Sleeping* or *Blocked* state, or the thread gets interrupted by a higher priority thread) before other threads of equal priority get a chance to execute. With timeslicing, each thread receives a brief burst of processor time, called a *quantum*, during which the thread can execute. When the quantum expires, even if the thread has not finished executing, the processor is taken away from that thread and given to the next thread of equal priority, if one is available.

The job of the *thread scheduler* is to keep the highest-priority thread *Running* at all times and, if there is more than one highest-priority thread, to ensure that all such threads execute for a quantum each in round-robin fashion. Figure 16.2 illustrates Java's multilevel priority queue for threads. In the figure, assuming a single-processor computer, threads *A* and *B* each execute for a quantum in round-robin fashion until both threads complete execution. This means that *A* gets a quantum of time to run. Then *B* gets a quantum. Then *A* gets another quantum. Then *B* gets another quantum. This continues until one thread completes. The processor then devotes all its power to the thread that remains (unless another thread of that priority is ready). Next, thread *C* runs to completion. Threads *D*, *E* and *F* each execute for a quantum in round-robin fashion until they all complete execution. This process continues until all threads run to completion. Note that, depending on the operating system, new higher-priority threads could postpone—possibly indefinitely—the execution of lower-priority threads. Such *indefinite postponement* often is referred to more colorfully as *starvation*. A thread's priority can be adjusted with Thread method *setPriority*, which accepts an int argument. If the argument is not in the range 1 through 10, setPriority throws an *IllegalArgumentException*. Thread method *getPriority* returns the thread's priority.

A thread can call Thread method *yield* to give other threads a chance to execute. However, whenever a higher priority thread enters the *Ready* state, the operating system preempts the current thread (an operation known as *preemptive scheduling*). So, a thread cannot yield to a higher priority thread, because the first thread would have been preempted when the higher priority thread became ready. If only lower priority threads are ready at the time of a yield call, the current thread will be the highest priority thread and will continue executing. Therefore, a thread yields to give threads of equal priority a chance to run. On a timesliced system this is unnecessary, because threads of equal priority will each execute for their quantum (or until they lose the processor for some other reason), and other threads of equal priority will execute in round-robin fashion. Thus yield is helpful for non timesliced systems in which a thread would ordinarily run to completion before another thread of equal priority would have an opportunity to run.

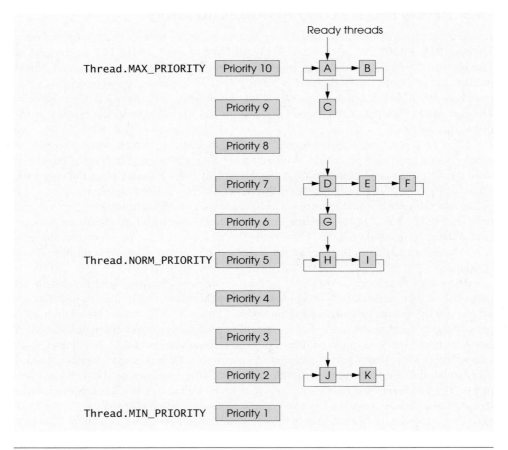

Fig. 16.2   Thread priority scheduling example.

Performance Tip 16.2

On non timesliced systems, cooperating threads of equal priority should periodically call yield *to enable their peers to proceed smoothly.*

Portability Tip 16.3

Java applets and applications should be programmed to work on all Java platforms to realize Java's goal of true portability. When designing applets and applications that use threads, you must consider the threading capabilities of all the platforms on which the applets and applications will execute.

A thread executes until it dies; becomes blocked for input/output (or some other reason); calls sleep, wait or yield; is preempted by a thread of higher priority; or has its quantum expire. A thread with a higher priority than the *Running* thread can become ready (and hence preempt the *Running* thread) if such a thread is started; if such a thread is sleeping and subsequently wakes up; if I/O completes for such a thread that was blocked for that I/O; or if either method notify or method notifyAll is called on an object on which wait was previously called.

16.4 Creating and Executing Threads

Figure 16.3 demonstrates basic threading techniques, such as constructing Thread objects and using Thread method sleep. The program creates three threads of execution, each with the default priority Thread.NORM_PRIORITY. Each thread displays a message indicating that it is going to sleep for a random interval from 0 to 5000 milliseconds, then goes to sleep. When each thread awakens, the thread displays its name, indicates that it is done sleeping, terminates and enters the *Dead* state. You will see that method main (i.e., the *main thread of execution*) terminates before the application terminates. The program consists of two classes—ThreadTester (lines 4–23), which creates the three threads, and PrintThread (lines 26–59), which contains in its run method the actions each Print-Thread will perform.

```java
1   // Fig. 16.3: ThreadTester.java
2   // Multiple threads printing at different intervals.
3
4   public class ThreadTester {
5
6      public static void main( String [] args )
7      {
8         // create and name each thread
9         PrintThread thread1 = new PrintThread( "thread1" );
10        PrintThread thread2 = new PrintThread( "thread2" );
11        PrintThread thread3 = new PrintThread( "thread3" );
12
13        System.err.println( "Starting threads" );
14
15        thread1.start(); // start thread1 and place it in ready state
16        thread2.start(); // start thread2 and place it in ready state
17        thread3.start(); // start thread3 and place it in ready state
18
19        System.err.println( "Threads started, main ends\n" );
20
21     } // end main
22
23   } // end class ThreadTester
24
25   // class PrintThread controls thread execution
26   class PrintThread extends Thread {
27      private int sleepTime;
28
29      // assign name to thread by calling superclass constructor
30      public PrintThread( String name )
31      {
32         super( name );
33
34         // pick random sleep time between 0 and 5 seconds
35         sleepTime = ( int ) ( Math.random() * 5001 );
36      }
37
```

Fig. 16.3   Threads sleeping and printing. (Part 1 of 2.)

```
38        // method run is the code to be executed by new thread
39        public void run()
40        {
41            // put thread to sleep for sleepTime amount of time
42            try {
43                System.err.println(
44                    getName() + " going to sleep for " + sleepTime );
45
46                Thread.sleep( sleepTime );
47            }
48
49            // if thread interrupted during sleep, print stack trace
50            catch ( InterruptedException exception ) {
51                exception.printStackTrace();
52            }
53
54            // print thread name
55            System.err.println( getName() + " done sleeping" );
56
57        } // end method run
58
59    } // end class PrintThread
```

```
Starting threads
Threads started, main ends

thread1 going to sleep for 1217
thread2 going to sleep for 3989
thread3 going to sleep for 662
thread3 done sleeping
thread1 done sleeping
thread2 done sleeping
```

```
Starting threads
thread1 going to sleep for 314
thread2 going to sleep for 1990
Threads started, main ends

thread3 going to sleep for 3016
thread1 done sleeping
thread2 done sleeping
thread3 done sleeping
```

Fig. 16.3 Threads sleeping and printing. (Part 2 of 2.)

Class PrintThread (lines 26–59) extends Thread, so that each PrintThread object can execute concurrently. The class consists of field sleepTime (line 27), a constructor (lines 30–36) and a run method (lines 39–57). Variable sleepTime stores a random integer value chosen when a new PrintThread object's constructor is called. Each thread controlled by a PrintThread object sleeps for the amount of time specified by the corresponding PrintThread object's sleepTime, then outputs its name.

The `PrintThread` constructor (lines 30–36) initializes `sleepTime` to a random integer from 0 to 5000. When a `PrintThread` is assigned a processor for the first time, its `run` method begins execution. Lines 43–44 display a message indicating the name of the currently executing thread and stating that the thread is going to sleep for a certain number of milliseconds. Note that line 44 uses the currently executing thread's `getName` method to obtain the thread's name, which was specified as a string argument to the `PrintThread` constructor and passed to the superclass `Thread` constructor at line 32. Line 46 invokes static `Thread` method `sleep` to place the thread into the *Sleeping* state. At this point, the thread loses the processor, and the system allows another thread to execute. When the thread awakens, it reenters the *Ready* state, where it waits until the system assigns a processor to the thread. When the `PrintThread` object enters the *Running* state again, line 55 outputs the thread's name in a message that indicates the thread is done sleeping; then method `run` terminates. This places the thread in the *Dead* state.

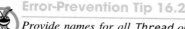

Error-Prevention Tip 16.2

Provide names for all Thread objects. When debugging a multithreaded program, these names identify which threads are executing.

`ThreadTester` method `main` (lines 6–21) creates and names three `PrintThread` objects (lines 9–11). Lines 15–17 invoke each thread's `start` method to transition all three `PrintThread` objects from the *Born* state to the *Ready* state. Method `start` returns immediately from each invocation; then line 19 outputs a message indicating that the threads were started. Note that all code in this program, except for the code in method `run`, executes in the main thread. The `PrintThread` constructor also executes in the main thread, since each `PrintThread` object is created in method `main`. When method `main` terminates (line 21), the program itself continues running because there are still threads that are alive (i.e., the threads were started and have not reached the *Dead* state yet). The program will not terminate until its last thread dies. When the system assigns a processor to a `Print-Thread` for the first time, the thread enters the *Running* state, and the thread's `run` method begins execution.

The sample outputs for this program show each thread's name and sleep time as the thread goes to sleep. The thread with the shortest sleep time normally awakens first, indicates that it is done sleeping and terminates. In Section 16.8, we discuss multithreading issues that could prevent the thread with the shortest sleep time from awakening first. Note in the second sample output that `thread1` and `thread2` each output their name and sleep time before method `main` completed its execution. This situation demonstrates that, once multiple threads are in the *Ready* state, any thread can be assigned the processor.

16.5 Thread Synchronization

Often, multiple threads of execution manipulate a shared object. If threads with access to the shared object simply read that object, then there is no need to prevent the shared object from being accessed by more than one thread at a time. However, when multiple threads share an object and that object is modified by one or more of the threads, indeterminate results may occur unless the shared object is managed properly. If one thread is in the process of updating the object and another thread tries to update it too, the object will reflect the update that occurs second. If the object is an array or other data structure in which the threads could update separate parts of the object concurrently, it is possible that part of the object will reflect the information from one thread while another part of the object will reflect information from a different thread. When this happens, the program's behavior cannot be determined. Sometimes the program will produce the correct results. Other times the program will produce incorrect results. In either case there will be no error message to indicate that the shared object was manipulated incorrectly.

The problem can be solved by giving one thread at a time exclusive access to code that manipulates the shared object. During that time, other threads desiring to manipulate the object should be kept waiting. When the thread with exclusive access to the object finishes manipulating the object, one of the threads that was kept waiting should be allowed to proceed. In this fashion, each thread accessing the shared object excludes all other threads from doing so simultaneously. This is called *mutual exclusion* or *thread synchronization*.

Java uses *monitors* to perform synchronization. Every object has a monitor. The monitor allows one thread at a time to execute inside a *synchronized statement* on the object. This is accomplished by *locking* the object when the program enters the synchronized statement—also known as *obtaining the lock*. If there are several synchronized statements trying to synchronize on the object at the same time, only one synchronized `statement` may be active on an object at once; all other threads attempting to enter a synchronized statement on the same object are placed in the *Blocked* state. When a synchronized statement finishes executing, the lock on the object is released and the monitor lets the highest priority blocked thread attempting to enter a synchronized statement proceed. Java also allows *synchronized methods*, which are used in the examples of Section 16.7 and Section 16.8. A synchronized method is equivalent to a synchronized statement that encloses the entire body of the method.

Once a thread obtains the lock on an object, if the thread determines that it cannot continue with its task on that object until some condition is satisfied, the thread can call `Object` method `wait`, thus removing the thread from contention for the processor and releasing the lock on the object. The thread releases the lock on the object and waits in the *Waiting* state while the other threads try to enter the object's synchronized statement(s). When a thread executing a synchronized statement completes or satisfies the condition on which another thread may be waiting, the thread can call `Object` method `notify` to allow a waiting thread to transition to the *Ready* state again. At this point, the thread that transitioned from the *wait* state to the *Ready* state can attempt to reacquire the lock on the object. Even if the thread is able to reacquire the lock, the thread still might not be able to perform its task at this time—in which case the thread will reenter the *Waiting* state and release the lock. If a thread calls `notifyAll`, then all threads waiting for the monitor object become eligible to reacquire the lock (that is, they all transition to the *Ready* state). Remember that only one of those threads can obtain the lock on the object at a time—other threads that attempt to acquire the same lock will be blocked by the operating system until the lock becomes available again (i.e., until no other thread is executing in a synchronized statement on that object). Methods `wait`, `notify`, and `notifyAll` are inherited by all classes from class `Object`. Every object has a monitor.

Common Programming Error 16.1

Deadlock occurs when a waiting thread (let us call this thread1*) cannot proceed because it is waiting for another thread (let us call this* thread2*) to proceed. Similarly,* thread2 *cannot proceed because it is waiting for* thread1 *to proceed. The two threads are waiting for each other; therefore, the actions that would enable each thread to continue execution never occur.*

Error-Prevention Tip 16.3

When multiple threads manipulate a shared object using monitors, ensure that if one thread calls method wait *to enter the* Waiting *state for the shared object, a separate thread eventually will call method* notify *to transition the thread waiting on the shared object back to the* Ready *state. If multiple threads may be waiting for the shared object, a separate thread can call method* notifyAll *as a safeguard to ensure that all waiting threads have another opportunity to perform their tasks.*

Performance Tip 16.3

Synchronization to achieve correctness in multithreaded programs can make programs run more slowly, as a result of monitor overhead and the frequent transition of threads among the Running, Waiting *and* Ready *states. There is not much to say, however, for highly efficient, incorrect multithreaded programs!*

Software Engineering Observation 16.2

The locking that occurs with the execution of synchronized *methods could lead to deadlock if the locks are never released. When exceptions occur, Java's exception mechanism coordinates with Java's synchronization mechanism to release locks and avoid these kinds of deadlocks.*

Common Programming Error 16.2

It is an error if a thread issues a wait, *a* notify, *or a* notifyAll *on an object without having acquired a lock for the object. This causes an* IllegalMonitorStateException.

16.6 Producer/Consumer Relationship without Synchronization

In a *producer/consumer relationship*, the *producer* portion of an application generates data and stores it in a shared object, and the *consumer* portion of an application reads data from the shared object. In a multithreaded producer/consumer relationship, a *producer thread* generates data and places it into a shared object, called a *buffer*. A *consumer thread* reads data from the buffer. If the producer waiting to put the next data into the buffer examines a condition and determines that the consumer has not yet read the previous data from the buffer, the producer thread should call wait so the consumer gets a chance to read the data before further updates; otherwise, the consumer never sees the previous data and that data is lost to the application. When the consumer thread reads the data, it should call notify to allow a waiting producer to store the next value. If a consumer thread finds the buffer empty or finds that the previous data has already been read, the consumer should call wait; otherwise, the consumer might read old data from the buffer. When the producer places the next data into the buffer, the producer should call notify to allow the consumer thread to proceed, so the consumer can read the new data.

Let us consider how logic errors can arise if we do not synchronize access among multiple threads manipulating shared data. Our next example (Fig. 16.4–Fig. 16.8) implements a producer/consumer relationship in which a producer thread writes a sequence of numbers (we use 1–4) into a shared buffer—a memory location shared between two threads (a single int variable called buffer in Fig. 16.7 of this example). The consumer thread reads this data from the shared buffer and displays the data. The program's output shows the values that the producer writes (produces) into the shared buffer and the values that the consumer reads (consumes) from the shared buffer.

Each value the producer thread writes to the shared buffer must be consumed exactly once by the consumer thread. However, the threads in this example are not synchronized. Therefore, data can be lost if the producer places new data into the shared buffer before the consumer consumes the previous data. Also, data can be incorrectly duplicated if the consumer consumes data again before the producer produces the next value. To show these possibilities, the consumer thread in the following example keeps a total of all the values it reads. The producer thread produces values from 1 to 4. If the consumer reads each value produced once and only once, the total will be 10. However, if you execute this program several times, you will see that the total is rarely, if ever, 10. Also, to emphasize our point, the producer and consumer threads in the example each sleep for random intervals of up to three seconds between performing their tasks, simulating some lengthy process such as waiting for user input. Thus, we do not know exactly when the producer thread will attempt to write a new value, nor do we know when the consumer thread will attempt to read a value.

The program consists of interface `Buffer` (Fig. 16.4) and four classes—`Producer` (Fig. 16.5), `Consumer` (Fig. 16.6), `UnsynchronizedBuffer` (Fig. 16.7) and `SharedBufferTest` (Fig. 16.8). Interface `Buffer` declares methods `set` and `get` that a `Buffer` must implement to enable a `Producer` thread to place a value in the `Buffer` and enable the `Consumer` thread to retrieve a value from the `Buffer`, respectively. We will see the implementation of this interface in Fig. 16.7.

Class `Producer` (Fig. 16.5)—a subclass of `Thread`—contains field `sharedLocation` (line 6), a constructor (lines 9–13) and a `run` method (lines 16–36). The constructor initializes `Buffer` reference `sharedLocation` with an object that implements the `Buffer` interface created in `main` (Fig. 16.8) and passed to the constructor as the parameter `shared`. As we will see, this is an `UnsynchronizedBuffer` object that implements interface `Buffer` without synchronizing access to the shared object. The producer thread in this program executes the tasks specified in method `run` (lines 16–36). The loop at lines 18–31 loops four times. Each iteration of the loop invokes `Thread` method `sleep` (line 22) to place the producer thread into the *Sleeping* state for a random time interval between 0 and 3 seconds (to simulate a lengthy process). When the thread awakens, line 23 passes the value of control variable `count` to the `Buffer` object's `set` method to set the shared buffer's value. When the loop completes, lines 33–34 display a message in the console window indicating that the thread finished producing data and that the thread is terminating. Next, method `run` terminates and the producer thread enters the *Dead* state. It is important to note that any method called from a thread's `run` method (such as `Buffer` method `set`) executes as part of that thread of execution. In fact, each thread has its own method-call stack. This fact becomes important in Section 16.7 when we add synchronization to the producer/consumer relationship.

```
1   // Fig. 16.4: Buffer.java
2   // Buffer interface specifies methods called by Producer and Consumer.
3
4   public interface Buffer {
5      public void set( int value );   // place value into Buffer
6      public int get();               // return value from Buffer
7   }
```

Fig. 16.4 `Buffer` interface used in producer/consumer examples.

```
1    // Fig. 16.5: Producer.java
2    // Producer's run method controls a thread that
3    // stores values from 1 to 4 in sharedLocation.
4
5    public class Producer extends Thread {
6       private Buffer sharedLocation; // reference to shared object
7
8       // constructor
9       public Producer( Buffer shared )
10      {
11         super( "Producer" );
12         sharedLocation = shared;
13      }
14
15      // store values from 1 to 4 in sharedLocation
16      public void run()
17      {
18         for ( int count = 1; count <= 4; count++ ) {
19
20            // sleep 0 to 3 seconds, then place value in Buffer
21            try {
22               Thread.sleep( ( int ) ( Math.random() * 3001 ) );
23               sharedLocation.set( count );
24            }
25
26            // if sleeping thread interrupted, print stack trace
27            catch ( InterruptedException exception ) {
28               exception.printStackTrace();
29            }
30
31         } // end for
32
33         System.err.println( getName() + " done producing." +
34            "\nTerminating " + getName() + "." );
35
36      } // end method run
37
38   } // end class Producer
```

Fig. 16.5   Producer represents the producer thread in a producer/consumer relationship.

Class Consumer (Fig. 16.6) contains instance variable sharedLocation (line 6), a constructor (lines 9–13) and a run method (lines 16–37). The constructor initializes Buffer reference sharedLocation with an object that implements the Buffer interface created in main (Fig. 16.8) and passed to the constructor as the parameter shared. As we will see, this is the same UnsynchronizedBuffer object that is used to initialize the Producer object; thus, the two threads share the object. The consumer thread in this program performs the tasks specified in method run method (lines 16–37). The loop at lines 20–32 loops four times. Each iteration of the loop invokes Thread method sleep (line 24) to put the consumer thread into the *Sleeping* state for a random time interval between 0 and 3 seconds. Next, line 25 uses the Buffer's get method to retrieve the value in the shared buffer and adds the value to variable sum. When the loop completes, lines 34–35 display a

```
1    // Fig. 16.6: Consumer.java
2    // Consumer's run method controls a thread that loops four
3    // times and reads a value from sharedLocation each time.
4
5    public class Consumer extends Thread {
6       private Buffer sharedLocation; // reference to shared object
7
8       // constructor
9       public Consumer( Buffer shared )
10      {
11         super( "Consumer" );
12         sharedLocation = shared;
13      }
14
15      // read sharedLocation's value four times and sum the values
16      public void run()
17      {
18         int sum = 0;
19
20         for ( int count = 1; count <= 4; count++ ) {
21
22            // sleep 0 to 3 seconds, read value from Buffer and add to sum
23            try {
24               Thread.sleep( ( int ) ( Math.random() * 3001 ) );
25               sum += sharedLocation.get();
26            }
27
28            // if sleeping thread interrupted, print stack trace
29            catch ( InterruptedException exception ) {
30               exception.printStackTrace();
31            }
32         }
33
34         System.err.println( getName() + " read values totaling: " + sum +
35            ".\nTerminating " + getName() + "." );
36
37      } // end method run
38
39   } // end class Consumer
```

Fig. 16.6   Consumer represents the consumer thread in a producer/consumer relationship.

line in the console window indicating the sum of the consumed values. Then, method run terminates, which places the consumer thread in the *Dead* state. Once both threads enter the *Dead* state, the program terminates.

[*Note*: We use method sleep in method run of both the Producer and Consumer classes to emphasize the fact that, in multithreaded applications, it is unclear when each thread will perform its task and for how long it will perform that task when it has the processor. Normally, these thread-scheduling issues are the job of the computer's operating system. In this program, our thread's tasks are quite simple—for the producer, loop four times and perform an assignment statement; for the consumer, loop four times and add a value to variable sum. Without the sleep method call, and if the producer executes first, the producer most likely would complete its task before the consumer ever gets a chance to execute. If the consumer executes first, it most likely would consume –1 four times, then terminate before the producer can produce the first real value.]

Class UnsynchronizedBuffer (Fig. 16.7) implements interface Buffer (line 4) and declares the type of object shared between the Producer and Consumer. Line 5 declares instance variable buffer and initializes it with the value –1. This value is used to demonstrate the case in which the Consumer attempts to consume a value before the Producer ever places a value in buffer. Methods set (lines 8–14) and get (lines 17–23) do not synchronize access to field buffer. Method set simply assigns its argument to buffer (line 13) and method get simply returns the value of buffer (line 22). Note that each method uses class Thread's static method currentThread to obtain a reference to the currently executing thread, then uses that thread's method getName to obtain the thread's name for output purposes.

Class SharedBufferTest contains method main (lines 6–18), which launches the application. Line 9 instantiates a shared UnsynchronizedBuffer object and assigns it to Buffer reference sharedLocation. This object stores the data that will be shared between the producer and consumer threads. Lines 12–13 create a Producer object and a Consumer object. Each constructor call passes sharedLocation as the argument to the constructor, so each object is initialized with a reference to the same Buffer. Next, lines 15–16 invoke method start on the producer and consumer threads to place them in the *Ready* state. This launches these threads and sets up the initial call to each thread's run

```
1   // Fig. 16.7: UnsynchronizedBuffer.java
2   // UnsynchronizedBuffer represents a single shared integer.
3
4   public class UnsynchronizedBuffer implements Buffer {
5      private int buffer = -1; // shared by producer and consumer threads
6
7      // place value into buffer
8      public void set( int value )
9      {
10         System.err.println( Thread.currentThread().getName() +
11            " writes " + value );
12
13         buffer = value;
14      }
15
16      // return value from buffer
17      public int get()
18      {
19         System.err.println( Thread.currentThread().getName() +
20            " reads " + buffer );
21
22         return buffer;
23      }
24
25   } // end class UnsynchronizedBuffer
```

Fig. 16.7 UnsynchronizedBuffer maintains the shared integer that is accessed by a producer thread and a consumer thread via methods set and get.

method, which will begin execution when each thread is assigned a processor. Finally, method main terminates and the main thread of execution dies.

```
1    // Fig. 16.8: SharedBufferTest.java
2    // SharedBufferTest creates producer and consumer threads.
3
4    public class SharedBufferTest {
5
6       public static void main( String [] args )
7       {
8          // create shared object used by threads
9          Buffer sharedLocation = new UnsynchronizedBuffer();
10
11         // create producer and consumer objects
12         Producer producer = new Producer( sharedLocation );
13         Consumer consumer = new Consumer( sharedLocation );
14
15         producer.start();  // start producer thread
16         consumer.start();  // start consumer thread
17
18      } // end main
19
20   } // end class SharedCell
```

```
Consumer reads -1
Producer writes 1
Consumer reads 1
Consumer reads 1
Consumer reads 1
Consumer read values totaling: 2.
Terminating Consumer.
Producer writes 2
Producer writes 3
Producer writes 4
Producer done producing.
Terminating Producer.
```

```
Producer writes 1
Producer writes 2
Consumer reads 2
Producer writes 3
Consumer reads 3
Producer writes 4
Producer done producing.
Terminating Producer.
Consumer reads 4
Consumer reads 4
Consumer read values totaling: 13.
Terminating Consumer.
```

Fig. 16.8 Threads modifying a shared object without synchronization. (Part 1 of 2.)

```
Producer writes 1
Consumer reads 1
Producer writes 2
Consumer reads 2
Producer writes 3
Consumer reads 3
Producer writes 4
Producer done producing.
Terminating Producer.
Consumer reads 4
Consumer read values totaling: 10.
Terminating Consumer.
```

Fig. 16.8 Threads modifying a shared object without synchronization. (Part 2 of 2.)

Recall from the overview of this example that we would like the Producer thread to execute first and every value produced by the producer to be consumed exactly once by the consumer. However, when we study the first output of Fig. 16.8, we see that the consumer retrieved a value (−1) before the producer ever placed a value in the buffer and that the value 1 was consumed three times. The consumer finished executing before the producer had an opportunity to produce the values 2, 3 and 4. Therefore, those three values were lost. In the second output, we see that the value 1 was lost, because the values 1 and 2 were produced before the consumer thread could read the value 1. Also, the value 4 was consumed twice. The last sample output demonstrates that it is possible, with some luck, to get a proper output in which each value the producer produces is consumed once and only once by the consumer, but this behavior cannot be guaranteed. This example clearly demonstrates that access to a shared object by concurrent threads must be controlled carefully; otherwise, a program may produce incorrect results.

To solve the problems of lost data and data consumed more than once, Section 16.7 presents an example in which we use keyword synchronized and Object methods wait and notify to synchronize access to the code that manipulates the shared object. When a method declared synchronized is running on an object, the object is *locked* so no other synchronized method can run on that object at the same time.

16.7 Producer/Consumer Relationship with Synchronization

The application in Fig. 16.9 and Fig. 16.10 demonstrates a producer and a consumer accessing a shared buffer with synchronization. In this case, the consumer consumes only after the producer produces a value, and the producer produces a new value only after the consumer consumes the previous value produced. In this example, we reuse interface Buffer (Fig. 16.4) and classes Producer (Fig. 16.5) and Consumer (Fig. 16.6) from the example of Section 16.6. This approach enables us to demonstrate that the threads accessing the shared object are unaware that they are being synchronized. The code that performs the synchronization is placed in the set and get methods of class SynchronizedBuffer (Fig. 16.9), which implements interface Buffer (line 4). Thus, the Producer's and Consumer's run methods simply call the shared object's set and get methods as in the example of Section 16.6.

Class `SynchronizedBuffer` (Fig. 16.9) contains two fields—`buffer` (line 5) and `occupiedBufferCount` (line 6). Method `set` (lines 9–41) and method `get` (lines 44–76) are now `synchronized` methods; thus, only one thread can call any of these methods at a time on a particular `SynchronizedBuffer` object. Field `occupiedBufferCount` is known as a *condition variable*—the methods uses this `int` in conditional expressions to determine whether it is the producer's or the consumer's turn to perform a task. If `occupiedBufferCount` is equal to zero, `buffer` is empty and the producer can call method `set` to place a value into variable `buffer`. This condition also means that the consumer cannot call `SynchronizedBuffer`'s `get` method to read the value of `buffer` (again, because it is empty). If `occupiedBufferCount` is equal to one, the consumer can call `SynchronizedBuffer`'s `get` method to read a value from variable `buffer`, because the variable does contain new information. This condition also means that the producer cannot call `SynchronizedBuffer`'s `set` method to place a value into `buffer`, because the buffer is currently full.

```java
1    // Fig. 16.9: SynchronizedBuffer.java
2    // SynchronizedBuffer synchronizes access to a single shared integer.
3
4    public class SynchronizedBuffer implements Buffer {
5       private int buffer = -1; // shared by producer and consumer threads
6       private int occupiedBufferCount = 0; // count of occupied buffers
7
8       // place value into buffer
9       public synchronized void set( int value )
10      {
11         // for output purposes, get name of thread that called this method
12         String name = Thread.currentThread().getName();
13
14         // while there are no empty locations, place thread in waiting state
15         while ( occupiedBufferCount == 1 ) {
16
17            // output thread information and buffer information, then wait
18            try {
19               System.err.println( name + " tries to write." );
20               displayState( "Buffer full. " + name + " waits." );
21               wait();
22            }
23
24            // if waiting thread interrupted, print stack trace
25            catch ( InterruptedException exception ) {
26               exception.printStackTrace();
27            }
28
29         } // end while
30
31         buffer = value; // set new buffer value
32
33         // indicate producer cannot store another value
34         // until consumer retrieves current buffer value
35         ++occupiedBufferCount;
```

Fig. 16.9   `SynchronizedBuffer` synchronizes access to a shared integer. (Part 1 of 2.)

```
36
37          displayState( name + " writes " + buffer );
38
39          notify(); // tell waiting thread to enter ready state
40
41      } // end method set; releases lock on SynchronizedBuffer
42
43      // return value from buffer
44      public synchronized int get()
45      {
46          // for output purposes, get name of thread that called this method
47          String name = Thread.currentThread().getName();
48
49          // while no data to read, place thread in waiting state
50          while ( occupiedBufferCount == 0 ) {
51
52              // output thread information and buffer information, then wait
53              try {
54                  System.err.println( name + " tries to read." );
55                  displayState( "Buffer empty. " + name + " waits." );
56                  wait();
57              }
58
59              // if waiting thread interrupted, print stack trace
60              catch ( InterruptedException exception ) {
61                  exception.printStackTrace();
62              }
63
64          } // end while
65
66          // indicate that producer can store another value
67          // because consumer just retrieved buffer value
68          --occupiedBufferCount;
69
70          displayState( name + " reads " + buffer );
71
72          notify(); // tell waiting thread to become ready to execute
73
74          return buffer;
75
76      } // end method get; releases lock on SynchronizedBuffer
77
78      // display current operation and buffer state
79      public void displayState( String operation )
80      {
81          StringBuffer outputLine = new StringBuffer( operation );
82          outputLine.setLength( 40 );
83          outputLine.append( buffer + "\t\t" + occupiedBufferCount );
84          System.err.println( outputLine );
85          System.err.println();
86      }
87
88  } // end class SynchronizedBuffer
```

Fig. 16.9 SynchronizedBuffer synchronizes access to a shared integer. (Part 2 of 2.)

When the `Producer` thread's `run` method invokes synchronized method `set` (from line 23 of Fig. 16.5), the thread attempts to acquire a lock on the `SynchronizedBuffer` monitor object. If the lock is available, the `Producer` thread acquires the lock. Then the `while` loop at lines 15–29 determines whether `occupiedBufferCount` is equal to one. If so, the buffer is full, so line 19 outputs a message indicating that the `Producer` thread is trying to write a value, and line 20 invokes method `displayState` (lines 79–86) to output another message indicating that the buffer is full and that the `Producer` thread is in the *Waiting* state. Line 21 invokes method `wait` (inherited from `Object` by `Synchronized-Buffer`) to place the thread that called method `set` (i.e., the `Producer` thread) in the *Waiting* state for the `SynchronizedBuffer` object. The call to `wait` causes the calling thread to release the lock on the `SynchronizedBuffer` object. This is important because the thread cannot currently perform its task and because other threads should be allowed to access the object at this time to allow the condition (`occupiedBufferCount == 1`) to change. Now another thread can attempt to acquire the `SynchronizedBuffer` object's lock and invoke the object's `set` or `get` methods.

The producer thread remains in the *Waiting* state until the thread is notified by another thread that it may proceed—at which point the producer thread returns to the *Ready* state and waits for the system to assign a processor to the thread. When the producer thread returns to the *Running* state, the thread implicitly attempts to reacquire the lock on the `Syn-chronizedBuffer` object. If the lock is available, the producer thread reacquires the lock and method `set` continues executing with the next statement after `wait`. Because `wait` is called in a loop (lines 15–29), the loop continuation condition is tested again to determine whether the thread can proceed with its execution. If not, `wait` is invoked again; otherwise, method `set` continues with the next statement after the loop.

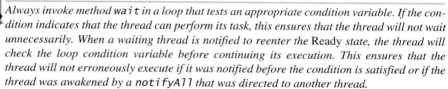

Software Engineering Observation 16.3

Always invoke method `wait` in a loop that tests an appropriate condition variable. If the condition indicates that the thread can perform its task, this ensures that the thread will not wait unnecessarily. When a waiting thread is notified to reenter the Ready *state, the thread will check the loop condition variable before continuing its execution. This ensures that the thread will not erroneously execute if it was notified before the condition is satisfied or if the thread was awakened by a `notifyAll` that was directed to another thread.*

Line 31 in method `set` assigns `value` to `buffer`. Line 35 increments the `occupied-BufferCount` to indicate that the `buffer` now contains a value (i.e., a consumer can read the value, and a producer cannot yet put another value there). Line 37 invokes method `dis-playState` to output a line to the console window indicating that the producer is writing a new value into the `buffer`. Line 39 invokes method `notify` (inherited from `Object`). If there are any waiting threads, the first waiting thread enters the *Ready* state, indicating that the thread can now attempt its task again (as soon as the thread is assigned a processor). Method `notify` returns immediately and method `set` returns to its caller.[4] When method `set` returns, it implicitly releases the lock on the shared memory.

---

4.   Invoking method `notify` works correctly in this program because only one thread calls method `get` at any time (the `ConsumerThread`). Programs that have multiple threads waiting on a condition should invoke `notifyAll` to ensure that multiple threads receive notifications properly.

Common Programming Error 16.3

Forgetting to notify a thread that is waiting for a condition is a logic error. The thread will remain in the Waiting state, which will prevent the thread from doing any further work. Such waiting can lead to indefinite postponement or deadlock.

Methods `get` and `set` are implemented similarly. When the `Consumer` thread's `run` method invokes synchronized method `get` (from line 25 of Fig. 16.6), the thread attempts to acquire a lock on the `SynchronizedBuffer` object. If the lock is available, the `Consumer` thread acquires the lock. Then the `while` loop at lines 50–64 determines whether `occupiedBufferCount` is equal to 0. If so, the buffer is empty, so line 54 outputs a message indicating that the `Consumer` thread is trying to read a value, and line 55 invokes method `displayState` to output another message indicating that the buffer is empty and that the `Consumer` thread waits. Line 56 invokes method `wait` to place the thread that called method `get` (i.e., the `Consumer` thread) in the *Waiting* state for the `SynchronizedBuffer` object. Again, the call to `wait` causes the calling thread to release the lock on the `SynchronizedBuffer` object, so another thread can attempt to acquire the `SynchronizedBuffer` object's lock and invoke the object's `set` or `get` method. If the lock on the `SynchronizedBuffer` was not available (e.g., if the `ProducerThread` had not yet returned from method `set`) the `ConsumerThread` is blocked until the lock becomes available.

The consumer thread object remains in the *Waiting* state until the thread is notified by another thread that it may proceed—at which point the consumer thread returns to the *Ready* state and waits for the system to assign a processor to the thread. When the thread returns to the *Running* state, the thread implicitly attempts to reacquire the lock on the `SynchronizedBuffer` object. If the lock is available, the consumer thread reacquires the lock and method `get` continues executing with the next statement after `wait`. Because `wait` is called in a loop (lines 50–64), the loop continuation condition is tested again to determine whether the thread can proceed with its execution. If not, `wait` is invoked again; otherwise, method `get` continues with the next statement after the loop. Line 68 of Fig. 16.9 decrements `occupiedBufferCount` to indicate that `buffer` is now empty (i.e., a consumer cannot read the value, but a producer can place another value into `buffer`), line 70 outputs a line to the console window indicating the value the consumer is reading and line 72 invokes method `notify`. If there are any threads waiting for the lock on this `SynchronizedBuffer` object, one waiting thread enters the *Ready* state, indicating that, as soon as the thread is assigned a processor, the thread can now attempt to reacquire the lock and continue performing its task. Method `notify` returns immediately, then method `get` returns the value of `buffer` to its caller.[5] When method `get` returns, the lock on the `SynchronizedBuffer` object is implicitly released.

Class `SharedBufferTest2` (Fig. 16.10) is similar to class `SharedBufferTest` (Fig. 16.8). `SharedBufferTest2` contains method `main` (lines 6–28), which launches the application. Line 11 instantiates a shared `SynchronizedBuffer` and assigns its reference to `SynchronizedBuffer` variable `sharedLocation`. We use a `SynchronizedBuffer` variable rather than a `Buffer` variable, so that main can invoke `SynchronizedBuffer` method `displayState`, which is not declared in interface `Buffer`. The `Synchronized-`

---

5.   Invoking method `notify` works correctly in this program because only one thread calls method `set` at any time (the `ProducerThread`). Programs that have multiple threads waiting on a condition should invoke `notifyAll` to ensure that multiple threads receive notifications properly.

`Buffer` object stores the data that will be shared between the producer and consumer threads. Lines 14–19 display the column heads for the output. Lines 22–23 create a `Pro-ducer` object and a `Consumer` object. Each constructor call passes `sharedLocation` as the argument to the constructor, so each object is initialized with a reference to the same `Buffer`. Next, lines 25–26 invoke method `start` on the `producer` and `consumer` threads to place them in the *Ready* state. This launches these threads and sets up the initial call to each thread's `run` method, which will begin execution when each thread is assigned a processor. Finally, method `main` terminates and the `main` thread of execution dies.

Study the outputs in Fig. 16.10. Observe that every integer produced is consumed exactly once—no values are lost, and no values are consumed more than once. The synchronization and condition variable ensure that the producer and consumer cannot perform their tasks unless it is their turn. The producer must go first; the consumer must wait if the producer has not produced since the consumer last consumed; and the producer must wait if the consumer has not yet consumed the value that the producer most recently produced. Execute this program several times to confirm that every integer produced is consumed exactly once. In the first and second sample outputs, notice the lines indicating when the producer and consumer must wait to perform their respective tasks. In the third sample output, notice that the producer and consumer were able to perform their tasks without waiting.

```
1   // Fig. 16.10: SharedBufferTest2.java
2   // SharedBufferTest2creates producer and consumer threads.
3
4   public class SharedBufferTest2 {
5
6      public static void main( String [] args )
7      {
8         // create shared object used by threads; we use a SynchronizedBuffer
9         // reference rather than a Buffer reference so we can invoke
10        // SynchronizedBuffer method displayState from main
11        SynchronizedBuffer sharedLocation = new SynchronizedBuffer();
12
13        // Display column heads for output
14        StringBuffer columnHeads = new StringBuffer( "Operation" );
15        columnHeads.setLength( 40 );
16        columnHeads.append( "Buffer\t\tOccupied Count" );
17        System.err.println( columnHeads );
18        System.err.println();
19        sharedLocation.displayState( "Initial State" );
20
21        // create producer and consumer objects
22        Producer producer = new Producer( sharedLocation );
23        Consumer consumer = new Consumer( sharedLocation );
24
25        producer.start();  // start producer thread
26        consumer.start();  // start consumer thread
27
28     } // end main
29
30  } // end class SharedBufferTest2
```

Fig. 16.10 Threads modifying a shared object with synchronization. (Part 1 of 3.)

Operation	Buffer	Occupied Count
Initial State	-1	0
Consumer tries to read. Buffer empty. Consumer waits.	-1	0
Producer writes 1	1	1
Consumer reads 1	1	0
Consumer tries to read. Buffer empty. Consumer waits.	1	0
Producer writes 2	2	1
Consumer reads 2	2	0
Producer writes 3	3	1
Consumer reads 3	3	0
Consumer tries to read. Buffer empty. Consumer waits.	3	0
Producer writes 4	4	1
Consumer reads 4 Producer done producing. Terminating Producer.	4	0
Consumer read values totaling: 10. Terminating Consumer.		

Operation	Buffer	Occupied Count
Initial State	-1	0
Consumer tries to read. Buffer empty. Consumer waits.	-1	0
Producer writes 1	1	1
Consumer reads 1	1	0
Producer writes 2	2	1
Producer tries to write. Buffer full. Producer waits.	2	1
Consumer reads 2	2	0
Producer writes 3	3	1
Consumer reads 3	3	0

(continued on next page)

Fig. 16.10 Threads modifying a shared object with synchronization. (Part 2 of 3.)

(continued from previous page)

Producer writes 4	4	1
Producer done producing. Terminating Producer. Consumer reads 4	4	0
Consumer read values totaling: 10. Terminating Consumer.		

Operation	Buffer	Occupied Count
Initial State	-1	0
Producer writes 1	1	1
Consumer reads 1	1	0
Producer writes 2	2	1
Consumer reads 2	2	0
Producer writes 3	3	1
Consumer reads 3	3	0
Producer writes 4	4	1
Producer done producing. Terminating Producer. Consumer reads 4	4	0
Consumer read values totaling: 10. Terminating Consumer.		

Fig. 16.10 Threads modifying a shared object with synchronization. (Part 3 of 3.)

16.8 Producer/Consumer Relationship: Circular Buffer

The program of Section 16.7 uses thread synchronization to guarantee that two threads manipulate data in a shared buffer correctly. However, the application may not perform optimally. If the two threads operate at different speeds, one of the threads will spend more (or most) of its time waiting. For example, in the program of Section 16.7 we shared a single integer variable between the two threads. If the producer thread produces values faster than the consumer can consume those values, then the producer thread waits for the consumer, because there are no other locations in memory to place the next value. Similarly, if the consumer consumes faster than the producer can produce values, the consumer waits until the producer places the next value into the shared location in memory. Even when we have threads that operate at the same relative speeds, over a period of time, those threads may become "out of sync," causing one of the threads to wait for the other. We cannot make assumptions about the relative speeds of asynchronous concurrent threads. There are too many interactions that occur with the operating system, the network, the user and other components, which can cause the threads to operate at different speeds. When this happens, threads wait. When threads wait, programs become less efficient, user-interactive programs become less responsive and applications suffer longer delays because the processor is not used efficiently.

To minimize the amount of waiting time for threads that share resources and operate at the same average speeds, we can implement a *circular buffer* that provides extra buffer space into which the producer can place values and from which the consumer can retrieve those values. Let us assume the buffer is implemented as an array. The producer and consumer work from the beginning of the array. When either thread reaches the end of the array, it simply returns to the first element of the array to perform its next task. If the producer temporarily produces values faster than the consumer can consume them, the producer can write additional values into the extra buffer space (if any are available). This capability enables the producer to perform its task even though the consumer is not ready to receive the current value being produced. Similarly, if the consumer consumes faster than the producer produces new values, the consumer can read additional values from the buffer (if there are any). This enables the consumer to perform its task even though the producer is not ready to produce additional values.

Note that the circular buffer would be inappropriate if the producer and consumer operate consistently at different speeds. If the consumer always executes faster than the producer, then a buffer containing one location is enough. Additional locations would waste memory. If the producer always executes faster, a buffer with an infinite number of locations would be required to absorb the extra production.

The key to using a circular buffer is to provide it with enough locations to handle the anticipated "extra" production. If, over a period of time, we determine that the producer often produces as many as three more values than the consumer can consume, we can provide a buffer of at least three cells to handle the extra production. We do not want the buffer to be too small, because that would cause threads to wait more. On the other hand, we do not want the buffer to be too large, because that would waste memory.

Performance Tip 16.4

Even when using a circular buffer, it is possible that a producer thread could fill the buffer, which would force the producer thread to wait until a consumer consumes a value to free an element in the buffer. Similarly, if the buffer is empty at any given time, the consumer thread must wait until the producer produces another value. The key to using a circular buffer is optimizing the buffer size to minimize the amount of thread-wait time.

The program of Fig. 16.11–Fig. 16.15 demonstrates a producer and a consumer accessing a circular buffer (in this case, a shared array of three cells) with synchronization. In this version of the producer/consumer relationship, the consumer consumes a value only when the array is not empty and the producer produces a value only when the array is not full. This program is implemented as a windowed application that sends its output to a JTextArea. The statements that created and started the thread objects in the main method of class SharedBufferTest2 (Fig. 16.10) now appear in class CircularBufferTest (Fig. 16.15). Classes Producer (Fig. 16.12) and Consumer (Fig. 16.13) perform the same tasks as in Fig. 16.5 and Fig. 16.6 respectively, except that they output messages to the JTextArea in the application window.

This is the first program that uses separate threads to modify the content displayed in a Swing GUI. The nature of multithreaded programming prevents the programmer from knowing exactly when a thread will execute. Swing components are not *thread-safe*—if multiple threads manipulate a Swing GUI component, the results may not be correct. All interactions with Swing GUI components should be performed one thread at a time. Normally, this thread is the *event-dispatching thread* (also known as the *event-handling thread*). Class *SwingUtilities* (package `javax.swing`) provides static method *invokeLater* to help with this process. Method `invokeLater` specifies GUI-processing statements to execute later as part of the event-dispatching thread. Method `invokeLater` receives as its argument an object that implements interface *Runnable* (package `java.lang`). Every class that implements `Runnable` must declare a `run` method with the header

```
public void run()
```

In fact, every `Thread` is a `Runnable` object, so each `Thread` object has a `run` method. The threads in this example that display their output in the GUI pass objects of class `RunnableOutput` (Fig. 16.11) to method `invokeLater`. Each `RunnableOutput` object receives a reference to the `JTextArea` in which outputs are displayed and a string representing the message to display. `RunnableOutput` method `run` (lines 47–50) appends the message to the `JTextArea`. When the program calls `invokeLater`, the GUI component update will be queued for execution in the event-dispatching thread. `RunnableOutput` method `run` will then be invoked as part of the event-dispatching thread to perform the output and ensure that the GUI component is updated in a thread-safe manner.

```java
31    // Fig. 16.11: RunnableOutput.java
32    // Class RunnableOutput updates JTextArea with output
33    import javax.swing.*;
34
35    public class RunnableOutput implements Runnable {
36       private JTextArea outputArea;
37       private String messageToAppend;
38
39       // initialize outputArea and message
40       public RunnableOutput( JTextArea output, String message )
41       {
42          outputArea = output;
43          messageToAppend = message;
44       }
45
46       // method called by SwingUtilities.invokeLater to update outputArea
47       public void run()
48       {
49          outputArea.append( messageToAppend );
50       }
51
52    } // end class RunnableOutput
```

Fig. 16.11 RunnableOutput objects are passed to SwingUtilities method invokeLater to process GUI updates in the event-dispatching thread.

Class `Producer` (Fig. 16.12) is slightly modified from the version presented in Fig. 16.5. Line 8 declares a `JTextArea` that will be used to output a message at the end of method `run`. This reference is initialized in the constructor (lines 11–16). Method `run` (lines 19–39) now produces values from 11 through 20. Also, lines 36–37 output a message in the GUI indicating that the thread is done producing values and is terminating. Note the use of a `RunnableObject` with `SwingUtilities` method `invokeLater` to ensure that the text is appended to the textarea in the event-dispatching thread.

```java
1   // Fig. 16.12: Producer.java
2   // Producer's run method controls a thread that
3   // stores values from 11 to 20 in sharedLocation.
4   import javax.swing.*;
5
6   public class Producer extends Thread {
7      private Buffer sharedLocation;
8      private JTextArea outputArea;
9
10     // constructor
11     public Producer( Buffer shared, JTextArea output )
12     {
13        super( "Producer" );
14        sharedLocation = shared;
15        outputArea = output;
16     }
17
18     // store values from 11-20 and in sharedLocation's buffer
19     public void run()
20     {
21        for ( int count = 11; count <= 20; count ++ ) {
22
23           // sleep 0 to 3 seconds, then place value in Buffer
24           try {
25              Thread.sleep( ( int ) ( Math.random() * 3000 ) );
26              sharedLocation.set( count );
27           }
28
29           // if sleeping thread interrupted, print stack trace
30           catch ( InterruptedException exception ) {
31              exception.printStackTrace();
32           }
33        }
34
35        String name = getName();
36        SwingUtilities.invokeLater( new RunnableOutput( outputArea, "\n" +
37           name + " done producing.\n" + name + " terminated.\n" ) );
38
39     } // end method run
40
41  } // end class Producer
```

Fig. 16.12 `Producer` represents the producer in a producer/consumer relationship.

Class **Consumer** (Fig. 16.13) is slightly modified from the version in Fig. 16.4. Line 8 declares a **JTextArea** that will display a message at the end of method **run**. This reference is initialized in the constructor (lines 11–16). Method **run** (lines 19–42) loops 10 times. Lines 38–40 display a message indicating that the thread is done producing values and is terminating. Again, note the use of a **RunnableObject** with **SwingUtilities** method **invokeLater** to ensure that the GUI is updated in the event-dispatching thread.

```java
1   // Fig. 16.13: Consumer.java
2   // Consumer's run method controls a thread that loops ten
3   // times and reads a value from sharedLocation each time.
4   import javax.swing.*;
5
6   public class Consumer extends Thread {
7      private Buffer sharedLocation; // reference to shared object
8      private JTextArea outputArea;
9
10     // constructor
11     public Consumer( Buffer shared, JTextArea output )
12     {
13        super( "Consumer" );
14        sharedLocation = shared;
15        outputArea = output;
16     }
17
18     // read sharedLocation's value ten times and sum the values
19     public void run()
20     {
21        int sum = 0;
22
23        for ( int count = 1; count <= 10; count++ ) {
24
25           // sleep 0 to 3 seconds, read value from Buffer and add to sum
26           try {
27              Thread.sleep( ( int ) ( Math.random() * 3001 ) );
28              sum += sharedLocation.get();
29           }
30
31           // if sleeping thread interrupted, print stack trace
32           catch ( InterruptedException exception ) {
33              exception.printStackTrace();
34           }
35        }
36
37        String name = getName();
38        SwingUtilities.invokeLater( new RunnableOutput( outputArea,
39           "\nTotal " + name + " consumed: " + sum + ".\n" +
40           name + " terminated.\n ") );
41
42     } // end method run
43
44  } // end class Consumer
```

Fig. 16.13 Consumer represents the consumer in a producer/consumer relationship.

The significant changes to the example in Section 16.7 occur in `CircularBuffer` (Fig. 16.14), which replaces `SynchronizedBuffer` (Fig. 16.9). `CircularBuffer` contains five fields. Array `buffers` (line 8) is a three-element integer array that represents the circular buffer. Variable `occupiedBufferCount` (line 11) is the condition variable that can be used to determine whether a producer can write into the circular buffer (i.e., `occupiedBufferCount` is less than the number of elements in `buffers`) and whether a consumer can read from the circular buffer (i.e., `occupiedBufferCount` is greater than 0). Variable `readLocation` (line 14) indicates the position from which the next value can be read by a consumer. Variable `writeLocation` (line 14) indicates the next location in which a value can be placed by a producer. All outputs are displayed in `outputArea` (line 17).

```java
1   // Fig. 16.14: CircularBuffer.java
2   // CircularBuffer synchronizes access to an array of shared buffers.
3   import javax.swing.*;
4
5   public class CircularBuffer implements Buffer {
6
7      // each array element is a buffer
8      private int buffers[] = { -1, -1, -1 };
9
10     // occupiedBufferCount maintains count of occupied buffers
11     private int occupiedBufferCount = 0;
12
13     // variables that maintain read and write buffer locations
14     private int readLocation = 0, writeLocation = 0;
15
16     // reference to GUI component that displays output
17     private JTextArea outputArea;
18
19     // constructor
20     public CircularBuffer( JTextArea output )
21     {
22        outputArea = output;
23     }
24
25     // place value into buffer
26     public synchronized void set( int value )
27     {
28        // for output purposes, get name of thread that called this method
29        String name = Thread.currentThread().getName();
30
31        // while there are no empty locations, place thread in waiting state
32        while ( occupiedBufferCount == buffers.length ) {
33
34           // output thread information and buffer information, then wait
35           try {
36              SwingUtilities.invokeLater( new RunnableOutput( outputArea,
37                 "\nAll buffers full. " + name + " waits." ) );
38              wait();
39           }
```

Fig. 16.14 `SynchronizedBuffer` monitors access to a shared array of integers. (Part 1 of 4.)

```
40
41        // if waiting thread interrupted, print stack trace
42        catch ( InterruptedException exception )
43        {
44            exception.printStackTrace();
45        }
46
47     } // end while
48
49     // place value in writeLocation of buffers
50     buffers[ writeLocation ] = value;
51
52     // update Swing GUI component with produced value
53     SwingUtilities.invokeLater( new RunnableOutput( outputArea,
54        "\n" + name + " writes " + buffers[ writeLocation ] + " ") );
55
56     // just produced a value, so increment number of occupied buffers
57     ++occupiedBufferCount;
58
59     // update writeLocation for future write operation
60     writeLocation = ( writeLocation + 1 ) % buffers.length;
61
62     // display contents of shared buffers
63     SwingUtilities.invokeLater( new RunnableOutput(
64        outputArea, createStateOutput() ) );
65
66     notify(); // return waiting thread (if there is one) to ready state
67
68  } // end method set
69
70  // return value from buffer
71  public synchronized int get()
72  {
73     // for output purposes, get name of thread that called this method
74     String name = Thread.currentThread().getName();
75
76     // while no data to read, place thread in waiting state
77     while ( occupiedBufferCount == 0 ) {
78
79        // output thread information and buffer information, then wait
80        try {
81            SwingUtilities.invokeLater( new RunnableOutput( outputArea,
82               "\nAll buffers empty. " + name + " waits.") );
83            wait();
84        }
85
86        // if waiting thread interrupted, print stack trace
87        catch ( InterruptedException exception ) {
88            exception.printStackTrace();
89        }
90
91     } // end while
```

Fig. 16.14 SynchronizedBuffer monitors access to a shared array of integers. (Part 2 of 4.)

```
92
93        // obtain value at current readLocation
94        int readValue = buffers[ readLocation ];
95
96        // update Swing GUI component with consumed value
97        SwingUtilities.invokeLater( new RunnableOutput( outputArea,
98           "\n" + name + " reads " + readValue + " ") );
99
100       // just consumed a value, so decrement number of occupied buffers
101       --occupiedBufferCount;
102
103       // update readLocation for future read operation
104       readLocation = ( readLocation + 1 ) % buffers.length;
105
106       // display contents of shared buffers
107       SwingUtilities.invokeLater( new RunnableOutput(
108          outputArea, createStateOutput() ) );
109
110       notify(); // return waiting thread (if there is one) to ready state
111
112       return readValue;
113
114    } // end method get
115
116    // create state output
117    public String createStateOutput()
118    {
119       // first line of state information
120       String output =
121          "(buffers occupied: " + occupiedBufferCount + ")\nbuffers: ";
122
123       for ( int i = 0; i < buffers.length; i++ )
124          output += " " + buffers[ i ] + "  ";
125
126       // second line of state information
127       output += "\n          ";
128
129       for ( int i = 0; i < buffers.length; i++ )
130          output += "---- ";
131
132       // third line of state information
133       output += "\n          ";
134
135       // append readLocation (R) and writeLocation (W)
136       // indicators below appropriate buffer locations
137       for ( int i = 0; i < buffers.length; i++ )
138
139          if ( i == writeLocation && writeLocation == readLocation )
140             output += " WR  ";
141          else if ( i == writeLocation )
142             output += " W   ";
```

Fig. 16.14 SynchronizedBuffer monitors access to a shared array of integers. (Part 3 of 4.)

```
143              else if ( i == readLocation )
144                  output += "  R  ";
145              else
146                  output += "     ";
147
148          output += "\n";
149
150          return output;
151
152      } // end method createStateOutput
153
154  } // end class CircularBuffer
```

Fig. 16.14 SynchronizedBuffer monitors access to a shared array of integers. (Part 4 of 4.)

CircularBuffer method set (lines 26–68) performs the same tasks that it did in Fig. 16.9, with a few modifications. The while loop at lines 32–47 determines whether the producer must wait (i.e., all buffers are full). If so, lines 36–37 invoke SwingUtilities method invokeLater to update the output and indicate that the consumer is waiting to perform its task. Then line 38 invokes method wait to place the producer thread in the *Waiting* state for the CircularBuffer object. When execution eventually continues at line 50 after the while loop, the value written by the producer is placed in the circular buffer at location writeLocation. Next, lines 53–54 invoke SwingUtilities method invokeLater to update the GUI output with the value produced. Line 57 increments occupiedBufferCount, because there is now at least one value in the buffer that the consumer can read. Then, line 60 updates writeLocation for the next call to Circular-Buffer method set. The output continues at lines 63–64 by invoking method createStateOutput (declared at lines 117–152), which outputs the number of occupied buffers, the contents of the buffers and the current writeLocation and readLocation. Finally, line 66 invokes method notify to indicate that a thread waiting on the Synchro-nizedBuffer object (if there is a waiting thread) should transition to the *Ready* state.

Method get (lines 71–114) of class CircularBuffer also performs the same tasks as it did in Fig. 16.9, with a few minor modifications. The while loop at lines 77–91 determines whether the consumer must wait (i.e., all buffers are empty). If the consumer thread must wait, lines 81–82 invoke SwingUtilities method invokeLater to update the output and indicate that the consumer is waiting to perform its task. Then, line 83 invokes method wait to place the consumer thread in the *Waiting* state for the CircularBuffer object. When execution eventually continues at line 94 after the while loop, readValue is assigned the value at location readLocation in the circular buffer. Lines 97–98 invoke SwingUtilities method invokeLater to update the GUI output with the consumed value. Line 101 decrements the occupiedBufferCount, because there is at least one open position in the buffer in which the producer thread can place a value. Then, line 104 updates readLocation for the next call to CircularBuffer method get. Lines 107–108 invoke method createStateOutput to output the number of occupied buffers, the contents of the buffers and the current writeLocation and readLocation. Finally, line 110 invokes method notify to transition the next thread waiting for the CircularBuffer object into the *Ready* state, and line 112 returns the consumed value to the calling method.

Class `CircularBufferTest` (Fig. 16.15) contains the `main` method that launches the application. Line 43 creates a `CircularBufferTest` object. The constructor creates the application's GUI (lines 16–21), creates the `Buffer` object of class `CircularBuffer` (line

```
1   // Fig. 16.15: CircularBufferTest.java
2   // CircularBufferTest shows two threads manipulating a circular buffer.
3   import java.awt.*;
4   import java.awt.event.*;
5   import javax.swing.*;
6
7   // set up the producer and consumer threads and start them
8   public class CircularBufferTest extends JFrame {
9      JTextArea outputArea;
10
11      // set up GUI
12      public CircularBufferTest()
13      {
14         super( "Demonstrating Thread Synchronizaton" );
15
16         outputArea = new JTextArea( 20,30 );
17         outputArea.setFont( new Font( "Monospaced", Font.PLAIN, 12 ) );
18         getContentPane().add( new JScrollPane( outputArea ) );
19
20         setSize( 310, 500 );
21         setVisible( true );
22
23         // create shared object used by threads; we use a CircularBuffer
24         // reference rather than a Buffer reference so we can invoke
25         // CircularBuffer method createStateOutput
26         CircularBuffer sharedLocation = new CircularBuffer( outputArea );
27
28         // display initial state of buffers in CircularBuffer
29         SwingUtilities.invokeLater( new RunnableOutput( outputArea,
30            sharedLocation.createStateOutput() ) );
31
32         // set up threads
33         Producer producer = new Producer( sharedLocation, outputArea );
34         Consumer consumer = new Consumer( sharedLocation, outputArea );
35
36         producer.start();  // start producer thread
37         consumer.start();  // start consumer thread
38
39      } // end constructor
40
41      public static void main ( String args[] )
42      {
43         CircularBufferTest application = new CircularBufferTest();
44         application.setDefaultCloseOperation( JFrame.EXIT_ON_CLOSE );
45      }
46
47   } // end class CircularBufferTest
```

Fig. 16.15 `CircularBufferTest` sets up a producer/consumer GUI application and instantiates producer and consumer threads. (Part 1 of 3.)

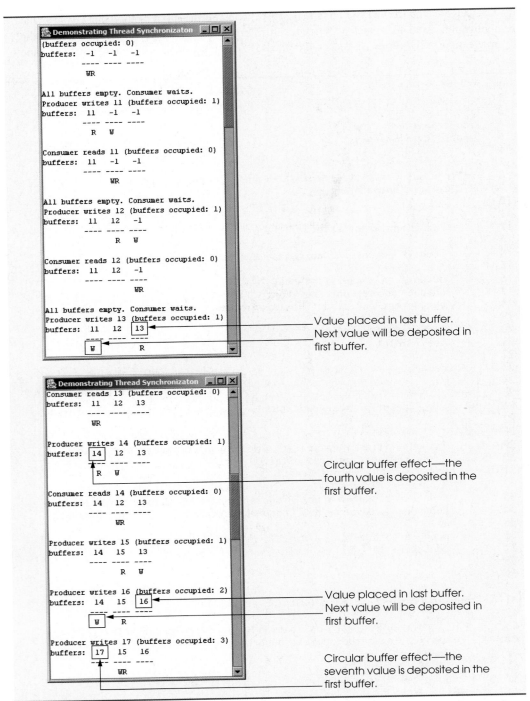

Fig. 16.15 CircularBufferTest sets up a producer/consumer GUI application and instantiates producer and consumer threads. (Part 2 of 3.)

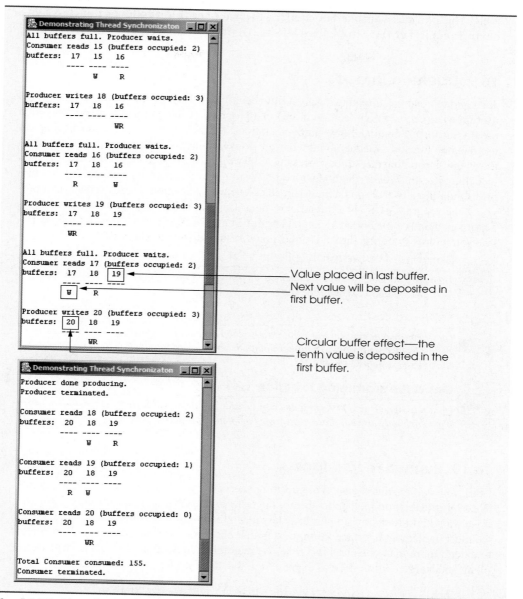

Fig. 16.15 `CircularBufferTest` sets up a producer/consumer GUI application and instantiates producer and consumer threads. (Part 3 of 3.)

26) and creates the threads (lines 33–34), then starts the threads (lines 36–37). The outputs include the current `occupiedBufferCount`, the contents of the buffers and the current `writeLocation` and `readLocation`. In the output, the letters W and R represent the current `writeLocation` and `readLocation`, respectively. Notice that, after the third value is placed in the third element of the buffer, the fourth value is inserted at the beginning of the

array. This provides a circular buffer effect. Method `createStateOutput` of class `SynchronizedBuffer` (Fig. 16.14, lines 117–152) formats the contents of the array `buffers`.

16.9 Daemon Threads

A daemon thread is a thread that runs for the benefit of other threads. Unlike conventional user threads (i.e., any non-daemon thread in a program), daemon threads do not prevent a program from terminating. Some implementations of Java's garbage-collection mechanism use daemon threads. Nondaemon threads are conventional user threads or threads such as the event-dispatching thread for processing GUI events. We designate a thread as a daemon by calling its *setDaemon* method with a `true` argument. A program can include a mixture of daemon threads and non daemon threads. When only daemon threads remain in a program, the program exits. If a thread is to be a daemon, it must be set as such before its `start` method is called or an `IllegalThreadStateException` is thrown. Method `isDaemon` returns `true` if a thread is a daemon thread and `false` otherwise.

Common Programming Error 16.4

Attempting to make a thread a daemon thread after it has already been started causes an `IllegalThreadStateException`.

Software Engineering Observation 16.4

The event-dispatching thread is an infinite loop and is not a daemon thread. As such, the event-dispatching thread will not terminate in a windowed application until the application calls System *method* `exit`.

Good Programming Practice 16.1

Do not assign critical tasks to a daemon thread. The tasks will be terminated without warning, which may prevent those tasks from completing properly.

16.10 Runnable Interface

Until now, we extended class `Thread` to create new classes that support multithreading. We overrode the `run` method to specify the tasks to be performed concurrently. However, if we want multithreading support in a class that already extends a class other than `Thread`, we must implement interface `Runnable` in that class, because Java does not allow a class to extend more than one class at a time. As mentioned in Section 16.7, class `Thread` implements interface `Runnable` as expressed in the class header

```
public class Thread extends Object implements Runnable
```

Implementing the `Runnable` interface in a class enables a program to manipulate objects of that class as `Runnable` objects. As is the case for extending the `Thread` class, the code that executes the thread is placed in method `run`.

A program that uses a `Runnable` object to control a thread creates a `Thread` object and associates the `Runnable` object with that `Thread`. Class `Thread` provides five constructors that can receive references to `Runnable` objects as arguments. For example, the constructor

```
public Thread( Runnable runnableObject )
```

specifies that method `run` of `runnableObject` is the method to be invoked when the thread begins execution. The constructor

```
public Thread( Runnable runnableObject, String threadName )
```

constructs a `Thread` with the name `threadName` and specifies that method `run` of its `runnableObject` argument is the method to be invoked when the thread begins execution. As always, the thread object's `start` method must be called to begin the thread's execution.

Software Engineering Observation 16.5

Favor implementing interface `Runnable` *over extending class* `Thread`. `Runnable` *objects can be used in many situations where* `Thread` *objects are cumbersome.*

Figure 16.16 demonstrates an applet with two inner classes that each implement interface `Runnable`—one that controls threads created in the applet and one that is used with `SwingUtilities` method `invokeLater` to ensure that the GUI is updated properly. This example also demonstrates how to suspend a thread (i.e., temporarily prevent it from executing), how to resume a suspended thread and how to terminate a thread that executes until a condition becomes false. [*Note:* Class `Thread` actually provides methods `suspend`, `resume` and `stop`; however, these methods are *deprecated* and should no longer be used in Java programs. Programs that use these methods could encounter problems such as deadlock with `suspend` and data corruption with `stop`, because methods `suspend`, `resume` and `stop` do not work properly with monitors. For these reasons, we demonstrate coding techniques for suspending, resuming and stopping threads. As we will demonstrate, these mechanisms rely on synchronized statements, loops and `boolean` flag variables.]

```java
1   // Fig. 16.16: RandomCharacters.java
2   // Class RandomCharacters demonstrates the Runnable interface
3   import java.awt.*;
4   import java.awt.event.*;
5   import javax.swing.*;
6
7   public class RandomCharacters extends JApplet implements ActionListener {
8      private String alphabet = "ABCDEFGHIJKLMNOPQRSTUVWXYZ";
9      private final static int SIZE = 3;
10     private JLabel outputs[];
11     private JCheckBox checkboxes[];
12     private Thread threads[];
13     private boolean suspended[];
14
15     // set up GUI and arrays
16     public void init()
17     {
18        outputs = new JLabel[ SIZE ];
19        checkboxes = new JCheckBox[ SIZE ];
20        threads = new Thread[ SIZE ];
21        suspended = new boolean[ SIZE ];
22
23        Container container = getContentPane();
24        container.setLayout( new GridLayout( SIZE, 2, 5, 5 ) );
```

Fig. 16.16 `Runnable` interface, suspending threads and resuming threads. (Part 1 of 4.)

```
25
26          // create GUI components, register listeners and attach
27          // components to content pane
28          for ( int count = 0; count < SIZE; count++ ) {
29             outputs[ count ] = new JLabel();
30             outputs[ count ].setBackground( Color.GREEN );
31             outputs[ count ].setOpaque( true );
32             container.add( outputs[ count ] );
33
34             checkboxes[ count ] = new JCheckBox( "Suspended" );
35             checkboxes[ count ].addActionListener( this );
36             container.add( checkboxes[ count ] );
37          }
38
39       } // end method init
40
41       // create and start threads each time start is called (i.e., after
42       // init and when user revists Web page containing this applet)
43       public void start()
44       {
45          for ( int count = 0; count < threads.length; count++ ) {
46
47             // create Thread; initialize object that implements Runnable
48             threads[ count ] =
49                new Thread( new RunnableObject(), "Thread " + ( count + 1 ) );
50
51             threads[ count ].start(); // begin executing Thread
52          }
53       }
54
55       // determine thread location in threads array
56       private int getIndex( Thread current )
57       {
58          for ( int count = 0; count < threads.length; count++ )
59             if ( current == threads[ count ] )
60                return count;
61
62          return -1;
63       }
64
65       // called when user switches Web pages; stops all threads
66       public synchronized void stop()
67       {
68          // set references to null to terminate each thread's run method
69          for ( int count = 0; count < threads.length; count++ )
70             threads[ count ] = null;
71
72          notifyAll(); // notify all waiting threads, so they can terminate
73       }
74
75       // handle button events
76       public synchronized void actionPerformed( ActionEvent event )
77       {
```

Fig. 16.16 Runnable interface, suspending threads and resuming threads. (Part 2 of 4.)

```
78        for ( int count = 0; count < checkboxes.length; count++ ) {
79
80           if ( event.getSource() == checkboxes[ count ] ) {
81              suspended[ count ] = !suspended[ count ];
82
83              // change label color on suspend/resume
84              outputs[ count ].setBackground(
85                 suspended[ count ] ? Color.RED : Color.GREEN );
86
87              // if thread resumed, make sure it starts executing
88              if ( !suspended[ count ] )
89                 notifyAll();
90
91              return;
92           }
93        }
94
95     } // end method actionPerformed
96
97     // private inner class that implements Runnable to control threads
98     private class RunnableObject implements Runnable {
99
100        // place random characters in GUI, variables currentThread and
101        // index are final so can be used in an anonymous inner class
102        public void run()
103        {
104           // get reference to executing thread
105           final Thread currentThread = Thread.currentThread();
106
107           // determine thread's position in array
108           final int index = getIndex( currentThread );
109
110           // loop condition determines when thread should stop; loop
111           // terminates when reference threads[ index ] becomes null
112           while ( threads[ index ] == currentThread ) {
113
114              // sleep from 0 to 1 second
115              try {
116                 Thread.sleep( ( int ) ( Math.random() * 1000 ) );
117
118                 // determine whether thread should suspend execution;
119                 // synchronize on RandomCharacters applet object
120                 synchronized( RandomCharacters.this ) {
121
122                    while ( suspended[ index ] &&
123                       threads[ index ] == currentThread ) {
124
125                       // temporarily suspend thread execution
126                       RandomCharacters.this.wait();
127                    }
128                 } // end synchronized statement
129
130              } // end try
```

Fig. 16.16 Runnable interface, suspending threads and resuming threads. (Part 3 of 4.)

```
131
132                // if thread interrupted during wait/sleep, print stack trace
133                catch ( InterruptedException exception ) {
134                   exception.printStackTrace();
135                }
136
137                // display character on corresponding JLabel
138                SwingUtilities.invokeLater(
139                   new Runnable() {
140
141                      // pick random character and display it
142                      public void run()
143                      {
144                         char displayChar =
145                            alphabet.charAt( ( int ) ( Math.random() * 26 ) );
146
147                         outputs[ index ].setText(
148                            currentThread.getName()  + ": " + displayChar );
149                      }
150
151                   } // end inner class
152
153                ); // end call to SwingUtilities.invokeLater
154
155             } // end while
156
157             System.err.println( currentThread.getName() + " terminating" );
158
159          } // end method run
160
161       } // end private inner class RunnableObject
162
163    } // end class RandomCharacters
```

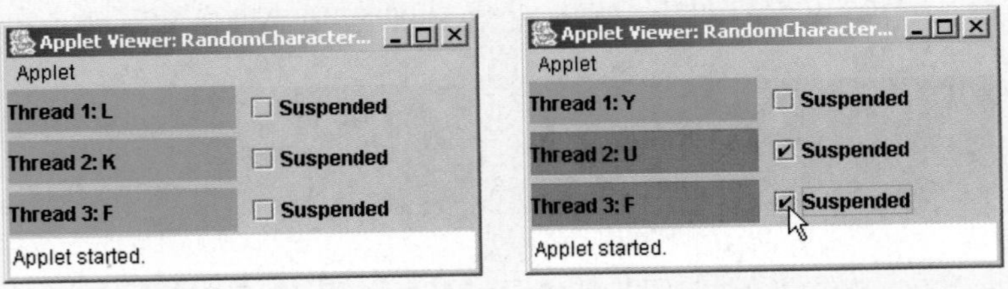

Fig. 16.16 Runnable interface, suspending threads and resuming threads. (Part 4 of 4.)

Applet class RandomCharacters displays three JLabels and three JCheckBoxes. A separate thread of execution is associated with each JLabel and JCheckBox pair. Each thread randomly displays letters from the alphabet in its corresponding JLabel object. The applet declares the string alphabet (line 8) containing the letters from A to Z. This string is shared among the three threads. Typically, when threads are used in an applet, the applet's start method creates the threads and places them in the *Ready* state, and the applet's stop method terminates the threads. This applet's start method (lines 43–53) instantiates three Thread objects (lines 48–49) and initializes each with an instance of class RunnableObject (declared at lines 98–161), which implements interface Runnable. Line 51 invokes each Thread's start method to place the threads in the *Ready* state.

Class RunnableObject (lines 98–161) implements interface Runnable's run method (lines 102–159). The method declares two local variables. Line 105 uses static Thread method currentThread to determine the currently executing Thread object. Line 108 calls the applet's utility method getIndex (declared at lines 56–63) to determine the index of the currently executing thread in array threads, which contains references to the threads in the applet. The current thread displays a random character in the JLabel object with the same index in array outputs (the array of JLabels). The loop at lines 112–155 continues to execute as long as threads[index] refers to the currently executing thread (currentThread). As we will see, threads[index] becomes null when it is time for the thread to terminate. At that point, threads[index] and currentThread no longer refer to the same object, so the loop terminates and the thread dies. In each iteration of the loop, the thread sleeps for a random interval from 0 to 1 second (line 116).

When the user clicks the JCheckBox to the right of a particular JLabel, the corresponding Thread should be *suspended* (temporarily prevented from executing) or *resumed* (allowed to continue executing). Suspending and resuming of a thread can be implemented by using thread synchronization and Object methods wait and notify. Lines 120–128 declare a synchronized statement for suspending the currently executing Thread. When the Thread reaches the synchronized statement, the applet object is locked and the loop condition (lines 122–123) tests suspended[index] to determine whether the Thread should be suspended. If so, and if the thread has not been terminated, line 126 invokes method wait on the applet object to place the Thread in the *Waiting* state for the applet's lock. When the Thread should resume, the program tells all waiting threads to become ready to execute (discussed shortly). However, suspended[index] will be false only for the resumed thread, so only that thread will get a chance to execute. The other suspended threads (if any) will reenter the *Waiting* state because of the loop at lines 122–127). Lines 138–153 use SwingUtilities method invokeLater to update the JLabel for the appropriate thread. This example uses an inner class (lines 139–151) to implement interface Runnable and passes the inner-class object to invokeLater. Lines 144–145 choose a random character from alphabet. Lines 147–148 display the character on the appropriate JLabel object. In lines 120 and 126, note the use of RandomCharacters.this to access the applet class's this reference from the inner class

If the user clicks the **Suspended** checkbox next to a particular JLabel, the program invokes method actionPerformed (lines 76–95) to determine which checkbox generated the event. Using the index of that checkbox in array outputs, line 81 toggles the corresponding boolean in array suspended. Lines 84–85 set the background color of the JLabel to red if the thread is being suspended and green if the thread is being resumed. If the appropriate boolean variable is false, the program calls Object method notifyAll (line 89) on the applet. This moves all the applet's waiting threads into the *Ready* state and prepares them to resume execution. When each thread is dispatched to the processor to resume execution, the while condition at lines 122–123 in RunnableObject method run fails for the resumed thread and the loop terminates, which allows that thread to continue executing from line 138. For any other threads that became ready, but still are suspended, the condition at lines 122–123 remains true and the threads reenter the *Waiting* state.

Recall from Section 6.10 that the applet's `stop` method is invoked when the user browses to another Web page. This applet overrides method `stop` (lines 66–73) to terminate all three threads if the user leaves the Web page on which this applet resides.

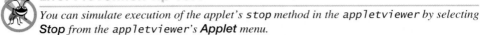

Error-Prevention Tip 16.4

*You can simulate execution of the applet's `stop` method in the `appletviewer` by selecting **Stop** from the `appletviewer`'s **Applet** menu.*

The `for` loop at lines 69–70 sets each `Thread` reference in array `threads` to `null`. Line 72 invokes `Object` method `notifyAll` to ensure that all waiting threads get ready to execute. Any threads that were previously suspended will get out of the loop at lines 122–127 and complete their iteration of the `while` loop that starts at line 112. When each thread encounters the `while` loop condition at line 112, the condition fails and method `run` terminates. Thus, each thread dies. If the user returns to the Web page, the applet container calls the applet's `start` method to instantiate and start three new threads.

Performance Tip 16.5

Stopping applet threads when leaving a Web page is a polite programming practice because it prevents your applet from using processor time (which can reduce performance) on the browser's machine when the applet is not being viewed. The threads can be restarted from the applet's `start` method, which is invoked by the browser when the Web page is revisited by the user.

Error-Prevention Tip 16.5

*You can simulate execution of the applet's `start` method in the `appletviewer` by selecting **Start** from the `appletviewer`'s **Applet** menu).*

This chapter presented Java's built in multithreading capabilities and demonstrated the powerful technique of thread synchronization. In addition, this chapter demonstrated how synchronization techniques can be used to suspend, resume and stop threads of execution. Multithreading is an advanced topic that could be the subject of an entire book. For more examples of Java multithreading visit

        developer.java.sun.com/developer/technicalArticles/Threads

There are numerous articles that discuss multithreading in the context of other Java technologies at

        developer.java.sun.com/developer/technicalArticles

Also, the archives of the online Java magazine *JavaWorld* (www.javaworld.com) provide many articles on Java multithreading. We use multithreading again in Chapter 18, Networking, to help build multithreaded servers that can interact with multiple clients concurrently.

16.11 (Optional Case Study) Thinking About Objects: Multithreading

Real-world objects perform their operations independently of one another and concurrently (in parallel). As you learned in this chapter, Java is a multithreaded programming language that facilitates the implementation of concurrent activities. The UML also supports the modeling of concurrent systems, as we will see shortly. In this section, we discuss how our simulation benefits from multithreading.

In Section 11.9, we encountered a problem with the collaboration diagram of Fig. 11.28—the waitingPassenger (the Person waiting to ride the Elevator) incorrectly enters the Elevator before the ridingPassenger (the Person riding the Elevator) exits. Proper use of multithreading in Java avoids this problem by guaranteeing that the waitingPassenger will wait for the ridingPassenger to exit the Elevator—as would happen in real life. We use Java's thread-synchronization mechanisms to enforce this polite behavior, to guarantee that only one Person may occupy the Elevator at a time and to ensure that the doors will not injure Persons by closing prematurely.

Threads, Active Classes and Modeling Sequences

Java uses threads—flows of program control independent of other flows—to execute independent, concurrent activities. The UML provides the notion of an *active class* to represent a thread or process. Classes Elevator and Person are active classes, because their objects must be able to operate concurrently and independently of one another and of other objects in the system. For example, the Elevator must be able to move between Floors while a Person is walking on a Floor.

To model this, and to model interactions between objects, we now present the *sequence diagram*. Like the collaboration diagram, the sequence diagram shows interactions among objects; however, the sequence diagram emphasizes how messages are sent between objects *over time*. Both diagrams model interactions in a system. Collaboration diagrams emphasize which objects interact in a system, and sequence diagrams emphasize when these interactions occur.

Figure 16.17 and Fig. 16.18 model the sequence of interactions for a Person changing floors. The dotted line extending down from an object's rectangle is that object's *lifeline*, which represents the progression of time. Actions occur along an object's lifeline in chronological order from top to bottom—an action near the top of a lifeline happens before an action near the bottom.

Message passing in sequence diagrams is similar to that in collaboration diagrams (Section 11.9). An arrow extending from the object sending the message to the object receiving the message represents a message between two objects. The arrowhead points to an *activation* on the receiving object's lifeline. An activation, which is shown as a thin rectangle, indicates that an object controls the program flow. When an object returns control, a return message—represented as a dashed line with an arrowhead—extends from the activation of the object returning control to the activation of the object that initially sent the message. To eliminate clutter, we omit the return-message arrows.

The sequence in Fig. 16.17 begins when a Person requests the Elevator by sending a pressButton message to the Button on the Floor. The Button then sends message requestElevator to the ElevatorShaft, which requests the Elevator's service. As indicated by the condition in square brackets, the Person presses the Button only if the floorDoor is not open already.

Note the split in flow for the Elevator after being requested; the flow of execution depends on which Floor generated the request. If the Elevator is on a different Floor than the request, the Elevator must travel to the Floor on which the Person is waiting. To save space, the note indicating that the Elevator moves to the other Floor represents this sequence. When the Elevator travels to the other Floor, the branched activation merges with the original activation in the Elevator's lifeline, and the Elevator sends an elevatorArrived message to the elevatorDoor. If the Elevator is on the same Floor as the request, the elevatorDoor immediately sends an elevatorArrived message to the elevatorDoor. The elevatorDoor receives the arrival message and opens the Door on the arrival Floor.

The Person must wait for the Floor's Door to open before entering the Elevator. The interactions among the Person threads in the simulation, the Elevator and the Doors are quite complex. The Person and Elevator objects each execute in separate threads of execution, so when they interact we must ensure they are properly synchronized for the simulation to work properly. To ensure that the Floor Door does not close while a Person is trying to walk on or off the Elevator, we require each Person to wait for exclusive access to the floor door. This waiting takes place by invoking floorDoor method wait in a while loop that terminates when floorDoor has opened. An asterisk in front of the condition [!floorDoor.isDoorOpen()] models this loop. When the floorDoor opens, it invokes its own notify method, the waiting Person thread is notified and method wait terminates. The Person then implicitly acquires a lock on the floorDoor and ensures that the floorDoor is open. The Person enters the Elevator by invoking Person method setLocation with the Elevator as the Location argument. By holding the lock on the floorDoor, the Person ensures that the floorDoor will not close and thus avoids injury. In the Java implementation, we will see that the Person also acquires a lock on the Elevator. This lock will not be available to the waiting Person until the passenger (if one exists) has exited the Elevator.[6] The sequence continues in Fig. 16.18.

Once the Person has entered the elevator, the Person must instruct the Elevator to move to the opposite floor. We model this sequence in Fig. 16.18. The Person begins by pressing the Elevator's Button. In response to the buttonPressed message, the Elevator begins the process of traveling to the opposite floor by invoking its own setMoving method with an argument of true. The Elevator then closes the ElevatorDoor. After five seconds of traveling, the Elevator stops moving by invoking method setMoving with a false argument, calls its own changeFloors method to reflect the new Floor location of the Elevator and sends an elevatorArrived message to the elevator-Door. In response to the elevatorArrived message, the elevatorDoor opens itself and the floorDoor (not shown in Fig. 16.18).

The Person riding the Elevator must wait for the elevatorDoor to open, so the Person sends a wait message to the elevatorDoor. When the elevatorDoor opens in response to the elevatorArrived message, the elevatorDoor will notify itself, the Person's invocation of wait will terminate and the Person will check whether the elevatorDoor is open. The Person then sets its Location to the destination Floor and exits the simulation. Note the large "X" at the bottom of the Person's lifeline. In a sequence diagram, this "X" indicates that the associated object destroys itself. (In Java, the Person object becomes eligible for garbage collection.)

---

6.   We discuss the details of this locking in our implementation discussion of Appendix E.

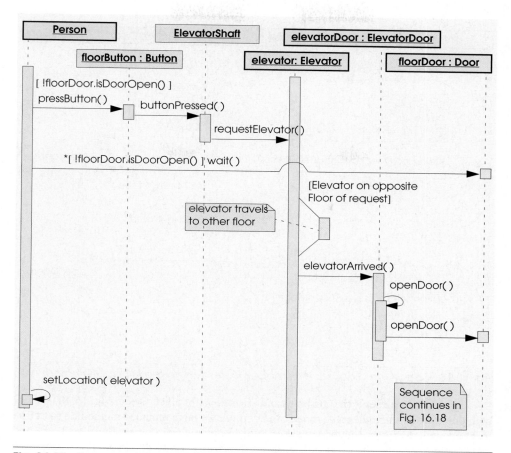

Fig. 16.17 Sequence diagram that models a `Person` requesting and entering an `Elevator`.

Our Final Class Diagram

The integration of multithreading in our elevator model concludes the design of the model. We implement this model in Appendix E. Figure 16.19 presents a revised class diagram. Note that the major difference between the class diagrams of Fig. 16.19 and Section 11.31 is the presence of active classes in Fig. 16.19. We have established that classes `Elevator` and `Person` are active classes. However, the problem statement mentioned that "if a person neither enters nor requests the elevator, the elevator closes its door." Having discussed multithreading, we believe that a better requirement would be for the `Doors` to close automatically (using a thread) if they have been open for more than a brief period (e.g., three seconds). In addition, although not mentioned in the problem statement, the `Lights` should turn off automatically—currently, the `Lights` turn off only when the `Elevator` departs from a `Floor`. We mark the `Doors` and `Lights` as active classes to model this change. We implement this change in Appendix E.

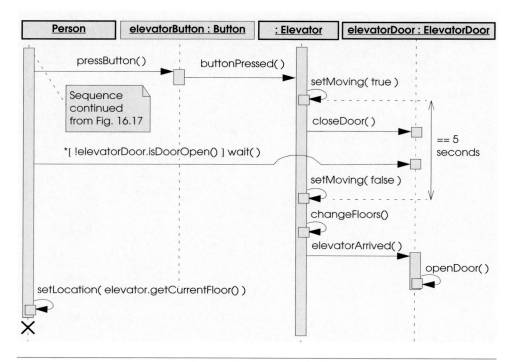

Fig. 16.18 Sequence diagram that models a `Person` traveling in an `Elevator`.

Figure 16.20 presents the attributes and operations for all classes in Fig. 16.19. We use both diagrams to implement the model. In addition, we have replaced method `departEl-evator` with `private` method `setMoving`, because according to Fig. 16.18, method `setMoving` provides the service that allows the `Elevator` to depart from a `Floor`. We will use these class diagrams to implement our Java code in Appendix E, but we will continue making subtle "Java-specific" adjustments to code. In the appendices, for each class, we create methods that access object references and implement interface methods.

In Section 19.7, we design the view—the display of our model. When we implement this display in Appendix E, we will have a fully functional elevator simulation.

16.12 (Optional) Discovering Design Patterns: Concurrent Design Patterns

Many additional design patterns have been discovered since the publication of the Gang of Four book, which introduced patterns involving object-oriented systems. Some of these new patterns involve specific object-oriented systems, such as concurrent, distributed or parallel systems. In this section, we discuss concurrency patterns to conclude our discussion of multithreaded programming.

Concurrency Design Patterns

Multithreaded programming languages such as Java allow designers to specify concurrent activities—that is, those that operate in parallel with one another. Designing concurrent

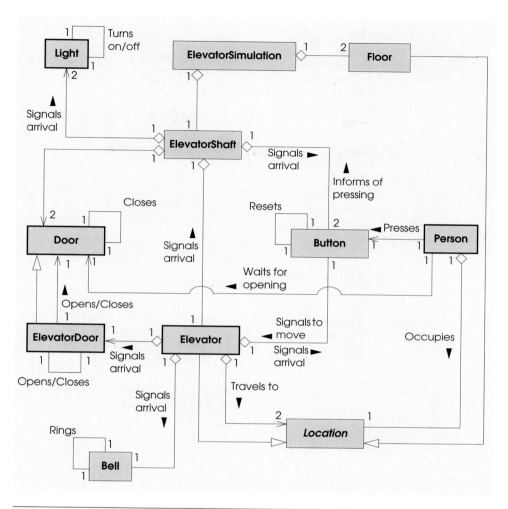

Fig. 16.19 Revised class diagram of the elevator simulation

systems improperly can introduce concurrency problems. For example, two objects attempting to alter shared data at the same time could corrupt that data. In addition, if two objects wait for one another to finish tasks, and if neither can complete their task, these objects could potentially wait forever—a situation called *deadlock*. Using Java, Doug Lea[7] and Mark Grand[8] documented *concurrency patterns* for multithreaded design architectures to prevent various problems associated with multithreading. We provide a partial list of these design patterns:

7. Lea, D. *Concurrent Programing in Java, Second Edition: Design Principles and Patterns.* Massachusetts: Addison-Wesley, 2000.
8. Grand, M. *Patterns in Java; A Catalog of Reusable Design Patterns Illustrated with UML, Second Edition, Volume I.* New York: John Wiley and Sons, 2002.

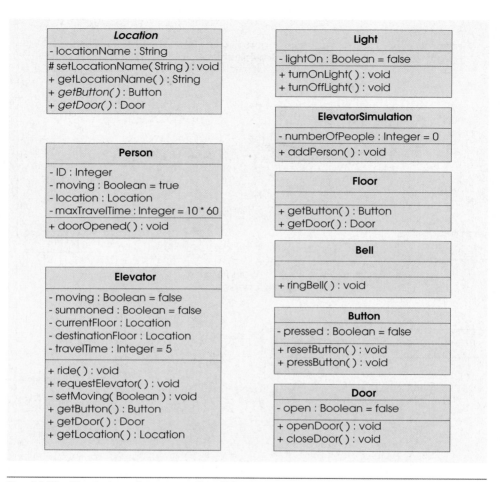

Fig. 16.20 Final class diagram with attributes and operations.

- The *Single-Threaded Execution design pattern* (Grand, 2002) prevents several threads from executing the same method of another object concurrently. In Java, the `synchronized` keyword (discussed in Chapter 15) can be used to apply this pattern.

- The *Guarded Suspension design pattern* (Lea, 2000) suspends a thread's activity and resumes that thread's activity when some condition is satisfied. Lines 137–147 and lines 95–109 of class `RandomCharacters` (Fig. 16.16) use this design pattern—methods `wait` and `notify` suspend and resume the program threads, and line 98 toggles the guard variable that the condition evaluates.

- The *Balking design pattern* (Lea, 2000) ensures that a method will *balk*—that is, return without performing any actions—if an object occupies a state that cannot execute that method. A variation of this pattern is that the method throws an exception describing why that method is unable to execute—for example, a method throwing an exception when accessing a data structure that does not exist.

- The *Read/Write Lock design pattern* (Lea, 2000) allows multiple threads to obtain concurrent read access on an object but prevents multiple threads from obtaining concurrent write access on that object. Only one thread at a time may obtain write access to an object—when that thread obtains write access, the object is *locked* to all other threads.

- The *Two-Phase Termination design pattern* (Grand, 98) uses a two-phase termination process for a thread to ensure that a thread has the opportunity to free resources—such as other spawned threads—in memory (phase one) before termination (phase two). In Java, a `Thread` object can use this pattern in method `run`. For instance, method `run` can contain an infinite loop that is terminated by some state change—upon termination, method `run` can invoke a `private` method responsible for stopping any other spawned threads (phase one). The thread then terminates after method `run` terminates (phase two).

In "Discovering Design Patterns" Section 18.12, we return to the Gang of Four design patterns. Using the material introduced in Chapter 17 and Chapter 18, we identify those classes in package `java.io` and `java.net` that use design patterns.

SUMMARY

- Computers perform operations concurrently, such as compiling programs, printing files and receiving electronic mail messages over a network.

- Programming languages generally provide only a simple set of control structures that enable programmers to perform one action at a time and proceed to the next action.

- Historically, concurrency has been implemented with operating system "primitives" available only to "systems programmers."

- Java makes concurrency primitives available to the programmer. The programmer specifies that applications contain threads of execution—each thread designating a portion of a program that may execute concurrently with other threads. This capability is called multithreading.

- A thread's `run` method contains the code that controls a thread's execution.

- A program launches a thread's execution by calling the thread's `start` method, which sets up the initial call to the thread's `run` method.

- Thread method `currentThread` returns a reference to the currently executing `Thread`.

- A thread that was just created is in the *Born* state. The thread remains in this state until the thread's `start` method is called; this causes the thread to enter the *Ready* state.

- A thread in the *Ready* state enters the *Running* state when the system assigns a processor to the thread. The system assigns the processor to one of the highest-priority ready threads.

- A thread enters the *Dead* state when its `run` method terminates. The system eventually will dispose of a dead thread.

- A *Running* thread enters the *Blocked* state for one of several reasons, such as when the thread issues an input/output request. In this case, the blocked thread becomes ready when the I/O it is waiting for completes. A blocked thread cannot use a processor, even if one is available.

- If a thread called method `wait`, a corresponding call to method `notify` (if there is only one thread waiting) or `notifyAll` by another thread in the program will transition the original thread from the *Waiting* state to the *Ready* state.

- Thread method `sleep` causes a thread to sleep for the specified number of milliseconds. A thread wakes up when the designated sleep interval expires.

- If a thread 1 cannot continue executing unless thread 2 terminates, thread 1 calls thread 2's `join` method to "join" the two threads. When the two threads are "joined," thread 1 leaves the *Waiting* state when thread 2 finishes execution (enters the *Dead* state).
- In thread synchronization, when a thread encounters code that it cannot yet run, the thread can call method `wait` to pause until certain actions occur that enable the thread to continue executing.
- Waiting can be dangerous; it can lead to two serious problems called deadlock and indefinite postponement. Indefinite postponement is also called starvation.
- Any thread in the *Waiting* or *Sleeping* state can leave that state if another thread invokes `Thread` method `interrupt` on the thread in the given state.
- Every Java thread has a priority between `MIN_PRIORITY` (1) and `MAX_PRIORITY` (10). By default, each thread is given priority `NORM_PRIORITY` (5). A thread's priority can be adjusted with method `setPriority`. Method `getPriority` returns a thread's priority.
- Some Java platforms support timeslicing. Without timeslicing, one thread of equal priority runs to completion before other threads of equal priority get a chance to execute. With timeslicing, each thread receives a brief burst of processor time called a quantum during which that thread can execute. At the completion of the quantum, even if that thread has not finished executing, the processor may be taken away from that thread and given to the next thread of equal priority, if one is available.
- The thread scheduler attempts to keep the highest-priority thread *Running* at all times and, if there is more than one highest-priority thread, ensures that all equally high-priority threads execute for a quantum at a time in round-robin fashion.
- A thread can call method `yield` to give other equal-priority threads a chance to execute.
- Every object has a monitor. The monitor lets only one thread at a time execute a synchronized statement or method on the object.
- A thread executing a synchronized statement may determine that it cannot proceed, so the thread voluntarily calls `wait`. This removes the thread from contention for the processor and places the thread in the *Waiting* state for that object.
- A thread that has called `wait` is awakened by a thread that calls `notify` or `notifyAll`. The notification acts as a signal to the waiting thread that the condition the waiting thread has been waiting for is now (or could be) satisfied, so it is acceptable for that thread to attempt to reenter the monitor.
- A daemon thread serves other threads. When only daemon threads remain in a program, the program terminates. If a thread is to be a daemon, this must be specified before it is started.
- To support multithreading in a class that is not a subclass of `Thread`, implement interface `Runnable` in that class.
- A `Runnable` thread is created by passing to the `Thread` class constructor a reference to a `Runnable` object. The `Thread` constructor specifies that method `run` of the `Runnable` object is the method to be invoked when the thread begins execution.

TERMINOLOGY

asynchronous threads
accessing shared data with synchronization
acquire the lock for an object
Blocked state
circular buffer
concurrency
concurrent producer and consumer threads

concurrent programming
condition variable
consumer
consumer thread
`currentThread` method of `Thread`
daemon thread
Dead state

deadlock
lock
garbage-collector thread
getName method of Thread
I/O completion
I/O request
IllegalArgumentException
IllegalMonitorStateException
IllegalThreadStateException
indefinite postponement
inherit thread priority
input/output blocking
interrupt method of Thread
interrupted method
InterruptedException
join method of Thread
kill a thread
life cycle of a thread
memory leak
monitor
multilevel priority queue
multiprocessing
multithreading
new state
notify method of Object
notifyAll method of Object
preemptive scheduling
priority of a thread
producer thread
producer/consumer relationship
quantum
Ready state
round-robin scheduling

run method of a thread
run method of Runnable
Runnable interface
Runnable state
Running state
scheduler
setDaemon method of Thread
setPriority method of Thread
shared buffer
single-threaded language
single-threaded program
sleep method of Thread
Sleeping state
start method of Thread
starvation
synchronization
synchronized statement
synchronized method
Thread class
thread of execution
thread safe
thread states
thread synchronization
Thread.MAX_PRIORITY
Thread.MIN_PRIORITY
Thread.NORM_PRIORITY
Thread.sleep()
ThreadDeath exception
timeslicing
wait method of Object
Waiting state
yield method of Thread

SELF-REVIEW EXERCISES

16.1   Fill in the blanks in each of the following statements:
a) C and C++ are _____-threaded languages whereas Java is a _____-threaded language.
b) Three reasons an alive thread might not be *Runnable* are that it is _____, _____ and _____.
c) A thread enters the *Dead* state when _____.
d) A thread's priority can be changed with method _____.
e) A thread may give up the processor to a thread of the same priority by calling Thread method _____.
f) To pause for a designated number of milliseconds and resume execution, a thread should call method _____.
g) Method _____ moves a single thread in an object's *Waiting* state to the *Ready* state.
h) Method _____ moves every thread in an object's *Waiting* state to the *Ready* state.

16.2   State whether each of the following is *true* or *false*. If *false*, explain why.
a) A thread is not *Runnable* if it is dead.

    b) In Java, a higher priority *Runnable* thread should preempt threads of lower priority.

    c) Some operating systems use timeslicing with threads. Therefore, they can enable threads to preempt threads of the same priority.

    d) Threads may `yield` to threads of lower priority.

ANSWERS TO SELF-REVIEW EXERCISES

16.1   a) single, multi. b) *Waiting, Sleeping, Blocked* for input/output. c) its `run` method terminates. d) `setPriority`. e) `yield`. f) `sleep`. g) `notify`. h) `notifyAll`.

16.2   a) True. b) True. c) False. Timeslicing allows a thread to execute until its timeslice (or quantum) expires. Then other threads of equal priority can execute. d) False. Threads can only yield to threads of equal priority.

EXERCISES

16.3   State whether each of the following is *true* or *false*. If *false*, explain why.

    a) Method `sleep` does not consume processor time while a thread sleeps.

    b) Declaring a method `synchronized` guarantees that deadlock cannot occur.

    c) `Thread` methods `suspend`, `resume` and `stop` are deprecated.

16.4   Define each of the following terms.

    a) thread

    b) multithreading

    c) *Ready* state

    d) *Blocked* state

    e) preemptive scheduling

    f) `Runnable` interface

    g) monitor

    h) `notify` method

    i) producer/consumer relationship

16.5   List each the reasons given in the text for entering the *Blocked* state. For each of these, describe how the program will normally leave the *Blocked* state and enter the *Ready* state.

16.6   What is timeslicing? Give a fundamental difference in how scheduling is performed on Java systems that support timeslicing vs. scheduling on Java systems that do not support timeslicing. Why would a thread ever want to call `yield`?

16.7   Distinguish among each of the following means of pausing threads:

    a) sleep

    b) blocking I/O

16.8   Discuss each of the following terms in the context of Java's threading mechanisms:

    a) monitor

    b) producer

    c) consumer

    d) `wait`

    e) `notify`

    f) `InterruptedException`

    g) `synchronized`

16.9   Write a Java program to demonstrate that as a high-priority thread executes, it will delay the execution of all lower priority threads.

16.10 If your system supports timeslicing, write a Java program that demonstrates timeslicing among several equal-priority threads. Show that a lower priority thread's execution is deferred by the timeslicing of the higher-priority threads.

16.11 Write a Java program that demonstrates a high priority thread using `sleep` to give lower priority threads a chance to run.

16.12 If your system does not support timeslicing, write a Java program that demonstrates two threads using `yield` to enable one another to execute.

16.13 Two problems that can occur in systems like Java, that allow threads to wait, are deadlock, in which one or more threads will wait forever for an event that cannot occur, and indefinite postponement, in which one or more threads will be delayed for some unpredictably long time. Give an example of how each of these problems can occur in a multithreaded Java program.

16.14 (Readers and Writers) This exercise asks you to develop a Java monitor to solve a famous problem in concurrency control. This problem was first discussed and solved by P. J. Courtois, F. Heymans and D. L. Parnas in their research paper, "Concurrent Control with Readers and Writers," *Communications of the ACM*, Vol. 14, No. 10, October 1971, pp. 667–668. The interested student might also want to read C. A. R. Hoare's seminal research paper on monitors, "Monitors: An Operating System Structuring Concept," *Communications of the ACM*, Vol. 17, No. 10, October 1974, pp. 549–557. Corrigendum, *Communications of the ACM*, Vol. 18, No. 2, February 1975, p. 95. [The Readers and Writers problem is discussed at length in Chapter 5 of the author's book: Deitel, H. M., *Operating Systems*, Reading, MA: Addison-Wesley, 1990.]

  a) With multithreading, many threads can access shared objects; as we have seen, access to shared objects needs to be synchronized carefully to avoid corrupting the objects.

  b) Consider an airline-reservation system in which many clients are attempting to book seats on particular flights between particular cities. All of the information about flights and seats is stored in a common database in memory. The database consists of many entries, each representing a seat on a particular flight for a particular day between particular cities. In a typical airline-reservation scenario, the client will probe around in the database looking for the "optimal" flight to meet that client's needs. So a client may probe the database many times before deciding to book a particular flight. A seat that was available during this probing phase could easily be booked by someone else before the client has a chance to book it. In that case, when the client attempts to make the reservation, the client will discover that the data has changed and the flight is no longer available.

  c) The client probing around the database is called a reader. The client attempting to book the flight is called a writer. Clearly, any number of readers can be probing the shared object at once, but each writer needs exclusive access to the shared object to prevent the object from being corrupted.

  d) Write a multithreaded Java program that launches multiple reader threads and multiple writer threads, each attempting to access a single reservation record. A writer thread has two possible transactions, `makeReservation` and `cancelReservation`. A reader has one possible transaction, `queryReservation`.

  e) First implement a version of your program that allows unsynchronized access to the reservation record. Show how the integrity of the database can be corrupted. Next implement a version of your program that uses Java monitor synchronization with `wait` and `notify` to enforce a disciplined protocol for readers and writers accessing the shared reservation data. In particular, your program should allow multiple readers to access the shared object simultaneously when no writer is active. But if a writer is active, then no readers should be allowed to access the shared object.

  f) Be careful. This problem has many subtleties. For example, what happens when there are several active readers and a writer wants to write? If we allow a steady stream of readers to arrive and share the object, they could indefinitely postpone the writer (who may become tired of waiting and take his or her business elsewhere). To solve this problem, you might decide to favor writers over readers. But here, too, there is a trap, because a steady stream of writers could then indefinitely postpone the waiting readers, and they, too, might choose to take their business elsewhere! Implement your monitor with the following methods: `startReading`, which is called by any reader who wants to begin accessing a reservation; `stopReading` to be called by any reader who has finished reading a reservation; `startWriting` to be called by any writer who wants to make a reservation and `stopWriting` to be called by any writer who has finished making a reservation.

16.15 Write a program that bounces a blue ball inside an applet. The ball should begin moving with a `mousePressed` event. When the ball hits the edge of the applet, the ball should bounce off the edge and continue in the opposite direction.

16.16 Modify the program of Exercise 16.15 to add a new ball each time the user clicks the mouse. Provide for a minimum of 20 balls. Randomly choose the color for each new ball.

16.17 Modify the program of Exercise 16.16 to add shadows. As a ball moves, draw a solid black oval at the bottom of the applet. You may consider adding a 3-D effect by increasing or decreasing the size of each ball when a ball hits the edge of the applet.`

16.18 Modify the program of Exercise 16.15 or Exercise 16.16 to bounce the balls off each other when they collide.

17

Files and Streams

Objectives

- To be able to create, read, write and update files.
- To be able to use class `File`.
- To understand the Java streams class hierarchy.
- To be able to use the `FileInputStream` and `FileOutputStream` classes.
- To be able to use a `JFileChooser` dialog to access files and directories.
- To be able to use the `ObjectInputStream` and `ObjectOutputStream` classes.
- To be able to use class `RandomAccessFile`.
- To become familiar with sequential-access and random-access file processing.

I can only assume that a "Do Not File" document is filed in a "Do Not File" file.
Senator Frank Church
Senate Intelligence Subcommittee Hearing, 1975

Consciousness … does not appear to itself chopped up in bits. … A "river" or a "stream" are the metaphors by which it is most naturally described.
William James

I read part of it all the way through.
Samuel Goldwyn

It is quite a three-pipe problem.
Sir Arthur Conan Doyle

17.1 Introduction

Storage of data in variables and arrays is temporary—the data is lost when a local variable goes out of scope or when the program terminates. Computers use *files* for long-term retention of large amounts of data, even after programs that create the data terminate. We refer to data maintained in files as *persistent data*, because the data exists beyond the duration of program execution. Computers store files on *secondary storage devices* such as magnetic disks, optical disks and magnetic tapes. In this chapter, we explain how Java programs create, update and process data files. We consider both sequential-access files and "random-access files and discuss typical applications for each. We also introduce the New I/O APIs introduced with J2SE 1.4. In Chapter 23, Java Database Connectivity with JDBC™, we continue our discussion of long-term data retention by creating programs that interact with databases.

File processing is one of the most important capabilities a language must have to support commercial applications, which typically process massive amounts of persistent data. In this chapter, we discuss Java's powerful file-processing and stream input/output features. File processing is a subset of Java's stream-processing capabilities, which enable a program to read and write bytes in memory, in files and over network connections. We have two goals in this chapter—to introduce file-processing paradigms and to provide the reader with sufficient stream-processing capabilities to support the networking features introduced in Chapter 18.

Software Engineering Observation 17.1

It would be dangerous to enable applets arriving from anywhere on the World Wide Web to be able to read and write files on the client system. By default, Web browsers prevent applets from performing file processing on the client system. Therefore, file-processing programs generally are implemented as Java applications.[1]

---

1. For information on accessing files from an applet, visit `developer.java.sun.com/developer/technicalArticles/Security/Signed`.

17.2 Data Hierarchy

Ultimately, a computer processes all data items as combinations of zeros and ones, because it is simple and economical for engineers to build electronic devices that can assume two stable states—one state represents 0, and the other state represents 1. It is remarkable that the impressive functions performed by computers involve only the most fundamental manipulations of 0s and 1s.

The smallest data item in a computer can assume the value 0 or the value 1. Such a data item is called a *bit* (short for "*bi*nary dig*it*"—a digit that can assume one of two values). Computer circuitry performs various simple bit manipulations, such as examining the value of a bit, setting the value of a bit and reversing the value of a bit (from 1 to 0 or from 0 to 1).

It is cumbersome for programmers to work with data in the low-level form of bits. Instead, programmers prefer to work with data in such forms as *decimal digits* (0–9), *letters* (A–Z and a–z), and *special symbols* (e.g., $, @, %, &, *, (,), -, +, ", :, ? and /). Digits, letters and special symbols are known as *characters*. The computer's *character set* is the set of all characters used to write programs and represent data items. Computers can process only 1s and 0s, so a computer's character set represents every character as a pattern of 1s and 0s. Characters in Java are *Unicode* characters composed of two *bytes*. Each byte is composed of eight bits. See Appendix G for more information on Unicode.

Just as characters are composed of bits, *fields* are composed of characters or bytes. A field is a group of characters or bytes that conveys meaning. For example, a field consisting of uppercase and lowercase letters can be used to represent a person's name.

Data items processed by computers form a *data hierarchy* in which data items become larger and more complex in structure as we progress from bits to characters to fields, etc.

Typically, several fields compose a *record* (implemented as a `class` in Java). In a payroll system, for example, a record for a particular employee might consist of the following fields (possible types for these fields are shown in parentheses following each field):

- Employee identification number (`int`)
- Name (`String`)
- Address (`String`)
- Hourly pay rate (`double`)
- Number of exemptions claimed (`int`)
- Year-to-date earnings (`int` or `double`)
- Amount of taxes withheld (`int` or `double`)

Thus, a record is a group of related fields. In the preceding example, each of the fields belongs to the same employee. Of course, a particular company might have many employees and thus will have a payroll record for each employee. A *file* is a group of related records.[2] A company's payroll file normally contains one record for each employee. Thus, a payroll file for a small company might contain only 22 records, whereas a payroll file for a large company might contain 100,000 records. It is not unusual for a company to have many files,

---

2. More generally, a file contains arbitrary data in arbitrary formats. At the operating-system level, a file is viewed as nothing more than a collection of bytes. Any organization of the bytes in a file (such as organizing the data into records) is a view created by the applications programmer.

some containing billions, or even trillions, of characters of information. Figure 17.1 illustrates the *data hierarchy*.

To facilitate the retrieval of specific records from a file, at least one field in each record is chosen as a *record key*. A record key identifies a record as belonging to a particular person or entity and is unique each record. This field typically is used to search and sort records. In the payroll record described previously, the employee identification number normally would be chosen as the record key.

There are many ways to organize records in a file. The most common organization is called a *sequential file*, in which records are stored in order by the record-key field. In a payroll file, records are placed in order by employee identification number. The first employee record in the file contains the lowest employee identification number, and subsequent records contain increasingly higher employee identification numbers.

Most businesses store data in many different files. For example, companies might have payroll files, accounts receivable files (listing money due from clients), accounts payable files (listing money due to suppliers), inventory files (listing facts about all the items handled by the business) and many other file types. Often, a group of related files is called a *database*. A collection of programs designed to create and manage databases is called a *database management system* (DBMS). We discuss databases in Chapter 23.

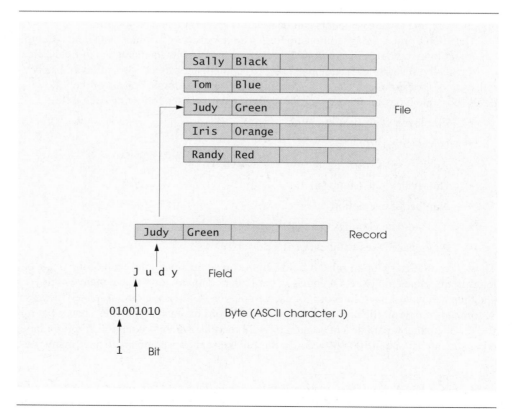

Fig. 17.1   Data hierarchy.

17.3 Files and Streams

Java views each file as a sequential *stream* of bytes (Fig. 17.2). Each operating system provides a mechanism to determine the end of a file, such as an *end-of-file marker* or count of the total bytes in the file that is recorded in a system-maintained administrative data structure. Java abstracts this concept from the programmer. A Java program processing a stream of bytes simply receives an indication from the operating system when the program reaches the end of the stream—the program does not need to know how the underlying platform represents files or streams. In some cases, the end-of-file indication occurs as an exception. In other cases, the indication is a return value from a method invoked on a stream-processing object. We demonstrate both cases in this chapter.

A Java program *opens* a file by creating an object and associating a stream of bytes with the object. Java also can associate streams of bytes with different devices. In fact, Java creates three stream objects that are associated with devices when a Java program begins executing—`System.in`, `System.out` and `System.err`. Object `System.in` (the *standard input stream object*) normally enables a program to input bytes from the keyboard; object `System.out` (the *standard output stream object*) normally enables a program to output data to the screen; and object `System.err` (the *standard error stream object*) normally enables a program to output error messages to the screen. Each of these streams can be *redirected*. For `System.in`, this capability enables the program to read bytes from a different source. For `System.out` and `System.err`, this capability enables the output to be sent to a different location, such as a file on disk. Class `System` provides methods `setIn`, `setOut` and `setErr` to redirect the standard input, output and error streams, respectively.

Java programs perform file processing by using classes from package `java.io`. This package includes definitions for stream classes, such as `FileInputStream` (for byte-based input from a file), `FileOutputStream` (for byte-based output to a file), `FileReader` (for character-based input from a file) and `FileWriter` (for character-based output to a file). Files are opened by creating objects of these stream classes that inherit from classes `InputStream`, `OutputStream`, `Reader` and `Writer`, respectively. Thus, the methods of these stream classes can all be applied to file streams as well. To perform input and output of data types, objects of classes `ObjectInputStream`, `DataInputStream`, `ObjectOutputStream` and `DataOutputStream` will be used together with the byte-based file stream classes `FileInputStream` and `FileOutputStream`. The hierarchy of classes in package `java.io` can be viewed in the online documentation at

    java.sun.com/j2se/1.4.1/docs/api/java/io/package-tree.html

In the hierarchy, each indentation level indicates that the indented class extends the class under which it is indented. For example, class `InputStream` is a subclass of `Object`. Click a class's name in the hierarchy to view the details of that class.

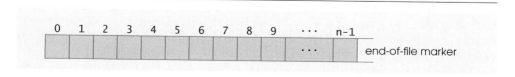

Fig. 17.2   Java's view of a file of *n* bytes.

As you can see in the hierarchy, Java offers many classes for performing input/output operations. This section briefly overviews many of these classes and explains how they relate to one another. We use several of these stream classes in this chapter as we implement a number of file-processing programs that create, manipulate and destroy sequential-access files and random-access files. We also include a detailed example on class `File`, which is useful for obtaining information about files and directories. In Chapter 18, Networking, we use stream classes extensively to implement networking applications.

Byte-Based Input and Output Classes

InputStream and *OutputStream* (subclasses of `Object`) are `abstract` classes that declare methods for performing byte-based input and output, respectively. We use classes `FileInputStream` (a subclass of `InputStream`) and `FileOutputStream` (a subclass of `OutputStream`) extensively to manipulate files in this chapter.

Pipes are synchronized communication channels between threads or processes. Java provides *PipedOutputStream* (a subclass of `OutputStream`) and *PipedInputStream* (a subclass of `InputStream`) to establish pipes between two threads. One thread sends data to another by writing to a `PipedOutputStream`. The target thread reads information from the pipe via a `PipedInputStream`.

A `FilterInputStream` *filters* an `InputStream`, and a `FilterOutputStream` filters an `OutputStream`; filtering means simply that the filter stream provides additional functionality, such as buffering, monitoring line numbers or aggregating data bytes into meaningful primitive-type units. `FilterInputStream` and `FilterOutputStream` are `abstract` classes, so additional functionality is provided by their subclasses.

A *PrintStream* (a subclass of `FilterOutputStream`) performs text output to the specified stream. Actually, we have been using `PrintStream` output throughout the text to this point—`System.out` is a `PrintStream` object, as is `System.err`.

Reading data as raw bytes is fast, but crude. Usually, programs read data as aggregates of bytes that form an `int`, a `float`, a `double` and so on. Java programs can use several classes to input and output data in aggregate form.

A *RandomAccessFile* is useful for direct-access applications, such as transaction-processing applications (e.g., airline-reservations systems and point-of-sale systems). With a sequential-access file, each successive input/output request reads or writes the next consecutive set of data in the file. With a random-access file, each successive input/output request could be directed to any part of the file—perhaps a section widely separated from the part of the file referenced in the previous request. Direct-access applications provide rapid access to specific data items in large files; often, such applications require users to wait for answers—these answers must be made available quickly, or the people might become impatient and take their business elsewhere.

Interface `DataInput` describes methods for reading primitive types from an input stream. Classes `DataInputStream` and `RandomAccessFile` each implement this interface to read sets of bytes and view them as primitive-type values. Interface `DataInput` includes methods `readLine` (for `byte` arrays), `readBoolean`, `readByte`, `readChar`, `readDouble`, `readFloat`, `readFully` (for `byte` arrays), `readInt`, `readLong`, `readShort`, `readUnsignedByte`, `readUnsignedShort`, `readUTF` (for strings) and `skipBytes`.

Interface `DataOutput` describes a set of methods for writing primitive types to an output stream. Classes `DataOutputStream` (a subclass of `FilterOutputStream`) and `RandomAccessFile` each implement this interface to write primitive-type values as bytes.

Interface `DataOutput` includes methods `write` (for a byte), `write` (for a byte array), `writeBoolean`, `writeByte`, `writeBytes`, `writeChar`, `writeChars` (for Unicode Strings), `writeDouble`, `writeFloat`, `writeInt`, `writeLong`, `writeShort` and `writeUTF`.

Buffering is an I/O-performance-enhancement technique. With a *BufferedOutput-Stream* (a subclass of class `FilterOutputStream`), each output statement does not necessarily result in an actual physical transfer of data to the output device. Rather, each output operation is directed to a region in memory called a buffer that is large enough to hold the data of many output operations. Then, actual transfer to the output device is performed in one large *physical output operation* each time the buffer fills. The output operations directed to the output buffer in memory are often called *logical output operations*. With a `BufferedOutputStream`, a partially filled buffer can be forced out to the device at any time by invoking the stream object's `flush` method.

With a *BufferedInputStream* (a subclass of class `FilterInputStream`), many "logical" chunks of data from a file are read as one large *physical input operation* into a memory buffer. As a program requests each new chunk of data, it is taken from the buffer. (This procedure is sometimes referred to as a *logical input operation*.) When the buffer is empty, the next actual physical input operation from the input device is performed to read in the next group of "logical" chunks of data. Thus, the number of actual physical input operations is small compared with the number of read requests issued by the program.

Performance Tip 17.1

Typical input/output operations are extremely slow compared with the speed of accessing computer memory. Buffered inputs and outputs normally yield significant performance improvements over unbuffered inputs and outputs.

When instance variables are output to a disk file, we lose the object's type information, in a sense. We have only data, not type information, on a disk. If the program that is going to read this data "knows" what object type the data correspond to, then the data are simply read into objects of that type. Sometimes, we would like to read or write an entire object to a file. Classes *ObjectInputStream* and *ObjectOutputStream*, which respectively implement the *ObjectInput* and *ObjectOutput* interfaces, enable an entire object to be read from or written to a file (or other stream type). We often wrap `FileInputStreams` in `ObjectInputStreams`. (We also wrap `FileOutputStreams` in `ObjectOutput-Streams`.) The `ObjectOutput` interface contains method `writeObject`, which takes an `Object` that implements interface *Serializable* as an argument and writes its information to the `OutputStream`. Correspondingly, the `ObjectInput` interface requires method `readObject`, which reads and returns an `Object` from an `InputStream`. After an object has been read, it can be cast to the desired type. In addition, these interfaces include other `Object`-centric methods as well as the same methods as `DataInput` and `DataOutput` for reading and writing primitive types.

Java stream I/O includes capabilities for inputting from byte arrays in memory and outputting to byte arrays in memory. A `ByteArrayInputStream` (a subclass of `Input-Stream`) reads from a byte array in memory. A `ByteArrayOutputStream` (a subclass of `OutputStream`) outputs to a byte array in memory. One application of byte-array I/O is data validation. A program can input an entire line at a time from the input stream into a byte array. Then a validation routine can scrutinize the contents of the byte array and correct the data, if necessary. Finally, the program can proceed to input from the byte array, "knowing" that the input data are in the proper format. Outputting to a `byte` array is a nice way to take advantage of the powerful output-formatting capabilities of Java streams. For example, data can be prepared in a `byte` array, using the same formatting that will be displayed at a later time, and output to a disk file to preserve the screen image.

A `SequenceInputStream` (a subclass of `InputStream`) enables concatenation of several `InputStream`s, so that the program sees the group as one continuous `Input-Stream`. When the program reaches the end of an input stream, that stream closes, and the next stream in the sequence opens.

Character-Based Input and Output Streams

In addition to the byte-based streams, Java provides *Reader* and *Writer* classes, which are Unicode two-byte, character-based streams. Most of the byte-based streams have corresponding character-based `Reader` or `Writer` classes.

Classes *BufferedReader* (a subclass of `abstract` class `Reader`) and *Buffered-Writer* (a subclass of `abstract` class `Writer`) enable efficient buffering for character-based streams. Character-based streams use Unicode characters—such streams can process data in any language that the Unicode character set represents.

Classes *CharArrayReader* and *CharArrayWriter* read and write, respectively, a stream of characters to a character array. A *LineNumberReader* (a subclass of *BufferedReader*) is a buffered character stream that keeps track of line numbers (i.e., a newline, a return or a carriage-return–line-feed combination).

Class *FileReader* (a subclass of *InputStreamReader*) and class *FileWriter* (a subclass of *OutputStreamWriter*) read characters from and write characters to a file, respectively. Class *PipedReader* and class *PipedWriter* implement piped-character streams that can be used to transfer information between threads. Class *StringReader* and *StringWriter* read and write characters, respectively, to `Strings`. A *PrintWriter* writes characters to a stream.

17.4 Class `File`

This section presents class `File`, which is particularly useful for retrieving information about a file or a directory from a disk. Objects of class `File` do not open files or provide any file-processing capabilities. However, `File` objects are used frequently with objects of other `java.io` classes to specify files or directories to manipulate.

Class `File` provides four constructors. The constructor

```
public File( String name )
```

specifies the `name` of a file or directory to associate with the `File` object. The `name` can contain *path information* as well as a file or directory name. A file or directory's path specifies the location of the file or directory on disk. The path includes some or all of the directories leading to the file or directory. An *absolute path* contains all the directories, starting with the *root directory*, that lead to a specific file or directory. Every file or directory on a particular disk drive has the same root directory in its path. A *relative path* contains a subset of the directories leading to a specific file or directory. Relative paths normally start from the directory in which the application began executing.

The constructor

```
public File( String pathToName, String name )
```

uses argument `pathToName` (an absolute or relative path) to locate the file or directory specified by `name`.

The constructor

```
public File( File directory, String name )
```

uses an existing `File` object `directory` (an absolute or relative path) to locate the file or directory specified by `name`. Figure 17.3 discusses some common `File` methods. The complete list of `File` methods can be viewed at `java.sun.com/j2se/1.4.1/docs/api/java/io/File.html`.

The constructor

```
public File( URI uri )
```

uses the given URI object to locate the file. A *Uniform Resource Identifier* (*URI*) is a more general form of a *Uniform Resource Locator* (*URL*), which commonly are used to locate Web sites. For example, `http://www.deitel.com/` is the URL for the Deitel & Associates' Web site. URIs for locating files vary across operating systems. On Windows platforms, the URI

```
file:/C:/data.txt
```

identifies the file `data.txt` stored in the root directory of the C: drive.

Good Programming Practice 17.1

Use `File` method `isFile` to determine that a `File` object represents a file (not a directory) before attempting to open a file.

Method	Description
`boolean canRead()`	Returns `true` if a file is readable; `false` otherwise.
`boolean canWrite()`	Returns `true` if a file is writable; `false` otherwise.
`boolean exists()`	Returns `true` if the name specified as the argument to the `File` constructor is a file or directory in the specified path; `false` otherwise.
`boolean isFile()`	Returns `true` if the name specified as the argument to the `File` constructor is a file; `false` otherwise.
`boolean isDirectory()`	Returns `true` if the name specified as the argument to the `File` constructor is a directory; `false` otherwise.
`boolean isAbsolute()`	Returns `true` if the arguments specified to the `File` constructor indicate an absolute path to a file or directory; `false` otherwise.
`String getAbsolutePath()`	Returns a string with the absolute path of the file or directory.
`String getName()`	Returns a string with the name of the file or directory.
`String getPath()`	Returns a string with the path of the file or directory.

Fig. 17.3   File methods. (Part 1 of 2.)

Method	Description
`String getParent()`	Returns a string with the parent directory of the file or directory—that is, the directory in which the file or directory can be found.
`long length()`	Returns the length of the file, in bytes. If the `File` object represents a directory, 0 is returned.
`long lastModified()`	Returns a platform-dependent representation of the time at which the file or directory was last modified. The value returned is useful only for comparison with other values returned by this method.
`String[] list()`	Returns an array of strings representing the contents of a directory. Returns `null` if the `File` object is not a directory.

Fig. 17.3   `File` methods. (Part 2 of 2.)

Figure 17.4 demonstrates class `File`. The `FileTest` application creates a GUI containing a `JTextField` for entering a file name or directory name and a `JTextArea` for displaying information about the file name or directory name input.

```
1   // Fig. 17.4: FileTest.java
2   // Demonstrating the File class.
3   import java.awt.*;
4   import java.awt.event.*;
5   import java.io.*;
6   import javax.swing.*;
7
8   public class FileTest extends JFrame
9      implements ActionListener {
10
11     private JTextField enterField;
12     private JTextArea outputArea;
13
14     // set up GUI
15     public FileTest()
16     {
17        super( "Testing class File" );
18
19        enterField = new JTextField( "Enter file or directory name here" );
20        enterField.addActionListener( this );
21        outputArea = new JTextArea();
22
23        JScrollPane scrollPane = new JScrollPane();
24        scrollPane.add( outputArea );
25
26        Container container = getContentPane();
27        container.add( enterField, BorderLayout.NORTH );
28        container.add( scrollPane, BorderLayout.CENTER );
```

Fig. 17.4   `File` class used to obtain file and directory information. (Part 1 of 3.)

```
29
30          setSize( 400, 400 );
31          setVisible( true );
32
33      } // end constructor
34
35      // display information about file user specifies
36      public void actionPerformed( ActionEvent actionEvent )
37      {
38          File name = new File( actionEvent.getActionCommand() );
39
40          // if name exists, output information about it
41          if ( name.exists() ) {
42              outputArea.setText( name.getName() + " exists\n" +
43                  ( name.isFile() ? "is a file\n" : "is not a file\n" ) +
44                  ( name.isDirectory() ? "is a directory\n" :
45                      "is not a directory\n" ) +
46                  ( name.isAbsolute() ? "is absolute path\n" :
47                      "is not absolute path\n" ) + "Last modified: " +
48                  name.lastModified() + "\nLength: " + name.length() +
49                  "\nPath: " + name.getPath() + "\nAbsolute path: " +
50                  name.getAbsolutePath() + "\nParent: " + name.getParent() );
51
52              // output information if name is a file
53              if ( name.isFile() ) {
54
55                  // append contents of file to outputArea
56                  try {
57                      BufferedReader input = new BufferedReader(
58                          new FileReader( name ) );
59                      StringBuffer buffer = new StringBuffer();
60                      String text;
61                      outputArea.append( "\n\n" );
62
63                      while ( ( text = input.readLine() ) != null )
64                          buffer.append( text + "\n" );
65
66                      outputArea.append( buffer.toString() );
67                  }
68
69                  // process file processing problems
70                  catch ( IOException ioException ) {
71                      JOptionPane.showMessageDialog( this, "FILE ERROR",
72                          "FILE ERROR", JOptionPane.ERROR_MESSAGE );
73                  }
74
75              } // end if
76
77              // output directory listing
78              else if ( name.isDirectory() ) {
79                  String directory[] = name.list();
80
81                  outputArea.append( "\n\nDirectory contents:\n");
```

Fig. 17.4   File class used to obtain file and directory information. (Part 2 of 3.)

```
82
83                for ( int i = 0; i < directory.length; i++ )
84                    outputArea.append( directory[ i ] + "\n" );
85            }
86
87        } // end outer if
88
89        // not file or directory, output error message
90        else {
91            JOptionPane.showMessageDialog( this,
92                actionEvent.getActionCommand() + " Does Not Exist",
93                "ERROR", JOptionPane.ERROR_MESSAGE );
94        }
95
96    } // end method actionPerformed
97
98    public static void main( String args[] )
99    {
100        FileTest application = new FileTest();
101        application.setDefaultCloseOperation( JFrame.EXIT_ON_CLOSE );
102    }
103
104 } // end class FileTest
```

Testing class File

c:\j2sdk1.4.1\demo/jfc

```
jfc exists
is not a file
is a directory
is absolute path
Last modified: 1032795938388
Length: 0
Path: c:\j2sdk1.4.1\demo\jfc
Absolute path: c:\j2sdk1.4.1\demo\jfc
Parent: c:\j2sdk1.4.1\demo

Directory contents:
FileChooserDemo
Font2DTest
Java2D
Metalworks
Notepad
SampleTree
Stylepad
SwingApplet
SwingSet2
TableExample
```

Testing class File

c:\j2sdk1.4.1\demo/jfc\Java2d\readme.txt

```
readme.txt exists
is a file
is not a directory
is absolute path
Last modified: 1030601450000
Length: 7489
Path: c:\j2sdk1.4.1\demo\jfc\Java2d\readme.txt
Absolute path: c:\j2sdk1.4.1\demo\jfc\Java2d\readme.txt
Parent: c:\j2sdk1.4.1\demo\jfc\Java2d

The classes for the Java2D demo are contained in the Java2Demo.j
To run the Java2D demo:

% java -jar Java2Demo.jar
  - or -
% appletviewer Java2Demo.html

Although it's not necessary to unpack the Java2Demo.jar file to run
the demo, you may want to extract its contents if you plan to modify
any of the demo source code. To extract the contents of Java2Demo.
run this command from the Java2D directory:
```

Fig. 17.4   File class used to obtain file and directory information. (Part 3 of 3.)

The user types a file name or directory name into the text field and presses the *Enter* key to invoke method actionPerformed (lines 36–96), which creates a new File object (line 38) and assigns its reference to name. Line 41 invokes File method exists to determine whether the name input by the user exists (either as a file or as a directory) on the disk.

If the name input by the user does not exist, the `actionPerformed` method proceeds to lines 90–94 and displays a message dialog containing the name the user typed, followed by "Does Not Exist." Otherwise, the body of the `if` statement (lines 42–86) executes. The program outputs the name of the file or directory, followed by the results of testing the `File` object with `isFile` (line 43), `isDirectory` (line 44) and `isAbsolute` (line 46). Next, the program displays the values returned by `lastModified` (line 48), `length` (line 48), `getPath` (line 49), `getAbsolutePath` (line 50) and `getParent` (line 50).

If the `File` object represents a file (line 53), the program reads the contents of the file and displays them in the `JTextArea` (lines 56–73). For the purpose of this program, we would like to read lines of text from a file. Class `FileReader` can be used to open a file for reading Unicode characters. Unfortunately, class `FileReader` does not know how to read lines of text. Class `BufferedReader` provides the functionality of reading lines of text, but does not know how to open a file for input. So, we need to combine the functionality of these two classes. The solution to this problem is a technique called *wrapping of stream objects*—the ability to add the services of one stream to another. To wrap a `FileReader` in a `BufferedReader`, we pass the `FileReader` object to the `BufferedReader`'s constructor (lines 57–58). The constructor could throw an *IOException* if a problem occurs during opening of the file (e.g., when a nonexistent file is opened for reading). If so, the program displays an error-message dialog (lines 70–73). If construction of the two streams does not throw an `IOException`, the file is open. Then reference `input` can be used to read from the file. Line 59 creates a `StringBuffer` to store the contents of the file in memory. Lines 63–64 use `BufferedReader` method `readLine` to read one line at a time as a string and append that string to the `StringBuffer`. Method `readLine` returns null when the end of file is reached.

If the `File` object represents a directory (line 78), the program reads the contents of the directory into the program by using `File` method `list` and displays the directory contents in the `JTextArea`.

The first output of this program demonstrates a `File` object associated with the `jfc` directory from the Java 2 Software Development Kit. The second output demonstrates a `File` object associated with the `readme.txt` file from the Java 2D example that comes with the Java 2 Software Development Kit. In both cases, we specified an absolute path on our personal computer.

A *separator character* is used to separate directories and files in the path. On a Windows computer, the separator character is a backslash (\) character. On a UNIX workstation, the separator character is a forward slash (/) character. Java processes both characters identically in a path name. For example, although the sample output uses the path

```
c:\j2sdk1.4.1\demo/jfc
```

which employs one of each separator character, Java still processes the path properly.

Common Programming Error 17.1

Using \ as a directory separator rather than \\ in a string literal is a logic error. A single \ indicates that the \ and the next character represent an escape sequence. To insert a \ in a string literal, you must use \\.

Good Programming Practice 17.2

When building strings that represent path information, use `File.pathSeparator` to obtain the local computer's proper separator character, rather than explicitly using / or \.

17.5 Creating a Sequential-Access File

Java imposes no structure on a file, so concepts such as a record do not exist in Java files. Therefore, programmers must structure files to meet the requirements of their applications. In the next example, we see how the programmer can impose a simple record structure on a file. First we present the program; then we analyze it in detail.

The program of Fig. 17.5–Fig. 17.7 creates a simple sequential-access file that might be used in an accounts-receivable system to help manage the money owed by a company's credit clients. For each client, the program obtains an account number, the client's first name, the client's last name and the client's balance (i.e., the amount the client still owes the company for goods and services received in the past). The data obtained for each client constitutes a record for that client. The program uses the account number as the record key, the file will be created and maintained in account-number order. [*Note*: This program assumes that the user enters the records in account-number order. In a comprehensive accounts receivable system, a sorting capability would be provided so the user could enter the records in any order—the records would then be sorted and written to the file.]

Most of the programs in this chapter have a similar GUI to the one used in this program, so this program declares class BankUI (Fig. 17.5) to encapsulate the GUI. (See the first and third sample-output screens in Fig. 17.7.) Also, the program declares class AccountRecord (Fig. 17.6) to encapsulate the client record information (i.e., account, first name, etc.) used by the examples in this chapter. For reuse, classes BankUI and AccountRecord are declared in package com.deitel.jhtp5.ch17.

When you compile classes BankUI and AccountRecord, or any others that will be reused in this chapter, you should place the classes in a common directory (e.g., c:\examples\ch17). When you compile or execute classes that use BankUI and Account-Record, be sure to specify the -classpath command-line argument to both javac and java, as in

```
javac -classpath .;c:\examples\ch17 CreateSequentialFile.java
java -classpath .;c:\examples\ch17 CreateSequentialFile
```

where classes of the package com.deitel.jhtp5.ch17 are compiled with

```
javac -d c:\examples\ch17 com\deitel\jhtp5\ch17\BankUI.java
javac -d c:\examples\ch17 com\deitel\jhtp5\ch17\AccountRecord.java
```

so that their class files reside in a directory structure that begins in c:\examples\ch17. Be sure to include the current directory (specified with .) in the classpath. Also, the path separator should be appropriate for your platform—e.g., a semicolon (;) on Windows and a colon (:) on UNIX/Linux/Mac OS X.

Class BankUI (Fig. 17.5) contains two JButtons and arrays of JLabels and JText-Fields. The number of JLabels and JTextFields is set with the constructor declared at

```
1   // Fig. 17.5: BankUI.java
2   // A reusable GUI for the examples in this chapter.
3   package com.deitel.jhtp5.ch17;
4
5   import java.awt.*;
```

Fig. 17.5   BankUI contains a reusable GUI for several programs. (Part 1 of 4.)

```
6   import javax.swing.*;
7
8   public class BankUI extends JPanel {
9
10      // label text for GUI
11      protected final static String names[] = { "Account number",
12         "First name", "Last name", "Balance", "Transaction Amount" };
13
14      // GUI components; protected for future subclass access
15      protected JLabel labels[];
16      protected JTextField fields[];
17      protected JButton doTask1, doTask2;
18      protected JPanel innerPanelCenter, innerPanelSouth;
19
20      protected int size; // number of text fields in GUI
21
22      // constants representing text fields in GUI
23      public static final int ACCOUNT = 0, FIRSTNAME = 1, LASTNAME = 2,
24         BALANCE = 3, TRANSACTION = 4;
25
26      // Set up GUI. Constructor argument size determines the number of
27      // rows of GUI components.
28      public BankUI( int mySize )
29      {
30         size = mySize;
31         labels = new JLabel[ size ];
32         fields = new JTextField[ size ];
33
34         // create labels
35         for ( int count = 0; count < labels.length; count++ )
36            labels[ count ] = new JLabel( names[ count ] );
37
38         // create text fields
39         for ( int count = 0; count < fields.length; count++ )
40            fields[ count ] = new JTextField();
41
42         // create panel to lay out labels and fields
43         innerPanelCenter = new JPanel();
44         innerPanelCenter.setLayout( new GridLayout( size, 2 ) );
45
46         // attach labels and fields to innerPanelCenter
47         for ( int count = 0; count < size; count++ ) {
48            innerPanelCenter.add( labels[ count ] );
49            innerPanelCenter.add( fields[ count ] );
50         }
51
52         // create generic buttons; no labels or event handlers
53         doTask1 = new JButton();
54         doTask2 = new JButton();
55
56         // create panel to lay out buttons and attach buttons
57         innerPanelSouth = new JPanel();
58         innerPanelSouth.add( doTask1 );
```

Fig. 17.5   BankUI contains a reusable GUI for several programs. (Part 2 of 4.)

```
59            innerPanelSouth.add( doTask2 );
60
61            // set layout of this container and attach panels to it
62            setLayout( new BorderLayout() );
63            add( innerPanelCenter, BorderLayout.CENTER );
64            add( innerPanelSouth, BorderLayout.SOUTH );
65
66            validate(); // validate layout
67
68         } // end constructor
69
70         // return reference to generic task button doTask1
71         public JButton getDoTask1Button()
72         {
73            return doTask1;
74         }
75
76         // return reference to generic task button doTask2
77         public JButton getDoTask2Button()
78         {
79            return doTask2;
80         }
81
82         // return reference to fields array of JTextFields
83         public JTextField[] getFields()
84         {
85            return fields;
86         }
87
88         // clear content of text fields
89         public void clearFields()
90         {
91            for ( int count = 0; count < size; count++ )
92               fields[ count ].setText( "" );
93         }
94
95         // set text field values; throw IllegalArgumentException if
96         // incorrect number of Strings in argument
97         public void setFieldValues( String strings[] )
98            throws IllegalArgumentException
99         {
100           if ( strings.length != size )
101              throw new IllegalArgumentException( "There must be " +
102                 size + " Strings in the array" );
103
104           for ( int count = 0; count < size; count++ )
105              fields[ count ].setText( strings[ count ] );
106        }
107
108        // get array of Strings with current text field contents
109        public String[] getFieldValues()
110        {
111           String values[] = new String[ size ];
```

Fig. 17.5   BankUI contains a reusable GUI for several programs. (Part 3 of 4.)

```
112
113        for ( int count = 0; count < size; count++ )
114            values[ count ] = fields[ count ].getText();
115
116        return values;
117     }
118
119 } // end class BankUI
```

Fig. 17.5   BankUI contains a reusable GUI for several programs. (Part 4 of 4.)

lines 28–68. Methods getFieldValues (lines 109–117), setFieldValues (lines 97–106) and clearFields (lines 89–93) manipulate the text of the JTextFields. Methods getFields (lines 83–86), getDoTask1Button (lines 71–74) and getDoTask2Button (lines 77–80) return individual GUI components, so that, for example, a client program can add ActionListeners.

Defining the Serializable *AccountRecord* Class

Class AccountRecord (Fig. 17.6) implements interface *Serializable*, which allows objects of AccountRecord to be used with ObjectInputStreams and ObjectOutputStreams. An ObjectOutputStream enables object to be *serialized*—i.e., converted to a series (stream) of bytes. Similarly, an ObjectInputStream enables data to be *deserialized*—i.e., converted from a series of bytes to the original object. Interface Serializable is a *tagging interface*. Such an interface contains no methods. A class that implements this interface is *tagged* as being a Serializable object, which is important because an ObjectOutputStream will not output an object unless it *is a* Serializable object. In a class that implements Serializable, the programmer must ensure that every instance variable of the class is a Serializable type, or must declare particular instance variables as *transient* to indicate that those variables are not Serializable and they should be ignored during the serialization process. By default, all primitive-type variables are serializable. For variables of reference types, you must check the definition of the class (and possibly its superclasses) to ensure that the type is Serializable. Class AccountRecord contains private data members account, firstName, lastName and balance. This class also provides public *get* and *set* methods for accessing the private fields.

```
1   // Fig. 17.6: AccountRecord.java
2   // A class that represents one record of information.
3   package com.deitel.jhtp5.ch17;
4
5   import java.io.Serializable;
6
7   public class AccountRecord implements Serializable {
8      private int account;
9      private String firstName;
10     private String lastName;
11     private double balance;
12
```

Fig. 17.6   AccountRecord maintains information for one account. (Part 1 of 3.)

```java
13      // no-argument constructor calls other constructor with default values
14      public AccountRecord()
15      {
16          this( 0, "", "", 0.0 );
17      }
18
19      // initialize a record
20      public AccountRecord( int acct, String first, String last, double bal )
21      {
22          setAccount( acct );
23          setFirstName( first );
24          setLastName( last );
25          setBalance( bal );
26      }
27
28      // set account number
29      public void setAccount( int acct )
30      {
31          account = acct;
32      }
33
34      // get account number
35      public int getAccount()
36      {
37          return account;
38      }
39
40      // set first name
41      public void setFirstName( String first )
42      {
43          firstName = first;
44      }
45
46      // get first name
47      public String getFirstName()
48      {
49          return firstName;
50      }
51
52      // set last name
53      public void setLastName( String last )
54      {
55          lastName = last;
56      }
57
58      // get last name
59      public String getLastName()
60      {
61          return lastName;
62      }
63
```

Fig. 17.6   AccountRecord maintains information for one account. (Part 2 of 3.)

```
64        // set balance
65        public void setBalance( double bal )
66        {
67            balance = bal;
68        }
69
70        // get balance
71        public double getBalance()
72        {
73            return balance;
74        }
75
76    } // end class AccountRecord
```

Fig. 17.6   AccountRecord maintains information for one account. (Part 3 of 3.)

Now let us discuss the code that creates the sequential-access file (Fig. 17.7). In this example, we introduce class *JFileChooser* (package `javax.swing`) for selecting files (as shown in the second output window). Line 94 creates a `JFileChooser` and assigns its reference to `fileChooser`. Line 95 calls method *setFileSelectionMode* to specify what the user can select from the `fileChooser`. For this program, we use `JFileChooser` static constant *FILES_ONLY* to indicate that only files can be selected. Other static constants include *FILES_AND_DIRECTORIES* and *DIRECTORIES_ONLY*.

```
1     // Fig. 17.7: CreateSequentialFile.java
2     // Writing objects sequentially to a file with class ObjectOutputStream.
3     import java.io.*;
4     import java.awt.*;
5     import java.awt.event.*;
6     import javax.swing.*;
7
8     import com.deitel.jhtp5.ch17.BankUI;
9     import com.deitel.jhtp5.ch17.AccountRecord;
10
11    public class CreateSequentialFile extends JFrame {
12        private ObjectOutputStream output;
13        private BankUI userInterface;
14        private JButton enterButton, openButton;
15
16        // set up GUI
17        public CreateSequentialFile()
18        {
19            super( "Creating a Sequential File of Objects" );
20
21            // create instance of reusable user interface
22            userInterface = new BankUI( 4 );  // four textfields
23            getContentPane().add( userInterface, BorderLayout.CENTER );
24
25            // configure button doTask1 for use in this program
26            openButton = userInterface.getDoTask1Button();
27            openButton.setText( "Save into File ..." );
```

Fig. 17.7   Sequential file created using `ObjectOutputStream`. (Part 1 of 6.)

```
28
29          // register listener to call openFile when button pressed
30          openButton.addActionListener(
31
32              // anonymous inner class to handle openButton event
33              new ActionListener() {
34
35                  // call openFile when button pressed
36                  public void actionPerformed( ActionEvent event )
37                  {
38                      openFile();
39                  }
40
41              } // end anonymous inner class
42
43          ); // end call to addActionListener
44
45          // configure button doTask2 for use in this program
46          enterButton = userInterface.getDoTask2Button();
47          enterButton.setText( "Enter" );
48          enterButton.setEnabled( false );   // disable button
49
50          // register listener to call addRecord when button pressed
51          enterButton.addActionListener(
52
53              // anonymous inner class to handle enterButton event
54              new ActionListener() {
55
56                  // call addRecord when button pressed
57                  public void actionPerformed( ActionEvent event )
58                  {
59                      addRecord();
60                  }
61
62              } // end anonymous inner class
63
64          ); // end call to addActionListener
65
66          // register window listener to handle window closing event
67          addWindowListener(
68
69              // anonymous inner class to handle windowClosing event
70              new WindowAdapter() {
71
72                  // add current record in GUI to file, then close file
73                  public void windowClosing( WindowEvent event )
74                  {
75                      if ( output != null )
76                          addRecord();
77
78                      closeFile();
79                  }
80
```

Fig. 17.7   Sequential file created using `ObjectOutputStream`. (Part 2 of 6.)

```
81                } // end anonymous inner class
82
83          ); // end call to addWindowListener
84
85          setSize( 300, 200 );
86          setVisible( true );
87
88      } // end CreateSequentialFile constructor
89
90      // allow user to specify file name
91      private void openFile()
92      {
93          // display file dialog, so user can choose file to open
94          JFileChooser fileChooser = new JFileChooser();
95          fileChooser.setFileSelectionMode( JFileChooser.FILES_ONLY );
96
97          int result = fileChooser.showSaveDialog( this );
98
99          // if user clicked Cancel button on dialog, return
100         if ( result == JFileChooser.CANCEL_OPTION )
101             return;
102
103         File fileName = fileChooser.getSelectedFile(); // get selected file
104
105         // display error if invalid
106         if ( fileName == null || fileName.getName().equals( "" ) )
107             JOptionPane.showMessageDialog( this, "Invalid File Name",
108                 "Invalid File Name", JOptionPane.ERROR_MESSAGE );
109
110         else {
111
112             // open file
113             try {
114                 output = new ObjectOutputStream(
115                     new FileOutputStream( fileName ) );
116
117                 openButton.setEnabled( false );
118                 enterButton.setEnabled( true );
119             }
120
121             // process exceptions from opening file
122             catch ( IOException ioException ) {
123                 JOptionPane.showMessageDialog( this, "Error Opening File",
124                     "Error", JOptionPane.ERROR_MESSAGE );
125             }
126
127         } // end else
128
129     } // end method openFile
130
131     // close file and terminate application
132     private void closeFile()
133     {
```

Fig. 17.7   Sequential file created using `ObjectOutputStream`. (Part 3 of 6.)

```
134          // close file
135          try {
136             output.close();
137             System.exit( 0 );
138          }
139
140          // process exceptions from closing file
141          catch( IOException ioException ) {
142             JOptionPane.showMessageDialog( this, "Error closing file",
143                "Error", JOptionPane.ERROR_MESSAGE );
144             System.exit( 1 );
145          }
146
147       } // end method closeFile
148
149       // add record to file
150       public void addRecord()
151       {
152          int accountNumber = 0;
153          AccountRecord record;
154          String fieldValues[] = userInterface.getFieldValues();
155
156          // if account field value is not empty
157          if ( ! fieldValues[ BankUI.ACCOUNT ].equals( "" ) ) {
158
159             // output values to file
160             try {
161                accountNumber = Integer.parseInt(
162                   fieldValues[ BankUI.ACCOUNT ] );
163
164                if ( accountNumber > 0 ) {
165
166                   // create new record
167                   record = new AccountRecord( accountNumber,
168                      fieldValues[ BankUI.FIRSTNAME ],
169                      fieldValues[ BankUI.LASTNAME ],
170                      Double.parseDouble( fieldValues[ BankUI.BALANCE ] ) );
171
172                   // output record and flush buffer
173                   output.writeObject( record );
174                   output.flush();
175                }
176
177                else {
178                   JOptionPane.showMessageDialog( this,
179                      "Account number must be greater than 0",
180                      "Bad account number", JOptionPane.ERROR_MESSAGE );
181                }
182
183                // clear textfields
184                userInterface.clearFields();
185
186             } // end try
```

Fig. 17.7   Sequential file created using `ObjectOutputStream`. (Part 4 of 6.)

```
187
188            // process invalid account number or balance format
189            catch ( NumberFormatException formatException ) {
190               JOptionPane.showMessageDialog( this,
191                  "Bad account number or balance", "Invalid Number Format",
192                  JOptionPane.ERROR_MESSAGE );
193            }
194
195            // process exceptions from file output
196            catch ( IOException ioException ) {
197               JOptionPane.showMessageDialog( this, "Error writing to file",
198                  "IO Exception", JOptionPane.ERROR_MESSAGE );
199               closeFile();
200            }
201
202         } // end if
203
204      } // end method addRecord
205
206      public static void main( String args[] )
207      {
208         new CreateSequentialFile();
209      }
210
211 } // end class CreateSequentialFile
```

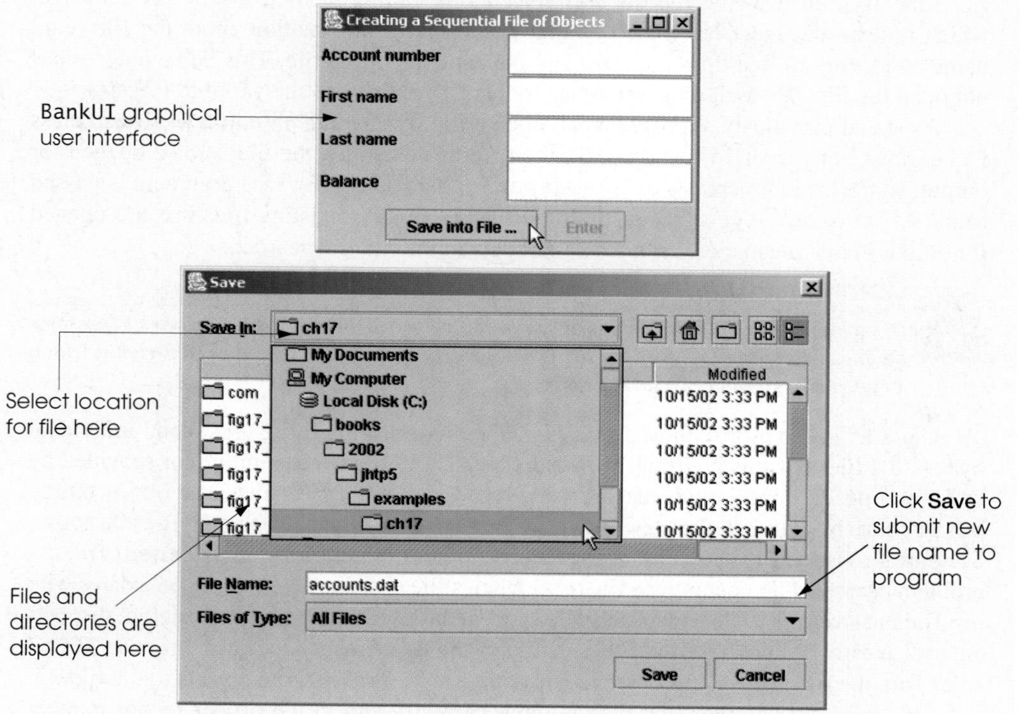

Fig. 17.7   Sequential file created using `ObjectOutputStream`. (Part 5 of 6.)

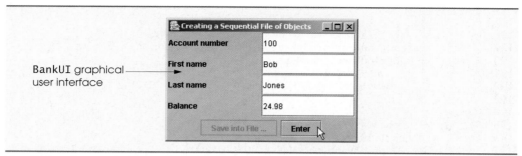

Fig. 17.7   Sequential file created using `ObjectOutputStream`. (Part 6 of 6.)

Line 97 calls method *showSaveDialog* to display the `JFileChooser` dialog titled **Save**. Argument `this` specifies the `JFileChooser` dialog's *parent* window, which determines the position of the dialog on the screen. If `null` is passed, the dialog is displayed in the center of the screen; otherwise, the dialog is centered over the application window. A `JFileChooser` dialog is a modal dialog that does not allow the user to interact with any other program window until the user closes the `JFileChooser` by clicking **Save** or **Cancel**. The user selects the drive, directory and file name, then clicks **Save**. Method `showSaveDialog` returns an integer specifying which button (**Save** or **Cancel**) the user clicked to close the dialog. Line 100 tests whether the user clicked **Cancel** by comparing `result` with `static` constant *CANCEL_OPTION*. If they are equals, the method returns.

Line 103 retrieves the file the user selected by calling method *getSelectedFile*, which returns an object of type `File` that encapsulates information about the file (e.g., name and location), but does not represent the contents of the file. This `File` object does not open the file. We assign the reference to this `File` object to the variable `fileName`.

As stated previously, a program can open a file by creating an object of stream class `FileInputStream` or `FileOutputStream`. In this example, the file is to be opened for output, so the program creates a `FileOutputStream` (line 115). One argument is passed to the `FileOutputStream`'s constructor—a `File` object. Existing files that are opened for output in this manner are *truncated*—all data in the file is discarded.

Common Programming Error 17.2

It is a logic error to open an existing file for output when, in fact, the user wishes to preserve the file. To append to a file, use the two-argument FileOutputStream constructor with a true second argument.

Class `FileOutputStream` provides methods for writing `byte` arrays and individual `byte`s to a file. For this program, we write objects to a file—a capability not provided by `FileOutputStream`. For this reason, we wrap a `FileOutputStream` in an `ObjectOutputStream` by passing the new `FileOutputStream` object to the `ObjectOutputStream`'s constructor (lines 114–115). The constructor might throw an *IOException* if a problem occurs while opening the file (e.g., when a file is opened for writing on a drive with insufficient space or when a read-only file is opened for writing). If so, the program displays an error message (lines 122–125). If creation of the two streams does not throw an *IOException*, the file is open and reference `output` can be used to write objects to the file.

This program assumes that data is input correctly and in the proper record number order. The user types data into the `JTextField`s and clicks **Enter** to write the data to the file. The **Enter** button's `actionPerformed` method (lines 57–60) calls our method `addRecord` (lines 150–204) to perform the write operation. Line 173 calls method *writeObject* to write the `record` object to the output file. Line 174 calls method *flush* to ensure that any data stored in memory is written to the file immediately.

When the user closes the application window, the program calls method `windowClosing` (lines 73–79), which compares `output` with `null` (line 75). If `output` is not `null`, the stream is open, and methods `addRecord` (lines 150–204) and `closeFile` (lines 132–147) are called. Method `closeFile` calls method *close* on `output` to close the file. Notice that the call to method `close` is contained in a `try` block. Method `close` throws an `IOException` if the file cannot be closed properly. In this case, it is important to notify the user that the information in the file might be corrupted.

Performance Tip 17.2

Always release resources explicitly and at the earliest possible moment at which it is determined that the resources are no longer needed. This procedure makes the resources immediately available to be reused by your program or by another program, thus improving resource utilization.

When using wrapped streams, the outermost stream (the `ObjectOutputStream` in this example) should be used to close the file.

Performance Tip 17.3

Explicitly close each file as soon as it is known that the program will not reference the file again. This practice can reduce resource usage in a program that will continue executing long after it no longer needs to be referencing a particular file. This practice also improves program clarity.

In the sample execution for the program of Fig. 17.7, we entered information for five accounts. (See Fig. 17.8.) The program does not show how the data records actually appear in the file. To verify that the file has been created successfully, the next section presents a program to read the file's contents.

17.6　Reading Data from a Sequential-Access File

Data are stored in files so that they may be retrieved for processing when needed. The previous section has demonstrated how to create a file for sequential access. In this section, we discuss how to read data sequentially from a file.

Sample Data			
100	Bob	Jones	24.98
200	Steve	Doe	-345.67
300	Pam	White	0.00
400	Sam	Stone	-42.16
500	Sue	Rich	224.62

Fig. 17.8　Sample data for the program of Fig. 17.7.

The program of Fig. 17.9 reads records from a file created by the program of Fig. 17.7 and displays the contents of the records. The program opens the file for input by creating a `FileInputStream` object. The program specifies the name of the file to open as an argument to the `FileInputStream` constructor. In Fig. 17.7, we wrote objects to the file, using an `ObjectOutputStream` object. Data must be read from the file in the same format in which it was written to the file. Therefore, we use an `ObjectInputStream` wrapped around a `FileInputStream` in this program. Note that the third sample screen capture shows the GUI displaying the last record in the file.

```java
1   // Fig. 17.9: ReadSequentialFile.java
2   // This program reads a file of objects sequentially
3   // and displays each record.
4   import java.io.*;
5   import java.awt.*;
6   import java.awt.event.*;
7   import javax.swing.*;
8
9   import com.deitel.jhtp5.ch17.*;
10
11  public class ReadSequentialFile extends JFrame {
12     private ObjectInputStream input;
13     private BankUI userInterface;
14     private JButton nextButton, openButton;
15
16     // Constructor -- initialize the Frame
17     public ReadSequentialFile()
18     {
19        super( "Reading a Sequential File of Objects" );
20
21        // create instance of reusable user interface
22        userInterface = new BankUI( 4 );  // four textfields
23        getContentPane().add( userInterface, BorderLayout.CENTER );
24
25        // get reference to generic task button doTask1 from BankUI
26        openButton = userInterface.getDoTask1Button();
27        openButton.setText( "Open File" );
28
29        // register listener to call openFile when button pressed
30        openButton.addActionListener(
31
32           // anonymous inner class to handle openButton event
33           new ActionListener() {
34
35              // get filename from user and open file
36              public void actionPerformed( ActionEvent event )
37              {
38                 openFile();
39              }
40
```

Fig. 17.9   Sequential file read using an `ObjectInputStream`. (Part 1 of 5.)

```
41                } // end anonymous inner class
42
43          ); // end call to addActionListener
44
45          // register window listener for window closing event
46          addWindowListener(
47
48              // anonymous inner class to handle windowClosing event
49              new WindowAdapter() {
50
51                  // close file and terminate application
52                  public void windowClosing( WindowEvent event )
53                  {
54                      if ( input != null )
55                          closeFile();
56
57                      System.exit( 0 );
58                  }
59
60              } // end anonymous inner class
61
62          ); // end call to addWindowListener
63
64          // get reference to generic task button doTask2 from BankUI
65          nextButton = userInterface.getDoTask2Button();
66          nextButton.setText( "Next Record" );
67          nextButton.setEnabled( false );
68
69          // register listener to call readRecord when button pressed
70          nextButton.addActionListener(
71
72              // anonymous inner class to handle nextRecord event
73              new ActionListener() {
74
75                  // call readRecord when user clicks nextRecord
76                  public void actionPerformed( ActionEvent event )
77                  {
78                      readRecord();
79                  }
80
81              } // end anonymous inner class
82
83          ); // end call to addActionListener
84
85          pack();
86          setSize( 300, 200 );
87          setVisible( true );
88
89      } // end ReadSequentialFile constructor
90
91      // enable user to select file to open
92      private void openFile()
93      {
```

Fig. 17.9   Sequential file read using an `ObjectInputStream`. (Part 2 of 5.)

```
94          // display file dialog so user can select file to open
95          JFileChooser fileChooser = new JFileChooser();
96          fileChooser.setFileSelectionMode( JFileChooser.FILES_ONLY );
97
98          int result = fileChooser.showOpenDialog( this );
99
100         // if user clicked Cancel button on dialog, return
101         if ( result == JFileChooser.CANCEL_OPTION )
102            return;
103
104         // obtain selected file
105         File fileName = fileChooser.getSelectedFile();
106
107         // display error if file name invalid
108         if ( fileName == null || fileName.getName().equals( "" ) )
109            JOptionPane.showMessageDialog( this, "Invalid File Name",
110               "Invalid File Name", JOptionPane.ERROR_MESSAGE );
111
112         else {
113
114            // open file
115            try {
116               input = new ObjectInputStream(
117                  new FileInputStream( fileName ) );
118
119               openButton.setEnabled( false );
120               nextButton.setEnabled( true );
121            }
122
123            // process exceptions opening file
124            catch ( IOException ioException ) {
125               JOptionPane.showMessageDialog( this, "Error Opening File",
126                  "Error", JOptionPane.ERROR_MESSAGE );
127            }
128
129         } // end else
130
131      } // end method openFile
132
133      // read record from file
134      public void readRecord()
135      {
136         AccountRecord record;
137
138         // input the values from the file
139         try {
140            record = ( AccountRecord ) input.readObject();
141
142            // create array of Strings to display in GUI
143            String values[] = { String.valueOf( record.getAccount() ),
144               record.getFirstName(), record.getLastName(),
145               String.valueOf( record.getBalance() ) };
146
```

Fig. 17.9   Sequential file read using an `ObjectInputStream`. (Part 3 of 5.)

```
147            // display record contents
148            userInterface.setFieldValues( values );
149         }
150
151      // display message when end-of-file reached
152      catch ( EOFException endOfFileException ) {
153         nextButton.setEnabled( false );
154
155         JOptionPane.showMessageDialog( this, "No more records in file",
156            "End of File", JOptionPane.ERROR_MESSAGE );
157      }
158
159      // display error message if class is not found
160      catch ( ClassNotFoundException classNotFoundException ) {
161         JOptionPane.showMessageDialog( this, "Unable to create object",
162            "Class Not Found", JOptionPane.ERROR_MESSAGE );
163      }
164
165      // display error message if cannot read due to problem with file
166      catch ( IOException ioException ) {
167         JOptionPane.showMessageDialog( this,
168            "Error during read from file",
169            "Read Error", JOptionPane.ERROR_MESSAGE );
170      }
171
172   } // end method readRecord
173
174   // close file and terminate application
175   private void closeFile()
176   {
177      // close file and exit
178      try {
179         input.close();
180         System.exit( 0 );
181      }
182
183      // process exception while closing file
184      catch ( IOException ioException ) {
185         JOptionPane.showMessageDialog( this, "Error closing file",
186            "Error", JOptionPane.ERROR_MESSAGE );
187
188         System.exit( 1 );
189      }
190
191   } // end method closeFile
192
193   public static void main( String args[] )
194   {
195      new ReadSequentialFile();
196   }
197
198 } // end class ReadSequentialFile
```

Fig. 17.9   Sequential file read using an `ObjectInputStream`. (Part 4 of 5.)

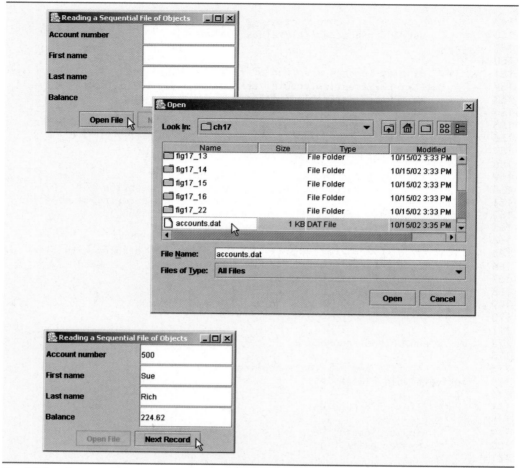

Fig. 17.9   Sequential file read using an `ObjectInputStream`. (Part 5 of 5.)

Most of the code in this example is similar to that in Fig. 17.7, so we discuss only the key lines of code that are different. Line 98 calls `JFileChooser` method *show-OpenDialog* to display the **Open** dialog (the second screen capture in Fig. 17.9). The behavior and GUI are the same as those of the dialog displayed by `showSaveDialog`, except that the title of the dialog and the **Save** button are both replaced with **Open**.

Lines 116–117 create an `ObjectInputStream` object and assign its reference to `input`. The `File` containing the file name the user selected is passed to the `FileInput-Stream` constructor to open the file.

The program reads a record from the file each time the user clicks **Next Record**. Line 78 in **Next Record**'s `actionPerformed` method calls method `readRecord` (lines 134–172) to read one record from the file. Line 140 calls method *readObject* to read an `Object` from the `ObjectInputStream`. To use `AccountRecord`-specific methods, we cast the returned `Object` to type `AccountRecord`. If the end-of-file marker is reached during reading, `readObject` throws an *EndOfFileException*.

Credit-Inquiry Program

To retrieve data sequentially from a file, programs normally start reading from the beginning of the file and read all the data consecutively until the desired information is found. It might be necessary to process the file sequentially several times (from the beginning of the file) during the execution of a program. Class FileInputStream does not provide the ability to reposition to the beginning of the file to read the file again unless the program closes the file and reopens it. RandomAccessFile objects can reposition to the beginning of the file. Class RandomAccessFile (Section 17.8–Section 17.12) provides all the capabilities of the classes FileInputStream, FileOutputStream, DataInputStream and DataOutputStream and adds several other methods, including a *seek* method that repositions the *file-position pointer* (the byte number of the next byte in the file to be read or written to) to any position in the file. However, class RandomAccessFile cannot read and write entire objects. For this reason, we will need to close and reopen the file to enable our program to read data from the beginning of the file repeatedly.

Performance Tip 17.4

> *The process of closing and reopening a file for the purpose of positioning the file-position pointer back to the beginning of a file is a time-consuming task for the computer. If this operation is done frequently, it can slow the performance of your program. If your program requires frequent repositioning of this nature to occur, consider using a random-access file.*

The program of Fig. 17.10 enables a credit manager to display the account information for those customers with zero balances (i.e., customers who do not owe the company any money), credit balances (i.e., customers to whom the company owes money) and debit balances (i.e., customers who owe the company money for goods and services received in the past). The program displays buttons that allow a credit manager to obtain credit information. The **Credit balances** button produces a list of accounts with credit balances. The **Debit balances** button produces a list of accounts with debit balances. The **Zero balances** button produces a list of accounts with zero balances.

Records are displayed in a JTextArea called recordDisplayArea. The record information is collected by reading through the entire file and determining, for each record, whether it satisfies the criteria for the account type selected by the credit manager. Clicking one of the balance buttons sets variable accountType (line 242) to the clicked button's text (e.g., **Zero balances**) and invokes method readRecords (lines 167–214), which loops through the file and reads every record. Line 189 of method readRecords calls method shouldDisplay (lines 217–229) to determine whether the current record satisfies the account type requested. If shouldDisplay returns true, the program appends the account information for the current record to the textarea recordDisplay. When the end-of-file marker is reached, line 199 calls method closeFile to close the file.

```
1   // Fig. 17.10: CreditInquiry.java
2   // This program reads a file sequentially and displays the contents in a
3   // text area based on the type of account the user requests
4   // (credit balance, debit balance or zero balance).
5   import java.io.*;
6   import java.awt.*;
```

Fig. 17.10   Credit inquiry program. (Part 1 of 7.)

```
 7   import java.awt.event.*;
 8   import java.text.DecimalFormat;
 9   import javax.swing.*;
10
11   import com.deitel.jhtp5.ch17.AccountRecord;
12
13   public class CreditInquiry extends JFrame {
14      private JTextArea recordDisplayArea;
15      private JButton openButton, creditButton, debitButton, zeroButton;
16      private JPanel buttonPanel;
17
18      private ObjectInputStream input;
19      private FileInputStream fileInput;
20      private File fileName;
21      private String accountType;
22
23      static private DecimalFormat twoDigits = new DecimalFormat( "0.00" );
24
25      // set up GUI
26      public CreditInquiry()
27      {
28         super( "Credit Inquiry Program" );
29
30         Container container = getContentPane();
31
32         buttonPanel = new JPanel(); // set up panel for buttons
33
34         // create and configure button to open file
35         openButton = new JButton( "Open File" );
36         buttonPanel.add( openButton );
37
38         // register openButton listener
39         openButton.addActionListener(
40
41            // anonymous inner class to handle openButton event
42            new ActionListener() {
43
44               // open file for processing
45               public void actionPerformed( ActionEvent event )
46               {
47                  openFile();
48               }
49
50            } // end anonymous inner class
51
52         ); // end call to addActionListener
53
54         // create and configure button to get accounts with credit balances
55         creditButton = new JButton( "Credit balances" );
56         buttonPanel.add( creditButton );
57         creditButton.addActionListener( new ButtonHandler() );
58
```

Fig. 17.10 Credit inquiry program. (Part 2 of 7.)

```
59        // create and configure button to get accounts with debit balances
60        debitButton = new JButton( "Debit balances" );
61        buttonPanel.add( debitButton );
62        debitButton.addActionListener( new ButtonHandler() );
63
64        // create and configure button to get accounts with zero balances
65        zeroButton = new JButton( "Zero balances" );
66        buttonPanel.add( zeroButton );
67        zeroButton.addActionListener( new ButtonHandler() );
68
69        // set up display area
70        recordDisplayArea = new JTextArea();
71        JScrollPane scroller = new JScrollPane( recordDisplayArea );
72
73        // attach components to content pane
74        container.add( scroller, BorderLayout.CENTER );
75        container.add( buttonPanel, BorderLayout.SOUTH );
76
77        creditButton.setEnabled( false ); // disable creditButton
78        debitButton.setEnabled( false );  // disable debitButton
79        zeroButton.setEnabled( false );   // disable zeroButton
80
81        // register window listener
82        addWindowListener(
83
84           // anonymous inner class for windowClosing event
85           new WindowAdapter() {
86
87              // close file and terminate program
88              public void windowClosing( WindowEvent event )
89              {
90                 closeFile();
91                 System.exit( 0 );
92              }
93
94           } // end anonymous inner class
95
96        ); // end call to addWindowListener
97
98        pack(); // pack components and display window
99        setSize( 600, 250 );
100       setVisible( true );
101
102    } // end CreditInquiry constructor
103
104    // enable user to choose file to open
105    private void openFile()
106    {
107       // display dialog, so user can choose file
108       JFileChooser fileChooser = new JFileChooser();
109       fileChooser.setFileSelectionMode( JFileChooser.FILES_ONLY );
110
111       int result = fileChooser.showOpenDialog( this );
```

Fig. 17.10 Credit inquiry program. (Part 3 of 7.)

```
112
113        // if user clicked Cancel button on dialog, return
114        if ( result == JFileChooser.CANCEL_OPTION )
115           return;
116
117        fileName = fileChooser.getSelectedFile(); // obtain selected file
118
119        // display error if file name invalid
120        if ( fileName == null || fileName.getName().equals( "" ) )
121           JOptionPane.showMessageDialog( this, "Invalid File Name",
122              "Invalid File Name", JOptionPane.ERROR_MESSAGE );
123
124        // open file
125        try {
126
127           // close file from previous operation
128           if ( input != null )
129              input.close();
130
131           fileInput = new FileInputStream( fileName );
132           input = new ObjectInputStream( fileInput );
133           openButton.setEnabled( false );
134           creditButton.setEnabled( true );
135           debitButton.setEnabled( true );
136           zeroButton.setEnabled( true );
137        }
138
139        // catch problems manipulating file
140        catch ( IOException ioException ) {
141           JOptionPane.showMessageDialog( this, "File does not exist",
142              "Invalid File Name", JOptionPane.ERROR_MESSAGE );
143        }
144
145     } // end method openFile
146
147     // close file before application terminates
148     private void closeFile()
149     {
150        // close file
151        try {
152           if ( input != null )
153              input.close();
154        }
155
156        // process exception from closing file
157        catch ( IOException ioException ) {
158           JOptionPane.showMessageDialog( this, "Error closing file",
159              "Error", JOptionPane.ERROR_MESSAGE );
160
161           System.exit( 1 );
162        }
163
164     } // end method closeFile
```

Fig. 17.10 Credit inquiry program. (Part 4 of 7.)

```
165
166     // read records from file and display only records of appropriate type
167     private void readRecords()
168     {
169        AccountRecord record;
170
171        // read records
172        try {
173
174           if ( input != null )
175              input.close();
176
177           fileInput = new FileInputStream( fileName );
178           input = new ObjectInputStream( fileInput );
179
180           recordDisplayArea.setText( "The accounts are:\n" );
181
182           // input the values from the file
183           while ( true ) {
184
185              // read one AccountRecord
186              record = ( AccountRecord ) input.readObject();
187
188              // if proper acount type, display record
189              if ( shouldDisplay( record.getBalance() ) )
190                 recordDisplayArea.append( record.getAccount() + "\t" +
191                    record.getFirstName() + "\t" + record.getLastName() +
192                    "\t" + twoDigits.format( record.getBalance() ) + "\n" );
193           }
194
195        } // end try
196
197        // close file when end-of-file reached
198        catch ( EOFException eofException ) {
199           closeFile();
200        }
201
202        // display error if cannot read object because class not found
203        catch ( ClassNotFoundException classNotFound ) {
204           JOptionPane.showMessageDialog( this, "Unable to create object",
205              "Class Not Found", JOptionPane.ERROR_MESSAGE );
206        }
207
208        // display error if cannot read because problem with file
209        catch ( IOException ioException ) {
210           JOptionPane.showMessageDialog( this, "Error reading from file",
211              "Error", JOptionPane.ERROR_MESSAGE );
212        }
213
214     } // end method readRecords
215
```

Fig. 17.10 Credit inquiry program. (Part 5 of 7.)

```
216        // use record type to determine if record should be displayed
217        private boolean shouldDisplay( double balance )
218        {
219           if ( accountType.equals( "Credit balances" ) && balance < 0 )
220              return true;
221
222           else if ( accountType.equals( "Debit balances" ) && balance > 0 )
223              return true;
224
225           else if ( accountType.equals( "Zero balances" ) && balance == 0 )
226              return true;
227
228           return false;
229        }
230
231        public static void main( String args[] )
232        {
233           new CreditInquiry();
234        }
235
236        // class for creditButton, debitButton and zeroButton event handling
237        private class ButtonHandler implements ActionListener {
238
239           // read records from file
240           public void actionPerformed( ActionEvent event )
241           {
242              accountType = event.getActionCommand();
243              readRecords();
244           }
245
246        } // end class ButtonHandler
247
248  } // end class CreditInquiry
```

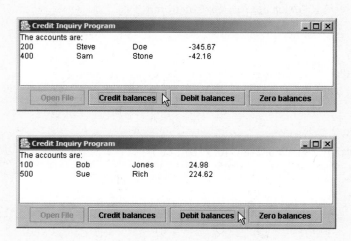

Fig. 17.10 Credit inquiry program. (Part 6 of 7.)

Fig. 17.10 Credit inquiry program. (Part 7 of 7.)

17.7 Updating Sequential-Access Files

Data that is formatted and written to a sequential-access file as shown in Section 17.5 cannot be modified without reading and writing all the data in the file. For example, if the name White needs to be changed to Worthington, the old name cannot simply be overwritten. Such updating can be done, but it is awkward. To make the preceding name change, the records before White in a sequential-access file are copied to a new file. The updated record is then written to the new file, and the records after White are copied to the new file. This operation requires processing of every record in the file in order to update one record. If many records are being updated in one pass of the file, this technique can be acceptable.

17.8 Random-Access Files

So far, we have seen how to create sequential-access files and to search through them to locate particular information. Sequential-access files are inappropriate for so-called *instant-access applications*, in which a particular record of information must be located immediately. Some popular instant-access applications are airline-reservation systems, banking systems, point-of-sale systems, automated-teller machines and other kinds of *transaction-processing systems* that require rapid access to specific data. The bank at which you have your account might have hundreds of thousands, or even millions, of other customers; yet, when you use an automated teller machine, the bank determines in seconds whether your account has sufficient funds for the transaction. This kind of instant access is possible with *random-access files* and with databases (Chapter 23). A program can access individual records of a random-access file directly (and quickly) without searching through other records. Random-access files are sometimes called *direct-access files*.

Recall from Section 17.5 that Java does not impose structure on a file, so an application that wants to use random-access files must specify the format of those files. Several techniques can be used to create random-access files. Perhaps the simplest is to require that all records in a file be of the same fixed length. Using fixed-length records makes it easy for a program to calculate (as a function of the record size and the record key) the exact location of any record relative to the beginning of the file. We will soon see how this capability facilitates direct access to specific records, even in large files.

Figure 17.11 illustrates Java's view of a random-access file composed of fixed-length records. (Each record in this figure is 100 bytes long.) A random-access file is like a railroad train with many cars—some are empty, and some have contents.

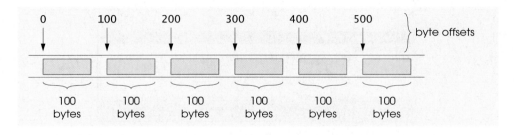

Fig. 17.11 Java's view of a random-access file.

A program can insert data in a random-access file without destroying other data in the file. Also, a program can update or delete data stored previously without rewriting the entire file. In the following sections, we explain how to create a random-access file, enter data, read the data both sequentially and randomly, update the data and delete the data.

17.9 Creating a Random-Access File

RandomAccessFile objects have all the capabilities of classes FileInputStream, FileOutputStream, DataInputStream and DataOutputStream. When a program associates an object of class RandomAccessFile with a file, the program reads or writes data, beginning at the location in the file specified by the *file-position pointer*, and manipulates all data as primitive types. When writing an int value, four bytes are output to the file. When reading a double value, eight bytes are input from the file. The size of the types is guaranteed, because Java has fixed representations and sizes for all primitive types, regardless of the computing platform.

Random-access file-processing programs rarely write a single field to a file. Normally, they write one object at a time, as we show in the upcoming examples. Consider the following problem:

> *Create a transaction-processing program capable of storing up to 100 fixed-length records for a company that can have up to 100 customers. Each record should consist of an account number that will be used as the record key, a last name, a first name and a balance. The program should be able to update an account, insert a new account and delete an account.*

The next several sections introduce the techniques necessary to create this credit-processing program. Figure 17.12 contains the RandomAccessAccountRecord class that is used by the next four programs for both reading records from and writing records to a file. Class RandomAccessAccountRecord inherits AccountRecord's (Fig. 17.6) implementation, which includes private fields—account, lastName, firstName and balance—as well as *set* and *get* methods for each field.

Line 9 declares the constant SIZE to represent the size, in bytes, of a record. A RandomAccessAccountRecord contains an int (4 bytes), two strings that we restrict to 15 characters (30 bytes) each for this example and a double (8 bytes), for a total of 72 bytes.

Method read (lines 25–31) reads one record from the RandomAccessFile specified as its argument. RandomAccessFile methods *readInt* (line 27) and *readDouble* (line 30) read the account and balance, respectively. Method read calls utility method readName (lines 34–44) twice to obtain the first and last names. Method readName reads 15 characters from the RandomAccessFile and returns a String. If a name is shorter than 15 characters, the program fills each extra character with a null byte ('\0'). Swing components, such as JTextFields, cannot display null-byte characters; instead, they display these characters as rectangles). Line 43 solves this problem by replacing null bytes with spaces.

Method write (lines 47–53) outputs one record to the RandomAccessFile specified as its argument. This method uses RandomAccessFile method *writeInt* to output the integer account, method *writeChars* (called from utility method writeName) to output the firstName and lastName character arrays, and method *writeDouble* to output the double balance. [*Note*: To ensure that all records in the RandomAccessFile have the same size, we write exactly 15 characters for the first name and exactly 15 characters for the last name.] Method writeName (lines 56–68) performs the write operations for the first and last name. Note that the class is in package com.deitel.jhtp5.ch17.

```java
1   // Fig. 17.12: RandomAccessAccountRecord.java
2   // Subclass of AccountRecord for random access file programs.
3   package com.deitel.jhtp5.ch17;
4
5   import java.io.*;
6
7   public class RandomAccessAccountRecord extends AccountRecord {
8
9      public static final int SIZE = 72;  // bytes in one record
10
11     // no-argument constructor calls other constructor with default values
12     public RandomAccessAccountRecord()
13     {
14        this( 0, "", "", 0.0 );
15     }
16
17     // initialize a RandomAccessAccountRecord
18     public RandomAccessAccountRecord( int account, String firstName,
19        String lastName, double balance )
20     {
21        super( account, firstName, lastName, balance );
22     }
23
24     // read a record from specified RandomAccessFile
25     public void read( RandomAccessFile file ) throws IOException
26     {
27        setAccount( file.readInt() );
28        setFirstName( readName( file ) );
29        setLastName( readName( file ) );
30        setBalance( file.readDouble() );
31     }
32
33     // ensure that name is proper length
34     private String readName( RandomAccessFile file ) throws IOException
35     {
36        char name[] = new char[ 15 ], temp;
37
```

Fig. 17.12 RandomAccessAccountRecord class used in the random-access file programs. (Part 1 of 2.)

```
38          for ( int count = 0; count < name.length; count++ ) {
39             temp = file.readChar();
40             name[ count ] = temp;
41          }
42
43          return new String( name ).replace( '\0', ' ' );
44       }
45
46       // write a record to specified RandomAccessFile
47       public void write( RandomAccessFile file ) throws IOException
48       {
49          file.writeInt( getAccount() );
50          writeName( file, getFirstName() );
51          writeName( file, getLastName() );
52          file.writeDouble( getBalance() );
53       }
54
55       // write a name to file; maximum of 15 characters
56       private void writeName( RandomAccessFile file, String name )
57          throws IOException
58       {
59          StringBuffer buffer = null;
60
61          if ( name != null )
62             buffer = new StringBuffer( name );
63          else
64             buffer = new StringBuffer( 15 );
65
66          buffer.setLength( 15 );
67          file.writeChars( buffer.toString() );
68       }
69
70    } // end class RandomAccessAccountRecord
```

Fig. 17.12 RandomAccessAccountRecord class used in the random-access file
programs. (Part 2 of 2.)

Figure 17.13 illustrates the process of opening a random-access file and writing data
to the disk. This program writes 100 blank RandomAccessAccountRecords. Each
RandomAccessAccountRecord object contains 0 for the account number, null for the
last name, null for the first name and 0.0 for the balance. The file is initialized to create
the proper amount of "empty" space in which the account data will be stored and to enable
us to determine in subsequent programs whether each record is empty or contains data.

```
1    // Fig. 17.13: CreateRandomFile.java
2    // Creates random access file by writing 100 empty records to disk.
3    import java.io.*;
4    import javax.swing.*;
5
6    import com.deitel.jhtp5.ch17.RandomAccessAccountRecord;
7
```

Fig. 17.13 Random-access file created sequentially. (Part 1 of 3.)

```
8   public class CreateRandomFile {
9
10    private static final int NUMBER_RECORDS = 100;
11
12    // enable user to select file to open
13    private void createFile()
14    {
15       // display dialog so user can choose file
16       JFileChooser fileChooser = new JFileChooser();
17       fileChooser.setFileSelectionMode( JFileChooser.FILES_ONLY );
18
19       int result = fileChooser.showSaveDialog( null );
20
21       // if user clicked Cancel button on dialog, return
22       if ( result == JFileChooser.CANCEL_OPTION )
23          return;
24
25       // obtain selected file
26       File fileName = fileChooser.getSelectedFile();
27
28       // display error if file name invalid
29       if ( fileName == null || fileName.getName().equals( "" ) )
30          JOptionPane.showMessageDialog( null, "Invalid File Name",
31             "Invalid File Name", JOptionPane.ERROR_MESSAGE );
32
33       else {
34
35          // open file
36          try {
37             RandomAccessFile file =
38                new RandomAccessFile( fileName, "rw" );
39
40             RandomAccessAccountRecord blankRecord =
41                new RandomAccessAccountRecord();
42
43             // write 100 blank records
44             for ( int count = 0; count < NUMBER_RECORDS; count++ )
45                blankRecord.write( file );
46
47             file.close(); // close file
48
49             // display message that file was created
50             JOptionPane.showMessageDialog( null, "Created file " +
51                fileName, "Status", JOptionPane.INFORMATION_MESSAGE );
52
53             System.exit( 0 );  // terminate program
54
55          } // end try
56
57          // process exceptions during open, write or close file operations
58          catch ( IOException ioException ) {
59             JOptionPane.showMessageDialog( null, "Error processing file",
60                "Error processing file", JOptionPane.ERROR_MESSAGE );
```

Fig. 17.13 Random-access file created sequentially. (Part 2 of 3.)

```
61
62                System.exit( 1 );
63             }
64
65          } // end else
66
67       } // end method createFile
68
69       public static void main( String args[] )
70       {
71          CreateRandomFile application = new CreateRandomFile();
72          application.createFile();
73       }
74
75    } // end class CreateRandomFile
```

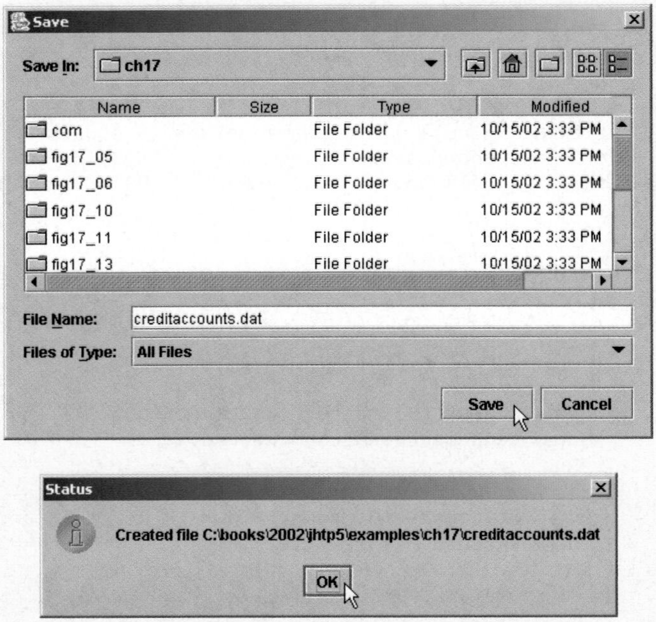

Fig. 17.13　Random-access file created sequentially. (Part 3 of 3.)

Lines 37–38 attempt to open a RandomAccessFile for use in this program. The RandomAccessFile constructor accepts two arguments—the file name and the *file-open mode*. The file-open mode for a RandomAccessFile is either *"r"* (to open the file for reading) or *"rw"* (to open the file for reading and writing).

If an IOException occurs during the open process, the program displays a message dialog and terminates. If the file opens properly, the program uses a for structure (lines 44–45) to invoke RandomAccessAccountRecord method write 100 times. This statement causes the fields of object blankRecord to be written to the file associated with RandomAccessFile object file.

17.10 Writing Data Randomly to a Random-Access File

Figure 17.14 writes data to a file that is opened with the "rw" mode (for reading and writing). It uses RandomAccessFile method *seek* to determine the exact location in the file at which a record of information is stored. Method seek sets the file-position pointer to a specific position in the file relative to the beginning of the file, and RandomAccessAccountRecord method write outputs the data. This program assumes that the user does not enter duplicate account numbers and that the user enters appropriate data in each textfield.

```java
1   // Fig. 17.14: WriteRandomFile.java
2   // This program uses textfields to get information from the user at the
3   // keyboard and writes the information to a random-access file.
4   import java.awt.*;
5   import java.awt.event.*;
6   import java.io.*;
7   import javax.swing.*;
8
9   import com.deitel.jhtp5.ch17.*;
10
11  public class WriteRandomFile extends JFrame {
12      private RandomAccessFile output;
13      private BankUI userInterface;
14      private JButton enterButton, openButton;
15
16      private static final int NUMBER_RECORDS = 100;
17
18      // set up GUI
19      public WriteRandomFile()
20      {
21          super( "Write to random access file" );
22
23          // create instance of reusable user interface BankUI
24          userInterface = new BankUI( 4 );  // four textfields
25          getContentPane().add( userInterface,
26              BorderLayout.CENTER );
27
28          // get reference to generic task button doTask1 in BankUI
29          openButton = userInterface.getDoTask1Button();
30          openButton.setText( "Open..." );
31
32          // register listener to call openFile when button pressed
33          openButton.addActionListener(
34
35              // anonymous inner class to handle openButton event
36              new ActionListener() {
37
38                  // allow user to select file to open
39                  public void actionPerformed( ActionEvent event )
40                  {
41                      openFile();
42                  }
43
```

Fig. 17.14 Writing data to a random-access file. (Part 1 of 5.)

```
44            } // end anonymous inner class
45
46         ); // end call to addActionListener
47
48         // register window listener for window closing event
49         addWindowListener(
50
51            // anonymous inner class to handle windowClosing event
52            new WindowAdapter() {
53
54               // add record in GUI, then close file
55               public void windowClosing( WindowEvent event )
56               {
57                  if ( output != null )
58                     addRecord();
59
60                  closeFile();
61               }
62
63            } // end anonymous inner class
64
65         ); // end call to addWindowListener
66
67         // get reference to generic task button doTask2 in BankUI
68         enterButton = userInterface.getDoTask2Button();
69         enterButton.setText( "Enter" );
70         enterButton.setEnabled( false );
71
72         // register listener to call addRecord when button pressed
73         enterButton.addActionListener(
74
75            // anonymous inner class to handle enterButton event
76            new ActionListener() {
77
78               // add record to file
79               public void actionPerformed( ActionEvent event )
80               {
81                  addRecord();
82               }
83
84            } // end anonymous inner class
85
86         ); // end call to addActionListener
87
88         setSize( 300, 150 );
89         setVisible( true );
90      }
91
92      // enable user to choose file to open
93      private void openFile()
94      {
95         // display file dialog so user can select file
96         JFileChooser fileChooser = new JFileChooser();
```

Fig. 17.14   Writing data to a random-access file. (Part 2 of 5.)

```
97              fileChooser.setFileSelectionMode( JFileChooser.FILES_ONLY );
98
99              int result = fileChooser.showOpenDialog( this );
100
101             // if user clicked Cancel button on dialog, return
102             if ( result == JFileChooser.CANCEL_OPTION )
103                 return;
104
105             // obtain selected file
106             File fileName = fileChooser.getSelectedFile();
107
108             // display error if file name invalid
109             if ( fileName == null || fileName.getName().equals( "" ) )
110                 JOptionPane.showMessageDialog( this, "Invalid File Name",
111                     "Invalid File Name", JOptionPane.ERROR_MESSAGE );
112
113             else {
114
115                 // open file
116                 try {
117                     output = new RandomAccessFile( fileName, "rw" );
118                     enterButton.setEnabled( true );
119                     openButton.setEnabled( false );
120                 }
121
122                 // process exception while opening file
123                 catch ( IOException ioException ) {
124                     JOptionPane.showMessageDialog( this, "File does not exist",
125                         "Invalid File Name", JOptionPane.ERROR_MESSAGE );
126                 }
127
128             } // end else
129
130         } // end method openFile
131
132         // close file and terminate application
133         private void closeFile()
134         {
135             // close file and exit
136             try {
137                 if ( output != null )
138                     output.close();
139
140                 System.exit( 0 );
141             }
142
143             // process exception while closing file
144             catch( IOException ioException ) {
145                 JOptionPane.showMessageDialog( this, "Error closing file",
146                     "Error", JOptionPane.ERROR_MESSAGE );
147
148                 System.exit( 1 );
149             }
```

Fig. 17.14 Writing data to a random-access file. (Part 3 of 5.)

```
150
151     } // end method closeFile
152
153     // add one record to file
154     private void addRecord()
155     {
156        String fields[] = userInterface.getFieldValues();
157
158        // ensure account field has a value
159        if ( ! fields[ BankUI.ACCOUNT ].equals( "" ) ) {
160
161           // output values to file
162           try {
163              int accountNumber =
164                 Integer.parseInt( fields[ ACCOUNT ] );
165
166              if ( accountNumber > 0 && accountNumber <= NUMBER_RECORDS ) {
167                 RandomAccessAccountRecord record
168                    new RandomAccessAccountRecord();
169
170                 record.setAccount( accountNumber );
171                 record.setFirstName( fields[ BankUI.FIRSTNAME ] );
172                 record.setLastName( fields[ BankUI.LASTNAME ] );
173                 record.setBalance( Double.parseDouble(
174                    fields[ BankUI.BALANCE ] ) );
175
176                 output.seek( ( accountNumber - 1 ) *
177                    RandomAccessAccountRecord.SIZE );
178                 record.write( output );
179              }
180
181              else {
182                 JOptionPane.showMessageDialog( this,
183                    "Account must be between 1 and 100",
184                    "Invalid account number", JOptionPane.ERROR_MESSAGE );
185              }
186
187              userInterface.clearFields();  // clear TextFields
188
189           } // end try
190
191           // process improper account number or balance format
192           catch ( NumberFormatException formatException ) {
193              JOptionPane.showMessageDialog( this,
194                 "Bad account number or balance",
195                 "Invalid Number Format", JOptionPane.ERROR_MESSAGE );
196           }
197
198           // process exceptions while writing to file
199           catch ( IOException ioException ) {
200              JOptionPane.showMessageDialog( this,
201                 "Error writing to the file", "IO Exception",
202                 JOptionPane.ERROR_MESSAGE );
```

Fig. 17.14 Writing data to a random-access file. (Part 4 of 5.)

```
203                 closeFile();
204            }
205
206        } // end if
207
208    } // end method addRecord
209
210    public static void main( String args[] )
211    {
212        new WriteRandomFile();
213    }
214
215 } // end class WriteRandomFile
```

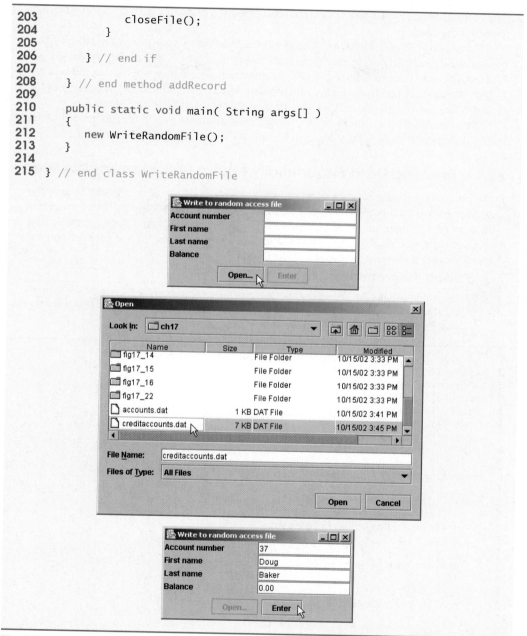

Fig. 17.14   Writing data to a random-access file. (Part 5 of 5.)

The user enters values for the account number, first name, last name and balance. When the user clicks the **Enter** button, the program calls WriteRandomFile method addRecord (154–208) to retrieve the data from the BankAccountUI's textfields, store the data in RandomAccessAccountRecord object record and call record's write method to output the data.

Lines 176–177 call RandomAccessFile method *seek* to position the file-position pointer for object output to the byte location calculated by (accountNumber - 1) * RandomAccessAccountRecord.SIZE. Account numbers in this program should be from 1–100. We subtract one from the account number when calculating the byte location of the record. Thus, for record one, the file-position pointer is set to byte zero of the file.

When the user closes the window, the program attempts to add the last record to the file (if there is one in the GUI waiting to be output), closes the file and terminates.

17.11 Reading Data Sequentially from a Random-Access File

In the previous sections, we created a random-access file and wrote data to that file. In this section, we develop a program (Fig. 17.15) that opens a RandomAccessFile for reading with the "r" file-open mode, reads through the file sequentially and displays only those records containing data. This program produces an additional benefit. See whether you can determine what it is; we will reveal it at the end of this section.

Good Programming Practice 17.3

Open a file with the "r" file-open mode for input if the contents of the file should not be modified. This practice prevents unintentional modification of the file's contents. This is another example of the principle of least privilege.

```
1   // Fig. 17.15: ReadRandomFile.java
2   // This program reads a random-access file sequentially and
3   // displays the contents one record at a time in text fields.
4   import java.awt.*;
5   import java.awt.event.*;
6   import java.io.*;
7   import java.text.DecimalFormat;
8   import javax.swing.*;
9
10  import com.deitel.jhtp5.ch17.*;
11
12  public class ReadRandomFile extends JFrame {
13     private BankUI userInterface;
14     private RandomAccessFile input;
15     private JButton nextButton, openButton;
16
17     private static DecimalFormat twoDigits = new DecimalFormat( "0.00" );
18
19     // set up GUI
20     public ReadRandomFile()
21     {
22        super( "Read Client File" );
23
24        // create reusable user interface instance
25        userInterface = new BankUI( 4 );  // four textfields
26        getContentPane().add( userInterface );
27
```

Fig. 17.15 Reading data sequentially from a random-access file. (Part 1 of 5.)

```
28        // configure generic doTask1 button from BankUI
29        openButton = userInterface.getDoTask1Button();
30        openButton.setText( "Open File for Reading..." );
31
32        // register listener to call openFile when button pressed
33        openButton.addActionListener(
34
35           // anonymous inner class to handle openButton event
36           new ActionListener() {
37
38              // enable user to select file to open
39              public void actionPerformed( ActionEvent event )
40              {
41                 openFile();
42              }
43
44           } // end anonymous inner class
45
46        ); // end call to addActionListener
47
48        // configure generic doTask2 button from BankUI
49        nextButton = userInterface.getDoTask2Button();
50        nextButton.setText( "Next" );
51        nextButton.setEnabled( false );
52
53        // register listener to call readRecord when button pressed
54        nextButton.addActionListener(
55
56           // anonymous inner class to handle nextButton event
57           new ActionListener() {
58
59              // read a record when user clicks nextButton
60              public void actionPerformed( ActionEvent event )
61              {
62                 readRecord();
63              }
64
65           } // end anonymous inner class
66
67        ); // end call to addActionListener
68
69        // register listener for window closing event
70        addWindowListener(
71
72           // anonymous inner class to handle windowClosing event
73           new WindowAdapter() {
74
75              // close file and terminate application
76              public void windowClosing( WindowEvent event )
77              {
78                 closeFile();
79              }
80
```

Fig. 17.15 Reading data sequentially from a random-access file. (Part 2 of 5.)

```
81              } // end anonymous inner class
82
83          ); // end call to addWindowListener
84
85          setSize( 300, 150 );
86          setVisible( true );
87
88      } // end constructor
89
90      // enable user to select file to open
91      private void openFile()
92      {
93          // display file dialog so user can select file
94          JFileChooser fileChooser = new JFileChooser();
95          fileChooser.setFileSelectionMode( JFileChooser.FILES_ONLY );
96
97          int result = fileChooser.showOpenDialog( this );
98
99          // if user clicked Cancel button on dialog, return
100         if ( result == JFileChooser.CANCEL_OPTION )
101             return;
102
103         // obtain selected file
104         File fileName = fileChooser.getSelectedFile();
105
106         // display error is file name invalid
107         if ( fileName == null || fileName.getName().equals( "" ) )
108             JOptionPane.showMessageDialog( this, "Invalid File Name",
109                 "Invalid File Name", JOptionPane.ERROR_MESSAGE );
110
111         else {
112
113             // open file
114             try {
115                 input = new RandomAccessFile( fileName, "r" );
116                 nextButton.setEnabled( true );
117                 openButton.setEnabled( false );
118             }
119
120             // catch exception while opening file
121             catch ( IOException ioException ) {
122                 JOptionPane.showMessageDialog( this, "File does not exist",
123                     "Invalid File Name", JOptionPane.ERROR_MESSAGE );
124             }
125
126         } // end else
127
128     } // end method openFile
129
130     // read one record
131     private void readRecord()
132     {
133         RandomAccessAccountRecord record = new RandomAccessAccountRecord();
```

Fig. 17.15 Reading data sequentially from a random-access file. (Part 3 of 5.)

```
134
135        // read a record and display
136        try {
137
138           do {
139              record.read( input );
140           } while ( record.getAccount() == 0 );
141
142           String values[] = { String.valueOf( record.getAccount() ),
143              record.getFirstName(), record.getLastName(),
144              String.valueOf( record.getBalance() ) };
145           userInterface.setFieldValues( values );
146        }
147
148        // close file when end-of-file reached
149        catch ( EOFException eofException ) {
150           JOptionPane.showMessageDialog( this, "No more records",
151              "End-of-file reached", JOptionPane.INFORMATION_MESSAGE );
152           closeFile();
153        }
154
155        // process exceptions from problem with file
156        catch ( IOException ioException ) {
157           JOptionPane.showMessageDialog( this, "Error Reading File",
158              "Error", JOptionPane.ERROR_MESSAGE );
159
160           System.exit( 1 );
161        }
162
163   } // end method readRecord
164
165   // close file and terminate application
166   private void closeFile()
167   {
168      // close file and exit
169      try {
170         if ( input != null )
171            input.close();
172
173         System.exit( 0 );
174      }
175
176      // process exception closing file
177      catch( IOException ioException ) {
178         JOptionPane.showMessageDialog( this, "Error closing file",
179            "Error", JOptionPane.ERROR_MESSAGE );
180
181         System.exit( 1 );
182      }
183
184   } // end method closeFile
185
```

Fig. 17.15 Reading data sequentially from a random-access file. (Part 4 of 5.)

```
186    public static void main( String args[] )
187    {
188        new ReadRandomFile();
189    }
190
191 } // end class ReadRandomFile
```

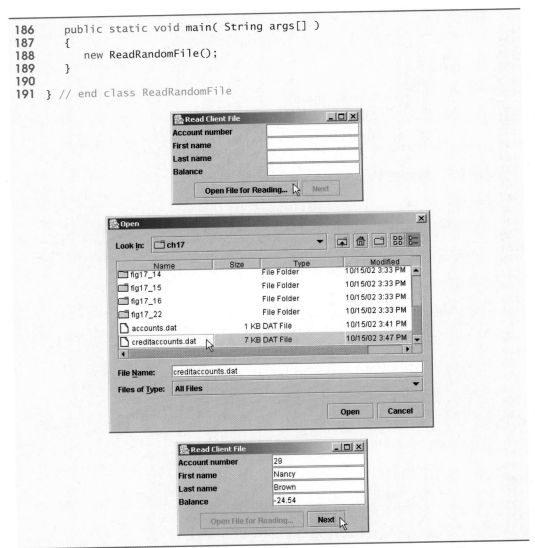

Fig. 17.15   Reading data sequentially from a random-access file. (Part 5 of 5.)

When the user clicks the **Next** button to read the next record in the file, the program invokes class ReadRandomFile's readRecord method (lines 131–163). This method invokes class RandomAccessAccountRecord's read method (line 139) to read one record's data into RandomAccessAccountRecord object record. Method readRecord reads from the file until it encounters a record with a nonzero account number (zero is the account number for empty records), at which point the loop terminates and readRecord displays the record data in the textfields. When the user clicks the **Done** button or when the end-of-file marker is encountered while reading, method closeFile is invoked to close the file and terminate the program.

What about that additional benefit we promised? If you examine the GUI as the program executes, you will notice that the records are displayed in sorted order (by account number)! This ordering is a simple consequence of the way we stored these records in the file, using direct-access techniques. Compared with the bubble sort we have seen (Chapter 7), sorting with direct-access techniques is blazingly fast. The speed is achieved by making the file large enough to hold every possible record that might be created, which enables the program to insert a record between other records without having to reorganize the file. This configuration, of course, means that the file could be sparsely occupied most of the time, a waste of storage. So this situation is another example of the space/time trade-off. By using large amounts of space, we are able to develop a much faster sorting algorithm.

17.12 Case Study: A Transaction-Processing Program

We now present a substantial transaction-processing program (Fig. 17.21 and Fig. 17.22), using a random-access file to achieve instant-access processing. The program maintains a bank's account information. The program updates existing accounts, adds new accounts and deletes accounts. We assume that the program of Fig. 17.13 has been executed to create a file and that the program of Fig. 17.14 has been executed to insert initial data. The techniques used in this example have been presented in the earlier RandomAccessFile examples.

This program's GUI consists of a window with a menu bar containing a **File** menu and text fields that enable the user to perform insert, update- and delete-record operations on the file. Buttons are provided to initiate the actions and to clear the fields. The **File** menu has five menu items for selecting various tasks, as shown in Fig. 17.16.

When the user selects **Update Record**, **Delete Record** or **New Record** from the **File** menu, the GUI is updated to represent each view (Fig. 17.17–Fig. 17.20). This enables certain text fields for editing, disables others, and changes the text of the action button. If the user enters a number into the account field and presses the *Enter* key, line 80 of Fig. 17.21 calls method displayRecord to input the record into the text fields.

Method performAction (Fig. 17.21, lines 323–366) is responsible for three actions. It takes the information from the text fields and sends this information to the appropriate method of class FileEditor (Fig. 17.22), which encapsulates the file-processing operations in this example. The method to call is determined by comparing performAction's

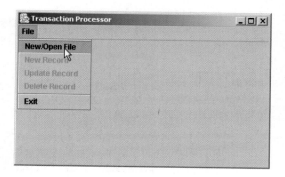

Fig. 17.16 Transaction Processor *window*.

string argument with the strings "Create", "Update" and "Delete". These strings come from the label on the action button in the GUI (the left button in each of the screen captures of Fig. 17.17–Fig. 17.20). Method performAction also handles any exceptions that might be thrown from FileEditor's methods.

Method displayRecord (Fig. 17.21, lines 369–412) finds a record from the file and displays it in the text fields. This method also takes a string as its input. This string represents a transaction. When the method is called from the account field's action listener (line 80), the string is "0". When the method is called from the transaction field's action listener (line 98), the string in the transaction field is passed as the argument. [*Note*: The transaction field is enabled only in update-record mode.]

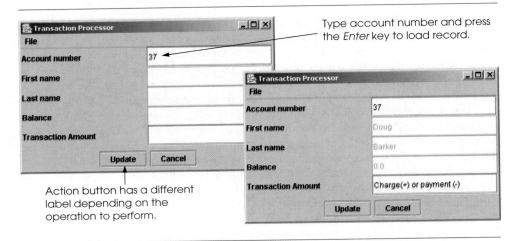

Fig. 17.17 **Update Record**: Loading a record to update.

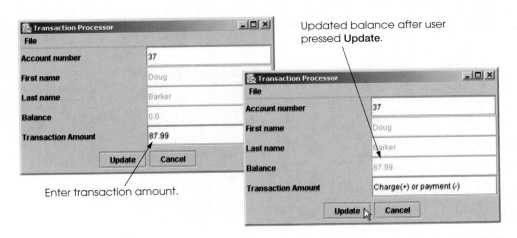

Fig. 17.18 **Update Record**: Inputting a transaction.

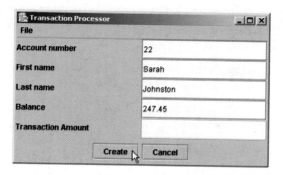

Fig. 17.19 New Record: Adding a record to the file.

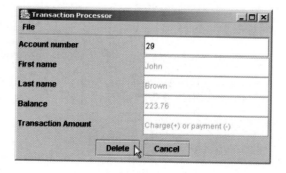

Fig. 17.20 Delete Record: Removing a record from the file.

```
1   // Fig. 17.21: TransactionProcessor.java
2   // A transaction processing program using random-access files.
3   import java.awt.*;
4   import java.awt.event.*;
5   import java.io.*;
6   import java.text.DecimalFormat;
7   import javax.swing.*;
8
9   import com.deitel.jhtp5.ch17.*;
10
11  public class TransactionProcessor extends JFrame {
12
13     private BankUI userInterface;
14     private JMenuItem newItem, updateItem, deleteItem, openItem, exitItem;
15     private JTextField fields[];
16     private JTextField accountField, transactionField;
17     private JButton actionButton, cancelButton;
18     private FileEditor dataFile;
19     private RandomAccessAccountRecord record;
```

Fig. 17.21 Transaction-processing program. (Part 1 of 9.)

```
20
21      public TransactionProcessor()
22      {
23         super( "Transaction Processor" );
24
25         // set up desktop, menu bar and File menu
26         userInterface = new BankUI( 5 );
27         getContentPane().add( userInterface );
28         userInterface.setVisible( false );
29
30         // set up the action button
31         actionButton = userInterface.getDoTask1Button();
32         actionButton.setText( "Save Changes" );
33         actionButton.setEnabled( false );
34
35         // register action button listener
36         actionButton.addActionListener(
37
38            new ActionListener() { // anonymous inner class
39
40               public void actionPerformed( ActionEvent event )
41               {
42                  String action = event.getActionCommand();
43                  performAction( action );
44
45               } // end method actionPerformed
46
47            } // end anonymous inner class
48
49         ); // end call to addActionListener
50
51         // set up the cancel button
52         cancelButton = userInterface.getDoTask2Button();
53         cancelButton.setText( "Cancel" );
54         cancelButton.setEnabled( false );
55
56         // register cancel button listener
57         cancelButton.addActionListener(
58
59            new ActionListener() { // anonymous inner class
60
61               // clear the fields
62               public void actionPerformed( ActionEvent event )
63               {
64                  userInterface.clearFields();
65               }
66
67            } // end anonymous inner class
68
69         ); // end call to addActionListener
70
71         // set up the listener for the account field
72         fields = userInterface.getFields();
```

Fig. 17.21   Transaction-processing program. (Part 2 of 9.)

```
73          accountField = fields[ BankUI.ACCOUNT ];
74          accountField.addActionListener(
75
76             new ActionListener() { // anonymous inner class
77
78                public void actionPerformed( ActionEvent event )
79                {
80                   displayRecord( "0" );
81                }
82
83             } // end anonymous inner class
84
85          ); // end call to addActionListener
86
87          // create reference to the transaction field
88          transactionField = fields[ BankUI.TRANSACTION ];
89
90          // register transaction field listener
91          transactionField.addActionListener(
92
93             new ActionListener() { // anonymous inner class
94
95                // update the GUI fields
96                public void actionPerformed( ActionEvent event )
97                {
98                   displayRecord( transactionField.getText() );
99                }
100
101            } // end anonymous inner class
102
103         ); // end call to addActionListener
104
105         JMenuBar menuBar = new JMenuBar(); // set up the menu
106         setJMenuBar( menuBar );
107
108         JMenu fileMenu = new JMenu( "File" );
109         menuBar.add( fileMenu );
110
111         // set up menu item for adding a record
112         newItem = new JMenuItem( "New Record" );
113         newItem.setEnabled( false );
114
115         // register new item listener
116         newItem.addActionListener(
117
118            new ActionListener() { // anonymous inner class
119
120               public void actionPerformed( ActionEvent event )
121               {
122
123                  // set up the GUI fields for editing
124                  fields[ BankUI.ACCOUNT ].setEnabled( true );
125                  fields[ BankUI.FIRSTNAME ].setEnabled( true );
```

Fig. 17.21 Transaction-processing program. (Part 3 of 9.)

```
126                    fields[ BankUI.LASTNAME ].setEnabled( true );
127                    fields[ BankUI.BALANCE ].setEnabled( true );
128                    fields[ BankUI.TRANSACTION ].setEnabled( false );
129
130                    actionButton.setEnabled( true );
131                    actionButton.setText( "Create" );
132                    cancelButton.setEnabled( true );
133
134                    userInterface.clearFields(); // reset the textfields
135
136                } // end method actionPerformed
137
138            } // end anonymous inner class
139
140        ); // end call to addActionListener
141
142        // set up menu item for updating a record
143        updateItem = new JMenuItem( "Update Record" );
144        updateItem.setEnabled( false );
145
146        // register update item listener
147        updateItem.addActionListener(
148
149            new ActionListener() { // anonymous inner class
150
151                public void actionPerformed( ActionEvent event )
152                {
153                    // set up the GUI fields for editing
154                    fields[ BankUI.ACCOUNT ].setEnabled( true );
155                    fields[ BankUI.FIRSTNAME ].setEnabled( false );
156                    fields[ BankUI.LASTNAME ].setEnabled( false );
157                    fields[ BankUI.BALANCE ].setEnabled( false );
158                    fields[ BankUI.TRANSACTION ].setEnabled( true );
159
160                    actionButton.setEnabled( true );
161                    actionButton.setText( "Update" );
162                    cancelButton.setEnabled( true );
163
164                    userInterface.clearFields(); // reset the textfields
165
166                } // end method actionPerformed
167
168            } // end anonymous inner class
169
170        ); // end call to addActionListener
171
172        // set up menu item for deleting a record
173        deleteItem = new JMenuItem( "Delete Record" );
174        deleteItem.setEnabled( false );
175
176        // register delete item listener
177        deleteItem.addActionListener(
178
```

Fig. 17.21   Transaction-processing program. (Part 4 of 9.)

```
179                     new ActionListener() { // anonymous inner class
180
181                         public void actionPerformed( ActionEvent event )
182                         {
183                             // set up the GUI fields for editing
184                             fields[ BankUI.ACCOUNT ].setEnabled( true );
185                             fields[ BankUI.FIRSTNAME ].setEnabled( false );
186                             fields[ BankUI.LASTNAME ].setEnabled( false );
187                             fields[ BankUI.BALANCE ].setEnabled( false );
188                             fields[ BankUI.TRANSACTION ].setEnabled( false );
189
190                             actionButton.setEnabled( true );
191                             actionButton.setText( "Delete" );
192                             cancelButton.setEnabled( true );
193
194                             userInterface.clearFields(); // reset the textfields
195
196                         } // end method actionPerformed
197
198                     } // end anonymous inner class
199
200                 ); // end call to addActionListener
201
202                 // set up menu item for opening file
203                 openItem = new JMenuItem( "New/Open File" );
204
205                 // register open item listener
206                 openItem.addActionListener(
207
208                     new ActionListener() { // anonymous inner class
209
210                         public void actionPerformed( ActionEvent event )
211                         {
212                             // try to open the file
213                             if ( !openFile() )
214                                 return;
215
216                             // set up the menu items
217                             newItem.setEnabled( true );
218                             updateItem.setEnabled( true );
219                             deleteItem.setEnabled( true );
220                             openItem.setEnabled( false );
221
222                             // set the interface
223                             userInterface.setVisible( true );
224                             fields[ BankUI.ACCOUNT ].setEnabled( false );
225                             fields[ BankUI.FIRSTNAME ].setEnabled( false );
226                             fields[ BankUI.LASTNAME ].setEnabled( false );
227                             fields[ BankUI.BALANCE ].setEnabled( false );
228                             fields[ BankUI.TRANSACTION ].setEnabled( false );
229
230                         } // end method actionPerformed
231
```

Fig. 17.21 Transaction-processing program. (Part 5 of 9.)

```
232              } // end anonymous inner class
233
234         ); // end call to addActionListener
235
236         // set up menu item for exiting program
237         exitItem = new JMenuItem( "Exit" );
238
239         // register exit item listener
240         exitItem.addActionListener(
241
242            new ActionListener() { // anonyomus inner class
243
244               public void actionPerformed( ActionEvent event )
245               {
246                  try {
247                     dataFile.closeFile(); // close the file
248                  }
249
250                  catch ( IOException ioException ) {
251                     JOptionPane.showMessageDialog(
252                        TransactionProcessor.this, "Error closing file",
253                        "IO Error", JOptionPane.ERROR_MESSAGE );
254                  }
255
256                  finally {
257                     System.exit( 0 ); // exit the program
258                  }
259
260               } // end method actionPerformed
261
262            } // end anonymous inner class
263
264         ); // end call to addActionListener
265
266         // attach menu items to File menu
267         fileMenu.add( openItem );
268         fileMenu.add( newItem );
269         fileMenu.add( updateItem );
270         fileMenu.add( deleteItem );
271         fileMenu.addSeparator();
272         fileMenu.add( exitItem );
273
274         setSize( 400, 250  );
275         setVisible( true );
276
277      } // end constructor
278
279      public static void main( String args[] )
280      {
281         new TransactionProcessor();
282      }
283
```

Fig. 17.21   Transaction-processing program. (Part 6 of 9.)

```
284      // get the file name and open the file
285      private boolean openFile()
286      {
287         // display dialog so user can select file
288         JFileChooser fileChooser = new JFileChooser();
289         fileChooser.setFileSelectionMode( JFileChooser.FILES_ONLY );
290
291         int result = fileChooser.showOpenDialog( this );
292
293         // if user clicked Cancel button on dialog, return
294         if ( result == JFileChooser.CANCEL_OPTION )
295            return false;
296
297         // obtain selected file
298         File fileName = fileChooser.getSelectedFile();
299
300         // display error if file name invalid
301         if ( fileName == null || fileName.getName().equals( "" ) ) {
302            JOptionPane.showMessageDialog( this, "Invalid File Name",
303               "Bad File Name", JOptionPane.ERROR_MESSAGE );
304            return false;
305         }
306
307         try {
308            // call the helper method to open the file
309            dataFile = new FileEditor( fileName );
310         }
311
312         catch( IOException ioException ) {
313            JOptionPane.showMessageDialog( this, "Error Opening File",
314               "IO Error", JOptionPane.ERROR_MESSAGE );
315            return false;
316         }
317
318         return true;
319
320      } // end method openFile
321
322      // create, update or delete the record
323      private void performAction( String action )
324      {
325         try {
326
327            // get the textfield values
328            String[] values = userInterface.getFieldValues();
329
330            int accountNumber = Integer.parseInt( values[ BankUI.ACCOUNT ] );
331            String firstName = values[ BankUI.FIRSTNAME ];
332            String lastName = values[ BankUI.LASTNAME ];
333            double balance = Double.parseDouble( values[ BankUI.BALANCE ] );
334
335            if ( action.equals( "Create" ) )
336               dataFile.newRecord( accountNumber, // create a new record
```

Fig. 17.21 Transaction-processing program. (Part 7 of 9.)

```
337                     firstName, lastName, balance );
338
339           else if ( action.equals( "Update" ) )
340              dataFile.updateRecord( accountNumber, // update record
341                 firstName, lastName, balance );
342
343           else if ( action.equals( "Delete" ) )
344              dataFile.deleteRecord( accountNumber ); // delete record
345
346           else
347              JOptionPane.showMessageDialog( this, "Invalid Action",
348                 "Error executing action", JOptionPane.ERROR_MESSAGE );
349
350        } // end try
351
352        catch( NumberFormatException format ) {
353           JOptionPane.showMessageDialog( this, "Bad Input",
354              "Number Format Error", JOptionPane.ERROR_MESSAGE );
355        }
356
357        catch( IllegalArgumentException badAccount ) {
358           JOptionPane.showMessageDialog( this, badAccount.getMessage(),
359              "Bad Account Number", JOptionPane.ERROR_MESSAGE );
360        }
361        catch( IOException ioException ) {
362           JOptionPane.showMessageDialog( this, "Error writing to the file",
363              "IO Error", JOptionPane.ERROR_MESSAGE );
364        }
365
366     } // end method performAction
367
368     //  input a record in the textfields and update the balance
369     private void displayRecord( String transaction )
370     {
371        try {
372           // get the account number
373           int accountNumber = Integer.parseInt(
374              userInterface.getFieldValues()[ BankUI.ACCOUNT ] );
375
376           // get the associated record
377           RandomAccessAccountRecord record =
378              dataFile.getRecord( accountNumber );
379
380           if ( record.getAccount() == 0 )
381              JOptionPane.showMessageDialog( this, "Record does not exist",
382                 "Bad Account Number",  JOptionPane.ERROR_MESSAGE );
383
384           // get the transaction
385           double change = Double.parseDouble( transaction );
386
387           // create a string array to send to the textfields
388           String[] values = { String.valueOf( record.getAccount() ),
389              record.getFirstName(), record.getLastName(),
```

Fig. 17.21   Transaction-processing program. (Part 8 of 9.)

```
390                   String.valueOf( record.getBalance() + change ),
391                   "Charge(+) or payment (-)" };
392
393              userInterface.setFieldValues( values );
394
395          } // end try
396
397          catch( NumberFormatException format ) {
398              JOptionPane.showMessageDialog( this, "Bad Input",
399                  "Number Format Error", JOptionPane.ERROR_MESSAGE );
400          }
401
402          catch ( IllegalArgumentException badAccount ) {
403              JOptionPane.showMessageDialog( this, badAccount.getMessage(),
404                  "Bad Account Number", JOptionPane.ERROR_MESSAGE );
405          }
406
407          catch( IOException ioException ) {
408              JOptionPane.showMessageDialog( this, "Error reading the file",
409                  "IO Error", JOptionPane.ERROR_MESSAGE );
410          }
411
412      } // end method displayRecord
413
414  } // end class TransactionProcessor
```

Fig. 17.21   Transaction-processing program. (Part 9 of 9.)

Class `FileEditor` (Fig. 17.22) declares methods for manipulating records in a random-access file. Method `getRecord` (lines 26–41) reads the record with the given account number and stores its information in a `RandomAccessAccountRecord` object. Method `updateRecord` (lines 44–60) modifies the record with the given account number using the given `firstName`, `lastName` and `balance`. Method `newRecord` (lines 63–80) adds a new record to the file using the provided account number, first name, last name and balance. Method `deleteRecord` (lines 83–98) deletes the record with the given account number from the file.

```
1   // Fig. 17.22: FileEditor.java
2   // This class declares methods that manipulate bank account
3   // records in a random access file.
4   import java.io.*;
5
6   import com.deitel.jhtp5.ch17.RandomAccessAccountRecord;
7
8   public class FileEditor {
9
10      RandomAccessFile file; // reference to the file
11
```

Fig. 17.22   `FileEditor` class that encapsulates the file-processing capabilities required in Fig. 17.21. (Part 1 of 3.)

```
12      // open the file
13      public FileEditor( File fileName ) throws IOException
14      {
15          file = new RandomAccessFile( fileName, "rw" );
16      }
17
18      // close the file
19      public void closeFile() throws IOException
20      {
21          if ( file != null )
22              file.close();
23      }
24
25      // get a record from the file
26      public RandomAccessAccountRecord getRecord( int accountNumber )
27          throws IllegalArgumentException, NumberFormatException, IOException
28      {
29          RandomAccessAccountRecord record = new RandomAccessAccountRecord();
30
31          if ( accountNumber < 1 || accountNumber > 100 )
32              throw new IllegalArgumentException( "Out of range" );
33
34          // seek appropriate record in file
35          file.seek( ( accountNumber - 1 ) * RandomAccessAccountRecord.SIZE );
36
37          record.read( file );
38
39          return record;
40
41      } // end method getRecord
42
43      // update record in file
44      public void updateRecord( int accountNumber, String firstName,
45          String lastName, double balance )
46          throws IllegalArgumentException, IOException
47      {
48          RandomAccessAccountRecord record = getRecord( accountNumber );
49          if ( accountNumber == 0 )
50              throw new IllegalArgumentException( "Account does not exist" );
51
52          // seek appropriate record in file
53          file.seek( ( accountNumber - 1 ) * RandomAccessAccountRecord.SIZE );
54
55          record = new RandomAccessAccountRecord( accountNumber,
56              firstName, lastName, balance );
57
58          record.write( file ); // write updated record to file
59
60      } // end method updateRecord
61
```

Fig. 17.22 FileEditor class that encapsulates the file-processing capabilities required in Fig. 17.21. (Part 2 of 3.)

```
62   // add record to file
63   public void newRecord( int accountNumber, String firstName,
64      String lastName, double balance )
65      throws IllegalArgumentException, IOException
66   {
67      RandomAccessAccountRecord record = getRecord( accountNumber );
68
69      if ( record.getAccount() != 0 )
70         throw new IllegalArgumentException( "Account already exists" );
71
72      // seek appropriate record in file
73      file.seek( ( accountNumber - 1 ) * RandomAccessAccountRecord.SIZE );
74
75      record = new RandomAccessAccountRecord( accountNumber,
76         firstName, lastName, balance );
77
78      record.write( file ); // write record to file
79
80   } // end method newRecord
81
82   // delete record from file
83   public void deleteRecord( int accountNumber )
84      throws IllegalArgumentException, IOException
85   {
86      RandomAccessAccountRecord record = getRecord( accountNumber );
87
88      if ( record.getAccount() == 0 )
89         throw new IllegalArgumentException( "Account does not exist" );
90
91      // seek appropriate record in file
92      file.seek( ( accountNumber - 1 ) * RandomAccessAccountRecord.SIZE );
93
94      // create a blank record to write to the file
95      record = new RandomAccessAccountRecord();
96      record.write( file );
97
98   } // end method deleteRecord
99
100 } // end class EditFile
```

Fig. 17.22 FileEditor class that encapsulates the file-processing capabilities required in Fig. 17.21. (Part 3 of 3.)

17.13 New I/O APIs for the Java Platform

The newest release of Java (version 1.4) introduces many new features. Arguably the most important additions are the new I/O APIs found in package *java.nio* which make I/O more efficient. The main concepts of the new IO APIs are buffers, channels, regular expressions, file locks, character sets and non-blocking IO. We introduced regular expressions in Section 11.8. We discuss buffers, channels, file locks and character sets here. We will discuss non-blocking I/O in Chapter 18, Networking.

Buffers

Input and output operations are considerably slower than most other operations. *Buffers* speed up input and output operations by combining many slow, small I/O operations into a single large I/O operation. When reading data, a large chunk is read into a buffer. The program uses that data in smaller pieces without calling multiple input operations. When writing data, multiple pieces of data are written to a buffer. That buffer can be output with a single operation. Buffers replace many slow I/O operations with many fast operations on the buffer and a single slow I/O operation. A buffer is similar to an array in that it contains a fixed number of items of a certain primitive type. In fact many buffers store their data in a *backing array*.

Each buffer has four properties: *capacity*, *limit*, *position* and *mark*. The *capacity* of the buffer indicates how much data the buffer can hold. This value is set when the buffer is created and cannot be changed. It must be a non-negative integer.

The *limit* of a buffer is the current end of the buffer. The limit allows a buffer to be resized without creating a new buffer. Items cannot be read or written past this value. This property is useful for buffers that are reused. For example, a buffer with capacity 100 is filled with data. The program then reuses the buffer, but only writes 10 new items to it. The limit can be set to 10 so that data from the previous use is not accessed. The limit must always be a non-negative integer value, but can never be more than the capacity of the buffer.

The *position* of a buffer indicates the next element of the buffer that will be read or written. This value changes each time an item is read from or written to a buffer. The position must be a non-negative integer and will always be less than or equal to the limit of the buffer.

The *mark* is a remembered place in the buffer. The value of the mark is undefined when the buffer is created, but can be set at a later point. The mark is always a non-negative integer and must be less than or equal to the position. The mark allows the programmer to go back to a previous point in the buffer. The mark is used to remember a position in the buffer that the program may want to return to later.

There are eight buffer classes. The simplest buffer is a `ByteBuffer`. ByteBuffers are sequences of bytes. One example of this is a *wrapped byte array*, which is a `Byte-Buffer` implemented as a byte array. With a *direct buffer*, the Java Virtual Machine attempts to use native operating system I/O operations directly on the buffer which makes these operations faster. Direct buffers are more expensive to allocate so they should be used only when the buffer is large, long-lived or will be reused often.

Buffers also exist for each of the primitive types except `boolean`. There are classes `CharBuffer`, `DoubleBuffer`, `FloatBuffer`, `IntBuffer`, `LongBuffer` and `Short-Buffer`. The last buffer is class `MappedByteBuffer` which is a type of direct `Byte-Buffer` that is mapped directly to a region of a file.

Data is written to a buffer with a *put* operation and read from a buffer with a *get* operation. These operations can be *relative* or *absolute*. A relative *get* or *put* operation starts with the element at the buffer's current position. If the operation completes successfully, the position is updated to the element after the last item that was read or written. An absolute *get* or *put* operation takes the index of the starting element for that operation as an additional argument and does not update the buffer's position.

Buffers have four more operations that alter the state of the buffer. None of these operations modify the data in the buffer; they only affect the four buffer properties. A *clear* operation sets the buffer's position to 0 and the limit to the capacity. This operation is often used to make the buffer ready to read or write more data. A *flip* operation sets the limit to the current position and sets the position to 0. After data has been written to a buffer with a relative put, the position will point to the item immediately following the last item written. A flip operation will set the limit to the position (the end of the data) and the position to 0 (the beginning of the data), making the buffer ready to be read. A *rewind* operation sets the position to 0 without altering the limit. This operation is often used to prepare a buffer so that the data can be re-read. A *reset* operation sets the position to the mark. This operation is used to go back to a previous point in the buffer.

Channels

The second part of the new I/O API introduces *channels*. A channel is a connection to an I/O device that is designed to interact efficiently with buffers. Interface *Channel* declares only two methods `close` and `isOpen`. A channel is opened when it is created and cannot be reopened once it is closed.

The two most important subinterfaces of Channel are *ReadableByteChannel* and *WritableByteChannel*. Interface ReadableByteChannel declares method *read*; interface WritableByteChannel declares method *write*. Interface *ByteChannel* is a convenience interface that extends both ReadableByteChannel and Writeable-ByteChannel and therefore allows both reading and writing. Method `read` takes a Byte-Buffer argument which is filled with bytes from the channel. Method `write` takes a ByteBuffer whose contents are written to the channel.

Interface ScatteringByteChannel implements ReadableByteChannel and allows *scattering reads*. A scattering read is a read that populates a number of buffers with a single read operation. For example, a program needs to read two integers, three characters and one double from a channel. Instead of reading two `ints` into an IntBuffer, then reading three `chars` into a CharBuffer, then reading one `double` into a DoubleBuffer, the program can perform all three reads at once with a scattering read. Interface GatheringByteChannel implements WritableByteChannel and allows *gathering writes*. A gathering write takes data from a number of buffers and writes them to the channel in a single operation. Scattering reads and gathering writes further speed up input and output operations.

Class FileChannel represents a channel connected to a file. This class implements ByteChannel, ScatteringByteChannel and GatheringByteChannel. It allows read operations, write operations, scattering reads and gathering writes. A FileChannel is created by calling method getChannel on a FileInputStream object, a FileOutputStream object or a RandomAccessFile object. SocketChannels and ServerSocketChannels enable socket-based network communication. These are discussed in Chapter 18.

File Locks

A *file lock* restricts access to a portion of a file. Each file lock has an associated file channel, position within the file and a size. The file channel is a conduit to a physical file on disk. This is the file that will be locked. The position is the starting byte owned by the lock and the size is the number of bytes owned by the lock. These two variables define the portion of the file owned by that lock. Two locks are said to *overlap* if there is a byte that is owned by both locks.

A file lock can be *exclusive* or *shared*. An exclusive lock does not allow any overlapping locks to be created on its portion of the file. Exclusive locks are typically created by processes that write to a file. Shared locks can overlap portions of a file, but do not allow any exclusive locks that overlap that portion. Shared locks allow multiple processes to read the same file.

There are two methods that can be called by a `FileChannel` to acquire a file lock: `lock` and `tryLock`. Method `lock` is a *blocking* operation. This means that the method will return only when the lock has been acquired. Method `tryLock` is a *non-blocking* operation. Method `tryLock` will immediately return when it is called, but it does not guarantee that the lock has been acquired. If the lock cannot be acquired, the method returns `null`. We discuss other non-blocking operations in more detail in Chapter 18.

Software Engineering Observation 17.2

Operating systems handle file locks by process not by thread. This means that file locks cannot be used to coordinate access to a file between multiple Java threads. A different mechanism must be used.

Charsets

A character is a member of a set of symbols that are combined to express information. A *coded character set* is an assignment of numeric values to a set of characters. Unicode is one example of this and it is the set that Java uses. This means that the character 'A' is mapped to the number 65; the character 'r' is mapped to the number 114; and the character 'ñ' is mapped to the number 257. A *character-encoding scheme* is a mapping of members of a coded character set to a sequence of bytes. A *charset* is a combination of a coded character set and a character-encoding scheme. A charset maps a sequence of bytes to a sequence of characters.

Unicode is not the only way to map characters. For many years the standard in the United States was the ASCII coded character set. This coded character set contains only those characters used in the English language and certain special characters (e.g. the newline and tab character). Some character files are still stored with an ASCII charset, others with a Unicode charset and others with a different charset. Converting between two or more charsets is often difficult.

The new I/O API contains package `java.nio.charset` to deal with this problem. Most of the functionality is in three classes. An object of class *Charset* represents a particular charset. Method *decode* converts bytes in the charset (input as a `ByteBuffer`) to a `CharBuffer` containing Unicode characters. Two *encode* methods convert either a `CharBuffer` or a string of Unicode characters into bytes in the `Charset` (output as a `ByteBuffer`).

The other two classes in this package are *CharsetDecoder* and *CharsetEncoder*. Class `CharsetDecoder` represents a decoding object for transforming bytes of a particular charset to Unicode characters. It declares method `decode` and provides additional functionality. Class `CharsetEncoder` represents an encoding object for transforming Unicode characters to bytes of a particular charset. It declares method `encode` and provides additional functionality.

Charsets can only be decoded to and encoded from Unicode. To convert between two non-Unicode charsets requires two steps: decoding from one charset to Unicode then encoding from Unicode to another charset.

Examples

In this section, we present one example that uses the capabilities of NIO. The example (Fig. 17.23) demonstrates how to read and write data in a FileChannel using buffers. With the new I/O APIs, each stream has an underlying channel associated with it. We cannot instantiate a FileChannel directly, instead we must invoke method getChannel (declared in classes FileOutputStream, FileInputStream and RandomAccessFile).

Figure 17.23 uses ByteBuffers to read and write data in a FileChannel. The constructor (lines 11–22) creates a RandomAccessFile and gets the file channel by invoking RandomAccessFile method getChannel. The write operation is done in method writeToFile (lines 25–38). Line 28 creates a ByteBuffer with capacity 14 by invoking static method allocate of ByteBuffer. Line 31 invokes method putInt of Byte-Buffer to write the integer 100 to the buffer at its current position. After the writing, the buffer's current position increments by four. Line 32 invokes method putChar of Byte-Buffer to write the character 'A' to the buffer at its current position. After the writing, the buffer's current position increments by two. Line 33 invokes method putDouble of Byte-Buffer to write the double 12.34 to the buffer at its current position. After the writing, the buffer's current position increments by eight. To write the buffer to the channel, line 36 invokes method flip of ByteBuffer to set the limit to current position and the position to zero, and line 37 invokes method write of FileChannel to write bytes into the file channel. Method write takes a ByteBuffer, writes the bytes contained in the buffer to the channel and returns the number of bytes written. The file position is updated to the file position before writing plus the number of bytes written.

```
1   // Fig. 17.23: FileChannelTest.java
2   // Demonstrates FileChannel and ByteBuffer.
3   import java.io.*;
4   import java.nio.*;
5   import java.nio.channels.*;
6
7   public class FileChannelTest {
8      private FileChannel fileChannel;
9
10     // no-arg constructor
11     public FileChannelTest()
12     {
13        // create random access file and get file channel
14        try {
15           RandomAccessFile file = new RandomAccessFile( "Test", "rw" );
16           fileChannel = file.getChannel();
17        }
18        catch ( IOException ioException ) {
19           ioException.printStackTrace();
20        }
21
22     } // end constructor FileChannelTest
23
```

Fig. 17.23   Write buffers to and read buffers from FileChannel. (Part 1 of 3.)

```java
24    // write to writeChannel
25    public void writeToFile() throws IOException
26    {
27       // create buffer for writing
28       ByteBuffer buffer = ByteBuffer.allocate( 14 );
29
30       // write an int, a char and a double to buffer
31       buffer.putInt( 100 );
32       buffer.putChar( 'A' );
33       buffer.putDouble( 12.34 );
34
35       // flip buffer and write buffer to fileChannel
36       buffer.flip();
37       fileChannel.write( buffer );
38    }
39
40    // read from readChannel
41    public void readFromFile() throws IOException
42    {
43       String content = "";
44
45       // create buffer for read
46       ByteBuffer buffer = ByteBuffer.allocate( 14 );
47
48       // read buffer from fileChannel
49       fileChannel.position( 0 );
50       fileChannel.read( buffer );
51
52       // flip buffer for reading
53       buffer.flip();
54
55       // obtain content
56       content += buffer.getInt() + ", " + buffer.getChar() + ", " +
57          buffer.getDouble();
58
59       System.out.println( "File contains: " + content );
60
61       // close fileChannel
62       fileChannel.close();
63
64    } // end method readFromFile
65
66    public static void main( String[] args )
67    {
68       FileChannelTest application = new FileChannelTest();
69
70       // write to file and then read from file
71       try {
72          application.writeToFile();
73          application.readFromFile();
74       }
75       catch ( IOException ioException ) {
76          ioException.printStackTrace();
```

Fig. 17.23   Write buffers to and read buffers from FileChannel. (Part 2 of 3.)

```
77            }
78         }
79
80      } // end class FileChannelTest
```

```
File contains: 100, A, 12.34
```

Fig. 17.23 Write buffers to and read buffers from `FileChannel`. (Part 3 of 3.)

The read operation is done in method `readFromFile` (lines 41–64). Line 46 creates a buffer with capacity 14. Remember that after writing, the channel is positioned after the last written byte. To read from the beginning, line 49 invokes method `position` of `FileChannel` to set the file position to 0. This is equivalent to calling method `seek` of a `RandomAccessFile`. Line 50 invokes method `read` of `FileChannel` to read bytes from the channel into a byte buffer. Method `read` fills its `ByteBuffer` argument with bytes from the channel and returns the number of bytes read. After the reading, the position in each byte buffer is set to the place after the last read byte. To read the buffer from the beginning, line 53 invokes method `flip` of `ByteBuffer` to set the position to zero. Lines 56–57 invoke method `getInt` to obtain an integer from the byte buffer, method `getChar` to obtain a character from the byte buffer and method `getDouble` to obtain a double from the byte buffer. Line 62 invokes method `close` of `FileChannel` to close the file channel.

New I/O API Web Resources

This section presented several of Java's New I/O capabilities. For more information on these APIs, visit the following Web sites:

`http://www.onjava.com/pub/a/onjava/2002/10/02/javanio.html`
This *OnJava* article lists the top ten new things you can do with the new I/O APIs.

`http://www.javaworld.com/javaworld/jw-09-2001/jw-0907-merlin.html`
This *JavaWorld* article details some of the new I/O capabilities.

`http://developer.java.sun.com/developer/technicalArticles/releases/nio/`
This article discusses the new I/O functionality found in the new I/O APIs.

`http://java.sun.com/j2se/1.4.1/docs/api/java/nio/package-summary.html`
This web site contains the API documentation for package `java.nio`.

SUMMARY

- All data items processed by a computer are reduced to combinations of zeros and ones. The smallest data item in a computer (a bit) can assume the value 0 or the value 1.

- Digits, letters and special symbols are called characters. The set of all characters used to write programs and represent data items on a particular computer is called that computer's character set. Every character in a computer's character set is represented as a pattern of 1s and 0s. (Characters in Java are Unicode characters composed of two bytes.)

- A field is a group of characters (or bytes) that conveys meaning.

- A record is a group of related fields.

- Class `File` enables programs to obtain information about a file or directory.

- Java views each file as a sequential stream of bytes. The programmer must structure a file appropriately to meet the requirements of an application.

- Each file ends in some machine-dependent form of end-of-file marker.

- Streams provide communication connections between programs and files, memory or other programs across a network.

- Programs use classes from package `java.io` to perform input and output.

- Files are opened by instantiating stream classes `FileInputStream`, `FileOutputStream`, `RandomAccessFile`, `FileReader` and `FileWriter`.

- `InputStream` and `OutputStream` are `abstract` classes that declare methods for performing input and output, respectively. File input/output can be performed with `FileInputStream` (a subclass of `InputStream`) and `FileOutputStream` (a subclass of `OutputStream`).

- Pipes are synchronized communication connections between threads. A pipe is established between two threads. One thread sends data to another by writing to a `PipedOutputStream`. The target thread reads information from the pipe via a `PipedInputStream`.

- A `PrintStream` is a text-based output stream. `System.out` and `System.err` are `PrintStream`s.

- Reading data as raw bytes is fast but crude. Usually, programs read data as aggregates of bytes that form objects or values of primitive types, such as `int` and `double`.

- Interface `DataInput` is implemented by classes `DataInputStream` and `RandomAccessFile`; each reads primitive-type values from a stream.

- The `DataOutput` interface is implemented by classes `DataOutputStream` and `RandomAccessFile`; each writes primitive-type values to an `OutputStream`.

- Buffering is an I/O-performance-enhancement technique. With a `BufferedOutputStream`, each output statement does not necessarily result in an actual physical transfer of data to the output device. Rather, each output operation is directed to a region in memory called a buffer that is large enough to hold the data of many output operations. Then, actual output to the output device is performed in one large physical output operation each time the buffer fills. The output operations directed to the output buffer in memory are often called logical output operations.

- With a `BufferedInputStream`, many "logical" chunks of data from a file are read as one large physical input operation into a memory buffer. As a program requests each new chunk of data, it is taken from the buffer. (This procedure is sometimes referred to as a logical input operation.) When the buffer is empty, the next physical input operation from the input device is performed to read in the next group of "logical" chunks of data. Thus, the number of physical input operations is small compared with the number of read requests issued by the program.

- With a `BufferedOutputStream`, a partially filled buffer can be forced out to the device at any time with an explicit call to method `flush`.

- Stream objects can be wrapped to create stream objects with combined functionality, such as writing objects to a file.

- The `ObjectInput` interface is similar to the `DataInput` interface, but includes additional methods to read `Object`s from `InputStream`s.

- The `ObjectOutput` interface is similar to the `DataOutput` interface, but includes additional methods to write `Object`s to `OutputStream`s.

- The `ObjectInputStream` and `ObjectOutputStream` classes implement the `ObjectInput` and `ObjectOutput` interfaces, respectively.

- A `RandomAccessFile` is useful for direct-access applications such as transaction-processing applications, airline-reservations systems and point-of-sale systems.

- With a sequential-access file, each successive input/output request reads or writes the next consecutive set of data in the file.

- With a random-access file, each successive input/output request might be directed to any part of the file, perhaps a section widely separated from the part of the file referenced in the previous request.

- A ByteArrayInputStream performs its inputs from a byte array in memory. A ByteArray-OutputStream outputs to a byte array in memory.

- A StringBufferInputStream (a subclass of abstract class InputStream) inputs from a StringBuffer object.

- A SequenceInputStream enables several InputStreams to be concatenated so that the program will see the group as one continuous InputStream. As the end of each input stream is reached, the stream is closed, and the next stream in the sequence is opened.

- Classes BufferedReader and BufferedWriter enable efficient buffering for character-based streams. Classes CharArrayReader and CharArrayWriter read and write, respectively, a stream of characters to a character array. Classes FileReader and FileWriter read and write, respectively, characters to a file. Classes PipedReader and PipedWriter are piped-character streams. Classes StringReader and StringWriter read and write, respectively, characters to strings. A PrintWriter writes characters to a stream.

- Files are opened for output by creating a FileOutputStream class object. One argument is passed to the constructor—the filename. Existing files are truncated, and all data in the files are lost. Nonexistent files are created.

- A program can process no files, one file or several files. Each file has a unique name and is associated with an appropriate file stream object. All file-processing methods must refer to a file with the appropriate object.

- A file-position pointer indicates the position in the file from which the next input is to occur or at which the next output is to be placed.

- A convenient way to implement random-access files is by using only fixed-length records. Using this technique, a program can quickly calculate the exact location of a record relative to the beginning of the file. Data can be inserted in a random-access file without destroying other data in the file. Data can also be updated or deleted without rewriting the entire file.

- Many buffers store their data in a backing array.

- Each buffer has four fundamental properties—capacity, limit, position and mark.

- The capacity of the buffer indicates how much data the buffer can hold.

- The limit of a buffer is the current end of the valid data in a buffer. Items cannot be read or written past this value.

- The position of a buffer is the next element of the buffer that will be read or written. This value will change each time an item is read from or written to a buffer.

- The mark is a remembered place in the buffer. The value of mark is undefined when the buffer is created, but can be set at a later point.

- The simplest buffer is a ByteBuffer. A non-direct ByteBuffer is backed by an array. With a direct ByteBuffer, the JVM attempts to use native operating system I/O operations.

- Buffers also exist for each of the primitive types other than boolean. There are classes CharBuffer, DoubleBuffer, FloatBuffer, IntBuffer, LongBuffer and ShortBuffer.

- MappedByteBuffers are a type of direct buffer which is mapped directly to a region of a file.

- Data is written to a buffer with a put operation and read from a buffer with a get operation.

- A relative get or put operation starts with the element at the buffer's position and the position is updated to the element after the last item that was read or written.

- An absolute get or put operation takes an index which is the starting element for that operation. An absolute get or put operation does not update the buffer's position.

- A clear operation sets the buffer's state to the original configuration. The buffer's limit is set to its capacity and the buffer's position is set to 0.
- A flip operation sets the limit to the current position and sets the position to 0.
- A rewind operation sets the position to 0 without altering the limit.
- A reset operation sets the position to the mark.
- A channel is a connection to an I/O device that is designed to interact efficiently with buffers. A channel is automatically opened when it is created and cannot be reopened once it is closed.
- Interface `ReadableByteChannel` declares method `read`; interface `WritableByteChannel` declares method `write`. Interface `ByteChannel` is a convenience interface that extends both `ReadableByteChannel` and `WriteableByteChannel`.
- Method `read` takes a `ByteBuffer` argument which is filled with bytes from the channel.
- Method `write` takes a `ByteBuffer` whose content is written to the channel.
- Interface `ScatteringByteChannel` implements `ReadableByteChannel` and allows scattering reads. A scattering read is a read that populates a number of buffers with a single read operation.
- Interface `GatheringByteChannel` implements `WritableByteChannel` and allows gathering writes. A gathering write takes data from a number of buffers and writes them to the channel in a single operation.
- Class `FileChannel` represents a channel connected to a file.
- A file lock restricts access to a portion of a file. The position is the starting byte owned by the lock and the size is the number of bytes owned by the lock.
- An exclusive lock does not allow any overlapping locks to be created on its portion of the file.
- Shared locks can overlap portions of a file, but do not allow any exclusive locks that overlap that portion.
- Method `lock` is a blocking operation. This means that the method will return only when the lock has been acquired.
- Method `tryLock` is a non-blocking operation. Method `tryLock` will immediately return when it is called, but it does not guarantee that the lock has been acquired.
- A charset maps a sequence of bytes to a sequence of characters.
- An object of class `CharSet` represents one of the charsets.
- Method `decode` converts bytes in the charset (input as a `ByteBuffer`) to a `CharBuffer` containing Unicode characters.
- Two `encode` methods convert either a `CharBuffer` or a string of Unicode characters into bytes in the `Charset` (output as a `ByteBuffer`).
- Class `CharsetDecoder` represents a decoding object for transforming a particular character set to Unicode characters.
- Class `CharsetEncoder` represents an encoding object for transforming Unicode characters to a particular character set.
- To convert between two non-Unicode character sets requires two steps: encoding from one character set to Unicode then decoding from Unicode to another character set.

TERMINOLOGY

absolute *get* operation
absolute path
absolute *put* operation

alphabetic field
alphanumeric field
backing array

output stream
OutputStream class
OutputStreamWriter class
overlapping locks
partially filled buffer
persistent data
pipe
PipedInputStream class
PipedOutputStream class
PipedReader class
PipedWriter class
position
PrintStream class
PrintWriter class
random-access file
RandomAccessFile class
read method
ReadableByteChannel
"r" file-open mode
readBoolean method
readByte method
readChar method
readDouble method
Reader class
readFloat method
readFully method
readInt method
readLong method
readObject method
readShort method
readUnsignedByte method
readUnsignedShort method
record
record key
relative *get* operation
relative path
relative *put* operation
reset operation

rewind operation
"rw" file-open mode
scattering read
ScatteringByteChannel
seek method
SequenceInputStream class
sequential-access file
Serializable interface
setFileSelectionMode method
shared lock
ShortBuffer
showOpenDialog method
showSaveDialog method
standard output
StringReader class
StringWriter class
System.err (standard error stream)
System.in (standard input stream)
System.out (standard output stream)
transaction-processing systems
truncate an existing file
tryLock
Unicode character set
wrapping streams
WritableByteChannel
write method
writeBoolean method
writeByte method
writeBytes method
writeChar method
writeChars method
writeDouble method
writeFloat method
writeInt method
writeLong method
writeObject method
Writer class
writeShort method

SELF-REVIEW EXERCISES

17.1 Fill in the blanks in each of the following statements:

a) Ultimately, all data items processed by a computer are reduced to combinations of _____ and _____.

b) The smallest data item a computer can process is called a(n) _____.

c) A(n) _____ is a group of related records.

d) Digits, letters and special symbols are referred to as _____.

e) A group of related files is called a _____.

f) Method _____ of the file stream classes FileOutputStream, FileInput-Stream, and RandomAccessFile closes a file.

g) RandomAccessFile method _____ reads an integer from the specified stream.

h) RandomAccessFile method _____ reads a line of text from the specified stream.

i) RandomAccessFile method _____ sets the file-position pointer to a specific location in a file for input or output.

17.2 Determine which of the given statements are *true* and which are *false*. If *false*, explain why.

a) The programmer must explicitly create System.in, System.out and System.err.

b) If the file-position pointer points to a location in a sequential file other than the beginning of the file, the file must be closed and reopened to read from the beginning of the file.

c) It is not necessary to search all the records in a random-access file in order to find a record.

d) Records in random-access files must be of uniform length.

e) Method seek must seek relative to the beginning of a file.

17.3 Complete the following tasks, assume that each applies to the same program:

a) Write a statement that opens file "oldmast.dat" for input; use ObjectInputStream object inOldMaster to wrap a FileInputStream object.

b) Write a statement that opens file "trans.dat" for input; use ObjectInputStream object inTransaction to wrap a FileInputStream object.

c) Write a statement that opens file "newmast.dat" for output (and creation); use ObjectOutputStream object outNewMaster to wrap a FileOutputStream.

d) Write a statement that reads a record from the file "oldmast.dat". The record is an object of class AccountRecord; use ObjectInputStream object inOldMaster.

e) Write a statement that reads a record from the file "trans.dat". The record is an object of class TransactionRecord; use ObjectInputStream object inTransaction.

f) Write a statement that outputs a record to the file "newmast.dat". The record is an object of type AccountRecord; use ObjectOutputStream object outNewMaster.

17.4 Find the error in each block of codes and show how to correct it.

a) Assume account, company and amount are declared.

```
ObjectOutputStream outputStream;

outputStream.writeInt( account );
outputStream.writeChars( company );
outputStream.writeDouble( amount );
```

b) The given statements should read a record from the file "payables.dat". The ObjectInputStream object inPayable refers to this file, and FileInputStream object inReceivable refers to the file "receivables.dat".

```
account = inReceivable.readInt();
companyID = inReceivable.readLong();
amount = inReceivable.readDouble();
```

ANSWERS TO SELF-REVIEW EXERCISES

17.1 a) ones, zeros.   b) bit.   c) file.   d) characters.   e) database.   f) close.   g) readInt.
h) readLine. i) seek.

17.2 a) False. These three streams are created automatically for the programmer.

b) True.

c) True.

d) False. Records in a random-access file are normally of uniform length.

e) True.

17.3 a) `ObjectInputStream inOldMaster = new ObjectInputStream(`
`        new FileInputStream( "oldmast.dat" ) );`

b) `ObjectInputStream inTransaction = new ObjectInputStream(`
    `new FileInputStream( "trans.dat" ) );`
c) `ObjectOutputStream outNewMaster = new ObjectOutputStream(`
    `new FileOutputStream( "newmast.dat" ) );`
d) `accountRecord = ( AccountRecord ) inOldMaster.getObject();`
e) `transactionRecord = (TransactionRecord) inTransaction.getObject();`
f) `outNewMaster.writeObject( newAccountRecord );`

17.4 a) Error: The file has not been opened before the attempt is made to output data to the stream.
       Correction: Create a new `ObjectOutputStream` object wrapping a
       `FileOutputStream` object in order to open the file for output.
   b) Error: The incorrect `FileInputStream` object is being used to read from file "pay-
       ables.dat".
       Correction: Use object `inPayable` to refer to "payables.dat".

EXERCISES

17.5 Fill in the blanks in each of the following statements:
   a) Computers store large amounts of data on secondary storage devices as _____.
   b) A(n) _____ is composed of several fields.
   c) To facilitate the retrieval of specific records from a file, one field in each record is chosen
       as a(n) _____.
   d) The majority of information stored in computer systems is stored in _____ files.
   e) The standard stream objects are _____, _____ and _____.

17.6 Determine which of the given statements are *true* and which are *false*. If *false*, explain why.
   a) The impressive functions performed by computers essentially involve the manipulation
       of zeros and ones.
   b) People specify programs and data items as characters; computers then manipulate and
       process these characters as groups of zeros and ones.
   c) A person's five-digit zip code is an example of a numeric field.
   d) A person's street address is generally considered to be an alphabetic field.
   e) Data items represented in computers form a data hierarchy in which data items become
       larger and more complex as we progress from fields to characters to bits and so on.
   f) A record key identifies a record as belonging to a particular field.
   g) Companies store all their information in a single file in order to facilitate computer pro-
       cessing of the information. When a program creates a file, the file is automatically re-
       tained by the computer for future reference.

17.7 Self-Review Exercise 17.3 asks the reader to write a series of single statements. Actually,
these statements form the core of an important type of file-processing program, namely, a file-matching program. In commercial data processing, it is common to have several files in each application
system. In an accounts receivable system, for example, there is generally a master file containing detailed information about each customer, such as the customer's name, address, telephone number,
outstanding balance, credit limit, discount terms, contract arrangements and possibly a condensed history of recent purchases and cash payments.
   a) As transactions occur (i.e., sales are made and payments arrive in the mail), information
       about them is entered into a file. At the end of each business period (i.e., a month for some
       companies, a week for others, and a day in some cases), the file of transactions (called
       "trans.dat" in Self-Review Exercise 17.3) is applied to the master file (called "old-
       mast.dat" in Self-Review Exercise 17.3) to update each account's purchase and payment
       record. During an update, the master file is rewritten as the file "newmast.dat", which is
       then used at the end of the next business period to begin the updating process again.

b) File-matching programs must deal with certain problems that do not exist in single-file programs. For example, a match does not always occur. A customer on the master file might not have made any purchases or cash payments in the current business period; therefore, no record for this customer will appear on the transaction file. Similarly, a customer who did make some purchases or cash payments could have just moved to this community, and the company might not have had a chance to create a master record for this customer.

c) Use the statements in Self-Review Exercise 17.3 as a basis for writing a complete file-matching accounts receivable program. Use the account number on each file as the record key for matching purposes. Assume that each file is a sequential file with records stored in increasing account-number order.

d) When a match occurs (i.e., records with the same account number appear on both the master file and the transaction file), add the dollar amount on the transaction file to the current balance on the master file, and write the `"newmast.dat"` record. (Assume that purchases are indicated by positive amounts on the transaction file and payments by negative amounts.) When there is a master record for a particular account, but no corresponding transaction record, merely write the master record to `"newmast.dat"`. When there is a transaction record, but no corresponding master record, print to a log file the message `"Unmatched transaction record for account number …"` (fill in the account number from the transaction record).

e) The log file should be a text file named `"log.txt"`. This file should be created using `PrintStream` object `logFile` to wrap a `FileOutputStream`. Error messages can be output to this file, using method `println` of class `PrintStream`.

17.8　　After writing the program of Exercise 17.7, write a simple program to create some test data for checking out the program. Use the sample account data in Fig. 17.24 and Fig. 17.25. Run the program of Exercise 17.7, using the files of test data created in this exercise. Print the new master file. Check that the accounts have been updated correctly.

Master file Account number	Name	Balance
100	Alan Jones	348.17
300	Mary Smith	27.19
500	Sam Sharp	0.00
700	Suzy Green	-14.22

Fig. 17.24 Sample data for master file.

Transaction file Account number	Transaction amount
100	27.14
300	62.11
400	100.56
900	82.17

Fig. 17.25 Sample data for transaction file.

17.9   It is possible (and actually common) to have several transaction records with the same record key. This situation occurs when a particular customer makes several purchases and cash payments during a business period. Rewrite your accounts receivable file-matching program of Exercise 17.7 to provide for the possibility of handling several transaction records with the same record key. Modify the test data of Exercise 17.8 to include the additional transaction records in Fig. 17.26.

17.10   You are the owner of a hardware store and need to keep an inventory that can tell you what different tools you have, how many of each you have on hand and the cost of each one. Write a program that initializes the random-access file `"hardware.dat"` to 100 empty records, lets you input the data concerning each tool, enables you to list all your tools, lets you delete a record for a tool that you no longer have and lets you update *any* information in the file. The tool identification number should be the record number. Use the information in Fig. 17.27 to start your file.

17.11   (*Telephone-Number Word Generator*) Standard telephone keypads contain the digits zero through nine. The numbers two through nine each have three letters associated with them. (See Fig. 17.28.) Many people find it difficult to memorize phone numbers, so they use the correspondence between digits and letters to develop seven-letter words that correspond to their phone numbers. For example, a person whose telephone number is 686-2377 might use the correspondence indicated in Fig. 17.28 to develop the seven-letter word "NUMBERS." Each seven-letter word corresponds to exactly one seven-digit telephone number. The restaurant wishing to increase its takeout business could surely do so with the number 825-3688 (i.e., "TAKEOUT").

Each seven-letter phone number corresponds to many separate seven-letter words. Unfortunately, most of these words represent unrecognizable juxtapositions of letters. It is possible, however, that the owner of a barbershop would be pleased to know that the shop's telephone number, 424-7288, corresponds to "HAIRCUT." The owner of a liquor store would, no doubt, be delighted to find that the

Account number	Dollar amount	
300	83.89	
700	80.78	
700	1.53	

Fig. 17.26   Additional transaction records.

Record #	Tool name	Quantity	Cost
3	Electric sander	18	35.99
19	Hammer	128	10.00
26	Jigsaw	16	14.25
39	Lawn mower	10	79.50
56	Power saw	8	89.99
76	Screwdriver	236	4.99
81	Sledgehammer	32	19.75
88	Wrench	65	6.48

Fig. 17.27   Data for Exercise 17.10.

Digit	Letters
2	A B C
3	D E F
4	G H I
5	J K L
6	M N O
7	P R S
8	T U V
9	W X Y

Fig. 17.28 Telephone keypad digits and letters.

store's number, 233-7226, corresponds to "BEERCAN." A veterinarian with the phone number 738-2273 would be pleased to know that the number corresponds to the letters "PETCARE." An automotive dealership would be pleased to know that the dealership number, 639-2277, corresponds to "NEW-CARS."

Write a program that, given a seven-digit number, uses a PrintStream object to write to a file every possible seven-letter word combination corresponding to that number. There are 2187 (3^7) such combinations. Avoid phone numbers with the digits 0 and 1.

17.12 Figure 7.8 contains an array of survey responses that is hard coded into the program. Suppose we wish to process survey results that are stored in a file. This exercise requires two separate programs. First, create an application that prompts the user for survey responses and outputs each response to a file. Use a DataOutputStream wrapping a FileOutputStream to create a file called numbers.dat. Each integer should be written using DataOutputStream method writeInt. Then modify the program of Fig. 7.8 to read the survey responses from numbers.dat. The responses should be read from the file by using a DataInputStream wrapping a FileInputStream. Method readInt from class DataInputStream should be used to input one integer from the file at a time. The program should continue to read responses until it reaches the end of file, at which point method readInt throws an EOFException. The results should be output to a text file and displayed in a window. Use a PrintWriter object wrapping a FileWriter to write to the file "output.txt". Use method print from class PrintWriter to output a string to the file.

17.13 Modify Exercise 14.17 to allow the user to output the array of MyShape objects to a file and to read in a file. Use an ObjectOutputStream wrapping a FileOutputStream to write to the file and an ObjectInputStream wrapping a FileInputStream to read from the file. Output the number of shapes currently stored in the array with method writeInt. Then output the array of shapes. The integer will be used to keep track of the next available position in the array so that more shapes can be added when the array is read back from the file. When reading from the file, read the integer with method readInt. Note that the integer and array must be read in the same order as they are written.

18

Networking

Objectives

- To understand Java networking with URLs, sockets and datagrams.
- To implement Java networking applications by using sockets and datagrams.
- To understand how to implement Java clients and servers that communicate with one another.
- To understand how to implement network-based collaborative applications.
- To construct a multithreaded server.

If the presence of electricity can be made visible in any part of a circuit, I see no reason why intelligence may not be transmitted instantaneously by electricity.
Samuel F. B. Morse

Mr. Watson, come here, I want to see you.
Alexander Graham Bell

What networks of railroads, highways and canals were in another age, the networks of telecommunications, information and computerization ... are today.
Bruno Kreisky

Science may never come up with a better office-communication system than the coffee break.
Earl Wilson

It's currently a problem of access to gigabits through punybaud.
J. C. R. Licklider

Outline

18.1 Introduction

There is much excitement over the Internet and the World Wide Web. The Internet ties the "information world" together. The World Wide Web makes the Internet easy to use and gives it the flair and sizzle of multimedia. Organizations see the Internet and the Web as crucial to their information-systems strategies. Java provides a number of built-in networking capabilities that make it easy to develop Internet-based and Web-based applications. Java can enable programs to search the world for information and to collaborate with programs running on other computers internationally, nationally or just within an organization. Java can enable applets and applications to communicate with one another (subject to security constraints).

Networking is a massive and complex topic. Computer science and computer engineering students will typically take a full-semester, upper level course in computer networking and continue with further study at the graduate level. Java provides a rich complement of networking capabilities and will likely be used as an implementation vehicle in computer networking courses. In *Java How to Program, Fifth Edition*, we introduce a portion of Java's networking concepts and capabilities. For more advanced networking capabilities, refer to our book *Advanced Java 2 Platform How to Program*.

Java's networking capabilities are grouped into several packages. The fundamental networking capabilities are declared by classes and interfaces of package *java.net*, through which Java offers *stream-based communications* that enable applications to view networking as streams of data. The classes and interfaces of package java.net also offer *packet-based communications* for transmitting individual *packets* of information—this is commonly used to transmit audio and video over the Internet. In this chapter, we show how to create and manipulate sockets and how to communicate with packets of data.

Our discussion of networking focuses on both sides of a *client-server relationship*. The *client* requests that some action be performed, and the *server* performs the action and responds to the client. A common implementation of the request-response model is between World Wide Web browsers and World Wide Web servers. When a user selects a Web site to browse through a browser (the client application), a request is sent to the appropriate Web server (the server application). The server normally responds to the client by sending an appropriate HTML Web page.

We introduce Java's *socket-based communications,* which enable applications to view networking as if it were file I/O—a program can read from a *socket* or write to a socket as simply as reading from a file or writing to a file. We show how to create and manipulate sockets. Java provides *stream sockets* and *datagram sockets*. With *stream sockets*, a process establishes a *connection* to another process. While the connection is in place, data flows between the processes in continuous *streams*. Stream sockets are said to provide a *connection-oriented service*. The protocol used for transmission is the popular *TCP (Transmission Control Protocol)*.

With *datagram sockets*, individual *packets* of information are transmitted. This is not the right protocol for everyday programmers, because, unlike TCP, the protocol used—*UDP*, the *User Datagram Protocol*—is a *connectionless service*, and it does not guarantee that packets arrive in any particular order. In fact, packets can be lost, can be duplicated and can even arrive out of sequence. So, with UDP, significant extra programming is required on the programmer's part to deal with these problems (if the programmer chooses to do so). UDP is most appropriate for network applications that do not require the error checking and reliability of TCP. Stream sockets and the TCP protocol will be more desirable for the vast majority of Java programmers.

Performance Tip 18.1

Connectionless services generally offer greater performance, but less reliability than connection-oriented services.

Portability Tip 18.1

TCP, UDP and related protocols enable a great variety of heterogeneous computer systems (i.e., computer systems with different processors and different operating systems) to intercommunicate.

The chapter includes a case study in which we implement a client/server chat application similar to the instant-messaging services popular on the Web today. The program incorporates many networking techniques introduced in this chapter. The program also introduces *multicasting*, in which a server can *publish* information and clients can *subscribe* to that information. Each time the server publishes more information, all subscribers receive that information. Throughout the examples of this chapter, we will see that many of the networking details are handled by the Java classes we use.

18.2 Manipulating URLs

The Internet offers many protocols. The *Hypertext Transfer Protocol* (*HTTP*) that forms the basis of the World Wide Web uses *URIs* (*Uniform Resource Identifiers*) to identify data on the Internet. URIs that specify the locations of documents are called *URLs* (*Uniform Resource Locators*). Common URLs refer to files or directories and can reference objects that perform complex tasks, such as database lookups and Internet searches. If you know the URL of publicly available HTML documents anywhere on the Web, you can access that data through HTTP. Java makes it easy to manipulate URLs. Using a URL that refers to the exact location of a resource (such as a Web page) as an argument to the *showDocument* method of interface *AppletContext* causes the browser in which the applet is executing to display the resource at the specified URL. The applet of Fig. 18.1 and Fig. 18.2 demonstrates simple networking capabilities. The applet enables the user to select a Web page from a JList and causes the browser to display the corresponding page. In this example, the networking is performed by the browser.

This applet takes advantage of *applet parameters* specified in the HTML document that invokes the applet. When browsing the World Wide Web, often you will come across applets that are in the public domain—you can use them free of charge on your own Web pages (normally in exchange for crediting the applet's creator). One common feature of such applets is the ability to customize the applet via parameters that are supplied from the HTML file that invokes the applet. For example, Fig. 18.1 contains the HTML that invokes the applet SiteSelector in Fig. 18.2.

The HTML document contains eight parameters specified with the *param element*—these lines must appear between the starting and ending applet tags. The applet can read these values and use them to customize itself. Any number of param tags can appear between the starting and ending applet tags. Each parameter has a *name* and a *value*. Applet method *getParameter* retrieves the value associated with a specific parameter name and returns the value as a string. The argument passed to getParameter is a string containing the name of the parameter in the param element. In this example, parameters represent the title of each Web site the user can select and the location of each site. Any number of parameters can be specified for this applet. However, these parameters must be

```
1   <html>
2   <title>Site Selector</title>
3   <body>
4      <applet code = "SiteSelector.class" width = "300" height = "75">
5         <param name = "title0" value = "Java Home Page">
6         <param name = "location0" value = "http://java.sun.com/">
7         <param name = "title1" value = "Deitel">
8         <param name = "location1" value = "http://www.deitel.com/">
9         <param name = "title2" value = "JGuru">
10        <param name = "location2" value = "http://www.jGuru.com/">
11        <param name = "title3" value = "JavaWorld">
12        <param name = "location3" value = "http://www.javaworld.com/">
13     </applet>
14  </body>
15  </html>
```

Fig. 18.1   HTML document to load SiteSelector applet.

named `title#`, where the value of # starts at 0 and increments by one for each new title. Each title should have a corresponding location parameter of the form `location#`, where the value of # starts at 0 and increments by one for each new location. The statement

```
String title = getParameter( "title0" );
```

gets the value associated with parameter `"title0"` and assigns it to reference `title`. If there is not a `param` tag containing the specified parameter, `getParameter` returns `null`.

The applet (Fig. 18.2) obtains from the HTML document (Fig. 18.1) the choices that will be displayed in the applet's `JList`. Class `SiteSelector` uses a *HashMap* (package *java.util*) to store the World Wide Web site names and URLs. A `HashMap` stores *key/value pairs*. The program uses the *key* to store and retrieve the associated *value* in the `HashMap`. In this example, the *key* is the string in the `JList` that represents the Web site name, and the value is a URL object that stores the location of the Web site to display in the browser. Class `HashMap` provides two methods of importance in this example—*put* and *get*. Method `put` takes two arguments—a key and its associated value—and places the value in the `HashMap` at a location determined by the key. Method `get` takes one argument—a key—and returns an `Object` reference to the corresponding value. Class `Site-Selector` also contains a `Vector` (package `java.util`) in which the site names are placed so they can be used to initialize the `JList` (one version of the `JList` constructor receives a `Vector` object). A `Vector` is a dynamically resizable array of `Object` references. Class `Vector` provides method *add* to add a new element to the end of the `Vector`. (We discuss class `Vector` in detail in Chapter 21 and we discuss class `HashMap` in detail in Chapter 22.)

```
1   // Fig. 18.2: SiteSelector.java
2   // This program uses a button to load a document from a URL.
3   import java.net.*;
4   import java.util.*;
5   import java.awt.*;
6   import java.applet.AppletContext;
7   import javax.swing.*;
8   import javax.swing.event.*;
9
10  public class SiteSelector extends JApplet {
11     private HashMap sites;      // site names and URLs
12     private Vector siteNames;   // site names
13     private JList siteChooser;  // list of sites to choose from
14
15     // read HTML parameters and set up GUI
16     public void init()
17     {
18        // create HashMap and Vector
19        sites = new HashMap();
20        siteNames = new Vector();
21
22        // obtain parameters from HTML document
23        getSitesFromHTMLParameters();
24
```

Fig. 18.2   Loading a document from a URL into a browser. (Part 1 of 3.)

```
25        // create GUI components and layout interface
26        Container container = getContentPane();
27        container.add( new JLabel( "Choose a site to browse" ),
28           BorderLayout.NORTH );
29
30        siteChooser = new JList( siteNames );
31        siteChooser.addListSelectionListener(
32
33           new ListSelectionListener() {
34
35              // go to site user selected
36              public void valueChanged( ListSelectionEvent event )
37              {
38                 // get selected site name
39                 Object object = siteChooser.getSelectedValue();
40
41                 // use site name to locate corresponding URL
42                 URL newDocument = ( URL ) sites.get( object );
43
44                 // get reference to applet container
45                 AppletContext browser = getAppletContext();
46
47                 // tell applet container to change pages
48                 browser.showDocument( newDocument );
49              }
50
51           } // end inner class
52
53        ); // end call to addListSelectionListener
54
55        container.add( new JScrollPane( siteChooser ),
56           BorderLayout.CENTER );
57
58     } // end method init
59
60     // obtain parameters from HTML document
61     private void getSitesFromHTMLParameters()
62     {
63        // look for applet parameters in HTML document and add to HashMap
64        String title, location;
65        URL url;
66        int counter = 0;
67
68        title = getParameter( "title" + counter ); // get first site title
69
70        // loop until no more parameters in HTML document
71        while ( title != null ) {
72
73           // obtain site location
74           location = getParameter( "location" + counter );
75
76           // place title/URL in HashMap and title in Vector
77           try {
```

Fig. 18.2   Loading a document from a URL into a browser. (Part 2 of 3.)

```
78              url = new URL( location ); // convert location to URL
79              sites.put( title, url );   // put title/URL in HashMap
80              siteNames.add( title );    // put title in Vector
81           }
82
83           // process invalid URL format
84           catch ( MalformedURLException urlException ) {
85              urlException.printStackTrace();
86           }
87
88           ++counter;
89           title = getParameter( "title" + counter ); // get next site title
90
91        } // end while
92
93     } // end method getSitesFromHTMLParameters
94
95  } // end class SiteSelector
```

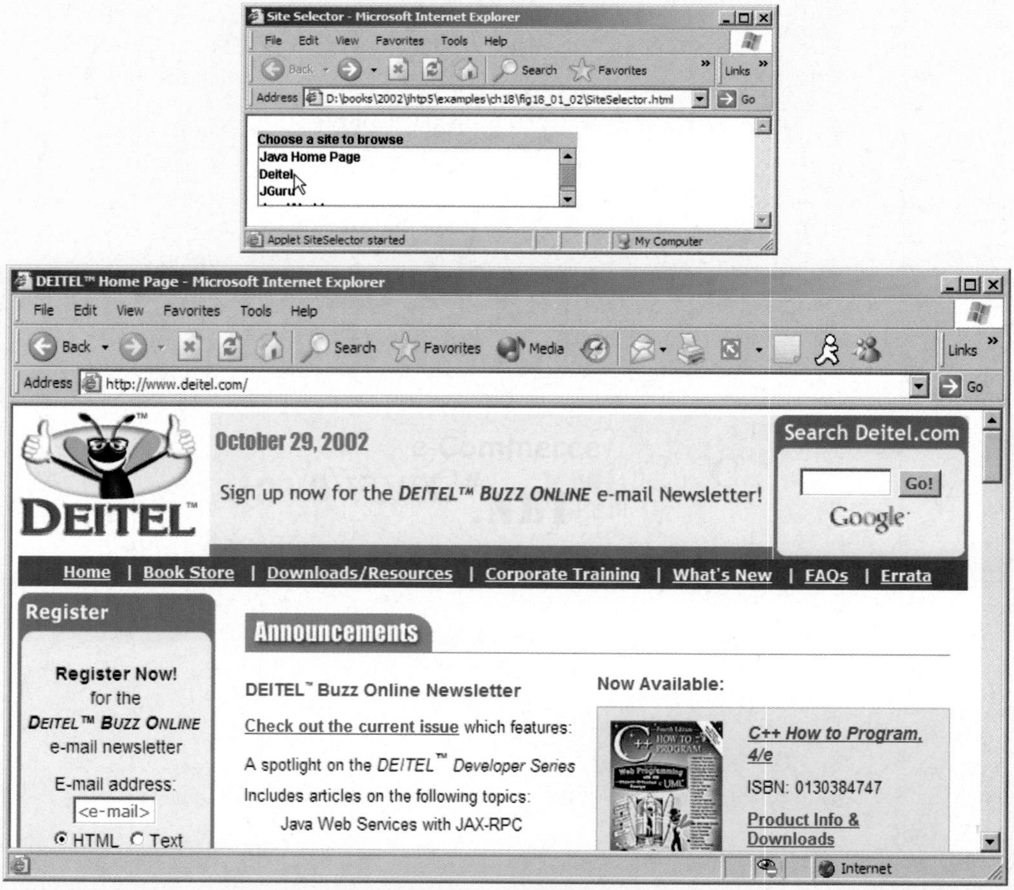

Fig. 18.2   Loading a document from a URL into a browser. (Part 3 of 3.)

Lines 19–20 in the applet's init method (lines 16–58) create a HashMap object and a Vector object. Line 23 calls our utility method getSitesFromHTMLParameters (declared at lines 61–93) to obtain the HTML parameters from the HTML document that invoked the applet.

In method getSitesFromHTMLParameters, line 68 uses Applet method getParameter to obtain a Web site title. If the title is not null, the loop at lines 71–91 begins executing. Line 74 uses Applet method getParameter to obtain the Web site location. Line 78 uses the location as the value of a new URL object. The URL constructor determines whether its argument represents a valid URL. If not, the URL constructor throws a *MalformedURLException*. Notice that the URL constructor must be called in a try block. If the URL constructor generates a MalformedURLException, the call to printStack-Trace (line 85) causes the program to display a stack trace. Then the program attempts to obtain the next Web site title. The program does not add the site for the invalid URL to the HashMap, so the title will not be displayed in the JList.

For a proper URL, line 79 places the title and URL into the HashMap, and line 80 adds the title to the Vector. Line 89 gets the next title from the HTML document. When the call to getParameter at line 89 returns null, the loop terminates.

When method getSitesFromHTMLParameters returns to init, lines 26–56 construct the applet's GUI. Lines 27–28 add the JLabel "Choose a site to browse" to the NORTH of the content pane's BorderLayout. Lines 31–53 register a ListSelection-Listener to handle the siteChooser's events. Lines 55–56 add siteChooser to the CENTER of the content pane's BorderLayout.

When the user selects one of the Web sites listed in siteChooser, the program calls method valueChanged (lines 36–49). Line 39 obtains the selected site name from the JList. Line 42 passes the selected site name (the *key*) to HashMap method get, which locates and returns an Object reference to the corresponding URL object (the *value*). The URL cast operator converts the reference to a URL that can be assigned to reference new-Document.

Line 45 uses Applet method getAppletContext to get a reference to an Applet-Context object that represents the applet container. Line 48 uses the AppletContext reference browser to invoke method *showDocument*, which receives a URL object as an argument and passes it to the AppletContext (i.e., the browser). The browser displays in the current browser window the World Wide Web resource associated with that URL. In this example, all the resources are HTML documents.

For programmers familiar with *HTML frames*, there is a second version of Applet-Context method showDocument that enables an applet to specify the so-called *target frame* in which to display the World Wide Web resource. The second version of showDoc-ument takes two arguments—a URL object specifying the resource to display and a string representing the target frame. There are some special target frames that can be used as the second argument. The target frame *_blank* results in a new Web browser window to display the content from the specified URL. The target frame *_self* specifies that the content from the specified URL should be displayed in the same frame as the applet (the applet's HTML page is replaced in this case). The target frame *_top* specifies that the browser should remove the current frames in the browser window, then display the content from the specified URI in the current window. For more information on HTML and frames, see the *World Wide Web Consortium (W3C)* Web site www.w3.org.

The applet in Fig. 18.2 must be run from a World Wide Web browser, such as Netscape or Microsoft Internet Explorer, to see the results of displaying another Web page. The `appletviewer` *is capable only of executing applets—it ignores all other HTML tags. If the Web sites in the program contained Java applets, only those applets would appear in the* `appletviewer` *when the user selects a Web site. Each applet would execute in a separate* `appletviewer` *window.*

18.3 Reading a File on a Web Server

Our next example, once again hides the networking details from us. The application of Fig. 18.3 uses Swing GUI component *JEditorPane* (from package `javax.swing`) to display the contents of a file on a Web server. The user inputs a URL in the `JTextField` at the top of the window, and the program displays the corresponding document (if it exists) in the `JEditorPane`. Class `JEditorPane` is able to render both plain text and HTML-formatted text, so this application acts as a simple Web browser. The application also demonstrates how to process *HyperlinkEvents* when the user clicks a hyperlink in the HTML document. The screen captures in Fig. 18.3 illustrate that the `JEditorPane` can display both simple text (the first screen) and HTML text (the second screen). The techniques shown in this example also can be used in applets. However, applets are allowed to read files only on the server from which the applet was downloaded.

```
1   // Fig. 18.3: ReadServerFile.java
2   // Use a JEditorPane to display the contents of a file on a Web server.
3   import java.awt.*;
4   import java.awt.event.*;
5   import java.net.*;
6   import java.io.*;
7   import javax.swing.*;
8   import javax.swing.event.*;
9
10  public class ReadServerFile extends JFrame {
11     private JTextField enterField;
12     private JEditorPane contentsArea;
13
14     // set up GUI
15     public ReadServerFile()
16     {
17        super( "Simple Web Browser" );
18
19        Container container = getContentPane();
20
21        // create enterField and register its listener
22        enterField = new JTextField( "Enter file URL here" );
23        enterField.addActionListener(
24           new ActionListener() {
25
26              // get document specified by user
27              public void actionPerformed( ActionEvent event )
28              {
```

Fig. 18.3   Reading a file by opening a connection through a URL. (Part 1 of 3.)

```
29                    getThePage( event.getActionCommand() );
30               }
31
32          } // end inner class
33
34      ); // end call to addActionListener
35
36      container.add( enterField, BorderLayout.NORTH );
37
38      // create contentsArea and register HyperlinkEvent listener
39      contentsArea = new JEditorPane();
40      contentsArea.setEditable( false );
41      contentsArea.addHyperlinkListener(
42          new HyperlinkListener() {
43
44              // if user clicked hyperlink, go to specified page
45              public void hyperlinkUpdate( HyperlinkEvent event )
46              {
47                  if ( event.getEventType() ==
48                      HyperlinkEvent.EventType.ACTIVATED )
49                      getThePage( event.getURL().toString() );
50              }
51
52          } // end inner class
53
54      ); // end call to addHyperlinkListener
55
56      container.add( new JScrollPane( contentsArea ),
57          BorderLayout.CENTER );
58      setSize( 400, 300 );
59      setVisible( true );
60
61   } // end constructor ReadServerFile
62
63   // load document
64   private void getThePage( String location )
65   {
66      // load document and display location
67      try {
68          contentsArea.setPage( location );
69          enterField.setText( location );
70      }
71      catch ( IOException ioException ) {
72          JOptionPane.showMessageDialog( this,
73              "Error retrieving specified URL", "Bad URL",
74              JOptionPane.ERROR_MESSAGE );
75      }
76
77   } // end method getThePage
78
79   public static void main( String args[] )
80   {
81       ReadServerFile application = new ReadServerFile();
```

Fig. 18.3   Reading a file by opening a connection through a URL. (Part 2 of 3.)

```
82          application.setDefaultCloseOperation( JFrame.EXIT_ON_CLOSE );
83       }
84
85    } // end class ReadServerFile
```

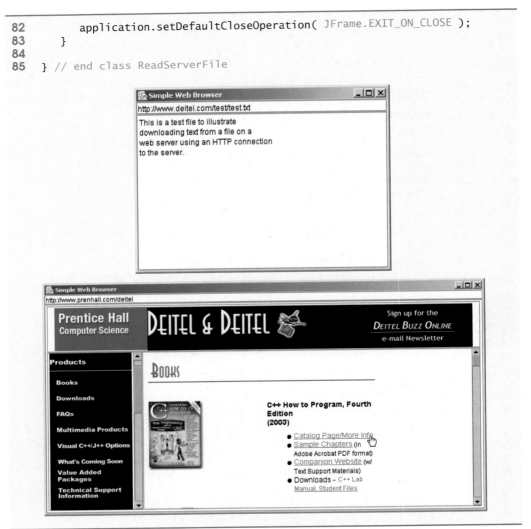

Fig. 18.3   Reading a file by opening a connection through a URL. (Part 3 of 3.)

The application class `ReadServerFile` contains `JTextField enterField`, in which the user enters the URL of the file to read and `JEditorPane contentsArea` to display the contents of the file. When the user presses the *Enter* key in `enterField`, the program calls method `actionPerformed` (lines 27–30). Line 29 uses `ActionEvent` method `getActionCommand` to get the string the user input in the `JTextField` and passes that string to utility method `getThePage` (lines 64–77).

Line 68 uses `JEditorPane` method *setPage* to download the document specified by `location` and display it in the `JEditorPane`. If there is an error downloading the document, method `setPage` throws an `IOException`. Also, if an invalid URL is specified, a `MalformedURLException` (a subclass of `IOException`) occurs. If the document loads successfully, line 69 displays the current location in `enterField`.

Typically, an HTML document contains *hyperlinks*—text, images or GUI components which, when clicked, provide quick access to another document on the Web. If a `JEditor-Pane` contains an HTML document and the user clicks a hyperlink, the `JEditorPane` generates a *HyperlinkEvent* (package `javax.swing.event`) and notifies all registered *HyperlinkListeners* (package `javax.swing.event`) of that event. Lines 41–54 register a `HyperlinkListener` to handle `HyperlinkEvents`. When a `HyperlinkEvent` occurs, the program calls method `hyperlinkUpdate` (lines 45–50). Lines 47–48 use `HyperlinkEvent` method *getEventType* to determine the type of the `HyperlinkEvent`. Class `HyperlinkEvent` contains `public` a nested class called *EventType* that declares three static `EventType` objects, which represent the hyperlink event types. *ACTIVATED* indicates that the user clicked a hyperlink to change Web pages, *ENTERED* indicates that the user moved the mouse over a hyperlink and *EXITED* indicates that the user moved the mouse away from a hyperlink. If a hyperlink was `ACTIVATED`, line 49 uses `HyperlinkEvent` method *getURL* to obtain the URL represented by the hyperlink. Method `toString` converts the returned URL to a string that can be passed to utility method `getThePage`.

Software Engineering Observation 18.1

A JEditorPane generates HyperlinkEvents only if it is uneditable.

18.4 Establishing a Simple Server Using Stream Sockets

The two examples discussed so far use high-level Java networking capabilities to communicate between applications. In those examples, it was not the Java programmer's responsibility to establish the connection between a client and a server. The first program relied on the Web browser to communicate with a Web server. The second program relied on a `JEditorPane` to perform the connection. This section begins our discussion of creating your own applications that can communicate with one another.

Establishing a simple server in Java requires five steps. Step 1 is to create a *Server-Socket* object. A call to the `ServerSocket` constructor such as

```
ServerSocket server = new ServerSocket( port, queueLength );
```

registers an available *port number* and specifies a maximum number of clients that can wait to connect to the server (i.e., the *queueLength*). The port number is used by clients to locate the server application on the server computer. This often is called the *handshake point*. If the queue is full, the server refuses client connections. The constructor establishes the port where the server waits for connections from clients—a process known as *binding the server to the port*. Each client will ask to connect to the server on this *port*. Only one application can be bound to a specific port on the server at a time.

Software Engineering Observation 18.2

Port numbers can be between 0 and 65,535. Some operating systems reserve port numbers below 1024 for system services (such as e-mail and World Wide Web servers). Generally, these ports should not be specified as connection ports in user programs. In fact, some operating systems require special access privileges to bind to port numbers below 1024.

Programs manage each client connection with a *Socket* object. In Step 2, the server listens indefinitely (or *blocks*) for an attempt by a client to connect. To listen for a client connection, the program calls `ServerSocket` method *accept*, as in

```
Socket connection = server.accept();
```

which returns a Socket when a connection with a client is established. The socket allows the server to interact with the client. The port specified in Step 1 can be used again in a multithreaded server to accept another client connection. We demonstrate this concept in Section 18.8.

Step 3 is to get the OutputStream and InputStream objects that enable the server to communicate with the client by sending and receiving bytes. The server sends information to the client via an OutputStream. The server receives information from the client via an InputStream. The server invokes method getOutputStream on the Socket to get a reference to the Socket's OutputStream and invokes method getInputStream on the Socket to get a reference to the Socket's InputStream.

The stream objects can be used to send or receive individual bytes or sets of bytes with the OutputStream's method write and the InputStream's method read, respectively. Often it is useful to send or receive values of primitive types (such as int and double) or Serializable objects (such as Strings or other serializable types) rather than sending bytes. In this case, we can use the techniques of Chapter 17 to wrap other stream types (such as ObjectOutputStream and ObjectInputStream) around the OutputStream and InputStream associated with the Socket. For example,

```
ObjectInputStream input =
    new ObjectInputStream( connection.getInputStream() );

ObjectOutputStream output =
    new ObjectOutputStream( connection.getOutputStream() );
```

The beauty of establishing these relationships is that whatever the server writes to the ObjectOutputStream is sent via the OutputStream and is available at the client's InputStream and whatever the client writes to its OutputStream (with a corresponding ObjectOutputStream) is available via the server's InputStream. The transmission of the data over the network is seamless and is handled completely by Java.

Step 4 is the *processing* phase, in which the server and the client communicate via the OutputStream and InputStream objects. In Step 5, when the transmission is complete, the server closes the connection by invoking the close method on the streams and on the Socket.

Software Engineering Observation 18.3

With sockets, network I/O appears to Java programs to be similar to sequential file I/O. Sockets hide much of the complexity of network programming from the programmer.

Software Engineering Observation 18.4

With Java's multithreading, we can create multithreaded servers that can manage many simultaneous connections with many clients; this multithreaded-server architecture is precisely what popular network servers use.

Software Engineering Observation 18.5

A multithreaded server can take the Socket returned by each call to accept and create a new thread that manages network I/O across that Socket, or a multithreaded server can maintain a pool of threads (a set of already existing threads) ready to manage network I/O across the new Sockets as they are created.

Performance Tip 18.2

In high-performance systems in which memory is abundant, a multithreaded server can be implemented to create a pool of threads that can be assigned quickly to handle network I/O across each new Socket *as it is created. Thus, when the server receives a connection, the server need not incur the overhead of thread creation. When the connection is closed, the thread is returned to the pool for reuse.*

18.5 Establishing a Simple Client Using Stream Sockets

Establishing a simple client in Java requires four steps. In Step 1, we create a Socket to connect to the server. The Socket constructor establishes the connection to the server. For example, the statement

```
Socket connection = new Socket( serverAddress, port );
```

uses the Socket constructor with two arguments—the server's IP address (*serverAddress*) and the *port* number. If the connection attempt is successful, this statement returns a Socket. A connection attempt that fails throws an instance of a subclass of IOException, so many programs simply catch IOException. An *UnknownHostException* occurs when the system is unable to resolve the server address specified in the call to the Socket constructor. A *ConnectException* is thrown when an error occurs while attempting to connect to a server.

In Step 2, the client uses Socket methods getInputStream and getOutputStream to obtain references to the Socket's InputStream and OutputStream. As we mentioned in the preceding section, we can use the techniques of Chapter 17 to wrap other stream types around the InputStream and OutputStream associated with the Socket. If the server is sending information in the form of actual types, the client should receive the information in the same format. Thus, if the server sends values with an ObjectOutputStream, the client should read those values with an ObjectInputStream.

Step 3 is the processing phase in which the client and the server communicate via the InputStream and OutputStream objects. In Step 4, the client closes the connection when the transmission is complete by invoking the close method on the streams and on the Socket. When processing information sent by a server, the client must determine when the server is finished sending information so the client can call close to close the Socket connection. For example, the InputStream method read returns the value –1 when it detects end-of-stream (also called EOF—end-of-file). If an ObjectInputStream is used to read information from the server, an EOFException occurs when the client attempts to read a value from a stream on which end-of-stream is detected.

18.6 Client/Server Interaction with Stream Socket Connections

Figure 18.4 and Fig. 18.5 use *stream sockets* to demonstrate a simple *client/server chat application*. The server waits for a client connection attempt. When a client connects to the server, the server application sends a String object (recall that Strings are Serializable objects) indicating that the connection was successful to the client. Then the client displays the message. Both the client and the server applications provide textfields that allow the user to type a message and send it to the other application. When the client or the server sends the string "TERMINATE", the connection between the client and the server terminates. Then the server waits for the next client to connect. The declaration of class Server appears in Fig. 18.4. The declaration of class Client appears in Fig. 18.5. The screen captures showing the execution between the client and the server are shown as part of Fig. 18.5.

Server Class

Server's constructor (lines 20–51) creates the server's GUI, which contains a JText-Field and a JTextArea. Server displays its output in the JTextArea. When the main method (lines 210–215) executes, it creates a Server object, specifies the window's default close operation and calls method runServer (declared at lines 54–89).

```
1   // Fig. 18.4: Server.java
2   // Set up a Server that will receive a connection from a client, send
3   // a string to the client, and close the connection.
4   import java.io.*;
5   import java.net.*;
6   import java.awt.*;
7   import java.awt.event.*;
8   import javax.swing.*;
9
10  public class Server extends JFrame {
11     private JTextField enterField;
12     private JTextArea displayArea;
13     private ObjectOutputStream output;
14     private ObjectInputStream input;
15     private ServerSocket server;
16     private Socket connection;
17     private int counter = 1;
18
19     // set up GUI
20     public Server()
21     {
22        super( "Server" );
23
24        Container container = getContentPane();
25
26        // create enterField and register listener
27        enterField = new JTextField();
28        enterField.setEditable( false );
29        enterField.addActionListener(
30           new ActionListener() {
31
32              // send message to client
33              public void actionPerformed( ActionEvent event )
34              {
35                 sendData( event.getActionCommand() );
36                 enterField.setText( "" );
37              }
38           }
39        );
40
41        container.add( enterField, BorderLayout.NORTH );
42
```

Fig. 18.4   Server portion of a client/server stream-socket connection. (Part 1 of 5.)

```
43          // create displayArea
44          displayArea = new JTextArea();
45          container.add( new JScrollPane( displayArea ),
46             BorderLayout.CENTER );
47
48          setSize( 300, 150 );
49          setVisible( true );
50
51       } // end Server constructor
52
53       // set up and run server
54       public void runServer()
55       {
56          // set up server to receive connections; process connections
57          try {
58
59             // Step 1: Create a ServerSocket.
60             server = new ServerSocket( 12345, 100 );
61
62             while ( true ) {
63
64                try {
65                   waitForConnection(); // Step 2: Wait for a connection.
66                   getStreams();        // Step 3: Get input & output streams.
67                   processConnection(); // Step 4: Process connection.
68                }
69
70                // process EOFException when client closes connection
71                catch ( EOFException eofException ) {
72                   System.err.println( "Server terminated connection" );
73                }
74
75                finally {
76                   closeConnection();   // Step 5: Close connection.
77                   ++counter;
78                }
79
80             } // end while
81
82          } // end try
83
84          // process problems with I/O
85          catch ( IOException ioException ) {
86             ioException.printStackTrace();
87          }
88
89       } // end method runServer
90
91       // wait for connection to arrive, then display connection info
92       private void waitForConnection() throws IOException
93       {
94          displayMessage( "Waiting for connection\n" );
95          connection = server.accept(); // allow server to accept connection
```

Fig. 18.4   Server portion of a client/server stream-socket connection. (Part 2 of 5.)

```
96          displayMessage( "Connection " + counter + " received from: " +
97             connection.getInetAddress().getHostName() );
98       }
99
100      // get streams to send and receive data
101      private void getStreams() throws IOException
102      {
103         // set up output stream for objects
104         output = new ObjectOutputStream( connection.getOutputStream() );
105         output.flush(); // flush output buffer to send header information
106
107         // set up input stream for objects
108         input = new ObjectInputStream( connection.getInputStream() );
109
110         displayMessage( "\nGot I/O streams\n" );
111      }
112
113      // process connection with client
114      private void processConnection() throws IOException
115      {
116         // send connection successful message to client
117         String message = "Connection successful";
118         sendData( message );
119
120         // enable enterField so server user can send messages
121         setTextFieldEditable( true );
122
123         do { // process messages sent from client
124
125            // read message and display it
126            try {
127               message = ( String ) input.readObject();
128               displayMessage( "\n" + message );
129            }
130
131            // catch problems reading from client
132            catch ( ClassNotFoundException classNotFoundException ) {
133               displayMessage( "\nUnknown object type received" );
134            }
135
136         } while ( !message.equals( "CLIENT>>> TERMINATE" ) );
137
138      } // end method processConnection
139
140      // close streams and socket
141      private void closeConnection()
142      {
143         displayMessage( "\nTerminating connection\n" );
144         setTextFieldEditable( false ); // disable enterField
145
146         try {
147            output.close();
148            input.close();
```

Fig. 18.4   Server portion of a client/server stream-socket connection. (Part 3 of 5.)

```
149            connection.close();
150        }
151        catch( IOException ioException ) {
152            ioException.printStackTrace();
153        }
154    }
155
156    // send message to client
157    private void sendData( String message )
158    {
159        // send object to client
160        try {
161            output.writeObject( "SERVER>>> " + message );
162            output.flush();
163            displayMessage( "\nSERVER>>> " + message );
164        }
165
166        // process problems sending object
167        catch ( IOException ioException ) {
168            displayArea.append( "\nError writing object" );
169        }
170    }
171
172    // utility method called from other threads to manipulate
173    // displayArea in the event-dispatch thread
174    private void displayMessage( final String messageToDisplay )
175    {
176        // display message from event-dispatch thread of execution
177        SwingUtilities.invokeLater(
178            new Runnable() {  // inner class to ensure GUI updates properly
179
180                public void run() // updates displayArea
181                {
182                    displayArea.append( messageToDisplay );
183                    displayArea.setCaretPosition(
184                        displayArea.getText().length() );
185                }
186
187            }  // end inner class
188
189        ); // end call to SwingUtilities.invokeLater
190    }
191
192    // utility method called from other threads to manipulate
193    // enterField in the event-dispatch thread
194    private void setTextFieldEditable( final boolean editable )
195    {
196        // display message from event-dispatch  thread of execution
197        SwingUtilities.invokeLater(
198            new Runnable() {  // inner class to ensure GUI updates properly
199
200                public void run()  // sets enterField's editability
201                {
```

Fig. 18.4   Server portion of a client/server stream-socket connection. (Part 4 of 5.)

```
202                    enterField.setEditable( editable );
203                }
204
205            }  // end inner class
206
207        );  // end call to SwingUtilities.invokeLater
208    }
209
210    public static void main( String args[] )
211    {
212        Server application = new Server();
213        application.setDefaultCloseOperation( JFrame.EXIT_ON_CLOSE );
214        application.runServer();
215    }
216
217 }  // end class Server
```

Fig. 18.4   Server portion of a client/server stream-socket connection. (Part 5 of 5.)

Method `runServer` sets up the server to receive a connection and processes one connection at a time. Line 60 creates a `ServerSocket` called `server` to wait for connections. The `ServerSocket` listens for a connection from a client at port `12345`. The second argument to the constructor is the number of connections that can wait in a queue to connect to the server (`100` in this example). If the queue is full when a client attempts to connect, the server refuses the connection.

Common Programming Error 18.1

Specifying a port that is already in use or specifying an invalid port number when creating a ServerSocket results in an IllegalArgumentException.

Line 65 calls method `waitForConnection` (declared at lines 92–98) to wait for a client connection. After the connection is established, line 66 calls method `getStreams` (declared at lines 101–111) to obtain references to the streams for the connection. Line 67 calls method `processConnection` (declared at lines 114–138) to send the initial connection message to the client and to process all messages received from the client. The `finally` block (lines 75–78) terminates the client connection by calling method `closeConnection` (lines 135–142) even if an exception occurred. Method `displayMessage` (lines 174–190) is called from these methods to use the event-dispatch thread to display messages in the application's textarea. Lines 183–184 of method `displayArea` use `JTextComponent` method *setCaretPosition* to position the input cursor in the textarea after the last character in the textarea. This scrolls the textarea as text is appended to it.

In method `waitForConnection` (lines 92–98), line 95 uses `ServerSocket` method `accept` to wait for a connection from a client. When a connection occurs, the resulting `Socket` is assigned to `connection`. Method `accept` blocks until a connection is received (i.e., the thread in which `accept` is called stops executing until a client connects). Lines 96–97 output the host name of the computer that made the connection. `Socket` method *getInetAddress* returns an *InetAddress* (package `java.net`) containing information about the client computer. `InetAddress` method *getHostName* returns the host name of the client computer. For example, there is a special IP address (`127.0.0.1`) and host name (localhost) that is useful for testing networking applications on your local computer. If getHostName is called on an InetAddress containing 127.0.0.1, the corresponding host name returned by the method would be localhost.

Method getStreams (lines 101–111) obtains references to the Socket's streams and uses them to initialize an ObjectOutputStream (line 104) and an ObjectInputStream (line 108), respectively. Notice the call to ObjectOutputStream method flush at line 105. This statement causes the ObjectOutputStream on the server to send a *stream header* to the corresponding client's ObjectInputStream. The stream header contains information such as the version of object serialization being used to send objects. This information is required by the ObjectInputStream so it can prepare to receive those objects correctly.

> **Software Engineering Observation 18.6**
>
> *When using an ObjectOutputStream and ObjectInputStream to send and receive data over a network connection, always create the ObjectOutputStream first and flush the stream so the client's ObjectInputStream can prepare to receive the data. This is required only for networking applications that communicate using ObjectOutputStream and ObjectInputStream.*

> **Performance Tip 18.3**
>
> *Output buffers typically are used to increase the efficiency of an application by sending larger amounts of data fewer times. The input and output components of a computer are typically much slower than the memory of the computer.*

Line 118 of method processConnection (lines 114–138) calls method sendData to send "SERVER>>> Connection successful" as a string to the client. The loop at lines 123–136 executes until the server receives the message "CLIENT>>> TERMINATE." Line 127 uses ObjectInputStream method readObject to read a String from the client. Line 128 invokes method displayMessage to append the message to the JTextArea.

When the transmission is complete, method processConnection returns and the program calls method closeConnection (lines 141–154) to close the streams associated with the Socket and close the Socket. Then, the server waits for the next connection attempt from a client by continuing with line 65 at the beginning of the while loop.

When the user of the server application enters a string in the textfield and presses the *Enter* key, the program calls method actionPerformed (lines 33–37), which reads the string from the textfield and calls utility method sendData (lines 157–170) to send the string to the client. Method sendData writes the object, flushes the output buffer and appends the same string to the textarea in the server window. It is not necessary to invoke displayMessage to modify the textarea here because method sendData is called from an event handler; thus, sendData executes as part of the event-dispatch thread.

Notice that the Server receives a connection, processes the connection, closes the connection and waits for the next connection. A more likely scenario would be a Server that receives a connection, sets up that connection to be processed as a separate thread of execution, then immediately waits for new connections. The separate threads that process existing connections can continue to execute while the Server concentrates on new connection requests. This makes the server more efficient as multiple client requests can be processed concurrently. We demonstrate a multithreaded server in Section 18.8.

Client Class

Like class `Server`, class `Client`'s (Fig. 18.5) constructor creates the GUI of the application (a `JTextField` and a `JTextArea`). `Client` displays its output in the textarea. When method `main` (lines 199–210) executes, it creates an instance of class `Client`, specifies the window's default close operation and calls method `runClient` (declared at lines 55–78). In this example, you can execute the client from any computer on the Internet and specify the IP address or host name of the server computer as a command-line argument to the program. For example, the command

```
java Client 192.168.1.15
```

attempts to connect to the `Server` on the computer with IP address 192.168.1.15.

```
1   // Fig. 18.5: Client.java
2   // Client that reads and displays information sent from a Server.
3   import java.io.*;
4   import java.net.*;
5   import java.awt.*;
6   import java.awt.event.*;
7   import javax.swing.*;
8
9   public class Client extends JFrame {
10     private JTextField enterField;
11     private JTextArea displayArea;
12     private ObjectOutputStream output;
13     private ObjectInputStream input;
14     private String message = "";
15     private String chatServer;
16     private Socket client;
17
18     // initialize chatServer and set up GUI
19     public Client( String host )
20     {
21        super( "Client" );
22
23        chatServer = host; // set server to which this client connects
24
25        Container container = getContentPane();
26
27        // create enterField and register listener
28        enterField = new JTextField();
29        enterField.setEditable( false );
30        enterField.addActionListener(
31           new ActionListener() {
32
33              // send message to server
34              public void actionPerformed( ActionEvent event )
35              {
36                 sendData( event.getActionCommand() );
```

Fig. 18.5   Client portion of a stream-socket connection between a client and a server. (Part 1 of 5.)

```
37                        enterField.setText( "" );
38                    }
39                }
40          );
41
42          container.add( enterField, BorderLayout.NORTH );
43
44          // create displayArea
45          displayArea = new JTextArea();
46          container.add( new JScrollPane( displayArea ),
47             BorderLayout.CENTER );
48
49          setSize( 300, 150 );
50          setVisible( true );
51
52       } // end Client constructor
53
54       // connect to server and process messages from server
55       private void runClient()
56       {
57          // connect to server, get streams, process connection
58          try {
59             connectToServer(); // Step 1: Create a Socket to make connection
60             getStreams();       // Step 2: Get the input and output streams
61             processConnection(); // Step 3: Process connection
62          }
63
64          // server closed connection
65          catch ( EOFException eofException ) {
66             System.err.println( "Client terminated connection" );
67          }
68
69          // process problems communicating with server
70          catch ( IOException ioException ) {
71             ioException.printStackTrace();
72          }
73
74          finally {
75             closeConnection(); // Step 4: Close connection
76          }
77
78       } // end method runClient
79
80       // connect to server
81       private void connectToServer() throws IOException
82       {
83          displayMessage( "Attempting connection\n" );
84
85          // create Socket to make connection to server
86          client = new Socket( InetAddress.getByName( chatServer ), 12345 );
87
```

Fig. 18.5   Client portion of a stream-socket connection between a client and a server. (Part 2 of 5.)

```
88          // display connection information
89          displayMessage( "Connected to: " +
90              client.getInetAddress().getHostName() );
91      }
92
93      // get streams to send and receive data
94      private void getStreams() throws IOException
95      {
96          // set up output stream for objects
97          output = new ObjectOutputStream( client.getOutputStream() );
98          output.flush(); // flush output buffer to send header information
99
100         // set up input stream for objects
101         input = new ObjectInputStream( client.getInputStream() );
102
103         displayMessage( "\nGot I/O streams\n" );
104     }
105
106     // process connection with server
107     private void processConnection() throws IOException
108     {
109         // enable enterField so client user can send messages
110         setTextFieldEditable( true );
111
112         do { // process messages sent from server
113
114             // read message and display it
115             try {
116                 message = ( String ) input.readObject();
117                 displayMessage( "\n" + message );
118             }
119
120             // catch problems reading from server
121             catch ( ClassNotFoundException classNotFoundException ) {
122                 displayMessage( "\nUnknown object type received" );
123             }
124
125         } while ( !message.equals( "SERVER>>> TERMINATE" ) );
126
127     } // end method processConnection
128
129     // close streams and socket
130     private void closeConnection()
131     {
132         displayMessage( "\nClosing connection" );
133         setTextFieldEditable( false ); // disable enterField
134
135         try {
136             output.close();
137             input.close();
138             client.close();
139         }
```

Fig. 18.5   Client portion of a stream-socket connection between a client and a server. (Part 3 of 5.)

```
140          catch( IOException ioException ) {
141              ioException.printStackTrace();
142          }
143      }
144
145      // send message to server
146      private void sendData( String message )
147      {
148          // send object to server
149          try {
150              output.writeObject( "CLIENT>>> " + message );
151              output.flush();
152              displayMessage( "\nCLIENT>>> " + message );
153          }
154
155          // process problems sending object
156          catch ( IOException ioException ) {
157              displayArea.append( "\nError writing object" );
158          }
159      }
160
161      // utility method called from other threads to manipulate
162      // displayArea in the event-dispatch thread
163      private void displayMessage( final String messageToDisplay )
164      {
165          // display message from GUI thread of execution
166          SwingUtilities.invokeLater(
167              new Runnable() {  // inner class to ensure GUI updates properly
168
169                  public void run() // updates displayArea
170                  {
171                      displayArea.append( messageToDisplay );
172                      displayArea.setCaretPosition(
173                          displayArea.getText().length() );
174                  }
175
176              }  // end inner class
177
178          ); // end call to SwingUtilities.invokeLater
179      }
180
181      // utility method called from other threads to manipulate
182      // enterField in the event-dispatch thread
183      private void setTextFieldEditable( final boolean editable )
184      {
185          // display message from GUI thread of execution
186          SwingUtilities.invokeLater(
187              new Runnable() {  // inner class to ensure GUI updates properly
188
189                  public void run()  // sets enterField's editability
190                  {
191                      enterField.setEditable( editable );
```

Fig. 18.5   Client portion of a stream-socket connection between a client and a
server. (Part 4 of 5.)

```
192              }
193
194          } // end inner class
195
196      ); // end call to SwingUtilities.invokeLater
197      }
198
199      public static void main( String args[] )
200      {
201          Client application;
202
203          if ( args.length == 0 )
204              application = new Client( "127.0.0.1" );
205          else
206              application = new Client( args[ 0 ] );
207
208          application.setDefaultCloseOperation( JFrame.EXIT_ON_CLOSE );
209          application.runClient();
210      }
211
212  } // end class Client
```

Fig. 18.5   Client portion of a stream-socket connection between a client and a server. (Part 5 of 5.)

Client method runClient (lines 55–78) sets up the connection to the server, processes messages received from the server and closes the connection when communication is complete. Line 59 calls method connectToServer (declared at lines 81–91) to perform the connection. After connecting, line 60 calls method getStreams (declared at lines 94–104) to obtain references to the Socket's stream objects. Then line 61 calls method processConnection (declared at lines 107–127) to receive and display messages sent from the server. The finally block (lines 74–76) calls closeConnection (lines 130–143) to close the streams and the Socket even if an exception occurred. Method displayMessage (lines 163–179) is called from these methods to use the event-dispatch thread to display messages in the application's textarea.

Method connectToServer (lines 81–91) creates a Socket called client (line 86) to establish a connection. The method passes two arguments to the Socket constructor—the IP address of the server computer and the port number (12345) where the server application is awaiting client connections. In the first argument, InetAddress static method getByName returns an InetAddress object containing the IP address specified as a command-line argument to the application (or 127.0.0.1 if no command-line arguments are specified). Method getByName can receive a string containing either the actual IP address or the host name of the server. The first argument also could have been written other ways. For the localhost address 127.0.0.1, the first argument could be

```
InetAddress.getByName( "localhost" )
```

or

```
InetAddress.getLocalHost()
```

Also, there are versions of the Socket constructor that receive a string for the IP address or host name. The first argument could have been specified as "127.0.0.1" or "localhost".[1] The Socket constructor's second argument is the server port number. This number must match the port number at which the server is waiting for connections (called the handshake point). Once the connection is made, lines 89–90 display a message in the textarea indicating the name of the server computer to which the client connected.

The Client uses an ObjectOutputStream to send data to the server and an ObjectInputStream to receive data from the server. Method getStreams (lines 94–104) creates the ObjectOutputStream and ObjectInputStream objects that use the streams associated with the client socket.

Method processConnection (lines 107–127) contains loop that executes until the client receives the message "SERVER>>> TERMINATE". Line 116 reads a String object from the server. Line 117 invokes displayMessage to append the message to the textarea.

When the transmission is complete, method closeConnection (lines 130–143) closes the streams and the Socket.

When the user of the client application enters a string in the textfield and presses the *Enter* key, the program calls method actionPerformed (lines 34–38) to read the string from the textfield and invoke utility method sendData (146–159)to send the string to the

---

1. We chose to demonstrate the client/server relationship by connecting between programs executing on the same computer (localhost). Normally, this first argument would be the IP address of another computer. The InetAddress object for another computer can be obtained by specifying the IP address or host name of the other computer as the argument to InetAddress method getByName.

server. Method `sendData` writes the object, flushes the output buffer and appends the same string to the textarea in the client window. Once again, it is not necessary to invoke utility method `displayMessage` to modify the textarea here because method `sendData` is called from an event handler.

18.7 Connectionless Client/Server Interaction with Datagrams

We have been discussing *connection-oriented, streams-based transmission*. Now we consider *connectionless transmission with datagrams*. Connection-oriented transmission is like the telephone system in which you dial and are given a *connection* to the telephone of the person with whom you wish to communicate. The connection is maintained for the duration of your phone call, even when you are not talking.

Connectionless transmission with *datagrams* is more like the way mail is carried via the postal service. If a large message will not fit in one envelope, you break it into separate message pieces that you place in separate, sequentially numbered envelopes. Each of the letters is then mailed at the same time. The letters could arrive in order, out of order or not at all (although the last case is rare, it does happen). The person at the receiving end reassembles the message pieces into sequential order before attempting to make sense of the message. If your message is small enough to fit in one envelope, you do not have to worry about the "out-of-sequence" problem, but it is still possible that your message might not arrive. One difference between datagrams and postal mail is that duplicates of datagrams can arrive at the receiving computer.

Figure 18.6 and Fig. 18.7 use datagrams to send packets of information via the User Datagram Protocol (*UDP*) between a client application and a server application. In the `Client` application (Fig. 18.7), the user types a message into a textfield and presses *Enter*. The program converts the message into a `byte` array and places it in a datagram packet that is sent to the server. The `Server` (Fig. 18.6) receives the packet and displays the information in the packet, then *echoes* the packet back to the client. When the client receives the packet, the client displays the information in the packet. In this example, the `Client` and `Server` classes are implemented similarly.

Server Class

Class `Server` (Fig. 18.6) declares two *DatagramPackets* that the server uses to send and receive information and one *DatagramSocket* that sends and receives these packets. The `Server` constructor (lines 14–35) creates the graphical user interface in which the packets of information will be displayed. Next, line 26 creates the `DatagramSocket` in a `try` block. Line 26 uses the `DatagramSocket` constructor that takes an integer port number argument (5000 in this example) to bind the server to a port where the server can receive packets from clients. `Clients` sending packets to this `Server` specify the same port number in the packets they send. A *SocketException* is thrown if the `DatagramSocket` constructor fails to bind the `DatagramSocket` to the specified port.

> **Common Programming Error 18.2**
>
> *Specifying a port that is already in use or specifying an invalid port number when creating a DatagramSocket results in a SocketException.*

`Server` method `waitForPackets` (lines 38–71) uses an infinite loop to wait for packets to arrive at the `Server`. Lines 47–48 create a `DatagramPacket` in which a received packet of information can be stored. The DatagramPacket constructor for this purpose receives two arguments—a byte array in which the data will be stored and the length of the array. Line 50 uses DatagramSocket method *receive* to wait for a packet to arrive at the Server. Method receive blocks until a packet arrives, then stores the packet in its DatagramPacket argument. The method throws an IOException if an error occurs while receiving a packet.

```java
1   // Fig. 18.6: Server.java
2   // Server that receives and sends packets from/to a client.
3   import java.io.*;
4   import java.net.*;
5   import java.awt.*;
6   import java.awt.event.*;
7   import javax.swing.*;
8
9   public class Server extends JFrame {
10      private JTextArea displayArea;
11      private DatagramSocket socket;
12
13      // set up GUI and DatagramSocket
14      public Server()
15      {
16         super( "Server" );
17
18         displayArea = new JTextArea();
19         getContentPane().add( new JScrollPane( displayArea ),
20            BorderLayout.CENTER );
21         setSize( 400, 300 );
22         setVisible( true );
23
24         // create DatagramSocket for sending and receiving packets
25         try {
26            socket = new DatagramSocket( 5000 );
27         }
28
29         // process problems creating DatagramSocket
30         catch( SocketException socketException ) {
31            socketException.printStackTrace();
32            System.exit( 1 );
33         }
34
35      } // end Server constructor
36
37      // wait for packets to arrive, display data and echo packet to client
38      private void waitForPackets()
39      {
40         while ( true ) { // loop forever
41
42            // receive packet, display contents, return copy to client
43            try {
```

Fig. 18.6   Server side of connectionless client/server computing with datagrams. (Part 1 of 3.)

```
44
45          // set up packet
46          byte data[] = new byte[ 100 ];
47          DatagramPacket receivePacket =
48             new DatagramPacket( data, data.length );
49
50          socket.receive( receivePacket ); // wait for packet
51
52          // display information from received packet
53          displayMessage( "\nPacket received:" +
54             "\nFrom host: " + receivePacket.getAddress() +
55             "\nHost port: " + receivePacket.getPort() +
56             "\nLength: " + receivePacket.getLength() +
57             "\nContaining:\n\t" + new String( receivePacket.getData(),
58                0, receivePacket.getLength() ) );
59
60          sendPacketToClient( receivePacket ); // send packet to client
61       }
62
63       // process problems manipulating packet
64       catch( IOException ioException ) {
65          displayMessage( ioException.toString() + "\n" );
66          ioException.printStackTrace();
67       }
68
69    } // end while
70
71 } // end method waitForPackets
72
73 // echo packet to client
74 private void sendPacketToClient( DatagramPacket receivePacket )
75    throws IOException
76 {
77    displayMessage( "\n\nEcho data to client..." );
78
79    // create packet to send
80    DatagramPacket sendPacket = new DatagramPacket(
81       receivePacket.getData(), receivePacket.getLength(),
82       receivePacket.getAddress(), receivePacket.getPort() );
83
84    socket.send( sendPacket ); // send packet
85    displayMessage( "Packet sent\n" );
86 }
87
88 // utility method called from other threads to manipulate
89 // displayArea in the event-dispatch thread
90 private void displayMessage( final String messageToDisplay )
91 {
92    // display message from event-dispatch thread of execution
93    SwingUtilities.invokeLater(
94       new Runnable() { // inner class to ensure GUI updates properly
95
```

Fig. 18.6   Server side of connectionless client/server computing with datagrams. (Part 2 of 3.)

```
96                 public void run() // updates displayArea
97                 {
98                     displayArea.append( messageToDisplay );
99                     displayArea.setCaretPosition(
100                        displayArea.getText().length() );
101                 }
102
103             }  // end inner class
104
105          );  // end call to SwingUtilities.invokeLater
106      }
107
108      public static void main( String args[] )
109      {
110          Server application = new Server();
111          application.setDefaultCloseOperation( JFrame.EXIT_ON_CLOSE );
112          application.waitForPackets();
113      }
114
115 } // end class Server
```

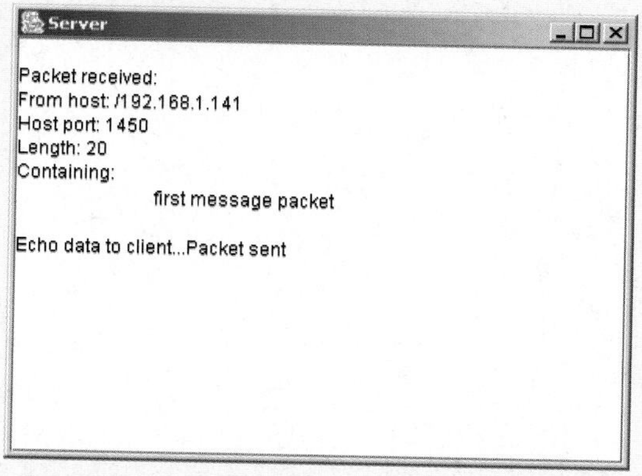

Server window after packet
of data is received from Client

Fig. 18.6   Server side of connectionless client/server computing with datagrams. (Part 3 of 3.)

When a packet arrives, lines 53–58 call method displayMessage (declared at lines 90–106) to append the packet's contents to the textarea. DatagramPacket method *getAddress* (line 54) returns an InetAddress object containing the host name of the computer from which the packet was sent. Method *getPort* (line 55) returns an integer specifying the port number through which the host computer sent the packet. Method *getLength* (line 56) returns an integer representing the number of bytes of data that were sent. Method *getData* (line 57) returns a byte array containing the data that was sent. The program uses the byte array to initialize a String object, which is then appended to the text to display.

After displaying a packet, line 60 calls method sendPacketToClient (declared at lines 74–86) to create a new packet and send it to the client. Lines 80–82 create a DatagramPacket and pass four arguments to its constructor. The first argument specifies the byte array to send. The second argument specifies the number of bytes to send. The third argument specifies the client computer's Internet address, to which the packet will be sent.

The fourth argument specifies the port where the client is waiting to receive packets. Line 83 sends the packet over the network. Method *send* throws an IOException if an error occurs while sending a packet.

Client Class

Class Client (Fig. 18.7) works similarly to class Server, except that the Client sends packets only when the user types a message in a textfield and presses the *Enter* key. When this occurs, the program calls method actionPerformed (lines 24–51), which converts the string the user entered into a byte array (line 33). Lines 36–37 create a DatagramPacket and initialize it with the byte array, the length of the string that was entered by the user, the IP address to which the packet is to be sent (InetAddress.getLocalHost() in this example) and the port number at which the Server is waiting for packets (5000 in this example). Line 39 sends the packet. Note that the client in this example must know that the server is receiving packets at port 5000; otherwise, the server will not receive the packets.

```
1   // Fig. 18.7: Client.java
2   // Client that sends and receives packets to/from a server.
3   import java.io.*;
4   import java.net.*;
5   import java.awt.*;
6   import java.awt.event.*;
7   import javax.swing.*;
8
9   public class Client extends JFrame {
10     private JTextField enterField;
11     private JTextArea displayArea;
12     private DatagramSocket socket;
13
14     // set up GUI and DatagramSocket
15     public Client()
16     {
17        super( "Client" );
18
19        Container container = getContentPane();
20
21        enterField = new JTextField( "Type message here" );
22        enterField.addActionListener(
23           new ActionListener() {
24              public void actionPerformed( ActionEvent event )
25              {
26                 // create and send packet
27                 try {
28                    displayArea.append( "\nSending packet containing: " +
29                       event.getActionCommand() + "\n" );
30
31                    // get message from textfield and convert to byte array
32                    String message = event.getActionCommand();
33                    byte data[] = message.getBytes();
34
```

Fig. 18.7 Client side of connectionless client/server computing with datagrams. (Part 1 of 4.)

```
35              // create sendPacket
36              DatagramPacket sendPacket = new DatagramPacket( data,
37                 data.length, InetAddress.getLocalHost(), 5000 );
38
39              socket.send( sendPacket ); // send packet
40              displayArea.append( "Packet sent\n" );
41              displayArea.setCaretPosition(
42                 displayArea.getText().length() );
43           }
44
45           // process problems creating or sending packet
46           catch ( IOException ioException ) {
47              displayMessage( ioException.toString() + "\n" );
48              ioException.printStackTrace();
49           }
50
51        } // end actionPerformed
52
53     } // end inner class
54
55  ); // end call to addActionListener
56
57  container.add( enterField, BorderLayout.NORTH );
58
59  displayArea = new JTextArea();
60  container.add( new JScrollPane( displayArea ),
61     BorderLayout.CENTER );
62
63  setSize( 400, 300 );
64  setVisible( true );
65
66  // create DatagramSocket for sending and receiving packets
67  try {
68     socket = new DatagramSocket();
69  }
70
71  // catch problems creating DatagramSocket
72  catch( SocketException socketException ) {
73     socketException.printStackTrace();
74     System.exit( 1 );
75  }
76
77  } // end Client constructor
78
79  // wait for packets to arrive from Server, display packet contents
80  private void waitForPackets()
81  {
82     while ( true ) { // loop forever
83
84        // receive packet and display contents
85        try {
86
```

Fig. 18.7   Client side of connectionless client/server computing with datagrams. (Part 2 of 4.)

```
87              // set up packet
88              byte data[] = new byte[ 100 ];
89              DatagramPacket receivePacket = new DatagramPacket(
90                 data, data.length );
91
92              socket.receive( receivePacket ); // wait for packet
93
94              // display packet contents
95              displayMessage( "\nPacket received:" +
96                 "\nFrom host: " + receivePacket.getAddress() +
97                 "\nHost port: " + receivePacket.getPort() +
98                 "\nLength: " + receivePacket.getLength() +
99                 "\nContaining:\n\t" + new String( receivePacket.getData(),
100                    0, receivePacket.getLength() ) );
101           }
102
103           // process problems receiving or displaying packet
104           catch( IOException exception ) {
105              displayMessage( exception.toString() + "\n" );
106              exception.printStackTrace();
107           }
108
109        } // end while
110
111     } // end method waitForPackets
112
113     // utility method called from other threads to manipulate
114     // displayArea in the event-dispatch thread
115     private void displayMessage( final String messageToDisplay )
116     {
117        // display message from event-dispatch thread of execution
118        SwingUtilities.invokeLater(
119           new Runnable() {  // inner class to ensure GUI updates properly
120
121              public void run() // updates displayArea
122              {
123                 displayArea.append( messageToDisplay );
124                 displayArea.setCaretPosition(
125                    displayArea.getText().length() );
126              }
127
128           } // end inner class
129
130        ); // end call to SwingUtilities.invokeLater
131     }
132
133     public static void main( String args[] )
134     {
135        Client application = new Client();
136        application.setDefaultCloseOperation( JFrame.EXIT_ON_CLOSE );
137        application.waitForPackets();
138     }
```

Fig. 18.7   Client side of connectionless client/server computing with datagrams. (Part 3 of 4.)

139
140 } // end class Client

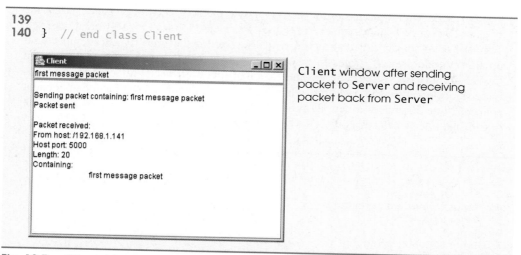

Client window after sending
packet to Server and receiving
packet back from Server

Fig. 18.7   Client side of connectionless client/server computing with datagrams. (Part 4 of 4.)

Notice that the DatagramSocket constructor call (line 68) in this application does not specify any arguments. This constructor allows the computer to select the next available port number for the DatagramSocket. The client does not need a specific port number, because the server receives the client's port number as part of each DatagramPacket sent by the client. Thus, the server can send packets back to the same computer and port number from which the server receives a packet of information.

Client method waitForPackets (lines 80–111) uses an infinite loop to wait for packets from the server. Line 92 blocks until a packet arrives. Note that this does not prevent the user from sending a packet, because the GUI events are handled in the event dispatch thread. It only prevents the while loop from continuing until a packet arrives at the Client. When a packet arrives, line 92 stores the packet in receivePacket, and lines 95–100 call method displayMessage (declared at lines 115–131) to display the packet's contents in the textarea.

18.8 Client/Server Tic-Tac-Toe Using a Multithreaded Server

In this section, we present the popular game Tic-Tac-Toe implemented by using client/server techniques with stream sockets. The program consists of a TicTacToeServer application (Fig. 18.8) that allows two TicTacToeClient applets (Fig. 18.9) to connect to the server and play Tic-Tac-Toe. Sample outputs are shown in Fig. 18.10.

TicTacToeServer Class

As the TicTacToeServer receives each client connection, it creates an instance of inner-class Player (lines 163–280 of Fig. 18.8) to process the client in a separate thread. These threads enable the clients to play the game independently. The first client to connect to the server is player X and the second client to connect is player O. Player X makes the first move. The server maintains the information about the board so it can determine whether a player's move is a valid or invalid move.

We begin with a discussion of the server side of the Tic-Tac-Toe game. When the TicTacToeServer application executes, the main method (lines 155–160) creates a Tic-TacToeServer object called application. The constructor (lines 19–46) attempts to set up a ServerSocket. If successful, the program displays the server window, then main invokes the TicTacToeServer method execute (lines 49–74). Method execute loops twice, blocking at line 56 each time while waiting for a client connection. When a client connects, line 56 creates a new Player object to manage the connection as a separate thread, and line 57 calls that object's start method to begin executing the thread.

```java
1   // Fig. 18.8: TicTacToeServer.java
2   // This class maintains a game of Tic-Tac-Toe for two client applets.
3   import java.awt.*;
4   import java.awt.event.*;
5   import java.net.*;
6   import java.io.*;
7   import javax.swing.*;
8
9   public class TicTacToeServer extends JFrame {
10     private char[] board;
11     private JTextArea outputArea;
12     private Player[] players;
13     private ServerSocket server;
14     private int currentPlayer;
15     private final int PLAYER_X = 0, PLAYER_O = 1;
16     private final char X_MARK = 'X', O_MARK = 'O';
17
18     // set up tic-tac-toe server and GUI that displays messages
19     public TicTacToeServer()
20     {
21        super( "Tic-Tac-Toe Server" );
22
23        board = new char[ 9 ];
24        players = new Player[ 2 ];
25        currentPlayer = PLAYER_X;
26
27        // set up ServerSocket
28        try {
29           server = new ServerSocket( 12345, 2 );
30        }
31
32        // process problems creating ServerSocket
33        catch( IOException ioException ) {
34           ioException.printStackTrace();
35           System.exit( 1 );
36        }
37
38        // set up JTextArea to display messages during execution
39        outputArea = new JTextArea();
40        getContentPane().add( outputArea, BorderLayout.CENTER );
41        outputArea.setText( "Server awaiting connections\n" );
42
```

Fig. 18.8   Server side of client/server Tic-Tac-Toe program. (Part 1 of 6.)

```
43          setSize( 300, 300 );
44          setVisible( true );
45
46      } // end TicTacToeServer constructor
47
48      // wait for two connections so game can be played
49      public void execute()
50      {
51          // wait for each client to connect
52          for ( int i = 0; i < players.length; i++ ) {
53
54              // wait for connection, create Player, start thread
55              try {
56                  players[ i ] = new Player( server.accept(), i );
57                  players[ i ].start();
58              }
59
60              // process problems receiving connection from client
61              catch( IOException ioException ) {
62                  ioException.printStackTrace();
63                  System.exit( 1 );
64              }
65          }
66
67          // Player X is suspended until Player O connects.
68          // Resume player X now.
69          synchronized ( players[ PLAYER_X ] ) {
70              players[ PLAYER_X ].setSuspended( false );
71              players[ PLAYER_X ].notify();
72          }
73
74      } // end method execute
75
76      // utility method called from other threads to manipulate
77      // outputArea in the event-dispatch thread
78      private void displayMessage( final String messageToDisplay )
79      {
80          // display message from event-dispatch thread of execution
81          SwingUtilities.invokeLater(
82              new Runnable() {  // inner class to ensure GUI updates properly
83
84                  public void run() // updates outputArea
85                  {
86                      outputArea.append( messageToDisplay );
87                      outputArea.setCaretPosition(
88                          outputArea.getText().length() );
89                  }
90
91              } // end inner class
92
93          ); // end call to SwingUtilities.invokeLater
94      }
95
```

Fig. 18.8   Server side of client/server Tic-Tac-Toe program. (Part 2 of 6.)

```
96      // Determine if a move is valid. This method is synchronized because
97      // only one move can be made at a time.
98      public synchronized boolean validateAndMove( int location, int player )
99      {
100        boolean moveDone = false;
101
102        // while not current player, must wait for turn
103        while ( player != currentPlayer ) {
104
105           // wait for turn
106           try {
107              wait();
108           }
109
110           // catch wait interruptions
111           catch( InterruptedException interruptedException ) {
112              interruptedException.printStackTrace();
113           }
114        }
115
116        // if location not occupied, make move
117        if ( !isOccupied( location ) ) {
118
119           // set move in board array
120           board[ location ] = currentPlayer == PLAYER_X ? X_MARK : O_MARK;
121
122           // change current player
123           currentPlayer = ( currentPlayer + 1 ) % 2;
124
125           // let new current player know that move occurred
126           players[ currentPlayer ].otherPlayerMoved( location );
127
128           notify(); // tell waiting player to continue
129
130           // tell player that made move that the move was valid
131           return true;
132        }
133
134        // tell player that made move that the move was not valid
135        else
136           return false;
137
138     } // end method validateAndMove
139
140     // determine whether location is occupied
141     public boolean isOccupied( int location )
142     {
143        if ( board[ location ] == X_MARK || board [ location ] == O_MARK )
144           return true;
145        else
146           return false;
147     }
148
```

Fig. 18.8   Server side of client/server Tic-Tac-Toe program. (Part 3 of 6.)

```
149        // place code in this method to determine whether game over
150        public boolean isGameOver()
151        {
152           return false;  // this is left as an exercise
153        }
154
155        public static void main( String args[] )
156        {
157           TicTacToeServer application = new TicTacToeServer();
158           application.setDefaultCloseOperation( JFrame.EXIT_ON_CLOSE );
159           application.execute();
160        }
161
162        // private inner class Player manages each Player as a thread
163        private class Player extends Thread {
164           private Socket connection;
165           private DataInputStream input;
166           private DataOutputStream output;
167           private int playerNumber;
168           private char mark;
169           protected boolean suspended = true;
170
171           // set up Player thread
172           public Player( Socket socket, int number )
173           {
174              playerNumber = number;
175
176              // specify player's mark
177              mark = ( playerNumber == PLAYER_X ? X_MARK : O_MARK );
178
179              connection = socket;
180
181              // obtain streams from Socket
182              try {
183                 input = new DataInputStream( connection.getInputStream() );
184                 output = new DataOutputStream( connection.getOutputStream() );
185              }
186
187              // process problems getting streams
188              catch( IOException ioException ) {
189                 ioException.printStackTrace();
190                 System.exit( 1 );
191              }
192
193           } // end Player constructor
194
195           // send message that other player moved
196           public void otherPlayerMoved( int location )
197           {
198              // send message indicating move
199              try {
200                 output.writeUTF( "Opponent moved" );
201                 output.writeInt( location );
```

Fig. 18.8   Server side of client/server Tic-Tac-Toe program. (Part 4 of 6.)

```
202              }
203
204         // process problems sending message
205         catch ( IOException ioException ) {
206            ioException.printStackTrace();
207         }
208      }
209
210      // control thread's execution
211      public void run()
212      {
213         // send client message indicating its mark (X or O),
214         // process messages from client
215         try {
216            displayMessage( "Player " + ( playerNumber ==
217               PLAYER_X ? X_MARK : O_MARK ) + " connected\n" );
218
219            output.writeChar( mark ); // send player's mark
220
221            // send message indicating connection
222            output.writeUTF( "Player " + ( playerNumber == PLAYER_X ?
223               "X connected\n" : "O connected, please wait\n" ) );
224
225            // if player X, wait for another player to arrive
226            if ( mark == X_MARK ) {
227               output.writeUTF( "Waiting for another player" );
228
229               // wait for player O
230               try {
231                  synchronized( this ) {
232                     while ( suspended )
233                        wait();
234                  }
235               }
236
237               // process interruptions while waiting
238               catch ( InterruptedException exception ) {
239                  exception.printStackTrace();
240               }
241
242               // send message that other player connected and
243               // player X can make a move
244               output.writeUTF( "Other player connected. Your move." );
245            }
246
247            // while game not over
248            while ( ! isGameOver() ) {
249
250               // get move location from client
251               int location = input.readInt();
252
253               // check for valid move
254               if ( validateAndMove( location, playerNumber ) ) {
```

Fig. 18.8   Server side of client/server Tic-Tac-Toe program. (Part 5 of 6.)

```
255              displayMessage( "\nlocation: " + location );
256              output.writeUTF( "Valid move." );
257           }
258           else
259              output.writeUTF( "Invalid move, try again" );
260        }
261
262        connection.close(); // close connection to client
263
264     } // end try
265
266     // process problems communicating with client
267     catch( IOException ioException ) {
268        ioException.printStackTrace();
269        System.exit( 1 );
270     }
271
272  } // end method run
273
274  // set whether or not thread is suspended
275  public void setSuspended( boolean status )
276  {
277     suspended = status;
278  }
279
280  } // end class Player
281
282 } // end class TicTacToeServer
```

Fig. 18.8   Server side of client/server Tic-Tac-Toe program. (Part 6 of 6.)

When the TicTacToeServer creates a Player, the Player constructor (lines 172–193) receives the Socket object representing the connection to the client and gets the associated input and output streams. The Player's run method (lines 211–272) controls the information that is sent to the client and the information that is received from the client. First, it passes to the client the character that the client will place on the board when a move is made (line 219). Then, it tells the client that the client's connection has been made (lines 222–223). Lines 231–234 suspend player X's thread as it starts executing, because player X can move only after player O connects.

At this point, the game can be played, and the `run` method begins executing its `while` structure (lines 248–260). Each iteration of this loop reads an integer (line 250) representing the location where the client wants to place a mark, and line 254 invokes the `Tic-TacToeServer` method `validateAndMove` (declared at lines 98–138) to check the move. If the move is valid line 256 sends a message to the client indicating that the move was valid; otherwise, line 259 sends a message to the client indicating that the move was invalid. The program maintains board locations as numbers from 0 to 8 (0 through 2 for the first row, 3 through 5 for the second row and 6 through 8 for the third row).

Method `validateAndMove` (lines 98–138 in class `TicTacToeServer`) is a `synchronized` method that allows only one player at a time to move. Synchronizing `validMove` prevents both players from modifying the state information of the game simultaneously. If the `Player` attempting to validate a move is not the current player (i.e., the one allowed to make a move), the `Player` is placed in a *wait* state until it is that `Player`'s turn to move. If the position for the move being validated is already occupied on the board, `validMove` returns `false`. Otherwise, the server places a mark for the player in its local representation of the board (line 120), notifies the other `Player` object (line 126) that a move has been made (so the client can be sent a message), invokes method `notify` (line 128) so the waiting `Player` (if there is one) can validate a move and returns `true` (line 131) to indicate that the move is valid.

TicTacToeClient Applet Class

Each `TicTacToeClient` applet (Fig. 18.9) maintains its own GUI version of the Tic-Tac-Toe board on which it displays the state of the game. The clients can place a mark only in an empty square on the board. Inner-class `Square` (lines 226–281 of Fig. 18.9) implements each of the nine squares on the board. When a `TicTacToeClient` applet begins execution, it creates a `JTextArea` in which messages from the server and a representation of the board using nine `Square` objects are displayed. The applet's `start` method (lines 67–89) opens a connection to the server and gets the associated input and output streams from the `Socket` object. Line 73 makes a connection to the applet host. The host name is obtained by calling method `getCodeBase` of `JApplet` to get the URL of the applet and then calling method `getHost` of the URL to get the host name of the URL. Class `TicTacToeClient` implements interface `Runnable` so that a separate thread can read messages from the server. This approach enables the user to interact with the board (in the event-dispatch thread) while waiting for messages from the server. After establishing the connection to the server, line 86 creates `Thread` object `outputThread` and initializes it with `this` applet (a `Runnable` object), then line 88 calls the thread's `start` method. The applet's `run` method (lines 92–122) controls the separate thread of execution. The method first reads the mark character (X or O) from the server (line 96), then loops continuously (lines 111–113) and reads messages from the server (line 112). Each message is passed to the applet's `processMessage` method (lines 125–166) for processing.

If the message received is `"Valid move."`, lines 129–130 display the message `"Valid move, please wait."` and call method `setMark` (lines 189–199) to set the client's mark in the current square (the one in which the user clicked) using `SwingUtilities` method `invokeLater` to ensure that the GUI updates occur in the event-dispatch

thread. If the message received is "Invalid move, try again.", line 135 displays the
message so the user can click a different square. If the message received is "Opponent
moved.", lines 144–151 read an integer from the server indicating where the opponent
moved and place a mark in that square of the board (again using SwingUtilities method
invokeLater to ensure that the GUI updates occur in the event dispatch thread). If any
other message is received, line 164 simply displays the message. Figure 18.10 shows
sample screen captures of two applets interacting via the TicTacToeServer.

```java
1   // Fig. 18.9: TicTacToeClient.java
2   // Client that let a user play Tic-Tac-Toe with another across a network.
3   import java.awt.*;
4   import java.awt.event.*;
5   import java.net.*;
6   import java.io.*;
7   import javax.swing.*;
8
9   public class TicTacToeClient extends JApplet implements Runnable {
10      private JTextField idField;
11      private JTextArea displayArea;
12      private JPanel boardPanel, panel2;
13      private Square board[][], currentSquare;
14      private Socket connection;
15      private DataInputStream input;
16      private DataOutputStream output;
17      private char myMark;
18      private boolean myTurn;
19      private final char X_MARK = 'X', O_MARK = 'O';
20
21      // Set up user-interface and board
22      public void init()
23      {
24         Container container = getContentPane();
25
26         // set up JTextArea to display messages to user
27         displayArea = new JTextArea( 4, 30 );
28         displayArea.setEditable( false );
29         container.add( new JScrollPane( displayArea ), BorderLayout.SOUTH );
30
31         // set up panel for squares in board
32         boardPanel = new JPanel();
33         boardPanel.setLayout( new GridLayout( 3, 3, 0, 0 ) );
34
35         // create board
36         board = new Square[ 3 ][ 3 ];
37
38         // When creating a Square, the location argument to the constructor
39         // is a value from 0 to 8 indicating the position of the Square on
40         // the board. Values 0, 1, and 2 are the first row, values 3, 4,
41         // and 5 are the second row. Values 6, 7, and 8 are the third row.
42         for ( int row = 0; row < board.length; row++ ) {
43
```

Fig. 18.9   Client side of client/server Tic-Tac-Toe program. (Part 1 of 6.)

```
44            for ( int column = 0; column < board[ row ].length; column++ ) {
45
46                // create Square
47                board[ row ][ column ] = new Square( ' ', row * 3 + column );
48                boardPanel.add( board[ row ][ column ] );
49            }
50        }
51
52        // textfield to display player's mark
53        idField = new JTextField();
54        idField.setEditable( false );
55        container.add( idField, BorderLayout.NORTH );
56
57        // set up panel to contain boardPanel (for layout purposes)
58        panel2 = new JPanel();
59        panel2.add( boardPanel, BorderLayout.CENTER );
60        container.add( panel2, BorderLayout.CENTER );
61
62    } // end method init
63
64    // Make connection to server and get associated streams.
65    // Start separate thread to allow this applet to
66    // continually update its output in textarea display.
67    public void start()
68    {
69        // connect to server, get streams and start outputThread
70        try {
71
72            // make connection
73            connection = new Socket( getCodeBase().getHost(), 12345 );
74
75            // get streams
76            input = new DataInputStream( connection.getInputStream() );
77            output = new DataOutputStream( connection.getOutputStream() );
78        }
79
80        // catch problems setting up connection and streams
81        catch ( IOException ioException ) {
82            ioException.printStackTrace();
83        }
84
85        // create and start output thread
86        Thread outputThread = new Thread( this );
87        outputThread.start();
88
89    } // end method start
90
91    // control thread that allows continuous update of displayArea
92    public void run()
93    {
94        // get player's mark (X or O)
95        try {
96            myMark = input.readChar();
```

Fig. 18.9   Client side of client/server Tic-Tac-Toe program. (Part 2 of 6.)

```
97
98              // display player ID in event-dispatch thread
99              SwingUtilities.invokeLater(
100                 new Runnable() {
101                    public void run()
102                    {
103                       idField.setText( "You are player \"" + myMark + "\"" );
104                    }
105                 }
106              );
107
108              myTurn = ( myMark == X_MARK ? true : false );
109
110              // receive messages sent to client and output them
111              while ( true ) {
112                 processMessage( input.readUTF() );
113              }
114
115           } // end try
116
117           // process problems communicating with server
118           catch ( IOException ioException ) {
119              ioException.printStackTrace();
120           }
121
122        } // end method run
123
124        // process messages received by client
125        private void processMessage( String message )
126        {
127           // valid move occurred
128           if ( message.equals( "Valid move." ) ) {
129              displayMessage( "Valid move, please wait.\n" );
130              setMark( currentSquare, myMark );
131           }
132
133           // invalid move occurred
134           else if ( message.equals( "Invalid move, try again" ) ) {
135              displayMessage( message + "\n" );
136              myTurn = true;
137           }
138
139           // opponent moved
140           else if ( message.equals( "Opponent moved" ) ) {
141
142              // get move location and update board
143              try {
144                 int location = input.readInt();
145                 int row = location / 3;
146                 int column = location % 3;
147
148                 setMark( board[ row ][ column ],
149                    ( myMark == X_MARK ? O_MARK : X_MARK ) );
```

Fig. 18.9   Client side of client/server Tic-Tac-Toe program. (Part 3 of 6.)

```
150                displayMessage( "Opponent moved. Your turn.\n" );
151                myTurn = true;
152
153             } // end try
154
155             // process problems communicating with server
156             catch ( IOException ioException ) {
157                ioException.printStackTrace();
158             }
159
160          } // end else if
161
162          // simply display message
163          else
164             displayMessage( message + "\n" );
165
166       } // end method processMessage
167
168       // utility method called from other threads to manipulate
169       // outputArea in the event-dispatch thread
170       private void displayMessage( final String messageToDisplay )
171       {
172          // display message from event-dispatch thread of execution
173          SwingUtilities.invokeLater(
174             new Runnable() {  // inner class to ensure GUI updates properly
175
176                public void run() // updates displayArea
177                {
178                   displayArea.append( messageToDisplay );
179                   displayArea.setCaretPosition(
180                      displayArea.getText().length() );
181                }
182
183             }  // end inner class
184
185          ); // end call to SwingUtilities.invokeLater
186       }
187
188       // utility method to set mark on board in event-dispatch thread
189       private void setMark( final Square squareToMark, final char mark )
190       {
191          SwingUtilities.invokeLater(
192             new Runnable() {
193                public void run()
194                {
195                   squareToMark.setMark( mark );
196                }
197             }
198          );
199       }
200
```

Fig. 18.9   Client side of client/server Tic-Tac-Toe program. (Part 4 of 6.)

```
201        // send message to server indicating clicked square
202        public void sendClickedSquare( int location )
203        {
204           if ( myTurn ) {
205
206              // send location to server
207              try {
208                 output.writeInt( location );
209                 myTurn = false;
210              }
211
212              // process problems communicating with server
213              catch ( IOException ioException ) {
214                 ioException.printStackTrace();
215              }
216           }
217        }
218
219        // set current Square
220        public void setCurrentSquare( Square square )
221        {
222           currentSquare = square;
223        }
224
225        // private inner class for the squares on the board
226        private class Square extends JPanel {
227           private char mark;
228           private int location;
229
230           public Square( char squareMark, int squareLocation )
231           {
232              mark = squareMark;
233              location = squareLocation;
234
235              addMouseListener(
236                 new MouseAdapter() {
237                    public void mouseReleased( MouseEvent e )
238                    {
239                       setCurrentSquare( Square.this );
240                       sendClickedSquare( getSquareLocation() );
241                    }
242                 }
243              );
244
245           } // end Square constructor
246
247           // return preferred size of Square
248           public Dimension getPreferredSize()
249           {
250              return new Dimension( 30, 30 );
251           }
252
```

Fig. 18.9   Client side of client/server Tic-Tac-Toe program. (Part 5 of 6.)

```
253        // return minimum size of Square
254        public Dimension getMinimumSize()
255        {
256            return getPreferredSize();
257        }
258
259        // set mark for Square
260        public void setMark( char newMark )
261        {
262            mark = newMark;
263            repaint();
264        }
265
266        // return Square location
267        public int getSquareLocation()
268        {
269            return location;
270        }
271
272        // draw Square
273        public void paintComponent( Graphics g )
274        {
275            super.paintComponent( g );
276
277            g.drawRect( 0, 0, 29, 29 );
278            g.drawString( String.valueOf( mark ), 11, 20 );
279        }
280
281    } // end inner-class Square
282
283 } // end class TicTacToeClient
```

Fig. 18.9   Client side of client/server Tic-Tac-Toe program. (Part 6 of 6.)

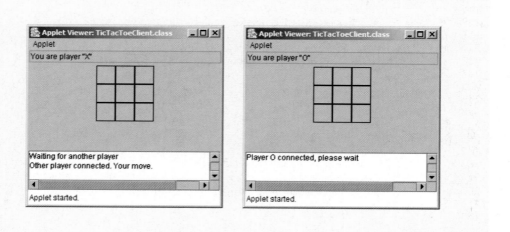

Fig. 18.10   Sample outputs from the client/server Tic-Tac-Toe program. (Part 1 of 2.)

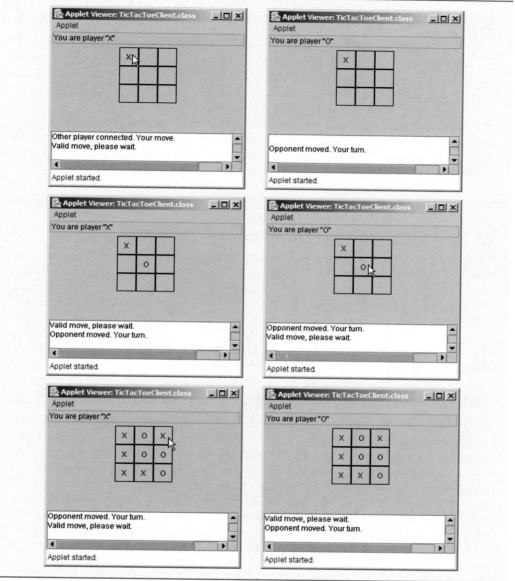

Fig. 18.10 Sample outputs from the client/server Tic-Tac-Toe program. (Part 2 of 2.)

18.9 Security and the Network

As much as we look forward to writing a great variety of powerful network-based applications, our efforts may be limited because of security concerns. Many Web browsers, such as Netscape and Microsoft Internet Explorer, by default prohibit Java applets from doing file processing on the machines on which they execute. Think about it. A Java applet is designed to be sent to your browser via an HTML document that could be downloaded from any Web server in the world. Often you will know very little about the sources of Java applets that will execute on your system. To allow these applets free rein with your files could be disastrous.

A more subtle situation occurs with limiting the machines to which executing applets can make network connections. To build truly collaborative applications, we would ideally like to have our applets communicate with machines almost anywhere. The Java security manager in a Web browser often restricts an applet so that it can communicate only with the machine from which it was originally downloaded.

These restrictions might seem too harsh. However, the Java Security API now provides capabilities for digitally signed applets that will enable browsers to determine whether an applet is downloaded from a *trusted source*. In cases where an applet is trusted, the applet can be given additional access to the computer on which the applet is executing. The features of the Java Security API and additional networking capabilities are discussed in our text *Advanced Java 2 Platform How to Program*.

18.10 DeitelMessenger Chat Server and Client

Chat rooms have become quite common on the Internet. Chat rooms provide a central location where users can chat with each other via short text messages. Each participant in a chat room can see all messages that other users post, and each user can post messages in the chat room. This section presents our capstone networking case study that integrates many of the Java networking, multithreading and Swing GUI features we have learned thus far to build an online chat system. We also introduce *multicast*, which enables an application to send `DatagramPacket`s to groups of clients. After reading this section, you will be able to build more significant networking applications.

18.10.1 DeitelMessengerServer and Supporting Classes

`DeitelMessengerServer` (Fig. 18.11) is the heart of the online chat system. This class appears in package `com.deitel.messenger.sockets.server`. Chat clients can participate in a chat by connecting to the `DeitelMessengerServer`. Method `startServer` (lines 16–51) launches `DeitelMessengerServer`. Lines 22–23 create a `ServerSocket` to accept incoming network connections. Recall that the `ServerSocket` constructor takes as its first argument the port on which the server should listen for incoming connections. Interface `SocketMessengerConstants` (Fig. 18.12) declares the port number as the constant `SERVER_PORT` to ensure that the server and the clients use the correct port number.

```
1   // Fig. 18.11: DeitelMessengerServer.java
2   // DeitelMessengerServer is a multi-threaded, socket- and
3   // packet-based chat server.
4   package com.deitel.messenger.sockets.server;
5
6   import java.util.*;
7   import java.net.*;
8   import java.io.*;
```

Fig. 18.11 `DeitelMessengerServer` for managing a chat room. (Part 1 of 3.)

```
9
10   import com.deitel.messenger.*;
11   import com.deitel.messenger.sockets.*;
12
13   public class DeitelMessengerServer implements MessageListener {
14
15      // start chat server
16      public void startServer()
17      {
18         // create server and manage new clients
19         try {
20
21            // create ServerSocket for incoming connections
22            ServerSocket serverSocket = new ServerSocket(
23               SocketMessengerConstants.SERVER_PORT, 100 );
24
25            System.out.println( "Server listening on port " +
26               SocketMessengerConstants.SERVER_PORT + " ..." );
27
28            // listen for clients constantly
29            while ( true ) {
30
31               // accept new client connection
32               Socket clientSocket = serverSocket.accept();
33
34               // create new ReceivingThread for receiving
35               // messages from client
36               new ReceivingThread( this, clientSocket ).start();
37
38               // print connection information
39               System.out.println( "Connection received from: " +
40                  clientSocket.getInetAddress() );
41
42            } // end while
43
44         } // end try
45
46         // handle exception creating server and connecting clients
47         catch ( IOException ioException ) {
48            ioException.printStackTrace();
49         }
50
51      } // end method startServer
52
53      // when new message is received, broadcast message to clients
54      public void messageReceived( String from, String message )
55      {
56         // create String containing entire message
57         String completeMessage = from +
58            SocketMessengerConstants.MESSAGE_SEPARATOR + message;
59
60         // create and start MulticastSendingThread to broadcast
61         // new messages to all clients
```

Fig. 18.11 DeitelMessengerServer for managing a chat room. (Part 2 of 3.)

```
62              new MulticastSendingThread( completeMessage.getBytes() ).start();
63         }
64
65         public static void main ( String args[] )
66         {
67              new DeitelMessengerServer().startServer();
68         }
69
70    } // end class DeitelMessengerServer
```

```
Server listening on port 5000 ...
Connection received from: SEANSANTRY/XXX.XXX.XXX.XXX
Connection received from: PJD/XXX.XXX.XXX.XXX
```

Fig. 18.11 DeitelMessengerServer for managing a chat room. (Part 3 of 3.)

Lines 29–42 listen continuously for new client connections. Line 32 invokes Server-Socket method accept to wait for and accept a new client connection. Line 36 creates and starts a new ReceivingThread for the client. Class ReceivingThread (Fig. 18.14) of package com.deitel.messenger.sockets.server is a Thread subclass that listens for incoming messages from a client. The first argument to the ReceivingThread constructor is a MessageListener (Fig. 18.13), to which messages from the client should be delivered. Class DeitelMessengerServer implements interface MessageListener (line 13) of package com.deitel.messenger and therefore can pass the this reference to the ReceivingThread constructor.

When each ReceivingThread receives a new message from a client, the ReceivingThread passes the message to a MessageListener through method messageReceived (lines 54–63). Lines 57–58 concatenate the from string with the separator >>> and the message body. Line 62 creates and starts a new MulticastSendingThread to deliver completeMessage to all clients. Class MulticastSendingThread (Fig. 18.15) of package com.deitel.messenger.sockets.server uses *multicast* as an efficient mechanism for sending one message to multiple clients. We discuss the details of multicasting shortly. Method main (lines 65–68) creates a new DeitelMessengerServer instance and starts the server.

Interface SocketMessengerConstants (Fig. 18.12) declares constants for use in the various classes that make up the Deitel messenger system. Classes can access these static constants by referencing the constants through interface SocketMessengerConstants (e.g., SocketMessengerConstants.SERVER_PORT).

```
1   // Fig. 18.12: SocketMessengerConstants.java
2   // SocketMessengerConstants declares constants for the port numbers
3   // and multicast address in DeitelMessenger
4   package com.deitel.messenger.sockets;
5
```

Fig. 18.12 SocketMessengerConstants declares constants for use in the DeitelMessengerServer and DeitelMessenger. (Part 1 of 2.)

```
6   public interface SocketMessengerConstants {
7
8       // address for multicast datagrams
9       public static final String MULTICAST_ADDRESS = "239.0.0.1";
10
11      // port for listening for multicast datagrams
12      public static final int MULTICAST_LISTENING_PORT = 5555;
13
14      // port for sending multicast datagrams
15      public static final int MULTICAST_SENDING_PORT = 5554;
16
17      // port for Socket connections to DeitelMessengerServer
18      public static final int SERVER_PORT = 5000;
19
20      // String that indicates disconnect
21      public static final String DISCONNECT_STRING = "DISCONNECT";
22
23      // String that separates the user name from the message body
24      public static final String MESSAGE_SEPARATOR = ">>>";
25
26      // message size (in bytes)
27      public static final int MESSAGE_SIZE = 512;
28   }
```

Fig. 18.12 SocketMessengerConstants declares constants for use in the DeitelMessengerServer and DeitelMessenger. (Part 2 of 2.)

Line 9 declares the String constant MULTICAST_ADDRESS, which contains the address to which a MulticastSendingThread (Fig. 18.15) should send messages. This address is one of the addresses reserved for multicast, which we describe in the discussion of Fig. 18.15. Line 12 declares the integer constant MULTICAST_LISTENING_PORT—the port on which clients should listen for new messages. Line 15 declares the integer constant MULTICAST_SENDING_PORT—the port to which a MulticastSendingThread should post new messages at the MULTICAST_ADDRESS. Line 18 declares the integer constant SERVER_PORT—the port on which DeitelMessengerServer listens for incoming client connections. Line 21 declares String constant DISCONNECT_STRING, which is the String that a client sends to DeitelMessengerServer when the user wishes to leave the chat room. Line 24 declares String constant MESSAGE_SEPARATOR, which separates the user name from the message body. Line 27 specifies the maximum message size in bytes.

Many different classes in the Deitel messenger system receive messages. For example, DeitelMessengerServer receives messages from clients and delivers those messages to all chat room participants. As we will see, the user interface for each client also receives messages and displays those messages to the users. Each of the classes that receives messages implements interface MessageListener (Fig. 18.13). The interface (from package com.deitel.messenger) declares method messageReceived, which allows an implementing class to receive chat messages. Method messageReceived takes two string arguments representing the name of sender and the message body, respectively.

```
1   // Fig. 18.13: MessageListener.java
2   // MessageListener is an interface for classes that wish to
3   // receive new chat messages.
4   package com.deitel.messenger;
5
6   public interface MessageListener {
7
8       // receive new chat message
9       public void messageReceived( String from, String message );
10  }
```

Fig. 18.13 MessageListener interface that declares method messageReceived for receiving new chat messages.

DeitelMessengerServer uses instances of class ReceivingThread (Fig. 18.14) from package com.deitel.messenger.sockets.server to listen for new messages from each client. Class ReceivingThread extends class Thread. This enables Deitel-MessengerServer to create an object of class ReceivingThread for each client, to handle messages from multiple clients at once. When DeitelMessengerServer receives a new client connection, DeitelMessengerServer creates a new ReceivingThread for the client, then continues listening for new client connections. The ReceivingThread listens for messages from a single client and passes those messages back to the Deitel-MessengerServer through method messageReceived.

```
1   // Fig. 18.14: ReceivingThread.java
2   // ReceivingThread is a Thread that listens for messages from a
3   // particular client and delivers messages to a MessageListener.
4   package com.deitel.messenger.sockets.server;
5
6   import java.io.*;
7   import java.net.*;
8   import java.util.StringTokenizer;
9
10  import com.deitel.messenger.*;
11  import com.deitel.messenger.sockets.*;
12
13  public class ReceivingThread extends Thread {
14
15      private BufferedReader input;
16      private MessageListener messageListener;
17      private boolean keepListening = true;
18
19      // ReceivingThread constructor
20      public ReceivingThread( MessageListener listener, Socket clientSocket )
21      {
22          // invoke superclass constructor to name Thread
23          super( "ReceivingThread: " + clientSocket );
24
25          // set listener to which new messages should be sent
26          messageListener = listener;
```

Fig. 18.14 ReceivingThread for listening for new messages from DeitelMessengerServer clients in separate threads. (Part 1 of 3.)

```
27
28        // set timeout for reading from clientSocket and create
29        // BufferedReader for reading incoming messages
30        try {
31           clientSocket.setSoTimeout( 5000 );
32
33           input = new BufferedReader( new InputStreamReader(
34              clientSocket.getInputStream() ) );
35        }
36
37        // handle exception creating BufferedReader
38        catch ( IOException ioException ) {
39           ioException.printStackTrace();
40        }
41
42     } // end ReceivingThread constructor
43
44     // listen for new messages and deliver them to MessageListener
45     public void run()
46     {
47        String message;
48
49        // listen for messages until stopped
50        while ( keepListening ) {
51
52           // read message from BufferedReader
53           try {
54              message = input.readLine();
55           }
56
57           // handle exception if read times out
58           catch ( InterruptedIOException interruptedIOException ) {
59
60              // continue to next iteration to keep listening
61              continue;
62           }
63
64           // handle exception reading message
65           catch ( IOException ioException ) {
66              ioException.printStackTrace();
67              break;
68           }
69
70           // ensure non-null message
71           if ( message != null ) {
72
73              // tokenize message to retrieve user name and message body
74              StringTokenizer tokenizer = new StringTokenizer(
75                 message, SocketMessengerConstants.MESSAGE_SEPARATOR );
76
77              // ignore messages that do not contain a user
78              // name and message body
```

Fig. 18.14 ReceivingThread for listening for new messages from DeitelMessengerServer clients in separate threads. (Part 2 of 3.)

```
79                  if ( tokenizer.countTokens() == 2 )
80
81                     // send message to MessageListener
82                  messageListener.messageReceived(
83                     tokenizer.nextToken(),    // user name
84                     tokenizer.nextToken() ); // message body
85
86             else
87
88                     // if disconnect message received, stop listening
89                  if ( message.equalsIgnoreCase(
90                     SocketMessengerConstants.MESSAGE_SEPARATOR +
91                     SocketMessengerConstants.DISCONNECT_STRING ) )
92                     stopListening();
93
94          } // end if
95
96       } // end while
97
98       // close BufferedReader (also closes Socket)
99       try {
100         input.close();
101      }
102
103      // handle exception closing BufferedReader
104      catch ( IOException ioException ) {
105         ioException.printStackTrace();
106      }
107
108   } // end method run
109
110   // stop listening for incoming messages
111   public void stopListening()
112   {
113      keepListening = false;
114   }
115
116 } // end class ReceivingThread
```

Fig. 18.14   ReceivingThread for listening for new messages from
DeitelMessengerServer clients in separate threads. (Part 3 of 3.)

The ReceivingThread constructor (lines 20–42) takes a MessageListener as its first argument. The ReceivingThread will deliver new messages to this listener by invoking its messageReceived method. The ReceivingThread constructor's Socket argument is the connection to a particular client. Line 23 invokes the Thread constructor to provide a unique name for each ReceivingThread instance. Recall that naming each thread can be useful when debugging an application. Line 26 sets the MessageListener to which the ReceivingThread should deliver new messages. Line 31 invokes Socket method *setSoTimeout* with an integer argument of 5000 milliseconds. Reading data from a Socket is a *blocking call*—the current thread is put in the blocked state (Fig. 16.1) while the thread waits for the read operation to complete. Method setSoTimeout specifies that, if no data is received in the given number of milliseconds, the Socket should issue an

InterruptedIOException, which the current thread can catch, then continue executing. This technique prevents the current thread from deadlocking if no more data is available from the Socket. Lines 33–34 create a new BufferedReader for the clientSocket's InputStream. The ReceivingThread uses this BufferedReader to read new messages from the client.

Method run (lines 45–108) listens continuously for new messages from the client. Lines 50–95 loop as long as the boolean variable keepListening is true. Line 54 invokes BufferedReader method readLine to read a line of text from the client. If more than 5000 milliseconds pass without reading any data, method readLine throws an InterruptedIOException, which indicates that the time-out set on line 31 has expired. Line 61 uses a continue statement to go to the next iteration of the while loop to continue listening for messages. Lines 65–68 catch an IOException, which indicates a more severe problem from method readLine. In this case, line 66 prints a stack trace to aid in debugging the application, and line 67 uses keyword break to terminate the loop.

When a client sends a message to the server, the client separates the user's name from the message body with the SocketMessengerConstants.MESSAGE_SEPARATOR. If there are no exceptions thrown when reading data from the client and the message is not null (line 71), lines 74–75 create a new StringTokenizer that uses delimiter SocketMessengerConstants.MESSAGE_SEPARATOR to separate each message into two tokens—the sender's user name and the message. Line 79 checks for the proper number of tokens, and lines 82–84 invoke method messageReceived of interface MessageListener to deliver the new message to the registered MessageListener. If the StringTokenizer does not produce two tokens, lines 89–91 check the message to see whether it matches the constant SockerMessengerConstants.DISCONNECT_STRING, which would indicate that the user wishes to leave the chat room. If the strings match, line 92 invokes ReceivingThread method stopListening to terminate the ReceivingThread.

Method stopListening (lines 111–114) sets boolean variable keepListening to false. This causes the while loop condition that starts at line 50 to fail and causes the ReceivingThread to close the client Socket (line 100). Then, method run returns, which terminates the ReceivingThread's execution.

MulticastSendingThread (Fig. 18.15) delivers DatagramPackets containing chat messages to a group of clients. Multicast is an efficient way to send data to many clients without the overhead of broadcasting that data to every host on the Internet. To understand multicast, let us look at a real-world analogy—the relationship between a magazine publisher and that magazine's subscribers. The magazine publisher produces a magazine and provides the magazine to a distributor. Customers interested in that magazine obtain a subscription and begin receiving the magazine in the mail from the distributor. This communication is quite different from a television broadcast. When a television station produces a television program, the station broadcasts that television show throughout a geographical region or perhaps throughout the world by using satellites. Broadcasting a television show for 10,000 viewers is no more expensive to the television station than broadcasting a television show for 100 viewers—the radio signal carrying the broadcast reaches a wide area. However, printing and delivering a magazine to 10,000 readers would be much more expensive than printing and delivering the magazine to 100 readers. Most magazine publishers could not stay in business if they had to broadcast their magazines to everyone, so magazine publishers multicast their magazines to a group of subscribers instead.

```java
1   // Fig. 18.15: MulticastSendingThread.java
2   // MulticastSendingThread is a Thread that broadcasts a chat
3   // message using a multicast datagram.
4   package com.deitel.messenger.sockets.server;
5
6   import java.io.*;
7   import java.net.*;
8
9   import com.deitel.messenger.sockets.*;
10
11  public class MulticastSendingThread extends Thread {
12
13     // message data
14     private byte[] messageBytes;
15
16     // MulticastSendingThread constructor
17     public MulticastSendingThread( byte[] bytes )
18     {
19        // invoke superclass constructor to name Thread
20        super( "MulticastSendingThread" );
21
22        messageBytes = bytes;
23     }
24
25     // deliver message to MULTICAST_ADDRESS over DatagramSocket
26     public void run()
27     {
28        // deliver message
29        try {
30
31           // create DatagramSocket for sending message
32           DatagramSocket socket = new DatagramSocket(
33              SocketMessengerConstants.MULTICAST_SENDING_PORT );
34
35           // use InetAddress reserved for multicast group
36           InetAddress group = InetAddress.getByName(
37              SocketMessengerConstants.MULTICAST_ADDRESS );
38
39           // create DatagramPacket containing message
40           DatagramPacket packet = new DatagramPacket( messageBytes,
41              messageBytes.length, group,
42              SocketMessengerConstants.MULTICAST_LISTENING_PORT );
43
44           // send packet to multicast group and close socket
45           socket.send( packet );
46           socket.close();
47        }
48
49        // handle exception delivering message
50        catch ( IOException ioException ) {
51           ioException.printStackTrace();
52        }
```

Fig. 18.15 MulticastSendingThread for delivering outgoing messages to a multicast group via DatagramPackets. (Part 1 of 2.)

```
53
54      } // end method run
55
56   } // end class MulticastSendingThread
```

Fig. 18.15 MulticastSendingThread for delivering outgoing messages to a multicast group via DatagramPackets. (Part 2 of 2.)

Using multicast, an application can "publish" DatagramPackets to be delivered to "subscriber" applications. An application multicasts DatagramPackets by sending the DatagramPackets to a *multicast address*, which is an IP address reserved for multicast. Multicast addresses are in the range from 224.0.0.0 to 239.255.255.255. Addresses starting with 239 are reserved for intranets, so we use one of these (239.0.0.1) in our case study. Clients that wish to receive these DatagramPackets can connect to the appropriate multicast address to join the group of subscribers—the *multicast group*. When an application sends a DatagramPacket to the multicast address, each client in the multicast group receives the DatagramPacket. Multicast DatagramPackets, like unicast Datagram-Packets (Fig. 18.7), are not reliable—packets are not guaranteed to reach any destination. Also, the order in which the particular clients receive the datagrams is not guaranteed.

Class MulticastSendingThread extends class Thread to enable Deitel-MessengerServer to send multicast messages in a separate thread. To send a multicast message, the DeitelMessengerServer creates a MulticastSendingThread with the contents of the message and starts the thread. The MulticastSendingThread constructor (lines 17–23) takes as an argument an array of bytes containing the message.

Method run (lines 26–54) delivers the message to the multicast address. Lines 32–33 create a new DatagramSocket. Recall from Section 18.7 that we use DatagramSockets to send *unicast* DatagramPackets—packets sent from one host directly to another host. Multicast DatagramPackets are sent the same way, except the address to which the packets are sent is a multicast address. Lines 36–37 create an InetAddress object for the multicast address, which is declared as a constant in interface SocketMessengerCon-stants. Lines 40–42 create the DatagramPacket containing the message. The first argument to the DatagramPacket constructor is the byte array containing the message. The second argument is the length of the byte array. The third argument specifies the InetAd-dress to which the packet should be sent, and the last argument specifies the port number at which the packet should be delivered to the multicast address. Line 45 sends the packet with DatagramSocket method send. All clients listening to the multicast address on the proper port will receive this DatagramPacket. Line 46 closes the DatagramSocket, and the run method returns, terminating the MulticastSendingThread.

Executing the *DeitelMessengerServer*

To execute the DeitelMessengerServer, open a command window and change directories to the location in which package com.deitel.messenger.sockets.server resides (i.e., the directory in which com is located). Then, type

```
java com.deitel.messenger.sockets.server.DeitelMessengerServer
```

to execute the server.

18.10.2 DeitelMessenger Client and Supporting Classes

The client for the DeitelMessengerServer has several components. A class that implements interface MessageManager (Fig. 18.16) manages communication with the server. A Thread subclass listens for messages at DeitelMessengerServer's multicast address. Another Thread subclass sends messages from the client to server. A JFrame subclass provides the client's GUI.

Interface MessageManager (Fig. 18.16) declares methods for managing communication with DeitelMessengerServer. We declare this interface to abstract the base functionality a client needs to interact with a chat server from the underlying communication mechanism needed to communicate with that chat server. This abstraction enables us to provide MessageManager implementations that use other network protocols to implement the communication details. For example, if we want to connect to a different chat server that does not use multicast DatagramPackets, we could implement the MessageManager interface with the appropriate network protocols for this alternate messaging server. We would not need to modify any other code in the client, because the other components of the client refer only to interface MessageManager, not a particular MessageManager implementation. Similarly, MessageManager methods refer to other components of the client only through interface MessageListener, so other client components can change without requiring changes in the MessageManager or its implementations. Method connect (line 10) connects a MessageManager to DeitelMessengerServer and routes incoming messages to the appropriate MessageListener. Method disconnect (line 14) disconnects a MessageManager from the DeitelMessengerServer and stops delivering messages to the given MessageListener. Method sendMessage (line 17) sends a new message to DeitelMessengerServer.

Class SocketMessageManager (Fig. 18.17) implements MessageManager (line 13), using Sockets and MulticastSockets to communicate with DeitelMessengerServer and receive incoming messages. Line 16 declares the Socket used to connect to

```
1   // Fig. 18.16: MessageManager.java
2   // MessageManager is an interface for objects capable of managing
3   // communications with a message server.
4   package com.deitel.messenger;
5
6   public interface MessageManager {
7
8      // connect to message server and route incoming messages
9      // to given MessageListener
10     public void connect( MessageListener listener );
11
12     // disconnect from message server and stop routing
13     // incoming messages to given MessageListener
14     public void disconnect( MessageListener listener );
15
16     // send message to message server
17     public void sendMessage( String from, String message );
18  }
```

Fig. 18.16 MessageManager interface that declares methods for communicating with a DeitelMessengerServer.

and send messages to DeitelMessengerServer. Line 22 declares a PacketReceivingThread (Fig. 18.19) that listens for new incoming messages. The connected flag (line 25) indicates whether the SocketMessageManager is currently connected to DeitelMessengerServer.

The SocketMessageManager constructor (lines 28–31) receives the address of the DeitelMessengerServer to which SocketMessageManager should connect. Method connect (lines 34–59) connects SocketMessageManager to DeitelMessengerServer. If SocketMessageManager was connected previously, line 38 returns from method connect. Lines 42–44 create a new Socket to communicate with the server. Line 43 creates an InetAddress object for the server's address and line 44 uses the constant SocketMessengerConstants.SERVER_PORT to specify the port on which the client should connect. Line 47 creates a new PacketReceivingThread, which listens for incoming multicast messages from the server, and line 48 starts the thread. Line 51 updates boolean variable connected to indicate that SocketMessageManager is connected to the server.

```java
1    // Fig. 18.17: SocketMessageManager.java
2    // SocketMessageManager communicates with a DeitelMessengerServer using
3    // Sockets and MulticastSockets.
4    package com.deitel.messenger.sockets.client;
5
6    import java.util.*;
7    import java.net.*;
8    import java.io.*;
9
10   import com.deitel.messenger.*;
11   import com.deitel.messenger.sockets.*;
12
13   public class SocketMessageManager implements MessageManager {
14
15      // Socket for outgoing messages
16      private Socket clientSocket;
17
18      // DeitelMessengerServer address
19      private String serverAddress;
20
21      // Thread for receiving multicast messages
22      private PacketReceivingThread receivingThread;
23
24      // flag indicating connection status
25      private boolean connected = false;
26
27      // SocketMessageManager constructor
28      public SocketMessageManager( String address )
29      {
30         serverAddress = address;
31      }
32
33      // connect to server and send messages to given MessageListener
```

Fig. 18.17 SocketMessageManager implementation of interface MessageManager for communicating via Sockets and multicast DatagramPackets. (Part 1 of 3.)

```
34      public void connect( MessageListener listener )
35      {
36         // if already connected, return immediately
37         if ( connected )
38            return;
39
40         // open Socket connection to DeitelMessengerServer
41         try {
42            clientSocket = new Socket(
43               InetAddress.getByName( serverAddress ),
44               SocketMessengerConstants.SERVER_PORT );
45
46            // create Thread for receiving incoming messages
47            receivingThread = new PacketReceivingThread( listener );
48            receivingThread.start();
49
50            // update connected flag
51            connected = true;
52         }
53
54         // handle exception connecting to server
55         catch ( IOException ioException ) {
56            ioException.printStackTrace();
57         }
58
59      } // end method connect
60
61      // disconnect from server and unregister given MessageListener
62      public void disconnect( MessageListener listener )
63      {
64         // if not connected, return immediately
65         if ( !connected )
66            return;
67
68         // stop listening thread and disconnect from server
69         try {
70
71            // notify server that client is disconnecting
72            Thread disconnectThread = new SendingThread( clientSocket, "",
73               SocketMessengerConstants.DISCONNECT_STRING );
74            disconnectThread.start();
75
76            // wait 10 seconds for disconnect message to be sent
77            disconnectThread.join( 10000 );
78
79            // stop receivingThread and remove given MessageListener
80            receivingThread.stopListening();
81
82            // close outgoing Socket
83            clientSocket.close();
84
85         } // end try
```

Fig. 18.17 SocketMessageManager implementation of interface MessageManager for communicating via Sockets and multicast DatagramPackets. (Part 2 of 3.)

```
86
87          // handle exception disconnecting from server
88          catch ( IOException ioException ) {
89             ioException.printStackTrace();
90          }
91
92          // handle exception joining disconnectThread
93          catch ( InterruptedException interruptedException ) {
94             interruptedException.printStackTrace();
95          }
96
97          // update connected flag
98          connected = false;
99
100     } // end method disconnect
101
102     // send message to server
103     public void sendMessage( String from, String message )
104     {
105        // if not connected, return immediately
106        if ( !connected )
107           return;
108
109        // create and start new SendingThread to deliver message
110        new SendingThread( clientSocket, from, message).start();
111     }
112
113  } // end method SocketMessageManager
```

Fig. 18.17   SocketMessageManager implementation of interface MessageManager for communicating via Sockets and multicast DatagramPackets. (Part 3 of 3.)

Method disconnect (lines 62–100) terminates the SocketMessageManager's connection to the server. If SocketMessageManager is not connected, line 66 returns from method disconnect. Lines 72–73 create a new SendingThread (Fig. 18.18) to send SocketMessengerConstants.DISCONNECT_STRING to DeitelMessengerServer. Class SendingThread delivers a message to DeitelMessengerServer over the SocketMessageManager's Socket connection. Line 74 starts the SendingThread to deliver the message. Line 77 invokes SendingThread method join (inherited from Thread) to wait for the disconnect message to be delivered. The integer argument 10000 specifies that the current thread should wait only 10 seconds to join the SendingThread before continuing. Once the disconnect message has been delivered, line 80 invokes PacketReceivingThread method stopListening to stop receiving incoming chat messages. Line 83 closes the Socket connection to DeitelMessengerServer.

Method sendMessage (lines 103–111) sends an outgoing message to the server. If SocketMessageManager is not connected, line 107 returns from method sendMessage. Line 110 creates and starts a new SendingThread (Fig. 18.18) to deliver the new message in a separate thread of execution.

Class SendingThread (Fig. 18.18), which extends Thread, delivers outgoing messages to the server in a separate thread of execution. SendingThread's constructor (lines 17–27) takes as arguments the Socket over which to send the message, the userName from

whom the message came and the message. Lines 25–26 concatenate these arguments to
build messageToSend. Constant SocketMessengerConstants.MESSAGE_SEPARATOR
enables the message recipient to parse the message into two parts—the sending user's name
and the message body—by using a StringTokenizer.

```java
1   // Fig. 18.18: SendingThread.java
2   // SendingThread sends a message to the chat server in a separate Thread.
3   package com.deitel.messenger.sockets.client;
4
5   import java.io.*;
6   import java.net.*;
7
8   import com.deitel.messenger.sockets.*;
9
10  public class SendingThread extends Thread {
11
12     // Socket over which to send message
13     private Socket clientSocket;
14     private String messageToSend;
15
16     // SendingThread constructor
17     public SendingThread( Socket socket, String userName, String message )
18     {
19        // invoke superclass constructor to name Thread
20        super( "SendingThread: " + socket );
21
22        clientSocket = socket;
23
24        // build the message to be sent
25        messageToSend = userName +
26           SocketMessengerConstants.MESSAGE_SEPARATOR + message;
27     }
28
29     // send message and exit Thread
30     public void run()
31     {
32        // send message and flush PrintWriter
33        try {
34           PrintWriter writer =
35              new PrintWriter( clientSocket.getOutputStream() );
36           writer.println( messageToSend );
37           writer.flush();
38        }
39
40        // handle exception sending message
41        catch ( IOException ioException ) {
42           ioException.printStackTrace();
43        }
44     }
45
46  } // end class SendingThread
```

Fig. 18.18   SendingThread for delivering outgoing messages to
              DeitelMessengerServer.

Method `run` (lines 30–44) delivers the complete message to the server, using the `Socket` provided to the `SendingThread` constructor. Lines 34–35 create a new `Print-Writer` for the `clientSocket`'s `OutputStream`. Line 36 invokes `PrintWriter` method `println` to send the message. Line 37 invokes method `flush` of class `PrintWriter` to ensure that the message is sent immediately. Note that class `SendingThread` does not close the `clientSocket`. Class `SocketMessageManager` uses a new object of class `SendingThread` for each message the client sends, so the `clientSocket` must remain open until the user disconnects from `DeitelMessengerServer`.

Class `PacketReceivingThread` (Fig. 18.19) extends class `Thread` to enable `SocketMessageManager` to listen for incoming messages in a separate thread of execution. Line 16 declares the `MessageListener` to which `PacketReceivingThread` will deliver incoming messages. Line 19 declares a `MulticastSocket` for receiving multicast `DatagramPackets`. Line 22 declares an `InetAddress` reference for the multicast address to which `DeitelMessengerServer` posts new chat messages. The `MulticastSocket` connects to this `InetAddress` to listen for incoming chat messages.

The `PacketReceivingThread` constructor (lines 28–56) takes as an argument the `MessageListener` to which the `PacketReceivingThread` should deliver incoming messages. Recall that interface `MessageListener` declares method `messageReceived`. When the `PacketReceivingThread` receives a new chat message over the `MulticastSocket`, `PacketReceivingThread` invokes `messageReceived` to deliver the new message to the `MessageListener`.

Lines 38–39 create a new `MulticastSocket` and pass to the `MulticastSocket` constructor the constant `MULTICAST_LISTENING_PORT` from interface `SocketMessengerConstants`. This argument specifies the port on which the `MulticastSocket` should listen for incoming chat messages. Lines 41–42 create an `InetAddress` object for the `SocketMessengerConstants.MULTICAST_ADDRESS`, to which `DeitelMessengerServer` multicasts new chat messages. Line 45 invokes `MulticastSocket` method *joinGroup* to register the `MulticastSocket` to receive messages sent to `MULTICAST_ADDRESS`. Line 48 invokes `MulticastSocket` method `setSoTimeout` to specify that, if no data is received in 5000 milliseconds, the `MulticastSocket` should issue an `InterruptedIOException`, which the current thread can catch, then continue executing. This approach prevents `PacketReceivingThread` from blocking indefinitely when waiting for incoming data. Also, if the `MulticastSocket` did not ever time out, the `while` loop would not be able to check the `keepListening` variable and would therefore prevent `PacketReceivingThread` from stopping if `keepListening` were set to `false`.

Method `run` (lines 59–122) listens for incoming multicast messages. Lines 69–70 create a `DatagramPacket` to store the incoming message. Line 74 invokes `MulticastSocket` method `receive` to read an incoming packet from the multicast address. If 5000 milliseconds pass without receipt of a packet, method `receive` throws an `InterruptedIOException`, because we previously set a 5000 millisecond time-out (line 48). Line 80 uses `continue` to proceed to the next loop iteration to listen for incoming messages. For other `IOExceptions`, line 87 `breaks` the `while` loop to terminate the `PacketReceivingThread`.

Line 91 invokes `DatagramPacket` method `getData` to retrieve the message data. Line 94 invokes method `trim` of class `String` to remove extra white space from the end of the message. Recall that `DatagramPackets` are a fixed size—512 bytes in this example—so, if the message is shorter than 512 bytes, there will be extra white space after the message. Lines 97–98 create a `StringTokenizer` to separate the message body from the name of the user who sent the message. Line 102 checks for the correct number of tokens. Lines 105–107 invoke method `messageReceived` of interface `MessageListener` to deliver the incoming message to the `PacketReceivingThread`'s `MessageListener`.

```java
1   // Fig. 18.19: PacketReceivingThread.java
2   // PacketReceivingThread listens for DatagramPackets containing
3   // messages from a DeitelMessengerServer.
4   package com.deitel.messenger.sockets.client;
5
6   import java.io.*;
7   import java.net.*;
8   import java.util.*;
9
10  import com.deitel.messenger.*;
11  import com.deitel.messenger.sockets.*;
12
13  public class PacketReceivingThread extends Thread {
14
15     // MessageListener to whom messages should be delivered
16     private MessageListener messageListener;
17
18     // MulticastSocket for receiving broadcast messages
19     private MulticastSocket multicastSocket;
20
21     // InetAddress of group for messages
22     private InetAddress multicastGroup;
23
24     // flag for terminating PacketReceivingThread
25     private boolean keepListening = true;
26
27     // PacketReceivingThread constructor
28     public PacketReceivingThread( MessageListener listener )
29     {
30        // invoke superclass constructor to name Thread
31        super( "PacketReceivingThread" );
32
33        // set MessageListener
34        messageListener = listener;
35
36        // connect MulticastSocket to multicast address and port
37        try {
38           multicastSocket = new MulticastSocket(
39              SocketMessengerConstants.MULTICAST_LISTENING_PORT );
40
41           multicastGroup = InetAddress.getByName(
42              SocketMessengerConstants.MULTICAST_ADDRESS );
43
44           // join multicast group to receive messages
45           multicastSocket.joinGroup( multicastGroup );
```

Fig. 18.19 PacketReceivingThread for listening for new multicast messages from DeitelMessengerServer in a separate thread. (Part 1 of 3.)

```
46
47            // set 5 second timeout when waiting for new packets
48            multicastSocket.setSoTimeout( 5000 );
49         }
50
51      // handle exception connecting to multicast address
52      catch ( IOException ioException ) {
53         ioException.printStackTrace();
54      }
55
56   } // end PacketReceivingThread constructor
57
58   // listen for messages from multicast group
59   public void run()
60   {
61      // listen for messages until stopped
62      while ( keepListening ) {
63
64         // create buffer for incoming message
65         byte[] buffer =
66            new byte[ SocketMessengerConstants.MESSAGE_SIZE ];
67
68         // create DatagramPacket for incoming message
69         DatagramPacket packet = new DatagramPacket( buffer,
70            SocketMessengerConstants.MESSAGE_SIZE );
71
72         // receive new DatagramPacket (blocking call)
73         try {
74            multicastSocket.receive( packet );
75         }
76
77         // handle exception when receive times out
78         catch ( InterruptedIOException interruptedIOException ) {
79
80            // continue to next iteration to keep listening
81            continue;
82         }
83
84         // handle exception reading packet from multicast group
85         catch ( IOException ioException ) {
86            ioException.printStackTrace();
87            break;
88         }
89
90         // put message data in a String
91         String message = new String( packet.getData() );
92
93         // trim extra white space from end of message
94         message = message.trim();
95
```

Fig. 18.19 PacketReceivingThread for listening for new multicast messages from
DeitelMessengerServer in a separate thread. (Part 2 of 3.)

```
96          // tokenize message to retrieve user name and message body
97          StringTokenizer tokenizer = new StringTokenizer(
98             message, SocketMessengerConstants.MESSAGE_SEPARATOR );
99
100         // ignore messages that do not contain a user
101         // name and message body
102         if ( tokenizer.countTokens() == 2 )
103
104            // send message to MessageListener
105            messageListener.messageReceived(
106               tokenizer.nextToken(),    // user name
107               tokenizer.nextToken() ); // message body
108
109      } // end while
110
111      // leave multicast group and close MulticastSocket
112      try {
113         multicastSocket.leaveGroup( multicastGroup );
114         multicastSocket.close();
115      }
116
117      // handle exception reading packet from multicast group
118      catch ( IOException ioException ) {
119         ioException.printStackTrace();
120      }
121
122   } // end method run
123
124   // stop listening for new messages
125   public void stopListening()
126   {
127      keepListening = false;
128   }
129
130 } // end class PacketReceivingThread
```

Fig. 18.19 PacketReceivingThread for listening for new multicast messages from DeitelMessengerServer in a separate thread. (Part 3 of 3.)

If the program invokes method stopListening (lines 125–128), the while loop in method run (lines 62–109) terminates. Line 113 invokes MulticastSocket method leaveGroup to stop receiving messages from the multicast address. Line 114 invokes MulticastSocket method close to close the MulticastSocket. When method run completes execution, the PacketReceivingThread terminates.

Class ClientGUI (Fig. 18.20) extends class JFrame to create a GUI for a user to send and receive chat messages. The GUI consists of a JTextArea for displaying incoming messages (line 19), a JTextArea for entering new messages (line 20), JButtons and JMenuItems for connecting to and disconnecting from the server (lines 23–26) and a JButton for sending messages (line 29). The GUI also contains a JLabel that displays whether the client is connected or disconnected (line 32).

```
1    // Fig. 18.20: ClientGUI.java
2    // ClientGUI provides a user interface for sending and receiving
3    // messages to and from the DeitelMessengerServer.
4    package com.deitel.messenger;
5
6    import java.io.*;
7    import java.net.*;
8    import java.awt.*;
9    import java.awt.event.*;
10   import javax.swing.*;
11   import javax.swing.border.*;
12
13   public class ClientGUI extends JFrame {
14
15      // JMenu for connecting/disconnecting server
16      private JMenu serverMenu;
17
18      // JTextAreas for displaying and inputting messages
19      private JTextArea messageArea;
20      private JTextArea inputArea;
21
22      // JButtons and JMenuItems for connecting and disconnecting
23      private JButton connectButton;
24      private JMenuItem connectMenuItem;
25      private JButton disconnectButton;
26      private JMenuItem disconnectMenuItem;
27
28      // JButton for sending messages
29      private JButton sendButton;
30
31      // JLabel for displaying connection status
32      private JLabel statusBar;
33
34      // userName to add to outgoing messages
35      private String userName;
36
37      // MessageManager for communicating with server
38      private MessageManager messageManager;
39
40      // MessageListener for receiving incoming messages
41      private MessageListener messageListener;
42
43      // ClientGUI constructor
44      public ClientGUI( MessageManager manager )
45      {
46         super( "Deitel Messenger" );
47
48         // set the MessageManager
49         messageManager = manager;
50
51         // create MyMessageListener for receiving messages
52         messageListener = new MyMessageListener();
```

Fig. 18.20   ClientGUI subclass of JFrame for presenting a GUI for viewing and sending chat messages. (Part 1 of 6.)

```
53
54       // create Server JMenu
55       serverMenu = new JMenu ( "Server" );
56       serverMenu.setMnemonic( 'S' );
57       JMenuBar menuBar = new JMenuBar();
58       menuBar.add( serverMenu );
59       setJMenuBar( menuBar );
60
61       // create ImageIcon for connect buttons
62       Icon connectIcon = new ImageIcon(
63          getClass().getResource( "images/Connect.gif" ) );
64
65       // create connectButton and connectMenuItem
66       connectButton = new JButton( "Connect", connectIcon );
67       connectMenuItem = new JMenuItem( "Connect", connectIcon );
68       connectMenuItem.setMnemonic( 'C' );
69
70       // create ConnectListener for connect buttons
71       ActionListener connectListener = new ConnectListener();
72       connectButton.addActionListener( connectListener );
73       connectMenuItem.addActionListener( connectListener );
74
75       // create ImageIcon for disconnect buttons
76       Icon disconnectIcon = new ImageIcon(
77          getClass().getResource( "images/Disconnect.gif" ) );
78
79       // create disconnectButton and disconnectMenuItem
80       disconnectButton = new JButton( "Disconnect", disconnectIcon );
81       disconnectMenuItem = new JMenuItem( "Disconnect", disconnectIcon );
82       disconnectMenuItem.setMnemonic( 'D' );
83
84       // disable disconnect buttons
85       disconnectButton.setEnabled( false );
86       disconnectMenuItem.setEnabled( false );
87
88       // create DisconnectListener for disconnect buttons
89       ActionListener disconnectListener = new DisconnectListener();
90       disconnectButton.addActionListener( disconnectListener );
91       disconnectMenuItem.addActionListener( disconnectListener );
92
93       // add connect and disconnect JMenuItems to fileMenu
94       serverMenu.add( connectMenuItem );
95       serverMenu.add( disconnectMenuItem );
96
97       // add connect and disconnect JButtons to buttonPanel
98       JPanel buttonPanel = new JPanel();
99       buttonPanel.add( connectButton );
100      buttonPanel.add( disconnectButton );
101
102      // create JTextArea for displaying messages
103      messageArea = new JTextArea();
104
```

Fig. 18.20 ClientGUI subclass of JFrame for presenting a GUI for viewing and sending chat messages. (Part 2 of 6.)

```
105        // disable editing and wrap words at end of line
106        messageArea.setEditable( false );
107        messageArea.setWrapStyleWord( true );
108        messageArea.setLineWrap( true );
109
110        // put messageArea in JScrollPane to enable scrolling
111        JPanel messagePanel = new JPanel();
112        messagePanel.setLayout( new BorderLayout( 10, 10 ) );
113        messagePanel.add( new JScrollPane( messageArea ),
114           BorderLayout.CENTER );
115
116        // create JTextArea for entering new messages
117        inputArea = new JTextArea( 4, 20 );
118        inputArea.setWrapStyleWord( true );
119        inputArea.setLineWrap( true );
120        inputArea.setEditable( false );
121
122        // create Icon for sendButton
123        Icon sendIcon = new ImageIcon(
124           getClass().getResource( "images/Send.gif" ) );
125
126        // create sendButton and disable it
127        sendButton = new JButton( "Send", sendIcon );
128        sendButton.setEnabled( false );
129        sendButton.addActionListener(
130
131           new ActionListener() {
132
133              // send new message when user activates sendButton
134              public void actionPerformed( ActionEvent event )
135              {
136                 messageManager.sendMessage( userName,
137                    inputArea.getText());
138
139                 // clear inputArea
140                 inputArea.setText( "" );
141              }
142           }
143        );
144
145        // lay out inputArea and sendButton in BoxLayout and
146        // add Box to messagePanel
147        Box box = new Box( BoxLayout.X_AXIS );
148        box.add( new JScrollPane( inputArea ) );
149        box.add( sendButton );
150        messagePanel.add( box, BorderLayout.SOUTH );
151
152        // create JLabel for statusBar with a recessed border
153        statusBar = new JLabel( "Not Connected" );
154        statusBar.setBorder( new BevelBorder( BevelBorder.LOWERED ) );
155
```

Fig. 18.20 ClientGUI subclass of JFrame for presenting a GUI for viewing and sending chat messages. (Part 3 of 6.)

```
156        // lay out components in JFrame
157        Container container = getContentPane();
158        container.add( buttonPanel, BorderLayout.NORTH );
159        container.add( messagePanel, BorderLayout.CENTER );
160        container.add( statusBar, BorderLayout.SOUTH );
161
162        // add WindowListener to disconnect when user quits
163        addWindowListener (
164
165           new WindowAdapter () {
166
167              // disconnect from server and exit application
168              public void windowClosing ( WindowEvent event )
169              {
170                 messageManager.disconnect( messageListener );
171                 System.exit( 0 );
172              }
173           }
174        );
175
176     } // end ClientGUI constructor
177
178     // ConnectListener listens for user requests to connect to server
179     private class ConnectListener implements ActionListener {
180
181        // connect to server and enable/disable GUI components
182        public void actionPerformed( ActionEvent event )
183        {
184           // connect to server and route messages to messageListener
185           messageManager.connect( messageListener );
186
187           // prompt for userName
188           userName = JOptionPane.showInputDialog(
189              ClientGUI.this, "Enter user name:" );
190
191           // clear messageArea
192           messageArea.setText( "" );
193
194           // update GUI components
195           connectButton.setEnabled( false );
196           connectMenuItem.setEnabled( false );
197           disconnectButton.setEnabled( true );
198           disconnectMenuItem.setEnabled( true );
199           sendButton.setEnabled( true );
200           inputArea.setEditable( true );
201           inputArea.requestFocus();
202           statusBar.setText( "Connected: " + userName );
203        }
204
205     } // end ConnectListener inner class
206
```

Fig. 18.20 ClientGUI subclass of JFrame for presenting a GUI for viewing and sending chat messages. (Part 4 of 6.)

```
207    // DisconnectListener listens for user requests to disconnect
208    // from DeitelMessengerServer
209    private class DisconnectListener implements ActionListener {
210
211       // disconnect from server and enable/disable GUI components
212       public void actionPerformed( ActionEvent event )
213       {
214          // disconnect from server and stop routing messages
215          // to messageListener
216          messageManager.disconnect( messageListener );
217
218          // update GUI components
219          sendButton.setEnabled( false );
220          disconnectButton.setEnabled( false );
221          disconnectMenuItem.setEnabled( false );
222          inputArea.setEditable( false );
223          connectButton.setEnabled( true );
224          connectMenuItem.setEnabled( true );
225          statusBar.setText( "Not Connected" );
226       }
227
228    } // end DisconnectListener inner class
229
230    // MyMessageListener listens for new messages from MessageManager and
231    // displays messages in messageArea using MessageDisplayer.
232    private class MyMessageListener implements MessageListener {
233
234       // when received, display new messages in messageArea
235       public void messageReceived( String from, String message )
236       {
237          // append message using MessageDisplayer and
238          // invokeLater, ensuring thread-safe access messageArea
239          SwingUtilities.invokeLater(
240             new MessageDisplayer( from, message ) );
241       }
242    }
243
244    // MessageDisplayer displays a new message by appending the message to
245    // the messageArea JTextArea. This Runnable object should be executed
246    // only on the Event thread, because it modifies a live Swing component
247    private class MessageDisplayer implements Runnable {
248       private String fromUser;
249       private String messageBody;
250
251       // MessageDisplayer constructor
252       public MessageDisplayer( String from, String body )
253       {
254          fromUser = from;
255          messageBody = body;
256       }
257
```

Fig. 18.20 ClientGUI subclass of JFrame for presenting a GUI for viewing and sending chat messages. (Part 5 of 6.)

```
258        // display new message in messageArea
259        public void run()
260        {
261           // append new message
262           messageArea.append( "\n" + fromUser + "> " + messageBody );
263
264           // move caret to end of messageArea to ensure new
265           // message is visible on screen
266           messageArea.setCaretPosition( messageArea.getText().length() );
267        }
268
269     } // end MessageDisplayer inner class
270
271 } // end class ClientGUI
```

Fig. 18.20 ClientGUI subclass of JFrame for presenting a GUI for viewing and sending chat messages. (Part 6 of 6.)

ClientGUI uses a MessageManager (line 38) to handle all communication with the chat server. Recall that MessageManager is an interface that enables ClientGUI to use any MessageManager implementation. Class ClientGUI also uses a MessageListener (line 41) to receive incoming messages from the MessageManager.

The ClientGUI constructor (lines 44–176) takes as an argument the Message-Manager for communicating with DeitelMessengerServer. Line 49 sets the ClientGUI's MessageManager. Line 52 creates an instance of MyMessageListener, which implements interface MessageListener. Lines 55–59 create a **Server** menu that contains JMenuItems for connecting to and disconnecting from the chat server. Lines 62–63 create an ImageIcon for connectButton and connectMenuItem.

Line 63 invokes method getClass (inherited from class Object) to retrieve the Class object that represents the ClientGUI class declaration. Line 63 then invokes Class method *getResource* to load the connect image. The Java virtual machine loads class declarations into memory, using a *class loader*. Method getResource uses the Class object's class loader to specify the location of a resource, such as an image file. Specifying resource locations in this manner enables programs to avoid hard-coded or absolute paths, which can make programs more difficult to deploy on multiple computers. Using the techniques described here enables an applet or application to load files from locations that are relative to the location of the .class file for a given class.

Lines 66–67 create connectButton and connectMenuItem, each with the label "Connect" and the Icon connectIcon. Line 68 invokes method setMnemonic to set the mnemonic character for keyboard access to connectMenuItem. Line 71 creates an instance of inner class ConnectListener (declared at lines 179–205), which implements interface ActionListener to handle ActionEvents from connectButton and connectMenuItem. Lines 72–73 add connectListener as an ActionListener for connectButton and connectMenuItem.

Lines 76–77 create an ImageIcon for the disconnectButton and disconnect-MenuItem components. Lines 80–81 create disconnectButton and disconnect-MenuItem, each with the label "Disconnect" and the Icon disconnectIcon. Line 82 invokes method setMnemonic to enable keyboard access to disconnectMenuItem. Lines 85–86 invoke method setEnabled with a false argument on disconnect-

Button and disconnectMenuItem to disable these components. This prevents the user from attempting to disconnect from the server because the client is not yet connected. Line 89 creates an instance of inner class DisconnectListener (declared at lines 209–228), which implements interface ActionListener to handle ActionEvents from disconnectButton and disconnectMenuItem. Lines 90–91 add disconnectListener as an ActionListener for disconnectButton and disconnectMenuItem.

Lines 94–95 add connectMenuItem and disconnectMenuItem to menu **Server**. Lines 98–100 create a JPanel and add connectButton and disconnectButton to that JPanel. Line 103 creates the textarea messageArea, in which the client displays incoming messages. Line 106 invokes method setEnabled with a false argument, to disable messageArea. Lines 107–108 invoke JTextArea methods setWrapStyleWord and setLineWrap to enable word wrapping in messageArea. If a message is longer than messageArea's width, the messageArea will wrap the text after the last word that fits on each line, making longer messages easier to read. Lines 113–114 create a JPanel for the messageArea and add the messageArea to the JPanel in a JScrollPane.

Line 117 creates the inputArea JTextArea for entering new messages. Lines 118–119 enable word and line wrapping, and line 120 disables editing the inputArea. When the client connects to the chat server, ConnectListener enables the inputArea to allow the user to type new messages.

Lines 123–124 create an ImageIcon for sendButton. Line 127 creates sendButton, which the user can click to send a message. Line 128 disables sendButton; the ConnectListener enables the sendButton when the client connects to the chat server. Lines 129–143 add an ActionListener to sendButton. Lines 136–137 invoke method sendMessage of interface MessageManager with the userName and inputArea text as arguments. This statement sends the user's name and message as a new chat message to DeitelMessengerServer. Line 140 clears the inputArea for the next message.

Lines 147–150 use a horizontal Box container to arrange components inputArea and sendButton. Line 148 places inputArea in a JScrollPane to enable scrolling of long messages. Line 150 adds the Box containing inputArea and sendButton to the SOUTH region of messagePanel. Line 153 creates the statusBar JLabel. This label displays whether the client is connected to or disconnected from the chat server. Line 154 invokes method setBorder of class JLabel and create a new BevelBorder of type BevelBorder.LOWERED. This border makes the label appear recessed, as is common with status bars in many applications. Lines 158–160 add buttonPanel, messagePanel and statusBar to the ClientGUI's content pane.

Lines 163–174 add a WindowListener to the ClientGUI. Line 170 invokes method disconnect of interface MessageManager to disconnect from the chat server in case the user quits while still connected. Then, line 171 terminates the application.

Inner class ConnectListener (lines 179–205) handles events from connectButton and connectMenuItem. Line 185 invokes MessageManager method connect to connect to the chat server. Line 185 passes as an argument to method connect the MessageListener to which new messages should be delivered. Lines 188-189 prompt the user for a user name, and line 198 clears the messageArea. Lines 195–200 enable the components for disconnecting from the server and for sending messages and disable components for connecting to the server. Line 201 invokes inputArea's requestFocus method to place the text-input cursor in the inputArea so the user can begin typing a message.

Inner class `DisconnectListener` (lines 209–228) handles events from `disconnectButton` and `disconnectMenuItem`. Line 216 invokes `MessageManager` method `disconnect` to disconnect from the chat server. Lines 219–224 disable the components for sending messages and the components for disconnecting then enable the components for connecting to the chat server.

Inner class `MyMessageListener` (lines 232–242) implements interface `MessageListener` to receive incoming messages from the `MessageManager`. When a new message is received, the `MessageManager` invokes method `messageReceived` (lines 235–241) with the user name of the sender and the message body. Lines 239–240 invoke `SwingUtilities` method `invokeLater` with a `MessageDisplayer` object that appends the new message to `messageArea`. Recall, from Chapter 16, that Swing components should be accessed only from the event-dispatch thread. Method `messageReceived` is invoked by the `PacketReceivingThread` in class `SocketMessageManager` and therefore cannot append the message text to `messageArea` directly, as this would occur in `PacketReceivingThread`, not the event-dispatch thread.

Inner class `MessageDisplayer` (lines 247–269) implements interface `Runnable` to provide a thread-safe way to append text to the `messageArea`. The `MessageDisplayer` constructor (lines 252–256) takes as arguments the user name and message to send. Method `run` (lines 259–267) appends the user name, `"> "` and `messageBody` to `messageArea`. Line 266 scrolls `messageArea` to the bottom to display the most recently received message.

Class `DeitelMessenger` (Fig. 18.21) launches the client for the `DeitelMessengerServer`. Lines 15–18 create a new `SocketMessageManager` to connect to the `DeitelMessengerServer` with the IP address specified as a command-line argument to the application (or localhost, if no address is provided). Lines 21–24 create a `ClientGUI` for the `MessageManager`, set the `ClientGUI` size and make the `ClientGUI` visible.

```
1   // Fig. 18.21 DeitelMessenger.java
2   // DeitelMessenger is a chat application that uses a ClientGUI
3   // and SocketMessageManager to communicate with DeitelMessengerServer.
4   package com.deitel.messenger.sockets.client;
5
6   import com.deitel.messenger.*;
7
8   public class DeitelMessenger {
9
10     public static void main( String args[] )
11     {
12        MessageManager messageManager;
13
14        // create new DeitelMessenger
15        if ( args.length == 0 )
16           messageManager = new SocketMessageManager( "localhost" );
17        else
18           messageManager = new SocketMessageManager( args[ 0 ] );
19
20        // create GUI for SocketMessageManager
21        ClientGUI clientGUI = new ClientGUI( messageManager );
```

Fig. 18.21 `DeitelMessenger` application for participating in a `DeitelMessengerServer` chat session. (Part 1 of 2.)

```
22          clientGUI.setSize( 300, 400 );
23          clientGUI.setResizable( false );
24          clientGUI.setVisible( true );
25       }
26
27    } // end class DeitelMessenger
```

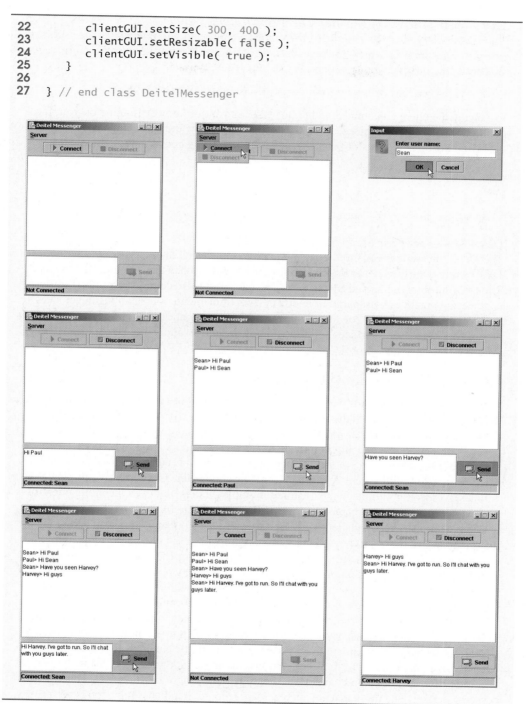

Fig. 18.21   DeitelMessenger application for participating in a
DeitelMessengerServer chat session. (Part 2 of 2.)

*Executing the **DeitelMessenger** Client Application*

To execute the DeitelMessenger client, open a command window and change directories to the location in which package com.deitel.messenger.sockets.client resides (i.e., the directory in which com is located). Then, type

```
java com.deitel.messenger.sockets.client.DeitelMessenger
```

to execute the client and connect to the DeitelMessengerServer running on your local computer. If the server resides on another computer, follow the preceding command with the hostname or IP address of that computer. The preceding command is equivalent to

```
java com.deitel.messenger.sockets.client.DeitelMessenger localhost
```

or

```
java com.deitel.messenger.sockets.client.DeitelMessenger 127.0.0.1
```

Deitel Messenger Case Study Summary

The Deitel messenger case study is a significant application that uses many intermediate Java features, such as networking with Sockets, DatagramPackets and MulticastSockets, multithreading and Swing GUI. The case study also demonstrates good software engineering practices by separating interface from implementation, enabling developers to build MessageManagers for different network protocols and MessageListeners that provide different user interfaces. You should now be able to apply these techniques to your own, more complex, Java projects.

18.11 NIO Networking Overview

Before J2SE 1.4, all I/O calls were blocking. When an input or output operation was called, the program would halt until the I/O operation completed, or for socket read operations, until the optionally configured timeout had expired. In the case of clients and servers this posed many problems. In a single-threaded, client-server application, if a client (Client B) tries to connect to the server while another client (Client A) is connected to the server, Client B is blocked until Client A disconnects from the server. Concurrent communication with a server from multiple clients required multiple threads. For each incoming client I/O request, a separate server thread was spawned to service the I/O request. For applications with large numbers of clients (e.g. web servers) this leads to thread overhead and reducing the scalability of these servers. The new I/O APIs in J2SE 1.4 enable developers to build *non-blocking I/O* into their applications. With non-blocking I/O, when an input or output operation is called, the operation returns immediately with whatever information is available and execution is not halted. Servers can now interact with multiple client connections simultaneously without creating a new thread for each connection.

Continuously attempting to read data from each connection wastes processor time. *Readiness selection* is a means of making the process of transferring data more efficient. Readiness selection is the simultaneous checking of multiple channels to determine which channel(s) are ready to perform I/O operations. Instead of querying each channel, the programmer determines which channels are ready with one step. Each ready channel is processed separately and those that are not ready are ignored. Readiness selection is performed with *selectors*. A selector monitors its registered channels, identifies channels that are ready for I/O and passes client requests to the corresponding channels.

Interface *SelectableChannel* (in package java.nio.channels) provides a framework for creating and using non-blocking channels. A SelectableChannel is a channel that supports readiness selection, which means that the channel can be queried to determine if it is ready to perform I/O operations. The most useful subclasses of SelectableChannel are ServerSocketChannel and SocketChannel. Objects of these classes carry on network communication between a server and a client and can work in non-blocking mode. Class *Selector* (also in package java.nio.channels) provides the selector functionality.

Non-blocking I/O DeitelMessenger Chat Program

In Section 18.10, we used multithreading to build a DeitelMessenger chat server that can handle many clients simultaneously. Here we create a single-threaded, non-blocking server using the new I/O API.

DeitelMessengerNonBlockingServer (Fig. 18.22) is the non-blocking DeitelMessenger server. Line 22 declares a Charset object that is used to encode and decode message sent between the server and the clients. Line 23 declares a ByteBuffer that is used to store bytes written to the socket channel. Line 23 declares and initializes a ByteBuffer with capacity 512 that is used to store bytes read from the socket channel. The constructor (lines 26–60) sets up the GUI and closes the ServerSocketChannel and Selector when the window is closed. Method runServer (lines 63–87) specifies a Charset for encoding and decoding messages, creates a ServerSocketChannel and calls method getConnection (lines 90–154) to wait for a client connection. Line 69 invokes static method forName of class Charset to obtain a Charset object for "UTF-8", a variable-width encoding form that requires one to four bytes to express each Unicode character. For more information on Unicode, see Appendix G. A ServerSocketChannel performs the same task as ServerSocket—it listens for socket connections. The major difference between ServerSocket and ServerSocketChannel is that ServerSocketChannel can work in non-blocking mode. A ServerSocketChannel is created by invoking static method open of class ServerSocketChannel (line 72). Lines 73–74 bind a port to the ServerSocket associated with the ServerSocketChannel. Method socket of class ServerSocketChannel returns the ServerSocket associated with the channel. Line 75 passes false to method configureBlocking to make the ServerSocketChannel operate in non-blocking mode, so that multiple clients can connect to the server concurrently.

```
1   // Fig. 18.22: DeitelMessengerNonBlockingServer.java
2   // Set up a nonblocking chatServer that will receive a connection from a
3   // client and echo client's message to all connected clients.
4   package com.deitel.messenger.sockets.server;
5
6   import java.io.*;
7   import java.nio.*;
8   import java.nio.channels.*;
9   import java.nio.channels.spi.*;
10  import java.nio.charset.*;
11  import java.net.*;
12  import java.util.*;
13  import java.awt.event.*;
```

Fig. 18.22 Nonblocking messenger server. (Part 1 of 6.)

```
14   import javax.swing.*;
15
16   public class DeitelMessengerNonBlockingServer extends JFrame {
17      private ServerSocketChannel serverSocketChannel;
18      private Selector selector;
19      private Vector sockets = new Vector();
20      private int counter = 0;
21      private JTextArea displayArea;
22      private Charset charSet;
23      private ByteBuffer writeBuffer;
24      private ByteBuffer readBuffer = ByteBuffer.allocate( 512 );
25
26      public DeitelMessengerNonBlockingServer()
27      {
28         super( "DeitelMessenger Server" );
29
30         displayArea = new JTextArea();
31         getContentPane().add( new JScrollPane( displayArea ) );
32
33         setSize( 200, 300 );
34         setVisible( true );
35
36         // close server socket channel and selector when closing window
37         addWindowListener(
38
39            new WindowAdapter() {
40
41               public void windowClosing( WindowEvent windowEvent )
42               {
43                  // close server socket channel and selector
44                  try {
45                     serverSocketChannel.close();
46                     selector.close();
47                  }
48                  catch( IOException ioException ) {
49                     ioException.printStackTrace();
50                  }
51                  finally {
52                     System.exit( 0 );
53                  }
54               }
55
56            } // end inner class WindowAdapter
57
58         ); // end addWindowListener
59
60      } // end constructor
61
62      // set up and run server
63      public void runServer()
64      {
65         // set up server to receive connections; process connections
66         try {
```

Fig. 18.22 Nonblocking messenger server. (Part 2 of 6.)

```
67
68          // specify the char set used to encode/decode messages
69          charSet = Charset.forName( "UTF-8" );
70
71          // create a ServerSocketChannel
72          serverSocketChannel = ServerSocketChannel.open();
73          serverSocketChannel.socket().bind(
74             new InetSocketAddress( 12345 ) );
75          serverSocketChannel.configureBlocking( false );
76
77          // wait for a connection
78          getConnection();
79
80       } // end try
81
82       // process problems with I/O
83       catch ( Exception ioException ) {
84          ioException.printStackTrace();
85       }
86
87    } // end method runServer
88
89    // wait for connection to arrive, then display connection info
90    private void getConnection() throws Exception
91    {
92       // Selector for incoming requests
93       selector = SelectorProvider.provider().openSelector();
94       serverSocketChannel.register(
95          selector, SelectionKey.OP_ACCEPT, null );
96
97       // process incoming requests
98       while ( selector.select() > 0 ) {
99
100         // get channels ready for i/o
101         Set readyKeys = selector.selectedKeys();
102         Iterator iterator = readyKeys.iterator();
103
104         // for each ready channel, process request
105         while ( iterator.hasNext() ) {
106            SelectionKey key = ( SelectionKey )iterator.next();
107            iterator.remove();
108
109            if ( key.isAcceptable() ) {  // ready for connection
110
111               // create connection
112               ServerSocketChannel nextReady =
113                  ( ServerSocketChannel ) key.channel();
114               SocketChannel socketChannel = nextReady.accept();
115
116               if ( socketChannel != null ) {
117                  socketChannel.configureBlocking( false );
118                  sockets.add( socketChannel.socket() );
119                  counter++;
```

Fig. 18.22 Nonblocking messenger server. (Part 3 of 6.)

```
120
121                    SwingUtilities.invokeLater(
122
123                       new Runnable() {
124
125                          public void run()
126                          {
127                             displayArea.append(
128                                "\nConnection with Client " + counter );
129                          }
130                       }
131                    );
132
133                    // register read operation to socketChannel
134                    SelectionKey readKey = socketChannel.register(
135                       selector, SelectionKey.OP_READ, null );
136
137                 } // end if socketChannel != null
138
139              } // end if key.isAcceptable
140
141              else if ( key.isReadable() ) {  // ready for read
142
143                 // get socketChannel ready for read
144                 SocketChannel socketChannel =
145                    ( SocketChannel ) key.channel();
146
147                 readMessage( socketChannel );
148              }
149
150           } // end processing each channel
151
152        } // end processing incoming requests
153
154     } // end method getConnection
155
156     // send message to client
157     private void writeMessage( String message ) throws IOException
158     {
159        Socket socket;
160        SocketChannel socketChannel;
161
162        // echo message back to all connected clients
163        for ( int i = 0; i < sockets.size(); i++ ) {
164           socket = ( Socket ) sockets.elementAt( i );
165           socketChannel = socket.getChannel();
166
167           // send message to client
168           try {
169
170              // convert message to bytes in charSet
171              writeBuffer = charSet.encode( message );
172
```

Fig. 18.22   Nonblocking messenger server. (Part 4 of 6.)

```
173                // write message to socketChannel
174                socketChannel.write( writeBuffer );
175             }
176
177             // process problems sending object
178             catch ( IOException ioException ) {
179                ioException.printStackTrace();
180                socketChannel.close();
181                sockets.remove( socket );
182             }
183
184          } // end for
185
186       } // end method writeMessage
187
188       // read message from client
189       private void readMessage( SocketChannel socketChannel )
190          throws IOException
191       {
192          // read message
193          try {
194
195             if ( socketChannel.isOpen() ) {
196                readBuffer.clear();
197                socketChannel.read( readBuffer );
198                readBuffer.flip();
199                CharBuffer charMessage = charSet.decode( readBuffer );
200                String message = charMessage.toString().trim();
201
202                // remove and close the connection when client disconnects
203                if ( message.indexOf( "Disconnect" ) >= 0 ) {
204                   sockets.remove( socketChannel.socket() );
205                   socketChannel.close();
206                }
207                else
208                   writeMessage( message );
209
210             } // end if
211
212          } // end try
213
214          catch ( IOException ioException ) {
215             ioException.printStackTrace();
216             sockets.remove( socketChannel.socket() );
217             socketChannel.close();
218          }
219
220       } // end method readMessage
221
222       public static void main( String args[] )
223       {
224          DeitelMessengerNonBlockingServer application =
225             new DeitelMessengerNonBlockingServer();
```

Fig. 18.22 Nonblocking messenger server. (Part 5 of 6.)

```
226          application.runServer();
227      }
228
229  }  // end class DeitelMessengerNonBlockingServer
```

Fig. 18.22   Nonblocking messenger server. (Part 6 of 6.)

Method `getConnection` (lines 90–154) waits for client connections and manages the channels that are ready for I/O operations. Line 93 creates a `Selector` for incoming client requests by invoking static method `open` of class `Selector`. Lines 94–95 register the `serverSocketChannel` with the `selector`. Method `register` takes three arguments— a `Selector` with which the channel is registered, an integer that indicates the set of operations the channel is interested in and an `Object` (i.e., some application-specific data which can be `null`) that is an attachment to the `SelectionKey` which is returned by method `register`. A `SelectionKey` contains two sets: one contains information about which operations the registered channel are interested in and the other contains information about which operations the registered channel are ready to perform. A `ServerSocketChannel` would be interested in a socket connection operation, so the second argument passed to method `register` is `SelectionKey.OP_ACCEPT`, which stands for the socket-accept operation. The `while` structure (lines 98–152) listens for and processes client requests. Line 98 invokes method `select` of the `Selector` to select a set of `SelectionKeys` whose channels are ready for I/O operations. Lines 101–102 get the key set and obtain an iterator from the set. Method `selectedKeys` of class `Selector` returns a `Set` that represents the key set selected by the selector. All selected keys are acceptable, readable or writable.

The `while` structure (lines 105–150) processes the requests for each channel that is ready for I/O. Lines 106–107 get the next key in the iterator and remove the key because this key is being handled. Method `isAcceptable` of class `SelectionKey` returns true when the key's associated channel is ready to accept a new socket connection. Lines 112–137 create a socket connection `SocketChannel` (lines 112–114) and register the channel with the selector for read operations (lines 134–135) if method `isAcceptable` returns `true`. Lines 108–109 get the `ServerSocketChannel` for which the key was created by invoking method `channel` of `SelectionKey` key. Line 114 invokes method `accept` of `nextReady` to create a socket connection. The return value of method `accept` is a `SocketChannel` that is the channel for the new connection, or `null` if no client connection is pending. If method `accept` returns a `SocketChannel`, line 117 invokes method `configureBlocking` with boolean value `false` to indicate that the newly created `SocketChannel` works in non-blocking mode. Lines 118–131 get the `Socket` associated with the `SocketChannel` by invoking `SocketChannel` method `socket`, add the socket to a socket array and display that a connection is made. Lines 134–135 register the `SocketChannel` with the `selector` for a read operation using `SelectionKey.OP_READ`.

Method `isReadable` of class `SelectionKey` returns `true` when the `SelectionKey`'s channel is ready for reading. If method `isReadable` of the `SelectionKey` returns `true` in line 141, lines 144–145 get the `SocketChannel` associated with the key and line 147 calls method `readMessage` to process the message sent from the client.

Method `writeMessage` (lines 157–186) sends the message to all clients connected with the server. For each socket stored in vector `sockets` (lines 163–184), lines 154–165 get the `SocketChannel` for the socket, line 171 invokes method `encode` of class

Charset to convert the message into a ByteBuffer, and line 174 invokes method write of class SocketChannel to send the message (in bytes) to the client.

Method readMessage (lines 189–220) is invoked each time a channel is ready for reading. Line 195 checks whether the channel is open by invoking SocketChannel method isOpen. Line 196 invokes method clear of ByteBuffer to clear the buffer so that the following read operation can place the message starting at position zero. Line 197 invokes method read of the socketChannel to read a sequence of bytes (in this case, 512 bytes) into ByteBuffer readBuffer. After reading, the position in readBuffer is set to the place after the last read byte. Line 198 invokes method flip to set the limit to the position and the position to zero so that we can get the message from the buffer. Line 199 invokes method decode of charSet to get a CharBuffer that contains the message. Line 200 invokes method toString on the CharBuffer to get the string representation. If the client sends a disconnect request, line 204 removes the connection from Vector sockets and line 205 closes the socket connection. Otherwise line 208 calls method writeMessage to send the message to all currently connected clients.

We reuse ClientGUI (Fig. 18.20), MessageListener (Fig. 18.13) and MessageManager (Fig. 18.16) to build the client application. Class SocketMessageManager2 (Fig. 18.23) manages the connection, disconnection and communication for the client.

```java
1   // Fig. 18.23: SocketMessageManager2.java
2   // SocketMessageManager2 is a class for objects capable of managing
3   // communications with a message server.
4   package com.deitel.messenger.sockets.client;
5
6   import java.io.*;
7   import java.nio.*;
8   import java.nio.channels.*;
9   import java.nio.charset.*;
10  import java.net.*;
11  import java.util.*;
12
13  import com.deitel.messenger.*;
14
15  public class SocketMessageManager2 implements MessageManager {
16     private SocketChannel socketChannel;
17     private MessageListener messageListener;
18     private String serverAddress;
19     private ReceivingThread receiveMessage;
20     private boolean connected;
21     private Charset charSet = Charset.forName( "UTF-8" );
22     private ByteBuffer writeBuffer;
23     private ByteBuffer readBuffer = ByteBuffer.allocate( 512 );
24
25     public SocketMessageManager2( String host )
26     {
27        serverAddress = host;
28        connected = false;
29     }
```

Fig. 18.23 SocketMessageManager2 manages communications with the message server. (Part 1 of 4.)

```
30
31        // connect to message server and start receiving message
32        public void connect( MessageListener listener )
33        {
34            messageListener = listener;
35
36            // connect to server and start thread to receive message
37            try {
38
39                // create SocketChannel to make connection to server
40                socketChannel = SocketChannel.open();
41                socketChannel.connect( new InetSocketAddress(
42                    InetAddress.getByName( serverAddress ), 12345 ) );
43
44                // start ReceivingThread to receive messages sent by server
45                receiveMessage = new ReceivingThread();
46                receiveMessage.start();
47
48                connected = true;
49            }
50            catch ( Exception exception ) {
51                exception.printStackTrace();
52            }
53        }
54
55        // disconnect from message server and stop receiving message
56        public void disconnect( MessageListener listener )
57        {
58            if ( connected ) {
59
60                // send disconnect request and stop receiving
61                try {
62                    sendMessage( "", "Disconnect" );
63
64                    connected = false;
65
66                    // send interrupt signal to receiving thread
67                    receiveMessage.interrupt();
68                }
69                catch ( Exception exception ) {
70                    exception.printStackTrace();
71                }
72            }
73        }
74
75        // send message to message server
76        public void sendMessage( String userName, String messageBody )
77        {
78            String message = userName + "> " + messageBody;
79
80            // send message to server
81            try {
```

Fig. 18.23 SocketMessageManager2 manages communications with the message
server. (Part 2 of 4.)

```
82            writeBuffer = charSet.encode( message );
83            socketChannel.write( writeBuffer );
84         }
85      catch ( IOException ioException ) {
86         ioException.printStackTrace();
87
88         try {
89            socketChannel.close();
90         }
91         catch ( IOException exception ) {
92            exception.printStackTrace();
93         }
94      }
95
96   } // end method sendMessage
97
98   public class ReceivingThread extends Thread
99   {
100     public void run()
101     {
102        int messageLength = 0;
103        String message = "";
104
105        // read messages until server close the connection
106        try {
107
108           // process messages sent from server
109           do {
110              readBuffer.clear();
111              socketChannel.read( readBuffer );
112              readBuffer.flip();
113              CharBuffer charMessage = charSet.decode( readBuffer );
114              message = charMessage.toString().trim();
115
116              // tokenize message to retrieve user name and message body
117              StringTokenizer tokenizer =
118                 new StringTokenizer( message, ">" );
119
120              // ignore messages that do not contain a user
121              // name and message body
122              if ( tokenizer.countTokens() == 2 )
123
124                 // send message to MessageListener
125                 messageListener.messageReceived(
126                    tokenizer.nextToken(),   // user name
127                    tokenizer.nextToken() ); // message body
128
129           } while ( true );  // keep receiving messages
130
131        } // end try
132
```

Fig. 18.23 SocketMessageManager2 manages communications with the message server. (Part 3 of 4.)

```
133                // catch problems reading from server
134                catch ( IOException ioException ) {
135                   if ( ioException instanceof ClosedByInterruptException )
136                      System.out.println( "socket channel closed" );
137                   else {
138                      ioException.printStackTrace();
139
140                      try {
141                         socketChannel.close();
142                         System.out.println( "socket channel closed" );
143                      }
144                      catch ( IOException exception ) {
145                         exception.printStackTrace();
146                      }
147                   }
148
149                } // end catch
150
151             } // end method run
152
153       } // end inner class ReceivingThread
154
155 } // end class SocketMessageManager2
```

Fig. 18.23 SocketMessageManager2 manages communications with the message
server. (Part 4 of 4.)

Method connect (lines 32–53) establishes a connection to the server. Lines 40–42
create a socket connection. Line 40 opens a SocketChannel by invoking static method
open of class SocketChannel. Lines 41–42 connect this channel's socket by invoking
method connect of SocketChannel with the SocketAddress specified by chat-
Server and port number 12345. Lines 45–46 create a ReceivingThread for receiving
messages from the server and start the thread.

Method sendMessage (lines 76–96) is invoked when the user clicks **Send**. Line 82
invokes method encode of Charset to encode the message into bytes. Line 83 invokes
method write of SocketChannel to send the message to the server as bytes. In case an
IOException occurs, which usually indicates that future I/O operations on the channel
will not succeed, line 89 invokes method close of SocketChannel to close the channel.

Inner class ReceivingThread (lines 98–153) keeps reading messages sent from the
server until the thread is interrupted by method disconnect (lines 56–73) or until the
remote endpoint finishes or resets the connection. Lines 110–114 get the message. Lines
117–118 create a StringTokenizer to separate the message body from the name of the user
who sent the message. Line 122 checks for the correct number of tokens. Lines 125–127
invoke method messageReceived of interface MessageListener to deliver the
incoming message to the DeitelMessageManager2's MessengerListener.

When the user clicks the **Disconnect** button or selects **Disconnect** from the menu,
lines 62–67 send a disconnect request to the server and close the connection, if the client is
connected. Line 62 sends the disconnect request to the server and line 67 closes the SocketChannel by interrupting the receiving thread. When the receiving thread is interrupted, the
channel that is blocked for I/O is closed and a ClosedByInterruptException is thrown.

Class `DeitelMessenger2` (Fig. 18.24) launches a client for the DeitelMessenger-NonBlockingServer. Lines 15–18 create a new `SocketMessageManager2` object that connects to the `DeitelMessengerNonBlockingServer` using the IP address specified as an argument. Lines 21–24 create a `ClientGUI` for the `MessageManager`, set the `ClientGUI` size and make the `ClientGUI` visible.

```java
1   // Fig. 18.24: DeitelMessenger2.java
2   // DeitelMessenger2 is a chat application that uses a ClientGUI
3   // to communicate with chat server.
4   package com.deitel.messenger.sockets.client;
5
6   import com.deitel.messenger.*;
7
8   public class DeitelMessenger2 {
9
10     public static void main( String args[] )
11     {
12        MessageManager messageManager;
13
14        // create new DeitelMessenger
15        if ( args.length == 0 )
16           messageManager = new SocketMessageManager2( "localhost" );
17        else
18           messageManager = new SocketMessageManager2( args[ 0 ] );
19
20        // create GUI for SocketMessageManager
21        ClientGUI clientGUI = new ClientGUI( messageManager );
22        clientGUI.setSize( 300, 400 );
23        clientGUI.setResizable( false );
24        clientGUI.setVisible( true );
25     }
26
27   } // end class DeitelMessenger2
```

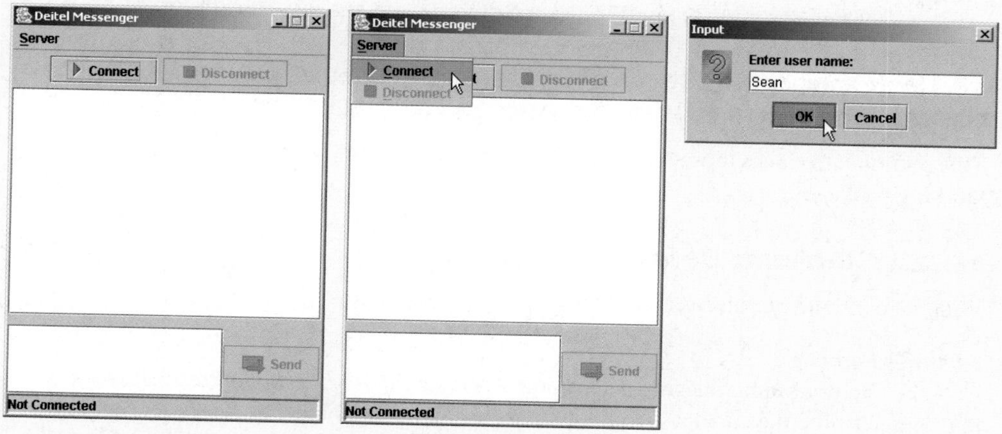

Fig. 18.24 `DeitelMessenger2` application for participating in a `DeitelMessengerNonBlockingServer` chat session. (Part 1 of 2.)

Fig. 18.24   `DeitelMessenger2` application for participating in a
`DeitelMessengerNonBlockingServer` chat session.   (Part 2 of 2.)

18.12 (Optional) Discovering Design Patterns: Design Patterns Used in Packages `java.io` and `java.net`

This section introduces those design patterns associated with the Java file, streams and networking packages.

18.12.1 Creational Design Patterns

We now continue our discussion of creational design patterns.

Abstract Factory
Like the Factory Method design pattern, the *Abstract Factory design pattern* allows a system to determine the subclass from which to instantiate an object at run time. Often, this subclass is unknown during development. However, Abstract Factory uses an object known as a *factory* that uses an interface to instantiate objects. A factory creates a product; in this case, that product is an object of a subclass determined at run time.

The Java socket library in package `java.net` uses the Abstract Factory design pattern. A socket describes a connection, or a stream of data, between two processes. Class `Socket` references an object of a `SocketImpl` subclass (Section 18.5). Class `Socket` also contains a `static` reference to an object implementing interface `SocketImplFactory`. The `Socket` constructor invokes method `createSocketImpl` of interface `SocketImpl-Factory` to create the `SocketImpl` object. The object that implements interface `Socket-ImplFactory` is the factory, and an object of a `SocketImpl` subclass is the product of that factory. The system cannot specify the `SocketImpl` subclass from which to instantiate until run time, because the system has no knowledge of what type of `Socket` implementation is required (e.g., a socket configured to the local network's security requirements). Method `createSocketImpl` decides the `SocketImpl` subclass from which to instantiate the object at run time.

18.12.2 Structural Design Patterns

This section concludes our discussion of structural design patterns.

Decorator

Let us reexamine class `CreateSequentialFile` (Fig. 17.7). Lines 114–115 of this class allow a `FileOutputStream` object, which writes bytes to a file, to gain the functionality of an `ObjectOutputStream`, which provides methods for writing entire objects to an `OutputStream`. Class `CreateSequentialFile` appears to "wrap" an `ObjectOutput-Stream` object around a `FileOutputStream` object. The fact that we can dynamically add the behavior of an `ObjectOutputStream` to a `FileOutputStream` prevents the need for a separate class called `ObjectFileOutputStream`, which would implement the behaviors of both classes.

Lines 127–128 of class `CreateSequentialFile` show an example of the *Decorator design pattern*, which allows an object to gain additional functionality dynamically. Using this pattern, designers do not have to create separate, unnecessary classes to add responsibilities to objects of a given class.

Let us consider a more complex example to discover how the Decorator design pattern can simplify a system's structure. Suppose that we wanted to enhance the I/O performance of the previous example by using a `BufferedOutputStream`. Using the Decorator design pattern, we would write

```
output = new ObjectOutputStream(
    new BufferedOutputStream(
        new FileOutputStream( fileName ) ) );
```

We can combine objects in this manner, because `ObjectOutputStream`, `BufferedOutputStream` and `FileOutputStream` extend abstract superclass `OutputStream`, and each subclass constructor takes an `OutputStream` object as a parameter. If the stream objects in package `java.io` did not use the Decorator pattern (i.e., did not satisfy these two requirements), package `java.io` would have to provide classes `BufferedFileOutputStream`, `ObjectBufferedOutputStream`, `ObjectBufferedFileOutputStream` and `ObjectFileOutputStream`. Consider how many classes we would have to create if we combined even more stream objects without applying the Decorator pattern.

Facade

When driving a car, you know that pressing the gas pedal accelerates your car, but you are unaware of exactly how the gas pedal causes your car to accelerate. This principle is the foundation of the *Facade design pattern*, which allows an object—called a *facade object*—to provide a simple interface for the behaviors of a *subsystem* (an aggregate of objects that comprise collectively a major system responsibility). The gas pedal, for example, is the facade object for the car's acceleration subsystem, the steering wheel is the facade object for the car's steering subsystem and the brake is the facade object for the car's deceleration subsystem. A *client object* uses the facade object to access the objects behind the facade. The client remains unaware of how the objects behind the facade fulfill responsibilities, so the subsystem complexity is hidden from the client. When you press the gas pedal you act as a client object. The Facade design pattern reduces system complexity, because a client interacts with only one object (the facade) to access the behaviors of the subsystem the facade represents. This pattern shields applications developers from subsystem complexities. Developers need to be familiar with only the operations of the facade object, rather than with the more detailed operations of the entire subsystem. The implementation behind the facade may be changed without changes to the clients.

In package `java.net`, an object of class URL is a facade object. This object contains a reference to an `InetAddress` object that specifies the host computer's IP address. The URL facade object also references an object from class `URLStreamHandler`, which opens the URL connection. The client object that uses the URL facade object accesses the `Inet-Address` object and the `URLStreamHandler` object through the facade object. However, the client object does not know how the objects behind the URL facade object accomplish their responsibilities.

18.12.3 Architectural Patterns

Design patterns allow developers to design specific parts of systems, such as abstracting object instantiations or aggregating classes into larger structures. Design patterns also promote loose coupling among objects. *Architectural patterns* promote loose coupling among subsystems. These patterns specify how subsystems interact with one another.[2] We introduce the popular Model-View-Controller and Layers architectural patterns.

MVC

Consider the design of a simple text editor. In this program, the user inputs text from the keyboard and formats this text using the mouse. Our program stores this text and format information into a series of data structures, then displays this information on screen for the user to read what has been inputted.

This program adheres to the *Model-View-Controller* (MVC) *architectural pattern*, which separates application data (contained in the *model*) from graphical presentation components (the *view*) and input-processing logic (the *controller*).[3] Figure 18.25 shows the relationships between components in MVC.

---

2. R. Hartman. "Building on Patterns." *Application Development Trends* May 2001: 19–26.
3. Section 13.17 also discussed Model-View-Controller architecture and its relevance to the elevator simulation case study.

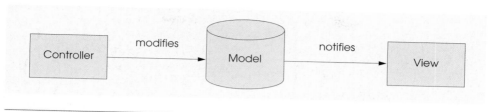

Fig. 18.25 Model-View-Controller Architecture.

The controller implements logic for processing user inputs. The model contains application data, and the view presents the data stored in the model. When a user provides some input, the controller modifies the model with the given input. The model contains the application data. With regards to the text-editor example, the model might contain only the characters that make up the document. When the model changes, it notifies the view of the change so the view can update its presentation with the changed data. The view in a word processor might display characters using a particular font, with a particular size, etc.

MVC does not restrict an application to a single view and a single controller. In a more sophisticated program (such as a word processor), there might be two views of a document model. One view might display an outline of the document and the other might display the complete document. The word processor also might implement multiple controllers—one for handling keyboard input and another for handling mouse selections. If either controller makes a change in the model, both the outline view and the print-preview window will show the change immediately when the model notifies all views of changes.

Another key benefit to the MVC architectural pattern is that developers can modify each component individually without having to modify the other components. For example, developers could modify the view that displays the document outline, but the developers would not have to modify either the model or other views or controllers.

Layers

Consider the design in Fig. 18.26, which presents the basic structure of a *three-tier application*, in which each tier contains a unique system component.

The *information tier* (also called the "bottom tier") maintains data for the application, typically storing the data in a database. The information tier for an online store may contain product information, such as descriptions, prices and quantities in stock and customer information, such as user names, billing addresses and credit-card numbers.

The *middle tier* acts as an intermediary between the information tier and the client tier. The middle tier processes client-tier requests, reads data from and writes data to the database. The middle tier then processes data from the information tier and presents the content to the client tier. This processing is the application's *business logic*, which handles such tasks as retrieving data from the information tier, ensuring that data is reliable before updating the database and presenting data to the client tier. For example, the business logic associated with the middle tier for the online store can verify a customer's credit card with the credit-card issuer before the warehouse ships the customer's order. This business logic could then store (or retrieve) the credit information in the database and notify the client tier that the verification was successful.

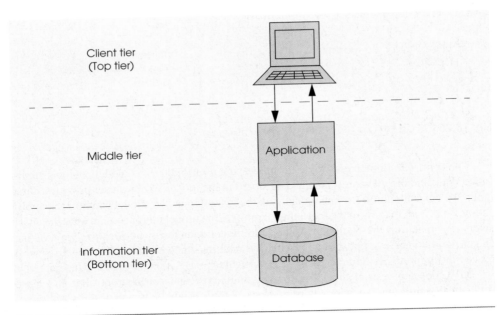

Fig. 18.26 Three-tier application model.

The *client tier* (also called the "top tier") is the application's user interface, such as a standard Web browser. Users interact directly with the application through the user interface. The client tier interacts with the middle tier to make requests and retrieve data from the information tier. The client tier then displays data retrieved from the middle tier.

Figure 18.26 is an implementation of the *Layers architectural pattern*, which divides functionality into separate *layers*. Each layer contains a set of system responsibilities and depends on the services of only the next lower layer. In Fig. 18.26, each tier corresponds to a layer. This architectural pattern is useful, because a designer can modify one layer without having to modify the other layers. For example, a designer could modify the information tier in Fig. 18.26 to accommodate a particular database product, but the designer would not have to modify either the client tier or the middle tier.

18.12.4 Conclusion

In this "Discovering Design Patterns" section, we discussed how packages java.io and java.net take advantage of specific design patterns and how developers can integrate design patterns with networking/file applications in Java. We also introduced the Model-View-Controller and Layers architectural patterns, which both assign system functionality to separate subsystems. These patterns make designing a system easier for developers. In "Discovering Design Patterns" Section 22.12, we conclude our presentation of design patterns by discussing those design patterns used in package java.util.

SUMMARY

- Java provides stream sockets and datagram sockets. With stream sockets, a process establishes a connection to another process. While the connection is in place, data flows between the processes in streams. Stream sockets are said to provide a connection-oriented service. The protocol used for transmission is the popular TCP (Transmission Control Protocol).

- With datagram sockets, individual packets of information are transmitted. UDP—the User Datagram Protocol—is a connectionless service that does not guarantee that packets arrive in a specific order. Packets can be lost, duplicated and even arrive out of sequence. Extra programming is required on the programmer's part to deal with these problems.

- The HTTP protocol (Hypertext Transfer Protocol) that forms the basis of the Web uses URIs (Uniform Resource Identifiers) to locate data on the Internet. Common URIs represent files or directories and can represent complex tasks such as database lookups and Internet searches. A URI that represents a document is called a URL (Uniform Resource Locator).

- Web browsers often restrict an applet so that it can communicate only with the machine from which it was originally downloaded.

- A HashMap stores key/value pairs. A program uses a key to store and retrieve an associated value in the HashMap. HashMap method put takes two arguments—a key and its associated value—and places the value in the HashMap at a location determined by the key. HashMap method get takes one argument—a key—and retrieves the value (as an Object reference) associated with the key.

- A Vector is a dynamically resizable array of Objects. Vector method add adds a new element to the end of the Vector.

- Applet method getAppletContext returns a reference to an AppletContext object that represents the applet's environment (i.e., the browser in which the applet is executing). AppletContext method showDocument receives a URL as an argument and passes it to the AppletContext (i.e., the browser), which displays the Web resource associated with that URL. A second version of showDocument enables an applet to specify the target frame in which to display a Web resource. Special target frames include _blank (display in a new Web browser window), _self (display in the same frame as the applet) and _top (remove the current frames, then display in the current window).

- JEditorPane method setPage downloads the document specified by its argument and displays it in the JEditorPane.

- Typically, an HTML document contains hyperlinks—text, images or GUI components that, when clicked, link to another document on the Web. If an HTML document is displayed in a JEditorPane and the user clicks a hyperlink, the JEditorPane generates a HyperlinkEvent and notifies all registered HyperlinkListeners of that event.

- HyperlinkEvent method getEventType determines the event type. HyperlinkEvent contains nested class EventType, which declares three hyperlink event types: ACTIVATED (hyperlink clicked), ENTERED (mouse over a hyperlink) and EXITED (mouse moved away from a hyperlink). HyperlinkEvent method getURL obtains the URL represented by the hyperlink.

- Stream-based connections are managed with Socket objects.

- A ServerSocket object establishes the port where a server waits for connections from clients. The second argument to the ServerSocket constructor is the number of connections that can wait in a queue to connect to the server. If the queue of clients is full, client connections are refused. The ServerSocket method accept waits indefinitely (i.e., blocks) for a connection from a client and returns a Socket object when a connection is established.

- Socket methods getOutputStream and getInputStream get references to the OutputStream and InputStream associated with a Socket, respectively. Socket method close terminates a connection.

- A Socket object connects a client to a server by specifying the server name and port number when creating the Socket object. A failed connection attempt throws an IOException.

- `InetAddress` method `getByName` returns an `InetAddress` object containing the host name of the computer for which the host name or IP address is specified as an argument. `InetAddress` method `getLocalHost` returns an `InetAddress` object containing the host name of the local computer executing the program.

- Connection-oriented transmission is like the telephone system—you dial and are given a connection to the telephone of the person with whom you wish to communicate. The connection is maintained for the duration of your phone call, even when you are not talking.

- Connectionless transmission with datagrams is similar to mail carried via the postal service. A large message that will not fit in one envelope can be broken into separate message pieces that are placed in separate, sequentially numbered envelopes. Each of the letters is then mailed at once. The letters could arrive in order, out of order or not at all.

- `DatagramPacket` objects store packets of data for sending or store packets of data received by an application. `DatagramSocket`s send and receive `DatagramPacket`s.

- The `DatagramSocket` constructor that takes no arguments binds the application to a port chosen by the computer on which the program executes. The `DatagramSocket` constructor that takes an integer port number argument binds the application to the specified port. If a `DatagramSocket` constructor fails to bind the application to a port, a `SocketException` occurs. `DatagramSocket` method `receive` blocks (waits) until a packet arrives, then stores the packet in its argument.

- `DatagramPacket` method `getAddress` returns an `InetAddress` object containing information about the host computer from which the packet was sent. Method `getPort` returns an integer specifying the port number through which the host computer sent the `DatagramPacket`. Method `getLength` returns an integer representing the number of bytes of data in a `DatagramPacket`. Method `getData` returns a byte array containing the data in a `DatagramPacket`.

- The `DatagramPacket` constructor for a packet to be sent takes four arguments—the byte array to be sent, the number of bytes to be sent, the client address to which the packet will be sent and the port number where the client is waiting to receive packets.

- `DatagramSocket` method `send` sends a `DatagramPacket` out over the network.

- If an error occurs when receiving or sending a `DatagramPacket`, an `IOException` occurs.

- Reading data from a `Socket` is a blocking call—the current thread is put in the blocked state while the thread waits for the read operation to complete. Method `setSoTimeout` specifies that, if no data is received in the given number of milliseconds, the `Socket` should issue an `Interrupted-IOException`, which the current thread can catch, then continue executing. This prevents the current thread from blocking indefinitely if there is no more data available from the `Socket`.

- Multicast is an efficient way to send data to many clients without the overhead of broadcasting that data to every host on the Internet. Using multicast, an application can "publish" `Datagram-Packet`s to be delivered to subscriber applications. An application multicasts `DatagramPacket`s by sending the `DatagramPacket`s to a multicast address—an IP address in the range from 224.0.0.0 to 239.255.255.255, reserved for multicast.

- Clients that wish to receive `DatagramPacket`s can join the multicast group that will receive the `DatagramPacket`s published to the multicast address.

- Multicast `DatagramPacket`s are not reliable—packets are not guaranteed to reach any destination. Also, the order in which clients receive the datagrams is not guaranteed.

- The `MulticastSocket` constructor takes as an argument the port to which the `MulticastSocket` should connect to receive incoming `DatagramPacket`s.

- Method `joinGroup` of class `MulticastSocket` takes as an argument the `InetAddress` of the multicast group to join. Method receive of class `MulticastSocket` reads an incoming `DatagramPacket` from a multicast address.

- Prior to J2SE 1.4, to allow two or more clients communication with the server concurrently using sockets, usually a multithreaded server is used. One server thread handles each client's I/O, which causes enormous thread overhead and hence reduces scalability. J2SE 1.4 solves this problem by introducing the non-blocking I/O mechanism.

- With non-blocking I/O technology, a server can interact with multiple client connections simultaneously without creating a new thread for each connection. The communication between server and client is done through *channels*, which can work in non-blocking mode.

- Non-blocking technology is achieved with SelectableChannels in conjunction with Selectors. Both classes are part of the java.nio.channels package.

- A SelectableChannel represents a communication channel that can manage multiple I/O channels simultaneously, which is also called multiplexing, when work together with a Selector.

- A Selector, a multiplexor of SelectableChannels, enables checking ready channels simultaneously.

- A ServerSocketChannel performs the same task as ServerSocket—listens for socket connections. The major difference between ServerSocket and ServerSocketChannel is that ServerSocketChannel can work in non-blocking mode.

- A SelectionKey represents the registration of a channel with a selector.

- Method selectedKeys of class Selector returns a Set that represents the key set selected by the selector. All selected keys are either acceptable, readable or writable.

- Method write of class SocketChannel takes a ByteBuffer which specifies the buffer from which the bytes are written and returns an int that indicates how many bytes are written to the channel.

- Method read of class SocketChannel takes a ByteBuffer which specifies the buffer to which the bytes are read and returns an int that indicates how many bytes are read from the channel.

TERMINOLOGY

accept a connection
accept method of ServerSocket
accept method of ServerSocketChannel
add method of Vector
allocate static method of ByteBuffer
AppletContext interface
bind to a port
ByteBuffer
channel method of SelectionKey
channels
CharBuffer
client
client connects to a server
client/server relationship
client-side socket
close a connection
close method of Selector
close method of ServerSocketChannel
close method of Socket
ClosedByInterruptException

collaborative computing
computer networking
configureBlocking method
connect method of SocketChannel
connect to a port
connect to a Web site
ConnectException class
connection
connection request
connectionless service
connectionless transmission with datagrams
connection-oriented service
datagram
datagram socket
DatagramPacket class
DatagramSocket class
deny a connection
duplicated packets
flip method of ByteBuffer
get method of class HashMap

SELF-REVIEW EXERCISES

18.1   Fill in the blanks in each of the following statements:

a) Exception _____ occurs when an input/output error occurs when closing a socket.

b) Exception _____ occurs when a host name indicated by a client cannot be resolved to an address.

c) If a `DatagramSocket` constructor fails to set up a `DatagramSocket` properly, an exception of type _____ occurs.

d) Many of Java's networking classes are contained in package _____.

e) Class _____ binds the application to a port for datagram transmission.

f) An object of class _____ contains an IP address.

g) The two types of sockets we discussed in this chapter are _____ and _____.

h) The acronym URL stands for _____.

i) The acronym URI stands for _____.

j) The key protocol that forms the basis of the World Wide Web is _____.

k) `AppletContext` method _____ receives a URL object as an argument and displays in a browser the World Wide Web resource associated with that URL.

l) Method `getLocalHost` returns a(n) _____ object containing the local host name of the computer on which the program is executing.

m) `MulticastSocket` method _____ subscribes a `MulticastSocket` to a multicast group.

n) The URL constructor determines whether its string argument is a valid URL. If so, the URL object is initialized with that location; otherwise, a(n) _____ exception occurs.

18.2   State whether each of the following is *true or false.* *If* false, explain why.

a) Multicast broadcasts `DatagramPacket`s to every host on the Internet.

b) UDP is a connection-oriented protocol.

c) With stream sockets a process establishes a connection to another process.

d) A server waits at a port for connections from a client.

e) Datagram packet transmission over a network is reliable—packets are guaranteed to arrive in sequence.

f) For security reasons, many Web browsers such as Netscape allow Java applets to do file processing only on the machines on which they execute.

g) Web browsers often restrict an applet so that it can only communicate with the machine from which it was originally downloaded.

h) IP addresses from `224.0.0.0` to `239.255.255.255` are reserved for multicast.

ANSWERS TO SELF-REVIEW EXERCISES

18.1   a) `IOException`. b) `UnknownHostException`. c) `SocketException`. d) `java.net`. e) `DatagramSocket`. f) `InetAddress`. g) stream sockets, datagram sockets. h) Uniform Resource Locator.   i) Uniform Resource Identifier.   j) HTTP.   k) `showDocument`.   l) `InetAddress`. m) `joinGroup`. n) `MalformedURLException`.

18.2   a) False; multicast sends `DatagramPacket`s only to hosts that have joined the multicast group. b) False; UDP is a connectionless protocol and TCP is a connection-oriented protocol. c) True. d) True. e) False; packets could be lost and packets can arrive out of order. f) False; most browsers prevent applets from doing file processing on the client machine. g) True. h) True.

EXERCISES

18.3   Distinguish between connection-oriented and connectionless network services.

18.4   How does a client determine the host name of the client computer?

18.5   Under what circumstances would a `SocketException` be thrown?

18.6   How can a client get a line of text from a server?

18.7   Describe how a client connects to a server.

18.8   Describe how a server sends data to a client.

18.9   Describe how to prepare a server to receive a stream-based connection request from a single client.

18.10   Describe how to prepare a server to receive connection requests from multiple clients if each client that connects should be processed concurrently with all other connected clients.

18.11   How does a server listen for streams-based socket connections at a port?

18.12   What determines how many connect requests from clients can wait in a queue to connect to a server?

18.13   As described in the text, what reasons might cause a server to refuse a connection request from a client?

18.14   Use a socket connection to allow a client to specify a file name and have the server send the contents of the file or indicate that the file does not exist.

18.15   Modify Exercise 18.14 to allow the client to modify the contents of the file and send the file back to the server for storage. The user can edit the file in a `JTextArea`, then click a *save changes* button to send the file back to the server.

18.16   Modify program of Fig. 18.2 to allow users to add their own sites to the list and remove sites from the list.

18.17   Multithreaded servers are quite popular today, especially because of the increasing use of multiprocessing servers. Modify the simple server application presented in Section 18.6 to be a multithreaded server. Then use several client applications and have each of them connect to the server simultaneously. Use a `Vector` to store the client threads. `Vector` provides several methods of use in this exercise. Method `size` determines the number of elements in a `Vector`. Method `get` returns the element (as an `Object` reference) in the location specified by its argument. Method `add` places its argument at the end of the `Vector`. Method `remove` deletes its argument from the `Vector`. Method `lastElement` returns an `Object` reference to the last object you inserted in the `Vector`.

18.18   In the text, we presented a tic-tac-toe program controlled by a multithreaded server. Develop a checkers program modeled after the tic-tac-toe program. The two users should alternate making moves. Your program should mediate the players' moves, determining whose turn it is and allowing only valid moves. The players themselves will determine when the game is over.

18.19   Develop a chess-playing program modeled after the checkers program in the Exercise 18.18.

18.20   Develop a Blackjack card game program in which the server application deals cards to each of the client applets. The server should deal additional cards (as per the rules of the game) to each player as requested.

18.21   Develop a Poker card game in which the server application deals cards to each of the client applets. The server should deal additional cards (as per the rules of the game) to each player as requested.

18.22   (*Modifications to the Multithreaded Tic-Tac-Toe Program*) The programs of Fig. 18.8 and Fig. 18.9 implemented a multithreaded, client/server version of the game Tic-Tac-Toe. Our goal in developing this game was to demonstrate a multithreaded server that could process multiple connections from clients at the same time. The server in the example is really a mediator between the two client applets—it makes sure that each move is valid and that each client moves in the proper order.

The server does not determine who won or lost or if there was a draw. Also, there is no capability to allow a new game to be played or to terminate an existing game.

The following is a list of suggested modifications to Fig. 18.8 and Fig. 18.9:

a) Modify the TicTacToeServer class to test for a win, loss or draw on each move in the game. Send a message to each client applet that indicates the result of the game when the game is over.

b) Modify the TicTacToeClient class to display a button that when clicked allows the client to play another game. The button should be enabled only when a game completes. Note that both class TicTacToeClient and class TicTacToeServer must be modified to reset the board and all state information. Also, the other TicTacToeClient should be notified that a new game is about to begin so its board and state can be reset.

c) Modify the TicTacToeClient class to provide a button that allows a client to terminate the program at any time. When the user clicks the button, the server and the other client should be notified. The server should then wait for a connection from another client so a new game can begin.

d) Modify the TicTacToeClient class and the TicTacToeServer class so the winner of a game can choose game piece X or O for the next game. Remember: X always goes first.

e) If you would like to be ambitious, allow a client to play against the server while the server waits for a connection from another client.

18.23 *(3-D Multithreaded Tic-Tac-Toe)* Modify the multithreaded, client/server Tic-Tac-Toe program to implement a three-dimensional 4-by-4-by-4 version of the game. Implement the server application to mediate between the two clients. Display the three-dimensional board as four boards containing four rows and four columns each. If you would like to be ambitious, try the following modifications:

a) Draw the board in a three-dimensional manner.

b) Allow the server to test for a win, loss or draw. Beware! There are many possible ways to win on a 4-by-4-by-4 board!

18.24 *(Networked Morse Code)* Modify your solution to Exercise 11.27 to enable two applets to send Morse Code messages to each other through a multithreaded server application. Each applet should allow the user to type normal characters in JTextAreas, translate the characters into Morse Code and send the coded message through the server to the other client. When messages are received, they should be decoded and displayed as normal characters and as Morse Code. The applet should have two JTextAreas: one for displaying the other client's messages and one for typing.

19

Multimedia: Images, Animation and Audio

Objectives

- To understand how to get and display images.
- To create animations from sequences of images.
- To create image maps.
- To be able to get, play, loop and stop sounds, using an `AudioClip`.

The wheel that squeaks the loudest … gets the grease.
John Billings (Henry Wheeler Shaw)

We'll use a signal I have tried and found far-reaching and easy to yell. Waa-hoo!
Zane Grey

There is a natural hootchy-kootchy motion to a goldfish.
Walt Disney

Between the motion and the act falls the shadow.
Thomas Stearns Eliot

Outline

Summary • Terminology • Self-Review Exercises • Answers to Self-Review Exercises • Exercises • Special Section: Challenging Multimedia Projects

19.1 Introduction

Welcome to what may be the largest revolution in the history of the computer industry. Those of us who entered the field decades ago were interested in using computers primarily to perform arithmetic calculations at high speed. As the computer field evolves, we are beginning to realize that the data-manipulation capabilities of computers are now equally important. The "sizzle" of Java is *multimedia*—the use of *sound, images, graphics* and *video* to make applications "come alive." Today, many people consider two-dimensional color video to be the "ultimate" in multimedia. We expect all kinds of exciting new three-dimensional applications. Java programmers already can use the *Java3D API* to create substantial 3D graphics applications.

Multimedia programming offers many new challenges. The field is already enormous and will grow rapidly. People are rushing to equip their computers for multimedia. Most new computers sold today are "multimedia ready," with CD or DVD drives, audio boards and, sometimes, special video capabilities.

Among users who want graphics, two-dimensional graphics no longer suffice. Many people now want three-dimensional, high-resolution, color graphics. True three-dimensional imaging may become available within the next decade. Imagine having high-resolution, "theater-in-the-round," three-dimensional television. Sporting and entertainment events will seem to take place on your living room floor! Medical students worldwide will see operations being performed thousands of miles away, as if they were occurring in the same room. People will be able to learn how to drive with extremely realistic driving simulators in their homes before they get behind the wheel. The possibilities are exciting and endless.

Multimedia demands extraordinary computing power. Until recently, affordable computers with that kind of power were not available. Today's ultrafast processors, like the SPARC Ultra from Sun Microsystems, the Pentium and Itanium from Intel, the Alpha from Hewlett-Packard Company and the processors from MIPS/Silicon Graphics (among others) make effective multimedia possible. The computer and communications industries will be primary beneficiaries of the multimedia revolution. Users will be willing to pay for the faster processors, larger memories and wider communications bandwidths that support demanding multimedia applications. Ironically, users may not have to pay more as fierce competition in these industries drives prices down.

We need programming languages that make creating multimedia applications easy. Most programming languages do not have built-in multimedia capabilities. However, Java provides extensive multimedia facilities that enable you to start developing powerful multimedia applications immediately.

This chapter presents several examples of interesting multimedia features you will need to build useful applications, including the following:

1. the basics of manipulating images

2. creating smooth animations

3. playing audio files with the `AudioClip` interface

4. creating image maps that can sense when the cursor is over them, even without a mouse click

The exercises for this chapter suggest dozens of challenging and interesting projects. When we were creating these exercises, it seemed that the ideas just kept flowing. Multimedia leverages creativity in ways that we have not experienced with "conventional" computer capabilities.[1]

19.2 Loading, Displaying and Scaling Images

Java's multimedia capabilities include graphics, images, animations, sounds and video. We begin our discussion with images.

The applet of Fig. 19.1 demonstrates loading an *Image* (package `java.awt`) and loading an *ImageIcon* (package `javax.swing`). The applet displays the `Image` in its original size and scaled to a larger size, using two versions of `Graphics` method *drawImage*. The applet also draws the `ImageIcon`, using the icon's method *paintIcon*. Class `ImageIcon` is easier to use than `Image`, because its constructor can receive arguments of several different formats, including a `byte` array containing the bytes of an image, an `Image` already loaded in memory, a string representing the location of an image and a URL representing the location of an image.

```
1   // Fig. 19.1: LoadImageAndScale.java
2   // Load an image and display it in its original size and twice its
3   // original size. Load and display the same image as an ImageIcon.
4   import java.applet.Applet;
5   import java.awt.*;
6   import javax.swing.*;
7
8   public class LoadImageAndScale extends JApplet {
9      private Image logo1;
10     private ImageIcon logo2;
11
```

Fig. 19.1   Loading and displaying an image in an applet. (Part 1 of 2.)

---

1. Java's multimedia capabilities go far beyond those presented in this chapter. These capabilities include the Java Media Framework API, Java Sound API, Java 3D API, Java Advanced Imaging API, Java Speech API, Java 2D API and Java Image I/O API. Section 19.6 contains URLs for the home page of each of these APIs.

```
12        // load image when applet is loaded
13        public void init()
14        {
15            logo1 = getImage( getDocumentBase(), "logo.gif" );
16            logo2 = new ImageIcon( "logo.gif" );
17        }
18
19        // display image
20        public void paint( Graphics g )
21        {
22            g.drawImage( logo1, 0, 0, this ); // draw original image
23
24            // draw image to fit the width and the height less 120 pixels
25            g.drawImage( logo1, 0, 120, getWidth(), getHeight() - 120, this );
26
27            // draw icon using its paintIcon method
28            logo2.paintIcon( this, g, 180, 0 );
29        }
30
31    } // end class LoadImageAndScale
```

Fig. 19.1   Loading and displaying an image in an applet. (Part 2 of 2.)

Lines 9 and 10 declare an Image reference and an ImageIcon reference, respectively. Class Image is an abstract class; therefore, the applet cannot create an object of class Image directly. Rather, the applet must call a method that causes the applet container to load and return the Image for use in the program. Class Applet (the direct superclass of JApplet) provides method *getImage* (line 15 in method init) that loads an Image into an applet. This version of getImage takes two arguments—the location of the image file and the file name of the image. In the first argument, Applet method getDocumentBase returns a URL representing the location of the image on the Internet (or on your computer if the applet was loaded from your computer). The program assumes that the image is stored in the same directory as the HTML file that invoked the applet. Method `getDocument-Base` returns the location of the HTML file on the Internet as an object of class URL. The second argument specifies an image file name. Java supports several image formats, including *Graphics Interchange Format (GIF)*, *Joint Photographic Experts Group (JPEG)* and *Portable Network Graphics (PNG)*. File names for each of these types end with `.gif`, `.jpg` (or `.jpeg`) and `.png`, respectively.

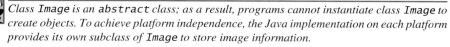

Portability Tip 19.1

*Class **Image** is an **abstract** class; as a result, programs cannot instantiate class **Image** to create objects. To achieve platform independence, the Java implementation on each platform provides its own subclass of **Image** to store image information.*

Line 15 begins loading the image from the local computer (or downloading the image from the Internet). When the image is required by the program, the image is loaded in a separate thread of execution. This enables the program to continue execution while the image loads. [*Note:* If the requested file is not available, method `getImage` does not indicate an error.]

Class `ImageIcon` is not an `abstract` class; therefore, a program can create an `ImageIcon` object. Line 16 in method `init` creates an `ImageIcon` object that loads the same `logo.gif` image. Class `ImageIcon` provides several constructors that enable programs to initialize `ImageIcon` objects with images from the local computer or with images stored on the Internet.

The applet's `paint` method (lines 20–29) displays the images. Line 22 uses `Graphics` method `drawImage` to display an `Image`. Method `drawImage` receives four arguments. The first argument is a reference to the `Image` object to display (`logo1`). The second and third arguments are the *x*- and *y*-coordinates at which to display the image on the applet; the coordinates indicate the location of the upper-left corner of the image. The last argument is a reference to an *ImageObserver* object. This argument is important when displaying large images that require a long time to download from the Internet. It is possible that a program will execute the code that displays the image before the image downloads completely. The `ImageObserver` is notified to update the displayed image as the remainder of the image loads. Normally, the `ImageObserver` is the object on which the program displays the image. An `ImageObserver` can be any object that implements interface `ImageObserver`. Class `Component` (one of class `JApplet`'s indirect superclasses) implements interface `ImageObserver`. Therefore, all `Components` (including our applet) are `ImageObservers`. When executing this applet, watch carefully as pieces of the image display while the image loads. [*Note:* On faster computers, you might not notice this effect.]

Line 25 uses another version of `Graphics` method `drawImage` to output a *scaled* version of the image. The fourth and fifth arguments specify the *width* and *height* of the image for display purposes. Method `drawImage` scales the image to fit the specified width and height. In this example, the fourth argument indicates that the width of the scaled image should be the width of the applet, and the fifth argument indicates that the height should be 120 pixels less than the height of the applet. The width and height of the applet are determined by calling methods `getWidth` and `getHeight` (inherited from class `Component`).

Line 28 uses `ImageIcon` method *paintIcon* to display the image. The method requires four arguments—a reference to the `Component` on which to display the image, a reference to the `Graphics` object that will render the image, the *x*-coordinate of the upper-left corner of the image and the *y*-coordinate of the upper-left corner of the image.

If you compare the two techniques for loading and displaying images in this example, you can see that using ImageIcon is simpler. You can create objects of class ImageIcon directly, and there is no need to use an ImageObserver reference when displaying the image. For this reason, we use class ImageIcon for the remainder of the chapter. [*Note:* Class ImageIcon's paintIcon method does not allow scaling of an image. However, class ImageIcon provides method getImage, which returns an Image reference that Graphics method drawImage can use to display a scaled image.]

19.3 Animating a Series of Images

The next example demonstrates animating a series of images that are stored in an array of ImageIcons. The animation presented in Fig. 19.2 is designed as a subclass of JPanel (called LogoAnimator) that can be attached to an application window or a JApplet. Class LogoAnimator also declares a main method (lines 85–99) to execute the animation as an application. Method main declares an instance of class JFrame and attaches a LogoAnimator object to the JFrame to display the animation.

```java
1   // Fig. 19.2: LogoAnimator.java
2   // Animation of a series of images.
3   import java.awt.*;
4   import java.awt.event.*;
5   import javax.swing.*;
6
7   public class LogoAnimator extends JPanel implements ActionListener {
8
9      private final static String IMAGE_NAME = "deitel"; // base image name
10     protected ImageIcon images[];        // array of images
11
12     private int totalImages = 30;       // number of images
13     private int currentImage = 0;       // current image index
14     private int animationDelay = 50;    // millisecond delay
15     private int width;                  // image width
16     private int height;                 // image height
17
18     private Timer animationTimer; // Timer drives animation
19
20     // initialize LogoAnimator by loading images
21     public LogoAnimator()
22     {
23        images = new ImageIcon[ totalImages ];
24
25        // load images
26        for ( int count = 0; count < images.length; ++count )
27           images[ count ] = new ImageIcon( getClass().getResource(
28              "images/" + IMAGE_NAME + count + ".gif" ) );
29
30        // this example assumes all images have the same width and height
31        width = images[ 0 ].getIconWidth();   // get icon width
32        height = images[ 0 ].getIconHeight(); // get icon height
33     }
```

Fig. 19.2 Animating a series of images. (Part 1 of 3.)

```
34
35      // display current image
36      public void paintComponent( Graphics g )
37      {
38         super.paintComponent( g );
39
40         images[ currentImage ].paintIcon( this, g, 0, 0 );
41
42         // move to next image only if timer is running
43         if ( animationTimer.isRunning() )
44            currentImage = ( currentImage + 1 ) % totalImages;
45      }
46
47      // respond to Timer's event
48      public void actionPerformed( ActionEvent actionEvent )
49      {
50         repaint(); // repaint animator
51      }
52
53      // start or restart animation
54      public void startAnimation()
55      {
56         if ( animationTimer == null ) {
57            currentImage = 0;
58            animationTimer = new Timer( animationDelay, this );
59            animationTimer.start();
60         }
61         else // continue from last image displayed
62            if ( ! animationTimer.isRunning() )
63               animationTimer.restart();
64      }
65
66      // stop animation timer
67      public void stopAnimation()
68      {
69         animationTimer.stop();
70      }
71
72      // return minimum size of animation
73      public Dimension getMinimumSize()
74      {
75         return getPreferredSize();
76      }
77
78      // return preferred size of animation
79      public Dimension getPreferredSize()
80      {
81         return new Dimension( width, height );
82      }
83
84      // execute animation in a JFrame
85      public static void main( String args[] )
86      {
```

Fig. 19.2 Animating a series of images. (Part 2 of 3.)

```
87          LogoAnimator animation = new LogoAnimator(); // create LogoAnimator
88
89          JFrame window = new JFrame( "Animator test" ); // set up window
90          window.setDefaultCloseOperation( JFrame.EXIT_ON_CLOSE );
91
92          Container container = window.getContentPane();
93          container.add( animation );
94
95          window.pack();   // make window just large enough for its GUI
96          window.setVisible( true );   // display window
97          animation.startAnimation();   // begin animation
98
99       } // end method main
100
101   } // end class LogoAnimator
```

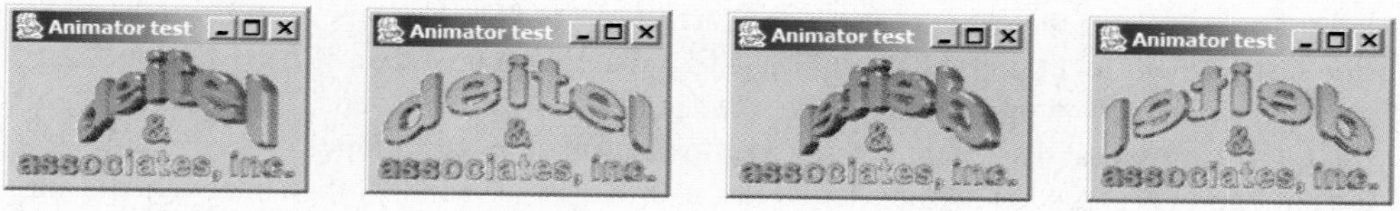

Fig. 19.2   Animating a series of images. (Part 3 of 3.)

Class `LogoAnimator` maintains an array of `ImageIcons` that are loaded in the constructor (lines 21–33). Lines 26–32 create each `ImageIcon` object and load the animation's 30 images. The constructor argument uses string concatenation to assemble the file name from the pieces `"images/"`, `IMAGE_NAME`, `count` and `".gif"`. Each of the images in the animation is in a file called `deitel#.gif`, where # is a value in the range 0–29 specified by the loop's control variable `count`. Lines 31–32 determine the width and height of the animation from the size of the first image in array `images`. We assume that all the images have the same width and height.

After the `LogoAnimator` constructor loads the images, method `main` sets up the window in which the animation will appear (lines 89–96), and line 97 calls the `Logo-Animator`'s `startAnimation` method (declared at lines 54–64) to begin the animation. The animation is driven by an instance of class *Timer* (from package `javax.swing`). A `Timer` generates `ActionEvents` at a fixed interval in milliseconds (normally specified as an argument to the `Timer`'s constructor) and notifies all of its `ActionListeners` that the event occurred. Lines 56–60 determine whether the `Timer` reference `animationTimer` is `null`. If so, line 57 sets `currentImage` to 0, which indicates that the animation should begin with the image in the first element of array `images`. Line 58 assigns a new `Timer` object to `animationTimer`. The `Timer` constructor receives two arguments—the delay in milliseconds (`animationDelay` is 50, as specified on line 14) and the `ActionListener` that will respond to the `Timer`'s `ActionEvents`. Class `LogoAnimator` implements `ActionListener`, so line 58 specifies `this` as the listener. Line 59 starts the `Timer` object. Once started, `animationTimer` will generate an `ActionEvent` every 50 milliseconds. Lines 62–63 enable the program to restart an animation that the program stopped previously. For example, to make an animation "browser friendly" in an applet, the animation should stop when the user switches Web pages. If the user returns to the Web page with the animation, method `startAnimation` can be called to restart the animation. The `if` condition at line 62 uses `Timer` method `isRunning` to determine whether the `Timer` is running (i.e., generating events). If it is not running, line 63 calls `Timer` method `restart` to indicate that the `Timer` should start generating events again.

In response to every `Timer` event in this example, the program calls method `actionPerformed` (lines 48–51). Line 50 calls `LogoAnimator`'s `repaint` method to schedule a call to `LogoAnimator`'s `paintComponent` method (lines 36–45). Remember that any subclass of `JComponent` that performs drawing should do so in its `paintComponent` method. Recall from Chapter 14 that the first statement in any `paintComponent` method should be a call to the superclass's `paintComponent` method, to ensure that Swing components are displayed correctly.

Line 40 paints the `ImageIcon` stored at element `currentImage` in the array. Lines 43–44 determine whether the `animationTimer` is running and, if so, prepare for the next image to be displayed by incrementing `currentImage` by 1. Notice the remainder calculation to ensure that the value of `currentImage` is set to 0 when it is incremented past 29 (the last element index in the array). The `if` statement ensures that, if `paintComponent` is called while the `Timer` is stopped, the same image will be displayed. This could be useful if a GUI is provided that enables the user to start and stop the animation. For example, if the animation is stopped and the user covers it with another window then uncovers the animation, method `paintComponent` will be called. In this case, we do not want the animation to show the next image.

Method `stopAnimation` (lines 67–70) stops the animation by calling `Timer` method *stop* to indicate that the `Timer` should stop generating events. This prevents `actionPerformed` from calling `repaint` to initiate the painting of the next image in the array.

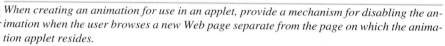

Software Engineering Observation 19.1

When creating an animation for use in an applet, provide a mechanism for disabling the animation when the user browses a new Web page separate from the page on which the animation applet resides.

Methods `getMinimumSize` (lines 73–76) and `getPreferredSize` (lines 79–82) override the corresponding methods inherited from class `Component` and enable layout managers to determine the appropriate size of a `LogoAnimator` in a layout. In this example, the images are 160 pixels wide and 80 pixels tall, so method `getPreferredSize` returns a `Dimension` object containing the numbers 160 and 80 (determined at lines 31–32). Method `getMinimumSize` simply calls `getPreferredSize` (a common programming practice) to indicate that the minimum size and preferred size are the same. Some layout managers ignore the dimensions specified by these methods. For example, a `BorderLayout`'s NORTH and SOUTH region use only the component's preferred height.

19.4 Image Maps

Image maps are a common technique used to create interactive Web pages. An image map is an image with *hot areas* that the user can click to accomplish a task, such as loading a different Web page into a browser. When the user positions the mouse pointer over a hot area, normally a descriptive message appears in the status area of the browser or in a tool tip.

Figure 19.3 loads an image containing several of the common tip icons used throughout this book. The program allows the user to position the mouse pointer over an

icon and display a descriptive message associated with the icon. Event handler mouse-
Moved (lines 37–41) takes the mouse coordinates and passes them to method translate-
Location (lines 59–70). Method translateLocation tests the coordinates to
determine the icon over which the mouse was positioned when the mouseMoved event
occurred; the method then returns a message indicating what the icon represents. This message is displayed in the applet container's status bar.

```java
1   // Fig. 19.3: ImageMap.java
2   // Demonstrating an image map.
3   import java.awt.*;
4   import java.awt.event.*;
5   import javax.swing.*;
6
7   public class ImageMap extends JApplet {
8      private ImageIcon mapImage;
9
10     private static final String captions[] = { "Common Programming Error",
11        "Good Programming Practice", "Graphical User Interface Tip",
12        "Performance Tip", "Portability Tip",
13        "Software Engineering Observation", "Error-Prevention Tip" };
14
15     // set up mouse listeners
16     public void init()
17     {
18        addMouseListener(
19
20           new MouseAdapter() { // anonymous inner class
21
22              // indicate when mouse pointer exits applet area
23              public void mouseExited( MouseEvent event )
24              {
25                 showStatus( "Pointer outside applet" );
26              }
27
28           } // end anonymous inner class
29
30        ); // end call to addMouseListener
31
32        addMouseMotionListener(
33
34           new MouseMotionAdapter() { // anonymous inner class
35
36              // determine icon over which mouse appears
37              public void mouseMoved( MouseEvent event )
38              {
39                 showStatus( translateLocation(
40                    event.getX(), event.getY() ) );
41              }
42
43           } // end anonymous inner class
44
45        ); // end call to addMouseMotionListener
```

Fig. 19.3 Image map. (Part 1 of 3.)

```
46
47        mapImage = new ImageIcon( "icons.png" );  // get image
48
49    }  // end method init
50
51    // display mapImage
52    public void paint( Graphics g )
53    {
54       super.paint( g );
55       mapImage.paintIcon( this, g, 0, 0 );
56    }
57
58    // return tip caption based on mouse coordinates
59    public String translateLocation( int x, int y )
60    {
61       // if coordinates outside image, return immediately
62       if ( x >= mapImage.getIconWidth() || y >= mapImage.getIconHeight() )
63          return "";
64
65       // determine icon number (0 - 6)
66       int iconWidth = mapImage.getIconWidth() / 7;
67       int iconNumber = x / iconWidth;
68
69       return captions[ iconNumber ]; // return appropriate icon caption
70    }
71
72 } // end class ImageMap
```

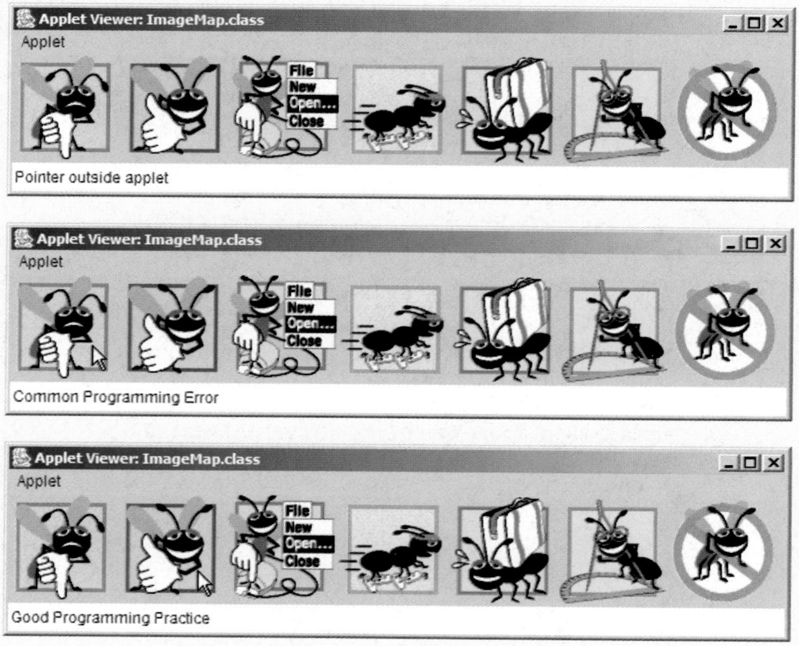

Fig. 19.3 Image map. (Part 2 of 3.)

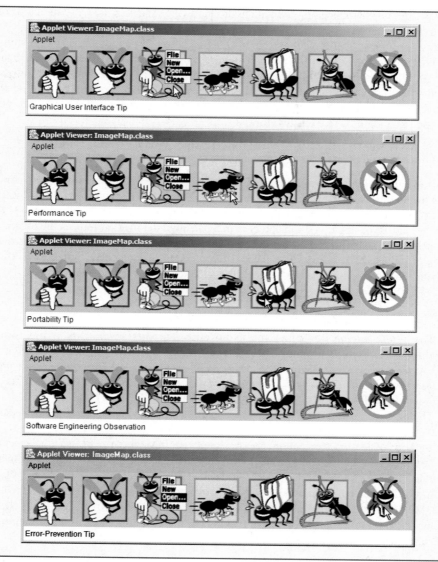

Fig. 19.3   Image map. (Part 3 of 3.)

Clicking in the applet of Fig. 19.3 will not cause any action. In Chapter 18, Networking, we discussed the techniques required to load another Web page into a browser via URLs and the `AppletContext` interface. Using those techniques, this applet could associate each icon with a URL that the browser would display when the user clicks the icon.

19.5 Loading and Playing Audio Clips

Java programs can manipulate and play *audio clips*. It is easy for users to capture their own audio clips, and there are many clips available in software products and over the Internet.

Your system needs to be equipped with audio hardware (speakers and a sound card) to be able to play the audio clips.

Java provides several mechanisms for playing sounds in an applet. The two simplest methods are the Applet's *play* method and the *play* method from the *AudioClip* interface. Additional audio capabilities are available in the Java Media Framework and JavaSound APIs. If you would like to play a sound once in a program, the Applet method play loads the sound and plays it once; the sound is marked for garbage collection after it plays. The Applet method play has two forms:

```
public void play( URL location, String soundFileName );
public void play( URL soundURL );
```

The first version loads the audio clip stored in file soundFileName from location and plays the sound. The first argument is normally a call to the applet's getDocumentBase or *getCodeBase* method. Method getDocumentBase returns the location of the HTML file that loaded the applet. (If the applet is in a package, the method returns the location of the package or JAR file containing the package.) Method getCodeBase indicates the location of the applet's .class file. The second version of method play takes a URL that contains the location and the file name of the audio clip. The statement

```
play( getDocumentBase(), "hi.au" );
```

loads the audio clip in file hi.au and plays the clip once.

The *sound engine* that plays the audio clips supports several audio file formats, including *Sun Audio file format* (.au *extension*), *Windows Wave file format* (.wav *extension*), *Macintosh AIFF file format* (.aif *or* .aiff *extension*) and *Musical Instrument Digital Interface (MIDI) file format* (.mid *or* .rmi *extensions*). The Java Media Framework (JMF) and Java Sound APIs support additional formats.

The program of Fig. 19.4 demonstrates loading and playing an *AudioClip* (package java.applet). This technique is more flexible than Applet method play. An applet can use an AudioClip to store audio for repeated use throughout a program's execution. Applet method *getAudioClip* has two forms that take the same arguments as method play described previously. Method getAudioClip returns a reference to an AudioClip. An AudioClip has three methods—*play*, *loop* and *stop*. Method play plays the audio once. Method loop continuously loops the audio clip in the background. Method stop terminates an audio clip that is currently playing. In the program, each of these methods is associated with a button on the applet.

```
1   // Fig. 19.4: LoadAudioAndPlay.java
2   // Load an audio clip and play it.
3
4   import java.applet.*;
5   import java.awt.*;
6   import java.awt.event.*;
7   import javax.swing.*;
8
9   public class LoadAudioAndPlay extends JApplet {
10      private AudioClip sound1, sound2, currentSound;
```

Fig. 19.4   Loading and playing an AudioClip. (Part 1 of 3.)

```
11      private JButton playSound, loopSound, stopSound;
12      private JComboBox chooseSound;
13
14      // load the image when the applet begins executing
15      public void init()
16      {
17         Container container = getContentPane();
18         container.setLayout( new FlowLayout() );
19
20         String choices[] = { "Welcome", "Hi" };
21         chooseSound = new JComboBox( choices );
22
23         chooseSound.addItemListener(
24
25            new ItemListener() {
26
27               // stop sound and change to sound to user's selection
28               public void itemStateChanged( ItemEvent e )
29               {
30                  currentSound.stop();
31
32                  currentSound =
33                     chooseSound.getSelectedIndex() == 0 ? sound1 : sound2;
34               }
35
36            } // end anonymous inner class
37
38         ); // end addItemListener method call
39
40         container.add( chooseSound );
41
42         // set up button event handler and buttons
43         ButtonHandler handler = new ButtonHandler();
44
45         playSound = new JButton( "Play" );
46         playSound.addActionListener( handler );
47         container.add( playSound );
48
49         loopSound = new JButton( "Loop" );
50         loopSound.addActionListener( handler );
51         container.add( loopSound );
52
53         stopSound = new JButton( "Stop" );
54         stopSound.addActionListener( handler );
55         container.add( stopSound );
56
57         // load sounds and set currentSound
58         sound1 = getAudioClip( getDocumentBase(), "welcome.wav" );
59         sound2 = getAudioClip( getDocumentBase(), "hi.au" );
60         currentSound = sound1;
61
62      } // end method init
63
```

Fig. 19.4 Loading and playing an `AudioClip`. (Part 2 of 3.)

```
64      // stop the sound when the user switches Web pages
65      public void stop()
66      {
67         currentSound.stop();
68      }
69
70      // private inner class to handle button events
71      private class ButtonHandler implements ActionListener {
72
73         // process play, loop and stop button events
74         public void actionPerformed( ActionEvent actionEvent )
75         {
76            if ( actionEvent.getSource() == playSound )
77               currentSound.play();
78
79            else if ( actionEvent.getSource() == loopSound )
80               currentSound.loop();
81
82            else if ( actionEvent.getSource() == stopSound )
83               currentSound.stop();
84         }
85
86      } // end class ButtonHandler
87
88   } // end class LoadAudioAndPlay
```

Fig. 19.4   Loading and playing an `AudioClip`. (Part 3 of 3.)

Lines 58–59 in the applet's `init` method use `getAudioClip` to load two audio files—a Windows Wave file (`welcome.wav`) and a Sun Audio file (`hi.au`). The user can select which audio clip to play from `JComboBox chooseSound`. Notice that the applet's `stop` method is overridden at lines 65–68. When the user switches Web pages, the applet container calls the applet's `stop` method. This enables the applet to stop playing the audio clip. Otherwise, the audio clip continues to play in the background—even if the applet is not displayed in the browser. This is not necessarily a problem, but it can be annoying to the user if the audio clip is looping. The `stop` method is provided here as a convenience to the user.

Look-and-Feel Observation 19.1

When playing audio clips in an applet or application, provide a mechanism for the user to disable the audio.

19.6 Internet and World Wide Web Resources

www.nasa.gov/gallery/index.html
The *NASA multimedia gallery* contains a wide variety of images, audio clips and video clips that you can download and use to test your Java multimedia programs.

`sunsite.sut.ac.jp/multimed/`
The *Sunsite Japan Multimedia Collection* also provides a wide variety of images, audio clips and video clips that you can download for educational purposes.

`www.anbg.gov.au/anbg/index.html`
The *Australian National Botanic Gardens* Web site provides links to sounds of many animals. Try, for example, the *Common Birds* link under the "Animals in the Botanic Gardens" section.

`www.thefreesite.com`
TheFreeSite.com has links to free sounds and clip art.

`www.soundcentral.com`
SoundCentral provides audio clips in WAV, AU, AIFF and MIDI formats.

`www.animationfactory.com`
The *Animation Factory* provides thousands of free GIF animations for personal use.

`www.clipart.com`
ClipArt.com is a subscription-based service for images and sounds.

`www.pngart.com`
PNGART.com provides over 50,000 free images in PNG format, in an effort to help this newer image format gain popularity.

`developer.java.sun.com/developer/techDocs/hi/repository`
The *Java Look-and-Feel Graphics Repository* provides standard images for use in a Swing GUI.

Java Multimedia API References

`java.sun.com/products/java-media/jmf/`
This is the *Java Media Framework (JMF) API* home page. Here you can download the latest Sun implementation of the JMF. The site also contains the documentation for the JMF.

`java.sun.com/products/java-media/sound/`
The *Java Sound API* home page. Java Sound provides capabilities for playing and recording audio.

`java.sun.com/products/java-media/3D/`
The *Java 3D API* home page. This API can be used to produce three-dimensional images typical of today's video games.

`developer.java.sun.com/developer/onlineTraining/java3d/`
This site provides a Java 3D API tutorial.

`java.sun.com/products/java-media/jai/`
The *Java Advanced Imaging API* home page. This API provides image-processing capabilities, such as contrast enhancement, cropping, scaling and geometric warping.

`java.sun.com/products/java-media/speech/`
This is the *Java Speech API* home page. This API enables programs to perform speech synthesis and speech recognition.

`freetts.sourceforge.net/docs/index.php`
FreeTTS is an implementation of the Java Speech API.

`java.sun.com/products/java-media/2D/`
This is the *Java 2D API* home page. This API (introduced in Chapter 12) provides complex two-dimensional graphics capabilities.

`java.sun.com/j2se/1.4.1/docs/guide/imageio/`
This site contains an overview of the *Java Image I/O API*, which enables programs to define custom image loading and saving of image formats that are not currently supported by the Java APIs.

19.7 (Optional Case Study) Thinking About Objects: Animation and Sound in the View

This case study has focused mainly on the MVC model for our elevator simulation. Now that we have completed our design of the model, we turn our attention to the *view*, which provides the visual presentation of the model. In our case study, the view—encapsulated in class `ElevatorView`—is a `JPanel` object containing other `JPanel` "child" objects, each representing a unique object in the MVC model (e.g. a `Person`, a `Button`, the `Elevator`). Class `ElevatorView` is the largest class in the case study. In this section, we discuss the graphics and sound classes used by class `ElevatorView`. We present and explain the remainder of the code in the view in Appendix E.

In Section 3.7, we constructed a class diagram for our model by locating the nouns and noun phrases from the problem statement of Section 2.9. We ignored several of these nouns, because they were not associated with the MVC model. Now, we list the nouns and noun phrases that apply to displaying the MVC model:

- display
- audio
- elevator music

The noun "display" corresponds to the view, or the visual presentation, of the MVC model. As described in Section 13.17, class `ElevatorView` aggregates several classes comprising the view. The "audio" refers to the sound effects that our simulation generates when various actions occur—we create class `SoundEffects` to generate these sound effects. The phrase "elevator music" refers to the music played as the `Person` rides in the `Elevator`—we will use class `SoundEffects` to play this music as well.

The view displays objects of the MVC model. We create class `ImagePanel` to represent stationary objects in the model, such as the `ElevatorShaft`. We create class `MovingPanel`, which extends `ImagePanel`, to represent moving objects, such as the `Elevator`. Lastly, we create class `AnimatedPanel`, which extends `MovingPanel`, to represent moving objects whose corresponding images change continuously, such as a `Person` (we use several frames of animation to show the `Person` walking then pressing a button). Using these classes, we present the class diagram of the view for our simulation in Fig. 19.5.

The notes indicate the roles that the classes play in the system. According to the class diagram, class `ElevatorView` represents the view, classes `ImagePanel`, `MovingPanel` and `AnimatedPanel` relate to the graphics, and class `SoundEffects` relates to the audio. Class `ElevatorView` contains several instances of classes `ImagePanel`, `MovingPanel` and `AnimatedPanel` and one instance of class `SoundEffects`. In Appendix F, we associate each object in the model with a corresponding class in the view.

In this section, we discuss classes `ImagePanel`, `MovingPanel` and `AnimatedPanel` to explain the graphics and animation. We then discuss class `SoundEffects` to explain the audio functionality.

ImagePanel

The `ElevatorView` uses objects from `JPanel` subclasses to represent and display each object in the model (such as the `Elevator`, a `Person`, the `ElevatorShaft`, etc.). Class `ImagePanel` (Fig. 19.6) is a `JPanel` subclass capable of displaying an image at a given screen position. The `ElevatorView` uses `ImagePanel` objects to represent stationary objects in the model, such as the `ElevatorShaft` and the two `Floors`. Class `ImagePanel` contains an integer attribute—ID (line 16)—that declares a unique identifier used to track the `ImagePanel` in the view if necessary. This tracking is useful when several objects of the same class exist in the model, such as several `Person` objects. Class `ImagePanel` contains `Point2D.Double` object `position` (line 19) to represent the `ImagePanel` screen position. We will see later that `MovingPanel`, which extends `ImagePanel`, declares velocity with `double`s. We cast the `position` coordinates to `int`s to place the `ImagePanel` on screen (Java represents screen coordinates as `int`s) in method `setPosition` (lines 90–94). Class `ImagePanel` also contains an `ImageIcon` object called `imageIcon` (line 22)—method `paintComponent` (lines 54–60) displays `imageIcon` on screen. Lines 41–42 initialize `imageIcon` using a `String` parameter holding the name of the image. Lastly, class `ImagePanel` contains `Set panelChildren` (line 25) that stores any child objects of class `ImagePanel` (or objects of a subclass of `ImagePanel`). The child objects are displayed on top of their parent `ImagePanel`—for example, a `Person` riding inside the `Elevator`. The first method `add` (lines 63–67) appends an object to `panelChildren`. The second method `add` (lines 70–74) inserts an object into `panelChildren` at a given index. Method `setIcon` (lines 84–87) sets `imageIcon` to a new image. Objects of class `AnimatedPanel` use method `setIcon` repeatedly to change the image displayed, which causes the animation for the view—we discuss animation later in the section.

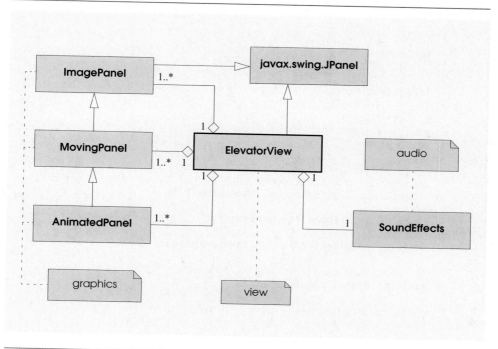

Fig. 19.5   Class diagram of elevator simulation view.

```
1   // ImagePanel.java
2   // JPanel subclass for positioning and displaying ImageIcon
3   package com.deitel.jhtp5.elevator.view;
4
5   // Java core packages
6   import java.awt.*;
7   import java.awt.geom.*;
8   import java.util.*;
9
10  // Java extension packages
11  import javax.swing.*;
12
13  public class ImagePanel extends JPanel {
14
15     // identifier
16     private int ID;
17
18     // on-screen position
19     private Point2D.Double position;
20
21     // imageIcon to paint on screen
22     private ImageIcon imageIcon;
23
24     // stores all ImagePanel children
25     private Set panelChildren;
26
27     // constructor initializes position and image
28     public ImagePanel( int identifier, String imageName )
29     {
30        super( null ); // specify null layout
31        setOpaque( false ); // make transparent
32
33        // set unique identifier
34        ID = identifier;
35
36        // set location
37        position = new Point2D.Double( 0, 0 );
38        setLocation( 0, 0 );
39
40        // create ImageIcon with given imageName
41        imageIcon = new ImageIcon(
42           getClass().getResource( imageName ) );
43
44        Image image = imageIcon.getImage();
45        setSize(
46           image.getWidth( this ), image.getHeight( this ) );
47
48        // create Set to store Panel children
49        panelChildren = new HashSet();
50
51     } // end ImagePanel constructor
52
```

Fig. 19.6   Class ImagePanel represents and displays a stationary object from the model. (Part 1 of 3.)

```
53    // paint Panel to screen
54    public void paintComponent( Graphics g )
55    {
56       super.paintComponent( g );
57
58       // if image is ready, paint it to screen
59       imageIcon.paintIcon( this, g, 0, 0 );
60    }
61
62    // add ImagePanel child to ImagePanel
63    public void add( ImagePanel panel )
64    {
65       panelChildren.add( panel );
66       super.add( panel );
67    }
68
69    // add ImagePanel child to ImagePanel at given index
70    public void add( ImagePanel panel, int index )
71    {
72       panelChildren.add( panel );
73       super.add( panel, index );
74    }
75
76    // remove ImagePanel child from ImagePanel
77    public void remove( ImagePanel panel )
78    {
79       panelChildren.remove( panel );
80       super.remove( panel );
81    }
82
83    // sets current ImageIcon to be displayed
84    public void setIcon( ImageIcon icon )
85    {
86       imageIcon = icon;
87    }
88
89    // set on-screen position
90    public void setPosition( double x, double y )
91    {
92       position.setLocation( x, y );
93       setLocation( ( int ) x,  ( int ) y );
94    }
95
96    // return ImagePanel identifier
97    public int getID()
98    {
99       return ID;
100   }
101
102   // get position of ImagePanel
103   public Point2D.Double getPosition()
104   {
```

Fig. 19.6   Class ImagePanel represents and displays a stationary object from the model. (Part 2 of 3.)

```
105          return position;
106       }
107
108       // get imageIcon
109       public ImageIcon getImageIcon()
110       {
111          return imageIcon;
112       }
113
114       // get Set of ImagePanel children
115       public Set getChildren()
116       {
117          return panelChildren;
118       }
119    }
```

Fig. 19.6 Class `ImagePanel` represents and displays a stationary object from the model. (Part 3 of 3.)

MovingPanel

Class `MovingPanel` (Fig. 19.7) is an `ImagePanel` subclass capable of changing its screen position according to its `xVelocity` and `yVelocity` (lines 20–21). The `ElevatorView` uses `MovingPanel` objects to represent moving objects from the model, such as the `Elevator`.

```
1    // MovingPanel.java
2    // JPanel subclass with on-screen moving capabilities
3    package com.deitel.jhtp5.elevator.view;
4
5    // Java core packages
6    import java.awt.*;
7    import java.awt.geom.*;
8    import java.util.*;
9
10   // Java extension packages
11   import javax.swing.*;
12
13   public class MovingPanel extends ImagePanel {
14
15      // should MovingPanel change position?
16      private boolean moving;
17
18      // number of pixels MovingPanel moves in both x and y values
19      // per animationDelay milliseconds
20      private double xVelocity;
21      private double yVelocity;
22
```

Fig. 19.7 Class `MovingPanel` represents and displays a moving object from the model (Part 1 of 3.).

```
23        // constructor initializes position, velocity and image
24        public MovingPanel( int identifier, String imageName )
25        {
26           super( identifier, imageName );
27
28           // set MovingPanel velocity
29           xVelocity = 0;
30           yVelocity = 0;
31
32        } // end MovingPanel constructor
33
34        // update MovingPanel position and animation frame
35        public void animate()
36        {
37           // update position according to MovingPanel velocity
38           if ( isMoving() ) {
39              double oldXPosition = getPosition().getX();
40              double oldYPosition = getPosition().getY();
41
42              setPosition( oldXPosition + xVelocity,
43                 oldYPosition + yVelocity );
44           }
45
46           // update all children of MovingPanel
47           Iterator iterator = getChildren().iterator();
48
49           while ( iterator.hasNext() ) {
50              MovingPanel panel = ( MovingPanel ) iterator.next();
51              panel.animate();
52           }
53        } // end method animate
54
55        // is MovingPanel moving on screen?
56        public boolean isMoving()
57        {
58           return moving;
59        }
60
61        // set MovingPanel to move on screen
62        public void setMoving( boolean move )
63        {
64           moving = move;
65        }
66
67        // set MovingPanel x and y velocity
68        public void setVelocity( double x, double y )
69        {
70           xVelocity = x;
71           yVelocity = y;
72        }
73
```

Fig. 19.7   Class MovingPanel represents and displays a moving object from the model (Part 2 of 3.).

```
74        // return MovingPanel x velocity
75        public double getXVelocity()
76        {
77           return xVelocity;
78        }
79
80        // return MovingPanel y velocity
81        public double getYVelocity()
82        {
83           return yVelocity;
84        }
85     }
```

Fig. 19.7   Class MovingPanel represents and displays a moving object from the model (Part 3 of 3.).

Method animate (lines 35–53) moves the MovingPanel according to the current values of fields xVelocity and yVelocity. If boolean variable moving (line 16) is true, lines 38–44 use fields xVelocity and yVelocity to determine the next location for the MovingPanel. Lines 47–52 repeat the process for any children. In our simulation, ElevatorView invokes method animate and method paintComponent of class ImagePanel every 50 milliseconds. These rapid, successive calls move the MovingPanel object.

AnimatedPanel

Class AnimatedPanel (Fig. 19.8), which extends class MovingPanel, represents an animated object from the model (i.e., moving objects whose corresponding images change continuously), such as a Person. The ElevatorView animates an AnimatedPanel object by changing the image associated with imageIcon.

```
1     // AnimatedPanel.java
2     // MovingPanel subclass with animation capabilities
3     package com.deitel.jhtp5.elevator.view;
4
5     // Java core packages
6     import java.awt.*;
7     import java.util.*;
8
9     // Java extension packages
10    import javax.swing.*;
11
12    public class AnimatedPanel extends MovingPanel {
13
14       // should ImageIcon cycle frames
15       private boolean animating;
16
17       // frame cycle rate (i.e., rate advancing to next frame)
18       private int animationRate;
```

Fig. 19.8   Class AnimatedPanel represents and displays an animated object from the model (Part 1 of 4.).

```
19      private int animationRateCounter;
20      private boolean cycleForward = true;
21
22      // individual ImageIcons used for animation frames
23      private ImageIcon imageIcons[];
24
25      // storage for all frame sequences
26      private java.util.List frameSequences;
27      private int currentAnimation;
28
29      // should loop (continue) animation at end of cycle?
30      private boolean loop;
31
32      // should animation display last frame at end of animation?
33      private boolean displayLastFrame;
34
35      // helps determine next displayed frame
36      private int currentFrameCounter;
37
38      // constructor takes array of filenames and screen position
39      public AnimatedPanel( int identifier, String imageName[] )
40      {
41         super( identifier, imageName[ 0 ] );
42
43         // creates ImageIcon objects from imageName string array
44         imageIcons = new ImageIcon[ imageName.length ];
45
46         for ( int i = 0; i < imageIcons.length; i++ ) {
47            imageIcons[ i ] = new ImageIcon(
48               getClass().getResource( imageName[ i ] ) );
49         }
50
51         frameSequences = new ArrayList();
52
53      } // end AnimatedPanel constructor
54
55      // update icon position and animation frame
56      public void animate()
57      {
58         super.animate();
59
60         // play next animation frame if counter > animation rate
61         if ( frameSequences != null && isAnimating() ) {
62
63            if ( animationRateCounter > animationRate ) {
64               animationRateCounter = 0;
65               determineNextFrame();
66            }
67            else
68               animationRateCounter++;
69         }
70      } // end method animate
```

Fig. 19.8　Class AnimatedPanel represents and displays an animated object from the model (Part 2 of 4.).

```
71
72     // determine next animation frame
73     private void determineNextFrame()
74     {
75        int frameSequence[] =
76           ( int[] ) frameSequences.get( currentAnimation );
77
78        // if no more animation frames, determine final frame,
79        // unless loop is specified
80        if ( currentFrameCounter >= frameSequence.length ) {
81           currentFrameCounter = 0;
82
83           // if loop is false, terminate animation
84           if ( !isLoop() ) {
85
86              setAnimating( false );
87
88              if ( isDisplayLastFrame() )
89
90                 // display last frame in sequence
91                 currentFrameCounter = frameSequence.length - 1;
92           }
93        }
94
95        // set current animation frame
96        setCurrentFrame( frameSequence[ currentFrameCounter ] );
97        currentFrameCounter++;
98
99     } // end method determineNextFrame
100
101    // add frame sequence (animation) to frameSequences ArrayList
102    public void addFrameSequence( int frameSequence[] )
103    {
104       frameSequences.add( frameSequence );
105    }
106
107    // ask if AnimatedPanel is animating (cycling frames)
108    public boolean isAnimating()
109    {
110       return animating;
111    }
112
113    // set AnimatedPanel to animate
114    public void setAnimating( boolean animate )
115    {
116       animating = animate;
117    }
118
119    // set current ImageIcon
120    public void setCurrentFrame( int frame )
121    {
122       setIcon( imageIcons[ frame ] );
```

Fig. 19.8   Class `AnimatedPanel` represents and displays an animated object from the model (Part 3 of 4.).

```
123       }
124
125           // set animation rate
126           public void setAnimationRate( int rate )
127           {
128               animationRate = rate;
129           }
130
131           // get animation rate
132           public int getAnimationRate()
133           {
134               return animationRate;
135           }
136
137           // set whether animation should loop
138           public void setLoop( boolean loopAnimation  )
139           {
140               loop = loopAnimation;
141           }
142
143           // get whether animation should loop
144           public boolean isLoop()
145           {
146               return loop;
147           }
148
149           // get whether to display last frame at animation end
150           private boolean isDisplayLastFrame()
151           {
152               return displayLastFrame;
153           }
154
155           // set whether to display last frame at animation end
156           public void setDisplayLastFrame( boolean displayFrame )
157           {
158               displayLastFrame = displayFrame;
159           }
160
161           // start playing animation sequence of given index
162           public void playAnimation( int frameSequence )
163           {
164               currentAnimation = frameSequence;
165               currentFrameCounter = 0;
166               setAnimating( true );
167           }
168       }
```

Fig. 19.8   Class AnimatedPanel represents and displays an animated object from the model (Part 4 of 4.).

Class AnimatedPanel chooses the ImageIcon object to be drawn on screen from among several ImageIcon objects stored in array imageIcons (line 23). Class AnimatedPanel determines the ImageIcon object according to a series of *frame sequence* references, stored in List frameSequences (line 26). A frame sequence is an array of integers holding the proper sequence to display the ImageIcon objects; specifically, each integer represents the index of an ImageIcon object in imageIcons. Figure 19.9 demonstrates the relationship between imageIcons and frameSequences. (This is not a diagram of the UML.) For example, frame sequence number

```
2 = { 2, 1, 0 }
```

refers to { imageIcon[2], imageIcon[1], imageIcon[0] }, which yields the image sequence { C, B, A }. In the view, each image is a unique .png file. Method addFrameSequence (lines 102–105) adds a frame sequence to List frameSequences. Method playAnimation (lines 162–167) starts the animation associated with the parameter frameSequence. For example, assume an AnimatedPanel object called personAnimatedPanel in class ElevatorView. The code segment

```
animatedPanel.playAnimation( 1 );
```

would generate the { A, B, D, B, A } image sequence using Fig. 19.9 as a reference.

Method animate (lines 56–70) overrides method animate of superclass MovingPanel. Lines 61–69 determine the next frame of animation depending on field animationRate, which is inversely proportional to the animation speed—a higher value for animationRate yields a slower frame rate. For example, if animationRate is 5, animate moves to the next frame of animation every fifth time it is invoked. Using this logic, the animation rate maximizes when animationRate has a value of 1, because the next frame is determined each time animate runs.

Method animate calls determineNextFrame (lines 73–99) to determine the next frame (image) to display—specifically, it calls method setCurrentFrame (lines 120–123), which sets imageIcon (the current image displayed) to the image returned from the current frame sequence. Lines 84–92 of determineNextFrame are used for "looping" purposes in the animation. If loop is false, the animation terminates after one iteration. The last frame in the sequence is displayed if displayLastFrame is true, and the first frame in the sequence is displayed if displayLastFrame is false. We explain in greater detail in Appendix F how ElevatorView uses displayLastFrame for the Person and Door AnimatedPanels to ensure the proper display of the image. If loop is true, the animation repeats until stopped explicitly.

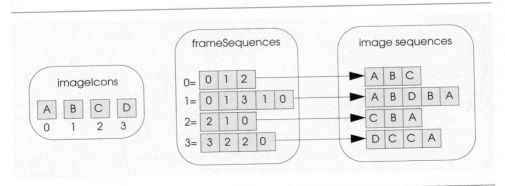

Fig. 19.9   Relationship between array imageIcons and List frameSequences.

Sound Effects

We now discuss how we generate audio in our elevator simulation. Class SoundEffects (Figure 19.10) transforms audio (.au), wave (.wav) and MIDI (.mid) files, containing such sounds as the bell ring, the person's footsteps and the elevator music, into java.applet.AudioClip objects. In Appendix I, we list all AudioClips used in our simulation. The ElevatorView object will play the AudioClip objects to generate sound. All sound files are in the directory structure

```
com/deitel/jhtp5/elevator/view/sounds
```

(i.e., in the sounds directory where the classes for the view are located in the file system). In our simulation, we use sounds and MIDI files provided free for download by Microsoft at the Web site:

```
msdn.microsoft.com/downloads/default.asp
```

To download these sounds, click "Graphics and Multimedia," "Multimedia (General)," then "Sounds."

Class SoundEffects contains method getAudioClip (lines 16–27), which uses static method newAudioClip (of class java.applet.Applet) to return an Audio-Clip object using the soundFile parameter. Method setPathPrefix (lines 30–33) allows for changing the directory of a sound file (useful if we want to partition our sounds among several directories).

```java
1   // SoundEffects.java
2   // Returns AudioClip objects
3   package com.deitel.jhtp5.elevator.view;
4
5   // Java core packages
6   import java.applet.*;
7
8   public class SoundEffects {
9
10     // location of sound files
11     private String prefix = "";
12
13     public SoundEffects() {}
14
15     // get AudioClip associated with soundFile
16     public AudioClip getAudioClip( String soundFile )
17     {
18        try {
19           return Applet.newAudioClip( getClass().getResource(
20              prefix + soundFile ) );
21        }
22
23        // return null if soundFile does not exist
24        catch ( NullPointerException nullPointerException ) {
25           return null;
26        }
27     }
```

Fig. 19.10 Class SoundEffects return AudioClip objects (Part 1 of 2.).

```
28
29        // set prefix for location of soundFile
30        public void setPathPrefix( String string )
31        {
32            prefix = string;
33        }
34    }
```

Fig. 19.10 Class `SoundEffects` return `AudioClip` objects (Part 2 of 2.).

Conclusion

You have completed a substantial object-oriented design (OOD) process that was intended to help prepare you for the challenges of "industrial-strength" projects. We hope you have found the optional "Thinking About Objects" sections informative and useful as a supplement to the material presented in the chapters. In addition, we hope you have enjoyed the experience designing the elevator system using the UML. The worldwide software industry has adopted the UML as the *de facto* standard for modeling object-oriented software.

Although we have completed the design process, we have merely "scratched the surface" of the implementation process. We urge you to read Appendices D, E and F on the accompanying CD, which fully implement the design. These appendices translate the UML diagrams into a complete Java program for the elevator simulation. In these appendices, we present all code that we did not cover in the "Thinking About Objects" sections and a complete "walkthrough" of this code.

1. Appendix D presents the Java files that implement events and listeners
2. Appendix E presents the Java files that implement the model
3. Appendix F presents the Java files that implement the view

We do not introduce an abundance of new material or UML design in these appendices—they simply serve to implement the UML-based diagram we have presented in previous chapters into a fully functional program. Studying the implementation in the appendices should hone the programming skills you have developed throughout the book and reinforce your understanding of the design process.

SUMMARY

- `Applet` method `getImage` loads an `Image`.

- `Applet` method `getDocumentBase` returns the location of the applet's HTML file on the Internet as an object of class URL (package `java.net`).

- Java supports several image formats, including Graphics Interchange Format (GIF), Joint Photographic Experts Group (JPEG) and Portable Network Graphics (PNG). File names for each of these types end with `.gif`, `.jpg` (or `.jpeg`) and `.png`, respectively.

- Class `ImageIcon` provides constructors that allow an `ImageIcon` object to be initialized with an image from the local computer or with an image stored on a Web server on the Internet.

- `Graphics` method `drawImage` receives four arguments—a reference to the `Image` object in which the image is stored, the *x*- and *y*-coordinates where the image should be displayed and a reference to an `ImageObserver` object.

- Another version of Graphics method drawImage outputs a *scaled* image. The fourth and fifth arguments specify the width and height of the image for display purposes.

- Interface ImageObserver is implemented by class Component. ImageObservers are notified to update an image that was displayed as the remainder of the image is loaded.

- ImageIcon method paintIcon displays the ImageIcon's image. The method requires four arguments—a reference to the Component on which the image will be displayed, a reference to the Graphics object used to render the image, the *x*-coordinate of the upper-left corner of the image and the *y*-coordinate of the upper-left corner of the image.

- Class ImageIcon provides method getImage, which returns an Image reference that can be used with Graphics method drawImage to display a scaled version of an image.

- Timer objects generate ActionEvents at fixed intervals in milliseconds. The Timer constructor receives two arguments—the delay in milliseconds and the ActionListener. Timer method start indicates that the Timer should start generating events. Timer method stop indicates that the Timer should stop generating events. Timer method restart indicates that the Timer should start generating events again.

- An image map is an image that has hot areas that the user can click to accomplish a task, such as loading a different Web page into a browser.

- Applet method play has two forms:

```
public void play( URL location, String soundFileName );
public void play( URL soundURL );
```

One version loads the audio clip stored in file soundFileName from location and plays the sound; the other takes a URL that contains the location and the file name of the audio clip.

- Applet method getDocumentBase indicates the location of the HTML file that loaded the applet. Method getCodeBase indicates where the .class file for an applet is located.

- The sound engine that plays audio clips supports several audio file formats, including Sun Audio file format (.au extension), Windows Wave file format (.wav extension), Macintosh AIFF file format (.aif or .aiff extension) and Musical Instrument Digital Interface (MIDI) file format (.mid or .rmi extensions). The Java Media Framework (JMF) supports other additional formats.

- Applet method getAudioClip has two forms that take the same arguments as the play method. Method getAudioClip returns a reference to an AudioClip. AudioClips have three methods—play, loop and stop. Method play plays the audio once. Method loop continuously loops the audio clip. Method stop terminates an audio clip that is currently playing.

TERMINOLOGY

.aif file-name extension
.aiff file-name extension
.au file-name extension
.gif file-name extension
.jpeg file-name extension
.jpg file-name extension
.mid file-name extension
.rmi file-name extension
.wav file-name extension
animating a series of images
animation
audio clip

drawImage method of Graphics
getAudioClip method of Applet
getCodeBase method of Applet
getDocumentBase method of Applet
getHeight method of Component
getIconHeight method of ImageIcon
getIconWidth method of ImageIcon
getImage method of Applet
getImage method of ImageIcon
getWidth method of Component
Graphics Interchange Format (GIF)
height of an image

hot area of an image map
image
Image class
image map
ImageIcon class
ImageObserver interface
information button
Joint Photographic Experts Group (JPEG)
loop method of interface AudioClip
Macintosh AIFF file (.aif or .aiff)
multimedia
Musical Instrument Digital Interface (MIDI)
mute button
paintIcon method of class ImageIcon
play method of class Applet

play method of interface AudioClip
restart method of class Timer
scaling an image
sound
sound engine
start method of class Timer
stop method of class Timer
stop method of interface AudioClip
Sun Audio file format (.au)
Timer class
update method of class Component
volume control
width of an image
Windows Wave file (.wav)

SELF-REVIEW EXERCISES

19.1   Fill in the blanks in each of the following statements:
a)   Applet method _____ loads an image into an applet.
b)   Applet method _____ returns, as an object of class URL, the location on the Internet of the HTML file that invoked the applet.
c)   Graphics method _____ displays an image on an applet.
d)   Java provides two mechanisms for playing sounds in an applet—the Applet's play method and the play method from the _____ interface.
e)   A(n) _____ is an image that has *hot areas* that the user can click to accomplish a task such as loading a different Web page.
f)   Method _____ of class ImageIcon displays the ImageIcon's image.
g)   Java supports several image formats, including _____, _____ and _____.

19.2   Determine whether each of the following statements is true or false. If false, explain why.
a)   A sound will be garbage collected as soon as it has finished playing.
b)   Class ImageIcon provides constructors that allow an ImageIcon object to be initialized only with an image from the local computer.

ANSWERS TO SELF-REVIEW EXERCISES

19.1   a) getImage. b) getDocumentBase. c) drawImage. d) AudioClip. e) image map. f) paintIcon. g) Graphics Interchange Format (GIF), Joint Photographic Experts Group (JPEG) Portable Network Graphics (PNG).

19.2   a)   False. The sound will be eligible for garbage collection (if it is not referenced by an AudioClip) and will be garbage collected when the garbage collector is able to run. b) False. ImageIcon can load images from the Internet as well.

EXERCISES

19.3   Describe how to make an animation "browser friendly."

19.4   Describe the Java methods for playing and manipulating audio clips.

19.5   Explain how image maps are used. List several examples in which image maps are used.

19.6   *(Randomly Erasing an Image)* Suppose an image is displayed in a rectangular screen area. One way to erase the image is simply to set every pixel to the same color immediately, but this is a dull visual effect. Write a Java program that displays an image and then erases it by using random-number generation to select individual pixels to erase. After most of the image is erased, erase all of the remaining pixels at once. You can draw individual pixels as a line that starts and ends at the same coordinates. You might try several variants of this problem. For example, you might display lines randomly or display shapes randomly to erase regions of the screen.

19.7   *(Text Flasher)* Create a Java program that repeatedly flashes text on the screen. Do this by alternating the text with a plain background-color image. Allow the user to control the "blink speed" and the background color or pattern.

19.8   *(Image Flasher)* Create a Java program that repeatedly flashes an image on the screen. Do this by alternating the image with a plain background-color image.

19.9   *(Digital Clock)* Implement a program that displays a digital clock on the screen. You might add options to scale the clock; display the day, month and year; issue an alarm; play certain audios at designated times and the like.

19.10   *(Calling Attention to an Image)* If you want to emphasize an image, you might place a row of simulated light bulbs around your image. You can let the light bulbs flash in unison, or you can let them fire on and off in sequence one after the other.

19.11   *(Image Zooming)* Create a program that enables you to zoom in on or away from an image.

SPECIAL SECTION: CHALLENGING MULTIMEDIA PROJECTS

The preceding exercises are keyed to the text and designed to test the reader's understanding of fundamental multimedia concepts. This section includes a collection of advanced multimedia projects. The reader should find these problems challenging, yet entertaining. The problems vary considerably in difficulty. Some require an hour or two of program writing and implementation. Others are useful for lab assignments that might require two or three weeks of study and implementation. Some are challenging term projects. [*Note:* Solutions are not provided for these exercises.].

19.12   *(Animation)* Create a a general-purpose Java animation program. Your program should allow the user to specify the sequence of frames to be displayed, the speed at which the images are displayed, audios that should be played while the animation is running and so on.

19.13   *(Limericks)* Modify the limerick-writing program you wrote in Exercise 10.10 to sing the limericks your program creates.

19.14   *(Random Inter-Image Transition)* This provides a nice visual effect. If you are displaying one image in a given area on the screen and you would like to transition to another image in the same screen area, store the new screen image in an off-screen buffer and randomly copy pixels from the new image to the display area, overlaying the previous pixels at those locations. When the vast majority of the pixels have been copied, copy the entire new image to the display area to be sure you are displaying the complete new image. To implement this program, you may need to use the Pixel-Grabber and MemoryImageSource classes (see the Java API documentation for descriptions of these classes). You might try several variants of this problem. For example, try selecting all the pixels in a randomly selected straight line or shape in the new image, and overlay those pixels above the corresponding positions of the old image.

19.15   *(Background Audio)* Add background audio to one of your favorite applications by using the loop method of class AudioClip to play the sound in the background while you interact with your application in the normal way.

19.16 *(Scrolling Marquee Sign)* Create a Java program that scrolls dotted characters from right to left (or from left to right if that is appropriate for your language) across a Marquee-like display sign. As an option, display the text in a continuous loop, so that after the text disappears at one end, it reappears at the other end.

19.17 *(Scrolling Image Marquee)* Create a Java program that scrolls an image across a Marquee screen.

19.18 *(Analog Clock)* Create a Java program that displays an analog clock with hour, minute and second hands that move appropriately as the time changes.

19.19 *(Dynamic Audio and Graphical Kaleidoscope)* Write a kaleidoscope program that displays reflected graphics to simulate the popular children's toy. Incorporate audio effects that "mirror" your program's dynamically changing graphics.

19.20 *(Automatic Jigsaw Puzzle Generator)* Create a Java jigsaw puzzle generator and manipulator. The user specifies an image. Your program loads and displays the image. Your program then breaks the image into randomly selected shapes and shuffles the shapes. The user then uses the mouse to move the pieces around to solve the puzzle. Add appropriate audio sounds as the pieces are being moved around and snapped back into place. You might keep tabs on each piece and where it really belongs; then use audio effects to help the user get the pieces into the correct positions.

19.21 *(Maze Generator and Walker)* Develop a multimedia-based maze generator and traverser program based on the maze programs you wrote in Exercise 7.40–Exercise 7.42. Let the user customize the maze by specifying the number of rows and columns and by indicating the level of difficulty. Have an animated mouse walk the maze. Use audio to dramatize the movement of your mouse character.

19.22 *(One-Armed Bandit)* Develop a multimedia simulation of a one-armed bandit. Have three spinning wheels. Place various fruits and symbols on each wheel. Use true random-number generation to simulate the spinning of each wheel and the stopping of each wheel on a symbol.

19.23 *(Horse Race)* Create a Java simulation of a horse race. Have multiple contenders. Use audios for a race announcer. Play the appropriate audios to indicate the correct status of each of the contenders throughout the race. Use audios to announce the final results. You might try to simulate the kinds of horse-racing games that are often played at carnivals. The players get turns at the mouse and have to perform some skill-oriented manipulation with the mouse to advance their horses.

19.24 *(Shuffleboard)* Develop a multimedia-based simulation of the game of shuffleboard. Use appropriate audio and visual effects.

19.25 *(Game of Pool)* Create a multimedia-based simulation of the game of pool. Each player takes turns using the mouse to position a pool stick and to hit the stick against the ball at the appropriate angle to try to get other balls to fall into the pockets. Your program should keep score.

19.26 *(Artist)* Design a Java art program that will give an artist a great variety of capabilities to draw, use images, use animations, etc., to create a dynamic multimedia art display.

19.27 *(Fireworks Designer)* Create a Java program that someone might use to create a fireworks display. Create a variety of fireworks demonstrations. Then orchestrate the firing of the fireworks for maximum effect.

19.28 *(Floor Planner)* Develop a Java program that will help someone arrange furniture in his or her home. Add features that enable the person to achieve the best possible arrangement.

19.29 *(Crossword)* Crossword puzzles are among the most popular pastimes. Develop a multimedia-based crossword-puzzle program. Your program should enable the player to place and erase words easily. Tie your program to a large computerized dictionary. Your program also should be able to suggest words on which letters have already been filled in. Provide other features that will make the crossword-puzzle enthusiast's job easier.

19.30 *(15 Puzzle)* Write a multimedia-based Java program that enables the user to play the game of 15. The game is played on is a 4-by-4 board for a total of 16 slots. One of the slots is empty. The other slots are occupied by 15 tiles numbered 1 through 15. Any tile next to the currently empty slot can be moved into that slot by clicking on the tile. Your program should create the board with the tiles out of order. The goal is to arrange the tiles into sequential order, row by row.

19.31 *(Reaction Time/Reaction Precision Tester)* Create a Java program that moves a randomly created shape around the screen. The user moves the mouse to catch and click on the shape. The shape's speed and size can be varied. Keep statistics on how much time the user typically takes to catch a shape of a given size. The user will probably have more difficulty catching faster moving, smaller shapes.

19.32 *(Calendar/Tickler File)* Using both audio and images, create a general-purpose calendar and "tickler" file. For example, the program should sing "Happy Birthday" when you use it on your birthday. Have the program display images and play audios associated with important events. Also, have the program remind you in advance of these important events. It would be nice, for example, to have the program give you a week's notice so you can pick up an appropriate greeting card for that special person.

19.33 *(Rotating Images)* Create a Java program that lets you rotate an image through some number of degrees (out of a maximum of 360 degrees). The program should let you specify that you want to spin the image continuously. The program should let you adjust the spin speed dynamically.

19.34 *(Coloring Black-and-White Photographs and Images)* Create a Java program that lets you paint a black-and-white photograph with color. Provide a color palette for selecting colors. Your program should let you apply different colors to different regions of the image.

19.35 *(Multimedia-Based Simpletron Simulator)* Modify the Simpletron simulator that you developed in the exercises in the previous chapters to include multimedia features. Add computer-like sounds to indicate that the Simpletron is executing instructions. Add a breaking-glass sound when a fatal error occurs. Use flashing lights to indicate which cells of memory or which registers are currently being manipulated. Use other multimedia techniques, as appropriate, to make your Simpletron simulator more valuable to its users as an educational tool.

20

Data Structures

Objectives

- To be able to form linked data structures using references, self-referential classes and recursion.
- To be able to create and manipulate dynamic data structures, such as linked lists, queues, stacks and binary trees.
- To understand various important applications of linked data structures.
- To understand how to create reusable data structures with classes, inheritance and composition.

Much that I bound, I could not free;
Much that I freed returned to me.
Lee Wilson Dodd

'Will you walk a little faster?' said a whiting to a snail,
'There's a porpoise close behind us, and he's treading on my tail.'
Lewis Carroll

There is always room at the top.
Daniel Webster

Push on—keep moving.
Thomas Morton

I think that I shall never see
A poem lovely as a tree.
Joyce Kilmer

Outline

20.1 Introduction

We have studied such fixed-size *data structures* as one-dimensional and multidimensional arrays. This chapter introduces *dynamic data structures* that grow and shrink at execution time. *Linked lists* are collections of data items "lined up in a row"—insertions and deletions can be made anywhere in a linked list. *Stacks* are important in compilers and operating systems; insertions and deletions are made only at one end of a stack—its *top*. *Queues* represent waiting lines; insertions are made at the back (also referred to as the *tail*) of a queue and deletions are made from the front (also referred to as the *head*) of a queue. *Binary trees* facilitate high-speed searching and sorting of data, eliminating of duplicate data items efficiently, representing file system directories, compiling expressions into machine language and many other interesting applications.

We will discuss each of these major types of data structures and implement programs that create and manipulate them. We use classes, inheritance and composition to create and package these data structures for reusability and maintainability. In Chapter 21, Java Utilities Package and Bit Manipulation, and Chapter 22, Collections, we discuss Java's predefined classes that implement the data structures discussed in this chapter.

The examples presented here are practical programs that can be used in more advanced courses and in industrial applications. The exercises include a rich collection of useful applications.

We encourage you to attempt the major project described in the special section entitled *Building Your Own Compiler*. You have been using a Java compiler to translate your Java programs to bytecodes so that you could execute these programs on your computer. In this project, you will actually build your own compiler. It will read a file of statements written in a simple, yet powerful high-level language similar to early versions of the popular language Basic. Your compiler will translate these statements into a file of Simpletron Machine Language (SML) instructions—SML is the language you learned in the Chapter 7 special section, *Building Your Own Computer*. Your Simpletron Simulator program will then execute the SML program produced by your compiler! Implementing this project by using an object-oriented approach will give you a wonderful opportunity to exercise most of what you have learned in this book. The special section carefully walks you through the specifications of the high-level language and describes the algorithms you will need to convert each high-level language statement into machine language instructions. If you enjoy being challenged, you might attempt the many enhancements to both the compiler and the Simpletron Simulator suggested in the exercises.

20.2 Self-Referential Classes

A *self-referential class* contains an instance variable that refers to another object of the same class type. For example, the declaration

```
class Node {
   private int data;
   private Node nextNode;   // reference to next linked node

   public Node( int data )        { /* constructor body */ }
   public void setData( int data )  { /* method body */ }
   public int getData()             { /* method body */ }
   public void setNext( Node next ) { /* method body */ }
   public Node getNext()            { /* method body */ }
}
```

declares class Node, which has two private instance variables—integer data and Node reference nextNode. Field nextNode references an object of class Node, an object of the same class being declared here—hence, the term "self-referential class." Field nextNode is a *link*—it "links" an object of type Node to another object of the same type. Type Node also has five methods: a constructor that receives an integer to initialize data, a setData method to set the value of data, a getData method to return the value of data, a setNext method to set the value of nextNode and a getNext method to return a reference to the next node.

Programs can link self-referential objects together to form such useful data structures as lists, queues, stacks and trees. Figure 20.1 illustrates two self-referential objects linked together to form a list. A backslash—representing a null reference—is placed in the link member of the second self-referential object to indicate that the link does not refer to another object.[1] Normally, a null reference indicates the end of a data structure.[2]

20.3 Dynamic Memory Allocation

Creating and maintaining dynamic data structures requires *dynamic memory allocation*—the ability for a program to obtain more memory space at execution time to hold new nodes and to release space no longer needed. Remember that Java programs do not explicitly release dynamically allocated memory. Rather, Java performs automatic garbage collection of objects that are no longer referenced in a program.

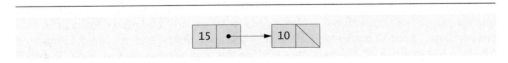

Fig. 20.1   Self-referential-class objects linked together.

1. The backslash is for illustration purposes; it does not correspond to the backslash character in Java.
2. There are other ways to represent the end of a data structure that are beyond the scope of this text.

The limit for dynamic memory allocation can be as large as the amount of available physical memory in the computer or the amount of available disk space in a virtual-memory system. Often, the limits are much smaller, because the computer's available memory must be shared among many applications.

The declaration and class-instance creation expression

```
Node nodeToAdd = new Node( 10 ); // 10 is nodeToAdd's data
```

allocates the memory to store a Node object and returns a reference to the object, which is assigned to nodeToAdd. If insufficient memory is available, the expression throws an OutOfMemoryError.

The following sections discuss lists, stacks, queues and trees that use dynamic memory allocation and self-referential classes to create dynamic data structures.

20.4 Linked Lists

A *linked list* is a linear collection (i.e., a sequence) of self-referential-class objects, called *nodes,* connected by reference *links*—hence, the term "linked" list. Typically, a program accesses a linked list via a reference to the first node in the list. The program accesses each subsequent node via the link reference stored in the previous node. By convention, the link reference in the last node of a list is set to null to mark the end of the list. Data is stored in a linked list dynamically—the program creates each node as necessary. A node can contain data of any type, including references to objects of other classes. Stacks and queues are also linear data structures and, as we will see, are constrained versions of linked lists. Trees are nonlinear data structures.

Lists of data can be stored in arrays, but linked lists provide several advantages. A linked list is appropriate when the number of data elements to be represented in the data structure is unpredictable. Linked lists are dynamic, so the length of a list can increase or decrease as necessary. The size of a "conventional" Java array, however, cannot be altered, because the array size is fixed at the time the program creates the array. "Conventional" arrays can become full. Linked lists become full only when the system has insufficient memory to satisfy dynamic storage allocation requests. Package java.util contains class LinkedList for implementing and manipulating linked lists that grow and shrink during program execution. We discuss class LinkedList in Chapter 22.

Performance Tip 20.1

An array can be declared to contain more elements than the number of items expected, but this wastes memory. Linked lists provide better memory utilization in these situations. Linked lists allow the program to adapt to storage needs at runtime.

Performance Tip 20.2

Insertion into a linked list is fast—only two references have to be modified (after locating the insertion point). All existing node objects remain at their current locations in memory.

Linked lists can be maintained in sorted order simply by inserting each new element at the proper point in the list. (It does, of course, take time to locate the proper insertion point.) Existing list elements do not need to be moved.

Performance Tip 20.3

Insertion and deletion in a sorted array can be time consuming—all the elements following the inserted or deleted element must be shifted appropriately.

Linked list nodes normally are not stored contiguously in memory. Rather, they are logically contiguous. Figure 20.2 illustrates a linked list with several nodes. This diagram presents a *singly-linked list*—each node contains one reference to the next node in the list. Often, linked lists are implemented as doubly-linked lists—each node contains a reference to the next node in the list and a reference to the previous node in the list. Java's `LinkedList` class is a doubly-linked list implementation.

 Performance Tip 20.4

Normally, the elements of an array are contiguous in memory. This allows immediate access to any array element, because the address of any element can be calculated directly as its offset from the beginning of the array. Linked lists do not afford such immediate access to their elements—an element can be accessed only by traversing the list from the front (or from the back in a doubly-linked list).

The program of Fig. 20.3–Fig. 20.5 uses an object of our `List` class to manipulate a list of miscellaneous objects. The program consists of four classes—`ListNode` (Fig. 20.3, lines 6–37), `List` (Fig. 20.3, lines 40–149), `EmptyListException` (Fig. 20.4) and `ListTest` (Fig. 20.5). The `List`, `ListNode` and `EmptyListException` classes are placed in package `com.deitel.jhtp5.ch20`,[3] so they can be reused throughout this chapter. Encapsulated in each `List` object is a linked list of `ListNode` objects.

Class `ListNode` (Fig. 20.3, lines 6–37) declares package-access fields `data` and `nextNode`. The `data` field is an `Object` reference, so it can refer to any object. `ListNode` member `nextNode` stores a reference to the next `ListNode` object in the linked list (or `null` if the node is the last node in the list).

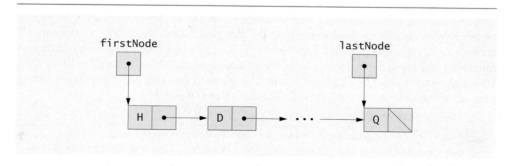

Fig. 20.2   Linked list graphical representation.

---

3. Many of the classes in this chapter are declared in the package `com.deitel.jhtp5.ch20`. Each such class should be compiled with the `-d` command-line option to `javac`. When compiling the classes that are not in this package and when running the programs, be sure to use the `-class-path` option to `javac` and `java`, respectively.

```
1   // Fig. 20.3: List.java
2   // ListNode and List class declarations.
3   package com.deitel.jhtp5.ch20;
4
5   // class to represent one node in a list
6   class ListNode {
7
8      // package access members; List can access these directly
9      Object data;
10     ListNode nextNode;
11
12     // create a ListNode that refers to object
13     ListNode( Object object )
14     {
15        this( object, null );
16     }
17
18     // create ListNode that refers to Object and to next ListNode
19     ListNode( Object object, ListNode node )
20     {
21        data = object;
22        nextNode = node;
23     }
24
25     // return reference to data in node
26     Object getObject()
27     {
28        return data; // return Object in this node
29     }
30
31     // return reference to next node in list
32     ListNode getNext()
33     {
34        return nextNode; // get next node
35     }
36
37  } // end class ListNode
38
39  // class List declaration
40  public class List {
41     private ListNode firstNode;
42     private ListNode lastNode;
43     private String name;  // string like "list" used in printing
44
45     // construct empty List with "list" as the name
46     public List()
47     {
48        this( "list" );
49     }
50
51     // construct an empty List with a name
52     public List( String listName )
53     {
```

Fig. 20.3   ListNode and List class declarations. (Part 1 of 3.)

```
54          name = listName;
55          firstNode = lastNode = null;
56       }
57
58       // insert Object at front of List
59       public synchronized void insertAtFront( Object insertItem )
60       {
61          if ( isEmpty() ) // firstNode and lastNode refer to same object
62             firstNode = lastNode = new ListNode( insertItem );
63
64          else // firstNode refers to new node
65             firstNode = new ListNode( insertItem, firstNode );
66       }
67
68       // insert Object at end of List
69       public synchronized void insertAtBack( Object insertItem )
70       {
71          if ( isEmpty() ) // firstNode and lastNode refer to same Object
72             firstNode = lastNode = new ListNode( insertItem );
73
74          else // lastNode's nextNode refers to new node
75             lastNode = lastNode.nextNode = new ListNode( insertItem );
76       }
77
78       // remove first node from List
79       public synchronized Object removeFromFront() throws EmptyListException
80       {
81          if ( isEmpty() ) // throw exception if List is empty
82             throw new EmptyListException( name );
83
84          Object removedItem = firstNode.data; // retrieve data being removed
85
86          // update references firstNode and lastNode
87          if ( firstNode == lastNode )
88             firstNode = lastNode = null;
89          else
90             firstNode = firstNode.nextNode;
91
92          return removedItem; // return removed node data
93
94       } // end method removeFromFront
95
96       // remove last node from List
97       public synchronized Object removeFromBack() throws EmptyListException
98       {
99          if ( isEmpty() ) // throw exception if List is empty
100            throw new EmptyListException( name );
101
102         Object removedItem = lastNode.data; // retrieve data being removed
103
104         // update references firstNode and lastNode
105         if ( firstNode == lastNode )
106            firstNode = lastNode = null;
```

Fig. 20.3 ListNode and List class declarations. (Part 2 of 3.)

```
107
108          else { // locate new last node
109             ListNode current = firstNode;
110
111             // loop while current node does not refer to lastNode
112             while ( current.nextNode != lastNode )
113                current = current.nextNode;
114
115             lastNode = current; // current is new lastNode
116             current.nextNode = null;
117          }
118
119          return removedItem; // return removed node data
120
121       } // end method removeFromBack
122
123       // determine whether list is empty
124       public synchronized boolean isEmpty()
125       {
126          return firstNode == null; // return true if List is empty
127       }
128
129       // output List contents
130       public synchronized void print()
131       {
132          if ( isEmpty() ) {
133             System.out.println( "Empty " + name );
134             return;
135          }
136
137          System.out.print( "The " + name + " is: " );
138          ListNode current = firstNode;
139
140          // while not at end of list, output current node's data
141          while ( current != null ) {
142             System.out.print( current.data.toString() + " " );
143             current = current.nextNode;
144          }
145
146          System.out.println( "\n" );
147       }
148
149    } // end class List
```

Fig. 20.3   ListNode and List class declarations. (Part 3 of 3.)

Lines 41–42 of class List (Fig. 20.3, lines 40–149) declare references to the first and last ListNodes in a List (firstNode and lastNode, respectively). The constructors (lines 46–49 and 52–56) initialize both references to null. The most important methods of class List are the synchronized methods insertAtFront (lines 59–66), insertAt-Back (lines 69–76), removeFromFront (lines 79–94) and removeFromBack (lines 97–121). These methods are declared synchronized so List objects can be thread safe when used in a multithreaded program. If one thread is modifying the contents of a List, no other thread should be able to modify the same List object at the same time. Method isEmpty (lines 124–127) is a *predicate method* that determines whether the list is empty (i.e., the reference to the first node of the list is null). Predicate methods typically test a condition and do not modify the object on which they are called. If the list is empty, method isEmpty returns true; otherwise, it returns false. Method print (lines 130–147) displays the list's contents. Both isEmpty and print are also synchronized methods to ensure that the list's state does not change while these methods are executing, which helps prevent incorrect results. A detailed discussion of List's methods follows Fig. 20.5.

Method main of class ListTest (Fig. 20.5) creates a list of objects, inserts objects at the beginning of the list using method insertAtFront, inserts objects at the end of the list using method insertAtBack, deletes objects from the front of the list using method removeFromFront and deletes objects from the end of the list using method removeFromBack. After each insert and remove operation, ListTest calls List method print to display the current list contents. If an attempt is made to remove an item from an empty list, an EmptyListException (Fig. 20.4) is thrown, so the method calls to removeFromFront and removeFromBack are placed in a try block that is followed by an appropriate exception handler.

```
1   // Fig. 20.4: EmptyListException.java
2   // Class EmptyListException declaration.
3   package com.deitel.jhtp5.ch20;
4
5   public class EmptyListException extends RuntimeException {
6
7      // no-argument constructor
8      public EmptyListException()
9      {
10        this( "List" );   // call other EmptyListException constructor
11     }
12
13     // constructor
14     public EmptyListException( String name )
15     {
16        super( name + " is empty" );  // call superclass constructor
17     }
18
19  } // end class EmptyListException
```

Fig. 20.4   EmptyListException class declaration.

```
1   // Fig. 20.5: ListTest.java
2   // ListTest class to demonstrate List capabilities.
3   import com.deitel.jhtp5.ch20.List;
4   import com.deitel.jhtp5.ch20.EmptyListException;
5
6   public class ListTest {
7
8      public static void main( String args[] )
9      {
```

Fig. 20.5   Linked list manipulations. (Part 1 of 3.)

```
10            List list = new List();   // create the List container
11
12            // objects to store in list
13            Boolean bool = Boolean.TRUE;
14            Character character = new Character( '$' );
15            Integer integer = new Integer( 34567 );
16            String string = "hello";
17
18            // insert references to objects in list
19            list.insertAtFront( bool );
20            list.print();
21            list.insertAtFront( character );
22            list.print();
23            list.insertAtBack( integer );
24            list.print();
25            list.insertAtBack( string );
26            list.print();
27
28            // remove objects from list; print after each removal
29            try {
30               Object removedObject = list.removeFromFront();
31               System.out.println( removedObject.toString() + " removed" );
32               list.print();
33
34               removedObject = list.removeFromFront();
35               System.out.println( removedObject.toString() + " removed" );
36               list.print();
37
38               removedObject = list.removeFromBack();
39               System.out.println( removedObject.toString() + " removed" );
40               list.print();
41
42               removedObject = list.removeFromBack();
43               System.out.println( removedObject.toString() + " removed" );
44               list.print();
45
46            } // end try block
47
48            // catch exception if remove is attempted on an empty List
49            catch ( EmptyListException emptyListException ) {
50               emptyListException.printStackTrace();
51            }
52         }
53
54   } // end class ListTest
```

```
The list is: true

The list is: $ true

The list is: $ true 34567

The list is: $ true 34567 hello                    (continued on next page)
```

Fig. 20.5   Linked list manipulations. (Part 2 of 3.)

```
$ removed                                    (continued from previous page)
The list is: true 34567 hello

true removed
The list is: 34567 hello

hello removed
The list is: 34567

34567 removed
Empty list
```

Fig. 20.5   Linked list manipulations. (Part 3 of 3.)

Now we discuss each of the methods of class List (Fig. 20.3) in detail and provide diagrams showing the reference manipulations performed by methods insertAtFront, insertAtBack, removeFromFront and removeFromBack. Method insertAtFront (lines 59–66 of Fig. 20.3) places a new node at the front of the list. The steps are:

1. Call isEmpty to determine whether the list is empty (line 61).

2. If the list is empty, assign firstNode and lastNode to the new ListNode that was initialized with insertItem (line 62). The ListNode constructor at lines 13–16 calls the ListNode constructor at lines 19–23 to set instance variable data to refer to the insertItem passed as an argument and to set reference nextNode to null, because this is the first and last node in the list.

3. If the list is not empty, the new node is "linked" into the list by setting firstNode to a new ListNode object and initializing that object with insertItem and firstNode (line 65). When the ListNode constructor (lines 19–23) executes, it sets instance variable data to refer to the insertItem passed as an argument and performs the insertion by setting the nextNode reference of the new node to the ListNode passed as an argument, which previously was the first node.

In Fig. 20.6, part (a) shows a list and a new node during the insertAtFront operation and before the program links the new node into the list. The dotted arrows in part (b) illustrate step 3 of the insertAtFront operation that enables the node containing 12 to become the new first node in the list.

Method insertAtBack (lines 69–76 of Fig. 20.3) places a new node at the back of the list. The steps are:

1. Call isEmpty to determine whether the list is empty (line 71).

2. If the list is empty, assign firstNode and lastNode to the new ListNode that was initialized with insertItem (line 72). The ListNode constructor at lines 13–16 calls the constructor at lines 19–23 to set instance variable data to refer to the insertItem passed as an argument and to set reference nextNode to null.

3. If the list is not empty, line 75 links the new node into the list by assigning last-Node and lastNode.nextNode the reference to the new ListNode that was initialized with insertItem. ListNode's constructor (lines 13–16), sets instance variable data to refer to the insertItem passed as an argument and sets reference nextNode to null, because this is the last node in the list.

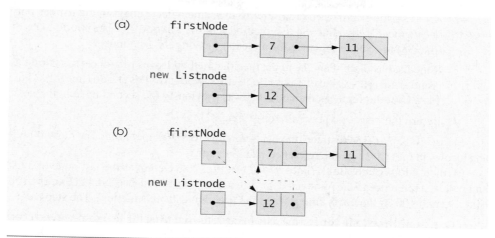

Fig. 20.6　Graphical representation of operation `insertAtFront`.

In Fig. 20.7, part (a) shows a list and a new node during the `insertAtBack` operation and before the program links the new node into the list. The dotted arrows in part (b) illustrate step 3 of method `insertAtBack`, which adds the new node to the end of a list that is not empty.

Method `removeFromFront` (lines 79–94 of Fig. 20.3) removes the first node of the list and returns a reference to the removed data. The method throws an `EmptyList-Exception` (lines 81–82) if the list is empty when the program calls this method. Otherwise, the method returns a reference to the removed data. The steps are:

1. Assign `firstNode.data` (the data being removed from the list) to reference `removedItem` (line 84).

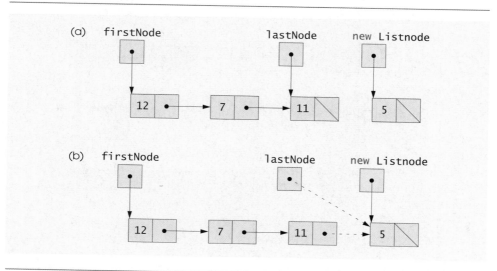

Fig. 20.7　Graphical representation of operation `insertAtBack`.

2. If `firstNode` and `lastNode` refer to the same object (line 87), the list has only one element at this time. So, the method sets `firstNode` and `lastNode` to `null` (line 88) to remove the node from the list (leaving the list empty).

3. If the list has more than one node, then the method leaves reference `lastNode` as is and assigns the value of `firstNode.nextNode` to `firstNode` (line 90). Thus, `firstNode` references the node that was previously the second node in the list.

4. Return the `removedItem` reference (line 92).

In Fig. 20.8, part (a) illustrates the list before the removal operation. The dashed lines and arrows in part (b) show the reference manipulations.

Method `removeFromBack` (lines 97–121 of Fig. 20.3) removes the last node of a list and returns a reference to the removed data. The method throws an `EmptyListException` (lines 99 and 100) if the list is empty when the program calls this method. The steps are:

1. Assign `lastNode.data` (the data being removed from the list) to `removedItem` (line 102).

2. If the `firstNode` and `lastNode` refer to the same object (line 105), the list has only one element at this time. So, line 106 sets `firstNode` and `lastNode` to `null` to remove that node from the list (leaving the list empty).

3. If the list has more than one node, create the `ListNode` reference `current` and assign it `firstNode` (line 109).

4. Now "walk the list" with `current` until it references the node before the last node. The `while` loop (lines 112–113) assigns `current.nextNode` to `current` as long as `current.nextNode` (the next node in the list) is not `lastNode`.

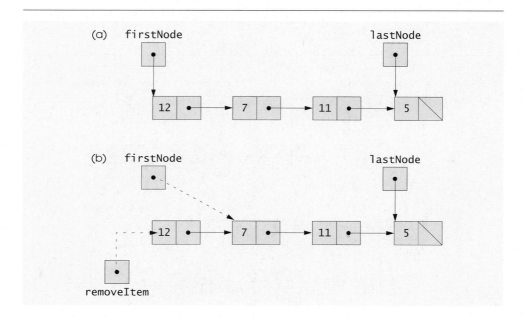

Fig. 20.8   Graphical representation of operation `removeFromFront`.

5. After locating the second-to-last node, assign `current` to `lastNode` (line 115) to update which node is last in the list.

6. Set the `current.nextNode` to `null` (line 116) to remove the last node from the list and terminate the list at the current node.

7. Return the `removedItem` reference (line 119).

In Fig. 20.9, part (a) illustrates the list before the removal operation. The dashed lines and arrows in part (b) show the reference manipulations.

Method `print` (lines 130–147) first determines whether the list is empty (lines 132–135). If so, `print` displays a message indicating that the list is empty and returns control to the calling method. Otherwise, `print` outputs the data in the list. Line 138 creates `List-Node` reference `current` and initializes it with `firstNode`. While `current` is not `null`, there are more items in the list. Therefore, line 142 outputs a string representation of `current.data`. Line 143 moves to the next node in the list by assigning the value of reference `current.nextNode` to `current`. This printing algorithm is identical for linked lists, stacks and queues.

20.5 Stacks

A *stack* is a constrained version of a linked list[4]—new nodes can be added to a stack and removed from a stack only at the top. For this reason, a stack is referred to as a *last-in, first-out (LIFO)* data structure. The link member in the bottom (i.e., last) node of the stack is set to `null` to indicate the bottom of the stack.

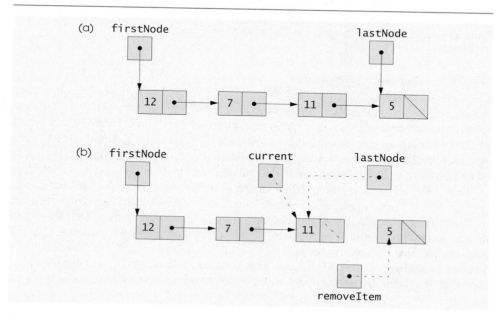

Fig. 20.9   Graphical representation of operation `removeFromBack`.

---

4. A stack does not have to be implemented using a linked list.

The primary methods for manipulating a stack are *push* and *pop*. Method `push` adds a new node to the top of the stack. Method `pop` removes a node from the top of the stack and returns the data from the popped node.

Stacks have many interesting applications. For example, when a program calls a method, the called method must know how to return to its caller, so the return address of the calling method is pushed onto the *program execution stack*. If a series of method calls occurs, the successive return addresses are pushed onto the stack in last-in, first-out order so that each method can return to its caller. Stacks support recursive method calls in the same manner as they do conventional nonrecursive method calls.

The program execution stack also contains the memory for local variables on each invocation of a method during a program's execution. When the method returns to its caller, the memory for that method's local variables is popped off the stack and those variables are no longer known to the program.[5]

Compilers use stacks to evaluate arithmetic expressions and generate machine language code to process the expressions. The exercises in this chapter explore several applications of stacks, including using them to develop a complete working compiler. Also, package `java.util` contains class `Stack` (see Chapter 21) for implementing and manipulating stacks that can grow and shrink during program execution.

We take advantage of the close relationship between lists and stacks to implement a stack class by reusing a list class. We demonstrate two different forms of reusability. First, we implement the stack class by extending class `List` of Fig. 20.3. Then we implement an identically performing stack class through composition by including a reference to a `List` object as a private instance variable of a stack class. The list, stack and queue data structures in this chapter are implemented to store `Object` references to encourage further reusability. Thus, any object type can be stored in a list, stack or queue.

Stack Class that Inherits from `List`

The application of Fig. 20.10 and Fig. 20.11 creates a stack class by extending class `List` of Fig. 20.3. We want the stack to have methods `push`, `pop`, `isEmpty` and `print`. Essentially, these are the methods `insertAtFront`, `removeFromFront`, `isEmpty` and `print` of class `List`. Of course, class `List` contains other methods (such as `insertAtBack` and `removeFromBack`) that we would rather not make accessible through the `public` interface to the stack class. It is important to remember that all methods in the `public` interface of class `List` class also are `public` methods of the subclass `StackInheritance` (Fig. 20.10). When we implement the stack's methods, we have each `StackInheritance` method call the appropriate `List` method—method `push` calls `insertAtFront` and method `pop` calls `removeFromFront`. Clients of class `StackInheritance` can call methods `isEmpty` and `print` because they are inherited from `List`. Class `StackInheritance` is declared as part of package `com.deitel.jhtp5.ch20` for reuse purposes. Note that `StackInheritance` does not import `List`, because both classes are in the same package.

---

5. If the local variable is a reference, the reference count for the object to which it referred is decremented by 1. If the reference count becomes zero, the object can be garbage collected.

```
1   // Fig. 20.10: StackInheritance.java
2   // Derived from class List.
3   package com.deitel.jhtp5.ch20;
4
5   public class StackInheritance extends List {
6
7      // construct stack
8      public StackInheritance()
9      {
10         super( "stack" );
11      }
12
13      // add object to stack
14      public synchronized void push( Object object )
15      {
16         insertAtFront( object );
17      }
18
19      // remove object from stack
20      public synchronized Object pop() throws EmptyListException
21      {
22         return removeFromFront();
23      }
24
25   } // end class StackInheritance
```

Fig. 20.10 StackInheritance extends class List.

Class StackInheritanceTest's method main (Fig. 20.11) creates an object of class StackInheritance called stack (line 10). The program pushes onto the stack (lines 19, 21, 23 and 25) a Boolean object containing true, a Character object containing $, an Integer object containing 34567 and a String object containing hello. Lines 32–36 pop the objects from the stack in an infinite while loop. If method pop is invoked on an empty stack, the method throws an EmptyListException. In this case, the program displays the exception's stack trace, which shows the methods on the program execution stack at the time the exception occurred. Note that the program uses method print (inherited from List) to output the contents of the stack.

```
1   // Fig. 20.11: StackInheritanceTest.java
2   // Class StackInheritanceTest.
3   import com.deitel.jhtp5.ch20.StackInheritance;
4   import com.deitel.jhtp5.ch20.EmptyListException;
5
6   public class StackInheritanceTest {
7
8      public static void main( String args[] )
9      {
10         StackInheritance stack = new StackInheritance();
11
12         // create objects to store in the stack
13         Boolean bool = Boolean.TRUE;
```

Fig. 20.11 Stack manipulation program. (Part 1 of 3.)

```
14          Character character = new Character( '$' );
15          Integer integer = new Integer( 34567 );
16          String string = "hello";
17
18          // use push method
19          stack.push( bool );
20          stack.print();
21          stack.push( character );
22          stack.print();
23          stack.push( integer );
24          stack.print();
25          stack.push( string );
26          stack.print();
27
28          // remove items from stack
29          try {
30             Object removedObject = null;
31
32             while ( true ) {
33                removedObject = stack.pop(); // use pop method
34                System.out.println( removedObject.toString() + " popped" );
35                stack.print();
36             }
37          }
38
39          // catch exception if stack is empty when item popped
40          catch ( EmptyListException emptyListException ) {
41             emptyListException.printStackTrace();
42          }
43       }
44
45    } // end class StackInheritanceTest
```

```
The stack is: true

The stack is: $ true

The stack is: 34567 $ true

The stack is: hello 34567 $ true

hello popped
The stack is: 34567 $ true

34567 popped
The stack is: $ true

$ popped
The stack is: true

true popped
Empty stack                                    (continued on next page)
```

Fig. 20.11 Stack manipulation program. (Part 2 of 3.)

```
com.deitel.jhtp5.ch20.EmptyListException: stack is empty
        at com.deitel.jhtp5.ch20.List.removeFromFront(List.java:82)
        at com.deitel.jhtp5.ch20.StackInheritance.pop(
           StackInheritance.java:22)
        at StackInheritanceTest.main(StackInheritanceTest.java:33)
```

Fig. 20.11 Stack manipulation program. (Part 3 of 3.)

Stack Class that Contains a Reference to a List

Another way to implement a stack class is by reusing a list class through composition. Figure 20.12 uses a private reference to an object of class List (line 6) in the declaration of class StackComposition. Composition enables us to hide the methods of class List that should not be in our stack's public interface by providing public interface methods only to the required List methods. This technique of implementing each stack method as a call to a List method is called *delegation*—the stack method invoked *delegates* the call to the appropriate List method. In particular, StackComposition delegates calls to List methods insertAtFront, removeFromFront, isEmpty and print. In this example, we do not show class StackCompositionTest, because the only difference in this example is that we change the type of the stack from StackInheritance to StackComposition (lines 3 and 10 of Fig. 20.11). The output is identical using either version of the stack.

```java
1   // Fig. 20.12: StackComposition.java
2   // Class StackComposition declaration with composed List object.
3   package com.deitel.jhtp5.ch20;
4
5   public class StackComposition {
6      private List stackList;
7
8      // construct stack
9      public StackComposition()
10     {
11        stackList = new List( "stack" );
12     }
13
14     // add object to stack
15     public synchronized void push( Object object )
16     {
17        stackList.insertAtFront( object );
18     }
19
20     // remove object from stack
21     public synchronized Object pop() throws EmptyListException
22     {
23        return stackList.removeFromFront();
24     }
25
26     // determine if stack is empty
27     public synchronized boolean isEmpty()
28     {
```

Fig. 20.12 StackComposition uses a composed List object. (Part 1 of 2.)

```
29            return stackList.isEmpty();
30      }
31
32      // output stack contents
33      public synchronized void print()
34      {
35            stackList.print();
36      }
37
38  } // end class StackComposition
```

Fig. 20.12 StackComposition uses a composed List object. (Part 2 of 2.)

20.6 Queues

Another commonly used data structure is the *queue*. A queue is similar to a checkout line in a supermarket—the cashier services the person at the beginning of the line first. Other customers enter the line only at the end and wait for service. Queue nodes are removed only from the *head* (or front) of the queue and are inserted only at the *tail* (or end) of the queue. For this reason, a queue is a *first-in, first-out (FIFO)* data structure. The insert and remove operations are known as *enqueue* and *dequeue*.

Queues have many applications in computer systems. Most computers have only a single processor, so only one application at a time can be serviced. Each application requiring processor time is placed in a queue. The application at the front of the queue is the next to receive service. Each application gradually advances to the front of the queue as the applications before it receive service.

Queues are also used to support *print spooling*. For example, a single printer might be shared by all users of a network. Many users can send print jobs to the printer, even when the printer is already busy. These print jobs are placed in a queue until the printer becomes available. A program called a *spooler* manages the queue to ensure that as each print job completes, the next print job is sent to the printer.

Information packets also wait in queues in computer networks. Each time a packet arrives at a network node, it must be routed to the next node on the network along the path to the packet's final destination. The routing node routes one packet at a time, so additional packets are enqueued until the router can route them.

A file server in a computer network handles file-access requests from many clients throughout the network. Servers have a limited capacity to service requests from clients. When that capacity is exceeded, client requests wait in queues.

Figure 20.13 creates a queue class that contains an object of class List (Fig. 20.3). Class Queue (Fig. 20.13) provides methods enqueue, dequeue, isEmpty and print. Class List contains other methods (e.g., insertAtFront and removeFromBack) that we would rather not make accessible through the public interface of class Queue. By using composition, these methods in the public interface of class List are not accessible to clients of class Queue. Each method of class Queue calls an appropriate List method—method enqueue calls List method insertAtBack, method dequeue calls List method removeFromFront, method isEmpty calls List method isEmpty and method print calls List method print. For reuse purposes, class Queue is declared in package com.deitel.jhtp5.ch20.

```
1   // Fig. 20.13: Queue.java
2   // Class Queue.
3   package com.deitel.jhtp5.ch20;
4
5   public class Queue {
6      private List queueList;
7
8      // construct queue
9      public Queue()
10     {
11        queueList = new List( "queue" );
12     }
13
14     // add object to queue
15     public synchronized void enqueue( Object object )
16     {
17        queueList.insertAtBack( object );
18     }
19
20     // remove object from queue
21     public synchronized Object dequeue() throws EmptyListException
22     {
23        return queueList.removeFromFront();
24     }
25
26     // determine if queue is empty
27     public synchronized boolean isEmpty()
28     {
29        return queueList.isEmpty();
30     }
31
32     // output queue contents
33     public synchronized void print()
34     {
35        queueList.print();
36     }
37
38  } // end class Queue
```

Fig. 20.13 Queue uses class List.

Class QueueCompositionTest (Fig. 20.14) method main creates an object of class QueueComposition called queue. Lines 19, 21, 23 and 25 enqueue a Boolean object containing true, a Character object containing $, an Integer object containing 34567 and a String object containing hello. Lines 32–36 use an infinite while loop to dequeue the objects in first-in, first-out order. When the queue is empty, method dequeue throws an EmptyListException, and the program displays the exception's stack trace.

```
1   // Fig. 20.14: QueueTest.java
2   // Class QueueTest.
3   import com.deitel.jhtp5.ch20.Queue;
```

Fig. 20.14 Queue processing program. (Part 1 of 3.)

```java
4    import com.deitel.jhtp5.ch20.EmptyListException;
5
6    public class QueueTest {
7
8       public static void main( String args[] )
9       {
10          Queue queue = new Queue();
11
12          // create objects to store in queue
13          Boolean bool = Boolean.TRUE;
14          Character character = new Character( '$' );
15          Integer integer = new Integer( 34567 );
16          String string = "hello";
17
18          // use enqueue method
19          queue.enqueue( bool );
20          queue.print();
21          queue.enqueue( character );
22          queue.print();
23          queue.enqueue( integer );
24          queue.print();
25          queue.enqueue( string );
26          queue.print();
27
28          // remove objects from queue
29          try {
30             Object removedObject = null;
31
32             while ( true ) {
33                removedObject = queue.dequeue(); // use dequeue method
34                System.out.println( removedObject.toString() + " dequeued" );
35                queue.print();
36             }
37          }
38
39          // process exception if queue is empty when item removed
40          catch ( EmptyListException emptyListException ) {
41             emptyListException.printStackTrace();
42          }
43       }
44
45    } // end class QueueCompositionTest
```

```
The queue is: true

The queue is: true $

The queue is: true $ 34567

The queue is: true $ 34567 hello

true dequeued
The queue is: $ 34567 hello
```

(continued on next page...)

Fig. 20.14 Queue processing program. (Part 2 of 3.)

```
$ dequeued                                          (continued from previous page...)
The queue is: 34567 hello

34567 dequeued
The queue is: hello

hello dequeued
Empty queue
com.deitel.jhtp5.ch20.EmptyListException: queue is empty
        at com.deitel.jhtp5.ch20.List.removeFromFront(List.java:88)
        at com.deitel.jhtp5.ch20.Queue.dequeue(Queue.java:23)
        at QueueTest.main(QueueTest.java:33)
```

Fig. 20.14 Queue processing program. (Part 3 of 3.)

20.7 Trees

Linked lists, stacks and queues are *linear data structures* (i.e., *sequences*). A tree is a non-linear, two-dimensional data structure with special properties. Tree nodes contain two or more links. This section discusses *binary trees* (Fig. 20.15)—trees whose nodes all contain two links (one or both of which may be null). The *root node* is the first node in a tree. Each link in the root node refers to a *child*. The *left child* is the first node in the *left subtree* (also known as the root node of the left subtree), and the *right child* is the first node in the *right subtree* (also known as the root node of the right subtree). The children of a specific node are called *siblings*. A node with no children is called a *leaf node*. Computer scientists normally draw trees from the root node down—exactly the opposite of the way most trees grow in nature.

In our binary tree example, we create a special binary tree called a *binary search tree*. A binary search tree (with no duplicate node values) has the characteristic that the values in any left subtree are less than the value in that subtree's parent node, and the values in any right subtree are greater than the value in that subtree's parent node. Figure 20.16 illustrates a binary search tree with 12 integer values. Note that the shape of the binary search tree that corresponds to a set of data can vary, depending on the order in which the values are inserted into the tree.

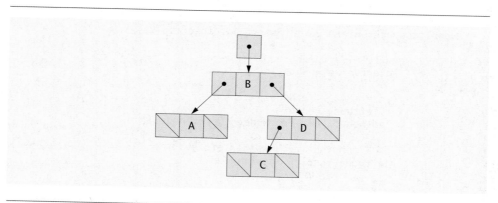

Fig. 20.15 Binary tree graphical representation.

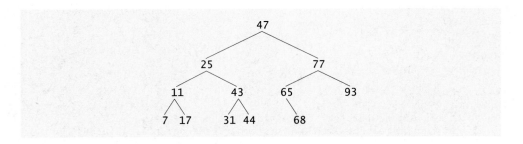

Fig. 20.16 Binary search tree containing 12 values.

The application of Fig. 20.17 and Fig. 20.18 creates a binary search tree of integers and traverses it (i.e., walks through all its nodes) three ways—using recursive *inorder, preorder* and *postorder traversals*. The program generates 10 random numbers and inserts each into the tree. Class **Tree** is declared in package **com.deitel.jhtp5.ch20** for reuse purposes.

```java
1   // Fig. 20.17: Tree.java
2   // Declaration of class TreeNode and class Tree.
3   package com.deitel.jhtp5.ch20;
4
5   // class TreeNode declaration
6   class TreeNode {
7
8      // package access members
9      TreeNode leftNode;
10     int data;
11     TreeNode rightNode;
12
13     // initialize data and make this a leaf node
14     public TreeNode( int nodeData )
15     {
16        data = nodeData;
17        leftNode = rightNode = null;   // node has no children
18     }
19
20     // locate insertion point and insert new node; ignore duplicate values
21     public synchronized void insert( int insertValue )
22     {
23        // insert in left subtree
24        if ( insertValue < data ) {
25
26           // insert new TreeNode
27           if ( leftNode == null )
28              leftNode = new TreeNode( insertValue );
29
30           else // continue traversing left subtree
31              leftNode.insert( insertValue );
32        }
33
```

Fig. 20.17 TreeNode and Tree class declarations for a binary search tree. (Part 1 of 3.)

```
34              // insert in right subtree
35              else if ( insertValue > data ) {
36
37                  // insert new TreeNode
38                  if ( rightNode == null )
39                      rightNode = new TreeNode( insertValue );
40
41                  else // continue traversing right subtree
42                      rightNode.insert( insertValue );
43              }
44
45      } // end method insert
46
47  } // end class TreeNode
48
49  // class Tree declaration
50  public class Tree {
51      private TreeNode root;
52
53      // construct an empty Tree of integers
54      public Tree()
55      {
56          root = null;
57      }
58
59      // insert a new node in the binary search tree
60      public synchronized void insertNode( int insertValue )
61      {
62          if ( root == null )
63              root = new TreeNode( insertValue ); // create the root node here
64
65          else
66              root.insert( insertValue ); // call the insert method
67      }
68
69      // begin preorder traversal
70      public synchronized void preorderTraversal()
71      {
72          preorderHelper( root );
73      }
74
75      // recursive method to perform preorder traversal
76      private void preorderHelper( TreeNode node )
77      {
78          if ( node == null )
79              return;
80
81          System.out.print( node.data + " " ); // output node data
82          preorderHelper( node.leftNode );      // traverse left subtree
83          preorderHelper( node.rightNode );     // traverse right subtree
84      }
85
```

Fig. 20.17 TreeNode and Tree class declarations for a binary search tree. (Part 2 of 3.)

```
86      // begin inorder traversal
87      public synchronized void inorderTraversal()
88      {
89          inorderHelper( root );
90      }
91
92      // recursive method to perform inorder traversal
93      private void inorderHelper( TreeNode node )
94      {
95          if ( node == null )
96              return;
97
98          inorderHelper( node.leftNode );      // traverse left subtree
99          System.out.print( node.data + " " ); // output node data
100         inorderHelper( node.rightNode );     // traverse right subtree
101     }
102
103     // begin postorder traversal
104     public synchronized void postorderTraversal()
105     {
106         postorderHelper( root );
107     }
108
109     // recursive method to perform postorder traversal
110     private void postorderHelper( TreeNode node )
111     {
112         if ( node == null )
113             return;
114
115         postorderHelper( node.leftNode );    // traverse left subtree
116         postorderHelper( node.rightNode );   // traverse right subtree
117         System.out.print( node.data + " " ); // output node data
118     }
119
120 } // end class Tree
```

Fig. 20.17   TreeNode and Tree class declarations for a binary search tree. (Part 3 of 3.)

Let us walk through the binary tree program. Method main of class TreeTest
(Fig. 20.18) begins by instantiating an empty Tree object and assigning its reference to
variable tree (line 9). Lines 15–19 randomly generate 10 integers, each of which is
inserted into the binary tree through a call to synchronized method insertNode (line
18). The program then performs preorder, inorder and postorder traversals (these will be
explained shortly) of tree (lines 22, 25 and 28, respectively).

```
1   // Fig. 20.18: TreeTest.java
2   // This program tests class Tree.
3   import com.deitel.jhtp5.ch20.Tree;
4
5   public class TreeTest {
6
```

Fig. 20.18   Binary-tree test program. (Part 1 of 2.)

```
 7      public static void main( String args[] )
 8      {
 9         Tree tree = new Tree();
10         int value;
11
12         System.out.println( "Inserting the following values: " );
13
14         // insert 10 random integers from 0-99 in tree
15         for ( int i = 1; i <= 10; i++ ) {
16            value = ( int ) ( Math.random() * 100 );
17            System.out.print( value + " " );
18            tree.insertNode( value );
19         }
20
21         System.out.println ( "\n\nPreorder traversal" );
22         tree.preorderTraversal(); // perform preorder traversal of tree
23
24         System.out.println ( "\n\nInorder traversal" );
25         tree.inorderTraversal(); // perform inorder traversal of tree
26
27         System.out.println ( "\n\nPostorder traversal" );
28         tree.postorderTraversal(); // perform postorder traversal of tree
29         System.out.println();
30      }
31
32   } // end class TreeTest
```

```
Inserting the following values:
39 69 94 47 50 72 55 41 97 73

Preorder traversal
39 69 47 41 50 55 94 72 73 97

Inorder traversal
39 41 47 50 55 69 72 73 94 97

Postorder traversal
41 55 50 47 73 72 97 94 69 39
```

Fig. 20.18   Binary-tree test program. (Part 2 of 2.)

Class `Tree` (Fig. 20.17, lines 50–120) has `private` field `root` (line 51)—a `TreeNode` reference to the root node of the tree. `Tree`'s constructor (lines 54–57) initializes `root` to `null` to indicate that the tree is empty. The class contains method `insertNode` (lines 60–67) to insert a new node in the tree and methods `preorderTraversal` (lines 70–73), `inorderTraversal` (lines 87–90) and `postorderTraversal` (lines 104–107) to begin traversals of the tree. Each of these methods calls a recursive utility method to perform the traversal operations on the internal representation of the tree.

Class `Tree`'s `synchronized` method `insertNode` (lines 60–67) first determines whether the tree is empty. If so, line 63 allocates a new `TreeNode`, initializes the node with the integer being inserted in the tree and assigns the new node to reference `root`. If the tree is not empty, line 66 calls `TreeNode` method `insert` (lines 21–45). This method uses recursion to determine the location for the new node in the tree and inserts the node at that location. *A node can be inserted only as a leaf node in a binary search tree.*

TreeNode method insert compares the value to insert with the data value in the root node. If the insert value is less than the root node data (line 24), the program determines if the left subtree is empty (line 27). If so, line 28 allocates a new TreeNode, initializes it with the integer being inserted and assigns the new node to reference leftNode. Otherwise, line 31 recursively calls insert for the left subtree to insert the value into the left subtree. If the insert value is greater than the root node data (line 35), the program determines if the right subtree is empty (line 38). If so, line 39 allocates a new TreeNode, initializes it with the integer being inserted and assigns the new node to reference rightNode. Otherwise, line 42 recursively calls insert for the right subtree to insert the value in the right subtree. If the insertValue is already in the tree, it is simply ignored.

Methods inorderTraversal, preorderTraversal and postorderTraversal call Tree helper methods inorderHelper (lines 93–101), preorderHelper (lines 76–84) and postorderHelper (lines 110–118), respectively, to traverse the tree and print the node values. The helper methods in class Tree enable the programmer to start a traversal without having to pass the root node to the method. Reference root is an implementation detail that a programmer should not be able to access. Methods inorderTraversal, preorderTraversal and postorderTraversal simply take the private root reference and pass it to the appropriate helper method to initiate a traversal of the tree. The base case for each helper method determines whether the reference it receives is null and, if so, returns immediately.

Method inorderHelper (lines 93–101) defines the steps for an inorder traversal:

1. Traverse the left subtree with a call to inorderHelper (line 98).

2. Process the value in the node (line 99).

3. Traverse the right subtree with a call to inorderHelper (line 100).

The inorder traversal does not process the value in a node until the values in that node's left subtree are processed. The inorder traversal of the tree in Fig. 20.19 is

        6 13 17 27 33 42 48

Note that the inorder traversal of a binary search tree prints the node values in ascending order. The process of creating a binary search tree actually sorts the data; thus, this process is called the *binary tree sort*.

Method preorderHelper (lines 76–84) defines the steps for a preorder traversal:

1. Process the value in the node (line 81).

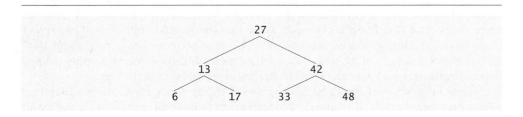

Fig. 20.19 Binary search tree with seven values.

2. Traverse the left subtree with a call to `preorderHelper` (line 82).

3. Traverse the right subtree with a call to `preorderHelper` (line 83).

The preorder traversal processes the value in each node as the node is visited. After processing the value in a given node, the preorder traversal processes the values in the left subtree, then the values in the right subtree. The preorder traversal of the tree in Fig. 20.19 is

```
27 13 6 17 42 33 48
```

Method `postorderHelper` (lines 110–118) defines the steps for a postorder traversal:

1. Traverse the left subtree with a call to `postorderHelper` (line 115).

2. Traverse the right subtree with a call to `postorderHelper` (line 116).

3. Process the value in the node (line 117).

The postorder traversal processes the value in each node after the values of all that node's children are processed. The `postorderTraversal` of the tree in Fig. 20.19 is

```
6 17 13 33 48 42 27
```

The binary search tree facilitates *duplicate elimination*. While building a tree, the insertion operation recognizes attempts to insert a duplicate value, because a duplicate follows the same "go left" or "go right" decisions on each comparison as the original value did. Thus, the insertion operation eventually compares the duplicate with a node containing the same value. At this point, the insertion operation can decide to discard the duplicate value (as we do in this example).

Searching a binary tree for a value that matches a key value is fast, especially for *tightly packed* (or *balanced*) trees. In a tightly packed tree, each level contains about twice as many elements as the previous level. Figure 20.19 is a tightly packed binary tree. A tightly packed binary search tree with n elements has $\log_2 n$ levels. Thus, at most $\log_2 n$ comparisons are required either to find a match or to determine that no match exists. Searching a (tightly packed) 1000-element binary search tree requires at most 10 comparisons, because $2^{10} > 1000$. Searching a (tightly packed) 1,000,000-element binary search tree requires at most 20 comparisons, because $2^{20} > 1,000,000$.

The chapter exercises present algorithms for several other binary tree operations, such as deleting an item from a binary tree, printing a binary tree in a two-dimensional tree format and performing a *level-order traversal of a binary tree*. The level-order traversal of a binary tree visits the nodes of the tree row-by-row, starting at the root node level. On each level of the tree, a level-order traversal visits the nodes from left to right. Other binary tree exercises include allowing a binary search tree to contain duplicate values, inserting string values in a binary tree and determining how many levels are contained in a binary tree. Chapter 21 and Chapter 22 continue our discussion of data structures by presenting the data structures in the Java API.

SUMMARY

- Dynamic data structures can grow and shrink at execution time.
- Linked lists are collections of data items "lined up in a row"—insertions and deletions can be made anywhere in a linked list.

- Stacks are important in compilers and operating systems—insertions and deletions are made only at one end of a stack, its top.

- Queues represent waiting lines; insertions are made at the tail of a queue and deletions are made from the head of a queue.

- Binary trees facilitate high-speed searching and sorting of data, eliminating duplicate data items efficiently, representing file system directories and compiling expressions into machine language.

- A self-referential class contains a reference that refers to another object of the same class type. Self-referential objects can be linked together to form dynamic data structures.

- The limit for dynamic memory allocation can be as large as the available physical memory in the computer or the amount of available disk space in a virtual-memory system. Often, the limits are much smaller because the computer's available memory must be shared among many users.

- If no memory is available, an `OutOfMemoryError` is thrown.

- A linked list is accessed via a reference to the first node of the list. Each subsequent node is accessed via the link-reference member stored in the previous node.

- By convention, the link reference in the last node of a list is set to `null` to mark the end of the list.

- A node can contain data of any type, including objects of other classes.

- A linked list is appropriate when the number of data elements to be stored is unpredictable. Linked lists are dynamic, so the length of a list can increase or decrease as necessary.

- The size of a "conventional" Java array cannot be altered—the size is fixed at creation time.

- Linked lists can be maintained in sorted order simply by inserting each new element at the proper point in the list.

- List nodes normally are not stored contiguously in memory. Rather, they are logically contiguous.

- Methods that manipulate the contents of a list should be declared `synchronized` so list objects can be *thread safe* when used in a multithreaded program. If one thread is modifying the contents of a list, no other thread is allowed to modify the same list at the same time.

- A stack is referred to as a last-in, first-out (LIFO) data structure. The primary methods used to manipulate a stack are `push` and `pop`. Method `push` adds a new node to the top of the stack. Method `pop` removes a node from the top of the stack and returns the `data` object from the popped node.

- Stacks have many interesting applications. When a method call is made, the called method must know how to return to its caller, so the return address is pushed onto the program execution stack. If a series of method calls occurs, the successive return values are pushed onto the stack in last-in, first-out order so that each method can return to its caller. The program execution stack contains the space created for local variables on each invocation of a method. When the method returns to its caller, the space for that method's local variables is popped off the stack, and those variables are no longer available to the program.

- Stacks are used by compilers to evaluate arithmetic expressions and generate machine language code to process the expressions.

- The technique of implementing each stack method as a call to a `List` method is called delegation—the stack method invoked delegates the call to the appropriate `List` method.

- A queue is similar to a checkout line in a supermarket—the first person in line is serviced first, and other customers enter the line only at the end and wait to be serviced.

- Queue nodes are removed only from the head of the queue and are inserted only at the tail of the queue. For this reason, a queue is referred to as a first-in, first-out (FIFO) data structure.

- The insert and remove operations for a queue are known as `enqueue` and `dequeue`.

- Queues have many applications in computer systems. Most computers have only a single processor, so only one user at a time can be serviced. Entries for the other users are placed in a queue. The entry at the front of the queue is the next to receive service. Each entry gradually advances to the front of the queue as users receive service.

- A tree is a nonlinear, two-dimensional data structure. Tree nodes contain two or more links.

- A binary tree is a tree whose nodes all contain two links. The root node is the first node in a tree.

- Each link in the root node refers to a child. The left child is the first node in the left subtree, and the right child is the first node in the right subtree.

- The children of a node are called siblings. A node with no children is called a leaf node.

- A binary search tree (with no duplicate node values) has the characteristic that the values in any left subtree are less than the value in its parent node, and the values in any right subtree are greater than the value in its parent node. A node can be inserted only as a leaf node in a binary search tree.

- An inorder traversal of a binary search tree processes the node values in ascending order.

- In a preorder traversal, the value in each node is processed as the node is visited. Then, the values in the left subtree are processed, then the values in the right subtree are processed.

- In a postorder traversal, the value in each node is processed after the values of its children.

- The binary search tree facilitates duplicate elimination. As the tree is created, attempts to insert a duplicate value are recognized because a duplicate follows the same "go left" or "go right" decisions on each comparison as the original value did. Thus, the duplicate eventually is compared with a node containing the same value. The duplicate value can be discarded at this point.

- Searching a binary tree for a value that matches a key value is also fast, especially for tightly packed trees. In a tightly packed tree, each level contains about twice as many elements as the previous level. So a tightly packed binary search tree with n elements has $\log_2 n$ levels, and thus at most $\log_2 n$, comparisons would have to be made either to find a match or to determine that no match exists. Searching a (tightly packed) 1000-element binary search tree requires at most 10 comparisons, because $2^{10} > 1000$. Searching a (tightly packed) 1,000,000-element binary search tree requires at most 20 comparisons, because $2^{20} > 1,000,000$.

TERMINOLOGY

balanced tree
binary search tree
binary tree
binary tree sort
child node
children of a node
delegate a method call
delete a node
dequeue
duplicate elimination
dynamic data structure
enqueue
FIFO (first-in, first-out)
head of a queue
inorder traversal of a binary tree
insert a node
leaf node
left child

left subtree
level-order traversal of a binary tree
LIFO (last-in, first-out)
linear data structure
linked list
node
nonlinear data structure
null reference
OutOfMemoryError
packed tree
parent node
pop
postorder traversal of a binary tree
predicate method
preorder traversal of a binary tree
program execution stack
push
queue

recursive tree traversal algorithms
right child
right subtree
root node
self-referential class
stack

subtree
tail of a queue
top of a stack
traversal
tree
visiting a node

SELF-REVIEW EXERCISES

20.1 Fill in the blanks in each of the following statements:
a) A self-_____ class is used to form dynamic data structures that can grow and shrink at execution time.
b) A _____ is a constrained version of a linked list in which nodes can be inserted and deleted only from the start of the list.
c) A method that does not alter a linked list, but simply looks at the list to determine whether it is empty is referred to as a _____ method.
d) A queue is referred to as a _____ data structure because the first nodes inserted are the first nodes removed.
e) The reference to the next node in a linked list is referred to as a _____.
f) Automatically reclaiming dynamically allocated memory in Java is called _____.
g) A _____ is a constrained version of a linked list in which nodes can be inserted only at the end of the list and deleted only from the start of the list.
h) A _____ is a nonlinear, two-dimensional data structure that contains nodes with two or more links.
i) A stack is referred to as a _____ data structure because the last node inserted is the first node removed.
j) The nodes of a _____ tree contain two link members.
k) The first node of a tree is the _____ node.
l) Each link in a tree node refers to a _____ or _____ of that node.
m) A tree node that has no children is called a _____ node.
n) The three traversal algorithms we mentioned in the text for binary search trees are _____, _____ and _____.

20.2 What are the differences between a linked list and a stack?

20.3 What are the differences between a stack and a queue?

20.4 Perhaps a more appropriate title for this chapter would have been "Reusable Data Structures." Comment on how each of the following entities or concepts contributes to the reusability of data structures:
a) classes
b) inheritance
c) composition

20.5 Manually provide the inorder, preorder and postorder traversals of the binary search tree of Fig. 20.20.

ANSWERS TO SELF-REVIEW EXERCISES

20.1   a)   referential. b) stack. c) predicate. d) first-in, first-out (FIFO). e) link. f) garbage collection. g) queue. h) tree i) last-in, first-out (LIFO). j) binary. k) root. l) child or subtree. m) leaf. n) inorder, preorder, postorder.

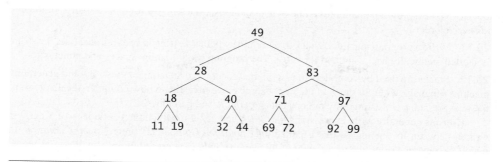

Fig. 20.20 Binary search tree with 15 nodes.

20.2   It is possible to insert a node anywhere in a linked list and remove a node from anywhere in a linked list. Nodes in a stack may only be inserted at the top of the stack and removed from the top of a stack.

20.3   A queue is a FIFO data structure that has references to both its head and its tail so that nodes may be inserted at the tail and deleted from the head. A stack is a LIFO data structure that has a single reference to the top of the stack where both insertion and deletion of nodes are performed.

20.4   a) Classes allow us to instantiate as many data structure objects of a certain type (i.e., class) as we wish.

   b) Inheritance enables a subclass to reuse the functionality from a superclass. Public methods of a superclass can be accesed through a subclass to eliminate duplicate logic.
   c) Composition enables a class to reuse code by storing an instance an instance of another class in a field. Public methods of the member class can be called by methods in the composite class.

20.5   The inorder traversal is

   11 18 19 28 32 40 44 49 69 71 72 83 92 97 99

The preorder traversal is

   49 28 18 11 19 40 32 44 83 71 69 72 97 92 99

The postorder traversal is

   11 19 18 32 44 40 28 69 72 71 92 99 97 83 49

EXERCISES

20.6   Write a program that concatenates two linked-list objects of characters. Class `ListConcatenate` should include a method `concatenate` that takes references to both list objects as arguments and concatenates the second list to the first list.

20.7   Write a program that merges two ordered-list objects of integers into a single ordered list object of integers. Method `merge` of class `ListMerge` should receive references to each of the list objects to be merged and should return a reference to the merged list object.

20.8   Write a program that inserts 25 random integers from 0 to 100 in order into a linked list object. The program should calculate the sum of the elements and the floating-point average of the elements.

20.9   Write a program that creates a linked list object of 10 characters, then creates a second list object containing a copy of the first list, but in reverse order.

20.10 Write a program that inputs a line of text and uses a stack object to print the words of the line in reverse order.

20.11 Write a program that uses a stack to determine whether a string is a palindrome (i.e., the string is spelled identically backward and forward). The program should ignore spaces and punctuation.

20.12 Stacks are used by compilers to help in the process of evaluating expressions and generating machine language code. In this and the next exercise, we investigate how compilers evaluate arithmetic expressions consisting only of constants, operators and parentheses.

Humans generally write expressions like 3 + 4 and 7 / 9 in which the operator (+ or / here) is written between its operands—this is called *infix notation*. Computers "prefer" *postfix notation*, in which the operator is written to the right of its two operands. The preceding infix expressions would appear in postfix notation as 3 4 + and 7 9 /, respectively.

To evaluate a complex infix expression, a compiler would first convert the expression to postfix notation and evaluate the postfix version of the expression. Each of these algorithms requires only a single left-to-right pass of the expression. Each algorithm uses a stack object in support of its operation, and in each algorithm, the stack is used for a different purpose.

In this exercise, you will write a Java version of the infix-to-postfix conversion algorithm. In the next exercise, you will write a Java version of the postfix expression evaluation algorithm. In a later exercise, you will discover that code you write in this exercise can help you implement a complete working compiler.

Write class `InfixToPostfixConverter` to convert an ordinary infix arithmetic expression (assume a valid expression is entered) with single-digit integers such as

    (6 + 2) * 5 - 8 / 4

to a postfix expression. The postfix version of the preceding infix expression is (note that no parentheses are needed)

    6 2 + 5 * 8 4 / -

The program should read the expression into `StringBuffer infix` and use one of the stack classes implemented in this chapter to help create the postfix expression in `StringBuffer postfix`. The algorithm for creating a postfix expression is as follows:

    a) Push a left parenthesis '(' on the stack.
    b) Append a right parenthesis ')' to the end of `infix`.
    c) While the stack is not empty, read `infix` from left to right and do the following:
        If the current character in `infix` is a digit, append it to `postfix`.
        If the current character in `infix` is a left parenthesis, push it onto the stack.
        If the current character in `infix` is an operator:
            Pop operators (if there are any) at the top of the stack while they have equal or higher precedence than the current operator, and append the popped operators to `postfix`.
            Push the current character in `infix` onto the stack.
        If the current character in `infix` is a right parenthesis:
            Pop operators from the top of the stack and append them to `postfix` until a left parenthesis is at the top of the stack.
            Pop (and discard) the left parenthesis from the stack.

The following arithmetic operations are allowed in an expression:

    +   addition
    –   subtraction
    *   multiplication
    /   division
    ^   exponentiation
    %   remainder

The stack should be maintained with stack nodes that each contain an instance variable and a reference to the next stack node. Some of the methods you may want to provide are as follows:

a) Method `convertToPostfix`, which converts the infix expression to postfix notation.
b) Method `isOperator`, which determines whether c is an operator.
c) Method `precedence`, which determines if the precedence of `operator1` (from the infix expression) is less than, equal to or greater than the precedence of `operator2` (from the stack). The method returns `true` if `operator1` has lower precedence than `operator2`. Otherwise, `false` is returned.
d) Method `stackTop` (this should be added to the stack class), which returns the top value of the stack without popping the stack.

20.13   Write class `PostfixEvaluator`, which evaluates a postfix expression such as

        6 2 + 5 * 8 4 / -

The program should read a postfix expression consisting of digits and operators into a `String-Buffer`. Using modified versions of the stack methods implemented earlier in this chapter, the program should scan the expression and evaluate it (assume it is valid) . The algorithm is as follows:

a) Append a right parenthesis (`')'`) to the end of the postfix expression. When the right-parenthesis character is encountered, no further processing is necessary.
b) When the right-parenthesis character has not been encountered, read the expression from left to right.

  If the current character is a digit do the following:

    Push its integer value on the stack (the integer value of a digit character is its value in the computer's character set minus the value of `'0'` in Unicode).

  Otherwise, if the current character is an *operator*:

    Pop the two top elements of the stack into variables x and y.
    Calculate y *operator* x.
    Push the result of the calculation onto the stack.

c) When the right parenthesis is encountered in the expression, pop the top value of the stack. This is the result of the postfix expression.

[*Note*: In b) above (based on the sample expression at the beginning of this exercises), if the operator is `'/'`, the top of the stack is 2 and the next element in the stack is 8, then pop 2 into x, pop 8 into y, evaluate 8 / 2 and push the result, 4, back on the stack. This note also applies to operator `'-'`.] The arithmetic operations allowed in an expression are:

    +   addition
    -   subtraction
    *   multiplication
    /   division
    ^   exponentiation
    %   remainder

The stack should be maintained with one of the stack classes introduced in this chapter. You may want to provide the following methods:

a) Method `evaluatePostfixExpression`, which evaluates the postfix expression.
b) Method `calculate`, which evaluates the expression op1 operator op2.
c) Method `push`, which pushes a value onto the stack.
d) Method `pop`, which pops a value off the stack.
e) Method `isEmpty`, which determines whether the stack is empty.
f) Method `printStack`, which prints the stack.

20.14   Modify the postfix evaluator program of Exercise 20.13 so that it can process integer operands larger than 9.

20.15 *(Supermarket Simulation)* Write a program that simulates a checkout line at a supermarket. The line is a queue object. Customers (i.e., customer objects) arrive in random integer intervals of from 1 to 4 minutes. Also, each customer is serviced in random integer intervals of from 1 to 4 minutes. Obviously, the rates need to be balanced. If the average arrival rate is larger than the average service rate, the queue will grow infinitely. Even with "balanced" rates, randomness can still cause long lines. Run the supermarket simulation for a 12-hour day (720 minutes), using the following algorithm:

    a) Choose a random integer between 1 and 4 to determine the minute at which the first customer arrives.

    b) At the first customer's arrival time, do the following:
        Determine customer's service time (random integer from 1 to 4).
        Begin servicing the customer.
        Schedule arrival time of next customer (random integer 1 to 4 added to the current time).

    c) For each minute of the day, consider the following:
        If the next customer arrives, proceed as follows:
            Say so.
            Enqueue the customer.
            Schedule the arrival time of the next customer.
        If service was completed for the last customer, do the following:
            Say so.
            Dequeue next customer to be serviced.
            Determine customer's service completion time (random integer from 1 to 4
                added to the current time).

Now run your simulation for 720 minutes and answer each of the following:

    a) What is the maximum number of customers in the queue at any time?

    b) What is the longest wait any one customer experiences?

    c) What happens if the arrival interval is changed from 1 to 4 minutes to 1 to 3 minutes?

20.16 Modify Fig. 20.17 and Fig. 20.18 to allow the binary tree to contain duplicates.

20.17 Write a program based on the program of Fig. 20.17 and Fig. 20.18 that inputs a line of text, tokenizes the sentence into separate words (you might want to use the `StreamTokenizer` class from the `java.io` package), inserts the words in a binary search tree and prints the inorder, preorder and post-order traversals of the tree.

20.18 In this chapter, we saw that duplicate elimination is straightforward when creating a binary search tree. Describe how you would perform duplicate elimination when using only a one-dimensional array. Compare the performance of array-based duplicate elimination with the performance of binary-search-tree-based duplicate elimination.

20.19 Write a method `depth` that receives a binary tree and determines how many levels it has.

20.20 *(Recursively Print a List Backwards)* Write a method `printListBackwards` that recursively outputs the items in a linked list object in reverse order. Write a test program that creates a sorted list of integers and prints the list in reverse order.

20.21 *(Recursively Search a List)* Write a method `searchList` that recursively searches a linked list object for a specified value. Method `searchList` should return a reference to the value if it is found; otherwise, `null` should be returned. Use your method in a test program that creates a list of integers. The program should prompt the user for a value to locate in the list.

20.22 *(Binary Tree Delete)* In this exercise, we discuss deleting items from binary search trees. The deletion algorithm is not as straightforward as the insertion algorithm. There are three cases that are encountered when deleting an item—the item is contained in a leaf node (i.e., it has no children), the item is contained in a node that has one child or the item is contained in a node that has two children.

If the item to be deleted is contained in a leaf node, the node is deleted and the reference in the parent node is set to null.

If the item to be deleted is contained in a node with one child, the reference in the parent node is set to reference the child node and the node containing the data item is deleted. This causes the child node to take the place of the deleted node in the tree.

The last case is the most difficult. When a node with two children is deleted, another node in the tree must take its place. However, the reference in the parent node cannot simply be assigned to reference one of the children of the node to be deleted. In most cases, the resulting binary search tree would not adhere to the following characteristic of binary search trees (with no duplicate values): *The values in any left subtree are less than the value in the parent node, and the values in any right subtree are greater than the value in the parent node.*

Which node is used as a *replacement node* to maintain this characteristic? It is either the node containing the largest value in the tree less than the value in the node being deleted, or the node containing the smallest value in the tree greater than the value in the node being deleted. Let us consider the node with the smaller value. In a binary search tree, the largest value less than a parent's value is located in the left subtree of the parent node and is guaranteed to be contained in the rightmost node of the subtree. This node is located by walking down the left subtree to the right until the reference to the right child of the current node is null. We are now referencing the replacement node, which is either a leaf node or a node with one child to its left. If the replacement node is a leaf node, the steps to perform the deletion are as follows:

a) Store the reference to the node to be deleted in a temporary reference variable.
b) Set the reference in the parent of the node being deleted to reference the replacement node.
c) Set the reference in the parent of the replacement node to null.
d) Set the reference to the right subtree in the replacement node to reference the right subtree of the node to be deleted.
e) Set the reference to the left subtree in the replacement node to reference the left subtree of the node to be deleted.

The deletion steps for a replacement node with a left child are similar to those for a replacement node with no children, but the algorithm also must move the child into the replacement node's position in the tree. If the replacement node is a node with a left child, the steps to perform the deletion are as follows:

a) Store the reference to the node to be deleted in a temporary reference variable.
b) Set the reference in the parent of the node being deleted to reference the replacement node.
c) Set the reference in the parent of the replacement node reference to the left child of the replacement node.
d) Set the reference to the right subtree in the replacement node reference to the right subtree of the node to be deleted.
e) Set the reference to the left subtree in the replacement node to reference the left subtree of the node to be deleted.

Write method deleteNode, which takes as its argument the value to delete. Method delete-Node should locate in the tree the node containing the value to delete and use the algorithms discussed here to delete the node. If the value is not found in the tree, the method should print a message that indicates whether the value is deleted. Modify the program of Fig. 20.17 and Fig. 20.18 to use this method. After deleting an item, call the methods inorderTraversal, preorderTraversal and postorderTraversal to confirm that the delete operation was performed correctly.

20.23 (*Binary Tree Search*) Write method binaryTreeSearch, which attempts to locate a specified value in a binary search tree object. The method should take as an argument a search key to be located. If the node containing the search key is found, the method should return a reference to that node; otherwise, the method should return a null reference.

20.24 (*Level-Order Binary Tree Traversal*) The program of Fig. 20.17 and Fig. 20.18 illustrated three recursive methods of traversing a binary tree—inorder, preorder and postorder traversals. This exercise presents the *level-order traversal* of a binary tree, in which the node values are printed level-by-level, starting at the root node level. The nodes on each level are printed from left to right. The level-order traversal is not a recursive algorithm. It uses a queue object to control the output of the nodes. The algorithm is as follows:

> a) Insert the root node in the queue.
> b) While there are nodes left in the queue, do the following:
> > Get the next node in the queue.
> > Print the node's value.
> > If the reference to the left child of the node is not null:
> > > Insert the left child node in the queue.
> > If the reference to the right child of the node is not null:
> > > Insert the right child node in the queue.

Write method `levelOrder` to perform a level-order traversal of a binary tree object. Modify the program of Fig. 20.17 and Fig. 20.18 to use this method. [*Note*: You will also need to use queue-processing methods of Fig. 20.13 in this program.]

20.25 (*Printing Trees*) Write a recursive method `outputTree` to display a binary tree object on the screen. The method should output the tree row-by-row, with the top of the tree at the left of the screen and the bottom of the tree toward the right of the screen. Each row is output vertically. For example, the binary tree illustrated in Fig. 20.20 is output as shown in Fig. 20.21.

Note that the rightmost leaf node appears at the top of the output in the rightmost column and the root node appears at the left of the output. Each column of output starts five spaces to the right of the preceding column. Method `outputTree` should receive an argument `totalSpaces` representing the number of spaces preceding the value to be output. (This variable should start at zero so the root node is output at the left of the screen.) The method uses a modified inorder traversal to output the tree—it starts at the rightmost node in the tree and works back to the left. The algorithm is as follows:

> While the reference to the current node is not null, perform the following:
> > Recursively call `outputTree` with the right subtree of the current node and
> > > `totalSpaces + 5`.
> > Use a `for` statement to count from 1 to `totalSpaces` and output spaces.
> > Output the value in the current node.
> > Set the reference to the current node to refer to the left subtree of the current node.
> > Increment `totalSpaces` by 5.

SPECIAL SECTION: BUILDING YOUR OWN COMPILER

In Exercise 7.43 and Exercise 7.44, we introduced Simpletron Machine Language (SML), and you implemented a Simpletron computer simulator to execute programs written in SML. In this section, we build a compiler that converts programs written in a high-level programming language to SML. This section "ties" together the entire programming process. You will write programs in this new high-level language, compile these programs on the compiler you build and run the programs on the simulator you built in Exercise 7.44. You should make every effort to implement your compiler in an object-oriented manner.

20.26 (*The Simple Language*) Before we begin building the compiler, we discuss a simple, yet powerful high-level language similar to early versions of the popular language Basic. We call the language *Simple*. Every Simple *statement* consists of a *line number* and a Simple *instruction*. Line numbers must appear in ascending order. Each instruction begins with one of the following Simple *commands*: `rem`, `input`, `let`, `print`, `goto`, `if/goto` or `end` (see Fig. 20.22). All commands except

```
                       99
                  97
                       92
              83
                       72
                  71
                       69
         49
                       44
                  40
                       32
              28
                       19
                  18
                       11
```

Fig. 20.21 Sample output of recursive method `outputTree`.

end can be used repeatedly. Simple evaluates only integer expressions using the +, -, * and / operators. These operators have the same precedence as in Java. Parentheses can be used to change the order of evaluation of an expression.

Our Simple compiler recognizes only lowercase letters. All characters in a Simple file should
be lowercase. (Uppercase letters result in a syntax error unless they appear in a rem statement, in
which case they are ignored.) A *variable name* is a single letter. Simple does not allow descriptive
variable names, so variables should be explained in remarks to indicate their use in a program. Simple uses only integer variables. Simple does not have variable declarations—merely mentioning a

Command	Example statement	Description
rem	50 rem this is a remark	Any text following the command rem is for documentation purposes only and is ignored by the compiler.
input	30 input x	Display a question mark to prompt the user to enter an integer. Read that integer from the keyboard and store the integer in x.
let	80 let u = 4 * (j - 56)	Assign u the value of 4 * (j - 56). Note that an arbitrarily complex expression can appear to the right of the equal sign.
print	10 print w	Display the value of w.
goto	70 goto 45	Transfer program control to line 45.
if/goto	35 if i == z goto 80	Compare i and z for equality and transfer program control to line 80 if the condition is true; otherwise, continue execution with the next statement.
end	99 end	Terminate program execution.

Fig. 20.22 Simple commands.

variable name in a program causes the variable to be declared and initialized to zero. The syntax of Simple does not allow string manipulation (reading a string, writing a string, comparing strings etc.). If a string is encountered in a Simple program (after a command other than rem), the compiler generates a syntax error. The first version of our compiler assumes that Simple programs are entered correctly. Exercise 20.29 asks the reader to modify the compiler to perform syntax error checking.

Simple uses the conditional if/goto and unconditional goto statements to alter the flow of control during program execution. If the condition in the if/goto statement is true, control is transferred to a specific line of the program. The following relational and equality operators are valid in an if/goto statement: <, >, <=, >=, == or !=. The precedence of these operators is the same as in Java.

Let us now consider several programs that demonstrate Simple's features. The first program (Fig. 20.23) reads two integers from the keyboard, stores the values in variables a and b and computes and prints their sum (stored in variable c).

The program of Fig. 20.24 determines and prints the larger of two integers. The integers are input from the keyboard and stored in s and t. The if/goto statement tests the condition s >= t. If the condition is true, control is transferred to line 90 and s is output; otherwise, t is output and control is transferred to the end statement in line 99, where the program terminates.

Simple does not provide a repetition statement (such as Java's for, while or do...while). However, Simple can simulate each of Java's repetition statements by using the if/goto and goto statements. Figure 20.25 uses a sentinel-controlled loop to calculate the squares of several integers. Each integer is input from the keyboard and stored in variable j. If the value entered is the sentinel value −9999, control is transferred to line 99, where the program terminates. Otherwise, k is assigned the square of j, k is output to the screen and control is passed to line 20, where the next integer is input.

```
 1    10 rem     determine and print the sum of two integers
 2    15 rem
 3    20 rem     input the two integers
 4    30 input a
 5    40 input b
 6    45 rem
 7    50 rem     add integers and store result in c
 8    60 let c = a + b
 9    65 rem
10    70 rem     print the result
11    80 print c
12    90 rem     terminate program execution
13    99 end
```

Fig. 20.23 Simple program that determines the sum of two integers.

```
 1    10 rem     determine and print the larger of two integers
 2    20 input s
 3    30 input t
 4    32 rem
 5    35 rem     test if s >= t
 6    40 if s >= t goto 90
 7    45 rem
 8    50 rem     t is greater than s, so print t
 9    60 print t
10    70 goto 99
```

Fig. 20.24 Simple program that finds the larger of two integers. (Part 1 of 2.)

```
11    75 rem
12    80 rem    s is greater than or equal to t, so print s
13    90 print s
14    99 end
```

Fig. 20.24 Simple program that finds the larger of two integers. (Part 2 of 2.)

```
 1    10 rem    calculate the squares of several integers
 2    20 input j
 3    23 rem
 4    25 rem    test for sentinel value
 5    30 if j == -9999 goto 99
 6    33 rem
 7    35 rem    calculate square of j and assign result to k
 8    40 let k = j * j
 9    50 print k
10    53 rem
11    55 rem    loop to get next j
12    60 goto 20
13    99 end
```

Fig. 20.25 Calculate the squares of several integers.

Using the sample programs of Fig. 20.23–Fig. 20.25 as your guide, write a Simple program to accomplish each of the following:

a) Input three integers, determine their average and print the result.

b) Use a sentinel-controlled loop to input 10 integers and compute and print their sum.

c) Use a counter-controlled loop to input 7 integers, some positive and some negative, and compute and print their average.

d) Input a series of integers and determine and print the largest. The first integer input indicates how many numbers should be processed.

e) Input 10 integers and print the smallest.

f) Calculate and print the sum of the even integers from 2 to 30.

g) Calculate and print the product of the odd integers from 1 to 9.

20.27 (*Building A Compiler; Prerequisites: Complete Exercise 7.43, Exercise 7.44, Exercise 20.12, Exercise 20.13 and Exercise 20.26*) Now that the Simple language has been presented (Exercise 20.26), we discuss how to build a Simple compiler. First, we consider the process by which a Simple program is converted to SML and executed by the Simpletron simulator (see Fig. 20.26). A file containing a Simple program is read by the compiler and converted to SML code. The SML code is output to a file on disk, in which SML instructions appear one per line. The SML file is then loaded into the Simpletron simulator, and the results are sent to a file on disk and to the screen. Note that the Simpletron program developed in Exercise 7.44 took its input from the keyboard. It must be modified to read from a file so it can run the programs produced by our compiler.

The Simple compiler performs two *passes* of the Simple program to convert it to SML. The first pass constructs a *symbol table* (object) in which every *line number* (object), *variable name* (object) and *constant* (object) of the Simple program is stored with its type and corresponding location in the final SML code (the symbol table is discussed in detail below). The first pass also produces the corresponding SML instruction object(s) for each of the Simple statements (object, etc.). If the Simple program contains statements that transfer control to a line later in the program, the first pass results in an SML program containing some "unfinished" instructions. The second pass of the compiler locates and completes the unfinished instructions and outputs the SML program to a file.

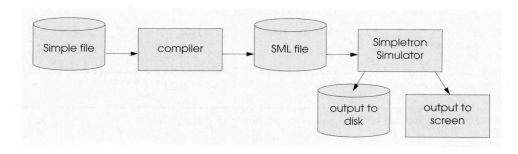

Fig. 20.26   Writing, compiling and executing a Simple language program.

First Pass

The compiler begins by reading one statement of the Simple program into memory. The line must be separated into its individual *tokens* (i.e., "pieces" of a statement) for processing and compilation. (The `StreamTokenizer` class from the `java.io` package can be used.) Recall that every statement begins with a line number followed by a command. As the compiler breaks a statement into tokens, if the token is a line number, a variable or a constant, it is placed in the symbol table. A line number is placed in the symbol table only if it is the first token in a statement. The `symbolTable` object is an array of `tableEntry` objects representing each symbol in the program. There is no restriction on the number of symbols that can appear in the program. Therefore, the `symbolTable` for a particular program could be large. Make the `symbolTable` a 100-element array for now. You can increase or decrease its size once the program is working.

Each `tableEntry` object contains three fields. Field `symbol` is an integer containing the Unicode representation of a variable (remember that variable names are single characters), a line number or a constant. Field `type` is one of the following characters indicating the symbol's type: `'C'` for constant, `'L'` for line number or `'V'` for variable. Field `location` contains the Simpletron memory location (00 to 99) to which the symbol refers. Simpletron memory is an array of 100 integers in which SML instructions and data are stored. For a line number, the location is the element in the Simpletron memory array at which the SML instructions for the Simple statement begin. For a variable or constant, the location is the element in the Simpletron memory array in which the variable or constant is stored. Variables and constants are allocated from the end of Simpletron's memory backwards. The first variable or constant is stored at location 99, the next at location 98, etc.

The symbol table plays an integral part in converting Simple programs to SML. We learned in Chapter 7 that an SML instruction is a four-digit integer comprised of two parts—the *operation code* and the *operand*. The operation code is determined by commands in Simple. For example, the simple command `input` corresponds to SML operation code 10 (read), and the Simple command `print` corresponds to SML operation code 11 (write). The operand is a memory location containing the data on which the operation code performs its task (e.g., operation code 10 reads a value from the keyboard and stores it in the memory location specified by the operand). The compiler searches `symbolTable` to determine the Simpletron memory location for each symbol, so the corresponding location can be used to complete the SML instructions.

The compilation of each Simple statement is based on its command. For example, after the line number in a `rem` statement is inserted in the symbol table, the remainder of the statement is ignored by the compiler because a remark is for documentation purposes only. The `input`, `print`, `goto` and `end` statements correspond to the SML *read, write, branch* (to a specific location) and *halt* instructions. Statements containing these Simple commands are converted directly to SML. (*Note*: A `goto` statement may contain an unresolved reference if the specified line number refers to a statement further into the Simple program file; this is sometimes called a *forward reference*.)

When a goto statement is compiled with an unresolved reference, the SML instruction must be *flagged* to indicate that the second pass of the compiler must complete the instruction. The flags are stored in a 100-element array flags of type int in which each element is initialized to -1. If the memory location to which a line number in the Simple program refers is not yet known (i.e., it is not in the symbol table), the line number is stored in array flags in the element with the same index as the incomplete instruction. The operand of the incomplete instruction is set to 00 temporarily. For example, an unconditional branch instruction (making a forward reference) is left as +4000 until the second pass of the compiler. The second pass of the compiler will be described shortly.

Compilation of if/goto and let statements is more complicated than other statements—they are the only statements that produce more than one SML instruction. For an if/goto statement, the compiler produces code to test the condition and to branch to another line if necessary. The result of the branch could be an unresolved reference. Each of the relational and equality operators can be simulated by using SML's *branch zero* and *branch negative* instructions (or possibly a combination of both).

For a let statement, the compiler produces code to evaluate an arbitrarily complex arithmetic expression consisting of integer variables and/or constants. Expressions should separate each operand and operator with spaces. Exercise 20.12 and Exercise 20.13 presented the infix-to-postfix conversion algorithm and the postfix evaluation algorithm used by compilers to evaluate expressions. Before proceeding with your compiler, you should complete each of these exercises. When a compiler encounters an expression, it converts the expression from infix notation to postfix notation, then evaluates the postfix expression.

How is it that the compiler produces the machine language to evaluate an expression containing variables? The postfix evaluation algorithm contains a "hook" where the compiler can generate SML instructions rather than actually evaluating the expression. To enable this "hook" in the compiler, the postfix evaluation algorithm must be modified to search the symbol table for each symbol it encounters (and possibly insert it), determine the symbol's corresponding memory location and *push the memory location on the stack (instead of the symbol)*. When an operator is encountered in the postfix expression, the two memory locations at the top of the stack are popped, and machine language for effecting the operation is produced by using the memory locations as operands. The result of each subexpression is stored in a temporary location in memory and pushed back onto the stack so the evaluation of the postfix expression can continue. When postfix evaluation is complete, the memory location containing the result is the only location left on the stack. This is popped, and SML instructions are generated to assign the result to the variable at the left of the let statement.

Second Pass

The second pass of the compiler performs two tasks: Resolve any unresolved references and output the SML code to a file. Resolution of references occurs as follows:

    a) Search the flags array for an unresolved reference (i.e., an element with a value other than -1).

    b) Locate the object in array symbolTable containing the symbol stored in the flags array (be sure that the type of the symbol is 'L' for line number).

    c) Insert the memory location from field location into the instruction with the unresolved reference (remember that an instruction containing an unresolved reference has operand 00).

    d) Repeat steps (a), (b) and (c) until the end of the flags array is reached.

After the resolution process is complete, the entire array containing the SML code is output to a disk file with one SML instruction per line. This file can be read by the Simpletron for execution (after the simulator is modified to read its input from a file). Compiling your first Simple program into an SML file and executing that file should give you a real sense of personal accomplishment.

A Complete Example

The following example illustrates complete conversion of a Simple program to SML as it will be performed by the Simple compiler. Consider a Simple program that inputs an integer and sums the values from 1 to that integer. The program and the SML instructions produced by the first pass of the Simple compiler are illustrated in Fig. 20.27. The symbol table constructed by the first pass is shown in Fig. 20.28.

Most Simple statements convert directly to single SML instructions. The exceptions in this program are remarks, the if/goto statement in line 20 and the let statements. Remarks do not translate into machine language. However, the line number for a remark is placed in the symbol table in case the line number is referenced in a goto statement or an if/goto statement. Line 20 of the program specifies that, if the condition y == x is true, program control is transferred to line 60. Since line 60 appears later in the program, the first pass of the compiler has not as yet placed 60 in the symbol table. (Statement line numbers are placed in the symbol table only when they appear as the first token in a statement.) Therefore, it is not possible at this time to determine the operand of the SML *branch zero* instruction at location 03 in the array of SML instructions. The compiler places 60 in location 03 of the flags array to indicate that the second pass completes this instruction.

Simple program	SML location and instruction		Description
5 rem sum 1 to x	*none*		rem ignored
10 input x	00	+1099	read x into location 99
15 rem check y == x	*none*		rem ignored
20 if y == x goto 60	01	+2098	load y (98) into accumulator
	02	+3199	sub x (99) from accumulator
	03	+4200	branch zero to unresolved location
25 rem increment y	*none*		rem ignored
30 let y = y + 1	04	+2098	load y into accumulator
	05	+3097	add 1 (97) to accumulator
	06	+2196	store in temporary location 96
	07	+2096	load from temporary location 96
	08	+2198	store accumulator in y
35 rem add y to total	*none*		rem ignored
40 let t = t + y	09	+2095	load t (95) into accumulator
	10	+3098	add y to accumulator
	11	+2194	store in temporary location 94
	12	+2094	load from temporary location 94
	13	+2195	store accumulator in t
45 rem loop y	*none*		rem ignored
50 goto 20	14	+4001	branch to location 01
55 rem output result	*none*		rem ignored
60 print t	15	+1195	output t to screen
99 end	16	+4300	terminate execution

Fig. 20.27 SML instructions produced after the compiler's first pass.

Symbol	Type	Location
5	L	00
10	L	00
'x'	V	99
15	L	01
20	L	01
'y'	V	98
25	L	04
30	L	04
1	C	97
35	L	09
40	L	09
't'	V	95
45	L	14
50	L	14
55	L	15
60	L	15
99	L	16

Fig. 20.28 Symbol table for program of Fig. 20.27.

We must keep track of the next instruction location in the SML array because there is not a one-to-one correspondence between Simple statements and SML instructions. For example, the if/goto statement of line 20 compiles into three SML instructions. Each time an instruction is produced, we must increment the *instruction counter* to the next location in the SML array. Note that the size of Simpletron's memory could present a problem for Simple programs with many statements, variables and constants. It is conceivable that the compiler will run out of memory. To test for this case, your program should contain a *data counter* to keep track of the location at which the next variable or constant will be stored in the SML array. If the value of the instruction counter is larger than the value of the data counter, the SML array is full. In this case, the compilation process should terminate, and the compiler should print an error message indicating that it ran out of memory during compilation. This serves to emphasize that, although the programmer is freed from the burdens of managing memory by the compiler, the compiler itself must carefully determine the placement of instructions and data in memory and must check for such errors as memory being exhausted during the compilation process.

A Step-by-Step View of the Compilation Process

Let us now walk through the compilation process for the Simple program in Fig. 20.27. The compiler reads the first line of the program

```
5 rem sum 1 to x
```

into memory. The first token in the statement (the line number) is determined using the String-Tokenizer class. (See Chapter 11 for a discussion of this class.) The token returned by the StringTokenizer is converted to an integer by using static method Integer.parseInt(), so the symbol 5 can be located in the symbol table. If the symbol is not found, it is inserted in the symbol table.

We are at the beginning of the program and this is the first line, and no symbols are in the table yet. Therefore, 5 is inserted into the symbol table as type L (line number) and assigned the first location in the SML array (00). Although this line is a remark, a space in the symbol table is still allocated for the line number (in case it is referenced by a `goto` or an `if/goto`). No SML instruction is generated for a `rem` statement, so the instruction counter is not incremented.

```
10 input x
```

is tokenized next. The line number 10 is placed in the symbol table as type L and assigned the first location in the SML array (00 because a remark began the program, so the instruction counter is currently 00). The command `input` indicates that the next token is a variable (only a variable can appear in an `input` statement). `input` corresponds directly to an SML operation code; therefore, the compiler simply has to determine the location of x in the SML array. Symbol x is not found in the symbol table. So, it is inserted into the symbol table as the Unicode representation of x, given type V and assigned location 99 in the SML array (data storage begins at 99 and is allocated backwards). SML code can now be generated for this statement. Operation code 10 (the SML read operation code) is multiplied by 100, and the location of x (as determined in the symbol table) is added to complete the instruction. The instruction is then stored in the SML array at location 00. The instruction counter is incremented by one, because a single SML instruction was produced.

The statement

```
15 rem    check y == x
```

is tokenized next. The symbol table is searched for line number 15 (which is not found). The line number is inserted as type L and assigned the next location in the array, 01. (Remember that `rem` statements do not produce code, so the instruction counter is not incremented.)

The statement

```
20 if y == x goto 60
```

is tokenized next. Line number 20 is inserted in the symbol table and given type L at the next location in the SML array 01. The command `if` indicates that a condition is to be evaluated. The variable y is not found in the symbol table, so it is inserted and given the type V and the SML location 98. Next, SML instructions are generated to evaluate the condition. There is no direct equivalent in SML for the `if/goto`; it must be simulated by performing a calculation using x and y and branching according to the result. If y is equal to x, the result of subtracting x from y is zero, so the *branch zero* instruction can be used with the result of the calculation to simulate the `if/goto` statement. The first step requires that y be loaded (from SML location 98) into the accumulator. This produces the instruction 01 +2098. Next, x is subtracted from the accumulator. This produces the instruction 02 +3199. The value in the accumulator may be zero, positive or negative. The operator is ==, so we want to *branch zero*. First, the symbol table is searched for the branch location (60 in this case), which is not found. So, 60 is placed in the `flags` array at location 03, and the instruction 03 +4200 is generated. (We cannot add the branch location because we have not yet assigned a location to line 60 in the SML array.) The instruction counter is incremented to 04.

The compiler proceeds to the statement

```
25 rem    increment y
```

The line number 25 is inserted in the symbol table as type L and assigned SML location 04. The instruction counter is not incremented.

When the statement

```
30 let y = y + 1
```

is tokenized, the line number 30 is inserted in the symbol table as type L and assigned SML location 04. Command let indicates that the line is an assignment statement. First, all the symbols on the line are inserted in the symbol table (if they are not already there). The integer 1 is added to the symbol table as type C and assigned SML location 97. Next, the right side of the assignment is converted from infix to postfix notation. Then the postfix expression (y 1 +) is evaluated. Symbol y is located in the symbol table, and its corresponding memory location is pushed onto the stack. Symbol 1 is also located in the symbol table, and its corresponding memory location is pushed onto the stack. When the operator + is encountered, the postfix evaluator pops the stack into the right operand of the operator and pops the stack again into the left operand of the operator, then produces the SML instructions

```
04  +2098    (load y)
05  +3097    (add 1)
```

The result of the expression is stored in a temporary location in memory (96) with instruction

```
06  +2196    (store temporary)
```

and the temporary location is pushed onto the stack. Now that the expression has been evaluated, the result must be stored in y (i.e., the variable on the left side of =). So, the temporary location is loaded into the accumulator and the accumulator is stored in y with the instructions

```
07  +2096    (load temporary)
08  +2198    (store y)
```

The reader should immediately notice that SML instructions appear to be redundant. We will discuss this issue shortly.

When the statement

```
35  rem    add y to total
```

is tokenized, line number 35 is inserted in the symbol table as type L and assigned location 09.

The statement

```
40  let t = t + y
```

is similar to line 30. The variable t is inserted in the symbol table as type V and assigned SML location 95. The instructions follow the same logic and format as line 30, and the instructions 09 +2095, 10 +3098, 11 +2194, 12 +2094 and 13 +2195 are generated. Note that the result of t + y is assigned to temporary location 94 before being assigned to t (95). Once again, the reader should note that the instructions in memory locations 11 and 12 appear to be redundant. Again, we will discuss this shortly.

The statement

```
45  rem    loop y
```

is a remark, so line 45 is added to the symbol table as type L and assigned SML location 14.

The statement

```
50  goto 20
```

transfers control to line 20. Line number 50 is inserted in the symbol table as type L and assigned SML location 14. The equivalent of goto in SML is the *unconditional branch* (40) instruction that transfers control to a specific SML location. The compiler searches the symbol table for line 20 and finds that it corresponds to SML location 01. The operation code (40) is multiplied by 100, and location 01 is added to it to produce the instruction 14 +4001.

The statement

```
55 rem    output result
```

is a remark, so line 55 is inserted in the symbol table as type L and assigned SML location 15.
   The statement

```
60 print t
```

is an output statement. Line number 60 is inserted in the symbol table as type L and assigned SML location 15. The equivalent of print in SML is operation code 11 (*write*). The location of t is determined from the symbol table and added to the result of the operation code multiplied by 100.
   The statement

```
99 end
```

is the final line of the program. Line number 99 is stored in the symbol table as type L and assigned SML location 16. The end command produces the SML instruction +4300 (43 is *halt* in SML), which is written as the final instruction in the SML memory array.
   This completes the first pass of the compiler. We now consider the second pass. The flags array is searched for values other than –1. Location 03 contains 60, so the compiler knows that instruction 03 is incomplete. The compiler completes the instruction by searching the symbol table for 60, determining its location and adding the location to the incomplete instruction. In this case, the search determines that line 60 corresponds to SML location 15, so the completed instruction 03 +4215 is produced, replacing 03 +4200. The Simple program has now been compiled successfully.
   To build the compiler, you will have to perform each of the following tasks:

   a) Modify the Simpletron simulator program you wrote in Exercise 7.44 to take its input from a file specified by the user (see Chapter 17). The simulator should output its results to a disk file in the same format as the screen output. Convert the simulator to be an object-oriented program. In particular, make each part of the hardware an object. Arrange the instruction types into a class hierarchy using inheritance. Then execute the program polymorphically simply by telling each instruction to execute itself with an executeInstruction message.

   b) Modify the infix-to-postfix evaluation algorithm of Exercise 20.12 to process multidigit integer operands and single-letter variable name operands. (*Hint*: Class StringTokenizer can be used to locate each constant and variable in an expression, and constants can be converted from strings to integers by using Integer class method parseInt.) [*Note*: The data representation of the postfix expression must be altered to support variable names and integer constants.]

   c) Modify the postfix evaluation algorithm to process multidigit integer operands and variable name operands. Also, the algorithm should now implement the "hook" discussed earlier so that SML instructions are produced rather than directly evaluating the expression. (*Hint*: Class StringTokenizer can be used to locate each constant and variable in an expression, and constants can be converted from strings to integers by using Integer class method parseInt.) [*Note*: The data representation of the postfix expression must be altered to support variable names and integer constants.]

   d) Build the compiler. Incorporate parts b) and c) for evaluating expressions in let statements. Your program should contain a method that performs the first pass of the compiler and a method that performs the second pass of the compiler. Both methods can call other methods to accomplish their tasks. Make your compiler as object oriented as possible.

20.28 (*Optimizing the Simple Compiler*) When a program is compiled and converted into SML, a set of instructions is generated. Certain combinations of instructions often repeat themselves, usually in triplets called *productions*. A production normally consists of three instructions, such as *load*, *add* and *store*. For example, Fig. 20.29 illustrates five of the SML instructions that were produced in the compilation of the program in Fig. 20.27. The first three instructions are the production that adds 1 to y. Note that instructions 06 and 07 store the accumulator value in temporary location 96, then load the value back into the accumulator so instruction 08 can store the value in location 98. Often a production is followed by a load instruction for the same location that was just stored. This code can be *optimized* by eliminating the store instruction and the subsequent load instruction that operate on the same memory location, thus enabling the Simpletron to execute the program faster. Figure 20.30 illustrates the optimized SML for the program of Fig. 20.27. Note that there are four fewer instructions in the optimized code—a memory-space savings of 25%.

1	04	+2098	*(load)*
2	05	+3097	*(add)*
3	06	+2196	*(store)*
4	07	+2096	*(load)*
5	08	+2198	*(store)*

Fig. 20.29 Unoptimized code from the program of Fig. 19.25.

Simple program	SML location and instruction		Description
5 rem sum 1 to x	*none*		rem ignored
10 input x	00	+1099	read x into location 99
15 rem check y == x	*none*		rem ignored
20 if y == x goto 60	01	+2098	load y (98) into accumulator
	02	+3199	sub x (99) from accumulator
	03	+4211	branch to location 11 if zero
25 rem increment y	*none*		rem ignored
30 let y = y + 1	04	+2098	load y into accumulator
	05	+3097	add 1 (97) to accumulator
	06	+2198	store accumulator in y (98)
35 rem add y to total	*none*		rem ignored
40 let t = t + y	07	+2096	load t from location (96)
	08	+3098	add y (98) accumulator
	09	+2196	store accumulator in t (96)
45 rem loop y	*none*		rem ignored
50 goto 20	10	+4001	branch to location 01
55 rem output result	*none*		rem ignored
60 print t	11	+1196	output t (96) to screen
99 end	12	+4300	terminate execution

Fig. 20.30 Optimized code for the program of Fig. 20.27.

20.29 (*Modifications to the Simple Compiler*) Perform the following modifications to the Simple compiler. Some of these modifications might also require modifications to the Simpletron simulator program written in Exercise 7.44.

 a) Allow the remainder operator (%) to be used in `let` statements. Simpletron Machine Language must be modified to include a remainder instruction.

 b) Allow exponentiation in a `let` statement using ^ as the exponentiation operator. Simpletron Machine Language must be modified to include an exponentiation instruction.

 c) Allow the compiler to recognize uppercase and lowercase letters in Simple statements (e.g., `'A'` is equivalent to `'a'`). No modifications to the Simpletron simulator are required.

 d) Allow `input` statements to read values for multiple variables such as `input x, y`. No modifications to the Simpletron simulator are required to perform this enhancement to the Simple compiler.

 e) Allow the compiler to output multiple values from a single `print` statement, such as `print a, b, c`. No modifications to the Simpletron simulator are required to perform this enhancement.

 f) Add syntax-checking capabilities to the compiler so error messages are output when syntax errors are encountered in a Simple program. No modifications to the Simpletron simulator are required.

 g) Allow arrays of integers. No modifications to the Simpletron simulator are required to perform this enhancement.

 h) Allow subroutines specified by the Simple commands `gosub` and `return`. Command `gosub` passes program control to a subroutine and command `return` passes control back to the statement after the `gosub`. This is similar to a method call in Java. The same subroutine can be called from many `gosub` commands distributed throughout a program. No modifications to the Simpletron simulator are required.

 i) Allow repetition statements of the form

```
for x = 2 to 10 step 2
    Simple statements
next
```

 This `for` statement loops from 2 to 10 with an increment of 2. The `next` line marks the end of the body of the `for` line. No modifications to the Simpletron simulator are required.

 j) Allow repetition statements of the form

```
for x = 2 to 10
    Simple statements
next
```

 This `for` statement loops from 2 to 10 with a default increment of 1. No modifications to the Simpletron simulator are required.

 k) Allow the compiler to process string input and output. This requires the Simpletron simulator to be modified to process and store string values. [*Hint*: Each Simpletron word (i.e., memory location) can be divided into two groups, each holding a two-digit integer. Each two-digit integer represents the Unicode decimal equivalent of a character. Add a machine-language instruction that will print a string beginning at a certain Simpletron memory location. The first half of the Simpletron word at that location is a count of the number of characters in the string (i.e., the length of the string). Each succeeding half word contains one Unicode character expressed as two decimal digits. The machine language instruction checks the length and prints the string by translating each two-digit number into its equivalent character.]

 l) Allow the compiler to process floating-point values in addition to integers. The Simpletron Simulator must also be modified to process floating-point values.

20.30　(*A Simple Interpreter*) An interpreter is a program that reads a high-level language program statement, determines the operation to be performed by the statement and executes the operation immediately. The high-level language program is not converted into machine language first. Interpreters execute more slowly than compilers do, because each statement encountered in the program being interpreted must first be deciphered at execution time. If statements are contained in a loop, the statements are deciphered each time they are encountered in the loop. Early versions of the Basic programming language were implemented as interpreters. Most Java programs are run interpretively.

　　Write an interpreter for the Simple language discussed in Exercise 20.26. The program should use the infix-to-postfix converter developed in Exercise 20.12 and the postfix evaluator developed in Exercise 20.13 to evaluate expressions in a `let` statement. The same restrictions placed on the Simple language in Exercise 20.26 should be adhered to in this program. Test the interpreter with the Simple programs written in Exercise 20.26. Compare the results of running these programs in the interpreter with the results of compiling the Simple programs and running them in the Simpletron simulator built in Exercise 7.44.

20.31　(*Insert/Delete Anywhere in a Linked List*) Our linked-list class allowed insertions and deletions at only the front and the back of the linked list. These capabilities were convenient for us when we used inheritance or composition to produce a stack class and a queue class with a minimal amount of code simply by reusing the list class. Linked lists are normally more general than those we provided. Modify the linked-list class we developed in this chapter to handle insertions and deletions anywhere in the list.

20.32　(*Lists and Queues without Tail References*) Our implementation of a linked list (Fig. 20.3) used both a `firstNode` and a `lastNode`. The `lastNode` was useful for the `insertAtBack` and `removeFromBack` methods of the `List` class. The `insertAtBack` method corresponds to the `enqueue` method of the `Queue` class.

　　Rewrite the `List` class so that it does not use a `lastNode`. Thus, any operations on the tail of a list must begin searching the list from the front. Does this affect our implementation of the `Queue` class (Fig. 20.13)?

20.33　(*Performance of Binary Tree Sorting and Searching*) One problem with the binary tree sort is that the order in which the data is inserted affects the shape of the tree—for the same collection of data, different orderings can yield binary trees of dramatically different shapes. The performance of the binary tree sorting and searching algorithms is sensitive to the shape of the binary tree. What shape would a binary tree have if its data were inserted in increasing order? in decreasing order? What shape should the tree have to achieve maximal searching performance?

20.34　(*Indexed Lists*) As presented in the text, linked lists must be searched sequentially. For large lists, this can result in poor performance. A common technique for improving list-searching performance is to create and maintain an index to the list. An index is a set of references to key places in the list. For example, an application that searches a large list of names could improve performance by creating an index with 26 entries—one for each letter of the alphabet. A search operation for a last name beginning with 'Y' would then first search the index to determine where the 'Y' entries begin, then "jump into" the list at that point and search linearly until the desired name is found. This would be much faster than searching the linked list from the beginning. Use the `List` class of Fig. 20.3 as the basis of an `IndexedList` class.

　　Write a program that demonstrates the operation of indexed lists. Be sure to include methods `insertInIndexedList`, `searchIndexedList` and `deleteFromIndexedList`.

20.35　In Section 20.5, we created a stack class from class `List` with inheritance (Fig. 20.10) and with composition (Fig. 20.12). In Section 20.6 we created a queue class from class `List` with composition (Fig. 20.13). Create a queue class by inheriting from class `List`. What are the differences between this class and the one we created with composition?

21

Java Utilities Package and Bit Manipulation

Objectives

- To understand containers, such as classes `Vector` and `Stack`, and the `Enumeration` interface.
- To be able to use `Hashtable` objects.
- To be able to use persistent hash tables manipulated with objects of class `Properties`.
- To use bit manipulation to process the individual bits in integer data.
- To be able to use `BitSet` objects.

Nothing can have value without being an object of utility.
Karl Marx

O! many a shaft at sent
Finds mark the archer little meant!
Sir Walter Scott

There was the Door to which I found no Key;
There was the Veil through which I might not see.
Edward Fitzgerald

"It's a poor sort of memory that only works backwards," the
Queen remarked.
Lewis Carroll [Charles Lutwidge Dodgson]

Not by age but by capacity is wisdom acquired.
Titus Maccius Plautus

21.1 Introduction

This chapter discusses several utility classes and interfaces in package java.util, including class *Vector*, interface *Enumeration*, class *Stack*, class *Hashtable*, class *Properties*, and class *BitSet*.

Programs use class Vector to create array-like objects that can grow and shrink dynamically as a program's data storage requirements change. We consider interface Enumeration, which enables a program to iterate through the elements of a container such as a Vector. Class Stack, a subclass of Vector, offers conventional stack operations push and pop, as well as others we did not consider in Chapter 20.

Class Hashtable provides a framework for storing keyed data in tables and retrieving that data. The chapter explains the theory of "hashing," a technique for rapidly storing and retrieving information from tables, and demonstrates Java's Hashtable class. Also, the chapter considers class Properties, which provides support for persistent hash tables—hash tables that can be written to a file via an output stream and read from a file via an input stream.

The chapter presents an extensive discussion of bit-manipulation operators, followed by a discussion of class BitSet, which enables the creation of bit-array-like objects for setting and getting individual bit values.

Chapter 22, Collections, introduces a framework for manipulating groups of objects called *collections*. Objects of type Vector, Stack and Hashtable are collections. It is recommended that new programs use the classes and interfaces presented in Chapter 22. However, many of the classes and interfaces presented in this chapter are used throughout the Java API and in third-party APIs. For this reason, it is good to be familiar with the classes and interfaces presented here. Also, classes such as Vector and Hashtable have been enhanced with the capabilities presented in Chapter 22.

21.2 Vector Class and Enumeration Interface

In most programming languages, including Java, conventional arrays are fixed in size—they cannot grow or shrink in response to an application's changing storage requirements. Class *Vector* provides the capabilities of array-like data structures that can resize themselves dynamically.

At any time, a `Vector` contains a number of elements that is less than or equal to its *capacity*. The capacity is the space that has been reserved for the `Vector`'s elements. If a `Vector` requires additional capacity, it grows by a *capacity increment* that you specify or by a default capacity increment. If you do not specify a capacity increment, the system will double the size of a `Vector` each time additional capacity is needed.

Performance Tip 21.1

Inserting additional elements into a `Vector` whose current size is less than its capacity is a relatively fast operation.

Performance Tip 21.2

It is a relatively slow operation to insert an element into a `Vector` that needs to grow larger to accommodate the new element.

Performance Tip 21.3

The default capacity increment doubles the size of the `Vector`. This may seem a waste of storage, but it is actually an efficient way for many `Vector`s to grow quickly to be "about the right size." This operation is much more efficient than growing the `Vector` each time by only as much space as it takes to hold a single element. The disadvantage is that the `Vector` might occupy more space than it requires.

Performance Tip 21.4

If storage is at a premium, use `Vector` method `trimToSize` to trim a `Vector`'s capacity to the `Vector`'s exact size. This operation optimizes a `Vector`'s use of storage. However, adding another element to the `Vector` will force the `Vector` to grow dynamically—trimming leaves no room for growth.

`Vector`s store references to `Object`s. Thus, a program can store references to any object in a `Vector`. To store values of primitive types in `Vector`s, use the type-wrapper classes (e.g., `Integer` and `Double`) from package `java.lang` to create objects that contain the primitive-type values. Figure 21.1 demonstrates class `Vector` and several of its methods. For complete information on class `Vector`, visit `java.sun.com/j2se/1.4.1/docs/api/java/util/Vector.html`.

```
1   // Fig. 21.1: VectorTest.java
2   // Using the Vector class.
3   import java.util.*;
4
5   public class VectorTest {
6      private static final String colors[] = { "red", "white", "blue" };
7
8      public VectorTest()
9      {
10        Vector vector = new Vector();
11        printVector( vector ); // print vector
12
13        // add elements to the vector
14        vector.add( "magenta" );
15
```

Fig. 21.1   `Vector` class of package `java.util`. (Part 1 of 3.)

```
16          for ( int count = 0; count < colors.length; count++ )
17             vector.add( colors[ count ] );
18
19          vector.add( "cyan" );
20          printVector( vector ); // print vector
21
22          // output the first and last elements
23          try {
24             System.out.println( "First element: " + vector.firstElement() );
25             System.out.println( "Last element: " + vector.lastElement() );
26          }
27
28          // catch exception if vector is empty
29          catch ( NoSuchElementException exception ) {
30             exception.printStackTrace();
31          }
32
33          // does vector contain "red"?
34          if ( vector.contains( "red" ) )
35             System.out.println( "\n\"red\" found at index " +
36                vector.indexOf( "red" ) + "\n" );
37          else
38             System.out.println( "\n\"red\" not found\n" );
39
40          vector.remove( "red" ); // remove the string "red"
41          System.out.println( "\"red\" has been removed" );
42          printVector( vector ); // print vector
43
44          // does vector contain "red" after remove operation?
45          if ( vector.contains( "red" ) )
46             System.out.println( "\"red\" found at index " +
47                vector.indexOf( "red" ) );
48          else
49             System.out.println( "\"red\" not found" );
50
51          // print the size and capacity of vector
52          System.out.println( "\nSize: " + vector.size() +
53             "\nCapacity: " + vector.capacity() );
54
55       } // end constructor
56
57       private void printVector( Vector vectorToOutput )
58       {
59          if ( vectorToOutput.isEmpty() )
60             System.out.print( "vector is empty" ); // vectorToOutput is empty
61
62          else { // iterate through the elements
63             System.out.print( "vector contains: " );
64             Enumeration items = vectorToOutput.elements();
65
66             while ( items.hasMoreElements() )
67                System.out.print( items.nextElement() + " " );
68          }
```

Fig. 21.1   Vector class of package java.util. (Part 2 of 3.)

```
69
70        System.out.println( "\n" );
71     }
72
73     public static void main( String args[] )
74     {
75        new VectorTest(); // create object and call its constructor
76     }
77
78  } // end class VectorTest
```

```
vector is empty

vector contains: magenta red white blue cyan

First element: magenta
Last element: cyan

"red" found at index 1

"red" has been removed
vector contains: magenta white blue cyan

"red" not found

Size: 4
Capacity: 10
```

Fig. 21.1   Vector class of package `java.util`. (Part 3 of 3.)

The application's constructor creates a Vector (line 10) with an initial capacity of 10 elements and capacity increment of zero (the defaults for a Vector). This Vector will double in size each time it needs to grow to accommodate more elements. Class Vector provides three other constructors. The constructor that takes one integer argument creates an empty Vector with the *initial capacity* specified by that argument. The constructor that takes two arguments creates a Vector with the initial capacity specified by the first argument and the *capacity increment* specified by the second argument. Each time the Vector needs to grow, it will add space for the specified number of elements in the capacity increment. The constructor that takes a `Collection` creates a copy of a collection's elements and stores them in the Vector. Chapter 22 discusses `Collections`.

Lines 14, 17 and 19 call Vector method *add* to add objects (strings in this program) to the end of the Vector. If necessary, the Vector increases its capacity to accommodate the new element. Class Vector also provides a method add that takes two arguments. This method takes an object and an integer and inserts the object at the specified index in the Vector. Method *set* will replace the element at a specified position in the Vector with a specified element. Method `insertElementAt` makes room for the new element by shifting elements.

Line 24 calls Vector method *firstElement* to return a reference to the first element in the Vector. Line 25 calls Vector method *lastElement* to return a reference to the last element in the Vector. Each of these methods throws a NoSuchElementException if there are no elements in the Vector when these methods are called.

Line 34 calls Vector method *contains* to determine whether the Vector contains "red". The method returns true if its argument is in the Vector; otherwise, the method returns false. Method contains uses Object method equals to determine whether the searchKey is equal to one of the Vector's elements. Many classes override method equals to perform the comparisons in a manner specific to those classes. For example, class String declares equals to compare the individual characters in the two Strings being compared. If method equals is not overridden, the original version of method equals inherited from class Object is used. This version performs comparisons that use operator == to determine whether two references refer to the same object in memory.

Line 36 calls Vector method *indexOf* to determine the index of the first location in the Vector that contains the argument. The method returns –1 if the argument is not found in the Vector. An overloaded version of this method takes a second argument specifying the index in the Vector at which the search should begin.

Performance Tip 21.5

Vector methods contains *and* indexOf *perform linear searches of a Vector's contents; these structures are inefficient for large Vectors. If a program frequently searches for elements in a collection, consider using a* Hashtable *(Section 21.4) or one of the Java Collection API's* Map *implementations (Chapter 22).*

Line 40 calls Vector method *remove* to remove the first occurrence of its argument from the Vector. The method returns true if it finds the element in the Vector; otherwise, the method returns false. If the element is removed, all elements after that element in the Vector shift one position toward the beginning of the Vector to fill in the position of the removed element. Class Vector also provides method *removeAllElements* to remove every element from a Vector and method *removeElementAt* to remove the element at a specified index.

Lines 52–53 use Vector methods *size* and *capacity* to determine the number of elements currently in the Vector and the number of elements that can be stored in the Vector without allocating more memory, respectively.

Line 59 calls Vector method *isEmpty* to determine whether the Vector is empty. The method returns true if there are no elements in the Vector; otherwise, the method returns false.

Line 64 calls Vector method *elements* to return an *Enumeration* that enables the program to iterate through the Vector's elements. An Enumeration provides two methods—*hasMoreElements* and *nextElement*.[1] In line 66, method hasMoreElements returns true if there are more elements in the Vector. In line 67, method nextElement returns a reference to the next Object in the Vector. If there are no more elements, method nextElement throws a NoSuchElementException.

21.3 Stack Class of Package java.util

In Chapter 20, Data Structures, we learned how to build such fundamental data structures as linked lists, stacks, queues and trees. In a world of software reuse, rather than building

---

1. In Chapter 22, we introduce a similar interface called Iterator, which is more flexible than Enumeration and is generally preferred. We demonstrate Enumerations here because they are used with some of the older classes in the Java API.

data structures as we need them, we can often take advantage of existing data structures. In this section, we investigate class *Stack* in the Java utilities package (`java.util`).

Section 21.2 discussed class `Vector`, which implements a dynamically resizable array. Class `Stack` extends class `Vector` to implement a stack data structure that stores references to `Objects`. To store primitive types, use the appropriate type-wrapper class from package `java.util` to create an object containing the primitive-type value. Figure 21.2 demonstrates several `Stack` methods. For complete information on class `Stack`, visit `java.sun.com/j2se/1.4.1/docs/api/java/util/Stack.html`.

```java
1   // Fig. 21.2: StackTest.java
2   // Program to test java.util.Stack.
3   import java.util.*;
4
5   public class StackTest {
6
7       public StackTest()
8       {
9           Stack stack = new Stack();
10
11          // create objects to store in the stack
12          Boolean bool = Boolean.TRUE;
13          Character character = new Character( '$' );
14          Integer integer = new Integer( 34567 );
15          String string = "hello";
16
17          // use push method
18          stack.push( bool );
19          printStack( stack );
20          stack.push( character );
21          printStack( stack );
22          stack.push( integer );
23          printStack( stack );
24          stack.push( string );
25          printStack( stack );
26
27          // remove items from stack
28          try {
29              Object removedObject = null;
30
31              while ( true ) {
32                  removedObject = stack.pop(); // use pop method
33                  System.out.println( removedObject.toString() + " popped" );
34                  printStack( stack );
35              }
36          }
37
38          // catch exception if stack is empty when item popped
39          catch ( EmptyStackException emptyStackException ) {
40              emptyStackException.printStackTrace();
41          }
42      }
```

Fig. 21.2 Stack class of package `java.util`. (Part 1 of 2.)

```
43
44      private void printStack( Stack stack )
45      {
46         if ( stack.isEmpty() )
47            System.out.print( "stack is empty" ); // the stack is empty
48
49         else {
50            System.out.print( "stack contains: " );
51            Enumeration items = stack.elements();
52
53            // iterate through the elements
54            while ( items.hasMoreElements() )
55               System.out.print( items.nextElement() + " " );
56         }
57
58         System.out.println( "\n" ); // go to the next line
59      }
60
61      public static void main( String args[] )
62      {
63         new StackTest();
64      }
65
66   } // end class StackTest
```

```
stack contains: true

stack contains: true $

stack contains: true $ 34567

stack contains: true $ 34567 hello

hello popped
stack contains: true $ 34567

34567 popped
stack contains: true $

$ popped
stack contains: true

true popped
stack is empty

java.util.EmptyStackException
        at java.util.Stack.peek(Stack.java:79)
        at java.util.Stack.pop(Stack.java:61)
        at StackTest.<init>(StackTest.java:32)
        at StackTest.main(StackTest.java:63)
```

Fig. 21.2   Stack class of package java.util. (Part 2 of 2.)

Line 9 of the constructor creates an empty `Stack`. Lines 18, 20, 22 and 24 each call `Stack` method *push* to add objects to the top of the stack.

Line 32 in the infinite `while` loop calls `Stack` method *pop* to remove the top element of the stack. The method returns an `Object` reference to the removed element. If there are no elements in the `Stack`, method pop throws an *EmptyStackException*, which will terminate the loop in this program. Class `Stack` also declares method *peek*. This method returns the top element of the stack without popping the element off the stack.

Line 46 calls `Stack` method `isEmpty` (inherited by `Stack` from class `Vector`) to determine whether the stack is empty. If it is empty, the method returns `true`; otherwise, the method returns `false`.

Method `printStack` (lines 44–59) uses an `Enumeration` to iterate through the elements in the stack. The current top of the stack (the last value pushed onto the stack) is the last value printed. Because class `Stack` extends class `Vector`, the entire `public` interface of class `Vector` is available to clients of class `Stack`. For example, method `printStack` invokes method `elements` (line 51) to get an `Enumeration` of the stack.

Error-Prevention Tip 21.1

A program can perform on Stack objects Vector operations that are ordinarily not allowed on conventional stack data structures. This could "corrupt" the elements of the Stack and destroy the integrity of the Stack. When manipulating a Stack, only methods push and pop should be used to add elements to and remove elements from the Stack.

21.4 Hashtable Class

Object-oriented programming languages facilitate creating new types. When a program creates objects of new or existing types, it needs to manage those objects efficiently. This task includes storing and retrieving objects. Storing and retrieving information with arrays is efficient if some aspect of your data directly matches a numerical key value and if those keys are unique and tightly packed. If you have 100 employees with nine-digit Social Security numbers and you want to store and retrieve employee data by using the Social Security number as a key, the task would require an array with one billion elements, because there are one billion unique nine-digit numbers (000,000,000–999,999,999). This is impractical for virtually all applications that use Social Security numbers as keys. If the program could have an array that large, the program could get high performance for both storing and retrieving employee records by simply using the Social Security number as the array index.

There are numerous applications that have this problem, namely, that either the keys are of the wrong type (e.g., not positive integers) or they are of the right type, but sparsely spread over a huge range. What is needed is a high-speed scheme for converting keys such as Social Security numbers, inventory part numbers and the like into unique array indices. Then, when an application needs to store something, the scheme could convert the application's key rapidly into an index, and the record of information could be stored at that slot in the array. Retrieval is accomplished the same way: Once the application has a key for which it wants to retrieve a data record, the application simply applies the conversion to the key—this produces the array index where the data is stored, and the data is retrieved.

The scheme we describe here is the basis of a technique called *hashing*. Why the name? When we convert a key into an array index, we literally scramble the bits, forming a kind of "mishmashed," or hashed, number. The number actually has no real significance beyond its usefulness in storing and retrieving a particular data record.

A glitch in the scheme occurs when *collisions* occur—i.e., when two different keys "hash into" the same cell (or element) in the array. We cannot store two values in the same space, so we need to find an alternative home for all values beyond the first that hash to a particular array index. There are many schemes for doing this. One is to "hash again" (i.e., to apply another hashing transformation to the key to provide a next candidate cell in the array). The hashing process is designed to distribute the values throughout the table, so the assumption is that, with just a few hashes, an available cell will be found.

Another scheme uses one hash to locate the first candidate cell. If that cell is occupied, successive cells are searched linearly until an available cell is found. Retrieval works the same way: The key is hashed once to determine the initial location and check whether it contains the desired data. If it does, the search is finished. If it does not, successive cells are searched linearly until the desired data is found.

The most popular solution to hash-table collisions is to have each cell of the table be a hash "bucket," typically a linked list of all the key–value pairs that hash to that cell. This is the solution that Java's Hashtable class (from package java.util) implements. A *Hashtable* maps *keys* to *values*.

A hash table's *load factor* affects the performance of hashing schemes. The load factor is the ratio of the number of occupied cells in the hash table to the size of the hash table. The closer this ratio gets to 1.0, the greater the chance of collisions.

Performance Tip 21.6

The load factor in a hash table is a classic example of a memory-space/execution-time trade-off: By increasing the load factor, we get better memory utilization, but the program runs slower, due to increased hashing collisions. By decreasing the load factor, we get better program speed, because of reduced hashing collisions, but we get poorer memory utilization, because a larger portion of the hash table remains empty.

The complexity of programming hash tables properly is high for most casual programmers. Computer science students study hashing schemes thoroughly in courses called "Data Structures" and "Algorithms." Recognizing the value of hashing to most programmers, Java's designers provided class Hashtable to enable programmers to use hashing without having to implement the messy details.[2]

Figure 21.3 provides a GUI that uses several Hashtable methods. Line 21 creates an empty Hashtable with a default capacity (11 elements) and a default load factor (0.75). When the number of occupied slots in the Hashtable becomes greater than the capacity times the load factor, the table grows larger. Class Hashtable also provides a constructor that takes one argument specifying the capacity and a constructor that takes two arguments specifying the capacity and the load factor, respectively.

---

2. This concept is profoundly important in our study of object-oriented programming. As discussed in earlier chapters, classes encapsulate and hide complexity (i.e., implementation details) and offer user-friendly interfaces. Properly crafting classes to exhibit such behavior is one of the most valued skills in the field of object-oriented programming.

```
1    // Fig. 21.3: WordTypeCount.java
2    // Count the number of occurrences of each word in a string.
3    import java.awt.*;
4    import java.awt.event.*;
5    import java.util.*;
6    import javax.swing.*;
7
8    public class WordTypeCount extends JFrame {
9       private JTextArea inputField;
10      private JLabel prompt;
11      private JTextArea display;
12      private JButton goButton;
13
14      private Hashtable table;
15
16      public WordTypeCount()
17      {
18         super( "Word Type Count" );
19         inputField = new JTextArea( 3, 20 );
20
21         table = new Hashtable();
22
23         goButton = new JButton( "Go" );
24         goButton.addActionListener(
25
26            new ActionListener() { // anonymous inner class
27
28               public void actionPerformed( ActionEvent event )
29               {
30                  createTable();
31                  display.setText( createOutput() );
32               }
33
34            }  // end anonymous inner class
35
36         ); // end call to addActionListener
37
38         prompt = new JLabel( "Enter a string:" );
39         display = new JTextArea( 15, 20 );
40         display.setEditable( false );
41
42         JScrollPane displayScrollPane = new JScrollPane( display );
43
44         // add components to GUI
45         Container container = getContentPane();
46         container.setLayout( new FlowLayout() );
47         container.add( prompt );
48         container.add( inputField );
49         container.add( goButton );
50         container.add( displayScrollPane );
51
52         setSize( 400, 400 );
53         setVisible( true );
```

Fig. 21.3   Hashtable class of package java.util. (Part 1 of 3.)

```
54
55        } // end constructor
56
57        // create table from user input
58        private void createTable() {
59           String input = inputField.getText();
60           StringTokenizer words = new StringTokenizer( input, " \n\t\r" );
61
62           while ( words.hasMoreTokens() ) {
63              String word = words.nextToken().toLowerCase(); // get word
64
65              // if the table contains the word
66              if ( table.containsKey( word ) ) {
67
68                 Integer count = (Integer) table.get( word ); // get value
69
70                 // and increment it
71                 table.put( word, new Integer( count.intValue() + 1 ) );
72              }
73              else // otherwise add the word with a value of 1
74                 table.put( word, new Integer( 1 ) );
75
76           } // end while
77
78        } // end method createTable
79
80        // create string containing table values
81        private String createOutput() {
82           String output = "";
83           Enumeration keys = table.keys();
84
85           // iterate through the keys
86           while ( keys.hasMoreElements() ) {
87              Object currentKey = keys.nextElement();
88
89              // output the key-value pairs
90              output += currentKey + "\t" + table.get( currentKey ) + "\n";
91           }
92
93           output += "size: " + table.size() + "\n";
94           output += "isEmpty: " + table.isEmpty() + "\n";
95
96           return output;
97
98        } // end method createOutput
99
100       public static void main( String args[] )
101       {
102          WordTypeCount application = new WordTypeCount();
103          application.setDefaultCloseOperation( JFrame.EXIT_ON_CLOSE );
104       }
105
106  } // end class WordTypeCount
```

Fig. 21.3   Hashtable class of package `java.util`. (Part 2 of 3.)

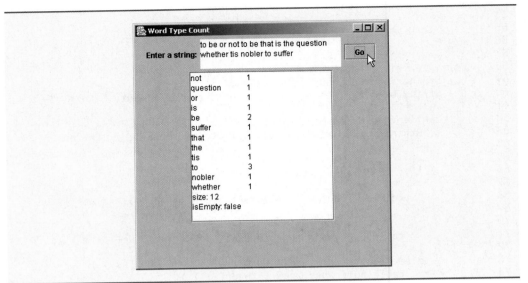

Fig. 21.3   Hashtable class of package java.util. (Part 3 of 3.)

When the user enters a string and presses **Go**, line 30 calls method createTable (lines 58–78). Line 66 calls Hashtable method *containsKey* to determine whether the key specified as an argument is in the hash table (i.e., a value is associated with that key).[3] If so, the method returns true; otherwise, the method returns false. If the key is not in the hash table, line 74 calls Hashtable method put to add a *key* (the word) and a *value* (an Integer object containing 1) into the hash-table. Method put returns the original value for that key in the hash table, or null if key has not been inserted in the hash table previously; this procedure helps the program manage cases in which it intends to replace the value stored for a given key. If either the key or the value is null, a NullPointerException occurs.

If the key is in the hash table, Line 68 calls Hashtable method get to locate the value associated with the key specified as an argument. If the key is not present in the table, the method will return null. Line 71 calls Hashtable method put to replace the count for the word in the hash table.

Method createOutput (lines 81–98) uses an Enumeration to output every value in the table. Line 93 calls method size to return the number of key–value pairs in the hash table. Line 94 calls method isEmpty to determine whether the hash table is empty. For more information on class Hashtable and its methods, visit java.sun.com/j2se/ 1.4.1/docs/api/java/util/Hashtable.html.

21.5 Properties Class

A *Properties* object is a persistent Hashtable that normally stores key–value pairs of strings—assuming that you use methods *setProperty* and *getProperty* to manipulate the table rather than inherited Hashtable methods put and get. By "persistent," we mean

---

3.   Class Hashtable also provides method *contains* to determine whether the Object specified as its argument is in the Hashtable.

that the `Properties` object can be written to an output stream (possibly a file) and read back in through an input stream. In fact, most objects in Java can be output and input with Java's object serialization, presented in Chapter 17.

A common use of `Properties` objects in prior versions of Java was to maintain application-configuration data or user preferences for applications. A new feature of the Java 2 Platform Standard Edition, Version 1.4, is the *Preferences API*, which is meant to replace the use of class `Properties` with a more robust mechanism for maintaining configuration and preference data. For more information on the Preferences API, visit `java.sun.com/j2se/1.4.1/docs/guide/lang/preferences.html`.

Class `Properties` extends class `Hashtable`, so `Properties` objects have the methods discussed in Fig. 21.3. Class `Properties` provides additional methods that are demonstrated in Fig. 21.4.

```java
1   // Fig. 21.4: PropertiesTest.java
2   // Demonstrates class Properties of the java.util package.
3   import java.awt.*;
4   import java.awt.event.*;
5   import java.io.*;
6   import java.util.*;
7   import javax.swing.*;
8
9   public class PropertiesTest extends JFrame {
10      private JLabel statusLabel;
11      private Properties table;
12      private JTextArea displayArea;
13      private JTextField valueField, nameField;
14
15      // set up GUI to test Properties table
16      public PropertiesTest()
17      {
18         super( "Properties Test" );
19
20         table = new Properties(); // create Properties table
21
22         Container container = getContentPane();
23
24         // set up NORTH of window's BorderLayout
25         JPanel northSubPanel = new JPanel();
26
27         northSubPanel.add( new JLabel( "Property value" ) );
28         valueField = new JTextField( 10 );
29         northSubPanel.add( valueField );
30
31         northSubPanel.add( new JLabel( "Property name (key)" ) );
32         nameField = new JTextField( 10 );
33         northSubPanel.add( nameField );
34
35         JPanel northPanel = new JPanel();
36         northPanel.setLayout( new BorderLayout() );
37         northPanel.add( northSubPanel, BorderLayout.NORTH );
```

Fig. 21.4   `Properties` class of package `java.util`. (Part 1 of 6.)

```
38
39          statusLabel = new JLabel();
40          northPanel.add( statusLabel, BorderLayout.SOUTH );
41
42          container.add( northPanel, BorderLayout.NORTH );
43
44          // set up CENTER of window's BorderLayout
45          displayArea = new JTextArea( 4, 35 );
46          container.add( new JScrollPane( displayArea ),
47             BorderLayout.CENTER );
48
49          // set up SOUTH of window's BorderLayout
50          JPanel southPanel = new JPanel();
51          southPanel.setLayout( new GridLayout( 1, 5 ) );
52
53          // button to put a name-value pair in Properties table
54          JButton putButton = new JButton( "Put" );
55          southPanel.add( putButton );
56
57          putButton.addActionListener(
58
59             new ActionListener() { // anonymous inner class
60
61                // put name-value pair in Properties table
62                public void actionPerformed( ActionEvent event )
63                {
64                   Object value = table.setProperty(
65                      nameField.getText(), valueField.getText() );
66
67                   if ( value == null )
68                      showstatus( "Put: " + nameField.getText() +
69                         " " + valueField.getText() );
70
71                   else
72                      showstatus( "Put: " + nameField.getText() + " " +
73                         valueField.getText() + "; Replaced: " + value );
74
75                   listProperties();
76                }
77
78             } // end anonymous inner class
79
80          ); // end call to addActionListener
81
82          // button to empty contents of Properties table
83          JButton clearButton = new JButton( "Clear" );
84          southPanel.add( clearButton );
85
86          clearButton.addActionListener(
87
88             new ActionListener() { // anonymous inner class
89
```

Fig. 21.4   Properties class of package java.util. (Part 2 of 6.)

```
90                // use method clear to empty table
91                public void actionPerformed( ActionEvent event )
92                {
93                   table.clear();
94                   showstatus( "Table in memory cleared" );
95                   listProperties();
96                }
97
98           } // end anonymous inner class
99
100    ); // end call to addActionListener
101
102    // button to get value of a property
103    JButton getPropertyButton = new JButton( "Get property" );
104    southPanel.add( getPropertyButton );
105
106    getPropertyButton.addActionListener(
107
108        new ActionListener() { // anonymous inner class
109
110                // use method getProperty to obtain a property value
111                public void actionPerformed( ActionEvent event )
112                {
113                   Object value = table.getProperty(
114                      nameField.getText() );
115
116                   if ( value != null )
117                      showstatus( "Get property: " + nameField.getText() +
118                         " " + value.toString() );
119
120                   else
121                      showstatus( "Get: " + nameField.getText() +
122                         " not in table" );
123
124                   listProperties();
125                }
126
127           } // end anonymous inner class
128
129    ); // end call to addActionListener
130
131    // button to save contents of Properties table to file
132    JButton saveButton = new JButton( "Save" );
133    southPanel.add( saveButton );
134
135    saveButton.addActionListener(
136
137        new ActionListener() { // anonymous inner class
138
139                // use method save to place contents in file
140                public void actionPerformed( ActionEvent event )
141                {
```

Fig. 21.4   Properties class of package java.util. (Part 3 of 6.)

```
142                    // save contents of table
143                    try {
144                       FileOutputStream output =
145                          new FileOutputStream( "props.dat" );
146
147                       table.store( output, "Sample Properties" );
148                       output.close();
149
150                       listProperties();
151                    }
152
153                    // process problems with file output
154                    catch( IOException ioException ) {
155                       ioException.printStackTrace();
156                    }
157                 }
158
159           } // end anonymous inner class
160
161        ); // end call to addActionListener
162
163        // button to load contents of Properties table from file
164        JButton loadButton = new JButton( "Load" );
165        southPanel.add( loadButton );
166
167        loadButton.addActionListener(
168
169           new ActionListener() { // anonymous inner class
170
171              // use method load to read contents from file
172              public void actionPerformed( ActionEvent event )
173              {
174                 // load contents of table
175                 try {
176                    FileInputStream input =
177                       new FileInputStream( "props.dat" );
178
179                    table.load( input );
180                    input.close();
181                    listProperties();
182                 }
183
184                 // process problems with file input
185                 catch( IOException ioException ) {
186                    ioException.printStackTrace();
187                 }
188              }
189
190           } // end anonymous inner class
191
192        ); // end call to addActionListener
193
194        container.add( southPanel, BorderLayout.SOUTH );
```

Fig. 21.4   Properties class of package java.util. (Part 4 of 6.)

```
195
196          setSize( 550, 225 );
197          setVisible( true );
198
199     } // end constructor
200
201     // output property values
202     public void listProperties()
203     {
204          StringBuffer buffer = new StringBuffer();
205          String name, value;
206
207          Enumeration enumeration = table.propertyNames();
208
209          while ( enumeration.hasMoreElements() ) {
210             name = enumeration.nextElement().toString();
211             value = table.getProperty( name );
212
213             buffer.append( name ).append( '\t' );
214             buffer.append( value ).append( '\n' );
215          }
216
217          displayArea.setText( buffer.toString() );
218     }
219
220     // display String in statusLabel label
221     public void showstatus( String s )
222     {
223          statusLabel.setText( s );
224     }
225
226     public static void main( String args[] )
227     {
228          PropertiesTest application = new PropertiesTest();
229          application.setDefaultCloseOperation( JFrame.EXIT_ON_CLOSE );
230     }
231
232 } // end class PropertiesTest
```

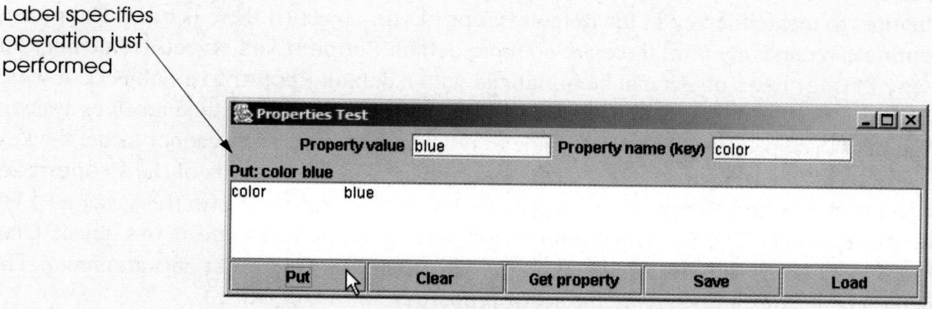

Label specifies operation just performed

Fig. 21.4   Properties class of package java.util. (Part 5 of 6.)

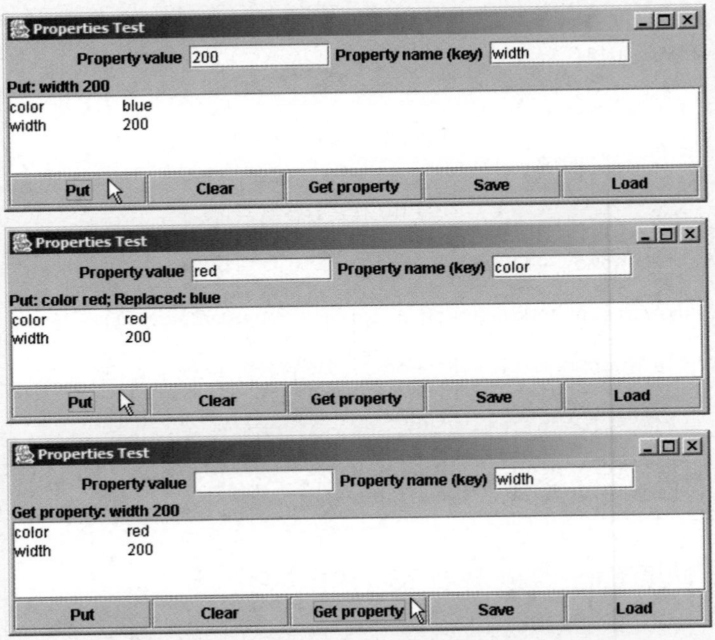

Fig. 21.4   `Properties` class of package `java.util`. (Part 6 of 6.)

Line 20 uses the no-argument constructor to create an empty `Properties` table with no default properties. Class `Properties` also provides an overloaded constructor that receives a reference to a `Properties` object containing default property values.

Lines 64–65 call `Properties` method `setProperty` to store a value for the specified key. If the key does not exist in the table, `setProperty` returns `null`; otherwise, it returns the previous value for that key.

Lines 113–114 call `Properties` method `getProperty` to locate the value associated with the specified key. If the key is not found in this `Properties` object, `getProperty` attempts to locate the key in the default `Properties` object (if there is one). The process continues recursively until there are no more default `Properties` objects (remember that every `Properties` object can be initialized with a default `Properties` object), at which point `getProperty` returns `null`. An overloaded version of this method receives a second argument that specifies the default value to return if `getProperty` cannot locate the key.

Line 147 calls `Properties` method *store* to save the contents of the `Properties` object to the `OutputStream` object specified as the first argument (in this case, a `File-OutputStream`). The `String` argument is a description of the `Properties` object. Class `Properties` also provides method *list*, which takes a `PrintStream` argument. This method is useful for displaying the set of properties.

Error-Prevention Tip 21.2

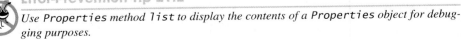

Use `Properties` method list to display the contents of a `Properties` object for debugging purposes.

Line 179 calls `Properties` method *load* to restore the contents of the `Properties` object from the `InputStream` specified as the first argument (in this case, a `FileInputStream`). Line 207 calls `Properties` method *propertyNames* to obtain an `Enumeration` of the property names. The value of each property can be determined by using method `getProperty`.

21.6 Bit Manipulation and the Bitwise Operators

Java provides extensive bit-manipulation capabilities for programmers who need to get down to the "bits-and-bytes" level. Operating systems, test equipment software, networking software and many other kinds of software require that the programmer communicate "directly with the hardware." We now discuss Java's bit-manipulation capabilities and bitwise operators.

Computers represent all data internally as sequences of bits. Each bit can assume the value 0 or the value 1. On most systems, a sequence of eight bits forms a byte—the standard storage unit for a variable of type `byte`. Other types are stored in larger numbers of bytes. The bitwise operators can manipulate the bits of integral operands (i.e., operations of type `byte`, `char`, `short`, `int` and `long`), but not floating-point operands.

Note that the discussions of bitwise operators in this section show the binary representations of the integer operands. For a detailed explanation of the binary (also called base 2) number system, see Appendix C, Number Systems.

The bitwise operators are *bitwise AND (&)*, *bitwise inclusive OR (|)*, *bitwise exclusive OR (^)*, *left shift (<<)*, *signed right shift (>>)*, *unsigned right shift (>>>)* and *bitwise complement (~)*. The bitwise AND, bitwise inclusive OR and bitwise exclusive OR operators compare their two operands bit by bit. The bitwise AND operator sets each bit in the result to 1 if and only if the corresponding bit in both operands is 1. The bitwise inclusive OR operator sets each bit in the result to 1 if the corresponding bit in either (or both) operand(s) is 1. The bitwise exclusive OR operator sets each bit in the result to 1 if the corresponding bit in exactly one operand is 1. The left-shift operator shifts the bits of its left operand to the left by the number of bits specified in its right operand. The signed right shift operator shifts the bits in its left operand to the right by the number of bits specified in its right operand—if the left operand is negative, 1s are shifted in from the left; otherwise, 0s are shifted in from the left. The unsigned right shift operator shifts the bits in its left operand to the right by the number of bits specified in its right operand—0s are shifted in from the left. The bitwise complement operator sets all 0 bits in its operand to 1 in the result and sets all 1 bits in this operation to 0 in the result. The bitwise operators are summarized in Fig. 21.5.

Operator	Name	Description
&	bitwise AND	The bits in the result are set to 1 if the corresponding bits in the two operands are both 1.
|	bitwise inclusive OR	The bits in the result are set to 1 if at least one of the corresponding bits in the two operands is 1.

Fig. 21.5   Bitwise operators. (Part 1 of 2.)

Operator	Name	Description
^	bitwise exclusive OR	The bits in the result are set to 1 if exactly one of the corresponding bits in the two operands is 1.
<<	left shift	Shifts the bits of the first operand left by the number of bits specified by the second operand; fill from the right with 0.
>>	signed right shift	Shifts the bits of the first operand right by the number of bits specified by the second operand. If the first operand is negative, 1s are filled in from the left; otherwise, 0s are filled in from the left.
>>>	unsigned right shift	Shifts the bits of the first operand right by the number of bits specified by the second operand; 0s are filled in from the left.
~	bitwise complement	All 0 bits are set to 1, and all 1 bits are set to 0.

Fig. 21.5   Bitwise operators. (Part 2 of 2.)

When using the bitwise operators, it is useful to display values in their binary representation to illustrate the effects of these operators. The application of Fig. 21.6 allows the user to enter an integer into a JTextField. Method actionPerformed (lines 29–33) reads the string from the JTextField, converts it to an integer and invokes method getBits (lines 52–73) to obtain a string representation of the integer, in bits. The result is displayed in outputField. The integer is displayed in its binary representation in groups of eight bits each. Line 63 of method getBits uses the bitwise AND operator to combine variable value with variable displayMask. Often, the bitwise AND operator is used with an operand called a *mask*—an integer value with specific bits set to 1. Masks are used to hide some bits in a value while selecting other bits. In getBits, mask variable displayMask is assigned the value 1 << 31, or

    10000000 00000000 00000000 00000000

The left-shift operator shifts the value 1 from the low-order (rightmost) bit to the high-order (leftmost) bit in displayMask and fills in 0 from the right.

```
1   // Fig. 21.6: PrintBits.java
2   // Printing an unsigned integer in bits.
3   import java.awt.*;
4   import java.awt.event.*;
5   import javax.swing.*;
6
7   public class PrintBits extends JFrame {
8      private JTextField outputField;
9
10     // set up GUI
11     public PrintBits()
12     {
13        super( "Printing bit representations for numbers" );
```

Fig. 21.6   Printing the bits in an integer. (Part 1 of 3.)

```
14
15          Container container = getContentPane();
16          container.setLayout( new FlowLayout() );
17
18          container.add( new JLabel( "Enter an integer " ) );
19
20          // textfield to read value from user
21          JTextField inputField = new JTextField( 10 );
22          container.add( inputField );
23
24          inputField.addActionListener(
25
26             new ActionListener() { // anonymous inner class
27
28                // read integer and get bitwise representation
29                public void actionPerformed( ActionEvent event )
30                {
31                   int value = Integer.parseInt( event.getActionCommand() );
32                   outputField.setText( getBits( value ) );
33                }
34
35             } // end anonymous inner class
36
37          ); // end call to addActionListener
38
39          container.add( new JLabel( "The integer in bits is" ) );
40
41          // textfield to display integer in bitwise form
42          outputField = new JTextField( 33 );
43          outputField.setEditable( false );
44          container.add( outputField );
45
46          setSize( 720, 70 );
47          setVisible( true );
48
49       } // end constructor
50
51       // display bit representation of specified int value
52       private String getBits( int value )
53       {
54          // create int value with 1 in leftmost bit and 0s elsewhere
55          int displayMask = 1 << 31;
56
57          StringBuffer buffer = new StringBuffer( 35 ); // buffer for output
58
59          // for each bit append 0 or 1 to buffer
60          for ( int bit = 1; bit <= 32; bit++ ) {
61
62             // use displayMask to isolate bit
63             buffer.append( ( value & displayMask ) == 0 ? '0' : '1' );
64
65             value <<= 1; // shift value one position to left
66
```

Fig. 21.6   Printing the bits in an integer. (Part 2 of 3.)

```
67                if ( bit % 8 == 0 )
68                    buffer.append( ' ' ); // append space to buffer every 8 bits
69            }
70
71            return buffer.toString();
72
73        } // end method getBits
74
75        public static void main( String args[] )
76        {
77            PrintBits application = new PrintBits();
78            application.setDefaultCloseOperation( JFrame.EXIT_ON_CLOSE );
79        }
80
81    } // end class PrintBits
```

Printing bit representations for numbers		_ □ ×
Enter an integer 0	The integer in bits is	00000000 00000000 00000000 00000000

Printing bit representations for numbers		_ □ ×
Enter an integer -1	The integer in bits is	11111111 11111111 11111111 11111111

Printing bit representations for numbers		_ □ ×
Enter an integer 65535	The integer in bits is	00000000 00000000 11111111 11111111

Fig. 21.6   Printing the bits in an integer. (Part 3 of 3.)

Line 63 determines whether the current leftmost bit of variable value is a 1 or 0 and appends '1' or '0', respectively, to buffer. Assume that value contains 2000000000 (01110111 00110101 10010100 00000000). When value and displayMask are combined using &, all the bits except the high-order (leftmost) bit in variable value are "masked off" (hidden), because any bit "ANDed" with 0 yields 0. If the leftmost bit is 1, the expression value & displayMask evaluates to a nonzero, value and line 63 appends '1'; otherwise, line 63 appends '0'. Then line 65 left shifts variable value to the left by one bit with the expression value <<= 1. (This expression is equivalent to value = value << 1.) These steps are repeated for each bit in variable value. At the end of method getBits, line 71 converts the StringBuffer to a String and returns the String. [*Note:* Class Integer provides method *toBinaryString*, which returns a string containing the binary representation of an integer.] Figure 21.7 summarizes the results of combining two bits with the bitwise AND (&) operator.

Common Programming Error 21.1

Using the conditional AND operator (&&) instead of the bitwise AND operator (&).

Bit 1	Bit 2	Bit 1 & Bit 2
0	0	0
1	0	0
0	1	0
1	1	1

Fig. 21.7   Bitwise AND operator (&) combining two bits.

Figure 21.8 demonstrates the bitwise AND operator, the bitwise inclusive OR operator, the bitwise exclusive OR operator and the bitwise complement operator. The program uses method getBits (lines 160–181) to get a string representation of the integer values. The program allows users to enter values into JTextFields (for the binary operators, two values must be entered) and press the button representing the operation they would like to test. The program displays the result of each operation in both integer and bitwise representations.

```
1   // Fig. 21.8: MiscBitOps.java
2   // Using the bitwise operators.
3   import java.awt.*;
4   import java.awt.event.*;
5   import javax.swing.*;
6
7   public class MiscBitOps extends JFrame {
8      private JTextField input1Field, input2Field,
9         bits1Field, bits2Field, bits3Field, resultField;
10     private int value1, value2;
11
12     // set up GUI
13     public MiscBitOps()
14     {
15        super( "Bitwise operators" );
16
17        JPanel inputPanel = new JPanel();
18        inputPanel.setLayout( new GridLayout( 4, 2 ) );
19
20        inputPanel.add( new JLabel( "Enter 2 ints" ) );
21        inputPanel.add( new JLabel( "" ) );
22
23        inputPanel.add( new JLabel( "Value 1" ) );
24        input1Field = new JTextField( 8 );
25        inputPanel.add( input1Field );
26
27        inputPanel.add( new JLabel( "Value 2" ) );
28        input2Field = new JTextField( 8 );
29        inputPanel.add( input2Field );
30
```

Fig. 21.8   Bitwise AND, bitwise inclusive OR, bitwise exclusive OR and bitwise complement operators. (Part 1 of 5.)

```
31          inputPanel.add( new JLabel( "Result" ) );
32          resultField = new JTextField( 8 );
33          resultField.setEditable( false );
34          inputPanel.add( resultField );
35
36          JPanel bitsPanel = new JPanel();
37          bitsPanel.setLayout( new GridLayout( 4, 1 ) );
38          bitsPanel.add( new JLabel( "Bit representations" ) );
39
40          bits1Field = new JTextField( 33 );
41          bits1Field.setEditable( false );
42          bitsPanel.add( bits1Field );
43
44          bits2Field = new JTextField( 33 );
45          bits2Field.setEditable( false );
46          bitsPanel.add( bits2Field );
47
48          bits3Field = new JTextField( 33 );
49          bits3Field.setEditable( false );
50          bitsPanel.add( bits3Field );
51
52          JPanel buttonPanel = new JPanel();
53
54          // button to perform bitwise AND
55          JButton andButton = new JButton( "AND" );
56          buttonPanel.add( andButton );
57
58          andButton.addActionListener(
59
60             new ActionListener() { // anonymous inner class
61
62                // perform bitwise AND and display results
63                public void actionPerformed( ActionEvent event )
64                {
65                   setFields();
66                   resultField.setText( Integer.toString( value1 & value2 ) );
67                   bits3Field.setText( getBits( value1 & value2 ) );
68                }
69
70             } // end anonymous inner class
71
72          ); // end call to addActionListener
73
74          // button to perform bitwise inclusive OR
75          JButton inclusiveOrButton = new JButton( "Inclusive OR" );
76          buttonPanel.add( inclusiveOrButton );
77
78          inclusiveOrButton.addActionListener(
79
80             new ActionListener() { // anonymous inner class
81
```

Fig. 21.8   Bitwise AND, bitwise inclusive OR, bitwise exclusive OR and bitwise complement operators. (Part 2 of 5.)

```
82              // perform bitwise inclusive OR and display results
83              public void actionPerformed( ActionEvent event )
84              {
85                 setFields();
86                 resultField.setText( Integer.toString( value1 | value2 ) );
87                 bits3Field.setText( getBits( value1 | value2 ) );
88              }
89
90           } // end anonymous inner class
91
92        ); // end call to addActionListener
93
94        // button to perform bitwise exclusive OR
95        JButton exclusiveOrButton = new JButton( "Exclusive OR" );
96        buttonPanel.add( exclusiveOrButton );
97
98        exclusiveOrButton.addActionListener(
99
100          new ActionListener() { // anonymous inner class
101
102             // perform bitwise exclusive OR and display results
103             public void actionPerformed( ActionEvent event )
104             {
105                setFields();
106                resultField.setText( Integer.toString( value1 ^ value2 ) );
107                bits3Field.setText( getBits( value1 ^ value2 ) );
108             }
109
110          } // end anonymous inner class
111
112       ); // end call to addActionListener
113
114       // button to perform bitwise complement
115       JButton complementButton = new JButton( "Complement" );
116       buttonPanel.add( complementButton );
117
118       complementButton.addActionListener(
119
120          new ActionListener() { // anonymous inner class
121
122             // perform bitwise complement and display results
123             public void actionPerformed( ActionEvent event )
124             {
125                input2Field.setText( "" );
126                bits2Field.setText( "" );
127
128                int value = Integer.parseInt( input1Field.getText() );
129
130                resultField.setText( Integer.toString( ~value ) );
131                bits1Field.setText( getBits( value ) );
132                bits3Field.setText( getBits( ~value ) );
133             }
```

Fig. 21.8 Bitwise AND, bitwise inclusive OR, bitwise exclusive OR and bitwise complement operators. (Part 3 of 5.)

```
134
135               } // end anonymous inner class
136
137          ); // end call to addActionListener
138
139          Container container = getContentPane();
140          container.add( inputPanel, BorderLayout.WEST );
141          container.add( bitsPanel, BorderLayout.EAST );
142          container.add( buttonPanel, BorderLayout.SOUTH );
143
144          setSize( 600, 150 );
145          setVisible( true );
146
147       } // end constructor
148
149       // display numbers and their bit form
150       private void setFields()
151       {
152          value1 = Integer.parseInt( input1Field.getText() );
153          value2 = Integer.parseInt( input2Field.getText() );
154
155          bits1Field.setText( getBits( value1 ) );
156          bits2Field.setText( getBits( value2 ) );
157       }
158
159       // display bit representation of specified int value
160       private String getBits( int value )
161       {
162          // create int value with 1 in leftmost bit and 0s elsewhere
163          int displayMask = 1 << 31;
164
165          StringBuffer buffer = new StringBuffer( 35 ); // buffer for output
166
167          // for each bit append 0 or 1 to buffer
168          for ( int bit = 1; bit <= 32; bit++ ) {
169
170             // use displayMask to isolate bit
171             buffer.append( ( value & displayMask ) == 0 ? '0' : '1' );
172
173             value <<= 1; // shift value one position to left
174
175             if ( bit % 8 == 0 )
176                buffer.append( ' ' ); // append space to buffer every 8 bits
177          }
178
179          return buffer.toString();
180
181       } // end method getBits
182
183       public static void main( String args[] )
184       {
185          MiscBitOps application = new MiscBitOps();
```

Fig. 21.8   Bitwise AND, bitwise inclusive OR, bitwise exclusive OR and bitwise complement operators. (Part 4 of 5.)

```
186            application.setDefaultCloseOperation( JFrame.EXIT_ON_CLOSE );
187        }
188
189    } // end class MiscBitOps
```

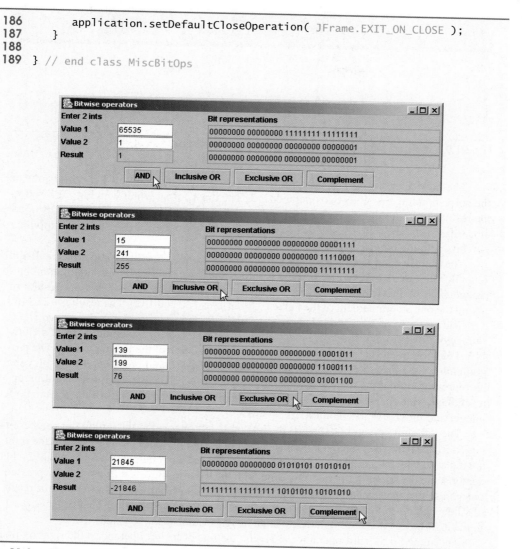

Fig. 21.8   Bitwise AND, bitwise inclusive OR, bitwise exclusive OR and bitwise complement operators. (Part 5 of 5.)

The first output window in Fig. 21.8 shows the results of combining the value 65535 and the value 1 with the bitwise AND operator (&; lines 66–67). All the bits except the low-order bit in the value 65535 are "masked off" (hidden) by "ANDing" with the value 1.

The bitwise inclusive OR operator (|)sets specific bits to 1 in an operand. The second output window in Fig. 21.8 shows the results of combining the value 15 and the value 241 by using the bitwise OR operator (lines 86–87)—the result is 255. Figure 21.9 summarizes the results of combining two bits with the bitwise inclusive OR operator.

Bit 1	Bit 2	Bit 1 | Bit 2
0	0	0
1	0	1
0	1	1
1	1	1

Fig. 21.9   Bitwise inclusive OR operator (|) combining two bits.

The bitwise exclusive OR operator (^) sets each bit in the result to 1 if *exactly* one of the corresponding bits in its two operands is 1. The third output window in Fig. 21.8 shows the results of combining the value 139 and the value 199 by using the exclusive OR operator (lines 106–107)—the result is 76. Figure 21.10 summarizes the results of combining two bits with the bitwise exclusive OR operator.

The *bitwise* complement operator (~) sets all 1 bits in its operand to 0 in the result and sets all 0 bits in its operand to 1 in the result—otherwise referred to as "taking the *one's complement* of the value." The fourth output window in Fig. 21.8 shows the results of taking the one's complement of the value 21845 (lines 130 and 132). The result is -21846.

The program of Fig. 21.11 demonstrates the *left-shift operator* (<<), the *signed right-shift operator* (>>) and the *unsigned right-shift operator* (>>>). Method getBits (lines 114–135) obtains a String containing the bit representation of the integer values. The program allows the user to enter an integer into a JTextField and press *Enter* to display the bit representation of the integer in a second JTextField. The user can press a button representing a shift operation to perform a one-bit shift and view the results of the shift in both integer and bitwise representation.

The left-shift operator (<<) shifts the bits of its left operand to the left by the number of bits specified in its right operand (performed at line 56 in Fig. 21.11). Bits vacated to the right are replaced with 0s; 1s shifted off the left are lost. The first four output windows in Fig. 21.11 demonstrate the left-shift operator. Starting with the value 1, the left shift button was pressed twice, resulting in the values 2 and 4, respectively. The fourth output window shows the result of value 1 being shifted 31 times. Note that the result is a negative value. That is because a 1 in the high-order bit is used to indicate in an integer with a negative value.

The signed right-shift operator (>>) shifts the bits of its left operand to the right by the number of bits specified in its right operand (performed at line 77 in Fig. 21.11). Performing

Bit 1	Bit 2	Bit 1 ^ Bit 2
0	0	0
1	0	1
0	1	1
1	1	0

Fig. 21.10   Bitwise exclusive OR operator (^) combining two bits.

a right shift causes the vacated bits at the left to be replaced by 0s if the number is positive or by 1s if the number is negative. Any 1s shifted off the right are lost. The fifth and sixth output windows in Fig. 21.11 show the results of right shifting (with sign extension) the value in the fourth output window two times.

The unsigned right-shift operator (>>>) shifts the bits of its left operand to the right by the number of bits specified in its right operand (performed at line 98 Fig. 21.11). Performing an unsigned right shift causes the vacated bits at the left to be replaced by 0s. Any 1s shifted off the right are lost. The eighth and ninth output windows of Fig. 21.11 show the results of unsigned right shifting the value in the seventh output window two times. Each bitwise operator (except the bitwise complement operator) has a corresponding assignment operator. These *bitwise assignment operators* are shown in Fig. 21.12.

```java
1   // Fig. 21.11: BitShift.java
2   // Using the bitwise shift operators.
3   import java.awt.*;
4   import java.awt.event.*;
5   import javax.swing.*;
6
7   public class BitShift extends JFrame {
8      private JTextField bitsField, valueField;
9
10     // set up GUI
11     public BitShift()
12     {
13        super( "Shifting bits" );
14
15        Container container = getContentPane();
16        container.setLayout( new FlowLayout() );
17
18        container.add( new JLabel( "Integer to shift " ) );
19
20        // textfield for user to input integer
21        valueField = new JTextField( 12 );
22        container.add( valueField );
23
24        valueField.addActionListener(
25
26           new ActionListener() { // anonymous inner class
27
28              // read value and display its bitwise representation
29              public void actionPerformed( ActionEvent event )
30              {
31                 int value = Integer.parseInt( valueField.getText() );
32                 bitsField.setText( getBits( value ) );
33              }
34
35           } // end anonymous inner class
36
37        ); // end call to addActionListener
```

Fig. 21.11　Bitwise shift operators. (Part 1 of 5.)

```
38
39         // textfield to display bitwise representation of an integer
40         bitsField = new JTextField( 33 );
41         bitsField.setEditable( false );
42         container.add( bitsField );
43
44         // button to shift bits left by one position
45         JButton leftButton = new JButton( "<<" );
46         container.add( leftButton );
47
48         leftButton.addActionListener(
49
50            new ActionListener() { // anonymous inner class
51
52               // left shift one position and display new value
53               public void actionPerformed( ActionEvent event )
54               {
55                  int value = Integer.parseInt( valueField.getText() );
56                  value <<= 1;
57                  valueField.setText( Integer.toString( value ) );
58                  bitsField.setText( getBits( value ) );
59               }
60
61            } // end anonymous inner class
62
63         ); // end call to addActionListener
64
65         // button to signed right shift value one position
66         JButton rightSignButton = new JButton( ">>" );
67         container.add( rightSignButton );
68
69         rightSignButton.addActionListener(
70
71            new ActionListener() { // anonymous inner class
72
73               // right shift one position and display new value
74               public void actionPerformed( ActionEvent event )
75               {
76                  int value = Integer.parseInt( valueField.getText() );
77                  value >>= 1;
78                  valueField.setText( Integer.toString( value ) );
79                  bitsField.setText( getBits( value ) );
80               }
81
82            } // end anonymous inner class
83
84         ); // end call to addActionListener
85
86         // button to unsigned right shift value one position
87         JButton rightZeroButton = new JButton( ">>>" );
88         container.add( rightZeroButton );
89
90         rightZeroButton.addActionListener(
```

Fig. 21.11 Bitwise shift operators. (Part 2 of 5.)

```
 91
 92                   new ActionListener() { // anonymous inner class
 93
 94                      // right shift one position and display new value
 95                      public void actionPerformed( ActionEvent event )
 96                      {
 97                         int value = Integer.parseInt( valueField.getText() );
 98                         value >>>= 1;
 99                         valueField.setText( Integer.toString( value ) );
100
101                         bitsField.setText( getBits( value ) );
102                      }
103
104                   } // end anonymous inner class
105
106               ); // end call to addActionListener
107
108            setSize( 400, 120 );
109            setVisible( true );
110
111         } // end constructor
112
113         // display bit representation of specified int value
114         private String getBits( int value )
115         {
116            // create int value with 1 in leftmost bit and 0s elsewhere
117            int displayMask = 1 << 31;
118
119            StringBuffer buffer = new StringBuffer( 35 ); // buffer for output
120
121            // for each bit append 0 or 1 to buffer
122            for ( int bit = 1; bit <= 32; bit++ ) {
123
124               // use displayMask to isolate bit
125               buffer.append( ( value & displayMask ) == 0 ? '0' : '1' );
126
127               value <<= 1; // shift value one position to left
128
129               if ( bit % 8 == 0 )
130                  buffer.append( ' ' ); // append space to buffer every 8 bits
131            }
132
133            return buffer.toString();
134
135         } // end method getBits
136
137         public static void main( String args[] )
138         {
139            BitShift application = new BitShift();
140            application.setDefaultCloseOperation( JFrame.EXIT_ON_CLOSE );
141         }
142
143      } // end class BitShift
```

Fig. 21.11 Bitwise shift operators. (Part 3 of 5.)

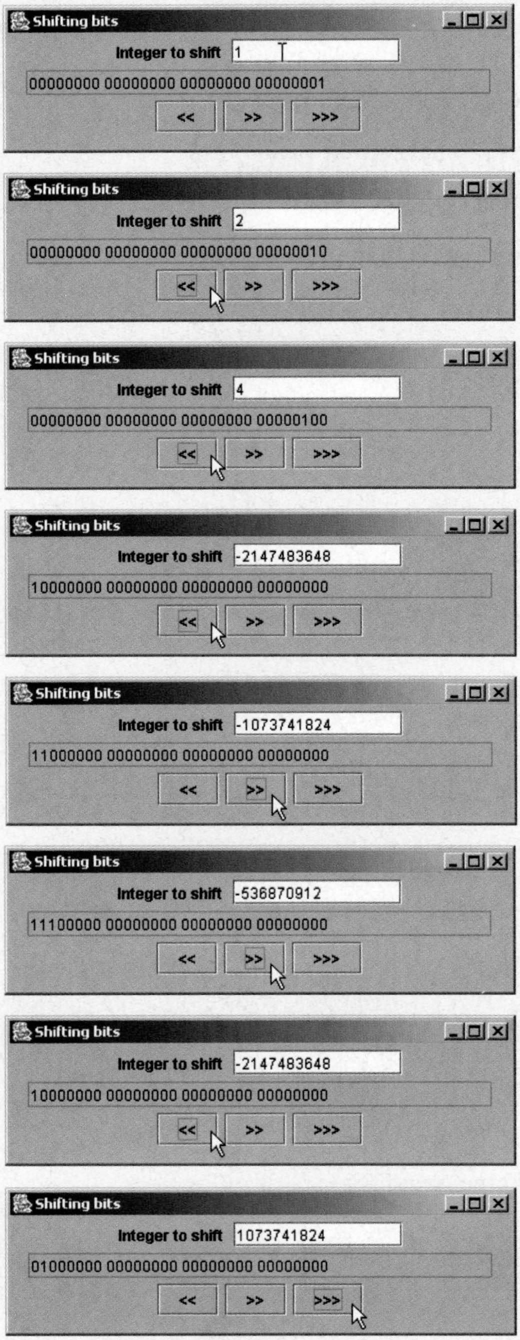

Start with integer 1.

Left shift one position.

Left shift one position.

Start with integer –2147483648.

Signed right shift one position.

Signed right shift one position.

Start with integer –2147483648.

Unsigned right shift one position.

Fig. 21.11 Bitwise shift operators. (Part 4 of 5.)

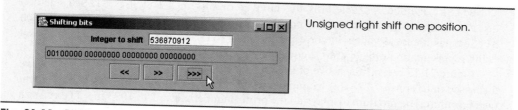

Unsigned right shift one position.

Fig. 21.11 Bitwise shift operators. (Part 5 of 5.)

Bitwise assignment operators	
&=	Bitwise AND assignment operator.
|=	Bitwise inclusive OR assignment operator.
^=	Bitwise exclusive OR assignment operator.
<<=	Left-shift assignment operator.
>>=	Signed right-shift assignment operator.
>>>=	Unsigned right-shift assignment operator.

Fig. 21.12 Bitwise assignment operators.

21.7 BitSet Class

Class *BitSet* makes it easy to create and manipulate *bit sets*, which are useful for representing sets of `boolean` flags. `BitSet`s are dynamically resizable—more bits can be added as needed, and a `BitSet` will grow to accommodate the additional bits. Class `BitSet` provides two constructors—a no-argument constructor that creates an empty `BitSet` and a constructor that receives an integer representing the number of bits in the `BitSet`. By default, each bit in a `BitSet` has a `false` value—the underlying bit has the value 0. A bit is set to `true` (also called "on") with a call to `BitSet` method *set*, which receives the index of the bit to set as an argument. This makes the underlying value of that bit 1. Note that bit indices are zero based, like arrays. A bit is set to `false` (also called "off") by calling `Bit-Set` method *clear*. This makes the underlying value of that bit 0. To obtain the value of a bit, use `BitSet` method *get*, which receives the index of the bit to get and returns a boolean value representing whether the bit at that index is on (`true`) or off (`false`).

   Class `BitSet` also provides methods for combining the bits in two `BitSet`s, using bitwise logical AND (*and*), bitwise logical inclusive OR (*or*), and bitwise logical exclusive OR (*xor*). Assuming that b1 and b2 are `BitSet`s, the statement

```
b1.and( b2 );
```

performs a bit-by-bit logical AND operation between `BitSet`s b1 and b2. The result is stored in b1. Bitwise logical inclusive OR and bitwise logical XOR are performed by the statements

```
b1.or( b2 );
b1.xor( b2 );
```

BitSet method *size* returns the number of bits in a BitSet. BitSet method *equals* compares two BitSets for equality. Two BitSets are equal if and only if each BitSet has identical values in corresponding bits. BitSet method *toString* creates a string representation of a BitSet's contents.

Figure 21.13 revisits the Sieve of Eratosthenes (for finding prime numbers), which we discussed in Exercise 7.27. This example uses a BitSet rather than an array to implement the algorithm. The program displays all the prime numbers from 2 to 1023 in a JTextArea and provides a JTextField in which the user can type any number from 2 to 1023 to determine whether that number is prime. (The result is displayed in a JLabel at the bottom of the window.)

```
 1   // Fig. 21.13: BitSetTest.java
 2   // Using a BitSet to demonstrate the Sieve of Eratosthenes.
 3   import java.awt.*;
 4   import java.awt.event.*;
 5   import java.util.*;
 6   import javax.swing.*;
 7
 8   public class BitSetTest extends JFrame {
 9      private BitSet sieve;
10      private JLabel statusLabel;
11      private JTextField inputField;
12
13      // set up GUI
14      public BitSetTest()
15      {
16         super( "BitSets" );
17
18         sieve = new BitSet( 1024 );
19
20         Container container = getContentPane();
21
22         statusLabel = new JLabel( "" );
23         container.add( statusLabel, BorderLayout.SOUTH );
24
25         JPanel inputPanel = new JPanel();
26         inputPanel.add( new JLabel( "Enter a value from 2 to 1023" ) );
27
28         // textfield for user to input a value from 2 to 1023
29         inputField = new JTextField( 10 );
30         inputPanel.add( inputField );
31         container.add( inputPanel, BorderLayout.NORTH );
32
33         inputField.addActionListener(
34
35            new ActionListener() { // inner class
36
37               // determine whether value is prime number
38               public void actionPerformed( ActionEvent event )
39               {
```

Fig. 21.13 Sieve of Eratosthenes, using a BitSet. (Part 1 of 3.)

```
40          int value = Integer.parseInt( inputField.getText() );
41
42             if ( sieve.get( value ) )
43                statusLabel.setText( value + " is a prime number" );
44
45             else
46                statusLabel.setText( value + " is not a prime number" );
47          }
48
49       } // end inner class
50
51    ); // end call to addActionListener
52
53    JTextArea primesArea = new JTextArea();
54
55    container.add( new JScrollPane( primesArea ), BorderLayout.CENTER );
56
57    int size = sieve.size(); // set all bits from 2 to 1023
58
59    for ( int i = 2; i < size; i++ )
60       sieve.set( i );
61
62    // perform Sieve of Eratosthenes
63    int finalBit = ( int ) Math.sqrt( size );
64
65    for ( int i = 2; i < finalBit; i++ )
66
67       if ( sieve.get( i ) )
68
69          for ( int j = 2 * i; j < size; j += i )
70             sieve.clear( j );
71
72    int counter = 0; // display prime numbers from 2 to 1023
73
74    for ( int i = 2; i < size; i++ )
75
76       if ( sieve.get( i ) ) {
77          primesArea.append( String.valueOf( i ) );
78          primesArea.append( ++counter % 7 == 0 ? "\n" : "\t" );
79       }
80
81    setSize( 600, 450 );
82    setVisible( true );
83
84    } // end constructor
85
86    public static void main( String args[] )
87    {
88       BitSetTest application = new BitSetTest();
89       application.setDefaultCloseOperation( JFrame.EXIT_ON_CLOSE );
90    }
91
92 } // end class BitSetTest
```

Fig. 21.13 Sieve of Eratosthenes, using a BitSet. (Part 2 of 3.)

BitSets

Enter a value from 2 to 1023 `773`

2	3	5	7	11	13	17
19	23	29	31	37	41	43
47	53	59	61	67	71	73
79	83	89	97	101	103	107
109	113	127	131	137	139	149
151	157	163	167	173	179	181
191	193	197	199	211	223	227
229	233	239	241	251	257	263
269	271	277	281	283	293	307
311	313	317	331	337	347	349
353	359	367	373	379	383	389
397	401	409	419	421	431	433
439	443	449	457	461	463	467
479	487	491	499	503	509	521
523	541	547	557	563	569	571
577	587	593	599	601	607	613
617	619	631	641	643	647	653
659	661	673	677	683	691	701
709	719	727	733	739	743	751
757	761	769	773	787	797	809
811	821	823	827	829	839	853
857	859	863	877	881	883	887
907	911	919	929	937	941	947

773 is a prime number

Fig. 21.13 Sieve of Eratosthenes, using a `BitSet`. (Part 3 of 3.)

Line 18 creates a `BitSet` of 1024 bits. We ignore the bits at indices zero and one in this program. Lines 59–60 set all the bits in the `BitSet` to "on" with `BitSet` method `set`. Lines 65–70 determine all the prime numbers from 2 to 1023. The integer `finalBit` specifies when the algorithm is complete. The basic algorithm is that a number is prime if it has no divisors other than 1 and itself. Starting with the number 2, once we know That a number is prime, we can eliminate all multiples of that number. The number 2 is divisible only by 1 and itself, so it is prime. Therefore, we can eliminate 4, 6, 8 and so on. Elimination of a value consists of setting its bit to "off" with `BitSet` method `clear` (line 70). The number 3 is divisible by 1 and itself. Therefore, we can eliminate all multiples of 3. (Keep in mind that all even numbers have already been eliminated.) After the list of primes is displayed, the user can type a value from 2 to 1023 in the textfield and press *Enter* to determine whether the number is prime. Method `actionPerformed` (lines 38–47) uses `BitSet` method `get` (line 42) to determine whether the bit for the number the user entered is set. If so, line 43 displays a message indicating that the number is prime. Otherwise, line 46 displays a message indicating that the number is not prime.

SUMMARY

- Class `Vector` manages dynamically resizable arrays. At any time, a `Vector` contains a number of elements that is less than or equal to its capacity. If a `Vector` needs to grow, it grows by its capacity increment. If no capacity increment is specified, Java doubles the size of the `Vector` each time additional capacity is required. The default capacity is ten elements.

- `Vectors` store references to `Objects`. To store values of primitive types in `Vectors`, use the type-wrapper classes (`Byte`, `Short`, `Integer`, `Long`, `Float`, `Double`, `Boolean` and `Character`) to create objects containing the primitive-type values.

- Class Vector provides four constructors. The no-argument constructor creates an empty Vector. The constructor that takes one argument creates a Vector with an initial capacity specified by the argument if it is an int, or based on the number of elements if it is a Collection. The constructor that takes two arguments creates a Vector with an initial capacity specified by the first argument and a capacity increment specified by the second argument.

- Vector method add adds its argument to the end of the Vector. Method insertElementAt inserts an element at the specified position. Method set sets the element at a specific position.

- Vector method remove removes the first occurrence of its argument. Method removeAllElements removes every element from the Vector. Method removeElementAt removes the element at the specified index.

- Vector method firstElement returns a reference to the first element. Method lastElement returns a reference to the last element.

- Vector method contains determines whether the Vector contains the searchKey specified as an argument. Vector method indexOf gets the index of the first location of its argument. The method returns –1 if the argument is not found in the Vector.

- Vector method isEmpty determines whether the Vector is empty. Methods size and capacity determine the number of elements currently in the Vector and the number of elements that can be stored in the Vector without allocating more memory, respectively.

- Vector method elements returns an Enumeration for the elements of a Vector. Enumeration method hasMoreElements determines whether there are elements that have not yet been visited to be enumerated. Method nextElement returns a reference to the next element.

- Class Stack extends Vector. Stack method push adds its argument to the top of the stack. Method pop removes the top element of the stack. Method peek returns a reference to the top element without removing the element. Stack method empty determines whether the stack is empty.

- A Hashtable maps keys to values.

- Hashing is a high-speed scheme for converting keys into unique array indices for storage and retrieval of information.

- The no-argument Hashtable constructor creates a Hashtable with a default capacity of 11 elements and a default load factor of 0.75. The Hashtable constructor that takes one argument specifies the initial capacity; the constructor that takes two arguments specifies the initial capacity and load factor, respectively.

- Hashtable method put adds a key and a value into a Hashtable. Method get locates the value associated with the specified key. Method remove deletes the key and its associated value. Method isEmpty determines whether the table is empty.

- Hashtable method containsKey determines whether the key specified as its argument is in the Hashtable. Method contains uses the Object method equals to determine whether the Object specified as its argument is in the Hashtable. Method clear empties the Hashtable. Method elements obtains an Enumeration of the values. Method keys obtains an Enumeration of the keys.

- A Properties object is a persistent Hashtable object. Class Properties extends Hashtable.

- The Properties no-argument constructor creates an empty Properties table with no default properties. There is also an overloaded constructor that is passed a reference to a default Properties object containing default property values.

- Properties method setProperty specifies the value associated with the key specified as an argument. Properties method getProperty locates the value of the key specified as an argument. Method store saves the contents of the Properties object to the OutputStream object specified as the first argument. Method load restores the contents of the Properties object from the `InputStream` object specified as the argument. Method `propertyNames` obtains an `Enumeration` of the property names.

- The bitwise AND (&) operator sets each bit in the result to 1 if the corresponding bit in both operands is 1.

- The bitwise inclusive OR (|) operator sets each bit in the result to 1 if the corresponding bit in either (or both) operand(s) is 1.

- The bitwise exclusive OR (^) operator sets each bit in the result to 1 if the corresponding bit in exactly one operand is 1.

- The left-shift (<<) operator shifts the bits of its left operand to the left by the number of bits specified in its right operand.

- The signed right-shift operator (>>) shifts the bits in its left operand to the right by the number of bits specified in its right operand—if the left operand is negative, 1s are filled in from the left; otherwise, 0s are shifted in from the left.

- The unsigned right-shift operator (>>>) shifts the bits in its left operand to the right by the number of bits specified in its right operand—0s are filled in from the left.

- The bitwise complement (~) operator sets all 0 bits in its operand to 1 in the result and sets all 1 bits in its operand to 0 in the result.

- Each bitwise operator (except complement) has a corresponding assignment operator.

- The no-argument `BitSet` constructor creates an empty `BitSet`. The one-argument `BitSet` constructor creates a `BitSet` with the number of bits specified by its argument.

- `BitSet` method `set` sets the specified bit "on." Method `clear` sets the specified bit "off." Method `get` returns `true` if the bit is on and `false` if the bit is off.

- `BitSet` method `and` performs a bit-by-bit logical AND between `BitSet`s. The result is stored in the `BitSet` that invoked the method. Similarly, bitwise logical OR and bitwise logical XOR are performed by methods `or` and `xor`, respectively. `BitSet` method `size` returns the size of a `BitSet`. Method `toString` converts a `BitSet` to a `String`.

TERMINOLOGY

add method of class `Vector`	capacity increment of a `Vector`
and method of class `BitSet`	`capacity` method of class `Vector`
bit set	capacity of a `Vector`
`BitSet` class	`clear` method of class `BitSet`
bitwise assignment operators	collision in hashing
&= (bitwise AND)	`contains` method of class `Vector`
^= (bitwise exclusive OR)	`containsKey` method of class `Hashtable`
|= (bitwise inclusive OR)	defaults
<<= (left shift)	dynamically resizable array
>>= (signed right shift)	`elementAt` method of class `Vector`
>>>= (unsigned right shift)	`elements` method of class `Hashtable`
bitwise manipulation operators	`elements` method of class `Vector`
& (bitwise AND)	`EmptyStackException` class
^ (bitwise exclusive OR)	enumerate successive elements
	(bitwise inclusive OR)	`Enumeration` interface
~ (bitwise complement)	`equals` method of class `Object`
<< (left shift)	`firstElement` method of class `Vector`
>> (signed right shift)	`get` method of class `BitSet`
>>> (unsigned right shift)	`get` method of class `Hashtable`

getProperty method of class Properties

hashing

Hashtable class

hasMoreElements method of Enumeration

indexOf method of class Vector

initial capacity of a Vector

insertElementAt method of class Vector

isEmpty method of class Hashtable

isEmpty method of class Vector

iterate through container elements

java.util package

key in a Hashtable

key/value pair

keys method of class Hashtable

lastElement method of class Vector

list method of class Properties

load factor in hashing

load method of class Properties

nextElement method of Enumeration

NoSuchElementException class

NullPointerException

or method of class BitSet

peek method of class Stack

persistent hash table

pop method of class Stack

Properties class

propertyNames method of Properties

push method of class Stack

put method of class Hashtable

remove method of class Hashtable

removeAllElements method of Vector

removeElement method of class Vector

removeElementAt method of class Vector

set method of class BitSet

set method of class Vector

setSize method of class Vector

size method of class Hashtable

size method of class Vector

Stack class

store method of class Properties

Vector class

xor method of class BitSet

SELF-REVIEW EXERCISES

21.1 Fill in the blanks in each of the following statements:

   a) Java class _____ provides the capabilities of array-like data structures that can re-size themselves dynamically.

   b) If you do not specify a capacity increment, the system will _____ the size of the Vector each time additional capacity is needed.

   c) Bits in the result of an expression using operator _____ are set to 1 if the corresponding bits in each operand are set to 1. Otherwise, the bits are set to zero.

   d) Bits in the result of an expression using operator _____ are set to 1 if at least one of the corresponding bits in either operand is set to 1. Otherwise, the bits are set to 0.

   e) Bits in the result of an expression using operator _____ are set to 1 if exactly one of the corresponding bits in either operand is set to 1. Otherwise, the bits are set to 0.

   f) The bitwise AND operator (&) is often used to _____ bits, that is, to select certain bits from a bit string while setting others to 0.

   g) The _____ operator is used to shift the bits of a value to the left.

   h) The _____ operator shifts the bits of a value to the right with sign extension, and the _____ operator shifts the bits of a value to the right with zero extension.

21.2 Determine whether each of the given statements is *true* or *false*. If *false*, explain why.

   a) Values of primitive types may be stored directly in a Vector.

   b) With hashing, as the load factor increases, the chance of collisions decreases.

21.3 Under what circumstances is an EmptyStackException thrown?

ANSWERS TO SELF-REVIEW EXERCISES

21.1   a) Vector. b) double. c) &. d) |. e) ^. f) mask. g) <<. h) >>, >>>.

21.2   a) False; a Vector stores only Objects. A program must use the type-wrapper classes (Byte, Short, Integer, Long, Float, Double, Boolean and Character) from package `java.lang` to create `Objects` containing the primitive type values. b) False; as the load factor increases, there are fewer available slots relative to the total number of slots, so the chance of selecting an occupied slot (a collision) with a hashing operation increases.

21.3   When a program calls `pop` or `peek` on an empty `Stack`, an `EmptyStackException` occurs.

EXERCISES

21.4   Define each of the following terms in the context of hashing:
   a) key
   b) collision
   c) hashing transformation
   d) load factor
   e) space/time trade-off
   f) `Hashtable` class
   g) capacity of a `Hashtable`

21.5   Explain briefly the operation of each of the following methods of class `Vector`:
   a) `add`
   b) `insertElementAt`
   c) `set`
   d) `remove`
   e) `removeAllElements`
   f) `removeElementAt`
   g) `firstElement`
   h) `lastElement`
   i) `isEmpty`
   j) `contains`
   k) `indexOf`
   l) `size`
   m) `capacity`

21.6   Explain why inserting additional elements into a `Vector` object whose current size is less than its capacity is a relatively fast operation and why inserting additional elements into a `Vector` object whose current size is at capacity is a relatively slow operation.

21.7   Explain the use of the `Enumeration` interface with objects of class `Vector`.

21.8   By extending class `Vector`, Java's designers were able to create class `Stack` quickly. What are the negative aspects of this use of inheritance, particularly for class `Stack`?

21.9   Explain briefly the operation of each of the following methods of class `Hashtable`:
   a) `put`
   b) `get`
   c) `isEmpty`
   d) `containsKey`
   e) `contains`
   f) `keys`

21.10   Use a `Hashtable` to create a reusable class for choosing one of the 13 predefined colors in class `Color`. The names of the colors should be used as keys, and the predefined `Color` objects should be used as values. Place this class in a package that can be imported into any Java program. Use your new class in an application that allows the user to select a color and draw a shape in that color.

21.11   Modify your solution to Exercise 14.17—the polymorphic painting program—to store every shape the user draws in a `Vector` of `MyShape` objects. For the purpose of this exercise, create your own `Vector` subclass called `ShapeVector` that manipulates only `MyShape` objects. Provide the following capabilities in your program:

a) Allow the user of the program to remove any number of shapes from the `Vector` by clicking an **Undo** button.

b) Allow the user to select any shape on the screen and move it to a new location. This operation requires the addition of a new method to the `MyShape` hierarchy. The method's header should be

```
public boolean isInside()
```

This method should be overridden for each subclass of `MyShape` in order to determine whether the coordinates where the user pressed the mouse button are inside the shape.

c) Allow the user to select any shape on the screen and change its color.

d) Allow the user to select any shape on the screen that can be filled or unfilled and change its fill state.

21.12 What does it mean when we state that a `Properties` object is a "persistent" `Hashtable` object? Explain the operation of each of the following methods of the `Properties` class:

a) `load`
b) `store`
c) `getProperty`
d) `propertyNames`
e) `list`

21.13 Why might you want to use objects of class `BitSet`? Explain the operation of each of the following methods of class `BitSet`:

a) `set`
b) `clear`
c) `get`
d) `and`
e) `or`
f) `xor`
g) `size`
h) `equals`
i) `toString`

21.14 Write a program that right shifts an integer variable four bits to the right with sign extension, then shifts the same integer variable four bits to the right with zero extension. The program should print the integer in bits before and after each shift operation. Run your program once with a positive integer and once with a negative integer.

21.15 Show how shifting an integer left by one can be used to perform multiplication by two and how shifting an integer right by one can be used to perform division by two. Be careful to consider issues related to the sign of an integer.

21.16 Write a program that reverses the order of the bits in an integer value. The program should input the value from the user and call method `reverseBits` to print the bits in reverse order. Print the value in bits both before and after the bits are reversed to confirm that the bits are reversed properly. You might want to implement both a recursive and an iterative solution.

21.17 Modify your solution to Exercise 20.10 to use class `Stack`.

21.18 Modify your solution to Exercise 20.12 to use class `Stack`.

21.19 Modify your solution to Exercise 20.13 to use class `Stack`.

22

Collections

Objectives

- To understand what collections are.
- To be able to use class `Arrays` for common array manipulations
- To use the collections-framework implementations.
- To be able to use collections-framework algorithms to manipulate various collections.
- To be able to use the collections-framework interfaces to program polymorphically.
- To be able to use iterators to "walk" through the elements of a collection.
- To understand synchronization wrappers and modifiability wrappers.

I think this is the most extraordinary collection of talent, of human knowledge, that has ever been gathered together at the White House—with the possible exception of when Thomas Jefferson dined alone.
John F. Kennedy

The shapes a bright container can contain!
Theodore Roethke

Journey over all the universe in a map.
Miguel de Cervantes

It is an immutable law in business that words are words, explanations are explanations, promises are promises — but only performance is reality.
Harold S. Green

Outline

22.1 Introduction

In Chapter 20, we discussed how to create and manipulate data structures. The discussion was "low level," in the sense that we painstakingly created each element of each data structure dynamically and modified the data structures by directly manipulating their elements and references to their elements. In this chapter, we consider the Java *collections framework*, which contains prepackaged data structures, interfaces and algorithms for manipulating those data structures. Some examples of collections are the cards you hold in a card game, your favorite music stored in your computer and the real-estate records in your local registry of deeds (which map book numbers and page numbers to property owners).

With collections, programmers use existing data structures, without concern for how the data structures are implemented. This is a marvelous example of code reuse. Programmers can code faster and can expect excellent performance, maximizing execution speed and minimizing memory consumption. In this chapter, we discuss the collections-framework interfaces that describe the capabilities of each collection type, the implementation classes, the algorithms that process the collections and the *iterators* that "walk" through them.[1]

---

1. This chapter provides an introduction to the collections framework. For the complete details of the collections framework, visit java.sun.com/j2se/1.4.1/docs/guide/collections.

The Java collections framework provides ready-to-go, reusable componentry;[2] you do not need to write your own collection classes. The collections are standardized so applications can share them easily, without being concerned with the details of their implementation. These collections are written for broad reuse. They are tuned for rapid execution as well as efficient use of memory. The collections framework encourages further reusability. As new data structures and algorithms are developed that fit this framework, a large base of programmers already will be familiar with the interfaces and algorithms implemented by those data structures.

22.2 Collections Overview

A collection is a data structure—actually, an object—that can hold references to other objects. The collection interfaces declare the operations that a program can perform on each type of collection. The collection implementations execute the operations in particular ways, some more appropriate than others for specific kinds of applications. The collection implementations are carefully constructed for rapid execution and efficient use of memory. Collections encourage software reuse by providing convenient functionality.

The collections-framework interfaces declare the operations to be performed generically on various types of collections. Some of the interfaces are Collection, Set, List and Map. Several implementations of these interfaces are provided within the framework. Programmers may also provide implementations specific to their own requirements.

The collections framework includes a number of other features that minimize the amount of coding programmers need to do to create and manipulate collections.

The classes and interfaces of the collections framework are members of package java.util. In the next section, we begin our discussion by examining the collections-framework capabilities for array manipulation.

22.3 Class Arrays

Class *Arrays* provides static methods for manipulating arrays. In Chapter 7, our discussion of array manipulation was low level, in the sense that we wrote the actual code to sort and search arrays. Class Arrays provides high-level methods, such as *sort* for sorting an array, *binarySearch* for searching a sorted array, *equals* for comparing arrays and *fill* for placing values into an array. These methods are overloaded for primitive-type arrays and Object arrays. Figure 22.1 demonstrates these methods.

```
1  // Fig. 22.1: UsingArrays.java
2  // Using Java arrays.
3  import java.util.*;
4
5  public class UsingArrays {
6     private int intValues[] = { 1, 2, 3, 4, 5, 6 };
7     private double doubleValues[] = { 8.4, 9.3, 0.2, 7.9, 3.4 };
```

Fig. 22.1   Arrays class methods. (Part 1 of 3.)

2. If you know C++, you will be familiar with its collections framework, which is called the Standard Template Library (STL). See Chapter 21 of *C++ How to Program, Fourth Edition*, by H. M. Deitel and P. J. Deitel, ©2003, Prentice Hall.

```
 8      private int filledInt[], intValuesCopy[];
 9
10      // initialize arrays
11      public UsingArrays()
12      {
13         filledInt = new int[ 10 ];
14         intValuesCopy = new int[ intValues.length ];
15
16         Arrays.fill( filledInt, 7 );    // fill with 7s
17
18         Arrays.sort( doubleValues );    // sort doubleValues ascending
19
20         // copy array intValues into array intValuesCopy
21         System.arraycopy( intValues, 0, intValuesCopy,
22            0, intValues.length );
23      }
24
25      // output values in each array
26      public void printArrays()
27      {
28         System.out.print( "doubleValues: " );
29
30         for ( int count = 0; count < doubleValues.length; count++ )
31            System.out.print( doubleValues[ count ] + " " );
32
33         System.out.print( "\nintValues: " );
34
35         for ( int count = 0; count < intValues.length; count++ )
36            System.out.print( intValues[ count ] + " " );
37
38         System.out.print( "\nfilledInt: " );
39
40         for ( int count = 0; count < filledInt.length; count++ )
41            System.out.print( filledInt[ count ] + " " );
42
43         System.out.print( "\nintValuesCopy: " );
44
45         for ( int count = 0; count < intValuesCopy.length; count++ )
46            System.out.print( intValuesCopy[ count ] + " " );
47
48         System.out.println();
49
50      } // end method printArrays
51
52      // find value in array intValues
53      public int searchForInt( int value )
54      {
55         return Arrays.binarySearch( intValues, value );
56      }
57
58      // compare array contents
59      public void printEquality()
60      {
```

Fig. 22.1   Arrays class methods. (Part 2 of 3.)

```
61        boolean b = Arrays.equals( intValues, intValuesCopy );
62
63        System.out.println( "intValues " + ( b ? "==" : "!=" ) +
64           " intValuesCopy" );
65
66        b = Arrays.equals( intValues, filledInt );
67
68        System.out.println( "intValues " + ( b ? "==" : "!=" ) +
69           " filledInt" );
70     }
71
72     public static void main( String args[] )
73     {
74        UsingArrays usingArrays = new UsingArrays();
75
76        usingArrays.printArrays();
77        usingArrays.printEquality();
78
79        int location = usingArrays.searchForInt( 5 );
80        System.out.println( ( location >= 0 ? "Found 5 at element " +
81           location : "5 not found" ) + " in intValues" );
82
83        location = usingArrays.searchForInt( 8763 );
84        System.out.println( ( location >= 0 ? "Found 8763 at element " +
85           location : "8763 not found" ) + " in intValues" );
86     }
87
88  } // end class UsingArrays
```

```
doubleValues: 0.2 3.4 7.9 8.4 9.3
intValues: 1 2 3 4 5 6
filledInt: 7 7 7 7 7 7 7 7 7
intValuesCopy: 1 2 3 4 5 6
intValues == intValuesCopy
intValues != filledInt
Found 5 at element 4 in intValues
8763 not found in intValues
```

Fig. 22.1 Arrays class methods. (Part 3 of 3.)

Line 16 calls static `Arrays` method `fill` to populate all 10 elements of array `filledInt` with 7s. Overloaded versions of `fill` allow the programmer to populate a specific range of elements with the same value.

Line 18 sorts the elements of array `doubleValues`. Overloaded versions of `sort` allow the programmer to sort a specific range of elements. `Arrays` static method `sort` orders the array's elements in ascending order by default. We discuss how to sort in descending order later in the chapter.

Lines 21–22 copy array `intValues` into array `intValuesCopy`. The first argument (`intValues`) passed to `System` method *arraycopy* is the array from which elements are copied. The second argument (0) is the index that specifies the starting point in the range of elements to copy from the array. This value can be any valid array index. The third argument (`intValuesCopy`) specifies the destination array that will store the copy. The fourth argument (0) specifies the index in the destination array where the first copied element should be stored. The last argument specifies the number of elements to copy from the array in the first argument. In this case, we copy all the elements in the array.

Line 55 calls static `Arrays` method `binarySearch` to perform a binary search on `intValues`, using `value` as the key. If `value` is found, `binarySearch` returns the index of the element. If `value` is not found, `binarySearch` returns a negative value. The negative value returned is based on the search key's *insertion point*—the index where the key would be inserted in the binary search tree if we were performing an insert operation. After `binarySearch` determines the insertion point, it changes the insertion point's sign to negative and subtracts 1 to obtain the return value. For example, in Fig. 22.1, the insertion point for the value 8763 is the element with index 6 in the array. Method `binarySearch` changes the insertion point to -6, subtracts 1 from it and returns the value -7. This return value is useful for adding elements to a sorted array.

Common Programming Error 22.1

Passing an unsorted array to `binarySearch` is a logic error. The value returned by `binarySearch` is undefined in such a case.

Lines 61 and 66 call static `Arrays` method `equals` to determine whether the elements of two arrays are equivalent. If the arrays are equal, the method returns `true`; otherwise, it returns `false`.

Viewing an Array as a `List`

One of the most important features of the collections framework is the ability to manipulate the elements of one collection type through a different collection type, regardless of the collection's internal implementation. The public set of methods through which collections are manipulated is called a *view*.

Class `Arrays` provides static method `asList` to view an array as a `List` collection (which encapsulates behavior similar to that of the linked lists created in Chapter 20; we will say more about `List`s in Section 22.5). A `List` view allows the programmer to manipulate the array programmatically as if it were a `List` by calling `List` methods. Any modifications made through the `List` view change the array, and any modifications made to the array change the `List` view. Figure 22.2 demonstrates method `asList`.

```
1   // Fig. 22.2: UsingAsList.java
2   // Using method asList.
3   import java.util.*;
4
5   public class UsingAsList {
6      private static final String values[] = { "red", "white", "blue" };
7      private List list;
8
9      // initialize List and set value at location 1
10     public UsingAsList()
11     {
12        list = Arrays.asList( values );   // get List
13        list.set( 1, "green" );           // change a value
14     }
```

Fig. 22.2   Arrays static method `asList`. (Part 1 of 2.)

```
15
16        // output List and array
17        public void printElements()
18        {
19           System.out.print( "List elements : " );
20
21           for ( int count = 0; count < list.size(); count++ )
22              System.out.print( list.get( count ) + " " );
23
24           System.out.print( "\nArray elements: " );
25
26           for ( int count = 0; count < values.length; count++ )
27              System.out.print( values[ count ] + " " );
28
29           System.out.println();
30        }
31
32        public static void main( String args[] )
33        {
34           new UsingAsList().printElements();
35        }
36
37     } // end class UsingAsList
```

```
List elements : red green blue
Array elements: red green blue
```

Fig. 22.2   Arrays static method asList. (Part 2 of 2.)

Line 7 declares a List reference called list. Line 12 uses static Arrays method asList to obtain a fixed-size List view of array values.

Performance Tip 22.1

Arrays.asList creates a fixed-size List that operates faster than any of the provided List implementations.

Common Programming Error 22.2

A List created with Arrays.asList is fixed in size; calling methods add or remove throws an UnsupportedOperationException.

Line 13 calls List method *set* to change the contents of List element 1 to "green". The program views the array as a List, so line 13 changes array element values[1] from "white" to "green". Any changes made to the List view are made to the underlying array object.

Software Engineering Observation 22.1

With the collections framework, there are many methods that apply to Lists and Collections that you would like to be able to use for arrays. Arrays.asList allows you to pass an array into a method that expects a List or Collection parameter.

Line 21 calls List method *size* to get the number of items in the List. Line 22 calls List method *get* to retrieve an individual item from the List. Note that the value returned by size is equal to the number of elements in array values (i.e., values.length) and that the items returned by get are the elements of array values.

22.4 Interface Collection and Class Collections

Interface *Collection* is the root interface in the collections hierarchy from which interfaces Set (a collection that does not contain duplicates—discussed in Section 22.7) and List are derived. Interface Collection contains *bulk operations* (i.e., operations performed on the entire collection) for adding, clearing, comparing and retaining objects (also called *elements*) in the collection. A Collection can also be converted to an array. In addition, interface Collection provides a method that returns an *Iterator*, which is similar to an Enumeration (introduced in Chapter 21). One difference is that an Iterator can remove elements from a collection, whereas an Enumeration cannot. Other methods of interface Collection enable a program to determine a collection's size and whether a collection is empty.

Good Programming Practice 22.1

An Iterator is more flexible than an Enumeration, so consider using an Iterator when it is necessary to traverse a Collection.

Software Engineering Observation 22.2

Collection is used commonly as a method parameter type to allow polymorphic processing of all objects that implement interface Collection.

Software Engineering Observation 22.3

Most collection implementations provide a constructor that takes a Collection argument, thereby allowing one collection type to be treated as another collection type.

Class *Collections* provides static methods that manipulate collections polymorphically. These methods implement algorithms for searching, sorting and so on. You will learn more about these algorithms in Section 22.6. Other Collections methods include *wrapper methods* that return new collections. We discuss wrapper methods in Section 22.9 and Section 22.10.

22.5 Lists

A List (sometimes called a *sequence*) is an ordered Collection that can contain duplicate elements. Like array indices, List indices are zero based (i.e., the first element's index is zero). In addition to the interface methods inherited from Collection, List provides methods for manipulating elements via their indices, manipulating a specified range of elements, searching for elements and getting a *ListIterator* to access the elements.

Interface List is implemented by several classes, including classes *ArrayList*, *LinkedList* and Vector. Class ArrayList is a resizable-array implementation of a List. Class ArrayList's behavior and capabilities are similar to those of class Vector, introduced in Chapter 21. A LinkedList is a linked-list implementation of a List.

Performance Tip 22.2

ArrayLists behave like unsynchronized Vectors and therefore execute faster than Vectors, because ArrayLists do not have the overhead of thread synchronization.

Software Engineering Observation 22.4

LinkedLists can be used to create stacks, queues, trees and deques (double-ended queues).

Figure 22.3 uses an `ArrayList` to demonstrate several `Collection` interface capabilities. The program places `Strings` and `Colors` in an `ArrayList` and uses an `Iterator` to remove the `Strings` from the `ArrayList` collection.

```
1   // Fig. 22.3: CollectionTest.java
2   // Using the Collection interface.
3   import java.awt.Color;
4   import java.util.*;
5
6   public class CollectionTest {
7      private static final String colors[] = { "red", "white", "blue" };
8
9      // create ArrayList, add objects to it and manipulate it
10     public CollectionTest()
11     {
12        List list = new ArrayList();
13
14        // add objects to list
15        list.add( Color.MAGENTA );      // add a color object
16
17        for ( int count = 0; count < colors.length; count++ )
18           list.add( colors[ count ] );
19
20        list.add( Color.CYAN );         // add a color object
21
22        // output list contents
23        System.out.println( "\nArrayList: " );
24
25        for ( int count = 0; count < list.size(); count++ )
26           System.out.print( list.get( count ) + " " );
27
28        // remove all String objects
29        removeStrings( list );
30
31        // output list contents
32        System.out.println( "\n\nArrayList after calling removeStrings: " );
33
34        for ( int count = 0; count < list.size(); count++ )
35           System.out.print( list.get( count ) + " " );
36
37     } // end constructor CollectionTest
38
39     // remove String objects from Collection
40     private void removeStrings( Collection collection )
41     {
42        Iterator iterator = collection.iterator(); // get iterator
43
```

Fig. 22.3 `Collection` interface demonstrated via an `ArrayList` object. (Part 1 of 2.)

```
44              // loop while collection has items
45              while ( iterator.hasNext() )
46
47                  if ( iterator.next() instanceof String )
48                      iterator.remove();   // remove String object
49              }
50
51          public static void main( String args[] )
52          {
53              new CollectionTest();
54          }
55
56      } // end class CollectionTest
```

```
ArrayList:
java.awt.Color[r=255,g=0,b=255] red white blue java.awt.Color
[r=0,g=255,b=255]

ArrayList after calling removeStrings:
java.awt.Color[r=255,g=0,b=255] java.awt.Color[r=0,g=255,b=255]
```

Fig. 22.3   Collection interface demonstrated via an ArrayList object. (Part 2 of 2.)

Line 12 creates an instance of an ArrayList and assigns its reference to variable list. Lines 15–20 populate list with Color and String objects. Lines 23–26 output each element of list. Line 25 calls List method size to get the number of ArrayList elements. Line 26 uses List method get to retrieve individual element values. Line 29 calls method removeStrings (declared on lines 40–49), passing list to it as an argument. Method removeStrings deletes Strings from a collection. Lines 32–35 print the elements of list after removeStrings removes the String objects from the list. The output in Fig. 22.3 contains only Colors after the Strings are removed.

Method removeStrings declares one parameter of type Collection (line 40) that allows any Collection to be passed as an argument to this method. The method accesses the elements of the Collection via an Iterator. Line 42 calls Collection method *iterator* to get an Iterator for the Collection. The loop condition (line 45) calls Iterator method *hasNext* to determine whether the Collection contains any more elements. Method hasNext returns true if another element exists and false otherwise.

The if condition at line 47 calls Iterator method *next* to obtain a reference to the next element, then uses instanceof to determine whether the object is a String. If so, line 48 calls Iterator method *remove* to remove the String from the Collection.

Common Programming Error 22.3

When iterating through a collection with an Iterator, use Iterator method remove to delete an element from the collection. Iterators are "fail fast"—if the collection is modified by one of the collection's methods after an iterator is created for that collection, each iterator operation will throw a ConcurrentModificationException.

Figure 22.4 demonstrates operations on LinkedLists. The program creates two LinkedLists that each contain Strings. The elements of one List are added to the other. Then all the Strings are converted to uppercase, and a range of elements is deleted.

Lines 14–15 create `LinkedLists` `link` and `link2`, respectively. Lines 18–21 call `List` method `add` to append elements from arrays `colors` and `colors2` to the end of `link` and `link2`, respectively.

```
1   // Fig. 22.4: ListTest.java
2   // Using LinkLists.
3   import java.util.*;
4
5   public class ListTest {
6      private static final String colors[] = { "black", "yellow",
7         "green", "blue", "violet", "silver" };
8      private static final String colors2[] = { "gold", "white",
9         "brown", "blue", "gray", "silver" };
10
11     // set up and manipulate LinkedList objects
12     public ListTest()
13     {
14        List link = new LinkedList();
15        List link2 = new LinkedList();
16
17        // add elements to each list
18        for ( int count = 0; count < colors.length; count++ ) {
19           link.add( colors[ count ] );
20           link2.add( colors2[ count ] );
21        }
22
23        link.addAll( link2 );              // concatenate lists
24        link2 = null;                      // release resources
25
26        printList( link );
27
28        uppercaseStrings( link );
29
30        printList( link );
31
32        System.out.print( "\nDeleting elements 4 to 6..." );
33        removeItems( link, 4, 7 );
34
35        printList( link );
36
37        printReversedList( link );
38
39     } // end constructor ListTest
40
41     // output List contents
42     public void printList( List list )
43     {
44        System.out.println( "\nlist: " );
45
46        for ( int count = 0; count < list.size(); count++ )
47           System.out.print( list.get( count ) + " " );
48
```

Fig. 22.4 Lists and ListIterators. (Part 1 of 2.)

```
49            System.out.println();
50         }
51
52         // locate String objects and convert to uppercase
53         private void uppercaseStrings( List list )
54         {
55            ListIterator iterator = list.listIterator();
56
57            while ( iterator.hasNext() ) {
58               Object object = iterator.next();   // get item
59
60               if ( object instanceof String )    // check for String
61                  iterator.set( ( ( String ) object ).toUpperCase() );
62            }
63         }
64
65         // obtain sublist and use clear method to delete sublist items
66         private void removeItems( List list, int start, int end )
67         {
68            list.subList( start, end ).clear();   // remove items
69         }
70
71         // print reversed list
72         private void printReversedList( List list )
73         {
74            ListIterator iterator = list.listIterator( list.size() );
75
76            System.out.println( "\nReversed List:" );
77
78            // print list in reverse order
79            while( iterator.hasPrevious() )
80               System.out.print( iterator.previous() + " " );
81         }
82
83         public static void main( String args[] )
84         {
85            new ListTest();
86         }
87
88      } // end class ListTest
```

```
list:
black yellow green blue violet silver gold white brown blue gray silver

list:
BLACK YELLOW GREEN BLUE VIOLET SILVER GOLD WHITE BROWN BLUE GRAY SILVER

Deleting elements 4 to 6...
list:
BLACK YELLOW GREEN BLUE WHITE BROWN BLUE GRAY SILVER

Reversed List:
SILVER GRAY BLUE BROWN WHITE BLUE GREEN YELLOW BLACK
```

Fig. 22.4   Lists and ListIterators. (Part 2 of 2.)

Line 23 calls List method *addAll* to append all elements of link2 to the end of link. Line 24 sets link2 to null, so the LinkedList to which link2 referred can be garbage collected. Line 26 calls method printList (lines 42–50) to output list link's contents. Line 28 calls method uppercaseStrings (lines 53–63) to convert each String element to uppercase; then line 30 calls printList again to display the modified Strings. Line 33 calls method removeItems (lines 66–69) to remove the elements starting at index 4 up to, but not including, index 7 of the list. Line 37 calls method print-ReversedList (lines 72–81) to print the list in reverse order.

Method uppercaseStrings (lines 53–63) changes lowercase String elements in its List argument to uppercase Strings. Line 55 calls List method *listIterator* to get a *bidirectional iterator* (i.e., an iterator that can traverse a List backward or forward) for the List. The while condition (line 57) calls method hasNext to determine whether the List contains another element. Line 58 gets the next Object in the List and assigns its reference to object. Line 60 determines whether object points to a String. If so, line 61 casts object to a String, calls String method toUpperCase to get an uppercase version of the String and calls Iterator method *set* to replace the current String to which iterator refers with the String returned by method toUpperCase.

Method removeItems (lines 66–69) removes a range of items from the list. Line 68 calls List method *subList* to obtain a portion of the List (called a *sublist*). The sublist is simply a view into the List on which subList is called. Method subList takes two arguments—the beginning index for the sublist and the ending index for the sublist. Note that the ending index is not part of the range of the sublist. In this example, we pass 4 for the beginning index and 7 for the ending index to subList. The sublist returned is the set of elements with indices 4 through 6. Next, the program calls List method *clear* on the sublist to remove the elements of the sublist from the List. Any changes made to a sublist are actually made to the original List.

Method printReversedList (lines 72–81) prints the list backward. Line 74 calls List method listIterator with one argument that specifies the starting position (in our case, the last element in the list) to get a bidirectional iterator for the list. The while condition (line 79) calls method hasPrevious to determine whether there are more elements while traversing the list backward. Line 80 gets the previous Object from the list and outputs it to the standard output stream.

Figure 22.5 uses method *toArray* to get an array from a LinkedList collection. The program adds a series of strings to a LinkedList and calls method toArray to obtain an array containing references to those strings.

```
1   // Fig. 22.5: UsingToArray.java
2   // Using method toArray.
3   import java.util.*;
4
5   public class UsingToArray {
6
7      // create LinkedList, add elements and convert to array
8      public UsingToArray()
9      {
```

Fig. 22.5   List method toArray. (Part 1 of 2.)

```
10        String colors[] = { "black", "blue", "yellow" };
11
12        LinkedList links = new LinkedList( Arrays.asList( colors ) );
13
14        links.addLast( "red" );    // add as last item
15        links.add( "pink" );       // add to the end
16        links.add( 3, "green" );   // add at 3rd index
17        links.addFirst( "cyan" );  // add as first item
18
19        // get LinkedList elements as an array
20        colors = ( String [] ) links.toArray( new String[ links.size() ] );
21
22        System.out.println( "colors: " );
23
24        for ( int count = 0; count < colors.length; count++ )
25           System.out.println( colors[ count ] );
26     }
27
28     public static void main( String args[] )
29     {
30        new UsingToArray();
31     }
32
33  } // end class UsingToArray
```

```
colors:
cyan
black
blue
yellow
green
red
pink
```

Fig. 22.5   List method toArray. (Part 2 of 2.)

Line 12 constructs a LinkedList containing the elements of array colors and assigns the LinkedList reference to links. Note the use of Arrays method asList to initialize the LinkedList with a Collection. Line 14 calls method *addLast* to add "red" to the end of links. Lines 15–16 call method *add* to add "pink" as the last element and "green" as the element at index 3 (i.e., the fourth element). Line 17 calls *addFirst* to add "cyan" as the new first item in the LinkedList. [*Note*: When "cyan" is added as the first element, "green" becomes the fifth element in the LinkedList.]

Line 20 calls List method toArray to get a String array from links. The array is a copy of the list's elements—modifying the contents of the array does not modify the list. The array passed to method toArray is of the same type as you would like method toArray to return. If the number of elements in the array is greater than the number of elements in the LinkedList, toArray copies the list's elements into its array argument and returns that array. If the LinkedList has more elements than the number of elements in the array passed to toArray, toArray allocates a new array of the same type it receives as an argument, copies the list's elements into the new array and returns the new array.

Common Programming Error 22.4

Passing an array that contains data to **toArray** *can create logic errors. If the number of elements in the array is smaller than the number of elements in the object calling* **toArray**, *new memory is allocated to store the object's elements—without preserving the array's elements. If the number of elements in the array is greater than the number of elements in the object, the elements of the array (starting at index zero) are overwritten with the object's elements. Array elements that are not overwritten retain their values.*

22.6 Algorithms

The collections framework provides several high-performance algorithms for manipulating collection elements. These algorithms are implemented as static methods of class `Collections`. Algorithms *sort, binarySearch, reverse, shuffle, fill* and *copy* operate on `List`s. Algorithms *min* and *max* operate on `Collection`s.

Algorithm *reverse* reverses the elements of a `List`; *fill* sets every `List` element to refer to a specified `Object`; and *copy* copies references from one `List` into another.

Software Engineering Observation 22.5

The collections-framework algorithms are polymorphic. That is, each algorithm can operate on objects that implement specific interfaces, regardless of the underlying implementations.

22.6.1 Algorithm sort

Algorithm `sort` sorts the elements of a `List`. The order is determined by the natural order of the elements' type as implemented by that object's `compareTo` method. Method `compareTo` is declared in interface *Comparable* and is sometimes called the *natural comparison method*. The `sort` call may specify as a second argument a *Comparator* object that determines an alternate ordering of the elements.

Algorithm `sort` uses a *stable sort*—a sort that does not reorder equivalent elements. The `sort` algorithm is fast. For readers who have studied some complexity theory in data structures or algorithms courses, this sort runs in $n \log(n)$ time. (Readers not familiar with complexity theory may rest assured that this algorithm is extremely fast.)

Software Engineering Observation 22.6

The Java API documentation sometimes provides implementation details. For example, sort *is implemented as a modified merge sort. Avoid writing code that is dependent on implementation details, because they can change.*

Figure 22.6 uses algorithm `sort` to order the elements of a `List` into ascending order (line 18). Note that lines 16 and 21 each use an implicit call to the list's `toString` method to output the list contents in the format shown on the second and fourth lines of the output.

```
1   // Fig. 22.6: Sort1.java
2   // Using algorithm sort.
3   import java.util.*;
4
5   public class Sort1 {
```

Fig. 22.6   `Collections` method `sort`. (Part 1 of 2.)

```
6      private static final String suits[] =
7         { "Hearts", "Diamonds", "Clubs", "Spades" };
8
9      // display array elements
10     public void printElements()
11     {
12        // create ArrayList
13        List list = new ArrayList( Arrays.asList( suits ) );
14
15        // output list
16        System.out.println( "Unsorted array elements:\n" + list );
17
18        Collections.sort( list ); // sort ArrayList
19
20        // output list
21        System.out.println( "Sorted array elements:\n" + list );
22     }
23
24     public static void main( String args[] )
25     {
26        new Sort1().printElements();
27     }
28
29  } // end class Sort1
```

```
Unsorted array elements:
[Hearts, Diamonds, Clubs, Spades]
Sorted array elements:
[Clubs, Diamonds, Hearts, Spades]
```

Fig. 22.6   Collections method sort. (Part 2 of 2.)

Figure 22.7 sorts the same list of strings used in Fig. 22.6 into descending order. The example introduces the Comparator object, which is used for sorting a Collection's elements in a different order.

```
1      // Fig. 22.7: Sort2.java
2      // Using a Comparator object with algorithm sort.
3      import java.util.*;
4
5      public class Sort2 {
6         private static final String suits[] =
7            { "Hearts", "Diamonds", "Clubs", "Spades" };
8
9         // output List elements
10        public void printElements()
11        {
12           List list = Arrays.asList( suits ); // create List
13
14           // output List elements
15           System.out.println( "Unsorted array elements:\n" + list );
```

Fig. 22.7   Collections method sort with a Comparator object. (Part 1 of 2.)

```
16
17            // sort in descending order using a comparator
18            Collections.sort( list, Collections.reverseOrder() );
19
20            // output List elements
21            System.out.println( "Sorted list elements:\n" + list );
22        }
23
24        public static void main( String args[] )
25        {
26            new Sort2().printElements();
27        }
28
29    } // end class Sort2
```

```
Unsorted array elements:
[Hearts, Diamonds, Clubs, Spades]
Sorted list elements:
[Spades, Hearts, Diamonds, Clubs]
```

Fig. 22.7   Collections method sort with a Comparator object. (Part 2 of 2.)

Line 18 calls Collections's method sort to order the List in descending order. Static Collections method *reverseOrder* returns a Comparator object that represents the collection's reverse order. For sorting a List view of a String array, the reverse order is a *lexicographical comparison*—the comparator compares the Unicode values that represent each element—in descending order. It is possible to create a custom Comparator by defining a class that implements interface Comparator.

Figure 22.8 creates a custom Comparator. This program creates five Time objects and declares a custom TimeComparator class to compare the objects.

```
1   // Fig. 22.8: Sort3.java
2   // Creating a custom Comparator class.
3   import java.util.*;
4
5   public class Sort3 {
6
7       public void printElements()
8       {
9           List list = new ArrayList(); // create List
10
11          list.add( new Time2(  6, 24, 34 ) );
12          list.add( new Time2( 18, 14, 05 ) );
13          list.add( new Time2(  8, 05, 00 ) );
14          list.add( new Time2( 12, 07, 58 ) );
15          list.add( new Time2(  6, 14, 22 ) );
16
17          // output List elements
18          System.out.println( "Unsorted array elements:\n" + list );
```

Fig. 22.8   Collections method sort with a custom Comparator object. (Part 1 of 2.)

```
19
20        // sort in order using a comparator
21        Collections.sort( list, new TimeComparator() );
22
23        // output List elements
24        System.out.println( "Sorted list elements:\n" + list );
25     }
26
27     public static void main( String args[] )
28     {
29        new Sort2().printElements();
30     }
31
32     private class TimeComparator implements Comparator {
33        int hourCompare, minuteCompare, secondCompare;
34        Time2 time1, time2;
35
36        public int compare(Object object1, Object object2)
37        {
38           // cast the objects
39           time1 = (Time2)object1;
40           time2 = (Time2)object2;
41
42           hourCompare = new Integer( time1.getHour() ).compareTo(
43                         new Integer( time2.getHour() ) );
44
45           // test the hour first
46           if ( hourCompare != 0 )
47              return hourCompare;
48
49           minuteCompare = new Integer( time1.getMinute() ).compareTo(
50                         new Integer( time2.getMinute() ) );
51
52           // then test the minute
53           if ( minuteCompare != 0 )
54              return minuteCompare;
55
56           secondCompare = new Integer( time1.getSecond() ).compareTo(
57                         new Integer( time2.getSecond() ) );
58
59           return secondCompare; // return result of comparing seconds
60        }
61
62     } // end class TimeComparator
63
64  } // end class Sort3
```

```
Unsorted array elements:
[06:24:34, 18:14:05, 08:05:00, 12:07:58, 06:14:22]
Sorted list elements:
[06:14:22, 06:24:34, 08:05:00, 12:07:58, 18:14:05]
```

Fig. 22.8   Collections method sort with a custom Comparator object. (Part 2 of 2.)

Line 9 creates an `ArrayList`. Lines 11–15 create five `Time2` objects and add them to this list. Line 21 calls method `sort`, passing it an object of our `TimeComparator` class.

Lines 32–62 declare class `TimeComparator` which implements interface `Comparator`. Method `compare` (lines 36–60) performs comparisons between `Time2` objects. Lines 39–40 assign `Time2` references to the two objects in variables `time1` and `time2`. Lines 42–43 compare the two hours of the `Time2` objects using `Integer` method `compareTo`. If the hours are different (line 45), then we return this value. If this value is positive, then the first hour is greater than the second and the first time is greater than the second. If this value is negative, then the first hour is less than the second and the first time is less than the second. If this value is zero, the hours are the same and we must test the minute (and maybe the second) in order to determine which time is greater.

22.6.2 Algorithm `shuffle`

Algorithm `shuffle` randomly orders a `List`'s elements. In Chapter 11, we presented a card shuffling and dealing simulation that used a loop to shuffle a deck of cards. In Fig. 22.9, we use algorithm `shuffle` to shuffle the deck of cards. Much of the code is the same as in Fig. 11.19. The shuffling of the deck occurs at line 59, which calls static `Collections` method `shuffle` to shuffle the array through the array's `List` view.

```
1    // Fig. 22.9: Cards.java
2    // Using algorithm shuffle.
3    import java.util.*;
4
5    // class to represent a Card in a deck of cards
6    class Card {
7       private String face;
8       private String suit;
9
10      // initialize a Card
11      public Card( String initialface, String initialSuit )
12      {
13         face = initialface;
14         suit = initialSuit;
15      }
16
17      // return face of Card
18      public String getFace()
19      {
20         return face;
21      }
22
23      // return suit of Card
24      public String getSuit()
25      {
```

Fig. 22.9   Card shuffling and dealing example with `Collections` method `shuffle`. (Part 1 of 3.)

```
26            return suit;
27        }
28
29        // return String representation of Card
30        public String toString()
31        {
32            StringBuffer buffer = new StringBuffer( face + " of " + suit );
33            buffer.setLength( 20 );
34
35            return buffer.toString();
36        }
37
38    } // end class Card
39
40    // class Cards declaration
41    public class Cards {
42        private static final String suits[] =
43            { "Hearts", "Clubs", "Diamonds", "Spades" };
44        private static final String faces[] = { "Ace", "Deuce", "Three",
45            "Four", "Five", "Six", "Seven", "Eight", "Nine", "Ten",
46            "Jack", "Queen", "King" };
47        private List list;
48
49        // set up deck of Cards and shuffle
50        public Cards()
51        {
52            Card deck[] = new Card[ 52 ];
53
54            for ( int count = 0; count < deck.length; count++ )
55                deck[ count ] = new Card( faces[ count % 13 ],
56                    suits[ count / 13 ] );
57
58            list = Arrays.asList( deck );    // get List
59            Collections.shuffle( list );     // shuffle deck
60        }
61
62        // output deck
63        public void printCards()
64        {
65            int half = list.size() / 2 - 1;
66
67            for ( int i = 0, j = half + 1; i <= half; i++, j++ )
68                System.out.println( list.get( i ).toString() + list.get( j ) );
69        }
70
71        public static void main( String args[] )
72        {
73            new Cards().printCards();
74        }
75
76    } // end class Cards
```

Fig. 22.9   Card shuffling and dealing example with `Collections` method `shuffle`.
(Part 2 of 3.)

King of Diamonds   Jack of Spades
Four of Diamonds   Six of Clubs
King of Hearts   Nine of Diamonds
Three of Spades   Four of Spades
Four of Hearts   Seven of Spades
Five of Diamonds   Eight of Hearts
Queen of Diamonds   Five of Hearts
Seven of Diamonds   Seven of Hearts
Nine of Hearts   Three of Clubs
Ten of Spades   Deuce of Hearts
Three of Hearts   Ace of Spades
Six of Hearts   Eight of Diamonds
Six of Diamonds   Deuce of Clubs
Ace of Clubs   Ten of Diamonds
Eight of Clubs   Queen of Hearts
Jack of Clubs   Ten of Clubs
Seven of Clubs   Queen of Spades
Five of Clubs   Six of Spades
Nine of Spades   Nine of Clubs
King of Spades   Ace of Diamonds
Ten of Hearts   Ace of Hearts
Queen of Clubs   Deuce of Spades
Three of Diamonds   King of Clubs
Four of Clubs   Jack of Diamonds
Eight of Spades   Five of Spades
Jack of Hearts   Deuce of Diamonds

Fig. 22.9   Card shuffling and dealing example with `Collections` method `shuffle`. (Part 3 of 3.)

22.6.3 Algorithms reverse, fill, copy, max and min

Class `Collections` provides algorithms for reversing, filling and copying `List`s. Algorithm `reverse` reverses the order of the elements in a `List`, and algorithm `fill` overwrites elements in a `List` with a specified value. (The `fill` operation is useful for reinitializing a `List`.) Algorithm `copy` takes two arguments—a destination `List` and a source `List`. Each source `List` element is copied to the destination `List`. The destination `List` must be at least as long as the source `List`; otherwise, an `IndexOutOfBoundsException` occurs. If the destination `List` is longer, the elements not overwritten are unchanged.

Each of the algorithms we have seen so far operates on `List`s. Algorithms `min` and `max` each operate on any `Collection`. Algorithm `min` returns the smallest element in a `List` (remember that a `List` is a `Collection`), and algorithm `max` returns the largest element in a `List`. Both of these algorithms can be called with a `Comparator` object as a second argument to perform custom comparisons of objects. Figure 22.10 demonstrates the use of algorithms `reverse`, `fill`, `copy`, `min` and `max`.

Line 19 calls `Collections` method *reverse* to reverse the order of `list`. Method `reverse` takes one `List` argument. (In this case, `list` is a `List` view of array `letters`.) Array `letters` now has its elements in reverse order.

Line 23 copies the elements of list into copyList, using Collections method copy. Changes to copyList do not change letters—copyList is a separate List that is not a List view for letters. Method copy requires two List arguments.

Line 27 calls Collections method fill to place the string "R" in each element of list. Because list is a List view of letters, this operation changes each element in letters to "R". Method fill requires a List for the first argument and an Object for the second argument.

Lines 41 and 42 call Collection methods max and min to find the largest element and the smallest element, respectively.

```
1   // Fig. 22.10: Algorithms1.java
2   // Using algorithms reverse, fill, copy, min and max.
3   import java.util.*;
4
5   public class Algorithms1 {
6      private String letters[] = { "P", "C", "M" }, lettersCopy[];
7      private List list, copyList;
8
9      // create a List and manipulate it with methods from Collections
10     public Algorithms1()
11     {
12        list = Arrays.asList( letters );      // get List
13        lettersCopy = new String[ 3 ];
14        copyList = Arrays.asList( lettersCopy );
15
16        System.out.println( "Initial list: " );
17        output( list );
18
19        Collections.reverse( list );          // reverse order
20        System.out.println( "\nAfter calling reverse: " );
21        output( list );
22
23        Collections.copy( copyList, list );   // copy List
24        System.out.println( "\nAfter copying: " );
25        output( copyList );
26
27        Collections.fill( list, "R" );        // fill list with Rs
28        System.out.println( "\nAfter calling fill: " );
29        output( list );
30
31     } // end constructor
32
33     // output List information
34     private void output( List listRef )
35     {
36        System.out.print( "The list is: " );
37
38        for ( int k = 0; k < listRef.size(); k++ )
39           System.out.print( listRef.get( k ) + " " );
40
41        System.out.print( "\nMax: " + Collections.max( listRef ) );
```

Fig. 22.10 Collections methods reverse, fill, copy, max and min. (Part 1 of 2.)

```
42            System.out.println( "  Min: " + Collections.min( listRef ) );
43        }
44
45        public static void main( String args[] )
46        {
47            new Algorithms1();
48        }
49
50    } // end class Algorithms1
```

```
Initial list:
The list is: P C M
Max: P  Min: C

After calling reverse:
The list is: M C P
Max: P  Min: C

After copying:
The list is: M C P
Max: P  Min: C

After calling fill:
The list is: R R R
Max: R  Min: R
```

Fig. 22.10 Collections methods reverse, fill, copy, max and min. (Part 2 of 2.)

22.6.4 Algorithm binarySearch

In Section 7.8, we studied the high-speed binary-search algorithm. This algorithm is built into the Java collections framework as a static method of class Collections. The binarySearch algorithm locates an Object in a List (i.e., a LinkedList, a Vector or an ArrayList) If the Object is found, the index of that Object is returned. If the Object is not found, binarySearch returns a negative value. Algorithm binarySearch determines this negative value by first calculating the insertion point and changing the insertion point's sign to negative. Finally, binarySearch subtracts one from the insertion point to obtain the return value. If multiple elements in the list match the search key, there is no guarantee which one will be located first. Figure 22.11 uses the binarySearch algorithm to search for a series of strings in an ArrayList.

Before searching with binary search, the list's elements must be sorted in ascending order, so line 14 in the constructor sorts the list with Collections method sort. Line 15 outputs the sorted list. Method printSearchResults (lines 19–27) is called from main to perform the searches. Each search calls method printSearchResultsHelper (lines 30–38) to perform the search and output the results. Line 35 calls Collections method binarySearch to search list for the specified key. Method binarySearch takes a List as the first argument and an Object as the second argument. Lines 36–37 output the results of the search. An overloaded version of binarySearch takes a Comparator object as its third argument, which specifies how binarySearch should compare elements.

```
1    // Fig. 22.11: BinarySearchTest.java
2    // Using algorithm binarySearch.
3    import java.util.*;
4
5    public class BinarySearchTest {
6       private static final String colors[] = { "red", "white",
7          "blue", "black", "yellow", "purple", "tan", "pink" };
8       private List list;          // List reference
9
10      // create, sort and output list
11      public BinarySearchTest()
12      {
13         list = new ArrayList( Arrays.asList( colors ) );
14         Collections.sort( list );    // sort the ArrayList
15         System.out.println( "Sorted ArrayList: " + list );
16      }
17
18      // search list for various values
19      private void printSearchResults()
20      {
21         printSearchResultsHelper( colors[ 3 ] ); // first item
22         printSearchResultsHelper( colors[ 0 ] ); // middle item
23         printSearchResultsHelper( colors[ 7 ] ); // last item
24         printSearchResultsHelper( "aardvark" );  // below lowest
25         printSearchResultsHelper( "goat" );      // does not exist
26         printSearchResultsHelper( "zebra" );     // does not exist
27      }
28
29      // helper method to perform searches
30      private void printSearchResultsHelper( String key )
31      {
32         int result = 0;
33
34         System.out.println( "\nSearching for: " + key );
35         result = Collections.binarySearch( list, key );
36         System.out.println( ( result >= 0 ? "Found at index " + result :
37            "Not Found (" + result + ")" ) );
38      }
39
40      public static void main( String args[] )
41      {
42         new BinarySearchTest().printSearchResults();
43      }
44
45   } // end class BinarySearchTest
```

```
Sorted ArrayList: [black, blue, pink, purple, red, tan, white, yellow]

Searching for: black
Found at index 0
```

(continued on next page)

Fig. 22.11 Collections method binarySearch. (Part 1 of 2.)

(continued from previous page)

```
Searching for: red
Found at index 4

Searching for: pink
Found at index 2

Searching for: aardvark
Not Found (-1)

Searching for: goat
Not Found (-3)

Searching for: zebra
Not Found (-9)
```

Fig. 22.11 `Collections` method `binarySearch`. (Part 2 of 2.)

22.7 Sets

A *Set* is a `Collection` that contains unique elements (i.e., no duplicate elements). The collections framework contains several `Set` implementations, including *HashSet* and *TreeSet*. HashSet stores its elements in a hash table, and `TreeSet` stores its elements in a tree. Figure 22.12 uses a `HashSet` to remove duplicate strings from an `ArrayList`.

```
1   // Fig. 22.12: SetTest.java
2   // Using a HashSet to remove duplicates.
3   import java.util.*;
4
5   public class SetTest {
6      private static final String colors[] = { "red", "white", "blue",
7         "green", "gray", "orange", "tan", "white", "cyan",
8         "peach", "gray", "orange" };
9
10     // create and output ArrayList
11     public SetTest()
12     {
13        List list = new ArrayList( Arrays.asList( colors ) );
14        System.out.println( "ArrayList: " + list );
15        printNonDuplicates( list );
16     }
17
18     // create set from array to eliminate duplicates
19     private void printNonDuplicates( Collection collection )
20     {
21        // create a HashSet and obtain its iterator
22        Set set = new HashSet( collection );
23        Iterator iterator = set.iterator();
24
25        System.out.println( "\nNonduplicates are: " );
```

Fig. 22.12 `HashSet` used to remove duplicate values from array of strings. (Part 1 of 2.)

```
26            while ( iterator.hasNext() )
27                System.out.print( iterator.next() + " " );
28
29
30            System.out.println();
31        }
32
33        public static void main( String args[] )
34        {
35            new SetTest();
36        }
37
38    } // end class SetTest
```

```
ArrayList: [red, white, blue, green, gray, orange, tan, white, cyan, peach,
gray, orange]

Nonduplicates are:
red cyan white tan gray green orange blue peach
```

Fig. 22.12 HashSet used to remove duplicate values from array of strings. (Part 2 of 2.)

Method `printNonDuplicates` (lines 19–31), which is called from the constructor, takes a `Collection` argument. Line 22 constructs a `HashSet` from the `Collection` argument. By definition, `Set`s do not contain any duplicates. So, when the `HashSet` is constructed, it removes any duplicates in the `Collection`. Line 23 gets an `Iterator` for the `Set`. The loop at lines 27–28 calls `Iterator` methods `hasNext` and `next` to access the `Set` elements and output their values.

Sorted Sets

The collections framework also includes interface *SortedSet* (which extends `Set`) for sets that maintain their elements in sorted order—either the elements' natural order (e.g., numbers are in ascending order) or an order specified by a `Comparator`. Class `TreeSet` implements `SortedSet`. The program of Fig. 22.13 places strings into a `TreeSet`. The strings are sorted as they are added to the `TreeSet`. This example also demonstrates *range-view methods*, which enable a program to view a portion of a collection.

```
1    // Fig. 22.13: SortedSetTest.java
2    // Using TreeSet and SortedSet.
3    import java.util.*;
4
5    public class SortedSetTest {
6        private static final String names[] = { "yellow", "green",
7            "black", "tan", "grey", "white", "orange", "red", "green" };
8
9        // create a sorted set with TreeSet, then manipulate it
10       public SortedSetTest()
11       {
```

Fig. 22.13 Using SortedSets and TreeSets. (Part 1 of 2.)

```
12          SortedSet tree = new TreeSet( Arrays.asList( names ) );
13
14          System.out.println( "set: " );
15          printSet( tree );
16
17          // get headSet based upon "orange"
18          System.out.print( "\nheadSet (\"orange\"):   " );
19          printSet( tree.headSet( "orange" ) );
20
21          // get tailSet based upon "orange"
22          System.out.print( "tailSet (\"orange\"):   " );
23          printSet( tree.tailSet( "orange" ) );
24
25          // get first and last elements
26          System.out.println( "first: " + tree.first() );
27          System.out.println( "last : " + tree.last() );
28       }
29
30       // output set
31       private void printSet( SortedSet set )
32       {
33          Iterator iterator = set.iterator();
34
35          while ( iterator.hasNext() )
36             System.out.print( iterator.next() + " " );
37
38          System.out.println();
39       }
40
41       public static void main( String args[] )
42       {
43          new SortedSetTest();
44       }
45
46    } // end class SortedSetTest
```

```
set:
black green grey orange red tan white yellow

headSet ("orange"):   black green grey
tailSet ("orange"):   orange red tan white yellow
first: black
last : yellow
```

Fig. 22.13 Using SortedSets and TreeSets. (Part 2 of 2.)

Line 12 of the constructor creates a TreeSet object containing the elements of array names and assigns the SortedSet to reference tree. Line 15 outputs the initial set of strings using method printSet (lines 31–39), which we discuss momentarily. Line 19 calls TreeSet method *headSet* to get a subset of the TreeSet in which every element is less than "orange". The view returned from headSet is then output with printSet. If any changes are made to the subset, those changes will also be made to the original TreeSet. Thus, the subset returned by headSet is a view of the TreeSet.

Line 23 calls TreeSet method *tailSet* to get a subset in which each element is greater than or equal to "orange". The subset returned by tailSet is then output. Any changes made through the tailSet view are made to the original TreeSet. Lines 26–27 call SortedSet methods *first* and *last* to get the smallest and largest elements of the set, respectively.

Method printSet (lines 31–39) receives a SortedSet as an argument and prints it. Line 33 gets an Iterator for the Set, which is used in lines 35–36 to print each element of the SortedSet.

22.8 Maps

Maps associate keys to values and cannot contain duplicate keys (i.e., each key can map to only one value; this type of mapping is called *one-to-one mapping*). Maps differ from Sets in that Maps contain keys and values, whereas Sets contain only values. Two of the several classes that implement interface Map are *HashMap* and *TreeMap*. HashMaps store elements in hash tables, and TreeMaps store elements in trees. Interface *SortedMap* extends Map and maintains its keys in sorted order—either the elements' natural order or an order specified by a Comparator. Class TreeMap implements SortedMap. Figure 22.14 uses a HashMap to count the number of occurrences of each word in a string. Class HashMap allows a null key and null values.

```
1    // Fig. 21.14: WordTypeCount.java
2    // Program counts the number of occurrences of each word in a string
3    import java.awt.*;
4    import java.awt.event.*;
5    import java.util.*;
6    import javax.swing.*;
7
8    public class WordTypeCount extends JFrame {
9        private JTextArea inputField;
10       private JLabel prompt;
11       private JTextArea display;
12       private JButton goButton;
13
14       private Map map;
15
16       public WordTypeCount()
17       {
18           super( "Word Type Count" );
19           inputField = new JTextArea( 3, 20 );
20
21           map = new HashMap();
22
23           goButton = new JButton( "Go" );
24           goButton.addActionListener(
25
26               new ActionListener() { // inner class
27
28                   public void actionPerformed( ActionEvent event )
29                   {
```

Fig. 22.14 HashMaps and Maps. (Part 1 of 3.)

```
30                    createMap();
31                    display.setText( createOutput() );
32               }
33
34           } // end inner class
35
36      ); // end call to addActionListener
37
38      prompt = new JLabel( "Enter a string:" );
39      display = new JTextArea( 15, 20 );
40      display.setEditable( false );
41
42      JScrollPane displayScrollPane = new JScrollPane( display );
43
44      // add components to GUI
45      Container container = getContentPane();
46      container.setLayout( new FlowLayout() );
47      container.add( prompt );
48      container.add( inputField );
49      container.add( goButton );
50      container.add( displayScrollPane );
51
52      setSize( 400, 400 );
53      show();
54
55   } // end constructor
56
57   // create map from user input
58   private void createMap()
59   {
60      String input = inputField.getText();
61      StringTokenizer tokenizer = new StringTokenizer( input );
62
63      while ( tokenizer.hasMoreTokens() ) {
64         String word = tokenizer.nextToken().toLowerCase(); // get word
65
66         // if the map contains the word
67         if ( map.containsKey( word ) ) {
68
69            Integer count = (Integer) map.get( word ); // get value
70
71            // increment value
72            map.put( word, new Integer( count.intValue() + 1 ) );
73         }
74         else // otherwise add word with a value of 1 to map
75            map.put( word, new Integer( 1 ) );
76
77      } // end while
78
79   } // end method createMap
80
81   // create string containing map values
82   private String createOutput() {
```

Fig. 22.14 HashMaps and Maps. (Part 2 of 3.)

```
83          StringBuffer output = new StringBuffer( "" );
84          Iterator keys = map.keySet().iterator();
85
86          // iterate through the keys
87          while ( keys.hasNext() ) {
88             Object currentKey = keys.next();
89
90             // output the key-value pairs
91             output.append( currentKey + "\t" +
92                               map.get( currentKey ) + "\n" );
93          }
94
95          output.append( "size: " + map.size() + "\n" );
96          output.append( "isEmpty: " + map.isEmpty() + "\n" );
97
98          return output.toString();
99
100      } // end method createOutput
101
102      public static void main( String args[] )
103      {
104         WordTypeCount application = new WordTypeCount();
105         application.setDefaultCloseOperation( JFrame.EXIT_ON_CLOSE );
106      }
107
108   } // end class WordTypeCount
```

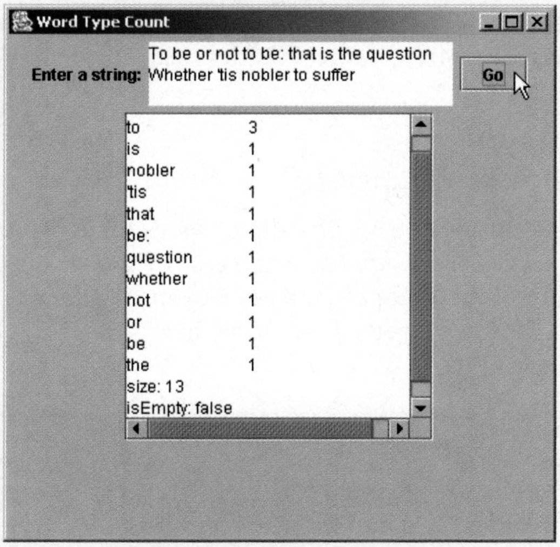

Fig. 22.14   HashMaps and Maps. (Part 3 of 3.)

Line 21 creates a HashMap and assigns it to map. The user enters a sentence in the text-area at the top of the window, then presses the **Go** button to invoke actionPerformed (lines 28–32). Line 30 calls method createMap (lines 58–79), which uses a map to store the number of occurrences of each word in the sentence. Line 60 obtains the user input, and line 61 creates a StringTokenizer to tokenize the string. While there are more tokens, line 64 converts the next token to lowercase letters. Then line 67 calls Map method *containsKey* to determine whether the word is in the map (and thus has occurred previously in the string). If the Map does not contain a mapping for the word, line 75 uses Map method *put* to create a new entry in the map, with the word as the key and an Integer object containing 1 as the value. If the word does exist in the map, line 69 use Map method get to obtain the key's associated value in the map. Line 72 increments that value and uses put to replace the key's associated value in the map. Method put returns the prior value associated with the key, or null if the key was not in the map.

Method createOutput (lines 82–100) creates a string with all the entries in the map. It uses HashMap method *keySet* (line 84) to get a set of the keys. It then uses an iterator for that set in a loop (lines 87–93) to access each key in the map. Line 91 appends each key and its associated value to string output. Lines 95–96 call Map methods *size* and *isEmpty* to get the number of key-value pairs in the Map and a boolean indicating whether the Map is empty, respectively.

22.9 Synchronization Wrappers

In Chapter 16, we discussed multithreading. The collections in the collections framework are unsynchronized by default, so they can operate efficiently. Because they are unsynchronized, however, concurrent access to a Collection by multiple threads could cause indeterminate results or fatal errors. To prevent potential threading problems, synchronization wrappers are used for collections that might be accessed by multiple threads. A *wrapper class* receives method calls, adds thread synchronization for thread safety and delegates the calls to the wrapped class. The Collections API provides a set of static methods for converting collections to synchronized versions. Method headers for the synchronization wrappers are listed in Fig. 22.15.

22.10 Unmodifiable Wrappers

The Collections API provides a set of static methods for converting collections to unmodifiable versions (called *unmodifiable wrappers*) of those collections. Unmodifiable wrappers throw UnsupportedOperationExceptions if attempts are made to modify the collection. Headers for these methods are listed in Fig. 22.16.

---

public static method header

```
Collection synchronizedCollection( Collection c )
List synchronizedList( List aList )
Set synchronizedSet( Set s )
SortedSet synchronizedSortedSet( SortedSet s )
Map synchronizedMap( Map m )
SortedMap synchronizedSortedMap( SortedMap m )
```

Fig. 22.15 Synchronization wrapper methods.

public static method header

```
Collection unmodifiableCollection( Collection c )
List unmodifiableList( List aList )
Set unmodifiableSet( Set s )
SortedSet unmodifiableSortedSet( SortedSet s )
Map unmodifiableMap( Map m )
SortedMap unmodifiableSortedMap( SortedMap m )
```

Fig. 22.16 Unmodifiable wrapper methods.

Software Engineering Observation 22.7

You can use an unmodifiable wrapper to create a collection that offers read-only access to others, while allowing read–write access to yourself. You do this simply by giving others a reference to the unmodifiable wrapper while retaining for yourself a reference to the wrapped collection itself.

22.11 Abstract Implementations

The collections framework provides various abstract implementations of collection interfaces from which the programmer can quickly "flesh out" complete customized implementations. These abstract implementations are a thin `Collection` implementation called an *AbstractCollection*, a thin `List` implementation with random-access backing called an *AbstractList*, a thin Map implementation called an *AbstractMap*, a thin `List` implementation with sequential-access backing called an *AbstractSequentialList* and a thin Set implementation called an *AbstractSet*.

To write a custom implementation, begin by extending the abstract-implementation class that best meets your needs. Next, implement each of the class's `abstract` methods. Then, if your collection is to be modifiable, override any concrete methods that prevent modification.

22.12 (Optional) Discovering Design Patterns: Design Patterns Used in Package `java.util`

In this section, we use the material on data structures and collections discussed in Chapters 20–22 to identify classes from package **java.util** that use design patterns. This section concludes our treatment of design patterns.

22.12.1 Creational Design Patterns

We conclude our discussion of creational design patterns by discussing the Prototype design pattern.

Prototype

Sometimes a system must make a copy of an object, but will not "know" that object's class until run time. For example, consider the drawing program design of Exercise 10.9—classes MyLine, MyOval and MyRect represent "shape" classes that extend abstract superclass MyShape. We could modify this exercise to allow the user to create, copy and paste new instances of class MyLine into the program. The *Prototype design pattern* allows an object—called a *prototype*—to return a copy of that prototype to a requesting object—called a *client*. Every prototype must belong to a class that implements a common interface that allows the prototype to clone itself. For example, the Java API provides method clone from class java.lang.Object and interface java.lang.Cloneable—any object from a class implementing Cloneable can use method clone to copy itself. Specifically, method clone creates a copy of an object, then returns a reference to that object. If we designate class MyLine as the prototype for Exercise 10.9, then class MyLine must implement interface Cloneable. To create a new line in our drawing, we clone the MyLine prototype. To copy a preexisting line, we clone that object. Method clone also is useful in methods that return a reference to an object, but the developer does not want that object to be altered through that reference—method clone returns a reference to the copy of the object instead of returning that object's reference. For more information on interface Cloneable, visit

    www.java.sun.com/j2se/1.4/docs/api/java/lang/Cloneable.html

22.12.2 Behavioral Design Patterns

We conclude our discussion of behavioral design patterns by discussing the Iterator design pattern.

Iterator

Designers use data structures such as arrays, linked lists and hash tables to organize data in a program. The *Iterator design pattern* allows objects to access individual objects from any data structure without "knowing" the data structure's behavior (such as traversing the structure or removing an element from that structure) or how that data structure stores objects. Instructions for traversing the data structure and accessing its elements are stored in a separate object called an *iterator*. Each data structure can create an iterator—each iterator implements methods of a common interface to traverse the data structure and access its data. A client can traverse two differently structured data structures—such as a linked list and a hash table—in the same manner, because both data structures provide an iterator object that belongs to a class implementing a common interface. Java provides interface Iterator from package java.util, which we discussed in Section 22.5—class CollectionTest (Fig. 22.3) uses an Iterator object.

22.12.3 Conclusion

In our optional "Discovering Design Patterns" sections, we have introduced the importance, usefulness and prevalence of design patterns. We have mentioned that in their book *Design Patterns, Elements of Reusable Object-Oriented Software*, the "Gang of Four" described 23 design patterns that provide proven strategies for building systems. Each pattern belongs to one of three pattern categories: creational, which address issues related to object creation; structural, which provide ways to organize classes and objects in a system; and behavioral, which offer strategies for modeling how objects collaborate with one another in a system.

Of the 23 design patterns, we discussed 18 of the more popular ones used by the Java community. In Section 10.12, Section 14.14, Section 16.12, Section 18.12 and Section 22.12, we divided the discussion according to how certain Java packages—such as package `java.awt`, `javax.swing`, `java.io`, `java.net` and `java.util`—use these design patterns. We also discussed patterns not described by the "Gang of Four," such as concurrency patterns, which are useful in multithreaded systems, and architectural patterns, which help designers assign functionality to various subsystems in a system. We have motivated each pattern—that is, explained why that pattern is important and how it may be used. When appropriate, we supplied several examples in the form of real-world analogies (e.g., the adapter in the Adapter design pattern is similar to an adapter for a plug on an electrical device). We also gave examples of how Java packages take advantage of design patterns (e.g., Swing GUI components use the Observer design pattern to collaborate with their listeners to respond to user interactions). We also provided examples of how certain programs in *Java How to Program, Fifth edition* used design patterns (e.g., the elevator-simulation case study in our optional "Thinking About Objects" sections uses the State design pattern to represent a `Person` object's location in the simulation).

We hope that you view our "Discovering Design Patterns" sections as a beginning to further study of design patterns. If you have not done so already, we recommend that you visit the many URLs we have provided in Section 10.12.5, Internet and World Wide Web Resources. We recommend that you then read the Gang of Four book. This information will help you build better systems using the collective wisdom of the object-technology industry.

If you have studied the optional sections in this book, you have been introduced to more substantial Java systems. If you have read our optional "Thinking about Objects" sections, you have immersed yourself in a substantial design and Java implementation experience learning a disciplined approach to object-oriented design with the UML. If you have read our optional "Discovering Design Patterns" sections, you have raised your awareness of the more advanced topic of design patterns.

We hope you continue your study of design patterns, and we would be most grateful if you would send your comments, criticisms and suggestions for improvement of *Java How to Program* to deitel@deitel.com. Good luck!

SUMMARY

- The Java collections framework gives the programmer access to prepackaged data structures, as well as algorithms for manipulating those data structures.

- A collection is an object that can hold references to other objects. The collection interfaces declare the operations that can be performed on each type of collection.

- The classes and interfaces of the collections framework are in package `java.util`.

- Class `Arrays` provides static methods for manipulating arrays, including `sort` for sorting an array, `binarySearch` for searching a sorted array, `equals` for comparing arrays and `fill` for placing items in an array.

- `Arrays` method `asList` returns a `List` view of an array, which enables a program to manipulate the array as if it were a `List`. Any modifications made through the `List` view change the array, and any modifications to the array change the `List` view.

- Method `size` gets the number of items in a `List`, and method `get` returns a `List` element.

- Interface `Collection` is the root interface in the collections hierarchy from which interfaces `Set` and `List` are derived. Interface `Collection` contains bulk operations for adding, clearing, comparing and retaining objects in a collection. Interface `Collection` provides a method `iterator` for getting an `Iterator`.

- Class `Collections` provides static methods for manipulating collections. Many of the methods are implementations of polymorphic algorithms for searching, sorting and so on.

- A `List` is an ordered `Collection` that can contain duplicate elements.

- Interface `List` is implemented by classes `ArrayList`, `LinkedList` and `Vector`. Class `Array-List` is a resizable-array implementation of a `List`. A `LinkedList` is a linked-list implementation of a `List`.

- `Iterator` method `hasNext` determines whether a `Collection` contains another element. Method `next` returns a reference to the next object in the `Collection` and advances the `Iterator`.

- Method `subList` returns a view of a portion of a `List`. Any changes made to a sublist are also made to the `List`.

- Method `clear` removes elements from a `List`.

- Method `toArray` returns the contents of a collection as an array.

- Algorithms `sort`, `binarySearch`, `reverse`, `shuffle`, `fill` and `copy` operate on `List`s. Algorithms `min` and `max` operate on `Collections`. Algorithm `reverse` reverses the elements of a `List`; `fill` sets every `List` element to a specified `Object`; and `copy` copies elements from one `List` into another `List`. Algorithm `sort` sorts the elements of a `List`.

- Algorithms `min` and `max` find the smallest item and the largest item in a `Collection`.

- The `Comparator` object provides a means of sorting a `Collection`'s elements in an order other than the natural order of the elements.

- `Collections` method `reverseOrder` returns a `Comparator` object that can be used with `sort` to sort elements of a collection in reverse order.

- Algorithm `shuffle` randomly orders the elements of a `List`.

- Algorithm `binarySearch` locates an `Object` in a sorted `List`.

- A `Set` is a `Collection` that contains no duplicate elements. `HashSet` stores its elements in a hash table. `TreeSet` stores its elements in a tree.

- Interface `SortedSet` extends `Set` and represents a set that maintains its elements in sorted order. Class `TreeSet` implements `SortedSet`.

- `TreeSet` method `headSet` gets a subset of a `TreeSet` that is less than a specified element. Method `tailSet` gets a subset that is greater than or equal to a specified element. Any changes made to the subset are made to the `TreeSet`.

- Maps map keys to values and cannot contain duplicate keys. Maps differ from `Sets` in that `Maps` contain both keys and values, whereas `Sets` contain only values. `HashMaps` store elements in a hash table, and `TreeMaps` store elements in a tree.

- Interface `SortedMap` extends `Map` and represents a map that maintains its keys in sorted order. Class `TreeMap` implements `SortedMap`.

- Collections from the collections framework are unsynchronized. Synchronization wrappers are provided for collections that might be accessed by multiple threads.

- The `Collections` API provides a set of `public static` methods for converting collections to unmodifiable versions. Unmodifiable wrappers throw `UnsupportedOperationExceptions` if attempts are made to modify the collection.

- The collections framework provides various abstract implementations of collection interfaces from which the programmer can quickly "flesh out" complete customized implementations.

TERMINOLOGY

AbstractCollection class
AbstractList class
AbstractMap class
AbstractSequentialList class
AbstractSet class
add method of List
addFirst method of List
addLast method of List
algorithms
ArrayList
arrays
arrays as collections
asList method of Arrays
bidirectional iterator
binarySearch method of Arrays
binarySearch method of Collections
clear method of List
Collection interface
collection
Collections class
collections framework
collections placed in arrays
Comparable interface
Comparator object
compareTo method of Comparable
copy method of Collections
delete an element from a collection
double-ended queue (deque)
duplicate elements
Enumeration interface
fill method of Arrays
fill method of Collections
HashMap class
HashSet class
hasNext method of Iterator
insert an element into a collection
isEmpty method of Map
iterator
Iterator interface

key
lexicographical comparison
LinkedList class
List interface
ListIterator interface
map
Map collection interface
mapping keys to values
mappings
max method of Collections
min method of Collections
modifiable collections
natural comparison method
natural ordering
next method of Iterator
one-to-one mapping
ordered collection
ordering
queue
range-view methods
reverse method of Collections
reverseOrder method of Collections
sequence
Set interface
shuffle method of Collections
sort a List
sort method of Arrays
sort method of Collections
SortedMap collection interface
SortedSet collection interface
stable sort
synchronization wrappers
TreeMap class
TreeSet class
unmodifiable collections
view
view an array as a List
wrapper class

SELF-REVIEW EXERCISES

22.1 Fill in the blanks in each of the following statements:
   a) Objects in a collection are called _____.
   b) An element in a List can be accessed by using the element's _____.
   c) Lists are sometimes called _____.
   d) You can use a(n) _____ to create a collection that offers only read-only access to others while allowing read–write access to yourself.
   e) _____ can be used to create stacks, queues, trees and deques (double-ended queues).

22.2   Determine whether each statement is *true* or *false*. If *false*, explain why.
   a) A Set can contain duplicate values.
   b) A Map can contain duplicate keys.
   c) A LinkedList can contain duplicate values.
   d) Collections is an interface.
   e) Iterators can remove elements, while Enumerations cannot.

ANSWERS TO SELF-REVIEW EXERCISES

22.1   a) elements. b) index. c) sequences. d) unmodifiable wrapper. e) LinkedLists.

22.2   a) False. A Set cannot contain duplicate values.
   b) False. A Map cannot contain duplicate keys.
   c) True.
   d) False. Collections is a class, and Collection is an interface.
   e) True.

EXERCISES

22.3   Define each of the following terms:
   a) Collection
   b) Collections
   c) Comparator
   d) List

22.4   Briefly answer the following questions:
   a) What is the primary difference between a Set and a Map?
   b) Can a two-dimensional array be passed to Arrays method asList? If yes, how would an individual element be accessed?
   c) What must you do before adding a primitive type (e.g., double) to a collection?

22.5   Explain briefly the operation of each of the following Iterator-related methods:
   a) iterator
   b) hasNext
   c) next

22.6   Determine whether each statement is *true* or *false*. If *false*, explain why.
   a) Elements in a Collection must be sorted in ascending order before a binarySearch may be performed.
   b) Method first gets the first element in a TreeSet.
   c) A List created with Arrays method asList is resizable.
   d) Class Arrays provides static method sort for sorting array elements.

22.7   Rewrite method printList of Fig. 22.4 to use a ListIterator.

22.8   Rewrite lines 14–21 in Fig. 22.4 to be more concise by using the asList method and the LinkedList constructor that takes a Collection argument.

22.9   Write a program that reads in a series of first names and stores them in a LinkedList. Do not store duplicate names. Allow the user to search for a first name.

22.10   Modify the program of Fig. 22.14 to count the number of occurrences of each letter rather than of each word. For example, the string "HELLO THERE" contains two Hs, three Es, two Ls, one O, one T and one R. Display the results.

22.11   Write a program that determines and prints the number of duplicate words in a sentence. Treat uppercase and lowercase letters the same. Ignore punctuation.

22.12 Rewrite your solution to Exercise 20.8 to use a LinkedList collection.

22.13 Rewrite your solution to Exercise 20.9 to use a LinkedList collection.

22.14 Write a program that takes a whole-number input from a user and determines whether it is prime. If the number is prime, add it to a JTextArea. If the number is not prime, display the prime factors of the number in a JLabel. Remember that a prime number's factors are only 1 and the prime number itself. Every number that is not prime has a unique prime factorization. For example, consider the number 54. The prime factors of 54 are 2, 3, 3 and 3. When the values are multiplied together, the result is 54. For the number 54, the prime factors output should be 2 and 3. Use Sets as part of your solution.

22.15 Rewrite your solution to Exercise 20.21 to use a LinkedList.

22.16 Write a program that uses a StringTokenizer to tokenize a line of text input by the user and places each token in a tree. Print the elements of the sorted tree.

23

Java Database Connectivity with JDBC™

Objectives

- To understand relational databases.
- To understand basic database queries using SQL.
- To use the classes and interfaces of package `java.sql` to manipulate databases.

It is a capital mistake to theorize before one has data.
Arthur Conan Doyle

Now go, write it before them in a table, and note it in a book, that it may be for the time to come for ever and ever.
The Holy Bible, Isaiah 30:8

Get your facts first, and then you can distort them as much as you please.
Mark Twain

I like two kinds of men: domestic and foreign.
Mae West

23.1 Introduction

A *database* is an organized collection of data. There are many different strategies for organizing data to facilitate easy access and manipulation. A *database management system*
(*DBMS*) provides mechanisms for storing and organizing data in a manner consistent with
the database's format. Database management systems allow for the access and storage of
data without concern for the internal representation of data.

Today's most popular database systems are *relational databases*. A language called
SQL—pronounced as its individual letters, or as "sequel"—is the international standard
language used almost universally with relational databases to perform *queries* (i.e., to
request information that satisfies given criteria) and to manipulate data. [*Note*: In this
chapter, we assume that SQL is pronounced as its individual letters. For this reason, we
often precede SQL with the article "an," as in "an SQL statement."]

Some popular *relational database management systems (RDBMSs)* are Microsoft SQL
Server, Oracle, Sybase, DB2, Informix and MySQL. In this chapter, we present examples
using *Cloudscape 5.0.4*—a pure-Java RDBMS from IBM. Cloudscape 5.0.4 is on the CD
that accompanies this book and can be downloaded from www.ibm.com/software/
data/cloudscape. [*Note*: We discuss basic Cloudscape features required to execute the
examples in this chapter. Please refer to the detailed Cloudscape documentation for complete information on using Cloudscape.]

Java programs communicate with databases and manipulate their data using the
JDBC™ API. A *JDBC driver* implements the interface to a particular database. This sepa-

ration of the API from particular drivers enables developers to change the underlying database without modifying Java code that accesses the database. Most popular database management systems now include JDBC drivers. There are also many third-party JDBC drivers available. In this chapter, we introduce JDBC and use it to manipulate a Cloudscape database. The techniques demonstrated here also can be used to manipulate other databases that have JDBC drivers. Check your system's documentation to determine whether your DBMS comes with a JDBC driver. Even if your DBMS does not come with a JDBC driver, many third-party vendors provide JDBC drivers for a wide variety of databases. For more information on JDBC, visit

```
java.sun.com/products/jdbc/
```

This site contains information concerning JDBC, including the JDBC specifications, FAQs on JDBC, a learning resource center, software downloads and other important information. For a list of available JDBC drivers, visit

```
industry.java.sun.com/products/jdbc/drivers/
```

This site provides a search engine to help you locate drivers appropriate to your DBMS.

23.2 Relational Databases

A *relational database* is a logical representation of data that allows the data to be accessed without consideration of the physical structure of the data. A relational database stores data in *tables*. Figure 23.1 illustrates a sample table that might be used in a personnel system. The table name is Employee, and its primary purpose is to store the attributes of an employee. Tables are composed of *rows*, and rows are composed of *columns* in which values are stored. This table consists of six rows. The Number column of each row in this table is the *primary key* for the table. A primary key is a column (or group of columns) in a table that have a unique value that cannot be duplicated in other rows. This guarantees that each row can be identified by its primary key. Good examples of primary key columns are a Social Security number, an employee ID number and a part number in an inventory system, as values in each of these columns are guaranteed to be unique. The rows of Fig. 23.1 are displayed in order by primary key. In this case, the rows are listed in increasing order; we could also use decreasing order. Rows in tables are not guaranteed to be stored in any particular order. As we will demonstrate in an upcoming example, programs can specify ordering criteria when requesting data from a database.

Each column of the table represents a different data attribute. Rows are normally unique (by primary key) within a table, but particular column values may be duplicated between rows. For example, three different rows in the Employee table's Department column contain number 413.

Different users of a database often are interested in different data and different relationships among those data. Most users require only subsets of the rows and columns. To obtain these subsets, we use SQL statements to specify which data to *select* from a table. SQL provides a complete set of statements (including *SELECT*) that enable programmers to define complex *queries* that select data from a table. For example, we might select data from the table in Fig. 23.1 to create a result that shows where departments are located. This result is shown in Fig. 23.2. SQL queries are discussed in Section 23.4.

	Number	Name	Department	Salary	Location
	23603	Jones	413	1100	New Jersey
	24568	Kerwin	413	2000	New Jersey
Row	34589	Larson	642	1800	Los Angeles
	35761	Myers	611	1400	Orlando
	47132	Neumann	413	9000	New Jersey
	78321	Stephens	611	8500	Orlando
	Primary key		Column		

Fig. 23.1   Employee table sample data.

Department	Location
413	New Jersey
611	Orlando
642	Los Angeles

Fig. 23.2   Result of selecting distinct Department and Location data from the Employee table.

23.3 Relational Database Overview: The books Database

This section gives an overview of relational databases in the context of a sample books database we created for this chapter. Before we discuss SQL, we overview the tables of the books database. We use this to introduce various database concepts, including the use of SQL to obtain information from the database and to manipulate the data. We provide a script to create the database. You can find the script in the examples directory for this chapter on the CD that accompanies this book. Section 23.5 explains how to use this script.

The database consists of four tables: authors, publishers, authorISBN and titles. The authors table (described in Fig. 23.3) consists of three columns that maintain each author's unique ID number, first name and last name. Figure 23.4 contains sample data from the authors table of the books database.

Column	Description
authorID	Author's ID number in the database. In the books database, this integer column is defined as *autoincremented*. For each row inserted in this table, the database automatically increments the authorID value to ensure that each row has a unique authorID. This column represents the table's primary key.
firstName	Author's first name (a string).
lastName	Author's last name (a string).

Fig. 23.3   authors table from books.

authorID	firstName	lastName
1	Harvey	Deitel
2	Paul	Deitel
3	Tem	Nieto
4	Sean	Santry

Fig. 23.4   Sample data from the `authors` table.

The `publishers` table (described in Fig. 23.5) consists of two columns representing each publisher's unique ID and name. Figure 23.6 contains the data from the `publishers` table of the `books` database.

The `titles` table (described in Fig. 23.7) consists of six columns that maintain general information about each book in the database, including the ISBN, title, edition number, copyright year, publisher's ID number, name of a file containing an image of the book cover and the price. The `publisherID` column is a *foreign key*—a key that matches the primary key in another table (e.g., `publisherID` in the `publishers` table). Foreign keys are specified when creating a table. The foreign key helps maintain the *Rule of Referential Integrity*: Every foreign key must appear as another table's primary key. Foreign keys enable rows from multiple tables to be *joined* for analysis purposes. There is a one-to-many relationship between a primary key and a corresponding foreign key. This means that a foreign key can appear many times in its own table, but can only appear once (as the primary key) in another table. Figure 23.8 contains sample data from the `titles` table.

Column	Description
publisherID	The publisher's ID number in the database. This autoincremented integer is the table's primary key.
publisherName	The name of the publisher (a string).

Fig. 23.5   `publishers` table from `books`.

publisherID	publisherName
1	Prentice Hall
2	Prentice Hall PTG

Fig. 23.6   Data from the `publishers` table.

Column	Description
isbn	ISBN of the book (a string). The table's primary key.
title	Title of the book (a string).
editionNumber	Edition number of the book (an integer).
copyright	Copyright year of the book (a string).
publisherID	Publisher's ID number (an integer). A foreign key to the publishers table.
imageFile	Name of the file containing the book's cover image (a string).
price	Suggested retail price of the book (a real number). [*Note*: The prices shown in this book are for example purposes only.]

Fig. 23.7   titles table from books.

isbn	title	edition-Number	copy-right	publish-erID	imageFile	price
0130895725	C How to Program	3	2001	1	chtp3.jpg	74.95
0130384747	C++ How to Program	4	2002	1	cpphtp4.jpg	74.95
0130461342	Java Web Services for Experienced Programmers	1	2002	1	jwsfep1.jpg	54.95
0131016210	Java How to Program	5	2003	1	jhtp5.jpg	74.95
0130852473	The Complete Java 2 Training Course	5	2002	2	javactc5.jpg	109.95
0130895601	Advanced Java 2 Platform How to Program	1	2002	1	advjhtp1.jpg	74.95

Fig. 23.8   Sample data from the titles table of books .

The authorISBN table (described in Fig. 23.9) consists of two columns that maintain each ISBN and its corresponding author's ID number. This table associates authors with their books. Together, these foreign keys represent the relationship between authors and books—one row in table authors may be associated with many rows in table titles and vice versa. Figure 23.10 contains the data from the authorISBN table of the books database. ISBN is an abbreviation for "International Standard Book Number"—a numbering scheme that publishers worldwide use to give every book a unique identification number. [*Note*: To save space, we have split the contents of this table into two columns, each containing the authorID and isbn columns.]

Column	Description
authorID	The author's ID number, a foreign key to the authors table.
isbn	The ISBN for a book, a foreign key to the titles table..

Fig. 23.9   authorISBN table from books.

authorID	isbn	authorID	isbn
1	0130895725	2	0139163050
2	0130895725	3	0130829293
2	0132261197	3	0130284173
2	0130895717	3	0130284181
2	0135289106	4	0130895601

Fig. 23.10 Sample data from the `authorISBN` table of `books`.

Figure 23.11 is an *entity-relationship* (*ER*) *diagram* for the `books` database. This diagram shows the various tables in the database as well as the relationships among those tables. The first compartment in each box contains the table's name. The names in green are primary keys. A table's primary key uniquely identifies each row in the table. Every row must have a value in the primary key, and the value of the key must be unique in the table. This is known as the *Rule of Entity Integrity*.

Common Programming Error 23.1

Not providing a value for every column in a primary key breaks the Rule of Entity Integrity and causes the DBMS to report an error.

Common Programming Error 23.2

Providing the same value for the primary key in multiple rows causes the DBMS to report an error.

The lines connecting the tables in Fig. 23.11 represent the *relationships* between the tables. Consider the line between the `publishers` and `titles` tables. On the `publishers` end of the line, there is a 1, and on the `titles` end, there is an infinity symbol (∞), indicating a *one-to-many relationship* in which every publisher in the `publishers` table can have an arbitrarily large number of books in the `titles` table. Note that the relationship line links the `publisherID` column in the table `publishers` to the `publisherID` column in table `titles`. The `publisherID` column in the `titles` table is a *foreign key*.

Common Programming Error 23.3

Providing a foreign-key value that does not appear as a primary-key value in another table breaks the Rule of Referential Integrity and causes the DBMS to report an error.

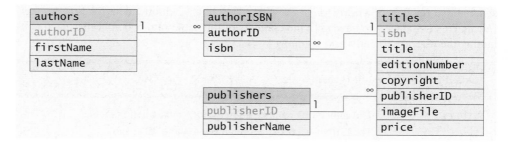

Fig. 23.11 Table relationships in `books`.

The line between the `authorISBN` and `authors` tables indicates that for each author in the `authors` table, there can be an arbitrary number of ISBNs for books written by that author in the `authorISBN` table. The `authorID` column in the `authorISBN` table is a foreign key matching the `authorID` column (the primary key) of the `authors` table. Note again that the line between the tables links the foreign key in table `authorISBN` to the corresponding primary key in table `authors`. The `authorISBN` table associates rows in the `titles` and `authors` tables.

Finally, the line between the `titles` and `authorISBN` tables illustrates a one-to-many relationship; a title can be written by any number of authors. In fact, the sole purpose of the `authorISBN` table is to provide a many-to-many relationship between the `authors` and `titles` tables; an author can write any number of books and a book can have any number of authors.

23.4 SQL

In this section, we provide an overview of SQL in the context of our `books` sample database. You will be able to use the SQL queries discussed here in the examples later in the chapter.

The SQL keywords listed in Fig. 23.12 are discussed in the context of complete SQL queries in the next several subsections; other SQL keywords are beyond the scope of this text. [*Note*: For more information on SQL, please refer to the World Wide Web resources in Section 23.8 and the bibliography at the end of this chapter.]

23.4.1 Basic SELECT Query

Let us consider several SQL queries that extract information from database `books`. An SQL query "selects" rows and columns from one or more tables in a database. Such selections are performed by *SELECT queries*. The basic form of a SELECT query is

```
SELECT * FROM tableName
```

SQL keyword	Description
SELECT	Retrieves data from one or more tables.
FROM	Tables involved in the query. Required in every SELECT.
WHERE	Criteria for selection that determine the rows to be retrieved, deleted or updated.
GROUP BY	Criteria for grouping rows.
ORDER BY	Criteria for ordering rows.
INNER JOIN	Merge rows from multiple tables.
INSERT	Insert rows into a specified table.
UPDATE	Update rows in a specified table.
DELETE	Delete rows from a specified table.

Fig. 23.12 SQL query keywords.

In the preceding query, the asterisk (*) indicates that all columns from the *tableName* table should be retrieved. For example, to retrieve all the data in the `authors` table, we would use the query

```
SELECT * FROM authors
```

To retrieve only specific columns from a table, replace the asterisk (*) with a comma-separated list of the column names. For example, to retrieve only the columns `authorID` and `lastName` for all rows in the `authors` table, use the query

```
SELECT authorID, lastName FROM authors
```

This query returns the data listed in Fig. 23.13.

Software Engineering Observation 23.1

For most SQL statements, the asterisk (*) should not be used to specify column names. In general, programmers process results by knowing in advance the order of the columns in the result—e.g., selecting `authorID` and `lastName` from table `authors` ensures that the columns will appear in the result with `authorID` as the first column and `lastName` as the second column. Programs typically process result columns by specifying the column number in the result (starting from number 1 for the first column).

Software Engineering Observation 23.2

Specifying the column names to select guarantees that the columns are always returned in the specified order and also avoids returning unneeded columns, even if the actual order of the columns in the table(s) changes.

Common Programming Error 23.4

If a programmer assumes that the columns in a result are always returned in the same order from an SQL statement that uses the asterisk (*), the program may process the result incorrectly. If the column order in the table(s) changes, the order of the columns in the result would change accordingly.

Performance Tip 23.1

If the order of columns in a result is unknown, a program must process the columns by name. Specifying the column names to select from tables enables the application receiving the result to know the order of the columns in advance. In this case, the program can process the data more efficiently, because columns can be accessed by column number.

authorID	lastName
1	Deitel
2	Deitel
3	Nieto
4	Santry

Fig. 23.13 Sample `authorID` and `lastName` data from the `authors` table.

23.4.2 WHERE Clause

In most cases, it is necessary to locate rows in a database that satisfy certain *selection criteria*. Only rows that satisfy the selection criteria (formally called *predicates*) are selected. SQL uses the optional *WHERE clause* in a SELECT query to specify the selection criteria for the query. The basic form of a SELECT query with selection criteria is

SELECT *columnName1*, *columnName2*, ... FROM *tableName* WHERE *criteria*

For example, to select the title, editionNumber and copyright columns from table titles for which the copyright date is greater than 2000, use the query

```
SELECT title, editionNumber, copyright
   FROM titles
   WHERE copyright > 2000
```

Figure 23.14 shows the result of the preceding query.

The WHERE clause criteria can contain operators <, >, <=, >=, =, <> and LIKE. Operator LIKE is used for *pattern matching* with wildcard characters *percent* (%) and *underscore* (_). Pattern matching allows SQL to search for strings that match a given pattern.

A pattern that contains a percent character (%) searches for strings that have zero or more characters at the percent character's position in the pattern. For example, the following query locates the rows of all the authors whose last name starts with the letter D:

```
SELECT authorID, firstName, lastName
   FROM authors
   WHERE lastName LIKE 'D%'
```

The preceding query selects the two rows shown in Fig. 23.15, because two of the four authors in our database have a last name starting with the letter D (followed by zero or more characters). The % in the WHERE clause's LIKE pattern indicates that any number of characters can appear after the letter D in the lastName column. Notice that the pattern string is surrounded by single-quote characters.

title	editionNumber	copyright
C How to Program	3	2001
C++ How to Program	4	2002
The Complete C++ Training Course	4	2002
Internet and World Wide Web How to Program	2	2002
Java How to Program	5	2003
XML How to Program	1	2001
Perl How to Program	1	2001
Advanced Java 2 Platform How to Program	1	2002

Fig. 23.14 Sampling of titles with copyrights after 2000 from table titles.

authorID	firstName	lastName
1	Harvey	Deitel
2	Paul	Deitel

Fig. 23.15 Authors whose last name starts with D from the `authors` table.

Portability Tip 23.1

See the documentation for your database system to determine whether SQL is case sensitive on your system and to determine the syntax for SQL keywords (i.e., should they be all upper-case letters, all lowercase letters or some combination of the two?).

Portability Tip 23.2

Not all database systems support the LIKE operator, so be sure to read your database system's documentation carefully.

Portability Tip 23.3

*Some databases use the * character in place of the % character in a pattern.*

An underscore (_) in the pattern string indicates a single wildcard character at that position in the pattern. For example, the following query locates the rows of all the authors whose last name starts with any character (specified by _), followed by the letter i, followed by any number of additional characters (specified by %):

```
SELECT authorID, firstName, lastName
    FROM authors
    WHERE lastName LIKE '_i%'
```

The preceding query produces the row shown in Fig. 23.16, because only one author in our database has a last name that contains the letter i as its second letter.

Portability Tip 23.4

Some databases use the ? character in place of the _ character in a pattern.

23.4.3 ORDER BY Clause

The result of a query can be sorted into ascending or descending order by using the optional *ORDER BY clause*. The basic form of a SELECT statement with an ORDER BY clause is

```
SELECT columnName1, columnName2, ... FROM tableName ORDER BY column ASC
SELECT columnName1, columnName2, ... FROM tableName ORDER BY column DESC
```

authorID	firstName	lastName
3	Tem	Nieto

Fig. 23.16 The only author from the `authors` table whose last name contains i as the second letter.

where ASC specifies ascending order (lowest to highest), DESC specifies descending order (highest to lowest) and *column* specifies the column on which the sort is based. For example, to obtain the list of authors in ascending order by last name (Fig. 23.17), use the query

```
SELECT authorID, firstName, lastName
    FROM authors
    ORDER BY lastName ASC
```

Note that the default sorting order is ascending, so ASC is optional. To obtain the same list of authors in descending order by last name (Fig. 23.18), use the query

```
SELECT authorID, firstName, lastName
    FROM authors
    ORDER BY lastName DESC
```

Multiple columns can be used for sorting with an ORDER BY clause of the form

```
ORDER BY column1 sortingOrder, column2 sortingOrder, ...
```

where *sortingOrder* is either ASC or DESC. Note that the *sortingOrder* does not have to be identical for each column. The query

```
SELECT authorID, firstName, lastName
    FROM authors
    ORDER BY lastName, firstName
```

sorts in ascending order all the rows by last name, then by first name. If any rows have the same last name value, they are returned sorted by first name (Fig. 23.19).

authorID	firstName	lastName
2	Paul	Deitel
1	Harvey	Deitel
3	Tem	Nieto
4	Sean	Santry

Fig. 23.17 Sample data from table authors in ascending order by lastName.

authorID	firstName	lastName
4	Sean	Santry
3	Tem	Nieto
2	Paul	Deitel
1	Harvey	Deitel

Fig. 23.18 Sample data from table authors in descending order by lastName.

authorID	firstName	lastName
1	Harvey	Deitel
2	Paul	Deitel
3	Tem	Nieto
4	Sean	Santry

Fig. 23.19 Sample author data from table `authors` in ascending order by `lastName` and by `firstName`.

The WHERE and ORDER BY clauses can be combined in one query. For example, the query

```
SELECT isbn, title, editionNumber, copyright, price
    FROM titles
    WHERE title
    LIKE '%How to Program'
    ORDER BY title ASC
```

returns the `isbn`, `title`, `editionNumber`, `copyright` and `price` of each book in the `titles` table that has a `title` ending with "How to Program" and sorts them in ascending order by `title`. The result of the query are shown in Fig. 23.20. Note that the title "e-Business and e-Commerce How to Program" appears at the end of the list, because Cloudscape uses the Unicode numeric values of the characters for comparison purposes. Remember that lowercase letters have larger numeric values than uppercase letters.

isbn	title	edition-Number	copy-right	price
0130895601	Advanced Java 2 Platform How to Program	1	2002	74.95
0130895725	C How to Program	3	2001	74.95
0130384747	C++ How to Program	4	2002	74.95
0130308978	Internet and World Wide Web How to Program	2	2002	74.95
0130284181	Perl How to Program	1	2001	74.95
0134569555	Visual Basic 6 How to Program	1	1999	74.95
0130284173	XML How to Program	1	2001	74.95
013028419x	e-Business and e-Commerce How to Program	1	2001	74.95

Fig. 23.20 Sampling of books from table `titles` whose titles end with How to Program in ascending order by `title`.

23.4.4 Merging Data from Multiple Tables: INNER JOIN

Database designers often split related data into separate tables to ensure that a database does not store data redundantly. For example, the Books database has tables authors and titles. We use an authorISBN table to store the relationship data between authors and their corresponding titles. If we did not separate this information into individual tables, we would need to include author information with each entry in the titles table. This would result in the database storing duplicate author information for authors who wrote multiple books. Often, it is necessary to merge data from multiple tables into a single result. Referred to as *joining* the tables, this is specified by an INNER JOIN operator in the SELECT query. An INNER JOIN merges rows from two tables by matching values in columns that are common to the tables. The basic form of an INNER JOIN is:

```
SELECT columnName1, columnName2, ...
FROM table1
INNER JOIN table2
    ON table1.columnName = table2.columnName
```

The ON clause of the INNER JOIN specifies the columns from each table that are compared to determine which rows are merged. For example, the following query produces a list of authors accompanied by the ISBNs for books written by each author:

```
SELECT firstName, lastName, isbn
FROM authors
INNER JOIN authorISBN
    ON authors.authorID = authorISBN.authorID
ORDER BY lastName, firstName
```

The query merges data from the firstName and lastName columns from table authors with the isbn column from table authorISBN, sorting the result in ascending order by lastName and firstName. Notice the use of the syntax *tableName*.*columnName* in the ON clause. This syntax (called a *qualified name*) specifies the columns from each table that should be compared to join the tables. The "*tableName*." syntax is required if the columns have the same name in both tables. The same syntax can be used in any query to distinguish among columns in different tables that have the same name. In some systems, table names qualified with the database name can be used to perform cross-database queries.

Software Engineering Observation 23.3

If an SQL statement includes columns from multiple tables that have the same name, the statement must precede those column names with their table names and the dot operator (e.g., authors.authorID).

Common Programming Error 23.5

In a query, failure to qualify names for columns that have the same name in two or more tables is an error.

As always, the query can contain an ORDER BY clause. Figure 23.21 depicts the result of the preceding query, ordered by lastName and firstName. [*Note*: To save space, we split the result of the query into two columns, each containing the firstName, lastName and isbn columns.]

firstName	lastName	isbn	firstName	lastName	isbn
Harvey	Deitel	0130895601	Paul	Deitel	0130895717
Harvey	Deitel	0130284181	Paul	Deitel	0132261197
Harvey	Deitel	0134569555	Paul	Deitel	0130895725
Harvey	Deitel	0139163050	Paul	Deitel	0130829293
Harvey	Deitel	0135289106	Paul	Deitel	0134569555
Harvey	Deitel	0130895717	Paul	Deitel	0130829277
Harvey	Deitel	0130284173	Tem	Nieto	0130161438
Harvey	Deitel	0130829293	Tem	Nieto	013028419x
Paul	Deitel	0130852473	Sean	Santry	0130895601

Fig. 23.21   Sampling of authors and ISBNs for the books they have written in ascending order by `lastName` and `firstName`.

23.4.5 INSERT Statement

The *INSERT* statement inserts a row into a table. The basic form of this statement is

```
INSERT INTO tableName ( columnName1, columnName2, ..., columnNameN )
    VALUES ( value1, value2, ..., valueN )
```

where *tableName* is the table in which to insert the row. The *tableName* is followed by a comma-separated list of column names in parentheses (this list is not required if the IN-SERT operation specifies a value for every column of the table in the correct order). The list of column names is followed by the SQL keyword VALUES and a comma-separated list of values in parentheses. The values specified here must match the columns specified after the table name in both order and type (e.g., if *columnName1* is supposed to be the `firstName` column, then *value1* should be a string in single quotes representing the first name). Always explicitly list the columns when inserting rows. If the order of the columns changes in the table, using only VALUES may cause an error. The INSERT statement

```
INSERT INTO authors ( firstName, lastName )
    VALUES ( 'Sue', 'Smith' )
```

inserts a row into the `authors` table. The statement indicates that values are provided for the `firstName` and `lastName` columns. The corresponding values are `'Sue'` and `'Smith'`. We do not specify an `authorID` in this example, because `authorID` is an *autoincremented column* in the `authors` table. For every row added to this table, Cloudscape assigns a unique `authorID` value that is the next value in the autoincremented sequence (i.e., 1, 2, 3 and so on). In this case, Sue Smith would be assigned `authorID` number 5. Figure 23.22 shows the `authors` table after the INSERT operation.

Common Programming Error 23.6

It is an error to specify a value for an autoincrement column.

authorID	firstName	lastName
1	Harvey	Deitel
2	Paul	Deitel
3	Tem	Nieto
4	Sean	Santry
5	Sue	Smith

Fig. 23.22 Sample data from table `Authors` after an `INSERT` operation.

Common Programming Error 23.7

SQL statements use the single-quote (') character as a delimiter for strings. To specify a string containing a single quote (such as O'Malley) in an SQL statement, the string must have two single quotes in the position where the single-quote character appears in the string (e.g., 'O''Malley'). The first of the two single-quote characters acts as an escape character for the second. Not escaping single-quote characters in a string that is part of an SQL statement is an SQL syntax error.

23.4.6 UPDATE Statement

An *UPDATE* statement modifies data in a table. The basic form of the UPDATE statement is

```
UPDATE tableName
    SET columnName1 = value1, columnName2 = value2, ..., columnNameN = valueN
    WHERE criteria
```

where *tableName* is the table to update. The *tableName* is followed by keyword *SET* and a comma-separated list of column name/value pairs in the format *columnName = value*. The WHERE clause provides criteria that determine which rows to update. The UPDATE statement

```
UPDATE authors
    SET lastName = 'Jones'
    WHERE lastName = 'Smith' AND firstName = 'Sue'
```

updates a row in the `authors` table. The statement indicates that `lastName` will be assigned the value `Jones` for the row in which `lastName` is equal to `Smith` and `firstName` is equal to `Sue`. [*Note:* If there are multiple rows with the first name "Sue" and the last name "Smith," this statement will modify all such rows to have the last name "Jones."] If we know the `authorID` in advance of the UPDATE operation (possibly because we searched for it previously), the WHERE clause could be simplified as follows:

```
WHERE AuthorID = 5
```

Figure 23.23 shows the `authors` table after the UPDATE operation has taken place.

23.4.7 DELETE Statement

An SQL *DELETE* statement removes rows from a table. The basic form of a DELETE statement is

```
DELETE FROM tableName WHERE criteria
```

authorID	firstName	lastName
1	Harvey	Deitel
2	Paul	Deitel
3	Tem	Nieto
4	Sean	Santry
5	Sue	Jones

Fig. 23.23 Sample data from table `authors` after an UPDATE operation.

where *tableName* is the table from which to delete. The WHERE clause specifies the criteria used to determine which rows to delete. The DELETE statement

```
DELETE FROM authors
    WHERE lastName = 'Jones' AND firstName = 'Sue'
```

deletes the row for Sue Jones in the `authors` table. If we know the `authorID` in advance of the DELETE operation, the WHERE clause can be simplified as follows:

```
WHERE authorID = 5
```

Figure 23.24 shows the `authors` table after the DELETE operation has taken place.

23.5 Creating Database books in Cloudscape

The CD that accompanies this book includes Cloudscape 5.0.4—a pure-Java embedded database management system from IBM. Complete information about Cloudscape is available from

```
www.ibm.com/software/data/cloudscape
```

Follow the provided instructions to install Cloudscape. Cloudscape executes on many platforms, including Windows, Solaris, Linux, Macintosh and others. For a complete list of platforms on which Cloudscape has been tested, visit

```
www.ibm.com/software/data/cloudscape/requirements.html
```

authorID	firstName	lastName
1	Harvey	Deitel
2	Paul	Deitel
3	Tem	Nieto
4	Sean	Santry

Fig. 23.24 Sample data from table `authors` after a DELETE operation.

Several Cloudscape JAR files must be in your program's classpath before you can create and manipulate databases in Cloudscape. To include the proper JAR files in the classpath, execute the `setCP.bat` batch file (or `setCP.ksh` shell script for UNIX) from the `Cloudscape_5.0\bin` directory.

For each Cloudscape database we discuss in this book, we provide an SQL script that will set up the database and its tables. These scripts can be executed with an interactive command line tool, called `ij`, that is part of Cloudscape. We provide a batch file (`create-Database.bat`) and a shell script (`createDatabase.ksh`) that you can use to start `ij` and execute the SQL scripts. In the examples directory for this chapter on the CD that accompanies this book, you will find the `createDatabase` scripts and the SQL script `books.sql`. To create database `books`, first execute the `setCP.bat` batch file (or `setCP.ksh` shell script for UNIX) from the `Cloudscape_5.0\bin` directory. This sets the environment variables required by our `createDatabase` script. Next, change to the directory where you installed Cloudscape on your computer (e.g., `C:\Cloudscape_5.0`) and type

```
createDatabase books.sql
```

to execute the SQL script. After completing this task, a new directory that contains the database information will be created in the current directory. Then you are ready to proceed to the first JDBC example. [*Note:* We wrote this script such that you can execute the script again at any time to restore the database's original contents. When you run this script the first time, it will generate four error messages as it tries to delete the four tables in the books database. This occurs because the database does not exist, so there are no tables to delete. You can simply ignore these messages.]

23.6 Manipulating Databases with JDBC

In this section, we present two examples that introduce how to connect to a database, query the database and display the result of the query.

23.6.1 Connecting to and Querying a Database

The example of Fig. 23.25 performs a simple query on the books database that retrieves the entire `authors` table and displays the data in a `JTextArea`. The program illustrates connecting to the database, querying the database and processing the result. The following discussion presents the key JDBC aspects of the program. [*Note:* Section 23.5 demonstrates how to prepare the Cloudscape database and how to create the books database. The steps in Section 23.5 must be performed before executing the program of Fig. 23.25.]

Line 5 imports package `java.sql`, which contains classes and interfaces for the JDBC API. Line 12 declares a `String` constant that contains the JDBC driver class name for the Cloudscape database. The program will use this value to load the proper driver into memory. Line 13 declares a string constant for the database URL. This identifies the name of the database to connect to, as well as information about the protocol used by the JDBC driver. The `DisplayAuthors` constructor (lines 22–108) connects to the books database, queries the database, displays the result of the query and closes the database connection.

```java
1   // Fig. 23.26: DisplayAuthors.java
2   // Displaying the contents of the authors table.
3
4   import java.awt.*;
5   import java.sql.*;
6   import java.util.*;
7   import javax.swing.*;
8
9   public class DisplayAuthors extends JFrame {
10
11      // JDBC driver name and database URL
12      static final String JDBC_DRIVER = "com.ibm.db2j.jdbc.DB2jDriver";
13      static final String DATABASE_URL = "jdbc:db2j:books";
14
15      // declare Connection and Statement for accessing
16      // and querying database
17      private Connection connection;
18      private Statement statement;
19
20      // constructor connects to database, queries database, processes
21      // results and displays results in window
22      public DisplayAuthors()
23      {
24         super( "Authors Table of Books Database" );
25
26         // connect to database books and query database
27         try {
28
29            // specify location of database on filesystem
30            System.setProperty( "db2j.system.home", "C:/Cloudscape_5.0" );
31
32            // load database driver class
33            Class.forName( JDBC_DRIVER );
34
35            // establish connection to database
36            connection = DriverManager.getConnection( DATABASE_URL );
37
38            // create Statement for querying database
39            statement = connection.createStatement();
40
41            // query database
42            ResultSet resultSet =
43               statement.executeQuery( "SELECT * FROM authors" );
44
45            // process query results
46            StringBuffer results = new StringBuffer();
47            ResultSetMetaData metaData = resultSet.getMetaData();
48            int numberOfColumns = metaData.getColumnCount();
49
50            for ( int i = 1; i <= numberOfColumns; i++ )
51               results.append( metaData.getColumnName( i ) + "\t" );
52
53            results.append( "\n" );
```

Fig. 23.25 Displaying the `authors` table from the `books` database (Part 1 of 3.).

```
54
55          while ( resultSet.next() ) {
56
57              for ( int i = 1; i <= numberOfColumns; i++ )
58                  results.append( resultSet.getObject( i ) + "\t" );
59
60              results.append( "\n" );
61          }
62
63          // set up GUI and display window
64          JTextArea textArea = new JTextArea( results.toString() );
65          Container container = getContentPane();
66
67          container.add( new JScrollPane( textArea ) );
68
69          setSize( 300, 100 );  // set window size
70          setVisible( true );   // display window
71
72      }  // end try
73
74      // detect problems interacting with the database
75      catch ( SQLException sqlException ) {
76          JOptionPane.showMessageDialog( null, sqlException.getMessage(),
77              "Database Error", JOptionPane.ERROR_MESSAGE );
78
79          System.exit( 1 );
80      }
81
82      // detect problems loading database driver
83      catch ( ClassNotFoundException classNotFound ) {
84          JOptionPane.showMessageDialog( null, classNotFound.getMessage(),
85              "Driver Not Found", JOptionPane.ERROR_MESSAGE );
86
87          System.exit( 1 );
88      }
89
90      // ensure statement and connection are closed properly
91      finally {
92
93          try {
94              statement.close();
95              connection.close();
96          }
97
98          // handle exceptions closing statement and connection
99          catch ( SQLException sqlException ) {
100             JOptionPane.showMessageDialog( null,
101                 sqlException.getMessage(), "Database Error",
102                 JOptionPane.ERROR_MESSAGE );
103
104             System.exit( 1 );
105         }
106     }
```

Fig. 23.25 Displaying the authors table from the books database (Part 2 of 3.).

```
107
108    } // end DisplayAuthors constructor
109
110    // launch the application
111    public static void main( String args[] )
112    {
113       DisplayAuthors window = new DisplayAuthors();
114       window.setDefaultCloseOperation( JFrame.EXIT_ON_CLOSE );
115    }
116
117 } // end class DisplayAuthors
```

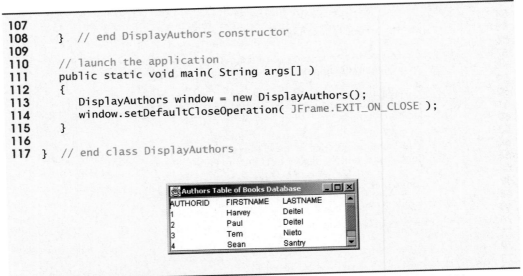

Fig. 23.25 Displaying the `authors` table from the `books` database (Part 3 of 3.).

The program must load the database driver before the program can connect to the database. Line 33 loads the class for the database driver. This line throws a checked exception of type *java.lang.ClassNotFoundException* if the class loader cannot locate the driver class. The Cloudscape JDBC driver determines the locations of database files using system property `db2j.system.home`. Line 30 sets this property to the location where we created the `books` database.

JDBC supports four categories of drivers: *JDBC-to-ODBC bridge driver* (Type 1), *Native-API, partly Java driver* (Type 2); *JDBC-Net pure Java driver* (Type 3) and *Native-Protocol pure Java driver* (Type 4). A description of each driver type is shown in Fig. 23.26. The Cloudscape driver `com.ibm.db2j.jdbc.DB2jDriver` is a Type-4 driver.

Type	Description
1	The *JDBC-to-ODBC bridge driver* connects Java programs to Microsoft ODBC (Open Database Connectivity) data sources. The Java 2 Software Development Kit from Sun Microsystems, Inc. includes the JDBC-to-ODBC bridge driver (`sun.jdbc.odbc.JdbcOdbcDriver`). This driver typically requires the ODBC driver to be installed on the client computer and normally requires configuration of the ODBC data source. The bridge driver was introduced primarily for development purposes and should not be used for production applications.
2	*Native-API, partly Java drivers* enable JDBC programs to use database-specific APIs (normally written in C or C++) that allow client programs to access databases via the Java Native Interface. This driver type translates JDBC into database-specific code. Type 2 drivers were introduced for reasons similar to the Type 1 ODBC bridge driver.

Fig. 23.26 JDBC driver types. (Part 1 of 2.)

Type	Description
3	*JDBC-Net pure Java drivers* take JDBC requests and translate them into a network protocol that is not database specific. These requests are sent to a server, which translates the database requests into a database-specific protocol.
4	*Native-protocol pure Java drivers* convert JDBC requests to database-specific network protocols, so that Java programs can connect directly to a database.

Fig. 23.26   JDBC driver types. (Part 2 of 2.)

Software Engineering Observation 23.4

Most major database vendors provide their own JDBC database drivers, and many third-party vendors provide JDBC drivers as well. For more information on JDBC drivers, visit the Sun Microsystems JDBC Web site, java.sun.com/products/jdbc.

Software Engineering Observation 23.5

On the Microsoft Windows platform, most databases support access via Open Database Connectivity (ODBC). ODBC is a technology developed by Microsoft to allow generic access to disparate database systems on the Windows platform (and some UNIX platforms). The Java 2 Software Development Kit (J2SDK) comes with the JDBC-to-ODBC-bridge database driver to allow any Java program to access any ODBC data source. The driver is class JdbcOdbcDriver in package sun.jdbc.odbc.

Line 36 of Fig. 23.25 creates a *Connection* object (package *java.sql*) referenced by connection. An object that implements interface Connection manages the connection between the Java program and the database. Connection objects enable programs to create SQL statements that manipulate databases. The program initializes connection with the result of a call to static method *getConnection* of class *DriverManager* (package java.sql), which attempts to connect to the database specified by its URL argument. The URL locates the database (possibly on a network or in the local file system of the computer). The URL jdbc:db2j:books specifies the protocol for communication (jdbc), the *subprotocol* for communication (db2j) and the name of the database (books). The subprotocol db2j indicates that the program uses an IBM-specific subprotocol to connect to the Cloudscape database. If the DriverManager cannot connect to the database, method getConnection throws an *SQLException* (package java.sql).

Software Engineering Observation 23.6

Most database management systems require the user to log in before accessing the database contents. DriverManager method getConnection is overloaded with versions that enable the program to supply the user name and password to gain access.

Line 39 invokes Connection method *createStatement* to obtain an object that implements interface Statement (package java.sql). The program uses the Statement object to submit SQL to the database.

Lines 42–43 use the Statement object's *executeQuery* method to submit a query that selects all the author information from table authors. This method returns an object that implements interface *ResultSet* and contains the result of the query. The ResultSet methods enable the program to manipulate the query result.

Lines 47–61 process the ResultSet. Line 47 obtains the *metadata* for the ResultSet and assigns it to a *ResultSetMetaData* (package java.sql) reference. The metadata describes the ResultSet's contents. Programs can use metadata programmatically to obtain information about the ResultSet's column names and types. Line 48 uses ResultSetMetaData method *getColumnCount* to retrieve the number of columns in the ResultSet. Lines 50–51 append the column names to the StringBuffer results.

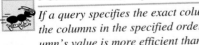

Software Engineering Observation 23.7

Metadata enables programs to process ResultSet contents dynamically when detailed information about the ResultSet is not known in advance.

Lines 55–61 append the data in each ResultSet row to the StringBuffer results. Before processing the ResultSet, the program positions the ResultSet *cursor* to the first row in the ResultSet with method **next** (line 55). The cursor points to the current row. Method next returns boolean value true if it is able to position to the next row; otherwise the method returns false.

Common Programming Error 23.8

Initially, a ResultSet cursor is positioned before the first row. Attempting to access a ResultSet's contents before positioning the ResultSet cursor to the first row with method next causes an SQLException.

If there are rows in the ResultSet, line 58 extracts the contents of the current row. When processing a ResultSet, it is possible to extract each column of the ResultSet as a specific Java type. In fact, ResultSetMetaData method *getColumnType* returns a constant integer from class *Types* (package java.sql) indicating the type of a specified column. Programs can use these values in a switch structure to invoke ResultSet methods that return the column values as appropriate Java types. If the type of a column is Types.INT, ResultSet method *getInt* returns the column value as an int. ResultSet *get* methods typically receive as an argument either a *column number* (as an int) or a *column name* (as a String) indicating which column's value to obtain. Visit

```
java.sun.com/j2se/1.4.1/docs/guide/jdbc/getstart/
    GettingStartedTOC.fm.html
```

for detailed mappings of SQL types to Java types and to determine the appropriate ResultSet method to call for each SQL type.

Performance Tip 23.2

If a query specifies the exact columns to select from the database, the ResultSet contains the columns in the specified order. In this case, using the column number to obtain the column's value is more efficient than using the column name. The column number provides direct access to the specified column. Using the column name requires a linear search of the column names to locate the appropriate column.

For simplicity, this example treats each value as an Object. The program retrieves each column value with ResultSet method *getObject* (line 58) and appends the String representation of the Object to results. Notice that, unlike array indices, which start at 0, ResultSet column numbers start at 1.

Common Programming Error 23.9

Specifying column number 0 when obtaining values from a ResultSet causes an SQLException.

Common Programming Error 23.10

Attempting to manipulate a ResultSet after closing the Statement that created the ResultSet causes an SQLException. The program discards the ResultSet when the corresponding Statement is closed.

Software Engineering Observation 23.8

Each Statement object can open only one ResultSet object at a time. When a Statement returns a new ResultSet, the Statement closes the prior ResultSet. To use multiple ResultSets in parallel, separate Statement objects must return the ResultSets.

Lines 64–70 create the GUI that displays the StringBuffer results, set the size of the application window and show the application window. The finally block (lines 91–106) closes the Statement (line 94) and the database Connection (line 95).

To run this example as well as the others in the chapter, first execute the setCP.bat batch file (or setCP.ksh shell script for UNIX) from the Cloudscape_5.0\bin directory to set the proper class path.

23.6.2 Querying the books Database

The next example (Fig. 23.27 and Fig. 23.30) enhances the example of Fig. 23.25 by allowing the user to enter any query into the program. The example displays the result of a query in a JTable, using a TableModel object to provide the ResultSet data to the JTable. Class ResultSetTableModel (Fig. 23.27) performs the connection to the database and maintains the ResultSet. Class DisplayQueryResults (Fig. 23.30) creates the GUI and specifies an instance of class ResultSetTableModel to provide data for the JTable.

Class ResultSetTableModel (Fig. 23.27) extends class *AbstractTableModel* (package javax.swing.table), which implements interface TableModel. Class ResultSetTableModel overrides TableModel methods getColumnClass, getColumnCount, getColumnName, getRowCount and getValueAt. The default implementations of TableModel methods isCellEditable and setValueAt (provided by AbstractTableModel) are not overridden, because this example does not support editing the JTable cells. Also, the default implementations of TableModel methods addTableModelListener and removeTableModelListener (provided by AbstractTableModel) are not overridden, because the implementations of these methods from AbstractTableModel properly add and remove event listeners.

```
1   // Fig. 23.27: ResultSetTableModel.java
2   // A TableModel that supplies ResultSet data to a JTable.
3
4   import java.sql.*;
5   import java.util.*;
6   import javax.swing.table.*;
```

Fig. 23.27 ResultSetTableModel enables a JTable to display the contents of a ResultSet. (Part 1 of 5.)

```
 7
 8    // ResultSet rows and columns are counted from 1 and JTable
 9    // rows and columns are counted from 0. When processing
10    // ResultSet rows or columns for use in a JTable, it is
11    // necessary to add 1 to the row or column number to manipulate
12    // the appropriate ResultSet column (i.e., JTable column 0 is
13    // ResultSet column 1 and JTable row 0 is ResultSet row 1).
14    public class ResultSetTableModel extends AbstractTableModel {
15       private Connection connection;
16       private Statement statement;
17       private ResultSet resultSet;
18       private ResultSetMetaData metaData;
19       private int numberOfRows;
20
21       // keep track of database connection status
22       private boolean connectedToDatabase = false;
23
24       // initialize resultSet and obtain its meta data object;
25       // determine number of rows
26       public ResultSetTableModel( String driver, String url,
27          String query ) throws SQLException, ClassNotFoundException
28       {
29          // load database driver class
30          Class.forName( driver );
31
32          // connect to database
33          connection = DriverManager.getConnection( url );
34
35          // create Statement to query database
36          statement = connection.createStatement(
37             ResultSet.TYPE_SCROLL_INSENSITIVE,
38             ResultSet.CONCUR_READ_ONLY );
39
40          // update database connection status
41          connectedToDatabase = true;
42
43          // set query and execute it
44          setQuery( query );
45       }
46
47       // get class that represents column type
48       public Class getColumnClass( int column ) throws IllegalStateException
49       {
50          // ensure database connection is available
51          if ( !connectedToDatabase )
52             throw new IllegalStateException( "Not Connected to Database" );
53
54          // determine Java class of column
55          try {
56             String className = metaData.getColumnClassName( column + 1 );
57
```

Fig. 23.27 ResultSetTableModel enables a JTable to display the contents of a ResultSet. (Part 2 of 5.)

```
58              // return Class object that represents className
59              return Class.forName( className );
60          }
61
62          // catch SQLExceptions and ClassNotFoundExceptions
63          catch ( Exception exception ) {
64              exception.printStackTrace();
65          }
66
67          // if problems occur above, assume type Object
68          return Object.class;
69      }
70
71      // get number of columns in ResultSet
72      public int getColumnCount() throws IllegalStateException
73      {
74          // ensure database connection is available
75          if ( !connectedToDatabase )
76              throw new IllegalStateException( "Not Connected to Database" );
77
78          // determine number of columns
79          try {
80              return metaData.getColumnCount();
81          }
82
83          // catch SQLExceptions and print error message
84          catch ( SQLException sqlException ) {
85              sqlException.printStackTrace();
86          }
87
88          // if problems occur above, return 0 for number of columns
89          return 0;
90      }
91
92      // get name of a particular column in ResultSet
93      public String getColumnName( int column ) throws IllegalStateException
94      {
95          // ensure database connection is available
96          if ( !connectedToDatabase )
97              throw new IllegalStateException( "Not Connected to Database" );
98
99          // determine column name
100         try {
101             return metaData.getColumnName( column + 1 );
102         }
103
104         // catch SQLExceptions and print error message
105         catch ( SQLException sqlException ) {
106             sqlException.printStackTrace();
107         }
108
```

Fig. 23.27 ResultSetTableModel enables a JTable to display the contents of a ResultSet. (Part 3 of 5.)

```
109          // if problems, return empty string for column name
110          return "";
111       }
112
113       // return number of rows in ResultSet
114       public int getRowCount() throws IllegalStateException
115       {
116          // ensure database connection is available
117          if ( !connectedToDatabase )
118             throw new IllegalStateException( "Not Connected to Database" );
119
120          return numberOfRows;
121       }
122
123       // obtain value in particular row and column
124       public Object getValueAt( int row, int column )
125          throws IllegalStateException
126       {
127          // ensure database connection is available
128          if ( !connectedToDatabase )
129             throw new IllegalStateException( "Not Connected to Database" );
130
131          // obtain a value at specified ResultSet row and column
132          try {
133             resultSet.absolute( row + 1 );
134
135             return resultSet.getObject( column + 1 );
136          }
137
138          // catch SQLExceptions and print error message
139          catch ( SQLException sqlException ) {
140             sqlException.printStackTrace();
141          }
142
143          // if problems, return empty string object
144          return "";
145       }
146
147       // set new database query string
148       public void setQuery( String query )
149          throws SQLException, IllegalStateException
150       {
151          // ensure database connection is available
152          if ( !connectedToDatabase )
153             throw new IllegalStateException( "Not Connected to Database" );
154
155          // specify query and execute it
156          resultSet = statement.executeQuery( query );
157
158          // obtain meta data for ResultSet
159          metaData = resultSet.getMetaData();
160
```

Fig. 23.27 ResultSetTableModel enables a JTable to display the contents of a ResultSet. (Part 4 of 5.)

```
161          // determine number of rows in ResultSet
162          resultSet.last();                      // move to last row
163          numberOfRows = resultSet.getRow();     // get row number
164
165          // notify JTable that model has changed
166          fireTableStructureChanged();
167      }
168
169      // close Statement and Connection
170      public void disconnectFromDatabase()
171      {
172          // close Statement and Connection
173          try {
174              statement.close();
175              connection.close();
176          }
177
178          // catch SQLExceptions and print error message
179          catch ( SQLException sqlException ) {
180              sqlException.printStackTrace();
181          }
182
183          // update database connection status
184          finally {
185              connectedToDatabase = false;
186          }
187      }
188
189  }  // end class ResultSetTableModel
```

Fig. 23.27   ResultSetTableModel enables a JTable to display the contents of a
ResultSet. (Part 5 of 5.)

The ResultSetTableModel constructor (lines 26–45) receives three String arguments—the driver class name, the URL of the database and the default query to perform. The
constructor throws any exceptions that occur in its body back to the application that created
the ResultSetTableModel object, so that the application can determine how to handle the
exception (e.g., report an error and terminate the application). Line 30 loads the database
driver. Line 33 establishes a connection to the database. Lines 36–38 invoke Connection
method createStatement to create a Statement object. This example uses a version of
method createStatement that takes two arguments—the *result-set type* and the *result-set
concurrency*. The result-set type (Fig. 23.28) specifies whether the ResultSet's cursor is
able to scroll in both directions or forward only and whether the ResultSet is sensitive to
changes. ResultSets that are sensitive to changes reflect those changes immediately after
they are made with methods of interface ResultSet. If a ResultSet is insensitive to
changes, the query that produced the ResultSet must be executed again to reflect any
changes made. The result-set concurrency (Fig. 23.29) specifies whether the ResultSet
can be updated with ResultSet's update methods. This example uses a ResultSet that is
scrollable, insensitive to changes and read only. Line 44 invokes ResultSetTableModel
method setQuery (lines 148–167) to perform the default query.

ResultSet static type constant	Description
TYPE_FORWARD_ONLY	Specifies that a ResultSet's cursor can move only in the forward direction (i.e., from the first row to the last row in the ResultSet).
TYPE_SCROLL_INSENSITIVE	Specifies that a ResultSet's cursor can scroll in either direction and that the changes made to the ResultSet during ResultSet processing are not reflected in the ResultSet unless the program queries the database again.
TYPE_SCROLL_SENSITIVE	Specifies that a ResultSet's cursor can scroll in either direction and that the changes made to the ResultSet during ResultSet processing are reflected immediately in the ResultSet.

Fig. 23.28   ResultSet constants for specifying ResultSet type .

ResultSet static concurrency constant	Description
CONCUR_READ_ONLY	Specifies that a ResultSet cannot be updated (i.e., changes to the ResultSet contents cannot be reflected in the database with ResultSet's *update* methods).
CONCUR_UPDATABLE	Specifies that a ResultSet can be updated (i.e., changes to the ResultSet contents can be reflected in the database with ResultSet's *update* methods).

Fig. 23.29   ResultSet constants for specifying result properties.

Portability Tip 23.5

Some JDBC drivers do not support scrollable ResultSets. In such cases, typically the driver returns a ResultSet in which the cursor can move only forward. For more information, see your database-driver documentation.

Portability Tip 23.6

Some JDBC drivers do not support updatable ResultSets. In such cases, typically the driver returns a read-only ResultSet. For more information, see your database-driver documentation.

Common Programming Error 23.11

Attempting to update a ResultSet when the database driver does not support updatable ResultSets causes SQLExceptions.

Common Programming Error 23.12

Attempting to move the cursor backwards through a ResultSet when the database driver does not support backwards scrolling causes an SQLException.

Method `getColumnClass` (lines 48–69) returns a `Class` object that represents the superclass of all objects in a particular column. The `JTable` uses this information to configure the default cell renderer and cell editor for that column in the `JTable`. Line 56 use `ResultSetMetaData` method *getColumnClassName* to obtain the fully qualified class name for the specified column. Line 59 loads the class and returns the corresponding `Class` object. If an exception occurs, the `catch` at lines 63–65 prints a stack trace and line 68 returns `Object.class`—the `Class` instance that represents class `Object`—as the default type. [*Note*: Line 56 uses the argument `column + 1`. Like arrays, `JTable` row and column numbers are counted from 0. However, `ResultSet` row and column numbers are counted from 1. Thus, when processing `ResultSet` rows or columns for use in a `JTable`, it is necessary to add 1 to the row or column number to manipulate the appropriate `ResultSet` row or column.]

Method `getColumnCount` (lines 72–90) returns the number of columns in the model's underlying `ResultSet`. Line 80 uses `ResultSetMetaData` method *getColumnCount* to obtain the number of columns in the `ResultSet`. If an exception occurs, the `catch` at lines 84–86 prints a stack trace and line 89 returns 0 as the default number of columns.

Method `getColumnName` (lines 93–111) returns the name of the column in the model's underlying `ResultSet`. Line 101 uses `ResultSetMetaData` method *getColumnName* to obtain the column name from the `ResultSet`. If an exception occurs, the `catch` at lines 105–107 prints a stack trace and line 110 returns the empty string as the default column name.

Method `getRowCount` (lines 114–121) returns the number of rows in the model's underlying `ResultSet`. When method `setQuery` (lines 148–167) performs a query, it stores the number of rows in variable `numberOfRows`.

Method `getValueAt` (lines 124–145) returns the `Object` in a particular row and column of the model's underlying `ResultSet`. Line 133 uses `ResultSet` method *absolute* to position the `ResultSet` cursor at a specific row. Line 135 uses `ResultSet` method `getObject` to obtain the `Object` in a specific column of the current row. If an exception occurs, the `catch` at lines 139–141 prints a stack trace and line 144 returns the empty string object as the default value.

Method `setQuery` (lines 148–167) executes the query it receives as an argument to obtain a new `ResultSet` (line 156). Line 159 gets the `ResultSetMetaData` for the new `ResultSet`. Line 162 uses `ResultSet` method *last* to position the `ResultSet` cursor at the last row in the `ResultSet`. Line 163 uses `ResultSet` method *getRow* to obtain the row number for the current row in the `ResultSet`. Line 166 invokes method *fireTableStructureChanged* (inherited from class `AbstractTableModel`) to notify any `JTable` using this `ResultSetTableModel` object as its model that the structure of the model has changed. This causes the `JTable` to repopulate its rows and columns with the new `ResultSet` data. Method `setQuery` throws any exceptions that occur in its body back to the application that invoked `setQuery`.

Method `disconnectFromDatabase` (lines 170–187) implements an appropriate termination method for class `ResultSetTableModel`. Recall from Chapter 8 that use of `Object` method `finalize` to "clean up" after objects is discouraged, since there is no guarantee that method `finalize` will ever be called. Instead, a class designer should provide a public method that clients of the class must invoke explicitly to free resources that an object has used. In this case, method `disconnectFromDatabase` closes the database statement and connection (lines 174–175), which are considered limited resources. Clients of the `ResultSetTableModel` class should always invoke this method when the instance of this class is no longer needed. In addition, note that each other method in the class throws an `IllegalStateException` if the boolean field `connectedToDatabase` is `false`. Method `disconnectFromDatabase` sets `connectedToDatabase` to `false` (line 185) to ensure that clients do not use an instance of `ResultSetTableModel` after that instance has already been terminated. `IllegalStateException` is an exception from the Java libraries that is appropriate for indicating this error condition.

The `DisplayQueryResults` (Fig. 23.30) constructor (lines 25–159) creates a `ResultSetTableModel` object and the GUI for the application. Lines 15, 16 and 19 declare the database driver class name, database URL and default query that are passed to the `ResultSetTableModel` constructor to make the initial connection to the database and perform the default query. Line 58 creates the `JTable` object and passes a `ResultSetTableModel` object to the `JTable` constructor, which then registers the `JTable` as a listener for `TableModelEvents` generated by the `ResultSetTableModel`. Lines 66–110 register an event handler for the `submitButton` that the user clicks to submit a query to the database. When the user clicks the button, method `actionPerformed` (lines 71–106) invokes `ResultSetTableModel` method `setQuery` to execute the new query. If the user's query fails (e.g., because of a syntax error in the user's input), lines 87–88 execute the default query. If the default query also fails, there could be a more serious error, so line 98 ensures that the database connection is closed and line 100 exits the program. The screen captures in Fig. 23.30 show the results of two queries. The first screen capture shows the default query that retrieves all the data from table `authors` of database `books`. The second screen capture shows a query that selects each author's first name and last name from the `authors` table and combines that information with the title and edition number from the `titles` table. Try entering your own queries in the text area and clicking the **Submit Query** button to execute the query.

```
1    // Fig. 23.30: DisplayQueryResults.java
2    // Display the contents of the Authors table in the
3    // Books database.
4
5    import java.awt.*;
6    import java.awt.event.*;
7    import java.sql.*;
8    import java.util.*;
9    import javax.swing.*;
10   import javax.swing.table.*;
11
12   public class DisplayQueryResults extends JFrame {
13
14      // JDBC driver and database URL
15      static final String JDBC_DRIVER = "com.ibm.db2j.jdbc.DB2jDriver";
16      static final String DATABASE_URL = "jdbc:db2j:books";
17
18      // default query selects all rows from authors table
19      static final String DEFAULT_QUERY = "SELECT * FROM authors";
```

Fig. 23.30 `DisplayQueryResults` for querying database `books`. (Part 1 of 5.)

```
20
21      private ResultSetTableModel tableModel;
22      private JTextArea queryArea;
23
24      // create ResultSetTableModel and GUI
25      public DisplayQueryResults()
26      {
27         super( "Displaying Query Results" );
28
29         // create ResultSetTableModel and display database table
30         try {
31
32            // specify location of database on filesystem
33            System.setProperty( "db2j.system.home", "C:/Cloudscape_5.0" );
34
35            // create TableModel for results of query SELECT * FROM authors
36            tableModel = new ResultSetTableModel( JDBC_DRIVER, DATABASE_URL,
37               DEFAULT_QUERY );
38
39            // set up JTextArea in which user types queries
40            queryArea = new JTextArea( DEFAULT_QUERY, 3, 100 );
41            queryArea.setWrapStyleWord( true );
42            queryArea.setLineWrap( true );
43
44            JScrollPane scrollPane = new JScrollPane( queryArea,
45               ScrollPaneConstants.VERTICAL_SCROLLBAR_AS_NEEDED,
46               ScrollPaneConstants.HORIZONTAL_SCROLLBAR_NEVER );
47
48            // set up JButton for submitting queries
49            JButton submitButton = new JButton( "Submit Query" );
50
51            // create Box to manage placement of queryArea and
52            // submitButton in GUI
53            Box box = Box.createHorizontalBox();
54            box.add( scrollPane );
55            box.add( submitButton );
56
57            // create JTable delegate for tableModel
58            JTable resultTable = new JTable( tableModel );
59
60            // place GUI components on content pane
61            Container c = getContentPane();
62            c.add( box, BorderLayout.NORTH );
63            c.add( new JScrollPane( resultTable ), BorderLayout.CENTER );
64
65            // create event listener for submitButton
66            submitButton.addActionListener(
67
68               new ActionListener() {
69
70                  // pass query to table model
71                  public void actionPerformed( ActionEvent event )
72                  {
```

Fig. 23.30 DisplayQueryResults for querying database books. (Part 2 of 5.)

```
73              // perform a new query
74              try {
75                  tableModel.setQuery( queryArea.getText() );
76              }
77
78              // catch SQLExceptions when performing a new query
79              catch ( SQLException sqlException ) {
80                  JOptionPane.showMessageDialog( null,
81                      sqlException.getMessage(), "Database error",
82                      JOptionPane.ERROR_MESSAGE );
83
84                  // try to recover from invalid user query
85                  // by executing default query
86                  try {
87                      tableModel.setQuery( DEFAULT_QUERY );
88                      queryArea.setText( DEFAULT_QUERY );
89                  }
90
91                  // catch SQLException when performing default query
92                  catch ( SQLException sqlException2 ) {
93                      JOptionPane.showMessageDialog( null,
94                          sqlException2.getMessage(), "Database error",
95                          JOptionPane.ERROR_MESSAGE );
96
97                      // ensure database connection is closed
98                      tableModel.disconnectFromDatabase();
99
100                     System.exit( 1 );   // terminate application
101
102                 }  // end inner catch
103
104             }  // end outer catch
105
106         }  // end actionPerformed
107
108     }  // end ActionListener inner class
109
110     ); // end call to addActionListener
111
112     // set window size and display window
113     setSize( 500, 250 );
114     setVisible( true );
115
116 }  // end try
117
118 // catch ClassNotFoundException thrown by
119 // ResultSetTableModel if database driver not found
120 catch ( ClassNotFoundException classNotFound ) {
121     JOptionPane.showMessageDialog( null,
122         "Cloudscape driver not found", "Driver not found",
123         JOptionPane.ERROR_MESSAGE );
124
125     System.exit( 1 );   // terminate application
```

Fig. 23.30 DisplayQueryResults for querying database books. (Part 3 of 5.)

```
126          } // end catch
127
128          // catch SQLException thrown by ResultSetTableModel
129          // if problems occur while setting up database
130          // connection and querying database
131          catch ( SQLException sqlException ) {
132             JOptionPane.showMessageDialog( null, sqlException.getMessage(),
133                "Database error", JOptionPane.ERROR_MESSAGE );
134
135             // ensure database connection is closed
136             tableModel.disconnectFromDatabase();
137
138             System.exit( 1 );   // terminate application
139          }
140
141          // dispose of window when user quits application (this overrides
142          // the default of HIDE_ON_CLOSE)
143          setDefaultCloseOperation( DISPOSE_ON_CLOSE );
144
145          // ensure database connection is closed when user quits application
146          addWindowListener(
147
148             new WindowAdapter() {
149
150                // disconnect from database and exit when window has closed
151                public void windowClosed( WindowEvent event )
152                {
153                   tableModel.disconnectFromDatabase();
154                   System.exit( 0 );
155                }
156             }
157          );
158
159       } // end DisplayQueryResults constructor
160
161       // execute application
162       public static void main( String args[] )
163       {
164          new DisplayQueryResults();
165       }
166
167 }  // end class DisplayQueryResults
```

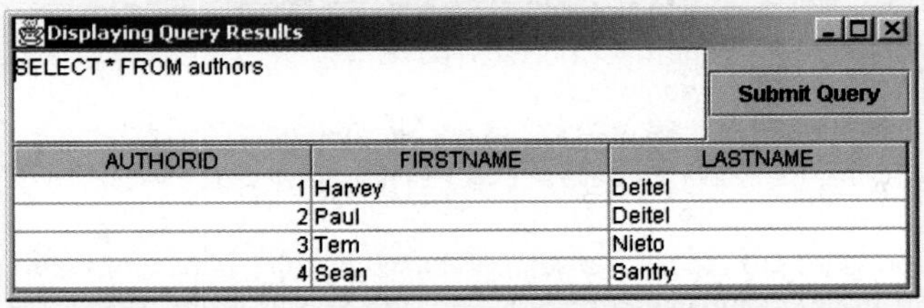

Fig. 23.30 DisplayQueryResults for querying database **books**. (Part 4 of 5.)

Displaying Query Results _ □ x

SELECT lastName, firstName, title, editionNumber FROM authors, titles, authorISBN WHERE authors.authorID = authorISBN.authorID AND titles.isbn = authorISBN.isbn   **Submit Query**

LASTNAME	FIRSTNAME	TITLE	EDITIONNUMBER
Deitel	Harvey	C How to Program	3
Deitel	Harvey	C How to Program	2
Deitel	Harvey	C++ How to Program	3
Deitel	Harvey	C++ How to Program	2
Deitel	Harvey	The Complete C++ ...	3
Deitel	Harvey	e-Business and e-...	1
Deitel	Harvey	Internet and World ...	1
Deitel	Harvey	The Complete Inter...	1
Deitel	Harvey	Java How to Progra...	3

Fig. 23.30 `DisplayQueryResults` for querying database `books`. (Part 5 of 5.)

23.7 Stored Procedures

Many database management systems can store individual SQL statements or sets of SQL statements in a database, so that programs accessing that database can invoke them. Such SQL statements are called *stored procedures*. JDBC enables programs to invoke stored procedures using objects that implement interface `CallableStatement`. `Callable-Statement`s can receive arguments specified with the methods inherited from interface `PreparedStatement`. In addition, `CallableStatement`s can specify *output parameters* in which a stored procedure can place return values. Interface `CallableStatement` includes methods to specify which parameters in a stored procedure are output parameters. The interface also includes methods to obtain the values of output parameters returned from a stored procedure.

Portability Tip 23.7

Although the syntax for creating stored procedures differs across database management systems, interface `CallableStatement` provides a uniform interface for specifying input and output parameters for stored procedures and for invoking stored procedures.

Portability Tip 23.8

According to the Java API documentation for interface `CallableStatement`, for maximum portability between database systems, programs should process the update counts or ResultSets returned from a `CallableStatement` before obtaining the values of any output parameters.

23.8 Internet and World Wide Web Resources

`java.sun.com/products/jdbc`
Sun Microsystems, Inc.'s JDBC home page.

`java.sun.com/docs/books/tutorial/jdbc/index.html`
The Sun Microsystems, Inc., Java Tutorial's JDBC track.

`www.sql.org`
This SQL portal provides links to many resources, including SQL syntax, tips, tutorials, books, magazines, discussion groups, companies with SQL services, SQL consultants and free software.

`industry.java.sun.com/products/jdbc/drivers`
Sun Microsystems, Inc., search engine for locating JDBC drivers.

`java.sun.com/j2se/1.3/docs/guide/jdbc/index.html`
Sun Microsystems, Inc.'s JDBC API documentation.

`java.sun.com/products/jdbc/faq.html`
Sun Microsystems, Inc.'s frequently asked questions on JDBC.

`www.jguru.com/jguru/faq/faqpage.jsp?name=JDBC`
The JGuru JDBC FAQs.

`www.cloudscape.com`
This site is Informix's Cloudscape database home page. Here, you can download the latest version of Cloudscape and access all of its documentation on line.

`java.sun.com/products/jdbc/articles/package2.html`
An overview of the JDBC 2.0 optional package API.

`developer.java.sun.com/developer/earlyAccess/crs`
Early access to the Sun RowSet implementations. [*Note*: You may need to register at the Java Developer Connection (`developer.java.sun.com/developer/index.html`) before downloading from this site.]

`developer.java.sun.com/developer/Books/JDBCTutorial/chapter5.html`
Chapter 5 (RowSet Tutorial) of the book *The JDBC 2.0 API Tutorial and Reference, Second Edition.*

SUMMARY

- A database is an integrated collection of data. A database management system (DBMS) provides mechanisms for storing and organizing data.
- Today's most popular database management systems are relational database systems.
- SQL is a language used almost universally with relational database systems to perform queries and manipulate data.
- Programs connect to, and interact with, relational databases via an interface—software that facilitates communications between a database management system and a program.
- Java programmers communicate with databases and manipulate their data using the JDBC API. A JDBC driver implements the interface to a particular database.
- A relational database stores data in tables. Tables are composed of rows and rows are composed of columns in which values are stored.
- A primary key provides a unique value that cannot be duplicated in other rows.
- Each column of the table represents a different attribute.
- The primary key can be composed of more than one column.
- SQL provides a complete set of statements that enable programmers to define complex queries to retrieve data from a database.
- Every column in a primary key must have a value and the value of the primary key must be unique. This is known as the Rule of Entity Integrity.
- A one-to-many relationship between tables indicates that a row in one table can have many rows in a separate table.
- A foreign key must match the value of the primary key in another table.
- The foreign key helps maintain the Rule of Referential Integrity: Every foreign key column value must appear in another table's primary key column. Foreign keys enable information from multiple tables to be joined together for analysis purposes. There is a one-to-many relationship between a primary key and its corresponding foreign key.

- The basic form of a SELECT query is

      SELECT * FROM *tableName*

  where the asterisk (*) indicates that all columns from *tableName* should be selected and *tableName* specifies the table in the database from which data will be retrieved.

- To retrieve specific columns from a table, replace the asterisk (*) with a comma-separated list of the column names.

- Programmers process query results by knowing in advance the order of the columns in the result. Specifying columns explicitly guarantees that they are always returned in the specified order, even if the actual order in the table(s) is different.

- The optional WHERE clause in a SELECT query specifies the selection criteria for the query. The basic form of a SELECT query with selection criteria is

      SELECT *columnName1*, *columnName2*, ... FROM *tableName* WHERE *criteria*

- The WHERE clause can contain operators <, >, <=, >=, =, <> and LIKE. Operator LIKE is used for pattern matching with wildcard characters percent (%) and underscore (_).

- A percent character (%) in a pattern indicates that a string matching the pattern can have zero or more characters at the percent character's location in the pattern.

- An underscore (_) in the pattern string indicates a single character at that position in the pattern.

- The result of a query can be sorted in ascending or descending order using the optional ORDER BY clause. The simplest form of an ORDER BY clause is

      SELECT *columnName1*, *columnName2*, ... FROM *tableName* ORDER BY *column* ASC
      SELECT *columnName1*, *columnName2*, ... FROM *tableName* ORDER BY *column*
      DESC

  where ASC specifies ascending order, DESC specifies descending order and *column* specifies the column on which the sort is based. The default sorting order is ascending, so ASC is optional.

- Multiple columns can be used for ordering purposes with an ORDER BY clause of the form

      ORDER BY *column1 sortingOrder*, *column2 sortingOrder*, ...

- The WHERE and ORDER BY clauses can be combined in one query. If used, ORDER BY must be the last clause in the query.

- An INNER JOIN merges rows from two tables by matching values in a column that is common to the tables. The basic form for the INNER JOIN oeprator is:

      SELECT *columnName1, columnName2, ...*
      FROM *table1*
      INNER JOIN *table2*
         ON *table1.columnName* = *table2.columnName*

  The ON clause specifies the columns from each table that are compared to determine which rows are joined.If an SQL statement uses columns with the same name from multiple tables, the column names must be fully qualified with its table name and a dot operator (.).

- An INSERT statement inserts a new row in a table. The basic form of this statement is

      INSERT INTO *tableName* (*columnName1*, *columnName2*, ..., *columnNameN*)
         VALUES (*value1*, *value2*, ..., *valueN*)

  where *tableName* is the table in which to insert the row. The *tableName* is followed by a comma-separated list of column names in parentheses. The list of column names is followed by the SQL keyword VALUES and a comma-separated list of values in parentheses.

- SQL statements use single quotes (') as a delimiter for strings. To specify a string containing a single quote in an SQL statement, the single quote must be escaped with another single quote.

- An UPDATE statement modifies data in a table. The basic form of an UPDATE statement is

      UPDATE *tableName*
          SET *columnName1* = *value1*, *columnName2* = *value2*, …, *columnNameN* = *valueN*
          WHERE *criteria*

  where *tableName* is the table in which to update data. The *tableName* is followed by keyword SET and a comma-separated list of column name/value pairs in the format *columnName = value*. The WHERE clause *criteria* determines the rows to update.

- A DELETE statement removes rows from a table. The simplest form for a DELETE statement is

      DELETE FROM *tableName* WHERE *criteria*

  where *tableName* is the table from which to delete a row (or rows). The WHERE *criteria* determines which row(s) to delete.

- Package java.sql contains classes and interfaces for manipulating relational databases in Java.

- A program must load the database driver class before the program can connect to the database.

- JDBC supports four categories of drivers: JDBC-to-ODBC bridge driver (Type 1); Native-API, partly Java driver (Type 2); JDBC-Net pure Java driver (Type 3) and Native-Protocol pure Java driver (Type 4). Type 3 and 4 drivers are preferred, because they are pure Java solutions.

- An object that implements interface Connection manages the connection between the Java program and the database. Connection objects enable programs to create SQL statements that manipulate data and to perform transaction processing.

- Method getConnection of class DriverManager attempts to connect to a database specified by its URL argument. The URL helps the program locate the database. The URL includes the protocol for communication, the subprotocol for communication and the name of the database.

- Connection method createStatement creates an object of type Statement. The program uses the Statement object to submit SQL statements to the database.

- Statement method executeQuery executes a query and returns an object that implements interface ResultSet containing the query result. ResultSet methods enable a program to manipulate query result.

- A ResultSetMetaData object describes a ResultSet's contents. Programs can use metadata programmatically to obtain information about the ResultSet column names and types.

- ResultSetMetaData method getColumnCount retrieves the number of ResultSet columns.

- ResultSet method next positions the ResultSet cursor to the next row in the ResultSet. The cursor points to the current row. Method next returns boolean value true if it is able to position to the next row; otherwise, the method returns false. This method must be called to begin processing a ResultSet.

- When processing ResultSets, it is possible to extract each column of the ResultSet as a specific Java type. ResultSetMetaData method getColumnType returns a constant integer from class Types (package java.sql) indicating the type of the data for a specific column.

- ResultSet *get* methods typically receive as an argument either a column number (as an int) or a column name (as a String) indicating which column's value to obtain.

- ResultSet row and column numbers start at 1.

- Each Statement object can open only one ResultSet object at a time. When a Statement returns a new ResultSet, the Statement closes the prior ResultSet.

- Connection method createStatement has an overloaded version that takes two arguments: the result type and the result concurrency. The result type specifies whether the ResultSet's cursor is able to scroll in both directions or forward only and whether the ResultSet is sensitive to changes. The result concurrency specifies whether the ResultSet can be updated with ResultSet's update methods.

- Some JDBC drivers do not support scrollable and/or updatable ResultSets.

- TableModel method getColumnClass returns a Class object that represents the superclass of all objects in a particular column. JTable uses this information to set up the default cell renderer and cell editor for that column in a JTable.

- ResultSetMetaData method getColumnClassName obtains the fully qualified class name of the specified column.

- TableModel method getColumnCount returns the number of columns in the model's underlying ResultSet.

- TableModel method getColumnName returns the name of the column in the model's underlying ResultSet.

- ResultSetMetaData method getColumnName obtains the column name from the ResultSet.

- TableModel method getRowCount returns the number of rows in the model's underlying ResultSet.

- TableModel method getValueAt returns the Object at a particular row and column of the model's underlying ResultSet.

- ResultSet method absolute positions the ResultSet cursor at a specific row.

- AbstractTableModel method fireTableStructureChanged notifies any JTable using a particular TableModel object as its model that the data in the model has changed.

- JDBC enables programs to invoke stored procedures using objects that implement interface CallableStatement.

- CallableStatements can receive arguments specified with the methods inherited from interface PreparedStatement. In addition, CallableStatements can specify output parameters in which a stored procedure can place return values.

TERMINOLOGY

% SQL wildcard character
_ SQL wildcard character
absolute method of ResultSet
AbstractTableModel class
addTableModelListener method of
    TableModel
CallableStatement interface
close method of Connection
close method of Statement
Cloudscape database
com.ibm.db2j.jdbc.DB2jDriver
column
connect to a database
Connection interface
createStatement method of Connection
database
database driver

DELETE SQL statement
deleteRow method of ResultSet
DriverManager class
execute method of Statement
executeQuery method of Statement
executeUpdate method of Statement
fireTableStructureChanged method of
    AbstractTableModel
foreign key
getColumnClass method of TableModel
getColumnClassName method of
    ResultSetMetaData
getColumnCount method of
    ResultSetMetaData
getColumnCount method of TableModel
getColumnName method of
    ResultSetMetaData

getColumnName method of TableModel
getColumnType method of
    ResultSetMetaData
getConnection method of DriverManager
getMetaData method of ResultSet
getMoreResults method of Statement
getObject method of ResultSet
getResultSet method of Statement
getRow method of ResultSet
getRowCount method of TableModel
getUpdateCount method of Statement
getValueAt method of TableModel
INNER JOIN SQL operator
INSERT SQL statement
insertRow method of ResultSet
java.sql package
javax.swing.table package
JDBC
JDBC driver
JdbcOdbcDriver
join
last method of ResultSet
metadata
moveToCurrentRow method of ResultSet
moveToInsertRow method of ResultSet
next method of ResultSet
one-to-many relationship
ORDER BY clause of an SQL statement
ordering rows
output parameter
pattern matching
primary key

query a database
relational database
removeTableModelListener method of
    TableModel
result
ResultSet interface
ResultSet types
ResultSetMetaData interface
row
Rule of Entity Integrity
Rule of Referential Integrity
SELECT SQL statement
selection criteria
setString method of PreparedStatement
SQL
SQL script
SQLException class
Statement interface
stored procedure
TableModel interface
TableModelEvent class
table
Type 1 (JDBC-to-ODBC bridge) driver
Type 2 (Native-API, partly Java) driver
Type 3 (JDBC-Net pure Java) driver
Type 4 (Native-Protocol pure Java) driver
Types class
updatable ResultSet
UPDATE SQL statement
updateRow method of ResultSet
WHERE clause of an SQL statement

SELF-REVIEW EXERCISES

23.1 Fill in the blanks in each of the following statements:
   a) The industry standard database query language is _____.
   b) A table in a database consists of _____ and _____.
   c) SQL query results are manipulated in Java as _____ objects.
   d) The _____ uniquely identifies each row in a table.
   e) SQL keyword _____ is followed by the selection criteria that specify the rows to select in a query.
   f) SQL keywords _____ specify the order in which rows are sorted in a query.
   g) Merging rows from multiple database tables is called _____ the tables.
   h) A(n) _____ is an organized collection of data.
   i) A(n) _____ is a set of columns whose values match the primary key valkues of another table.
   j) Package _____ contains classes and interfaces for manipulating relational databases in Java.
   k) Interface _____ helps manage the connection between a Java program and a database.
   l) A(n) _____ object is used to submit a query to a database.

ANSWERS TO SELF-REVIEW EXERCISES

23.1   a) SQL. b) rows, columns. c) `ResultSet`. d) primary key. e) `WHERE`. f) `ORDER BY`. g) joining. h) database. i) foreign key. j) `java.sql`. k) `Connection`. l) `Statement`.

EXERCISES

23.2   Using the techniques shown in this chapter, define a complete query application for the books database. Provide a series of predefined queries, with an appropriate name for each query, displayed in a `JComboBox`. Also allow users to supply their own queries and add them to the `JComboBox`. Provide the following predefined queries:

   a) Select all authors from the `authors` table.
   b) Select all publishers from the `publishers` table.
   c) Select a specific author and list all books for that author. Include the title, year and ISBN. Order the information alphabetically by the author's last name and first name.
   d) Select a specific publisher and list all books published by that publisher. Include the title, year and ISBN. Order the information alphabetically by title.
   e) Provide any other queries you feel are appropriate.

23.3   Modify Exercise 23.2 to define a complete database manipulation application for the books database. In addition to the querying, the user should be able to edit existing data and add new data to the database (obeying referential and entity integrity constraints). Allow the user to edit the database in the following ways:

   a) Add a new author.
   b) Edit the existing information for an author.
   c) Add a new title for an author. (Remember that the book must have an entry in the `authorISBN` table.) Be sure to specify the publisher of the title.
   d) Add a new publisher.
   e) Edit the existing information for a publisher.
   f) For each of the preceding database manipulations, design an appropriate GUI to allow the user to perform the data manipulation.

23.4   In Section 10.7, we introduced an employee-payroll hierarchy to calculate each employee's payroll. In this exercise, we provide a database of employees that corresponds to the employee-payroll hierarchy. (A SQL script to create the employee database is provided with the examples for this chapter on the CD that accompanies this text and on our Web site www.deitel.com.) Write an application that allows:

   a) Add employees to the Employee table.
   b) For each employee added to the table, add payroll to the corresponding table. For example, for a salaried employee add the payroll information to the salariedEmployees table.

23.5   Write an application that provides a `JComboBox` and a `JTextArea` to allow the user to perform a query that is either selected from the `JComboBox` or defined in the `JTextArea`. Sample predefined querys are:

   a) Select all employees working in Department SALES.
   b) Select hourly employees working over 30 hours.
   c) Select all comission employees in descending order of the comission rate.

23.6   Modify Exercise 23.5 to perform the following tasks:

   a) Increase base salary by 10% for all base plus comission employees.
   b) If the employee's birthday is in current month, add $100 bonus.
   c) For all comission employee whose gross sales over 10000, add $100 bonus.

BIBLIOGRAPHY

Ashmore, D. C. "Best Practices for JDBC Programming." *Java Developers Journal*, 5: no. 4 (2000): 42–54.

Blaha, M. R., W. J. Premerlani and J. E. Rumbaugh. "Relational Database Design Using an Object-Oriented Methodology." *Communications of the ACM*, 31: no. 4 (1988): 414–427.

Brunner, R. J. "The Evolution of Connecting." *Java Developers Journal*, 5: no. 10 (2000): 24–26.

Brunner, R. J. "After the Connection." *Java Developers Journal*, 5: no. 11 (2000): 42–46.

Callahan, T. "So You Want a Stand-Alone Database for Java." *Java Developers Journal*, 3: no. 12 (1998): 28–36.

Codd, E. F. "A Relational Model of Data for Large Shared Data Banks." *Communications of the ACM*, June 1970.

Codd, E. F. "Further Normalization of the Data Base Relational Model." *Courant Computer Science Symposia*, Vol. 6, *Data Base Systems*. Upper Saddle River, NJ: Prentice Hall, 1972.

Codd, E. F. "Fatal Flaws in SQL." *Datamation*, 34: no. 16 (1988): 45–48.

Cooper, J. W. "Making Databases Easier for Your Users." *Java Pro*, 4: no. 10 (2000): 47–54.

Date, C. J. *An Introduction to Database Systems, Seventh Edition*. Reading, MA: Addison Wesley, 2000.

Deitel, H. M. *Operating Systems, Second Edition*. Reading, MA: Addison Wesley, 1990.

Duguay, C. "Electronic Mail Merge." *Java Pro*, Winter 1999/2000, 22–32.

Ergul, S. "Transaction Processing with Java." *Java Report*, January 2001, 30–36.

Fisher, M. "JDBC Database Access," (a trail in *The Java Tutorial*), <`java.sun.com/docs/books/tutorial/jdbc/index.html`>.

Harrison, G., "Browsing the JDBC API," *Java Developers Journal*, 3: no. 2 (1998): 44–52.

Jasnowski, M. "Persistence Frameworks," *Java Developers Journal*, 5: no. 11 (2000): 82–86.

"JDBC API Documentation," <`java.sun.com/j2se/1.3/docs/guide/jdbc/index.html`>.

Jordan, D. "An Overview of Sun's Java Data Objects Specification," *Java Pro*, 4: no. 6 (2000): 102–108.

Khanna, P. "Managing Object Persistence with JDBC," *Java Pro*, 4: no. 5 (2000): 28–33.

Reese, G. *Database Programming with JDBC and Java, Second Edition*. Cambridge, MA: O'Reilly, 2001.

Spell, B. "Create Enterprise Applications with JDBC 2.0," *Java Pro*, 4: no. 4 (2000): 40–44.

Stonebraker, M. "Operating System Support for Database Management," *Communications of the ACM*, 24: no. 7 (1981): 412–418.

Taylor, A. *JDBC Developer's Resource: Database Programming on the Internet*. Upper Saddle River, NJ: Prentice Hall, 1999.

Thilmany, C. "Applying Patterns to JDBC Development," *Java Developers Journal*, 5: no. 6 (2000): 80–90.

Venugopal, S. 2000. "Cross-Database Portability with JDBC, *Java Developers Journal*, 5: no. 1 (2000): 58–62.

White, S., M. Fisher, R. Cattell, G. Hamilton and M. Hapner. *JDBC API Tutorial and Reference, Second Edition*. Boston, MA: Addison Wesley, 1999.

Winston, A. "A Distributed Database Primer," *UNIX World*, April 1988, 54–63.

24

Servlets

Objectives

- To execute servlets with the Apache Tomcat server.
- To be able to respond to HTTP requests from an `HttpServlet`.
- To be able to redirect requests to static and dynamic Web resources.

A fair request should be followed by the deed in silence.
Dante Alighieri

The longest part of the journey is said to be the passing of the gate.
Marcus Terentius Varro

If nominated, I will not accept; if elected, I will not serve.
General William T. Sherman

Friends share all things.
Pythagoras

24.1 Introduction

There is much excitement over the Internet and the World Wide Web. The Internet ties the "information world" together. The World Wide Web makes the Internet easy to use and gives it the flair and sizzle of multimedia. Organizations see the Internet and the Web as crucial to their information systems strategies. Java provides a number of built-in networking capabilities that make it easy to develop Internet-based and Web-based applications. Not only can Java specify parallelism through multithreading, but it can enable programs to search the world for information and to collaborate with programs running on other computers internationally, nationally or just within an organization. Java can even enable applets and applications running on the same computer to communicate with one another, subject to security constraints.

Networking is a massive and complex topic. Computer science and computer engineering students typically take a full-semester, upper-level course in computer networking and continue with further study at the graduate level. Java provides a rich complement of networking capabilities that are used as implementation vehicles in computer networking courses and industry.

Java's networking capabilities are grouped into several packages. The fundamental networking capabilities are defined by classes and interfaces of package *java.net*. This package offers *socket-based communications* that enable applications to view networking as streams of data—a program can read from a *socket* or write to a socket as simply as reading from a file or writing to a file. The classes and interfaces of package java.net also offer *packet-based communications* that enable individual *packets* of information to be transmitted—commonly used to transmit audio and video over the Internet. Chapter 18 shows how to create and manipulate sockets and how to communicate with packets of data.

Higher-level views of networking are provided by classes and interfaces in the *java.rmi* packages (five packages) for *Remote Method Invocation (RMI)* and *org.omg* packages (seven packages) for *Common Object Request Broker Architecture (CORBA)* that are part of the Java 2 API. The RMI packages allow Java objects running on separate Java virtual machines (normally on separate computers) to communicate via remote method calls. Such calls appear to invoke methods on an object in the same program, but actually have built-in networking (based on the capabilities of package *java.net*) that communicates the method calls to another object on a separate computer. The CORBA packages provide similar functionality to the RMI packages. A key difference between RMI and CORBA is that RMI can only be used between Java objects, whereas CORBA can be used between any two applications that understand CORBA—including applications written in other programming languages.[1] In Chapter 13 of our book *Advanced Java 2 Platform How to Program*, we present Java's RMI capabilities. Chapters 26–27 of *Advanced Java 2 Platform How to Program* discuss the basic CORBA concepts and present a case study that implements a distributed system in CORBA.

Our discussion of networking focuses on both sides of a *client-server relationship*. The *client* requests that some action be performed and the *server* performs the action and responds to the client. This request-response model of communication is the foundation for the highest-level views of networking in Java—*servlets* and *JavaServer Pages (JSP)*. A servlet extends the functionality of a server, such as a Web server. Packages *javax.servlet* and *javax.servlet.http* provide the classes and interfaces to define servlets. Packages *javax.servlet.jsp* and *javax.servlet.jsp.tagext* provide the classes and interfaces that extend the servlet capabilities for JavaServer Pages. Using special syntax, JSP allows Web-page implementors to create pages that use encapsulated Java functionality and even to write *scriptlets* of actual Java code directly in the page.

A common implementation of the request-response model is between World Wide Web browsers and World Wide Web servers. When a user selects a Web site to browse through their browser (the client application), a request is sent to the appropriate Web server (the server application). The server normally responds to the client by sending the appropriate XHTML Web page.[2] Servlets are effective for developing Web-based solutions that help provide secure access to a Web site, interact with databases on behalf of a client, dynamically generate custom XHTML documents to be displayed by browsers and maintain unique session information for each client.

This chapter begins our networking discussions with servlets that enhance the functionality of World Wide Web servers—the most common form of servlet today. Chapter 25 discusses JSPs, which are translated into servlets. JSPs are a convenient and powerful way to implement the request/response mechanism of the Web without getting into the lower-level details of servlets. Together, servlets and JSPs form the Web tier of the Java 2 Enterprise Edition (J2EE).

Many developers feel that servlets are the right solution for database-intensive applications that communicate with so-called *thin clients*—applications that require minimal

---

1.   *Remote Method Invocation over the Internet Inter-Orb Protocol* (*RMI-IIOP*) enables the integration of Java with non-Java distributed objects by using CORBA IIOP.

2.   If you are not familiar with XHTML and CSS, refer to the PDF documents *Introduction to XHTML* and *Cascading Style Sheets (CSS)* on the CD that accompanies this book. These also are available at our Web site, www.deitel.com.

client-side support. The server is responsible for database access. Clients connect to the server using standard protocols available on most client platforms. Thus, the presentation-logic code for generating dynamic content can be written once and reside on the server for access by clients, to allow programmers to create efficient thin clients.

In this chapter, our servlet examples demonstrate the Web's request/response mechanism (primarily with `get` and `post` requests), redirecting requests to other resources and interacting with databases through JDBC. We placed this chapter after our discussion of JDBC and databases intentionally, so that we can build multi-tier, client–server applications that access databases.

Sun Microsystems, through the *Java Community Process*, is responsible for the development of the servlet and JavaServer Pages specifications. The reference implementation of both these standards is under development by the *Apache Software Foundation* (`www.apache.org`) as part of the *Jakarta Project* (`jakarta.apache.org`). As stated on the Jakarta Project's home page, "The goal of the Jakarta Project is to provide commercial-quality server solutions based on the Java Platform that are developed in an open and cooperative fashion." There are many subprojects under the Jakarta project to help commercial server-side developers. The servlet and JSP part of the Jakarta Project is called *Tomcat*. This is the official reference implementation of the JSP and servlet standards. We use Tomcat to demonstrate the servlets in this chapter. The most recent implementation of Tomcat at the time of this writing was version 4.1.12. For your convenience, Tomcat 4.1.12 is included on the CD that accompanies this book. However, the most recent version always can be downloaded from the Apache Group's Web site. To execute the servlets in this chapter, you must install Tomcat or an equivalent servlet and JavaServer Pages implementation. We discuss the set up and configuration of Tomcat in Section 24.3.1 and Section 24.3.2 after we introduce our first example.

In our directions for testing each of the examples in this chapter, we indicate that you should copy files into specific Tomcat directories. All the example files for this chapter are located on the CD that accompanies this book and on our Web site `www.deitel.com`.

[*Note*: At the end of Section 24.8, we provide a list of Internet specifications (as discussed in the Servlet 2.2 Specification) for technologies related to servlet development. Each is listed with its RFC (Request for Comments) number. We provide the URL of a Web site that allows you to locate each specification for your review.]

24.2 Servlet Overview and Architecture

In this section, we overview Java servlet technology. We discuss at a high level the servlet-related classes, methods and exceptions. The next several sections present examples in which we build multi-tier client–server systems using servlet and JDBC technology.

The Internet offers many protocols. The HTTP (*Hypertext Transfer Protocol*) that forms the basis of the World Wide Web uses *URLs* (*Uniform Resource Locators*) to locate resources on the Internet. Common URLs represent files or directories and can represent complex tasks such as database lookups and Internet searches. For more information on URL formats, visit `www.w3.org/Addressing`. For more information on the HTTP protocol, visit `www.w3.org/Protocols/HTTP`. For information on a variety of World Wide Web topics, visit `www.w3.org`.

JavaServer Pages technology is an extension of servlet technology. Normally, JSPs are used when most of the content sent to the client is static text and markup, and only a small portion of the content is generated dynamically with Java code. Servlets commonly are used when a small portion of the content sent to the client is static text or markup. In fact, some servlets do not produce content. Rather, they perform a task on behalf of the client, then invoke other servlets or JSPs to provide a response. Note that in most cases servlet and JSP technologies are interchangeable. The server that executes a servlet is referred to as the *servlet container* or *servlet engine*.

Servlets and JavaServer Pages have become so popular that they are now supported directly or with third-party plug-ins by most major Web servers and application servers, including the Sun ONE Application Server, Microsoft's Internet Information Services (IIS), the Apache HTTP Server, BEA's WebLogic application server, IBM's WebSphere application server, the World Wide Web Consortium's Jigsaw Web server, and many more.

The servlets in this chapter demonstrate communication between clients and servers via the HTTP protocol. A client sends an HTTP request to the server. The servlet container receives the request and directs it to be processed by the appropriate servlet. The servlet does its processing, which may include interacting with a database or other server-side components such as other servlets, JSPs or Enterprise JavaBeans. The servlet returns its results to the client—normally in the form of an HTML, XHTML or XML document to display in a browser, but other data formats, such as images and binary data, can be returned.

24.2.1 Interface `Servlet` and the Servlet Life Cycle

Architecturally, all servlets must implement the *Servlet* interface. As with the key applet methods, the methods of interface `Servlet` are invoked by the servlet container. This interface defines five methods described in Fig. 24.1.

Software Engineering Observation 24.1

All servlets must implement the Servlet interface of package `javax.servlet`.

Method	Description
void init(ServletConfig config)	
	The servlet container calls this method once during a servlet's execution cycle to initialize the servlet. The `ServletConfig` argument is supplied by the servlet container that executes the servlet.
ServletConfig getServletConfig()	
	This method returns a reference to an object that implements interface `ServletConfig`. This object provides access to the servlet's configuration information such as servlet initialization parameters and the servlet's `ServletContext`, which provides the servlet with access to its environment (i.e., the servlet container in which the servlet executes).
String getServletInfo()	
	This method is defined by a servlet programmer to return a string containing servlet information such as the servlet's author and version.

Fig. 24.1   Methods of interface `Servlet` (package `javax.servlet`). (Part 1 of 2.)

Method	Description

`void service( ServletRequest request, ServletResponse response )`

The servlet container calls this method to respond to a client request to the servlet.

`void destroy()`

This "cleanup" method is called when a servlet is terminated by its servlet container. Resources used by the servlet, such as an open file or an open database connection, should be deallocated here.

Fig. 24.1   Methods of interface `Servlet` (package `javax.servlet`). (Part 2 of 2.)

A servlet's life cycle begins when the servlet container loads the servlet into memory—normally, in response to the first request that the servlet receives. Before the servlet can handle that request, the servlet container invokes the servlet's *init* method. After `init` completes execution, the servlet can respond to its first request. All requests are handled by a servlet's *service* method, which receives the request, processes the request and sends a response to the client. During a servlet's life cycle, method `service` is called once per request. Each new request typically results in a new thread of execution (created by the servlet container) in which method `service` executes. When the servlet container terminates the servlet, the servlet's `destroy` method is called to release servlet resources.

Performance Tip 24.1

Starting a new thread for each request is more efficient than starting an entirely new process, as is the case in some other server-side technologies such as CGI. [Note: Like servlets, Fast CGI eliminates the overhead of starting a new process for each request.]

The servlet packages define two `abstract` classes that implement the interface `Servlet`—class *GenericServlet* (from the package `javax.servlet`) and class *HttpServlet* (from the package `javax.servlet.http`). These classes provide default implementations of all the `Servlet` methods. Most servlets extend either `Generic-Servlet` or `HttpServlet` and override some or all of their methods.

The examples in this chapter all extend class `HttpServlet`, which defines enhanced processing capabilities for servlets that extend the functionality of a Web server. The key method in every servlet is `service`, which receives both a *ServletRequest* object and a *ServletResponse* object. These objects provide access to input and output streams that allow the servlet to read data from the client and send data to the client. These streams can be either byte based or character based. If problems occur during the execution of a servlet, either `ServletException`s or `IOException`s are thrown to indicate the problem.

Software Engineering Observation 24.2

Servlets can implement tagging interface SingleThreadModel to indicate that only one thread of execution at a time may enter method service on a particular servlet instance. When a servlet implements SingleThreadModel, the servlet container can create multiple instances of the servlet to handle multiple requests to the servlet in parallel. In this case, you may need to provide synchronized access to shared resources used by method service.

24.2.2 HttpServlet Class

Web-based servlets typically extend class HttpServlet. Class HttpServlet overrides method service to distinguish between the typical requests received from a client Web browser. The two most common *HTTP request types* (also known as *request methods*) are *get* and *post*. A get request *gets* (or *retrieves*) information from a server. Common uses of get requests are to retrieve an HTML document or an image. A post request *posts* (or *sends*) data to a server. Common uses of post requests typically send information, such as authentication information or data from a *form* that gathers user input, to a server.

Class HttpServlet defines methods *doGet* and *doPost* to respond to get and post requests from a client, respectively. These methods are called by method service, which is called when a request arrives at the server. Method service first determines the request type, then calls the appropriate method for handling such a request. Other less common request types are beyond the scope of this book. Methods of class HttpServlet that respond to the other request types are shown in Fig. 24.2. They all receive parameters of type HttpServletRequest and HttpServletResponse and return void. The methods of Fig. 24.2 are not frequently used. For more information on the HTTP protocol, visit

> www.w3.org/Protocols

Software Engineering Observation 24.3

Do not override method service *in an* HttpServlet *subclass. Doing so prevents the servlet from distinguishing between request types.*

Methods doGet and doPost receive as arguments an HttpServletRequest object and an HttpServletResponse object that enable interaction between the client and the server. The methods of HttpServletRequest make it easy to access the data supplied as part of the request. The HttpServletResponse methods make it easy to return the servlet's results to the Web client. Interfaces HttpServletRequest and HttpServlet-Response are discussed in the next two sections.

Method	Description
doDelete	Called in response to an HTTP *delete* request. Such a request is normally used to delete a file from a server. This may not be available on some servers, because of its inherent security risks (e.g., the client could delete a file that is critical to the execution of the server or an application).
doHead	Called in response to an HTTP *head* request. Such a request is normally used when the client only wants the headers of a response, such as the content type and content length of the response.
doOptions	Called in response to an HTTP *options* request. This returns information to the client indicating the HTTP options supported by the server, such as the version of HTTP (1.0 or 1.1) and the request methods the server supports.

Fig. 24.2   Other methods of class HttpServlet. (Part 1 of 2.)

Method	Description
doPut	Called in response to an HTTP *put* request. Such a request is normally used to store a file on the server. This may not be available on some servers, because of its inherent security risks (e.g., the client could place an executable application on the server, which, if executed, could damage the server— perhaps by deleting critical files or occupying resources).
doTrace	Called in response to an HTTP *trace* request. Such a request is normally used for debugging. The implementation of this method automatically returns an HTML document to the client containing the request header information (data sent by the browser as part of the request).

Fig. 24.2　Other methods of class `HttpServlet`. (Part 2 of 2.)

24.2.3 HttpServletRequest Interface

Every call to doGet or doPost for an HttpServlet receives an object that implements interface HttpServletRequest. The Web server that executes the servlet creates an HttpServletRequest object and passes this to the servlet's service method (which, in turn, passes it to doGet or doPost). This object contains the request from the client. A variety of methods are provided to enable the servlet to process the client's request. Some of these methods are from interface *ServletRequest*—the interface that HttpServletRequest extends. A few key methods used in this chapter are presented in Fig. 24.3. You can view a complete list of HttpServletRequest methods online at

```
java.sun.com/j2ee/j2sdkee/techdocs/api/javax/servlet/http/
HttpServletRequest.html
```

or you can download and install Tomcat (discussed in Section 24.3.1) and view the documentation on your local computer.

Method	Description
String getParameter(String name)	Obtains the value of a parameter sent to the servlet as part of a get or post request. The **name** argument represents the parameter name.
Enumeration getParameterNames()	Returns the names of all the parameters sent to the servlet as part of a post request.
String[] getParameterValues(String name)	For a parameter with multiple values, this method returns an array of strings containing the values for a specified servlet parameter.

Fig. 24.3　Some methods of interface `HttpServletRequest`. (Part 1 of 2.)

Method	Description
`Cookie[] getCookies()`	Returns an array of `Cookie` objects stored on the client by the server. `Cookie` objects can be used to uniquely identify clients to the servlet.
`HttpSession getSession( boolean create )`	Returns an `HttpSession` object associated with the client's current browsing session. This method can create an `HttpSession` object (`true` argument) if one does not already exist for the client. `HttpSession` objects are used in similar ways to `Cookie`s for uniquely identifying clients.

Fig. 24.3   Some methods of interface `HttpServletRequest`. (Part 2 of 2.)

24.2.4 `HttpServletResponse` Interface

Every call to `doGet` or `doPost` for an `HttpServlet` receives an object that implements interface `HttpServletResponse`. The Web server that executes the servlet creates an `HttpServletResponse` object and passes it to the servlet's `service` method (which, in turn, passes it to `doGet` or `doPost`). This object provides a variety of methods that enable the servlet to formulate the response to the client. Some of these methods are from interface *ServletResponse*—the interface that `HttpServletResponse` extends. A few key methods used in this chapter are presented in Fig. 24.4. You can view a complete list of `HttpServletResponse` methods online at

> `java.sun.com/j2ee/j2sdkee/techdocs/api/javax/servlet/http/`
> `HttpServletResponse.html`

or you can download and install Tomcat (discussed in Section 24.3.1) and view the documentation on your local computer.

Method	Description
`void addCookie( Cookie cookie )`	Used to add a `Cookie` to the header of the response to the client. The `Cookie`'s maximum age and whether `Cookie`s are enabled on the client determine if `Cookie`s are stored on the client.
`ServletOutputStream getOutputStream()`	Obtains a byte-based output stream for sending binary data to the client.
`PrintWriter getWriter()`	Obtains a character-based output stream for sending text data to the client.

Fig. 24.4   Some methods of interface `HttpServletResponse`. (Part 1 of 2.)

Method	Description

void setContentType(String type)

> Specifies the MIME type of the response to the browser. The MIME type helps the browser determine how to display the data (or possibly what other application to execute to process the data). For example, MIME type "text/html" indicates that the response is an HTML document, so the browser displays the HTML page.

Fig. 24.4   Some methods of interface `HttpServletResponse`. (Part 2 of 2.)

24.3 Handling HTTP get Requests

The primary purpose of an HTTP get request is to retrieve the content of a specified URL—normally the content is an HTML or XHTML document (i.e., a Web page). The servlet of Fig. 24.5 and the XHTML document of Fig. 24.6 demonstrate a servlet that handles HTTP get requests. When the user clicks the **Get HTML Document** button (Fig. 24.6), a get request is sent to the servlet WelcomeServlet (Fig. 24.5). The servlet responds to the request by generating dynamically an XHTML document for the client that displays "Welcome to Servlets!". Figure 24.5 shows the WelcomeServlet source code. Figure 24.6 shows the XHTML document the client loads to access the servlet and shows screen captures of the client's browser window before and after the interaction with the servlet. [*Note*: Section 24.3.1 discusses how to set up and configure Tomcat to execute this example.]

```
1   // Fig. 24.5: WelcomeServlet.java
2   // A simple servlet to process get requests.
3
4   import javax.servlet.*;
5   import javax.servlet.http.*;
6   import java.io.*;
7
8   public class WelcomeServlet extends HttpServlet {
9
10     // process "get" requests from clients
11     protected void doGet( HttpServletRequest request,
12        HttpServletResponse response )
13         throws ServletException, IOException
14   {
15        response.setContentType( "text/html" );
16        PrintWriter out = response.getWriter();
17
18        // send XHTML page to client
19
20        // start XHTML document
21        out.println( "<?xml version = \"1.0\"?>" );
22
```

Fig. 24.5   `WelcomeServlet` that responds to a simple HTTP get request. (Part 1 of 2.)

```
23        out.println( "<!DOCTYPE html PUBLIC \"-//W3C//DTD " +
24            "XHTML 1.0 Strict//EN\" \"http://www.w3.org" +
25            "/TR/xhtml1/DTD/xhtml1-strict.dtd\">" );
26
27        out.println( "<html xmlns = \"http://www.w3.org/1999/xhtml\">" );
28
29        // head section of document
30        out.println( "<head>" );
31        out.println( "<title>A Simple Servlet Example</title>" );
32        out.println( "</head>" );
33
34        // body section of document
35        out.println( "<body>" );
36        out.println( "<h1>Welcome to Servlets!</h1>" );
37        out.println( "</body>" );
38
39        // end XHTML document
40        out.println( "</html>" );
41        out.close();  // close stream to complete the page
42     }
43  }
```

Fig. 24.5   `WelcomeServlet` that responds to a simple HTTP `get` request. (Part 2 of 2.)

Lines 4 and 5 import the `javax.servlet` and `javax.servlet.http` packages. We use several data types from these packages in the example.

Package `javax.servlet.http` provides superclass `HttpServlet` for servlets that handle HTTP `get` requests and HTTP `post` requests. This class implements interface `javax.servlet.Servlet` and adds methods that support HTTP protocol requests. Class `WelcomeServlet` extends `HttpServlet` (line 8) for this reason.

Superclass `HttpServlet` provides method *doGet* to respond to `get` requests. Its default functionality is to indicate a "Method not allowed" error. Typically, this error is indicated in Internet Explorer with a Web page that states "This page cannot be displayed" and in Netscape Navigator with a Web page that states "Error: 405." Lines 11–42 override method *doGet* to provide custom `get` request processing. Method *doGet* receives two arguments—an `HttpServletRequest` object and an `HttpServletResponse` object (both from package `javax.servlet.http`). The `HttpServletRequest` object represents the client's request, and the `HttpServletResponse` object represents the server's response to the client. If method *doGet* is unable to handle a client's request, it throws an exception of type *javax.servlet.ServletException*. If doGet encounters an error during stream processing (reading from the client or writing to the client), it throws a *java.io.IOException*.

To demonstrate a response to a `get` request, our servlet creates an XHTML document containing the text "`Welcome to Servlets!`". The text of the XHTML document is the response to the client. The response is sent to the client through the `PrintWriter` object obtained from the `HttpServletResponse` object.

Line 15 uses the `response` object's *setContentType* method to specify the content type of the data to be sent as the response to the client. This enables the client browser to understand and handle the content. The content type also is known as the *MIME* type (*Multipurpose Internet Mail Extension*) of the data. In this example, the content type is *text/*

html to indicate to the browser that the response is an XHTML document. The browser knows that it must read the XHTML tags in the document, format the document according to the tags and display the document in the browser window.

Line 16 uses the `response` object's *getWriter* method to obtain a reference to the `PrintWriter` object that enables the servlet to send content to the client. [*Note*: If the response is binary data, such as an image, method *getOutputStream* is used to obtain a reference to a `ServletOutputStream` object.]

Lines 21–40 create the XHTML document by writing strings with the `out` object's *println* method. This method outputs a newline character after its `String` argument. When rendering the Web page, the browser does not use the newline character. Rather, the newline character appears in the XHTML source that you can see by selecting **Source** from the **View** menu in Internet Explorer or **Page Source** from the **View** menu in Netscape Navigator. Line 41 closes the output stream, flushes the output buffer and sends the information to the client. This commits the response to the client.

The XHTML document in Fig. 24.6 provides a `form` that invokes the servlet defined in Fig. 24.5. The `form`'s `action` (/jhtp5/welcome1) specifies the URL path that invokes the servlet, and the `form`'s `method` indicates that the browser sends a `get` request to the server, which results in a call to the servlet's `doGet` method. The URL specified as the `action` in this example is discussed in detail in Section 24.3.2 after we show how to set up and configure the *Apache Tomcat server* to execute the servlet in Fig. 24.5.

Note that the sample screen captures show a URL containing the server name *localhost*—a well-known server *host name* on most computers that support TCP/IP-based networking protocols such as HTTP. We often use `localhost` to demonstrate networking programs on the local computer, so that readers without a network connection can still learn network programming concepts. In this example, `localhost` indicates that the server on

```
1   <?xml version = "1.0"?>
2   <!DOCTYPE html PUBLIC "-//W3C//DTD XHTML 1.0 Strict//EN"
3      "http://www.w3.org/TR/xhtml1/DTD/xhtml1-strict.dtd">
4
5   <!-- Fig. 24.6: WelcomeServlet.html -->
6
7   <html xmlns = "http://www.w3.org/1999/xhtml">
8   <head>
9      <title>Handling an HTTP Get Request</title>
10  </head>
11
12  <body>
13     <form action = "/jhtp5/welcome1" method = "get">
14
15        <p><label>Click the button to invoke the servlet
16           <input type = "submit" value = "Get HTML Document" />
17        </label></p>
18
19     </form>
20  </body>
21  </html>
```

Fig. 24.6   HTML document in which the `form`'s `action` invokes `WelcomeServlet` through the alias `welcome1` specified in `web.xml`. (Part 1 of 2.)

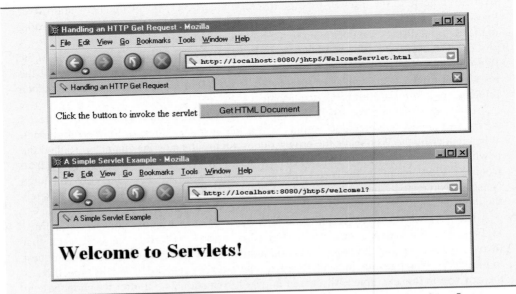

Fig. 24.6   HTML document in which the form's action invokes WelcomeServlet through the alias welcome1 specified in web.xml. (Part 2 of 2.)

which the servlet is installed is running on the local machine. The server host name is followed by :8080, specifying the TCP port number at which the Tomcat server awaits requests from clients. Web browsers assume TCP port 80 by default as the server port at which clients make requests, but the Tomcat server awaits client requests at TCP port 8080. This allows Tomcat to execute on the same computer as a standard Web server application without affecting the Web server application's ability to handle requests. If we do not explicitly specify the port number in the URL, the servlet never will receive our request and an error message will be displayed in the browser.

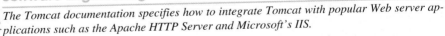

Software Engineering Observation 24.4

The Tomcat documentation specifies how to integrate Tomcat with popular Web server applications such as the Apache HTTP Server and Microsoft's IIS.

Ports in this case are not physical hardware ports to which you attach cables; rather, they are logical locations named with integer values that allow clients to request different services on the same server. The port number specifies the logical location where a server waits for and receives connections from clients—this is also called the *handshake point*. When a client connects to a server to request a service, the client must specify the port number for that service; otherwise, the client request cannot be processed. Port numbers are positive integers with values up to 65,535, and there are separate sets of these port numbers for both the TCP and UDP protocols. Many operating systems reserve port numbers below 1024 for system services (such as email and World Wide Web servers). Generally, these ports should not be specified as connection ports in your own server programs. In fact, some operating systems require special access privileges to use port numbers below 1024.

With so many ports from which to choose, how does a client know which port to use when requesting a service? The term *well-known port number* often is used when describing popular services on the Internet such as Web servers and email servers. For example, a Web server waits for clients to make requests at port 80 by default. All Web browsers know this number as the well-known port on a Web server where requests for HTML documents are made. So when you type a URL into a Web browser, the browser normally connects to port 80 on the server. Similarly, the Tomcat server uses port 8080 as its port number. Thus, requests to Tomcat for Web pages or to invoke servlets and Java-Server Pages must specify that the Tomcat server waiting for requests on port 8080.

The client can access the servlet only if the servlet is installed on a server that can respond to servlet requests. In some cases, servlet support is built directly into the Web server, and no special configuration is required to handle servlet requests. In other cases, it is necessary to integrate a servlet container with a Web server (as can be done with Tomcat and the Apache or IIS Web servers). Web servers that support servlets normally have an installation procedure for servlets. If you intend to execute your servlet as part of a Web server, please refer to your Web server's documentation on how to install a servlet. For our examples, we demonstrate servlets with the Apache Tomcat server. Section 24.3.1 discusses the setup and configuration of Tomcat for use with this chapter. Section 24.3.2 discusses the deployment of the servlet in Fig. 24.5.

24.3.1 Setting Up the Apache Tomcat Server

Tomcat is a fully functional implementation of the JSP and servlet standards. It includes a Web server, so it can be used as a standalone test container for JSPs and servlets. Tomcat also can be specified as the handler for JSP and servlet requests received by popular Web servers such as the Apache Software Foundation's Apache HTTP server or Microsoft's Internet Information Services (IIS). Tomcat is integrated into the Java 2 Enterprise Edition reference implementation from Sun Microsystems.

The most recent release of Tomcat (version 4.1.12) can be downloaded from

```
jakarta.apache.org/builds/jakarta-tomcat-4.0/release/v4.1.12/bin
```

where there are a number of archive files. The complete Tomcat implementation is contained in the files that begin with the name `jakarta-tomcat-4.1.12`. Zip, exe, tar and compressed tar files are provided.

Extract the contents of the archive file to a directory on your hard disk. For the examples in this book, we use the directory `jakarta-tomcat-4.1.12`. For Tomcat to work correctly, you must define environment variables JAVA_HOME and CATALINA_HOME. JAVA_HOME should point to the directory containing your Java installation (ours is `c:\j2sdk1.4.1`), and CATALINA_HOME should point to the directory that contains Tomcat (ours is `c:\jakarta-tomcat-4.1.12`).

Error-Prevention Tip 24.1

On some platforms you may need to restart your computer for the new environment variables to take effect.

After setting the environment variables, you can start the Tomcat server. Open a command prompt (or shell) and change to the `bin` directory in `jakarta-tomcat-4.1.12`. In this directory are the files *startup.bat*, *shutdown.bat*, *startup.sh* and *shut-*

down.sh, for starting and stopping the Tomcat server on Windows and UNIX/Linux/Mac OS X, respectively. To start the server, type

```
startup
```

This launches the Tomcat server, which executes on TCP port 8080 to prevent conflicts with standard Web servers that typically execute on TCP port 80. To verify that Tomcat is executing and can respond to requests, open your Web browser and enter the URL

```
http://localhost:8080/
```

This should display the Tomcat documentation home page (Fig. 24.7). The host `local-host` indicates to the Web browser that it should request the home page from the Tomcat server on the local computer.

If the Tomcat documentation home page does not display, try the URL

```
http://127.0.0.1:8080/
```

The host `localhost` translates to the IP address `127.0.0.1`.

Error-Prevention Tip 24.2

If the host name `localhost` does not work on your computer, substitute the IP address `127.0.0.1` instead.

To shut down the Tomcat server, issue the command

```
shutdown
```

from a command prompt (or shell).

Fig. 24.7   Tomcat documentation home page. (Courtesy of The Apache Software Foundation.)

24.3.2 Deploying a Web Application

JSPs, servlets and their supporting files are deployed as part of *Web applications*. Normally, Web applications are deployed in the *webapps* subdirectory of `jakarta-tomcat-4.1.12`. A Web application has a well-known directory structure in which all the files that are part of the application reside. This directory structure can be created by the server administrator in the `webapps` directory, or the entire directory structure can be archived in a *Web application archive file*. Such an archive is known as a *WAR file* and ends with the `.war` file extension. If a WAR file is placed in the `webapps` directory, then, when the Tomcat server begins execution, it extracts the contents of the WAR file into the appropriate `webapps` subdirectory structure. For simplicity as we teach servlets and JavaServer Pages, we create the already expanded directory structure for all the examples in this chapter.

The Web application directory structure contains a *context root*—the top-level directory for an entire Web application—and several subdirectories. These are described in Fig. 24.8.

Common Programming Error 24.1

Using "servlet" or "servlets" as a context root may prevent a servlet from working correctly on some servers.

Configuring the context root for a Web application in Tomcat requires creating a subdirectory in the `webapps` directory. When Tomcat begins execution, it creates a context root for each subdirectory of `webapps`, using each subdirectory's name as a context root name. To test the examples in this chapter, create the directory `jhtp5` in Tomcat's `webapps` directory.

Directory	Description
context root	This is the root directory for the Web application. All the JSPs, HTML documents, servlets and supporting files such as images and class files reside in this directory or its subdirectories. The name of this directory is specified by the Web application creator. To provide structure in a Web application, subdirectories can be placed in the context root. For example, if your application uses many images, you might place an images subdirectory in this directory. The examples of this chapter use `jhtp5` as the context root.
WEB-INF	This directory contains the Web application *deployment descriptor* (`web.xml`).
WEB-INF/classes	This directory contains the servlet class files and other supporting class files used in a Web application. If the classes are part of a package, the complete package directory structure would begin here.
WEB-INF/lib	This directory contains Java archive (JAR) files. The JAR files can contain servlet class files and other supporting class files used in a Web application.

Fig. 24.8   Web application standard directories.

After configuring the context root, we must configure our Web application to handle the requests. This configuration occurs in a *deployment descriptor*, which is stored in a file called *web.xml*. The deployment descriptor specifies various configuration parameters such as the name used to invoke the servlet (i.e., its *alias*), a description of the servlet, the servlet's fully qualified class name and a *servlet mapping* (i.e., the path or paths that cause the servlet container to invoke the servlet). You must create the web.xml file for this example. Many Java Web-application deployment tools create the web.xml file for you. The web.xml file for the first example in this chapter is shown in Fig. 24.9. We enhance this file as we add other servlets to the Web application throughout this chapter.

Lines 1–3 specify the document type for the Web application deployment descriptor and the location of the DTD for this XML file. Element *web-app* (lines 5–37) defines the configuration of each servlet in the Web application and the servlet mapping for each

```
1   <!DOCTYPE web-app PUBLIC
2       "-//Sun Microsystems, Inc.//DTD Web Application 2.2//EN"
3       "http://java.sun.com/j2ee/dtds/web-app_2_2.dtd">
4
5   <web-app>
6
7       <!-- General description of your Web application -->
8       <display-name>
9           Java How to Program JSP
10          and Servlet Chapter Examples
11      </display-name>
12
13      <description>
14          This is the Web application in which we
15          demonstrate our JSP and Servlet examples.
16      </description>
17
18      <!-- Servlet definitions -->
19      <servlet>
20          <servlet-name>welcome1</servlet-name>
21
22          <description>
23              A simple servlet that handles an HTTP get request.
24          </description>
25
26          <servlet-class>
27              WelcomeServlet
28          </servlet-class>
29      </servlet>
30
31      <!-- Servlet mappings -->
32      <servlet-mapping>
33          <servlet-name>welcome1</servlet-name>
34          <url-pattern>/welcome1</url-pattern>
35      </servlet-mapping>
36
37  </web-app>
```

Fig. 24.9   Deployment descriptor (web.xml) for the jhtp5 Web application.

servlet. Element *display-name* (lines 8–11) specifies a name that can be displayed to the administrator of the server on which the Web application is installed. Element *description* (lines 13–16) specifies a description of the Web application that might be displayed to the administrator of the server.

Element servlet (lines 19–29) describes a servlet. Element *servlet-name* (line 20) is the name we chose for the servlet (welcome1). Element *description* (lines 22–24) specifies a description for this particular servlet. Again, this can be displayed to the administrator of the Web server. Element servlet-class (lines 26–28) specifies compiled servlet's fully qualified class name. Thus, the servlet welcome1 is defined by class WelcomeServlet.

Element *servlet-mapping* (lines 32–35) specifies *servlet-name* and *url-pattern* elements. The *URL pattern* helps the server determine which requests are sent to the servlet (welcome1). Our Web application will be installed as part of the jhtp5 context root discussed in Section 24.3.2. Thus, the relative URL we supply to the browser to invoke the servlet in this example is

    /jhtp5/welcome1

where /jhtp5 specifies the context root that helps the server determine which Web application handles the request and /welcome1 specifies the URL pattern that is mapped to servlet welcome1 to handle the request. Note that the server on which the servlet resides is not specified here, although it is possible to do so as follows:

    http://localhost:8080/jhtp5/welcome1

If the explicit server and port number are not specified as part of the URL, the browser assumes that the form handler (i.e., the servlet specified in the action property of the form element) resides at the same server and port number from which the browser downloaded the Web page containing the form.

There are several URL pattern formats that can be used. The /welcome1 URL pattern requires an exact match of the pattern. You can also specify *path mappings*, extension mappings and a *default servlet* for a Web application. A path mapping begins with a / and ends with a /*. For example, the URL pattern

    /jhtp5/example/*

indicates that any URL path beginning with /jhtp5/example/ will be sent to the servlet that has the preceding URL pattern. An extension mapping begins with *. and ends with a file name extension. For example, the URL pattern

    *.jsp

indicates that any request for a file with extension .jsp will be sent to the servlet that handles JSP requests. In fact, servers with JSP containers have an implicit mapping of the .jsp extension to a servlet that handles JSP requests. The URL pattern / represents the default servlet for the Web application. This is similar to the default document of a Web server. For example, if you type the URL www.deitel.com into your Web browser, the document you receive from our Web server is the default document index.html. If the URL pattern matches the default servlet for a Web application, that servlet is invoked to return a default response to the client. This can be useful for personalizing Web content to specific users.

Finally, we are ready to place our files into the appropriate directories to complete the deployment of our first servlet for testing. There are three files we must place in the appro-

priate directories—WelcomeServlet.html, WelcomeServlet.class and web.xml. In
the webapps subdirectory of your jakarta-tomcat-4.1.12 directory, create subdirectory
jhtp5—the context root for our Web application. In this directory, create subdirectories
named servlets and WEB-INF. We place our HTML files for this servlets chapter in the
servlets directory. Copy the WelcomeServlet.html file into the servlets directory.
In the WEB-INF directory, create the subdirectory classes, then copy the web.xml file into
the WEB-INF directory, and copy the WelcomeServlet.class file into the classes directory. [*Note:* To compile your servlet, you will need to use javac's -classpath option to
specify the name and location of the file servlet.jar, which is located in Tomcat's
common\libs directory.] Thus, the directory and file structure under the webapps directory
should be as shown in Fig. 24.10 (file names are in italics).

Error-Prevention Tip 24.3

Restart the Tomcat server after modifying the **web.xml** *deployment descriptor file. Otherwise, Tomcat will not recognize your new Web application.*

After the files are placed in the proper directories, start the Tomcat server, open your
browser and type the following URL

    http://localhost:8080/jhtp5/servlets/WelcomeServlet.html

to load WelcomeServlet.html into the Web browser. Then, click the **Get HTML Document** button to invoke the servlet. You should see the results shown in Fig. 24.6. You can
try this servlet from several different Web browsers to demonstrate that the results are the
same across Web browsers.

Common Programming Error 24.2

*Not placing servlet or other class files in the appropriate directory structure prevents the
server from locating those classes properly. This results in an error response to the client
Web browser. This error response normally is "Not Found (404)" in Netscape Navigator
and "The page cannot be found" plus an explanation in Microsoft Internet Explorer.*

Actually, the HTML file in Fig. 24.6 was not necessary to invoke this servlet. A get
request can be sent to a server simply by typing the URL in a browser—exactly as you do
when you request a Web page in the browser. In this example, you can type

    http://localhost:8080/jhtp5/welcome1

in the **Address** or **Location** field of your browser to invoke the servlet directly.

WelcomeServlet Web application directory and file structure

```
jhtp5
   servlets
      WelcomeServlet.html
   WEB-INF
      web.xml
      classes
         WelcomeServlet.class
```

Fig. 24.10 Web application directory and file structure for WelcomeServlet.

24.4 Handling HTTP get Requests Containing Data

When requesting a document or resource from a Web server, it is possible to supply data as part of the request. The servlet `WelcomeServlet2` of Fig. 24.11 responds to an HTTP get request that contains a name supplied by the user. The servlet uses the name as part of the response to the client.

```java
1   // Fig. 24.11: WelcomeServlet2.java
2   // Processing HTTP get requests containing data.
3
4   import javax.servlet.*;
5   import javax.servlet.http.*;
6   import java.io.*;
7
8   public class WelcomeServlet2 extends HttpServlet {
9
10     // process "get" request from client
11     protected void doGet( HttpServletRequest request,
12        HttpServletResponse response )
13           throws ServletException, IOException
14     {
15        String firstName = request.getParameter( "firstname" );
16
17        response.setContentType( "text/html" );
18        PrintWriter out = response.getWriter();
19
20        // send XHTML document to client
21
22        // start XHTML document
23        out.println( "<?xml version = \"1.0\"?>" );
24
25        out.println( "<!DOCTYPE html PUBLIC \"-//W3C//DTD " +
26           "XHTML 1.0 Strict//EN\" \"http://www.w3.org" +
27           "/TR/xhtml1/DTD/xhtml1-strict.dtd\">" );
28
29        out.println( "<html xmlns = \"http://www.w3.org/1999/xhtml\">" );
30
31        // head section of document
32        out.println( "<head>" );
33        out.println(
34           "<title>Processing get requests with data</title>" );
35        out.println( "</head>" );
36
37        // body section of document
38        out.println( "<body>" );
39        out.println( "<h1>Hello " + firstName + ",<br />" );
40        out.println( "Welcome to Servlets!</h1>" );
```

Fig. 24.11 `WelcomeServlet2` responds to a get request containing data. (Part 1 of 2.)

```
41          out.println( "</body>" );
42
43          // end XHTML document
44          out.println( "</html>" );
45          out.close();  // close stream to complete the page
46       }
47    }
```

Fig. 24.11 `WelcomeServlet2` responds to a `get` request containing data. (Part 2 of 2.)

Parameters are passed as name/value pairs in a `get` request. Line 15 demonstrates how to obtain information that was passed to the servlet as part of the client request. The `request` object's *getParameter* method receives the parameter name as an argument and returns the corresponding `String` value, or `null` if the parameter is not part of the request. Line 39 uses the result of line 15 as part of the response to the client.

The `WelcomeServlet2.html` document (Fig. 24.12) provides a `form` in which the user can input a name in the text `input` element `firstname` (line 17) and click the **Submit** button to invoke `WelcomeServlet2`. When the user presses the **Submit** button, the values of the `input` elements are placed in name/value pairs as part of the request to the server. In the second screen capture of Fig. 24.12, notice that the browser appended

> `?firstname=Paul`

to the end of the `action` URL. The ? separates the *query string* (i.e., the data passed as part of the `get` request) from the rest of the URL in a `get` request. The name/value pairs are passed with the name and the value separated by =. If there is more than one name/value pair, each name/value pair is separated by &.

```
1    <?xml version = "1.0"?>
2    <!DOCTYPE html PUBLIC "-//W3C//DTD XHTML 1.0 Strict//EN"
3       "http://www.w3.org/TR/xhtml1/DTD/xhtml1-strict.dtd">
4
5    <!-- Fig. 24.12: WelcomeServlet2.html -->
6
7    <html xmlns = "http://www.w3.org/1999/xhtml">
8    <head>
9       <title>Processing get requests with data</title>
10   </head>
11
12   <body>
13      <form action = "/jhtp5/welcome2" method = "get">
14
15         <p><label>
16            Type your first name and press the Submit button
17            <br /><input type = "text" name = "firstname" />
18            <input type = "submit" value = "Submit" />
19         </p></label>
20
21      </form>
```

Fig. 24.12 HTML document in which the form's `action` invokes `WelcomeServlet2` through the alias `welcome2` specified in `web.xml`. (Part 1 of 2.)

```
22    </body>
23    </html>
```

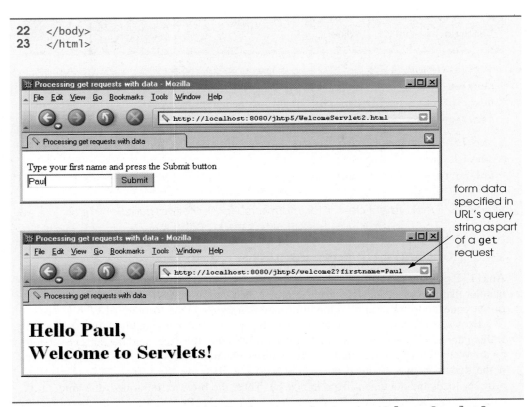

Fig. 24.12   HTML document in which the form's `action` invokes `WelcomeServlet2` through the alias `welcome2` specified in `web.xml`. (Part 2 of 2.)

Once again, we use our `jhtp5` context root to demonstrate the servlet of Fig. 24.11. Place `WelcomeServlet2.html` in the `servlets` directory created in Section 24.3.2. Place `WelcomeServlet2.class` in the `classes` subdirectory of WEB-INF in the `jhtp5` context root. Remember that classes in a package must be placed in the appropriate package directory structure. Then, edit the `web.xml` deployment descriptor in the WEB-INF directory to include the information specified in Fig. 24.13. This table contains the information for the `servlet` and `servlet-mapping` elements that you will add to the `web.xml` deployment descriptor. You should not type the italic text into the deployment descriptor. Restart Tomcat and type the following URL in your Web browser:

```
http://localhost:8080/jhtp5/servlets/WelcomeServlet2.html
```

Type your name in the text field of the Web page, then click **Submit** to invoke the servlet.

Once again, note that the `get` request could have been typed directly into the browser's **Address** or **Location** field as follows:

```
http://localhost:8080/jhtp5/welcome2?firstname=Paul
```

Try it with your own name.

Descriptor element	Value
servlet element	
servlet-name	welcome2
description	Handling HTTP get requests with data.
servlet-class	WelcomeServlet2
servlet-mapping element	
servlet-name	welcome2
url-pattern	/welcome2

Fig. 24.13 Deployment descriptor information for servlet WelcomeServlet2.

24.5 Handling HTTP post Requests

An HTTP post request often is used to send data from an HTML form to a server-side form handler that processes the data. For example, when you respond to a Web-based survey, a post request normally supplies the information you type in the form to the Web server.

Browsers often *cache* (save on disk) Web pages so they can quickly reload the pages. If there are no changes between the last version stored in the cache and the current version on the Web, this helps speed up your browsing experience. The browser first asks the server if the document has changed or expired since the date the file was cached. If not, the browser loads the document from the cache. Thus, the browser minimizes the amount of data that must be downloaded for you to view a Web page. Browsers typically do not cache the server's response to a post request, because the next post might not return the same result. For example, in a survey, many users could visit the same Web page and respond to a question. The survey results could then be displayed for the user. Each new response changes the overall results of the survey.

When you use a Web-based search engine, the browser normally supplies the information you specify in an HTML form to the search engine with a get request. The search engine performs the search, then returns the results to you as a Web page. Such pages are often cached by the browser in case you perform the same search again. As with post requests, get requests can supply parameters as part of the request to the Web server.

The WelcomeServlet3 servlet of Fig. 24.14 is identical to the servlet of Fig. 24.11, except that it defines a doPost method (line 11) to respond to post requests rather than a doGet method. The default functionality of doPost is to indicate a "Method not allowed" error. We override this method to provide custom post request processing. Method doPost receives the same two arguments as doGet—an object that implements interface HttpServletRequest to represent the client's request and an object that implements interface HttpServletResponse to represent the servlet's response. As with doGet, method doPost throws a ServletException if it is unable to handle a client's request and throws an IOException if a problem occurs during stream processing.

WelcomeServlet3.html (Fig. 24.15) provides a form (lines 13–21) in which the user can input a name in the text input element firstname (line 17), then click the Submit button to invoke WelcomeServlet3. When the user presses the Submit button, the values of the input elements are sent to the server as part of the request. However, note that the values are not appended to the request URL. Note that the form's method in this example is post. Also, note that a post request cannot be typed into the browser's **Address** or **Location** field and users cannot bookmark post requests in their browsers.

```java
1   // Fig. 24.14: WelcomeServlet3.java
2   // Processing post requests containing data.
3
4   import javax.servlet.*;
5   import javax.servlet.http.*;
6   import java.io.*;
7
8   public class WelcomeServlet3 extends HttpServlet {
9
10      // process "post" request from client
11      protected void doPost( HttpServletRequest request,
12         HttpServletResponse response )
13            throws ServletException, IOException
14      {
15         String firstName = request.getParameter( "firstname" );
16
17         response.setContentType( "text/html" );
18         PrintWriter out = response.getWriter();
19
20         // send XHTML page to client
21
22         // start XHTML document
23         out.println( "<?xml version = \"1.0\"?>" );
24
25         out.println( "<!DOCTYPE html PUBLIC \"-//W3C//DTD " +
26            "XHTML 1.0 Strict//EN\" \"http://www.w3.org" +
27            "/TR/xhtml1/DTD/xhtml1-strict.dtd\">" );
28
29         out.println( "<html xmlns = \"http://www.w3.org/1999/xhtml\">" );
30
31         // head section of document
32         out.println( "<head>" );
33         out.println(
34            "<title>Processing post requests with data</title>" );
35         out.println( "</head>" );
36
37         // body section of document
38         out.println( "<body>" );
39         out.println( "<h1>Hello " + firstName + ",<br />" );
40         out.println( "Welcome to Servlets!</h1>" );
41         out.println( "</body>" );
42
43         // end XHTML document
44         out.println( "</html>" );
45         out.close();  // close stream to complete the page
46      }
47   }
```

Fig. 24.14 WelcomeServlet3 responds to a post request containing data.

```
1   <?xml version = "1.0"?>
2   <!DOCTYPE html PUBLIC "-//W3C//DTD XHTML 1.0 Strict//EN"
3      "http://www.w3.org/TR/xhtml1/DTD/xhtml1-strict.dtd">
4
5   <!-- Fig. 24.15: WelcomeServlet3.html -->
6
7   <html xmlns = "http://www.w3.org/1999/xhtml">
8   <head>
9      <title>Handling an HTTP Post Request with Data</title>
10  </head>
11
12  <body>
13     <form action = "/jhtp5/welcome3" method = "post">
14
15        <p><label>
16           Type your first name and press the Submit button
17           <br /><input type = "text" name = "firstname" />
18           <input type = "submit" value = "Submit" />
19        </label></p>
20
21     </form>
22  </body>
23  </html>
```

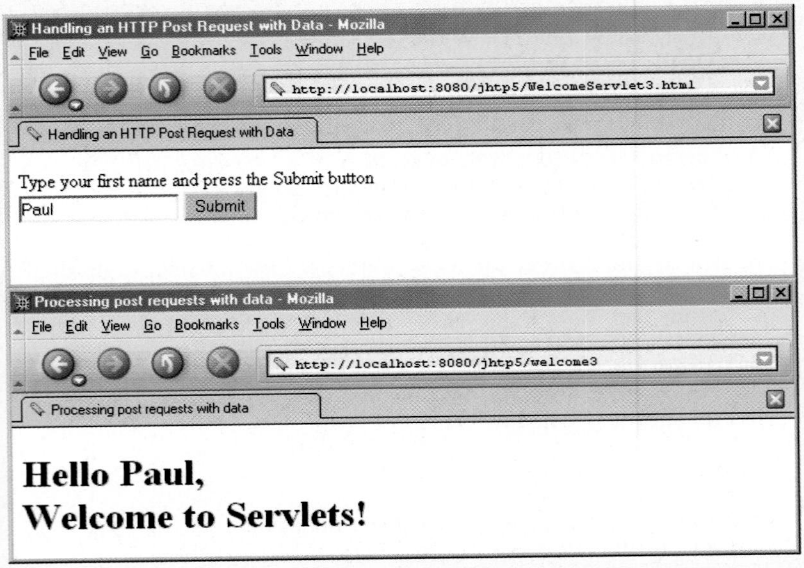

Fig. 24.15 HTML document in which the form's `action` invokes `WelcomeServlet3` through the alias `welcome3` specified in `web.xml`.

We use our `jhtp5` context root to demonstrate the servlet of Fig. 24.14. Place `WelcomeServlet3.html` in the `servlets` directory created in Section 24.3.2. Place `WelcomeServlet3.class` in the `classes` subdirectory of WEB-INF in the `jhtp5` context root. Then, using the information specified in Fig. 24.16, edit the `web.xml` deployment

Descriptor element	Value
servlet element	
servlet-name	welcome3
description	Handling HTTP post requests with data.
servlet-class	WelcomeServlet3
servlet-mapping element	
servlet-name	welcome3
url-pattern	/welcome3

Fig. 24.16 Deployment descriptor information for servlet WelcomeServlet3.

descriptor in the WEB-INF directory. Restart Tomcat and type the following URL in your Web browser:

> http://localhost:8080/jhtp5/servlets/WelcomeServlet3.html

Type your name in the text field of the Web page, then click **Submit** to invoke the servlet.

24.6 Redirecting Requests to Other Resources

Sometimes it is useful to redirect a request to a different resource. For example, a servlet could determine the type of the client browser and redirect the request to a Web page that was designed specifically for that browser. The RedirectServlet of Fig. 24.17 receives a page parameter as part of a get request, then uses that parameter to redirect the request to a different resource.

```
1   // Fig. 24.17: RedirectServlet.java
2   // Redirecting a user to a different Web page.
3
4   import javax.servlet.*;
5   import javax.servlet.http.*;
6   import java.io.*;
7
8   public class RedirectServlet extends HttpServlet {
9
10      // process "get" request from client
11      protected void doGet( HttpServletRequest request,
12          HttpServletResponse response )
13              throws ServletException, IOException
14      {
15          String location = request.getParameter( "page" );
16
17          if ( location != null )
18
19              if ( location.equals( "deitel" ) )
20                  response.sendRedirect( "http://www.deitel.com" );
```

Fig. 24.17 Redirecting requests to other resources. (Part 1 of 2.)

```
21              else
22                 if ( location.equals( "welcome1" ) )
23                    response.sendRedirect( "welcome1" );
24
25        // code that executes only if this servlet
26        // does not redirect the user to another page
27
28        response.setContentType( "text/html" );
29        PrintWriter out = response.getWriter();
30
31        // start XHTML document
32        out.println( "<?xml version = \"1.0\"?>" );
33
34        out.println( "<!DOCTYPE html PUBLIC \"-//W3C//DTD " +
35           "XHTML 1.0 Strict//EN\" \"http://www.w3.org" +
36           "/TR/xhtml1/DTD/xhtml1-strict.dtd\">" );
37
38        out.println(
39           "<html xmlns = \"http://www.w3.org/1999/xhtml\">" );
40
41        // head section of document
42        out.println( "<head>" );
43        out.println( "<title>Invalid page</title>" );
44        out.println( "</head>" );
45
46        // body section of document
47        out.println( "<body>" );
48        out.println( "<h1>Invalid page requested</h1>" );
49        out.println( "<p><a href = " +
50           "\"servlets/RedirectServlet.html\">" );
51        out.println( "Click here to choose again</a></p>" );
52        out.println( "</body>" );
53
54        // end XHTML document
55        out.println( "</html>" );
56        out.close();   // close stream to complete the page
57     }
58  }
```

Fig. 24.17   Redirecting requests to other resources. (Part 2 of 2.)

Line 15 obtains the page parameter from the request. If the value returned is not null, the if…else structure at lines 19–23 determines if the value is either "deitel" or "welcome1." If the value is "deitel," the response object's *sendRedirect* method (line 20) redirects the request to www.deitel.com. If the value is "welcome1," line 23 redirect the request to the servlet of Fig. 24.5. Note that line 23 does not explicitly specify the jhtp5 context root for our Web application. When a servlet uses a relative path to reference another static or dynamic resource, the servlet assumes the same base URL and context root as the one that invoked the servlet—unless a complete URL is specified for the resource. So, line 23 actually is requesting the resource located at

```
http://localhost:8080/jhtp5/welcome1
```

Similarly, line 50 actually is requesting the resource located at

> http://localhost:8080/jhtp5/servlets/RedirectServlet.html

 Software Engineering Observation 24.5

Using relative paths to reference resources in the same context root makes your Web application more flexible. For example, you can change the context root without making changes to the static and dynamic resources in the application.

Once method `sendRedirect` executes, processing of the original request by the `RedirectServlet` terminates. If method `sendRedirect` is not called, the remainder of method `doGet` outputs a Web page indicating that an invalid request was made. The page allows the user to try again by returning to the XHTML document of Fig. 24.18. Note that one of the redirects is sent to a static XHTML Web page and the other is sent to a servlet.

`RedirectServlet.html` (Fig. 24.18) provides two hyperlinks (lines 15–16 and 17–18) that allow the user to invoke the servlet `RedirectServlet`. Note that each hyperlink specifies a `page` parameter as part of the URL. To demonstrate passing an invalid page, you can type the URL into your browser with no value for the `page` parameter.

We use our `jhtp5` context root to demonstrate the servlet of Fig. 24.17. Place `RedirectServlet.html` in the `servlets` directory created in Section 24.3.2. Place `RedirectServlet.class` in the `classes` subdirectory of WEB-INF in the `jhtp5` context root. Then, edit the `web.xml` deployment descriptor in the WEB-INF directory to include the information specified in Fig. 24.19. Restart Tomcat, and type the following URL in your Web browser:

> http://localhost:8080/jhtp5/servlets/RedirectServlet.html

Click a hyperlink in the Web page to invoke the servlet.

```
1   <?xml version = "1.0"?>
2   <!DOCTYPE html PUBLIC "-//W3C//DTD XHTML 1.0 Strict//EN"
3       "http://www.w3.org/TR/xhtml1/DTD/xhtml1-strict.dtd">
4
5   <!-- Fig. 24.18: RedirectServlet.html -->
6
7   <html xmlns = "http://www.w3.org/1999/xhtml">
8   <head>
9       <title>Redirecting a Request to Another Site</title>
10  </head>
11
12  <body>
13      <p>Click a link to be redirected to the appropriate page</p>
14      <p>
15      <a href = "/jhtp5/redirect?page=deitel">
16          www.deitel.com</a><br />
17      <a href = "/jhtp5/redirect?page=welcome1">
18          Welcome servlet</a>
19      </p>
20  </body>
21  </html>
```

Fig. 24.18 `RedirectServlet.html` document to demonstrate redirecting requests to other resources. (Part 1 of 2.)

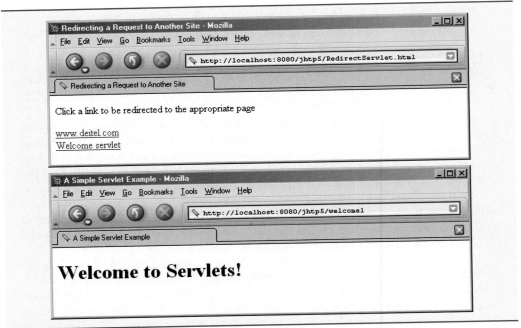

Fig. 24.18   RedirectServlet.html document to demonstrate redirecting requests to other resources. (Part 2 of 2.)

Descriptor element	Value
servlet element	
servlet-name	redirect
description	Redirecting to static Web pages and other servlets.
servlet-class	com.deitel.jhtp5.servlets.RedirectServlet
servlet-mapping element	
servlet-name	redirect
url-pattern	/redirect

Fig. 24.19   Deployment descriptor information for servlet RedirectServlet.

When redirecting requests, the request parameters from the original request are passed as parameters to the new request. Additional request parameters also can be passed. For example, the URL passed to sendRedirect could contain name/value pairs. New parameters are added to the existing parameters. A new parameter with the same name as an existing parameter takes precedence over the original value. However, all the values are still passed. In this case, the complete set of values for a given parameter name can be obtained by callings method *getParameterValues* from interface HttpServletRequest. This method receives the parameter name as an argument and returns an array of strings containing the parameter values in most recent to least recent order.

24.7 Multi-Tier Applications: Using JDBC from a Servlet

Servlets can communicate with databases via JDBC. As we discussed in Chapter 23, JDBC provides a uniform way for Java programs to connect with a variety of databases in a general manner without having to deal with the specifics of those database systems.

Many of today's applications are *three-tier distributed applications*, consisting of a *user interface, business logic* and a *database*. The user interface in such an application is often created using HTML, XHTML (as shown in this chapter) or Dynamic HTML. HTML and XHTML are the preferred mechanisms for representing the user interface in systems where portability is a concern. Because HTML is supported by all browsers, designing the user interface to be accessed through a Web browser guarantees portability across all platforms that have browsers. Using the networking provided by the browser, the user interface can communicate with the middle-tier business logic. The middle tier can then access the database to manipulate the data. The three tiers can reside on separate computers that are connected to a network.

In multi-tier architectures, Web servers often are used in the middle tier. Server-side components, such as servlets, execute in an *application server* along-side the Web server. These components provide the business logic that manipulates data from databases and that communicates with client Web browsers. Servlets, through JDBC, can interact with popular database systems. Developers use SQL-based queries and JDBC drivers handle the specifics of interacting with each database system.

The SurveyServlet of Fig. 24.20 and the Survey.html document of Fig. 24.21 implement portions of a three-tier distributed application. The middle tier is SurveyServlet, which handles requests from the client browser and provides access to the third tier—a Cloudscape database accessed via JDBC. The servlet in this example allows users to vote for their favorite animals. When the servlet receives a post request from the web browser, the servlet uses JDBC to update the total number of votes for that animal in the database and returns a dynamically generated XHTML document containing the survey results to the client.

```java
1   // Fig. 24.20: SurveyServlet.java
2   // A Web-based survey that uses JDBC from a servlet.
3   package com.deitel.jhtp5.servlets;
4
5   import java.io.*;
6   import java.text.*;
7   import java.sql.*;
8   import javax.servlet.*;
9   import javax.servlet.http.*;
10
11  public class SurveyServlet extends HttpServlet {
12     private Connection connection;
13     private Statement statement;
14
15     // set up database connection and create SQL statement
16     public void init( ServletConfig config ) throws ServletException
17     {
```

Fig. 24.20 Multi-tier Web-based survey using XHTML, servlets and JDBC. (Part 1 of 4.)

```
18          // attempt database connection and create Statements
19          try {
20             System.setProperty( "db2j.system.home",
21                config.getInitParameter( "databaseLocation" ) );
22
23             Class.forName( config.getInitParameter( "databaseDriver" ) );
24             connection = DriverManager.getConnection(
25                config.getInitParameter( "databaseName" ) );
26
27             // create Statement to query database
28             statement = connection.createStatement();
29          }
30
31          // for any exception throw an UnavailableException to
32          // indicate that the servlet is not currently available
33          catch ( Exception exception ) {
34             exception.printStackTrace();
35             throw new UnavailableException(exception.getMessage());
36          }
37
38       } // end of init method
39
40       // process survey response
41       protected void doPost( HttpServletRequest request,
42          HttpServletResponse response )
43             throws ServletException, IOException
44       {
45          // set up response to client
46          response.setContentType( "text/html" );
47          PrintWriter out = response.getWriter();
48          DecimalFormat twoDigits = new DecimalFormat( "0.00" );
49
50          // start XHTML document
51          out.println( "<?xml version = \"1.0\"?>" );
52
53          out.println( "<!DOCTYPE html PUBLIC \"-//W3C//DTD " +
54             "XHTML 1.0 Strict//EN\" \"http://www.w3.org" +
55             "/TR/xhtml1/DTD/xhtml1-strict.dtd\">" );
56
57          out.println(
58             "<html xmlns = \"http://www.w3.org/1999/xhtml\">" );
59
60          // head section of document
61          out.println( "<head>" );
62
63          // read current survey response
64          int value =
65             Integer.parseInt( request.getParameter( "animal" ) );
66          String query;
67
68          // attempt to process a vote and display current results
69          try {
70
```

Fig. 24.20 Multi-tier Web-based survey using XHTML, servlets and JDBC. (Part 2 of 4.)

```
71              // update total for current surevy response
72              query = "UPDATE surveyresults SET votes = votes + 1 " +
73                  "WHERE id = " + value;
74              statement.executeUpdate( query );
75
76              // get total of all survey responses
77              query = "SELECT sum( votes ) FROM surveyresults";
78              ResultSet totalRS = statement.executeQuery( query );
79              totalRS.next();
80              int total = totalRS.getInt( 1 );
81
82              // get results
83              query = "SELECT surveyoption, votes, id FROM surveyresults " +
84                  "ORDER BY id";
85              ResultSet resultsRS = statement.executeQuery( query );
86              out.println( "<title>Thank you!</title>" );
87              out.println( "</head>" );
88
89              out.println( "<body>" );
90              out.println( "<p>Thank you for participating." );
91              out.println( "<br />Results:</p><pre>" );
92
93              // process results
94              int votes;
95
96              while ( resultsRS.next() ) {
97                  out.print( resultsRS.getString( 1 ) );
98                  out.print( ": " );
99                  votes = resultsRS.getInt( 2 );
100                 out.print( twoDigits.format(
101                     ( double ) votes / total * 100 ) );
102                 out.print( "%  responses: " );
103                 out.println( votes );
104             }
105
106             resultsRS.close();
107
108             out.print( "Total responses: " );
109             out.print( total );
110
111             // end XHTML document
112             out.println( "</pre></body></html>" );
113             out.close();
114
115         } // end try
116
117         // if database exception occurs, return error page
118         catch ( SQLException sqlException ) {
119             sqlException.printStackTrace();
120             out.println( "<title>Error</title>" );
121             out.println( "</head>" );
122             out.println( "<body><p>Database error occurred. " );
123             out.println( "Try again later.</p></body></html>" );
```

Fig. 24.20 Multi-tier Web-based survey using XHTML, servlets and JDBC. (Part 3 of 4.)

```
124              out.close();
125          }
126
127      }  // end of doPost method
128
129      // close SQL statements and database when servlet terminates
130      public void destroy()
131      {
132          // attempt to close statements and database connection
133          try {
134              statement.close();
135              connection.close();
136          }
137
138          // handle database exceptions by returning error to client
139          catch ( SQLException sqlException ) {
140              sqlException.printStackTrace();
141          }
142      }
143
144  } // end class SurveyServlet
```

Fig. 24.20 Multi-tier Web-based survey using XHTML, servlets and JDBC. (Part 4 of 4.)

Lines 12 and 13 begin by declaring a `Connection` reference to manage the database connection and a `Statement` reference for updating the vote count for an animal, totalling all the votes and obtaining the complete survey results.

Servlets are initialized by method *init*, which we override in `SurveyServlet` (lines 16–38). Method `init` is called exactly once in a servlet's lifetime, before any client requests are accepted. Method `init` takes *ServletConfig* argument and throws a `ServletException`. The argument provides the servlet with information about its *initialization parameters* (i.e., parameters not associated with a request, but passed to the servlet for initializing the servlet's state). These parameters are specified in the `web.xml` deployment descriptor file as part of a `servlet` element. Each parameter appears in an *init-param* element of the following form:

```
<init-param>
    <param-name>parameter name</param-name>
    <param-value>parameter value</param-value>
</init-param>
```

Servlets can obtain initialization parameter values by invoking `ServletConfig` method *getInitParameter*, which receives a string representing the name of the parameter.

In this example, the servlet's `init` method (lines 16–38) performs the connection to the Cloudscape database. Lines 20–21 invoke `System` method `setProperty` to set the property `"db2j.system.home"` to the location of the database in the file system. Line 21 invokes method `getInitParameter` to get the initialization parameter value for parameter `"databaseLocation"`. (For this example, we create the database in the folder `C:\CloudScape_5.0`.) Line 23 loads the driver (`com.ibm.db2j.jdbc.DB2jDriver`, which is specified in the initialization parameter `"databaseDriver"`). Lines 24–25 attempt to open a connection to the `animalsurvey` database. The database name is specified in the initialization parameter "databaseName". The database contains one table (surveyresults) that consists of three fields—a unique integer to identify each record (id), a string representing the survey option (surveyoption) and an integer representing the number of votes for a survey option (votes). [*Note*: The examples folder for this chapter contains an SQL script (animalsurvey.sql) with which you can create the animalsurvey database for this example. For information on executing the SQL script, please refer to Chapter 23.]

When a user submits a survey response, method doPost (lines 41–127) handles the request. Lines 64–65 obtain the survey response, then lines 69–115 attempt to process the response. Lines 72–73 specify a query to increment the votes value for the record with the specified ID and update the database. Lines 78–80 execute the query specified in line 77 to retrieve the total number of votes received using SQL's built-in sum capability to total all the votes in the surveyresults table. Then, lines 85–113 execute the query (returns all the data in the surveyresults table) specified in lines 83–84 and process the ResultSet to create the survey summary for the client. When the servlet container terminates the servlet, method *destroy* (lines 130–142) closes the Statement, then closes the database connection. Figure 24.21 shows survey.html, which invokes SurveyServlet through alias animalsurvey when the user submits the form.

```
1   <?xml version = "1.0"?>
2   <!DOCTYPE html PUBLIC "-//W3C//DTD XHTML 1.0 Strict//EN"
3      "http://www.w3.org/TR/xhtml1/DTD/xhtml1-strict.dtd">
4
5   <!-- Fig. 24.21: Survey.html -->
6
7   <html xmlns = "http://www.w3.org/1999/xhtml">
8   <head>
9      <title>Survey</title>
10  </head>
11
12  <body>
13  <form method = "post" action = "/jhtp5/animalsurvey">
14
15     <p>What is your favorite pet?</p>
16
17     <p>
18        <input type = "radio" name = "animal"
19           value = "1" />Dog<br />
20        <input type = "radio" name = "animal"
21           value = "2" />Cat<br />
22        <input type = "radio" name = "animal"
23           value = "3" />Bird<br />
24        <input type = "radio" name = "animal"
25           value = "4" />Snake<br />
26        <input type = "radio" name = "animal"
27           value = "5" checked = "checked" />None
28     </p>
29
```

Fig. 24.21   Survey.html document that allows users to submit survey responses to SurveyServlet. (Part 1 of 2.)

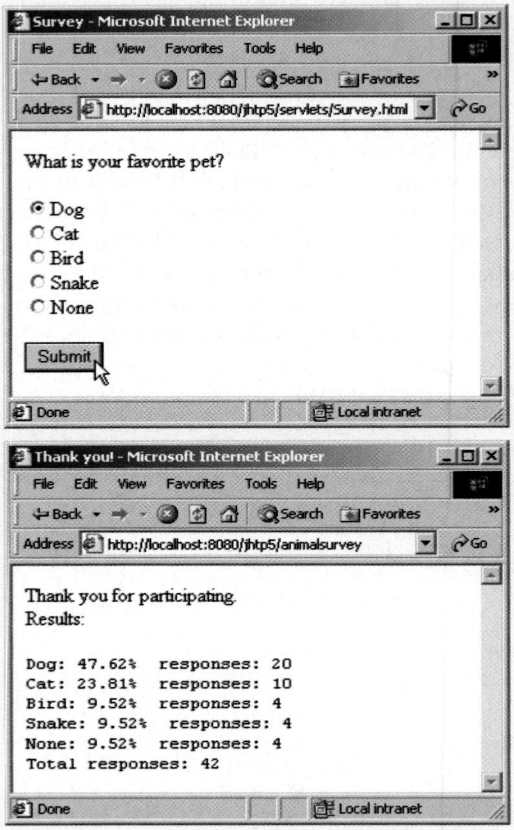

```
30          <p><input type = "submit" value = "Submit" /></p>
31
32      </form>
33      </body>
34      </html>
```

Fig. 24.21   Survey.html document that allows users to submit survey responses to SurveyServlet. (Part 2 of 2.)

We use our jhtp5 context root to demonstrate the servlet of Fig. 24.20. Place Survey.html in the servlets directory created previously. Place SurveyServlet.class (with the complete package structure) in the classes subdirectory of WEB-INF in the jhtp5 context root. Then, edit the web.xml deployment descriptor in the WEB-INF directory to include the information specified in Fig. 24.22. Also, this program cannot execute in Tomcat unless the Web application has access to the JAR files that contain the Cloudscape database driver and its supporting classes. These JAR files can be found in your Cloudscape installation's lib directory. Place *copies* of these JAR files in the WEB-INF subdirectory lib to make them available to the Web application. Please refer to Chapter 23 for more information on how to configure Cloudscape.

Descriptor element	Value
servlet element	
servlet-name	animalsurvey
description	Connecting to a database from a servlet.
servlet-class	com.deitel.jhtp5.servlets.SurveyServlet
init-param	
param-name	databaseLocation
param-value	C:/CloudScape_5.0
init-param	
param-name	databaseDriver
param-value	com.ibm.db2j.jdbc.DB2jDriver
init-param	
param-name	databaseName
param-value	jdbc:db2j:animalsurvey
servlet-mapping element	
servlet-name	animalsurvey
url-pattern	/animalsurvey

Fig. 24.22 Deployment descriptor information for servlet `SurveyServlet`.

After copying these files, restart Tomcat and type the following URL in your Web browser:

```
http://localhost:8080/jhtp5/servlets/Survey.html
```

Select an animal and press the **Submit** button to invoke the servlet.

24.8 Internet and World Wide Web Resources

This section lists a variety of servlet resources available on the Internet and provides a brief description of each.

`java.sun.com/products/servlet/index.html`
The servlet page at the Sun Microsystems, Inc., Java Web site provides access to the latest servlet information and servlet resources.

`jakarta.apache.org`
This is the Apache Project's home page for the *Jakarta Project. Tomcat*—the servlets and JavaServer Pages reference implementation— is one of many subprojects of the Jakarta Project.

`jakarta.apache.org/tomcat/index.html`
Home page for the Tomcat servlets and JavaServer Pages reference implementation.

`java.apache.org`
This is the Apache Project's home page for all Java-related technologies. This site provides access to many Java packages useful to servlet and JSP developers.

`www.servlets.com`
This is the Web site for the book *Java Servlet Programming* published by O'Reilly. The book provides a variety of resources. This book is an excellent resource for programmers who are learning servlets.

`theserverside.com`
TheServerSide.com is dedicated to information and resources for J2EE.

`www.servletsource.com`
ServletSource.com is a general servlet resource site containing code, tips, tutorials and links to many other Web sites with information on servletswww.cookiecentral.com
A good all-around resource site for cookies.

`developer.netscape.com/docs/manuals/communicator/jsguide4/cookies.htm`
A description of Netscape cookies.

`www.javacorporate.com`
Home of the open-source *Expresso Framework*, which includes a library of extensible servlet components to help speed Web application development.

`www.servlet.com/srvdev.jhtml`
ServletInc's Servlet Developers Forum provides resources for server-side Java developers and information about Web servers that support servlet technologies.

`www.servletforum.com`
ServletForum.com is a newsgroup where you can post questions and have them answered by your peers.

`www.coolservlets.com`
Provides free open-source Java servlets.

`www.cetus-links.org/oo_java_servlets.html`
Provides a list of links to resources on servlets and other technologies.

`www.javaskyline.com`
Java Skyline is an online magazine for servlet developers.

`www.rfc-editor.org`
The RFC Editor provides a search engine for RFCs (Request for Comments). Many of these RFCs provide details of Web-related technologies. RFCs of interest to servlet developers include *URI in WWW* (RFC 1630), *URI: generic syntax* (RFC 2396), *HTTP State Management Mechanism* (RFC 2109), *Use and Interpretation of HTTP Version Numbers* (RFC 2145), *Hyper Text Coffee Pot Control Protocol* (RFC 2324), HTTP/1.1 (RFC 2616) and *HTTP Authentication: Basic and Digest Authentication* (RFC 2617).

SUMMARY

- The classes and interfaces used to define servlets are found in packages `javax.servlet` and `javax.servlet.http`.

- The Internet offers many protocols. The HTTP protocol (Hypertext Transfer Protocol) that forms the basis of the World Wide Web uses URLs (Uniform Resource Locators) to locate resources on the Internet.

- URLs represent files or directories and can represent complex tasks such as database lookups and Internet searches.

- JavaServer Pages technology is an extension of servlet technology.

- Servlets are normally executed by the servlet container component of a Web application server.

- Servlets and JavaServer Pages have become so popular that they are now supported by most major Web servers and application servers.

- All servlets must implement the `Servlet` interface. The methods of interface `Servlet` are invoked automatically by the servlet container.

- A servlet's life cycle begins when the servlet container loads the servlet into memory—normally in response to the first request to that servlet. Before the servlet can handle the first request, the servlet container invokes the servlet's `init` method. After `init` completes execution, the servlet can respond to its first request. All requests are handled by a servlet's `service` method, which may be called many times during the life cycle of a servlet. When the servlet container terminates the servlet, the servlet's `destroy` method is called to release servlet resources.

- The servlet packages define two `abstract` classes that implement the interface `Servlet`—class `GenericServlet` and class `HttpServlet`. Most servlets extend one of these classes and override some or all of their methods with appropriate customized behaviors.

- The key method in every servlet is method `service`, which receives both a `ServletRequest` object and a `ServletResponse` object. These objects provide access to input and output streams that allow the servlet to read data from the client and send data to the client.

- Web-based servlets typically extend class `HttpServlet`. Class `HttpServlet` overrides method `service` to distinguish between the typical requests received from a client Web browser. The two most common HTTP request types (also known as request methods) are `get` and `post`.

- Class `HttpServlet` defines methods `doGet` and `doPost` to respond to `get` and `post` requests from a client, respectively. These methods are called by the `HttpServlet` class's `service` method, which is called when a request arrives at the server.

- Methods `doGet` and `doPost` receive as arguments an `HttpServletRequest` object and an `HttpServletResponse` object that enable interaction between the client and the server.

- A response is sent to the client through a `PrintWriter` object returned by the `getWriter` method of the `HttpServletResponse` object.

- The `HttpServletResponse` object's `setContentType` method specifies the MIME type of the response to the client. This enables the client browser to understand and handle the content.

- The server `localhost` (IP address `127.0.0.1`) is a well-known host name on computers that support TCP/IP-based networking protocols such as HTTP. This host name can be used to test TCP/IP applications on the local computer.

- The Tomcat server awaits requests from clients on port 8080. This port number must be specified as part of the URL to request a servlet running in Tomcat.

- The client can access a servlet only if that servlet is installed on a server that can respond to servlet requests. Web servers that support servlets normally have an installation procedure for servlets.

- Tomcat is a fully functional implementation of the JSP and servlet standards. It includes a Web server, so it can be used as a stand-alone test container for JSPs and servlets.

- Tomcat can be specified as the handler for JSP and servlet requests received by popular Web servers such as Apache and IIS. Tomcat also is integrated into the Java 2 Enterprise Edition reference implementation from Sun Microsystems.

- JSPs, servlets and their supporting files are deployed as part of Web applications. In Tomcat, Web applications are deployed in the `webapps` subdirectory of the Tomcat installation.

- A Web application has a well-known directory structure in which all the files that are part of the application reside. This directory structure can be set up by the Tomcat server administrator in the `webapps` directory, or the entire directory structure can be archived in a Web application archive file. Such an archive is known as a WAR file and ends with the `.war` file extension.

- If a WAR file is placed in the `webapps` directory, when the Tomcat server starts up it extracts the contents of the WAR file into the appropriate `webapps` subdirectory structure.

- The Web application directory structure is separated into a context root—the top-level directory for an entire Web application—and several subdirectories. The context root is the root directory for the Web application. All the JSPs, HTML documents, servlets and supporting files such as images and class files reside in this directory or its subdirectories. The `WEB-INF` directory contains the Web application deployment descriptor (`web.xml`). The `WEB-INF/classes` directory contains the servlet class files and other supporting class files used in a Web application. The WEB-INF/lib directory contains Java archive (JAR) files that may include servlet class files and other supporting class files used in a Web application.

- Before deploying a Web application, the servlet container must be made aware of the context root for the Web application. In Tomcat, this can be done simply by placing a directory in the webapps subdirectory. Tomcat uses the directory name as the context name.

- Deploying a Web application requires the creation of a deployment descriptor (web.xml).

- HTTP get requests can be typed directly into your browser's Address or Location field.

- Parameters are passed as name/value pairs in a get request. A ? separates the URL from the data passed as part of a get request. Name/value pairs are passed with the name and the value separated by =. If there is more than one name/value pair, each name/value pair is separated by &.

- Method getParameter of interface HttpServletRequest receives the parameter name as an argument and returns the corresponding String value, or null if the parameter is not part of the request.

- An HTTP post request is often used to post data from a Web-page form to a server-side form handler that processes the data.

- Browsers often cache (save on disk) Web pages so they can quickly reload the pages. Browsers do not cache the server's response to a post request.

- Method doPost receives the same two arguments as doGet—an object that implements interface HttpServletRequest to represent the client's request and an object that implements interface HttpServletResponse to represent the servlet's response.

- Method sendRedirect of HttpServletResponse redirects a request to the specified URL.

- When a servlet uses a relative path to reference another static or dynamic resource, the servlet assumes the same context root unless a complete URL is specified for the resource.

- Once method sendRedirect executes, processing of the request by the servlet that called sendRedirect terminates.

- When redirecting requests, the request parameters from the original request are passed as parameters to the new request. Additional request parameters also can be passed.

- New parameters are added to the existing request parameters. If a new parameter has the same name as an existing parameter, the new parameter value takes precedence over the original value. However, all the values are still passed.

- The complete set of values for a given request-parameter name can be obtained by calling method getParameterValues from interface HttpServletRequest, which receives the parameter name as an argument and returns an array of Strings containing the parameter values in order from the most recently added value for that parameter to the least recently added.

- Many of today's applications are three-tier distributed applications, consisting of a user interface, business logic and database access.

- In multi-tier architectures, Web servers often are used in the middle tier. Server-side components, such as servlets, execute in an application server along-side with Web server. These components provide the business logic that manipulates data from databases and that communicates with client Web browsers.

- Servlet method init takes a ServletConfig argument and throws a ServletException. The argument provides the servlet with information about its initialization parameters that are specified in a servlet element in the deployment descriptor. Each parameter appears in an init-param element with child elements param-name and param-value.

TERMINOLOGY

Apache Tomcat server
cache a Web page
`CATALINA_HOME` environment variable
commit a response
context root
deploy a Web application
deployment descriptor
`destroy` method of `Servlet`
`doGet` method of `HttpServlet`
`doPost` method of `HttpServlet`
`GenericServlet` class from `javax.servlet`
get request
`getCookies` method of
   `HttpServletRequest`
`getOutputStream` method of
   `HTTPServletResponse`
`getParameter` method of
   `HttpServletRequest`
`getParameterNames` method of
   `HttpServletRequest`
`getParameterValues` method of
   `HttpServletRequest`
`getWriter` method of
   `HTTPServletResponse`
host name
HTTP request
`HttpServlet` interface
`HttpServletRequest` interface
`HttpServletResponse` interface
HTTP (Hypertext Transfer Protocol)
HTTP header
`init` method of `Servlet`
initialization parameter
Jakarta project
`JAVA_HOME` environment variable
`javax.servlet` package
`javax.servlet.http` package

`localhost (127.0.0.1)`
MIME type
`path` attribute
port
`post` request
`put` request
redirect a request
request method
request parameter
`sendRedirect` method of
   `HttpServletResponse`
`service` method of `Servlet`
servlet
servlet container
`Servlet` interface
servlet life cycle
servlet mapping
`ServletException` class
`ServletOutputStream` class
`ServletRequest` interface
`ServletResponse` interface
`setContentType` method of
   `HttpServletResponse`
`text/html` MIME type
thin client
`trace` request
URL pattern
WAR (Web application archive) file
Web application
Web application deployment
   descriptor (`web.xml`)
`webapps` directory
`WEB-INF` directory
`WEB-INF/classes` directory
`WEB-INF/lib` directory
well-known port number

SELF-REVIEW EXERCISES

24.1 Fill in the blanks in each of the following statements:

a) Classes `HttpServlet` and `GenericServlet` implement the _____ interface.

b) Class `HttpServlet` defines the methods _____ and _____ to respond to `get` and `post` requests from a client.

c) `HttpServletResponse` method _____ obtains a character-based output stream that enables text data to be sent to the client.

d) The `form` attribute _____ specifies the server-side *form handler,* i.e., the program that handles the request.

e) _____ is the well-known host name that refers to your own computer.

24.2   State whether each of the following is *true* or *false*. If *false*, explain why.
  a) Servlets usually are used on the client side of a networking application.
  b) Servlet methods are executed by the servlet container.
  c) The two most common HTTP requests are get and put.
  d) The well-known port number for Web requests is 55.

ANSWERS TO SELF-REVIEW EXERCISES

24.1   a) Servlet. b) doGet, doPost. c) getWriter. d) action. e) localhost.

24.2   a) False. Servlets are usually used on the server side.
  b) True.
  c) False. The two most common HTTP request types are get and post.
  d) False. The well-known port number for Web requests is 80.

EXERCISES

24.3   Create a Web application for dynamic FAQs. The application should obtain the information to create the dynamic FAQ Web page from a database that consists of a Topics table and an FAQ table. The Topics table should have two fields—a unique integer ID for each topic (topicID) and a name for each topic (topicName). The FAQ table should have three fields—the topicID (a foreign key), a string representing the question (question) and the answer to the question (answer). When the servlet is invoked, it should read the data from the database and return a dynamically created Web page containing each question and answer, sorted by topic.

24.4   Modify the Web application of Exercise 24.3 so that the initial request to the servlet returns a Web page of topics in the FAQ database. Then, the user can hyperlink to another servlet that returns only the frequently asked questions for a particular topic.

24.5   Modify the Web application of Fig. 24.20 to allow the user to see the survey results without responding to the survey.

24.6   Modify the Web application of Fig. 24.20 to make it generic for use with any survey of the appropriate form. Use servlet parameters (as discussed in Section 24.7) to specify the survey options. When the user requests the survey, dynamically generate a form containing the survey options. Deploy this Web application twice using different context roots. *Note*: You may need to modify the database in this example so that it can store multiple surveys at once.

24.7   Write a Web application that consists of a servlet (DirectoryServlet) and several Web documents. Document index.html should be the first document the user sees. In that document, you should have a series of hyperlinks for other Web pages in your site. When clicked, each hyperlink should invoke the servlet with a get request that contains a page parameter. The servlet should obtain parameter page and redirect the request to the appropriate document.

JavaServer Pages (JSP)

Objectives

- To be able to create and deploy JavaServer Pages.
- To use JSP's implicit objects and scriptlets to create dynamic Web pages.
- To specify global JSP information with directives.
- To use actions to manipulate JavaBeans in a JSP, to include resources dynamically and to forward requests to other JSPs.

A tomato does not communicate with a tomato, we believe. We could be wrong.
Gustav Eckstein

A donkey appears to me like a horse translated into Dutch.
Georg Christoph Licthtenberg

Talent is a question of quantity. Talent does not write one page: it writes three hundred.
Jules Renard

Every action must be due to one or other of seven causes: chance, nature, compulsion, habit, reasoning, anger, or appetite.
Aristotle

25.1 Introduction

Our discussion of client–server networking continues in this chapter with *JavaServer Pages (JSP)*—an extension of servlet technology. JavaServer Pages simplify the delivery of dynamic Web content. They enable Web application programmers to create dynamic content by reusing predefined components and by interacting with components using server-side scripting. JavaServer Page programmers can reuse JavaBeans and create custom tag libraries that encapsulate complex, dynamic functionality. Custom-tag libraries even enable Web-page designers who are not familiar with Java to enhance Web pages with powerful dynamic content and processing capabilities.

In addition to the types for programming servlets (Chapter 24), classes and interfaces specific to JavaServer Pages programming are located in packages `javax.servlet.jsp` and `javax.servlet.jsp.tagext`. We discuss many of these classes and interfaces throughout this chapter as we present JavaServer Pages fundamentals. For a complete description of JavaServer Pages, see the JavaServer Pages 1.2 specification, which can be downloaded from `java.sun.com/products/jsp/download.html`. We also include other JSP resources in Section 25.9. [*Note:* The source code and images the examples in this chapter can be found on the CD that accompanies this book and at `www.deitel.com`.]

25.2 JavaServer Pages Overview

There are four key components to JSPs: *directives*, *actions*, *scriptlets* and *tag libraries*. Directives are messages to the JSP container that enable the programmer to specify page settings, to include content from other resources and to specify custom tag libraries for use in a JSP. Actions encapsulate functionality in predefined tags that programmers can embed in a JSP. Actions often are performed based on the information sent to the server as part of a particular client request. They also can create Java objects for use in JSP scriptlets. Scriptlets, or *scripting elements*, enable programmers to insert Java code that interacts with components in a JSP (and possibly other Web application components) to perform request processing. Tag libraries are part of the *tag extension mechanism* that enables programmers to create custom tags. Such tags enable programmers to manipulate JSP content. These JSP component types are discussed in detail in subsequent sections.

In some ways, Java Server Pages look like standard XHTML or XML documents. In fact, JSPs normally include XHTML or XML markup. Such markup is known as *fixed-template data* or *fixed-template text*. Fixed-template data often help a programmer decide whether to use a servlet or a JSP. Programmers tend to use JSPs when most of the content sent to the client is fixed template data and only a small portion of the content is generated dynamically with Java code. Programmers typically use servlets when only a small portion of the content sent to the client is fixed-template data. In fact, some servlets do not produce content. Rather, they perform a task on behalf of the client, then invoke other servlets or JSPs to provide a response. Note that in most cases, servlet and JSP technologies are interchangeable. As with servlets, JSPs normally execute as part of a Web server. The server component that executes them often is referred to as the *JSP container*.

Software Engineering Observation 25.1

Literal text in a JSP becomes string literals in the servlet that represents the translated JSP.

When a JSP-enabled server receives the first request for a JSP, the JSP container translates that JSP into a Java servlet that handles the current request and future requests to the JSP. If there are any errors compiling the new servlet, these errors result in *translation-time errors*. The JSP container places the Java statements that implement the JSP's response in method `_jspService` at translation time. If the new servlet compiles properly, the JSP container invokes method `_jspService` to process the request. The JSP may respond directly to the request or may invoke other Web application components to assist in processing the request. Any errors that occur during request processing are known as *request-time errors*.

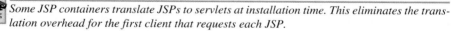

Performance Tip 25.1

Some JSP containers translate JSPs to servlets at installation time. This eliminates the translation overhead for the first client that requests each JSP.

Overall, the request/response mechanism and life cycle of a JSP is the same as that of a servlet. JSPs can define methods `jspInit` and `jspDestroy` (similar to servlet methods `init` and `destroy`), which the JSP container invokes when initializing a JSP and terminating a JSP, respectively. JSP programmers can define these methods using JSP *declarations*—part of the JSP scripting mechanism.

25.3 First JavaServer Page Example

We begin our introduction to JavaServer Pages with a simple example (Fig. 25.1) in which the current date and time are inserted into a Web page using a JSP expression.

As you can see, most of `clock.jsp` consists of XHTML markup. In cases like this, JSPs are easier to implement than servlets. In a servlet that performs the same task as this JSP, each line of XHTML markup typically is a separate Java statement that outputs the string representing the markup as part of the response to the client. Writing code to output markup can often lead to errors. Most JSP editors provide syntax coloring to help programmers check that their markup follows proper syntax.

Software Engineering Observation 25.2

JavaServer Pages are easier to implement than servlets when the response to a client request consists primarily of markup that remains constant between requests.

```
1   <?xml version = "1.0"?>
2   <!DOCTYPE html PUBLIC "-//W3C//DTD XHTML 1.0 Strict//EN"
3      "http://www.w3.org/TR/xhtml1/DTD/xhtml1-strict.dtd">
4
5   <!-- Fig. 25.1: clock.jsp -->
6
7   <html xmlns = "http://www.w3.org/1999/xhtml">
8
9      <head>
10        <meta http-equiv = "refresh" content = "60" />
11
12        <title>A Simple JSP Example</title>
13
14        <style type = "text/css">
15           .big { font-family: helvetica, arial, sans-serif;
16                  font-weight: bold;
17                  font-size: 2em; }
18        </style>
19     </head>
20
21     <body>
22        <p class = "big">Simple JSP Example</p>
23
24        <table style = "border: 6px outset;">
25           <tr>
26              <td style = "background-color: black;">
27                 <p class = "big" style = "color: cyan;">
28
29                    <!-- JSP expression to insert date/time -->
30                    <%= new java.util.Date() %>
31
32                 </p>
33              </td>
34           </tr>
35        </table>
36     </body>
37
38  </html>
```

Fig. 25.1   JSP expression inserting the date and time into a Web page. (Part 1 of 2.)

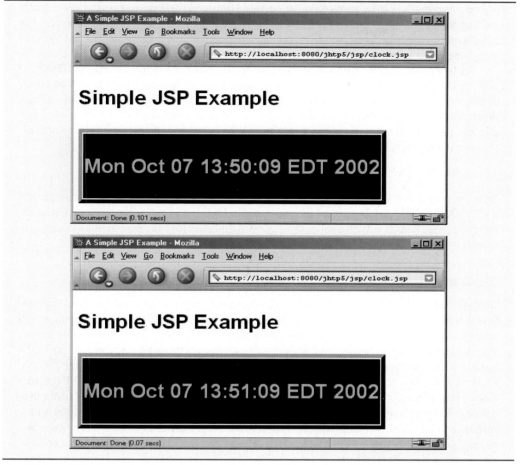

Fig. 25.1   JSP expression inserting the date and time into a Web page. (Part 2 of 2.)

The JSP of Fig. 25.1 generates an XHTML document that displays the current date and time. The key line in this JSP (line 30) is the expression

```
<%= new java.util.Date() %>
```

JSP expressions are delimited by <%= and %>. The preceding expression creates a new instance of class Date (package java.util). When the client requests this JSP, the preceding expression inserts the String representation of the date and time in the response to the client. [Note: Proper internationalization requires that the JSP return the date in the client locale's format. In this example, the server's locale determines the String representation of the Date. In Fig. 25.9, clock2.jsp demonstrates how to determine the client's locale and uses a DateFormat (package java.text) object to format the date using that locale.]

Software Engineering Observation 25.3

The JSP container converts the result of every JSP expression into a string that is output as part of the response to the client.

We use the XHTML *meta element* on line 10 to set a *refresh interval* of 60 seconds for the document. This causes the browser to request `clock.jsp` every 60 seconds. For each request to `clock.jsp`, the JSP container reevaluates the expression on line 30, creating a new `Date` object with the server's current date and time.

As in Chapter 24, we use Apache Tomcat to test our JSPs in the `jhtp5` Web application we created previously. For details on creating and configuring the `jhtp5` Web application, review Section 24.3.1 and Section 24.3.2. To test `clock.jsp`, create a new directory called `jsp` in the `jhtp5` subdirectory of Tomcat's `webapps` directory. Next, copy `clock.jsp` into the `jsp` directory. Open your Web browser and enter the following URL to test `clock.jsp`:

    http://localhost:8080/jhtp5/jsp/clock.jsp

When you first invoke the JSP, notice the delay as Tomcat translates the JSP into a servlet and invokes the servlet to respond to your request. [*Note:* It is not necessary to create a directory named `jsp` in a Web application. We use this directory to separate the examples in this chapter from the servlet examples in Chapter 24.]

25.4 Implicit Objects

Implicit objects provide programmers with access to many servlet capabilities in the context of a JavaServer Page. Implicit objects have four scopes: *application*, *page*, *request* and *session*. The JSP and servlet container application owns objects with *application scope*. Any servlet or JSP can manipulate such objects. Objects with *page scope* exist only in the page that defines them. Each page has its own instances of the page-scope implicit objects. Objects with *request scope* exist for the duration of the request. For example, a JSP can partially process a request, then forward the request to another servlet or JSP for further processing. Request-scope objects go out of scope when request processing completes with a response to the client. Objects with *session scope* exist for the client's entire browsing session. Figure 25.2 describes the JSP implicit objects and their scopes. This chapter demonstrates several of these objects.

Implicit object	Description
Application Scope	
application	This `javax.servlet.ServletContext` object represents the container in which the JSP executes.
Page Scope	
config	This `javax.servlet.ServletConfig` object represents the JSP configuration options. As with servlets, configuration options can be specified in a Web application descriptor.
exception	This `java.lang.Throwable` object represents the exception that is passed to the JSP error page. This object is available only in a JSP error page.

Fig. 25.2   JSP implicit objects. (Part 1 of 2.)

Implicit object	Description
out	This `javax.servlet.jsp.JspWriter` object writes text as part of the response to a request. This object is used implicitly with JSP expressions and actions that insert string content in a response.
page	This `java.lang.Object` object represents the `this` reference for the current JSP instance.
pageContext	This `javax.servlet.jsp.PageContext` object hides the implementation details of the underlying servlet and JSP container and provides JSP programmers with access to the implicit objects discussed in this table.
response	This object represents the response to the client and is normally an instance of a class that implements `HttpServletResponse` (package `javax.servlet.http`). If a protocol other than HTTP is used, this object is an instance of a class that implements `javax.servlet.ServletResponse`.
Request Scope	
request	This object represents the client request. The object normally is an instance of a class that implements `HttpServletRequest` (package `javax.servlet.http`). If a protocol other than HTTP is used, this object is an instance of a subclass of `javax.servlet.ServletRequest`.
Session Scope	
session	This `javax.servlet.http.HttpSession` object represents the client session information if such a session has been created. This object is available only in pages that participate in a session.

Fig. 25.2   *JSP implicit objects. (Part 2 of 2.)*

Note that many of the implicit objects extend classes or implement interfaces discussed in Chapter 24. Thus, JSPs can use the same methods that servlets use to interact with such objects, as described in Chapter 24. Most of the examples in this chapter use one or more of the implicit objects in Fig. 25.2.

25.5 Scripting

JavaServer Pages often present dynamically generated content as part of an XHTML document that is sent to the client in response to a request. In some cases, the content is static, but is output only if certain conditions are met during a request (such as providing values in a `form` that submits a request). JSP programmers can insert Java code and logic in a JSP using scripting.

25.5.1 Scripting Components

JSP scripting components include scriptlets, comments, expressions, declarations and escape sequences. This section describes each of these scripting components. Many of these scripting components are demonstrated in Fig. 25.4 at the end of Section 25.5.2.

Scriptlets are blocks of code delimited by `<%` and `%>`. They contain Java statements that the container places in method `_jspService` at translation time.

JSPs support three comment styles: JSP comments, XHTML comments and scripting-language comments. *JSP comments* are delimited by *<%--* and *--%>*. These can be placed throughout a JSP, but not inside scriptlets. *XHTML comments* are delimited with *<!--* and *-->*. These comments can be placed throughout a JSP, but not inside scriptlets. Scripting language comments are currently Java comments, because Java is the only JSP scripting language at the present time. Scriptlets can use Java's end-of-line *//* comments and traditional comments (delimited by */** and **/*). JSP comments and scripting-language comments are ignored and do not appear in the response to a client. When clients view the source code of a JSP response, they will see only the XHTML comments in the source code. The different comment styles are useful for separating comments that the user should be able to see from comments that document logic processed on the server.

Common Programming Error 25.1

Placing a JSP comment or XHTML comment inside a scriptlet is a translation-time syntax error that prevents the JSP from being translated properly.

A JSP expression, delimited by *<%=* and *%>*, contains a Java expression that is evaluated when a client requests the JSP containing the expression. The container converts the result of a JSP expression to a `String` object, then outputs the `String` as part of the response to the client.

Declarations (delimited by *<%!* and *%>*) enable a JSP programmer to define variables and methods for use in a JSP. Variables become instance variables of the servlet class that represents the translated JSP. Similarly, methods become members of the class that represents the translated JSP. Declarations of variables and methods in a JSP use Java syntax. Thus, a variable declaration must end in a semicolon, as in

```
<%! int counter = 0; %>
```

Common Programming Error 25.2

Declaring a variable without using a terminating semicolon is a syntax error.

Software Engineering Observation 25.4

JSPs should not store client state information in instance variables. Rather, JSPs should use the JSP implicit `session` object.

Special characters or character sequences that the JSP container normally uses to delimit JSP code can be included in a JSP as literal characters in scripting elements, fixed template data and attribute values using *escape sequences*. Figure 25.3 shows the literal character or characters and the corresponding escape sequences and discusses where to use the escape sequences.

Literal	Escape sequence	Description
<%	<\%	The character sequence <% normally indicates the beginning of a scriptlet. The <\% escape sequence places the literal characters <% in the response to the client.

Fig. 25.3 JSP escape sequences. (Part 1 of 2.)

Literal	Escape sequence	Description
%>	%\>	The character sequence %> normally indicates the end of a scriptlet. The %\> escape sequence places the literal characters %> in the response to the client.
' " \	\' \" \\	As with string literals in a Java program, the escape sequences for characters ', " and \ allow these characters to appear in attribute values. Remember that the literal text in a JSP becomes string literals in the servlet that represents the translated JSP.

Fig. 25.3   JSP escape sequences. (Part 2 of 2.)

25.5.2 Scripting Example

The JSP of Fig. 25.4 demonstrates responding to get requests with basic scripting capabilities. The JSP enables the user to input a first name, then outputs that name in the response. Using scripting, the JSP determines whether a firstName parameter was passed as part of the request; if not, the JSP returns an XHTML document containing a form through which the user can input a first name. Otherwise, the JSP obtains the firstName value and uses it as part of an XHTML document that welcomes the user to JavaServer Pages.

```
1   <?xml version = "1.0"?>
2   <!DOCTYPE html PUBLIC "-//W3C//DTD XHTML 1.0 Strict//EN"
3      "http://www.w3.org/TR/xhtml1/DTD/xhtml1-strict.dtd">
4
5   <!-- Fig. 25.4: welcome.jsp -->
6   <!-- JSP that processes a "get" request containing data. -->
7
8   <html xmlns = "http://www.w3.org/1999/xhtml">
9
10     <!-- head section of document -->
11     <head>
12        <title>Processing "get" requests with data</title>
13     </head>
14
15     <!-- body section of document -->
16     <body>
17        <% // begin scriptlet
18
19           String name = request.getParameter( "firstName" );
20
21           if ( name != null ) {
22
23        %> <%-- end scriptlet to insert fixed template data --%>
24
25           <h1>
26              Hello <%= name %>, <br />
```

Fig. 25.4   Scripting a JavaServer Page—welcome.jsp. (Part 1 of 2.)

```
27                    Welcome to JavaServer Pages!
28              </h1>
29
30        <% // continue scriptlet
31
32              }  // end if
33          else {
34
35        %> <%-- end scriptlet to insert fixed template data --%>
36
37              <form action = "welcome.jsp" method = "get">
38                  <p>Type your first name and press Submit</p>
39
40                  <p><input type = "text" name = "firstName" />
41                      <input type = "submit" value = "Submit" />
42                  </p>
43              </form>
44
45        <% // continue scriptlet
46
47              }  // end else
48
49          %> <%-- end scriptlet --%>
50      </body>
51
52  </html>   <!-- end XHTML document -->
```

Fig. 25.4   Scripting a JavaServer Page—welcome.jsp. (Part 2 of 2.)

Notice that the majority of the code in Fig. 25.4 is XHTML markup (i.e., fixed template data). Throughout the body element are several scriptlets (lines 17–23, 30–35 and 45–

49) and a JSP expression (line 26). Note that three comment styles appear in this JSP (at line 5, line17 and line 23).

The scriptlets define an `if...else` structure that determines whether the JSP received a value for the first name as part of the request. Line 19 uses method `getParameter` of JSP implicit object `request` (an `HttpServletRequest` object) to obtain the value for parameter `firstName` and assigns the result to variable `name`. Line 21 determines if `name` is not `null`, (i.e., a value for the first name was passed to the JSP as part of the request). If this condition is `true`, the scriptlet terminates temporarily so the fixed template data at lines 25–28 can be output. The JSP expression in line 26 outputs the value of variable `name` (i.e., the first name passed to the JSP as a request parameter. The scriptlet continues at lines 30–35 with the closing brace of the `if` structure's body and the beginning of the `else` part of the `if...else` structure. If the condition at line 21 is `false`, lines 25–28 are not output. Instead, lines 37–43 output a `form` element. The user can type a first name in the `form` and press the **Submit** button to request the JSP again and execute the `if` structure's body (lines 25–28).

Software Engineering Observation 25.5

Scriptlets, expressions and fixed template data can be intermixed in a JSP to create different responses based on information in a request to a JSP.

Error-Prevention Tip 25.1

It is sometimes difficult to debug errors in a JSP, because the line numbers reported by a JSP container normally refer to the servlet that represents the translated JSP, not the original JSP line numbers. Program development environments such as Sun Microsystems, Inc.'s Sun One Studio 4 enable JSPs to be compiled in the environment, so you can see syntax error messages. These messages include the statement in the servlet that represents the translated JSP, which can be helpful in determining the error.

Error-Prevention Tip 25.2

Many JSP containers store the servlets representing the translated JSPs. For example, the Tomcat installation directory contains a subdirectory called **work** *in which you can find the source code for the servlets translated by Tomcat.*

To test Fig. 25.4 in Tomcat, copy `welcome.jsp` into the `jsp` directory created in Section 25.3. Open your Web browser and enter the following URL to test `welcome.jsp`:

```
http://localhost:8080/jhtp5/jsp/welcome.jsp
```

When you first execute the JSP, it displays the `form` in which you can enter your first name, because the preceding URL does not pass a `firstName` parameter to the JSP. After you submit your first name, your browser should appear as shown in the second screen capture of Fig. 25.4. *Note*: As with servlets, it is possible to pass `get` request arguments as part of the URL. The following URL supplies the `firstName` parameter to `welcome.jsp`:

```
http://localhost:8080/jhtp5/jsp/welcome.jsp?firstName=Paul
```

25.6 Standard Actions

We continue our JSP discussion with the *JSP standard actions* (Fig. 25.5). These actions provide JSP implementors with access to several of the most common tasks performed in a JSP, such as including content from other resources, forwarding requests to other resources and interacting with JavaBeans. JSP containers process actions at request time. Actions

Action	Description
`<jsp:include>`	Dynamically includes another resource in a JSP. As the JSP executes, the referenced resource is included and processed.
`<jsp:forward>`	Forwards request processing to another JSP, servlet or static page. This action terminates the current JSP's execution.
`<jsp:plugin>`	Allows a plug-in component to be added to a page in the form of a browser-specific `object` or `embed` HTML element. In the case of a Java applet, this action enables the downloading and installation of the *Java Plug-in*, if it is not already installed on the client computer.
`<jsp:param>`	Used with the `include`, `forward` and `plugin` actions to specify additional name/value pairs of information for use by these actions.
JavaBean Manipulation	
`<jsp:useBean>`	Specifies that the JSP uses a JavaBean instance. This action specifies the scope of the bean and assigns it an ID that scripting components can use to manipulate the bean.
`<jsp:setProperty>`	Sets a property in the specified JavaBean instance. A special feature of this action is automatic matching of request parameters to bean properties of the same name.
`<jsp:getProperty>`	Gets a property in the specified JavaBean instance and converts the result to a string for output in the response.

Fig. 25.5   JSP standard actions.

are delimited by `<jsp:`*action*`>` and `</jsp:`*action*`>`, where *action* is the standard action name. In cases where nothing appears between the starting and ending tags, the XML empty element syntax `<jsp:`*action* `/>` can be used. Figure 25.5 summarizes the JSP standard actions. We use the actions in the next several subsections.

25.6.1 `<jsp:include>` Action

JavaServer Pages support two include mechanisms—the *`<jsp:include>` action* and the *`include` directive*. Action `<jsp:include>` enables dynamic content to be included in a JavaServer Page at request time (not translation time as with the include directive). If the included resource changes between requests, the next request to the JSP containing the `<jsp:include>` action includes the new content of the resource. On the other hand, the `include` directive copies the content into the JSP once, at JSP translation time. If the included resource changes, the new content will not be reflected in the JSP that used the `include` directive unless that JSP is recompiled. Figure 25.6 describes the attributes of action `<jsp:include>`.

Software Engineering Observation 25.6

According to the JavaServer Pages 1.1 specification, a JSP container is allowed to determine whether a resource included with the `include` directive has changed. If so, the container can recompile the JSP that included the resource. However, the specification does not provide a mechanism to indicate a change in an included resource to the container.

Attribute	Description
page	Specifies the relative URI path of the resource to include. The resource must be part of the same Web application.
flush	Specifies whether the buffer should be flushed after the include is performed. In JSP 1.1, this attribute is required to be true.

Fig. 25.6   Action `<jsp:include>` attributes.

Performance Tip 25.2

The `<jsp:include>` action is more flexible than the include directive, but requires more overhead when page contents change frequently. Use the `<jsp:include>` action only when dynamic content is necessary.

Common Programming Error 25.3

Setting the `<jsp:include>` action's flush attribute to false is a translation-time error. Currently, the flush attribute supports only true values.

Common Programming Error 25.4

Not specifying the `<jsp:include>` action's flush attribute is a translation-time error. Specifying this attribute is mandatory.

Common Programming Error 25.5

Specifying in a `<jsp:include>` action a page that is not part of the same Web application is a request-time error—the `<jsp:include>` action will not include any content.

The next example demonstrates action `<jsp:include>` using four XHTML and JSP resources that represent both static and dynamic content. JavaServer Page include.jsp (Fig. 25.10) includes three other resources: banner.html (Fig. 25.7), toc.html (Fig. 25.8) and clock2.jsp (Fig. 25.9). JavaServer Page include.jsp creates an XHTML document containing a table in which banner.html spans two columns across the top of the table, toc.html is the left column of the second row and clock2.jsp (a simplified version of Fig. 25.1) is the right column of the second row. Figure 25.10 uses three `<jsp:include>` actions (lines 38–39, 48 and 55–56) as the content in td elements of the table. Using two XHTML documents and a JSP in Fig. 25.10 demonstrates that JSPs can include both static and dynamic content. The output window in Fig. 25.10 demonstrates the result of one request to include.jsp.

```
1   <!-- Fig. 25.7: banner.html              -->
2   <!-- banner to include in another document -->
3   <div style = "width: 580px">
4       <p>
5           Java(TM), C, C++, Visual Basic(R),
```

Fig. 25.7   Banner (banner.html) to include across the top of the XHTML document created by Fig. 25.10 (Part 1 of 2.).

```
 6              Object Technology, and <br /> Internet and
 7              World Wide Web Programming Training <br />
 8              On-Site Seminars Delivered Worldwide
 9         </p>
10
11         <p>
12            <a href = "mailto:deitel@deitel.com">deitel@deitel.com</a>
13            <br />978.461.5880<br />12 Clock Tower Place, Suite 200,
14            Maynard, MA 01754
15         </p>
16    </div>
```

Fig. 25.7   Banner (`banner.html`) to include across the top of the XHTML document
created by Fig. 25.10 (Part 2 of 2.).

```
 1    <!-- Fig. 25.8: toc.html                          -->
 2    <!-- contents to include in another document -->
 3
 4    <p><a href = "http://www.deitel.com/books/index.html">
 5       Publications/BookStore
 6    </a></p>
 7
 8    <p><a href = "http://www.deitel.com/whatsnew.html">
 9       What's New
10    </a></p>
11
12    <p><a href = "http://www.deitel.com/books/downloads.html">
13       Downloads/Resources
14    </a></p>
15
16    <p><a href = "http://www.deitel.com/faq/index.html">
17       FAQ (Frequently Asked Questions)
18    </a></p>
19
20    <p><a href = "http://www.deitel.com/intro.html">
21       Who we are
22    </a></p>
23
24    <p><a href = "http://www.deitel.com/index.html">
25       Home Page
26    </a></p>
27
28    <p>Send questions or comments about this site to
29       <a href = "mailto:deitel@deitel.com">
30          deitel@deitel.com
31       </a><br />
32       Copyright 1995-2003 by Deitel &amp; Associates, Inc.
33       All Rights Reserved.
34    </p>
```

Fig. 25.8   Table of contents (`toc.html`) to include down the left side of the XHTML
document created by Fig. 25.10.

Figure 25.9 (clock2.jsp) demonstrates how to determine the client's Locale (package java.util) and uses that Locale to format a Date with a *DateFormat* (package java.text) object. Line 14 invokes the request object's getLocale method, which returns the client's Locale. Lines 17–20 invoke DateFormat static method getDateTimeInstance to obtain a DateFormat object. The first two arguments indicate that the date and time formats should each be LONG format (other options are FULL, MEDIUM, SHORT and DEFAULT). The third argument specifies the Locale for which the DateFormat object should format the date. Line 25 invokes the DateFormat object's format method to produce a String representation of the Date. The DateFormat object formats this String for the Locale specified on lines 17–20. [*Note*: This example works for Western languages that use the ISO-8859-1 character set. However, for languages that do not use this character set, the JSP must specify the proper character set using the JSP page directive (Section 25.7.1). At the site java.sun.com/j2se/1.3/docs/guide/intl/encoding.doc.html, Sun provides a list of character encodings. The response's content type defines the character set to use in the response. The content type has the form: "*mimeType*;charset=*encoding*" (e.g., "text/html;charset=ISO-8859-1".]

```
1   <!-- Fig. 25.9: clock2.jsp                        -->
2   <!-- date and time to include in another document -->
3
4   <table>
5      <tr>
6         <td style = "background-color: black;">
7            <p class = "big" style = "color: cyan; font-size: 3em;
8               font-weight: bold;">
9
10              <%-- script to determine client local and --%>
11              <%-- format date accordingly              --%>
12              <%
13                 // get client locale
14                 java.util.Locale locale = request.getLocale();
15
16                 // get DateFormat for client's Locale
17                 java.text.DateFormat dateFormat =
18                    java.text.DateFormat.getDateTimeInstance(
19                       java.text.DateFormat.LONG,
20                       java.text.DateFormat.LONG, locale );
21
22              %>  <%-- end script --%>
23
24              <%-- output date --%>
25              <%= dateFormat.format( new java.util.Date() ) %>
26           </p>
27        </td>
28     </tr>
29  </table>
```

Fig. 25.9   JSP clock2.jsp to include as the main content in the XHTML document created by Fig. 25.10.

To test Fig. 25.10 in Tomcat, copy `banner.html`, `toc.html`, `clock2.jsp`, `include.jsp` and the `images` directory into the `jsp` directory created in Section 25.3. Open your Web browser and enter the following URL to test `include.jsp`:

```
http://localhost:8080/jhtp5/jsp/include.jsp
```

```
1    <?xml version = "1.0"?>
2    <!DOCTYPE html PUBLIC "-//W3C//DTD XHTML 1.0 Strict//EN"
3       "http://www.w3.org/TR/xhtml1/DTD/xhtml1-strict.dtd">
4
5    <!-- Fig. 25.10: include.jsp -->
6
7    <html xmlns = "http://www.w3.org/1999/xhtml">
8
9       <head>
10         <title>Using jsp:include</title>
11
12         <style type = "text/css">
13            body {
14               font-family: tahoma, helvetica, arial, sans-serif;
15            }
16
17            table, tr, td {
18               font-size: .9em;
19               border: 3px groove;
20               padding: 5px;
21               background-color: #dddddd;
22            }
23         </style>
24      </head>
25
26      <body>
27         <table>
28            <tr>
29               <td style = "width: 160px; text-align: center">
30                  <img src = "images/logotiny.png"
31                     width = "140" height = "93"
32                     alt = "Deitel & Associates, Inc. Logo" />
33               </td>
34
35               <td>
36
37                  <%-- include banner.html in this JSP --%>
38                  <jsp:include page = "banner.html"
39                     flush = "true" />
40
41               </td>
42            </tr>
43
44            <tr>
45               <td style = "width: 160px">
46
```

Fig. 25.10 JSP `include.jsp` Includes resources with `<jsp:include>`. (Part 1 of 2.)

```
47              <%-- include toc.html in this JSP --%>
48              <jsp:include page = "toc.html" flush = "true" />
49
50          </td>
51
52          <td style = "vertical-align: top">
53
54              <%-- include clock2.jsp in this JSP --%>
55              <jsp:include page = "clock2.jsp"
56                  flush = "true" />
57
58          </td>
59      </tr>
60   </table>
61   </body>
62 </html>
```

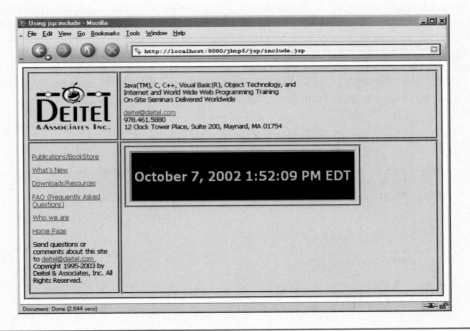

Fig. 25.10 JSP `include.jsp` Includes resources with `<jsp:include>`. (Part 2 of 2.)

25.6.2 `<jsp:forward>` Action

Action `<jsp:forward>` enables a JSP to forward request processing to a different re-source. Request processing by the original JSP terminates as soon as the JSP forwards the request. Action `<jsp:forward>` has only a `page` attribute that specifies the relative URL of the resource (in the same Web application) to which the request should be forwarded.

Software Engineering Observation 25.7

When using the `<jsp:forward>` action, the resource to which the request will be forwarded must be in the same context (Web application) as the JSP that originally received the request.

JavaServer Page `forward1.jsp` (Fig. 25.11) is a modified version of `welcome.jsp` (Fig. 25.4). The primary difference is in lines 22–25 in which JavaServer Page `forward1.jsp` forwards the request to JavaServer Page `forward2.jsp` (Fig. 25.12). Notice the `<jsp:param>` action in lines 23–24. This action adds a request parameter representing the date and time at which the initial request was received to the request object that is forwarded to `forward2.jsp`.

The `<jsp:param>` action specifies name/value pairs of information that are passed to the `<jsp:include>`, `<jsp:forward>` and `<jsp:plugin>` actions. Every `<jsp:param>` action has two required attributes: `name` and `value`. If a `<jsp:param>` action specifies a parameter that already exists in the request, the new value for the parameter takes precedence over the original value. All values for that parameter can be obtained by using the JSP implicit object `request`'s `getParameterValues` method, which returns an array of `String`s.

JSP `forward2.jsp` uses the `name` specified in the `<jsp:param>` action (`"date"`) to obtain the date and time. It also uses the `firstName` parameter originally passed to `forward1.jsp` to obtain the user's first name. JSP expressions in Fig. 25.12 (lines 23 and 31) insert the request parameter values in the response to the client. The screen capture in Fig. 25.11 shows the initial interaction with the client. The screen capture in Fig. 25.12 shows the results returned to the client after the request was forwarded to `forward2.jsp`.

To test Fig. 25.11 and Fig. 25.12 in Tomcat, copy `forward1.jsp` and `forward2.jsp` into the `jsp` directory created in Section 25.3. Open your Web browser and enter the following URL to test `forward1.jsp`:

```
http://localhost:8080/jhtp5/jsp/forward1.jsp
```

```
1   <?xml version = "1.0"?>
2   <!DOCTYPE html PUBLIC "-//W3C//DTD XHTML 1.0 Strict//EN"
3      "http://www.w3.org/TR/xhtml1/DTD/xhtml1-strict.dtd">
4
5   <!-- Fig. 25.11: forward1.jsp -->
6
7   <html xmlns = "http://www.w3.org/1999/xhtml">
8
9   <head>
10     <title>Forward request to another JSP</title>
11  </head>
12
13  <body>
14     <% // begin scriptlet
15
16        String name = request.getParameter( "firstName" );
17
18        if ( name != null ) {
19
20     %> <%-- end scriptlet to insert fixed template data --%>
21
```

Fig. 25.11 JSP `forward1.jsp` receives a `firstName` parameter, adds a date to the request parameters and forwards the request to `forward2.jsp` for further processing. (Part 1 of 2.)

```
22              <jsp:forward page = "forward2.jsp">
23                 <jsp:param name = "date"
24                     value = "<%= new java.util.Date() %>" />
25              </jsp:forward>
26
27     <% // continue scriptlet
28
29        }  // end if
30        else {
31
32     %> <%-- end scriptlet to insert fixed template data --%>
33
34              <form action = "forward1.jsp" method = "get">
35                 <p>Type your first name and press Submit</p>
36
37                 <p><input type = "text" name = "firstName" />
38                    <input type = "submit" value = "Submit" />
39                 </p>
40              </form>
41
42     <% // continue scriptlet
43
44        }  // end else
45
46     %> <%-- end scriptlet --%>
47  </body>
48
49  </html>  <!-- end XHTML document -->
```

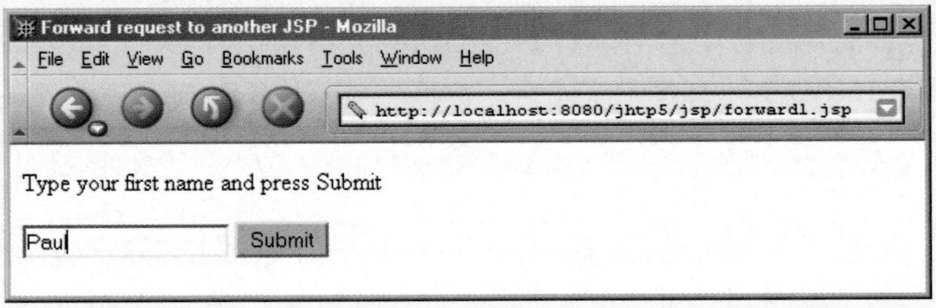

Fig. 25.11 JSP forward1.jsp receives a firstName parameter, adds a date to the request parameters and forwards the request to forward2.jsp for further processing. (Part 2 of 2.)

```
1   <?xml version = "1.0"?>
2   <!DOCTYPE html PUBLIC "-//W3C//DTD XHTML 1.0 Strict//EN"
3       "http://www.w3.org/TR/xhtml1/DTD/xhtml1-strict.dtd">
4
5   <!-- forward2.jsp -->
6
```

Fig. 25.12 JSP forward2.jsp receives a request (from forward1.jsp in this example) and uses the request parameters as part of the response to the client. (Part 1 of 2.)

```
 7   <html xmlns = "http://www.w3.org/1999/xhtml"v
 8
 9   <head>
10      <title>Processing a forwarded request</title>
11
12      <style type = "text/css">
13          .big {
14              font-family: tahoma, helvetica, arial, sans-serif;
15              font-weight: bold;
16              font-size: 2em;
17          }
18      </style>
19   </head>
20
21   <body>
22      <p class = "big">
23          Hello <%= request.getParameter( "firstName" ) %>, <br />
24          Your request was received <br /> and forwarded at
25      </p>
26
27      <table style = "border: 6px outset;">
28          <tr>
29              <td style = "background-color: black;">
30                  <p class = "big" style = "color: cyan;">
31                      <%= request.getParameter( "date" ) %>
32                  </p>
33              </td>
34          </tr>
35      </table>
36   </body>
37
38   </html>
```

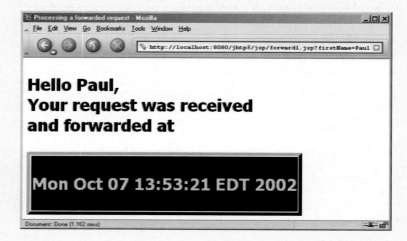

Fig. 25.12   JSP `forward2.jsp` receives a request (from `forward1.jsp` in this example) and uses the request parameters as part of the response to the client. (Part 2 of 2.)

25.6.3 `<jsp:useBean>` Action

Action `<jsp:useBean>` enables a JSP to manipulate a Java object. This action creates a Java object or locates an existing object for use in the JSP. Figure 25.13 summarizes action `<jsp:useBean>`'s attributes. If attributes `class` and `beanName` are not specified, the JSP container attempts to locate an existing object of the type specified in attribute `type`. Like JSP implicit objects, objects specified with action `<jsp:useBean>` have `page`, `request`, `session` or `application` scope that indicates where they can be used in a Web application. Objects with `page` scope are accessible only by the page in which they are defined. Multiple JSP pages potentially can access objects in other scopes. For example, all JSPs that process a single request can access an object in `request` scope.

Common Programming Error 25.6

One or both of the `<jsp:useBean>` attributes `class` and `type` must be specified; otherwise, a translation-time error occurs.

Many Web sites place rotating advertisements on their Web pages. Each visit to one of these pages typically results in a different advertisement being displayed in the user's Web browser. Typically, clicking an advertisement takes you to the Web site of the company that placed the advertisement. Our first example of `<jsp:useBean>` demonstrates a simple advertisement rotator bean that cycles through a list of five advertisements. In this example, the advertisements are covers for some of our books. Clicking a cover takes you to the Amazon.com Web site where you can read about and possibly order the book.

The `Rotator` bean (Fig. 25.14) has three methods: `getImage`, `getLink` and `nextAd`. Method `getImage` returns the image file name for the book cover image. Method `getLink` returns the hyperlink to the book at Amazon.com. Method `nextAd` updates the `Rotator` so the next calls to `getImage` and `getLink` return information for a different advertisement. Methods `getImage` and `getLink` each represent a read-only JavaBean property—`image` and `link`, respectively. `Rotator` keeps track of the current advertisement with its `selectedIndex` variable, which is updated by invoking method `nextAd`.

Attribute	Description
id	The name used to manipulate the Java object with actions `<jsp:setProperty>` and `<jsp:getProperty>`. A variable of this name is also declared for use in JSP scripting elements. The name specified here is case sensitive.
scope	The scope in which the Java object is accessible—`page`, `request`, `session` or `application`. The default scope is `page`.
class	The fully qualified class name of the Java object.
beanName	The name of a bean that can be used with method `instantiate` of class `java.beans.Beans` to load a JavaBean into memory.
type	The type of the JavaBean. This can be the same type as the `class` attribute, a superclass of that type or an interface implemented by that type. The default value is the same as for attribute `class`. A `ClassCastException` occurs if the Java object is not of the type specified with attribute `type`.

Fig. 25.13 Attributes of the `<jsp:useBean>` action.

```
1   // Fig. 25.14: Rotator.java
2   // A JavaBean that rotates advertisements.
3   package com.deitel.jhtp5.jsp;
4
5   public class Rotator {
6      private String images[] = { "images/advjHTP1.jpg",
7         "images/cppHTP4.jpg", "images/iw3HTP2.jpg",
8         "images/jwsFEP1.jpg", "images/vbnetHTP2.jpg" };
9
10     private String links[] = {
11        "http://www.amazon.com/exec/obidos/ASIN/0130895601/" +
12           "deitelassociatin",
13        "http://www.amazon.com/exec/obidos/ASIN/0130384747/" +
14           "deitelassociatin",
15        "http://www.amazon.com/exec/obidos/ASIN/0130308978/" +
16           "deitelassociatin",
17        "http://www.amazon.com/exec/obidos/ASIN/0130461342/" +
18           "deitelassociatin",
19        "http://www.amazon.com/exec/obidos/ASIN/0130293636/" +
20           "deitelassociatin" };
21
22     private int selectedIndex = 0;
23
24     // returns image file name for current ad
25     public String getImage()
26     {
27        return images[ selectedIndex ];
28     }
29
30     // returns the URL for ad's corresponding Web site
31     public String getLink()
32     {
33        return links[ selectedIndex ];
34     }
35
36     // update selectedIndex so next calls to getImage and
37     // getLink return a different advertisement
38     public void nextAd()
39     {
40        selectedIndex = ( selectedIndex + 1 ) % images.length;
41     }
42   }
```

Fig. 25.14   Rotator bean that maintains a set of advertisements.

Lines 7–8 of JavaServer Page adrotator.jsp (Fig. 25.15) obtain a reference to an instance of class Rotator. The id for the bean is rotator. The JSP uses this name to manipulate the bean. The scope of the object is session, so that each individual client will see the same sequence of ads during their browsing session. When adrotator.jsp receives a request from a new client, the JSP container creates the bean and stores it in JSP that client's session (an HttpSession object). In each request to this JSP, line 22 uses the rotator reference created in line 7 to invoke the Rotator bean's nextAd method. Thus, each request will receive the next advertisement selected by the Rotator bean. Lines

29–34 define a hyperlink to the Amazon.com site for a particular book. Lines 29–30 introduce action *<jsp:getProperty>* to obtain the value of the Rotator bean's link property. Action <jsp:getProperty> has two attributes—name and property—that specify the bean object to manipulate and the property to get. If the JavaBean object uses standard JavaBean naming conventions, the method used to obtain the link property value from the bean should be getLink. Action <jsp:getProperty> invokes getLink on the bean referenced with rotator, converts the return value into a String and outputs the String as part of the response to the client. The link property becomes the value of the hyperlink's href attribute. The hyperlink is represented in the resulting Web page as the book cover image. Lines 32–33 create an img element and use another <jsp:getProperty> action to obtain the Rotator bean's image property value.

```
1   <?xml version = "1.0"?>
2   <!DOCTYPE html PUBLIC "-//W3C//DTD XHTML 1.0 Strict//EN"
3      "http://www.w3.org/TR/xhtml1/DTD/xhtml1-strict.dtd">
4
5   <!-- Fig. 25.15: adrotator.jsp -->
6
7   <jsp:useBean id = "rotator" scope = "application"
8      class = "com.deitel.jhtp5.jsp.Rotator" />
9
10  <html xmlns = "http://www.w3.org/1999/xhtml">
11
12     <head>
13        <title>AdRotator Example</title>
14
15        <style type = "text/css">
16           .big { font-family: helvetica, arial, sans-serif;
17                  font-weight: bold;
18                  font-size: 2em }
19        </style>
20
21        <%-- update advertisement --%>
22        <% rotator.nextAd(); %>
23     </head>
24
25     <body>
26        <p class = "big">AdRotator Example</p>
27
28        <p>
29           <a href = "<jsp:getProperty name = "rotator"
30              property = "link" />">
31
32              <img src = "<jsp:getProperty name = "rotator"
33                 property = "image" />" alt = "advertisement" />
34           </a>
35        </p>
36     </body>
37  </html>
```

Fig. 25.15 JSP adrotator.jsp uses a Rotator bean to display a different advertisement on each request for the page. (Part 1 of 2.)

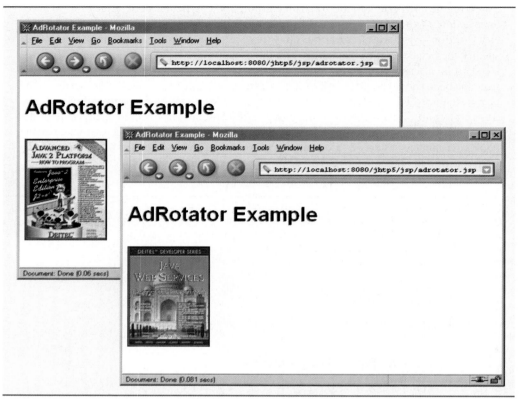

Fig. 25.15 JSP `adrotator.jsp` uses a `Rotator` bean to display a different advertisement on each request for the page. (Part 2 of 2.)

The link and image properties also can be obtained with JSP expressions. For example, action `<jsp:getProperty>` in lines 29–30 can be replaced with the expression

```
<%= rotator.getLink() %>
```

Similarly, action `<jsp:getProperty>` in lines 32–33 can be replaced with the expression

```
<%= rotator.getImage() %>
```

To test `adrotator.jsp` in Tomcat, copy `adrotator.jsp` into the `jsp` directory created in Section 25.3. You should have copied the `images` directory into the `jsp` directory when you tested Fig. 25.10. If not, you must copy the `images` directory there now. Copy `Rotator.class` into the `jhtp5` Web application's `WEB-INF\classes` directory in Tomcat. [*Note:* This example will work only if the proper package directory structure for `Rotator` is defined in the `classes` directory. `Rotator` is defined in package `com.deitel.jhtp5.jsp`.] Open your Web browser and enter the following URL to test `adrotator.jsp`:

```
http://localhost:8080/jhtp5/jsp/adrotator.jsp
```

Try reloading this JSP several times in your browser to see the advertisement change with each request.

Action *<jsp:setProperty>* sets JavaBean property values and is particularly useful for mapping request parameter values to JavaBean properties. Request parameters can be used to set properties of primitive types boolean, byte, char, int, long, float and double and java.lang types String, Boolean, Byte, Character, Integer, Long, Float and Double. Figure 25.16 summarizes the <jsp:setProperty> attributes.

Common Programming Error 25.7

Use action <jsp:setProperty>'s value attribute to set JavaBean property types that cannot be set with request parameters; otherwise, conversion errors occur.

Software Engineering Observation 25.8

Action <jsp:setProperty> can use request-parameter values to set JavaBean properties only for properties of the following types: Strings, primitive types (boolean, byte, char, short, int, long, float and double) and type wrapper classes (Boolean, Byte, Character, Short, Integer, Long, Float and Double).

25.7 Directives

Directives are messages to the JSP container that enable the programmer to specify page settings (such as the error page), to include content from other resources and to specify custom-tag libraries for use in a JSP. Directives (delimited by *<%@* and *%>*) are processed at translation time. Thus, directives do not produce any immediate output, because they are

Attribute	Description
name	The ID of the JavaBean for which a property (or properties) will be set.
property	The name of the property to set. Specifying "*" for this attribute causes the JSP to match the request parameters to the properties of the bean. For each request parameter that matches (i.e., the name of the request parameter is identical to the bean's property name), the corresponding property in the bean is set to the value of the parameter. If the value of the request parameter is "", the property value in the bean remains unchanged.
param	If request parameter names do not match bean property names, this attribute can be used to specify which request parameter should be used to obtain the value for a specific bean property. This attribute is optional. If this attribute is omitted, the request parameter names must match bean property names.
value	The value to assign to a bean property. The value typically is the result of a JSP expression. This attribute is particularly useful for setting bean properties that cannot be set using request parameters. This attribute is optional. If this attribute is omitted, the JavaBean property must be of a type that can be set using request parameters.

Fig. 25.16 Attributes of the <jsp:setProperty> action.

processed before the JSP accepts any requests. Figure 25.17 summarizes the three directive types. These directives are discussed in the next several subsections.

25.7.1 page Directive

The *page directive* specifies global settings for the JSP in the JSP container. There can be many page directives, provided that there is only one occurrence of each attribute. The only exception to this is the import attribute, which can be used repeatedly to import Java packages used in the JSP. Figure 25.18 summarizes the attributes of the page directive.

Directive	Description
page	Defines page settings for the JSP container to process.
include	Causes the JSP container to perform a translation-time insertion of another resource's content. As the JSP is translated into a servlet and compiled, the referenced file replaces the include directive and is translated as if it were originally part of the JSP.
taglib	Allows programmers to define new tags in the form of *tag libraries*, which can be used to encapsulate functionality and simplify the coding of a JSP.

Fig. 25.17 JSP directives.

Attribute	Description
language	The scripting language used in the JSP. Currently, the only valid value for this attribute is java.
extends	Specifies the class from which the translated JSP will be inherited. This attribute must be a fully qualified class name.
import	Specifies a comma-separated list of fully qualified type names and/or packages that will be used in the current JSP. When the scripting language is java, the default import list is java.lang.*, javax.servlet.*, javax.servlet.jsp.* and javax.servlet.http.*. If multiple import properties are specified, the package names are placed in a list by the container.
session	Specifies whether the page participates in a session. The values for this attribute are true (participates in a session—the default) or false (does not participate in a session). When the page is part of a session, implicit object session is available for use in the page. Otherwise, session is not available, and using session in the scripting code results in a translation-time error.
buffer	Specifies the size of the output buffer used with the implicit object out. The value of this attribute can be none for no buffering, or a value such as 8kb (the default buffer size). The JSP specification indicates that the buffer used must be at least the size specified.

Fig. 25.18 Attributes of the page directive. (Part 1 of 2.)

Attribute	Description
autoFlush	When set to `true` (the default), this attribute indicates that the output buffer used with implicit object `out` should be flushed automatically when the buffer fills. If set to `false`, an exception occurs if the buffer overflows. This attribute's value must be `true` if the buffer attribute is set to `none`.
isThreadSafe	Specifies if the page is thread safe. If `true` (the default), the page is considered to be thread safe, and it can process multiple requests at the same time. If `false`, the servlet that represents the page implements interface `java.lang.SingleThreadModel` and only one request can be processed by that JSP at a time. The JSP standard allows multiple instances of a JSP to exists for JSPs that are not thread safe. This enables the container to handle requests more efficiently. However, this does not guarantee that resources shared across JSP instances are accessed in a thread-safe manner.
info	Specifies an information string that describes the page. This string is returned by the `getServletInfo` method of the servlet that represents the translated JSP. This method can be invoked through the JSP's implicit `page` object.
errorPage	Any exceptions in the current page that are not caught are sent to the error page for processing. The error page implicit object `exception` references the original exception.
isErrorPage	Specifies if the current page is an error page that will be invoked in response to an error on another page. If the attribute value is `true`, the implicit object `exception` is created and references the original exception that occurred. If `false` (the default), any use of the `exception` object in the page results in a translation-time error.
contentType	Specifies the MIME type of the data in the response to the client. The default type is `text/html`.

Fig. 25.18 Attributes of the **page** directive. (Part 2 of 2.)

Common Programming Error 25.8

*Providing multiple **page** directives with one or more repeated attributes in common is a JSP translation-time error. Also, providing a **page** directive with an attribute or value that is not recognized is a JSP translation-time error.*

Software Engineering Observation 25.9

*According to the JSP specification section 2.7.1, the **extends** attribute "should not be used without careful consideration as it restricts the ability of the JSP container to provide specialized superclasses that may improve on the quality of rendered service." Rememeber that a Java class can extend exactly one other class. If your JSP specifies an explicit superclass, the JSP container cannot translate your JSP into a sublcass of one of the container application's own enhanced servlet classes.*

Common Programming Error 25.9

*Using JSP implicit object **session** in a JSP that does not have its **page** directive attribute **session** set to **true** is a translation-time error.*

25.7.2 `include` Directive

The *include directive* includes the content of another resource once, at JSP translation time. The `include` directive has only one attribute—`file`—that specifies the URL of the resource to include. The difference between directive `include` and action `<jsp:in-clude>` is noticeable only if the included content changes. For example, if the definition of an XHTML document changes after it is included with directive `include`, future invocations of the JSP will show the original content of the XHTML document, not the new content. In contrast, action `<jsp:include>` is processed in each request to the JSP. Therefore, changes to included content would be apparent in the next request to the JSP that uses action `<jsp:include>`.

JSP `includeDirective.jsp` (Fig. 25.19) reimplements `include.jsp` (Fig. 25.10) using `include` directives. To test `includeDirective.jsp` in Tomcat, copy `include-Directive.jsp` into the `jsp` directory created in Section 25.3. Open your Web browser and enter the following URL to test `includeDirective.jsp`:

```
http://localhost:8080/jhtp5/jsp/includeDirective.jsp
```

```
1   <?xml version = "1.0"?>
2   <!DOCTYPE html PUBLIC "-//W3C//DTD XHTML 1.0 Strict//EN"
3      "http://www.w3.org/TR/xhtml1/DTD/xhtml1-strict.dtd">
4
5   <!-- Fig. 25.19: includeDirective.jsp -->
6
7   <html xmlns = "http://www.w3.org/1999/xhtml">
8
9      <head>
10        <title>Using the include directive</title>
11
12        <style type = "text/css">
13           body {
14              font-family: tahoma, helvetica, arial, sans-serif;
15           }
16
17           table, tr, td {
18              font-size: .9em;
19              border: 3px groove;
20              padding: 5px;
21              background-color: #dddddd;
22           }
23        </style>
24     </head>
25
26     <body>
27        <table>
28           <tr>
29              <td style = "width: 160px; text-align: center">
30                 <img src = "images/logotiny.png"
31                    width = "140" height = "93"
32                    alt = "Deitel & Associates, Inc. Logo" />
```

Fig. 25.19 JSP `includeDirective.jsp` demonstrates including content at translation-time with directive `include`. (Part 1 of 2.)

```
33                </td>
34
35                <td>
36
37                    <%-- include banner.html in this JSP --%>
38                    <%@ include file = "banner.html" %>
39
40                </td>
41            </tr>
42
43            <tr>
44                <td style = "width: 160px">
45
46                    <%-- include toc.html in this JSP --%>
47                    <%@ include file = "toc.html" %>
48
49                </td>
50
51                <td style = "vertical-align: top">
52
53                    <%-- include clock2.jsp in this JSP --%>
54                    <%@ include file = "clock2.jsp" %>
55
56                </td>
57            </tr>
58        </table>
59    </body>
60 </html>
```

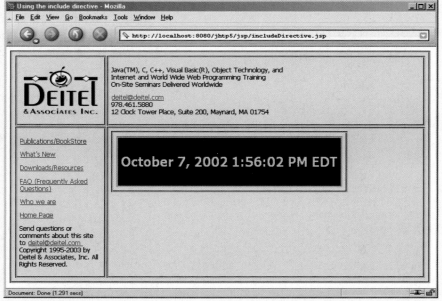

Fig. 25.19 JSP `includeDirective.jsp` demonstrates including content at translation-time with directive `include`. (Part 2 of 2.)

25.8 Case Study: Guest Book

Our next example is a guest book that enables users to place their first name, last name and e-mail address into a guest-book database. After submitting their information, users see a Web page containing all the users in the guest book. Each person's e-mail address is displayed as a hyperlink that allows the user to send an e-mail message to the person. The example demonstrates action <jsp:setProperty>, the JSP page directive, JSP error pages, and the use of JDBC.

The guest book example consists of JavaBeans GuestBean (Fig. 25.20) and Guest-DataBean (Fig. 25.21), and JSPs guestBookLogin.jsp (Fig. 25.22), guestBook-View.jsp (Fig. 25.23) and guestBookErrorPage.jsp (Fig. 25.24). Sample outputs from this example are shown in Fig. 25.25. JavaBean GuestBean (Fig. 25.20) defines three guest properties: firstName, lastName and email. Each is a read/write property with *set* and *get* methods to manipulate the property.

```java
1  // Fig. 25.20: GuestBean.java
2  // JavaBean to store data for a guest in the guest book.
3  package com.deitel.jhtp5.jsp.beans;
4
5  public class GuestBean {
6     private String firstName, lastName, email;
7
8     // set the guest's first name
9     public void setFirstName( String name )
10    {
11       firstName = name;
12    }
13
14    // get the guest's first name
15    public String getFirstName()
16    {
17       return firstName;
18    }
19
20    // set the guest's last name
21    public void setLastName( String name )
22    {
23       lastName = name;
24    }
25
26    // get the guest's last name
27    public String getLastName()
28    {
29       return lastName;
30    }
31
32    // set the guest's email address
33    public void setEmail( String address )
34    {
35       email = address;
36    }
```

Fig. 25.20   GuestBean stores information for one guest. (Part 1 of 2.)

```
37
38       // get the guest's email address
39       public String getEmail()
40       {
41          return email;
42       }
43    }
```

Fig. 25.20 GuestBean stores information for one guest. (Part 2 of 2.)

JavaBean `GuestDataBean` (Fig. 25.21) connects to the `guestbook` database and provides methods `getGuestList` and `addGuest` to manipulate the database. The guest-book database has a single table (`guests`) containing three columns (`firstName`, `last-Name` and `email`). We provide an SQL script (`guestbook.sql`) with this example that can be used with the Cloudscape DBMS to create the `guestbook` database. For further details on creating a database with Cloudscape, refer back to Chapter 23.

```
1    // Fig. 25.21: GuestDataBean.java
2    // Class GuestDataBean makes a database connection and supports
3    // inserting and retrieving data from the database.
4    package com.deitel.jhtp5.jsp.beans;
5
6    // Java core packages
7    import java.io.*;
8    import java.sql.*;
9    import java.util.*;
10
11   public class GuestDataBean {
12      private Connection connection;
13      private PreparedStatement addRecord, getRecords;
14
15      // construct TitlesBean object
16      public GuestDataBean() throws Exception
17      {
18         System.setProperty( "db2j.system.home", "C:/Cloudscape_5.0" );
19
20         // load the Cloudscape driver
21         Class.forName( "com.ibm.db2j.jdbc.DB2jDriver" );
22
23         // connect to the database
24         connection = DriverManager.getConnection(
25            "jdbc:db2j:guestbook" );
26
27         statement = connection.createStatement();
28      }
29
30      // return an ArrayList of GuestBeans
31      public ArrayList getGuestList() throws SQLException
32      {
33         ArrayList guestList = new ArrayList();
```

Fig. 25.21 GuestDataBean performs database access on behalf of guestBookLogin.jsp. (Part 1 of 2.)

```
34
35        // obtain list of titles
36        ResultSet results = statement.executeQuery(
37           "SELECT firstName, lastName, email FROM guests" );
38
39        // get row data
40        while ( results.next() ) {
41           GuestBean guest = new GuestBean();
42
43           guest.setFirstName( results.getString( 1 ) );
44           guest.setLastName( results.getString( 2 ) );
45           guest.setEmail( results.getString( 3 ) );
46
47           guestList.add( guest );
48        }
49
50        return guestList;
51     }
52
53     // insert a guest in guestbook database
54     public void addGuest( GuestBean guest ) throws SQLException
55     {
56        statement.executeUpdate( "INSERT INTO guests ( firstName, " +
57           "lastName, email ) VALUES ( '" + guest.getFirstName() + "', '" +
58           guest.getLastName() + "', '" + guest.getEmail() + "' )" );
59     }
60
61     // close statements and terminate database connection
62     protected void finalize()
63     {
64        // attempt to close database connection
65        try {
66           statement.close();
67           connection.close();
68        }
69
70        // process SQLException on close operation
71        catch ( SQLException sqlException ) {
72           sqlException.printStackTrace();
73        }
74     }
75  }
```

Fig. 25.21 `GuestDataBean` performs database access on behalf of
`guestBookLogin.jsp`. (Part 2 of 2.)

`GuestDataBean` method `getGuestList` (lines 31–51) returns an `ArrayList` of `GuestBean` objects representing the guests in the database. Method `getGuestList` creates the `GuestBean` objects from the `ResultSet` returned by `Statement` method `executeQuery` (lines 36–37).

`GuestDataBean` method `addGuest` (lines 54–59) receives a `GuestBean` as an argument and uses the `GuestBean`'s properties as the arguments to `Statement` method `executeUpdate` (lines 56–58). This `Statement` inserts a new guest in the database.

Note that the `GuestDataBean`'s constructor, `getGuestList` and `addGuest` methods do not process potential exceptions. In the constructor, line 21 can throw a `ClassNotFoundException`, and the other statements can throw `SQLExceptions`. Similarly, `SQLExceptions` can be thrown from the bodies of methods `getGuestList` and `addGuest`. In this example, we purposely let any exceptions that occur get passed back to the JSP that invokes the `GuestDataBean`'s constructor or methods. This enables us to demonstrate JSP error pages. When a JSP performs an operation that causes an exception, the JSP can include scriptlets that catch the exception and process it. Exceptions that are not caught can be forwarded to a JSP error page for handling.

JavaServer Page `guestBookLogin.jsp` (Fig. 25.22) is a modified version of `forward1.jsp` (Fig. 25.11) that displays a `form` in which users can enter their first name, last name and e-mail address. When the user submits the `form`, `guestBookLogin.jsp` is requested again, so it can ensure that all the data values were entered. If not, the `guestBookLogin.jsp` responds with the `form` again, so the user can fill in missing field(s). If the user supplies all three pieces of information, `guestBookLogin.jsp` forwards the request to `guestBookView.jsp`, which displays the guest book contents.

```
1    <?xml version = "1.0"?>
2    <!DOCTYPE html PUBLIC "-//W3C//DTD XHTML 1.0 Strict//EN"
3       "http://www.w3.org/TR/xhtml1/DTD/xhtml1-strict.dtd">
4
5    <!-- Fig. 25.22: guestBookLogin.jsp -->
6
7    <%-- page settings --%>
8    <%@ page errorPage = "guestBookErrorPage.jsp" %>
9
10   <%-- beans used in this JSP --%>
11   <jsp:useBean id = "guest" scope = "page"
12      class = "com.deitel.jhtp5.jsp.beans.GuestBean" />
13   <jsp:useBean id = "guestData" scope = "request"
14      class = "com.deitel.jhtp5.jsp.beans.GuestDataBean" />
15
16   <html xmlns = "http://www.w3.org/1999/xhtml">
17
18   <head>
19      <title>Guest Book Login</title>
20
21      <style type = "text/css">
22         body {
23            font-family: tahoma, helvetica, arial, sans-serif;
24         }
25
26         table, tr, td {
27            font-size: .9em;
28            border: 3px groove;
29            padding: 5px;
30            background-color: #dddddd;
31         }
```

Fig. 25.22   JavaServer page `guestBookLogin.jsp` enables the user to submit a first name, a last name and an e-mail address to be placed in the guest book. (Part 1 of 3.)

```
32        </style>
33    </head>
34
35    <body>
36        <jsp:setProperty name = "guest" property = "*" />
37
38        <% // start scriptlet
39
40           if ( guest.getFirstName() == null ||
41                guest.getLastName() == null ||
42                guest.getEmail() == null ) {
43
44        %> <%-- end scriptlet to insert fixed template data --%>
45
46              <form method = "post" action = "guestBookLogin.jsp">
47                 <p>Enter your first name, last name and email
48                    address to register in our guest book.</p>
49
50                 <table>
51                    <tr>
52                       <td>First name</td>
53
54                       <td>
55                          <input type = "text" name = "firstName" />
56                       </td>
57                    </tr>
58
59                    <tr>
60                       <td>Last name</td>
61
62                       <td>
63                          <input type = "text" name = "lastName" />
64                       </td>
65                    </tr>
66
67                    <tr>
68                       <td>Email</td>
69
70                       <td>
71                          <input type = "text" name = "email" />
72                       </td>
73                    </tr>
74
75                    <tr>
76                       <td colspan = "2">
77                          <input type = "submit"
78                             value = "Submit" />
79                       </td>
80                    </tr>
81                 </table>
82              </form>
```

Fig. 25.22 JavaServer page `guestBookLogin.jsp` enables the user to submit a first name, a last name and an e-mail address to be placed in the guest book. (Part 2 of 3.)

```
83
84      <% // continue scriptlet
85
86         }  // end if
87         else {
88             guestData.addGuest( guest );
89
90      %> <%-- end scriptlet to insert jsp:forward action --%>
91
92             <%-- forward to display guest book contents --%>
93             <jsp:forward page = "guestBookView.jsp" />
94
95      <% // continue scriptlet
96
97         }  // end else
98
99      %> <%-- end scriptlet --%>
100  </body>
101
102  </html>
```

Fig. 25.22   JavaServer page `guestBookLogin.jsp` enables the user to submit a first
              name, a last name and an e-mail address to be placed in the guest book.
              (Part 3 of 3.)

Line 8 of `guestBookLogin.jsp` uses the *page directive*, which defines information
that is globally available in a JSP. Directives are delimited by *<%@* and *%>*. In this case, the
page directive's *errorPage attribute* is set to `guestBookErrorPage.jsp` (Fig. 25.24),
indicating that all uncaught exceptions are forwarded to `guestBookErrorPage.jsp` for
processing.

Lines 11–14 define two `<jsp:useBean>` actions. Lines 11–12 create an instance of
`GuestBean` called `guest`. This bean has `page` scope—it exists for use only in this page.
Lines 13–14 create an instance of `GuestDataBean` called `guestData`. This bean has
`request` scope—it exists for use in this page and any other page that helps process a single
client request. Thus, when `guestBookLogin.jsp` forwards a request to `guestBook-
View.jsp`, the same `GuestDataBean` instance is still available for use in `guestBook-
View.jsp`.

Line 36 demonstrates setting properties of the `GuestBean` called `guest` with request
parameter values. The `input` elements on lines 55, 63 and 71 have the same names as the
`GuestBean` properties. So, we use action `<jsp:setProperty>`'s ability to match request
parameters to properties by specifying `"*"` for attribute `property`. Line 36 also can set the
properties individually with the following lines:

```
<jsp:setProperty name = "guest" property = "firstName"
   param = "firstName" />

<jsp:setProperty name = "guest" property = "lastName"
   param = "lastName" />

<jsp:setProperty name = "guest" property = "email"
   param = "email" />
```

If the request parameters had names that differed from GuestBean's properties, the param attribute in each of the preceding <jsp:setProperty> actions could be changed to the appropriate request parameter name.

JavaServer Page guestBookView.jsp (Fig. 25.23) outputs an XHTML document containing the guest-book entries in tabular format. Lines 8–10 define three page directives. Line 8 specifies that the error page for this JSP is guestBookErrorPage.jsp. Line 9 indicates that classes from package java.util are used in this JSP, and line 10 indicates that classes from our package com.deitel.advjhtp1.jsp.beans also are used.

Lines 13–14 specify a <jsp:useBean> action that declares a reference to a GuestDataBean object. If a GuestDataBean object already exists, the action returns a reference to the existing object. Otherwise, the action creates a GuestDataBean for use in this JSP. Lines 50–59 define a scriptlet that gets the guest list from the GuestDataBean and begin a loop to output the entries. Lines 61–70 combine fixed template text with JSP expressions to create rows in the table of guest book data that will be displayed on the client. The scriptlet at lines 72–76 terminates the loop.

```
1   <?xml version = "1.0"?>
2   <!DOCTYPE html PUBLIC "-//W3C//DTD XHTML 1.0 Strict//EN"
3      "http://www.w3.org/TR/xhtml1/DTD/xhtml1-strict.dtd">
4
5   <!-- Fig. 25.23: guestBookView.jsp -->
6
7   <%-- page settings --%>
8   <%@ page errorPage = "guestBookErrorPage.jsp" %>
9   <%@ page import = "java.util.*" %>
10  <%@ page import = "com.deitel.jhtp5.jsp.beans.*" %>
11
12  <%-- GuestDataBean to obtain guest list --%>
13  <jsp:useBean id = "guestData" scope = "request"
14     class = "com.deitel.jhtp5.jsp.beans.GuestDataBean" />
15
16  <html xmlns = "http://www.w3.org/1999/xhtml">
17
18     <head>
19        <title>Guest List</title>
20
21        <style type = "text/css">
22           body {
23              font-family: tahoma, helvetica, arial, sans-serif;
24           }
25
26           table, tr, td, th {
27              text-align: center;
28              font-size: .9em;
29              border: 3px groove;
30              padding: 5px;
```

Fig. 25.23   JavaServer page guestBookView.jsp displays the contents of the guest book. (Part 1 of 2.)

```
31                   background-color: #dddddd;
32               }
33           </style>
34       </head>
35
36       <body>
37           <p style = "font-size: 2em;">Guest List</p>
38
39           <table>
40               <thead>
41                   <tr>
42                       <th style = "width: 100px;">Last name</th>
43                       <th style = "width: 100px;">First name</th>
44                       <th style = "width: 200px;">Email</th>
45                   </tr>
46               </thead>
47
48               <tbody>
49
50                   <% // start scriptlet
51
52                       List guestList = guestData.getGuestList();
53                       Iterator guestListIterator = guestList.iterator();
54                       GuestBean guest;
55
56                       while ( guestListIterator.hasNext() ) {
57                           guest = ( GuestBean ) guestListIterator.next();
58
59                   %> <%-- end scriptlet; insert fixed template data --%>
60
61                       <tr>
62                           <td><%= guest.getLastName() %></td>
63
64                           <td><%= guest.getFirstName() %></td>
65
66                           <td>
67                               <a href = "mailto:<%= guest.getEmail() %>">
68                                   <%= guest.getEmail() %></a>
69                           </td>
70                       </tr>
71
72                   <% // continue scriptlet
73
74                       } // end while
75
76                   %> <%-- end scriptlet --%>
77
78               </tbody>
79           </table>
80       </body>
81
82   </html>
```

Fig. 25.23   JavaServer page guestBookView.jsp displays the contents of the guest book. (Part 2 of 2.)

JavaServer Page `guestBookErrorPage.jsp` (Fig. 25.24) outputs an XHTML document containing an error message based on the type of exception that causes this error page to be invoked. Lines 8–10 define several `page` directives. Line 8 sets `page` directive attribute *isErrorPage*. Setting this attribute to `true` makes the JSP an error page and enables access to the JSP implicit object `exception` that refers to an exception object indicating the problem that occurred.

Common Programming Error 25.10

JSP implicit object **exception** *can be used only in error pages. Using this object in other JSPs results in a translation-time error.*

Lines 29–46 define scriptlets that determine the type of exception that occurred and begin outputting an appropriate error message with fixed template data. The actual error message from the exception is output at line 56.

```
1   <?xml version = "1.0"?>
2   <!DOCTYPE html PUBLIC "-//W3C//DTD XHTML 1.0 Strict//EN"
3      "http://www.w3.org/TR/xhtml1/DTD/xhtml1-strict.dtd">
4
5   <!-- Fig. 25.24: guestBookErrorPage.jsp -->
6
7   <%-- page settings --%>
8   <%@ page isErrorPage = "true" %>
9   <%@ page import = "java.util.*" %>
10  <%@ page import = "java.sql.*" %>
11
12  <html xmlns = "http://www.w3.org/1999/xhtml">
13
14     <head>
15        <title>Error!</title>
16
17        <style type = "text/css">
18           .bigRed {
19              font-size: 2em;
20              color: red;
21              font-weight: bold;
22           }
23        </style>
24     </head>
25
26     <body>
27        <p class = "bigRed">
28
29           <% // scriptlet to determine exception type
30              // and output beginning of error message
31              if ( exception instanceof SQLException )
32           %>
33
34              An SQLException
35
```

Fig. 25.24   JavaServer page `guestBookErrorPage.jsp` responds to exceptions in `guestBookLogin.jsp` and `guestBookView.jsp`. (Part 1 of 2.)

```
36        <%
37            else if ( exception instanceof ClassNotFoundException )
38        %>
39
40                A ClassNotFoundException
41
42        <%
43            else
44        %>
45
46                An exception
47
48        <%-- end scriptlet to insert fixed template data --%>
49
50            <%-- continue error message output --%>
51            occurred while interacting with the guestbook database.
52        </p>
53
54        <p class = "bigRed">
55            The error message was:<br />
56            <%= exception.getMessage() %>
57        </p>
58
59        <p class = "bigRed">Please try again later</p>
60    </body>
61
62 </html>
```

Fig. 25.24   JavaServer page `guestBookErrorPage.jsp` responds to exceptions in `guestBookLogin.jsp` and `guestBookView.jsp`. (Part 2 of 2.)

Figure 25.25 shows sample interactions between the user and the JSPs in the guest book example. In the first two rows of output, separate users entered their first name, last name and e-mail. In each case, the current contents of the guest book are returned and displayed for the user. In the final interaction, a third user specified an e-mail address that already existed in the database. The e-mail address is the primary key in the `guests` table of the `guestbook` database, so its values must be unique. Thus, the database prevents the new record from being inserted, and an exception occurs. The exception is forwarded to `guestBookErrorPage.jsp` for processing, which results in the last screen capture.

To test the guest book in Tomcat, copy `guestBookLogin.jsp`, `guestBook-View.jsp` and `guestBookErrorPage.jsp` into the `jsp` directory created in Section 25.3. Copy `GuestBean.class` and `GuestDataBean.class` into the `jhtp5` Web application's `WEB-INF\classes` directory in Tomcat. [*Note:* This example will work only if the proper package directory structure for `GuestBean` and `GuestDataBean` is defined in the `classes` directory. These classes are defined in package `com.deitel.jhtp5.jsp.beans`.] Create the database by running the **guestbook.sql** script. Open your Web browser and enter the following URL to test `guestBook-Login.jsp`:

```
http://localhost:8080/jhtp5/jsp/guestBookLogin.jsp
```

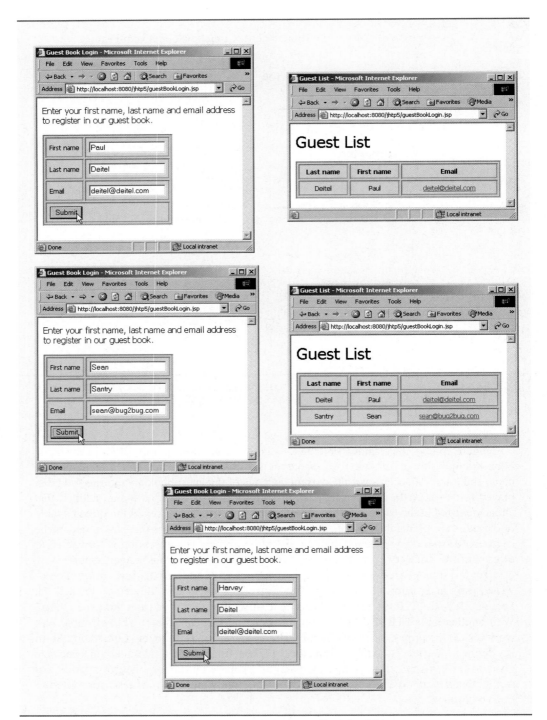

Fig. 25.25 JSP guest book sample output windows (Part 1 of 2.).

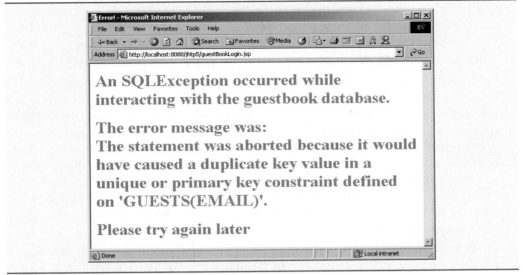

Fig. 25.25 JSP guest book sample output windows (Part 2 of 2.).

25.9 Internet and World Wide Web Resources

`java.sun.com/products/jsp`
The home page for information about JavaServer Pages at the Sun Microsystems Java site.

`java.sun.com/products/servlet`
The home page for information about servlets at the Sun Microsystems Java site.

`java.sun.com/j2ee`
The home page for the Java 2 Enterprise Edition at the Sun Microsystems Java site.

`www.w3.org`
The World Wide Web Consortium home page. This site provides information about current and developing Internet and Web standards, such as XHTML, XML and CSS.

`jsptags.com`
This site includes tutorials, tag libraries, software and other resources for JSP programmers.

`jspinsider.com`
This Web programming site concentrates on resources for JSP programmers. It includes software, tutorials, articles, sample code, references and links to other JSP and Web programming resources.

SUMMARY

- JavaServer Pages (JSPs) are an extension of servlet technology.
- JavaServer Pages enable Web application programmers to create dynamic content by reusing predefined components and by interacting with components using server-side scripting.
- JSP programmers can create custom tag libraries that enable Web-page designers who are not familiar with Java programming to enhance their Web pages with powerful dynamic content and processing capabilities.
- Classes and interfaces specific to JavaServer Pages programming are located in packages `javax.servlet.jsp` and `javax.servlet.jsp.tagext`.

- The JavaServer Pages 1.1 specification can be downloaded from `java.sun.com/products/jsp/download.html`.
- There are four key components to JSPs—directives, actions, scriptlets and tag libraries.
- Directives specify global information that is not associated with a particular JSP request.
- Actions encapsulate functionality in predefined tags that programmers can embed in a JSP.
- Scriptlets, or scripting elements, enable programmers to insert Java code that interacts with components in a JSP (and possibly other Web application components) to perform request processing.
- Tag libraries are part of the tag extension mechanism that enables programmers to create new tags that encapsulate complex Java functionality.
- JSPs normally include XHTML or XML markup. Such markup is known as fixed template data or fixed template text.
- Programmers tend to use JSPs when most of the content sent to the client is fixed template data and only a small portion of the content is generated dynamically with Java code.
- Programmers use servlets when a small portion of the content is fixed template data.
- JSPs normally execute as part of a Web server. The server often is referred to as the JSP container.
- When a JSP-enabled server receives the first request for a JSP, the JSP container translates that JSP into a Java servlet that handles the current request and future requests to the JSP.
- The JSP container places the Java statements that implement a JSP's response in method `_jspService` at translation time.
- The request/response mechanism and life cycle of a JSP are the same as those of a servlet.
- JSPs can define methods `jspInit` and `jspDestroy` that are invoked when the container initializes a JSP and when the container terminates a JSP, respectively.
- JSP expressions are delimited by <%= and %>. Such expressions are converted to `Strings` by the JSP container and are output as part of the response.
- The XHTML `meta` element can set a refresh interval for a document that is loaded into a browser. This causes the browser to request the document repeatedly at the specified interval in seconds.
- When you first invoke a JSP in Tomcat, there is a delay as Tomcat translates the JSP into a servlet and invokes the servlet to respond to your request.
- Implicit objects provide programmers with servlet capabilities in the context of a JavaServer Page.
- Implicit objects have four scopes—application, page, request and session.
- Objects with application scope are part of the JSP and servlet container application. Objects with page scope exist only as part of the page in which they are used. Each page has its own instances of the page-scope implicit objects. Objects in request scope exist for the duration of the request. Request-scope objects go out of scope when request processing completes with a response to the client. Objects in session scope exist for the client's entire browsing session.
- JSP scripting components include scriptlets, comments, expressions, declarations and escape sequences.
- Scriptlets are blocks of code delimited by <% and %>. They contain Java statements that are placed in method `_jspService` when the container translates a JSP into a servlet.
- JSP comments are delimited by <%-- and --%>. XHTML comments are delimited by <!-- and -->. Java's end-of-line comments (//) and traditional comments (delimited by /* and */) can be used inside scriptlets.
- JSP comments and scripting language comments are ignored and do not appear in the response.

- A JSP expression, delimited by <%= and %>, contains a Java expression that is evaluated when a client requests the JSP containing the expression. The container converts the result of a JSP expression to a `String` object, then outputs the `String` as part of the response to the client.

- Declarations, delimited by <%! and %>, enable a JSP programmer to define variables and methods. Variables become instance variables of the class that represents the translated JSP. Similarly, methods become members of the class that represents the translated JSP.

- Special characters or character sequences that the JSP container normally uses to delimit JSP code can be included in a JSP as literal characters in scripting elements, fixed template data and attribute values by using escape sequences.

- JSP standard actions provide JSP implementors with access to several of the most common tasks performed in a JSP. JSP containers process actions at request time.

- JavaServer Pages support two include mechanisms—the `<jsp:include>` action and the `include` directive.

- Action `<jsp:include>` enables dynamic content to be included in a JavaServer Page. If the included resource changes between requests, the next request to the JSP containing the `<jsp:include>` action includes the new content of the resource.

- The `include` directive is processed once, at JSP translation time, and causes the content to be copied into the JSP. If the included resource changes, the new content will not be reflected in the JSP that used the include directive unless that JSP is recompiled.

- Action `<jsp:forward>` enables a JSP to forward the processing of a request to a different resource. Processing of the request by the original JSP terminates as soon as the request is forwarded.

- Action `<jsp:param>` specifies name/value pairs of information that are passed to the `include`, `forward` and `plugin` actions. Every `<jsp:param>` action has two required attributes—`name` and `value`. If a `param` action specifies a parameter that already exists in the request, the new value for the parameter takes precedence over the original value. All values for that parameter can be obtained with the JSP implicit object `request`'s `getParameterValues` method, which returns an array of `Strings`.

- Action `<jsp:useBean>` enables a JSP to manipulate a Java object. This action can be used to create a Java object for use in the JSP or to locate an existing object.

- Like JSP implicit objects, objects specified with action `<jsp:useBean>` have `page`, `request`, `session` or `application` scope that indicates where they can be used in a Web application.

- Action `<jsp:getProperty>` obtains the value of a JavaBean's property. Action `<jsp:getProperty>` has two attributes—`name` and `property`—that specify the bean object to manipulate and the property to get.

- JavaBean property values can be set with action `<jsp:setProperty>`, which is particularly useful for mapping request parameter values to JavaBean properties. Request parameters can be used to set properties of primitive types `boolean`, `byte`, `char`, `int`, `long`, `float` and `double` and java.lang types `String`, `Boolean`, `Byte`, `Character`, `Integer`, `Long`, `Float` and `Double`.

- The `page` directive defines information that is globally available in a JSP. Directives are delimited by <%@ and %>. The `page` directive's `errorPage` attribute indicates where all uncaught exceptions are forwarded for processing.

- Action `<jsp:setProperty>` has the ability to match request parameters to properties of the same name in a bean by specifying "*" for attribute `property`.

- Attribute `import` of the `page` directive enables programmers to specify Java classes and packages that are used in the context of a JSP.

- If the attribute `isErrorPage` of the `page` directive is set to `true`, the JSP is an error page. This condition enables access to the JSP implicit object `exception` that refers to an exception object indicating the problem that occurred.

- Directives are messages to the JSP container that enable the programmer to specify page settings (such as the error page), to include content from other resources and to specify custom tag libraries that can be used in a JSP. Directives are processed at the time a JSP is translated into a servlet and compiled. Thus, directives do not produce any immediate output.

- The `page` directive specifies global settings for a JSP in the JSP container. There can be many `page` directives, provided that there is only one occurrence of each attribute. The exception to this rule is the `import` attribute, which can be used repeatedly to import Java packages.

TERMINOLOGY

%\> escape sequence for %>
<!-- and --> XHTML comment delimiters
<%-- and --%> JSP comment delimiters
<% and %> scriptlet delimiters
<%! and %> declaration delimiters
<%= and %> JSP expression delimiters
<%@ and %> directive delimiters
<\% escape sequence for <%
action
`autoFlush` attribute of `page` directive
`beanName` attribute of `<jsp:useBean>` action
`buffer` attribute of `page` directive
`class` attribute of `<jsp:useBean>` action
client-server networking
comment
`config` implicit object
container
`contentType` attribute of `page` directive
declaration
directive
dynamic content
error page
`errorPage` attribute of `page` directive
escape sequence
expression
`extends` attribute of `page` directive
`file` attribute of `include` directive
fixed template data
fixed template text
`flush` attribute of `<jsp:include>` action
forward a request
`getParameterValues` method of
    `request` object
`id` attribute of `<jsp:useBean>` action
implicit object
implicit object scopes
`import` attribute of `page` directive

include a resource
`include` directive
`info` attribute of `page` directive
`isErrorPage` attribute of `page` directive
`isThreadSafe` attribute of `page` directive
JavaServer Pages (JSPs)
JavaServer Pages 1.1 specification
`javax.servlet.jsp` package
`javax.servlet.jsp.tagext` package
`<jsp:forward>` action
`<jsp:getProperty>` action
`<jsp:include>` action
`<jsp:param>` action
`<jsp:setProperty>` action
`<jsp:useBean>` action
`jspDestroy` method
`jspInit` method
`_jspService` method
`JspWriter` (package `javax.servlet.jsp`)
`language` attribute of `page` directive
match request parameters
`meta` element
`name` attribute of `<jsp:param>`
`name` attribute of `<jsp:setProperty>`
name/value pair
`out` implicit object
`page` attribute of `<jsp:forward>`
`page` attribute of `<jsp:include>`
`page` directive
`page` implicit object
page scope
`param` attribute of `<jsp:setProperty>`
`prefix` attribute of `taglib` directive
`property` attribute of `<jsp:setProperty>`
refresh interval
`request` implicit object
request scope

request-time error
`response` implicit object
`scope` attribute of `<jsp:useBean>`
scope of a bean
scripting element
scriptlet
specify attributes of a custom tag

standard actions
translation-time error
translation-time include
`type` attribute of `<jsp:plugin>`
`type` attribute of `<jsp:useBean>`
`value` attribute of `<jsp:param>`
`value` attribute of `<jsp:setProperty>`

SELF-REVIEW EXERCISES

25.1 Fill in the blanks in each of the following statements:
   a) Action _____ has the ability to match request parameters to properties of the same name in a bean by specifying "*" for attribute `property`.
   b) There are four key components to JSPs: _____, _____, _____ and _____.
   c) The implicit objects have four scopes: _____, _____, _____ and _____.
   d) The _____ directive is processed once, at JSP translation time and causes content to be copied into the JSP.
   e) Classes and interfaces specific to JavaServer Pages programming are located in packages _____ and _____.
   f) JSPs normally execute as part of a Web server that is referred to as the _____.
   g) JSP scripting components include _____, _____, _____, _____ and _____.

25.2 State whether each of the following is *true* or *false*. If *false*, explain why.
   a) An object in page scope exists in every JSP of a particular Web application.
   b) Directives specify global information that is not associated with a particular JSP request.
   c) Action `<jsp:include>` is evaluated once at page translation time.
   d) Like XHTML comments, JSP comments and script language comments appear in the response to the client.
   e) Objects in application scope are part of a particular Web application.
   f) Each page has its own instances of the page-scope implicit objects.
   g) Action `<jsp:setProperty>` has the ability to match request parameters to properties of the same name in a bean by specifying "*" for attribute `property`.
   h) Objects in session scope exist for the client's entire browsing session.

ANSWERS TO SELF-REVIEW EXERCISES

25.1   a) `<jsp:setProperty>`. b) directives, actions, scriptlets, tag libraries. c) application, page, request and session. d) `include`. e) `javax.servlet.jsp`, `javax.servlet.jsp.tagext`. f) JSP container. g) scriptlets, comments, expressions, declarations, escape sequences.

25.2   a) False. Objects in page scope exist only as part of the page in which they are used. b) True. c) False. Action `<jsp:include>` enables dynamic content to be included in a JavaServer Page. d) False. JSP comments and script language comments are ignored and do not appear in the response. e) False. Objects in application scope are part of the JSP container application. f) True. g) True. h) True.

EXERCISES

25.3   Write a JSP page to output the string "Hello world!" ten times.

25.4   Modify Exercise 24.4 to run as a JSP page.

25.5   Rewrite Figure 25.15 to allow users to select the image. Use a JSP expression instead of the getProperty JSP tag.

25.6   Create a JSP and JDBC-based address book. Use the guest book example of Fig. 25.20 through Fig. 25.24 as a guide. Your address book should allow one to insert entries, delete entries and search for entries.

25.7   Reimplement the Web application of Fig. 24.20 (favorite animal survey) using JSPs.

25.8   Modify your solution to Exercise 25.7 to allow the user to see the survey results without responding to the survey.

Operator Precedence Chart

Operators are shown in decreasing order of precedence from top to bottom.

Operator	Description	Associativity
++ --	unary postincrement unary postdecrement	right to left
++ -- + - ! ~ (*type*)	unary preincrement unary predecrement unary plus unary minus unary logical negation unary bitwise complement unary cast	right to left
* / %	multiplication division remainder	left to right
+ -	addition or string concatenation subtraction	left to right
<< >> >>>	left shift signed right shift unsigned right shift	left to right
< <= > >= instanceof	less than less than or equal to greater than greater than or equal to type comparison	left to right

Fig. A.1 Operator precedence chart. (Part 1 of 2.)

Operator	Description	Associativity
==	is equal to	left to right
!=	is not equal to	
&	bitwise AND	left to right
	boolean logical AND	
^	bitwise exclusive OR	left to right
	boolean logical exclusive OR	
|	bitwise inclusive OR	left to right
	boolean logical inclusive OR	
&&	conditional AND	left to right
||	conditional OR	left to right
?:	conditional	right to left
=	assignment	right to left
+=	addition assignment	
-=	subtraction assignment	
*=	multiplication assignment	
/=	division assignment	
%=	remainder assignment	
&=	bitwise AND assignment	
^=	bitwise exclusive OR assignment	
|=	bitwise inclusive OR assignment	
<<=	bitwise left shift assignment	
>>=	bitwise signed-right-shift assignment	
>>>=	bitwise unsigned-right-shift assignment	

Fig. A.1   Operator precedence chart. (Part 2 of 2.)

ASCII Character Set

	0	1	2	3	4	5	6	7	8	9
0	nul	soh	stx	etx	eot	enq	ack	bel	bs	ht
1	nl	vt	ff	cr	so	si	dle	dc1	dc2	dc3
2	dc4	nak	syn	etb	can	em	sub	esc	fs	gs
3	rs	us	sp	!	"	#	$	%	&	'
4	(	)	*	+	,	-	.	/	0	1
5	2	3	4	5	6	7	8	9	:	;
6	<	=	>	?	@	A	B	C	D	E
7	F	G	H	I	J	K	L	M	N	O
8	P	Q	R	S	T	U	V	W	X	Y
9	Z	[	\	]	^	_	'	a	b	c
10	d	e	f	g	h	i	j	k	l	m
11	n	o	p	q	r	s	t	u	v	w
12	x	y	z	{	|	}	~	del		

Fig. B.1   ASCII character set.

The digits at the left of the table are the left digits of the decimal equivalent (0-127) of the character code, and the digits at the top of the table are the right digits of the character code. For example, the character code for "F" is 70, and the character code for "&" is 38.

Most users of this book are interested in the ASCII character set used to represent English characters on many computers. The ASCII character set is a subset of the Unicode character set used by Java to represent characters from most of the world's languages. For more information on the Unicode character set, see Appendix G.

Number Systems

Objectives

- To understand basic number systems concepts such as base, positional value and symbol value.
- To understand how to work with numbers represented in the binary, octal, and hexadecimal number systems
- To be able to abbreviate binary numbers as octal numbers or hexadecimal numbers.
- To be able to convert octal numbers and hexadecimal numbers to binary numbers.
- To be able to covert back and forth between decimal numbers and their binary, octal, and hexadecimal equivalents.
- To understand binary arithmetic and how negative binary numbers are represented using two's complement notation.

Here are only numbers ratified.
William Shakespeare

Nature has some sort of arithmetic-geometrical coordinate system, because nature has all kinds of models. What we experience of nature is in models, and all of nature's models are so beautiful.
It struck me that nature's system must be a real beauty, because in chemistry we find that the associations are always in beautiful whole numbers—there are no fractions.
Richard Buckminster Fuller

Outline

C.1 Introduction

In this appendix, we introduce the key number systems that Java programmers use, especially when they are working on software projects that require close interaction with "machine-level" hardware. Projects like this include operating systems, computer networking software, compilers, database systems and applications requiring high performance.

When we write an integer such as 227 or –63 in a Java program, the number is assumed to be in the decimal (base 10) number system. The digits in the decimal number system are 0, 1, 2, 3, 4, 5, 6, 7, 8 and 9. The lowest digit is 0 and the highest digit is 9—one less than the base of 10. Internally, computers use the binary (base 2) number system. The binary number system has only two digits, namely 0 and 1. Its lowest digit is 0 and its highest digit is 1—one less than the base of 2.

As we will see, binary numbers tend to be much longer than their decimal equivalents. Programmers who work in assembly languages and in high-level languages like Java that enable programmers to reach down to the "machine level," find it cumbersome to work with binary numbers. So two other number systems the octal number system (base 8) and the hexadecimal number system (base 16)—are popular primarily because they make it convenient to abbreviate binary numbers.

In the octal number system, the digits range from 0 to 7. Because both the binary number system and the octal number system have fewer digits than the decimal number system, their digits are the same as the corresponding digits in decimal.

The hexadecimal number system poses a problem because it requires sixteen digits—a lowest digit of 0 and a highest digit with a value equivalent to decimal 15 (one less than the base of 16). By convention, we use the letters A through F to represent the hexadecimal digits corresponding to decimal values 10 through 15. Thus in hexadecimal we can have numbers like 876 consisting solely of decimal-like digits, numbers like 8A55F consisting of digits and letters and numbers like FFE consisting solely of letters. Occasionally, a hexadecimal number spells a common word such as FACE or FEED—this can appear strange to programmers accustomed to working with numbers. The digits of the binary, octal, decimal and hexadecimal number systems are summarized in Fig. C.1–Fig. C.2.

Each of these number systems uses positional notation—each position in which a digit is written has a different positional value. For example, in the decimal number 937 (the 9, the 3 and the 7 are referred to as symbol values), we say that the 7 is written in the ones position, the 3 is written in the tens position and the 9 is written in the hundreds position. Notice that each of these positions is a power of the base (base 10) and that these powers begin at 0 and increase by 1 as we move left in the number (Fig. C.3).

Binary digit	Octal digit	Decimal digit	Hexadecimal digit
0	0	0	0
1	1	1	1
	2	2	2
	3	3	3
	4	4	4
	5	5	5
	6	6	6
	7	7	7
		8	8
		9	9
			A (decimal value of 10)
			B (decimal value of 11)
			C (decimal value of 12)
			D (decimal value of 13)
			E (decimal value of 14)
			F (decimal value of 15)

Fig. C.1   Digits of the binary, octal, decimal and hexadecimal number systems.

Attribute	Binary	Octal	Decimal	Hexadecimal
Base	2	8	10	16
Lowest digit	0	0	0	0
Highest digit	1	7	9	F

Fig. C.2   Comparing the binary, octal, decimal and hexadecimal number systems.

Positional values in the decimal number system			
Decimal digit	9	3	7
Position name	Hundreds	Tens	Ones
Positional value	100	10	1
Positional value as a power of the base (10)	10^2	10^1	10^0

Fig. C.3   Positional values in the decimal number system.

For longer decimal numbers, the next positions to the left would be the thousands position (10 to the 3rd power), the ten-thousands position (10 to the 4th power), the hundred-thousands position (10 to the 5th power), the millions position (10 to the 6th power), the ten-millions position (10 to the 7th power) and so on.

In the binary number 101, we say that the rightmost 1 is written in the ones position, the 0 is written in the twos position and the leftmost 1 is written in the fours position. Notice that each of these positions is a power of the base (base 2) and that these powers begin at 0 and increase by 1 as we move left in the number (Fig. C.4).

For longer binary numbers, the next positions to the left would be the eights position (2 to the 3rd power), the sixteens position (2 to the 4th power), the thirty-twos position (2 to the 5th power), the sixty-fours position (2 to the 6th power) and so on.

In the octal number 425, we say that the 5 is written in the ones position, the 2 is written in the eights position and the 4 is written in the sixty-fours position. Notice that each of these positions is a power of the base (base 8) and that these powers begin at 0 and increase by 1 as we move left in the number (Fig. C.5).

For longer octal numbers, the next positions to the left would be the five-hundred-and-twelves position (8 to the 3rd power), the four-thousand-and-ninety-sixes position (8 to the 4th power), the thirty-two-thousand-seven-hundred-and-sixty eights position (8 to the 5th power) and so on.

In the hexadecimal number 3DA, we say that the A is written in the ones position, the D is written in the sixteens position and the 3 is written in the two-hundred-and-fifty-sixes position. Notice that each of these positions is a power of the base (base 16) and that these powers begin at 0 and increase by 1 as we move left in the number (Fig. C.6).

Positional values in the binary number system			
Binary digit	1	0	1
Position name	Fours	Twos	Ones
Positional value	4	2	1
Positional value as a power of the base (2)	2^2	2^1	2^0

Fig. C.4   Positional values in the binary number system.

Positional values in the octal number system			
Decimal digit	4	2	5
Position name	Sixty-fours	Eights	Ones
Positional value	64	8	1
Positional value as a power of the base (8)	8^2	8^1	8^0

Fig. C.5   Positional values in the octal number system.

Positional values in the hexadecimal number system			
Decimal digit	3	D	A
Position name	Two-hundred-and-fifty-sixes	Sixteens	Ones
Positional value	256	16	1
Positional value as a power of the base (16)	16^2	16^1	16^0

Fig. C.6   Positional values in the hexadecimal number system.

For longer hexadecimal numbers, the next positions to the left would be the four-thousand-and-ninety-sixes position (16 to the 3rd power), the sixty-five-thousand-five-hundred-and-thirty-six position (16 to the 4th power) and so on.

C.2 Abbreviating Binary Numbers as Octal Numbers and Hexadecimal Numbers

The main use for octal and hexadecimal numbers in computing is for abbreviating lengthy binary representations. Figure C.7 highlights the fact that lengthy binary numbers can be expressed concisely in number systems with higher bases than the binary number system.

Decimal number	Binary representation	Octal representation	Hexadecimal representation
0	0	0	0
1	1	1	1
2	10	2	2
3	11	3	3
4	100	4	4
5	101	5	5
6	110	6	6
7	111	7	7
8	1000	10	8
9	1001	11	9
10	1010	12	A
11	1011	13	B
12	1100	14	C
13	1101	15	D
14	1110	16	E
15	1111	17	F
16	10000	20	10

Fig. C.7   Decimal, binary, octal and hexadecimal equivalents.

A particularly important relationship that both the octal number system and the hexa-decimal number system have to the binary system is that the bases of octal and hexadecimal (8 and 16 respectively) are powers of the base of the binary number system (base 2). Consider the following 12-digit binary number and its octal and hexadecimal equivalents. See if you can determine how this relationship makes it convenient to abbreviate binary numbers in octal or hexadecimal. The answer follows the numbers.

Binary Number	Octal equivalent	Hexadecimal equivalent
100011010001	4321	8D1

To see how the binary number converts easily to octal, simply break the 12-digit binary number into groups of three consecutive bits each and write those groups over the corresponding digits of the octal number as follows

100	011	010	001
4	3	2	1

Notice that the octal digit you have written under each group of thee bits corresponds precisely to the octal equivalent of that 3-digit binary number as shown in Fig. C.7.

The same kind of relationship can be observed in converting from binary to hexadecimal. Break the 12-digit binary number into groups of four consecutive bits each and write those groups over the corresponding digits of the hexadecimal number as follows

1000	1101	0001
8	D	1

Notice that the hexadecimal digit you wrote under each group of four bits corresponds precisely to the hexadecimal equivalent of that 4-digit binary number as shown in Fig. C.7.

C.3 Converting Octal Numbers and Hexadecimal Numbers to Binary Numbers

In the previous section, we saw how to convert binary numbers to their octal and hexadecimal equivalents by forming groups of binary digits and simply rewriting these groups as their equivalent octal digit values or hexadecimal digit values. This process may be used in reverse to produce the binary equivalent of a given octal or hexadecimal number.

For example, the octal number 653 is converted to binary simply by writing the 6 as its 3-digit binary equivalent 110, the 5 as its 3-digit binary equivalent 101 and the 3 as its 3-digit binary equivalent 011 to form the 9-digit binary number 110101011.

The hexadecimal number FAD5 is converted to binary simply by writing the F as its 4-digit binary equivalent 1111, the A as its 4-digit binary equivalent 1010, the D as its 4-digit binary equivalent 1101 and the 5 as its 4-digit binary equivalent 0101 to form the 16-digit 1111101011010101.

C.4 Converting from Binary, Octal, or Hexadecimal to Decimal

Because we are accustomed to working in decimal, it is often convenient to convert a binary, octal, or hexadecimal number to decimal to get a sense of what the number is "really" worth. Our diagrams in Section C.1 express the positional values in decimal. To convert a number to decimal from another base, multiply the decimal equivalent of each digit by its positional value and sum these products. For example, the binary number 110101 is converted to decimal 53 as shown in Fig. C.8.

Converting a binary number to decimal

Positional values:	32	16	8	4	2	1
Symbol values:	1	1	0	1	0	1
Products:	1*32=32	1*16=16	0*8=0	1*4=4	0*2=0	1*1=1
Sum:	= 32 + 16 + 0 + 4 + 0s + 1 = 53					

Fig. C.8   Converting a binary number to decimal.

To convert octal 7614 to decimal 3980, we use the same technique, this time using appropriate octal positional values as shown in Fig. C.9.

To convert hexadecimal AD3B to decimal 44347, we use the same technique, this time using appropriate hexadecimal positional values as shown in Fig. C.10.

C.5 Converting from Decimal to Binary, Octal, or Hexadecimal

The conversions in Section C.4 follow naturally from the positional notation conventions. Converting from decimal to binary, octal, or hexadecimal also follows these conventions.

Suppose we wish to convert decimal 57 to binary. We begin by writing the positional values of the columns right to left until we reach a column whose positional value is greater than the decimal number. We do not need that column, so we discard it. Thus, we first write:

Positional values:	64	32	16	8	4	2	1

Then we discard the column with positional value 64 leaving:

Positional values:		32	16	8	4	2	1

Converting an octal number to decimal

Positional values:	512	64	8	1
Symbol values:	7	6	1	4
Products	7*512=3584	6*64=384	1*8=8	4*1=4
Sum:	= 3584 + 384 + 8 + 4 = 3980			

Fig. C.9   Converting an octal number to decimal.

Converting a hexadecimal number to decimal

Positional values:	4096	256	16	1
Symbol values:	A	D	3	B
Products	A*4096=40960	D*256=3328	3*16=48	B*1=11
Sum:	= 40960 + 3328 + 48 + 11 = 44347			

Fig. C.10   Converting a hexadecimal number to decimal.

Next we work from the leftmost column to the right. We divide 32 into 57 and observe that there is one 32 in 57 with a remainder of 25, so we write 1 in the 32 column. We divide 16 into 25 and observe that there is one 16 in 25 with a remainder of 9 and write 1 in the 16 column. We divide 8 into 9 and observe that there is one 8 in 9 with a remainder of 1. The next two columns each produce quotients of zero when their positional values are divided into 1 so we write 0s in the 4 and 2 columns. Finally, 1 into 1 is 1 so we write 1 in the 1 column. This yields:

Positional values:	32	16	8	4	2	1
Symbol values:	1	1	1	0	0	1

and thus decimal 57 is equivalent to binary 111001.

To convert decimal 103 to octal, we begin by writing the positional values of the columns until we reach a column whose positional value is greater than the decimal number. We do not need that column, so we discard it. Thus, we first write:

Positional values:	512	64	8	1

Then we discard the column with positional value 512, yielding:

Positional values:	64	8	1

Next we work from the leftmost column to the right. We divide 64 into 103 and observe that there is one 64 in 103 with a remainder of 39, so we write 1 in the 64 column. We divide 8 into 39 and observe that there are four 8s in 39 with a remainder of 7 and write 4 in the 8 column. Finally, we divide 1 into 7 and observe that there are seven 1s in 7 with no remainder so we write 7 in the 1 column. This yields:

Positional values:	64	8	1
Symbol values:	1	4	7

and thus decimal 103 is equivalent to octal 147.

To convert decimal 375 to hexadecimal, we begin by writing the positional values of the columns until we reach a column whose positional value is greater than the decimal number. We do not need that column, so we discard it. Thus, we first write

Positional values:	4096	256	16	1

Then we discard the column with positional value 4096, yielding:

Positional values:	256	16	1

Next we work from the leftmost column to the right. We divide 256 into 375 and observe that there is one 256 in 375 with a remainder of 119, so we write 1 in the 256 column. We divide 16 into 119 and observe that there are seven 16s in 119 with a remainder of 7 and write 7 in the 16 column. Finally, we divide 1 into 7 and observe that there are seven 1s in 7 with no remainder so we write 7 in the 1 column. This yields:

Positional values:	256	16	1
Symbol values:	1	7	7

and thus decimal 375 is equivalent to hexadecimal 177.

C.6 Negative Binary Numbers: Two's Complement Notation

The discussion in this appendix has been focussed on positive numbers. In this section, we explain how computers represent negative numbers using *two's complement notation*. First we explain how the two's complement of a binary number is formed and then we show why it represents the negative value of the given binary number.

Consider a machine with 32-bit integers. Suppose

```
int value = 13;
```

The 32-bit representation of value is

```
00000000 00000000 00000000 00001101
```

To form the negative of value we first form its *one's complement* by applying Java's bit-wise complement operator (~):

```
onesComplementOfValue = ~value;
```

Internally, ~value is now value with each of its bits reversed—ones become zeros and zeros become ones as follows:

```
value:
00000000 00000000 00000000 00001101

~value  (i.e., value's ones complement):
11111111 11111111 11111111 11110010
```

To form the two's complement of value we simply add one to value's one's complement. Thus

```
Two's complement of value:
11111111 11111111 11111111 11110011
```

Now if this is in fact equal to –13, we should be able to add it to binary 13 and obtain a result of 0. Let us try this:

```
 00000000 00000000 00000000 00001101
+11111111 11111111 11111111 11110011
-------------------------------------
 00000000 00000000 00000000 00000000
```

The carry bit coming out of the leftmost column is discarded and we indeed get zero as a result. If we add the one's complement of a number to the number, the result would be all 1s. The key to getting a result of all zeros is that the twos complement is 1 more than the one's complement. The addition of 1 causes each column to add to 0 with a carry of 1. The carry keeps moving leftward until it is discarded from the leftmost bit and hence the resulting number is all zeros.

Computers actually perform a subtraction such as

```
x = a - value;
```

by adding the two's complement of value to a as follows:

```
x = a + (~value + 1);
```

Suppose a is 27 and value is 13 as before. If the two's complement of value is actually the negative of value, then adding the two's complement of value to a should produce the result 14. Let us try this:

```
a (i.e., 27)          00000000 00000000 00000000 00011011
+(~value + 1)        +11111111 11111111 11111111 11110011
                     -----------------------------------
                      00000000 00000000 00000000 00001110
```

which is indeed equal to 14.

SUMMARY

- An integer such as 19 or 227 or –63 in a Java program is assumed to be in the decimal (base 10) number system. The digits in the decimal number system are 0, 1, 2, 3, 4, 5, 6, 7, 8 and 9. The lowest digit is 0 and the highest digit is 9—one less than the base of 10.

- Internally, computers use the binary (base 2) number system. The binary number system has only two digits, namely 0 and 1. Its lowest digit is 0 and its highest digit is 1—one less than the base of 2.

- The octal number system (base 8) and the hexadecimal number system (base 16) are popular primarily because they make it convenient to abbreviate binary numbers.

- The digits of the octal number system range from 0 to 7.

- The hexadecimal number system poses a problem because it requires sixteen digits—a lowest digit of 0 and a highest digit with a value equivalent to decimal 15 (one less than the base of 16). By convention, we use the letters A through F to represent the hexadecimal digits corresponding to decimal values 10 through 15.

- Each number system uses positional notation—each position in which a digit is written has a different positional value.

- A particularly important relationship that both the octal number system and the hexadecimal number system have to the binary system is that the bases of octal and hexadecimal (8 and 16 respectively) are powers of the base of the binary number system (base 2).

- To convert an octal to a binary number, replace each octal digit with its three-digit binary equivalent.

- To convert a hexadecimal number to a binary number, simply replace each hexadecimal digit with its four-digit binary equivalent.

- Because we are accustomed to working in decimal, it is convenient to convert a binary, octal or hexadecimal number to decimal to get a sense of the number's "real" worth.

- To convert a number to decimal from another base, multiply the decimal equivalent of each digit by its positional value and sum these products.

- Computers represent negative numbers using two's complement notation.

- To form the negative of a value in binary, first form its one's complement by applying Java's bitwise complement operator (~). This reverses the bits of the value. To form the two's complement of a value, simply add one to the value's one's complement.

TERMINOLOGY

base	digit
base 2 number system	hexadecimal number system
base 8 number system	negative value
base 10 number system	octal number system
base 16 number system	one's complement notation
binary number system	positional notation
bitwise complement operator (~)	positional value
conversions	symbol value
decimal number system	two's complement notation

SELF-REVIEW EXERCISES

C.1   The bases of the decimal, binary, octal and hexadecimal number systems are _____, _____, _____ and _____ respectively.

C.2   In general, the decimal, octal and hexadecimal representations of a given binary number contain (more/fewer) digits than the binary number contains.

C.3   (True/False) A popular reason for using the decimal number system is that it forms a convenient notation for abbreviating binary numbers simply by substituting one decimal digit per group of four binary bits.

C.4   The (octal / hexadecimal / decimal) representation of a large binary value is the most concise (of the given alternatives).

C.5   (True/False) The highest digit in any base is one more than the base.

C.6   (True/False) The lowest digit in any base is one less than the base.

C.7   The positional value of the rightmost digit of any number in either binary, octal, decimal, or hexadecimal is always _____.

C.8   The positional value of the digit to the left of the rightmost digit of any number in binary, octal, decimal, or hexadecimal is always equal to _____.

C.9   Fill in the missing values in this chart of positional values for the rightmost four positions in each of the indicated number systems:

decimal	1000	100	10	1
hexadecimal	...	256	...	...
binary	...	...	...	...
octal	512	...	8	...

C.10   Convert binary 110101011000 to octal and to hexadecimal.

C.11   Convert hexadecimal FACE to binary.

C.12   Convert octal 7316 to binary.

C.13   Convert hexadecimal 4FEC to octal. (Hint: First convert 4FEC to binary then convert that binary number to octal.)

C.14   Convert binary 1101110 to decimal.

C.15   Convert octal 317 to decimal.

C.16   Convert hexadecimal EFD4 to decimal.

C.17   Convert decimal 177 to binary, to octal and to hexadecimal.

C.18   Show the binary representation of decimal 417. Then show the one's complement of 417 and the two's complement of 417.

C.19   What is the result when the one's complement of a number is added to itself?

ANSWERS TO SELF-REVIEW EXERCISES

C.1   10, 2, 8, 16.

C.2   Fewer.

C.3   False.

C.4   Hexadecimal.

C.5   False. The highest digit in any base is one less than the base.

C.6   False. The lowest digit in any base is zero.

C.7   1 (the base raised to the zero power).

C.8   The base of the number system.

C.9   Fill in the missing values in this chart of positional values for the rightmost four positions in each of the indicated number systems:

decimal	1000	100	10	1
hexadecimal	4096	256	16	1
binary	8	4	2	1
octal	512	64	8	1

C.10   Octal 6530; Hexadecimal D58.

C.11   Binary 1111 1010 1100 1110.

C.12   Binary 111 011 001 110.

C.13   Binary 0 100 111 111 101 100; Octal 47754.

C.14   Decimal 2+4+8+32+64=110.

C.15   Decimal 7+1*8+3*64=7+8+192=207.

C.16   Decimal 4+13*16+15*256+14*4096=61396.

C.17   Decimal 177
to binary:

```
256 128 64 32 16 8 4 2 1
128 64 32 16 8 4 2 1
(1*128)+(0*64)+(1*32)+(1*16)+(0*8)+(0*4)+(0*2)+(1*1)
10110001
```

to octal:

```
512 64 8 1
64 8 1
(2*64)+(6*8)+(1*1)
261
```

to hexadecimal:

```
256 16 1
16 1
(11*16)+(1*1)
(B*16)+(1*1)
B1
```

C.18   Binary:

```
512 256 128 64 32 16 8 4 2 1
256 128 64 32 16 8 4 2 1
(1*256)+(1*128)+(0*64)+(1*32)+(0*16)+(0*8)+(0*4)+(0*2)+
(1*1)
110100001
```

```
One's complement: 001011110
Two's complement: 001011111
Check: Original binary number + its two's complement

110100001
001011111
---------
000000000
```

C.19   Zero.

EXERCISES

C.20   Some people argue that many of our calculations would be easier in the base 12 number system because 12 is divisible by so many more numbers than 10 (for base 10). What is the lowest digit in base 12? What might the highest symbol for the digit in base 12 be? What are the positional values of the rightmost four positions of any number in the base 12 number system?

C.21   How is the highest symbol value in the number systems we discussed related to the positional value of the first digit to the left of the rightmost digit of any number in these number systems?

C.22   Complete the following chart of positional values for the rightmost four positions in each of the indicated number systems:

decimal	1000	100	10	1
base 6	...	...	6	...
base 13	...	169	...	...
base 3	27	...	...	...

C.23   Convert binary 100101111010 to octal and to hexadecimal.

C.24   Convert hexadecimal 3A7D to binary.

C.25   Convert hexadecimal 765F to octal. (Hint: First convert 765F to binary, then convert that binary number to octal.)

C.26   Convert binary 1011110 to decimal.

C.27   Convert octal 426 to decimal.

C.28   Convert hexadecimal FFFF to decimal.

C.29   Convert decimal 299 to binary, to octal and to hexadecimal.

C.30   Show the binary representation of decimal 779. Then show the one's complement of 779 and the two's complement of 779.

C.31   What is the result when the two's complement of a number is added to itself?

C.32   Show the two's complement of integer value −1 on a machine with 32-bit integers.

Elevator Events
and Listener Interfaces

D.1 Introduction

In Section 11.9, we discussed how event handling works in our elevator simulation. We mentioned that for an object to receive an event, that object must register as a listener for that event. Therefore, the class of that object must implement an appropriate listener interface that contains methods that receive an event object as a parameter. In this section, we present the events and listener interfaces used in our simulation.

D.2 Events

The next seven figures (Fig. D.1–Fig. D.7) contain the event classes of the system. Each event inherits from class `ElevatorSimulationEvent` in Fig. D.1. This class contains a `Location` reference (line 11) that represents where the event was generated—in our simulation, this reference is the `Elevator` object or either `Floor` object. Class `Elevator-SimulationEvent` also contains an `Object` reference (line 14) representing the source object that generated the event. Methods `getLocation` (lines 30–33) and `getSource` (lines 42–45) return the `Location` and `Object` references, respectively. Note that each subclass of `ElevatorSimulationEvent` (Fig. D.2–Fig. D.7) provides only a constructor calling the constructor of class `ElevatorSimulationEvent`. As we mentioned in Section 11.9, dividing class `ElevatorSimulationEvent` into several subclass events makes event handling easier to understand in our simulation.

```
1  // ElevatorSimulationEvent.java
2  // Basic event packet in Elevator simulation
3  package com.deitel.jhtp5.elevator.event;
4
```

Fig. D.1   `ElevatorSimulationEvent` superclass for events in the elevator simulation model. (Part 1 of 2.)

```
 5    // Deitel packages
 6    import com.deitel.jhtp5.elevator.model.*;
 7
 8    public class ElevatorSimulationEvent {
 9
10       // Location where ElevatorSimulationEvent was generated
11       private Location location;
12
13       // source Object that generated ElevatorSimulationEvent
14       private Object source;
15
16       // ElevatorSimulationEvent constructor sets Location
17       public ElevatorSimulationEvent( Object source, Location location )
18       {
19          setSource( source );
20          setLocation( location );
21       }
22
23       // set ElevatorSimulationEvent Location
24       public void setLocation( Location eventLocation )
25       {
26          location = eventLocation;
27       }
28
29       // get ElevatorSimulationEvent Location
30       public Location getLocation()
31       {
32          return location;
33       }
34
35       // set ElevatorSimulationEvent source
36       private void setSource( Object eventSource )
37       {
38          source = eventSource;
39       }
40
41       // get ElevatorSimulationEvent source
42       public Object getSource()
43       {
44          return source;
45       }
46    }
```

Fig. D.1   ElevatorSimulationEvent superclass for events in the elevator simulation model. (Part 2 of 2.)

```
1    // BellEvent.java
2    // Indicates that Bell has rung
3    package com.deitel.jhtp5.elevator.event;
4
```

Fig. D.2   BellEvent ElevatorSimulationEvent subclass indicating that the Bell has rung. (Part 1 of 2.)

```
5    // Deitel packages
6    import com.deitel.jhtp5.elevator.model.*;
7
8    public class BellEvent extends ElevatorSimulationEvent {
9
10       // BellEvent constructor
11       public BellEvent( Object source, Location location )
12       {
13           super( source, location );
14       }
15   }
```

Fig. D.2   BellEvent ElevatorSimulationEvent subclass indicating that the Bell has rung. (Part 2 of 2.)

```
1    // ButtonEvent.java
2    // Indicates that a Button has changed state
3    package com.deitel.jhtp5.elevator.event;
4
5    // Deitel packages
6    import com.deitel.jhtp5.elevator.model.*;
7
8    public class ButtonEvent extends ElevatorSimulationEvent {
9
10       // ButtonEvent constructor
11       public ButtonEvent( Object source, Location location )
12       {
13           super( source, location );
14       }
15   }
```

Fig. D.3   ButtonEvent ElevatorSimulationEvent subclass indicating that a Button has changed state.

```
1    // DoorEvent.java
2    // Indicates that a Door has changed state
3    package com.deitel.jhtp5.elevator.event;
4
5    // Deitel packages
6    import com.deitel.jhtp5.elevator.model.*;
7
8    public class DoorEvent extends ElevatorSimulationEvent {
9
10       // DoorEvent constructor
11       public DoorEvent( Object source, Location location )
12       {
13           super( source, location );
14       }
15   }
```

Fig. D.4   DoorEvent ElevatorSimulationEvent subclass indicating that a Door has changed state.

```
1   // ElevatorMoveEvent.java
2   // Indicates on which Floor the Elevator arrived or departed
3   package com.deitel.jhtp5.elevator.event;
4
5   // Deitel packages
6   import com.deitel.jhtp5.elevator.model.*;
7
8   public class ElevatorMoveEvent extends ElevatorSimulationEvent {
9
10     // ElevatorMoveEvent constructor
11     public ElevatorMoveEvent( Object source, Location location )
12     {
13        super( source, location );
14     }
15  }
```

Fig. D.5   ElevatorMoveEvent ElevatorSimulationEvent subclass indicating on which Floor the Elevator has either arrived or departed.

```
1   // LightEvent.java
2   // Indicates on which Floor the Light has changed state
3   package com.deitel.jhtp5.elevator.event;
4
5   // Deitel packages
6   import com.deitel.jhtp5.elevator.model.*;
7
8   public class LightEvent extends ElevatorSimulationEvent {
9
10     // LightEvent constructor
11     public LightEvent( Object source, Location location )
12     {
13        super( source, location );
14     }
15  }
```

Fig. D.6   LightEvent ElevatorSimulationEvent subclass indicating on which Floor the Light has changed state.

Class PersonMoveEvent (Fig. D.7) has a slightly different structure than that of the other event classes. Line 11 declares int field ID. We will discover in Appendix F that the ElevatorView obtains this field through method getID (lines 22–25) to determine which Person sent the event.

```
1   // PersonMoveEvent.java
2   // Indicates that a Person has moved
3   package com.deitel.jhtp5.elevator.event;
4
5   // Deitel packages
6   import com.deitel.jhtp5.elevator.model.*;
```

Fig. D.7   PersonMoveEvent ElevatorSimulationEvent subclass indicating that a Person has moved. (Part 1 of 2.)

```
7
8   public class PersonMoveEvent extends ElevatorSimulationEvent {
9
10      // identifier of Person sending Event
11      private int ID;
12
13      // PersonMoveEvent constructor
14      public PersonMoveEvent( Object source, Location location,
15         int identifier )
16      {
17         super( source, location );
18         ID = identifier;
19      }
20
21      // return identifier
22      public int getID()
23      {
24         return( ID );
25      }
26   }
```

Fig. D.7   PersonMoveEvent ElevatorSimulationEvent subclass indicating that a Person has moved. (Part 2 of 2.)

D.3 Listeners

The next seven figures (Fig. D.8–Fig. D.14) contain the listener interfaces for the elevator simulation. BellListener (Fig. D.8) provides method bellRang (lines 8), which is invoked when the Bell has rung. ButtonListener (Fig. D.9) provides methods buttonPressed (line 8) and buttonReset (line 11), which listen when a Button is pressed or reset. DoorListener (Fig. D.10) provides methods doorOpened (line 8) and doorClosed (line 11), which listen for a Door opening or closing. ElevatorMoveListener (Fig. D.11) provides methods elevatorDeparted (line 8) and elevatorArrived (line 11), which listen for Elevator departures and arrivals. LightListener (Fig. D.12) provides methods lightTurnedOn (line 8) and lightTurnedOff (line 11) that listen for Light state changes. PersonMoveListener (Fig. D.13) provides methods personCreated (line 8), personArrived (line 11), personDeparted (line 14), personPressedButton (line 17–18), personEntered (line 21) and personExited (line 24). These methods listen for when a Person has been created, has arrived at or departed from the Elevator, pressed a Button, entered the Elevator, or exited the simulation, respectively. Lastly, ElevatorSimulationListener (Fig. D.14) inherits behaviors from all listener interfaces. The ElevatorView uses interface ElevatorSimulationListener to receive events from the ElevatorModel.

```
1   // BellListener.java
2   // Method invoked when Bell has rung
3   package com.deitel.jhtp5.elevator.event;
4
```

Fig. D.8   Interface BellListener method when Bell has rung. (Part 1 of 2.)

```
5   public interface BellListener {
6
7      // invoked when Bell has rungs
8      public void bellRang( BellEvent bellEvent );
9   }
```

Fig. D.8 Interface BellListener method when Bell has rung. (Part 2 of 2.)

```
1   // ButtonListener.java
2   // Methods invoked when Button has been either pressed or reset
3   package com.deitel.jhtp5.elevator.event;
4
5   public interface ButtonListener {
6
7      // invoked when Button has been pressed
8      public void buttonPressed( ButtonEvent buttonEvent );
9
10     // invoked when Button has been reset
11     public void buttonReset( ButtonEvent buttonEvent );
12  }
```

Fig. D.9 Interface ButtonListener methods when Button has been either pressed or reset.

```
1   // DoorListener.java
2   // Methods invoked when Door has either opened or closed
3   package com.deitel.jhtp5.elevator.event;
4
5   public interface DoorListener {
6
7      // invoked when Door has opened
8      public void doorOpened( DoorEvent doorEvent );
9
10     // invoked when Door has closed
11     public void doorClosed( DoorEvent doorEvent );
12  }
```

Fig. D.10 Interface DoorListener methods when Door has either opened or closed.

```
1   // ElevatorMoveListener.java
2   // Methods invoked when Elevator has either departed or arrived
3   package com.deitel.jhtp5.elevator.event;
4
5   public interface ElevatorMoveListener {
6
7      // invoked when Elevator has departed
8      public void elevatorDeparted( ElevatorMoveEvent moveEvent );
9
```

Fig. D.11 Interface ElevatorMoveListener methods when Elevator has either departed from or arrived on a Floor. (Part 1 of 2.)

```
10      // invoked when Elevator has arrived
11      public void elevatorArrived( ElevatorMoveEvent moveEvent );
12   }
```

Fig. D.11 Interface `ElevatorMoveListener` methods when `Elevator` has either departed from or arrived on a `Floor`. (Part 2 of 2.)

```
1    // LightListener.java
2    // Methods invoked when Light has either turned on or off
3    package com.deitel.jhtp5.elevator.event;
4
5    public interface LightListener {
6
7        // invoked when Light has turned on
8        public void lightTurnedOn( LightEvent lightEvent );
9
10       // invoked when Light has turned off
11       public void lightTurnedOff( LightEvent lightEvent );
12   }
```

Fig. D.12 Interface `LightListener` method for when `Light` has either turned on or off.

```
1    // PersonMoveListener.java
2    // Methods invoked when Person moved
3    package com.deitel.jhtp5.elevator.event;
4
5    public interface PersonMoveListener {
6
7        // invoked when Person has been instantiated in model
8        public void personCreated( PersonMoveEvent moveEvent );
9
10       // invoked when Person arrived at elevator
11       public void personArrived( PersonMoveEvent moveEvent );
12
13       // invoked when Person departed from elevator
14       public void personDeparted( PersonMoveEvent moveEvent );
15
16       // invoked when Person pressed Button
17       public void personPressedButton(
18          PersonMoveEvent moveEvent );
19
20       // invoked when Person entered Elevator
21       public void personEntered( PersonMoveEvent moveEvent );
22
23       // invoked when Person exited simulation
24       public void personExited( PersonMoveEvent moveEvent );
25   }
```

Fig. D.13 Interface `PersonMoveListener` methods when `Person` has moved.

```
1   // ElevatorSimulationListener.java
2   // Listener for ElevatorView from ElevatorModel
3   package com.deitel.jhtp5.elevator.event;
4
5   // ElevatorSimulationListener inherits all Listener interfaces
6   public interface ElevatorSimulationListener extends BellListener,
7      ButtonListener, DoorListener, ElevatorMoveListener,
8      LightListener, PersonMoveListener {
9   }
```

Fig. D.14   Interface `ElevatorSimulationListener` allows the model to send all events to the view.

D.4 Artifacts Revisited

In Section 14.13, we introduced the artifacts for the elevator simulation. In our simulation, the `ElevatorView` and every object in the model import package `event`. Figure D.15 presents the artifacts in package `event`. Each artifact in package `event` maps to a class from Fig. D.1–Fig. D.14. According to the diagram, `ElevatorView.java` of package `view` imports package `event`. In Java, this translates to class `ElevatorView` importing package `event`. Also according to Fig. D.15, package `model` imports package `event`. (We show all artifacts of package `model` in a separate diagram in Appendix E.) In Java, this translates to each class in package `model` that imports package `event`.

This concludes the appendix on the events and listener interfaces of the elevator simulation. We hope you have found it a useful reference for the material on event handling discussed in Section 11.9. In the next two appendices, we implement the design for the MVC model and the view, and we provide the component diagrams for packages `model` and `view`.

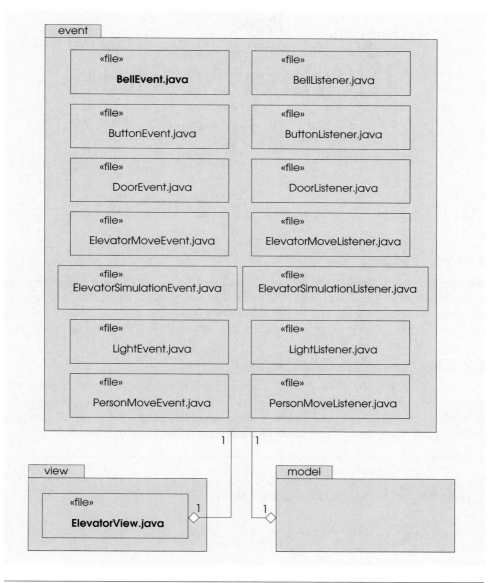

Fig. D.15   Artifacts for package event.

Elevator Model

E.1 Introduction

After reading the "Thinking About Objects" sections, you should have a comfortable grasp of the design process and of the UML diagrams that pertain to our simulation. This appendix presents the code for the classes that collectively implement the MVC model and concludes the discussion of its workings. We discuss each class separately and in detail.

E.2 Class ElevatorSimulation

As discussed in Section 14.13, class ElevatorSimulation (Fig. E.1) ties together the objects that comprise the elevator simulation model. The ElevatorSimulation sends events from the MVC model to the view. The ElevatorSimulation also instantiates new Persons and allows each Floor to obtain a reference to the ElevatorShaft.

```
1   // ElevatorSimulation.java
2   // Elevator simulation model with ElevatorShaft and two Floors
3   package com.deitel.jhtp5.elevator.model;
4
5   // Java core packages
6   import java.util.*;
7
8   // Deitel packages
9   import com.deitel.jhtp5.elevator.event.*;
10  import com.deitel.jhtp5.elevator.ElevatorConstants;
11
12  public class ElevatorSimulation implements ElevatorSimulationListener,
13     ElevatorConstants {
14
```

Fig. E.1 Class ElevatorSimulation represents the MVC model in our elevator simulation. (Part 1 of 7.)

```
15      // declare two-Floor architecture in simulation
16      private Floor firstFloor;
17      private Floor secondFloor;
18
19      // ElevatorShaft in simulation
20      private ElevatorShaft elevatorShaft;
21
22      // objects listening for events from ElevatorModel
23      private Set personMoveListeners;
24      private DoorListener doorListener;
25      private ButtonListener buttonListener;
26      private LightListener lightListener;
27      private BellListener bellListener;
28      private ElevatorMoveListener elevatorMoveListener;
29
30      // cumulative number of people in simulation
31      private int numberOfPeople = 0;
32
33      // constructor instantiates ElevatorShaft and Floors
34      public ElevatorSimulation()
35      {
36         // instantiate firstFloor and secondFloor objects
37         firstFloor = new Floor( FIRST_FLOOR_NAME );
38         secondFloor = new Floor( SECOND_FLOOR_NAME );
39
40         // instantiate ElevatorShaft object
41         elevatorShaft =
42            new ElevatorShaft( firstFloor, secondFloor );
43
44         // give elevatorShaft reference to first and second Floor
45         firstFloor.setElevatorShaft( elevatorShaft );
46         secondFloor.setElevatorShaft( elevatorShaft );
47
48         // register for events from ElevatorShaft
49         elevatorShaft.setDoorListener( this );
50         elevatorShaft.setButtonListener( this );
51         elevatorShaft.addElevatorMoveListener( this );
52         elevatorShaft.setLightListener( this );
53         elevatorShaft.setBellListener( this );
54
55         // instantiate Set for ElevatorMoveListener objects
56         personMoveListeners = new HashSet( 1 );
57
58      } // end ElevatorModel constructor
59
60      // return Floor with given name
61      private Floor getFloor( String name )
62      {
63         if ( name.equals( FIRST_FLOOR_NAME ) )
64            return firstFloor;
65         else
66
```

Fig. E.1   Class ElevatorSimulation represents the MVC model in our elevator
simulation. (Part 2 of 7.)

```
67              if ( name.equals( SECOND_FLOOR_NAME ) )
68                  return secondFloor;
69              else
70                  return null;
71
72      } // end method getFloor
73
74      // add Person to Elevator Simulator
75      public void addPerson( String floorName )
76      {
77          // instantiate new Person and place on Floor
78          Person person =
79              new Person( numberOfPeople, getFloor( floorName ) );
80          person.setName( Integer.toString( numberOfPeople ) );
81
82          // register listener for Person events
83          person.setPersonMoveListener( this );
84
85          // start Person thread
86          person.start();
87
88          // increment number of Person objects in simulation
89          numberOfPeople++;
90
91      } // end method addPerson
92
93      // invoked when Elevator has departed from Floor
94      public void elevatorDeparted( ElevatorMoveEvent moveEvent )
95      {
96          elevatorMoveListener.elevatorDeparted( moveEvent );
97      }
98
99      // invoked when Elevator has arrived at destination Floor
100     public void elevatorArrived( ElevatorMoveEvent moveEvent )
101     {
102         elevatorMoveListener.elevatorArrived( moveEvent );
103     }
104
105     // send PersonMoveEvent to listener, depending on event type
106     private void sendPersonMoveEvent(
107         int eventType, PersonMoveEvent event )
108     {
109         Iterator iterator = personMoveListeners.iterator();
110
111         while ( iterator.hasNext() ) {
112
113             PersonMoveListener listener =
114                 ( PersonMoveListener ) iterator.next();
115
116             // send Event to this listener, depending on eventType
117             switch ( eventType ) {
118
```

Fig. E.1   Class ElevatorSimulation represents the MVC model in our elevator simulation. (Part 3 of 7.)

```
119                  // Person has been created
120                  case Person.PERSON_CREATED:
121                     listener.personCreated( event );
122                     break;
123
124                  // Person arrived at Elevator
125                  case Person.PERSON_ARRIVED:
126                     listener.personArrived( event );
127                     break;
128
129                  // Person entered Elevator
130                  case Person.PERSON_ENTERING_ELEVATOR:
131                     listener.personEntered( event );
132                     break;
133
134                  // Person pressed Button object
135                  case Person.PERSON_PRESSING_BUTTON:
136                     listener.personPressedButton( event );
137                     break;
138
139                  // Person exited Elevator
140                  case Person.PERSON_EXITING_ELEVATOR:
141                     listener.personDeparted( event );
142                     break;
143
144                  // Person exited simulation
145                  case Person.PERSON_EXITED:
146                     listener.personExited( event );
147                     break;
148
149                  default:
150                     break;
151            }
152         }
153      } // end method sendPersonMoveEvent
154
155      // invoked when Person has been created in model
156      public void personCreated( PersonMoveEvent moveEvent )
157      {
158         sendPersonMoveEvent( Person.PERSON_CREATED, moveEvent );
159      }
160
161      // invoked when Person has arrived at Floor's Button
162      public void personArrived( PersonMoveEvent moveEvent )
163      {
164         sendPersonMoveEvent( Person.PERSON_ARRIVED, moveEvent );
165      }
166
167      // invoked when Person has pressed Button
168      public void personPressedButton( PersonMoveEvent moveEvent )
169      {
```

Fig. E.1   Class `ElevatorSimulation` represents the MVC model in our elevator simulation. (Part 4 of 7.)

```
170           sendPersonMoveEvent( Person.PERSON_PRESSING_BUTTON,
171              moveEvent );
172        }
173
174        // invoked when Person has entered Elevator
175        public void personEntered( PersonMoveEvent moveEvent )
176        {
177           sendPersonMoveEvent( Person.PERSON_ENTERING_ELEVATOR,
178              moveEvent );
179        }
180
181        // invoked when Person has departed from Elevator
182        public void personDeparted( PersonMoveEvent moveEvent )
183        {
184           sendPersonMoveEvent( Person.PERSON_EXITING_ELEVATOR,
185              moveEvent );
186        }
187
188        // invoked when Person has exited Simulation
189        public void personExited( PersonMoveEvent moveEvent )
190        {
191           sendPersonMoveEvent( Person.PERSON_EXITED, moveEvent );
192        }
193
194        // invoked when Door has opened
195        public void doorOpened( DoorEvent doorEvent )
196        {
197           doorListener.doorOpened( doorEvent );
198        }
199
200        // invoked when Door has closed
201        public void doorClosed( DoorEvent doorEvent )
202        {
203           doorListener.doorClosed( doorEvent );
204        }
205
206        // invoked when Button has been pressed
207        public void buttonPressed( ButtonEvent buttonEvent )
208        {
209           buttonListener.buttonPressed( buttonEvent );
210        }
211
212        // invoked when Button has been reset
213        public void buttonReset( ButtonEvent buttonEvent )
214        {
215           buttonListener.buttonReset( buttonEvent );
216        }
217
218        // invoked when Bell has rung
219        public void bellRang( BellEvent bellEvent )
220        {
221           bellListener.bellRang( bellEvent );
```

Fig. E.1   Class ElevatorSimulation represents the MVC model in our elevator
             simulation. (Part 5 of 7.)

```
222        }
223
224        // invoked when Light has turned on
225        public void lightTurnedOn( LightEvent lightEvent )
226        {
227            lightListener.lightTurnedOn( lightEvent );
228        }
229
230        // invoked when Light has turned off
231        public void lightTurnedOff( LightEvent lightEvent )
232        {
233            lightListener.lightTurnedOff( lightEvent );
234        }
235
236        // set listener for ElevatorModelListener
237        public void setElevatorSimulationListener(
238            ElevatorSimulationListener listener )
239        {
240            // ElevatorModelListener extends all interfaces below
241            addPersonMoveListener( listener );
242            setElevatorMoveListener( listener );
243            setDoorListener( listener );
244            setButtonListener( listener );
245            setLightListener( listener );
246            setBellListener( listener );
247        }
248
249        // set listener for PersonMoveEvents
250        public void addPersonMoveListener(
251            PersonMoveListener listener )
252        {
253            personMoveListeners.add( listener );
254        }
255
256        // set listener for DoorEvents
257        public void setDoorListener( DoorListener listener )
258        {
259            doorListener = listener;
260        }
261
262        // set listener for ButtonEvents
263        public void setButtonListener( ButtonListener listener )
264        {
265            buttonListener = listener;
266        }
267
268        // add listener for ElevatorMoveEvents
269        public void setElevatorMoveListener(
270            ElevatorMoveListener listener )
271        {
272            elevatorMoveListener = listener;
273        }
```

Fig. E.1   Class ElevatorSimulation represents the MVC model in our elevator simulation. (Part 6 of 7.)

```
274
275      // set listener for LightEvents
276      public void setLightListener( LightListener listener )
277      {
278          lightListener = listener;
279      }
280
281      // set listener for BellEvents
282      public void setBellListener( BellListener listener )
283      {
284          bellListener = listener;
285      }
286  }
```

Fig. E.1   Class ElevatorSimulation represents the MVC model in our elevator simulation. (Part 7 of 7.)

The class diagram in Fig. 16.19 shows that class ElevatorSimulation contains one instance of class ElevatorShaft and two instances of class Floor, so ElevatorSimulation declares variable elevatorShaft (line 20) and variables firstFloor and secondFloor (lines 16–17). Lines 37–46 instantiate these objects and give each Floor object a reference to the ElevatorShaft object. Figure 16.19 also shows that class ElevatorSimulation creates Person objects. According to Fig. 16.19, class ElevatorSimulation contains method addPerson (lines 75–91), which creates and places a Person on the specified Floor. Line 86 of method addPerson starts the Person's thread and line 89 increments the cumulative number of Person objects in the simulation.

As previously mentioned, class ElevatorSimulation sends events from the model to the view. The class declaration (lines 12–13) and lines 49–53 reveal that the ElevatorSimulation listens for several types of events from the ElevatorShaft—this is how the ElevatorSimulation receives events from the objects that comprise the model. Specifically, class ElevatorSimulation implements interface ElevatorSimulationListener, which implements all interfaces in package event. Lines 23–28 declare variables for the listener objects to which the ElevatorSimulation sends the events it receives from the ElevatorShaft. The ElevatorFrame (the application) registers the ElevatorView as a listener for events from the ElevatorSimulation—this is how the ElevatorSimulation sends events from the model to the view.

Lines 94–234 of class ElevatorSimulation implement all methods of interface ElevatorSimulationListener, and lines 237–285 provide addListener methods to register a listener (in this case, the listener is the ElevatorView) for all events. In fact, two-thirds of the class devotes itself to "bubbling up" messages from the model to the view.

We presented a class diagram that showed the realizations of the elevator model in Fig. 12.27. We alter this diagram to accommodate the fact that class ElevatorSimulation implements all interfaces through interface ElevatorSimulationListener. In addition, class ElevatorShaft must implement more interfaces to receive events from class Elevator so that ElevatorShaft can send these events to the ElevatorSimulation. We present the class diagram showing all realizations for the model in Fig. E.2 and Fig. E.3—Fig. E.2 shows the relationship between the classes in the model and the listener interfaces, and Fig. E.3 shows the relationship between the listener interfaces and interface

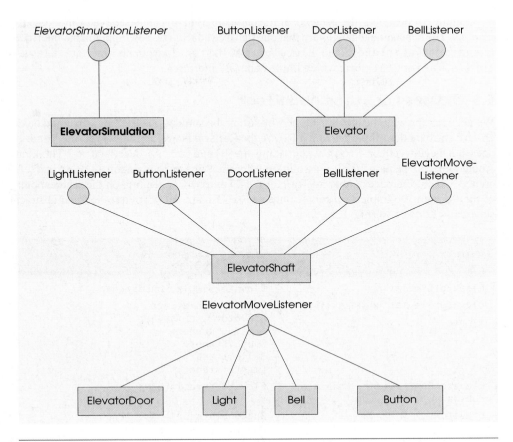

Fig. E.2   Class diagram showing realizations in the elevator model (Part 1).

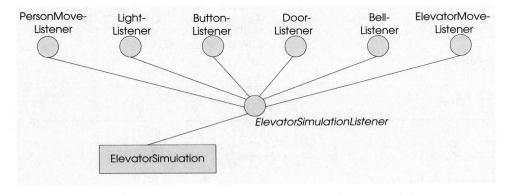

Fig. E.3   Class diagram showing realizations in the elevator model (Part 2).

ElevatorSimulationListener. (We could have created one class diagram showing both types of relationships, but the diagram would have been too cluttered.)

Figure E.4 describes the contents of the class diagram that shows elevator model realizations. The substantial changes are that class `ElevatorShaft` now implements interface `ElevatorMoveListener`, and `ElevatorSimulation` implements interface `ElevatorSimulationListener`, which implements all interfaces.

E.3 Classes `Location` and `Floor`

We need to represent the location of the `Person` in the simulation. The `Person` could have an `int` attribute describing on which `Floor` the `Person` is walking; however, the `Person` does not occupy either `Floor` when riding the `Elevator`. As described in "Thinking About Objects" Section 10.11, our solution is for the `Person` to maintain a `Location` reference, which references either a `Floor` or the `Elevator`, depending on the whereabouts of the `Person`. To implement this feature, classes `Floor` and `Elevator` extend abstract superclass `Location` (Fig. E.5).

Class	implements Listener
ElevatorSimulation	ElevatorSimulationListener
ElevatorSimulationListener	PersonMoveListener ElevatorMoveListener ButtonListener DoorListener BellListener LightListener
ElevatorDoor, Light, Bell, Button	ElevatorMoveListener
Elevator	ButtonListener DoorListener BellListener
ElevatorShaft	LightListener ButtonListener DoorListener BellListener ElevatorMoveListener
Person	DoorListener

Fig. E.4   Classes and implemented listener interfaces from Fig. E.2.

```
1  // Location.java
2  // Abstract superclass representing location in simulation
3  package com.deitel.jhtp5.elevator.model;
4
5  // Deitel packages
6  import com.deitel.jhtp5.elevator.event.*;
7
8  public abstract class Location {
9
```

Fig. E.5   `Location` superclass that represents a location in the simulation. (Part 1 of 2.)

```
10      // name of Location
11      private String locationName;
12
13      // set name of Location
14      protected void setLocationName( String name )
15      {
16          locationName = name;
17      }
18
19      // return name of Location
20      public String getLocationName()
21      {
22          return locationName;
23      }
24
25      // return Button at Location
26      public abstract Button getButton();
27
28      // return Door object at Location
29      public abstract Door getDoor();
30  }
```

Fig. E.5   Location superclass that represents a location in the simulation. (Part 2 of 2.)

Location contains String locationName (line 11), which may contain value firstFloor, secondFloor or elevator to describe the three locations the Person may occupy. Lines 26 and 29 declare abstract methods getButton and getDoor, respectively. Using these methods, a Floor returns references to objects associated with that Floor, and the Elevator returns references to the objects associated with the Elevator. The Location reference allows a Person to press a Button and to know when a Door has opened. For example, if we wish a Person to press a Button, we write

```
person.getLocation().getButton().pressButton();
```

Therefore, our use of an abstract superclass provides an alternate means for objects in our model to interact. Figure E.6 presents class Floor, a subclass of class Location. The Floor constructor (lines 15–18) takes as a String argument the value firstFloor or second-Floor to identify the Floor. Line 17 invokes method setLocationName to assign the value of this String to attribute locationName, inherited from superclass Location.

```
1   // Floor.java
2   // Represents a Floor located next to an ElevatorShaft
3   package com.deitel.jhtp5.elevator.model;
4
5   // Deitel packages
6   import com.deitel.jhtp5.elevator.ElevatorConstants;
7
8   public class Floor extends Location
9       implements ElevatorConstants {
```

Fig. E.6   Class Floor—a subclass of Location—represents a Floor across which a Person walks to the Elevator. (Part 1 of 2.)

```
10
11        // reference to ElevatorShaft object
12        private ElevatorShaft elevatorShaft;
13
14        // Floor constructor sets name of Floor
15        public Floor( String name )
16        {
17           setLocationName( name );
18        }
19
20        // get first or second Floor Button, using Location name
21        public Button getButton()
22        {
23           if ( getLocationName().equals( FIRST_FLOOR_NAME ) )
24              return getElevatorShaft().getFirstFloorButton();
25           else
26
27              if ( getLocationName().equals( SECOND_FLOOR_NAME ) )
28                 return getElevatorShaft().getSecondFloorButton();
29           else
30
31              return null;
32
33        } // end method getButton
34
35        // get first or second Floor Door, using Location name
36        public Door getDoor()
37        {
38           if ( getLocationName().equals( FIRST_FLOOR_NAME ) )
39              return getElevatorShaft().getFirstFloorDoor();
40           else
41
42              if ( getLocationName().equals( SECOND_FLOOR_NAME ) )
43                 return getElevatorShaft().getSecondFloorDoor();
44           else
45
46              return null;
47
48        } // end method getDoor
49
50        // get ElevatorShaft reference
51        public ElevatorShaft getElevatorShaft()
52        {
53           return elevatorShaft;
54        }
55
56        // set ElevatorShaft reference
57        public void setElevatorShaft( ElevatorShaft shaft )
58        {
59           elevatorShaft = shaft;
60        }
61    }
```

Fig. E.6   Class Floor—a subclass of Location—represents a Floor across which a Person walks to the Elevator. (Part 2 of 2.)

Class `Floor` provides concrete methods `getButton` (lines 21–33) and `getDoor` (lines 36–48). Methods `getButton` and `getDoor` return a `Button` and `Door` reference on either the first or the second `Floor`, depending on which `Floor` returns the reference. Lastly, method `getElevatorShaft` (lines 51–54) returns a reference to the `Elevator-Shaft`. We will see later how a `Person` uses this method, in conjunction with that `Person`'s `Location` reference, to enter the `Elevator`.

E.4 Classes Door and ElevatorDoor

The `Door`s are an essential part of the model, because they inform a `Person` when to enter and exit the `Elevator`—without the `Door`s, no `Person` would be able to ride the `Eleva-tor`. The collaboration diagrams of Fig. 7.19 and Fig. 11.28 presented the collaborations among the `Door`s, the `Elevator` and the `Person`. Now, we provide a walkthrough of class `Door` (Fig. E.7).

```java
1   // Door.java
2   // Sends DoorEvents to DoorListeners when opened or closed
3   package com.deitel.jhtp5.elevator.model;
4
5   // Java core packages
6   import java.util.*;
7
8   // Deitel packages
9   import com.deitel.jhtp5.elevator.event.*;
10
11  public class Door {
12
13     // represent whether Door is open or closed
14     private boolean open = false;
15
16     // time before Door closes automatically
17     public static final int AUTOMATIC_CLOSE_DELAY = 3000;
18
19     // Set of DoorListeners
20     private Set doorListeners;
21
22     // location where Door opened or closed
23     private Location doorLocation;
24
25     // Door constructor instantiates Set for DoorListeners
26     public Door()
27     {
28        doorListeners = new HashSet( 1 );
29     }
30
31     // add Door listener
32     public void addDoorListener( DoorListener listener )
33     {
```

Fig. E.7   Class `Door`, which represents a `Door` in the model, informs listeners when a `Door` has opened or closed. (Part 1 of 3.)

```
34          // prevent other objects from modifying doorListeners
35          synchronized( doorListeners )
36          {
37             doorListeners.add( listener );
38          }
39       }
40
41       // remove Door listener
42       public void removeDoorListener( DoorListener listener )
43       {
44          // prevent other objects from modifying doorListeners
45          synchronized( doorListeners )
46          {
47             doorListeners.remove( listener );
48          }
49       }
50
51       // open Door and send all listeners DoorEvent objects
52       public synchronized void openDoor( Location location )
53       {
54          if ( !open ) {
55
56             open = true;
57
58             // obtain iterator from Set
59             Iterator iterator;
60             synchronized( doorListeners )
61             {
62                iterator = new HashSet( doorListeners ).iterator();
63             }
64
65             // get next DoorListener
66             while ( iterator.hasNext() ) {
67                DoorListener doorListener =
68                   ( DoorListener ) iterator.next();
69
70                // send doorOpened event to this DoorListener
71                doorListener.doorOpened(
72                   new DoorEvent( this, location ) );
73             }
74
75             doorLocation = location;
76
77             // declare Thread that ensures automatic Door closing
78             Thread closeThread = new Thread(
79                new Runnable() {
80
81                   public void run()
82                   {
83                      // close Door if open for more than 3 seconds
84                      try {
85                         Thread.sleep( AUTOMATIC_CLOSE_DELAY );
```

Fig. E.7   Class **Door**, which represents a **Door** in the model, informs listeners when a **Door** has opened or closed. (Part 2 of 3.)

```
 86                                closeDoor( doorLocation );
 87                             }
 88
 89                             // handle exception if interrupted
 90                             catch ( InterruptedException exception ) {
 91                                exception.printStackTrace();
 92                             }
 93                          }
 94                       } // end anonymous inner class
 95                    );
 96
 97                    closeThread.start();
 98                 }
 99
100                 // notify all waiting threads that the door has opened
101                 notifyAll();
102
103              } // end method openDoor
104
105              // close Door and send all listeners DoorEvent objects
106              public synchronized void closeDoor( Location location )
107              {
108                 if ( open ) {
109
110                    open = false;
111
112                    // obtain iterator from Set
113                    Iterator iterator;
114                    synchronized( doorListeners )
115                    {
116                       iterator = new HashSet( doorListeners ).iterator();
117                    }
118
119                    // get next DoorListener
120                    while ( iterator.hasNext() ) {
121                       DoorListener doorListener =
122                          ( DoorListener ) iterator.next();
123
124                       // send doorClosed event to this DoorListener
125                       doorListener.doorClosed(
126                          new DoorEvent( this, location ) );
127                    }
128                 }
129
130              } // end method closeDoor
131
132              // return whether Door is open or closed
133              public synchronized boolean isDoorOpen()
134              {
135                 return open;
136              }
137           }
```

Fig. E.7   Class **Door**, which represents a **Door** in the model, informs listeners when a **Door** has opened or closed. (Part 3 of 3.)

Figure 16.20 indicates that class Door contains boolean attribute open (line 14) to represent the state of the Door (open or closed). Figure 16.20 also indicates that class Door contains methods openDoor (lines 52–103) and closeDoor (lines 106–130). Method openDoor sends a doorOpened event to all registered DoorListeners (the Door passes a DoorEvent object to the doorOpened method of each registered DoorListener), and method closeDoor sends a doorClosed event to all registered DoorListeners. Set doorListeners (line 20) stores all registered DoorListeners. A DoorListener wishing to receive DoorEvents from a Door must invoke method addDoorListener (lines 32–39); those listeners that no longer wish to be a DoorListener for that Door must invoke removeDoorListener (lines 42–49).

Line 56 of method openDoor opens the Door by setting open to true. Lines 66–73 iterate Set doorListeners and send each object a doorOpened event. Lines 60–63 use a synchronized block obtaining the Iterator from Set doorListeners, because a Person, at any time, can add or remove itself from this Set. If method openDoor iterates doorListeners as a Person adds or removes itself from doorListeners, the JVM throws a ConcurrentModificationException—the Person is modifying the Set as method openDoor is iterating the same Set. Method openDoor avoids this situation with the synchronized block.

Method openDoor receives as an argument a Location reference on what Floor that Door should open. Lines 71–72 send a DoorEvent using the Location reference to all registered DoorListeners. Method closeDoor sets open to false (thus closing the Door) and invokes the doorClosed method on all registered DoorListeners.

We decided in Section 16.11 to make class Door an active class, so that the Door closes itself after three seconds of being open. Lines 78–95 of method openDoor instantiate a thread that handles this responsibility. Method run (lines 81–93) puts this thread to sleep for three seconds then closes the Door. Line 97 of method openDoor starts the thread.

Each method related to the opening and closing of doors is marked as synchronized. Since multiple threads (i.e., Persons, Elevators and autoclosing threads) interact with the Doors, it is important for us to ensure proper synchronization among these threads. For example, a Door should not close when a Person is walking onto the Elevator as this could injure the Person. By marking these methods as synchronized, we ensure that multiple threads cannot open and close the door when it is not appropriate to do so. In addition, note that line 101 in method openDoor calls method notifyAll, which class Door inherited from class Object. As we will see in our discussion of the Person class (Fig. E.14), this notifies a waiting Person when the Door has opened.

Class ElevatorDoor (Fig. E.8) is a Door subclass that overrides methods openDoor and closeDoor and implements interface ElevatorMoveListener. An Elevator-Door has additional responsibilities over the Floor Doors. When the Elevator arrives at a Floor, it is the ElevatorDoor's reponsibility to process the elevatorArrived message (lines 35–38) and open the Door on that Floor (line 16). Additionally, when the Elevator closes the ElevatorDoor, the ElevatorDoor must close the Door on the departure Floor (line 25) before closing itself (line 27).

Method elevatorDeparted does not perform any action. At a first glance, you may wonder why this method does not call method closeDoor. The reason is that the Elevator-Door must be closed *before* the Elevator departs so the passenger will not be

```
1   // ElevatorDoor.java
2   // Opens and closes floor Door when elevator arrives and departs.
3   package com.deitel.jhtp5.elevator.model;
4
5   // Java core packages
6   import java.util.*;
7
8   // Deitel packages
9   import com.deitel.jhtp5.elevator.event.*;
10
11  public class ElevatorDoor extends Door implements ElevatorMoveListener {
12
13     // open ElevatorDoor and corresponding Floor Door
14     public synchronized void openDoor( Location location )
15     {
16        location.getDoor().openDoor( location );
17
18        super.openDoor( location );
19
20     } // end method openDoor
21
22     // close ElevatorDoor and Corresponding Floor Door
23     public synchronized void closeDoor( Location location )
24     {
25        location.getDoor().closeDoor( location );
26
27        super.closeDoor( location );
28
29     } // end method closeDoor
30
31     // invoked when Elevator has departed
32     public void elevatorDeparted( ElevatorMoveEvent moveEvent ) {}
33
34     // invoked when Elevator has arrived
35     public void elevatorArrived( ElevatorMoveEvent moveEvent )
36     {
37        openDoor( moveEvent.getLocation() );
38     }
39  }
```

Fig. E.8   Class ElevatorDoor opens in response to elevatorArrived messages
and opens and closes the Floor Doors.

injured—in our implementation, the Elevator calls ElevatorDoor method closeDoor
before calling elevatorDeparted.

E.5 Class Button

Buttons (Fig. E.9) are important to the model as well, because they signal the Elevator
to move between Floors. Figure 16.20 indicates that class Button contains boolean attribute pressed (Fig. E.9, line 14) to represent the state of the Button (pressed or reset).
Figure 16.20 also indicates that class Button contains methods pressButton (Fig. E.9,
lines 23–29) and resetButton (Fig. E.9, lines 32–38).

```java
1   // Button.java
2   // Sends ButtonEvents to ButtonListeners when accessed
3   package com.deitel.jhtp5.elevator.model;
4
5   // Deitel packages
6   import com.deitel.jhtp5.elevator.event.*;
7
8   public class Button implements ElevatorMoveListener {
9
10     // ButtonListener
11     private ButtonListener buttonListener = null;
12
13     // represent whether Button is pressed
14     private boolean pressed = false;
15
16     // set listener
17     public void setButtonListener( ButtonListener listener )
18     {
19         buttonListener = listener;
20     }
21
22     // press Button and send ButtonEvent
23     public void pressButton( Location location )
24     {
25         pressed = true;
26
27         buttonListener.buttonPressed(
28             new ButtonEvent( this, location ) );
29     }
30
31     // reset Button and send ButtonEvent
32     public void resetButton( Location location )
33     {
34         pressed = false;
35
36         buttonListener.buttonReset(
37             new ButtonEvent( this, location ) );
38     }
39
40     // return whether button is pressed
41     public boolean isButtonPressed()
42     {
43         return pressed;
44     }
45
46     // invoked when Elevator has departed
47     public void elevatorDeparted( ElevatorMoveEvent moveEvent ) {}
48
49     // invoked when Elevator has arrived
50     public void elevatorArrived( ElevatorMoveEvent moveEvent )
51     {
52         resetButton( moveEvent.getLocation() );
```

Fig. E.9 Class Button, which represents a Button in the model, informs listeners when a Button has been pressed or reset. (Part 1 of 2.)

```
53       }
54    }
```

Fig. E.9   Class Button, which represents a Button in the model, informs listeners when a Button has been pressed or reset. (Part 2 of 2.)

Method pressButton sends a buttonPressed event to the registered ButtonListener (line 11), and method resetButton sends a buttonReset event to the ButtonListener. Method setButtonListener (lines 17–20) allows an object to receive ButtonEvents by registering itself as the ButtonListener.

Line 25 of method pressButton sets attribute pressed to true, and lines 27–28 pass a ButtonEvent to method buttonPressed of the buttonListener. Line 34 of method resetButton sets attribute pressed to false, and lines 36–37 pass a ButtonEvent to method buttonReset of the buttonListener.

Lastly, according to Fig. E.2, class Button implements interface ElevatorMoveListener. Method elevatorArrived (lines 50–53) calls method resetButton to reset the Button.

E.6 Class ElevatorShaft

Class ElevatorShaft (Fig. E.10) represents the ElevatorShaft in which the Elevator travels in the model. Most methods in class ElevatorShaft access private variables, listen for messages from the Elevator and send "bubble up" events to the ElevatorSimulation, which sends them to the ElevatorView. According to the class diagram of Fig. 16.20, class ElevatorShaft contains one Elevator object, two Button objects, two Door objects and two Light objects. The Button, Door and Light objects refer to the buttons, doors and lights on each Floor. Line 15 declares the Elevator elevator. Lines 18–19 declare the Buttons firstFloorButton and secondFloorButton. Lines 22–23 declare the Doors firstFloorDoor and secondFloorDoor. Lines 26–27 declare the Lights firstFloorLight and secondFloorLight. Lines 169–208 provide methods to access references to these objects.

```
1    // ElevatorShaft.java
2    // Represents elevator shaft, which contains elevator
3    package com.deitel.jhtp5.elevator.model;
4
5    // Java core packages
6    import java.util.*;
7
8    // Deitel packages
9    import com.deitel.jhtp5.elevator.event.*;
10
11   public class ElevatorShaft implements ElevatorMoveListener,
12      LightListener, BellListener {
13
14      // Elevator
15      private Elevator elevator;
```

Fig. E.10   Class ElevatorShaft, which represents the ElevatorShaft, which sends events from the Elevator to the ElevatorSimulation. (Part 1 of 7.)

```
16
17       // Buttons on Floors
18       private Button firstFloorButton;
19       private Button secondFloorButton;
20
21       // Doors on Floors
22       private Door firstFloorDoor;
23       private Door secondFloorDoor;
24
25       // Lights on Floors
26       private Light firstFloorLight;
27       private Light secondFloorLight;
28
29       // listeners
30       private DoorListener doorListener;
31       private ButtonListener buttonListener;
32       private LightListener lightListener;
33       private BellListener bellListener;
34       private Set elevatorMoveListeners;
35
36       // constructor initializes aggregated components
37       public ElevatorShaft( Floor firstFloor, Floor secondFloor )
38       {
39          // instantiate Set for ElevatorMoveListeners
40          elevatorMoveListeners = new HashSet( 1 );
41
42          // anonymous inner class listens for ButtonEvents
43          ButtonListener floorButtonListener =
44             new ButtonListener() {
45
46             // called when Floor Button has been pressed
47             public void buttonPressed( ButtonEvent buttonEvent )
48             {
49                // request elevator move to location
50                Location location = buttonEvent.getLocation();
51                buttonListener.buttonPressed( buttonEvent );
52                elevator.requestElevator( location );
53             }
54
55             // called when Floor Button has been reset
56             public void buttonReset( ButtonEvent buttonEvent )
57             {
58                buttonListener.buttonReset( buttonEvent );
59             }
60          }; // end anonymous inner class
61
62          // instantiate Floor Buttons
63          firstFloorButton = new Button();
64          secondFloorButton = new Button();
65
```

Fig. E.10   Class ElevatorShaft, which represents the ElevatorShaft, which sends events from the Elevator to the ElevatorSimulation. (Part 2 of 7.)

```
66          // register anonymous ButtonListener with Floor Buttons
67          firstFloorButton.setButtonListener(
68             floorButtonListener );
69          secondFloorButton.setButtonListener(
70             floorButtonListener );
71
72          // Floor Buttons listen for ElevatorMoveEvents
73          addElevatorMoveListener( firstFloorButton );
74          addElevatorMoveListener( secondFloorButton );
75
76          // anonymous inner class listens for DoorEvents
77          DoorListener floorDoorListener = new DoorListener() {
78
79             // called when Floor Door has opened
80             public void doorOpened( DoorEvent doorEvent )
81             {
82                // forward event to doorListener
83                doorListener.doorOpened( doorEvent );
84             }
85
86             // called when Floor Door has closed
87             public void doorClosed( DoorEvent doorEvent )
88             {
89                // forward event to doorListener
90                doorListener.doorClosed( doorEvent );
91             }
92          }; // end anonymous inner class
93
94          // instantiate Floor Doors
95          firstFloorDoor = new Door();
96          secondFloorDoor = new Door();
97
98          // register anonymous DoorListener with Floor Doors
99          firstFloorDoor.addDoorListener( floorDoorListener );
100         secondFloorDoor.addDoorListener( floorDoorListener );
101
102         // instantiate Lights, then listen for LightEvents
103         firstFloorLight = new Light();
104         addElevatorMoveListener( firstFloorLight );
105         firstFloorLight.setLightListener( this );
106
107         secondFloorLight = new Light();
108         addElevatorMoveListener( secondFloorLight );
109         secondFloorLight.setLightListener( this );
110
111         // instantiate Elevator object
112         elevator = new Elevator( firstFloor, secondFloor );
113
114         // register for ElevatorMoveEvents from elevator
115         elevator.addElevatorMoveListener( this );
116
```

Fig. E.10   Class ElevatorShaft, which represents the ElevatorShaft, which sends events from the Elevator to the ElevatorSimulation. (Part 3 of 7.)

```
117          // listen for BellEvents from elevator
118          elevator.setBellListener( this );
119
120          // anonymous inner class listens for ButtonEvents from
121          // elevator
122          elevator.setButtonListener(
123             new ButtonListener() {
124
125                // invoked when button has been pressed
126                public void buttonPressed( ButtonEvent buttonEvent )
127                {
128                   // send event to listener
129                   buttonListener.buttonPressed( buttonEvent );
130                }
131
132                // invoked when button has been reset
133                public void buttonReset( ButtonEvent buttonEvent )
134                {
135                   // send event to listener
136                   buttonListener.buttonReset(
137                      new ButtonEvent( this, elevator ) );
138                }
139             } // end anonymous inner class
140          );
141
142          // anonymous inner class listens for DoorEvents from
143          // elevator
144          elevator.setDoorListener(
145             new DoorListener() {
146
147                // invoked when door has opened
148                public void doorOpened( DoorEvent doorEvent )
149                {
150                   // send event to listener
151                   doorListener.doorOpened( doorEvent );
152                }
153
154                // invoked when door has closed
155                public void doorClosed( DoorEvent doorEvent )
156                {
157                   // send event to listener
158                   doorListener.doorClosed( doorEvent );
159                }
160             } // end anonymous inner class
161          );
162
163          // start Elevator Thread
164          elevator.start();
165
166       } // end ElevatorShaft constructor
167
```

Fig. E.10   Class `ElevatorShaft`, which represents the `ElevatorShaft`, which sends events from the `Elevator` to the `ElevatorSimulation`. (Part 4 of 7.)

```
168        // get Elevator
169        public Elevator getElevator()
170        {
171           return elevator;
172        }
173
174        // get Door on first Floor
175        public Door getFirstFloorDoor()
176        {
177           return firstFloorDoor;
178        }
179
180        // get Door on second Floor
181        public Door getSecondFloorDoor()
182        {
183           return secondFloorDoor;
184        }
185
186        // get Button on first Floor
187        public Button getFirstFloorButton()
188        {
189           return firstFloorButton;
190        }
191
192        // get Button on second Floor
193        public Button getSecondFloorButton()
194        {
195           return secondFloorButton;
196        }
197
198        // get Light on first Floor
199        public Light getFirstFloorLight()
200        {
201           return firstFloorLight;
202        }
203
204        // get Light on second Floor
205        public Light getSecondFloorLight()
206        {
207           return secondFloorLight;
208        }
209
210        // invoked when Bell rings
211        public void bellRang( BellEvent bellEvent )
212        {
213           bellListener.bellRang( bellEvent );
214        }
215
216        // invoked when Light turns on
217        public void lightTurnedOn( LightEvent lightEvent )
218        {
219           lightListener.lightTurnedOn( lightEvent );
```

Fig. E.10   Class ElevatorShaft, which represents the ElevatorShaft, which sends events from the Elevator to the ElevatorSimulation. (Part 5 of 7.)

```
220        }
221
222        // invoked when Light turns off
223        public void lightTurnedOff( LightEvent lightEvent )
224        {
225            lightListener.lightTurnedOff( lightEvent );
226        }
227
228        // invoked when Elevator departs
229        public void elevatorDeparted( ElevatorMoveEvent moveEvent )
230        {
231            Iterator iterator = elevatorMoveListeners.iterator();
232
233            // iterate Set of ElevatorMoveEvent listeners
234            while ( iterator.hasNext() ) {
235
236                // get respective ElevatorMoveListener from Set
237                ElevatorMoveListener listener =
238                    ( ElevatorMoveListener ) iterator.next();
239
240                // send ElevatorMoveEvent to this listener
241                listener.elevatorDeparted( moveEvent );
242            }
243        } // end method elevatorDeparted
244
245        // invoked when Elevator arrives
246        public void elevatorArrived( ElevatorMoveEvent moveEvent )
247        {
248            // obtain iterator from Set
249            Iterator iterator = elevatorMoveListeners.iterator();
250
251            // get next DoorListener
252            while ( iterator.hasNext() ) {
253
254                // get next ElevatorMoveListener from Set
255                ElevatorMoveListener listener =
256                    ( ElevatorMoveListener ) iterator.next();
257
258                // send ElevatorMoveEvent to this listener
259                listener.elevatorArrived( moveEvent );
260
261            } // end while loop
262        } // end method elevatorArrived
263
264        // set listener to DoorEvents
265        public void setDoorListener( DoorListener listener )
266        {
267            doorListener = listener;
268        }
269
```

Fig. E.10 Class ElevatorShaft, which represents the ElevatorShaft, which sends events from the Elevator to the ElevatorSimulation. (Part 6 of 7.)

```
270    // set listener to ButtonEvents
271    public void setButtonListener( ButtonListener listener )
272    {
273        buttonListener = listener;
274    }
275
276    // add listener to ElevatorMoveEvents
277    public void addElevatorMoveListener(
278        ElevatorMoveListener listener )
279    {
280        elevatorMoveListeners.add( listener );
281    }
282
283    // set listener to LightEvents
284    public void setLightListener( LightListener listener )
285    {
286        lightListener = listener;
287    }
288
289    // set listener to BellEvents
290    public void setBellListener( BellListener listener )
291    {
292        bellListener = listener;
293    }
294 }
```

Fig. E.10   Class ElevatorShaft, which represents the ElevatorShaft, which sends events from the Elevator to the ElevatorSimulation. (Part 7 of 7.)

The main responsibility of the ElevatorShaft is to receive events from other objects then to send these events to the ElevatorSimulation. (The ElevatorSimulation then sends the events to the ElevatorView, which displays the workings of the model.) The ElevatorShaft contains references to several different listener objects, such as a DoorListener, a ButtonListener, a LightListener, a BellListener and several ElevatorMoveListeners. Lines 30–34 declare these listeners—line 34 declares a Set to hold multiple ElevatorMoveListeners, because the Buttons, Doors, Lights and the ElevatorSimulation are all ElevatorMoveListeners. Lines 265–293 provide methods allowing objects to register themselves as listeners for various events.

The constructor (lines 37–166) instantiates listener objects from several inner classes—these listener objects receive events from other objects, then resend the events to the listener objects defined in line 30–34. For example, lines 43–60 declare a ButtonListener object called floorButtonListener, which contains the logic for when a Button on a Floor has been pressed or reset. Lines 63–70 instantiate firstFloorButton and secondFloorButton, then register floorButtonListener as a ButtonListener for both Button objects. When either Button has been pressed, that Button invokes method buttonPressed (lines 47–53) of the floorButtonListener. When either Button has been reset, that Button invokes the floorButtonListener's method buttonReset (lines 56–59). Method buttonPressed requests the Elevator by invoking the Elevator's method requestElevator—method buttonPressed passes a Location reference of the Floor that generated the ButtonEvent. Both methods buttonPressed and buttonReset send the ButtonEvent to the ButtonListener defined in line 31 (which, in this case, is ElevatorSimulation).

Lines 77–92 declare a DoorListener object called floorDoorListener, which contains the logic for when a Door on a Floor has opened or closed. Lines 95–100 instantiate firstFloorDoor and secondFloorDoor, then register floorDoorListener as a DoorListener for both Door objects. When either Door has opened, that Door calls method doorOpened (lines 80–84) of the floorDoorListener. When either Door has closed, that Door calls method doorClosed (lines 87–91) of the floorDoorListener. Both methods send the DoorEvent to the DoorListener declared in line 30 (which, in this case, is ElevatorSimulation).

Lines 112–115 instantiate the Elevator and register the ElevatorShaft as an ElevatorMoveListener with the Elevator. When the Elevator has departed, the Elevator invokes method elevatorDeparted (lines 229–243), which informs all objects in elevatorMoveListeners of the departure. When the Elevator has arrived, the Elevator invokes method elevatorArrived (lines 246–262), which informs all objects in elevatorMoveListeners of the arrival.

E.7 Classes Light and Bell

Class Light (Fig. E.11) represents the Lights on the Floors in the model. Objects of class Light help decorate the view by sending events to the ElevatorView via the "bubble up" technique described previously. In our simulation, the ElevatorView turns the Light on and off in the view upon receiving a lightTurnedOn or lightTurnedOff event, respectively.

```java
1   // Light.java
2   // Light turns a light on or off
3   package com.deitel.jhtp5.elevator.model;
4
5   // Deitel packages
6   import com.deitel.jhtp5.elevator.event.*;
7
8   public class Light implements ElevatorMoveListener {
9
10      // Light state (on/off)
11      private boolean lightOn;
12
13      // time before Light turns off automatically (3 seconds)
14      public static final int AUTOMATIC_TURNOFF_DELAY = 3000;
15
16      // LightListener listens for when Light should turn on/off
17      private LightListener lightListener;
18
19      // location where Light turned on or off
20      private Location lightLocation;
21
```

Fig. E.11   Class Light represents a Light on the Floor in the model. (Part 1 of 3.)

```
22          // set LightListener
23          public void setLightListener( LightListener listener )
24          {
25             lightListener = listener;
26          }
27
28          // turn on Light
29          public void turnOnLight( Location location )
30          {
31             if ( !lightOn ) {
32
33                lightOn = true;
34
35                // send LightEvent to LightListener
36                lightListener.lightTurnedOn(
37                   new LightEvent( this, location ) );
38
39                lightLocation = location;
40
41                // declare Thread that ensures automatic Light turn off
42                Thread thread = new Thread(
43                   new Runnable() {
44
45                      public void run()
46                      {
47                         // turn off Light if on for more than 3 seconds
48                         try {
49                            Thread.sleep( AUTOMATIC_TURNOFF_DELAY );
50                            turnOffLight( lightLocation );
51                         }
52
53                         // handle exception if interrupted
54                         catch ( InterruptedException exception ) {
55                            exception.printStackTrace();
56                         }
57                      }
58                   } // end anonymous inner class
59                );
60
61                thread.start();
62             }
63          } // end method turnOnLight
64
65          // turn off Light
66          public void turnOffLight( Location location )
67          {
68             if ( lightOn ) {
69
70                lightOn = false;
71
72                // send LightEvent to LightListener
73                lightListener.lightTurnedOff(
74                   new LightEvent( this, location ) );
```

Fig. E.11   Class Light represents a Light on the Floor in the model. (Part 2 of 3.)

```
75          }
76      } // end method turnOffLight
77
78      // return whether Light is on or off
79      public boolean isLightOn()
80      {
81          return lightOn;
82      }
83
84      // invoked when Elevator has departed
85      public void elevatorDeparted(
86          ElevatorMoveEvent moveEvent )
87      {
88          turnOffLight( moveEvent.getLocation() );
89      }
90
91      // invoked when Elevator has arrived
92      public void elevatorArrived(
93          ElevatorMoveEvent moveEvent )
94      {
95          turnOnLight( moveEvent.getLocation() );
96      }
97  }
```

Fig. E.11   Class Light represents a Light on the Floor in the model. (Part 3 of 3.)

According to Fig. 16.20, class Light contains attribute lightOn (line 11), which represents the state of the Light (on or off). In addition, Fig. 16.20 specifies that class Light contains methods turnOnLight (lines 29–63) and turnOffLight (lines 66–76). Line 33 of method turnOnLight sets attribute lightOn to true, and lines 36–37 call method lightTurnedOn of the lightListener (line 17). In our model, the ElevatorShaft is the lightListener—the ElevatorShaft receives events from the Light and sends them to the ElevatorSimulation, which sends them to the ElevatorView. The ElevatorShaft uses method setLightListener (lines 23–26) to register for Light-Events. Method turnOffLight sets attribute lightOn to false, then calls method lightTurnedOff of the lightListener.

We decided in Section 16.11 to make class Light an active class, so that the Light turns itself off after three seconds of being illuminated. Lines 42–59 of method turnOnLight create a thread that handles this responsibility. Method run (lines 45–57) puts this thread to sleep for three seconds, then turns off the Light. Line 61 of method turnOnLight starts the thread.

According to Fig. E.2, class Light implements interface ElevatorMoveListener. Lines 85–89 and lines 92–96 declare methods elevatorDeparted and elevatorArrived, respectively. In our model, the Light turns off when the Elevator has departed, and the Light turns on when the Elevator has arrived.

Class Bell (Fig. E.12) represents the Bell in the model and sends a bellRang event to a BellListener when the Bell has rung. This event eventually "bubbles up" to the ElevatorView. The ElevatorView plays an audio clip of a bell ringing upon receiving a bellRang event.

```
1    // Bell.java
2    // Represents Bell in simulation
3    package com.deitel.jhtp5.elevator.model;
4
5    // Deitel packages
6    import com.deitel.jhtp5.elevator.event.*;
7
8    public class Bell implements ElevatorMoveListener {
9
10       // BellListener listens for BellEvent object
11       private BellListener bellListener;
12
13       // ring bell and send BellEvent object to listener
14       private void ringBell( Location location )
15       {
16          if ( bellListener != null )
17             bellListener.bellRang(
18                new BellEvent( this, location ) );
19       }
20
21       // set BellListener
22       public void setBellListener( BellListener listener )
23       {
24          bellListener = listener;
25       }
26
27       // invoked when Elevator has departed
28       public void elevatorDeparted( ElevatorMoveEvent moveEvent ) {}
29
30       // invoked when Elevator has arrived
31       public void elevatorArrived( ElevatorMoveEvent moveEvent )
32       {
33          ringBell( moveEvent.getLocation() );
34       }
35    }
```

Fig. E.12   Class Bell represents the Bell in the model.

According to Fig. 16.20, class Bell does not contain attributes, because the Bell does not change state. However, Fig. 16.20 specifies that class Bell contains method ringBell (lines 14–19), which rings the Bell by invoking method bellRang of the BellListener bellListener (line 11). In our simulation, the Elevator is the bellListener—the Elevator receives an event from the Bell, then sends the event to the ElevatorShaft, which sends the event to the ElevatorSimulation, which sends the event to the ElevatorView. The ElevatorView then plays an audio clip of a bell ringing. The Elevator uses method setBellListener (lines 22–25) to register for BellEvents from the Bell.

According to Fig. E.2, class Bell implements interface ElevatorMoveListener. Line 28 and lines 31–34 declare methods elevatorDeparted and elevatorArrived, respectively. In our simulation, the Bell rings when the Elevator has arrived.

E.8 Class Elevator

Class Elevator (Fig. E.13) represents the elevator car that travels between the two Floors in the ElevatorShaft while carrying a Person. According to the class diagram of Fig. 16.20, class Elevator contains one object each of classes Button, Door and Bell—lines 37–39 declare variables elevatorButton, elevatorDoor and bell. As discussed in Section 10.11, class Elevator extends Location, because the Elevator is a location that the Person can occupy. Class Elevator implements methods getButton (lines 200–203) and getDoor (lines 206–209) provided by class Location. Method get-Button returns the elevatorButton and method getDoor returns the elevatorDoor. According to Fig. 16.20, we also must include two Location objects—one named cur-rentFloorLocation (line 22), which represents the current Floor being serviced, and the other named destinationFloorLocation (line 25), which represents the Floor at which the Elevator will arrive. In addition, Fig. 16.20 specifies that class Elevator requires boolean variable moving (line 19), which describes whether the Elevator is moving or idle, and boolean variable summoned (line 28), which describes whether the Elevator has been summoned. Also, class Elevator uses int constant TRAVEL_TIME (line 44), which indicates the five second travel time between Floors.

```
1    // Elevator.java
2    // Travels between Floors in the ElevatorShaft
3    package com.deitel.jhtp5.elevator.model;
4
5    // Java core packages
6    import java.util.*;
7
8    // Deitel packages
9    import com.deitel.jhtp5.elevator.event.*;
10   import com.deitel.jhtp5.elevator.ElevatorConstants;
11
12   public class Elevator extends Location implements Runnable,
13      BellListener, ElevatorConstants {
14
15      // manages Elevator thread
16      private boolean elevatorRunning = false;
17
18      // describes Elevator state (idle or moving)
19      private boolean moving = false;
20
21      // current Floor
22      private Location currentFloorLocation;
23
24      // destination Floor
25      private Location destinationFloorLocation;
26
27      // Elevator needs to service other Floor
28      private boolean summoned;
29
```

Fig. E.13   Class Elevator represents the Elevator traveling between two Floors, operating asynchronously with other objects. (Part 1 of 8.)

```
30        // listener objects
31        private Set elevatorMoveListeners;
32        private BellListener bellListener;
33        private ButtonListener elevatorButtonListener;
34        private DoorListener elevatorDoorListener;
35
36        // ElevatorDoor, Button and Bell on Elevator
37        private ElevatorDoor elevatorDoor;
38        private Button elevatorButton;
39        private Bell bell;
40
41        public static final int ONE_SECOND = 1000;
42
43        // time needed to travel between Floors (5 seconds)
44        private static final int TRAVEL_TIME = 5 * ONE_SECOND;
45
46        // Elevator's thread to handle asynchronous movement
47        private Thread thread;
48
49        // constructor creates variables; registers for ButtonEvents
50        public Elevator( Floor firstFloor, Floor secondFloor )
51        {
52           setLocationName( ELEVATOR_NAME );
53
54           // instantiate Elevator's Door, Button and Bell
55           elevatorDoor = new ElevatorDoor();
56           elevatorButton = new Button();
57           bell = new Bell();
58
59           // register Elevator for BellEvents
60           bell.setBellListener( this );
61
62           // instantiate listener Set
63           elevatorMoveListeners = new HashSet( 1 );
64
65           // start Elevator on first Floor
66           currentFloorLocation = firstFloor;
67           destinationFloorLocation = secondFloor;
68
69           // register elevatorButton for ElevatorMoveEvents
70           addElevatorMoveListener( elevatorButton );
71
72           // register elevatorDoor for ElevatorMoveEvents
73           addElevatorMoveListener( elevatorDoor );
74
75           // register bell for ElevatorMoveEvents
76           addElevatorMoveListener( bell );
77
78           // anonymous inner class listens for ButtonEvents from
79           // elevatorButton
80           elevatorButton.setButtonListener(
81              new ButtonListener() {
```

Fig. E.13   Class Elevator represents the Elevator traveling between two Floors, operating asynchronously with other objects. (Part 2 of 8.)

```
82
83                    // invoked when elevatorButton has been pressed
84                    public void buttonPressed( ButtonEvent buttonEvent )
85                    {
86                       // send ButtonEvent to listener
87                       elevatorButtonListener.buttonPressed(
88                          buttonEvent );
89
90                       // start moving Elevator to destination Floor
91                       setMoving( true );
92                    }
93
94                    // invoked when elevatorButton has been reset
95                    public void buttonReset( ButtonEvent buttonEvent )
96                    {
97                       // send ButtonEvent to listener
98                       elevatorButtonListener.buttonReset(
99                          buttonEvent );
100                   }
101             } // end anonymous inner class
102          );
103
104          // anonymous inner class listens for DoorEvents from
105          // elevatorDoor
106          elevatorDoor.addDoorListener(
107             new DoorListener() {
108
109                // invoked when elevatorDoor has opened
110                public void doorOpened( DoorEvent doorEvent )
111                {
112                   // send DoorEvent to listener
113                   elevatorDoorListener.doorOpened( new DoorEvent(
114                      doorEvent.getSource(), Elevator.this ));
115                }
116
117                // invoked when elevatorDoor has closed
118                public void doorClosed( DoorEvent doorEvent )
119                {
120                   // send DoorEvent to listener
121                   elevatorDoorListener.doorClosed( new DoorEvent(
122                      doorEvent.getSource(), Elevator.this ));
123                }
124             } // end anonymous inner class
125          );
126       } // end Elevator constructor
127
128       // swaps current Floor Location with opposite Floor Location
129       private void changeFloors()
130       {
131          Location location = currentFloorLocation;
132          currentFloorLocation = destinationFloorLocation;
133          destinationFloorLocation = location;'
```

Fig. E.13   Class Elevator represents the Elevator traveling between two Floors, operating asynchronously with other objects. (Part 3 of 8.)

```
134     }
135
136     // start Elevator thread
137     public void start()
138     {
139        if ( thread == null )
140           thread = new Thread( this );
141
142        elevatorRunning = true;
143        thread.start();
144     }
145
146     // stop Elevator thread; method run terminates
147     public void stopElevator()
148     {
149        elevatorRunning = false;
150     }
151
152     // Elevator thread's run method
153     public void run()
154     {
155        while ( isElevatorRunning() ) {
156
157           // remain idle until awoken
158           while ( !isMoving() )
159              pauseThread( 10 );
160
161           // pause while passenger exits (if one exists)
162           pauseThread( ONE_SECOND );
163
164           // close elevatorDoor
165           getDoor().closeDoor( currentFloorLocation );
166
167           // closing Door takes one second
168           pauseThread( ONE_SECOND );
169
170           // issue elevatorDeparted Event
171           sendDepartureEvent( currentFloorLocation );
172
173           // Elevator needs 5 seconds to travel
174           pauseThread( TRAVEL_TIME );
175
176           // stop Elevator
177           setMoving( false );
178
179           // swap Floor Locations
180           changeFloors();
181
182           // issue elevatorArrived Event
183           sendArrivalEvent( currentFloorLocation );
184
185        } // end while loop
```

Fig. E.13   Class Elevator represents the Elevator traveling between two Floors,
operating asynchronously with other objects. (Part 4 of 8.)

```
186
187     } // end method run
188
189     // pause concurrent thread for number of milliseconds
190     private void pauseThread( int milliseconds )
191     {
192        try {
193           Thread.sleep( milliseconds );
194        }
195
196        // handle if interrupted while sleeping
197        catch ( InterruptedException exception ) {
198           exception.printStackTrace();
199        }
200     } // end method pauseThread
201
202     // return Button on Elevator
203     public Button getButton()
204     {
205        return elevatorButton;
206     }
207
208     // return Door on Elevator
209     public Door getDoor()
210     {
211        return elevatorDoor;
212     }
213
214     // set if Elevator should move
215     private void setMoving( boolean elevatorMoving )
216     {
217        moving = elevatorMoving;
218     }
219
220     // is Elevator moving?
221     public boolean isMoving()
222     {
223        return moving;
224     }
225
226     // is Elevator thread running?
227     private boolean isElevatorRunning()
228     {
229        return elevatorRunning;
230     }
231
232     // register ElevatorMoveListener for ElevatorMoveEvents
233     public void addElevatorMoveListener(
234        ElevatorMoveListener listener )
235     {
236        elevatorMoveListeners.add( listener );
237     }
```

Fig. E.13   Class Elevator represents the Elevator traveling between two Floors, operating asynchronously with other objects. (Part 5 of 8.)

```
238
239    // register BellListener fpr BellEvents
240    public void setBellListener( BellListener listener )
241    {
242       bellListener = listener;
243    }
244
245    // register ButtonListener for ButtonEvents
246    public void setButtonListener( ButtonListener listener )
247    {
248       elevatorButtonListener = listener;
249    }
250
251    // register DoorListener for DoorEvents
252    public void setDoorListener( DoorListener listener )
253    {
254       elevatorDoorListener = listener;
255    }
256
257    // notify all ElevatorMoveListeners of arrival
258    private void sendArrivalEvent( Location location )
259    {
260       // obtain iterator from Set
261       Iterator iterator = elevatorMoveListeners.iterator();
262
263       // get next DoorListener
264       while ( iterator.hasNext() ) {
265
266          // get next ElevatorMoveListener from Set
267          ElevatorMoveListener listener =
268             ( ElevatorMoveListener ) iterator.next();
269
270          // send event to listener
271          listener.elevatorArrived( new
272             ElevatorMoveEvent( this, location ) );
273
274       } // end while loop
275
276       // service queued request, if one exists
277       if ( summoned ) {
278          setMoving( true ); // start moving Elevator
279       }
280
281       summoned = false; // request has been serviced
282
283    } // end method sendArrivalEvent
284
285    // notify all ElevatorMoveListeners of departure
286    private void sendDepartureEvent( Location location )
287    {
288       // obtain iterator from Set
289       Iterator iterator = elevatorMoveListeners.iterator();
```

Fig. E.13   Class Elevator represents the Elevator traveling between two Floors, operating asynchronously with other objects. (Part 6 of 8.)

```
290
291          // get next DoorListener
292          while ( iterator.hasNext() ) {
293
294             // get next ElevatorMoveListener from Set
295             ElevatorMoveListener listener =
296                ( ElevatorMoveListener ) iterator.next();
297
298             // send ElevatorMoveEvent to this listener
299             listener.elevatorDeparted( new ElevatorMoveEvent(
300                this, currentFloorLocation ) );
301
302          } // end while loop
303       } // end method sendDepartureEvent
304
305       // request Elevator
306       public void requestElevator( Location location )
307       {
308          // if Elevator is idle
309          if ( !isMoving() ) {
310
311             // if Elevator is on same Floor of request
312             if ( location == currentFloorLocation )
313
314                // Elevator has already arrived; send arrival event
315                sendArrivalEvent( currentFloorLocation );
316
317             // if Elevator is on opposite Floor of request
318             else {
319                setMoving( true ); // move to other Floor
320             }
321          }
322          else // if Elevator is moving
323
324             // if Elevator departed from same Floor as request
325             if ( location == currentFloorLocation )
326                summoned = true;
327
328             // if Elevator is traveling to Floor of request,
329             // simply continue traveling
330
331       } // end method requestElevator
332
333       // invoked when bell has rung
334       public void bellRang( BellEvent bellEvent )
335       {
336          // send event to bellLirdstener
337          if ( bellListener != null )
338             bellListener.bellRang( bellEvent );
339       }
340
```

Fig. E.13   Class Elevator represents the Elevator traveling between two Floors, operating asynchronously with other objects. (Part 7 of 8.)

```
341        // get the currentFloorLocation of the Elevator
342        public Location getCurrentFloor()
343        {
344            return currentFloorLocation;
345        }
346    }
```

Fig. E.13 Class `Elevator` represents the `Elevator` traveling between two `Floors`, operating asynchronously with other objects. (Part 8 of 8.)

According to Fig. E.2, class `Elevator` implements interfaces `ButtonListener`, `DoorListener` and `BellListener` and therefore can listen for `ButtonEvents`, `DoorEvents` and `BellEvents`. Class `Elevator` must send these events to a listener (in this case, the `ElevatorShaft`), so that these events can "bubble up" to the `ElevatorView`. Class `Elevator` contains a `ButtonListener` called `elevatorButtonListener` (line 33), a `DoorListener` called `elevatorDoorListener` (line 34) and a `BellListener` called `bellListener` (line 32). Lines 237–252 declare methods `setButtonListener`, `setDoorListener` and `setBellListener` that allow an object—such as `ElevatorShaft`—to register as a listener for these events.

Class `Elevator` contains an anonymous `ButtonListener` (lines 81–101) that registers for `ButtonEvents` from the `elevatorButton`. When a `Person` has pressed the `elevatorButton`, the `ButtonListener` calls method `buttonPressed` (lines 84–92) of the `ButtonListener`. Lines 87–88 of this method call method `buttonPressed` of the `elevatorButtonListener`, and line 91 informs the `Elevator` to move using method `setMoving`. When the `Button` has been reset, the `ButtonListener` calls method `buttonReset` (lines 95–100) of the `ButtonListener`. Lines 98–99 of this method call method `buttonReset` of the `elevatorButtonListener`.

Class `Elevator` contains a `DoorListener` (lines 107–124) that registers for `DoorEvents` from the `elevatorDoor`. When the `elevatorDoor` has opened, the `DoorListener` calls method `doorOpened` (lines 110–115) of this `DoorListener`. Lines 113–114 call method `doorOpened` of the `elevatorDoorListener`. When the `elevatorDoor` has closed, the `DoorListener` calls method `doorClosed` (lines 118–123) of the `DoorListener`. Lines 121–122 call method `doorClosed` of the `elevatorDoorListener`.

Class `Elevator` is a thread because it implements interface `Runnable`. Method `run` (lines 153–184) handles the travel between `Floors`. The method begins with the `Elevator` remaining idle in a `while` loop (lines 158–159). The loop exits when method `buttonPressed` in the anonymous `ButtonListener` calls method `setMoving`.

When the `Elevator` exits the loop, the `Elevator` pauses for one second to let a passenger exit (line 162), closes the `elevatorDoor` (line 165), pauses while the door closes then calls `private` method `sendDepartureEvent` (lines 286–303) to inform all listeners—the `elevatorButton`, the `elevatorDoor`, the `bell` and the `ElevatorShaft`—of the `Elevator`'s departure. Class `Elevator` contains `Set elevatorMoveListeners` (line 34), which stores all registered `ElevatorMoveListeners`. Objects wishing to receive `ElevatorMoveEvents` from the `Elevator` must call method `addElevatorMoveListener` (lines 233–237), which appends that object to `elevatorMoveListeners`. Method `sendDepartureEvent` invokes method `elevatorDeparted` of each listener object in `Set elevatorMoveListeners`.

Line 174 of method run allows the Elevator to travel to the Floor by calling method pauseThread (lines 190–200)—this simulates travel by invoking method sleep of class Thread. The Elevator stops moving when its thread awakens after five seconds. Line 177 invokes setMoving with a false argument to stop the Elevator at the arrival Floor. Line 180 calls private method changeFloors (lines 132–137), which swaps currentFloorLocation and destinationFloorLocation. Line 183 calls private method sendArrivalEvent (lines 258–283), which invokes method elevatorArrived of all listeners in Set elevatorMoveListeners. Lines 277–281 of method sendArrivalEvent service any queued request (e.g., if a Person pressed a Button on the Floor from which the Elevator has departed). If a queued request exists, line 278 invokes method setMoving to move the Elevator to the opposite Floor.

Method requestElevator (lines 306–331) requests the Elevator and generates a queued request. In our model, the ButtonListener defined in the inner class of the ElevatorShaft calls this method when a Button on either Floor has been pressed. The activity diagram of Fig. 5.29 specifies the logic for method requestElevator. If the Elevator is idle and on the same Floor as the Floor of the request, line 315 calls method sendArrivalEvent, because the Elevator has already arrived. If the Elevator is idle but on the opposite Floor from the Floor of the request, line 319 moves the Elevator to the opposite Floor. If the Elevator is traveling to the Floor that generated the request, the Elevator should continue traveling to that Floor. If the Elevator is traveling away from the Floor that generated the request, the Elevator must remember to return to that Floor (lines 325–326).

E.9 Class Person

Class Person (Fig. E.14) represents a Person that walks across the Floors and rides the Elevator in our simulation. According to the class diagram of Fig. 16.20, class Person contains one object of class Location (line 20) that represents the Person's current location in the model (either on a Floor or in the Elevator). In addition, Fig. 16.20 specifies that Person requires int attribute ID (line 14) as a unique identifier and boolean attribute moving (line 17), which indicates whether Person is walking across the Floor or waiting for a Door to open.

```
1   // Person.java
2   // Person riding the elevator
3   package com.deitel.jhtp5.elevator.model;
4
5   // Java core packages
6   import java.util.*;
7
8   // Deitel packages
9   import com.deitel.jhtp5.elevator.event.*;
10
11  public class Person extends Thread {
12
```

Fig. E.14   Class Person represents the Person that rides the Elevator. The Person operates asynchronously with other objects. (Part 1 of 6.)

```
13        // identification number
14        private int ID = -1;
15
16        // represents whether Person is moving or waiting
17        private boolean moving;
18
19        // reference to Location (either on Floor or in Elevator)
20        private Location location;
21
22        // listener object for PersonMoveEvents
23        private PersonMoveListener personMoveListener;
24
25        // time in milliseconds to walk to Button on Floor
26        private static final int TIME_TO_WALK = 3000;
27
28        // types of messages Person may send
29        public static final int PERSON_CREATED = 1;
30        public static final int PERSON_ARRIVED = 2;
31        public static final int PERSON_ENTERING_ELEVATOR = 3;
32        public static final int PERSON_PRESSING_BUTTON = 4;
33        public static final int PERSON_EXITING_ELEVATOR = 5;
34        public static final int PERSON_EXITED = 6;
35
36        // Person constructor set initial location
37        public Person( int identifier, Location initialLocation )
38        {
39           super();
40
41           ID = identifier; // assign unique identifier
42           location = initialLocation; // set Floor Location
43           moving = true; // start moving toward Button on Floor
44        }
45
46        // set listener for PersonMoveEvents
47        public void setPersonMoveListener(
48           PersonMoveListener listener )
49        {
50           personMoveListener = listener;
51        }
52
53        // set Person Location
54        private void setLocation( Location newLocation )
55        {
56           location = newLocation;
57        }
58
59        // get current Location
60        private Location getLocation()
61        {
62           return location;
63        }
64
```

Fig. E.14   Class Person represents the Person that rides the Elevator. The Person operates asynchronously with other objects. (Part 2 of 6.)

```
65          // get identifier
66          public int getID()
67          {
68              return ID;
69          }
70
71          // set if Person should move
72          public void setMoving( boolean personMoving )
73          {
74              moving = personMoving;
75          }
76
77          // get if Person should move
78          public boolean isMoving()
79          {
80              return moving;
81          }
82
83          // Person either rides or waits for Elevator
84          public void run()
85          {
86              // indicate that Person thread was created
87              sendPersonMoveEvent( PERSON_CREATED );
88
89              // walk to Elevator
90              pauseThread( TIME_TO_WALK );
91
92              // stop walking at Elevator
93              setMoving( false );
94
95              // Person arrived at Elevator
96              sendPersonMoveEvent( PERSON_ARRIVED );
97
98              // get Door on current Floor
99              Door currentFloorDoor = location.getDoor();
100
101             // get Elevator
102             Elevator elevator =
103                 ( (Floor) getLocation() ).getElevatorShaft().getElevator();
104
105             // begin exclusive access to currentFloorDoor
106             synchronized ( currentFloorDoor ) {
107
108                 // check whether Floor Door is open
109                 if ( !currentFloorDoor.isDoorOpen() ) {
110
111                     sendPersonMoveEvent( PERSON_PRESSING_BUTTON );
112                     pauseThread( 1000 );
113
114                     // press Floor's Button to request Elevator
115                     Button floorButton = getLocation().getButton();
116                     floorButton.pressButton( getLocation() );
```

Fig. E.14   Class **Person** represents the **Person** that rides the **Elevator**. The **Person** operates asynchronously with other objects. (Part 3 of 6.)

```
117         }
118
119             // wait for Floor door to open
120             try {
121
122                 while ( !currentFloorDoor.isDoorOpen() )
123                     currentFloorDoor.wait();
124             }
125
126             // handle exception waiting for Floor door to open
127             catch ( InterruptedException interruptedException ) {
128                 interruptedException.printStackTrace();
129             }
130
131             // Floor Door takes one second to open
132             pauseThread( 1000 );
133
134             // implicitly wait for exclusive access to elevator
135             synchronized ( elevator ) {
136
137                 // Person enters Elevator
138                 sendPersonMoveEvent( PERSON_ENTERING_ELEVATOR );
139
140                 // set Person Location to Elevator
141                 setLocation( elevator );
142
143                 // Person takes one second to enter Elevator
144                 pauseThread( 1000 );
145
146                 // pressing Elevator Button takes one second
147                 sendPersonMoveEvent( PERSON_PRESSING_BUTTON );
148                 pauseThread( 1000 );
149
150                 // get Elevator's Button
151                 Button elevatorButton = getLocation().getButton();
152
153                 // press Elevator's Button
154                 elevatorButton.pressButton( location );
155
156                 // Door closing takes one second
157                 pauseThread( 1000 );
158             }
159
160         } // give up exclusive access to Floor door
161
162         // get exclusive access to Elevator
163         synchronized( elevator ) {
164
165             // get Elevator door
166             Door elevatorDoor = getLocation().getDoor();
167
```

Fig. E.14 Class `Person` represents the `Person` that rides the `Elevator`. The `Person` operates asynchronously with other objects. (Part 4 of 6.)

```
168              // wait for Elevator door to open
169              synchronized( elevatorDoor ) {
170
171                 try {
172
173                    while ( !elevatorDoor.isDoorOpen() )
174                       elevatorDoor.wait();
175                 }
176
177                 // handle exception waiting for Elevator door to open
178                 catch ( InterruptedException interruptedException ) {
179                    interruptedException.printStackTrace();
180                 }
181
182                 // waiting for Elevator's Door to open takes a second
183                 pauseThread( 1000 );
184
185                 // move Person onto Floor
186                 setLocation( elevator.getCurrentFloor() );
187
188                 // walk away from Elevator
189                 setMoving( true );
190
191                 // Person exiting Elevator
192                 sendPersonMoveEvent( PERSON_EXITING_ELEVATOR );
193
194              } // release elevatorDoor lock, allowing door to close
195
196           } // release elevator lock, allowing waiting Person to enter
197
198           // walking from elevator takes five seconds
199           pauseThread( 2 * TIME_TO_WALK );
200
201           // Person exits simulation
202           sendPersonMoveEvent( PERSON_EXITED );
203
204        } // end method run
205
206        // pause thread for desired number of milliseconds
207        private void pauseThread( int milliseconds )
208        {
209           try {
210              sleep( milliseconds );
211           }
212
213           // handle exception if interrupted when paused
214           catch ( InterruptedException interruptedException ) {
215              interruptedException.printStackTrace();
216           }
217        } // end method pauseThread
218
```

Fig. E.14   Class **Person** represents the **Person** that rides the **Elevator**. The **Person** operates asynchronously with other objects. (Part 5 of 6.)

```
219      // send PersonMoveEvent to listener, depending on event type
220      private void sendPersonMoveEvent( int eventType )
221      {
222         // create new event
223         PersonMoveEvent event =
224            new PersonMoveEvent( this, getLocation(), getID() );
225
226         // send Event to this listener, depending on eventType
227         switch ( eventType ) {
228
229            // Person has been created
230            case PERSON_CREATED:
231               personMoveListener.personCreated( event );
232               break;
233
234            // Person arrived at Elevator
235            case PERSON_ARRIVED:
236               personMoveListener.personArrived( event );
237               break;
238
239            // Person entered Elevator
240            case PERSON_ENTERING_ELEVATOR:
241               personMoveListener.personEntered( event );
242               break;
243
244            // Person pressed Button object
245            case PERSON_PRESSING_BUTTON:
246               personMoveListener.personPressedButton( event );
247               break;
248
249            // Person exited Elevator
250            case PERSON_EXITING_ELEVATOR:
251               personMoveListener.personDeparted( event );
252               break;
253
254            // Person exited simulation
255            case PERSON_EXITED:
256               personMoveListener.personExited( event );
257               break;
258
259            default:
260               break;
261         }
262      } // end method sendPersonMoveEvent
263   }
```

Fig. E.14   Class Person represents the Person that rides the Elevator. The Person operates asynchronously with other objects. (Part 6 of 6.)

Class Person is subclass of class Thread. The Person performs all actions, such as walking across Floors and riding the Elevator, in method run (lines 84–204). Method run represents the lifetime of a Person described in the sequence diagrams of Fig. 16.17

and Fig. 16.18. Class `Person` contains a `PersonMoveListener` object (line 23) to which the `Person` sends `PersonMoveEvents`. In our simulation, the `ElevatorSimulation` uses method `setPersonMoveListener` (lines 47–51) to register itself as the `Person-MoveListener`. The `ElevatorSimulation`, upon receiving a `PersonMoveEvent`, sends the event to the `ElevatorView`—therefore, the `ElevatorView` "knows" when a `Person` has performed certain actions discussed momentarily.

There are several types of actions a `Person` performs in its lifetime, so there exist several types of `PersonMoveEvents` that a `Person` may send to the `personMoveListener`. Lines 29–34 declare a set of constants in which each constant represents a unique type of `PersonMoveEvent`. The `Person` sends events to `personMoveListener` when

- the `Person` has been created

- the `Person` arrives at the `Elevator`

- the `Person` enters the `Elevator`

- the `Person` presses a `Button` (either in the `Elevator` or on a `Floor`)

- the `Person` exits the `Elevator`

- the `Person` exits the simulation

When the `Person` decides to send an event to its `PersonMoveListener`, the `Person` calls `private` method `sendPersonMoveEvent` and passes the desired constant as a parameter. This method sends the event associated with the constant. For example, line 111 calls

```
sendPersonMoveEvent( PERSON_PRESSING_BUTTON );
```

when the `Person` presses a `Button` on a `Floor`. In method `run`, the `Person` walks to the `Elevator`, then sends a `personArrived` event upon arrival at the `Elevator` (line 96). We use the activity diagram of Fig. 5.28 to determine the `Person`'s actions.

It is important for the `Person` to interact with the `Door` in a thread-safe manner to prevent injury to the `Person` and to avoid "missing" the `Door`'s opening. Line 106 begins a synchronized block in which the `Person` can have exclusive access to the `current-FloorDoor`. This will ensure that when the `Person` invokes method `isDoorOpen`, the result will still be valid when the `Person` decides the next step. If we did not interact with the `Door` in a synchronized block, it is possible that between the time when the `Person` determines whether the `Door` is open and the time when the `Person` enters the `Elevator`, the `Door` could open or close without the `Person` noticing. The `Person` would then have to wait unnecessarily long to travel in the `Elevator`.

In this synchronized block on the `currentFloorDoor` object, if the `Door` on the `Floor` is closed (line 109), the `Person` must press the button and wait for the `Door` to open. Lines 111–116 press the `floorButton` to request the `Elevator`. Lines 122–123 then `wait` for the `currentFloorDoor` to open. This releases the `Person`'s lock on the `currentFloorDoor` so that the `Elevator` can open the `currentFloorDoor` when it arrives. If the `Person` did not release the lock in this manner, the `ElevatorDoor` would not be able to invoke synchronized `Door` method `openDoor`. Recall that `Door` method `openDoor` calls `notifyAll` when the `Door` opens. That `notifyAll` invocation will terminate the `Person`'s call to `wait` on line 123. The `Person` will then reacquire the lock on the `Door` (to prevent it from closing) and ensure that the Door is open (line 122). If the Door is open after wait returns, the while loop terminates and the Person can attempt to enter the Elevator.

Recall that only one Person is allowed to occupy the Elevator at one time and that the waiting Person must allow the Elevator passenger to exit the Elevator first. The synchronized block on lines 135–158 enforces this restriction. If the Elevator is occupied when the waiting Person's thread reaches line 135, the waiting Person's thread must wait to acquire a lock on the Elevator. As we will see in a moment, the passenger releases the lock on the Elevator once the passenger has exited the Elevator. At that point in time, the waiting Person can acquire the lock and enter the Elevator. Line 141 sets the Person's location to the Elevator and line 154 presses the Elevator's button to instruct the Elevator to begin traveling. The synchronized blocks for the currentFloorDoor and the Elevator terminate on lines 158–160. This allows the ElevatorDoor to close the currentFloorDoor and the Elevator to begin traveling.

The Person now must hold a lock on the Elevator (to prevent a waiting Person on the opposite Floor from entering the Elevator) and wait for the ElevatorDoor to open. Line 163 reacquires the Elevator's lock and lines 173–174 invoke method wait on the elevatorDoor. When the elevatorDoor opens, ElevatorDoor method openDoor will invoke notifyAll to notify the passenger that the ElevatorDoor has opened. When the ElevatorDoor opens, the while loop on lines 173–174 terminates and the passenger obtains the new Floor location from the Elevator (line 186). The Person then begins walking away from the Elevator (line 189) and releases the locks on the elevatorDoor and Elevator (lines 194–196). Line 202 sends a PERSON_EXITED event, which indicates that the Person has left the simulation.

E.10 Artifacts Revisited

In Section 14.13, we introduced the component diagram for the elevator simulation. In our simulation, the each class in the model imports package event—we showed the components of package event in Fig. D.15. Figure E.15 presents the component diagram for package model. Each component in package model maps to a class from the class diagram of Fig. 16.20—package model imports package event.

E.11 Conclusion

This concludes our discussion of the case study model. We hope you have enjoyed the design process of our elevator simulation using the UML, along with the presentation of object-oriented fundamentals and Java-specific topics, such as event handling and multithreading. Using the concepts discussed in this case study, you should now be able to tackle even larger systems. We encourage you to read Appendix F, which implements the ElevatorView, which transforms the ElevatorSimulation that we have designed into a vibrant and interactive program abundant with graphics, animation and sound.

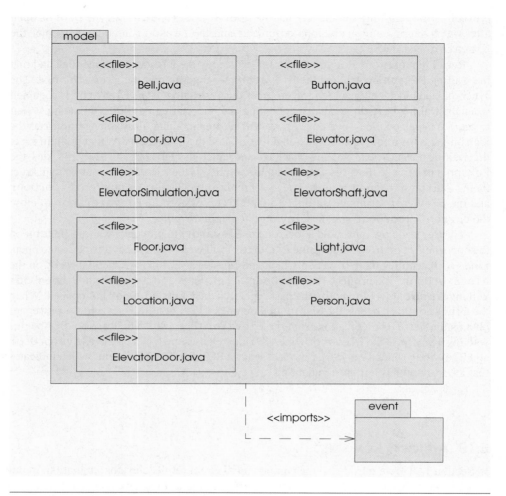

Fig. E.15   Artifacts for package **model**.

Elevator View (on CD)

F.1 Introduction

This appendix contains the implementation for class ElevatorView (Fig. F.1). Familiarity with the "Thinking About Objects" sections from all chapters (Chapter 19, in particular) is ncecessary for the understanding of material presented in this appendix. Class ElevatorView is the largest class in the simulation. To facilitate discussion, we have divided the discussion of the ElevatorView into five topics—*Class Objects*, *Class Constants*, *Class Constructor*, *Event Handling* and *Artifacts Revisited*.

```
1   // ElevatorView.java
2   // View for ElevatorSimulation
3   package com.deitel.jhtp5.elevator.view;
4
5   // Java core packages
6   import java.awt.*;
7   import java.awt.event.*;
8   import java.util.*;
9   import java.applet.*;
10
11  // Java extension package
12  import javax.swing.*;
13
14  // Deitel packages
15  import com.deitel.jhtp5.elevator.event.*;
16  import com.deitel.jhtp5.elevator.ElevatorConstants;
17
18  public class ElevatorView extends JPanel
19      implements ActionListener, ElevatorSimulationListener,
20          ElevatorConstants {
21
```

Fig. F.1   ElevatorView displays the elevator simulation model. (Part 1 of 18.)

```
22        // ElevatorView dimensions
23        private static final int VIEW_WIDTH = 800;
24        private static final int VIEW_HEIGHT = 435;
25
26        // offset for positioning Panels in ElevatorView
27        private static final int OFFSET = 10;
28
29        // Elevator repaints components every 50 ms
30        private static final int ANIMATION_DELAY = 50;
31
32        // horizontal distance constants
33        private static final int PERSON_TO_BUTTON_DISTANCE = 400;
34        private static final int BUTTON_TO_ELEVATOR_DISTANCE = 50;
35        private static final int PERSON_TO_ELEVATOR_DISTANCE =
36           PERSON_TO_BUTTON_DISTANCE + BUTTON_TO_ELEVATOR_DISTANCE;
37
38        // times walking to Floor's Button and Elevator
39        private static final int TIME_TO_BUTTON = 3000; // 3 seconds
40        private static final int TIME_TO_ELEVATOR = 1000; // 1 second
41
42        // time traveling in Elevator (5 seconds)
43        private static final int ELEVATOR_TRAVEL_TIME = 5000;
44
45        // Door images for animation
46        private static final String doorFrames[] = {
47           "images/door1.png", "images/door2.png", "images/door3.png",
48           "images/door4.png", "images/door5.png" };
49
50        // Person images for animation
51        private static final String personFrames[] = {
52           "images/bug1.png", "images/bug2.png", "images/bug3.png",
53           "images/bug4.png", "images/bug5.png", "images/bug6.png",
54           "images/bug7.png", "images/bug8.png" };
55
56        // Light images for animation
57        private static final String lightFrames[] = {
58           "images/lightOff.png", "images/lightOn.png" };
59
60        // Floor Light images for animation
61        private static final String firstFloorLightFrames[] = {
62           "images/firstFloorLightOff.png",
63           "images/firstFloorLightOn.png" };
64
65        private static final String secondFloorLightFrames[] = {
66           "images/secondFloorLightOff.png",
67           "images/secondFloorLightOn.png", };
68
69        // Floor Button images for animation
70        private static final String floorButtonFrames[] = {
71           "images/floorButtonUnpressed.png",
72           "images/floorButtonPressed.png",
73           "images/floorButtonLit.png" };
74
```

Fig. F.1   ElevatorView displays the elevator simulation model. (Part 2 of 18.)

```java
75      // Elevator Button images for animation
76      private static final String elevatorButtonFrames[] = {
77          "images/elevatorButtonUnpressed.png",
78          "images/elevatorButtonPressed.png",
79          "images/elevatorButtonLit.png" };
80
81      // Bell images for animation
82      private static final String bellFrames[] = {
83          "images/bell1.png", "images/bell2.png",
84          "images/bell3.png" };
85
86      private static final String floorImage =
87          "images/floor.png";
88      private static final String ceilingImage =
89          "images/ceiling.png";
90      private static final String elevatorImage =
91          "images/elevator.png";
92      private static final String wallImage =
93          "images/wall.jpg";
94      private static final String elevatorShaftImage =
95          "images/elevatorShaft.png";
96
97      // audio files
98      private static final String bellSound = "bell.wav";
99      private static final String doorOpenSound = "doorOpen.wav";
100     private static final String doorCloseSound = "doorClose.wav";
101     private static final String elevatorSound = "elevator.au";
102     private static final String buttonSound = "button.wav";
103     private static final String walkingSound = "walk.wav";
104     private static final String elevatorMusicSound = "liszt.mid";
105
106     // ImagePanels for Floors, ElevatorShaft, wall and ceiling
107     private ImagePanel firstFloorPanel;
108     private ImagePanel secondFloorPanel;
109     private ImagePanel elevatorShaftPanel;
110     private ImagePanel wallPanel;
111     private ImagePanel ceilingPanel;
112
113     // MovingPanels for Elevator
114     private MovingPanel elevatorPanel;
115
116     // AnimatedPanels for Buttons, Bell, Lights and Door
117     private AnimatedPanel firstFloorButtonPanel;
118     private AnimatedPanel secondFloorButtonPanel;
119     private AnimatedPanel elevatorButtonPanel;
120     private AnimatedPanel bellPanel;
121     private AnimatedPanel elevatorLightPanel;
122     private AnimatedPanel firstFloorLightPanel;
123     private AnimatedPanel secondFloorLightPanel;
124     private AnimatedPanel doorPanel;
125
126     // List containing AnimatedPanels for all Person objects
127     private java.util.List personAnimatedPanels;
```

Fig. F.1   ElevatorView displays the elevator simulation model. (Part 3 of 18.)

```
128
129      // AudioClips for sound effects
130      private AudioClip bellClip;
131      private AudioClip doorOpenClip;
132      private AudioClip doorCloseClip;
133      private AudioClip elevatorClip;
134      private AudioClip buttonClip;
135      private AudioClip walkClip;
136
137      // ElevatorMusic to play in Elevator
138      private AudioClip elevatorMusicClip;
139
140      // Timer for animation controller;
141      private javax.swing.Timer animationTimer;
142
143      // distance from top of screen to display Floors
144      private int firstFloorPosition;
145      private int secondFloorPosition;
146
147      // Elevator's velocity
148      private double elevatorVelocity;
149
150      // ElevatorView constructor
151      public ElevatorView()
152      {
153         // specifiy null Layout
154         super( null );
155
156         instantiatePanels();
157         placePanelsOnView();
158         initializeAudio();
159
160         // calculate distance Elevator travels
161         double floorDistance =
162            firstFloorPosition - secondFloorPosition;
163
164         // calculate time needed for travel
165         double time = ELEVATOR_TRAVEL_TIME / ANIMATION_DELAY;
166
167         // determine Elevator velocity (rate = distance / time)
168         elevatorVelocity = ( floorDistance + OFFSET ) / time;
169
170         // start animation Thread
171         startAnimation();
172
173      } // end ElevatorView constructor
174
175      // instantiate all Panels (Floors, Elevator, etc.)
176      private void instantiatePanels()
177      {
178         // instantiate ImagePanels representing Floors
179         firstFloorPanel = new ImagePanel( 0, floorImage );
180         secondFloorPanel = new ImagePanel( 0, floorImage );
```

Fig. F.1   ElevatorView displays the elevator simulation model. (Part 4 of 18.)

```
181
182        // calculate first and second Floor positions
183        firstFloorPosition =
184           VIEW_HEIGHT - firstFloorPanel.getHeight();
185        secondFloorPosition =
186           ( int ) ( firstFloorPosition / 2 ) - OFFSET;
187
188        firstFloorPanel.setPosition( 0, firstFloorPosition );
189        secondFloorPanel.setPosition( 0, secondFloorPosition );
190
191        wallPanel = new ImagePanel( 0, wallImage );
192
193        // create and position ImagePanel for ElevatorShaft
194        elevatorShaftPanel =
195           new ImagePanel( 0, elevatorShaftImage );
196
197        double xPosition = PERSON_TO_ELEVATOR_DISTANCE + OFFSET;
198        double yPosition =
199           firstFloorPosition - elevatorShaftPanel.getHeight();
200
201        elevatorShaftPanel.setPosition( xPosition, yPosition );
202
203        // create and position ImagePanel for ceiling
204        ceilingPanel = new ImagePanel( 0, ceilingImage );
205
206        yPosition = elevatorShaftPanel.getPosition().getY() -
207           ceilingPanel.getHeight();
208
209        ceilingPanel.setPosition( xPosition, yPosition );
210
211        // create and position MovingPanel for Elevator
212        elevatorPanel = new MovingPanel( 0, elevatorImage );
213
214        yPosition = firstFloorPosition - elevatorPanel.getHeight();
215
216        elevatorPanel.setPosition( xPosition, yPosition );
217
218        // create and position first Floor Button
219        firstFloorButtonPanel =
220           new AnimatedPanel( 0, floorButtonFrames );
221
222        xPosition = PERSON_TO_BUTTON_DISTANCE + 2 * OFFSET;
223        yPosition = firstFloorPosition - 5 * OFFSET;
224        firstFloorButtonPanel.setPosition( xPosition, yPosition );
225
226        int floorButtonPressedFrameOrder[] = { 0, 1, 2 };
227        firstFloorButtonPanel.addFrameSequence(
228           floorButtonPressedFrameOrder );
229
230        // create and position second Floor Button
231        secondFloorButtonPanel =
232           new AnimatedPanel( 1, floorButtonFrames );
233
```

Fig. F.1   ElevatorView displays the elevator simulation model. (Part 5 of 18.)

```
234        xPosition = PERSON_TO_BUTTON_DISTANCE + 2 * OFFSET;
235        yPosition = secondFloorPosition - 5 * OFFSET;
236        secondFloorButtonPanel.setPosition( xPosition, yPosition );
237
238        secondFloorButtonPanel.addFrameSequence(
239           floorButtonPressedFrameOrder );
240
241        // create and position Floor Lights
242        firstFloorLightPanel =
243           new AnimatedPanel( 0, firstFloorLightFrames );
244
245        xPosition = elevatorPanel.getLocation().x - 4 * OFFSET;
246        yPosition =
247           firstFloorButtonPanel.getLocation().y - 10 * OFFSET;
248        firstFloorLightPanel.setPosition( xPosition, yPosition );
249
250        secondFloorLightPanel =
251           new AnimatedPanel( 1, secondFloorLightFrames );
252
253        yPosition =
254           secondFloorButtonPanel.getLocation().y - 10 * OFFSET;
255        secondFloorLightPanel.setPosition( xPosition, yPosition );
256
257        // create and position Door AnimatedPanels
258        doorPanel = new AnimatedPanel( 0, doorFrames );
259        int doorOpenedFrameOrder[] = { 0, 1, 2, 3, 4 };
260        int doorClosedFrameOrder[] = { 4, 3, 2, 1, 0 };
261        doorPanel.addFrameSequence( doorOpenedFrameOrder );
262        doorPanel.addFrameSequence( doorClosedFrameOrder );
263
264        // determine where Door is located relative to Elevator
265        yPosition =
266           elevatorPanel.getHeight() - doorPanel.getHeight();
267
268        doorPanel.setPosition( 0, yPosition );
269
270        // create and position Light AnimatedPanel
271        elevatorLightPanel = new AnimatedPanel( 0, lightFrames );
272        elevatorLightPanel.setPosition( OFFSET, 5 * OFFSET );
273
274        // create and position Bell AnimatedPanel
275        bellPanel = new AnimatedPanel( 0, bellFrames );
276
277        yPosition = elevatorLightPanel.getPosition().getY() +
278           elevatorLightPanel.getHeight() + OFFSET;
279
280        bellPanel.setPosition( OFFSET, yPosition );
281        int bellRingAnimation[] = { 0, 1, 0, 2 };
282        bellPanel.addFrameSequence( bellRingAnimation );
283
284        // create and position Elevator's Button AnimatedPanel
285        elevatorButtonPanel =
286           new AnimatedPanel( 0, elevatorButtonFrames );
```

Fig. F.1   ElevatorView displays the elevator simulation model. (Part 6 of 18.)

```
287
288        yPosition = elevatorPanel.getHeight() - 6 * OFFSET;
289        elevatorButtonPanel.setPosition( 10 * OFFSET, yPosition );
290
291        int buttonPressedFrameOrder[] = { 0, 1, 2 };
292        elevatorButtonPanel.addFrameSequence(
293           buttonPressedFrameOrder );
294
295        // create List to store Person AnimatedPanels
296        personAnimatedPanels = new ArrayList();
297
298     } // end method instantiatePanels
299
300     // place all Panels on ElevatorView
301     private void placePanelsOnView()
302     {
303        // add Panels to ElevatorView
304        add( firstFloorPanel );
305        add( secondFloorPanel );
306        add( ceilingPanel );
307        add( elevatorPanel );
308        add( firstFloorButtonPanel );
309        add( secondFloorButtonPanel );
310        add( firstFloorLightPanel );
311        add( secondFloorLightPanel );
312        add( elevatorShaftPanel );
313        add( wallPanel );
314
315        // add Panels to Elevator's MovingPanel
316        elevatorPanel.add( doorPanel );
317        elevatorPanel.add( elevatorLightPanel );
318        elevatorPanel.add( bellPanel );
319        elevatorPanel.add( elevatorButtonPanel );
320
321     } // end method placePanelsOnView
322
323     // get sound effects and elevatorMusic
324     private void initializeAudio()
325     {
326        // create AudioClip sound effects from audio files
327        SoundEffects sounds = new SoundEffects();
328        sounds.setPathPrefix( "sounds/" );
329
330        bellClip = sounds.getAudioClip( bellSound );
331        doorOpenClip = sounds.getAudioClip( doorOpenSound );
332        doorCloseClip = sounds.getAudioClip( doorCloseSound );
333        elevatorClip = sounds.getAudioClip( elevatorSound );
334        buttonClip = sounds.getAudioClip( buttonSound );
335        walkClip = sounds.getAudioClip( walkingSound );
336        elevatorMusicClip = sounds.getAudioClip( elevatorMusicSound );
337
338     } // end method initializeAudio
339
```

Fig. F.1   ElevatorView displays the elevator simulation model. (Part 7 of 18.)

```
340     // starts animation by repeatedly drawing images to screen
341     public void startAnimation()
342     {
343        if ( animationTimer == null ) {
344           animationTimer =
345              new javax.swing.Timer( ANIMATION_DELAY, this );
346           animationTimer.start();
347        }
348        else
349
350           if ( !animationTimer.isRunning() )
351              animationTimer.restart();
352     }
353
354     // stop animation
355     public void stopAnimation()
356     {
357        animationTimer.stop();
358     }
359
360     // update AnimatedPanels animation in response to Timer
361     public void actionPerformed( ActionEvent actionEvent )
362     {
363        elevatorPanel.animate();
364
365        firstFloorButtonPanel.animate();
366        secondFloorButtonPanel.animate();
367
368        Iterator iterator = getPersonAnimatedPanelsIterator();
369
370        while ( iterator.hasNext() ) {
371
372           // get Person's AnimatedPanel from Set
373           AnimatedPanel personPanel =
374              ( AnimatedPanel ) iterator.next();
375
376           personPanel.animate(); // update panel
377        }
378
379        repaint(); // paint all Components
380
381     } // end method actionPerformed
382
383     private Iterator getPersonAnimatedPanelsIterator()
384     {
385        // obtain iterator from List
386        synchronized( personAnimatedPanels )
387        {
388           return new ArrayList( personAnimatedPanels ).iterator();
389        }
390     }
391
```

Fig. F.1   ElevatorView displays the elevator simulation model. (Part 8 of 18.)

```
392       // stop sound clip of Person walking
393       private void stopWalkingSound()
394       {
395          // stop playing walking sound
396          walkClip.stop();
397
398          Iterator iterator = getPersonAnimatedPanelsIterator();
399
400          // but if Person is still walking, then keep playing
401          while ( iterator.hasNext() ) {
402             AnimatedPanel panel = ( AnimatedPanel ) iterator.next();
403
404             if ( panel.getXVelocity() != 0 )
405                walkClip.loop();
406          }
407       } // end method stopWalkingSound
408
409       // returns Person AnimatedPanel with proper identifier
410       private AnimatedPanel getPersonPanel( PersonMoveEvent event )
411       {
412          Iterator iterator = getPersonAnimatedPanelsIterator();
413
414          while ( iterator.hasNext() ) {
415
416             // get next AnimatedPanel
417             AnimatedPanel personPanel =
418                ( AnimatedPanel ) iterator.next();
419
420             // return AnimatedPanel with identifier that matches
421             if ( personPanel.getID() == event.getID() )
422                return personPanel;
423          }
424
425          // return null if no match with correct identifier
426          return null;
427
428       } // end method getPersonPanel
429
430       // invoked when Elevator has departed from Floor
431       public void elevatorDeparted( ElevatorMoveEvent moveEvent )
432       {
433          String location =
434             moveEvent.getLocation().getLocationName();
435
436          // determine if Person is on Elevator
437          Iterator iterator = getPersonAnimatedPanelsIterator();
438
439          while ( iterator.hasNext() ) {
440
441             AnimatedPanel personPanel =
442                ( AnimatedPanel ) iterator.next();
443
444             double yPosition = personPanel.getPosition().getY();
```

Fig. F.1   ElevatorView displays the elevator simulation model. (Part 9 of 18.)

```
445            String panelLocation;
446
447        // determine on which Floor the Person entered
448        if ( yPosition > secondFloorPosition )
449            panelLocation = FIRST_FLOOR_NAME;
450        else
451            panelLocation = SECOND_FLOOR_NAME;
452
453        int xPosition =
454            ( int ) personPanel.getPosition().getX();
455
456        // if Person is inside Elevator
457        if ( panelLocation.equals( location )
458            && xPosition > PERSON_TO_BUTTON_DISTANCE + OFFSET ) {
459
460            // remove Person AnimatedPanel from ElevatorView
461            remove( personPanel );
462
463            // add Person AnimatedPanel to Elevator
464            elevatorPanel.add( personPanel, 1 );
465            personPanel.setLocation( 2 * OFFSET, 9 * OFFSET );
466            personPanel.setMoving( false );
467            personPanel.setAnimating( false );
468            personPanel.setVelocity( 0, 0 );
469            personPanel.setCurrentFrame( 1 );
470        }
471    } // end while loop
472
473    // determine Elevator velocity depending on Floor
474    if ( location.equals( FIRST_FLOOR_NAME ) )
475        elevatorPanel.setVelocity( 0, -elevatorVelocity );
476    else
477
478        if ( location.equals( SECOND_FLOOR_NAME ) )
479            elevatorPanel.setVelocity( 0, elevatorVelocity );
480
481    // begin moving Elevator and play Elevator music
482    elevatorPanel.setMoving( true );
483
484    if ( elevatorClip != null )
485        elevatorClip.play();
486
487    elevatorMusicClip.play();
488
489 } // end method elevatorDeparted
490
491 // invoked when Elevator has arrived at destination Floor
492 public void elevatorArrived( ElevatorMoveEvent moveEvent )
493 {
494    // stop Elevator and music
495    elevatorPanel.setMoving( false );
496    elevatorMusicClip.stop();
497
```

Fig. F.1   ElevatorView displays the elevator simulation model. (Part 10 of 18.)

```
498            double xPosition = elevatorPanel.getPosition().getX();
499            double yPosition;
500
501            // set Elevator's position to either first or second Floor
502            if ( elevatorPanel.getYVelocity() < 0 )
503               yPosition =
504                  secondFloorPosition - elevatorPanel.getHeight();
505            else
506               yPosition =
507                  firstFloorPosition - elevatorPanel.getHeight();
508
509            elevatorPanel.setPosition( xPosition, yPosition );
510
511        } // end method elevatorArrived
512
513        // invoked when Person has been created in model
514        public void personCreated( PersonMoveEvent personEvent )
515        {
516            int personID = personEvent.getID();
517
518            String floorLocation =
519               personEvent.getLocation().getLocationName();
520
521            // create AnimatedPanel representing Person
522            AnimatedPanel personPanel =
523               new AnimatedPanel( personID, personFrames );
524
525            // determine where Person should be drawn initially
526            // negative xPosition ensures Person drawn offscreen
527            double xPosition = - personPanel.getWidth();
528            double yPosition = 0;
529
530            if ( floorLocation.equals( FIRST_FLOOR_NAME ) )
531               yPosition = firstFloorPosition +
532                  ( firstFloorPanel.getHeight() / 2 );
533            else
534
535               if ( floorLocation.equals( SECOND_FLOOR_NAME ) )
536                  yPosition = secondFloorPosition +
537                     ( secondFloorPanel.getHeight() / 2 );
538
539            yPosition -= personPanel.getHeight();
540
541            personPanel.setPosition( xPosition, yPosition );
542
543            // add some animations for each Person
544            int walkFrameOrder[] = { 1, 0, 1, 2 };
545            int pressButtonFrameOrder[] = { 1, 3, 3, 4, 4, 1 };
546            int walkAwayFrameOrder[] = { 6, 5, 6, 7 };
547            personPanel.addFrameSequence( walkFrameOrder );
548            personPanel.addFrameSequence( pressButtonFrameOrder );
549            personPanel.addFrameSequence( walkAwayFrameOrder );
550
```

Fig. F.1   ElevatorView displays the elevator simulation model. (Part 11 of 18.)

```
551        // have Person begin walking to Elevator
552        personPanel.playAnimation( 0 );
553        personPanel.setLoop( true );
554        personPanel.setAnimating( true );
555        personPanel.setMoving( true );
556
557        // determine Person velocity
558        double time =
559           ( double ) ( TIME_TO_BUTTON / ANIMATION_DELAY );
560
561        double xDistance = PERSON_TO_BUTTON_DISTANCE -
562           2 * OFFSET + personPanel.getSize().width;
563        double xVelocity = xDistance / time;
564
565        personPanel.setVelocity( xVelocity, 0 );
566        personPanel.setAnimationRate( 1 );
567
568        walkClip.loop(); // play sound clip of Person walking
569
570        // store in personAnimatedPanels
571        synchronized( personAnimatedPanels )
572        {
573           personAnimatedPanels.add( personPanel );
574        }
575
576        add( personPanel, 0 );
577
578     } // end method personCreated
579
580     // invoked when Person has arrived at Elevator
581     public void personArrived( PersonMoveEvent personEvent )
582     {
583        // find Panel associated with Person that issued event
584        AnimatedPanel panel = getPersonPanel( personEvent );
585
586        if ( panel != null ) { // if Person exists
587
588           // Person stops at Floor Button
589           panel.setMoving( false );
590           panel.setAnimating( false );
591           panel.setCurrentFrame( 1 );
592           stopWalkingSound();
593
594           double xPosition = PERSON_TO_BUTTON_DISTANCE -
595              ( panel.getSize().width / 2 );
596           double yPosition = panel.getPosition().getY();
597
598           panel.setPosition( xPosition, yPosition );
599        }
600     } // end method personArrived
601
```

Fig. F.1   ElevatorView displays the elevator simulation model. (Part 12 of 18.)

```
602     // invoked when Person has pressed Button
603     public void personPressedButton( PersonMoveEvent personEvent )
604     {
605        // find Panel associated with Person that issued event
606        AnimatedPanel panel = getPersonPanel( personEvent );
607
608        if ( panel != null ) { // if Person exists
609
610           // Person stops walking and presses Button
611           panel.setLoop( false );
612           panel.playAnimation( 1 );
613
614           panel.setVelocity( 0, 0 );
615           panel.setMoving( false );
616           panel.setAnimating( true );
617           stopWalkingSound();
618        }
619     } // end method personPressedButton
620
621     // invoked when Person has started to enter Elevator
622     public void personEntered( PersonMoveEvent personEvent )
623     {
624        // find Panel associated with Person that issued event
625        AnimatedPanel panel = getPersonPanel( personEvent );
626
627        if ( panel != null ) {
628
629           // determine velocity
630           double time = TIME_TO_ELEVATOR / ANIMATION_DELAY;
631
632           double distance =
633              elevatorPanel.getPosition().getX() -
634              panel.getPosition().getX() + 2 * OFFSET;
635
636           panel.setVelocity( distance / time, -1.5 );
637
638           // Person starts walking
639           panel.setMoving( true );
640           panel.playAnimation( 0 );
641           panel.setLoop( true );
642        }
643     } // end method personEntered
644
645     // invoked when Person has departed from Elevator
646     public void personDeparted( PersonMoveEvent personEvent)
647     {
648        // find Panel associated with Person that issued event
649        AnimatedPanel panel = getPersonPanel( personEvent );
650
651        if ( panel != null ) { // if Person exists
652
653           // determine velocity (in opposite direction)
654           double time = TIME_TO_BUTTON / ANIMATION_DELAY;
```

Fig. F.1   ElevatorView displays the elevator simulation model. (Part 13 of 18.)

```
655            double xVelocity = - PERSON_TO_BUTTON_DISTANCE / time;
656
657            panel.setVelocity( xVelocity, 0 );
658
659            // remove Person from Elevator
660            elevatorPanel.remove( panel );
661
662            double xPosition =
663               PERSON_TO_ELEVATOR_DISTANCE + 3 * OFFSET;
664            double yPosition = 0;
665
666            String floorLocation =
667               personEvent.getLocation().getLocationName();
668
669            // determine Floor onto which Person exits
670            if ( floorLocation.equals( FIRST_FLOOR_NAME ) )
671               yPosition = firstFloorPosition +
672                  ( firstFloorPanel.getHeight() / 2 );
673            else
674
675               if ( floorLocation.equals( SECOND_FLOOR_NAME ) )
676                  yPosition = secondFloorPosition +
677                     ( secondFloorPanel.getHeight() / 2 );
678
679         yPosition -= panel.getHeight();
680
681         panel.setPosition( xPosition, yPosition );
682
683         // add Person to ElevatorView
684         add( panel, 0 );
685
686         // Person starts walking
687         panel.setMoving( true );
688         panel.setAnimating( true );
689         panel.playAnimation( 2 );
690         panel.setLoop( true );
691         walkClip.loop();
692      }
693   } // end method PersonDeparted
694
695   // invoked when Person has exited simulation
696   public void personExited( PersonMoveEvent personEvent)
697   {
698      // find Panel associated with Person that issued moveEvent
699      AnimatedPanel panel = getPersonPanel( personEvent );
700
701      if ( panel != null ) { // if Person exists
702
703         panel.setMoving( false );
704         panel.setAnimating( false );
705
```

Fig. F.1   ElevatorView displays the elevator simulation model. (Part 14 of 18.)

```
706          // remove Person permanently and stop walking sound
707          synchronized( personAnimatedPanels )
708          {
709             personAnimatedPanels.remove( panel );
710          }
711          remove( panel );
712          stopWalkingSound();
713       }
714    } // end method personExited
715
716    // invoked when Door has opened in model
717    public void doorOpened( DoorEvent doorEvent )
718    {
719       // get DoorEvent Location
720       String location =
721          doorEvent.getLocation().getLocationName();
722
723       // play animation of Door opening
724       doorPanel.playAnimation( 0 );
725       doorPanel.setAnimationRate( 2 );
726       doorPanel.setDisplayLastFrame( true );
727
728       // play sound clip of Door opening
729       if ( doorOpenClip != null )
730          doorOpenClip.play();
731
732    } // end method doorOpened
733
734    // invoked when Door has closed in model
735    public void doorClosed( DoorEvent doorEvent )
736    {
737       // get DoorEvent Location
738       String location =
739          doorEvent.getLocation().getLocationName();
740
741       // play animation of Door closing
742       doorPanel.playAnimation( 1 );
743       doorPanel.setAnimationRate( 2 );
744       doorPanel.setDisplayLastFrame( true );
745
746       // play sound clip of Door closing
747       if ( doorCloseClip != null )
748          doorCloseClip.play();
749
750    } // end method doorClosed
751
752    // invoked when Button has been pressed in model
753    public void buttonPressed( ButtonEvent buttonEvent )
754    {
755       // get ButtonEvent Location
756       String location =
757          buttonEvent.getLocation().getLocationName();
758
```

Fig. F.1   ElevatorView displays the elevator simulation model. (Part 15 of 18.)

```
759          // press Elevator Button if from Elevator
760          if ( location.equals( ELEVATOR_NAME ) ) {
761             elevatorButtonPanel.playAnimation( 0 );
762             elevatorButtonPanel.setDisplayLastFrame( true );
763          }
764
765          // press Floor Button if from Floor
766          else
767
768             if ( location.equals( FIRST_FLOOR_NAME ) ) {
769                firstFloorButtonPanel.playAnimation( 0 );
770                firstFloorButtonPanel.setDisplayLastFrame( true );
771             }
772          else
773
774             if ( location.equals( SECOND_FLOOR_NAME ) ) {
775                secondFloorButtonPanel.playAnimation( 0 );
776                secondFloorButtonPanel.setDisplayLastFrame( true );
777             }
778
779          if ( buttonClip != null )
780             buttonClip.play(); // play button press sound clip
781
782       } // end method buttonPressed
783
784       // invoked when Button has been reset in model
785       public void buttonReset( ButtonEvent buttonEvent )
786       {
787          // get ButtonEvent Location
788          String location =
789             buttonEvent.getLocation().getLocationName();
790
791          // reset Elevator Button if from Elevator
792          if ( location.equals( ELEVATOR_NAME ) ) {
793
794             // return to first frame if still animating
795             if ( elevatorButtonPanel.isAnimating() )
796                elevatorButtonPanel.setDisplayLastFrame( false );
797             else
798                elevatorButtonPanel.setCurrentFrame( 0 );
799          }
800
801          // reset Floor Button if from Floor
802          else
803
804             if ( location.equals( FIRST_FLOOR_NAME ) ) {
805
806                // return to first frame if still animating
807                if ( firstFloorButtonPanel.isAnimating() )
808                   firstFloorButtonPanel.setDisplayLastFrame( false );
809
```

Fig. F.1   ElevatorView displays the elevator simulation model. (Part 16 of 18.)

```
810                else
811                    firstFloorButtonPanel.setCurrentFrame( 0 );
812            }
813        else
814
815            if ( location.equals( SECOND_FLOOR_NAME ) ) {
816
817                // return to first frame if still animating
818                if ( secondFloorButtonPanel.isAnimating() )
819                    secondFloorButtonPanel.setDisplayLastFrame(
820                        false );
821                else
822                    secondFloorButtonPanel.setCurrentFrame( 0 );
823            }
824
825    } // end method buttonReset
826
827    // invoked when Bell has rung in model
828    public void bellRang( BellEvent bellEvent )
829    {
830        bellPanel.playAnimation( 0 ); // animate Bell
831
832        if ( bellClip != null ) // play Bell sound clip
833            bellClip.play();
834    }
835
836    // invoked when Light turned on in model
837    public void lightTurnedOn( LightEvent lightEvent )
838    {
839        // turn on Light in Elevator
840        elevatorLightPanel.setCurrentFrame( 1 );
841
842        String location =
843            lightEvent.getLocation().getLocationName();
844
845        // turn on Light on either first or second Floor
846        if ( location.equals( FIRST_FLOOR_NAME ) )
847            firstFloorLightPanel.setCurrentFrame( 1 );
848
849        else
850
851            if ( location.equals( SECOND_FLOOR_NAME ) )
852                secondFloorLightPanel.setCurrentFrame( 1 );
853
854    } // end method lightTurnedOn
855
856    // invoked when Light turned off in model
857    public void lightTurnedOff( LightEvent lightEvent )
858    {
859        // turn off Light in Elevator
860        elevatorLightPanel.setCurrentFrame( 0 );
861
```

Fig. F.1   ElevatorView displays the elevator simulation model. (Part 17 of 18.)

```
862        String location =
863            lightEvent.getLocation().getLocationName();
864
865        // turn off Light on either first or second Floor
866        if ( location.equals( FIRST_FLOOR_NAME ) )
867            firstFloorLightPanel.setCurrentFrame( 0 );
868
869        else
870
871            if ( location.equals( SECOND_FLOOR_NAME ) )
872                secondFloorLightPanel.setCurrentFrame( 0 );
873
874    } // end method lightTurnedOff
875
876    // return preferred size of ElevatorView
877    public Dimension getPreferredSize()
878    {
879        return new Dimension( VIEW_WIDTH, VIEW_HEIGHT );
880    }
881
882    // return minimum size of ElevatorView
883    public Dimension getMinimumSize()
884    {
885        return getPreferredSize();
886    }
887
888    // return maximum size of ElevatorView
889    public Dimension getMaximumSize()
890    {
891        return getPreferredSize();
892    }
893 }
```

Fig. F.1   ElevatorView displays the elevator simulation model. (Part 18 of 18.)

F.2 Class Objects

The ElevatorView is a JPanel with a series of other JPanel "children" added to it. Each JPanel provides a visual representation of an object from the model. For example, the ElevatorView contains ImagePanels, MovingPanels and AnimatedPanels to represent the Elevator, the Persons, the ElevatorShaft, the Buttons on the Floors, the Button in the Elevator, the Doors on the Floors, the Door in the Elevator, the Lights on the Floors, the two Floors and the Bell. Figure F.2 lists the ElevatorView's objects and their counterparts in the model.

Lines 107–127 of class ElevatorView declare the objects in the second column of Fig. F.2. The firstFloorPanel (line 107), secondFloorPanel (line 108) and elevatorShaftPanel (line 109) are ImagePanels, because neither the Floors nor the ElevatorShaft move in the simulation. The elevatorPanel (line 114) is a MovingPanel, because the Elevator's only function is to move between Floors. The firstFloorButtonPanel (line 117), secondFloorButtonPanel (line 118) and elevatorButtonPanel (line 119) are AnimatedPanels, because each object animates when the associated Button in the model is pressed or reset. The bellPanel (line 120) is an AnimatedPanel

The object (in model) of Class...	is represented by the object (in view)...	of Class...
Floor	firstFloorPanel secondFloorPanel	ImagePanel ImagePanel
ElevatorShaft	elevatorShaftPanel	ImagePanel
Elevator	elevatorPanel	MovingPanel
Button (on Floor)	firstFloorButtonPanel secondFloorButtonPanel	AnimatedPanel AnimatedPanel
Button (in Elevator)	elevatorButtonPanel	AnimatedPanel
Bell	bellPanel	AnimatedPanel
Light	firstFloorLightPanel secondFloorLightPanel	AnimatedPanel AnimatedPanel
Door (in Elevator)	doorPanel	AnimatedPanel
Door (on Floor)	<not represented>	<not represented>
Person	personAnimatedPanels	List (of AnimatedPanels)

Fig. F.2   Objects in the ElevatorView representing objects in the model.

to animate the ringing of the Bell. The firstFloorLightPanel (line 122) and second-FloorLightPanel (line 123) are AnimatedPanels, because these objects animate when the associated Light turns on or off. The doorPanel (line 124) is an AnimatedPanel to animate the opening and closing of the Door. Note that the ElevatorView shows only the Door in the Elevator. The ElevatorView does not show the Doors on the Floors, which enables us to show the Elevator's interior. (These Doors would obstruct the objects inside the Elevator.) Lastly, the personAnimatedPanels (line 127) is a List of AnimatedPanels, because there can exist several Person objects during execution—the ElevatorView must need to store dynamically the AnimatedPanels associated with Persons in the model.

We add to the ElevatorView three more elements that we assume to be parts of the Elevator (Fig. F.3), although the model does not represent these elements—a light inside the Elevator of type AnimatedPanel called elevatorLightPanel (line 121), a ceiling over the Elevator of type ImagePanel called ceilingPanel (line 111) and wallpaper inside the building of type ImagePanel called wallPanel (line 110).

The object (in model) of Class...	is represented by the object (in view)...	of Class...
<not represented>	elevatorLightPanel	AnimatedPanel
<not represented>	ceilingPanel	ImagePanel
<not represented>	wallPanel	ImagePanel

Fig. F.3   Objects in the ElevatorView not represented in the model.

In addition, the class diagram of Fig. 19.5 shows that the ElevatorView contains one instance of class SoundEffects. The SoundEffects object generates the AudioClips used to play sound effects, such as the Door opening and a Person walking. Lines 130–135 declare all AudioClips and line 327 (in method initializeAudio, which we discuss later in this section) creates the SoundEffects object.

F.3 Class Constants

The ElevatorView uses constants to specify or obtain such information as

- The initial placement of objects in the ElevatorView
- The rate at which the ElevatorView redraws the screen (animation rate)
- The names of image files used by the ImagePanels
- The names of sound files used by the SoundEffects object
- The distances in pixels the ImagePanels representing the Elevator and Person must travel
- The times needed to travel these distances

Lines 23–24 declare int constants VIEW_WIDTH and VIEW_HEIGHT, which specify the ElevatorView's dimensions. Method getPreferredSize (lines 877–880) returns this dimension. Method pack of class ElevatorCaseStudy uses this method to obtain the ElevatorView's dimension to place the ElevatorView in the GUI properly.

The ElevatorView has a null layout, so we may place ImagePanels in any x-y coordinate in the ElevatorView. Line 27 of class ElevatorView declares int constant OFFSET, which helps to determine the exact positions of objects in the ElevatorView. Line 30 declares int constant ANIMATION_DELAY, which specifies the number of milliseconds between animation frames. In our simulation, we initialize ANIMATION_DELAY to 50 milliseconds. Lines 46–95 declare String constants specifying the image files used to instantiate the ImagePanels. Lines 98–104 declare the String constant specifying the audio files used to instantiate the AudioClips.

Line 33 declares the int constant PERSON_TO_BUTTON_DISTANCE, which represents the horizontal distance between the on-screen location of the firstFloorButtonPanel or secondFloorButtonPanel and the initial on-screen location of an AnimatedPanel associated with Person. This AnimatedPanel uses this constant to calculate the travel distance to the firstFloorButtonPanel or secondFloorButtonPanel. The firstFloorButtonPanel and secondFloorButtonPanel use the constant to position themselves on screen. Line 34 declares the int constant BUTTON_TO_ELEVATOR_DISTANCE, describing the horizontal distance between the firstFloorButtonPanel or secondFloorButtonPanel and the elevatorPanel. The AnimatedPanel associated with a Person uses this constant to determine the travel distance when entering the elevatorPanel.

Line 39 declares int constant TIME_TO_BUTTON, which represents this AnimatedPanel's travel time to the firstFloorButtonPanel or secondFloorButtonPanel. Line 40 declares int constant TIME_TO_ELEVATOR, which represents the time the AnimatedPanel associated with a Person needs to enter the elevatorPanel from the firstFloorButtonPanel or secondFloorButtonPanel. Using the equation *rate = distance / time*, the AnimatedPanel associated with the Person can determine the velocity needed to travel. Similarly, line 43 declares int constant ELEVATOR_TRAVEL_TIME, which represents the elevatorPanel's travel time between the firstFloorPanel and sec-ondFloorPanel—lines 165–168 use this constant to determine double attribute eleva-torVelocity (line 148).

F.4 Class Constructor

The responsibilities of the ElevatorView constructor (lines 151–173) are

- To instantiate all ImagePanels
- To add all ImagePanels to the ElevatorView
- To initialize the audio objects
- To compute the elevatorPanel's initial velocity and distance traveled
- To start the animation Timer

Lines 156 calls method instantiatePanels (lines 176–298) to instantiate the ImagePanels in the ElevatorView. Lines 179–180 instantiate the firstFloorPanel and secondFloorPanel, and lines 183–189 set these objects' positions—the Elevator-View positions the firstFloorPanel on the bottom of the screen and positions the sec-ondFloorPanel in the vertical center of the screen. Line 191 instantiates the wallPanel ImagePanel. The ElevatorView does not need to calculate the position for the wall-Panel, because the wallPanel's default screen position (i.e., xPosition = 0, yPosi-tion = 0) is correct. Lines 194–201 and lines 204–209 instantiate and position the elevatorShaftPanel and ceilingPanel ImagePanels, respectively. The Eleva-torView positions the elevatorShaftPanel in the right of the screen and positions the ceilingPanel above the elevatorShaftPanel. Lines 212–216 instantiate the eleva-torPanel and position it over the elevatorShaftPanel above the firstFloorPanel. Lines 219–228 instantiate the firstFloorButtonPanel AnimatedPanel, place it next to the elevatorShaftPanel, then create a frame sequence Button pressed animation. Lines 231–239 perform the same actions on the secondFloorButtonPanel. Lines 242–248 instantiate the firstFloorLightPanel AnimatedPanel and place it to the left of the elevatorShaftPanel but above the firstFloorButtonPanel. Lines 250–255 position the secondFloorLightPanel above the secondFloorButtonPanel. Lines 258–268 instantiate the doorPanel AnimatedPanel, place it relative to the elevator-Panel's position (because the elevatorPanel will contain the doorPanel) and assign frame sequences describing the Door animation opening and closing. Lines 271–272 instantiate the elevatorLightPanel AnimatedPanel and position it over the eleva-torPanel and to the left of the doorPanel. Lines 275–282 instantiate the bellPanel, position it below the elevatorLightPanel, then assign a frame sequence describing the Bell ringing animation. Lines 285–293 instantiate the elevatorButtonPanel, position it in the center of the elevatorPanel and assign a frame sequence describing the Button pressed animation. Lastly, line 296 instantiates the ArrayList holding the Animated-Panels associated with the Persons in the model.

After the ElevatorView constructor calls instantiatePanels, the constructor calls method placePanelsOnView (lines 301–321), which adds all instantiated Panels to the ElevatorView. Lines 316–319 add the doorPanel, elevatorLightPanel, bellPanel and elevatorButtonPanel to the elevatorPanel. The ElevatorView constructor then calls method `initializeAudio` (lines 324–338). Lines 327–328 instantiate a Sound-Effects object, and lines 330–336 use method `getAudioClip` of the `SoundEffects` object to return the `AudioClip`s for the simulation. Method `play` of class `AudioClip` plays the `AudioClip`—the `ElevatorView` uses this method for sounds that do not repeat, such as the `Bell` ring. Method `loop` of class `AudioClip` plays the clip continually—the `ElevatorView` uses this method for sounds that repeat, such as the sound of footsteps.

Finally, lines 161–162 (in the `ElevatorView` constructor) calculate the distance between the two `Floor`s (i.e., the distance the `elevatorPanel` will travel). Lines 165–168 use the equation *rate = distance / time* to determine the `elevatorPanel`'s velocity when traveling. Finally, line 171 calls method `startAnimation`, which starts the animation timer.

The `ElevatorView` animates the `ImagePanel`s using `animationTimer` (line 141), an instance of class `javax.swing.Timer`. The `animationTimer` starts in the `ElevatorView` constructor through method `startAnimation` (lines 341–352). Class `ElevatorView` implements interface `ActionListener` to listen for `ActionEvent`s. The `animationTimer` sends an `ActionEvent` to the `ElevatorView` every 50 (`ANIMATION_DELAY`) milliseconds. When the `ElevatorView` receives an `ActionEvent`, the `ElevatorView` calls method `actionPerformed` (lines 361–381). Line 363 in this method updates the position and current image of the `elevatorPanel` and of the `elevatorPanel`'s children. Lines 365–366 allow the `firstFloorButtonPanel` and `secondFloorButtonPanel` to update themselves. Lines 370–377 iterate `List` `personAnimatedPanels` and update the position and current image of each `AnimatedPanel` associated with a `Person` in the model. Lastly, line 379 calls method `repaint` to redraw all `ImagePanel`s added to the `ElevatorView` on screen.

We present an object diagram that lists all objects in the `ElevatorView`. Recall that an object diagram provides a snapshot of the structure when the system is running. The object diagram of Fig. F.4 represents the `ElevatorView` after invoking the constructor.

The `ElevatorView` object links (contains an association) with all objects presented in Fig. F.4. The `elevatorPanel` links with objects `elevatorLightPanel`, `bellPanel`, `doorPanel` and `elevatorButtonPanel`. This association provides a visualization of what is happening in the model—the `Elevator` contains a `Light`, `Bell`, `Door` and `Button`. The `SoundEffects` object links with the `AudioClip` objects, because the `SoundEffects` object generates the `AudioClip` objects.

F.5 Event Handling

Figure 14.21 specified that `ElevatorView` implements `ElevatorSimulationListener`, which implements all interfaces in the simulation. The `ElevatorCaseStudy` registers the `ElevatorView` as a listener for events from the `ElevatorSimulation`; in other words, the `ElevatorSimulation` sends all events generated in the model to the `ElevatorView`.

Every method implementing an interface receives an event object of type `ElevatorSimulationEvent` (or a subclass) as a parameter. For example, the `doorOpened` method receives a `DoorEvent`. Appendix D contains further reference on events and listeners. The following sections discuss the types of events that the `ElevatorView` handles.

F.5.1 ElevatorMoveEvent types

The `ElevatorSimulation` sends an `ElevatorMoveEvent` when the `Elevator` has either departed or arrived in the model. The `ElevatorSimulation` invokes method `eleva-`

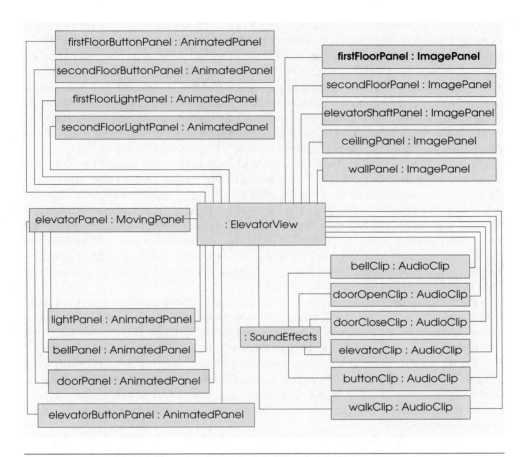

Fig. F.4   Object diagram for the `ElevatorView` after initialization.

torDeparted (lines 431–489) when the `Elevator` has departed from a `Floor`. Lines 437–471 determine whether an `AnimatedPanel` associated with a `Person` overlaps the `elevatorPanel` by iterating `personAnimatedPanels` and testing whether any `AnimatedPanel` in the `List` has an on-screen *x*-coordinate greater than that of the `elevatorPanel`. If this is the case, then the `Person` is inside the `Elevator`, and lines 464–469 add the `AnimatedPanel` associated with that `Person` to the `elevatorPanel`. Regardless of whether a `Person` is inside the `Elevator`, lines 474–479 set the `elevatorPanel`'s velocity according to the direction the `Elevator` must travel. Line 487 plays the `elevatorMusicClip`.

The `ElevatorSimulation` invokes method `elevatorArrived` (lines 492–511) when the `Elevator` has arrived at a `Floor`. Line 495 stops the `elevatorPanel`, and line 496 stops the `elevatorMusic`. Lines 502–509 change the direction of the `elevatorPanel` for the next travel.

F.5.2 PersonMoveEvent types

The `ElevatorSimulation` sends a `PersonMoveEvent` when a `Person` has performed some action in the model that the `ElevatorView` must represent. The `ElevatorSimula-`

tion invokes method `personCreated` (lines 514–578) when the model instantiates a new `Person`. Lines 522–523 instantiate an `AnimatedPanel` for a `Person`. Lines 527–541 determine on which `Floor` to situate the `AnimatedPanel`, depending on the `Floor` on which the event was generated. Lines 544–549 add frame sequences to the `AnimatedPanel` describing the `Person` walking and pressing a `Button`. Lines 552–568 animate the `Person` walking, determine the `Person`'s velocity necessary to reach the `Button` on the `Floor` and play the sound effect of footsteps. Lastly, lines 571–576 add the `AnimatedPanel` associated with the `Person` to `List personAnimatedPanels`, using a synchronized block (lines 571–574) to guarantee no other object can access the `List`.

The `ElevatorSimulation` invokes method `personArrived` (lines 581–600) when a `Person` has arrived at the `Elevator`. Line 584 calls method `getPersonPanel` (lines 410–428), which determines the `AnimatedPanel` associated with the `Person` that issued the event. Specifically, method `getPersonPanel` iterates `List personAnimatedPanels` and returns the `AnimatedPanel` whose identifier matches the identifier of the `PersonMoveEvent`. Lines 586–599 in method `personArrived` stop this `AnimatedPanel` from moving. Line 592 stops the sound of footsteps by calling method `stopWalkingSound` (lines 393–407), which stops the `AudioClip` playing the footstep sound only if no `Person`s are walking.

The `ElevatorSimulation` invokes method `personPressedButton` (lines 603–619) when a `Person` pressed a `Button`. Line 606 determines the `AnimatedPanel` associated with the `Person` who pressed the `Button`. Line 612 calls method `playAnimation`, which plays the animation sequence of that `Person` pressing the `Button`.

The `ElevatorSimulation` invokes method `personEntered` (lines 622–643) when a `Person` is about to enter the `Elevator`. Line 625 retrieves the `AnimatedPanel` associated with the `Person` entering the `Elevator`. Lines 630–636 determine the velocity needed to walk into the `Elevator`. Lines 639–641 animate this `AnimatedPanel` to walk in the `elevatorPanel`.

`ElevatorSimulation` invokes `personDeparted` (lines 646–693) when a `Person` is about to exit the `Elevator`. Line 649 determines the `AnimatedPanel` associated with the `Person` departing the `Elevator`. Lines 654–657 determine that `Person`'s velocity needed to walk to across the `Floor` to exit the simulation. Lines 660–684 position the `AnimatedPanel` for the `Person` on the `Floor` in front of the `Elevator` by removing the `AnimatedPanel` from the `elevatorPanel` and adding the `AnimatedPanel` to the `ElevatorView`. Lines 687–691 animate this `AnimatedPanel` to walk across either the `firstFloorPanel` or `secondFloorPanel` and start the sound of footsteps.

The `ElevatorSimulation` invokes `personExited` (lines 696–714) when a `Person` exits the simulation. Line 699 determines the `AnimatedPanel` associated with the `Person` who exited the simulation. Lines 707–712 remove the `AnimatedPanel` associated with that `Person` from the `ElevatorView` and stop the sound of footsteps.

F.5.3 DoorEvent types

The `ElevatorSimulation` sends a `DoorEvent` to the `ElevatorView` when a `Door` has opened or closed in the model. The `ElevatorSimulation` invokes method `doorOpened` (lines 717–732) when a `Door` has opened. Lines 720–726 animate the `doorPanel` opening, and lines 729–730 play the `doorOpenClip`, which is the sound effect associated with the `Door`'s opening.

The `ElevatorSimulation` invokes method `doorClosed` (lines 735–750) when a Door has closed. Lines 738–744 animate the `doorPanel` closing, and lines 747–748 plays the `doorClosedClip`, which is the sound effect associated with the Door's closing.

F.5.4 ButtonEvent types

The `ElevatorSimulation` sends a `ButtonEvent` to the `ElevatorView` when a Button has been pressed or reset in the model. The `ElevatorSimulation` invokes method `buttonPressed` (lines 753–782) when a `Button` has been pressed. Lines 756–757 determine the `Location` where the `Button` was pressed. If the `Location` is the `Elevator`, then lines 760–763 play the `Button` pressed animation inside the `Elevator`. If the `Location` is the first `Floor`, then lines 768–771 play the `Button` pressed animation on the first `Floor`. If the `Location` is the second `Floor`, then lines 774–777 play the `Button` pressed animation on the second `Floor` being pressed. Lines 779–780 play the `buttonClip`, which is the sound effect associated with the `Button` being pressed.

The `ElevatorSimulation` invokes method `buttonReset` (lines 785–825) when a Button has been reset. Lines 788–789 determine the `Location` where the `Button` was reset. If the `Location` is the `Elevator`, then lines 792–799 change the `elevatorButtonPanel`'s image to that of the `Button` reset. If the `Location` is the first `Floor`, then lines 804–812 change the `firstFloorButtonPanel`'s image associated with the `Button` reset. If the `Location` is the second `Floor`, then lines 815–823 change the `secondFloorButtonPanel`'s image associated with the `Button` reset.

F.5.5 BellEvent types

The `ElevatorSimulation` sends a `BellEvent` to the `ElevatorView` by invoking method `bellRang` (lines 828–834) when a `Bell` has rung in the model. Line 830 animates the `bellPanel`, and lines 832–833 play the `bellClip`, which is the sound effect associated with the `Bell` ringing.

F.5.6 LightEvent types

The `ElevatorSimulation` sends a `LightEvent` to the `ElevatorView` when a `Light` has changed state in the model. The `ElevatorSimulation` invokes method `lightTurnedOn` (lines 837–854) when a `Light` has turned on. Line 840 turns on `elevatorLightPanel`. Lines 842–852 determine on which `Floor` the `Light` has turned on, then illuminates the `AnimatedPanel` associated with that `Light` in the `ElevatorView`.

The `ElevatorSimulation` invokes method `lightTurnedOff` (lines 857–874) when a `Light` has turned off. Line 860 turns on `elevatorLightPanel`. Lines 862–872 determine on which `Floor` the `Light` has turned on, then turns off the `AnimatedPanel` associated with that `Light` in the `ElevatorView`.

F.6 Artifacts Revisited

In Section 14.13, we modeled the artifacts of the elevator simulation, and in Appendix D and Appendix E, we added artifacts to packages `event` and `model`, respectively. Figure F.5 presents the component diagram for package `view`, which contains artifacts `ElevatorView.java`, `ImagePanel.java`, `MovingPanel.java`, `AnimatedPanel.java`, `ElevatorMusic.java` and `SoundEffects.java`. `ElevatorView.java` imports packages `images`, `sounds` and `event`. Packages `images` and `sounds` contain all image files and sound files (artifacts) used by `ElevatorView.java`, respectively. The diagram does not show the contents of these directories, because there exist far too many graphics and audio files to represent on one page—the contents of these packages can be found in the directory structures

```
com/deitel/jhtp5/elevator/view/images
com/deitel/jhtp5/elevator/view/sounds
```

(i.e., in the `images` and `sounds` directories where the classes for the view are located in the file system).

F.7 Conclusion

Congratulations! You have completed an "industrial-strength" OOD/UML case study. You are well prepared to tackle more substantial design problems and to go on to deeper study of OOD with the UML. Hopefully you have developed a greater appreciation and understanding of design and implementation processes. Now, you can use Java to implement substantial object-oriented system designs generated by the UML. We hope you have enjoyed using Java and the UML to construct this case study while learning what features the two technologies have to offer. In addition, we hope you have enjoyed using Java's GUI, graphics and sound capabilities, while learning important object-oriented and Java-related concepts, such as classes, objects, GUI construction, inheritance, event handling and multithreading.

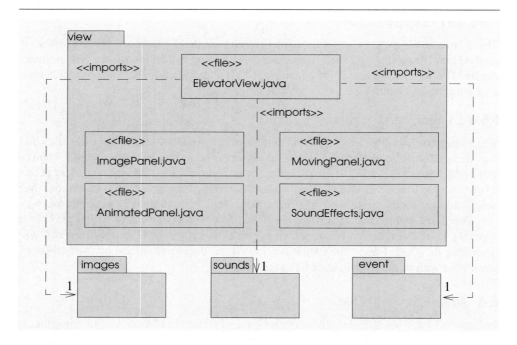

Fig. F.5   Component diagram for package view.

G
Unicode®

Objectives

- To become familiar with Unicode.
- To discuss the mission of the Unicode Consortium.
- To discuss the design basis of Unicode.
- To understand the three Unicode encoding forms:
  UTF-8, UTF-16 and UTF-32.
- To introduce characters and glyphs.
- To discuss the advantages and disadvantages of using
  Unicode.
- To provide a brief tour of the Unicode Consortium's
  Web site.

Outline

G.1 Introduction

The use of inconsistent character *encodings* (i.e., numeric values associated with characters) when developing global software products causes serious problems because computers process information using numbers. For instance, the character "a" is converted to a numeric value so that a computer can manipulate that piece of data. Many countries and corporations have developed their own encoding systems that are incompatible with the encoding systems of other countries and corporations. For example, the Microsoft Windows operating system assigns the value 0xC0 to the character "A with a grave accent" while the Apple Macintosh operating system assigns that same value to an upside-down question mark. This results in the misrepresentation and possible corruption of data because data is not processed as intended.

In the absence of a widely-implemented universal character encoding standard, global software developers had to *localize* their products extensively before distribution. Localization includes the language translation and cultural adaptation of content. The process of localization usually includes significant modifications to the source code (such as the conversion of numeric values and the underlying assumptions made by programmers), which results in increased costs and delays releasing the software. For example, some English-speaking programmers might design global software products assuming that a single character can be represented by one byte. However, when those products are localized in Asian markets, the programmer's assumptions are no longer valid, thus the majority, if not the entirety, of the code needs to be rewritten. Localization is necessary with each release of a version. By the time a software product is localized for a particular market, a newer version, which needs to be localized as well, is ready for distribution. As a result, it is cumbersome and costly to produce and distribute global software products in a market where there is no universal character encoding standard.

In response to this situation, the *Unicode Standard*, an encoding standard that facilitates the production and distribution of software, was created. The Unicode Standard outlines a specification to produce consistent encoding of the world's characters and *symbols*. Software products which handle text encoded in the Unicode Standard need to be localized, but the localization process is simpler and more efficient because the numeric values need not be converted and the assumptions made by programmers about the character encoding are universal. The Unicode Standard is maintained by a non-profit organization called the

Unicode Consortium, whose members include Apple, IBM, Microsoft, Oracle, Sun Microsystems, Sybase and many others.

When the Consortium envisioned and developed the Unicode Standard, they wanted an encoding system that was *universal, efficient, uniform* and *unambiguous*. A universal encoding system encompasses all commonly used characters. An efficient encoding system allows text files to be parsed easily. A uniform encoding system assigns fixed values to all characters. An unambiguous encoding system represents a given character in a consistent manner. These four terms are referred to as the Unicode Standard design basis.

G.2 Unicode Transformation Formats

Although Unicode incorporates the limited ASCII *character set* (i.e., a collection of characters), it encompasses a more comprehensive character set. In ASCII each character is represented by a byte containing 0s and 1s. One byte is capable of storing the binary numbers from 0 to 255. Each character is assigned a number between 0 and 255, thus ASCII-based systems can support only 256 characters, a tiny fraction of world's characters. Unicode extends the ASCII character set by encoding the vast majority of the world's characters. The Unicode Standard encodes all of those characters in a uniform numerical space from 0 to 10FFFF hexadecimal. An implementation will express these numbers in one of several transformation formats, choosing the one that best fits the particular application at hand.

Three such formats are in use, called *UTF-8, UTF-16* and *UTF-32*, depending on the size of the units—in *bits*—being used. UTF-8, a variable width encoding form, requires one to four bytes to express each Unicode character. UTF-8 data consists of 8-bit bytes (sequences of one, two, three or four bytes depending on the character being encoded) and is well suited for ASCII-based systems when there is a predominance of one-byte characters (ASCII represents characters as one-byte). Currently, UTF-8 is widely implemented in UNIX systems and in databases.

The variable width UTF-16 encoding form expresses Unicode characters in units of 16-bits (i.e., as two adjacent bytes, or a short integer in many machines). Most characters of Unicode are expressed in a single 16-bit unit. However, characters with values above FFFF hexadecimal are expressed with an ordered pair of 16-bit units called *surrogates*. Surrogates are 16-bit integers in the range D800 through DFFF, which are used solely for the purpose of "escaping" into higher numbered characters. Approximately one million characters can be expressed in this manner. Although a surrogate pair requires 32-bits to represent characters, it is space-efficient to use these 16-bit units. Surrogates are rare characters in current implementations. Many string-handling implementations are written in terms of UTF-16. [*Note*: Details and sample-code for UTF-16 handling are available on the Unicode Consortium Web site at `www.unicode.org`.]

Implementations that require significant use of rare characters or entire scripts encoded above FFFF hexadecimal, should use UTF-32, a 32-bit fixed-width encoding form that usually requires twice as much memory as UTF-16 encoded characters. The major advantage of the fixed-width UTF-32 encoding form is that it uniformly expresses all characters, so it is easy to handle in arrays.

There are few guidelines that state when to use a particular encoding form. The best encoding form to use depends on computer systems and business protocols, not on the data itself. Typically, the UTF-8 encoding form should be used where computer systems and business protocols require data to be handled in 8-bit units, particularly in legacy systems being upgraded because it often simplifies changes to existing programs. For this reason, UTF-8 has become the encoding form of choice on the Internet. Likewise, UTF-16 is the encoding form of choice on Microsoft Windows applications. UTF-32 is likely to become more widely used in the future as more characters are encoded with values above FFFF hexadecimal. Also, UTF-32 requires less sophisticated handling than UTF-16 in the presence of surrogate pairs.

Figure G.1 shows the different ways in which the three encoding forms handle character encoding.

G.3 Characters and Glyphs

The Unicode Standard consists of *characters*, written components (i.e., alphabets, numbers, punctuation marks, accent marks, etc.) that can be represented by numeric values. Examples of characters include: U+0041 LATIN CAPITAL LETTER A. In the first character representation, U+*yyyy* is a *code value*, in which U+ refers to Unicode code values, as opposed to other hexadecimal values. The *yyyy* represents a four-digit hexadecimal number of an encoded character. Code values are bit combinations that represent encoded characters. Characters are represented using *glyphs*, various shapes, fonts and sizes for displaying characters. There are no code values for glyphs in the Unicode Standard. Examples of glyphs are shown in Fig. G.2.

The Unicode Standard encompasses the alphabets, ideographs, syllabaries, punctuation marks, *diacritics*, mathematical operators, etc. that comprise the written languages and scripts of the world. A diacritic is a special mark added to a character to distinguish it from another letter or to indicate an accent (e.g., in Spanish, the tilde "~" above the character "n"). Currently, Unicode provides code values for 94,140 character representations, with more than 880,000 code values reserved for future expansion.

Character	UTF-8	UTF-16	UTF-32
LATIN CAPITAL LETTER A	0x41	0x0041	0x00000041
GREEK CAPITAL LETTER ALPHA	0xCD 0x91	0x0391	0x00000391
CJK UNIFIED IDEOGRAPH-4E95	0xE4 0xBA 0x95	0x4E95	0x00004E95
OLD ITALIC LETTER A	0xF0 0x80 0x83 0x80	0xDC00 0xDF00	0x00010300

Fig. G.1   Correlation between the three encoding forms.

Fig. G.2   Various glyphs of the character A.

G.4 Advantages/Disadvantages of Unicode

The Unicode Standard has several significant advantages that promote its use. One is the impact it has on the performance of the international economy. Unicode standardizes the characters for the world's writing systems to a uniform model that promotes transferring and sharing data. Programs developed using such a schema maintain their accuracy because each character has a single definition (i.e., *a* is always U+0061, % is always U+0025). This enables corporations to manage the high demands of international markets by processing different writing systems at the same time. Also, all characters can be managed in an identical manner, thus avoiding any confusion caused by different character code architectures. Moreover, managing data in a consistent manner eliminates data corruption, because data can be sorted, searched and manipulated using a consistent process.

Another advantage of the Unicode Standard is *portability* (i.e., software that can execute on disparate computers or with disparate operating systems). Most operating systems, databases, programming languages and Web browsers currently support, or are planning to support, Unicode.

A disadvantage of the Unicode Standard is the amount of memory required by UTF-16 and UTF-32. ASCII character sets are 8-bits in length, so they require less storage than the default 16-bit Unicode character set. However, the *double-byte character set (DBCS)* and the *multi-byte character set (MBCS)* that encode Asian characters (ideographs) require two to four bytes, respectively. In such instances, the UTF-16 or the UTF-32 encoding forms may be used with little hindrance on memory and performance.

Another disadvantage of Unicode is that although it includes more characters than any other character set in common use, it does not yet encode all of the world's written characters.

Another disadvantage of the Unicode Standard is that UTF-8 and UTF-16 are variable width encoding forms, so characters occupy different amounts of memory.

G.5 Unicode Consortium's Web Site

If you would like to learn more about the Unicode Standard, visit www.unicode.org. This site provides a wealth of information about the Unicode Standard that is insightful to those new to Unicode. Currently, the home page is organized into various sections—*New to Unicode*, *General Information*, *The Consortium*, *The Unicode Standard*, *Work in Progress* and *For Members*.

The *New to Unicode* section consists of two subsections: **What is Unicode** and **How to Use this Site**. The first subsection provides a technical introduction to Unicode by describing design principles, character interpretations and assignments, text processing and Unicode conformance. This subsection is recommended reading for anyone new to Unicode. Also, this subsection provides a list of related links that provide the reader with additional information about Unicode. The **How to Use this Site** subsection contains information about using and navigating the site as well hyperlinks to additional resources.

The *General Information* section contains six subsections: **Where is my Character**, **Display Problems**, **Useful Resources**, **Enabled Products**, **Mail Lists** and **Conferences**. The main areas covered in this section include a link to the Unicode code charts (a complete listing of code values) assembled by the Unicode Consortium as well as a detailed outline on how to locate an encoded character in the code chart. Also, the section contains advice on how to configure different operating systems and Web browsers so that the Unicode characters can be viewed properly. Moreover, from this section, the user can navigate to other sites that provide information on various topics such as, fonts, linguistics and other standards such as the *Armenian Standards Page* and the *Chinese GB 18030 Encoding Standard*.

The *Consortium* section consists of five subsections: **Who we are**, **Our Members**, **How to Join**, **Press Info** and **Contact Us**. This section provides a list of the current Unicode Consortium members as well as information on how to become a member. Privileges for each member type—*full*, *associate*, *specialist* and *individual*—and the fees assessed to each member are listed here.

The *Unicode Standard* section consists of nine subsections: **Start Here**, **Latest Version**, **Technical Reports**, **Code Charts**, **Unicode Data**, **Update & Errata**, **Unicode Policies**, **Glossary** and **Technical FAQ**. This section describes the updates applied to the latest version of the Unicode Standard as well as categorizing all defined encoding. The user can learn how the latest version has been modified to encompass more features and capabilities. For instance, one enhancement of Version 3.1 is that it contains additional encoded characters. Also, if users are unfamiliar with vocabulary terms used by the Unicode Consortium, then they can navigate to the **Glossary** subsection.

The *Work in Progress* section consists of three subsections: **Calendar of Meetings**, **Proposed Characters** and **Submitting Proposals**. This section presents the user with a catalog of the recent characters included into the Unicode Standard scheme as well as those characters being considered for inclusion. If users determine that a character has been overlooked, then they can submit a written proposal for the inclusion of that character. The **Submitting Proposals** subsection contains strict guidelines that must be adhered to when submitting written proposals.

The *For Members* section consists of two subsections: **Member Resources** and **Working Documents**. These subsections are password protected; only consortium members can access these links.

G.6 Using Unicode

Numerous programming languages (e.g., C, Java, JavaScript, Perl, Visual Basic, etc.) provide some level of support for the Unicode Standard. Figure G.3 shows a Java program that prints the text "Welcome to Unicode!" in eight different languages: English, Russian, French, German, Japanese, Portuguese, Spanish and Traditional Chinese. [*Note*: The Unicode Consortium's Web site contains a link to code charts that lists the 16-bit Unicode code values.]

```
1   // Fig. G.3: Unicode.java
2   // Demonstrating how to use Unicode in Java programs.
3
4   // Java core packages
5   import java.awt.*;
6
7   // Java extension packages
8   import javax.swing.*;
9
```

Fig. G.3   Java program that uses Unicode encoding (Part 1 of 3.).

```
10   public class Unicode extends JFrame {
11      private JLabel english, chinese, cyrillic, french, german,
12         japanese, portuguese, spanish;
13
14      // Unicode constructor
15      public Unicode()
16      {
17         super( "Demonstrating Unicode" );
18
19         // get content pane and set its layout
20         Container container = getContentPane();
21         container.setLayout( new GridLayout( 8, 1 ) );
22
23         // JLabel constructor with a string argument
24         english = new JLabel( "\u0057\u0065\u006C\u0063\u006F" +
25            "\u006D\u0065\u0020\u0074\u006F\u0020Unicode\u0021" );
26         english.setToolTipText( "This is English" );
27         container.add( english );
28
29         chinese = new JLabel( "\u6B22\u8FCE\u4F7F\u7528\u0020" +
30            "\u0020Unicode\u0021" );
31         chinese.setToolTipText( "This is Traditional Chinese" );
32         container.add( chinese );
33
34         cyrillic = new JLabel( "\u0414\u043E\u0431\u0440\u043E" +
35            "\u0020\u043F\u043E\u0436\u0430\u043B\u043E\u0432" +
36            "\u0430\u0422\u044A\u0020\u0432\u0020Unicode\u0021" );
37         cyrillic.setToolTipText( "This is Russian" );
38         container.add( cyrillic );
39
40         french = new JLabel( "\u0042\u0069\u0065\u006E\u0076" +
41            "\u0065\u006E\u0075\u0065\u0020\u0061\u0075\u0020" +
42            "Unicode\u0021" );
43         french.setToolTipText( "This is French" );
44         container.add( french );
45
46         german = new JLabel( "\u0057\u0069\u006C\u006B\u006F" +
47            "\u006D\u006D\u0065\u006E\u0020\u007A\u0075\u0020" +
48            "Unicode\u0021" );
49         german.setToolTipText( "This is German" );
50         container.add( german );
51
52         japanese = new JLabel( "Unicode\u3078\u3087\u3045\u3053" +
53            "\u305D\u0021" );
54         japanese.setToolTipText( "This is Japanese" );
55         container.add( hiragana );
56
57         portuguese = new JLabel( "\u0053\u00E9\u006A\u0061\u0020" +
58            "\u0042\u0065\u006D\u0076\u0069\u006E\u0064" +
59            "\u006F\u0020Unicode\u0021" );
60         portuguese.setToolTipText( "This is Portuguese" );
61         container.add( portuguese );
62
```

Fig. G.3   Java program that uses Unicode encoding (Part 2 of 3.).

```
63        spanish = new JLabel( "\u0042\u0069\u0065\u006E\u0076" +
64          "\u0065\u006E\u0069\u0064\u0061\u0020\u0061\u0020" +
65          "Unicode\u0021" );
66        spanish.setToolTipText( "This is Spanish" );
67        container.add( spanish );
68
69      } // end Unicode constructor
70
71      // execute application
72      public static void main( String args[] )
73      {
74        Unicode application = new Unicode();
75        application.setDefaultCloseOperation(
76          JFrame.EXIT_ON_CLOSE );
77        application.pack();
78        application.setVisible( true );
79
80      } // end method main
81
82    } // end class Unicode
```

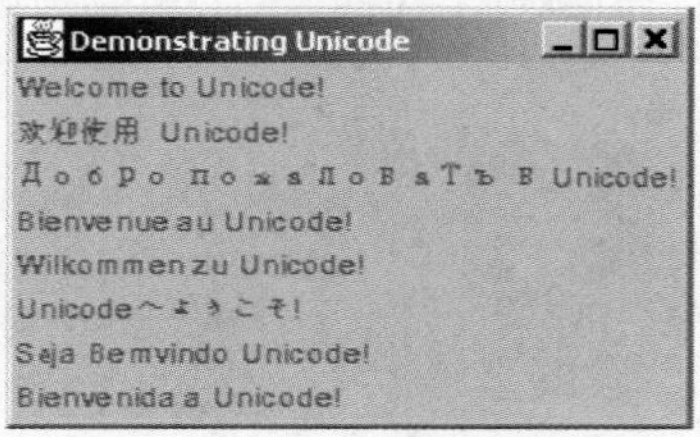

Fig. G.3   Java program that uses Unicode encoding (Part 3 of 3.).

The Unicode.java program uses *escape sequences* to represent characters. An escape sequence is in the form \u*yyyy, where yyyy* represents the four-digit hexadecimal code value. Lines 24 and 25 contain the series of escape sequences necessary to print "Welcome to Unicode!" in English. The first escape sequence (\u0057) equates to the character "W," the second escape sequence (\u0065) equates to the character "e," and so on. The \u0020 escape sequence (line 25) is the encoding for the *space* character. The \u0074 and \u006F escape sequences equate to the word "to." Note that "Unicode" is not encoded because it is a registered trademark and has no equivalent translation in most languages. Line 25 also contains the \u0021 escape sequence for the exclamation mark (!).

Lines 29–65 contain the escape sequences for the other seven languages. The English, French, German, Portuguese and Spanish characters are located in the **Basic Latin** block, the Japanese characters are located in the **Hiragana** block, the Russian characters are located in the **Cyrillic** block and the Traditional Chinese characters are located in the **CJK Unified Ideographs** block.

[*Note*: To display the output of Unicode.java properly, copy the font.properties.zh file to the font.properties files (located in the C:\Program Files\Java

\J2re1.4.1\lib and in the C:\j2sdk1.4.1\jre\lib directories). Save the contents of font.properties prior to overwriting them with the contents from font.proper-ties.zh.

G.7 Character Ranges

The Unicode Standard assigns code values, which range from 0000 (**Basic Latin**) to E007F (*Tags*), to the written characters of the world. Currently, there are code values for 94,140 characters. To simplify the search for a character and its associated code value, the Unicode Standard generally groups code values by *script* and function (i.e., Latin charac-ters are grouped in a block, mathematical operators are grouped in another block, etc.). As a rule, a script is a single writing system that is used for multiple languages (e.g., the Latin script is used for English, French, Spanish, etc.). The **Code Charts** page on the Unicode Consortium Web site lists all the defined blocks and their respective code values. Figure G.4 lists some blocks (scripts) from the Web site and their range of code values.

Script	Range of code values
Arabic	U+0600–U+06FF
Basic Latin	U+0000–U+007F
Bengali (India)	U+0980–U+09FF
Cherokee (Native America)	U+13A0–U+13FF
CJK Unified Ideographs (East Asia)	U+4E00–U+9FAF
Cyrillic (Russia and Eastern Europe)	U+0400–U+04FF
Ethiopic	U+1200–U+137F
Greek	U+0370–U+03FF
Hangul Jamo (Korea)	U+1100–U+11FF
Hebrew	U+0590–U+05FF
Hiragana (Japan)	U+3040–U+309F
Khmer (Cambodia)	U+1780–U+17FF
Lao (Laos)	U+0E80–U+0EFF
Mongolian	U+1800–U+18AF
Myanmar	U+1000–U+109F
Ogham (Ireland)	U+1680–U+169F
Runic (Germany and Scandinavia)	U+16A0–U+16FF
Sinhala (Sri Lanka)	U+0D80–U+0DFF
Telugu (India)	U+0C00–U+0C7F
Thai	U+0E00–U+0E7F

Fig. G.4   Some character ranges.

SUMMARY

- Before Unicode, software developers were plagued by the use of inconsistent character encoding (i.e., numeric values for characters). Most countries and organizations had their own encoding systems, which were incompatible. A good example is the individual encoding systems on the Windows and Macintosh platforms.

- Computers process data by converting characters to numeric values. For instance, the character "a" is converted to a numeric value so that a computer can manipulate that piece of data.

- Localization of global software requires significant modifications to the source code, which results in the increased cost and delays releasing the product.

- Localization is necessary with each release of a version. By the time a software product is localized for a particular market, a newer version, which needs to be localized as well, is ready for distribution. As a result, it is cumbersome and costly to produce and distribute global software products in a market where there is no universal character encoding standard.

- The Unicode Consortium developed the Unicode Standard in response to the serious problems created by multiple character encodings and the use of those encodings.

- The Unicode Standard facilitates the production and distribution of localized software. It outlines a specification for the consistent encoding of the world's characters and symbols.

- Software products which handle text encoded in the Unicode Standard need to be localized, but the localization process is simpler and more efficient because the numeric values need not be converted.

- The Unicode Standard is designed to be universal, efficient, uniform and unambiguous.

- A universal encoding system encompasses all commonly used characters; an efficient encoding system parses text files easily; a uniform encoding system assigns fixed values to all characters; and a unambiguous encoding system represents the same character for any given value.

- Unicode extends the limited ASCII character set to include all the major characters of the world.

- Unicode makes use of three Unicode Transformation Formats (UTF): UTF-8, UTF-16 and UTF-32, each of which may be appropriate for use in different contexts.

- UTF-8 data consists of 8-bit bytes (sequences of one, two, three or four bytes depending on the character being encoded) and is well suited for ASCII-based systems when there is a predominance of one-byte characters (ASCII represents characters as one-byte).

- UTF-8 is a variable width encoding form that is more compact for text involving mostly Latin characters and ASCII punctuation.

- UTF-16 is the default encoding form of the Unicode Standard. It is a variable width encoding form that uses 16-bit code units instead of bytes. Most characters are represented by a single 16-bit unit, but some characters require surrogate pairs.

- Without surrogate pairs, the UTF-16 encoding form can only encompass 65,000 characters, but with the surrogate pairs, this is expanded to include over a million characters.

- UTF-32 is a 32-bit encoding form. The major advantage of the fixed-width encoding form is that it uniformly expresses all characters, so that they are easy to handle in arrays and so forth.

- The Unicode Standard consists of characters. A character is any written component that can be represented by a numeric value.

- Characters are represented using glyphs, which are various shapes, fonts and sizes for displaying characters.

- Code values are bit combinations that represent encoded characters. The Unicode notation for a code value is U+*yyyy* in which U+ refers to the Unicode code values, as opposed to other hexadecimal values. The *yyyy* represents a four-digit hexadecimal number.

- Currently, the Unicode Standard provides code values for 94,140 character representations.

- An advantage of the Unicode Standard is its impact on the overall performance of the international economy. Applications that conform to an encoding standard can be processed easily by computers.

- Another advantage of the Unicode Standard is its portability. Applications written in Unicode can be easily transferred to different operating systems, databases, Web browsers, etc. Most companies currently support, or are planning to support Unicode.

- To obtain more information about the Unicode Standard and the Unicode Consortium, visit www.unicode.org. It contains a link to the code charts, which contain the 16-bit code values for the currently encoded characters.

- Numerous programming languages provide some level of support for the Unicode Standard.

- In Java programs, the \u*yyyy* escape sequence represents a character, where *yyyy* is the four-digit hexadecimal code value. The \u0020 escape sequence is the universal encoding for the *space* character.

TERMINOLOGY

\u*yyyy* escape sequence	portability
ASCII	script
block	surrogate
character	symbol
character set	unambiguous (Unicode design basis)
code value	Unicode Consortium
diacritic	Unicode design basis
double-byte character set (DBCS)	Unicode Standard
efficient (Unicode design basis)	Unicode Transformation Format (UTF)
encode	uniform (Unicode design basis)
escape sequence	universal (Unicode design basis)
glyph	UTF-8
hexadecimal notation	UTF-16
localization	UTF-32
multi-byte character set (MBCS)	

SELF-REVIEW EXERCISES

G.1 Fill in the blanks in each of the following.
  a) Global software developers had to _____ their products to a specific market before distribution.
  b) The Unicode Standard is a(n) _____ standard that facilitates the uniform production and distribution of software products.
  c) The four design basis that constitute the Unicode Standard are: _____, _____, _____ and _____.
  d) A(n) _____ is the smallest written component the can be represented with a numeric value.
  e) Software that can execute on different operating systems is said to be _____.

G.2 State whether each of the following is *true* or *false*. If *false*, explain why.
  a) The Unicode Standard encompasses all the world's characters.
  b) A Unicode code value is represented as U+*yyyy*, where *yyyy* represents a number in binary notation.
  c) A diacritic is a character with a special mark that emphasizes an accent.

   d) Unicode is portable.

   e) When designing Java programs, the escape sequence is denoted by/**u**yyyy.

ANSWERS TO SELF-REVIEW EXERCISES

G.1　a) localize. b) encoding. c) universal, efficient, uniform, unambiguous. d) character. e) portable.

G.2　a) False. It encompasses the majority of the world's characters. b) False. The yyyy represents a hexadecimal number. c) False. A diacritic is a special mark added to a character to distinguish it from another letter or to indicate an accent. d) True. e) False. The escape sequence is denoted by \uyyyy.

EXERCISES

G.3　Navigate to the Unicode Consortium Web site (www.unicode.org) and write the hexadecimal code values for the following characters. In which block were they located?

   a) Latin letter 'Z.'

   b) Latin letter 'n' with the 'tilde (~).'

   c) Greek letter 'delta.'

   d) Mathematical operator 'less than or equal to.'

   e) Punctuation symbol 'open quote (").'

G.4　Describe the Unicode Standard design basis.

G.5　Define the following terms:

   a) code value.

   b) surrogates.

   c) Unicode Standard.

G.6　Define the following terms:

   a) UTF-8.

   b) UTF-16.

   c) UTF-32.

G.7　Describe a scenario where it is optimal to store your data in UTF-16 format.

G.8　Using the Unicode Standard code values, write a Java program that prints your first and last name. The program should print your name in all uppercase letters and in all lowercase letters. If you know other languages, print your first and last name in those languages as well.

Bibliography

Sun Microsystems Resources

Block, J., "Tutorial: Collections," java.sun.com/docs/books/tutorial/collections/index.html

Fisher, M., "The JDBC Tutorial and Reference: Second Edition Chapter 3 Excerpt," developer.java.sun.com/developer/Books/JDBCTutorial/index.html

Gosling, B., B. Joy, G. Steele and G. Bracha, "The Java Language Specification: Second Edition," java.sun.com/docs/books/jls/second_edition/html/j.title.doc.html

Lindholm, T., and F. Yellin, "The Java Virtual Machine Specification: Second Edition," java.sun.com/docs/books/vmspec/2nd-edition/html/VMSpecTOC.doc.html

Meloan, M.D. "The Science Of Java Sound," developer.java.sun.com/developer/technicalArticles/Media/JavaSoundAPI/index.html

Sun Microsystems, "Java Technology and XML," java.sun.com/xml

Sun Microsystems, "Java 2D API Specifications and Tutorials," java.sun.com/products/java-media/2D/forDevelopers/2Dapi/index.html

Sun Microsystems, "Java Servlet Technology," java.sun.com/products/servlet/index.html

Sun Microsystems, "JavaServer Pages: Dynamically Generated Web Content," java.sun.com/products/jsp/index.html

Sun Microsystems, "Java Foundation Classes: White Paper," java.sun.com/marketing/collateral/foundation_classes.html

Sun Microsystems, "The Collections Framework Overview," java.sun.com/products/jdk/1.4.1/docs/guide/collections/overview.html

Sun Microsystems, "JDBC Data Access API," java.sun.com/products/jdbc/overview.html

Sun Microsystems, "Lesson: Getting Started with Swing," java.sun.com/docs/books/tutorial/uiswing/start/index.html

Sun Microsystems, "New to Java Training Center," developer.java.sun.com/developer/onlineTraining/new2java

Sun Microsystems, "The Java Tutorial," `java.sun.com/docs/books/tutorial`

Sun Microsystems "Lesson: Swing Features and Concepts," `java.sun.com/docs/books/tutorial/uiswing/overview/index.html`

Sun Microsystems "Lesson: Using Swing Components," `java.sun.com/docs/books/tutorial/uiswing/components/index.html`

Sun Microsystems "Lesson: Laying Out Components within a Container," `java.sun.com/docs/books/tutorial/uiswing/layout/index.html`

Other Resources

Arnold, K., J. Gosling, and D. Holmes. *The Java™ Programming Language: Third Edition*. Reading, MA: Addison-Wesley, 2000.

Barker, J. *Beginning Java Objects: From Concepts to Code*. Birmingham: Wrox Press, 2000.

Bennet, S., J. Skelton, and K. Lunn. *Schaum's Outline of UML*. New York, NY: McGraw Hill, 2001.

Berg, D. and Fritzinger, J.S., *Advanced Techniques for Java Developers,* New York, NY: John Wiley & Sons, Inc., 1998.

Bloch, J. *Effective Java™ Programming Language Guide*. Reading, MA: Addison-Wesley, 2001.

Booch, G. *Object-Oriented Analysis and Design with Applications*. Reading, MA: Addison-Wesley, 1994.

Booch, G., J. Rumbaugh, and I. Jacobson. *The Complete UML Training Course*. Upper Saddle River, NJ: Prentice Hall PTR, 2000.

Brodsky, S. and T. Grose. *Mastering XMI: Java Programming XMI, XML, and UML*. New York, NY: John Wiley & Sons, 2002.

Brogden, B., *Java 2 Exam Cram, Second Edition*, Scottsdale, AZ: The Coriolis Group, 2001.

Cheesman, J., and J. Daniels. *UML Components: A Simple Process for Specifying Component-Based Software (The Component Software Series)*. Reading, MA: Addison-Wesley, 2000.

Daconta, M. C., E. Monk, J. P. Keller, and K. Bohnenberger. *Java Pitfalls: Time-Saving Solutions and Workarounds to Improve Programs*. New York, NY: John Wiley & Sons, 2000.

Eckel, B. *Thinking In Java: 2nd Edition*. Upper Saddle River, NJ: Prentice Hall, 2000.

Flanagan, D. *Java Examples In A Nutshell*. Sabastopol, CA: O'Reilly and Associates, 2000.

Folwer, M. and K. Scott. *UML Distilled Second Edition; A Brief Guide to the Standard Object Modeling Language*. Reading, MA: Addison-Wesley, 1999.

Gamma, E., R. Helm, R. Johnson, and J. Vlissides. *Design Patterns; Elements of Reusable Object-Oriented Software.* Reading, MA: Addison-Wesley, 1995.

Gilbert, S., and McCarty, B., *Object-Oriented Design in Java,* Corte Madera, CA: Waite Group Press, 1998.

Grand, M. *Patterns in Java; A Catalog Reusable Design Patterns Illustrated with UML (Second Edition)*. New York, NY: John Wiley & Sons, 2002.

Horstmann, C. S. and G. Cornell. *Core Java 2: Volume 1-Fundamentals (Sixth Edition)*. Upper Saddle River, NJ: Prentice Hall, 2003.

Horstmann, C. S. and G. Cornell. *Core Java 2: Volume II-Advanced Features (Fifth Edition)*. Upper Saddle River, NJ; Prentice Hall, 2002.

Larman, C. *Applying UML and Patterns; An Introduction to Object-Oriented Analysis and Design and the Unified Process*. Upper Saddle River, NJ: Prentice Hall, 2002.

Lea, D. *Concurrent Programming in Java™ Second Edition Design Principles and Patterns*. Reading, MA: Addison-Wesley, 2000.

Lauinger, T., "Object-Oriented Software Development in Java," *Java Report,* February 1999, pp. 59-61

Malarvannan, M., "A Multithreaded Server in Java," *Web Techniques,* October 1998, pp. 47-51

Maruyama, H., A. Clark, M. Murata, M. Uramoto, K. Tamamura, Y. Nakamura, R. Neyama, K. Kisaka and S. Hada., *XML and JAVA: Developing Web Applications (Second Edition),* Reading, MA: Addison-Wesley Professional, 2002

Oaks, S., "How Do I Create My Own UI Component?" Java Report, March/April 1996, pp. 64, 63.

Oaks, S., "Two Techniques for Handling Events," *Java Report,* July/August, 1996. p. 80.

Page-Jones, M. *Fundamentals of Object-Oriented Design in UML*. Reading, MA: Addison-Wesley, 1999.

Penker, M. and E. Hans-Erik. *Business Modeling with UML: Business Patterns At Work*. New York, NY: John Wiley & Sons, 2000.

Roberts, Si., P. Heller, M. Ernest, and R. et al. *The Complete Java 2 Certification Study Guide (Third Edition)*. Alameda, CA: SYBEX, 2002.

Rodrigues, L., "On JavaBeans Customization," *Java Developer's Journal,* May 1999, pp.-21

Rumbaugh, J., I. Jacobson and G. Booch. The *Unified Modeling Language Reference Manual*. Reading, MA: Addison-Wesley, 1999.

Rumbaugh, J., I. Jacobson and G. Booch. *The Unified Modeling Language User Guide*. Reading, MA: Addison-Wesley, 1999.

Rumbaugh, J., I. Jacobson and G. Booch. *The Complete UML Training Course*. Upper Saddle River, NJ: Prentice Hall, 2000.

Rumbaugh, J., I. Jacobson and G. Booch. *The Unified Software Development Process*. Reading, MA: Addison-Wesley, 1999.

Rosenburg, D. and K. Scott. *Applying Use Case Driven Object Modeling with UML: An Annotated e-Commerce Example*. Reading, MA: Addison-Wesley, 2001.

Schach, S. *Object-Oriented and Classical Software Engineering*. New York, NY: McGraw Hill, 2001.

Schneider, G. and J. Winters. *Applying Use Cases*. Reading, MA: Addison-Wesley, 1998.

Scott, K. *UML Explained*. Reading, MA: Addison-Wesley, 2001.

Shirazi, J. *Java Performance Tuning*. Sebastopol, CA: O'Reilly and Associates, 2000.

Stevens, P. and R. J. Pooley. *Using UML: Software Engineering with Objects and Components Revised Edition*. Reading, MA: Addison-Wesley, 2000.

Sun Microsystems Inc. *Java™ Look and Feel Design Guidelines, Second Edition*. Reading, MA: Addison-Wesley, 2001.

Topley, K. *Core Swing: Advanced Programming*. Upper Saddle River, NJ: Prentice Hall, 2000.

Venners, B., *Inside the Java Virtual Machine*. New York, NY: McGraw-Hill, 2000.

Vlissides, J. *Pattern Hatching; Design Patterns Applied*. Reading, MA: Addison-Wesley, 1998.

Index

M

End User License Agreements

5. LIMITATION OF LIABILITY. TO THE EXTENT NOT PROHIBITED BY LAW, IN NO EVENT WILL SUN OR ITS LICENSORS BE LIABLE FOR ANY LOST REVENUE, PROFIT OR DATA, OR FOR SPECIAL, INDIRECT, CONSEQUENTIAL, INCIDENTAL OR PUNITIVE DAMAGES, HOWEVER CAUSED REGARDLESS OF THE THEORY OF LIABILITY, ARISING OUT OF OR RELATED TO THE USE OF OR INABILITY TO USE SOFTWARE, EVEN IF SUN HAS BEEN ADVISED OF THE POSSIBILITY OF SUCH DAMAGES. In no event will Sun's liability to you, whether in contract, tort (including negligence), or otherwise, exceed the amount paid by you for Software under this Agreement. The foregoing limitations will apply even if the above stated warranty fails of its essential purpose.

6. Termination. This Agreement is effective until terminated. You may terminate this Agreement at any time by destroying all copies of Software. This Agreement will terminate immediately without notice from Sun if you fail to comply with any provision of this Agreement. Upon Termination, you must destroy all copies of Software.

7. Export Regulations. All Software and technical data delivered under this Agreement are subject to US export control laws and may be subject to export or import regulations in other countries. You agree to comply strictly with all such laws and regulations and acknowledge that you have the responsibility to obtain such licenses to export, re-export, or import as may be required after delivery to you.

8. U.S. Government Restricted Rights. If Software is being acquired by or on behalf of the U.S. Government or by a U.S. Government prime contractor or subcontractor (at any tier), then the Government's rights in Software and accompanying documentation will be only as set forth in this Agreement; this is in accordance with 48 CFR 227.7201 through 227.7202-4 (for Department of Defense (DOD) acquisitions) and with 48 CFR 2.101 and 12.212 (for non-DOD acquisitions).

9. Governing Law. Any action related to this Agreement will be governed by California law and controlling U.S. federal law. No choice of law rules of any jurisdiction will apply.

10. Severability. If any provision of this Agreement is held to be unenforceable, this Agreement will remain in effect with the provision omitted, unless omission would frustrate the intent of the parties, in which case this Agreement will immediately terminate.

11. Integration. This Agreement is the entire agreement between you and Sun relating to its subject matter. It supersedes all prior or contemporaneous oral or written communications, proposals, representations and warranties and prevails over any conflicting or additional terms of any quote, order, acknowledgment, or other communication between the parties relating to its subject matter during the term of this Agreement. No modification of this Agreement will be binding, unless in writing and signed by an authorized representative of each party.

JAVA™ 2 SOFTWARE DEVELOPMENT KIT (J2SDK), STANDARD EDITION, VERSION 1.4.X SUPPLEMENTAL LICENSE TERMS

These supplemental license terms ("Supplemental Terms") add to or modify the terms of the Binary Code License Agreement (collectively, the "Agreement"). Capitalized terms not defined in these Supplemental Terms shall have the same meanings ascribed to them in the Agreement. These Supplemental Terms shall supersede any inconsistent or conflicting terms in the Agreement, or in any license contained within the Software.

1. Software Internal Use and Development License Grant. Subject to the terms and conditions of this Agreement, including, but not limited to Section 4 (Java Technology Restrictions) of these Supplemental Terms, Sun grants you a non-exclusive, non-transferable, limited license without fees to reproduce internally and use internally the binary form of the Software complete and unmodified for the sole purpose of designing, developing and testing your Java applets and applications intended to run on the Java platform ("Programs").

2. License to Distribute Software. Subject to the terms and conditions of this Agreement, including, but not limited to Section 4 (Java Technology Restrictions) of these Supplemental Terms, Sun grants you a non-exclusive, non-transferable, limited license without fees to reproduce and distribute the Software, provided that (i) you distribute the Software complete and unmodified (unless otherwise specified in the applicable README file) and only bundled as part of, and for the sole purpose of running, your Programs, (ii) the Programs add significant and primary functionality to the Software, (iii) you do not distribute additional software intended to replace any component(s) of the Software (unless otherwise specified in the applicable README file), (iv) you do not remove or alter any proprietary legends or notices contained in the Software, (v) you only distribute the Software subject to a license agreement that protects Sun's interests consistent with the terms contained in this Agreement, and (vi) you agree to defend and indemnify Sun and its licensors from and against any damages, costs, liabilities, settle-

ment amounts and/or expenses (including attorneys' fees) incurred in connection with any claim, lawsuit or action by any third party that arises or results from the use or distribution of any and all Programs and/or Software. (vi) include the following statement as part of product documentation (whether hard copy or electronic), as a part of a copyright page or proprietary rights notice page, in an "About" box or in any other form reasonably designed to make the statement visible to users of the Software: "This product includes code licensed from RSA Security, Inc.", and (vii) include the statement, "Some portions licensed from IBM are available at http://oss.software.ibm.com/icu4j/".

3. License to Distribute Redistributables. Subject to the terms and conditions of this Agreement, including but not limited to Section 4 (Java Technology Restrictions) of these Supplemental Terms, Sun grants you a non-exclusive, non-transferable, limited license without fees to reproduce and distribute those files specifically identified as redistributable in the Software "README" file ("Redistributables") provided that: (i) you distribute the Redistributables complete and unmodified (unless otherwise specified in the applicable README file), and only bundled as part of Programs, (ii) you do not distribute additional software intended to supersede any component(s) of the Redistributables (unless otherwise specified in the applicable README file), (iii) you do not remove or alter any proprietary legends or notices contained in or on the Redistributables, (iv) you only distribute the Redistributables pursuant to a license agreement that protects Sun's interests consistent with the terms contained in the Agreement, (v) you agree to defend and indemnify Sun and its licensors from and against any damages, costs, liabilities, settlement amounts and/or expenses (including attorneys' fees) incurred in connection with any claim, lawsuit or action by any third party that arises or results from the use or distribution of any and all Programs and/or Software, (vi) include the following statement as part of product documentation (whether hard copy or electronic), as a part of a copyright page or proprietary rights notice page, in an "About" box or in any other form reasonably designed to make the statement visible to users of the Software: "This product includes code licensed from RSA Security, Inc.", and (vii) include the statement, "Some portions licensed from IBM are available at http://oss.software.ibm.com/icu4j/".

4. Java Technology Restrictions. You may not modify the Java Platform Interface ("JPI", identified as classes contained within the "java" package or any subpackages of the "java" package), by creating additional classes within the JPI or otherwise causing the addition to or modification of the classes in the JPI. In the event that you create an additional class and associated API(s) which (i) extends the functionality of the Java platform, and (ii) is exposed to third party software developers for the purpose of developing additional software which invokes such additional API, you must promptly publish broadly an accurate specification for such API for free use by all developers. You may not create, or authorize your licensees to create, additional classes, interfaces, or subpackages that are in any way identified as "java", "javax", "sun" or similar convention as specified by Sun in any naming convention designation.

5. Notice of Automatic Software Updates from Sun. You acknowledge that the Software may automatically download, install, and execute applets, applications, software extensions, and updated versions of the Software from Sun ("Software Updates"), which may require you to accept updated terms and conditions for installation. If additional terms and conditions are not presented on installation, the Software Updates will be considered part of the Software and subject to the terms and conditions of the Agreement.

6. Notice of Automatic Downloads. You acknowledge that, by your use of the Software and/or by requesting services that require use of the Software, the Software may automatically download, install, and execute software applications from sources other than Sun ("Other Software"). Sun makes no representations of a relationship of any kind to licensors of Other Software. TO THE EXTENT NOT PROHIBITED BY LAW, IN NO EVENT WILL SUN OR ITS LICENSORS BE LIABLE FOR ANY LOST REVENUE, PROFIT OR DATA, OR FOR SPECIAL, INDIRECT, CONSEQUENTIAL, INCIDENTAL OR PUNITIVE DAMAGES, HOWEVER CAUSED REGARDLESS OF THE THEORY OF LIABILITY, ARISING OUT OF OR RELATED TO THE USE OF OR INABILITY TO USE OTHER SOFTWARE, EVEN IF SUN HAS BEEN ADVISED OF THE POSSIBILITY OF SUCH DAMAGES.

7. Distribution by Publishers. This section pertains to your distribution of the Software with your printed book or magazine (as those terms are commonly used in the industry) relating to Java technology ("Publication"). Subject to and conditioned upon your compliance with the restrictions and obligations contained in the Agreement, in addition to the license granted in Paragraph 1 above, Sun hereby grants to you a non-exclusive, nontransferable limited right to reproduce complete and unmodified copies of the Software on electronic media (the "Media") for the sole purpose of inclusion and distribution with your Publication(s), subject to the following terms: (i) You may not distribute the Software on a stand-alone basis; it must be distributed with your Publication(s); (ii) You are responsible for downloading the Software from the applicable Sun web site; (iii) You must refer to the Software as JavaTM 2 Software Development Kit, Standard Edition, Version 1.4.0; (iv) The Software

must be reproduced in its entirety and without any modification whatsoever (including, without limitation, the Binary Code License and Supplemental License Terms accompanying the Software and proprietary rights notices contained in the Software); (v) The Media label shall include the following information: Copyright 2002, Sun Microsystems, Inc. All rights reserved. Use is subject to license terms. Sun, Sun Microsystems, the Sun logo, Solaris, Java, the Java Coffee Cup logo, J2SE , and all trademarks and logos based on Java are trademarks or registered trademarks of Sun Microsystems, Inc. in the U.S. and other countries. This information must be placed on the Media label in such a manner as to only apply to the Sun Software; (vi) You must clearly identify the Software as Sun's product on the Media holder or Media label, and you may not state or imply that Sun is responsible for any third-party software contained on the Media; (vii) You may not include any third party software on the Media which is intended to be a replacement or substitute for the Software; (viii) You shall indemnify Sun for all damages arising from your failure to comply with the requirements of this Agreement. In addition, you shall defend, at your expense, any and all claims brought against Sun by third parties, and shall pay all damages awarded by a court of competent jurisdiction, or such settlement amount negotiated by you, arising out of or in connection with your use, reproduction or distribution of the Software and/or the Publication. Your obligation to provide indemnification under this section shall arise provided that Sun: (i) provides you prompt notice of the claim; (ii) gives you sole control of the defense and settlement of the claim; (iii) provides you, at your expense, with all available information, assistance and authority to defend; and (iv) has not compromised or settled such claim without your prior written consent; and (ix) You shall provide Sun with a written notice for each Publication; such notice shall include the following information: (1) title of Publication, (2) author(s), (3) date of Publication, and (4) ISBN or ISSN numbers. Such notice shall be sent to Sun Microsystems, Inc., 4150 Network Circle, M/S USCA12-110, Santa Clara, California 95054, U.S.A , Attention: Contracts Administration.

8. Trademarks and Logos. You acknowledge and agree as between you and Sun that Sun owns the SUN, SOLARIS, JAVA, JINI, FORTE, and iPLANET trademarks and all SUN, SOLARIS, JAVA, JINI, FORTE, and iPLANET-related trademarks, service marks, logos and other brand designations ("Sun Marks"), and you agree to comply with the Sun Trademark and Logo Usage Requirements currently located at http://www.sun.com/policies/trademarks. Any use you make of the Sun Marks inures to Sun's benefit.

9. Source Code. Software may contain source code that is provided solely for reference purposes pursuant to the terms of this Agreement. Source code may not be redistributed unless expressly provided for in this Agreement.

10. Termination for Infringement. Either party may terminate this Agreement immediately should any Software become, or in either party's opinion be likely to become, the subject of a claim of infringement of any intellectual property right.

For inquiries please contact: Sun Microsystems, Inc., 4150 Network Circle, Santa Clara, California 95054, U.S.A (LFI#111374/Form ID#011801)

SUN™ ONE STUDIO 4 UPDATE 1, COMMUNITY EDITION SUPPLEMENTAL LICENSE TERMS

These supplemental license terms ("Supplemental Terms") add to or modify the terms of the Binary Code License Agreement (collectively, the "Agreement"). Capitalized terms not defined in these Supplemental Terms shall have the same meanings ascribed to them in the Agreement. These Supplemental Terms shall supersede any inconsistent or conflicting terms in the Agreement, or in any license contained within the Software.

1. Software Internal Use and Development License Grant. Subject to the terms and conditions of this Agreement, including, but not limited to Section 4 (Java Technology Restrictions) of these Supplemental Terms, Sun grants you a non-exclusive, non-transferable, limited license to reproduce internally and use internally the binary form of the Software complete and unmodified for the sole purpose of designing, developing and testing your applets and applications ("Programs"). To the extent that you are designing, developing and testing Java applets and applications for a particular version of the Java platform, any executable output generated by a compiler that is contained in the Software must (a) only be compiled from source code that conforms to the corresponding version of the OEM Java Language Specification; (b) be in the class file format defined by the corresponding version of the OEM Java Virtual Machine Specification; and (c) execute properly on a reference runtime, as specified by Sun, associated with such version of the Java platform.

2. License to Distribute Software. Subject to the terms and conditions of this Agreement, including, but not limited to Section 4 (Java Technology Restrictions) of these Supplemental Terms, Sun grants you a non-exclusive, non-transferable, limited license to reproduce and distribute the Software in binary code form only, provided that

(i) you distribute the Software complete and unmodified, (ii) you do not distribute additional software intended to replace any component(s) of the Software, (iii) if you are distributing Java applets and applications for a particular version of the Java platform, any executable output generated by a compiler that is contained in the Software must (a) only be compiled from source code that conforms to the corresponding version of the OEM Java Language Specification; (b) be in the class file format defined by the corresponding version of the OEM Java Virtual Machine Specification; and (c) execute properly on a reference runtime, as specified by Sun, associated with such version of the Java platform, (iv) you do not remove or alter any proprietary legends or notices contained in the Software, (v) you only distribute the Software subject to a license agreement that protects Sun's interests consistent with the terms contained in this Agreement, and (vi) you agree to defend and indemnify Sun and its licensors from and against any damages, costs, liabilities, settlement amounts and/or expenses (including attorneys' fees) incurred in connection with any claim, lawsuit or action by any third party that arises or results from the use or distribution of any and all Programs and/or Software.

    3. License to Distribute Redistributables. Subject to the terms and conditions of this Agreement, including but not limited to Section 4 (Java Technology Restrictions) of these Supplemental Terms, Sun grants you a non-exclusive, non-transferable, limited license to reproduce and distribute the binary form of those files specifically identified as redistributable in the Software "RELEASE NOTES" file ("Redistributables") provided that: (i) you distribute the Redistributables complete and unmodified (unless otherwise specified in the applicable RELEASE NOTES file), and only bundled as part of Programs, (ii) you do not distribute additional software intended to supersede any component(s) of the Redistributables, (iii) you do not remove or alter any proprietary legends or notices contained in or on the Redistributables, (iv) if you are distributing Java applets and applications for a particular version of the Java platform, any executable output generated by a compiler that is contained in the Software must (a) only be compiled from source code that conforms to the corresponding version of the OEM Java Language Specification; (b) be in the class file format defined by the corresponding version of the OEM Java Virtual Machine Specification; and (c) execute properly on a reference runtime, as specified by Sun, associated with such version of the Java platform, (v) you only distribute the Redistributables pursuant to a license agreement that protects Sun's interests consistent with the terms contained in the Agreement, and (v) you agree to defend and indemnify Sun and its licensors from and against any damages, costs, liabilities, settlement amounts and/or expenses (including attorneys' fees) incurred in connection with any claim, lawsuit or action by any third party that arises or results from the use or distribution of any and all Programs and/or Software.

    4. Java Technology Restrictions. You may not modify the Java Platform Interface ("JPI", identified as classes contained within the "java" package or any subpackages of the "java" package), by creating additional classes within the JPI or otherwise causing the addition to or modification of the classes in the JPI. In the event that you create an additional class and associated API(s) which (i) extends the functionality of the Java platform, and (ii) is exposed to third party software developers for the purpose of developing additional software which invokes such additional API, you must promptly publish broadly an accurate specification for such API for free use by all developers. You may not create, or authorize your licensees to create, additional classes, interfaces, or subpackages that are in any way identified as "java", "javax", "sun" or similar convention as specified by Sun in any naming convention designation.

    5. Java Runtime Availability. Refer to the appropriate version of the Java Runtime Environment binary code license (currently located at http://www.java.sun.com/jdk/index.html) for the availability of runtime code which may be distributed with Java applets and applications.

    6. Distribution by Publishers. This section pertains to your distribution of the Software with your printed book or magazine (as those terms are commonly used in the industry) relating to Java technology ("Publication"). Subject to and conditioned upon your compliance with the restrictions and obligations contained in the Agreement, in addition to the license granted in Paragraph 1 above, Sun hereby grants to you a non-exclusive, nontransferable limited right to reproduce complete and unmodified copies of the Software on electronic media (the "Media") for the sole purpose of inclusion and distribution with your Publication(s), subject to the following terms: (i) you may not distribute the Software on a stand-alone basis; it must be distributed with your Publication(s); (ii) you are responsible for downloading the Software from the applicable Sun web site; (iii) you must refer to the Software as Sun ONE Studio 4, Community Edition; (iv) the Software must be reproduced in its entirety and without any modification whatsoever (including, without limitation, the Binary Code License and Supplemental License Terms accompanying the Software and proprietary rights notices contained in the Software); (v) the Media label shall include the following information: Copyright 2002, Sun Microsystems, Inc., 4150 Network Circle, Santa Clara, CA 95054. Java and SUN One and all trademarks and logos based on Java and SUN One are trademarks or registered trademarks of Sun Microsystems, Inc. in the U.S. and other countries. This information must be placed on the Media label in such a manner as to only apply to the Sun Software; (vi) you

must clearly identify the Software as Sun's product on the Media holder or Media label, and you may not state or imply that Sun is responsible for any third-party software contained on the Media; (vii) you may not include any third party software on the Media which is intended to be a replacement or substitute for the Software or which directly competes with the Software; (viii) you shall indemnify Sun for all damages arising from your failure to comply with the requirements of this Agreement. In addition, you shall defend, at your expense, any and all claims brought against Sun by third parties, and shall pay all damages awarded by a court of competent jurisdiction, or such settlement amount negotiated by you, arising out of or in connection with your use, reproduction or distribution of the Software and/or the Publication. Your obligation to provide indemnification under this section shall arise provided that Sun: (i) provides you prompt notice of the claim; (ii) gives you sole control of the defense and settlement of the claim; (iii) provides you, at your expense, with all available information, assistance and authority to defend; and (iv) has not compromised or settled such claim without your prior written consent; (ix) you shall provide Sun with a written notice for each Publication; such notice shall include the following information: (1) title of Publication, (2) author(s), (3) date of Publication, and (4) ISBN or ISSN numbers. Such notice shall be sent to Sun Microsystems, Inc., 4150 Network Circle, M/S USCA12-110, Palo Alto, CA 94303-4900, Attention: Contracts Administration; and (x) you shall provide Sun with quarterly written reports regarding the number of copies of the Software distributed during the prior quarter; such reports shall be sent to Sun Microsystems, Inc., 4150 Network Circle, Santa Clara, CA, 95054, Attn.: Sun ONE Studio Product Management Group, M/S UOAK01.

7. Trademarks and Logos. You acknowledge and agree as between you and Sun that Sun owns the SUN, SOLARIS, JAVA, JINI, FORTE, and iPLANET trademarks and all SUN, SOLARIS, JAVA, JINI, FORTE, and iPLANET-related trademarks, service marks, logos and other brand designations ("Sun Marks"), and you agree to comply with the Sun Trademark and Logo Usage Requirements currently located at http://www.sun.com/policies/trademarks. Any use you make of the Sun Marks inures to Sun's benefit.

8. Source Code. Software may contain source code that is provided solely for reference purposes pursuant to the terms of this Agreement. Source code may not be redistributed unless expressly provided for in this Agreement.

9. Termination for Infringement. Either party may terminate this Agreement immediately should any Software become, or in either party's opinion be likely to become, the subject of a claim of infringement of any intellectual property right.

For inquiries please contact: Sun Microsystems, Inc.
4150 Network Circle, Santa Clara, California 95054.
(LFI#117241/Form ID#011801)

IBM® CLOUDSCAPE™ SERVER EDITION, VERSION 5.0.4. INTERNATIONAL LICENSE AGREEMENT FOR EVALUATION OF PROGRAMS

Part 1 - General Terms
PLEASE READ THIS AGREEMENT CAREFULLY BEFORE USING THE PROGRAM. IBM WILL LICENSE THE PROGRAM TO YOU ONLY IF YOU FIRST ACCEPT THE TERMS OF THIS AGREEMENT. BY USING THE PROGRAM YOU AGREE TO THESE TERMS. IF YOU DO NOT AGREE TO THE TERMS OF THIS AGREEMENT, PROMPTLY RETURN THE UNUSED PROGRAM TO IBM.

The Program is owned by International Business Machines Corporation or one of its subsidiaries (IBM) or an IBM supplier, and is copyrighted and licensed, not sold.

The term "Program" means the original program and all whole or partial copies of it. A Program consists of machine-readable instructions, its components, data, audio-visual content (such as images, text, recordings, or pictures), and related licensed materials.

This Agreement includes Part 1 - General Terms and Part 2 - Country-unique Terms and is the complete agreement regarding the use of this Program, and replaces any prior oral or written communications between you and IBM. The terms of Part 2 may replace or modify those of Part 1.

1. License
Use of the Program
IBM grants you a nonexclusive, nontransferable license to use the Program.

You may 1) use the Program only for internal evaluation, testing or demonstration purposes, on a trial or "try-and-buy" basis and 2) make and install a reasonable number of copies of the Program in support of such use, unless IBM identifies a specific number of copies in the documentation accompanying the Program. The terms of this license apply to each copy you make. You will reproduce the copyright notice and any other legends of ownership on each copy, or partial copy, of the Program.

THE PROGRAM MAY CONTAIN A DISABLING DEVICE THAT WILL PREVENT IT FROM BEING USED UPON EXPIRATION OF THIS LICENSE. YOU WILL NOT TAMPER WITH THIS DISABLING DEVICE OR THE PROGRAM. YOU SHOULD TAKE PRECAUTIONS TO AVOID ANY LOSS OF DATA THAT MIGHT RESULT WHEN THE PROGRAM CAN NO LONGER BE USED.

You will 1) maintain a record of all copies of the Program and 2) ensure that anyone who uses the Program does so only for your authorized use and in compliance with the terms of this Agreement.

You may not 1) use, copy, modify or distribute the Program except as provided in this Agreement; 2) reverse assemble, reverse compile, or otherwise translate the Program except as specifically permitted by law without the possibility of contractual waiver; or 3) sublicense, rent, or lease the Program.

This license begins with your first use of the Program and ends 1) as of the duration or date specified in the documentation accompanying the Program or 2) when the Program automatically disables itself. Unless IBM specifies in the documentation accompanying the Program that you may retain the Program (in which case, an additional charge may apply), you will destroy the Program and all copies made of it within ten days of when this license ends.

2. No Warranty

SUBJECT TO ANY STATUTORY WARRANTIES WHICH CANNOT BE EXCLUDED, IBM MAKES NO WARRANTIES OR CONDITIONS EITHER EXPRESS OR IMPLIED, INCLUDING WITHOUT LIMITATION, THE WARRANTY OF NON-INFRINGEMENT AND THE IMPLIED WARRANTIES OF MERCHANTABILITY AND FITNESS FOR A PARTICULAR PURPOSE, REGARDING THE PROGRAM OR TECHNICAL SUPPORT, IF ANY. IBM MAKES NO WARRANTY REGARDING THE CAPABILITY OF THE PROGRAM TO CORRECTLY PROCESS, PROVIDE AND/OR RECEIVE DATE DATA WITHIN AND BETWEEN THE 20TH AND 21ST CENTURIES.

This exclusion also applies to any of IBM's subcontractors, suppliers or program developers (collectively called "Suppliers").

Manufacturers, suppliers, or publishers of non-IBM Programs may provide their own warranties.

3. Limitation of Liability

NEITHER IBM NOR ITS SUPPLIERS ARE LIABLE FOR ANY DIRECT OR INDIRECT DAMAGES, INCLUDING WITHOUT LIMITATION, LOST PROFITS, LOST SAVINGS, OR ANY INCIDENTAL, SPECIAL, OR OTHER ECONOMIC CONSEQUENTIAL DAMAGES, EVEN IF IBM IS INFORMED OF THEIR POSSIBILITY. SOME JURISDICTIONS DO NOT ALLOW THE EXCLUSION OR LIMITATION OF INCIDENTAL OR CONSEQUENTIAL DAMAGES, SO THE ABOVE EXCLUSION OR LIMITATION MAY NOT APPLY TO YOU.

4. General

Nothing in this Agreement affects any statutory rights of consumers that cannot be waived or limited by contract.

IBM may terminate your license if you fail to comply with the terms of this Agreement. If IBM does so, you must immediately destroy the Program and all copies you made of it.

You may not export the Program.

Neither you nor IBM will bring a legal action under this Agreement more than two years after the cause of action arose unless otherwise provided by local law without the possibility of contractual waiver or limitation.

Neither you nor IBM is responsible for failure to fulfill any obligations due to causes beyond its control.

There is no additional charge for use of the Program for the duration of this license.

IBM does not provide program services or technical support, unless IBM specifies otherwise.

The laws of the country in which you acquire the Program govern this Agreement, except 1) in Australia, the laws of the State or Territory in which the transaction is performed govern this Agreement; 2) in Albania, Armenia, Belarus, Bosnia/Herzegovina, Bulgaria, Croatia, Czech Republic, Georgia, Hungary, Kazakhstan, Kirghizia, Former Yugoslav Republic of Macedonia (FYROM), Moldova, Poland, Romania, Russia, Slovak Republic, Slovenia, Ukraine, and Federal Republic of Yugoslavia, the laws of Austria govern this Agreement; 3) in the United Kingdom, all disputes relating to this Agreement will be governed by English Law and will be submitted to the exclusive jurisdiction of the English courts; 4) in Canada, the laws in the Province of Ontario govern this Agreement; and 5) in the United States and Puerto Rico, and People's Republic of China, the laws of the State of New York govern this Agreement.

Part 2 - Country-unique Terms

AUSTRALIA:

No Warranty (Section 2):

The following paragraph is added to this Section:

Although IBM specifies that there are no warranties, you may have certain rights under the Trade Practices Act 1974 or other legislation and are only limited to the extent permitted by the applicable legislation.

Limitation of Liability (Section 3):

The following paragraph is added to this Section:

Where IBM is in breach of a condition or warranty implied by the Trade Practices Act 1974, IBM's liability is limited to the repair or replacement of the goods, or the supply of equivalent goods. Where that condition or warranty relates to right to sell, quiet possession or clear title, or the goods are of a kind ordinarily acquired for personal, domestic or household use or consumption, then none of the limitations in this paragraph apply.

GERMANY:

No Warranty (Section 2):

The following paragraphs are added to this Section:

The minimum warranty period for Programs is six months.

In case a Program is delivered without Specifications, we will only warrant that the Program information correctly describes the Program and that the Program can be used according to the Program information. You have to check the usability according to the Program information within the "money-back guaranty" period.

Limitation of Liability (Section 3):

The following paragraph is added to this Section:

The limitations and exclusions specified in the Agreement will not apply to damages caused by IBM with fraud or gross negligence, and for express warranty.

INDIA:

General (Section 4):

The following replaces the fourth paragraph of this Section:

If no suit or other legal action is brought, within two years after the cause of action arose, in respect of any claim that either party may have against the other, the rights of the concerned party in respect of such claim will be forfeited and the other party will stand released from its obligations in respect of such claim.

IRELAND:

No Warranty (Section 2):

The following paragraph is added to this Section:

Except as expressly provided in these terms and conditions, all statutory conditions, including all warranties implied, but without prejudice to the generality of the foregoing, all warranties implied by the Sale of Goods Act 1893 or the Sale of Goods and Supply of Services Act 1980 are hereby excluded.

ITALY:

Limitation of Liability (Section 3):

This Section is replaced by the following:

Unless otherwise provided by mandatory law, IBM is not liable for any damages which might arise.

NEW ZEALAND:

No Warranty (Section 2):

The following paragraph is added to this Section:

Although IBM specifies that there are no warranties, you may have certain rights under the Consumer Guarantees Act 1993 or other legislation which cannot be excluded or limited. The Consumer Guarantees Act 1993 will not apply in respect of any goods or services which IBM provides, if you require the goods and services for the purposes of a business as defined in that Act.

Limitation of Liability (Section 3):

The following paragraph is added to this Section:

Where Programs are not acquired for the purposes of a business as defined in the Consumer Guarantees Act 1993, the limitations in this Section are subject to the limitations in that Act.

UNITED KINGDOM:

Limitation of Liability (Section 3):

The following paragraph is added to this Section at the end of the first paragraph:

The limitation of liability will not apply to any breach of IBM's obligations implied by Section 12 of the Sales of Goods Act 1979 or Section 2 of the Supply of Goods and Services Act 1982.

Z125-5543-01 (10/97)

LICENSE INFORMATION

The Programs listed below are licensed under the following terms and conditions in addition to those of the International License Agreement for Evaluation of Programs.

Program Name:

IBM Cloudscape Server Edition Version 5.0.4

Specified Operating Environment

The Program Specifications and Specified Operating Environment information may be found in documentation accompanying the Program such as the Installation/Users Guide.

Evaluation Period

The license begins on the date you first use the Program and ends after 60 days.

Program-unique Terms

U.S. Government Users Restricted Rights

U.S. Government Users Restricted Rights - Use, duplication, or disclosure restricted by the GSA ADP Schedule Contract with the IBM Corporation.

IBM, DB2, and Cloudscape are trademarks of IBM Corporation in the United States, other countries, or both.

Java and all Java-based trademarks and logos, and Solaris are trademarks of Sun Microsystems, Inc. in the United States, other countries, or both.

Microsoft, Windows, and Windows NT are trademarks of Microsoft Corporation in the United States, other countries, or both.

UNIX is a registered trademark in the United States, other countries or both and is licensed exclusively through X/Open Company Limited.

THE APACHE SOFTWARE LICENSE, VERSION 1.1

Copyright (c) 2000 The Apache Software Foundation. All rights reserved.

Redistribution and use in source and binary forms, with or without modification, are permitted provided that the following conditions are met:

1. Redistributions of source code must retain the above copyright notice, this list of conditions and the following disclaimer.

2. Redistributions in binary form must reproduce the above copyright notice, this list of conditions and the following disclaimer in the documentation and/or other materials provided with the distribution.

3. The end-user documentation included with the redistribution, if any, must include the following acknowledgment: "This product includes software developed by the Apache Software Foundation (http://www.apache.org/)." Alternately, this acknowledgment may appear in the software itself, if and wherever such third-party acknowledgments normally appear.

4. The names "Apache" and "Apache Software Foundation" must not be used to endorse or promote products derived from this software without prior written permission. For written permission, please contact apache@apache.org.

5. Products derived from this software may not be called "Apache", nor may "Apache" appear in their name, without prior written permission of the Apache Software Foundation.

THIS SOFTWARE IS PROVIDED ``AS IS'' AND ANY EXPRESSED OR IMPLIED WARRANTIES, INCLUDING, BUT NOT LIMITED TO, THE IMPLIED WARRANTIES OF MERCHANTABILITY AND FITNESS FOR A PARTICULAR PURPOSE ARE DISCLAIMED. IN NO EVENT SHALL THE APACHE SOFTWARE FOUNDATION OR ITS CONTRIBUTORS BE LIABLE FOR ANY DIRECT, INDIRECT, INCIDENTAL, SPECIAL, EXEMPLARY, OR CONSEQUENTIAL DAMAGES (INCLUDING, BUT NOT LIMITED TO, PROCUREMENT OF SUBSTITUTE GOODS OR SERVICES; LOSS OF USE, DATA, OR PROFITS; OR BUSINESS INTERRUPTION) HOWEVER CAUSED AND ON ANY THEORY OF LIABILITY, WHETHER IN CONTRACT, STRICT LIABILITY, OR TORT (INCLUDING NEGLIGENCE OR OTHERWISE) ARISING IN ANY WAY OUT OF THE USE OF THIS SOFTWARE, EVEN IF ADVISED OF THE POSSIBILITY OF SUCH DAMAGE.

This software consists of voluntary contributions made by many individuals on behalf of the Apache Software Foundation. For more information on the Apache Software Foundation, please see <http://www.apache.org/>.

Portions of this software are based upon public domain software originally written at the National Center for Supercomputing Applications, University of Illinois, Urbana-Champaign.

PRENTICE HALL LICENSE AGREEMENT AND LIMITED WARRANTY

READ THE FOLLOWING TERMS AND CONDITIONS CAREFULLY BEFORE OPENING THIS SOFT-
WARE PACKAGE. THIS LEGAL DOCUMENT IS AN AGREEMENT BETWEEN YOU AND PRENTICE-
HALL, INC. (THE "COMPANY"). BY OPENING THIS SEALED SOFTWARE PACKAGE, YOU ARE
AGREEING TO BE BOUND BY THESE TERMS AND CONDITIONS. IF YOU DO NOT AGREE WITH
THESE TERMS AND CONDITIONS, DO NOT OPEN THE SOFTWARE PACKAGE. PROMPTLY RETURN
THE UNOPENED SOFTWARE PACKAGE AND ALL ACCOMPANYING ITEMS TO THE PLACE YOU
OBTAINED THEM FOR A FULL REFUND OF ANY SUMS YOU HAVE PAID.

1.   GRANT OF LICENSE: In consideration of your purchase of this book, and your agreement to abide
by the terms and conditions of this Agreement, the Company grants to you a nonexclusive right to use and
display the copy of the enclosed software program (hereinafter the "SOFTWARE") on a single computer (i.e.,
with a single CPU) at a single location so long as you comply with the terms of this Agreement. The Company
reserves all rights not expressly granted to you under this Agreement.

2.   OWNERSHIP OF SOFTWARE: You own only the magnetic or physical media (the enclosed
media) on which the SOFTWARE is recorded or fixed, but the Company and the software developers retain all
the rights, title, and ownership to the SOFTWARE recorded on the original media copy(ies) and all subsequent
copies of the SOFTWARE, regardless of the form or media on which the original or other copies may exist.
This license is not a sale of the original SOFTWARE or any copy to you.

3.   COPY RESTRICTIONS: This SOFTWARE and the accompanying printed materials and user
manual (the "Documentation") are the subject of copyright. The individual programs on the media are
copyrighted by the authors of each program. Some of the programs on the media include separate licensing
agreements. If you intend to use one of these programs, you must read and follow its accompanying license
agreement. You may not copy the Documentation or the SOFTWARE, except that you may make a single copy
of the SOFTWARE for backup or archival purposes only. You may be held legally responsible for any copying
or copyright infringement which is caused or encouraged by your failure to abide by the terms of this
restriction.

4.   USE RESTRICTIONS: You may not network the SOFTWARE or otherwise use it on more than one
computer or computer terminal at the same time. You may physically transfer the SOFTWARE from one
computer to another provided that the SOFTWARE is used on only one computer at a time. You may not
distribute copies of the SOFTWARE or Documentation to others. You may not reverse engineer, disassemble,
decompile, modify, adapt, translate, or create derivative works based on the SOFTWARE or the Documentation
without the prior written consent of the Company.

5.   TRANSFER RESTRICTIONS: The enclosed SOFTWARE is licensed only to you and may not be
transferred to any one else without the prior written consent of the Company. Any unauthorized transfer of the
SOFTWARE shall result in the immediate termination of this Agreement.

6.   TERMINATION: This license is effective until terminated. This license will terminate automatically
without notice from the Company and become null and void if you fail to comply with any provisions or
limitations of this license. Upon termination, you shall destroy the Documentation and all copies of the
SOFTWARE. All provisions of this Agreement as to warranties, limitation of liability, remedies or damages,
and our ownership rights shall survive termination.

7.   MISCELLANEOUS: This Agreement shall be construed in accordance with the laws of the United
States of America and the State of New York and shall benefit the Company, its affiliates, and assignees.

8.   LIMITED WARRANTY AND DISCLAIMER OF WARRANTY: The Company warrants that the
SOFTWARE, when properly used in accordance with the Documentation, will operate in substantial conformity
with the description of the SOFTWARE set forth in the Documentation. The Company does not warrant that the
SOFTWARE will meet your requirements or that the operation of the SOFTWARE will be uninterrupted or
error-free. The Company warrants that the media on which the SOFTWARE is delivered shall be free from
defects in materials and workmanship under normal use for a period of thirty (30) days from the date of your
purchase. Your only remedy and the Company's only obligation under these limited warranties is, at the
Company's option, return of the warranted item for a refund of any amounts paid by you or replacement of the
item. Any replacement of SOFTWARE or media under the warranties shall not extend the original warranty
period. The limited warranty set forth above shall not apply to any SOFTWARE which the Company
determines in good faith has been subject to misuse, neglect, improper installation, repair, alteration, or damage
by you. EXCEPT FOR THE EXPRESSED WARRANTIES SET FORTH ABOVE, THE COMPANY
DISCLAIMS ALL WARRANTIES, EXPRESS OR IMPLIED, INCLUDING WITHOUT LIMITATION, THE

IMPLIED WARRANTIES OF MERCHANTABILITY AND FITNESS FOR A PARTICULAR PURPOSE. EXCEPT FOR THE EXPRESS WARRANTY SET FORTH ABOVE, THE COMPANY DOES NOT WARRANT, GUARANTEE, OR MAKE ANY REPRESENTATION REGARDING THE USE OR THE RESULTS OF THE USE OF THE SOFTWARE IN TERMS OF ITS CORRECTNESS, ACCURACY, RELIABILITY, CURRENTNESS, OR OTHERWISE.

IN NO EVENT, SHALL THE COMPANY OR ITS EMPLOYEES, AGENTS, SUPPLIERS, OR CONTRACTORS BE LIABLE FOR ANY INCIDENTAL, INDIRECT, SPECIAL, OR CONSEQUENTIAL DAMAGES ARISING OUT OF OR IN CONNECTION WITH THE LICENSE GRANTED UNDER THIS AGREEMENT, OR FOR LOSS OF USE, LOSS OF DATA, LOSS OF INCOME OR PROFIT, OR OTHER LOSSES, SUSTAINED AS A RESULT OF INJURY TO ANY PERSON, OR LOSS OF OR DAMAGE TO PROPERTY, OR CLAIMS OF THIRD PARTIES, EVEN IF THE COMPANY OR AN AUTHORIZED REPRESENTATIVE OF THE COMPANY HAS BEEN ADVISED OF THE POSSIBILITY OF SUCH DAMAGES. IN NO EVENT SHALL LIABILITY OF THE COMPANY FOR DAMAGES WITH RESPECT TO THE SOFTWARE EXCEED THE AMOUNTS ACTUALLY PAID BY YOU, IF ANY, FOR THE SOFTWARE.

SOME JURISDICTIONS DO NOT ALLOW THE LIMITATION OF IMPLIED WARRANTIES OR LIABILITY FOR INCIDENTAL, INDIRECT, SPECIAL, OR CONSEQUENTIAL DAMAGES, SO THE ABOVE LIMITATIONS MAY NOT ALWAYS APPLY. THE WARRANTIES IN THIS AGREEMENT GIVE YOU SPECIFIC LEGAL RIGHTS AND YOU MAY ALSO HAVE OTHER RIGHTS WHICH VARY IN ACCORDANCE WITH LOCAL LAW.

ACKNOWLEDGMENT

YOU ACKNOWLEDGE THAT YOU HAVE READ THIS AGREEMENT, UNDERSTAND IT, AND AGREE TO BE BOUND BY ITS TERMS AND CONDITIONS. YOU ALSO AGREE THAT THIS AGREEMENT IS THE COMPLETE AND EXCLUSIVE STATEMENT OF THE AGREEMENT BETWEEN YOU AND THE COMPANY AND SUPERSEDES ALL PROPOSALS OR PRIOR AGREEMENTS, ORAL, OR WRITTEN, AND ANY OTHER COMMUNICATIONS BETWEEN YOU AND THE COMPANY OR ANY REPRESENTATIVE OF THE COMPANY RELATING TO THE SUBJECT MATTER OF THIS AGREEMENT.

Should you have any questions concerning this Agreement or if you wish to contact the Company for any reason, please contact in writing at the address below.

Robin Short
Prentice Hall PTR
One Lake Street
Upper Saddle River, New Jersey 07458

The DEITEL™ Suite of Products...

HOW TO PROGRAM BOOKS

C++
How to Program
Fourth Edition

BOOK / CD-ROM

©2003, 1400 pp., paper
(0-13-038474-7)

The world's best-selling C++ textbook is now even better! Designed for beginning through intermediate courses, this comprehensive, practical introduction to C++ includes hundreds of hands-on exercises, and uses 267 LIVE-CODE™ programs to demonstrate C++'s powerful capabilities. This edition includes a new chapter—Web Programming with CGI—that provides everything readers need to begin developing their own Web-based applications that will run on the Internet! Readers will learn how to build so-called *n*-tier applications, in which the functionality provided by each tier can be distributed to separate computers across the Internet or executed on the same computer. This edition uses a new code-highlighting style with a yellow background to focus the reader on the C++ features introduced in each program. The book provides a carefully designed sequence of examples that introduces inheritance and polymorphism and helps students understand the motivation and implementation of these key object-oriented programming concepts. In addition, the OOD/UML case study has been upgraded to UML 1.4 and all flowcharts and inheritance diagrams in the text have been converted to UML diagrams. The book presents an early introduction to strings and arrays as objects using standard C++ classes **string** and **vector**.
The book also covers key concepts and techniques standard C++ developers need to master, including control structures, functions, arrays, pointers and strings, classes and data abstraction, operator overloading, inheritance, virtual functions, polymorphism, I/O, templates, exception handling, file processing, data structures and more. The book includes a detailed introduction to Standard Template Library (STL) containers, container adapters, algorithms and iterators. It also features insight into good programming practices, maximizing performance, avoiding errors, and testing and debugging tips.

📖 Also available is *C++ in the Lab, Fourth Edition,* a lab manual designed to accompany this book. Use ISBN 0-13-038478-X to order.

Java™ How to Program Fifth Edition

BOOK / CD-ROM

©2003, 1500 pp., paper
(0-13-101621-0)

The Deitels' new Fifth Edition of *Java™ How to Program* is now even better! It now includes an updated, optional case study on object-oriented design with the UML, new coverage of JDBC, servlets and JSP and the most up-to-date Java coverage available.

The book includes substantial comments and enhanced syntax coloring of all the code. This edition uses a new code-highlighting style with a yellow background to focus the reader on the Java features introduced in each program. Red text is used to point out intentional errors and problematic areas in programs. Plus, user input is highlighted in output windows so that the user input can be distinguished from the text output by the program.

Updated throughout, the text now includes an enhanced presentation of inheritance and polymorphism. All flowcharts have been replaced with UML activity diagrams, and class hierarchy diagrams have been replaced with UML class diagrams.

📖 Also available is *Java in the Lab, Fifth Edition,* a lab manual designed to accompany this book. Use ISBN 0-13-101631-8 to order.

Advanced Java™ 2 Platform How to Program

BOOK / CD-ROM

©2002, 1811 pp., paper
(0-13-089560-1)

Expanding on the world's best-selling Java textbook—*Java™ How to Program*—*Advanced Java™ 2 Platform How To Program* presents advanced Java topics for developing sophisticated, user-friendly GUIs; significant, scalable enterprise applications; wireless applications and distributed systems. Primarily based on Java 2 Enterprise Edition (J2EE), this textbook integrates technologies such as XML, JavaBeans, security, JDBC™, JavaServer Pages (JSP™), servlets, Remote Method Invocation (RMI), Enterprise JavaBeans™ (EJB) and design patterns into a production-quality system that allows developers to benefit from the leverage and platform independence Java 2 Enterprise Edition provides. The book also features the development of a complete, end-to-end e-business solution using advanced Java technologies. Additional topics include Swing, Java 2D and 3D, XML, design patterns, CORBA, Jini™, JavaSpaces™, Jiro™, Java Management Extensions (JMX) and Peer-to-Peer networking with an introduction to JXTA. This textbook also introduces the Java 2 Micro Edition (J2ME™) for building applications for handheld and wireless devices using MIDP and MIDlets. Wireless technologies covered include WAP, WML and i-mode.

C# How to Program

BOOK / CD-ROM

©2002, 1568 pp., paper (0-13-062221-4)

An exciting addition to the *How to Program Series*, *C# How to Program* provides a comprehensive introduction to Microsoft's new object-oriented language. C# builds on the skills already mastered by countless C++ and Java programmers, enabling them to create powerful Web applications and components—ranging from XML-based Web services on Microsoft's .NET platform to middle-tier business objects and system-level applications. *C# How to Program* begins with a strong foundation in the introductory- and intermediate-programming principles students will need in industry. It then explores such essential topics as object-oriented programming and exception handling. Graphical user interfaces are extensively covered, giving readers the tools to build compelling and fully interactive programs. Internet technologies such as XML, ADO .NET and Web services are covered as well as topics including regular expressions, multithreading, networking, databases, files and data structures.

Visual Basic® .NET How to Program Second Edition

BOOK / CD-ROM

©2002, 1400 pp., paper (0-13-029363-6)

Learn Visual Basic .NET programming from the ground up! The introduction of Microsoft's .NET Framework marks the beginning of major revisions to all of Microsoft's programming languages. This book provides a comprehensive introduction to the next version of Visual Basic—Visual Basic .NET—featuring extensive updates and increased functionality. *Visual Basic .NET How to Program, Second Edition* covers introductory programming techniques as well as more advanced topics, featuring enhanced treatment of developing Web-based applications. Other topics discussed include an extensive treatment of XML and wireless applications, databases, SQL and ADO .NET, Web forms, Web services and ASP .NET.

C How to Program Third Edition

BOOK / CD-ROM

©2001, 1253 pp., paper (0-13-089572-5)

Highly practical in approach, the Third Edition of the world's best-selling C book introduces the fundamentals of structured programming and software engineering. This comprehensive book not only covers the full C language, but also reviews library functions and introduces object-based and object-oriented programming in C++ and Java and event-driven GUI programming in Java. *C How to Program, Third Edition* includes a new 346-page introduction to Java 2 and the basics of GUIs, and the 298-page introduction to C++ has been updated to be consistent with the most current ANSI/ISO C++ standards. Plus, icons throughout the book point out valuable programming tips such as Common Programming Errors, Portability Tips and Testing and Debugging Tips.

Getting Started with Microsoft® Visual C++™ 6 with an Introduction to MFC

BOOK / CD-ROM

©2000, 163 pp., paper (0-13-016147-0)

Internet & World Wide Web How to Program, Second Edition

BOOK / CD-ROM

©2002, 1428 pp., paper (0-13-030897-8)

The revision of this groundbreaking book in the Deitels' *How to Program Series* offers a thorough treatment of programming concepts that yield visible or audible results in Web pages and Web-based applications. This book discusses effective Web-based design, server- and client-side scripting, multitier Web-based applications development, ActiveX® controls and electronic commerce essentials. This book offers an alternative to traditional programming courses using markup languages (such as XHTML, Dynamic HTML and XML) and scripting languages (such as JavaScript, VBScript, Perl/CGI, Python and PHP) to teach the fundamentals of programming "wrapped in the metaphor of the Web." Updated material on **www.deitel.com** and **www.prenhall.com/deitel** provides additional resources for instructors who want to cover Microsoft® or non-Microsoft technologies. The Web site includes an extensive treatment of Netscape® 6 and alternate versions of the code from the Dynamic HTML chapters that will work with non-Microsoft environments as well.

Wireless Internet & Mobile Business How to Program

© 2002, 1292 pp., paper
(0-13-062226-5)

While the rapid expansion of wireless technologies, such as cell phones, pagers and personal digital assistants (PDAs), offers many new opportunities for businesses and programmers, it also presents numerous challenges related to issues such as security and standardization. This book offers a thorough treatment of both the management and technical aspects of this growing area, including coverage of current practices and future trends. The first half explores the business issues surrounding wireless technology and mobile business, including an overview of existing and developing communication technologies and the application of business principles to wireless devices. It also discusses location-based services and location-identifying technologies, a topic that is revisited throughout the book. Wireless payment, security, legal and social issues, international communications and more are also discussed. The book then turns to programming for the wireless Internet, exploring topics such as WAP (including 2.0), WML, WMLScript, XML, XHTML™, wireless Java programming (J2ME™), Web Clipping and more. Other topics covered include career resources, wireless marketing, accessibility, Palm™, PocketPC, Windows CE, i-mode, Bluetooth, MIDP, MIDlets, ASP, Microsoft .NET Mobile Framework, BREW™, multimedia, Flash™ and VBScript.

Python How to Program

BOOK / CD-ROM

©2002, 1376 pp., paper
(0-13-092361-3)

This exciting new textbook provides a comprehensive introduction to Python—a powerful object-oriented programming language with clear syntax and the ability to bring together various technologies quickly and easily. This book covers introductory-programming techniques and more advanced topics such as graphical user interfaces, databases, wireless Internet programming, networking, security, process management, multithreading, XHTML, CSS, PSP and multimedia. Readers will learn principles that are applicable to both systems development and Web programming. The book features the consistent and applied pedagogy that the *How to Program Series* is known for,

including the Deitels' signature LIVE-CODE™ Approach, with thousands of lines of code in hundreds of working programs; hundreds of valuable programming tips identified with icons throughout the text; an extensive set of exercises, projects and case studies; two-color four-way syntax coloring and much more.

e-Business & e-Commerce for Managers

©2001, 794 pp., cloth
(0-13-032364-0)

This comprehensive overview of building and managing e-businesses explores topics such as the decision to bring a business online, choosing a business model, accepting payments, marketing strategies and security, as well as many other important issues (such as career resources). The book features Web resources and online demonstrations that supplement the text and direct readers to additional materials. The book also includes an appendix that develops a complete Web-based shopping-cart application using HTML, JavaScript, VBScript, Active Server Pages, ADO, SQL, HTTP, XML and XSL. Plus, company-specific sections provide "real-world" examples of the concepts presented in the book.

XML How to Program

BOOK / CD-ROM

©2001, 934 pp., paper
(0-13-028417-3)

This book is a comprehensive guide to programming in XML. It teaches how to use XML to create customized tags and includes chapters that address markup languages for science and technology, multimedia, commerce and many other fields. Concise introductions to Java, JavaServer Pages, VBScript, Active Server Pages and Perl/CGI provide readers with the essentials of these programming languages and server-side development technologies to enable them to work effectively with XML. The book also covers cutting-edge topics such as XSL, DOM™ and SAX, plus a real-world e-commerce case study and a complete chapter on Web accessibility that addresses Voice XML. It includes tips such as Common Programming Errors, Software Engineering Observations, Portability Tips and Debugging Hints. Other topics covered include XHTML, CSS, DTD, schema, parsers, XPath, XLink, namespaces, XBase, XInclude, XPointer, XSLT, XSL Formatting Objects, JavaServer Pages, XForms, topic maps, X3D, MathML, OpenMath, CML, BML, CDF, RDF, SVG, Cocoon, WML, XBRL and BizTalk™ and SOAP™ Web resources.

Perl How to Program

BOOK / CD-ROM

©2001, 1057 pp., paper (0-13-028418-1)

This comprehensive guide to Perl programming emphasizes the use of the Common Gateway Interface (CGI) with Perl to create powerful, dynamic multi-tier Web-based client/server applications. The book begins with a clear and careful introduction to programming concepts at a level suitable for beginners, and proceeds through advanced topics such as references and complex data structures. Key Perl topics such as regular expressions and string manipulation are covered in detail. The authors address important and topical issues such as object-oriented programming, the Perl database interface (DBI), graphics and security. Also included is a treatment of XML, a bonus chapter introducing the Python programming language, supplemental material on career resources and a complete chapter on Web accessibility. The text includes tips such as Common Programming Errors, Software Engineering Observations, Portability Tips and Debugging Hints.

e-Business & e-Commerce How to Program

BOOK / CD-ROM

©2001, 1254 pp., paper (0-13-028419-X)

This innovative book explores programming technologies for developing Web-based e-business and e-commerce solutions, and covers e-business and e-commerce models and business issues. Readers learn a full range of options, from "build-your-own" to turnkey solutions. The book examines scores of the top e-businesses (examples include Amazon, eBay, Priceline, Travelocity, etc.), explaining the technical details of building successful e-business and e-commerce sites and their underlying business premises. Learn how to implement the dominant e-commerce models—shopping carts, auctions, name-your-own-price, comparison shopping and bots/ intelligent agents—by using markup languages (HTML, Dynamic HTML and XML), scripting languages (JavaScript, VBScript and Perl), server-side technologies (Active Server Pages and Perl/CGI) and database (SQL and ADO), security and online payment technologies. Updates are regularly posted to **www.deitel.com** and the book includes a CD-ROM with software tools, source code and live links.

Visual Basic® 6 How to Program

BOOK / CD-ROM

©1999, 1015 pp., paper (0-13-456955-5)

Visual Basic® 6 How to Program was developed in cooperation with Microsoft to cover important topics such as graphical user interfaces (GUIs), multimedia, object-oriented programming, networking, database programming, VBScript®, COM/DCOM and ActiveX®.

ORDER INFORMATION

SINGLE COPY SALES:
Visa, Master Card, American Express, Checks, or Money Orders only
Toll-Free: 800-643-5506; Fax: 800-835-5327

GOVERNMENT AGENCIES:
Prentice Hall Customer Service
(#GS-02F-8023A)
Phone: 201-767-5994; Fax: 800-445-6991

COLLEGE PROFESSORS:
For desk or review copies, please visit us on the World Wide Web at www.prenhall.com

CORPORATE ACCOUNTS:
Quantity, Bulk Orders totaling 10 or more books. Purchase orders only — No credit cards.
Tel: 201-236-7156; Fax: 201-236-7141
Toll-Free: 800-382-3419

CANADA:
Pearson Technology Group Canada
10 Alcorn Avenue, suite #300
Toronto, Ontario, Canada M4V 3B2
Tel.: 416-925-2249; Fax: 416-925-0068
E-mail: phcinfo.pubcanada@pearsoned.com

UK/IRELAND:
Pearson Education
Edinburgh Gate
Harlow, Essex CM20 2JE UK
Tel: 01279 623928; Fax: 01279 414130
E-mail: enq.orders@pearsoned-ema.com

EUROPE, MIDDLE EAST & AFRICA:
Pearson Education
P.O. Box 75598
1070 AN Amsterdam, The Netherlands
Tel: 31 20 5755 800; Fax: 31 20 664 5334
E-mail: amsterdam@pearsoned-ema.com

ASIA:
Pearson Education Asia
317 Alexandra Road #04-01
IKEA Building
Singapore 159965
Tel: 65 476 4688; Fax: 65 378 0370

JAPAN:
Pearson Education
Nishi-Shinjuku, KF Building 101
8-14-24 Nishi-Shinjuku, Shinjuku-ku
Tokyo, Japan 160-0023
Tel: 81 3 3365 9001; Fax: 81 3 3365 9009

INDIA:
Pearson Education Indian Liaison Office
90 New Raidhani Enclave, Ground Floor
Delhi 110 092, India
Tel: 91 11 2059850 & 2059851
Fax: 91 11 2059852

AUSTRALIA:
Pearson Education Australia
Unit 4, Level 2
14 Aquatic Drive
Frenchs Forest, NSW 2086, Australia
Tel: 61 2 9454 2200; Fax: 61 2 9453 0089
E-mail: marketing@pearsoned.com.au

NEW ZEALAND/FIJI:
Pearson Education
46 Hillside Road
Auckland 10, New Zealand
Tel: 649 444 4968; Fax: 649 444 4957
E-mail: sales@pearsoned.co.nz

SOUTH AFRICA:
Pearson Education
P.O. Box 12122
Mill Street
Cape Town 8010 South Africa
Tel: 27 21 686 6356; Fax: 27 21 686 4590

LATIN AMERICA:
Pearson Education Latinoamerica
815 NW 57th Street Suite 484
Miami, FL 33158
Tel: 305 264 8344; Fax: 305 264 7933

Visual C++ .NET
A Managed Code Approach
for Experienced Programmers

© 2003, 1600 pp., paper (0-13-045821-X)

Written by the authors of the world's best-selling introductory/intermediate C and C++ textbooks, this comprehensive book thoroughly examines Visual C++® .NET. It starts with a brief yet thorough introduction to computers and Visual C++ .NET programming, including fundamental topics such as arrays, functions and control structures. The text then moves on to more advanced topics such as graphical user interfaces (GUIs), multimedia, Web services, file processing, object-oriented programming, databases and networking. Readers learn how to create reusable software components with classes and assemblies, database connections using ADO .NET, Web-based applications using ATL Server and Web services using ASP .NET and ATL Server. Readers will learn the difference between managed and unmanaged code. The first 20 chapters focus on Microsoft®'s new managed extensions for C++ while Chapters 21–25 familiarize experienced programmers with new features of unmanaged code and interoperability between managed and unmanaged code.

Java™ Web Services
for Experienced Programmers

© 2003, 700 pp., paper (0-13-046134-2)

Java™ Web Services for Experienced Programmers from the DEITEL™ Developer Series provides the experienced Java programmer with 103 LIVE-CODE™ examples and covers industry standards including XML, SOAP, WSDL and UDDI. Learn how to build and integrate Web services using the Java API for XML RPC, the Java API for XML Messaging, Apache Axis and the Java Web Services Developer Pack. Develop and deploy Web services on several major Web services platforms. Register and discover Web services through public registries and the Java API for XML Registries. Build Web Services clients for several platforms, including J2ME. Significant Web Services case studies also are included.

Web Services:
A Technical Introduction

© 2003, 400 pp., paper (0-13-046135-0)

Web Services: A Technical Introduction from the DEITEL™ Developer Series familiarizes programmers, technical managers and project managers with key Web services concepts, including what Web services are and why they are revolutionary. The book covers the business case for Web services—the underlying technologies, ways in which Web services can provide competitive advantages and opportunities for Web services-related lines of business. Readers learn the latest Web-services standards, including XML, SOAP, WSDL and UDDI; learn about Web services implementations in .NET and Java; benefit from an extensive comparison of Web services products and vendors; and read about Web services security options. Although this is not a programming book, the appendices show .NET and Java code examples to demonstrate the structure of Web services applications and documents. In addition, the book includes numerous case studies describing ways in which organizations are implementing Web services to increase efficiency, simplify business processes, create new revenue streams and interact better with partners and customers.

BOOK/MULTIMEDIA PACKAGES

Complete Training Courses

Each complete package includes the corresponding *How to Program Series* book and interactive multimedia CD-ROM Cyber Classroom. *Complete Training Courses* are perfect for anyone interested in Web and e-commerce programming. They are affordable resources for college students and professionals learning programming for the first time or reinforcing their knowledge.

Each *Complete Training Course* is compatible with Windows 95, Windows 98, Windows NT, Windows 2000, Windows ME and Windows XP* and includes the following features:

Intuitive Browser-Based Interface

You'll love the *Complete Training Courses'* new browser-based interface, designed to be easy and accessible to anyone who's ever used a Web browser. Every *Complete Training Course* features the full text, illustrations and program listings of its corresponding *How to Program* book—all in full color—with full-text searching and hyperlinking.

Further Enhancements to the Deitels' Signature LIVE-CODE™ Approach

Every code sample from the main text can be found in the interactive, multimedia, CD-ROM-based *Cyber Classrooms* included in the *Complete Training Courses*. Syntax coloring of code is included for the *How to Program* books that are published in full color. Even the recent two-color and one-color books use effective syntax shading. The *Cyber Classroom* products always are in full color.

Audio Annotations

Hours of detailed, expert audio descriptions of thousands of lines of code help reinforce concepts.

Easily Executable Code

With one click of the mouse, you can execute the code or save it to your hard drive to manipulate using the programming environment of your choice. With selected *Complete Training Courses*, you can also load all of the code into a development environment such as Microsoft® Visual C++™, enabling you to modify and execute the programs with ease.

Abundant Self-Assessment Material

Practice exams test your understanding with hundreds of test questions and answers in addition to those found in the main text. Hundreds of self-review questions, all with answers, are drawn from the text; as are hundreds of programming exercises, half with answers.

The Complete Visual Basic 6 Training Course, Student Edition is not compatible with Windows 2000 or Windows XP. *The Complete C# Training Course, Student Edition, The Complete Visual Basic .NET Training Course, Student Edition* and *The Complete Python Training Course* are not compatible with Windows 95.

www.phptr.com/phptrinteractive

BOOK/MULTIMEDIA PACKAGES

Coming Soon!

The Complete C++ Training Course, Fourth Edition
(0-13-100252-X)

The Complete Python Training Course
(0-13-067374-9)

The Complete C# Training Course
(0-13-064584-2)

The Complete Visual Basic 6 Training Course
(0-13-082929-3)

The Complete e-Business & e-Commerce Programming Training Course
(0-13-089549-0)

The Complete Visual Basic .NET Training Course, Second Edition
(0-13-042530-3)

The Complete Internet & World Wide Web Programming Training Course, Second Edition
(0-13-089550-4)

The Complete Wireless Internet & Mobile Business Programming Training Course
(0-13-062335-0)

Coming Soon!

The Complete Java™ 2 Training Course, Fifth Edition
(0-13-102819-7)

The Complete XML Programming Training Course
(0-13-089557-1)

The Complete Perl Training Course
(0-13-089552-0)

All of these ISBNs are retail ISBNs. College and university instructors should contact your local Prentice Hall representative or write to cs@prenhall.com for the corresponding student edition ISBNs.

If you would like to purchase the Cyber Classrooms separately...

Prentice Hall offers Multimedia Cyber Classroom CD-ROMs to accompany the *How to Program Series* texts for the topics listed at right. If you have already purchased one of these books and would like to purchase a stand-alone copy of the corresponding *Multimedia Cyber Classroom,* you can make your purchase at the following Web site:

www.informit.com/cyberclassrooms

C++ Multimedia Cyber Classroom, 4/E, ISBN # 0-13-100253-8

C# Multimedia Cyber Classroom, ask for product number 0-13-064587-7

e-Business & e-Commerce Cyber Classroom, ISBN # 0-13-089540-7

Internet & World Wide Web Cyber Classroom, 2/E, ISBN # 0-13-089559-8

Java Multimedia Cyber Classroom, 5/E, ISBN # 0-13-101769-1

Perl Multimedia Cyber Classroom, ISBN # 0-13-089553-9

Python Multimedia Cyber Classroom, ISBN # 0-13-067375-7

Visual Basic 6 Multimedia Cyber Classroom, ISBN # 0-13-083116-6

Visual Basic .NET Multimedia Cyber Classroom, 2/E, ISBN # 0-13-065193-1

XML Multimedia Cyber Classroom, ISBN # 0-13-089555-5

Wireless Internet & Mobile Business Programming Multimedia Cyber Classroom, ISBN # 0-13-062337-7

Deitel & Associates, Inc. has partnered with Prentice Hall's parent company, Pearson PLC, and its information technology Web site, **InformIT.com**, to provide the Deitel InformIT kiosk at **www.InformIT.com/deitel**. The Deitel InformIT kiosk contains information on the continuum of Deitel products, including:

- **Free informational articles**
- **Books and e-Books**
- **Web-based training**

- **Instructor-led training by Deitel & Associates**
- *Complete Training Courses/Cyber Classrooms*

Deitel & Associates also contributes content to two InformIT e-mail newsletters.

The first is the InformIT promotional newsletter, which features weekly specials and discounts on most Pearson publications. Each week features information about our corporate instructor-led training courses and the opportunity to read about upcoming issues of our own e-mail newsletter, the *DEITEL™ BUZZ ONLINE*.

The second newsletter is the InformIT editorial newsletter, which contains approximately 50 new articles per week on various IT topics, including programming, advanced computing, networking, security, databases, creative media, business, Web development, software engineering, operating systems and more. Deitel & Associates regularly contributes articlees pulled from our extensive existing content base or material being created during our research and development process.

This publication is sent to over 1 million registered users worldwide (for opt-in registration, visit **www.informIT.com**).

Cyber Classrooms, Web-Based Training and Course Management Systems

DEITEL is committed to continuous research and development in e-Learning.

We are pleased to announce that we have incorporated examples of Web-based training, including a five-way Macromedia® Flash™ animation of a `for` loop in Java™, into the *Java 2 Multimedia Cyber Classroom, 5/e* (which is included in *The Complete Java 2 Training Course, 5/e*). Our instructional designers and Flash animation team are developing additional simulations that demonstrate key programming concepts.

We are enhancing the Multimedia Cyber Classroom products to include more audio, pre- and post-assessment questions and Web-based labs with solutions for the benefit of professors and students alike. In addition, our Multimedia Cyber Classroom products, currently available in CD-ROM format, are being ported to Pearson's CourseCompass course-management system—*a powerful e-platform for teaching and learning*. Many Deitel materials are available in WebCT, Blackboard and CourseCompass formats for colleges, and will soon be available for various corporate learning management systems.

Future Publications

Here are some new books we are considering for 2003/2004 release:

In 2003, we will wrap up the first book in our new Computer Science Series, **Operating Systems**. If you have been looking for a new kind of OS book and are interested in sharing your thoughts with us as a reviewer, please send an e-mail to deitel@deitel.com.

Other Books in the Computer Science Series: *Data Structures in C++, Data Structures in Java, Theory and Principles of Database Systems.*

Database Series: *Oracle, SQL Server, MySQL.*

Internet and Web Programming Series: *Internet and World Wide Web How to Program 3/e; Open Source Software Development: Linux, Apache, MySQL, Perl and PHP.*

Multimedia Programming Series: *Flash™.*

.NET Programming Series: *.NET A Technical Introduction, ASP .NET with Visual Basic .NET, ASP .NET with C#.*

Object Technology Series: *OOAD with the UML, Design Patterns, Java and XML.*

Advanced Java Series: *Advanced Java 2 Platform How to Program 2/e, Java 2 Enterprise Edition, Java Servlets, JavaServer Pages™ (JSP), Java 2 Micro Edition™ (J2ME).*

Turn the page to find out more about Deitel & Associates!

DEITEL™ BUZZ ONLINE Newsletter

We are proud to announce the launch of our official e-mail newsletter, the DEITEL™ BUZZ ONLINE. This free publication is designed to keep you updated on our publishing program, instructor-led corporate training courses, hottest industry trends and topics and more.

Issues of our newsletter include:

- **Technology Spotlights** that feature articles and information on the hottest industry topics drawn directly from our publications or written during the research and development process.

- **Anecdotes** and/or **challenges** that allow our readers to interact with our newsletter and with us. We always welcome and appreciate your comments, answers and feedback. We will summarize all responses we receive in future issues.

- **Announcements** on what's happening at Deitel as well as updated information on our publishing plans.

- **Highlights** and **Announcements** on current and upcoming products that are of interest to professionals, students and instructors.

- Information on our **instructor-led corporate training courses delivered at organizations worldwide**. Complete course listings and special course highlights provide readers with additional details on DEITEL™ training offerings.

- Our newsletter is available in both **full-color HTML** or **plain-text** formats depending on your viewing preferences and e-mail client capabilities.

- Learn about the history of Deitel & Associates, our brands, the bugs and more in the **Lore and Legends** section of the newsletter.

- **Hyperlinked Table of Contents** allows readers to navigate quickly through the newsletter by jumping directly to specific topics of interest.

To sign up for the Deitel™ Buzz Online newsletter, visit www.deitel.com/newsletter/subscribe.html.

License Agreement and Limited Warranty

Using the CD-ROM

The interface to the contents of this CD is designed to start automatically through the **AUTORUN.EXE** file. If a startup screen does not pop up automatically when you insert the CD into your computer, double click on the welcome.htm file to launch the Student CD or refer to the file **readme.txt** on the CD.

Contents of the CD-ROM

- Java™ 2 Platform, Software Development Kit Standard Edition Version1.4.1 for Windows and Linux (32-bit)
- Sun™ ONE Studio 4, Community Edition for Windows and Linux platforms
- IBM® Cloudscape™ Server Edition, Version 5.0.4 (60 day evaluation)
- Apache Tomcat version 4.1.12 from the Apache Software Foundation
- Live code examples from the book Java How to Program 5/e
- Web Resources -- Links to internet sites mentioned in the book Java How to Program, 5/e
- Additional Resources (in the Adobe® Acrobat® PDF format) not included in the book

Software and Hardware System Requirements

- 500 MHz (minimum) Pentium III or faster processor
- Microsoft Windows® NT (with Service Pack 6a), Windows 2000 Professional (with Service Pack 3 or greater), Windows XP, or
- Red Hat Linux 7.2
- 256 MB of RAM (minimum), 512 MB of RAM (recommended)
- CD-ROM drive
- Internet connection and web browser